Fodor's 2003

California

The Guide
for All Budgets

Completely
Updated

Where to Stay, Eat,
and Explore

On and Off
the Beaten Path

When to Go,
What to Pack

Maps, Travel Tips,
and Web Sites

Fodor's Travel Publications • New York, Toronto, London, Sydney, Auckland
www.fodors.com

Fodor's California 2003

EDITOR: Constance Jones

Editorial Contributors: Gregory Benchwick, Mary Beth Bohman, Tina Carr, Deke Castleman, Cheryl Crabtree, Steve Gerace, Lisa Hamilton, Veronica Hill, Satu Hummasti, Susan Lawson, Emmanuelle Morgen, Marty Olmstead, Reed Parsell, John Vlahides, Bobbi Zane

Editorial Production: Tom Holton

Maps: David Lindroth, *cartographer*; Robert Blake, Rebecca Baer, *map editors*

Design: Fabrizio La Rocca, *creative director*; Guido Caroti, *art director*; Jolie Novak, *senior photo editor*; Melanie Marin, *photo editor*

Cover Design: Pentagram

Production/Manufacturing: Yexenia (Jessie) Markland

Cover Photograph (Yosemite National Park): Darrell Gulin/Corbis

Copyright

ISBN 1–4000–1057–8

ISSN 0192–9925

Important Tip

Although all prices, opening times, and other details in this book are based on information supplied to us at press time, changes occur all the time in the travel world, and Fodor's cannot accept responsibility for facts that become outdated or for inadvertent errors or omissions. So **always confirm information when it matters,** especially if you're making a detour to visit a specific place.

Special Sales

Fodor's Travel Publications are available at special discounts for bulk purchases for sales promotions or premiums. Special editions, including personalized covers, excerpts of existing guides, and corporate imprints, can be created in large quantities for special needs. For more information, contact your local bookseller or write to Special Markets, Fodor's Travel Publications, 1745 Broadway, New York, NY 10019. Inquiries from Canada should be directed to your local Canadian bookseller or sent to Random House of Canada, Ltd., Marketing Department, 2775 Matheson Boulevard East, Mississauga, Ontario L4W 4P7. Inquiries from the United Kingdom should be sent to Fodor's Travel Publications, 20 Vauxhall Bridge Road, London SW1V 2SA, England.

PRINTED IN THE UNITED STATES OF AMERICA

10 9 8 7 6 5 4 3 2 1

CONTENTS

Maps

ON THE ROAD WITH FODOR'S

A TRIP TAKES YOU OUT OF YOURSELF. Concerns of life at home completely disappear, driven away by more immediate thoughts—about, say, what marvels will beguile the next day, or where you'll have dinner. That's where Fodor's comes in. We make sure that you know all your options, so that you don't miss something that's around the next bend just because you didn't know it was there. Mindful that the best memories of your trip might have nothing to do with what you came to California to see, we guide you to sights large and small all over the state. You might set out to see where the gold rush of 1849 started, but back at home you find yourself unable to forget the taste of the wine at that Santa Ynez vineyard or the otherworldly thrill of a hike in the Mojave National Preserve. With Fodor's at your side, serendipitous discoveries are never far away.

About Our Writers

Our success in showing you every corner of California is a credit to our extraordinary writers. Although there's no substitute for travel advice from a good friend who knows your style, our contributors are the next best thing—the kind of people you would poll for travel advice if you knew them.

San Francisco-based freelance writer **Gregory Benchwick** is a frequent Fodor's contributor. His work on the North Coast chapter took him up what he calls "the most memorable strip of highway I've ever seen."

For **Tina Carr,** growing up in Southern California meant hanging out in artsy Laguna Beach, trying her hand at surfing in San Clemente, and taking frequent trips to Disneyland. She put her pen to the page, or rather, her fingers to the keyboard for the Orange County chapter.

Deke Castleman, who updated the Lake Tahoe chapter, discovered the region's many wonders while engaged in a variety of occupations—door-to-door vacuum-cleaner salesman in northern California, tour guide at Alaska's Denali National Park, and travel writer from Reno.

Cheryl Crabtree, updater of the Central Coast chapter, has worked as a freelance writer since 1987, contributing to *Santa Barbara Magazine* and *Touring and Tasting: Great American Wineries*. She coauthored *The Insiders' Guide to Santa Barbara* in 1999.

Far north updater **Steve Gerace** is a native northern Californian. A longtime reporter and photographer for Southern Siskiyou Newspapers, he is now editor of the *Mount Shasta Herald, Weed Press,* and *Dunsmuir News.*

When not writing about California travel and outdoors, Central Valley updater **Lisa M. Hamilton** can be found at the beach. Accounts of the Marin County writer/photographer's food-related journeys have appeared in *National Geographic Traveler, Gastronomica,* and *Z Magazine.*

Southern California native **Veronica Hill** grew up in coastal Orange County and has traveled the state for 32 years. Nine years ago Hill moved to the tranquil Mojave Desert, where she is Features Editor at the *Daily Press.* She was a co-updater for the Death Valley and Mojave Desert chapter.

Susan D. Lawson, co-updater for the Death Valley and Mojave Desert chapter, has lived in the desert for more than 25 years. A full-time staffer for the *Daily Press* in Victorville since 1987, she is currently the paper's entertainment and travel magazine editor.

Wine Country and Peninsula updater **Marty Olmstead** has lived in Sonoma County since 1989. She covers the region for her weekly column in the *Marin Independent Journal* and other publications.

Reed Parsell, who updated Sacramento and the Gold Country, has been in the newspaper business for 20 years. He is currently a copy editor for the *Sacramento Bee* and a part-time travel writer.

Southern Sierra, Monterey Bay, and South Bay updater **John Andrew Vlahides** lives in San Francisco, spending his free time skiing the Sierra, touring California by motorcycle, and sunning on the beach beneath the Golden Gate Bridge. A columnist, essayist, and former *Clefs d'Or* concierge, he is a regular contributor to Fodor's guides.

Bobbi Zane, who updated the Southern California Desert chapter and Smart Travel Tips A to Z, has been visiting the region since her childhood. Her articles on Palm Springs have appeared in the *Orange County Register* and *Westways* magazine.

You can rest assured that you're in good hands—and that no property mentioned in the book has paid to be included. Each has been selected strictly on its merits, as the best of its type in its price range.

How to Use This Book

Up front are maps of northern and southern California and Smart Travel Tips A to Z, arranged alphabetically by topic and loaded with tips, Web sites, and contact information. Destination: California helps get you in the mood for your trip. Subsequent chapters in the guide are arranged regionally. All major-city chapters begin with exploring information, with a section for each neighborhood (each recommending a good tour and listing sights alphabetically). All regional chapters are divided geographically; within each area, towns are covered in logical geographical order, and attractive stretches of road between them are indicated by the designation En Route. To help you decide what you'll have time to visit, all chapters begin with our writers' favorite itineraries. (Mix itineraries from several chapters, and you can put together a really exceptional trip.) The A to Z section that ends every chapter lists additional resources.

Icons and Symbols

★ Our special recommendations
✕ Restaurant
🏠 Lodging establishment
✕🏠 Lodging establishment whose restaurant warrants a special trip
⚑ Campgrounds
🐤 Good for kids (rubber duck)
☞ Sends you to another section of the guide for more information

✉ Address
☎ Telephone number
🕐 Opening and closing times
💳 Admission prices (those we give apply to adults; substantially reduced fees are almost always available for children, students, and senior citizens)

Numbers in white and black circles ③ ❸ that appear on the maps, in the margins, and within the tours correspond to one another.

For hotels, you can assume that all rooms have private baths, phones, TVs, and air-conditioning unless otherwise noted and that all hotels operate on the European Plan (with no meals) if we don't specify another meal plan. We always list a property's facilities but not whether you'll be charged extra to use them, so when pricing accommodations, do ask what's included. For restaurants, it's always a good idea to book ahead; we mention reservations only when they're essential or are not accepted. All restaurants we list are open daily for lunch and dinner unless stated otherwise; dress is mentioned only when men are required to wear a jacket or a jacket and tie. Look for an overview of local dining-out habits in Smart Travel Tips A to Z and in the Pleasures and Pastimes section that follows each chapter introduction.

Don't Forget to Write

Your experiences—positive and negative—matter to us. If we have missed or misstated something, we want to hear about it. We follow up on all suggestions. Contact the California editor at editors@fodors.com or c/o Fodor's at 1745 Broadway, New York, NY 10019. And have a fabulous trip!

Karen Cure

Karen Cure
Editorial Director

Northern California

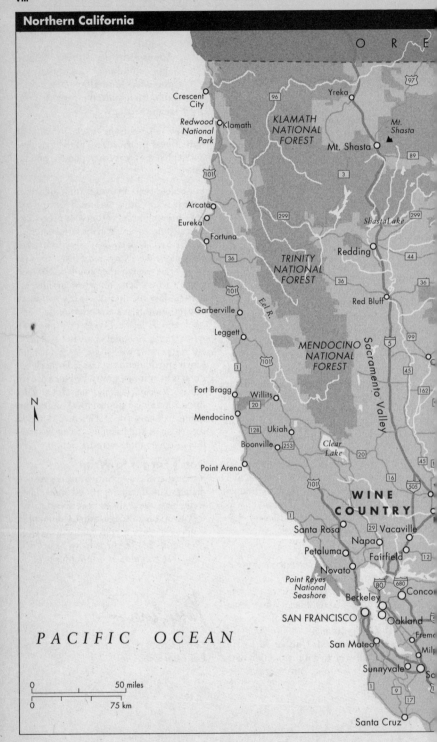

PACIFIC OCEAN

Crescent City
Redwood National Park
Klamath
Yreka
KLAMATH NATIONAL FOREST
Mt. Shasta
Mt. Shasta

ShastaLake

Arcata
Eureka
Fortuna
TRINITY NATIONAL FOREST
Redding
Red Bluff

Garberville
Leggett
MENDOCINO NATIONAL FOREST
Sacramento Valley

Fort Bragg
Willits
Mendocino
Ukiah
Boonville
Clear Lake
Point Arena

WINE COUNTRY

Santa Rosa
Vacaville
Napa
Petaluma
Fairfield
Novato
Point Reyes National Seashore
Berkeley
SAN FRANCISCO
Oakland
Concord
Fremont
San Mateo
Milpitas
Sunnyvale
Santa Cruz

Eel R.

O R E

0   50 miles
0   75 km

N

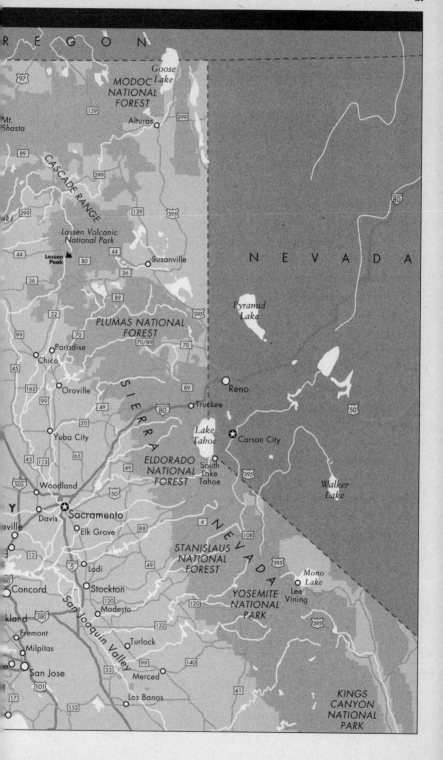

Southern California

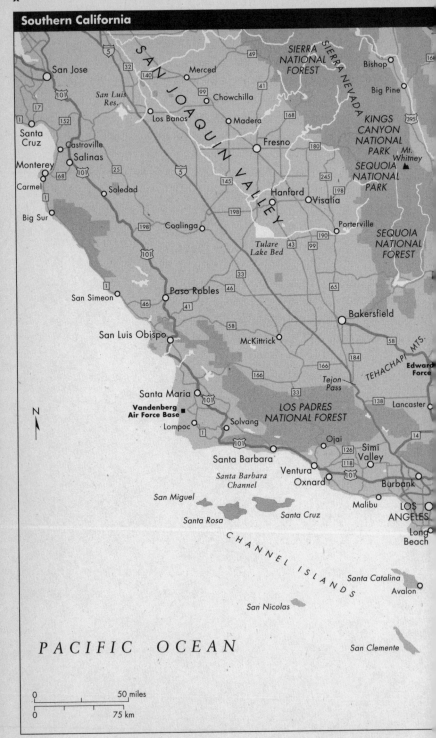

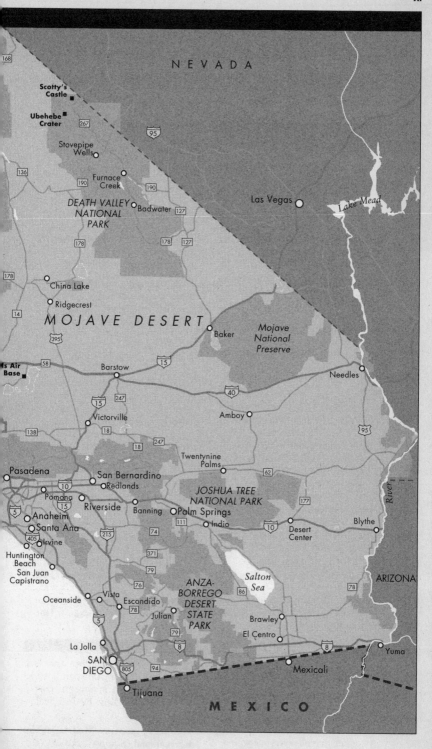

ESSENTIAL INFORMATION

AIR TRAVEL

BOOKING

When you book **look for nonstop flights** and **remember that "direct" flights stop at least once.** Try to avoid connecting flights, which require a change of plane. Because of frequent fog and weather delays there, **avoid booking tight connections in San Francisco.** For more booking tips and to check prices and make on-line flight reservations, log on to www.fodors.com.

CARRIERS

United, with hubs in San Francisco and Los Angeles, has the greatest number of flights into and within California. But most national and many international airlines fly here.

➤ MAJOR AIRLINES: **Air Canada** (☎ 888/247–2622). **Alaska** (☎ 800/426–0333). **America West** (☎ 800/235–9292). **American** (☎ 800/433–7300). **British Airways** (☎ 800/247–9297). **Cathay Pacific** (☎ 800/233–2742). **Continental** (☎ 800/231–0856). **Delta** (☎ 800/221–1212). **Japan Air Lines** (☎ 800/525–3663). **Northwest/KLM** (☎ 800/225–2525). **Qantas** (☎ 800/227–4500). **Southwest** (☎ 800/435–9792). **United** (☎ 800/241–6522). **US Airways** (☎ 800/428–4322).

➤ SMALLER AIRLINES: **American Trans Air** (☎ 800/435–9282). **Horizon** (☎ 800/547–9308. **Midwest Express** (☎ 800/452–2022). **Skywest** (☎ 800/453–9417).

➤ FROM THE U.K.: **American** (☎ 0345/789–789). **British Airways** (☎ 0345/222–111). **Delta** (☎ 0800/414–767). **United** (☎ 0800/888–555). **Virgin Atlantic** (☎ 01293/747–747).

CHECK-IN AND BOARDING

Assuming that not everyone with a ticket will show up, airlines routinely overbook planes. When everyone does, airlines ask for volunteers to give up their seats. In return, these volunteers usually get a certificate for a free flight and are rebooked on the next flight out. If there are not enough volunteers, the airline must choose who will be denied boarding. The first to get bumped are passengers who checked in late and those flying on discounted tickets, so **get to the gate and check in as early as possible,** especially during peak periods.

Always **bring a government-issued photo ID to the airport;** a passport is best. You may be asked to show it before you are allowed to check in.

FLYING TIMES

Flying time to California is roughly six hours from New York and four hours from Chicago. Travel from London to Los Angeles or San Francisco takes about 10 hours and from Sydney approximately 14. Flying between San Francisco and Los Angeles takes one hour.

HOW TO COMPLAIN

If your baggage goes astray or your flight goes awry, complain right away. Most carriers require that you **file a claim immediately.**

➤ AIRLINE COMPLAINTS: U.S. Department of Transportation **Aviation Consumer Protection Division** (✉ C-75, Room 4107, Washington, DC 20590, ☎ 202/366–2220, WEB www.dot.gov/airconsumer). **Federal Aviation Administration Consumer Hotline** (☎ 800/322–7873).

AIRPORTS

Major gateways to California are Los Angeles International Airport (LAX), San Francisco International Airport (SFO), and San Diego International Airport (SAN).

➤ AIRPORT INFORMATION: **Los Angeles International Airport** (☎ 310/646–5252). **San Diego International Air-**

port (☎ 619/231–2100). **San Francisco International Airport** (☎ 650/761–0800).

BIKE TRAVEL

There are beautiful places to bike throughout California. For each part of the state, please see the specific chapter on that area for biking ideas.

BIKES IN FLIGHT

Most airlines accommodate bikes as luggage, provided they are dismantled and boxed. Airlines sell bike boxes, which are often free at bike shops, for about $5 (it's at least $100 for bike bags). International travelers can sometimes substitute a bike for a piece of checked luggage at no charge; otherwise, the cost is about $100. Domestic and Canadian airlines charge $25–$50.

BUS TRAVEL

Because of the state's size, traveling by bus in California can be slow. But if you don't want to rent a car and wish to go where the train does not, a bus may be your only option. Greyhound is the major carrier for intermediate and long distances, though smaller, regional bus service is available in metropolitan areas. Check the specific chapters for the regions you plan to visit. Smoking is prohibited on all buses in California.

CUTTING COSTS

You can purchase an Ameripass through Greyhound up to 45 minutes prior to departure. Depending on which type you buy, an Ameripass offers unlimited travel on all routes for between one week and three months. Inquire also about seasonal advance-purchase fares. Reserving by phone with a credit card requires you have a U.S. billing address. Otherwise, you may purchase tickets only at a terminal.

➤ Bus Information: **Greyhound** (☎ 800/231–2222, WEB www.greyhound.com).

BUSINESS HOURS

Banks in California are typically open from 9 to 4 and are closed most holidays (☞ Holidays, *below*). Smaller shops usually operate from 10 to 6, with larger stores remaining open until 8 or later. Hours vary for museums and historical sites, and many are closed one or more days a week. It's a good idea to **check before you visit a tourist site.** Many gas stations are open 24 hours, especially on interstate highways. In rural areas many close early, so fill up before nightfall.

CAMERAS AND PHOTOGRAPHY

The pounding surf, glorious mountains, sprawling deserts, towering trees, and sparkling beaches—not to mention the cities and towns in between—make California a photographer's dream destination. Bring lots of film to capture the special moments of your trip. The *Kodak Guide to Shooting Great Travel Pictures* (available at bookstores everywhere) is loaded with tips.

➤ Photo Help: **Kodak Information Center** (☎ 800/242–2424).

EQUIPMENT PRECAUTIONS

Don't pack film and equipment in checked luggage, where it is much more susceptible to damage. X-ray machines used to view checked luggage are becoming much more powerful and therefore are much more likely to ruin your film. Always **keep film and tape out of the sun.** Carry an extra supply of batteries, and **be prepared to turn on your camera or camcorder** to prove to security personnel that the device is real. Always **ask for hand inspection of film,** which becomes clouded after repeated exposure to airport X-ray machines, and **keep videotapes away from metal detectors.**

CAR RENTAL

A car is essential in most parts of California. In compact San Francisco it's better to use public transportation to avoid parking headaches. In sprawling cities such as Los Angeles and San Diego, however, getting just about anywhere requires making use of the freeways.

Rates in Los Angeles begin at around $35 a day and $175 a week. This does not include tax on car rentals, which is 8¼%. In San Diego rates for an economy car with unlimited mileage begin around $30 a day and

$150 a week. The tax is an additional 7¾%. In San Francisco rates begin around $38 a day and $194 a week. The tax is 8½%. There is also a vehicle license fee, which varies with the value of the car, but you should expect to pay $1–$4 per day.

➤ MAJOR AGENCIES: **Alamo** (☎ 800/327–9633). **Avis** (☎ 800/331–1212; 800/879–2847 in Canada; 02/9353–9000 in Australia; 09/525–1982 in New Zealand; 0870/606–0100 in the U.K.). **Budget** (☎ 800/527–0700; 0144/227–6266 in the U.K., through affiliate Europcar). **Dollar** (☎ 800/800–4000; 0124/622–0111 in the U.K., where it is known as Sixt Kenning; 02/9223–1444 in Australia). **Hertz** (☎ 800/654–3131; 800/263–0600 in Canada; 020/8897–2072 in the U.K.; 02/9669–2444 in Australia; 09/256–8690 in New Zealand). **National Car Rental** (☎ 800/227–7368; 0845/722–2525 in the U.K., where it is known as National Europe).

CONVERTIBLES AND SUVS

If you dream of driving down the coast with the top down, or you want to explore the desert landscape not visible from the road, consider renting a specialty vehicle. Agencies that specialize in convertibles and sport-utility vehicles will often arrange airport delivery in larger cities.

➤ SPECIALTY CAR AGENCIES: In San Francisco, **SpecialtyRentals.com** (☎ 800/400–8412); in Los Angeles, **Budget of Beverly Hills** (☎ 800/729–7350); in San Diego, **Rent-a-Vette** (☎ 800/627–0808).

Do **look into wholesalers,** companies that do not own fleets but rent in bulk from those that do and often offer better rates than traditional car-rental operations. Payment must be made before you leave home.

INSURANCE

When driving a rented car you are generally responsible for any damage to or loss of the vehicle as well as for any property damage or personal injury that you may cause. Before you rent, see what coverage your personal auto-insurance policy and credit cards provide.

For $9 per day, rental companies sell protection, known as a collision- or loss-damage waiver (CDW or LDW), that eliminates your liability for damage to the car. Some states, including California, have capped the price of the CDW and LDW. In most states you don't need a CDW if you have personal auto insurance that covers rental cars. **Read your policy.** However, **make sure you have enough coverage to pay for the car.** If you do not have auto insurance or an umbrella policy that covers damage to third parties, purchasing liability insurance and a CDW or LDW is highly recommended.

REQUIREMENTS AND RESTRICTIONS

In California you must be 21 to rent a car, and rates may be higher if you're under 25. Some agencies will not rent to those between 21 and 24; check when you book. You'll pay extra for child seats (about $3 per day), which are compulsory for children under five. Children up to age six or 60 pounds must be placed in booster seats. There is no extra charge for an additional driver. Non–U.S. residents must have a license whose text is in the Roman alphabet, though it need not be in English. An international license is recommended but not required.

SURCHARGES

Before you pick up a car in one city and leave it in another, **ask about drop-off charges or one-way service fees,** which can be substantial. Note, too, that some rental agencies charge extra if you return the car before the time specified in your contract. To avoid a hefty refueling fee, **fill the tank just before you turn in the car,** but be aware that gas stations near the rental outlet may overcharge.

CAR TRAVEL

Three major highways—Interstate 5 (I–5), U.S. 101, and Highway 1—run north–south through California. The main routes into the state from the east are I–15 and I–10 in southern California and I–80 in northern California.

AUTO CLUBS

➤ IN AUSTRALIA: **Australian Automobile Association** (☎ 02/6247–7311).

➤ IN CANADA: **Canadian Automobile Association** (CAA; ☎ 613/247–0117).

➤ IN NEW ZEALAND: **New Zealand Automobile Association** (☎ 09/377–4660).

➤ IN THE U.K.: **Automobile Association** (AA; ☎ 0990/500–600). **Royal Automobile Club** (RAC, ☎ 0990/722–722 for membership; 0345/121–345 for insurance).

➤ IN THE U.S.: **American Automobile Association** (AAA; ☎ 800/564–6222).

EMERGENCIES

Dial 911 to report accidents on the road and to reach police, the California Highway Patrol, or the fire department. On some rural highways and on most interstates, look for emergency phones on the side of the road.

GASOLINE

Gasoline prices in California vary widely depending on location, oil company, and whether you buy it at a full-serve or self-serve pump. At press time regular unleaded gasoline cost about $1.60 a gallon. It is less expensive to buy fuel in the southern part of the state than in the north. If you are planning to travel near Nevada, you can save a lot by purchasing gas over the border.

Gas stations are plentiful throughout the state. Most stay open late (24 hours along large highways and in big cities), except in rural areas, where Sunday hours are limited and where you may drive long stretches without a refueling opportunity.

ROAD CONDITIONS

Rainy weather can make driving along the coast or in the mountains treacherous. Some of the smaller routes over the mountain ranges are prone to flash flooding. When the rains are severe, coastal Highway 1 can quickly become a slippery nightmare, buffeted by strong winds and obstructed by falling debris from the cliffs above. When the weather is particularly bad, Highway 1 may be closed. Drivers should **check road conditions before heading into stormy weather.**

Many smaller roads over the Sierra Nevada are closed in winter, and if it is snowing, tire chains may be required on routes that are open, most notably those to Yosemite and Lake Tahoe. If it is raining along the coast, it is usually snowing at higher elevations. **Do not wait until the highway patrol's chain-control checkpoint to look for chains;** you'll be unable to turn around, and you will get stuck and have to wait out the storm. Rent a four-wheel-drive vehicle or **purchase chains before you get to the mountains.** If you delay and purchase them in the vicinity of the chain-control area, the cost may double. Be aware that most rental-car companies prohibit chain installation on their vehicles. If you choose to risk it and do not tighten them properly, they may snap; insurance will not cover the damage that could result. Uniformed chain installers on I–80 and U.S. 50 will apply them at the checkpoint for $20 or take them off for $10. On smaller roads you are on your own. Always carry extra clothing, blankets, and food when driving to the mountains in the winter, and keep your gas tank full to prevent the fuel line from freezing.

In larger cities the biggest driving hazards are traffic jams. **Avoid major urban highways, especially at rush hour.**

➤ ROAD CONDITIONS: **Statewide hot line** (☎ 800/427–7623 from a touch-tone telephone; 916/445–1534 from a rotary-dial telephone).

ROAD MAPS

You can buy detailed maps in bookstores and gas stations and at some grocery and drugstores. The various California branches of the American Automobile Association (☞ *above*) have state and local maps that are free to members.

RULES OF THE ROAD

Always **strap children under age six and weighing 60 pounds or less into approved child-safety seats;** also children up to age six and weighing up to 60 pounds must be placed in booster seats designed to reduce seat belt injuries. Seat belts are required at all times; tickets can be given for failing to comply. Children must wear seat belts regardless of where they're seated (studies show that children are safest in the rear seats).

Unless otherwise indicated, right turns are allowed at red lights after you've come to a full stop. Left turns onto one-way streets are allowed at red lights after you've come to a full stop. Drivers with a blood-alcohol level higher than 0.08 who are stopped by police are subject to arrest, and police officers can detain those with a level of 0.05 if they appear impaired. California's drunk-driving laws are extremely tough. The licenses of violators may immediately be suspended, and offenders may have to spend the night in jail and pay hefty fines.

The speed limit on many rural highways is 70 mph. In the cities freeway speed limits are between 55 mph and 65 mph. Many city routes have commuter lanes, but the operating rules vary from city to city: in San Francisco, for example, you need three people in a car to use these lanes, in Los Angeles only two.

CHILDREN IN CALIFORNIA

California is made to order for traveling with children: youngsters love Disneyland; Legoland, in Carlsbad; the San Diego Zoo; the Monterey Aquarium; San Francisco cable cars; the gold mine in Placerville; Forestiere Underground Gardens, in Fresno, and the caverns near Lake Shasta. Fodor's *Where Should We Take the Kids? California,* Fodor's *Around Los Angeles with Kids,* and Fodor's *Around San Francisco with Kids* (available in bookstores everywhere) can help you plan your days together.

If you are renting a car, don't forget to **arrange for a car seat** when you reserve. For general advice about traveling with children, consult Fodor's *FYI: Travel with Your Baby* (available in bookstores everywhere).

LODGING

Most hotels in California allow children under a certain age to stay in their parents' room at no extra charge, but others charge for them as extra adults; be sure to **find out the cut-off age for children's discounts.**

SIGHTS AND ATTRACTIONS

Places that are especially appealing to children are indicated by a rubber-duckie icon (🦆) in the margin.

CONSUMER PROTECTION

Whenever shopping or buying travel services in California, **pay with a major credit card,** if possible, so you can cancel payment or get reimbursed if there's a problem. If you're doing business with a particular company for the first time, **contact your local Better Business Bureau and the attorney general's offices** in your state and (for U.S. businesses) the company's home state as well. Have any complaints been filed? Finally, if you're buying a package or tour, always **consider travel insurance** that includes default coverage (☞ Insurance, *below*).

➤ BBBs: **Council of Better Business Bureaus** (✉ 4200 Wilson Blvd., Suite 800, Arlington, VA 22203, ☎ 703/276–0100, FAX 703/525–8277, WEB www.bbb.org).

CUSTOMS AND DUTIES

When shopping, **keep receipts** for all purchases. Upon reentering the country, **be ready to show customs officials what you've bought.** If you feel a duty is incorrect or object to the way your clearance was handled, note the inspector's badge number and ask to see a supervisor. If the problem isn't resolved, write to the appropriate authorities, beginning with the port director at your point of entry.

IN AUSTRALIA

Australian residents who are 18 or older may bring home $A400 worth of souvenirs and gifts (including jewelry), 250 cigarettes or 250 grams of tobacco, and 1,125 ml of alcohol (including wine, beer, and spirits). Residents under 18 may bring back $A200 worth of goods. Prohibited items include meat products. Seeds, plants, and fruits need to be declared upon arrival.

➤ INFORMATION: **Australian Customs Service** (Regional Director, ✉ Box 8, Sydney, NSW 2001, Australia, ☎ 02/9213–2000 or 1300/363–263; 1800/020–504 quarantine-inquiry line, FAX 02/9213–4043, WEB www.customs.gov.au).

IN CANADA

Canadian residents who have been out of Canada for at least seven days may bring home C$500 worth of goods duty-free. If you've been away fewer than seven days but more than 48 hours, the duty-free allowance drops to C$200; if your trip lasts 24–48 hours, the allowance is C$50. You may not pool allowances with family members. Goods claimed under the C$500 exemption may follow you by mail; those claimed under the lesser exemptions must accompany you. Alcohol and tobacco products may be included in the seven-day and 48-hour exemptions but not in the 24-hour exemption. If you meet the age requirements of the province or territory through which you reenter Canada, you may bring in, duty-free, 1.14 liters (40 imperial ounces) of wine or liquor or 24 12-ounce cans or bottles of beer or ale. If you are 16 or older you may bring in, duty-free, 200 cigarettes and 50 cigars. Check ahead of time with Revenue Canada or the Department of Agriculture for policies regarding meat products, seeds, plants, and fruits.

You may send an unlimited number of gifts worth up to C$60 each duty-free to Canada. Label the package UNSOLICITED GIFT—VALUE UNDER $60. Alcohol and tobacco are excluded.

➤ INFORMATION: **Canada Customs and Revenue Agency** (⌧ 2265 St. Laurent Blvd. S, Ottawa, Ontario K1G 4K3, Canada, ☎ 613/993–0534 or 800/461–9999, FAX 613/991–4126, WEB www.ccra-adrc.gc.ca).

IN NEW ZEALAND

Homeward-bound residents 17 or older may bring back $700 worth of souvenirs and gifts. Your duty-free allowance also includes 4.5 liters of wine or beer; one 1,125-ml bottle of spirits; and either 200 cigarettes, 250 grams of tobacco, 50 cigars, or a combination of the three up to 250 grams. Prohibited items include meat products, seeds, plants, and fruits.

➤ INFORMATION: **New Zealand Customs** (Head office: ⌧ 50 Anzac Ave., Box 29, Auckland, New Zealand, ☎ 09/300–5399 or 0800/428–786, FAX 09/359–6730, WEB www.customs. govt.nz).

IN THE U.K.

From countries outside the EU, including the United States, you may bring home, duty-free, 200 cigarettes or 50 cigars; 1 liter of spirits or 2 liters of fortified or sparkling wine or liqueurs; 2 liters of still table wine; 60 ml of perfume; 250 ml of toilet water; plus £136 worth of other goods, including gifts and souvenirs. If returning from outside the EU, prohibited items include meat products, seeds, plants, and fruits.

➤ INFORMATION: **HM Customs and Excise** (⌧ Portcullis House, 21 Cowbridge Rd. E, Cardiff CF11 9SS, ☎ 029/2038–6423 or 0845/010–9000, WEB www.hmce.gov.uk).

IN THE U.S.

If you decide to cross the border into Mexico, bear in mind that U.S. residents who have been out of the country for at least 48 hours may bring home, for personal use, $400 worth of foreign goods duty-free, as long as they haven't used the $400 allowance or any part of it in the past 30 days. This exemption may include 1 liter of alcohol (for travelers 21 and older), 200 cigarettes, and 100 non-Cuban cigars. Family members from the same household who are traveling together may pool their $400 personal exemptions. For fewer than 48 hours, the duty-free allowance drops to $200, which may include 50 cigarettes, 10 non-Cuban cigars, and 150 milliliters of alcohol (or perfume containing alcohol). The $200 allowance cannot be combined with other individuals' exemptions, and if you exceed it, the full value of all the goods will be taxed. Antiques, which the U.S. Customs Service defines as objects more than 100 years old, enter duty-free, as do original works of art done entirely by hand, including paintings, drawings, and sculptures.

You may also send packages home duty-free, with a limit of one parcel per addressee per day (except alcohol or tobacco products or perfume worth more than $5). You can mail up to $200 worth of goods for personal use; label the package PERSONAL USE and attach a list of its contents and their retail value. If the package contains your used personal belongings, mark it PERSONAL GOODS RETURNED to avoid paying duties. You may send up to $100 worth of goods as a gift; mark the package UNSOLICITED GIFT. Mailed items do not affect your duty-free allowance on your return.

➤ INFORMATION: **U.S. Customs Service** (✉ 1300 Pennsylvania Ave. NW, Room 6.3D, Washington, DC 20229, ☎ 202/354–1000 inquiries, WEB www. customs.gov; complaints c/o ✉ Office of Regulations and Rulings; registration of equipment c/o ✉ Resource Management, ☎ 202/927–0540).

DINING

California has led the pack in bringing natural and organic foods to the forefront of American cooking. The Asian and Latin influences in California cooking are also strong. Wherever you go, you're likely to find the dishes are made with fresh produce and other local ingredients.

The restaurants we list are the cream of the crop in each price category. Properties indicated by an ✕☲ are lodging establishments whose restaurant warrants a special trip. Lunch is typically served 11:30–2:30, and dinner service in most restaurants begins at 5:30 and ends at 10. Some restaurants in larger cities stay open until midnight or later.

PRICES

CATEGORY	COST*
$$$$	over $30
$$$	$22–$30
$$	$15–$21
$	under $15

per person for a main course at dinner, excluding tip and tax

RESERVATIONS AND DRESS

Reservations are always a good idea; we mention them only when they're essential or not accepted. Book as far ahead as you can, and reconfirm as soon as you arrive. We mention dress only when men are required to wear a jacket or a jacket and tie.

WINE, BEER, AND SPIRITS

If you like wine, your trip to California won't be complete unless you try a few of the local vintages. Throughout the state, most famously in the Napa and Sonoma valleys, you can visit wineries, most of which have tasting rooms and many of which offer tours. The legal drinking age is 21.

DISABILITIES AND ACCESSIBILITY

California is a national leader in making attractions and facilities accessible to people with disabilities. The Americans with Disabilities Act (ADA) requires that all businesses make accommodations for individuals with any physical handicap, and state laws provide special privileges, such as license plates allowing special parking spaces, unlimited parking in time-limited spaces, and free parking in metered spaces. Insignia from other states are honored.

LODGING

When discussing accessibility with an operator or reservations agent, **ask hard questions.** Are there any stairs, inside *or* out? Are there grab bars next to the toilet *and* in the shower/tub? How wide is the doorway to the room? To the bathroom? For the most extensive facilities meeting the latest legal specifications, **opt for newer accommodations.**

PARKS

The National Park Service provides a Golden Access Passport for all national parks free of charge to those who are medically blind or have a permanent disability; the passport covers the entry fee for the holder and anyone accompanying the holder in the same private vehicle as well as a 50% discount on camping and various other user fees. Apply for the passport in person at a national recreation facility that charges an entrance fee; proof of disability is required.

TRANSPORTATION

Hertz and Avis (☞ Car Rental, *above*) are able to supply cars modified for those with disabilities, but they require one to two days' advance notice. Discounts are available for travelers with disabilities on Amtrak (☞ Train Travel, *below*). On Greyhound (☞ Bus Travel, *above*), your companion can ride free.

➤ COMPLAINTS: **Aviation Consumer Protection Division** (☞ Air Travel, *above*) for airline-related problems. **Departmental Office of Civil Rights** (✉ U.S. Department of Transportation, Departmental Office of Civil Rights, S-30, 400 7th St. SW, Room 10215, Washington, DC 20590, ☎ 202/366–4648, FAX 202/366–3571, WEB www.dot.gov/ost/docr/index.htm) for problems with surface transportation. **Disability Rights Section** (✉ NYAV, U.S. Department of Justice, Civil Rights Division, 950 Pennsylvania Ave. NW, Washington, DC 20530; ☎ ADA information line 202/514–0301, 800/514–0301, 202/514–0383 TTY, 800/514–0383 TTY, WEB www.usdoj.gov/crt/ada/adahom1.htm).

TRAVEL AGENCIES

In the United States, the Americans with Disabilities Act requires that travel firms serve the needs of all travelers. Some agencies specialize in working with people with disabilities.

➤ TRAVELERS WITH MOBILITY PROBLEMS: **Access Adventures** (✉ 206 Chestnut Ridge Rd., Scottsville, NY 14624, ☎ 716/889–9096, dltravel@prodigy.net), run by a former physical-rehabilitation counselor. **Accessible Vans of America** (✉ 9 Spielman Rd., Fairfield, NJ 07004, ☎ 877/282–8267, FAX 973/808–9713, WEB www.accessiblevans.com). **CareVacations** (✉ 5-5110 50th Ave., Leduc, Alberta T9E 6V4, Canada, ☎ 780/986–6404 or 877/478–7827, FAX 780/986–8332, WEB www.carevacations.com), for group tours and cruise vacations. **Flying Wheels Travel** (✉ 143 W. Bridge St., Box 382, Owatonna, MN 55060, ☎ 507/451–5005, FAX 507/451–1685, WEB www.flyingwheelstravel.com). **Wilderness Inquiry, Inc.** (✉ 808 14th Ave. SE, Minneapolis, MN 55414-1516, ☎ 612/676–9400 or 800/728–0719, FAX 612/676–9401 WEB www.wildernessinquiry.org) is a nonprofit organization that plans outdoor adventures for all ages, backgrounds, and abilities.

➤ TRAVELERS WITH DEVELOPMENTAL DISABILITIES: **New Directions** (✉ 5276 Hollister Ave., Suite 207, Santa Barbara, CA 93111, ☎ 805/967–2841 or 888/967–2841, FAX 805/964–7344,

WEB www.newdirectionstravel.com). **Sprout** (✉ 893 Amsterdam Ave., New York, NY 10025, ☎ 212/222–9575 or 888/222–9575, FAX 212/222–9768, WEB www.gosprout.org).

DISCOUNTS AND DEALS

Be a smart shopper and **compare all your options** before making decisions. A plane ticket bought with a promotional coupon from travel clubs, coupon books, and direct-mail offers or on the Internet may not be cheaper than the least expensive fare from a discount ticket agency. And always keep in mind that what you get is just as important as what you save.

DISCOUNT RESERVATIONS

To save money, **look into discount reservations services** with toll-free numbers, which use their buying power to get a better price on hotels, airline tickets, even car rentals. When booking a room, always **call the hotel's local toll-free number** (if one is available) rather than the central reservations number—you'll often get a better price. Always ask about special packages or corporate rates.

➤ AIRLINE TICKETS: ☎ 800/FLY-ASAP.

➤ HOTEL ROOMS: **Accommodations Express** (☎ 800/444–7666, WEB www.accommodationsexpress.com). **Central Reservation Service (CRS;** ☎ 800/548–3311). **Hotels.com** (☎ 800/246–8357, WEB www.hotels.com). **Players Express Vacations** (☎ 800/458–6161, WEB www.playersexpress.com). **Quikbook** (☎ 800/789–9887, WEB www.quikbook.com). **RMC Travel** (☎ 800/245–5738, WEB www.rmcwebtravel.com). **Steigenberger Reservation Service** (☎ 800/223–5652, WEB www.srs-worldhotels.com). **Turbotrip.com** (☎ 800/473–7829, WEB www.turbotrip.com).

PACKAGE DEALS

Don't confuse packages and guided tours. When you buy a package, you travel on your own, just as though you had planned the trip yourself. Fly-drive packages, which combine airfare and car rental, are often a good deal.

DIVERS' ALERT

Do not fly within 24 hours of scuba diving.

ECOTOURISM

When traveling in wilderness areas and parks, remember to tread lightly. Do not drive an SUV through sensitive habitats, and **pack out what you pack in.** Many remote camping areas do not provide waste disposal. It's a good idea to bring plastic bags to store refuse until you can dispose of it properly. Recycling programs are abundant in California, and trash at many state and national parks is sorted. Look for appropriately labeled garbage containers. Numerous ecotours are available in California (☞ Tours and Packages, *below*).

GAY AND LESBIAN TRAVEL

San Francisco, Los Angeles, West Hollywood, San Diego, and Palm Springs are among the California cities with visible lesbian and gay communities. Though it is usually safe to be visibly "out" in many areas, you should always use common sense when in unfamiliar places. Gay bashings still occur in both urban and rural areas. For details about the gay and lesbian scene, consult *Fodor's Gay Guide to the USA* (available in bookstores everywhere).

LOCAL INFORMATION

Many California cities large and small have lesbian and gay publications available in sidewalk racks and at bars, bookstores, and other social spaces; most have extensive events and information listings.

➤ COMMUNITY CENTERS: **Billy De-Frank Lesbian & Gay Community Center** (✉ 938 The Alameda, San Jose 95126, ☎ 408/293–2429). **Gay and Lesbian Community Services Center** (✉ 1625 N. Schrader Blvd., Los Angeles 90028, ☎ 323/993–7400). **Lambda Community Center** (✉ 1927 L St., Sacramento 95814, ☎ 916/442–0185). **Lavender Youth Recreation & Information Center** (✉ 127 Collingwood St., San Francisco 94114, ☎ 415/703–6150; 415/863–3636 for hot line). **Lesbian and Gay Men's Community Center** (✉ 3909 Centre St., San Diego 92103, ☎ 619/692–2077).

Pacific Center Lesbian, Gay and Bisexual Switchboard (✉ 2712 Telegraph Ave., Berkeley 94705, ☎ 510/548–8283).

➤ LOCAL PUBLICATIONS: *Bay Area Reporter* (✉ 395 9th St., San Francisco 94103, ☎ 415/861–5019). *Bottom Line* (✉ 120 E. Andreas, Suite C, Palm Springs 92262, ☎ 760/323–0552). *Frontiers* (✉ 8380 Santa Monica Blvd., Suite 200, West Hollywood 90069, ☎ 323/848–2222). *Mom Guess What* (✉ 1725 L St., Sacramento 95814, ☎ 916/441–6397). *Update* (✉ 2801 4th Ave., San Diego 92103, ☎ 619/299–0500).

➤ GAY- AND LESBIAN-FRIENDLY TRAVEL AGENCIES: **Different Roads Travel** (✉ 8383 Wilshire Blvd., Suite 902, Beverly Hills, CA 90211, ☎ 323/651–5557 or 800/429–8747, FAX 323/651–3678, lgernert@tzell.com). **Kennedy Travel** (✉ 314 Jericho Turnpike, Floral Park, NY 11001, ☎ 516/352–4888 or 800/237–7433, FAX 516/354–8849, WEB www.kennedytravel.com). **Now Voyager** (✉ 4406 18th St., San Francisco, CA 94114, ☎ 415/626–1169 or 800/255–6951, FAX 415/626–8626). **Flying Dutchmen Travel** (✉ 1006 Mendocino Ave., Santa Rosa, CA 95401, ☎ 707/546–9888 or 877/359–3882, FAX 707/545–2112, WEB www.flyingdutchmentravel.com), serving lesbian travelers.

GUIDEBOOKS

Plan well and you won't be sorry. Guidebooks are excellent tools—and you can take them with you. You may want to check out color-photo-illustrated *Fodor's Exploring California, Compass American Guide: Coastal California,* and *Compass American Guide: Wine Country,* all thorough on culture and history, and *Fodor's Road Guide USA: California,* for comprehensive restaurant, hotel, and attractions listings for driving vacations. For additional city coverage try *Fodor's San Francisco, Compass American Guide: San Francisco, Fodor's Exploring San Francisco, Fodor's CITYGUIDE San Francisco, Citypack San Francisco, Fodor's Flashmaps San Francisco, Fodor's Los Angeles, Fodor's CITYGUIDE Los Angeles, Citypack Los Angeles,* and *Fodor's San Diego.* All are available through on-line retailers and at bookstores everywhere.

HOLIDAYS

Most traditional businesses are closed these days, but tourist attractions and some restaurants are usually open except on Thanksgiving, Christmas, and New Year's Day.

Major national holidays include New Year's Day (Jan. 1); Martin Luther King Jr. Day (3rd Mon. in Jan.); President's Day (3rd Mon. in Feb.); Memorial Day (last Mon. in May); Independence Day (July 4); Labor Day (1st Mon. in Sept.); Thanksgiving Day (4th Thurs. in Nov.); Christmas Eve and Christmas Day; and New Year's Eve.

INSURANCE

The most useful travel-insurance plan is a comprehensive policy that includes coverage for trip cancellation and interruption, default, trip delay, and medical expenses (with a waiver for preexisting conditions).

Without insurance you will lose all or most of your money if you cancel your trip, regardless of the reason. Default insurance covers you if your tour operator, airline, or cruise line goes out of business. Trip-delay covers expenses that arise because of bad weather or mechanical delays. Study the fine print when comparing policies.

Always **buy travel policies directly from the insurance company**; if you buy them from a cruise line, airline, or tour operator that goes out of business, you probably will not be covered for the agency or operator's default, a major risk. Before making any purchase, **review your existing health and home-owner's policies** to find what they cover away from home.

➤ TRAVEL INSURERS: In the United States: **Access America** (✉ 6600 W. Broad St., Richmond, VA 23230, ☏ 804/285–3300 or 800/284–8300, FAX 804/673–1586, WEB www. accessamerica.com). **Travel Guard International** (✉ 1145 Clark St., Stevens Point, WI 54481, ☏ 715/345–0505 or 800/826–1300, FAX 800/955–8785, WEB www.noelgroup. com).

FOR INTERNATIONAL TRAVELERS

For information on customs restrictions, see Customs and Duties, above.

CAR RENTAL

When picking up a rental car, non-U.S. residents need a reservation voucher for any prepaid reservations that were made in the traveler's home country, a passport, a driver's license, and a travel policy that covers each driver.

CAR TRAVEL

Highways are well paved. Interstate highways—limited-access, multilane highways whose numbers are prefixed by "I–"—are the fastest routes. Interstates with three-digit numbers encircle urban areas, which may have other limited-access expressways, freeways, and parkways as well. Tolls may be levied on limited-access highways. So-called U.S. highways and state highways are not necessarily limited-access but may have several lanes.

Along larger highways, roadside stops with rest rooms, fast-food restaurants, and sundries stores are well spaced. State police and tow trucks patrol major highways and lend assistance. If your car breaks down on an interstate, pull onto the shoulder and wait for help, or have your passengers wait while you walk to an emergency phone. If you carry a cell phone, dial *55, noting your location on the small green roadside mileage markers.

Driving in the United States is on the right. Do **obey speed limits** posted along roads and highways. Watch for lower limits in small towns and on back roads. California requires front-seat passengers to wear seat belts. On weekdays between 6 and 10 AM and again between 4 and 7 PM **expect heavy traffic.** To encourage carpooling, some freeways have special lanes for so-called high-occupancy vehicles (HOV)—cars carrying more than one passenger.

In California you may turn right at a red light after stopping if there is no oncoming traffic unless a sign forbids you to do so. When in doubt, wait for the green. Be alert for one-way streets, "no left turn" intersections, and blocks closed to car traffic. Bookstores, gas stations, convenience stores, and rest stops sell maps (about $3) and multiregion road atlases (about $10). *For more information on driving in California, see Car Travel, above.*

CONSULATES AND EMBASSIES

➤ AUSTRALIA: ⊠ Century Plaza Towers, 2049 Century Park E, 19th floor, Los Angeles 90067, ☎ 310/229–4800; ⊠ 625 Market St., Suite 200, San Francisco 94105, ☎ 415/536–1970.

➤ CANADA: ⊠ 550 S. Hope St., 9th floor, Los Angeles 90071–2627, ☎ 213/346–2701.

➤ NEW ZEALAND: ⊠ 12400 Wilshire Blvd., Suite 1150, Los Angeles 90025, ☎ 310/207–1605; ⊠ Box 330455, San Francisco 94133–0455, ☎ 415/399–1255.

➤ UNITED KINGDOM: ⊠ 11766 Wilshire Blvd., Suite 400, Los Angeles 90025, ☎ 310/477–3322; ⊠ 1 Sansome St., Suite 850, San Francisco 94104, ☎ 415/981–3030.

CURRENCY

The dollar is the basic unit of U.S. currency. It has 100 cents. Coins include the copper penny (1¢); the silvery nickel (5¢), dime (10¢), quarter (25¢), and half-dollar (50¢); and the golden $1 coin, replacing a now-rare silver dollar. Bills are denominated $1, $5, $10, $20, $50, and $100, all green and identical in size; designs vary. The exchange rate at press time was US$1.46 per British pound, $.64 per Canadian dollar, $.54 per Australian dollar, and $.45 per New Zealand dollar.

ELECTRICITY

The U.S. standard is AC, 110 volts/60 cycles. Plugs have two flat pins set parallel to each other.

EMERGENCIES

For police, fire, or ambulance, **dial 911** (0 in rural areas).

INSURANCE

Britons and Australians need extra medical coverage when traveling overseas.

➤ INSURANCE INFORMATION: In the United Kingdom: **Association of British Insurers** (⊠ 51–55 Gresham St., London EC2V 7HQ, ☎ 020/7600–3333, FAX 020/7696–8999, WEB www.abi.org.uk). In Australia: **Insurance Council of Australia** (⊠ Level 3, 56 Pitt St., Sydney NSW 2000, ☎ 03/9614–1077, FAX 03/9614–7924). In Canada: **RBC Insurance** (⊠ 6880 Financial Dr., Mississauga, Ontario L5N 7Y5, ☎ 905/816–2400 or 800/668–4342 in Canada, FAX 905/816–2498, WEB www.royalbank.com). In New Zealand: **Insurance Council of New Zealand** (⊠ Box 474, Wellington, ☎ 04/472–5230, FAX 04/473–3011, WEB www.icnz.org.nz).

MAIL AND SHIPPING

You can buy stamps and aerograms and send letters and parcels in post offices. Stamp-dispensing machines can occasionally be found in airports, bus and train stations, office buildings, drugstores, and the like. You can also deposit mail in the stout, dark blue steel bins at strategic locations everywhere and in the mail chutes of large buildings; pickup schedules are posted.

For mail sent within the United States, you need a 37¢ stamp for first-class letters weighing up to 1 ounce (23¢ for each additional ounce) and 23¢ for postcards. You pay 80¢ for 1-ounce airmail letters and 70¢ for airmail postcards to most other countries; to Canada and Mexico, you need a 60¢ stamp for a 1-ounce letter and 50¢ for a postcard. An aerogram—a single sheet of lightweight blue paper that folds into its own envelope, stamped for overseas airmail—costs 70¢.

To receive mail on the road, have it sent c/o General Delivery at your destination's main post office (use the correct five-digit zip code). You must pick up mail in person within 30 days and show a driver's license or passport.

PASSPORTS AND VISAS

When traveling internationally, **carry your passport** even if you don't need one (it's always the best form of ID) and **make two photocopies of the data page** (one for someone at home and another for you, carried separately from your passport). If you lose your passport, promptly call the nearest embassy or consulate and the local police.

Visitor visas are not necessary for Canadian citizens, or for citizens of Australia and the United Kingdom who are staying fewer than 90 days.

➤ AUSTRALIAN CITIZENS: **Australian State Passport Office** (☎ 131–232, WEB www.passports.gov.au). **United States Consulate General** (✉ MLC Centre, 19–29 Martin Pl., 59th floor, Sydney, NSW 2000, ☎ 02/9373–9200; 1902/941–641 for fee-based visa-inquiry line, WEB www.usis-australia. gov/index.html).

➤ CANADIAN CITIZENS: **Passport Office** (☎ 819/994–3500; 800/567–6868 in Canada; to mail in applications: ✉ Department of Foreign Affairs and International Trade, Ottawa, Ontario K1A 0G3, ☎ 819/994–3500 or 800/ 567–6868, WEB www.dfait-maeci.gc. ca/passport).

➤ NEW ZEALAND CITIZENS: **New Zealand Passport Office** (☎ 04/474–8100 or 0800/22–5050). **Embassy of the United States** (✉ 29 Fitzherbert Terr., Thorndon, Wellington, ☎ 04/ 462–6000, WEB usembassy.org.nz). **U.S. Consulate General** (✉ Citibank Bldg., 23 Customs St. E, 3rd floor, Auckland, ☎ 09/303–2724, WEB usembassy. org.nz).

➤ U.K. CITIZENS: **London Passport Office** (☎ 0870/521–0410, WEB www. passport.gov.uk). **U.S. Consulate General** (✉ Queen's House, 14 Queen St., Belfast, Northern Ireland BT1 6EQ, ☎ 028/9032–8239, WEB www. usembassy.org.uk). **U.S. Embassy** (enclose a SASE to ✉ Consular Information Unit, 24 Grosvenor Sq., London W1 1AE, for general information; ✉ Visa Branch, 5 Upper Grosvenor St., London W1A 2JB, to submit an application via mail; ☎ 09068/200– 290 for recorded visa information; 09055/444–546 for operator service, both with per-minute charges; WEB www.usembassy.org.uk).

TELEPHONES

All U.S. telephone numbers consist of a three-digit area code and a seven-digit local number. Within most local calling areas, dial only the seven-digit number. Within some area codes, you must dial "1" first for calls outside the local area. To call between area-code regions, dial "1" then all 10 digits; the same goes for calls to numbers prefixed by "800," "888," and "877"—all toll-free. For calls to numbers preceded by "900" you must pay—usually dearly.

For international calls, dial "011" followed by the country code and the local number. For help, dial "0" and ask for an overseas operator. The country code is 61 for Australia, 64 for New Zealand, 44 for the United Kingdom. Calling Canada is the same as calling within the United States. Most local phone books list country codes and U.S. area codes. The country code for the United States is 1.

For operator assistance, dial "0." To obtain someone's phone number, call directory assistance, 555–1212 or occasionally 411 (free at public phones). To have the person you're calling foot the bill, phone collect; dial "0" instead of "1" before the 10-digit number.

At pay phones, instructions are usually posted. Usually you insert coins in a slot (10¢–50¢ for local calls) and wait for a steady tone before dialing. When you call long-distance, the operator will tell you how much to insert; prepaid phone cards, widely available in various denominations, are easier. Call the number on the back, punch in the card's personal identification number when prompted, then dial your number.

Competitive long-distance carriers make calling within the United States relatively convenient and let you avoid hotel surcharges. By dialing an 800 number, you can get connected to the long-distance company of your choice.

➤ LONG-DISTANCE CARRIERS: **AT&T** (☎ 800/225–5288). **MCI** (☎ 800/ 888–8000). **Sprint** (☎ 800/366– 2255).

LODGING

The lodgings we list are the cream of the crop in each price category. We always list the facilities that are available, but we don't specify whether they cost extra. When pricing accommodations, always ask what's included and what costs extra. Properties indicated by a ×⌨ are lodging establishments whose restaurant warrants a special trip.

Assume that hotels operate on the **European Plan** (EP, with no meals) unless we specify that they use the **Continental Plan** (CP, with a Continental breakfast), **Modified American Plan** (MAP, with breakfast and dinner), or the **Full American Plan** (FAP, with all meals).

PRICES

Properties are assigned price categories based on the range from their least-expensive standard double room at high season (excluding holidays) to the most expensive.

CATEGORY	COST*
$$$$	over $225
$$$	$160–$225
$$	$100–$159
$	under $100

All prices are for a standard double room, excluding tax.

Hotel taxes vary from city to city, but the average is around 10%, with higher rates in major urban areas.

APARTMENT AND VILLA RENTALS

If you want a home base that's roomy enough for a family and comes with cooking facilities, **consider a furnished rental.** These can save you money, especially if you're traveling with a group. Home-exchange directories sometimes list rentals as well as exchanges.

➤ INTERNATIONAL AGENTS: **Hideaways International** (✉ 767 Islington St., Portsmouth, NH 03801, ☎ 603/430–4433 or 800/843–4433, FAX 603/430–4444, WEB www.hideaways.com; membership $129). **Vacation Home Rentals Worldwide** (✉ 235 Kensington Ave., Norwood, NJ 07648, ☎ 201/767–9393 or 800/633–3284, FAX 201/767–5510, WEB www.vhrww.com).

CAMPING

California offers numerous camping options, from family campgrounds with all the amenities to secluded hike-in campsites with no facilities. Some are operated by the state, others are on federal land, and still others are private. Rules vary for each. You can camp anywhere in a National Forest, but in a National Park, you must use only specific sites. Whenever possible, **book well in advance,** especially if your trip will be in summer or on a weekend. Contact the National Parks Reservation Service to reserve a campsite in a national park. Reserveamerica and ReserveUSA handle reservations for many of the campgrounds in California state parks and in areas administered by the U.S. Forest Service and the U.S. Army Corps of Engineers. On their Web sites you can search for locations, view campground maps, check availability, learn rules and regulations, and find driving directions.

➤ INFORMATION: **California Travel Parks Association** (✉ Box 5648, Auburn, CA 95604, ☎ 530/885–1124, FAX 530/823–6331).

➤ RESERVATIONS: **National Parks Reservation Service** (☎ 800/436–7275 or 800/365–2267, WEB reservations.nps.gov). **ReserveAmerica/ReserveUSA** (✉ ☎ 877/444-6777 for U.S. Forest Service and U.S. Army Corps of Engineers camping facilities; 800/444–7275 for California state parks, WEB www.reserveamerica.com or www.reserveusa.com).

HOME EXCHANGES

If you would like to exchange your home for someone else's, **join a home-exchange organization,** which will send you its updated listings of available exchanges for a year and will include your own listing in at least one of them. It's up to you to make specific arrangements.

➤ EXCHANGE CLUBS: **HomeLink International** (✉ Box 47747, Tampa, FL 33647, ☎ 813/975–9825 or 800/638–3841, FAX 813/910–8144, WEB www.homelink.org; $98 per year). **Intervac U.S.** (✉ 30 Corte San Fernando, Tiburon, CA 94920, ☎ 800/756–4663, FAX 415/435–7440, WEB www.intervacus.com; $90 yearly fee for a listing, on-line access, and a catalog; $50 without catalog).

HOSTELS

No matter what your age, you can **save on lodging costs by staying at hostels.** In some 5,000 locations in more than 70 countries around the world, Hostelling International (HI), the umbrella group for a number of national youth-hostel associations, offers single-sex, dorm-style beds and, at many hostels, rooms for couples and family accommodations. Membership in any HI national hostel association, open to travelers of all ages, allows you to stay in HI-affiliated hostels at member rates; one-year membership is about $25 for adults (C$26.75 in Canada, £13 in the United Kingdom, $30 in Australia, and $30 in New Zealand); hostels run about $10–$30 per night. Members have priority if the hostel is full; they're also eligible for discounts around the world, even on rail and bus travel in some countries.

➤ ORGANIZATIONS: **Australian Youth Hostel Association** (✉ 10 Mallett St., Camperdown, NSW 2050, Australia, ☎ 02/9565-1699, FAX 02/9565-1325, WEB www.yha.com.au). **Hostelling International—American Youth Hostels** (✉ 733 15th St. NW, Suite 840, Washington, DC 20005, ☎ 202/783-6161, FAX 202/783-6171, WEB www.hiayh.org). **Hostelling International—Canada** (✉ 400-205 Catherine St., Ottawa, Ontario K2P 1C3, ☎ 613/237-7884 or 800/663-5777, FAX 613/237-7868, WEB www.hostellingintl.ca). **Youth Hostel Association of England and Wales** (✉ Dimple Rd., Matlock, Derbyshire DE4 3YH, ☎ 0870/870-8808, FAX 0169/592-702, WEB www.yha.org.uk). **Youth Hostels Association of New Zealand** (✉ Box 436, Christchurch, ☎ 03/379-9970, FAX 03/365-4476, WEB www.yha.org.nz).

HOTELS

Most major hotel chains are represented in California. All hotels listed have private bath unless otherwise noted. Make any special needs known when you book your reservation. Guarantee your room with a credit card, or many hotels will automatically cancel your reservations if you don't show up by 4 PM. Many hotels, like airlines, overbook. It is best to reconfirm your reservation directly with the hotel on the morning of your arrival date.

➤ TOLL-FREE NUMBERS: **Best Western** (☎ 800/528-1234, WEB www.bestwestern.com). **Choice** (☎ 800/424-6423, WEB www.hotelchoice.com). **Clarion** (☎ 800/424-6423, WEB www.choicehotels.com). **Colony** (☎ 800/777-1700, WEB www.colony.com). **Comfort** (☎ 800/424-6423, WEB www.choicehotels.com). **Days Inn** (☎ 800/325-2525, WEB www.daysinn.com). **Doubletree and Red Lion Hotels** (☎ 800/222-8733, WEB www.hilton.com). **Embassy Suites** (☎ 800/362-2779, WEB www.embassysuites.com). **Fairfield Inn** (☎ 800/228-2800, WEB www.marriott.com). **Hilton** (☎ 800/445-8667, WEB www.hilton.com). **Holiday Inn** (☎ 800/465-4329, WEB www.sixcontinentshotels.com). **Howard Johnson** (☎ 800/654-4656, WEB www.hojo.com). **Hyatt Hotels & Resorts** (☎ 800/233-1234, WEB www.hyatt.com). **Inter-Continental** (☎ 800/327-0200, WEB www.intercontinental.com). **La Quinta** (☎ 800/531-5900, WEB www.laquinta.com). **Marriott** (☎ 800/228-9290, WEB www.marriott.com). **Nikko Hotels International** (☎ 800/645-5687, WEB www.nikkohotels.com). **Omni** (☎ 800/843-6664, WEB www.omnihotels.com). **Quality Inn** (☎ 800/424-6423, WEB www.choicehotels.com). **Radisson** (☎ 800/333-3333, WEB www.radisson.com). **Ramada** (☎ 800/228-2828, WEB www.ramada.com). **Renaissance Hotels & Resorts** (☎ 800/468-3571, WEB www.renaissancehotels.com). **Ritz-Carlton** (☎ 800/241-3333, WEB www.ritzcarlton.com). **Sheraton** (☎ 800/325-3535, WEB www.starwood.com). **Sleep Inn** (☎ 800/424-6423, WEB www.choicehotels.com). **Westin Hotels & Resorts** (☎ 800/228-3000, WEB www.westin.com). **Wyndham Hotels & Resorts** (☎ 800/822-4200, WEB www.wyndham.com).

MEDIA

California's major daily newspapers, the *Los Angeles Times,* the *San Diego Union-Tribune,* and the *San Francisco Chronicle,* maintain up-to-the-minute Web sites. The state's weekly newspapers are a great source of arts and entertainment information, from what shows are on the boards to who's playing the clubs. Visit the Web sites of the *L.A. Weekly,* the *San Diego Reader,* the *San Francisco Bay Guardian,* the *San Jose Metro* (MetroActive), and *SF Weekly* for the latest info on events in your destination.

➤ WEB SITES: *L.A. Weekly* (WEB www. laweekly.com). *Los Angeles Times* (WEB www.latimes.com). MetroActive (WEB www.metroactive.com). *San Diego Reader* (WEB www.sdreader. com). *San Diego Union–Tribune* (WEB www.signonsandiego.com). *San Francisco Bay Guardian* (WEB www. sfbayguardian.com). *San Francisco Chronicle* (WEB www.sfchron.com). *SF Weekly* (WEB www.sfweekly.com).

MONEY MATTERS

Los Angeles and San Francisco tend to be expensive cities to visit, and rates at coastal and desert resorts are almost as high. A day's admission to a major theme park can run upwards of $40 a head, hotel rates average $150–$250 a night (though you can find cheaper places), and dinners at even moderately priced restaurants often cost $20–$40 per person. Costs in the Gold Country, the far north, and the Death Valley/Mojave Desert region are considerably less—many fine Gold Country B&Bs charge around $100 a night, and some motels in the far north and the Mojave charge $50–$70.

Prices throughout this guide are given for adults only; however, reduced fees are almost always available for children, students, and senior citizens. For information on taxes, *see* Taxes, *below.*

ATMS

ATMs are readily available throughout California. If you withdraw cash from a bank other than your own, expect to pay a fee of up to $2.50. If you're going to very remote areas of the mountains or deserts, take some extra cash with you or find out ahead of time if you can pay with credit cards.

CREDIT CARDS

Throughout this guide, the following abbreviations are used: **AE,** American Express; **D,** Discover; **DC,** Diners Club; **MC,** MasterCard; and **V,** Visa.

➤ REPORTING LOST CARDS: **American Express** (☎ 800/441–0519). **Discover** (☎ 800/347–2683). **Diners Club** (☎ 800/234–6377). **MasterCard** (☎ 800/ 622–7747). **Visa** (☎ 800/847–2911).

NATIONAL PARKS

Look into discount passes to save money on park entrance fees. For $50, the National Parks Pass admits you (and any passengers in your private vehicle) to all national parks, monuments, and recreation areas, as well as other sites run by the National Park Service, for a year. (In parks that charge per person, the pass admits you, your spouse and children, and your parents, when you arrive together.) Camping and parking are extra. The $15 Golden Eagle Pass, a hologram you affix to your National Parks Pass, functions as an upgrade, granting entry to all sites run by the NPS, the U.S. Fish and Wildlife Service, the U.S. Forest Service, and the Bureau of Land Management (BLM). The upgrade, which expires with the parks pass, is sold by most national-park, Fish-and-Wildlife, and BLM fee stations. A percentage of the proceeds from pass sales funds National Parks projects.

Both the Golden Age Passport ($10), for U.S. citizens or permanent residents who are 62 and older, and the Golden Access Passport (free), for those with disabilities, entitle holders (and any passengers in their private vehicles) to lifetime free entry to all national parks, plus 50% off fees for the use of many park facilities and services. (The discount doesn't always apply to companions.) To obtain them, you must show proof of age and of U.S. citizenship or permanent residency—such as a U.S. passport, driver's license, or birth certificate—and, if requesting Golden Access, proof of disability. The Golden Age and Golden Access passes, as well as the National Parks Pass, are available at any NPS-run site that charges an entrance fee. The National Parks Pass is also available by mail and via the Internet.

➤ INFORMATION: **National Park Foundation** (⊠ 1101 17th St. NW, Suite 1102, Washington, DC 20036, ☎ 202/785–4500, WEB www. nationalparks.org). **National Park Service** (⊠ National Park Service/ Department of Interior, 1849 C St. NW, Washington, DC 20240, ☎ 202/208–4747, WEB www.nps.gov). **National Parks Conservation Association** (⊠ 1300 19th St. NW, Suite 300, Washington, DC 20036, ☎ 202/223–6722, WEB www.npca.org.)

➤ PASSES BY MAIL: **National Park Foundation** (WEB www.nationalparks. org). **National Parks Pass** (⊠ 27540 Ave. Mentry, Valencia, CA 91355, ☎ 888/GO–PARKS or 888/467–2757, WEB www.nationalparks.org); include a check or money order payable to the National Park Service for the pass, plus $3.95 for shipping and handling.

OUTDOORS AND SPORTS

In California you can scale high peaks, hike through sequoia groves, fish, bike, sail, dive, ski, or golf. Whatever sport you love, you can do it in California.

FISHING

You'll need a license to fish in California. State residents pay $29 ($4.75 for senior citizens), but nonresidents are charged $77.75 for a one-year license or $28 for a 10-day license. Both residents and nonresidents can purchase a two-day license for $10.50. The no-frills site of the California Department of Fish and Game provides information on fishing zones, licenses, and schedules.

➤ INFORMATION: **Department of Fish and Game** (⊠ 3211 S St., Sacramento 95816, ☎ 916/227–2244 or 916/227–2242, WEB www.dfg.ca.gov).

STATE PARKS

➤ INFORMATION: **California State Park System** (⊠ Dept. of Parks and Recreation, Box 942896, Sacramento 94296, ☎ 916/653–6995, info@ parks.ca.gov, WEB www.parks.ca.gov).

PACKING

When packing for a California vacation, **prepare for changes in temperature.** Take along sweaters, jackets, and clothes for layering as your best insurance for coping with variations in temperature. **Know that San Francisco and other coastal towns can be chilly** at any time of the year, especially in summer when the fog descends in the afternoon. Always tuck in a bathing suit; many lodgings have pools, spas, and saunas. Casual dressing is a hallmark of the California lifestyle, but in the evening men will need a jacket and tie at more formal restaurants, and women will be most comfortable in something dressier than sightseeing garb. Check *Fodor's How to Pack* (available in bookstores everywhere) for more tips.

In your carry-on luggage, **pack an extra pair of eyeglasses or contact lenses and enough of any medication you take** to last a few days longer than the entire trip. You may also ask your doctor to write a spare prescription using the drug's generic name, since brand names may vary from country to country. In luggage to be checked, **never pack prescription drugs or valuables.** To avoid customs delays, carry medications in their original packaging. And don't forget to carry with you the addresses of offices that handle refunds of lost traveler's checks.

CHECKING LUGGAGE

How many carry-on bags you can bring with you is up to the airline. Most allow two, but not always, so make sure that everything you carry aboard will fit under your seat or in the overhead bin, and get to the gate early. Note that if you have a seat at the back of the plane, you'll probably board first, while the overhead bins are still empty.

If you are flying internationally, note that baggage allowances may be determined not by piece but by weight—generally 88 pounds (40 kilograms) in first class, 66 pounds (30 kilograms) in business class, and 44 pounds (20 kilograms) in economy.

Airline liability for baggage is limited to $1,250 per person on flights within the United States. On international flights it amounts to $9.07 per pound or $20 per kilogram for checked baggage (roughly $640 per 70-pound bag) and $400 per passenger for unchecked baggage. You can buy additional coverage at check-in for about $10 per $1,000 of coverage, but it excludes a rather extensive list of items, shown on your airline ticket.

Before departure, **itemize your bags' contents** and their worth, and label the bags with your name, address, and phone number. (If you use your home address, cover it so potential thieves can't see it readily.) Inside each bag, **pack a copy of your itinerary.** At check-in, **make sure that each bag is correctly tagged** with the destination airport's three-letter code. If your bags arrive damaged or fail to arrive at all, file a written report with the airline before leaving the airport.

SENIOR-CITIZEN TRAVEL

To qualify for age-related discounts, **mention your senior-citizen status up front** when booking hotel reservations (not when checking out) and before you're seated in restaurants (not when paying the bill). When renting a car, ask about promotional car-rental discounts, which can be cheaper than senior-citizen rates.

➤ EDUCATIONAL PROGRAMS: **Elderhostel** (✉ 11 Ave. de Lafayette, Boston, MA 02111-1746, ☎ 877/426–8056, FAX 877/426–2166, WEB www.elderhostel.org). **Interhostel** (✉ University of New Hampshire, 6 Garrison Ave., Durham, NH 03824, ☎ 603/862–1147 or 800/733–9753, FAX 603/862–1113, WEB www.learn.unh.edu).

SMOKING

Smoking is illegal in all California bars and restaurants. Though some bar owners have built outdoor patios or smoking rooms, others have refused to comply. This law is typically not well enforced, so take your cues from the locals. Hotels and motels are also decreasing their inventory of smoking rooms; inquire at the time you book your reservation if any are available. In addition, there is a selective tax on cigarettes sold in California, and prices can be as high as $4.50 per pack. You might want to bring a carton from home.

TAXES

Sales tax in California varies from about 7¼% to 8½% and applies to all purchases except for prepackaged food; restaurant food is taxed. Airlines include departure taxes in the price of the ticket.

TELEPHONES

Pay phones cost 35¢ in California.

TIME

California is in the Pacific time zone. Pacific daylight saving time is in effect from early April through late October; Pacific standard time the rest of the year. Clocks are set ahead one hour when daylight saving time begins, back one hour when it ends.

TIPPING

At restaurants, a 15% tip is standard for waiters; up to 20% may be expected at more expensive establishments. The same goes for taxi drivers, bartenders, and hairdressers. Coat-check operators usually expect $1; bellhops and porters should get $1–$2 per bag; hotel maids in upscale hotels should get about $2 per day of your stay. A concierge typically receives a tip of $5–$10, with an additional gratuity for special services or favors.

On package tours, conductors and drivers usually get $1 per person from the group as a whole; check whether this has already been figured into your cost. For local sightseeing tours, you may individually tip the driver-guide 10%–15% if he or she has been helpful or informative. Ushers in theaters do not expect tips.

TRAIN TRAVEL

Amtrak's *California Zephyr* train from Chicago via Denver terminates in Oakland. The *Coast Starlight* train travels between southern California and the state of Washington. The *Sunset Limited* heads west from Florida through New Orleans and Texas to Los Angeles.

➤ TRAIN INFORMATION: **Amtrak** (☎ 800/872–7245, WEB www.amtrak.com).

VISITOR INFORMATION

For general information about California, contact the California Division of Tourism. For the numbers of regional and city visitors bureaus and chambers of commerce *see* the A to Z section at the end of each chapter.

➤ TOURIST INFORMATION: **California Division of Tourism** (✉ 1102 Q St., Sacramento, CA 95814, ☎ 916/322–2881 or 800/862–2543, FAX 916/322–3402, WEB www.gocalif.ca.gov).

➤ IN THE U.K.: **California Tourist Office** (✉ ABC California, Box 35, Abingdon, Oxfordshire OX14 4TB, ☎ 0891/200–278, FAX 020/7242–2838).

WEB SITES

Do check out the World Wide Web when planning your trip. You'll find everything from weather forecasts to virtual tours of famous cities. Be sure to **visit Fodors.com** (www.fodors.com), a complete travel-planning site. You can research prices and book plane tickets, hotel rooms, rental cars, vacation packages, and more. In addition, you can post your pressing questions in the Travel Talk section and, in the site's Rants & Raves section, read comments about some of the restaurants and hotels in this book—and chime in yourself. Other planning tools include a currency converter and weather reports, and there are loads of links to travel resources.

The California Division of Tourism Web site has travel tips, events calendars, and other resources, and the site will link you—via the Regions icon—to the Web sites of city and regional tourism offices and attractions. The California Parks Department site has the lowdown on state-run parks and other recreational areas. A must-visit for outdoors and adventure travel enthusiasts, the Great Outdoor Recreation Page is arranged into easily navigated categories. The site of the Wine Institute, which is based in San Francisco, provides events listings and detailed information about the California wine industry and has links to the home pages of regional wine associations.

➤ WEB SITES: **California Division of Tourism** (WEB www.gocalif.ca.gov).

California Parks Department (WEB www.parks.ca.gov). **Great Outdoor Recreation Page** (WEB www.gorp.com). **Wine Institute** (WEB www.wineinstitute.org).

WHEN TO GO

Any time of the year is the right time to go to California. It's such a large state that when it's too hot in the southern parts, all you need do is head north for cooler temperatures. There won't be skiable snow in the mountains between Easter and Thanksgiving. It's likely to be too hot to enjoy Palm Springs or Death Valley in the summer. But San Francisco, Los Angeles, and San Diego are pleasant year-round.

CLIMATE

The climate varies amazingly in California, not only over distances of several hundred miles but occasionally within an hour's drive. A foggy, cool August day in San Francisco makes you grateful for a sweater, tweed jacket, or light wool coat. Head north 50 mi to the Napa Valley to check out the wine country, and you'll probably wear short sleeves and thin cottons.

Nighttime temperatures may vary greatly from daytime temperatures. Take Sacramento, a city that is at sea level but in California's Central Valley. In the summer afternoons can be very warm, in the 90s and occasionally more than 100°F. But the nights cool down, the temperature often dropping by 30 degrees.

Because the weather is so varied throughout the state, it's hard to generalize much about it. Rain comes in the winter, with snow at higher elevations. Summers are dry everywhere. As a rule, compared to the coastal areas, which are cool year-round, inland regions are warmer in summer and cooler in winter. As you climb into the mountains, the climate varies more distinctly with the seasons: winter brings snow, autumn is crisp, spring is variable, and summer is clear and warm, with only an occasional thundershower.

➤ FORECASTS: **Weather Channel Connection** (☎ 900/932–8437, 95¢ per minute from a Touch-Tone phone, WEB www.weather.com).

LOS ANGELES

Jan.	64F	18C	May	72F	22C	Sept.	81F	27C
	44	7		53	12		60	16
Feb.	64F	18C	June	76F	24C	Oct.	76F	24C
	46	8		57	14		55	13
Mar.	66F	19C	July	81F	27C	Nov.	71F	22C
	48	9		60	16		48	9
Apr.	70F	21C	Aug.	82F	28C	Dec.	66F	19C
	51	11		62	17		46	8

SAN DIEGO

Jan.	62F	17C	May	66F	19C	Sept.	73F	23C
	46	8		55	13		62	17
Feb.	62F	17C	June	69F	21C	Oct.	71F	22C
	48	9		59	15		57	14
Mar.	64F	18C	July	73F	23C	Nov.	69F	21C
	50	10		62	17		51	11
Apr.	66F	19C	Aug.	73F	23C	Dec.	64F	18C
	53	12		64	18		48	9

SAN FRANCISCO

Jan.	55F	13C	May	66F	19C	Sept.	73F	23C
	41	5		48	9		51	11
Feb.	59F	15C	June	69F	21C	Oct.	69F	21C
	42	6		51	11		50	10
Mar.	60F	16C	July	69F	21C	Nov.	64F	18C
	44	7		51	11		44	7
Apr.	62F	17C	Aug.	69F	21C	Dec.	57F	14C
	46	8		53	12		42	6

FESTIVALS AND SEASONAL EVENTS

➤ JANUARY: Palm Springs's annual **Nortel Networks International Film Festival** (☎ 800/927–7256) showcases the best of international cinema, with more than 100 screenings, lectures, and workshops. In Pasadena the annual **Tournament of Roses Parade** (☎ 626/449–7673) takes place on New Year's Day, with lavish flower-decked floats, marching bands, and equestrian teams, followed by the Rose Bowl game.

➤ FEBRUARY: The legendary **AT&T Pebble Beach National Pro-Am** (formerly the Bing Crosby Pro-Am) golf tournament (☎ 831/649–1533) begins in late January and ends in early February. San Francisco's Chinatown is the scene of parades and noisy fireworks, all part of a several-day **Chinese New Year celebration** (415/391–9680). Los Angeles also has a **Chinese New Year Parade** (☎ 213/617–0396). Indio's **Riverside County Fair and National Date Festival** (☎ 760/863–8247 or 800/811–3247) is an exotic event with an *Arabian Nights* theme; camel and ostrich races, date exhibits, and tastings are among the draws.

➤ MARCH: **Snowfest** in North Lake Tahoe (☎ 530/581–1283) is the largest winter carnival in the West, with skiing, food, fireworks, parades, and live music. The finest female golfers in the world compete for the richest purse on the LPGA circuit at the **Nabisco Championship** (☎ 760/324–4546), in Rancho Mirage. The **Mendocino/Fort Bragg Whale Festival** (☎ 800/726–2780) includes whale-watching excursions, marine art exhibits, wine and beer tastings, crafts displays, and a chowder contest.

➤ APRIL: The **Cherry Blossom Festival** (☎ 415/563–2313), an elaborate presentation of Japanese culture and customs, winds up with a colorful parade through San Francisco's Japantown. The **Toyota Grand Prix** (☎ 562/436–9953), in Long Beach, the largest street race in North America, draws top competitors from all over the world.

➤ MAY: Oxnard celebrates its big cash crop at the **California Strawberry Festival** (☎ 805/385–7545), with exhibitors preparing the fruit in every imaginable form—shortcake, jam, tarts, and pizza. Inspired by Mark Twain's story "The Notorious Jumping Frog of Calaveras County," the **Jumping Frog Jubilee** (☎ 209/736–2561), in Angels Camp, is for frogs and trainers who take their competition seriously. Sacramento hosts the four-day **Sacramento Jazz Jubilee** (☎ 916/372–5277); the late-May event is the world's largest Dixieland festival, with 125 bands from around the world. Thousands sign up to run the **San Francisco Bay to Breakers Race** (☎ 415/359–2707), a 7½-mi route from the bay side to the ocean side that's a hallowed San Francisco tradition. The **Santa Ysabel Art Festival** (☎ 760/765–1676) is a mountain art celebration with works by 50 San Diego area painters, sculptors, and fiber artists, plus a poetry fair and jazz and classical music.

➤ JUNE: Starting in late May and running into early June is a national ceramics competition and exhibition called **Feats of Clay,** in the historic Gladding-McBean factory in Lincoln (☎ 916/645–9713). The **Christopher Street West Gay & Lesbian Pride Festival** (☎ 323/969–8302) celebrates the diversity of the gay and lesbian community in West Hollywood with a parade, music, dancing, food, and merchandise. The **Napa Valley Wine Auction,** in St. Helena, is accompanied by open houses and a wine tasting. Preregistration by fax in early March is required (☎ 800/982–1371, FAX 707/963–3488). During the latter part of June, Ojai hosts a noted outdoor **classical music festival** (☎ 805/646–2094).

➤ JULY: During the first weekend in July Pasadena City Hall Plaza hosts the **Chalk It Up Festival.** Artists use the pavement as their canvas to create masterpieces that wash away when festivities have come to a close. There are also musical performances and exotic dining kiosks. The proceeds benefit arts and homeless organizations of the Light-Bringer Project (☎ 626/440–7379). During the three weeks of the **Carmel Bach Festival** (☎ 831/624–2046), the works of Johann Sebastian Bach and 18th-century contemporaries are performed; events include concerts, recitals, and seminars. During the last full weekend in July, Gilroy, the self-styled Garlic Capital of the World, self-styled "garlic capital of the world," celebrates its smelly but delicious product with the **Gilroy Garlic Festival** (☎ 408/842–1625), featuring such unusual concoctions as garlic ice cream. Late July through early August the **California Mid-State Fair** (805/239–0655) takes place in Paso Robles. Nearly a quarter-million people show up to see wine competitions, musical performances, carnival fun, and agricultural exhibits.

➤ AUGUST: The **Cabrillo Music Festival** (☎ 831/426–6966), in Santa Cruz, one of the longest-running contemporary orchestral festivals, brings in American and other composers for two weeks in early August. The **California State Fair** (☎ 916/263–3247) showcases the state's agricultural side, with a rodeo, horse racing, a carnival, and big-name entertainment. It runs 18 days from August to Labor Day in Sacramento. Santa Barbara's **Old Spanish Days' Fiesta** (☎ 805/962–8101) is a five-day citywide celebration held Wednesday through Sunday the first week in August. Two Mexican marketplaces, costumed dancers and singers, a carnival, and a rodeo entertain fiesta goers, and there are two parades, including the nation's largest all-equestrian parade, with horseback riders and 19th-century carriages.

➤ SEPTEMBER: On Catalina Island the **Pottery & Tile Extravaganza** (☎ 213/510–2414) showcases unique tile and pottery from private collections. There are displays, walking tours, demonstrations, and lectures. The **San Francisco Blues Festival** (☎ 415/979–5588) is held at Fort Mason in late September. The **Los Angeles County Fair** (☎ 909/623–3111), in Pomona, is the largest county fair in the world. It hosts entertainment, exhibits, livestock, horse racing, food, and more.

➤ OCTOBER: The **Grand National Rodeo, Horse, and Stock Show** (☎ 414/404–4100), at San Francisco's

Cow Palace, is a 10-day world-class competition straddling the end of October and the beginning of November. Near San Luis Obispo, speakers and poets gather for readings on the beach, seminars, a banquet, and a book signing at the **Pismo Beach Clam Festival** (☎ 805/773–4382), on the Central Coast. Restaurants along Pomeroy Avenue engage in a competition for the best clam chowder. The **Tor House Fall Festival** (☎ 831/624–1813) honors the late poet Robinson Jeffers, an area resident for many years.

➤ NOVEMBER: The **Death Valley '49er Encampment,** at Furnace Creek, commemorates the historic crossing of Death Valley in 1849, with a fiddlers' contest and an art show (☎ 760/786–2331). Pasadena's **Doo Dah Parade** (☎ 626/440–7379), a fun-filled spoof of the annual Rose Parade, brings out partiers such as the Lounge Lizards, who dress as reptiles and lip-synch to Frank Sinatra favorites, and West Hollywood men in cheerleader drag.

➤ DECEMBER: For the **Newport Harbor Christmas Boat Parade,** in Newport Beach (☎ 949/729–4400), more than 200 festooned boats glide through the harbor nightly December 17–23. In early December the **Miners' Christmas Celebration** in Columbia (☎ 209/536–1672), is an extravaganza of costumed carolers and children's piñatas. Related events include a Victorian Christmas feast at the City Hotel, lamplight tours, and Las Posados Nativity Procession. The internationally acclaimed **El Teatro Campesino** (☎ 831/623–2444) annually stages its nativity play *La Virgen del Tepeyac* in the Mission San Juan Bautista.

1   DESTINATION: CALIFORNIA

Restless Nirvana

What's Where

Pleasures and Pastimes

Fodor's Choice

Great Itineraries

Books and Movies

RESTLESS NIRVANA

COASTAL CALIFORNIA began its migration from somewhere far to the south millions of years ago. It's still moving north along the San Andreas Fault, but you have plenty of time for a visit before Santa Monica hits the Arctic Circle. If you've heard predictions that some of the state may fall into the Pacific, take the long view and consider that much of California has been in and out of the ocean throughout its history. The forces that raised its mountains and formed the Central Valley are still at work.

Upheaval has always been a fact of life in California—below ground and above. Floods, earthquakes, racial strife, immigration woes, and Hollywood scandals have been par for the course. Still, few states have grown as rapidly as California, which had a population of about 7 million as World War II came to a close and is now the home of more than 34 million people. For tourists, too, the Golden State has too many positives to be written off: dramatic coastline; rugged desert and mountain regions; Hollywood glitz and Palm Springs glamour; a potpourri of Pacific Rim, European, and Latin American influences; and a fabled history as a conduit for fame and fortune, hope and renewal.

California has always been a place where initiative—as opposed to class, family, or other connections—is honored above all else. The state has lured assertive types who metaphorically or otherwise have come seeking gold—in the Sacramento foothills, in Hollywood, and, more recently, in Silicon Valley. To be sure, not everyone achieves the mythical California dream—like the gold rush of an earlier era, the boom of the dot-com revolution has gone bust—but neither is it totally an illusion. The sense of infinite possibility, as much a by-product of the state's varied and striking land forms as media hype, is what most tourists notice on their first trip. It's why so many return—sometimes forever.

More so than most of its residents are willing to admit, California is a land of contradictions. Take for instance two volumes that can be found in many local libraries, books about the historic chain of 21 California missions established by Spanish Catholic priests, most notably Father Junípero Serra. One book is titled *California's Missions: Their Romance and Beauty*. Its author details Serra's strategy "to convert and civilize the Indians" who resided in late-18th-century California. The other tome, *The Missions of California: A Legacy of Genocide,* disputes the contentions of "mission apologists" and illustrates how on the physical and spiritual levels the mission system "was the first disaster for the Indian population of California" (the second being the gold rush of the mid-1800s).

The truth? It's likely somewhere in between, though recent scholarship has tended to show Serra and other missionaries in a less than favorable light. The treatment of other groups—from the Chinese who came to mine and build the railroads to Mexican farmworkers—has been equally problematic through the years. The scapegoating of foreigners—often by second-generation Californians with no sense of the irony of their protestations—is a cyclical blot on the state's conscience.

Right from the beginning California has seemed always to be in the thick of one controversy or another, whether over land rights, race relations, energy usage, or personal morality. This may be because of the state's great size and diversity, both geographic and demographic. Economic, political, and social circumstances here are more complex than they are in many other states in the union because California has a more diverse population than most other areas of the country. In any case, as with the taxpayer revolts of the 1970s and 1980s, the immigration debate, and managed health care, Californians by choice or by necessity tend to face issues head-on.

CALIFORNIA IS A RESTLESS nirvana. The sun shines, and all is beautiful; then the earth shakes, and all is shattered. It's time to rebuild. And the state bounces back—San Francisco from the 1906 and 1989 quakes, Los Angeles from ones in 1971 and 1994, much of the state from incredible flooding in 1997 and El Niño–induced storms of 1998. Billions were made during the cold war defense boom; then communism collapsed, military bases closed, and unemployment skyrocketed. It was time to diversify, and the state did, making overtures to Asia and Latin America and cultivating a huge technology industry. In a land of such duality, reality is a matter of opinion—which is why the cinema, an enterprise based wholly on the manipulation of reality, is the perfect signature industry for the state.

Tourists find that although the state (like most movies) isn't perfect, it's a source of endless diversion, natural and man-made. "Wow!" is a word you hear often here—at Half Dome in Yosemite, during the simulated earthquake at Universal Studios, driving through the Mojave Desert, or walking among the redwoods of Humboldt County. If Texans like things big and New Yorkers like a little style, what delights Californians most is drama—indoors or out.

California is too big, too diverse, too full of charming surprises to be a single state. You do not visit just one California—you choose a particular California. If you are looking for natural beauty, the Big Sur coastline isn't a bad place to start, but it's only one gem on a long, long list. If you favor worldly pleasures, San Francisco and the Wine Country beckon. Sybarites needing a fix are well advised to head to Palm Springs. Aficionados of the edgy love L.A. Wherever you go in the Golden State, there's plenty to fall in love with: very few go home unsmitten.

WHAT'S WHERE

Though most people mentally divide California into a northern and a southern region, the state might just as easily be conceived of as three long strips of land: coastal, central, and eastern. Roughly from Susanville in the far north to Kernville on the southeast fringes of the Central Valley, the state is divided north to south by the mighty Sierra Nevada. Likewise, along many stretches closer to the Pacific Ocean,

the Coast ranges separate the shore towns and cities from the interior of the state. Few roads cross the mountains, and those that do can be narrow and twisting, so getting from points west to points east or vice versa in central California often involves long, circuitous drives. Along the coast or through the central zone that parallels the coast, the north–south drive is long but direct.

California's biggest cities—Los Angeles, San Diego, and San Francisco—are all on the coast. San Diego is 136 mi south of Los Angeles on I–5, and San Francisco is 380 mi north of Los Angeles (I–5 to I–580 east to I–80 east). I–5 is the quickest route between Los Angeles and the San Francisco Bay Area, but many tourists travel the coastal route—a combination of U.S. 101 and Highway 1 (the Pacific Coast Highway)—between Los Angeles and San Francisco, making stops at Santa Barbara, Hearst Castle®, Big Sur, the Monterey Peninsula, and other points along the way.

The Far North
One of California's best-kept secrets is its far northeast corner. Away from the coast and north of Sacramento and the Gold Country via I–5, this is a region of soaring mountain peaks, wild rivers brimming with fish, and almost infinite recreational possibilities. The earth's molten inner cauldron shaped the far north, whose landscape is defined by reminders of ancient volcanic activity. Most notable is Mt. Shasta, a dormant volcano that tops 14,000 ft. Eerie folklore surrounds the peak, but its size and beauty are fantastical enough. Tramping up it in summer and schussing down it in winter are two of the joys of being here. Anglers and boaters flock to Lake Shasta for its many watery diversions, including houseboating. At Lassen Volcanic National Park steam is the theme, and hot springs, steam vents, and mud pots await discovery by hikers with a sense of wonder.

The North Coast
Migrating whales and other sea mammals swim past the dramatic bluffs of the 400 mi of shoreline between the Oregon state line and San Francisco. Redwood-studded Highway 1 travels close to the coast; U.S. 101 parallels the highway inland a bit. California's north coast is a place for retreat, for restoring the soul. But although its pleasures are low-key, they are

hardly unrefined. Elegant country inns, cozy Victorian B&Bs, and rustic lodges provide comfortable bases for touring. The architecture of Mendocino and other towns along the coast reflects the New England origins of their founders. But before the easterners, before the missionaries and the Hispanic settlers—even before the Native Americans—there was the land and its beauty. The north coast's majestic redwoods inspire awe, even reverence. If no gold rush had built San Francisco, if Los Angeles were still a bunch of orange groves in search of a freeway, this glory would still be worth the trip.

San Francisco

I–80 ends its westward jaunt across the United States in the country's most popular tourist destination, San Francisco. The graceful Golden Gate Bridge (a conduit for U.S. 101) provides access from the north, and U.S. 101 and I–280 are the routes into the city from the south. This is, arguably, the most beautiful city in the United States and one of the most beautiful in the world. Here you can rub elbows with those lucky enough to live here in the city's cable cars and stroll along thoroughfares like Lombard Street—the crookedest street in the United States—or lively Market Street. But sightseeing is only part of the San Francisco experience. The essence of the city is the diversity of its people. When you cross between neighborhoods—bohemian yet ethnic North Beach, busy and crowded Chinatown, prosperous Pacific Heights, transporting Japantown, the Castro with its gay denizens, the Haight with its countercultural legacy—you know it.

The Wine Country

America's answer to Tuscany, the wine country looks and feels like its Italian counterpart, complete with gentle green hills and a soft coastal climate. The wine-centered life in Napa and Sonoma counties makes them a vibrant destination for food and wine lovers. Don't think that you need a cultivated palate to enjoy yourself here, however. Local wine makers happily educate the uninitiated during tours and in their tasting rooms. If you're lucky, you might arrive in time to see the grape harvest, but whenever you visit, you will be greeted by row upon row of vines and wonderful food in scores of superb restaurants. You can get to the wine country by heading from San Francisco across the Golden Gate Bridge on U.S. 101, then east on Highway 37 and north on Highway 121. Do some sightseeing between wine tastings. The towns and countryside are gorgeous. Sonoma's historic Mission San Francisco Solano reflects the Spanish influence, but you'll find Victorian gems as well.

Sacramento and the Gold Country

California's capital, Sacramento, is 87 mi northeast of San Francisco on I–80, which continues into the northern part of the Gold Country in the Sierra Nevada foothills. Highway 49 travels north–south through the Gold Country. This is where modern-day California began, along the American River on a winter's day in 1848, when James Marshall first glimpsed something shiny in the bottom of a ditch. Besides making California, gold made Sacramento, paying for the state capitol. Many a museum and historic site commemorate the gold rush—reenactors make it come alive at Coloma's Marshall Gold Discovery State Historic Park, and mining towns have been gussied up. Sacramento's California State Railroad Museum is a must for train buffs.

Lake Tahoe

The largest alpine lake in North America lies 198 mi east of San Francisco via I–80 or U.S. 50. Deep, clear, intensely blue-green, and surrounded by forests, this lake straddling the California–Nevada border is one of North America's prettiest. That strict environmental controls have kept it pristine is no small feat, considering its popularity. If you're staying on the California side, you can golf, fish, hike, or ski at Squaw Valley USA. Pop in to see Vikingsholm, an authentic replica of a 1,200-year-old Viking castle, built in 1929 on the shore of jewel-like Emerald Bay. On the Nevada side gambling is king and casinos abound, but once you leave the bright lights of the gaming tables, natural wonders surround you again. Summer is generally cooler here than in the Sierra Nevada foothills, and the clean mountain air is bracingly crisp.

The Peninsula and South Bay

San Francisco lies at the tip of an approximately 35-mi peninsula bounded by San Francisco Bay on the east and the

Pacific Ocean on the west. Highway 1 runs down the rugged coast past Half Moon Bay to Año Nuevo State Reserve, while I–280 or U.S. 101 runs down the interior Peninsula through congested Silicon Valley to San Jose and the South Bay. In the prosperous interior Peninsula and South Bay cultural institutions glitter—from Stanford University's Iris and B. Gerald Cantor Center for Visual Arts to San Jose's Tech Museum of Innovation—and fine dining is abundant in cities such as Palo Alto. For quieter pursuits take the coast route and go tidepooling at Pescadero State Beach.

The Central Valley

The Central Valley, one of the world's most fertile agricultural zones, is California's heartland. I–5 runs north–south through the region, but the more scenic route is Highway 99, which runs more or less parallel to the interstate but farther east. This sunbaked region—whose anchors are Stockton in the north and Bakersfield, 226 mi to the south—contains a wealth of rivers, lakes, and waterways. The sun and the water nurture vineyards, dairy farms, orchards, fields, and pastures that stretch to the horizon. California's farm country is a face of the state worth knowing. The vast agricultural tracts of the valley can be beautiful, and markets and festivals celebrating their bounty are numerous. Munch on fresh strawberries and other fruit sold up and down the valley at roadside stands, and when you're fortified, take in attractions ranging from Victorian houses to the whitewater of the Kern River.

The Southern Sierra

The highlight for many California travelers is a visit to one of the national parks in the southern portion of the Sierra Nevada. At Yosemite, Kings Canyon, and Sequoia national parks, nature has outdone itself, carving magnificent glacial valleys out of a landscape sized for titans. Yosemite Valley is 214 mi southeast of San Francisco via I–80 to I–580 to I–205 to Highway 120; it's 330 mi northeast of Los Angeles via I–5 to Highway 99 to Highway 41. Grant Grove in Kings Canyon National Park is about 150 mi south of Yosemite Valley via Highway 41 to Highway 180. In summer and early fall (or whenever snows aren't blocking the Tioga Pass), you can continue east from Yosemite National Park on Highway 120 to see Mono Lake's tufa towers, resembling a giant's fingers. The Mammoth Lakes area, with skiing in winter and many outdoor sports in summer, is south of Mono Lake on U.S. 395.

Death Valley and the Mojave Desert

East of the Sierra Nevada, Death Valley is a 200-mi drive south of Mammoth Lakes through the forested Owens Valley via U.S. 395 and Highway 190. If you stay on U.S. 395 instead of taking the Death Valley turnoff, you will reach the Mojave Desert after another 80 mi. Interstates 15 and 40 cross the Mojave Desert east–west. For the discerning a trip to Death Valley and the Mojave Desert is a journey through the great empty spaces of a stirring wilderness with a colorful past. You can see history's trailings at the Mojave Desert's Calico Ghost Town, once a wealthy silver-mining center, and at the Harmony Borax Works in Death Valley. If it's vast scenery you're looking for, check out the sand dunes near Stovepipe Wells Village, the brilliantly colored Artists Palette, and the magnificently panoramic Dante's View, in Death Valley National Park, or the Trona Pinnacles, Red Rock Canyon State Park, or the Mojave National Preserve, all in the Mojave Desert.

Monterey Bay

Monterey Bay forms a crescent that begins near Santa Cruz, to the north, and ends near Carmel, to the south. Highway 1 follows this crescent; U.S. 101 travels inland a bit; and Highway 68 and Highway 156 connect U.S. 101 and Highway 1. For many the coast here is California at its best. The things that make the state so wonderful to visit converge here—from history, on view at the Carmel Mission, to natural splendor, unforgettable on 17-Mile Drive, to Pebble Beach, where golfing pilgrims come to perform their devotions. The coastal towns will charm you with pretty streets, great food, and occasional quirkiness. John Steinbeck immortalized Monterey's rough-and-tumble Cannery Row in his 1945 novel of the same name. Today the sardine canneries are gone, and the fantastic Monterey Bay Aquarium, re-creating the local marine habitat, stands on a street that Steinbeck would hardly recognize.

The Central Coast

The spectacular Central Coast stretches from Big Sur to Santa Barbara, with Highway 1 threading through a staggeringly scenic landscape between friendly small towns. The curving road demands an unhurried pace, but even if it didn't, you'd find yourself stopping often to take in the scenery. Wild Big Sur gives way to the hills above San Simeon, where newspaper baron William Randolph Hearst's Hearst Castle® sprawls above the sea. Farther south the velvety Coastal Range rises east of Highway 1; to the west the land drops precipitously into the Pacific, which spreads as far as the eye can see in stupendous vistas. Santa Barbara manages to blend sophistication and tranquillity, stimulation and repose, in perfect doses. Mission Santa Barbara is just one of the graceful sights here.

Los Angeles

It's hard to be indifferent to Los Angeles. Love it or hate it, it is a city unlike any other. You can reach the provocative megalopolis via I–5 from the north and south, via U.S. 101 also from the north, and via I–10 and I–210 from the east. Start forming your own impressions along Sunset Boulevard, which will take you through Hollywood all the way to the sea, through the city's multiple layers, including wealthy Bel-Air and Beverly Hills. When you get to the ocean, you can experience the beach culture that's so integral to life here. Check out Venice Boardwalk, where Angelenos surf, skate, bodybuild, and stage some of the wackiest street theater in the galaxy. Also pure L.A. are Universal Studios Hollywood, where you can live the movies, and Mann's Chinese Theatre, where celebrities press their hands and other body parts into cement for posterity. Amid the freeways and smog, the city's numerous beauty spots—the Getty Center, Griffith Park—sometimes come as a surprise. When you're ready for shopping (high-class or funky), nightlife (from alternative to swing), or dining (from tacos to Asian-fusion), you'll find it in L.A.

Orange County

If Orange County issued its own license plates, the slogan would have to read: "Quintessential Southern California." South of Los Angeles along I–5, I–405, and Highway 1, the glitz of L.A. drops off, and what remains is an uncomplicated lifestyle with a serious focus on fun in the sun. The biggest draw for most nonresidents is Disneyland, the only one of Disney's magic kingdoms built while Walt was still alive. With its diminutive, idyllic Main Street and moss-hung New Orleans Square, it has an ineffable charm, a certain softness that you don't find in other Disney realms. For thrill rides, head for another vintage theme park nearby, Knott's Berry Farm, whose founder also created the boysenberry. Meanwhile, the Pacific exerts an irresistible pull. Some neighborhoods in Orange County's beach towns could be sisters to Beverly Hills and are well worth a gawk. Between Laguna Beach and Huntington Beach are dozens of spots where you can work on your tan or learn to surf among masters.

San Diego

It's a straight shot 124 mi south on I–5 from Los Angeles to sunny, friendly San Diego, which is 18 mi north of Tijuana, Mexico, via I–5 or I–805. California's beautiful southernmost city is its most laid-back, rendered deliciously mellow, almost like a small town, by near-perfect weather. The sun shines perpetually on lush Balboa Park, on Shamu's SeaWorld home, on Pacific-pounded strands like Mission Beach and pretty La Jolla's Black's Beach. Residents of the San Diego Zoo, one of the world's greats, are at home in the warm climate. But it's not all fun in the sun here—there's history, too. The first of California's 21 Spanish missions was established in San Diego in 1769, and the city's links to its Spanish past remain strong. For natural beauty head east on I–8 into San Diego County, which covers a vast area, extending from the coast to mile-high mountains to a point near sea level farther east in the desert.

Palm Springs and the Southern California Desert

Striking scenery and the therapeutic benefits of a warm, arid climate lure people to the southern California desert. The drive from Los Angeles to Palm Springs and its neighbors—Palm Desert, Rancho Mirage, Indian Wells—takes about two hours via I–10 to Highway 111 going east. From San Diego I–15 connects with the Pomona Freeway (Highway 60), leading to I–10. In these improbably situated bastions of wealth and celebrity, Jaguars and Bentleys are as common as driveways, and worldly pleasure rules. So does golf. The area has close to 100 golf courses, many of them scenic stunners—no wonder thousands of people come to these parts just to hone their golf or tennis skills. Life here can be downright sybaritic, even if you're just on vacation, and especially if you're staying at one of the many luxury resorts, where you can guiltlessly abandon yourself to total pampering. Connecting with the desert's wild beauty at Joshua Tree National Park, Anza-Borrego Desert State Park, and the Salton Sea can be restorative as well. The slanting late-afternoon or early morning light sets the desert aglow, lending an otherworldly texture to the place.

PLEASURES AND PASTIMES

Beaches

With 1,264 mi of coastline, California is well supplied with beaches. You can walk, sun, and snooze on them, watch seabirds and hunt for shells, dig clams, or spot seals and sea otters at play. From December through March you can witness the migrations of gray whales. Access to beaches in California is generally excellent. The state park system includes many fine beaches, and ocean-side communities maintain public beaches. Through the work of the California Coastal Commission, many stretches of private property that would otherwise seal off a beach from outsiders have public-access paths. But you can't always swim at these beaches. From San Francisco northward the water is too cold for all but the hardiest souls. Even along the southern half of the coast some beaches are too dangerous for swimming because of the undertow. Look for signs and postings and take them seriously.

Dining

California's name has come to signify a certain type of healthful, sophisticated cuisine made from local ingredients, creatively combined and served in often stunning presentations. The state is also the North American edge of the Pacific Rim, so Asian flavors and preparations are part of the scene. San Francisco and Los Angeles contain top-notch restaurants—an expensive meal at one of these culinary shrines is often the high point of a trip to California. The wine country north of San Francisco is also known for superb restaurants, as is the city of Santa Barbara. In coastal areas most menus usually include some seafood fresh off the boat. Don't neglect the state's many ethnic eateries—among them Mexican, Chinese, Japanese, Scandinavian, Italian, French, Belgian, Vietnamese, English, Thai, and German.

Golf

Golf is a year-round sport in California. Pebble Beach and the Palm Springs desert resorts have the most famous links, but there are championship courses all over the state. *See* Outdoor Activities and Sports in each chapter for listings of area courses.

National and State Parks

There are eight national parks in California, some of them among the country's most awe-inspiring: Death Valley, Joshua Tree, Lassen Volcanic, Redwood, Sequoia, Kings Canyon, Yosemite, and the Channel Islands. National monuments include Cabrillo, in San Diego, and Muir Woods, north of San Francisco. California has three national recreation areas: Golden Gate, with 87,000 acres both north and south of the Golden Gate Bridge in San Francisco; the Santa Monica Mountains, with 150,000 acres from Griffith Park in Los Angeles to Point Mugu in Ventura County; and Whiskeytown-Shasta-Trinity, with 240,000 acres, including four major lakes, in the far north. The Point Reyes National Seashore is on a peninsula north of San Francisco.

California's state park system includes more than 200 sites; many are recreational and scenic, others historic or scientific. Among the most popular are Angel Island, in San Francisco Bay, reached by ferry from San Francisco or Tiburon; Anza-Borrego Desert, 600,000 acres northeast of San Diego; Humboldt Redwoods, with its tall trees; Empire Mine, one of the richest mines in the Mother Lode, in Grass Valley; Hearst Castle®, at San Simeon; and Leo Carrillo Beach, north of Malibu, with lively tidal pools and numerous secret coves. Most state parks are open year-round.

Skiing

Snow skiing at Lake Tahoe, Mammoth Mountain area, and elsewhere is generally limited to the period between Thanksgiving and late April, though in years of heavy snowfall skiers can hit some trails as late as July. Other ski options include Lassen Volcanic National Park and Mt. Shasta, in the far north; the San Bernardino Mountains, in southern California; and Badger Pass, in Yosemite National Park.

Water Sports

Swimming, surfing, and scuba diving in the Pacific Ocean are year-round pleasures in the southern part of the state and are seasonal sports on the coast from Santa Cruz northward. Sailboats are available for rent in many places along the coast and inland. River rafting—whitewater and otherwise—canoeing, and kayaking are popular, especially in the northern part of the state.

Wine Tasting

You can visit wineries in many parts of the state, and not only in the Sonoma and Napa valleys. Mendocino County, in the north, and the Monterey Bay and Central Coast regions, farther south, have become major players in the world of high-quality wine. Respected appellations now include the Anderson Valley, Arroyo Seco, the Santa Cruz Mountains, Edna Valley, Santa Ynez Valley, and many more—even the Gold Country is producing wine. Most winegrowing areas publish brochures with lists of local wineries that have tours or tastings. Wineries and good wine stores throughout the state will package your purchases for safe travel or shipping.

FODOR'S CHOICE

Even with so many special places in California, Fodor's writers and editors have their favorites. Here are a few that stand out.

Breathtaking Sights

El Capitan and Half Dome, Yosemite. El Capitan, the world's largest exposed-granite monolith, and Half Dome, rising 4,733 ft above the valley floor with a 2,000-ft cliff on its fractured west side, are nothing short of mesmerizing.

Emerald Bay, Lake Tahoe. Massive glaciers carved this fjordlike bay millions of years ago. Famed for its jewel-like shape and colors, it surrounds Fannette, Tahoe's only island. Survey the glorious scene from the lookout.

Golden Gate Bridge Vista Point, Marin County. On a clear day San Francisco glistens from this vantage point at the bridge's north end.

Huntington Library, Art Gallery, and Gardens, Pasadena. The botanical splendors here include the 12-acre Desert Garden and 1,500 varieties of camellias.

La Jolla Cove at sunset. Always beautiful, it's never more splendid than when the setting sun gilds the cove and backlights the towering palms.

Drives to Remember

Highway 1, Big Sur to San Simeon. This stretch of twisting coastal highway affords some of the world's most renowned ocean vistas.

Highway 49, the Gold Country. California's pioneer past comes to life in the many towns along this 325-mi highway at the base of the Sierra foothills.

Kings Canyon Highway. From late spring to early fall the stretch of Highway 180 in Kings Canyon National Park from Grant Grove to Cedar Grove is spectacular. Peer into the nation's deepest gorge and up to the High Sierra's gorgeous canyons.

Mulholland Drive, Los Angeles. One of L.A.'s most famous thoroughfares winds through the Hollywood Hills and across the spine of the Santa Monica Mountains almost to the Pacific. It's slow going, but the grand homes and the city and San Fernando Valley views are sensational.

17-Mile Drive, Pebble Beach. The wonders are both man-made and natural along this detour from Highway 1 between Pacific Grove and Carmel. Robert Louis Stevenson described the gnarled and twisted Monterey cypresses en route as "ghosts fleeing before the wind."

Historic Buildings

Coit Tower, San Francisco. A monument to the city's volunteer firefighters, the 210-ft-tall art deco tower commands unmatched views of San Francisco Bay. WPA-commissioned murals inside depict Depression-era life in San Francisco.

Hotel del Coronado, San Diego. Coronado's most prominent landmark was the world's first electrically lighted hotel. You'll instantly recognize the cluster of white Victorian buildings with red pitched and turreted roofs.

Mission Santa Barbara. Twin bell towers and Greco-Roman columns and statuary embellish the queen of the California missions. Established in 1786, it's still an active church.

State Capitol, Sacramento. With its lacy plasterwork, the rotunda of this 1869 structure is like a Fabergé egg. The 40-acre Capitol Park outside is one of the state's oldest gardens.

Weaverville Joss House, Weaverville. Chinese miners built this Taoist temple in 1874, and it is still in use today. This piece of California history is filled with intriguing artifacts of the Chinese experience in California.

Hotels

Château du Sureau, Oakhurst. This fairytale castle near Yosemite National Park pampers you with cheerful fires on the hearths and goose-down comforters on the beds. Your palate will be pleased by Erna's Elderberry House restaurant, one of California's best. *$$$$*

Hotel Bel-Air, Bel-Air. This ultraluxurious escape in a secluded wooded canyon feels like a grand country home. To splurge, request a room with its own hot tub on the patio. *$$$$*

Post Ranch Inn, Big Sur. In this indulgent hideaway each room has its own hot tub, stereo, private deck, and massage table—in addition to dizzying Pacific or mountain views. *$$$$*

Ritz-Carlton, Laguna Niguel. Hallmark Ritz-Carlton service and an unrivaled location on the edge of the Pacific have made a star of this grand hotel with the feel of a Mediterranean country villa. *$$$$*

Sherman House, San Francisco. The words *crème de la crème* best describe this French-Italianate mansion in Pacific Heights with a sumptuous European feel. *$$$$*

Hotel Monaco, San Francisco. The whimsical postmodern Monaco stands out for its snappy public areas, comfortable rooms, and devotion to all who cross its threshold. *$$$*

Restaurants

Patina, Hollywood. Here, in one of L.A.'s best restaurants, the spare, elegant room is as beguiling as Joachim Splichal's contemporary cuisine. *$$$$*

George's at the Cove, La Jolla. Come for the splendid cove view in the elegant main dining room and for the wonderful fresh seafood. *$$$–$$$$*

Jardinière, San Francisco. One of the city's most talked-about restaurants is also the hot ticket before symphony, opera, and theater events. Chef Traci Des Jardins provides the creative touch. *$$$–$$$$*

Café Beaujolais, Mendocino. Peaceful, backwoods Mendocino charm pervades this cottage, and the cooking is great, to boot. The cross-cultural menu may include corn crepes filled with barbecued rock shrimp and served with avocado and blood-orange *pico de gallo*. *$$–$$$*

Granita, Malibu. Wolfgang Puck's coastal outpost has striking interior details and a menu that favors seafood, along with the chef's signature California-inspired dishes. *$$–$$$*

Montrio, Monterey. If you like hearty cooking and clean, strong flavors, this European-inspired American bistro, a montage of brick, rawhide, and wrought iron, is the place to go. *$$*

GREAT ITINERARIES

Highlights of California

22 days

California encompasses so many different lands and people that to visit only one area would be to see only a single color in a rainbow. There is something tantalizing about life here that has as much to do with the silence of Yosemite as with the glitz of Hollywood. Tour some of the treasures of California, and you will soon understand why this is the Golden State. *You can split this tour in two, to spend 10 days in northern California (returning to San Francisco after touring Yosemite) or 14 days in southern California (starting your tour in Yosemite).*

Marin and the Wine Country. *2 days.* Head north from San Francisco over the Golden Gate Bridge and start at Point Reyes National Seashore, perhaps the quintessence of northern California's coast. Highway 121 will take you east into Napa County, where you can indulge in an afternoon of wine touring and an excellent evening meal. Driving north and west on Highway 128 you'll enter vineyard-blanketed Sonoma County and run right up against the Pacific Ocean. *Chapters 3 and 5.*

The North Coast. *2 days.* Drive Highway 1 up to Gualala and Mendocino, where the coast becomes tamer but no less striking. Year-round blooms and Victorian buildings filled with shops, restaurants, and B&Bs make Mendocino feel uniquely refined. Continue north past Eureka for a visit to the ancient giants of Redwood National and State Parks. *Chapter 3.*

Shasta and Tahoe. *3 days.* Scenic Highway 299 traverses Trinity National Forest eastward past Weaverville to Redding, north of which is magnificent Shasta—the lake, the mountain, and the caverns. Farther east via Highway 44 lies volcanic, almost lunar, Lassen National Park. Head south on Highway 89 into the Sierra Nevada to reach Lake Tahoe, a glistening blue alpine jewel. Cruise the lake on a sightseeing boat, or try your luck at the casinos on the Nevada side. *Chapters 1 and 7.*

Gold Country. *2 days.* I–80 or U.S. 50 will take you west into the Sierra Nevada foothills of Gold Country. Highway 49 runs through the heart of the territory, past Empire Mine State Historic Park, in Grass Valley, and Marshall Gold Discovery State Historic Park, in Coloma. Detour into Sacramento for a stop at the California State Railroad Museum, then drive southwest on Highways 16 and 49 to Columbia State Historic Park. *Chapter 6.*

Yosemite. *1 day.* From Gold Country Yosemite National Park is only a one- or two-hour drive east on Highway 120 or 140. The incomparable majesty of marvels like Half Dome and the sublime

smell of sweet meadow air make this a world unto itself. Yosemite Valley shelters the park's most picturesque creations: gushing Yosemite Falls, proud and mighty El Capitan, and untamed Bridalveil Falls. *Yosemite National Park in Chapter 10.*

Death Valley and the Mojave Desert. *2 days.* East of the Sierra Nevada, U.S. 395 leads south into Death Valley, where Highway 190 penetrates Death Valley National Park. Explore Scotty's Castle and ponder Badwater, then overnight in the park—it has the most and best accommodations for many miles around. Leaving the park on its east side, take Highway 127 south into the Mojave Desert and drive I–15 west toward Barstow and Victorville. The huge emptiness, geological oddities, and ghost towns are far more exciting than you might imagine. *Chapter 11.*

Palm Springs and Joshua Tree. *2 days.* Return to civilization via Highways 18, 247, and 62, which link Victorville with the desert resort of Palm Springs. Check into a resort and lounge by the pool or play a round of golf, or give your credit card a workout on Palm Canyon Drive. To the east lies Joshua Tree National Park, whose odd namesake shrubs cluster around desert oases. *Chapter 17.*

San Diego. *3 days.* You can make the trip from Palm Springs to San Diego entirely along official scenic routes: Highway 86 south to Highway 78 west to Highway 79 south to I–8 west. It'll take about 2½ hours, which will give you the afternoon to explore Balboa Park. There you can visit more than a dozen museums and art galleries while strolling through the gardens and lawns. Save a whole day for the famed San Diego Zoo. Visit SeaWorld for another adventure into the wild world of animals, meeting hammerhead sharks and starfish along the way. Admire the romantic pueblo architecture of Old Town and the elegant Victorian buildings of the Gaslamp Quarter. *Chapter 16.*

Anaheim. *1 day.* Get up early for the drive up I–5 to Disneyland (about 95 mi). Then step into Walt's fantasia for a day and experience the lightness of pure fun. *Disneyland in Chapter 15.*

Los Angeles. *2 days.* Spend some time soaking up the L.A. culture scene at the

Getty Center and the Museum of Contemporary Art, or hit Rodeo Drive to practice the art of shopping. Don't miss Hollywood's attractions or the Venice boardwalk, and spend an evening strolling the Santa Monica Pier or club-hopping on the Sunset Strip. *Chapter 14.*

Santa Barbara to San Simeon. *2 days.* Framed by ocher mountains and a lapis ocean, Santa Barbara is a pleasant place to shop, eat, and wander along the beach. As you drive the Pacific Coast Highway (Highway 1) northward you'll wind through grassy inland hills past San Luis Obispo to the cool breezes of Morro Bay. A half day at Hearst Castle®, in San Simeon, is a must, as is a drive through Big Sur, whose delicate waterfalls, dense redwood groves, and breathtaking coastal cliffs thrill all who pass this way. *Chapter 13.*

Monterey and Carmel. *1 day.* Earthly and artistic beauty is a way of life in Carmel and Monterey, where the crashing ocean and twisted splendor of cypresses provide a backdrop for galleries, shops, and restaurants. The 17-Mile Drive gives you a glimpse of the mansions and golf courses of Pebble Beach. At the end of your three-week trek through California, you'll find yourself back in San Francisco. *Chapter 12.*

California with Kids

12–15 days

As a real-world land of make-believe, California seems to have been created just for children. Fantasy comes to life in castles, museums, and exotic animals. New fairy tales are created daily in the studios and streets of Hollywood. Check local newspapers for seasonal children's events.

Sacramento. *2 days.* You won't strike it rich in the Gold Country, but you can catch the spirit of the Mother Lode at Marshall Gold Discovery State Historic Park. Along historic Highway 49 towns such as Sutter Creek maintain the charm of the area's colorful past. Save an afternoon to wander the streets of Old Sacramento. Ride a tugboat taxi and marvel at old locomotives in the California State Railroad Museum. *Chapter 6.*

San Francisco. *2 or 3 days.* Seeing the city from a cable car is sure to thrill, and Coit Tower offers a scenic panorama. But high above the bay, the Golden Gate Bridge wins for best photo opportunity. Along the water, sample the chocolates that made Ghirardelli Square famous and bark back at the sea lions lounging at Pier 39. Ride a ferry to Alcatraz to see the island prison. Golden Gate Park's pastures, woods, and water can offer a whole day of entertainment. If the weather doesn't cooperate, head inside to the Exploratorium or California Academy of Sciences for outrageous hands-on exhibits. *Chapter 4.*

San Simeon. *2 or 3 days.* Allow plenty of time to enjoy the Pacific Coast Highway's curves through temperate rain forests and salty seascapes as you drive south from San Francisco. While picnicking atop the craggy cliffs of Big Sur, keep your eyes peeled for otters, seals, and sea lions surfing the waves below. Spend at least one afternoon daydreaming at Hearst Castle®, a fantastical hilltop mansion. The drive from here to Los Angeles is long, so allow ample time. *San Simeon in Chapter 10.*

Los Angeles. *2 or 3 days.* No visit to LA-LA land is complete without a trip to Universal Studios for a behind-the-scenes look at the glamorous world of the movies. Night or day, stargaze for famous names along the Hollywood Walk of Fame. Haven't had your fill of celebrities yet? Seek out the rich and famous in Beverly Hills. Head to the Page Museum at La Brea Tar Pits to visit the onetime digs of woolly mammoths. *Chapter 14.*

Orange County. *2 days.* Disneyland fulfills every kid's dreams. Knott's Berry Farm also offers diversion for the imagination, complete with international cuisine and lively shows re-creating California history. *Chapter 15.*

San Diego. *2 days.* In San Diego your first stop should be the San Diego Zoo. Wander the landscaped grounds, and you're sure to find something you've never seen before, perhaps a two-headed corn snake or an East African bongo. Spend the next day at SeaWorld to see Shamu the killer whale and the world's largest collection of sharks. *Chapter 16.*

BOOKS AND MOVIES

San Francisco

BOOKS

While many novels have San Francisco settings, they don't come any better than *The Maltese Falcon*, by Dashiell Hammett, the founder of the hard-boiled school of detective fiction. First published in 1930, Hammett's books continue to be readily available in new editions, and the details about the fog, the hills, and the once-seedy offices south of Market continue to be accurate.

Another standout is Vikram Seth's *Golden Gate*, a novel in verse about life in San Francisco and Marin County in the early 1980s. Others are John Gregory Dunne's *The Red White and Blue*, Stephen Longstreet's *All or Nothing* and *Our Father's House*, and Alice Adams's *Rich Rewards*. Many of the short stories in Adams's collection, *To See You Again*, have Bay Area settings. *The Joy Luck Club* by Bay Area writer Amy Tan is a novel about four generations of Chinese American women in San Francisco.

Two books that are filled with interesting background information on the city are Richard H. Dillon's *San Francisco: Adventurers and Visionaries* and *San Francisco: As It Is, As It Was*, by Paul C. Johnson and Richard Reinhardt.

For anecdotes, gossip, and the kind of detail that will make you feel almost like a native San Franciscan, get hold of any of the books by the late and much-loved San Francisco *Chronicle* columnist Herb Caen: *Baghdad-by-the-Bay, Only in San Francisco, One Man's San Francisco*, and *San Francisco: City on Golden Hills*. Armistead Maupin's gay-themed soap opera–style *Tales of the City* stories are set in San Francisco; you can read them or watch them on video.

MOVIES

Films shot in San Francisco in the 1990s include *Mrs. Doubtfire, Basic Instinct, The Rock, Metro, The Presidio*, and *The Game*. Among the older films about the city, *San Francisco*, starring Clark Gable and Spencer Tracy, re-creates the 1906 earthquake with outstanding special effects. In *Escape from Alcatraz*, Clint Eastwood plays the prisoner who allegedly escaped from the famous jail on a rock in the San Francisco Bay. Eastwood also starred in the Dirty Harry film series, which takes place around the Bay Area. *The Times of Harvey Milk*, about San Francisco's first openly gay elected official, won the Academy Award for best documentary feature in 1984. Alfred Hitchcock immortalized Mission Dolores and the Golden Gate Bridge in *Vertigo*, the eerie story of a detective with a fear of heights, starring Jimmy Stewart and Kim Novak. A few other noteworthy films shot in San Francisco are *Dark Passage*, with Humphrey Bogart; *Foul Play*, with Chevy Chase and Goldie Hawn; the 1978 remake of *Invasion of the Body Snatchers*; and *Bullitt*, starring Steve McQueen, with a memorable car chase scene down San Francisco's infamous hills.

Los Angeles

BOOKS

Los Angeles: The Enormous Village, 1781–1981, by John D. Weaver, and *Los Angeles: Biography of a City*, by John and LaRee Caughey, will give you a fine background in how Los Angeles came to be the city it is today. The unique social and cultural life of the whole southern California area is explored in *Southern California: An Island on the Land*, by Carey McWilliams.

One of the most outstanding features of Los Angeles is its architecture. *Los Angeles: The Architecture of Four Ecologies*, by Reyner Banham, relates the city's physical environment to its buildings. *Architecture in Los Angeles: A Complete Guide*, by David Gebhard and Robert Winter, is also very useful.

Two controversial books by Mike Davis, *Ecology of Fear: Los Angeles and the Imagination of Disaster* and *City of Quartz: Excavating the Future in Los Angeles*, offer historical analyses of the City of Angels.

Many novels have been written with Los Angeles as the setting. One of the very best, Nathanael West's *Day of the Locust*, was first published in 1939 but still rings true. Budd Schulberg's *What Makes Sammy Run?*, Evelyn Waugh's *The Loved One*, and Joan Didion's *Play It as It Lays* and *The White Album* are unforgettable. Other novels that give a sense of contemporary life in Los Angeles are *Sex and Rage,* by Eve Babitz, and *Less Than Zero,* by Bret Easton Ellis. Raymond Chandler and Ross Macdonald have written many suspense novels with a Los Angeles background.

MOVIES AND TV

Billy Wilder's *Sunset Boulevard* (1950) is a classic portrait of a faded star and her attempt to recapture past glory. Roman Polanski's *Chinatown* (1974), arguably one of the best American films ever made, is a fictional account of the wheeling and dealing that helped make Los Angeles what it is today. Southern California's varied urban and rural landscapes are used to great effect (as is an all-star cast that includes Ethel Merman and Spencer Tracy) in Stanley Kramer's manic *It's a Mad, Mad, Mad, Mad World* (1963). *Rebel Without a Cause* (1955) offers a view from Griffith Observatory in the days before smog. *L.A. Story* (1991), written by and starring Steve Martin, gives a glimpse of modern-day Los Angeles, while *L.A. Confidential* (1997) provides a look at its seedy and salacious past.

San Diego

BOOKS

There is no better way to establish the mood for your visit to Old Town San Diego than by reading Helen Hunt Jackson's 19th-century romantic novel, *Ramona,* a steady seller for decades and still in print. The Casa de Estudillo, in Old Town, has been known for many years as Ramona's Marriage Place because of its close resemblance to the house described in the novel. Richard Henry Dana Jr.'s *Two Years Before the Mast* (1869), based on the author's experiences as a merchant sailor, provides a masculine perspective on early San Diego history.

Other novels with a San Diego backdrop include Raymond Chandler's mystery about the waterfront, *Playback*; Wade Miller's mystery, *On Easy Street;* Eric Higgs's thriller, *A Happy Man;* Tom Wolfe's satire of the La Jolla surfing scene, *The Pump House Gang;* and David Zielinski's modern-day story, *A Genuine Monster.*

MOVIES AND TV

Filmmakers have taken advantage of San Diego's diverse and amiable climate since the dawn of cinema. Westerns, comedy-westerns, and tales of the sea were early staples: *Cupid in Chaps, The Sagebrush Phrenologist,* the 1914 version of *The Virginian,* and Lon Chaney's *Tell It to the Marines* were among the silent films shot in the area. Easy-to-capture outdoor locales have lured many productions south from Hollywood over the years, including the following military-oriented talkies, all or part of which were shot in San Diego: James Cagney's *Here Comes the Navy* (1934), Errol Flynn's *Dive Bomber* (1941), John Wayne's *The Sands of Iwo Jima* (1949), Ronald Reagan's *Hellcats of the Navy* (1956, co-starring Nancy Davis, the future First Lady), Rock Hudson's *Ice Station Zebra* (1967), Tom Cruise's *Top Gun* (1986), Sean Connery's *Hunt for Red October,* Charlie Sheen's *Navy Seals* (1990), and Danny Glover's *Flight of the Intruder* (1991).

In a lighter military vein, the famous talking mule hit the high seas in *Francis Joins the Navy* (1955), in which a very young Clint Eastwood has a bit part. The Tom Hanks–Darryl Hannah hit *Splash* (1984), *Spaceballs* (1987), *Wayne's World II* (1993), and *Mr. Wrong* (1996) are comedies with scenes filmed here. Billy Wilder's *Some Like It Hot* (1959)—starring Marilyn Monroe, Jack Lemmon, and Tony Curtis—takes place at the Hotel del Coronado (standing in for a Miami resort).

The amusing low-budget *Attack of the Killer Tomatoes* (1976) makes good use of local scenery. The producers must have liked what they found in town, as they returned for three sequels: *Return of the Killer Tomatoes* (1988), *Killer Tomatoes Strike Back* (1990), and—proving just how versatile the region is as a film location—*Killer Tomatoes Go to France* (1991).

Television producers zip south for series and made-for-TV movies all the time. The alteration of San Diego's skyline in the 1980s was partially documented on the hit show *Simon & Simon.* San Diego is virtually awash in syndicated productions: *Silk Stalkings, Baywatch, High Tide,* and *Renegade* are among the shows that have been shot here. Reality and cop shows love the area, too: *Unsolved Mysteries, Rescue 911, America's Missing Children, Totally Hidden Video, America's Most Wanted,* and *America's Funniest People* have all taped in San Diego, making it one of the most seen—yet often uncredited—locales in movie and video land.

Around the State

John Steinbeck immortalized the Monterey-Salinas area in numerous books, including *Cannery Row* and *East of Eden*. Joan Didion captured the heat—solar, political, and otherwise—of the Sacramento Delta area in *Run River*. Mark Twain's *Roughing It* and Bret Harte's *The Luck of Roaring Camp* evoke life during the gold rush, and J. S. Holliday's *The World Rushed In* tells the story through excerpts from 49ers' journals and letters. For a window on the past and present of the Central Valley, see *Highway 99: A Literary Journey Through California's Great Central Valley,* edited by Stan Yogi. Marc Reiser's *Cadillac Desert* explores the history and significance of the state's water rights. In her 1903 classic, *Land of Little Rain,* Mary Austin offers a detailed account of the terrain between Death Valley and the High Sierra. For a telling of what befell the Donner Party, see George Stewart's *Ordeal by Hunger,* and for a source on pioneer California, William Brewer's *Up and Down California in 1860–1864* is outstanding. The hardship of life on the desert frontier is depicted in *Borrega Beginnings,* by Phil Brigandi, while the naturalist's appreciation of desert beauty shines through in Joseph Wood Krutch's *The Desert Year.*

John Steinbeck's *East of Eden* was a hit film starring James Dean and later a television movie. Buster Keaton's masterpiece *Steamboat Bill, Jr.* (1928) was shot in Sacramento. The exteriors in Alfred Hitchcock's *Shadow of a Doubt* (1943) were shot in Santa Rosa, and his creepy *The Birds* (1963) was shot in Bodega Bay, along the North Coast. *Shack Out on 101* is a loopy 1950s beware-the-Commies caper also set on the California coast. *Bagdad Café* (1988) captures the tedium of the Mojave Desert.

Erich von Stroheim used a number of northern California locations for his films: *Greed* takes place in San Francisco but includes excursions to Oakland and other points in the East Bay. Carmel is one of the locations for his *Foolish Wives*. The various *Star Trek* movies and Michelangelo Antonioni's *Zabriskie Point* are among the feature films that have made use of the eastern desert region. Initial footage of Sam Peckinpah's western *Ride the High Country* was shot in the Sierra Nevada before his studio yanked him back to southern California, where he blended the original shots with ones of the Santa Monica Mountains and the Hollywood Hills.

2 THE FAR NORTH

INCLUDING LAKE SHASTA,
MOUNT SHASTA, AND LASSEN
VOLCANIC NATIONAL PARK

Soaring mountain peaks, wild rivers
brimming with fish, and almost unlimited
recreational possibilities make the far north
the perfect destination for sports lovers. You
won't find many hot nightspots and cultural
enclaves, but you will find some of the best
hiking and fishing in the state. The region
offers a glimpse of old California—natural,
awesome, and inspiring.

Updated by
Steve Gerace

THE WONDROUS LANDSCAPE of California's northeastern corner, relatively unmarred by development, congestion, and traffic, is the product of volcanic activity. At the southern end of the Cascade Range, Lassen Volcanic National Park is the best place to witness the far north's fascinating geology. Beyond the sulfur vents and bubbling mud pots, the park owes much of its beauty to 10,457-ft Mt. Lassen and 50 wilderness lakes. But the enduring image of the region has to be Mt. Shasta: at 14,162 ft its snowcapped peak is visible for miles, beckoning outdoor adventurers of all kinds. There are many versions of Shasta to enjoy—the mountain, the lake, the river, the town, the dam, and the forest—all named after the Native Americans known as the Shatasla or Sastise who once inhabited the region.

Pleasures and Pastimes

Camping

In the vast expanses of the far north are hundreds of campgrounds: some small and remote with few facilities; others with nearly all the conveniences of home; and still others somewhere in between. Some campgrounds get booked as much as a year in advance for the Fourth of July, although that's not the norm. Still, it's a good idea to make reservations 2–3 months in advance during the peak summer tourist season. You can reserve a site at many of the campgrounds in the region through ReserveAmerica and ReserveUSA (*see* Lodging *in* Smart Travel Tips A to Z).

Dining

Redding, the urban center of the far north, has the greatest selection of restaurants. In the smaller towns cafés and simple restaurants are the rule, though trendy, innovative restaurants have been opening. Dress is always informal in the far north.

CATEGORY	COST*
$$$$	over $30
$$$	$22–$30
$$	$15–$21
$	under $15

*per person for a main course at dinner, excluding tip and 8¼% tax

Lodging

Aside from the large chain hotels and motels in the Redding area, most accommodations in the far north blend rusticity, simplicity, and coziness. That's just fine with most folks, as they spend much of their time outdoors anyway. Wilderness resorts close in fall and reopen after the snow season ends in May.

CATEGORY	COST*
$$$$	over $225
$$$	$160–$225
$$	$100–$159
$	under $100

*All prices are for a standard double room, excluding 8% tax.

Outdoor Activities and Sports

In the far north almost all the attractions are found outdoors. Cascading rivers, lakes of many shapes and sizes, and bountiful streams draw sportfishers. Hikers, backpackers, hunters, skiers, and other outdoor enthusiasts flock to Castle Crags State Park and Lassen Volcanic National Park. In winter the uncrowded slopes of Mt. Shasta tempt skiers. Pristine campgrounds throughout the region make overnighting in the great outdoors a singular pleasure.

Exploring the Far North

The far north encompasses all of four vast counties—Tehama, Shasta, Siskiyou, and Trinity—as well as part of Butte County. The area stretches from the valleys east of the Coast Range to the Nevada border and from the almond and olive orchards north of Sacramento to the Oregon border.

Numbers in the text correspond to numbers in the margin and on the Far North map.

Great Itineraries

IF YOU HAVE 3 DAYS

From I–5 north of Redding, head northeast on Highways 299 and 89 to **McArthur–Burney Falls Memorial State Park** ⑧. To appreciate the falls, take a short stroll to the overlook or hike down for a closer view. Continue north on Highway 89. Long before you arrive in the town of 🖼 **Mount Shasta** ⑦, you will spy the conical peak for which it is named. The central Mount Shasta exit east leads out of town along **Everitt Memorial Highway.** Take this scenic drive, which climbs to almost 8,000 ft. The views of the mountain and the valley below are extraordinary. Stay overnight in town. On the second day head south on I–5 toward **Lake Shasta** ⑤, visible on both sides of the highway. Have a look at **Lake Shasta Caverns** and the **Shasta Dam** ⑨ before heading west on Highway 299 to spend the night in 🖼 **Weaverville** ④ or south on I–5 to overnight in 🖼 **Redding** ③. The next day visit **Whiskeytown-Shasta-Trinity National Recreation Area** and **Weaverville Joss House,** on Highway 299.

IF YOU HAVE 5 OR 6 DAYS

Get a glimpse of the far north's heritage in **Red Bluff** ② before heading north on I–5 to the town of 🖼 **Mount Shasta** ⑦. On day two drop by the Forest Service ranger station to check on trail conditions on the mountain and to pick up maps. Pack a picnic lunch before taking **Everitt Memorial Highway** up the mountain. After exploring the mountain, head south on I–5 and spend the night in 🖼 **Dunsmuir** ⑥ at the **Railroad Car Resort,** where all the accommodations are old cabooses. On your third day take an early morning hike in nearby **Castle Crags State Park.** Continue south on I–5 to **Lake Shasta** ⑤ and tour **Shasta Dam.** Spend the night camping in the area or in 🖼 **Redding** ③. On your fourth morning head west on Highway 299, stopping at **Shasta State Historic Park** on your way to 🖼 **Weaverville** ④. Spend the night there or back in Redding. If you will be leaving the area on your fifth day but have a little time, zip north and visit **Lake Shasta Caverns.** If you're staying and it's between late May and early October, spend the next day and a half exploring **Lassen Volcanic National Park** ⑪. Highway 44 heads east from Redding into the park.

When to Tour the Far North

This region attracts the greatest number of tourists during the summer, which can be dry and scorching in the Sacramento Valley but milder in the mountains to the north and east. The valley around Redding is mild in the winter, with snow country in the higher elevations. In winter Mt. Shasta is a great place for downhill and cross-country skiing—and even ice fishing at the area's many high-elevation lakes. Snow closes the roads to some of the region's most awesome sights, including much of Lassen Volcanic National Park, from October until late May. During the off-season many restaurants and museums here have limited hours, sometimes closing for extended periods.

The Far North

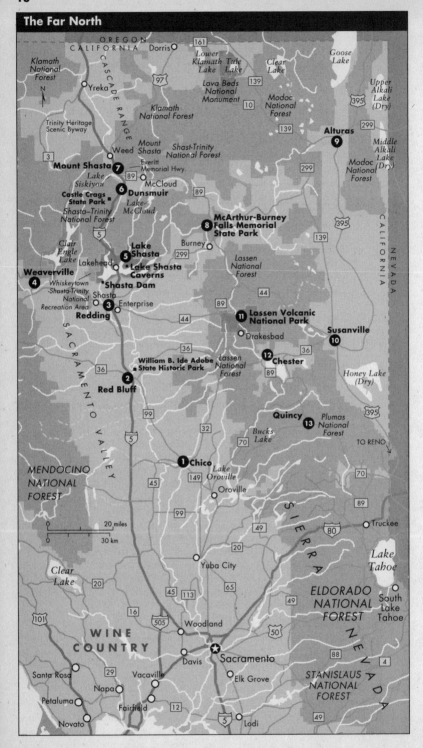

FROM CHICO TO MOUNT SHASTA
Along I–5

The far north is bisected, south to north, by I–5. Along this route you will find historic towns, museums, and state parks. Halfway to the Oregon border is Lake Shasta, a favorite recreation destination, and farther to the north stands the spectacular snowy peak of Mt. Shasta.

Chico

❶ *180 mi from San Francisco, east on I–80, north on I–505 to I–5, and east on Hwy. 32; 86 mi north of Sacramento on Hwy. 99.*

Chico sits just west of Paradise in the Sacramento Valley and offers a welcome break from the monotony of I–5. With California State University at Chico, scores of local artisans, and acres of almond orchards in the mix, the town of 55,000 successfully blends academics, the arts, and agriculture. It has many art galleries, but Chico's true claim to fame is the popular Sierra Nevada Brewery, which keeps locals and beer drinkers across the country happy with its distinctive microbrews.

★ The sprawling 3,670-acre **Bidwell Park** (✉ River Rd. south of Sacramento St., ☎ 530/895–4972), a community green space that straddles Big Chico Creek, is where scenes from *Gone with the Wind* and the 1938 version of *Robin Hood,* starring Errol Flynn, were filmed. It provides the region with a recreational oasis of playgrounds; a golf course; swimming areas; and paved biking, hiking, and in-line skating trails. The third-largest city-run park in the country starts as a slender strip downtown and expands eastward toward the Sierra foothills.

In **Bidwell Mansion State Historic Park** you can take a one-hour tour of approximately 20 of Bidwell Mansion's rooms. Built between 1865 and 1868 by General John Bidwell, the founder of Chico, the mansion was designed by Henry W. Cleaveland, a San Francisco architect. Bidwell and his wife welcomed many distinguished guests to the distinctive pink 26-room Italianate mansion, including President Rutherford B. Hayes, naturalist John Muir, suffragist Susan B. Anthony, and General William T. Sherman. ✉ *525 The Esplanade,* ☎ *530/895–6144.* 🎟 *$1.* ☉ *Daily noon–5, last tour at 4.*

★ The renowned **Sierra Nevada Brewing Company,** one of the pioneers of the microbrewery movement, still has a hands-on approach to beer making that makes touring its sparkling brewery a pleasure. You can enjoy a hearty lunch or dinner in the brewpub, which serves standard pub fare and interesting entrées. There is also a gift shop. The brewery is closed Monday. ✉ *1075 E. 20th St.,* ☎ *530/345–2739,* FAX *530/ 893–9358,* WEB *www.sierranevada.com.* 🎟 *Free.* ☉ *Tours Tues.–Fri. at 2:30, Sat. noon–3 on the ½ hr.*

Dining and Lodging

$–$$ ✕ **Red Tavern.** With its warm, butter-yellow walls and mellow lighting, this is Chico's most refined restaurant. The menu, often inspired by fresh local produce, changes frequently. If you're lucky, it might include lamb chops with a lemon–pine nut crust or stuffed Atlantic salmon with Swiss chard, bacon, and sage butter. Choose from the California wine list or full bar. ✉ *1250 The Esplanade, 95926,* ☎ *530/ 894–3463. AE, MC, V. No lunch.*

$ ✕ **Kramore Inn.** Crepes—from ham and avocado to crab cannelloni— are the inn's specialty. The menu also includes salads, stir-fries, Asian dishes, and pastas. Dinner is served by candlelight. Brunch is available on Sunday from 9 to 2. ✉ *1903 Park Ave.,* ☎ *530/343–3701. AE, D, MC, V.*

$-$$ ☷ **Johnson's Country Inn.** Nestled near an almond orchard five min-
utes from downtown, this Victorian-style farmhouse with a wraparound
veranda is a welcome change from motel row. It is full of antique furnishings and modern conveniences. ⊠ *3935 Morehead Ave., 95928,*
☎ FAX *530/345–7829,* WEB *www.chico.com/johnsonsinn. 4 rooms. AE,
MC, V. BP.*

Shopping

Made in Chico (⊠ 232 Main St., ☎ 530/894–7009) carries Woof and
Poof products and locally made goods, including handwoven scarves,
beautiful pottery, salad dressings, mustards, olives, and almonds. Beautiful custom-made stained, etched, and beveled glass is created at **Need-
ham Studios** (⊠ 237 Broadway, ☎ 530/345–4718). Shop and watch
demonstrations of glass blowing at the **Satava Art Glass Studio** (⊠ 819
Wall St., ☎ 530/345–7985).

Red Bluff

❷ *41 mi north of Chico on I–5.*

Historic Red Bluff is a gateway to Mount Lassen National Park. Established in the mid-19th century as a shipping center and named for
the color of its soil, the town is filled with dozens of restored Victorians, resulting in a downtown that resembles a stage set for a western
movie. It's a great home base for outdoor adventures in the area.

The **Kelly-Griggs House Museum,** a beautifully restored 1880s home,
holds an impressive collection of antique furniture, housewares, and clothing arranged as though a refined Victorian-era family were still in residence. A Venetian glass punch bowl sits on the dining room table. In
the upstairs parlor costumed mannequins seem eerily frozen in time (yes,
this could be the set of a horror film). The museum's collection includes
carved china cabinets and Native American basketry. *Persephone,* the
painting over the fireplace, is by Sarah Brown, daughter of abolition-
ist John Brown, whose family settled in Red Bluff. ⊠ *311 Washington
St.,* ☎ *530/527–1129.* ▤ *Donation suggested.* ☉ *Thurs.–Sun. 1–4.*

William B. Ide Adobe State Historic Park is named for the first and only
president of the short-lived California Republic of 1846. The Bear Flag
Party proclaimed California a sovereign nation, no longer under the
dominion of Mexico, and the republic existed for 25 days before it was
occupied by the United States. The flag concocted for the republic has
survived, with only minor refinements, as California's state flag. The
park's main attraction is an adobe home built in the 1850s and outfitted with period furnishings. There are also a carriage shed, a blacksmith shop, and a small visitor center. Home tours are available on
request. ⊠ *21659 Adobe Rd.,* ☎ *530/529–8599,* WEB *www.ideadobe.
tehama.k12.ca.us.* ▤ *$2 per vehicle.* ☉ *Park and picnic facilities daily
8 AM–sunset.*

Dining and Lodging

$-$$ ✕ **Crystal Steak & Seafood Co.** This place was voted one of the top
28 steak houses in California and no wonder—the meat is tender, flavorful, and cooked to perfection. ⊠ *343 S. Main St.,* ☎ *530/527–0880.
AE, D, MC, V. No lunch.*

$ ✕ **Snack Box.** Unabashedly corny pictures and knickknacks decorate
the renovated Victorian cottage that holds the family-owned Snack Box.
The breakfast and lunch food, however, is perfectly crafted, including
soups, omelets, country-fried steaks, and even simple items such as grilled-
cheese sandwiches. The portions are generous. ⊠ *257 Main St., 1 block
from Kelly-Griggs House Museum,* ☎ *530/529–0227. AE, MC, V. No
dinner.*

$ ⌘ **Lamplighter Lodge.** Simple rooms, some with refrigerators, are available. The pool area is a great place to relax on sweltering summer days. Continental breakfast is included. ✉ *210 S. Main St., 96080,* ☎ *530/527–1150. 50 rooms, 2 suites. Refrigerators (some), microwaves (some), pool. AE, D, MC, V. CP.*

Redding

❸ *32 mi north of Red Bluff on I–5.*

As the largest city in the far north, Redding is an ideal headquarters for exploring the surrounding countryside.

Dining and Lodging

$–$$$ ✕ **Hatch Cover.** This establishment's dark-wood paneling and views of the adjacent Sacramento River create the illusion of dining aboard a ship, especially on the outside deck with its views of Mt. Shasta. The menu emphasizes seafood, but you can also get steaks, chicken, pasta, and combination plates. The appetizer menu is extensive. ✉ *202 Hemsted Dr. (from Cypress Ave. exit off I–5, turn left, then right on Hemsted Dr.),* ☎ *530/223–5606. AE, D, MC, V. No lunch weekends.*

$–$$$ ✕ **Jack's Grill.** Although it's hard to tell from the outside, this steak house and bar is immensely popular for its 16-ounce steaks. Be prepared to eat meat; it's your only choice here. The place is usually jam-packed and noisy. ✉ *1743 California St.,* ☎ *530/241–9705. AE, D, MC, V. Closed Sun. No lunch.*

$–$$ ✕⌘ **The Red Lion.** Landscaped grounds and a large patio area with out-
★ door food service are the highlights here. Rooms are spacious and comfortable. There are irons, ironing boards, and hair dryers in the rooms and video games in the public areas. Waters Seafood Grill is a popular place for locals. Pets are allowed with advance notice. ✉ *1830 Hilltop Dr. (Hwy. 44/299 exit east from I–5), 96002,* ☎ *530/221–8700,* FAX *530/221–0324,* WEB *www.redlion.com. 192 rooms, 2 suites. Restaurant, coffee shop, room service, pool, wading pool, gym, hot tub, bar. AE, D, DC, MC, V.*

$$$–$$$$ ⌘ **Brigadoon Castle Bed & Breakfast.** Fifteen winding miles from I–5 is an 86-acre estate crowned with an Elizabethan-style castle. Marble baths, antiques, and luxurious fabrics make the Brigadoon an elegant retreat. A separate 1,250-square-ft cottage is available. In the game room are a fireplace, a 61-inch satellite, and DIRECTV, and a wall of videos. Evening snacks are included. ✉ *9036 Zogg Mine Rd., Igo 96047,* ☎ *530/396–2785 or 888/343–2836,* FAX *530/396–2784. 4 rooms. Hot tub; no room TVs. AE, MC, V. BP.*

$ ⌘ **Howard Johnson Express.** Here's a budget option off I–5's Cypress exit. There's complimentary coffee. ✉ *2731 Bechelli La.,* ☎ *530/223–1935 or 800/354–5222,* FAX *530/223–1176. 75 rooms, 2 suites. Cable TV with movies, pool. AE, D, MC, V.*

Outdoor Activities and Sports

The **Fly Shop** (✉ 4140 Churn Creek Rd., ☎ 530/222–3555) sells fishing licenses and has information about guides, conditions, and fishing packages.

En Route Six miles west of Redding on Highway 299, **Shasta State Historic Park** (☎ 530/243–8194; ✺ $1) stands where Shasta City thrived in the mid-to late 1800s. Its 19 acres of half-ruined brick buildings and overgrown graveyards, accessed via trails, are a reminder of the glory days of the California gold rush. The former county courthouse building, jail, and gallows have been restored to their 1860s appearance. The Courthouse Museum (Wednesday–Sunday 10–5) now houses a visitor center, information desk, and interactive exhibits, including a storytelling ghost locked in the jail. Art galleries display paintings created between 1850 and 1950. The Blumb Bakery, which operated in Shasta until 1918, has been revived and now offers free samples and period baking demonstrations. The Litsch General Store, in operation from 1850 to 1950, is now a general merchandise museum, with many of the actual items that were sold in the store.

Weaverville

❹ *46 mi west of Redding on Hwy. 299 (called Main St. in town).*

Weaverville is an enjoyable amalgam of gold-rush history and tourist kitsch. Named after John Weaver, who was one of three men who built the first cabin here in 1850, the town has an impressive downtown historic district. It's a popular headquarters for family vacations and biking, hiking, fishing, and gold-panning excursions.

★ Weaverville's real attraction is the **Weaverville Joss House**, a Taoist temple built in 1874 and called Won Lim Miao (The Temple of the Forest Beneath the Clouds) by Chinese miners. The oldest continuously used Chinese temple in California, it attracts worshipers from around the world. With its golden altar, carved wooden canopies, and intriguing artifacts, the Joss House is a piece of California history that can best be appreciated on a guided 40-minute tour. The original temple building and many of its furnishings—some of which had come from China—were burned in 1873, but members of the local Chinese community soon rebuilt it. ✉ *Oregon and Main Sts.,* ☎ *530/623–5284.* 🎫 *Museum free; guided tour $1.* ☉ *June–Aug., daily 10–5; Sept.–May, Wed.–Sun. 10–5.*

The **Trinity County Courthouse** (✉ Court and Main Sts.), built in 1856 as a store, office building, and hotel, was converted to county use in 1865. The Apollo Saloon, in the basement, became the county jail. It is the oldest courthouse still in use in California.

Trinity County Historical Park houses the **Jake Jackson Memorial Museum**, which has a blacksmith shop, a genuine stamp mill from the 1890s that is still in use, and the original jail cells of the Trinity County Courthouse. ✉ *508 Main St.,* ☎ *530/623–5211.* ☉ *May–Oct., daily noon–4; Nov.–Apr., Tues. and Sat. noon–4.*

OFF THE
BEATEN PATH

TRINITY HERITAGE SCENIC BYWAY – This road, shown on many maps as Highway 3, runs north from Weaverville for 120 mi up to its intersection with I-5, south of Yreka. The Trinity Alps and Lewiston Lake, formed by the Trinity Dam, are visible all along this beautiful, forest-lined road, which is often closed during the winter months. As it climbs from 2,000 ft to 6,500 ft, the route for the most part follows a path established by early miners and settlers.

Dining and Lodging

$–$$ ✕ **La Grange Café.** In two brick buildings dating from the 1850s (they're some of the oldest in town), this eatery always has buffalo, venison, pasta, and chicken on its menu. It lists 135 wines, a full premium bar, and farmers' market vegetables when available. La Grange serves plenty of vegetables and is open six days a week for lunch and seven days a week for dinner. ✉ *226 Main St.,* ☎ *530/623–5325. AE, D, MC, V. No lunch Sun.; call for winter hrs.*

$ ✕ **La Casita.** Here you'll find the traditional selection—all the quesadillas (including one with roasted chili peppers), tostadas, enchiladas, tacos, and tamales you could want, many of them available in a vegetarian version. This casual spot is open from late morning through early evening, so it's great for a midafternoon snack. ✉ *254 Main St.,* ☎ *530/623–5797. No credit cards.*

$ 🏠 **Red Hill Motel.** This is the best choice among Weaverville motels. One cozy cabin that has a full kitchen is popular with families. ✉ *Red Hill Rd., Box 234, 96093,* ☎ *530/623–4331,* WEB *www.redhillresorts.com. 4 rooms, 10 cabins. Cable TV. AE, D, MC, V.*

Outdoor Activities and Sports

Below the Lewiston Dam, east of Weaverville on Highway 299, is the **Fly Stretch** of the Trinity River, a world-class fly-fishing area. The **Pine Cove Boat Ramp,** on Lewiston Lake, provides quality fishing access for those with disabilities—decks here are built over prime trout-fishing water. Contact the **Weaverville Ranger Station** (☎ 530/623–2121) for maps and information about hiking trails in the Trinity Alps Wilderness.

Shopping

Hays Bookstore (✉ 106 Main St., ☎ 530/623–2516) is a general bookstore that includes books on the natural history, attractions, and sights of the far north.

Lake Shasta Area

★ ❺ *12 mi north of Redding on I–5.*

Twenty-one varieties of fish—from rainbow trout to salmon—inhabit **Lake Shasta.** The lake region also has the largest nesting population of bald eagles in California. You can rent fishing boats, ski boats, sailboats, canoes, paddleboats, Jet Skis, and windsurfing boards at one of the many marinas and resorts along the 370-mi shoreline. Lake Shasta is known as the houseboat capital of the world.

Stalagmites, stalactites, flowstone deposits, and crystals entice people of all ages to the **Lake Shasta Caverns.** A two-hour tour includes a catamaran ride across the McCloud arm of Lake Shasta and a bus ride up Grey Rock Mountain to the cavern entrance. The caverns are 58°F year-round, making them an enticingly cool retreat on a hot summer day. The high point is the awe-inspiring Cathedral Room. The guides are friendly, enthusiastic, and knowledgeable. A gift shop is open from 8 to 4:30. ✉ *Shasta Caverns Rd. exit from I–5,* ☎ *530/238–2341 or 800/795–2283,* WEB *www.lakeshastacaverns.com.* 💲 *$17, but subject to seasonal changes.* ☉ *Daily 9–4. Tours every ½ hr in summer, spring, and fall.*

Shasta Dam is the second-largest concrete dam in the United States (Grand Coulee in Washington is the largest). At dusk the sight is magical, with Mt. Shasta gleaming above the not-quite-dark water and deer frolicking on the nearby hillside. The dam is lighted after dark, but there is no access from 10 PM to 6 AM. The visitor center has computerized photographic tours of the dam construction, video presentations, fact sheets, and historic displays. The friendly staff is very knowledgeable about the area. ✉ *16349 Shasta Dam Blvd.,* ☎ *530/275–4463,* WEB *www.mp.usbr.gov/ncao.* ☉ *Dam daily 6 AM–10 PM; visitor center weekdays 8:30–4:30, weekends 8:30–5.*

Dining and Camping

$$–$$$ ✕ **Tail o' the Whale.** With a name like this, it's no surprise this restaurant overlooking Lake Shasta has a nautical theme. Seafood, pasta, prime rib, and poultry are the specialties. ✉ *10300 Bridge Bay Rd., Bridge Bay exit from I–5,* ☎ *530/275–3021. D, MC, V.*

⚠ **Antlers Campground.** On a level bluff above the Sacramento Arm of Lake Shasta, this campground stands in oak and pine forest. Some sites are near the lakeshore, but direct access to the water is difficult. The campground is adjacent to Antlers Boat Ramp, and a nearby marina resort has watercraft rentals, on-water fueling, and a small store. Reservations are taken mid-May–early September only. ⊠ *Antlers Rd., 1 mi east of I–5,* ☎ *530/275–8113,* FAX *530/275–8344. 59 sites. Flush toilets, vault toilets, drinking water, fire pits, picnic tables.*

Outdoor Activities and Sports

FISHING

The Fishin' Hole (⊠ 3844 Shasta Dam Blvd., Shasta Lake City, ☎ 530/ 275–4123) is a bait-and-tackle shop just a couple of miles from the lake. It sells fishing licenses and provides information about conditions.

HOUSEBOATING

Houseboats come in all sizes except small. As a rule, rentals are outfitted with cooking utensils, dishes, and most of the equipment you'll need—you just supply the food and the linens. When you rent a houseboat, you will receive a short course in how to maneuver your launch before you set out on your cruise. It's not difficult, as houseboats are slow moving. You can fish, swim, sunbathe on the flat roof, or sit on the deck and watch the world go by. The shoreline of Lake Shasta is beautifully ragged, with countless inlets; it's not hard to find privacy. Expect to spend a minimum of $300 a day for a craft that sleeps six. A three-day, two-night minimum is customary. Prices are often lower during the off-season. The **Shasta Cascade Wonderland Association** (⊠ 1699 Hwy. 273, Anderson 96007, ☎ 530/365–7500 or 800/326–6944) has information on houseboating on Lake Shasta. **Bridge Bay Resort** (⊠ 10300 Bridge Bay Rd., Redding, ☎ 800/752–9669) rents houseboats, Jet Skis, fishing boats, and patio boats.

Dunsmuir

❻ *10 mi south of Mt. Shasta on I–5.*

Castle Crags State Park surrounds the town of Dunsmuir, which was named for a 19th-century Scottish coal baron who offered to build a fountain if the town was renamed in his honor. The town's other major attraction is the Railroad Park Resort, where you can spend the night in restored railcars.

Named for its 6,000-ft glacier-polished crags, which tower over the Sacramento River, **Castle Crags State Park** offers wading and fishing in Castle Creek, hiking in the backcountry, and a view of Mt. Shasta. The crags draw climbers and hikers from around the world. The 4,350-acre park has 28 mi of hiking trails, including a 2¾-mi access trail to **Castle Crags Wilderness,** part of the **Shasta-Trinity National Forest.** There are excellent trails at lower altitudes, along with picnic areas, rest rooms, showers, and campsites. ⊠ ¼ *mi off I–5, 6 mi south of Dunsmuir,* ☎ *530/235–2684.* ☞ *$2 per vehicle (day use).*

Lodging and Camping

$ 🏨 **Railroad Park Resort.** The antique cabooses here were collected over ☺ more than three decades and have been converted into cozy motel rooms in honor of Dunsmuir's railroad legacy. The resort has a vaguely *Orient Express*–style dining room and a lounge fashioned from vintage railcars. The landscaped grounds contain a huge steam engine and a restored water tower. Rooms have satellite TV and coffeemakers. There's also an RV park. ⊠ *100 Railroad Park Rd., 96025,* ☎ *530/ 235–4440 or 800/974–7245,* FAX *530/235–4470,* WEB *www.rrpark.com. 23 cabooses, 4 cabins. Refrigerators, restaurant, pool, hot tub. AE, D, MC, V.*

🏕 **Castle Crags State Park Campground.** This campground stands amid tall evergreens at the base of the towering crags. It's a great base for hiking and rock climbing. The campground can accommodate RVs up to 27 ft long, although there are no hookups. Six environmental sites in relatively undisturbed areas are for tents only. You will need reservations during peak season (late May–early September). *Flush toilets, showers, picnic tables, swimming (river). 76 sites.* ⊠ *15 mi south of Mt. Shasta (Castella exit off I–5),* ☎ *530/235–2684. AE, D, MC, V.*

Mt. Shasta

❼ *34 mi north of Lake Shasta on I–5.*

The crown jewel of the 2.5-million-acre Shasta-Trinity National Forest, Mt. Shasta is popular with day hikers, especially in spring, when the fragrant Shasta lily and other flowers adorn the rocky slopes. A paved road travels only as high as the timberline of this 16-million-year-old dormant volcano, and the final 6,000 ft are a tough climb of rubble, ice, and snow (the summit is perennially ice-packed). Only a hardy few are qualified to make the trek to the top.

The town of Mount Shasta has real character and some fine restaurants. Lovers of the outdoors and backcountry skiers abound, and they are more than willing to offer advice on the most beautiful spots in the region, including out-of-the-way swimming holes, dozens of high mountain lakes, and a challenging 18-hole golf course with 360 degrees of spectacular views.

Dining, Lodging, and Camping

$–$$ ✕ **Lily's.** This restaurant in a white-clapboard home, framed by a picket fence and arched trellis, serves everything from steaks and pastas to Mexican and vegetarian dishes. The tasty salads include the Jalisco—marinated rib-eye steak slices with greens, tomatoes, and Asiago cheese. The *huevos rancheros* (scrambled eggs with salsa) are a delicious choice for brunch. ⊠ *1013 S. Mt. Shasta Blvd.,* ☎ *530/926–3372. AE, D, MC, V.*

$–$$ ✕ **Michael's Restaurant.** Wood paneling, candlelight, and wildlife prints by local artists create an unpretentious backdrop for such favorites as prime rib and Italian specialties such as stuffed calamari, filet mignon, scallopini, and linguine pesto. ⊠ *313 N. Mt. Shasta Blvd.,* ☎ *530/926–5288. AE, D, MC, V. Closed Sun.–Mon.*

$–$$ ✕ **Trinity Café.** This cozy little restaurant has gained popularity in the
★ area with California-style cuisine that changes weekly. Offerings range from roasted duck breast with seared foie gras to grilled ahi on a bed of chard with a red-wine vinaigrette. ⊠ *622 N. Mt. Shasta Blvd.,* ☎ *530/926–6200. MC, V. Closed Mon.–Tues.*

$ ✕ **Has Beans.** This coffee shop is a favorite gathering spot for locals. Fliers posted inside offer loads of insider information on life in Mount Shasta. The coffee beans are roasted on site. Enjoy the pastries made fresh daily. ⊠ *1011 S. Mt. Shasta Blvd.,* ☎ *530/926–3602. No credit cards.*

$–$$ ✕🏨 **Mount Shasta Resort.** Private chalets are nestled among tall pine
★ trees along the shore of Lake Siskiyou, all with gas-log fireplaces and hot tubs, some with complete kitchens. The resort's Highland House Restaurant, above the clubhouse of a spectacular 18-hole golf course, has uninterrupted views of Mt. Shasta. Large steaks and herb-crusted calamari are menu highlights. Take the Central Mount Shasta exit west from I–5, then go south on Old Stage Road. ⊠ *1000 Siskiyou Lake Blvd., 96067,* ☎ *530/926–3030 or 800/958–3363,* FAX *530/926–0333,* WEB *www.mountshastaresort.com. 65 units. Restaurant, kitchenettes (some), 18-hole golf course. AE, D, DC, MC, V.*

$ ⊞ **Best Western Tree House Motor Inn.** The clean standard rooms at this motel less than a mile from downtown Mount Shasta are decorated with natural-wood furnishings. Some rooms have vaulted ceilings and mountain views; most room rates include hot breakfast. ⊠ *111 Morgan Way, at I–5 and Lake St., 96067,* ☎ *530/926–3101 or 800/545–7164,* FAX *530/926–3542,* WEB *www.bestwestern.com. 98 rooms, 5 suites. Restaurant, refrigerators, indoor pool, hot tub. AE, D, DC, MC, V. BP.*

⚠ **Lake Siskiyou Camp Resort.** On the west side of 430-acre Lake Siskiyou, the sites in this 250-acre resort lie beneath tall pine trees that filter the light. With group sites, a marina, a free boat-launch ramp, fishing dock, fish cleaning station, power boat and kayak rentals, and evening movies, it's a great spot for families. Full hookups include TV. *Flush toilets, full hookups, showers, general store, swimming (lake). 200 tent sites, 150 RV sites.* ⊠ *4239 W. A. Barr Rd., 3 mi southwest of city of Mount Shasta,* ☎ *888/926–2618 or 530/926–2618,* WEB *www.lakesis.com. Reservations essential. D, MC, V.* ☽ *Apr.–Oct.*

Outdoor Activities and Sports

GOLF

At 6,100 yards the **Mount Shasta Resort** golf course isn't long, but it's beautiful and challenging, with narrow tree-lined fairways and several lakes and other waterways. From May through September it costs $64 to play 18 holes with a cart; the fee is $45 from October through April. ⊠ *1000 Siskiyou Lake Blvd.,* ☎ *530/926–3052.*

HIKING

The **Forest Service Ranger Station** (☎ 530/926–4511 or 530/926–9613) keeps tabs on trail conditions and offers avalanche reports.

MOUNTAIN CLIMBING

Fifth Season Mountaineering Shop (⊠ 300 N. Mt. Shasta Blvd., ☎ 530/926–3606 or 530/926–5555) rents skiing and climbing equipment and operates a recorded 24-hour climber-skier report. **Shasta Mountain Guides** (☎ 530/926–3117) leads hiking, climbing, and ski-touring groups to the summit of Mt. Shasta.

SKIING

�ృ On the southeast flank of Mt. Shasta **Mt. Shasta Board & Ski Park** has three lifts on 425 skiable acres. It's a great place for novices because three-quarters of the trails are for beginning or intermediate skiers. There are not many challenges for advanced skiers, however. The area's vertical drop is 1,390 ft, with a top elevation of 6,600 ft. The longest of the 31 trails is 1¾ mi. You can ski until 10 PM from Wednesday through Saturday. A package for beginners, available through the ski school, includes a lift ticket, ski rental, and a lesson. The school also runs the SKIwee program for children ages 4–7. Within the base lodge are food and beverage facilities, a ski shop, and a ski/snowboard rental shop. The park's Cross-Country Ski and Snowshoe Center, with 30 km (18 mi) of trails, is on the same road. ⊠ *Hwy. 89 exit east from I–5, south of Mt. Shasta,* ☎ *530/926–8686 or 800/754–7427.*

THE BACKCOUNTRY

Including Lassen Volcanic National Park

East of I–5, the far north's main corridor, dozens of scenic two-lane roads crisscross the wilderness, leading to dramatic mountain peaks and fascinating natural wonders. Small towns settled in the second half of the 19th century seem frozen in time, except that they are well equipped with tourist amenities.

McArthur–Burney Falls Memorial State Park

🖐 **8** *Hwy. 89, 52 mi southeast of Mount Shasta and 41 mi north of Lassen Volcanic National Park.*

Just inside the park's southern boundary, Burney Creek wells up from the ground and divides into two cascades that fall over a 129-ft cliff and into a pool below. Countless ribbonlike falls stream from hidden moss-covered crevices—an ethereal backdrop to the main cascades. Each day 100 million gallons of water rush over these falls. Legend has it that Theodore Roosevelt called them "the eighth wonder of the world." A self-guided nature trail descends to the foot of the falls. Resident bald eagles are frequently seen soaring overhead. You can swim at Lake Britton, lounge on the beach, or rent motorboats, paddleboats, and canoes. A campground, picnic sites, and other facilities are available. The camp store is open from early May to the end of October. ✉ *24898 Hwy. 89, Burney 96013,* ☎ *530/335–2777.* 🎫 *$2 per vehicle for day use.*

Camping

🏕 **McArthur–Burney Falls Memorial State Park.** Campsites here sit within evergreen forests near Burney Falls, some springs, a half dozen hiking trails, and Lake Britton. Boating and fishing are popular pursuits. Some sites can accommodate 35-ft RVs; two sites are handicapped accessible. Reservations are necessary during the peak months from Memorial Day to Labor Day. *Flush toilets, dump station, showers, picnic tables, general store, swimming (lake). 98 RV sites, 24 tent sites.* ✉ *McArthur–Burney Falls Memorial State Park, Hwy. 89,* ☎ *530/335–2777. AE, D, MC, V.*

Alturas

9 *86 mi northeast of McArthur–Burney Falls Memorial State Park on Hwy. 299.*

Alturas is the county seat and largest town in Modoc County in the remote upper reaches of northeastern California. The Dorris family arrived in the area in 1874, built Dorris Bridge over the Pit River, and later opened a small wayside stop for travelers. Today the Alturas area is a land of few people but much rugged natural beauty. Travelers come to see eagles and an abundance of other wildlife, geologic history in the Modoc National Forest, and active geothermal areas.

Modoc County Museum exhibits explore the development of the area from the 15th century through World War II. Featured are Native American artifacts, firearms, and a steam engine. ✉ *600 S. Main St.,* ☎ *530/233–6328.* 🎫 *Donations accepted.* 🕐 *May–Oct., Tues.–Sat. 10–4.*

Modoc National Forest encompasses 1.6 million acres and protects 300 species of wildlife. In spring and fall look for migratory waterfowl, as the Pacific Flyway crosses directly over the forest. Hiking trails lead to Petroglyph Point, one of the largest panels of rock art in the United States. ✉ *800 W. 12th St.,* ☎ *530/233–5811,* 📠 *530/233–8709,* 🌐 *www.r5.fs.fed.us/modoc.*

Canada geese, mallards, teal, wigeon, and pintail can be found everywhere in summer and fall within 6,280-acre **Modoc National Wildlife Refuge,** established to protect migratory waterfowl. In summer white pelicans, cormorants, and snowy egrets arrive. The park is open for hiking, bird observation, and photography. A portion of the refuge is set aside for hunters; regulations and seasons vary. ✉ ☎ *530/233–3572.* 🎫 *Free.* 🕐 *Daily dawn–dusk.*

LAVA BEDS NATIONAL MONUMENT – Volcanic activity created the rugged landscape of this intriguing monument. It is distinguished by cinder cones, lava flows, spatter cones, pit craters, and more than 400 underground lava tube caves. During the Modoc War (1872–73), the Modoc Indians under the leadership of Captain Jack took refuge in a natural lava fortress now known as Captain Jack's Stronghold. They managed to hold off U.S. army forces numbering as many as 20 times their strength for five months. When exploring, wear hard-sole boots, and pick up the necessary equipment (they loan lights and sell hard hats for $3.25 each) at the Indian Well Visitor Center, at the park's south end. Guided walks and cave tours, which take place during summer months, depart from the visitor center. Campfire programs are offered nightly in summer months. Bird-watching is popular in the spring and fall. ⊠ *Forest Service Rte. 10, 72 mi northwest of Alturas (Hwy. 299 west from Alturas to Hwy. 139 northwest to Forest Service Rte. 97 to Forest Service Rte. 10),* ☎ *530/667–2282,* WEB *www.nps.gov/labe.* ▨ *$5 per vehicle; $3 per person on foot, bicycle, or motorcycle.* ☉ *Visitor center Memorial Day–Labor Day, daily 8–6; Labor Day–Memorial Day, daily 8–5.*

Dining, Lodging, and Camping

$ ✕ **Black Bear Diner.** This is one of a chain of diners, with the big black bear standing in front, that have been sprouting up throughout the far north in recent years. The menu is basic, offering everything from spaghetti to barbecued pork ribs and prime rib. Serving sizes are generous. Breakfast is served any time of day. ⊠ *449 N. Main St.,* ☎ *530/ 233–3332. AE, D, DC, MC, V.*

$ ✕ **Brass Rail.** Formerly a whiskey distillery, this restaurant offers hearty meals in a comfortable space. Try the Basque lamb, the rib-eye steak, or the shrimp and scallops. There is a full bar and lounge. ⊠ *395 Lakeview Hwy.,* ☎ *530/233–2906. V. Closed Mon.*

$ ▥ **Best Western Trailside Inn.** This is the only lodging in town with a swimming pool. It's near local outdoor entertainment: 2 mi north of Rachael Doris Park, 3 mi south of Devils Garden, and 5 mi north of Modoc Wildlife Reserve. It's also five blocks south of the Modoc County Museum. You have access to a fax machine and a coffee machine here. ⊠ *343 N. Main St., 96101,* ☎ *530/233–4111,* FAX *530/233– 3180. 38 rooms. Kitchenettes (some), microwaves (some), cable TV, pool, Internet access, some pets allowed. AE, DC, MC, V.*

$ ▥ **Hacienda.** In the heart of farm country, this motel is marked with a large 19th-century wagon wheel out front. A gas station, fast-food restaurants, and a supermarket are all within five blocks. ⊠ *201 E. 12th St., 96101,* ☎ *530/233–3459. 20 rooms. Kitchenettes (some), microwaves (some), refrigerators, cable TV, pets allowed; no-smoking rooms. AE, D, DC, MC, V.*

⚠ **Medicine Lake Campground.** One of several small campgrounds on the shores of Medicine Lake, this spot lies at 6,700 ft, near the western border of Modoc National Forest. Sites can accommodate vehicles up to 22 ft. The lake, 14 mi south of Lava Beds National Monument, is a popular vacation spot for northern California residents and tourists alike. Fishing, boating, and waterskiing are among the activities here. *Vault toilets, drinking water, fire pits, picnic tables, swimming (lake). 22 sites.* ⊠ *Off Forest Service Rd. 44N38 (Hwy. 139 to County Rd. 97 west to Forest Service Rd. 44N38, follow signs),* ☎ *530/667–2246,* WEB *www.r5.fs.fed.us/modoc. Reservations not accepted.* ☉ *July–Oct.*

Susanville

❿ *104 mi south of Alturas via Rte. 395, 65 mi east of Lassen Volcanic National Park via Hwy. 36.*

Susanville wears its history on its walls, telling the tale of its rich history through murals painted on buildings in the historic uptown area. Established as a trading post in 1854, Susanville is the second-oldest town in the western Great Basin. Many of its original buildings remain and are now part of a self-guided tour. Historic buildings also house popular restaurants in town. Plenty of outdoor recreation awaits just outside town at such sites as the Bizz Johnson Trail and Eagle Lake.

Bizz Johnson Trail follows a defunct line of the Southern Pacific Railroad for 25 mi. Known to locals as the Bizz, the trail is open for hikers, walkers, mountain bikers, and horseback riders. It follows the Susan River through a scenic landscape of canyons, bridges, and forests abundant with wildlife. ⊠ *Trailhead: 601 Richmond Rd.,* ☏ *530/257-0456,* WEB *www.ca.blm.gov/eaglelake/bizztrail.html.* ☐ *Free.*

Anglers travel great distances to fish the waters of **Eagle Lake.** California's second-largest natural lake is surrounded by high desert to the north and alpine forests to the south. The Eagle Lake trout is prized for its size and fighting ability. The lake is also popular for picnicking, hiking boating, waterskiing, and windsurfing. Wildlife watchers can see ospreys, pelicans, western grebes, and many other waterfowl on the lake. On land, you'll see mule deer, small mammals, and even pronghorn antelope. ⊠ *20 mi north of Susanville on Eagle Lake Rd.,* ☏ *530/257-0456 for Eagle Lake Recreation Area; 530/825-3454 for Eagle Lake Marina,* WEB *shastacascade.org/blm/eagle/lake.htm.*

Dining, Lodging, and Camping

$-$$$ ✕ **St. Francis Champion Steakhouse.** On the ground floor of the historic St. Francis Hotel, this steak house is decorated in an Old West **★** theme and is all about meat. Those who succeed in finishing the "grand champion" 64-ounce steak dinner get their meal on the house; otherwise, it'll cost you $54.95. Prime rib is served on Saturday and all-you-can-eat Santa Maria–style Tri Tip on Thursday. ⊠ *830 Main St.,* ☏ *530/257-4820. AE, MC, V. No lunch weekends. No dinner Sun.*

$ ✕ **Grand Cafe.** Step back in time in this downtown coffee shop, which has been owned and operated by the same family since the 1920s. You can sit at the old-fashioned fountain counter or in a booth with its own nickel jukebox. The swiveling fountain seats have hat clips on the back, and wooden refrigerators are still in use. The chili is homemade, and so are the fruit cobblers. ⊠ *730 Main St.,* ☏ *530/257-4713. No credit cards. Closed Sun. No dinner.*

$ ✕ **Josefina's.** Popular with the locals, Josefina's makes its own salsas and tamales. The interior's Aztec accents are a perfect accompaniment to the menu's traditional Mexican fare of chile *rellenos,* enchiladas, tacos, and fajitas. ⊠ *1960 Main St.,* ☏ *530/257-9262. MC, V. Closed Mon.*

$ 🏨 **Best Western Trailside Inn.** This large business-friendly motel offers a meeting room, data lines, and Continental breakfast. Some rooms have wet bars, and there are some smoking rooms. ⊠ *2785 Main St., 96130,* ☏ *530/257-4123,* FAX *530/257-2665,* WEB *www.bestwesterncalifornia. com. 85 rooms. In-room data ports, refrigerators (some), cable TV, pool. AE, D, MC, V. CP.*

$ 🏨 **High Country Inn.** Spacious rooms open onto indoor corridors in this two-story colonial-style motel on the east edge of town. The hotel provides complimentary Continental breakfast; more extensive dining is available next door at the Country Chicken, a local outlet of the chain.

All rooms have hair dryers and coffeepots; business suites have in-room data ports. ⊠ *3015 Riverside Dr., 96130,* ☎ *530/257–3450,* FAX *530/257–2460. 66 rooms. Microwaves, refrigerators, cable TV with movies, pool, outdoor hot tub; no smoking. AE, D, MC, DC, V. CP.*

$ ★ 🏨 **St. Francis Hotel.** Susanville's oldest continuously operated guest house was built of brick in 1914. The rooms, furnished with wooden antiques, have the style of a bed-and-breakfast, albeit without the breakfast. ⊠ *830 Main St., 96130,* ☎ *530/257–4820. 4 rooms, 10 cabins. Cable TV. AE, D, MC, V.*

🏕 **Eagle Campground.** One of 11 campgrounds surrounding Eagle Lake, this site nestled amid pine trees has a boat ramp. *Flush toilets, dump station, drinking water, showers, picnic tables. 35 tent/RV sites, 14 tent-only sites.* ⊠ *County Rd. A-1, 14 mi north of Hwy. 36,* ☎ *530/825–3212. Reservations essential. AE, D, MC, V.* ☉ *Late May–mid-Oct.*

Lassen Volcanic National Park

🔟 *45 mi east of Redding on Hwy. 44, 48 mi east of Red Bluff on Hwy. 36.*

Lassen Volcanic National Park provides a look at three sides of one of the world's largest plug-dome volcanoes. Much of the park is inaccessible from late October to late May because of heavy snow. The Lassen Park Road (the continuation of Highway 89 within the park) is closed to cars in winter but open to intrepid cross-country skiers and snowshoers, conditions permitting. In the summer food service and gifts are available at the Lassen Chalet near the southwest entrance and at the Manzanita Lake Camper Store near the north entrance. Maps and road guides are available at the Loomis Museum, park headquarters, southwest information station, and park entrance and ranger stations. The park newspaper, *Peak Experiences,* available at the visitor contact stations, details these and other facilities. ⊠ *Park Headquarters: 38050 Hwy. 36E, Mineral 96063,* ☎ *530/595–4444,* WEB *www.nps.gov/lavo.* 🎫 *$10 per vehicle, $5 on foot or bicycle.* ☉ *Park headquarters weekdays 8–4:30.*

In 1914 the 10,457-ft Lassen Peak came to life, beginning what would become 300 eruptions over the next seven years. Molten rock overflowed the crater, and the mountain emitted clouds of smoke and hailstorms of rocks and volcanic cinders. Proof of the volcanic landscape's volatility becomes evident shortly after you enter the park at the **Sulphur Works Thermal Area.** Boardwalks take you over bubbling mud and boiling springs and through sulfur-emitting steam vents. ⊠ *Lassen Park Rd., south end of park.*

The **Lassen Peak Hike** winds 2½ mi to the mountaintop. It's a tough climb—2,000 ft uphill on a steady, steep grade—but the reward is a spectacular view. At the peak you can see into the rim and view the entire park (and much of the far north). Bring sunscreen and water. ⊠ *Off Lassen Park Rd., 7 mi north of southwest entrance.*

Along **Bumpass Hell Trail,** a scenic 3-mi round-trip hike to the park's most interesting thermal-spring area, you can view boiling springs, steam vents, and mud pots up close. There is a gradual climb of 500 ft during the first mile before a 250-ft descent to the basin. Stay on trails and boardwalks near the thermal areas. What appears to be firm ground may be only a thin crust over scalding mud. ⊠ *Off Lassen Park Rd., 6 mi north of southwest entrance.*

Hot Rock, a 400-ton boulder, tumbled down from the summit during the volcano's active period and was still hot to the touch when locals discovered it nearly two days later. Although cool now, it's still an impressive sight. ⊠ *Lassen Park Rd., north end of park.*

Lassen Volcanic National Park

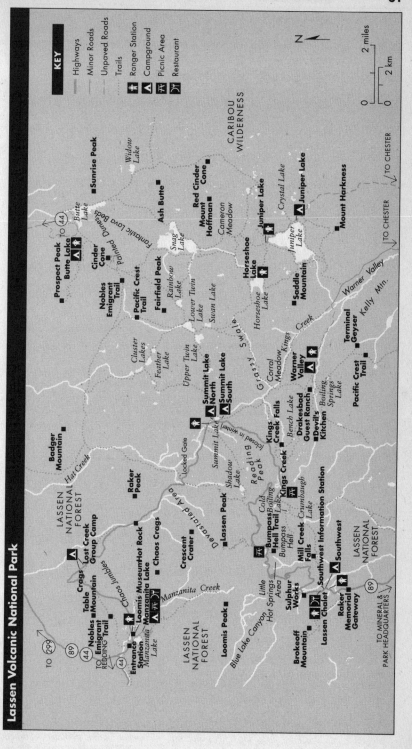

KEY

Highways
Minor Roads
Unpaved Roads
Trails
Ranger Station
Campground
Picnic Area
Restaurant

N

0   2 miles
0   2 km

TO 299

TO 89

44

89 TO MINERAL &
PARK HEADQUARTERS

TO CHESTER

TO CHESTER

CARIBOU WILDERNESS

Widow Lake

■ Sunrise Peak

■ Ash Butte

■ Red Cinder Cone

■ Mount Hoffman

Cameron Meadow

Fantastic Lava Beds

Snag Lake

Dunes Painted

Butte Lake

▲ ♦ Prospect Peak

■ Cinder Cone

Nobles Emigrant Trail

Pacific Crest Trail

■ Fairfield Peak

Rainbow Lake

Lower Twin Lake

Swan Lake

Grassy Swale

▲ Juniper Lake

♦ Juniper Lake

■ Mount Harkness

▲ Horseshoe Lake

Horseshoe Lake

Saddle Mountain ■

Kings Creek

Warner Valley

Kelly Mtn.

Terminal Geyser ■

Pacific Crest Trail

Boiling Springs Lake

▲ Warner Valley

♦

Corral Meadow

Bench Lake

Devil's Kitchen

Drakesbad Guest Ranch ♦

Kings Creek Falls

Kings Creek

■ Badger Mountain

Hat Creek

LASSEN NATIONAL FOREST

■ Raker Peak

Cluster Lakes

Feather Lake

Upper Twin Lake

Summit Lake ▲ North

Summit Lake ▲ South

♦

Summit Lake

Locked Gate

Shadow Lake

Devastated Area

Cold Boiling Lake

Reading Peak

■ Lassen Peak

Summit Lake (Closed in winter)

Lost Creek Group Camp ▲

Table Mountain ■

Chaos Jumbles

Nobles Emigrant Trail

REDDING TRAIL

Entrance Station

Manzanita Lake

Loomis Peak ■

Loomis Museum
Hot Rock
Manzanita Lake ▲ ♦

■ Chaos Crags

■ Crescent Crater

Manzanita Creek

Blue Lake Canyon

Little Hot Springs Area

Sulphur Works

Bumpass Hell Trail

Bumpass Hell

Mill Creek Falls

Crumbaugh Lake

Southwest Information Station

▲ Southwest

Lassen Chalet ♦

Raker Memorial Gateway ♦ ♦

■ Brokeoff Mountain

Chaos Jumbles was created 300 years ago when an avalanche from the Chaos Crags lava domes spread hundreds of thousands of rocks, many of them 2–3 ft in diameter, over a couple of square miles. ⊠ *Lassen Park Rd., north end of park.*

Dining, Lodging, and Camping

$$$ ✕🖭 **Drakesbad Guest Ranch.** This century-old guest ranch, at elevation 5,700 ft near Lassen Volcanic National Park's southern border, is isolated from most of the rest of the park. Rooms in the lodge, bungalows, and cabins don't have electricity, are lighted by kerosene lamps, have furnace heat, and either a half or full bath. They're clean and comfortable. Meals, which are rather elegant affairs in the evening, are included in the room rate. The waiting list for reservations can be up to two years long. ⊠ *Chester–Warner Valley Rd., north from Hwy. 36 (booking office: 2150 N. Main St., Suite 5, Red Bluff 96080),* ☎ *530/529–1512,* FAX *530/529–4511,* WEB *www.drakesbad.com. 19 rooms. Dining room, pool, fishing, badminton, horseback riding, horseshoes, Ping-Pong, volleyball. D, MC, V. Closed early Oct.–early June. FAP.*

$ ✕🖭 **Lassen Mineral Lodge.** Reserve rooms at this motel-style property, at 5,000 ft, as far ahead as possible. You can rent cross-country skis, snowshoes, and snowboards at the lodge's ski shop. There's also a general store. ⊠ *Hwy. 36 E, Mineral 96063,* ☎ *530/595–4422,* WEB *www.minerallodge.com. 20 rooms. Restaurant, bar. AE, D, MC, V.*

🏕 **Manzanita Lake Campground.** The largest of Lassen Volcanic National Park's eight campgrounds is near the northern entrance. It can accommodate vehicles up to 35 ft. A trail near the campground leads to Crags Lake. Summer reservations for group campgrounds can be made up to seven months in advance. From the end of September until snow closes the campground there is no running water. *Flush toilets, dump station, drinking water, showers, fire pits, picnic tables. 149 tent/RV sites, 31 tent sites.* ⊠ *Off Lassen Park Rd., 2 mi east of junction of Hwys. 44 and 89,* ☎ *530/595–4444,* WEB *www.nps.gov/lavo.* 🔳 *$14.* ☉ *Mid- to late May–Sept.*

Chester

🄬 *36 mi west of Susanville on Hwy 36.*

Chester's population swells from 2,500 to nearly 5,000 in the summer months as the small town at the edge of Lake Almanor comes alive with tourist activity. Perched along the Lassen Scenic Byway, the town serves as a gateway to Lassen Volcanic National Park.

Lake Almanor's 52 mi of shoreline lie in the shadow of Mt. Lassen. It's a popular draw for camping, swimming, boating, waterskiing, and fishing. At an elevation of 4,500 ft, the lake warms to above 70°F for about eight weeks in summer. Information is available at the Almanor Ranger District headquarters. ⊠ *900 W. Hwy. 36,* ☎ *530/258–2141.* ☉ *Open mid-May–mid-October.*

Lassen Scenic Byway is a 172-mi drive through the forested terrain, volcanic peaks, geothermal springs, and lava fields of Lassen National Forest and Lassen National Park. Along the way you'll pass through five rural communities in which refreshments and basic services are available. Information is available at Almanor Ranger District headquarters. ⊠ *900 W. Hwy. 36,* ☎ *530/258–2141.* 🔳 *$10 per vehicle within Lassen National Park. Partially inaccessible in winter; call for road conditions.*

Dining and Lodging

$$–$$$$ ✕ **Peninsula Station Bar and Grill.** Popular with outdoor recreationists, this spot stands next door to the Almanor Country Club and draws customers with its patio seating and full bar. You'll love the big meals of steak, prime rib, and seafood. ✉ *401 Peninsula Dr. on Lake Almanor Peninsula,* ☎ *530/596–3538. Closed Mon. No lunch. AE, DC, MC, V.*

$–$$ ✕ **Benassi's.** This popular restaurant on the north end of town is
★ small and nondescript from the outside, but homey inside. Specializing in northern Italian food, it serves everything homemade, including sauces, ravioli, and tortellini. You can't go wrong with seafood, chicken, or beef, and the vegetables are cooked to perfection. ✉ *159 Main St.,* ☎ *530/258–2600. Closed Mon. Oct.–Apr. No dinner Sun. MC, V.*

$–$$ ✕ **Cynthia's.** Formerly known as Creekside Grill, Cynthia's sits on the banks of a bubbling brook near the center of town and serves California home-style cuisine with a French touch. Specialties include light meat dishes, pastas, and salads, all made with fresh seasonal ingredients. Wines and microbrews are served at the bar. It also has a bakery that's well-known for rustic pizzas and artisan breads. Hours change frequently, so it's suggested you call ahead. ✉ *278 Main St.,* ☎ *530/ 258–1966. Closed Sun.–Mon. No dinner Tues.–Thurs. Labor Day– Memorial Day. MC, V.*

$–$$ ⊡ **Bidwell House.** This two-story 1901 ranch house sits on the southeastern slope of Mt. Lassen on 2 acres of cottonwood-studded lawns and gardens with a view of Lake Almanor. The front porch has chairs and swings, and there's a sunroom supplied with puzzles and games. Rooms are outfitted with such amenities as a Jacuzzi, wood-burning stove, claw-foot tub, hardwood floors, and antiques. A separate cottage is available for $170. The full breakfast features the inn's specialties—omelets and blueberry-walnut pancakes. ✉ *1 Main St., 96020,* ☎ *530/258–3338,* WEB *www.bidwellhouse.com. 14 rooms. Cable TV; no air-conditioning, no room phones, no smoking. MC, V. BP.*

$ ⊡ **Chester Manor Motel.** This remodeled 1950s-era one-story motel is within easy walking distance of restaurants and offers picnic tables among the pine groves on its 2½ acre lot. Six of their 18 rooms are two-bedroom suites; all rooms have hair dryers. ✉ *306 Main St., 96020,* ☎ *530/258–2441 or 888/571–4885,* FAX *530/258–3523. 18 rooms. Microwaves, refrigerators, cable TV with movies, Internet; no air-conditioning, no smoking. AE, MC, V.*

Quincy

⓭ *67 mi southwest of Susanville via Hwys. 36 and 89.*

A center for mining and logging in the 1850s, Quincy is nestled against the western slope of the Sierra Nevada. The county seat and largest community in Plumas County, the town is rich in historic buildings that have been the focus of preservation and restoration efforts. The four-story courthouse on Main Street, one of several stops on a self-guided tour, was built in 1921 with marble posts and staircases. The arts are alive and well in Quincy, too, as evidenced by public murals and the historic Town Hall Theatre.

Considered the centerpiece of recreation in central Plumas County, **Bucks Lake Recreation Area** is 17 mi southwest of Quincy at the 5,200-ft level. During the warm seasons the lake's 17 mi of shoreline attract fishermen and water-sports enthusiasts. It has two marinas and eight campgrounds. Hiking and horseback riding are also popular. In winter months much of the area remains open for snowmobiling and cross-country skiing. ✉ *Bucks Lake Rd.,* ☎ *800/326–2247 or 530/283–5465,* WEB *www.plumas.ca.us.*

Plumas County is known for its wide-open spaces, and the 1.2-million-acre **Plumas National Forest** is a large part of that. High alpine lakes and crystal-clear streams sparkle in this forest, which attracts outdoor enthusiasts year-round. Literally hundreds of campsites are maintained in the forest, and picnic areas and hiking trails abound. You can explore Gold Country history or ride the rapids in canoes, rafts, and inner tubes. Access to the forest can be found at numerous sites along Highways 70 and 89. ⊠ *159 Lawrence St.,* ☎ *530/283–2050,* FAX *530/283–4156,* WEB *www.r5.fs.fed.us/plumas.* ☉ *U.S. Forest Service office weekdays 8–4:30.*

The cultural, home arts, and industrial history displays at the **Plumas County Museum** contain artifacts dating to the 1850s. Highlights include collections of Maidu Indian basketry, pioneer weapons, and rooms depicting life in the early days of Plumas County. There are a blacksmith shop and gold-mining cabin outdoors, along with equipment from the early days of logging and a restored buggy. Also featured are railroad and mining exhibits. ⊠ *500 Jackson St.,* ☎ *530/283–6320,* FAX *530/283–6080.* 🎟 *$1.* ☉ *May–Sept., weekdays 8–5, weekends 10–4; Oct., daily 8–5; Nov.–Apr., weekdays 8–5.*

Dining, Lodging, and Camping

$–$$　✕ **Moon's.** This restored 1930 building houses a dinner-only restaurant that serves such delights as honey-almond chicken, prime rib (on weekends), ravioli, and Tuscan pasta. The pastas and breads are homemade, and the pizza is wonderful. Top off the meal with a slice of chocolate Kahlua pie for dessert. A verdant outdoor garden patio adds to Moon's allure. ⊠ *497 Lawrence St.,* ☎ *530/283–0765. AE, D, MC, V. Closed Mon.*

$–$$　✕ **Sweet Lorraine's Good Food Good Feelings.** You can choose to eat upstairs by candlelight or in the more casual downstairs bar and dining area. Sweet Lorraine's serves hearty fare such as Cajun meat loaf with roasted-garlic mashed potatoes, as well as lighter items; and it has a great assortment of microbrews and wine. ⊠ *384 Main St.,* ☎ *530/283–5300. Reservations essential. MC, V. Closed Sun.*

$–$$　🛏 **Feather Bed.** Housed in an 1893 Queen Anne Victorian, a stay at Feather Bed is a visit to a simpler time. The look of this bed-and-breakfast is Victorian, the furnishings antique, and the views (of the Sierra Nevada) spectacular. The five rooms in the main house have claw-foot tubs. Two private guest cottages have fireplaces and outside decks. Classical music plays softly in the morning, and breakfast begins with homegrown blackberry or raspberry smoothies. Fresh fruit or baked fruit crunch and home-baked bread or muffins accompany the hot entrée. ⊠ *542 Jackson St., 95971,* ☎ *800/696–8624 or 530/283–0102,* WEB *www.featherbed-inn.com. 7 rooms. Cable TV, bicycles, airport shuttle. AE, D, DC, MC, V. BP.*

$　🛏 **Lariat Lodge.** Built in 1956 out of cinder blocks, this small, quiet hotel in the Plumas National Forest is 2 mi west of downtown. The hotel serves a complimentary Continental breakfast. ⊠ *2370 E. Main St., 95971,* ☎ *530/283–1000 or 800/999–7199,* FAX *530/283–2154. 20 rooms. Refrigerators (some), cable TV, pool; no-smoking rooms. AE, D, MC, V. CP.*

$　🛏 **Ranchito.** Exposed log rafters make up the front exterior of this rustic Spanish-style motel, 1½ mi east of downtown. A brook runs through the mostly wooded 2½-acre grounds. ⊠ *2020 E. Main St., 95971,* ☎ *530/283–2265,* FAX *530/283–2316. 30 rooms. Picnic area, kitchenettes (some), cable TV; no air-conditioning in some rooms, no-smoking rooms. AE, D, MC, V.*

　　🛆 **Haskins Valley Campground.** At an elevation of 5,200 ft, this campground lies on the south shore of Bucks Lake. There is a boat ramp. *Vault toilets, dump station, drinking water. 65 sites.* ⊠ *Bucks Lake Rd., 16½ mi off Hwy. 70,* ☎ *800/743–5000. Reservations not accepted.* ☉ *Mid-May–mid-Oct.*

THE FAR NORTH A TO Z

To research prices, get advice from other travelers, and book travel arrangements, visit www.fodors.com.

AIR TRAVEL

Chico Municipal Airport and Redding Municipal Airport are served by United Express. Horizon Air also uses the airport in Redding. *See* Air Travel *in* Smart Travel Tips A to Z for airline phone numbers.

➤ AIRPORT INFORMATION: **Chico Municipal Airport** (✉ 150 Airpark Blvd., off Cohasset Rd., ☎ 800/241–6522). **Redding Municipal Airport** (✉ Airport Rd., ☎ 530/224–4320).

BUS TRAVEL

Greyhound buses travel I–5, serving Chico, Red Bluff, Redding, Dunsmuir, and Mount Shasta. Butte County Transit serves Chico, Oroville, and elsewhere. Chico Area Transit System provides bus service within Chico. The vehicles of the Redding Area Bus Authority operate daily except Sunday within Redding. STAGE buses travel on weekdays only from Yreka to Dunsmuir, stopping in Mount Shasta and other towns, and provide service in Scott Valley, Happy Camp, and the Klamath River area. Lassen Rural Bus serves the Susanville, northeast Lake Almanor, and south Lassen County areas, running weekdays except holidays. Lassen Rural Bus also connects with Plumas County Transit, which serves the Quincy area, and with Modoc County Sage Stage, which serves the Alturas area.

➤ BUS INFORMATION: **Butte County Transit** (☎ 530/342–0221, WEB www.bcag.org/transit). **Chico Area Transit System (CATS;** ☎ 530/342–0221, WEB www.bcag.org/transit). **Greyhound** (☎ 800/231–2222). **Lassen Rural Bus** (☎ 530/252–7433, WEB www.lrbs.com). **Modoc County Sage Stage** (☎ 530/233–3883, WEB www.billbra.com/modoc). **Plumas County Transit** (☎ 530/283–2538, WEB www.aworkforce.org/ptransit). **Redding Area Bus Authority** (☎ 530/241–2877, WEB http://ci.redding.ca.us). **STAGE** (☎ 530/842–8295, WEB www.co.siskiyou.ca.us).

CAR RENTAL

Avis and Hertz serve Redding Municipal Airport. Enterprise has branches in Red Bluff and Redding. *See* Car Rental *in* Smart Travel Tips A to Z for national rental agency phone numbers.

CAR TRAVEL

An automobile is virtually essential for touring the far north unless you arrive by bus, plane, or train and plan to stay put in one town or resort. I–5, an excellent four-lane divided highway, runs up the center of California through Red Bluff and Redding and continues north to Oregon. The other main roads in the area are good two-lane highways that are, with few exceptions, kept open year-round. Chico is east of I–5 on Highway 32. Lassen Volcanic National Park can be reached by Highway 36 from Red Bluff or (except in winter) Highway 44 from Redding. Highway 299 connects Redding and Alturas. Highway 139 leads from Susanville to Lava Beds National Monument. Highway 89 will take you from Mount Shasta to Quincy. Highway 36 links Chester and Susanville. If you are traveling through the far north in winter, always carry snow chains in your vehicle. For information on the condition of roads in northern California, call the Caltrans Highway Information Network's voice-activated system. At the prompt say the route number in which you are interested, and you'll hear a recorded message about current conditions.

➤ CONTACTS: **Caltrans Highway Information Network** (☎ 800/427–7623).

EMERGENCIES
In an emergency dial 911.
➤ HOSPITALS: **Enloe Medical Center** (✉ 1531 Esplanade, Chico, ☎ 530/891–7300). **Lassen Community Hospital** (✉ 560 Hospital Ln., Susanville, ☎ 916/257–5325). **Mercy Medical Center** (✉ 2175 Rosaline Ave., Redding, ☎ 530/225–6000).

LODGING
The far north is gaining popularity as a tourist destination, especially the mountainous backcountry. For summer holiday weekends make lodging reservations well in advance. The Web site of the California Association of Bed & Breakfast Inns lists numerous B&Bs in the far north region.
➤ CONTACTS: **California Association of Bed & Breakfast Inns** (WEB www.cabbi.com).

TRAIN TRAVEL
Amtrak has stations in Chico, Redding, and Dunsmuir and operates buses that connect to Greyhound service through Redding, Red Bluff, and Chico.
➤ CONTACTS: **Amtrak** (✉ W. 5th and Orange Sts., Chico; 1620 Yuba St., Redding; 5750 Sacramento Ave., Dunsmuir; ☎ 800/872–7245, WEB www.amtrak.com).

VISITOR INFORMATION
➤ CONTACTS: **Alturas Chamber of Commerce**(✉ 522 S. Main St., Alturas 96101, ☎ 530/233–4434, WEB www.alturaschamber.org). **Chester–Lake Almanor Chamber of Commerce** (✉ 529 Main St., Chester 96020, ☎ 530/258–2426 or 800/350–4838, WEB www.chester-lakealmanor.com). **Chico Chamber of Commerce** (✉ 300 Salem St., 95928, ☎ 530/891–5556 or 800/852–8570, WEB www.chicochamber.com). **Lassen County Chamber of Commerce (Susanville;** ✉ 84 N. Lassen St., Susanville 96130, ☎ 530/257–4323, WEB lassencountychamber.org). **Plumas County Visitors Bureau** (✉ Hwy. 70, ½ mi west of downtown, Quincy 95971, ☎ 530/283–6345 or 800/326–2247, WEB www.plumas.ca.us). **Quincy Chamber of Commerce** (✉ 464 Main St., Quincy 95971, ☎ 530/283–0188, WEB www.psln.com/qchamber). **Red Bluff–Tehama County Chamber of Commerce** (✉ 100 Main St., Red Bluff 96080, ☎ 530/527–6220 or 800/655–6225, FAX 530/527–2908, WEB www.redbluffchamberofcommerce.com). **Shasta Cascade Wonderland Association** (✉ 1699 Hwy. 273, Anderson 96007, ☎ 530/365–7500 or 800/326–6944, WEB www.shastacascade.org). **Siskiyou County Visitors Bureau (Mt. Shasta;** ✉ 508 Chestnut St., Mt. Shasta 96067, ☎ 530/926–3850 or 877/847–8777, FAX 530/926–3680, WEB www.visitsiskiyou.org).

3 THE NORTH COAST

FROM MUIR BEACH TO CRESCENT CITY

Migrating whales and other sea mammals swim past the dramatic bluffs that make the 400 mi of shoreline north of San Francisco among the most photographed landscapes in the country. Along cypress- and redwood-studded Highway 1 you will find many small inns, uncrowded beaches and parks, art galleries, and restaurants serving imaginative dishes that showcase locally produced ingredients.

T HE REDWOOD EMPIRE, that aptly named stretch of coast between
San Francisco Bay and the Oregon state line, is a land of spectacular scenery protected by numerous national, state, and local
Updated by parks. The shoreline's natural attributes are self-evident, but the area
Gregory is also rich in human history, having been the successive domain of the
Benchwick Native American Miwok and Pomo, Russian fur traders, Hispanic settlers, and more contemporary fishing folk and loggers. All have left
visible legacies. Only a handful of towns in this sparsely populated region have more than 1,000 inhabitants.

Pleasures and Pastimes

Beaches

The waters of the Pacific Ocean along the North Coast are fine for seals,
but most humans find the temperatures downright arctic. When it comes
to spectacular cliffs and seascapes, though, the North Coast beaches
are second to none. Explore tidal pools, watch for sea life, or dive for
abalone. Don't worry about crowds: on many of these beaches you will
have the sands largely to yourself.

Dining

Despite its small population, the North Coast lays claim to several well-
regarded restaurants. Seafood is abundant, as are locally grown vegetables and herbs. In general, dining options are more varied near the
coast than inland. Dress is usually informal, though dressy casual is
the norm at some of the pricier establishments listed below.

CATEGORY	COST*
$$$$	over $30
$$$	$22–$30
$$	$15–$21
$	under $15

per person for a main course at dinner, excluding tip and 7¼% tax

Fishing

Depending on the season, you can fish for rockfish, salmon, and steel-
head in the rivers. Charters leave from Fort Bragg, Eureka, and elsewhere for ocean fishing. There's particularly good abalone diving
around Jenner, Fort Ross, Point Arena, Westport, and Trinidad.

Lodging

Restored Victorians, rustic lodges, country inns, and chic hotels are
among the accommodations available along the North Coast. In several towns there are only one or two places to spend the night; some
of these lodgings are destinations in themselves. Make summer and weekend B&B reservations as far ahead as possible—rooms at the best inns
often sell out months in advance.

CATEGORY	COST*
$$$$	over $225
$$$	$160–$225
$$	$100–$159
$	under $100

All prices are for a standard double room, excluding 8%–10% tax.

Whale-Watching

From any number of excellent observation points along the coast, you
can watch gray whales during their annual winter migration season
or, in the summer and fall, blue or humpback whales. Another option
is a whale-watching cruise (☞ Tours *in* The North Coast A to Z, *below*).

Exploring the North Coast

Exploring the northern California coast is easiest by car. Highway 1 is a beautiful if sometimes slow and nerve-racking drive. You'll want to stop frequently to appreciate the views, and there are many portions of the highway along which you won't drive faster than 20–40 mph. You can still have a fine trip even if you don't have much time, but be realistic and don't plan to drive too far in one day. The itineraries below proceed north from San Francisco.

Numbers in the text correspond to numbers in the margin and on the North Coast maps.

Great Itineraries

IF YOU HAVE 3 DAYS

Some of the finest redwoods in California are found less than 20 mi north of San Francisco in **Muir Woods National Monument** ①. After walking through the woods, stop for an early lunch in **Inverness** ⑥ (on Sir Francis Drake Boulevard, northwest from Highway 1) or continue on Highway 1 to **Fort Ross State Historic Park** ⑧. Catch the sunset and stay the night in ⛺ **Gualala** ⑩. On day two drive to ⛺ **Mendocino** ⑫. Spend the next day and a half browsing in the many galleries and shops and visiting the historic sites, beaches, and parks of this cliff-side enclave. Return to San Francisco via Highway 1, or the quicker (3½ hours, versus up to five) and less winding route of Highway 128 east (off Highway 1 at the Navarro River, 10 mi south of Mendocino) to Route 101 south.

IF YOU HAVE 7 DAYS

Early on your first day, walk through **Muir Woods National Monument** ①. Then visit **Stinson Beach** ② for a walk on the shore and lunch. In springtime and early summer head north on Highway 1 to Bolinas Lagoon, where you can see bird nestings at **Audubon Canyon Ranch** ③. At other times of the year (or after you've visited the ranch) continue north on Highway 1. One-third of a mile beyond **Olema,** look for a sign marking the turnoff for the **Bear Valley Visitor Center,** the gateway to the **Point Reyes National Seashore.** Tour the reconstructed Miwok village near the visitor center. Spend the night in nearby ⛺ **Inverness** ⑥ or one of the other coastal Marin towns. The next day stop at Goat Rock State Beach and **Fort Ross State Historic Park** ⑧ on the way to ⛺ **Mendocino** ⑫. On your third morning head to **Fort Bragg** ⑬ for a visit to the **Mendocino Coast Botanical Gardens.** If you're in the mood to splurge, drive inland on Highway 1 to Route 101 north and spend the night at the Benbow Inn in ⛺ **Garberville.** Otherwise, linger in the Mendocino area and drive inland the next morning. On day four continue north through parts of **Humboldt Redwoods State Park** ⑭, including the Avenue of the Giants. Stop for the night in the Victorian village of ⛺ **Ferndale** ⑮ and visit the cemetery and the Ferndale Museum. On day five drive to ⛺ **Eureka** ⑯. Have lunch in Old Town, visit the shops, and get a feel for local marine life on a Humboldt Bay cruise. Begin day six by driving to **Patrick's Point State Park** ⑱ to enjoy stunning views of the Pacific from a point high above the surf. Have a late lunch overlooking the harbor in **Trinidad** before returning to Eureka for the night. Return to San Francisco on day seven. The drive back takes six hours on Route 101; it's nearly twice as long if you take Highway 1.

When to Tour the North Coast

The North Coast is a year-round destination, though when you go determines what you will see. The migration of the Pacific gray whales is a wintertime phenomenon, roughly from mid-December to early April.

The North Coast (San Francisco to Fort Bragg)

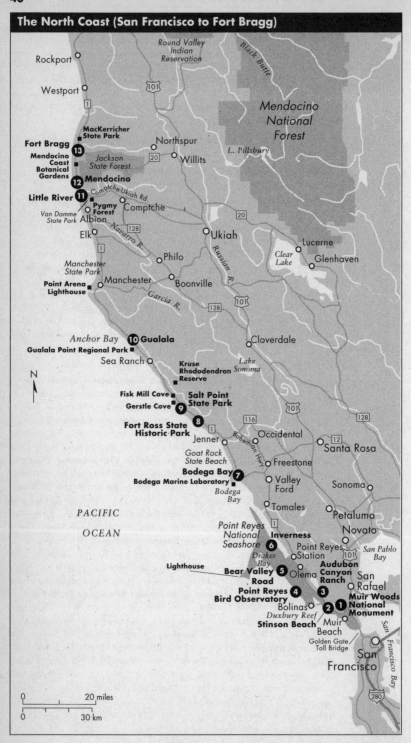

In July and August views are often obstructed by fog. The coastal climate is quite similar to San Francisco's, although winter nights are colder than in the city.

SOUTHERN COASTAL MARIN COUNTY

Much of the Marin County coastline is less than an hour from San Francisco, but the pace is slower. Most sights in the southern coastal Marin area can easily be done as day trips from the city.

Muir Woods National Monument

★ ❶ *17 mi from San Francisco, north on Rte. 101 and west on Hwy. 1 (take Mill Valley/Stinson Beach exit off Rte. 101 and follow signs).*

This grove of old-growth *Sequoia sempervirens* was one of the country's first national monuments. A number of easy hikes can be accomplished in an hour. There's even a short valley-floor trek, accessible to travelers with disabilities, that takes only 10 minutes to walk. The coast redwoods that grow here are mostly between 500 and 800 years old and as tall as 236 ft. Along Redwood Creek are other trees—live oak, madrone, and buckeye, as well as wildflowers (even in winter), ferns, and mushrooms. Parking is easier at Muir Woods before 10 and after 4. ⊠ *Panoramic Hwy. off Hwy. 1,* ☎ *415/388–2595,* WEB *www.nps. gov/muwo.* ⊠ *$3.* ☉ *Daily 8 AM–sunset.*

OFF THE BEATEN PATH

MUIR BEACH – Small but scenic, this patch of shoreline 3 mi south of Muir Woods off Highway 1 is a good place to stretch your legs and gaze out at the Pacific.

Dining and Lodging

$$$–$$$$ ✕🏠 **Pelican Inn.** This Tudor-style B&B is a five-minute walk from Muir
★ Beach. Rooms have Oriental rugs, English prints, hanging tapestries, and half-tester beds. Even the bathrooms are special, with Victorian-style hardware and hand-painted tiles in the shower. Locals and tourists compete at darts in the ground-floor pub, which has a wide selection of brews, sherries, and ports. The Pelican's restaurant ($–$$; no lunch Monday, November–April) serves sturdy English fare. ⊠ *10 Pacific Way, at Hwy. 1, 94965,* ☎ *415/383–6000,* FAX *415/383–3424,* WEB *www. pelicaninn.com. 7 rooms. Restaurant, pub. MC, V. BP.*

Stinson Beach

❷ *8 mi north of Muir Woods National Monument via Panoramic Hwy., 25 mi north of San Francisco, Rte. 101 to Hwy. 1.*

Stinson Beach has the most expansive sands in Marin County. It's as close (when the fog hasn't rolled in) as you'll get to the stereotypical feel of a southern California beach. On any hot summer weekend every road to Stinson Beach is jam-packed, so factor this into your plans.

Dining and Lodging

$–$$ ✕ **Sand Dollar.** This friendly, modest pub serves California-style pizza, hamburgers, and other sandwiches for lunch and decent seafood for dinner; there's an outdoor dining deck. ⊠ *3458 Hwy. 1,* ☎ *415/868– 0434. AE, D, MC, V.*

$–$$ ✕ **Stinson Beach Grill.** A great selection of beer and wine, art on the walls, and outdoor seating on a heated deck are among the draws here. The food is good, too. Seafood, including several types of oysters, is served at lunch and dinner. Pasta, lamb, chicken, and Mexican and Japanese specialties are on the evening menu. ⊠ *3465 Hwy. 1,* ☎ *415/868–2002. MC, V.*

$$$$ ⊡ **The Beach Cottage.** Stinson Beach's best accommodation is rented out by Darrellyn Morris, a friendly longtime local who built a pleasant studio next to her seaside house. With its peaked cedar ceiling, the room was designed to emulate a provincial French church that Morris visited years ago. Breakfast is served on your private patio, which sits, quite literally, above the sand. ⊠ *28 Calle del Sierra, 94970,* ☎ *415/868–0474,* WEB *www.stinsonbeachfront.com. 1 room. No credit cards.*

Audubon Canyon Ranch

❸ *12 mi northwest of Stinson Beach.*

The Audubon Canyon Ranch, a 1,000-acre wildlife sanctuary along the Bolinas Lagoon, is open to the public during nesting season. Among the 60 species of birds that can be spotted here with the aid of telescopes and hidden observation posts are great blue herons and egrets. There are many miles of hiking trails through the preserve that offer tremendous views of the Bolinas Lagoon and Stinson Beach. A small museum surveys the geology and natural history of the region. ⊠ *4900 Hwy. 1, along Bolinas Lagoon,* ☎ *415/868–9244,* WEB *www.egret. org.* ▦ *$10 donation requested.* ☉ *Mid-Mar.–mid-July, weekends 10– 4, Tues.–Fri. 2–4 (weekday visits by appointment only).*

An unmarked road running west from Highway 1 about 2 mi beyond Audubon Canyon Ranch leads to the sleepy town of **Bolinas.** Don't expect a warm welcome: some residents of Bolinas are so wary of tourism that whenever the state tries to post road signs, they take them down.

Nightlife
Smiley's Schooner Saloon (⊠ 41 Wharf Rd., ☎ 415/868–1311) hosts live music on Friday, Saturday, and Sunday.

POINT REYES NATIONAL SEASHORE

The Point Reyes National Seashore, which borders the northern reaches of the Golden Gate National Recreation Area (☞ Chapter 4), is a great place for hiking to secluded beaches, viewing wildlife, and driving through rugged, rolling grasslands. Highlights include the ½-mi Earthquake Trail, which passes by what is believed to be the epicenter of the 1906 quake that destroyed much of San Francisco, and the late-19th-century Point Reyes Lighthouse, a good spot to watch for whales. Horses and mountain bikes are permitted on some trails. The towns of Olema, Point Reyes Station, and Inverness, all in or near the national seashore area, have dining, lodging, and recreational facilities.

Point Reyes Bird Observatory

❹ *2 mi northwest of Bolinas off Mesa Rd.*

Birders love the Point Reyes Bird Observatory, a sanctuary and research center within the Point Reyes National Seashore but more easily accessible from Bolinas. The area harbors nearly 225 bird species. As you hike the trails, you're likely to see biologists banding the birds to aid in studying their life cycles. Trails pass waterfalls and a lake and lead to the national seashore. ⊠ *West on Mesa Rd. off Olema–Bolinas Rd.,* ☎ *415/868–0655,* WEB *www.prbo.org.* ▦ *Free.* ☉ *Visitor center daily 9–5.*

Mile-long **Duxbury Reef,** a nature preserve, is the largest shale intertidal reef in North America. Check a tide table if you plan to explore the reef, which is accessible only at low tide. Look for starfish, barnacles, sea anemones, purple urchins, limpets, sea mussels, and the occasional abalone. ⊠ *From Bolinas take Mesa Rd. off Olema–Bolinas Rd.; turn left on Overlook Dr. and right on Elm Ave. to beach parking lot.*

Bear Valley Road

⑤ *9 mi north of Bolinas on Hwy. 1.*

☾ ★ The Point Reyes National Seashore's **Bear Valley Visitor Center** has exhibits of park wildlife. The rangers here dispense advice about beaches, the Point Reyes Lighthouse, whale-watching, hiking trails, and camping. A reconstructed Miwok village, a short walk from the visitor center, provides insight into the daily lives of the region's first human inhabitants. ⊠ *Bear Valley Rd. west of Hwy. 1,* ☎ *415/464–5100,* WEB *www.nps.gov/pore.* ⊠ *Free.* ☉ *Weekdays 9–5, weekends 8–5.*

Outdoor Activities and Sports

Many of the beaches in Point Reyes National Seashore are accessible off Bear Valley Road. **Limantour Beach** (⊠ end of Limantour Beach Rd.) is one of the most beautiful of Point Reyes sands; trails lead to other beaches north and south of here. **Blue Waters Kayaking** (⊠ 12938 Sir Francis Drake Blvd., Inverness, ☎ 415/669–2600) rents kayaks and offers tours. **Five Brooks Stables** (⊠ 8001 Hwy. 1, ☎ 415/663–1570) rents horses and equipment. Trails from the stables wind through the Point Reyes woods and along the beaches.

Point Reyes Station

2 mi north of Olema on Hwy. 1.

The best place to find out what's going on in Point Reyes Station, a stop on the North Pacific Coast narrow-rauge railroad until 1933, is Toby's Feed Barn. Toby's sells offbeat gifts (many festooned with cows) to tourists and locals and feed and grain to local farmers. There's a market on Main Street for picking up picnic supplies.

Lodging

$ ☷ **Point Reyes Hostel.** These dorm-style lodgings in an old clapboard ranch house are a good deal for budget travelers. A family room is limited to those with children five and under and must be reserved well in advance. ⊠ *Off Limantour Rd., Box 247, 94956,* ☎ *415/663–8811. MC, V.*

Shopping

Gallery Route One (⊠ 11101 Hwy. 1, ☎ 415/663–1347), a nonprofit cooperative, shows the works of area artists.

Inverness

⑥ *4 mi from Point Reyes Station on Sir Francis Drake Blvd., northwest from Hwy. 1.*

Inverness boomed after the 1906 earthquake, when wealthy San Franciscans built summer homes in its hills. Today many structures serve as full-time residences or small inns. A deli, a grocery store, restaurants, and shops are along Sir Francis Drake Boulevard.

★ The **Point Reyes Lighthouse Visitor Center** is a 45-minute drive from Inverness, across rolling landscape that resembles Scottish heath. Parking near the lighthouse is difficult on weekends during summer. The view alone persuades most people to make the effort of walking down—and then back up—the hundreds of steps from the cliff tops to the lighthouse below. Rangers sometimes close the trail if the coastal winds are too strong. ⊠ *Western end of Sir Francis Drake Blvd.*, ☎ *415/669–1534,* WEB *www.nps.gov/pore.* ◷ *Thurs.–Mon. 10–4:30.*

Dining and Lodging

$ ✕ **Grey Whale.** This casual place is a good stop for pizza, sandwiches, salad, pastries, and espresso. ⊠ *12781 Sir Francis Drake Blvd.*, ☎ *415/669–1244. MC, V.*

$$$–$$$$ ✕🖬 **Manka's.** Rustic wood-paneled dining rooms glowing with candlelight are the backdrop for an evening of creative American cuisine. ★ Two of the four smallish guest rooms above the restaurant have private decks overlooking Tomales Bay. Rooms in the redwood annex and two cabins are also available. The restaurant, open for dinner only ($$$$), is closed on Tuesday and Wednesday year-round and from Sunday through Thursday January–March. ⊠ *30 Callendar Way, 94937,* ☎ *415/669–1034,* WEB *www.mankas.com. 14 rooms. Restaurant. MC, V. BP.*

$$$$ 🖬 **Blackthorne Inn.** There's no other inn quite like the Blackthorne, a combination of whimsy and sophistication in the woods. This imaginative structure has as its centerpiece a 3,500-square-ft deck. The solarium was made with timbers from San Francisco wharves; the outer walls are salvaged doors from a railway station. A glass-sheathed octagonal tower called the Eagle's Nest crowns the inn. ⊠ *266 Vallejo Ave., Box 712, Inverness Park 94937,* ☎ *415/663–8621,* WEB *www.blackthorneinn.com. 5 rooms, 3 with bath. Hot tub. MC, V. BP.*

$$–$$$ 🖬 **Ten Inverness Way.** This is the kind of place where you sit around after breakfast and share tips for hiking the nearby Point Reyes National Seashore. The living room of this low-key inn has a stone fireplace and library. The rooms contain such homespun touches as patchwork quilts, well-worn antiques, and dormer ceilings with skylights. ⊠ *Inverness Way, Box 63, 94937,* ☎ *415/669–1648,* FAX *415/669–7403,* WEB *www.teninvernessway.com. 5 rooms. Hot tub. D, MC, V. BP.*

Valley Ford

23 mi north of Point Reyes Station on Hwy. 1.

Bird-watching is a favorite pastime in Valley Ford, where blue herons, egrets, hawks, and owls nest.

Lodging

$ 🖬 **Inn at Valley Ford.** The rooms at this B&B, a Victorian farmhouse built in the late 1860s, are named after literary figures, characters, or periods. Books commemorating each chamber's theme grace the inn's bookshelves. The breakfast comes with old-fashioned cream scones. ⊠ *14395 Hwy. 1, Box 439, 94972,* ☎ FAX *707/876–3182. 4 rooms without bath. DC, MC, V. BP.*

FROM SONOMA TO FORT BRAGG

The gently rolling countryside of coastal Marin gives way to more dramatic scenery north of Bodega Bay. Cattle cling for their lives (or so it seems) to steep inclines alongside the increasingly curvy highway, now traveling right along the coast. The stunning vistas make this one of the most attractive stretches of coastline north of San Francisco.

Occidental

10 mi from Valley Ford, north on Hwy. 1, east on Hwy. 12 (Bodega Hwy.), and north on Bohemian Hwy.

A village in a clearing that's surrounded by the redwood forests, orchards, and vineyards of western Sonoma County, Occidental is so small that you might drive right through the town and barely take notice. A 19th-century logging hub with a present-day bohemian feel, Occidental has a top-notch B&B, good eats, and a handful of art galleries and crafts and clothing boutiques, all of which make the town an ideal base for day trips to Sonoma Coast beaches, Bodega Bay, Armstrong Redwoods Reserve, and Point Reyes National Seashore.

OFF THE
BEATEN PATH

OSMOSIS ENZYME BATHS – The tiny town of Freestone, 3 mi south of Occidental and 7½ mi east of Bodega Bay off Highway 12 (Bodega Highway), is famous regionally as the home of the unique Osmosis Enzyme Baths. This spa, in a two-story clapboard house on extensive grounds, specializes in several treatments, including a detoxifying "dry" bath in a blend of enzymes and fragrant wood shavings. After 20 minutes in the tub, opt for a 75-minute massage in one of the freestanding Japanese-style pagodas near the creek that runs through the property. ⊠ *209 Bohemian Hwy., Freestone,* ☎ *707/823–8231,* WEB *www.osmosis.com.*

Lodging

$$$$ ⊡ **The Inn at Occidental.** Jack Bullard had to open an inn to have a
★ place to show off his collections. Every room here showcases a collection of one sort or another. Antique English and Irish cut-glass jars decorate the Cut-Glass Room, which has its own sunny garden and outdoor whirlpool tub. A fireplace, fine Oriental rugs, and antique clocks create a cozy but dignified mood in the ground-floor living room. Antiques, quilts, and original artwork fill the guest rooms in the main house. This inn is a decidedly adult place. ⊠ *3657 Church St., Box 857, 95465,* ☎ *707/874–1047 or 800/522–6324,* FAX *707/874–1078,* WEB *www. innatoccidental.com. 18 rooms. AE, D, MC, V. BP.*

Bodega Bay

❼ *8 mi from Valley Ford on Hwy. 1, 65 mi north of San Francisco via Rte. 101 and Hwy. 1.*

Bodega Bay (where Alfred Hitchcock's film *The Birds* takes place) is one of the busiest harbors on the Sonoma County coast. Commercial boats pursue fish as well as the famed Dungeness crabs. T-shirt shops and galleries line both sides of Highway 1; a short drive around the harbor leads to the Pacific. This is the last stop, townwise, before Gualala, and a good spot for stretching your legs and taking in the salt air. Visit the **Bodega Marine Laboratory** (☎ 707/875–2211 for directions), on a 326-acre reserve on nearby Bodega Head. The lab gives one-hour tours and peeks at intertidal invertebrates, such as sea stars and sea anemones, on Friday from 2 to 3:45. ☜ $2 donation requested.

Dining and Lodging

$$–$$$ ✕⊡ **Inn at the Tides.** The condominium-style buildings at this complex have spacious rooms with high ceilings and an uncluttered feel. All rooms have views of the harbor, and some have fireplaces. The inn's two restaurants ($$) serve both old-style and more adventurous seafood dishes. In season you can buy a slab of salmon or live or cooked crab at a seafood market across the highway and have the kitchen prepare it for you. ⊠ *800 Hwy. 1, Box 640, 94923,* ☎ *707/875–2751 or 800/ 541–7788,* FAX *707/875–2669,* WEB *www.innatthetides.com. 86 rooms. 2 restaurants, room service, refrigerators, pool, hot tub, sauna, bar, laundry facilities. AE, D, MC, V. CP.*

$$$$ 🏠 **Sonoma Coast Villa.** In this secluded spot in the coastal hills between Valley Ford and Bodega Bay sits a most unusual inn. Founded as an Arabian horse ranch in 1976, the 60-acre property has two single-story rows of accommodations beside a swimming pool. Red-tile roofs, a stucco exterior, Mediterranean-style landscaping, and two courtyards create a European mood. Rooms have slate floors, French doors, beam ceilings, and wood-burning fireplaces. The dining room serves complimentary breakfast. ⊠ *16702 Hwy. 1, Bodega 94922,* 🕾 *707/876–9818 or 888/404–2255,* ℻ *707/876–9856,* 🕸 *www.scvilla.com. 16 rooms. Pool, hot tub, spa. AE, MC, V. BP.*

Outdoor Activities and Sports

Bodega Bay Sportfishing (⊠ Bay Flat Rd., 🕾 707/875–3344) charters ocean-fishing boats and rents equipment. The operators of the 700-acre **Chanslor Guest Ranch** (⊠ 2660 Hwy. 1, 🕾 707/875–2721) lead guided horseback rides.

Shopping

The **Ren Brown Gallery** (⊠ 1781 Hwy. 1, 🕾 707/875–2922), in the north end of town, is renowned for its selection of Asian arts, crafts, and furnishings. This two-floor gallery also represents a number of local artists worth checking out.

Jenner

10 mi north of Bodega Bay on Hwy. 1.

The Russian River empties into the Pacific Ocean at Jenner. The town has a couple of good restaurants and some shops. South of the Russian River is windy **Goat Rock State Beach,** where a colony of sea lions (walk north from the parking lot) resides most of the year. The beach is open daily from 8 AM to sunset; there's no day-use fee.

Dining

$$–$$$ ✕ **River's End.** At the right time of year diners at this rustic restaurant
★ can view sea lions lazing on the beach below. The creative fare is eclectic with seafood, venison, and duck dishes ranging in style from Continental to Indonesian. ⊠ *Hwy. 1, north end of Jenner,* 🕾 *707/865–2484. MC, V. Closed weekdays Jan.–Feb. and Tues.–Wed. Mar.–June.*

Fort Ross State Historic Park

🐾 ⑧ *9 mi north of Jenner on Hwy. 1.*

Fort Ross, completed in 1821, became Russia's major fur-trading outpost in California. The Russians brought Aleut hunters down from Alaska. By 1841 the area was depleted of seals and otters, and the Russians sold their post to John Sutter, later of gold-rush fame. After a local Anglo rebellion against the Mexicans, the land fell under U.S. domain, becoming part of California in 1850. The state park service has reconstructed Fort Ross, including its Russian Orthodox chapel, a redwood stockade, the officers' barracks, and a blockhouse. The excellent museum here documents the history of the fort and some of the North Coast. ⊠ *Hwy. 1,* 🕾 *707/847–3286,* 🕸 *www.parks.ca.gov. ▧ $3 per vehicle (day use).* ☉ *Daily 10–4:30. No dogs allowed past the parking lot.*

Lodging

$–$$$$ 🏠 **Fort Ross Lodge.** Conveniently located about 1½ mi north of the historic site, this lodge has a wind-bitten look. Some of the rooms have views of the shoreline; others have private hot tubs. Six hill units have saunas, hot tubs, and fireplaces. ⊠ *20705 Hwy. 1, 95450,* 🕾 *707/847–3333,* ℻ *707/847–3330,* 🕸 *www.fortrosslodge.com. 22 rooms. Refrigerators. AE, MC, V.*

Salt Point State Park

❾ *11 mi north of Jenner on Hwy. 1.*

Salt Point State Park yields a glimpse of nature virtually untouched by humans. At the 6,000-acre park's Gerstle Cove you'll probably catch sight of seals sunning themselves on the beach and deer roaming in the meadow. Don't miss the unusual *tafonis,* caverns in the sandstone caused by centuries of erosion by wind and rain. A very short drive leads to Fisk Mill Cove. A five-minute walk uphill brings you to a dramatic overview of Sentinel Rock and the pounding surf below. ⊠ *Hwy. 1,* ☎ *707/847–3221.* ⊞ *$2 per vehicle.* ☉ *Daily sunrise–sunset.*

Kruse Rhododendron Reserve, a peaceful 317-acre forested park, has thousands of rhododendrons that bloom in light shade in the late spring. ⊠ *Hwy. 1, north of Fisk Mill Cove.* ⊞ *Free.*

Lodging and Camping

$ ⊞ **Stillwater Cove Ranch.** Seventeen miles north of Jenner, this former boys' school overlooking Stillwater Cove has been transformed into a pleasant, if spartan, place to lodge. Group accommodations are also available in a bunkhouse and a dairy barn. ⊠ *22555 Hwy. 1, 95450,* ☎ *707/847–3227. 6 rooms. No credit cards.*

⚠ **Salt Point State Park Campgrounds.** There are two excellent campsites in the park. Gerstle Cove campground, on the west side of Highway 1, is set on a wooded hill with some sites overlooking the ocean. Woodside campground offers more trees and protection from the wind; it is on the east side of Highway 1. Woodside is closed December–March 15. *Flush toilets, drinking water, picnic tables, fire grates. Gerstle Cove, 29 sites; Woodside, 79 sites.* ⊠ *20705 Hwy. 1, 95450,* ☎ *800/444–7275. Reservations accepted Mar.–Oct.*

Sea Ranch

18 mi northwest of Fort Ross on Hwy. 1.

Sea Ranch is a dramatically positioned development of stylish homes on 5,000 acres overlooking the Pacific. To appease critics, the developers provided public beach-access trails off Highway 1 south of Gualala. Even some militant environmentalists deem the structures designed by William Turnbull and Charles Moore to be reasonably congruent with the surroundings; some folks find the weathered wooden buildings beautiful.

Dining and Lodging

$$$–$$$$ ✕⊞ **Sea Ranch Lodge.** High on a bluff with ocean views, the lodge is close to beaches, trails, and golf. Some rooms have fireplaces, while others have hot tubs. Handcrafted wood furnishings and quilts create an earthy, contemporary look. The restaurant ($$–$$$), which overlooks the Pacific, serves good seafood and homemade desserts. Try the five-course chef's dinner for a special treat. ⊠ *60 Sea Walk Dr., Box 44, 95497,* ☎ *707/785–2371 or 800/732–7262,* ℻ *707/785–2917,* ⟪WEB⟫ *www.searanchlodge.com. 20 rooms, 2 suites. Restaurant. AE, MC, V. BP.*

$$$$ ⊞ **Sea Ranch Escape.** The Sea Ranch houses, sparsely scattered on a grass meadow fronting a stretch of ocean, are a striking sight from Highway 1. Groups or families can rent fully furnished homes for two nights or more. Linen, housekeeping, and catering services are available for a fee. You can dine at superb nearby restaurants or stock up on provisions from one of the markets in Gualala and make use of the full kitchens. All homes have TVs and VCRs, some have hot tubs, and some allow pets. ⊠ *60 Sea Walk Dr., Box 238, 95497,* ☎ *707/785–2426 or 888/732–7262,* ℻ *707/785–1021. 71 houses. In-room VCRs. MC, V.*

Gualala

❿ *11 mi north of Sea Ranch on Hwy. 1*

This former lumber port remains a sleepy drive-through except for the several ocean-view motels that serve as headquarters for exploring the coast. The town lies north of the Gualala River—a good place for fishing. On the Gualala River's Sonoma side, **Gualala Point Regional Park** (✉ 1 mi south of Gualala on Hwy. 1, ☎ 707/785–2377), open daily from 8 AM until sunset, is an excellent whale-watching spot. The park has picnicking ($3 day-use fee) and camping.

Dining, Lodging, and Camping

$–$$$$ ✕▨ **St. Orres.** Two onion-dome towers evoke the area's Russian heritage at one of the North Coast's most eye-catching inns. The main house is further accented by balconies, stained-glass windows, and wood-inlaid towers. Two rooms overlook the sea, and the other six have views of the garden or a stand of pines. In the tranquil woods behind the house are 12 cottages. The inn's restaurant (closed on Tuesday and Wednesday from October through June) serves dinner only, a fixed-price meal ($$$$). ✉ *Hwy. 1, 2 mi north of Gualala, Box 523, 95445,* ☎ *707/884–3303,* FAX *707/884–1840,* WEB *www.saintorres.com. 8 rooms without bath, 13 cottages. Restaurant, hot tub, sauna, beach. MC, V. BP.*

$$$–$$$$ ▨ **Whale Watch Inn.** The largest accommodations at this inn are in the main house, but all have their merits. Most rooms do indeed have views (through cypress trees) down the coast, where whales often come close to shore on their northern migration in early spring. Year-round the scent of pine and salt-sea air fills the rooms, all of which have fireplaces and small decks. Some rooms have whirlpool baths or kitchens. A 132-step stairway leads down to a small, virtually private beach. Breakfast is served in your room. There is a two-night minimum Friday and Saturday. ✉ *35100 Hwy. 1, 95445,* ☎ *707/884–3667 or 800/942–5342,* FAX *707/884–4815,* WEB *www.whalewatchinn.com. 18 rooms. Kitchenettes (some), beach. AE, MC, V. BP.*

$$–$$$ ▨ **Old Milano Hotel.** This not-so-old hotel—the 1905 mansion burned in the spring of 2001—is one of the most beautiful sunset spots on the coast. You can stay in one five modern cottages or a train caboose. Some cottages have spa tubs; four have gas fireplaces. The caboose has a wood-burning stove and brakeman's seats. ✉ *38300 Hwy. 1, 95445,* ☎ *707/884–3256,* FAX *707/884–4249,* WEB *www.oldmilanohotel.com. 5 cottages, 1 caboose. Hot tub. MC, V. BP.*

$ ▨ **Gualala Hotel.** Gualala's oldest hotel, which once housed timber-mill workers, has small, no-nonsense rooms furnished with well-worn antiques. Most rooms share baths. Rooms in the front have ocean views (and some street noise). The rustic first-floor saloon was a haunt of Jack London's. ✉ *39301 Hwy. 1,* ☎ *707/884–3441,* FAX *707/884–3908. 19 rooms, 5 with bath. Restaurant, bar. AE, D, MC, V.*

△ **Gualala Point Regional Park Campground.** Right on the Gualala River, this campground offers riverfront campsites as well as more secluded sites that sit among the giants of a redwood forest. None of the sites has hookups. *Flush toilets, drinking water, showers, fire pits. 19 drive-in sites, 6 walk-in sites.* ✉ *Hwy. 1, one mi south of Gualala,* ☎ *707/565–2267 reservations,* WEB *www.sonoma-county.org/camping.* ☺ *Year-round.*

En Route   For a dramatic view of the surf and, in winter, migrating whales, take the marked road off Highway 1 north of the fishing village of Point Arena to the **Point Arena Lighthouse** (☎ 707/882–2777). First constructed in 1870, the lighthouse was destroyed by the 1906 earthquake that also devastated San Francisco. Rebuilt in 1907, it towers 115 ft from its base, which is 50 ft above the sea. The lighthouse is open for tours daily from 11 until 3:30, from 10 in summer; admission is $4. As you continue north on Highway 1 toward Mendocino, there are several beaches, most notably the one at **Manchester State Park,** 3 mi north of Point Arena. If you're driving directly to Mendocino from points south and want to grab a quick lunch or a good cup of coffee, visit the café at the **Greenwood Pier Inn** (✉ 5928 Hwy. 1, ☎ 707/877–9997), in Elk.

Elk

39 mi north of Gualala on Hwy. 1.

A former timber town, the village of Elk has two first class bed-and-breakfasts and a beautiful, rocky coastline.

Dining and Lodging

$$$$ ✕🏠 **Harbor House.** Constructed in 1916 by a timber company, this redwood ranch-style house has a dining room with a view of the Pacific. Five of the six rooms in the main house have fireplaces. There are also four smallish cottages with fireplaces and decks. The room rates include breakfast and a four-course dinner (except on weeknights during January and February, when the rates drop drastically as a result). The restaurant ($$$$, reservations essential), which serves California cuisine on a prix-fixe menu, is highly recommended; there's limited seating for those not spending the night. ✉ 5600 S. Hwy. 1, 95432, ☎ 707/877–3203 or 800/720–7474, 🖥 *www.theharborhouseinn.com.* 10 rooms. Restaurant. AE, MC, V. MAP.

$$–$$$$ ✕🏠 **Elk Cove Inn.** Perched on a bluff above the surf that pounds on a
★ virtually private beach, Elk Cove offers priceless views from most rooms. The plushest suites are in a stone-and-cedar-shingle arts and crafts–style building separate from the main house. All rooms have stereos and fireplaces; some have wood-burning stoves. The older accommodations range from a viewless but smartly furnished small room to a huge ocean-view suite with a whirlpool tub. The full bar is open daily. Ask about off-season discount packages. ✉ 6300 S. Hwy. 1, Box 367, 95432, ☎ 707/877–3321 or 800/275–2967, 🖷 707/877–1808, 🖥 *www.elkcoveinn.com. 11 rooms, 5 suites. Refrigerators, hot tub, beach, bar. AE, DC, D, MC, V. BP.*

Albion

4 mi north of Elk on Hwy. 1.

A tiny hamlet nestled next to its namesake river, Albion has played host to myriad visitors—from the Pomo Indians to Sir Francis Drake. With beautiful ocean views and a rich history, it is a good choice for relaxation and comfort.

Dining and Lodging

$$–$$$ ✕ **Ledford House.** There's nothing between this bluff-top wood-and-glass restaurant and the Pacific Ocean but a great view. Entrées are divided into hearty bistro dishes, mainly stews and pastas, and equally large-portion examples of California cuisine—*ahi* tuna, grilled meats, and the like. ✉ 3000 N. Hwy. 1, ☎ 707/937–0282. AE, DC, MC, V. Closed Mon.–Tues. No lunch.

$$$–$$$$ ✕🏠 **Albion River Inn.** Contemporary New England–style cottages at this inn overlook the dramatic bridge and seascape where the Albion River empties into the Pacific. All but two have decks facing the ocean. Six have hot tubs with ocean views. The rooms are filled with everything from antique furnishings to wide-back willow chairs. In the glassed-in dining room ($–$$), which serves grilled dishes and fresh seafood, the views are as captivating as the food. ✉ 3790 N. Hwy. 1,

Box 100, 95410, ☎ 707/937–1919; 800/479–7944 *in northern CA,* FAX 707/937–2604, WEB *www.albionriverinn.com. 20 rooms. Restaurant. AE, D, DC, MC, V. BP.*

Little River

⑪ *3 mi north of Albion on Hwy. 1.*

Van Damme State Park is one of the coast's best spots for abalone diving. The visitor center here has interesting displays on ocean life and Native American history. ✉ *Hwy. 1,* ☎ *707/937–5804 for park; 707/ 937–4016 for visitor center.*

The **Pygmy Forest** contains wizened trees, some more than a century old, that stand only 3–4 ft tall. Highly acidic soil and poor drainage have combined to stunt their growth. To reach the forest by car, turn east on Little River Airport Road ½ mi south of Van Damme State Park, and continue 3½ mi to the clearly marked parking area.

Dining and Lodging

$$–$$$ ✕ **Little River Inn Restaurant.** There are fewer than a dozen entrées on the inn's menu, but they're varied: loin of lamb, petrale sole, grilled polenta with vegetables. Main courses come with soup or salad. Less expensive appetizers, salads, and sandwiches are served in the ocean-view Ole's Whale Watch Bar. ✉ *7551 N. Hwy. 1,* ☎ *707/937–5942. AE, MC, V.*

$$–$$$$ ✕☲ **Heritage House.** The cottages at this resort have stunning ocean views. All the rooms contain plush furnishings and period antiques, and many have private decks, fireplaces, and whirlpool tubs. The dining room ($$$–$$$$), also with a Pacific panorama, serves breakfast, brunch, and dinner. Salmon, quail, sirloin, and elegant desserts are the standouts on the evening menu. The restaurant is closed from early December through mid-February. ✉ *Hwy. 1, 95456,* ☎ *707/937–5885 or 800/235–5885,* FAX *707/937–0318,* WEB *www.heritagehouseinn.com. 66 rooms. Restaurant. AE, MC, V.*

$$–$$$$ ☲ **Glendeven Inn.** The New England–style main house of this tranquil
★   inn has five rooms, all with private baths, three with fireplaces. A converted barn holds an art gallery and a two-bedroom suite with a kitchen. The 1986 Stevenscroft building, whose four rooms have fireplaces, has a high gable roof and weathered barnlike siding. A carriage-house suite makes for a romantic retreat. ✉ *8221 N. Hwy. 1, 95456,* ☎ *707/937– 0083 or 800/822–4536,* FAX *707/937–6108,* WEB *www.glendeven.com. 9 rooms, 2 suites. Kitchenettes. AE, MC, V. BP.*

Mendocino

★ **⑫** *2 mi north of Little River on Hwy. 1; 153 mi from San Francisco, north on Rte. 101, west on Hwy. 128, and north on Hwy. 1.*

Logging created the first boom in the windswept town of Mendocino, which flourished for most of the second half of the 19th century. As the timber industry declined during the early 20th century, many residents left, but the town's setting was too beautiful for it to remain neglected for long. Artists and craftspeople began flocking here in the 1950s, and in their wake came entrepreneurial types who opened restaurants, cafés, and inns. By the 1970s a full-scale revival was under way. A bit of the old town can be seen in such dives as Dick's Place, a bar near the Mendocino Hotel, but the rest of the small downtown area is devoted almost exclusively to contemporary restaurants and shops.

Mendocino may look familiar to fans of *Murder, She Wrote*; the town played the role of Cabot Cove, Maine, in the television show. The subterfuge worked because so many of the town's original settlers had come here from the Northeast and built houses in the New England style. The Blair House, at 45110 Little Lake Street, was the home of Jessica Fletcher (Angela Lansbury's character) in the series. Mendocino has also played a California town, most notably in the Elia Kazan film of John Steinbeck's novel *East of Eden*. The building on Main Street (at Kasten Street) that houses the astronomy-oriented Out of This World store was the Bay City Bank in the 1955 movie, which starred James Dean.

An 1861 structure holds the **Kelley House Museum,** whose artifacts include antique cameras, Victorian-era clothing, furniture, and historical photographs of Mendocino's logging days. ⊠ *45007 Albion St.,* ☎ *707/937–5791.* 🎫 *$2.* ☉ *June–Aug., daily 1–4; Sept.–May, Fri.–Mon. 1–4.*

The **Mendocino Art Center** (⊠ 45200 Little Lake St., ☎ 707/937–5818 or 800/653–3328), which hosts exhibits and art classes and contains a gallery and a theater, is the nexus of Mendocino's flourishing art scene.

The tiny green-and-red **Temple of Kwan Tai** (⊠ Albion St., west of Kasten St., ☎ 707/937–5123), the oldest Chinese temple on the North Coast, dates from 1852. It's open only by appointment, but you can peer in the window and see everything there is to see.

The restored **Ford House,** built in 1854, serves as the visitor center for Mendocino Headlands State Park. The house has a scale model of Mendocino as it looked in 1890, when the town had 34 water towers and a 12-seat public outhouse. History walks leave from Ford House on Saturday afternoon at 1. The park itself consists of the cliffs that border the town; access is free. ⊠ *Main St. west of Lansing St.,* ☎ *707/937–5397.* 🎫 *Free ($1 donation suggested).* ☉ *Daily 11–4, with possible midweek closings in winter.*

★ The **Mendocino Coast Botanical Gardens** offer something for nature lovers in every season. Even in winter, heather and Japanese tulips bloom. Along 2 mi of coastal trails, with ocean views and observation points for whale-watching, is a splendid profusion of flowers. The rhododendrons are at their peak from April through June, and fuchsias and azaleas are resplendent as well. ⊠ *18220 N. Hwy. 1, between Mendocino and Fort Bragg,* ☎ *707/964–4352,* WEB *www.gardenbythesea.com.* 🎫 *$6.* ☉ *Mar.–Oct., daily 9–5; Nov.–Feb., daily 9–4.*

Mendocino's ocean breezes might seem too cool for grape growing, but summer days can be quite warm just over the hills in the **Anderson Valley,** where the cool nights permit a longer ripening period. Chardonnays and pinot noirs find the valley's climate particularly hospitable. Tasting here is a decidedly more laid-back affair than in the Napa and Sonoma valleys. Most tasting rooms are open from 11 to 5 daily and charge a nominal fee (usually deducted if you purchase any wines) to sample a few vintages.

Husch (⊠ 4400 Hwy. 128, Philo, ☎ 707/895–3216 or 800/554–8724), one of the valley's oldest wineries, sells renowned chardonnays and a superb gewürztraminer. At the elegant tasting room at **Roederer Estate** (⊠ 4501 Hwy. 128, Philo, ☎ 707/895–2288), you can taste (for $3) sparkling wines produced by the American affiliate of the famous French champagne maker. **Pacific Echo** (⊠ 8501 Hwy. 128, Philo, ☎ 800/824–7754) was the first Anderson Valley winery to produce critically acclaimed sparkling wines. **Fetzer Vineyards** (⊠ Main St. between Lansing and Kasten Sts., Mendocino, ☎ 707/937–6191 or 800/653–3328) has a tasting room next to the Mendocino Hotel & Garden Suites.

To get to the Anderson Valley from Mendocino, take Highway 1 south to Highway 128 east.

Dining and Lodging

$$-$$$ ✕ **Cafe Beaujolais.** This famous restaurant is housed in a charming cot-
★ tage that makes it all the more appealing. The ever-evolving menu is cross-cultural, with duck, seafood, and free-range, hormone-free meats. Try the Yucatecan-Thai crab cakes. The restaurant typically closes for a month or more in winter. ⊠ *961 Ukiah St.,* ☎ *707/937–5614. D, MC, V.*

$-$$$ ✕ **955 Ukiah.** The interior of this smart restaurant is woodsy and the California cuisine creative. Specialties include fresh fish, duck cannel-loni, peppercorn New York steak, and pastas topped with the house sauce. ⊠ *955 Ukiah St.,* ☎ *707/937–1955. MC, V. Closed Tues. July–Nov. and Mon.–Wed. Dec.–June. No lunch.*

$$$$ ✕⊡ **Stanford Inn by the Sea.** This warm, family-run property is
★ spread among several buildings set back from the highway. The older rooms have wood paneling; the newer ones are quite chic, and suites have ocean-view decks, four-poster or sleigh beds, fireplaces or wood-stoves, and paintings by local artists. The inn is the only one on the North Coast with an organic garden *and* resident llamas. The inn's dining room ($–$$$) serves pizzas, salads, soups, pastas, and vege-tarian entrées, for dinner only. ⊠ *South of Mendocino, east on Comptche-Ukiah Rd. (off Hwy. 1), Box 487, 95460,* ☎ *707/937–5615 or 800/331–8884,* ℻ *707/937–0305,* ⑱ *www.stanfordinn.com. 23 rooms, 10 suites. Refrigerator, indoor pool, hot tub, sauna, bicycles. AE, D, DC, MC, V.*

$-$$$$ ✕⊡ **Mendocino Hotel & Garden Suites.** From the street this hotel looks like something out of the Wild West, with a period facade and balcony that overhangs the raised sidewalk. Stained-glass lamps, polished wood, and Persian carpets lend the hotel a swank 19th-century appeal. All but 14 of the rooms have private baths. Deluxe garden rooms have fireplaces and TVs. The wood-paneled dining room ($–$$$), fronted by a glassed-in solarium, serves fine fish entrées and the best deep-dish ollalieberry pie in California. ⊠ *45080 Main St., Box 587, 95460,* ☎ *707/937–0511 or 800/548–0513,* ℻ *707/937–0513,* ⑱ *www.mendocinohotel.com. 51 rooms, 37 with bath. Restaurant, room ser-vice, bar. AE, MC, V.*

$$-$$$ ✕⊡ **MacCallum House.** With the most meticulously restored Victorian exterior in Mendocino, this 1882 inn, complete with gingerbread trim, transports patrons to another era. Comfortable furnishings and antiques enhance the period feel. In addition to the main house, there are indi-vidual cottages and barn suites around a garden. The menu at the red-wood-paneled restaurant ($$–$$$$; reservations essential) changes quarterly. The focus is on local seafood and organic and free-range meats. The restaurant is closed mid-January through mid-February. ⊠ *45020 Albion St., Box 206, 95460,* ☎ *707/937–0289 or 800/609–0492,* ⑱ *www.maccallumhouse.com. 19 rooms, 3 suites. Restaurant, bar. AE, MC, V.*

$$$-$$$$ ⊡ **Whitegate Inn.** With a white picket fence, a latticework gazebo, and
★ a romantic garden, the Whitegate is a picture-book Victorian. High ceil-ings, floral fabrics, and pastel walls define the public spaces and the luxurious rooms, all of which have fireplaces. Best of all, you can watch the ocean breakers from the deck out back. ⊠ *499 Howard St., 95460,* ☎ *707/937–4892 or 800/531–7282,* ℻ *707/937–1131,* ⑱ *www.whitegateinn.com. 6 rooms. AE, D, DC, MC, V. BP.*

$$-$$$$ ⊡ **Agate Cove Inn.** Facing the Mendocino Headlands across a rocky cove, this inn is ideally situated for watching whales during the winter. Adirondack chairs are set on a small deck for just that purpose; borrow the inn's binoculars for a closer look. Each blue-and-white cottage unit is individually decorated. There are four single and four duplex cottages; two more rooms are in the 1860s farmhouse, where country breakfasts are prepared on an antique woodstove in a kitchen with a full view of the Pacific. ✉ *11201 N. Lansing St., 95460,* ☎ *707/937–0551 or 800/527–3111,* FAX *707/937–0550,* WEB *www.agatecove. com. 10 rooms. MC, V, AE. BP.*

$$–$$$$ 🏠 **C. O. Packard House.** One of four landmark homes on Executive Row, this Carpenter Gothic Victorian is run by a husband-and-wife team of interior decorators. Four oddly shaped rooms are dazzlingly sophisticated, with custom wall finishes, jet-massage baths, and a mix of French and English antiques. A garden cottage is large enough to accommodate four but is less elegant than the rooms in the main house. ✉ *45170 Little Lake St., 95460,* ☎ *707/937–2677 or 888/453– 2677,* FAX *707/937–1323,* WEB *www.packardhouse.com. 4 rooms, 1 suite. D, MC, V. BP.*

$$–$$$$ 🏠 **Joshua Grindle Inn.** The original farmhouse of this B&B on a 2-acre hilltop has five guest rooms, a parlor, and a dining room. Two other buildings, the Watertower (an upper room has windows on all four sides) and the Cottage, hold five additional rooms. Furnishings throughout are simple but comfortable American antiques: Salem rockers, wing chairs, steamer-trunk tables, painted pine beds. ✉ *44800 Little Lake Rd., 95460,* ☎ *707/937–4143, 800/474–6353,* WEB *www.joshgrin. com. 10 rooms. MC, V. BP.*

$$–$$$ 🏠 **Blackberry Inn.** Each single-story unit here has a false front, creating the image of a frontier town. There are a bank, a saloon, Belle's Place (of hospitality), and "offices" for doctors and sheriffs, as well as other themed accommodations. The rooms are cheery and spacious. Most have wood-burning stoves or fireplaces and at least partial ocean views. The inn is a short drive east of town down a quiet side street. Two rooms have kitchenettes. ✉ *44951 Larkin Rd., 95460,* ☎ *707/ 937–5281 or 800/950–7806,* WEB *www.mendocinomotel.com. 17 rooms. Kitchenettes (some). MC, V. CP.*

Nightlife and the Arts

Mendocino Theatre Company (✉ Mendocino Art Center, 42500 Little Lake St., ☎ 707/937–4477) has been around for more than two decades. The community theater's repertoire ranges from such classics as *Uncle Vanya* to more recent plays such as *Other People's Money.*

Patterson's Pub (✉ 10485 Lansing St., ☎ 707/937–4782), an Irish-style watering hole, is a friendly gathering place day or night, though it does become boisterous as the evening wears on. Bands entertain on Friday night.

Outdoor Activities and Sports

Catch-a-Canoe and Bicycles Too (✉ Stanford Inn by the Sea, Mendocino, ☎ 707/937–0273) rents regular and outrigger canoes as well as mountain and suspension bicycles.

Shopping

Many artists exhibit their wares in Mendocino, and the streets of this compact town are so easily walkable that you're sure to find a gallery with something that strikes your fancy. Start your gallery tour at the **Mendocino Art Center** (✉ 45200 Little Lake St., ☎ 707/937–5818 or 800/653–3328). **Old Gold** (✉ 6 Albion St., ☎ 707/937–5005) is a good place to look for locally crafted jewelry.

Fort Bragg

⑬ *10 mi north of Mendocino on Hwy. 1.*

Fort Bragg has changed more than any other coastal town in the past few years. The decline in what was the top industry, timber, is being offset in part by a boom in charter-boat excursions and other tourist pursuits. The city is also attracting many artists, some lured from Mendocino, where the cost of living is higher. This basically blue-collar town is the commercial center of Mendocino County.

The **Skunk Train,** a remnant of the region's logging days, dates from 1885 and travels a route—through redwood forests inaccessible to automobiles—from Fort Bragg to the town of Willits, 40 mi inland. A fume-spewing self-propelled train car that shuttled passengers along the railroad earned the nickname Skunk Train, and the entire line has been called that ever since. Excursions are now given on historic trains and replicas of the Skunk Train motorcar that smell less foul than the original. In summer you can go partway, to Northspur, a three-hour round-trip, or make the full seven-hour journey to Willits and back. ⊠ *Foot of Laurel St., Fort Bragg,* ☎ *707/964–6371 or 800/777–5865.* 🚂 *Fort Bragg–Willits $39; Fort Bragg–Northspur $29–$39.* ☉ *Departs Fort Bragg 9 and 2; departs Willits 8:45 and 1:45.*

★ **MacKerricher State Park** includes 10 mi of sandy beach and several square miles of dunes. Fishing (at two freshwater lakes, one stocked with trout), canoeing, hiking, jogging, bicycling, camping, and harbor-seal watching at Laguna Point are among the popular activities, many of which are accessible to travelers with disabilities. Whales can often be spotted from December to mid-April from the nearby headland. Rangers lead nature hikes throughout the year. ⊠ *Hwy. 1, 3 mi north of Fort Bragg,* ☎ *707/937–5804.* 🚂 *Free.*

Dining, Lodging, and Camping

$$ ✕ **The Restaurant.** The name may be generic, but this place isn't. California cuisine is served in a dining room that doubles as an art gallery. Under the same ownership since 1973, the Restaurant is one of the few places in town serving Sunday brunch. ⊠ *418 N. Main St.,* ☎ *707/964–9800. MC, V. Closed Wed. No lunch.*

$–$$ ✕ **Mendo Bistro.** On the second floor of the Company Store complex, downtown, the town's sole hip restaurant serves oodles of noodles, made fresh on the premises. You might find rotini with sun-dried tomatoes, shells stuffed with spinach, chard, and ricotta, and sweet-potato gnocchi with Gorgonzola sauce on the menu. ⊠ *301 N. Main St.,* ☎ *707/964–4974. AE, D, DC, MC, V. No lunch.*

$–$$ ✕ **Sharon's by the Sea.** The views of Noyo Harbor are up close and scenic at this one-story restaurant at the end of the pier. Seafood is the other reason to visit this unpretentious establishment, which replaced another restaurant at this site. ⊠ *32096 N. Harbor Dr., at south end of Fort Bragg,* ☎ *707/962–0680. AE, MC, V.*

$ ✕ **Headlands Coffee House.** The coffeehouse acts as a cultural center and local gathering place. Musicians perform most nights. ⊠ *120 E. Laurel St.,* ☎ *707/964–1987. D, MC, V.*

$ ✕ **Samraat Restaurant.** Soothing pastels and sitar music set the mood for good, inexpensive Indian dishes. Tandoori, curry, and seafood are specialties. ⊠ *546 S. Main St.,* ☎ *707/964–0386. MC, V.*

$–$$$ 🛏 **Surf and Sand Lodge.** You have to go north of Fort Bragg to find lodgings with unimpeded ocean views, and they're just what you'll get at this souped-up motel. As its name implies, it's practically on the beach. Right out the door are pathways down to the rock-strewn shore. The six cheaper rooms don't have views, but all the bright and fresh accommodations come with enough amenities to make you feel you're staying somewhere grander than a motel. The fancier of the second-story rooms have hot tubs and fireplaces. ⊠ *1131 N. Main St., 95437,* ☎ *707/964–9383 or 800/964–0184,* FAX *707/964–0314,* WEB *www. surfsandlodge.com. 30 rooms. Refrigerators, in-room VCRs, beach. AE, D, MC, V.*

$–$$$ 🏨 **Weller House Inn.** Guest accommodations in this 1886 mansion are decorated with Victorian-style wallpaper and furnishings; the baths have hand-painted tiles. The third floor has a 900-square-ft ballroom (now the breakfast room) paneled in rare California redwood. Newer accommodations are in a water tower on the property—at 51 ft the tallest building in town—topped by a hot tub with spectacular ocean views. ⊠ *524 Stewart St., 95437,* ☎ *707/964–4415 or 877/893–5537,* FAX *707/964–4198,* WEB *www.wellerhouse.com. 8 rooms. AE, D, DC, MC, V. BP.*

⚠ **MacKerricher State Park.** The campsites at MacKerricher are in woodsy spots a quarter mile or so from the ocean. There are no hookups. Make reservations for summer weekends as early as possible (reservations are taken April–mid-October), unless you want to try your luck getting one of the 25 sites that are available on a first-come, first-served basis each day. *Flush toilets, showers, drinking water, fire pits, picnic tables. 142 sites.* ⊠ *Hwy. 1, 3 mi north of Fort Bragg,* ☎ *800/444–7275 for reservations.*

Nightlife

Caspar Inn & Blues Cafe (⊠ 14957 Caspar Rd., ☎ 707/964–5565) presents blues, rock, and alternative rock from Thursday through Saturday.

Outdoor Activities and Sports

Matlick's *Tally Ho II* (⊠ 11845 N. Main St., ☎ 707/964–2079) operates whale-watching trips from December through mid-April, as well as fishing excursions all year. **Ricochet Ridge Ranch** (⊠ 24201 N. Hwy. 1, ☎ 707/964–7669) guides groups on horseback to the Mendocino–Fort Bragg beaches.

En Route   North on Highway 1 from Fort Bragg past the mill town of Westport, the road cuts inland around the **King Range,** a stretch of mountain so rugged it was impossible to build the intended major highway through it. Highway 1 joins Route 101 at the town of Leggett. **Richardson Grove State Park,** north of Leggett along Route 101, marks your first encounter with the truly giant redwoods, but there are even more magnificent stands farther north, in Humboldt and Del Norte counties.

REDWOOD COUNTRY
From Garberville to Crescent City

The majestic redwoods that grace California's coast become more plentiful as you head north. Their towering ancient presence defines the landscape.

Garberville

70 mi from Fort Bragg, north and east on Hwy. 1 and north on Rte. 101; 197 mi north of San Francisco on Rte. 101.

Although it's the largest town in the vicinity of Humboldt Redwoods State Park, Garberville hasn't changed a whole lot since timber was king. The town is a pleasant place to stop for lunch, pick up picnic provisions, or poke through arts-and-crafts stores. A few miles below

The North Coast (Leggett to Crescent City)

OREGON

KLAMATH NATIONAL FOREST

199

N

Smith R.

Klamath R.

Battery Point Lighthouse ■ ⓴
Crescent City

PACIFIC OCEAN

Klamath ○
169

SIX RIVERS NATIONAL FOREST

Prairie Creek Redwoods State Park ■

Klamath

Salmon R.

Redwood National and State Parks ⓳ Lady Bird Johnson Grove

Orick ○ 169

■ Tall Trees Grove

Redwood R.

Bald Hills Rd.
96

SHASTA-TRINITY NATIONAL FOREST

Patrick's Point State Park ⓲
○ Trinidad

101

Arcata Bay 255
Samoa ○ ⓱ **Arcata**

299

Eureka ⓰
Humboldt Bay

Trinity R.

101

Mud R.

TRINITY NATIONAL FOREST

Ferndale ⓯
211

36

Pepperwood ○

254

Humboldt Redwoods State Park ⓮ Weott ○

Mattole Rd.

Avenue of the Giants

101

KING MOUNTAIN RANGE

Garberville ○

Richardson Grove State Park ■

Shelter Cove ○

Eel R.

Leggett ○

101

0 ——— 20 miles
0 ——— 30 km

1

Rockport ○

Garberville is an elegant Tudor resort, the Benbow Inn. Even if you are not staying there, stop in for a drink or a meal and take a look at the architecture and gardens.

Dining and Lodging

$ ✕ **Woodrose Cafe.** This unpretentious eatery serves basic breakfast items on the weekends and healthy lunches every day. Dishes include chicken, pasta, and vegetarian specials. ⌧ *911 Redwood Dr.,* ☎ *707/923–3191. No credit cards. No dinner.*

$$–$$$$ ✕⌂ **Benbow Inn.** South of Garberville alongside the Eel River, this three-
★ story Tudor-style manor resort is the equal of any in the region. The most luxurious of the antiques-filled rooms are on the terrace, with fine river views; some rooms have fireplaces, and 18 have TVs with VCRs. You have canoeing, tennis, golf, and pool privileges at an adjacent property. The wood-panel dining room ($$–$$$) serves American cuisine, with the focus on fresh salmon and trout. ⌧ *445 Lake Benbow Dr., 95542,* ☎ *707/923–2124 or 800/355–3301,* 𝖥𝖠𝖷 *707/923–2897,* 𝖶𝖤𝖡 *www.benbowinn.com. 55 rooms, 1 cottage. Restaurant, refrigerators, in-room VCRs (some), golf privileges, lake, lobby lounge. AE, D, MC, V. Closed early Jan.–early Apr.*

Humboldt Redwoods State Park

🐾 ⑭ *15 mi north of Garberville on Rte. 101.*

At the **Humboldt Redwoods State Park Visitor Center** you can pick up information about the redwoods, waterways, and recreational activities in the more than 53,000-acre park. Brochures are available for a self-guided auto tour of the park. Stops on the auto tour include short and long hikes into redwood groves. ⌧ *Ave. of the Giants, 2 mi south of Weott,* ☎ *707/946–2409 (park); 707/946–2263 (visitor center).* 🈯 *Free; $2 day-use fee for parking and facilities in Williams Grove and Women's Federation Grove.* ☉ *Park daily; visitor center Mar.–Oct., daily 9–5; Nov.–Feb., daily 10–4.*

The **Avenue of the Giants** (Highway 254) begins about 7 mi north of Garberville and winds north, more or less parallel to Route 101, toward Pepperwood. Some of the tallest trees on the planet tower over this stretch of two-lane blacktop. The road follows the south fork of the Eel River and cuts through part of Humboldt Redwoods State Park. Reached via a ½-mi trail off Avenue of the Giants is **Founders Grove** (⌧ Hwy. 254, 4 mi north of Humboldt Redwoods State Park Visitor Center). One of the most impressive trees here—the 362-ft-long Dyerville Giant—fell to the ground in 1991; its root base points skyward 35 ft. **Rockefeller Forest** (⌧ Mattole Rd., 6 mi north of Humboldt Redwoods State Park Visitor Center) is the largest remaining coast redwood forest. It contains 40 of the 100 tallest trees in the world.

Ferndale

⑮ *30 mi from Weott, north on Rte. 101 to Hwy. 211 west.*

The residents of the stately town of Ferndale maintain some of the most sumptuous Victorian homes in California, many of them built by 19th-century Scandinavian, Swiss, and Portuguese dairy farmers who were drawn to the mild climate. The queen of them all is the Gingerbread Mansion. A beautiful sloped graveyard sits on Ocean Avenue west of Main Street. Many shops carry a map with self-guided tours of this lovingly preserved town.

The main building of the **Ferndale Museum** hosts changing exhibitions of Victoriana and has an old-style barbershop and a display of Wiyot

Indian baskets. In the annex are a horse-drawn buggy, a re-created black-smith's shop, and antique farming, fishing, and dairy equipment. ⊠ *515 Shaw Ave.,* ☎ *707/786–4466.* ☞ *$1.* ⊘ *June–Sept., Tues.–Sat. 11–4, Sun. 1–4; Oct.–Dec. and Feb.–May, Wed.–Sat. 11–4, Sun. 1–4.*

Lodging

$$–$$$$ 🏠 **Gingerbread Mansion.** This photogenic Victorian B&B rivals San Francisco's "painted ladies" for dazzle. The mansion's carved friezes set off its gables, and turrets delight the eye. The comfortable parlors and spacious bedrooms are laid out in flowery Victorian splendor. Some rooms have views of the mansion's English garden, and one has side-by-side bathtubs. One spectacular suite is the Veneto, with hand-painted scenes of Venice on the walls and ceiling as well as marble floors. Ask about off-season discounts. ⊠ *400 Berding St., off Brown St., Box 40, 95536,* ☎ *707/786–4000 or 800/952–4136,* WEB *www.gingerbread-mansion. com. 11 rooms, 4 suites. AE, MC, V. BP.*

Outdoor Activities and Sports

Eel River Delta Tours (⊠ 285 Morgan Slough Rd., ☎ 707/786–4187) conducts a two-hour boat trip that emphasizes the wildlife and history of the Eel River's estuary and salt marsh.

Shopping

Among the shops lined up along Main Street, **Golden Gait Mercantile** (⊠ 421 Main St., ☎ 707/786–4891) seems to be lost in a time warp, what with Burma Shave products and old-fashioned long johns as well as penny candy.

Eureka

 10 mi north of Ferndale and 269 mi north of San Francisco on Rte. 101.

Eureka, population 28,500, is the North Coast's largest city. It has gone through several cycles of boom and bust, first with mining and later with timber and fishing. There are nearly 100 Victorian buildings here, many of them well preserved. The splendid **Carson Mansion** (⊠ M and 2nd Sts.) was built in 1885 for timber baron William Carson. A private men's club now occupies the house. Don't miss the Victorian extravaganza popularly known as the **Pink Lady** (⊠ M and 2nd Sts.). For proof that contemporary architects have the skills to design lovely Victoriana, take a look at the **Carter House** B&B (⊠ 3rd and L Sts.) and keep in mind it was built in the 1980s, not the 1880s.

At the **Chamber of Commerce** you can pick up maps with self-guided driving tours of Eureka's architecture and find out about organized tours. ⊠ *2112 Broadway,* ☎ *707/442–3738 or 800/356–6381.* ⊘ *Weekdays 8:30–5.*

The **Clarke Memorial Museum** contains extraordinary northwestern California Native American basketry and artifacts of Eureka's Victorian, logging, and maritime eras. ⊠ *240 E St.,* ☎ *707/443–1947.* ☞ *Donations accepted.* ⊘ *Feb.–Dec., Tues.–Sat. 11–4.*

The structure that gave **Fort Humboldt State Historic Park** its name once protected white settlers from the Native Americans. Ulysses S. Grant was posted here in 1854. The old fort is no longer around, but on its grounds are a museum, some ancient steam engines (operators rev them up on the third Saturday of the month), and a logger's cabin. The park is a good place for a picnic. ⊠ *3431 Fort Ave.,* ☎ *707/445–6567 or 707/445–6547.* ☞ *Free.* ⊘ *Daily 9–5.*

To explore the waters around Eureka, take a **Humboldt Bay Harbor Cruise.** You can observe some of the region's bird life while sailing past fishing boats and decaying timber mills during a 75-minute narrated cruise. ⊠ *Pier at C St.,* ☎ *707/445–1910 or 707/444–9440.* ☞ *Harbor cruise $9.50; cocktail cruise $6.50.* ☉ *Harbor cruise departs May–Oct., Mon.–Sat. at 1, 2:30, and 4, Sun. 1 and 2:30. Cocktail cruise departs Tues.–Sat. at 5:30.*

Dining and Lodging

$$–$$$$ ✕ **Restaurant 301.** Mark and Christi Carter, owners of Eureka's fanciest hotels, also run the town's best restaurant. Most vegetables and herbs used here are grown at their greenhouse and nearby ranch. Try the sea scallops, roasted pork chop, spring rack of lamb, or local petrale sole, and don't skip the appetizers—especially if the vegetable ragouts or gnocchi are on the menu. The wine list is one of the finest in the country. ⊠ *301 L St.,* ☎ *707/444–8062. AE, D, DC, MC, V. No lunch.*

$–$$ ✕ **Cafe Waterfront.** This small eatery across from the marina has a long bar with a TV. Sandwiches and affordable seafood dishes are the menu mainstays. ⊠ *102 F St.,* ☎ *707/443–9190. MC, V.*

$ ✕ **Ramone's.** A casual bakery café, Ramone's serves light sandwiches from dawn to 6. ⊠ *209 E. St.,* ☎ *707/442–6082. MC, V. No dinner.*

$ ✕ **Samoa Cookhouse.** The recommendation here is for rustic fun, of
★ which there is plenty: this is a longtime loggers' hangout. The Samoa's cooks serve three substantial set meals family style at long wooden tables. Meat dishes predominate. Save room (if possible) for dessert. ⊠ *Cookhouse Rd. (from Rte. 101 cross Samoa Bridge, turn left onto Samoa Rd., then left 1 block later onto Cookhouse Rd.),* ☎ *707/442–1659. AE, D, MC, V.*

$$–$$$$ ▦ **Carter House.** Whether you like small inns, country hotels, or the
★ charm of a cottage, the Carter family has something to offer. The Carter House, built in 1982 following the floor plan of a San Francisco mansion, has large rooms with heirloom furniture. Two doors down, the three-room Victorian Bell Cottage is decorated in contemporary southwestern style. The three-story Hotel Carter, catercorner from the Carter House, has an elegant lobby and suites. Breakfast is served in the hotel's sunny corner dining room. ⊠ *301 L St., 95501,* ☎ *707/444–8062,* 𝔽𝔸𝕏 *707/444–8067,* 𝕎𝔼𝔹 *www.carterhouse.com. 21 rooms, 11 suites. Dining room. AE, D, DC, MC, V. BP.*

$–$$$ ▦ **An Elegant Victorian Mansion.** This meticulously restored Eastlake
★ mansion in a residential neighborhood east of the Old Town lives up to its name. Each room is completely decked out in period furnishings and wall coverings, down to the carved-wood beds, fringed lamp shades, and pull-chain commodes. The innkeepers may even greet you in vintage clothing and entertain you with silent movies on tape, croquet on the rose-encircled lawn, and guided tours of local Victoriana in their antique automobile. ⊠ *1406 C St., 95501,* ☎ *707/444–3144,* 𝔽𝔸𝕏 *707/442–3295,* 𝕎𝔼𝔹 *www.eureka-california.com. 4 rooms. Sauna, bicycles, croquet, laundry service. MC, V. BP.*

Nightlife

Lost Coast Brewery & Cafe (⊠ 617 4th St., ☎ 707/445–4480), a bustling microbrewery, is the best place in town to relax with a pint of ale or porter. Soups, salads, and light meals are served for lunch and dinner (about $15).

Outdoor Activities and Sports

Hum-Boats (⊠ 2 F St., ☎ 707/443–5157) provides sailing rides, sailboat rentals, guided kayak tours, and sea kayak rentals and lessons (year-round; by appointment only in winter). The company also runs a water-taxi service on Humboldt Bay.

Shopping

Eureka has several art galleries in the district running from C to I streets between 2nd and 3rd streets. Specialty shops in Eureka's Old Town include the original **Restoration Hardware** (⊠ 417 2nd St., ☎ 707/443–3152), a good place to find stylish yet functional home and garden accessories and clever polishing and cleaning products. The **Irish Shop** (⊠ 334 2nd St., ☎ 707/443–8343) carries imports from the Emerald Isle, mostly fine woolens.

Arcata

⑰ *9 mi north of Eureka on Rte. 101.*

The home of Humboldt State University is one of the few California burgs to retain a town square. A farmers' market takes place in the square on Saturday morning from May through November. For a self-guided tour of Arcata that includes some of its restored Victorian buildings, pick up a map from the **Chamber of Commerce** (⊠ 1635 Heindon Rd., ☎ 707/822–3619, WEB www.arcata.com/chamber), open daily from 9 to 5.

Dining and Lodging

$–$$$ ✕ **Abruzzi.** Salads and hefty pasta dishes take up most of the menu at this upscale Italian restaurant in the lower level of Jacoby's Storehouse, off the town square. One specialty is linguine *pescara*, with a spicy seafood-and-tomato sauce. ⊠ *H and 8th Sts.,* ☎ *707/826–2345. AE, D, MC, V. No lunch.*

$ ✕ **Crosswinds.** This restaurant serves Continental cuisine in a sunny Victorian room, at prices that attract students from Humboldt State University. ⊠ *10th and I Sts.,* ☎ *707/826–2133. MC, V. Closed Mon. No dinner.*

$–$$ 🏨 **Hotel Arcata.** Rooms are clean and modest, but flowered bedspreads and claw-foot bathtubs lend a bit of character to this historic landmark overlooking the town square. Tomo, the Japanese restaurant on the ground floor, serves sushi as well as cooked food. It is closed for lunch on weekends. ⊠ *708 9th St., 95521,* ☎ *707/826–0217 or 800/344–1221,* FAX *707/826–1737,* WEB *www.hotelarcata.com. 32 rooms. Restaurant. AE, D, DC, MC, V. CP.*

Shopping

Plaza Design (⊠ 808 G St., ☎ 707/822–7732), one of Arcata's impressive selection of book, housewares, clothing, fabric, and other shops, specializes in gifts, papers, and innovative furnishings.

Trinidad

14 mi north of Arcata on Rte. 101.

Trinidad got its name from the Spanish mariners who entered the bay on Trinity Sunday, June 9, 1775. The town became a principal trading post for the mining camps along the Klamath and Trinity rivers. As mining, and then whaling, faded, so did the luster of this former boomtown. Developers have overlooked this scenic spot for now, making it one of the quietest of the coastal towns that have inns and dining spots. Picturesque Trinidad Bay's harbor cove and rock formations look both raw and tranquil.

Dining and Lodging

$$–$$$ ✕ **Larrupin' Cafe.** Considered by many locals one of the best places to
★   eat on the North Coast, this restaurant has earned widespread fame for its mesquite-grilled ribs and fresh fish dishes, served in a bright yellow two-story house on a quiet country road 2 mi north of Trinidad. ⊠ *1658*

Patrick's Point Dr., ☎ *707/677–0230. Reservations essential. No credit cards. Closed Tues.–Wed. in winter, Tues. in summer. No lunch.*

$–$$ ✕ **Seascape.** With its glassed-in main room and deck for outdoor dining, this casual spot is an ideal place to take in the scenery of Trinidad Bay. The breakfasts are great, the lunches are substantial, and the dinners showcase local seafood, particularly Dungeness crab in season. ⊠ *At pier,* ☎ *707/677–3762. D, MC, V.*

$$$ 🏨 **Turtle Rocks Oceanfront Inn.** Unobstructed ocean views from most rooms make this inn a desirable choice for nature lovers. Named for some of the enormous formations within view offshore, this B&B has a two-tier Whale Watch Deck, where you can sit on rocking chairs or chaise lounges and take catnaps or scan the horizon. Contemporary and antique furnishings decorate the spacious rooms, all but one of which have decks. ⊠ *3392 Patrick's Point Dr., 95570,* ☎ *707/677–3707,* WEB *www.turtlerocksinn.com. 6 rooms, 1 suite. AE, D, MC, V. BP.*

$$–$$$ 🏨 **Trinidad Bay Bed & Breakfast.** This Cape Cod–style shingle house overlooks the harbor and the coastline to the south. The innkeepers provide a wealth of information about the nearby wilderness, beach, and fishing habitats. A crackling fire warms the living room in chilly weather; one room has its own fireplace. ⊠ *560 Edwards St., Box 849, 95570,* ☎ *707/677–0840,* FAX *707/677–9245,* WEB *www.trinidadbaybnb.com. 4 rooms. MC, V. Closed Dec.–Jan. BP.*

Patrick's Point State Park

⑱ *5 mi north of Trinidad and 25 mi north of Eureka on Rte. 101.*

Patrick's Point is the ultimate California coastal park. On a forested plateau almost 200 ft above the surf, it has stunning views of the Pacific, great whale and sea-lion watching in season, picnic areas, bike paths, and hiking trails through old-growth forest. There are tidal pools at Agate Beach and a small museum with natural-history exhibits. ☎ *707/677–3570.* 🎟 *$2 per vehicle.*

Camping

⚠ **Patrick's Point State Park Campground.** In a spruce and alder forest above the ocean, with just a handful of sites that have views of the ocean, Patrick's Point campground has all the amenities, save RV hookups. You should reserve in advance in summer. *Flush toilets, drinking water, showers, bear boxes, fire pits. 124 sites.* ⊠ *Rte. 101, 4150 Patrick's Point Dr.,* ☎ *800/444–7275.* ☉ *Year-round.*

Redwood National and State Parks

⑲ *22 mi north (Orick entrance) of Trinidad on Rte. 101.*

After 115 years of intensive logging, this 106,000-acre parcel of tall trees came under government protection in 1968, marking the California environmentalists' greatest victory over the timber industry. Redwood National and State Parks encompasses three state parks (Prairie Creek Redwoods, Del Norte Coast Redwoods, and Jedediah Smith Redwoods) and is more than 40 mi long. There is no admission fee to the national or state parks, but the state parks charge $2 to use facilities such as the beach or picnic areas. ⊠ *Park Headquarters: 1111 2nd St., Crescent City,* ☎ *707/464–6101 Ext. 5064.*

At the **Redwood Information Center** you can get brochures, advice, and a free permit to drive up the steep, 17-mi road (the last 6 mi are gravel) to reach the Tall Trees Grove. Whale-watchers will find the deck of the visitor center an excellent observation point, and birders will enjoy the nearby Freshwater Lagoon, a popular layover for migrating waterfowl. ⊠ *Off Rte. 101, Orick,* ☎ *707/464–6101 Ext. 5265.*

At **Tall Trees Grove** a 3-mi round-trip hiking trail leads to the world's tallest redwood, as well as its third- and fifth-tallest ones.

Within **Lady Bird Johnson Grove,** off Bald Hills Road, is a short circular trail to resplendent redwoods. This section of the park was dedicated by and named for the former first lady. For additional views take Davison Road to Fern Canyon. This gravel road winds through 4 mi of second-growth redwoods, then hugs a bluff 100 ft above the pounding Pacific surf for another 4 mi.

To reach the entrance to **Prairie Creek Redwoods State Park** (☎ 707/ 464–6101 Ext. 5300), take the Prairie Parkway exit off the Route 101 bypass. Extra space has been paved alongside the parklands, providing fine vantage points from which to observe an imposing herd of Roosevelt elk grazing in the adjoining meadow. Prairie Creek's Revelation Trail is fully accessible to those with disabilities.

Lodging and Camping

$ ⊞ **Hostelling International–Redwood National Park.** This century-old inn is a stone's throw from the ocean; hiking begins just beyond its doors. Lodging is dormitory style. Reserve in advance for the hostel's one private room. ⊠ *14480 Rte. 101, at Wilson Creek Rd. (20 mi north of Orick), Klamath 95548,* ☎ FAX *707/482–8265,* WEB *www.norcalhostels. org. D, MC, V.*

⚠ **Freshwater Lagoon.** A strip of sand between the ocean and Freshwater Lagoon holds a primitive unofficial campground with no water or hookups—but great views. From the parking lot head into the wilderness to stake your claim; the campground is full when the parking lot is. Use only the existing fire pits. *Pump toilets, fire pits.* ⊠ *West side of Rte. 101, 1½ mi south of Orick (¼ mi south of Redwood Information Center),* ☎ *707/464–6101 Ext. 5265. Reservations not accepted.* ☉ *Year-round.*

Crescent City

⑳ *40 mi north of Orick on Rte. 101.*

Del Norte County's largest town (population just under 5,000) is named for the shape of its harbor; during the 1800s this was an important steamship stop. At the bottom of B Street at **Popeye's Landing** you can rent a crab pot, buy some bait, and try your luck at crabbing. At low tide from April through September, you can walk from the pier across the ocean floor to the oldest lighthouse on the North Coast, **Battery Point Lighthouse** (☎ 707/464–3089). Tours ($2) of the 1856 structure are given from May through October, Wednesday through Sunday between 10 and 4, and by appointment the rest of the year.

Dining and Lodging

$–$$ ✕ **Harbor View Grotto.** This glassed-in dining hall overlooking the Pacific prides itself on its fresh fish entrées. The white two-story building is marked only by a neon sign that reads RESTAURANT. ⊠ *155 Starcross Way,* ☎ *707/464–3815. D, MC, V.*

$ ⊞ **Curly Redwood Lodge.** A single redwood tree produced the 57,000 board ft of lumber used to build this lodge. The rooms make the most of that tree, with paneling, platform beds, and dressers built into the walls. ⊠ *701 Rte. 101 S, 95531,* ☎ *707/464–2137,* FAX *707/464– 1655,* WEB *www.curlyredwoodlodge.com. 36 rooms. AE, DC, MC, V.*

En Route   Travelers continuing north to the **Smith River** near the Oregon state line will find fine trout and salmon fishing as well as a profusion of flowers. Ninety percent of America's lily bulbs are grown in this area.

THE NORTH COAST A TO Z

To research prices, get advice from other travelers, and book travel arrangements, visit www.fodors.com.

AIR TRAVEL

Arcata/Eureka Airport receives United Express flights from San Francisco to Arcata/Eureka. *See* Air Travel *in* Smart Travel Tips A to Z for airline phone numbers.

➤ AIRPORT INFORMATION: **Arcata/Eureka Airport** (✉ Off Rte. 101, McKinleyville, ☎ 707/839–5401).

BUS TRAVEL

Greyhound buses travel along Route 101 from San Francisco to Seattle, with regular stops in Eureka and Crescent City. Bus drivers will stop in other towns along the route if you specify your destination when you board.

Humboldt Transit Authority connects Eureka, Arcata, Scotia, Fortuna, and Trinidad.

➤ BUS INFORMATION: **Greyhound** (☎ 800/231–2222). **Humboldt Transit Authority** (☎ 707/443–0826).

CAR RENTAL

Hertz rents cars at the Arcata/Eureka Airport. *See* Car Rental *in* Smart Travel Tips A to Z for national rental agency phone numbers.

CAR TRAVEL

Although there are excellent services along Highway 1 and Route 101, the main routes through the North Coast, gas stations and mechanics are few and far between on the smaller roads. If you're running low on fuel and see a gas station, stop for a refill. Highway 1 and Route 101 are the main north–south coastal routes. Highway 1 is often curvy and difficult all along the coast. Driving directly to Mendocino from San Francisco is quicker if, instead of driving up the coast on Highway 1, you take Route 101 north to Highway 128 west (from Cloverdale) to Highway 1 north. Once it gets into Humboldt County, Route 101 itself becomes as twisting as Highway 1 as it continues on to the northernmost corner of the state.

For information on the condition of roads in northern California, call the Caltrans Highway Information Network's voice-activated system. At the prompt say the route number in which you are interested, and you'll hear a recorded message about current conditions.

➤ HIGHWAY INFORMATION: **Caltrans Highway Information Network** (☎ 800/427–7623).

EMERGENCIES

In an emergency dial 911. In state and national parks park rangers serve as police officers and will help you in any emergency. Bigger towns along the coast have their own hospitals, but for major medical emergencies you will need to go to San Francisco.

➤ EMERGENCY CONTACTS: **Central Hospital Health Direct** (✉ 2200 Harrison Ave., Eureka, ☎ 707/445–3121). **Del Norte County Hospital** (✉ 100 A St., Crescent City, ☎ 707/464–8511). **Eureka Police Department** (✉ 604 C St., Eureka, ☎ 707/441–4060). **Mendocino Coast District**

Hospital (⊠ 700 River Dr., Fort Bragg, ☎ 707/961–1234). **Mendo-cino County Sheriff** (⊠ 951 Low Gap Rd., Ukiah, ☎ 707/463–4411).

LODGING

For summer stays you should reserve your room well in advance, while during the winter you are likely to see reduced rates and nearly empty inns and bed-and-breakfasts. Unique Northwest Inns can lead you to some of the area's nicest lodging options.

➤ RESERVATIONS AGENCY: **Unique Northwest Inns** (WEB www. uniquenorthwestinns.com).

TRAIN TRAVEL

There is no Amtrak service to this region, but the historic Skunk Train offers chug-chug service from Fort Bragg to Willits. Trains depart Fort Bragg at 9 and 2; they depart Willits at 8:45 and 1:45. The fare from Fort Bragg to Willits is $39; from Fort Bragg to Northspur it's $29–$39.

➤ RAIL SERVICE: **Skunk Train** (⊠ Foot of Laurel St., Fort Bragg, ☎ 707/964–6371 or 800/777–5865).

TOURS

New Sea Angler and Jaws runs cruises and fishing charters daily, weather permitting. Oceanic Society Expeditions conducts whale-watching and other nature cruises north and west of San Francisco throughout much of the year.

➤ CONTACTS: **New Sea Angler and Jaws** (⊠ Bodega Bay, ☎ 707/875–3495). **Oceanic Society Expeditions** (☎ 415/474–3385).

VISITOR INFORMATION

➤ CONTACTS: **Eureka/Humboldt County Convention and Visitors Bu-reau** (⊠ 1034 2nd St., Eureka 95501, ☎ 707/443–5097 or 800/346–3482). **Fort Bragg–Mendocino Coast Chamber of Commerce** (⊠ Box 1141, Fort Bragg 95437, ☎ 707/961–6300 or 800/726–2780). **Red-wood Empire Association** (⊠ Cannery, 2801 Leavenworth St., San Fran-cisco 94133, ☎ 415/543–8334). **Sonoma County Tourism Program** (⊠ 2300 County Center Dr., Room B260, Santa Rosa 95405, ☎ 707/565–5383). **West Marin Chamber of Commerce** (⊠ Box 1045, Point Reyes Station 94956, ☎ 415/663–9232).

4 SAN FRANCISCO

WITH SIDE TRIPS TO MARIN COUNTY AND THE EAST BAY

Brace yourself for the brilliant colors of ornately painted, bay-window Victorians; the sounds of foghorns and cable car lines; and the crisp, salty smell of the bay. San Francisco's world-famous landmarks—the Golden Gate Bridge, Alcatraz, the Transamerica Pyramid—provide an unforgettable backdrop for its eclectic neighborhoods, from bustling Chinatown and bacchanalian North Beach to the left-of-center Castro district and the city's new cultural center, SoMa.

N ITS FIRST LIFE, SAN FRANCISCO was little more than a small, well-situated settlement. Founded by Spaniards in 1776, it was prized for its natural harbor, so commodious that "all the navies of the world might fit inside it," as one visitor wrote. Around 1849 the discovery of gold at John Sutter's sawmill in the nearby Sierra foothills transformed the sleepy little settlement into a city of 30,000. As millions of dollars' worth of gold was panned and blasted out of the hills, a "western Wall Street" sprang up. Just when gold production began to taper off, prospectors turned up a rich vein of silver in Virginia City, Nevada. San Francisco, the nearest financial center, saw its population soar to 342,000. But it was the 1869 completion of the transcontinental railway, linking the once-isolated western capital to the rest of the nation, that turned San Francisco into a major city.

Loose, tolerant, and even licentious are words that are used to describe San Francisco. Bohemian communities thrive here. As early as the 1860s, the Barbary Coast—a collection of taverns, whorehouses, and gambling joints along Pacific Avenue close to the waterfront—was famous, or infamous. North Beach, the city's Little Italy, became the home of the Beat movement in the 1950s (Herb Caen, the city's best-known columnist, coined the term "beatnik"). City Lights, a bookstore and publishing house that still stands on Columbus Avenue, brought out, among other titles, Allen Ginsberg's *Howl* and *Kaddish*. In the '60s, the Haight-Ashbury district became synonymous with hippiedom, giving rise to such legendary bands as Jefferson Airplane and the Grateful Dead. The Free Speech movement began across the Bay at the University of California at Berkeley, and Stanford University's David Harris, who went to prison for defying the draft, numbered among the nation's most famous student leaders. The '70s saw lesbians and gay men from around the country descend on the Castro, turning the one-time Irish neighborhood into the country's best-known gay enclave.

Technically speaking, San Francisco is only California's fourth-largest city, behind Los Angeles, San Diego, and nearby San Jose. But that statistic is misleading: the Bay Area, extending from the bedroom communities north of Oakland and Berkeley south through the peninsula and the San Jose area, is really one continuous megacity, with San Francisco at its heart.

EXPLORING SAN FRANCISCO

Revised by
Denise M. Leto

You could live in San Francisco a month and ask no greater entertainment than walking through it," wrote Inez Hayes Irwin, author of *The Californiacs*, an effusive 1921 homage to the state of California and the City by the Bay. Her claim remains true today: As in the 1920s, touring on foot is the best way to experience this diverse metropolis.

San Francisco is a relatively small city. About 800,000 residents live on a 46½-square-mi tip of land between San Francisco Bay and the Pacific Ocean. Yet this compact space is packed with sites of historical and architectural interest. San Franciscans cherish the city's colorful past—many older buildings have been nostalgically converted into modern offices and shops, and longtime locals still rue those that fell victim to acts of nature and the indifference of developers. In addition, the neighborhoods of San Francisco retain strong cultural, political, and ethnic identities. Locals know this pluralism is the real life of the city. Experiencing San Francisco means visiting the neighborhoods: the

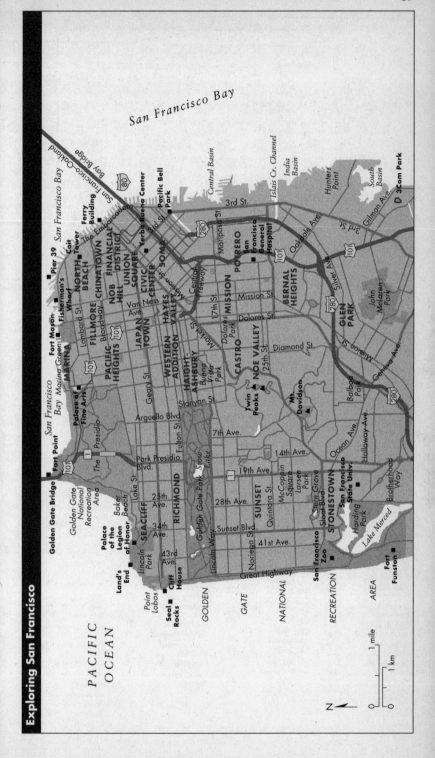

San Francisco Bay

PACIFIC
OCEAN

Golden Gate Bridge

San Francisco Bay

San Francisco-Oakland Bay Bridge

Pier 39

Fisherman's Wharf

Fort Mason

Marina Green

Coit Tower

The Embarcadero

Ferry Building

NORTH BEACH

CHINATOWN

FINANCIAL DISTRICT

Pacific Bell Park

Yerba Buena Center

Old St.

3rd St.

Central Basin

Islais Cr. Channel

India Basin

Hunters Point

South Basin

3Com Park

NOB HILL

UNION SQUARE

CIVIC CENTER

SOMA

Mission St.

Central Freeway

Mariposa St.

POTRERO

San Francisco General Hospital

Oakdale Ave.

Gilman Ave.

Silver Ave.

John McLaren Park

Geneva Ave.

Mission St.

Fort Point

San Francisco Bay

The Presidio

Palace of Fine Arts

MARINA

Lombard St.

Broadway

PACIFIC HEIGHTS

FILLMORE

JAPAN TOWN

HAYES VALLEY

WESTERN ADDITION

Van Ness Ave.

Market St.

17th St.

MISSION

Dolores St.

Dolores St.

BERNAL HEIGHTS

GLEN PARK

Mission St.

Golden Gate National Recreation Area

Baker Beach

Geary St.

Arguello Blvd.

HAIGHT-ASHBURY

Buena Vista Park

Stanyan St.

Fulton St.

7th Ave.

Park Presidio Blvd.

Lake St.

CASTRO

NOE VALLEY

25th St.

Diamond St.

Twin Peaks

Mt. Davidson

Balboa Park

Ocean Ave.

14th Ave.

19th Ave.

McCoppin Square

Larsen Park

Stern Grove

Sloat Blvd.

STONESTOWN

San Francisco State Univ.

Harding Park

Lake Merced

Brotherhood Way

Fort Point

Palace of the Legion of Honor

Lincoln Park

SEACLIFF

RICHMOND

25th Ave.

34th Ave.

43rd Ave.

28th Ave.

Golden Gate Park

Sunset Blvd.

Quintara St.

Noriega St.

41st Ave.

SUNSET

Stow Lake

Lincoln Way

Great Highway

Land's End

Point Lobos

Seal Rocks

Cliff House

GOLDEN

GATE

NATIONAL

RECREATION

AREA

San Francisco Zoo

Fort Funston

1 mile

1 km

N

68

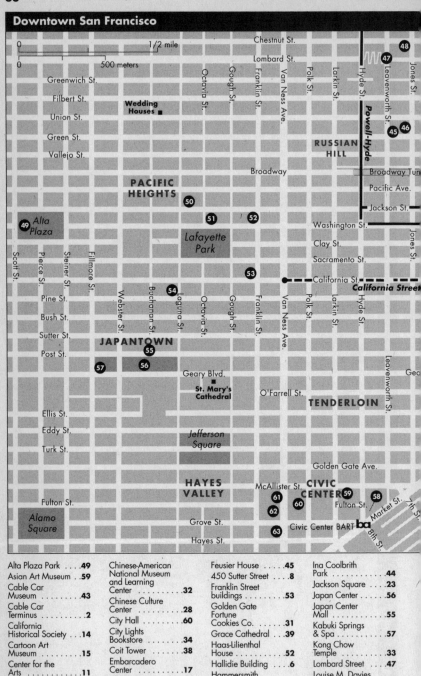

San Francisco Bay

colorful Mission District, the gay Castro, countercultural Haight Street, swank Pacific Heights, lively Chinatown, and ever bohemian North Beach.

Numbers in the text correspond to numbers in the margin and on the neighborhood maps.

Union Square

Much of San Francisco may feel like a collection of small towns strung together, but the Union Square area bristles with big-city bravado. The city's finest department stores—including Bloomingdale's, scheduled to open in spring 2003—do business here, along with exclusive emporiums like Tiffany & Co., Prada, and Coach and big-name franchises like Niketown, the Original Levi's Store, and Virgin Megastore. Several dozen hotels within a three-block walk of the square cater to visitors. The downtown theater district and many fine arts galleries are nearby.

A Good Walk

Begin three blocks south of Union Square at the **San Francisco Visitor Information Center** ①, on the lower level of Hallidie Plaza at Powell and Market streets. Up the escalators on the east side of the plaza, where Powell dead-ends into Market, lies the **cable car terminus** ② for two of the city's three lines. Head north on Powell from the terminus to Geary Street, where the sturdy and stately **Westin St. Francis Hotel** ③ dominates Powell between Geary and Post streets. **Union Square** ④ is across Powell from the hotel's main entrance. You can pick up discount and full-price event tickets at the TIX Bay Area booth in the square.

From the square head north on Stockton Street and make a right on **Maiden Lane** ⑤, a two-block alley directly across Stockton from Union Square that runs east parallel to Geary. When the lane ends at Kearny Street, turn left, walk 1½ blocks to Sutter Street, make a right, and walk a half block to the **Hallidie Building** ⑥. After viewing this historic building, reverse direction and head west 1½ blocks up Sutter to the fanciful beaux-arts–style **Hakmersmith Building** ⑦, on the southwest corner of Sutter Street and Grant Avenue. In the middle of the next block of Sutter stands a glorious Art Deco building at **No. 450** ⑧. From here, backtrack a half block east to Stockton Street and take a right. In front of the the Grand Hyatt hotel sits **Ruth Asawa's Fantasy Fountain** ⑨. Union Square is a half block south on Stockton.

TIMING

Allow two hours to see everything around Union Square. If you're a shopper, give yourself extra time.

Sights to See

🐾 ❷ **Cable car terminus.** San Francisco's signature red cable cars were declared National Landmarks—the only ones that move—in 1964. Two of the three operating lines begin and end their runs in Union Square. The more dramatic Powell–Mason line climbs up Nob Hill, then winds through North Beach to Fisherman's Wharf. The Powell–Hyde line also crosses Nob Hill but then continues up Russian Hill and down Hyde Street to Victorian Park, across from the Buena Vista Café and near Ghirardelli Square. Buy your ticket ($2 one-way) on board, at nearby hotels, or at the police/information booth near the turnaround. If it's just the experience of riding a cable car you're after, board the less-busy California line at Van Ness Avenue and ride it down to the Hyatt Regency Hotel. ⊠ *Powell and Market Sts., Union Square.*

8 450 Sutter Street. Handsome Maya-inspired designs adorn the exterior and interior surfaces of this 1928 Art Deco skyscraper, a masterpiece of terra-cotta and other detailing. ⊠ *Between Stockton and Powell Sts., Union Square.*

6 Hallidie Building. Named for cable car inventor Andrew S. Hallidie, this 1918 structure is best viewed from across the street. Willis Polk's revolutionary glass-curtain wall—believed to be the world's first such facade—hangs a foot beyond the reinforced concrete of the frame. The reflecting glass, decorative exterior fire escapes that appear to be metal balconies, and Venetian Gothic cornice are worth noting. ⊠ *130 Sutter St., between Kearny and Montgomery Sts., Union Square.*

7 Hammersmith Building. Glass walls and a colorful design distinguish this four-story beaux-arts–style structure, built in 1907. The Foundation for Architectural Heritage once described the building as a "commercial jewel box." Appropriately, it was originally designed for use as a jewelry store. ⊠ *301 Sutter St., at Grant Ave., Union Square.*

5 Maiden Lane. Known as Morton Street in the raffish Barbary Coast era, this former red-light district reported at least one murder a week during the late 19th century. After the 1906 fire destroyed the brothels, the street emerged as Maiden Lane, and it has since become a semi-chic pedestrian mall stretching two blocks, between Stockton and Kearny streets.

With its circular interior ramp and skylights, the handsome brick 1948 structure at **140 Maiden Lane,** the only Frank Lloyd Wright building in San Francisco, is said to have been his model for the Guggenheim Museum in New York. **Xanadu Tribal Arts** (☎ 415/392–9999), a gallery showcasing Baltic, Latin American, and African folk art, occupies the space. ⊠ *Between Stockton and Kearny Sts., Union Square.*

9 Ruth Asawa's Fantasy Fountain. Local artist Ruth Asawa's sculpture, a wonderland of real and mythical creatures, honors the city's hills, bridges, and architecture. Children and friends helped Asawa shape the hundreds of tiny figures from baker's clay; these were assembled on 41 large panels from which molds were made for the bronze casting. ⊠ *In front of Grand Hyatt at 345 Stockton St., Union Square.*

1 San Francisco Visitor Information Center. A multilingual staff operates this facility below the cable car terminus. They answer questions and provide maps and pamphlets. You can also pick up discount coupons and hotel brochures here. ⊠ *Hallidie Plaza, lower level, Powell and Market Sts., Union Square,* ☎ *415/391–2000 or 415/283–0177,* ⓦⒺⒷ *www.sfvisitor.org.* ☉ *Weekdays 9–5, weekends 9–3.*

4 Union Square. The heart of San Francisco's downtown since 1850, the 2½-acre square takes its name from the violent pro-union demonstrations staged here prior to the Civil War. At center stage, the *Victory Monument,* by Robert Ingersoll Aitken, commemorates Commodore George Dewey's victory over the Spanish fleet at Manila in 1898. The 97-ft Corinthian column, topped by a bronze figure symbolizing naval conquest, was dedicated by Theodore Roosevelt in 1903 and withstood the 1906 earthquake. Completely renovated in 2002, the once dowdy square now has an open-air stage and central plaza, an outdoor café, gardens, four sculptures by the artist R. M. Fischer, and a visitor information booth. ⊠ *Between Powell, Stockton, Post, and Geary Sts., Union Square.*

3 Westin St. Francis Hotel. The second-oldest hotel in the city, established in 1904, was conceived by railroad baron and financier Charles Crocker and his associates as a hostelry for their millionaire friends. After the hotel was ravaged by the 1906 fire, a larger, more luxurious Italian Renaissance–style residence was opened in 1907. The hotel's checkered past includes the ill-fated 1921 bash in the suite of the silent-film comedian Fatty Arbuckle, at which a woman became ill and later died. Arbuckle endured three sensational trials for rape and murder before being acquitted, by which time his career was kaput. In 1975 Sara Jane Moore, standing among a crowd outside the hotel, attempted to shoot then-president Gerald R. Ford. As might be imagined, no plaques in the lobby commemorate these events. ✉ *335 Powell St., at Geary St., Union Square,* ☎ *415/397–7000,* WEB *www.westin.com.*

South of Market (SoMa) and Embarcadero

South of Market was once known as South of the Slot, in reference to the cable car slot that ran up Market Street. Ever since gold-rush miners set up their tents in 1848, SoMa has played a major role in housing immigrants to the city; except for a brief flowering of elegance during the mid-19th century, these streets were reserved for newcomers who couldn't yet afford to move to another neighborhood. Industry took over most of the area when the 1906 earthquake collapsed most of the homes into their quicksand bases.

SoMa's emergence as a focal point of San Francisco's cultural life was more than three decades in the making. Huge sections of the industrial neighborhood were razed to make way for an ambitious multiuse redevelopment project in the 1960s and 70s. Key players in San Francisco's arts scene then migrated to the area in the 1990s. At the heart of the action are the San Francisco Museum of Modern Art (SF-MOMA) and the Center for the Arts at Yerba Buena Gardens. Today the gentrified South Park area, not long ago the buzzing epicenter of new-media activity, has lost much of its new-economy luster, but the recent influx of money from the cyber heyday has changed the face of SoMa forever. Glitzy projects like the Four Seasons Hotel and residential complex coexist uneasily with still-gritty stretches of Mission and Market streets. This juxtaposition creates a friction that keeps the neighborhood interesting.

A Good Walk

The **San Francisco Museum of Modern Art** ⑩ dominates a half block of 3rd Street between Howard and Mission streets. Use the crosswalk near SFMOMA's entrance to head across 3rd Street into Yerba Buena Gardens. To your right after you've walked a few steps, a sidewalk leads to the main entrance of the **Center for the Arts** ⑪. Straight ahead is the East Garden of Yerba Buena Gardens and beyond that, on the 4th Street side of the block, is the **Metreon** ⑫ entertainment, retail, and restaurant complex. A second-level walkway in the southern portion of the East Garden, above the Martin Luther King Jr. waterfall, arches over Howard Street, leading to the main (south) entrance to Moscone Convention Center and the **Rooftop@Yerba Buena Gardens** ⑬ facilities.

Exit the rooftop, head north on 4th Street, and then take a right on Mission Street. Walk east on Mission (toward SFMOMA) past the monolithic San Francisco Marriott, also known as the "jukebox" Marriott because of its exterior design. Just before St. Patrick's Catholic Church is the pedestrian walkway Yerba Buena Lane, due to open late in 2002. It will include a water course, shops, and restaurants. The new Mexican Museum and the Magnes Museum are also scheduled to open on this block of Mission Street in late 2003. A half block past 3rd Street on Mission is the headquarters of the **California Historical Society** ⑭. Across the street and a few steps farther east is the **Cartoon Art Museum** ⑮.

Continue east on Mission Street and turn left up New Montgomery Street to Market Street and the **Palace Hotel** ⑯. Enter via the Market Street entrance, checking out the Pied Piper Bar, Garden Court restaurant, and main lobby. Exit via the lobby onto New Montgomery Street and make a left, which will bring you back up to Market Street. Turn right and walk toward the waterfront. Toward the end of Market a three-tier pedestrian mall connects the five buildings of the **Embarcadero Center** ⑰ office-retail complex. Across the busy Embarcadero roadway from the plaza stands the port's trademark, the **Ferry Building** ⑱.

The ground floor of the ornate 1889 Audiffred Building, on the southwest corner of the Embarcadero and Mission Street, houses Boulevard restaurant. Head west on Mission Street along the side of Boulevard and cross Steuart Street. In the middle of the block is the entrance to the historic sections of **Rincon Center** ⑲, worth seeing for the famous murals and the old Rincon Annex Post Office. Continue south within the center to its newer portions and make a left as you exit through the doors near Chalkers Billiards. Across Steuart Street you'll see the Jewish Community Federation Building, which houses the **Magnes Museum** ⑳.

TIMING
The walk above takes a good two hours, more if you visit the museums and galleries. SFMOMA merits about two hours; the Center for the Arts and the Cartoon Art Museum, 45 minutes each.

Sights to See

⑭ **California Historical Society.** The society, founded in 1871, administers a vast repository of Californiana—500,000 photographs, 150,000 manuscripts, thousands of books, periodicals, and paintings as well as gold-rush paraphernalia. ⊠ *678 Mission St., South of Market,* ☎ *415/357–1848,* WEB *www.californiahistoricalsociety.org.* ☞ *$3, free 1st Tues. of month.* ☉ *Tues.–Sat. 11–5 (galleries close between exhibitions).*

⑮ **Cartoon Art Museum.** Krazy Kat, Zippy the Pinhead, Batman, and other colorful cartoon icons greet you at the Cartoon Art Museum. In addition to a 12,000-piece permanent collection, a 3,000-volume library, and a CD-ROM gallery, changing exhibits examine everything from the impact of underground comics to the output of women and African-American cartoonists. ⊠ *655 Mission St., South of Market,* ☎ *415/227–8666,* WEB *www.cartoonart.org.* ☞ *$5 (pay what you wish 1st Thurs. of month).* ☉ *Tues.–Fri. 11–5, Sat. 10–5, Sun. 1–5.*

⑪ **Center for the Arts.** The dance, music, theater, visual arts, films, and videos presented at this facility in Yerba Buena Gardens range from the community-based to the international and lean toward the cutting edge. ⊠ *701 Mission St., South of Market,* ☎ *415/978–2787,* WEB *www.yerbabuenaarts.org.* ☞ *Galleries $6, free 1st Tues. of month 5 PM–8 PM.* ☉ *Galleries and box office Tues.–Wed. and weekends 11–6, Thurs.–Fri. 11–8.*

⑰ **Embarcadero Center.** John Portman designed this five-block complex built during the 1970s and early 1980s. Shops and restaurants abound on the first three levels; there's ample office space on the floors above. Louise Nevelson's 54-ft-high black-steel sculpture, *Sky Tree*, stands guard over Building 3 and is among 20-plus artworks throughout the center. ⊠ *Clay St. between Battery St. (Embarcadero 1) and the Embarcadero (Embarcadero 5), Embarcadero,* ☎ *415/772–0734,* WEB *www.embarcaderocenter.com.*

⑱ **Ferry Building.** The beacon of the port area, erected in 1896, has a 230-ft clock tower modeled after the campanile of the cathedral in Seville,

Spain. On April 18, 1906, the four great clock faces on the tower, powered by the swinging of a 14-ft pendulum, stopped at 5:17—the moment the great earthquake struck—and stayed still for 12 months. Renovated in 2002 to the tune of $70 million, the Ferry Building now has a skilt market hall on street level bustling with restaurants, cafés, and local-food purveyors. A waterfront promenade that extends from the piers on the north side of the building south to the Bay Bridge is great for jogging, in-line skating, watching sailboats on the bay, or enjoying a picnic. Ferries behind the building sail to Sausalito, Larkspur, Tiburon, and the East Bay. ⊠ *The Embarcadero at the foot of Market St., Embarcadero.*

㉚ The Magnes Museum. The exhibits at this small museum survey Jewish art, history, and culture. Call ahead before visiting; the museum sometimes closes between exhibits. In late 2003 the museum plans to move into its new, state-of-the-art, Daniel Libeskind–designed quarters South of Market, on Mission Street between 3rd and 4th streets. ⊠ *121 Steuart St., Embarcadero,* ☎ *415/788–9990,* WEB *www.magnesmuseum.org.* 🖼 *$5, free 1st Mon. of month.* ☉ *Sun.–Thurs. noon–5.*

㉓ ⑫ Metreon. Child's play meets the 21st century at this Sony entertainment center with interactive play areas based on books like Maurice Sendak's *Where the Wild Things Are* and a three-screen, three-dimensional installation that illustrates principles discussed in architect David Macauley's *The Way Things Work.* In the Digital Solutions shop you can access the Internet for free. There are also a 15-screen multiplex, an IMAX theater, retail shops, and restaurants. ⊠ *4th St. between Mission and Howard Sts., South of Market,* ☎ *800/638–7366,* WEB *www.metreon.com.*

⑯ Palace Hotel. The city's oldest hotel, a Sheraton property, opened in 1875. Fire destroyed the original Palace following the 1906 earthquake despite the hotel's 28,000-gallon reservoir fed by four artesian wells; the current building dates from 1909. President Warren Harding died at the Palace while still in office in 1923, and the body of King Kalakaua of Hawaii spent a night chilling here after he died in San Francisco in 1891. The managers play up this ghoulish past with talk of a haunted guest room. Glass cases off the main lobby contain memorabilia of the hotel's glory days. ⊠ *2 New Montgomery St., South of Market,* ☎ *415/512–1111,* WEB *www.sfpalace.com.* ☉ *Tours Tues. and Sat. at 10 AM, Thurs. at 2 PM.*

⑲ Rincon Center. A sheer five-story column of water resembling a mini-rainstorm is the centerpiece of the indoor arcade at this mostly modern office-retail complex. The lobby of the streamline moderne–style former post office on the Mission Street side contains a Works Project Administration **mural by Anton Refregier.** The 27 panels depict California life from the days when Native Americans were the state's sole inhabitants through World War I. A permanent exhibit below the murals contains photographs and artifacts of life in the Rincon area in the 1800s. ⊠ *Between Steuart, Spear, Mission, and Howard Sts., South of Market.*

★ ㉓ ⑬ Rooftop@Yerba Buena Gardens. Fun is the order of the day among these brightly colored concrete and corrugated-metal buildings atop Moscone Convention Center South. The historic **Looff carousel** ($2 for two rides) that originally graced San Francisco's beloved Playland at the Beach twirls from Sunday through Friday between 10 and 6, Saturday between 10 and 8. South of the carousel is **Zeum** (☎ 415/777–2800, WEB www.zeum.org), a high-tech interactive arts and technology center ($7) geared to children ages eight and over. Kids can make Claymation videos, work in a computer lab, and view exhibits and performances. Zeum is open in summer from Wednesday through Sunday between 11 and 5, in winter on weekends and school holidays from 11 to 5. Also part of the rooftop complex are gardens, an ice-skating rink, and a bowling alley. ⊠ *4th St. between Howard and Folsom Sts., South of Market.*

★ ⑩ **San Francisco Museum of Modern Art (SFMOMA).** Mario Botta designed the striking SFMOMA facility, completed in early 1995, which consists of a sienna brick facade and a central tower of alternating bands of black and white stone. Inside, natural light from the tower floods the central atrium and some of the museum's galleries. A black-and-gray stone staircase leads from the atrium to four floors of galleries. Works by Matisse, Picasso, O'Keeffe, Kahlo, Pollock, and Warhol form the heart of the diverse permanent collection. The photography holdings are also strong. ⊠ *151 3rd St., South of Market,* ☎ *415/357–4000,* WEB *www. sfmoma.org.* ⌨ *$10, free 1st Tues. of each month, ½-price Thurs. 6– 9.* ☉ *Memorial Day–Labor Day, Fri.–Tues. 10–6, Thurs. 10–9; Labor Day–Memorial Day, Fri.–Tues. 11–6, Thurs. 11–9.*

★ **Yerba Buena Gardens.** The centerpiece of the SoMa redevelopment area, these two blocks encompass the Center for the Arts, Metreon, Moscone Center, and the Rooftop@Yerba Buena Gardens. A circular walkway lined with benches and sculptures surrounds the East Garden, a large patch of green amid this visually stunning complex. The waterfall memorial to Martin Luther King Jr. is the focal point of the East Garden. Powerful streams of water surge over large, jagged stone columns, mirroring the enduring force of King's words that are carved on the stone walls and on glass blocks behind the waterfall. Above the memorial are two restaurants and an overhead walkway to Moscone Convention Center's main entrance. ⊠ *Between 3rd, 4th, Mission, and Folsom Sts., South of Market.* ☉ *Daily sunrise–10 PM.* WEB *www.yerbabuena.org.*

Financial District (The Heart of the Barbary Coast)

It was on Montgomery Street, in the Financial District, that Sam Brannan proclaimed the historic gold discovery that took place at Sutter's Mill on January 24, 1848. The gold rush brought streams of people from across America and Europe, transforming the onetime frontier town into a cosmopolitan city almost overnight. The population of San Francisco jumped from a mere 800 in 1848 to more than 25,000 in 1850 and to nearly 150,000 in 1870. Along with the prospectors came many other fortune seekers. Saloon keepers, gamblers, and prostitutes all flocked to the so-called Barbary Coast (now Jackson Square and the Financial District). Underground dance halls, casinos, bordellos, and palatial homes sprung up as the city grew into a world-class metropolis. Along with the quick money came a wave of violence. In 1852 the city suffered an average of two murders and one major fire each day. Diarists commented that hardly a day would pass without bloodshed in the city's estimated 500 bars and 1,000 gambling dens.

By 1917 the excesses of the Barbary Coast had fallen victim to the Red-Light Abatement Act and the ire of church leaders. Since then the red-light establishments have edged upward to the Broadway strip of North Beach, and Jackson Square evolved into a sedate district of refurbished brick buildings decades ago. Only one remnant of the era remains. Below Montgomery Street between California Street and Broadway, underlying many building foundations along the former waterfront area (long since filled in), lay at least 100 ships abandoned by frantic crews and passengers caught up in gold fever.

A Good Walk

Bronze sidewalk plaques mark the street corners along the 50-sight, approximately 3¾-mi Barbary Coast Trail. The trail begins at the Old Mint, at 5th and Mission streets, and runs north through downtown, Chinatown, Jackson Square, North Beach, and Fisherman's Wharf, ending at Aquatic Park. For information about the sites on the trail, pick up a brochure at the San Francisco Visitor Information Center.

To catch the highlights of the Barbary Coast Trail and a glimpse of a few important Financial District structures, start on Montgomery Street, between California and Sacramento streets, at the **Wells Fargo Bank History Museum** ㉑.

Two blocks north on Montgomery from the Wells Fargo museum stands the **Transamerica Pyramid** ㉒, between Clay and Washington streets. A tranquil redwood grove graces the east side of the pyramid. Walk through it, and you'll exit on Washington Street, across which you can see Hotaling Place to your left. Walk west (left) to the corner, cross Washington Street, and walk back to Hotaling. This historic alley is your entrance to **Jackson Square** ㉓, the heart of the Barbary Coast. Of particular note here are the former A. P. Hotaling whiskey distillery, on the corner of Hotaling Place, and the 1850s structures around the corner in the **700 block of Montgomery Street.** To see these buildings, walk west on Jackson from the distillery and make a left on Montgomery. Continue south on Montgomery to Washington Street, make a right, and cross Columbus Avenue. Head north (to the right) up Columbus to the **San Francisco Brewing Company** ㉔, the last standing saloon of the Barbary Coast era and a place overflowing with freshly brewed beers and history.

TIMING

Two hours should be enough time to see everything on this tour. The Wells Fargo museum (open only on weekdays) deserves a half hour.

Sights to See

㉓ **Jackson Square.** Here was the heart of the Barbary Coast of the Gay '90s. Though most of the red-light district was destroyed in the 1906 fire, old redbrick buildings and narrow alleys recall the romance and rowdiness of the early days. Some of the city's earliest business buildings, survivors of the 1906 quake, still stand in Jackson Square, between Montgomery and Sansome streets. Restored 19th-century brick buildings line Hotaling Place, which connects Washington and Jackson streets. The lane is named for the head of the **A. P. Hotaling Company** whiskey distillery, which was the largest liquor repository on the West Coast in its day. A plaque on the side of the Italianate Hotaling building repeats a famous query about the structure's survival of the quake: IF, AS THEY SAY, GOD SPANKED THE TOWN FOR BEING OVER FRISKY, WHY DID HE BURN THE CHURCHES DOWN AND SAVE HOTALING'S WHISKEY?. The **Ghirardelli Chocolate Factory** once occupied 415 Jackson Street. By 1894 the enterprise had become large enough to necessitate the creation of what's now Ghirardelli Square, near Fisherman's Wharf. In the **700 block of Montgomery Street,** Bret Harte wrote his novel *The Luck of Roaring Camp* at No. 730. He toiled as a typesetter for the spunky *golden-era* newspaper, which occupied No. 732 (now part of the building at No. 744). ⊠ *Jackson Square district: between Broadway and Washington and Montgomery and Sansome Sts., Financial District.*

㉔ **San Francisco Brewing Company.** Built in 1907, this pub looks like a museum piece from the Barbary Coast days. An old upright piano sits in the corner under the original stained-glass windows. Take a seat at the mahogany bar and look down at the white-tile spittoon. In an adjacent room look for the handmade copper brewing kettle used to produce a dozen beers—with names like Pony Express—by means of old-fashioned gravity-flow methods. ✉ *155 Columbus Ave., North Beach,* ☎ *415/434–3344,* WEB *www.sfbrewing.com.*

㉒ **Transamerica Pyramid.** The city's most photographed high-rise is the 853-ft Transamerica Pyramid. Designed by William Pereira and Associates in 1972, the initially controversial icon has become more acceptable to most locals over time. A fragrant redwood grove along the east side of the building, replete with benches and a cheerful fountain, is a placid patch in which to unwind. ✉ *600 Montgomery St., Financial District,* WEB *www.tapyramid.com.*

㉑ **Wells Fargo Bank History Museum.** There were no formal banks in San Francisco during the early years of the gold rush, and miners often entrusted their gold dust to saloon keepers. In 1852 Wells Fargo opened its first bank in the city, and the company established banking offices in the mother-lode camps, using stagecoaches and pony express riders to service the burgeoning state. The museum displays samples of nuggets and gold dust from mines, a mural-size map of the Mother Lode, original art by western artists Charles M. Russell and Maynard Dixon, mementos of the poet bandit Black Bart ("Po8," as he signed his poems), and an old telegraph machine on which you can practice sending codes. The showpiece is the red Concord stagecoach, the likes of which carried passengers from St. Joseph, Missouri, to San Francisco in three weeks during the 1850s. ✉ *420 Montgomery St., Financial District,* ☎ *415/396–2619.* ▣ *Free.* ☺ *Weekdays 9–5.*

Chinatown

Prepare to have your senses assaulted in Chinatown. Pungent smells waft out of restaurants, fish markets, and produce stands. Good-luck banners of crimson and gold hang beside dragon-entwined lampposts, pagoda roofs, and street signs with Chinese calligraphy. Honking cars chime in with shoppers bargaining loudly in Cantonese or Mandarin. Add to this the sight of millions of Chinese-theme goods spilling out of the shops along Grant Avenue, and you get an idea of what Chinatown is all about.

Bordered roughly by Bush, Kearny, and Powell streets and Broadway, Chinatown has one of the largest Chinese communities outside Asia. The area is tightly packed, mostly because housing discrimination in the past kept residents from moving outside Chinatown. The two main drags of Chinatown are Grant Avenue, jammed with kitschy tourist shops, and Stockton Street, where the locals do business.

A Good Walk

While wandering through Chinatown's streets and alleys, don't forget to look up. Above street level, many older structures—mostly brick buildings that replaced rickety wooden ones destroyed during the 1906 earthquake—have ornate balconies and cornices. The architecture in the 900 block of Grant Avenue (at Washington Street) and Waverly Place (west of and parallel to Grant Avenue between Sacramento and Washington streets) is particularly noteworthy, though some locals decry it and similar examples as inauthentic adornment meant to make their neighborhood seem "more Chinese."

Enter Chinatown through the green-tile **Chinatown Gate** ㉕, on Grant Avenue at Bush Street. Shops selling souvenirs, jewelry, and home furnishings line Grant north past the gate. Pop into Dragon House, at No. 455. A veritable museum, the store sells centuries-old antiques rather than six-month-old goods made in Taiwan. **Old St. Mary's Cathe-**

dral ㉖ towers over the corner of Grant Avenue and California Street. Continue on Grant to Clay Street and turn right. A half block down on your left is **Portsmouth Square** ㉗. A walkway on the eastern edge of the park leads over Kearny Street to the third floor of the Holiday Inn, where you'll find the **Chinese Culture Center** ㉘.

Backtrack on the walkway to Portsmouth Square and head west up Washington Street a half block to the **Old Chinese Telephone Exchange** ㉙ (now the Bank of Canton), and then continue west on Washington Street. Cross Grant Avenue and look for Waverly Place a half block up on the left. One of the best examples of this alley's traditional architecture is the **Tin How Temple** ㉚. After visiting Waverly Place and Tin How, walk back to Washington Street. Several herb shops do business in this area. Two worth checking out are Superior Trading Company at No. 839 and the Great China Herb Co. at No. 857.

Across Washington Street from Superior is Ross Alley. Head north on Ross toward Jackson Street, stopping along the way to watch the bakers at the **Golden Gate Fortune Cookies Co.** ㉛. Turn right on Jackson. When you get to Grant Avenue, don't cross it. For some of Chinatown's best pastries, turn left and stop by No. 1029, the Golden Gate Bakery. The markets in the 1100 block of Grant Avenue carry intriguing delicacies, such as braised pig noses and ears, eels, and all manner of live game birds and fish.

Head west on Pacific Avenue to Stockton Street, turn left, and walk south past Stockton Street's markets. At Clay Street make a right and head halfway up the hill to the **Chinese-American National Museum and Learning Center** ㉜. Return to Stockton Street and make a right; a few doors down is the **Kong Chow Temple** ㉝, and next door is the elaborate **Chinese Six Companies** building.

TIMING

Allow at least two hours to see Chinatown. Brief stops will suffice at the cultural center and temples.

Sights to See

㉕ **Chinatown Gate.** Stone lions flank the base of the pagoda-topped gate, the official entrance to Chinatown. The male lion's right front paw rests playfully on a ball; the female's left front paw tickles a cub lying on its back. The lions and the glazed clay dragons atop the largest of the gate's three pagodas symbolize, among other things, wealth and prosperity. The four Chinese characters immediately beneath the pagoda represent the philosophy of Sun Yat-sen (1866–1925), the leader who unified China in the early 20th century. Sun Yat-sen, who lived in exile in San Francisco for a few years, promoted the notion of friendship and peace among all nations based on equality, justice, and goodwill. The vertical characters under the left pagoda read "peace" and "trust," the ones under the right pagoda "respect" and "love." ⊠ *Grant Ave. at Bush St., Chinatown.*

㉜ **Chinese-American National Museum and Learning Center.** This airy, light-filled gallery has displays about the Chinese-American experience from 19th-century agriculture to 21st-century food and fashion trends. A separate room hosts rotating exhibits by contemporary Chinese-American artists; another describes the building's time as the Chinatown YWCA, which served as a meeting place and residence for Chinese women in need of social services. Julia Morgan, the architect known for the famous Hearst Castle® and the first woman in California to be licensed as an architect, designed this handsome redbrick building. ⊠ *965 Clay St., Chinatown,* ☎ *415/391–1188,* WEB *www.chsa.org.* ⊡ *$3.* ☉ *Tues.–Fri. 11–4, weekends noon–4.*

28 **Chinese Culture Center.** The San Francisco Redevelopment Commission agreed to let Holiday Inn build in Chinatown if the chain provided room for a Chinese culture center. Inside the center are the works of Chinese and Chinese-American artists as well as traveling exhibits relating to Chinese culture. Walking tours ($12; make reservations one week ahead) of historic points in Chinatown take place on most days at 10 AM. ⊠ *Holiday Inn, 750 Kearny St., 3rd floor, Chinatown,* ☎ *415/986–1822,* WEB *www.c-c-c.org.* ⊠ *Free.* ⊙ *Tues.–Sun. 10–4.*

Chinese Six Companies. Several fine examples of Chinese architecture can be spotted along Stockton Street, but this is the most noteworthy. With its curved roof tiles and elaborate cornices, the imposing structure's oversize pagoda cheerfully calls attention to itself. The business leaders who ran the six companies, which still exist today, dominated Chinatown's political and economic life for decades. ⊠ *843 Stockton St., Chinatown.*

31 **Golden Gate Fortune Cookies Co.** Walk down Ross Alley and you'll likely be invited into this small cookie factory. The workers sit at circular motorized griddles and wait for dollops of batter to drop onto a tiny metal plate, which rotates into an oven. A few moments later out comes a cookie that's pliable and ready for folding. A bagful of cookies—with mildly racy "adult" fortunes or more benign ones—costs $2 or $3; personalized fortunes are also available. ⊠ *56 Ross Alley (west of and parallel to Grant Ave. between Washington and Jackson Sts.), Chinatown,* ☎ *415/781–3956.* ⊙ *Daily 10–7.*

33 **Kong Chow Temple.** The god to whom the members of this temple pray represents honesty and trust. You'll often see his image in Chinese stores and restaurants because he's thought to bring good luck in business. Take the elevator up to the fourth floor, where incense fills the air. Your party can show its respect by placing a dollar or two in the donation box. Amid the statuary, flowers, and richly colored altars (red wards off evil spirits and signifies virility, green symbolizes longevity, and gold majesty) are a couple of plaques announcing that MRS. HARRY S. TRUMAN CAME TO THIS TEMPLE IN JUNE 1948 FOR A PREDICTION ON THE OUTCOME OF THE ELECTION . . . THIS FORTUNE CAME TRUE. The temple's balcony has a good view of Chinatown. ⊠ *855 Stockton St., Chinatown,* ☎ *no phone.* ⊠ *Free.* ⊙ *Mon.–Sat. 9–4.*

29 **Old Chinese Telephone Exchange.** Most of Chinatown burned down after the 1906 earthquake, and this building set the style for the new Chinatown. The intricate three-tier pagoda was built in 1909. The exchange's operators were renowned for their prodigious memories, about which the San Francisco Chamber of Commerce boasted in 1914: "These girls respond all day with hardly a mistake to calls that are given (in English or one of five Chinese dialects) by the name of the subscriber instead of by his number—a mental feat that would be practically impossible to most high-schooled American misses." ⊠ *Bank of Canton, 743 Washington St., Chinatown.*

26 **Old St. Mary's Cathedral.** This building served as the city's Catholic cathedral until 1891. The church needs to undergo seismic retrofitting or be demolished and is in the process of raising funds for the procedure. Across California Street in **St. Mary's Park,** the late local sculptor Beniamino (Benny) Bufano's 12-ft-tall stainless-steel and rose-color granite statue of Sun Yat-sen towers over the site of the Chinese leader's favorite reading spot during his years in San Francisco. ⊠ *Grant Ave. and California St., Chinatown,* WEB *www.oldstmarys.org.*

27 **Portsmouth Square.** Captain John B. Montgomery raised the American flag here in 1846, claiming the area from Mexico. The square—a

former potato patch—was the plaza for Yerba Buena, the Mexican settlement that was renamed San Francisco. Robert Louis Stevenson, the
author of *Treasure Island,* lived on the edge of Chinatown in the late
19th century and often visited the square, chatting up the sailors who
hung out here. Bruce Porter designed the bronze galleon that sits on
top of a 9-ft granite shaft in the northwestern corner of the square in
honor of the writer. With its pagoda-shape structures, Portsmouth
Square is a favorite spot for morning tai chi and afternoon Chinese
chess. ⊠ *Bordered by Walter Lum Pl. and Kearny, Washington, and
Clay Sts., Chinatown.*

★ ③⓪ **Tin How Temple.** Day Ju, one of the first three Chinese to arrive in San
Francisco, dedicated this temple to the Queen of the Heavens and the
Goddess of the Seven Seas in 1852. In the third-floor temple's entry-
way, elderly ladies can often be seen preparing "money" to be burned
as offerings to various Buddhist gods or as funds for ancestors to use
in the afterlife. The gold-leaf wood carving suspended from the ceiling depicts the north and east sides of the sea, which Tin How (Tien
Hau or Tien Hou in Cantonese) and other gods protect. A statue of
Tin How sits in the middle of the back of the temple, flanked by a red
lesser god and by a green one. Photography is not permitted, and visitors are asked not to step onto the balcony. ⊠ *125 Waverly Pl., Chinatown,* ☎ *no phone.* 🎫 *Free (donations accepted).* ☉ *Daily 9–4.*

North Beach

Novelist and resident Herbert Gold calls North Beach "the longest-
running, most glorious American bohemian operetta outside Greenwich Village." Indeed, to anyone who's spent some time in its eccentric
old bars and cafés or wandered the neighborhood, North Beach evokes
everything from the Barbary Coast days to the no-less-rowdy beatnik
era. Italian bakeries appear frozen in time, homages to Jack Kerouac
and Allen Ginsberg pop up everywhere, and the modern equivalent of
the Barbary Coast's "houses of ill repute," strip joints, do business on
Broadway.

A Good Walk

Stand on the northwest corner of Broadway and Columbus Avenue to
get your bearings. To the south, the triangular Sentinel Building, where
Kearny Street and Columbus Avenue meet at an angle, grabs the eye
with its unusual shape and mellow green patina. (The building's owner,
filmmaker Francis Ford Coppola, has the penthouse office.) East across
Columbus is the Condor, where in 1964 local celeb Carol Doda became the nation's first dancer at a nightclub to go topless. Around the
same time, North Beach was a nexus of comedy. Bill Cosby, Phyllis Diller,
Dick Gregory, the Smothers Brothers, and other talents cut their teeth
at clubs like the hungry i and the Purple Onion. To the north of Broadway and Columbus is the heart of Italian North Beach.

Walk southeast across Columbus to **City Lights Bookstore** ㉞, where you
can pick up a book by one of the Beat writers. There are plenty of atmospheric bars near here, including Vesuvio, Specs, and Tosca, where
opera tunes stock the jukebox. For joltingly caffeinated espresso drinks,
also to the tune of opera, head north on Columbus a block and a half
on the same side of the avenue as City Lights to Caffè Puccini, at No.
411. By now, you've been in North Beach for a couple of hours and
hardly gone anywhere. There are sights to see, but relaxing and enjoying life is what North Beach is all about.

Head up the east side of Columbus Avenue (the same side as the Condor) past Grant Avenue. On the northeast corner of Columbus and

Vallejo Street is the Victorian-era **St. Francis of Assisi Church** ㉟. Go east on Vallejo Street to Grant Avenue and make another left. Check out the eclectic shops and old-time bars and cafés between Vallejo and Union streets.

Turn left at Union Street and head west to Washington Square, an oasis of green amid the tightly packed streets of North Beach. On the north side of the park, on Filbert, stands the double-turreted **Saints Peter and Paul Catholic Church** ㊱.

After you've had your fill of North Beach, head up **Telegraph Hill** ㊲ from Washington Square. Atop the hill is **Coit Tower** ㊳. People in poor health will not want to attempt the walk up the steep hill; Coit Tower can be reached by car (though parking is very tight) or public transportation. To walk, head east up Filbert Street at the park; turn left at Grant Avenue and go one block north, then right at Greenwich Street and ascend the steps on your right. Cross the street at the top of the first set of stairs and continue up the curving stone steps to Coit Tower.

On the other side of Coit Tower, the Greenwich steps take you down the east side of Telegraph Hill, with stunning views of the bay en route. At Montgomery Street, perched on the side of the hill, is Julius' Castle restaurant. A block to the right, the Filbert steps intersect. Descend the Filbert steps amid roses, fuchsias, irises, and trumpet flowers—courtesy of Grace Marchant, who labored for nearly 30 years to transform a dump into one of San Francisco's hidden treasures in the 1900s.

TIMING

It takes a little more than an hour to walk the tour, but the point in both North Beach and Telegraph Hill is to linger—set aside at least a few hours.

Sights to See

★ ㉞ **City Lights Bookstore.** Finally designated a city landmark in 2001, the hangout of Beat-era writers—Allen Ginsberg and Lawrence Ferlinghetti among them—remains a vital part of San Francisco's literary scene. Still leftist at heart, in 1999 the store unveiled a replica of a revolutionary mural destroyed in Chiapas, Mexico, by military forces. ⊠ *261 Columbus Ave., North Beach,* ☎ *415/362–8193,* WEB *www.citylights. com.*

★ ㊳ **Coit Tower.** Among San Francisco's most distinctive skyline sights, the 210-ft-tall Coit Tower stands as a monument to the city's volunteer firefighters. During the early days of the gold rush, Lillie Hitchcock Coit (known as Miss Lil) was said to have deserted a wedding party and chased down the street after her favorite engine, Knickerbocker No. 5, while clad in her bridesmaid finery. She was soon made an honorary member of the Knickerbocker Company and after that always signed her name as "Lillie Coit 5" in honor of her favorite fire engine. Lillie died in 1929 at the age of 86, leaving the city $125,000 to "expend in an appropriate manner . . . to the beauty of San Francisco." Inside the tower, 19 depression-era murals depict economic and political life in California. ⊠ *Telegraph Hill Blvd., at Greenwich St. or Lombard St., North Beach,* ☎ *415/362–0808.* ▣ *$3.75.* ☉ *Daily 10–6.*

㉟ **St. Francis of Assisi Church.** This 1860 building stands on the site of the frame parish church that served the Catholic community during the gold rush. Its solid terra-cotta facade complements the many brightly colored restaurants and cafés nearby. ⊠ *610 Vallejo St., North Beach,* ☎ *415/983–0405,* WEB *www.shrinesf.org.* ☉ *Daily 11–5.*

㊱ **Saints Peter and Paul Catholic Church.** Camera-toting tourists focus their lenses on the Romanesque splendor of what's often called the Italian Cathedral. Completed in 1924, the cathedral has Disneyesque stone-white towers that are local landmarks. ⊠ *666 Filbert St., at Washington Square, North Beach,* ☎ *415/421–0809,* ⓦⒺⒷ *www.stspeterpaul. san-francisco.ca.us/church.*

㊲ **Telegraph Hill.** Telegraph Hill got its name from one of its earliest functions—in 1853 it became the location of the first Morse Code Signal Station. Hill residents have some of the best views in the city, as well as the most difficult ascents to their aeries (the flower-lined steps flanking the hill make the climb more than tolerable for visitors, though). The Hill rises from the east end of Lombard Street to a height of 284 ft and is capped by Coit Tower. ⊠ *Between Lombard, Filbert, Kearny, and Sansome Sts., North Beach.*

Nob Hill and Russian Hill

Once called the Hill of Golden Promise, this area was officially dubbed Nob Hill during the 1870s when "the Big Four"—Charles Crocker, Leland Stanford, Mark Hopkins, and Collis Huntington, who were involved in the construction of the transcontinental railroad—built their hilltop estates. The lingo is thick from this era: those on the hilltop were referred to as "nabobs" (originally meaning a provincial governor from India) and "swells," and the hill itself was called Snob Hill, a term that survives to this day. By 1882 so many estates had sprung up on Nob Hill that Robert Louis Stevenson called it "the hill of palaces." But the 1906 earthquake and fire destroyed all the palatial mansions, except for portions of the Flood brownstone.

Just nine blocks or so from downtown and a few blocks north of Nob Hill, the old San Francisco families of Russian Hill were joined during the 1890s by bohemian artists and writers that included Charles Norris, George Sterling, and Maynard Dixon. Today, simple studios, spiffy pieds-à-terre, Victorian flats, Edwardian cottages, and boxlike condos rub elbows on the hill. The bay views here are some of the city's best.

A Good Walk

Begin on California and Taylor streets at the majestic **Grace Cathedral** ㊴. From the cathedral walk east (toward Mason Street and downtown) on California Street to the **Pacific Union Club** ㊵. Across Mason Street from the Pacific Union Club is the lush hotel **The Fairmont** ㊶, with its quirky Tonga Room tiki bar. Directly across California Street from the Fairmont is the **Mark Hopkins Inter-Continental Hotel** ㊷, famed for panoramic views from its Top of the Mark lounge. Head north on Mason Street to the **Cable Car Museum** ㊸, at Washington Street.

From the Cable Car Museum continue four blocks north on Mason Street to Vallejo Street, turn west, and start climbing the steps that lead to the multilevel **Ina Coolbrith Park** ㊹. At the top, you can see the **Vallejo steps area** across Taylor Street. The Flag House, one of several brown-shingle prequake buildings in this area, is to your left at Taylor Street. Cross Taylor Street and ascend the Vallejo steps; the view east takes in downtown and the Bay Bridge. Continue west from the top of the Vallejo steps to two secluded Russian Hill alleys. Down and to your left is Florence Place, an enclave of 1920s stucco homes, and down a bit farther on your right is Russian Hill Place, with a row of 1915 Mediterranean town houses designed by Willis Polk. After reemerging on Vallejo Street from the alleys, walk north (right) on Jones Street one short block to Green Street. Head west (left) halfway down the block to the octagonal **Feusier House** ㊺. Backtrack to Jones Street, and head north to **Macondray Lane** ㊻. Walk west (to the left) on Macondray and follow it to Leavenworth Street. Head north (to the right) on Leavenworth to the bottom of **Lombard Street** ㊼, the "Crookedest Street in the World." Continue north one block on Leavenworth and then east one block on Chestnut Street to the **San Francisco Art Institute** ㊽.

TIMING

The tour above covers a lot of ground, much of it steep. If you're in reasonably good shape you can complete this walk in 3½ to 4 hours, including 30-minute stops at Grace Cathedral and the Cable Car Museum. Add time for gazing at the bay from Ina Coolbrith Park or enjoying tea or a cocktail at one of Nob Hill's grand hotels.

Sights to See

★ ㊸ **Cable Car Museum.** San Francisco once had more than a dozen cable car barns and powerhouses. The only survivor, this 1907 redbrick structure, is an engaging stopover between Russian Hill and Nob Hill. Photographs, old cable cars, signposts, ticketing machines, and other memorabilia dating from 1873 document the history of these moving landmarks. The massive powerhouse wheels that move the entire cable car system steal the show; the design is so simple it seems almost unreal. You can also go downstairs to the sheave room and check out the innards of the system. A 15-minute video describes how it all works—cables must be replaced every three to six months—or you can opt to read the detailed placards. The gift shop sells cable car paraphernalia. ⊠ *1201 Mason St., at Washington St., Nob Hill,* ☎ *415/474–1887,* WEB *www.cablecarmuseum.com.* ▧ *Free.* ☉ *Oct.–Mar., daily 10–5; Apr.–Sept., daily 10–6.*

㊶ **The Fairmont.** The Fairmont's dazzling opening was delayed a year by the 1906 quake, but since then the marble palace has hosted presidents, royalty, movie stars (Valentino, Dietrich), and local nabobs. Things have changed since its early days, however: on the eve of World War I you could get a room for as low as $2.50 per night, meals included. Nowadays, prices go as high as $8,000, which buys a night in the eight-room, Persian art–filled penthouse suite that was showcased regularly in the 1980s TV series *Hotel.* ⊠ *950 Mason St., Nob Hill,* ☎ *415/772–5000,* WEB *www.fairmont.com.*

㊺ **Feusier House.** Octagonal houses were once thought to make the best use of space and enhance the physical and mental well-being of their occupants. A brief mid-19th-century craze inspired the construction of several in San Francisco. Only the Feusier House, built in 1857 and now a private residence surrounded by lush gardens, and the Octagon House remain standing. ⊠ *1067 Green St., Russian Hill.*

㊴ **Grace Cathedral.** The seat of the Episcopal Church in San Francisco, this soaring Gothic structure, erected on the site of Charles Crocker's mansion, took 53 years to build. The gilded bronze doors at the east entrance were taken from casts of Ghiberti's Gates of Paradise, which are on the baptistery in Florence, Italy. A black-and-bronze stone sculpture of St. Francis by Beniamino Bufano greets you as you enter. ⊠ *1100 California St., at Taylor St., Nob Hill,* ☎ *415/749–6300,* WEB *www.gracecathedral.org.* ☉ *Weekdays 7–5:45, weekends 7–5.*

㊹ **Ina Coolbrith Park.** This attractive park is unusual because it's vertical—that is, rather than being one open space, it's composed of a series of terraces up a very steep hill. A poet, Oakland librarian, and niece of Mormon prophet Joseph Smith, Ina Coolbrith (1842–1928) introduced Jack London and Isadora Duncan to the world of books. For years she entertained literary greats in her Macondray Lane home near the park. In 1915 she was named poet laureate of California. ✉ *Vallejo St. between Mason and Taylor Sts., Russian Hill.*

★ **㊼ Lombard Street.** The block-long "Crookedest Street in the World" makes eight switchbacks down the east face of Russian Hill between Hyde and Leavenworth streets. Residents bemoan the traffic jam outside their front doors, and occasionally the city attempts to discourage drivers by posting a traffic cop near the top of the hill, but the determined can find a way around. If no one is standing guard, join the line of cars waiting to drive down the steep hill, or avoid the whole morass and walk down the steps on either side of Lombard. You'll take in super views of North Beach and Coit Tower whether you walk or drive. ✉ *Lombard St. between Hyde and Leavenworth Sts., Russian Hill.*

㊻ Macondray Lane. Enter this "secret garden" under a lovely wooden trellis and walk down a quiet cobbled pedestrian street lined with Edwardian cottages and flowering plants and trees. A flight of steep wooden stairs at the end of the lane leads down to Taylor Street—on the way down you can't miss the bay views. If you've read any of Armistead Maupin's *Tales of the City* or sequels, you may find the lane vaguely familiar. It's the thinly disguised setting for part of the series's action. ✉ *Jones St. between Union and Green Sts., Russian Hill.*

㊷ Mark Hopkins Inter-Continental Hotel. Built on the ashes of railroad tycoon Mark Hopkins's grand estate (which was built at his wife's urging; Hopkins himself preferred to live frugally), this 19-story hotel went up in 1926. A combination of French château and Spanish Renaissance architecture, with noteworthy terra-cotta detailing, it has hosted statesmen, royalty, and Hollywood celebrities. From the 1920s through the 1940s, Benny Goodman, Tommy Dorsey, and other top-drawer entertainers appeared here regularly. The 11-room penthouse was turned into a glass-walled cocktail lounge in 1939: the **Top of the Mark** is remembered fondly by thousands of World War II veterans who jammed the lounge before leaving for overseas duty. Wives and sweethearts watching the ships depart gave the room's northwest nook its name—Weepers' Corner. With its 360° views, the lounge is a wonderful spot for a nighttime drink. ✉ *1 Nob Hill, at California and Mason Sts., Nob Hill,* ☎ *415/392–3434,* WEB *www.hotels.san-francisco.interconti.com.*

㊱ Pacific Union Club. The former home of silver baron James Flood cost a whopping $1.5 million in 1886, when even a stylish Victorian like the Haas-Lilienthal House cost less than $20,000. All that cash did buy some structural stability. The Flood residence (to be precise, its shell) was the only Nob Hill mansion to survive the 1906 earthquake and fire. The Pacific Union Club, a bastion of the wealthy and powerful, purchased the house in 1907 and commissioned Willis Polk to redesign it; the architect added the semicircular wings and third floor. (The ornate fence design dates from the mansion's construction.) ✉ *1000 California St., Nob Hill.*

㊽ San Francisco Art Institute. A Moorish-tile fountain in a tree-shaded courtyard immediately draws the eye as you enter the institute. The highlight of a visit is Mexican master Diego Rivera's *The Making of a Fresco Showing the Building of a City* (1931), in the student gallery to your immediate left once inside the entrance. Rivera himself is in the fresco—his back is to the viewer—and he's surrounded by his assistants. They in turn are surrounded by a construction scene, laborers, and city notables such as sculptor Robert Stackpole and architect Timothy Pfleuger. The older portions of the Art Institute were erected in 1926. Ansel Adams created the school's fine-arts photography department in 1946, and school directors established the country's first fine-arts film program. Notable faculty and alumni have included painter Richard Diebenkorn and photographers Dorothea Lange, Edward Weston, and Annie Leibovitz. The **Walter & McBean Galleries** (☎ 415/749–4563) exhibit the often provocative works of established artists. ✉ *800 Chestnut St., North Beach,* ☎ *415/771–7020,* WEB *www.sanfranciscoart.edu.* *Galleries free.* ⏲ *Walter & McBean Galleries Mon.–Sat. 11–6, student gallery daily 9–9.*

Vallejo steps area. Several Russian Hill buildings survived the 1906 earthquake and fire and remain standing. Alert firefighters saved what's come to be known as the **Flag House** (✉ 1652–56 Taylor St., Russian Hill) when they spotted the American flag on the property and doused the flames with seltzer water and wet sand. The owner, a flag collector, fearing the house would burn to the ground, wanted it to go down in style, with "all flags flying."

The Flag House, at the southwest corner of Ina Coolbrith Park, is one of a number of California Shingle–style homes in this neighborhood, several of which were designed by Willis Polk. Polk also laid out the Vallejo steps, which climb the steep ridge across Taylor Street from the Flag House. Polk designed the **Polk-Williams House** (✉ Taylor and Vallejo Sts., Russian Hill) and lived in one of its finer sections, and **1034–1036 Vallejo**, across the street. ✉ *Taylor and Vallejo Sts. (steps lead up toward Jones St.), Russian Hill.*

Pacific Heights and Japantown

Some of the city's most expensive and dramatic real estate—including mansions and town houses priced in the millions—is in Pacific Heights. Grand Victorians line the streets, and from almost any point in this neighborhood you get a magnificent view.

Japantown, or "Nihonmachi," is centered on the southern slope of Pacific Heights north of Geary Boulevard between Fillmore and Laguna streets. Around 1860 a wave of Japanese immigrants arrived in San Francisco, which they called Soko. After the 1906 earthquake and fire, many of these newcomers settled in the Western Addition. By the 1930s they had opened shops, markets, meeting halls, and restaurants and established Shinto and Buddhist temples. Known as Japantown, this area was virtually deserted during World War II when many of its residents, including second- and third-generation Americans, were forced into so-called relocation camps.

Though Japantown is a relatively safe area, the Western Addition, which lies to the south of Geary Boulevard, can be dangerous; after dark also avoid straying too far west of Fillmore Street just north of Geary.

A Good Walk

Pacific Heights lies on an east–west ridge along the city's northern flank from Van Ness Avenue to the Presidio and from California Street to the Marina. Begin your tour by taking in the views from **Alta Plaza Park** ㊾, at the intersection of Steiner and Jackson streets.

Walk east on Jackson Street several blocks to the **Whittier Mansion** ㊿, on the corner of Jackson and Laguna streets. Make a right on Laguna and a left at the next block, Washington Street. The patch of green that spreads southeast from here is Lafayette Park. Walk on Washington along the edge of Lafayette Park past the formal French **Spreckels Mansion** (51), at the corner of Octavia Street, and continue east two more blocks to Franklin Street. Turn left (north); halfway down the block stands the handsome **Haas-Lilienthal House** (52). Head back south on Franklin Street, stopping to view several **Franklin Street buildings** (53).

At California Street, turn right (west) to see more **noteworthy Victorians** ⑤ on that street and Laguna Street.

Continue west on California Street to begin the Japantown segment of your tour. When you reach Buchanan Street, turn left (south). The open-air **Japan Center Mall** ㊺ is a short block of shoji-screened buildings on Buchanan Street between Post and Sutter streets.

Cross Post Street and enter the three-block **Japan Center** ㊻ in the Kintetsu Building. There are usually several fine ikebana arrangements in the windows of the headquarters of the Ikenobo Ikebana Society of America. A few doors farther along at May's Coffee Stand you can pick up a lemonade and a tasty fish-shape waffle filled with red-bean paste. If you're hungrier, head to the noodle shop Mifune. A second-level bridge spans Webster Street, connecting the Kintetsu and Kinokuniya buildings. Among the shops of note in the Kinokuniya Building are the Kinokuniya Bookstore and Ma-Shi'-Ko Folk Craft, both on the second floor. Exit the Kinokuniya Building onto Post Street. Take a left on Fillmore Street and head south toward Geary Boulevard. **Kabuki Springs & Spa** ㊽ is on the northeast corner of Geary and Fillmore.

Several key components of San Francisco's history intersect at Geary Boulevard and Fillmore Street. Japan Center sits on a portion of the area settled by Japanese and Japanese-Americans in the early 20th century. The stretch of Fillmore on either side of Geary Boulevard was a center of African-American culture during the mid-20th century. The part to the south remains so today, though the many blues and other music clubs that once thrived here have closed.

Near the southwest corner of Geary and Fillmore is the entrance to the legendary Fillmore Auditorium, where 1960s bands like Jefferson Airplane and the Grateful Dead performed. Two doors west of the Fillmore was the People's Temple (since demolished), the headquarters of the cult run by the Reverend Jim Jones, whose flock participated in a mass suicide in Guyana in November 1978.

TIMING

Set aside about two hours for the Pacific Heights portion of the tour, not including the tour of the Haas-Lilienthal House. Although most of the attractions are walk-bys, you'll be covering a good bit of pavement. The Japantown tour, on the other hand, is very compact. Not including a visit to the Kabuki Springs, an hour will probably suffice.

Sights to See

㊾ Alta Plaza Park. Landscape architect John McLaren, who also created Golden Gate Park, designed Alta Plaza in 1910, modeling its terracing on the Grand Casino in Monte Carlo, Monaco. From the top you can see Marin to the north, downtown to the east, Twin Peaks to the south, and Golden Gate Park to the west. ⊠ *Between Clay, Steiner, Jackson, and Scott Sts., Pacific Heights.*

㊿ Franklin Street buildings. Don't be fooled by the **Golden Gate Church** (⊠ 1901 Franklin St., Pacific Heights)—what at first looks like a stone facade is actually redwood painted white. A Georgian-style residence built in the early 1900s for a coffee merchant sits at **1735 Franklin**. On the northeast corner of Franklin and California streets is a **Christian Science church**; built in the Tuscan Revival style, it's noteworthy for its terra-cotta detailing. The **Coleman House** (⊠ 1701 Franklin St., Pacific Heights) is an impressive twin-turreted Queen Anne mansion built for a gold-rush mining and lumber baron. Don't miss the large stained-glass window on the house's north side. ⊠ *Franklin St. between Washington and California Sts., Pacific Heights.*

52 Haas-Lilienthal House. A small display of photographs on the bottom floor of this elaborate 1886 Queen Anne house, which cost a mere $18,500 to build, makes clear that it was modest compared with some of the giants that fell victim to the 1906 earthquake and fire. The Foundation for San Francisco's Architectural Heritage operates the home, whose carefully kept rooms provide an intriguing glimpse into late-19th-century life. Volunteers conduct one-hour house tours two days a week and an informative two-hour tour of the eastern portion of Pacific Heights on Sunday afternoon. ⊠ *2007 Franklin St., between Washington and Jackson Sts., Pacific Heights,* ☎ *415/441–3004,* WEB *www.sfheritage.org/house.html.* ⊡ *$5.* ⊘ *Wed. noon–4 (last tour at 3), Sun. 11–5 (last tour at 4). Pacific Heights tours ($5) leave the house Sun. at 12:30.*

56 Japan Center. The noted American architect Minoru Yamasaki created this 5-acre complex, which opened in 1968. The development includes a hotel; a public garage with discounted validated parking; shops selling Japanese furnishings, clothing, cameras, tapes and records, porcelain, pearls, and paintings; an excellent spa; and a multiplex cinema. Between the Miyako Mall and Kintetsu Building are the five-tier, 100-ft-tall **Peace Pagoda** and the Peace Plaza. The pagoda, which draws on the 1,200-year-old tradition of miniature round pagodas dedicated to eternal peace, was designed by Yoshiro Taniguchi to convey the "friendship and goodwill" of the Japanese people to the people of the United States. ⊠ *Bordered by Geary Blvd. and Fillmore, Post, and Laguna Sts., Japantown,* ☎ *415/922–6776.*

55 Japan Center Mall. The buildings lining this open-air mall are of the shoji school of architecture. Seating in this area can be found on local artist Ruth Asawa's twin origami-style fountains, which sit in the middle of the mall; they're squat circular structures made of fieldstone, with three levels for sitting and a brick floor. ⊠ *Buchanan St. between Post and Sutter Sts., Japantown.*

★ **57 Kabuki Springs & Spa.** Japantown's house of tranquility offers a treatment regimen including facials, salt scrubs, and mud and seaweed wraps. You can take your massage in a private room with a bath or in a curtained-off area. The communal baths ($15 before 5 PM, $18 after 5 and all weekend) contain hot and cold tubs, a large Japanese-style bath, a sauna, a steam room, and showers. A package that includes a 50-minute massage and the use of the communal baths costs $75. ⊠ *1750 Geary Blvd., Japantown,* ☎ *415/922–6000,* WEB *www.kabukisprings.com.* ⊘ *Daily 10–10.*

54 Noteworthy Victorians. Two **Italianate Victorians** (⊠ 1818 and 1834 California St., Pacific Heights) stand out on the 1800 block of California. A block farther is the Victorian-era **Atherton House** (⊠ 1990 California St., Pacific Heights), whose mildly daffy design incorporates Queen Anne, Stick-Eastlake, and other architectural elements. The oft-photographed **Laguna Street Victorians,** on the west side of the 1800 block of Laguna Street, cost between $2,000 and $2,600 when they were built in the 1870s. ⊠ *California St. between Franklin and Octavia Sts., and Laguna St. between Pine and Bush Sts., Pacific Heights.*

51 Spreckels Mansion. This estate was built for sugar heir Adolph Spreckels and his wife, Alma. Mrs. Spreckels was so pleased with her house that she commissioned George Applegarth to design another building in a similar vein: the California Palace of the Legion of Honor. One of the city's great iconoclasts, Alma Spreckels was the model for the bronze figure atop the Victory Monument in Union Square. ⊠ *2080 Washington St., at Octavia St., Pacific Heights.*

(50) **Whittier Mansion.** This was one of the most elegant 19th-century houses in the state, with a Spanish-tile roof and scrolled bay windows on all four sides. An anomaly in a town that lost most of its grand mansions to the 1906 quake, the Whittier Mansion was built so solidly that only a chimney toppled over during the disaster. ✉ *2090 Jackson St., Pacific Heights.*

Civic Center

The Civic Center—the beaux-arts complex between McAllister and Grove streets and Franklin and Hyde streets that includes City Hall, the War Memorial Opera House, the Veterans Building, and the old Public Library (slated to become the Asian Art Museum and Cultural Center in early 2003)—is a product of the "City Beautiful" movement of the early 20th century. City Hall, completed in 1915 and renovated in 1999, is the centerpiece.

A Good Walk

Start at **United Nations Plaza** (58), set on an angle between Hyde and Market streets. BART and Muni trains stop here, and the Bus 5–Fulton, Bus 21–Hayes, and other lines serve the area. Walk west across the plaza toward Fulton Street, which dead-ends at Hyde Street, and cross Hyde. Towering over the block of Fulton between Hyde and Larkin streets is the Pioneers Monument. The new main branch of the San Francisco Public Library is south of the monument. North of it is the old library, in 2003 slated to become the **Asian Art Museum** (59). The patch of green west of the museum is Civic Center Plaza, and beyond that is **City Hall** (60). If City Hall is open, walk through it, exiting on Van Ness Avenue and turning right. If the building's closed, walk around it to the north—to the right as you're facing it—and make a left at McAllister. Either way you'll end up at McAllister Street and Van Ness Avenue. Looking south (to the left) across the street on Van Ness, you'll see three grand edifices, each of which takes up most of its block. On the southwestern corner of McAllister and Van Ness Avenue is the **Veterans Building** (61). A horseshoe-shape carriage entrance on its south side separates the building from the **War Memorial Opera House** (62). In the next block of Van Ness Avenue, across Grove Street from the opera house, is **Louise M. Davies Symphony Hall** (63). From Davies, head west (to the right) on Grove Street to Franklin Street, turn left (south), walk one block to Hayes Street, and turn right (west). A hip strip of galleries, shops, and restaurants lies between Franklin and Laguna streets. Like Japantown, the Civic Center borders the Western Addition; it's best not to stray west of Laguna at night.

TIMING

Walking around the Civic Center shouldn't take more than about 45 minutes. The Asian Art Museum merits an hour; another half hour or more can be spent browsing in the shops along Hayes Street. On Wednesday or Sunday allot some extra time to take in the farmers' market in United Nations Plaza.

Sights to See

★ (59) **Asian Art Museum.** In early 2003 the Asian Art Museum, one of the largest collections of Asian art in the world, opens in its new home. Holdings include more than 12,000 sculptures, paintings, and ceramics from 40 countries, illustrating major periods of Asian art. Though the bulk of the art and artifacts come from China, treasures from Korea, Iran, Turkey, Syria, India, Tibet, Nepal, Pakistan, India, Japan, Afghanistan, and Southeast Asia are also on view. ✉ *200 Larkin St., between McAllister and Fulton Sts., Civic Center,* ☎ *415/668–8921 or 415/379–8801,* WEB *www.asianart.org.*

60 **City Hall.** This masterpiece of granite and marble was modeled after St. Peter's cathedral in Rome. City Hall's bronze and gold-leaf dome, which is even higher than the U.S. Capitol's version, dominates the area. Arthur Brown Jr., who also designed Coit Tower and the War Memorial Opera House, was trained in Paris; his classical influences can be seen throughout the structure. Some noteworthy events that have taken place here include the marriage of Marilyn Monroe and Joe DiMaggio (1954); the hosing—down the central staircase—of civil-rights and freedom-of-speech protesters (1960); the murders of Mayor George Moscone and openly gay supervisor Harvey Milk (1978); the torching of the lobby by angry members of the gay community in response to the light sentence (8 years for manslaughter, eventually reduced to 5½ years) given to the former supervisor who killed them (1979); and the weddings of scores of gay couples in celebration of the passage of San Francisco's Domestic Partners Act (1991). Free tours are available weekdays at 10, noon, and 2 and weekends at 12:30. Inside City Hall, the **Museum of the City of San Francisco** (☎ 415/928–0289, WEB www.sfmuseum.org) displays historical items, maps, and photographs, as well as the 500-pound head of the Goddess of Progress statue, which crowned the City Hall building that crumbled during the 1906 earthquake. Admission to the museum is free. Across Polk Street is **Civic Center Plaza**, with lawns, walkways, seasonal flower beds, a playground, and an underground parking garage. ✉ *Between Van Ness Ave. and Polk, Grove, and McAllister Sts., Civic Center,* ☎ *415/554–6023.* WEB *www.ci.sf.ca.us/cityhall.*

63 **Louise M. Davies Symphony Hall.** Fascinating and futuristic looking, this 2,750-seat hall is the home of the San Francisco Symphony. The glass wraparound lobby and pop-out balcony high on the southeast corner are visible from the outside. Henry Moore created the bronze sculpture that sits on the sidewalk at Van Ness Avenue and Grove Street. The hall's 59 adjustable Plexiglas acoustical disks cascade from the ceiling like hanging windshields. Scheduled tours (75 minutes), which meet at the Grove Street entrance, take in Davies and the nearby opera house and Herbst Theatre. ✉ *201 Van Ness Ave., Civic Center,* ☎ *415/ 552–8338.* 🎫 *Tours $5.* ☉ *Tours Mon. on the hr 10–2.*

58 **United Nations Plaza.** Brick pillars listing various nations and the dates of their admittance into the United Nations line the plaza, and its floor is inscribed with the goals and philosophy of the United Nations charter, which was signed at the War Memorial Opera House in 1945. On Wednesday and Sunday a farmers' market fills the space with homegrown produce and plants. ✉ *Fulton St. between Hyde and Market Sts., Civic Center.*

61 **Veterans Building.** Performing and visual arts organizations occupy much of this 1930s structure. The **Herbst Theatre** (☎ 415/392–4400) hosts classical ensembles, dance performances, and City Arts and Lectures events. Past City Arts speakers have included author Salman Rushdie and veteran anchor Ted Koppel. Also in the building are two galleries that charge no admission. The street-level **San Francisco Arts Commission Gallery** (☎ 415/554–6080), open from Wednesday through Saturday between 11 and 5:30, displays the works of Bay Area artists. The **San Francisco Performing Arts Library and Museum** (☎ 415/255–4800) occupies part of the fourth floor. A small gallery hosts interesting exhibitions, though the organization functions mainly as a library and research center, collecting, documenting, and preserving the San Francisco Bay Area's rich performing arts legacy. The gallery is open Wednesday 11 to 7 and Thursday through Saturday 11 to 5. ✉ *401 Van Ness Ave., Civic Center.*

⑥ **War Memorial Opera House.** During San Francisco's Barbary Coast days, operagoers smoked cigars, didn't check their revolvers, and expressed their appreciation with "shrill whistles and savage yells," as one observer put it. All the old opera houses were destroyed in the 1906 quake, but lusty support for opera continued. The opera didn't have a permanent home until the War Memorial Opera House was inaugurated in 1932 with a performance of *Tosca*. Modeled after its European counterparts, the building has a vaulted and coffered ceiling, marble foyer, two balconies, and a huge silver art deco chandelier that resembles a sunburst. ⊠ *301 Van Ness Ave., Civic Center,* ☎ *415/621–6600.*

The Northern Waterfront

For the sights, sounds, and smells of the sea, hop the Powell–Hyde cable car from Union Square and take it to the end of the line. The views as you descend Hyde Street down to the bay are breathtaking—tiny sailboats bob in the whitecaps, Alcatraz hovers ominously in the distance, and the Marin Headlands form a rugged backdrop to the Golden Gate Bridge. Once you reach sea level at the cable car turnaround, Aquatic Park and the National Maritime Museum are immediately to the west, and the commercial attractions of the Fisherman's Wharf area are to the east. Bring good walking shoes and a jacket or sweater for mid-afternoon breezes or foggy mists.

A Good Walk

Begin at Polk and Beach streets at the **National Maritime Museum** ①. (Walk west from the cable car turnaround; Bus 19 stops at Polk and Beach streets, and Bus 47–Van Ness stops one block west at Van Ness Avenue and Beach Street.) Across Beach from the museum is **Ghirardelli Square** ②, a complex of shops, cafés, and galleries in an old chocolate factory. Continue east on Beach to Hyde Street and make a left. At the end of Hyde is the **Hyde Street Pier** ③. South on Hyde a block and a half is the former Del Monte **Cannery** ④, which holds more shops, cafés, and restaurants. Walk east from the Cannery on Jefferson Street to **Fisherman's Wharf** ⑤. A few blocks farther east is **Pier 39** ⑥.

TIMING
For the entire Northern Waterfront circuit, set aside three or four hours, not including boat tours, which will take from one to three hours or more. All the attractions here are open daily.

Sights to See

★ **Alcatraz Island.** The boat ride to the island is brief (15 minutes) but affords beautiful views of the city, Marin County, and the East Bay. The audio tour, highly recommended, includes observations of guards and prisoners about life in one of America's most notorious penal colonies. A separate ranger-led tour surveys the island's ecology. Plan your schedule to allow at least three hours for the visit and boat rides combined. Reservations, even in the off-season, are recommended. ⊠ *Pier 41, Northern Waterfront,* ☎ *415/773–1188 boat schedules and information; 415/705–5555; 800/426–8687 credit-card ticket orders; 415/705–1042 park information.* ⊡ *$13.25, $9.25 without audio ($20.75 evening tours, including audio); add $2.25 per ticket to charge by phone.* ☉ *Ferry departures Sept.–late May, daily 9:30–2:15 (4:20 for evening tour Thurs.–Sun. only); late May–Aug., daily 9:30–4:15 (6:30 and 7:30 for evening tour).* WEB *www.nps.gov/alcatraz.*

④ **Cannery.** This three-story structure was built in 1894 to house what became the Del Monte Fruit and Vegetable Cannery. Today the Can-

Northern Waterfront/Marina and the Presidio

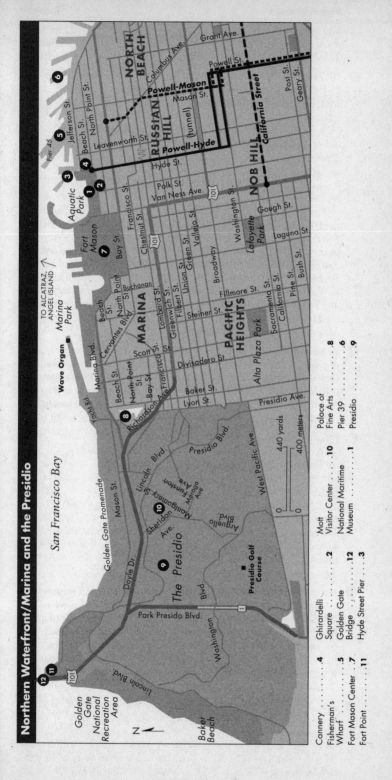

nery has shops, art galleries, a comedy club (Cobb's), and some unusual restaurants. ⊠ *2801 Leavenworth St., Northern Waterfront,* ☎ *415/771–3112.*

👆 **⑤** **Fisherman's Wharf.** Ships creak at their moorings; seagulls cry out for a handout. By mid-afternoon the fishing fleet is back to port. The chaotic streets of the wharf have numerous seafood restaurants, among them sidewalk stands where shrimp and crab cocktails are sold in disposable containers. T-shirts and sweats, gold chains galore, redwood furniture, acres of artwork (precious little of it original), and generally amusing street artists also beckon visitors. Everything's overpriced, especially the so-called novelty museums, which can provide a diversion if you're touring with antsy kids. The best of the lot, though mostly for their kitsch value, are **Ripley's Believe It or Not! Museum** (⊠ 175 Jefferson St., Northern Waterfront, ☎ 415/771–6188, WEB www. ripleysf.com) and the **Wax Museum** (⊠ 145 Jefferson St., Northern Waterfront, ☎ 415/439–4305), rebuilt in the late 1990s. For an intriguing if mildly claustrophobic glimpse into life on a submarine during World War II, drop by the **USS *Pampanito*** (⊠ Pier 45, Northern Waterfront, ☎ 415/775–1943). The sub, open Thursday–Tuesday 9–8, Wednesday 9–6 (October through Memorial Day open Sunday–Thursday 9–6, Friday–Saturday 9–8), sank six Japanese warships and damaged four others. Admission is $7. ⊠ *Jefferson St. between Leavenworth St. and Pier 39, Northern Waterfront.*

② **Ghirardelli Square.** Most of the redbrick buildings in this early 20th-century complex were part of the Ghirardelli chocolate factory. Now they house name-brand emporiums, tourist-oriented restaurants, and galleries that sell everything from crafts and knickknacks to sports memorabilia. Placards throughout the square describe the factory's history. ⊠ *900 N. Point St., Northern Waterfront,* ☎ *415/775–5500.*

③ **Hyde Street Pier.** The pier, one of the wharf area's best bargains, always crackles with activity. Depending on the time of day, you might see boatbuilders at work or children manning a ship as though it were still the early 1900s. The highlight of the pier is its collection of historic vessels, all of which can be boarded: the *Balclutha*, an 1886 full-rigged three-masted sailing vessel that sailed around Cape Horn 17 times; the *Eureka*, a side-wheel ferry; the *C. A. Thayer*, a three-masted schooner; and the *Hercules*, a steam-powered tugboat. ⊠ *Hyde and Jefferson Sts., Northern Waterfront,* ☎ *415/556–3002 or 415/556–0859,* WEB *www.maritime.org.* ⌷ *$6.* ⊙ *May 15–Sept. 15, daily 9:30–5:30, Sept. 16–May 14, daily 9:30–5.*

① **National Maritime Museum.** You'll feel as if you're out to sea when you step inside this sturdy, rounded structure. Part of the San Francisco Maritime National Historical Park, which includes Hyde Street Pier, the museum exhibits ship models, maps, and other artifacts chronicling the development of San Francisco and the West Coast through maritime history. ⊠ *Aquatic Park at the foot of Polk St., Northern Waterfront,* ☎ *415/556–3002,* WEB *www.nps.gov.* ⌷ *Donation suggested.* ⊙ *Daily 10–5.*

👆 **⑥** **Pier 39.** This is the most popular—and commercial—of San Francisco's waterfront attractions, drawing millions of visitors each year to browse through its dozens of shops. Ongoing free entertainment, accessible validated parking, and nearby public transportation ensure crowds most days. Check out the **Marine Mammal Store & Interpretive Center** (☎ 415/289–7373), a quality gift shop and education center whose proceeds benefit Sausalito's Marine Mammal Center, and the **National Park Store** (☎ 415/433–7221), with books, maps, and collectibles sold to support the National Park Service. Brilliant colors enliven the double-decker **Venetian Carousel,** often awhirl with happily howling children ($2 a ride). The din on the northwest side of the pier comes courtesy of the hundreds of sea lions that bask and play on the docks. At **Aquarium of the Bay** (☎ 415/623–5300 or 888/732–3483), moving walkways transport you through a space surrounded on three sides by water filled with indigenous San Francisco Bay marine life, from fish and plankton to sharks. The **California Welcome Center** (☎ 415/956–3493), inside the Citibank Cinemax Theater, is open from 10 to 6 daily. Parking is at the Pier 39 Garage, off Powell Street at the Embarcadero. ⊠ *Beach St. at the Embarcadero, Northern Waterfront,* WEB *www.pier39.com.*

Marina and the Presidio

The Marina district was a coveted place to live until the 1989 earthquake, when the area's homes suffered the worst damage in the city—largely because the Marina is built on landfill. Many homeowners and renters fled in search of more solid ground, but young professionals quickly replaced them, changing the tenor of this formerly low-key neighborhood. The number of upscale coffee emporiums skyrocketed. A bank became a Williams-Sonoma, and the local grocer gave way to a Pottery Barn.

West of the Marina is the sprawling Presidio, a former military base. The Presidio has superb views and the best hiking and biking areas in San Francisco.

A Good Drive

Though you can visit the sights below using public transportation, this is the place to use your car if you have one. You might even consider renting one for a day to cover the area, as well as Lincoln Park, Golden Gate Park, and the western shoreline.

Start at **Fort Mason Center** ⑦, whose entrance for automobiles is off Marina Boulevard at Buchanan Street. If you're coming by bus, take Bus 30–Stockton heading north (and later west); get off at Chestnut and Laguna streets and walk north three blocks to the pedestrian entrance at Marina Boulevard and Laguna. To get from Fort Mason to the **Palace of Fine Arts** ⑧ by car, make a right on Marina Boulevard. The road curves past a small marina and the Marina Green. Turn left at Divisadero Street, right on North Point Street, left on Baker Street, and right on Bay Street, which passes the palace's lagoon and dead-ends at the Lyon Street parking lot. Part of the palace complex is the **Exploratorium,** a hands-on science museum. (If you're walking from Fort Mason to the palace, the directions are easier: Follow Marina Boulevard to Scott Street. Cross to the south side of the street—away from the water—and continue past Divisadero Street to Baker Street, and turn left; you'll see the palace's lagoon on your right. To take Muni, walk back to Chestnut and Laguna streets and take Bus 30–Stockton continuing west; get off at North Point and Broderick streets and walk west on North Point.)

The least confusing way to drive to the **Presidio** ⑨ from the palace is to exit from the south end of the Lyon Street parking lot and head east (left) on Bay Street. Turn right (south) onto Baker Street, and right (west) on Francisco Street, taking it across Richardson Avenue to Lyon Street. Turn south (left) on Lyon and right (west) on Lombard Street, and go through the main gate to Presidio Boulevard. Turn right on Presidio, which becomes Lincoln Boulevard. Make a left at Montgomery Street; a half block up on the right is the Presidio's **Mott Visitor Center** ⑩. (To take the bus to the Presidio, walk north from the palace to Lombard Street and catch Bus 28 heading west; it stops on Lincoln near the visitor center.)

From the visitor center head north a half block to Sheridan Avenue, make a right, and make a left when Sheridan runs into Lincoln Boulevard. Lincoln winds through the Presidio past a large cemetery and some vista points. After a couple of miles you'll see a parking lot marked FORT POINT on the right. Park and follow the signs leading to **Fort Point** ⑪, walking downhill through a lightly wooded area. To walk the short distance to the **Golden Gate Bridge** ⑫, follow the signs from the Fort Point parking lot; to drive across the bridge, continue on Lincoln Boulevard a bit and watch for the turnoff on the right. Bus 28 serves stops fairly near these last two attractions; ask the driver to call them out.

TIMING

The time it takes to see this area will vary greatly depending on whether you'll be taking public transportation or driving. If you drive, plan to spend at least three hours, not including a walk across the Golden Gate Bridge or hikes along the shoreline—each of which will take a few hours. A great way to see the area is on bicycle; the folks at the Mott Visitor Center will help you find the closest rental outfit. With or without kids, you could easily pass two hours at the Exploratorium.

Sights to See

★ ♻ **Exploratorium.** The curious of all ages flock to this fascinating "museum of science, art, and human perception" within the Palace of Fine Arts. The more than 650 exhibits focus on sea and insect life, computers, electricity, patterns and light, language, the weather, and much more. Reservations are required to crawl through the pitch-black, touchy-feely **Tactile Dome**, an adventure of 15 minutes. The object is to crawl and climb through the space relying solely on the sense of touch. ⊠ *3601 Lyon St., at Marina Blvd., Marina,* ☎ *415/561–0360 general information; 415/561–0362 Tactile Dome reservations,* WEB *www. exploratorium.edu.* ⊡ *$10, free 1st Wed. of month; Tactile Dome $4 extra.* ☉ *Memorial Day–Labor Day, Sun.–Tues. and Thurs.–Sat. 10– 6, Wed. 10–9; Labor Day–Memorial Day, Tues. and Thurs.–Sun. 10– 5, Wed. 10–9.*

❼ **Fort Mason Center.** Originally a depot for the shipment of supplies to the Pacific during World War II, Fort Mason was converted into a cultural center in 1977. In business here are the popular vegetarian restaurant Greens and shops, galleries, and performance spaces, most of which are closed on Monday.

Two interesting small museums in Building C are the **Museo Italo-Americano** (☎ 415/673–2200) and the **San Francisco African-American Historical and Cultural Society** (☎ 415/441–0640).

In Building A is the **San Francisco Craft and Folk Art Museum** (☎ 415/ 775–0990), an airy space with exhibits of American folk art, tribal art, and contemporary crafts. Next door to the Craft and Folk Art Museum is the **SFMOMA Artists Gallery** (☎ 415/441–4777), where the art is available for sale or rent. Most of the museums and shops at Fort Mason close by 6 or 7. The museum admission fees range from pay-what-you-wish to $4. ⊠ *Buchanan St. and Marina Blvd., Marina,* ☎ *415/979–3010 event information.*

⓫ **Fort Point.** Designed to mount 126 cannons with a range of up to 2 mi, Fort Point was constructed between 1853 and 1861 to protect San Francisco from sea attack during the Civil War—but it was never used for that purpose. It was, however, used as a coastal defense fortification post during World War II, when soldiers stood watch here. This National Historic Site is a museum filled with military memorabilia. The building has a gloomy air and is suitably atmospheric. On days when Fort Point is staffed, guided group tours and cannon drills take place. The top floor affords a unique angle on the bay. Take care when walking along the front side of the building, as it's slippery and the waves have a dizzying effect. Just north of this structure is the cluster of buildings known as **Fort Point Mine Depot,** an army facility that functioned as the headquarters for underwater mining operations throughout World War II. ⊠ *Marine Dr. off Lincoln Blvd., Presidio,* ☎ *415/556–1693,* WEB *www.nps.gov/fopo.* ☜ *Free.* ☉ *Thurs.–Mon. 10–5.*

★ ⑫ **Golden Gate Bridge.** The suspension bridge that connects San Francisco with Marin County has long wowed sightseers with its rust-color beauty, 750-ft towers, and simple but powerful art deco design. At nearly 2 mi, the Golden Gate, completed in 1937 after four years of construction, was built to withstand winds of more than 100 mph. Though frequently gusty and misty (walkers should wear warm clothing), the bridge offers unparalleled views of the Bay Area. The east walkway yields a glimpse of the San Francisco skyline as well as the islands of the bay. The view west takes in the wild hills of the Marin Headlands, the curving coast south to Land's End, and the majestic Pacific Ocean. A vista point on the Marin side affords a spectacular view of the city. On sunny days sailboats dot the water, and brave windsurfers test the often-treacherous tides beneath the bridge. Muni Buses 28 and 29 make stops at the Golden Gate Bridge toll plaza, on the San Francisco side. ⊠ *Lincoln Blvd. near Doyle Dr. and Fort Point, Presidio,* ☎ *415/ 921–5858,* WEB *www.goldengatebridge.org.* ☉ *For pedestrians: In winter daily 6–6; in summer daily 5 AM–9 PM.*

⑩ **Mott Visitor Center.** National Park Service employees at the William P. Mott Jr. Visitor Center dispense maps, brochures, and schedules for guided walking and bicycle tours, along with information about the Presidio's past, present, and future. ⊠ *Montgomery St. between Lincoln Blvd. and Sheridan Ave., Presidio,* ☎ *415/561–4323.* ☜ *Free.* ☉ *Daily 9–5.*

★ ⑧ **Palace of Fine Arts.** San Francisco's rosy rococo Palace of Fine Arts is at the western end of the Marina. The palace is the sole survivor of the many tinted plaster buildings (a temporary classical city of sorts) built for the 1915 Panama-Pacific International Exposition, the world's fair that celebrated San Francisco's recovery from the 1906 earthquake and fire. The expo lasted for 288 days and the buildings extended about a mile along the shore. Bernard Maybeck designed this faux Roman Classic beauty, which was reconstructed in concrete and reopened in 1967. The massive columns, great rotunda (dedicated to the glory of Greek culture), and swan-filled lagoon have been used in countless fashion layouts and films. ⊠ *Baker and Beach Sts., Marina,* ☎ *415/561–0364 palace tours,* WEB *www.exploratorium.edu/palace.*

⑨ **Presidio.** Part of the Golden Gate National Recreation Area, the Presidio was a military post for more than 200 years. Don Juan Bautista de Anza and a band of Spanish settlers first claimed the area in 1776. It became a Mexican garrison in 1822 when Mexico gained its independence from Spain; U.S. troops forcibly occupied the Presidio in 1846. The U.S. Sixth Army was stationed here until October 1994, when the coveted space was transferred into civilian hands. Today, after much controversy, the area is being transformed into a self-sustaining national park with a combination of public, commercial, and residential projects. The more than 1,400 acres of hills, majestic woods, and redbrick army barracks include two beaches, a golf course, a visitor center, and picnic sites, and the views of the bay, the Golden Gate Bridge, and Marin County are sublime. ⊠ *Between the Marina and Lincoln Park, Presidio,* WEB *www.nps.gov/prsf.*

Golden Gate Park

William Hammond Hall conceived one of the nation's great city parks and began in 1870 to put into action his plan for a natural reserve with no reminders of urban life. Hammond began work in the Panhandle and eastern portions of Golden Gate Park, but it took John McLaren the length of his tenure as park superintendent, from 1890 to 1943, to complete the transformation of 1,000 desolate brush- and sand-covered acres into a rolling, landscaped oasis. Urban reality now encroaches on all sides, but the park remains a great getaway. On Sunday John F. Kennedy Drive is closed to cars and comes alive with joggers, cyclists, and in-line skaters. In addition to cultural and other attractions there are public tennis courts, baseball diamonds, soccer fields, and trails for horseback riding. The fog can sweep into the park with amazing speed; always bring a sweatshirt or jacket.

Because the park is so large, a car will come in handy if you're going to tour it from one end to the other—though you'll still do a fair amount of walking. Muni also serves the park. Buses 5–Fulton and 21–Hayes stop along its northern edge, and the N–Judah light-rail car stops a block south of the park between Stanyan Street and 9th Avenue, then two blocks south and the rest of the way west.

A Good Walk

Begin on the park's north side at Fulton Street and 6th Avenue, where the Bus 5–Fulton and Bus 21–Hayes from downtown stop. Walk south into the park at 6th Avenue. The road you'll come to is John F. Kennedy Drive. Turn left on the blacktop sidewalk and head east. Across the drive on your right is the Rhododendron Dell. (If it's springtime and the rhododendrons are in bloom, detour into the dell and return to John F. Kennedy Drive heading east.) Past the first stop sign you'll see the exterior gardens of the **Conservatory of Flowers** ① on your left. Explore the gardens; then walk south (back toward Kennedy Drive) from the conservatory entrance. Continue east on Kennedy Drive a short way to the three-way intersection and turn right (south) at Middle Drive East.

Less than a block away at the intersection of Middle and Bowling Green drives you'll see a sign for the National AIDS Memorial Grove. Before you enter the grove, follow the curve of Bowling Green Drive to the left, past the Bowling Green to the Children's Playground. If you've got kids in tow, you'll probably be spending time here. If not, still take a peek at the 1912 Herschell-Spillman Carousel.

Reverse direction on Bowling Green Drive and enter the **National AIDS Memorial Grove** ②, a sunken meadow that stretches west along Middle Drive East. At the end of the wheelchair-access ramp make a left to view the Circle of Friends; then continue west along the graded paths (ignore the staircase on the right halfway through the grove) to another circle with a poem by Thom Gunn. Exit north from this circle. As you're standing in the circle looking at the poem, the staircase to take is on your left. At the top of the staircase make a left and continue west on Middle Drive East. You'll come to the back entrance of the **California Academy of Sciences** ③.

A hundred feet shy of the Ninth Avenue and Lincoln Way entrance to Golden Gate Park is the main entrance to **Strybing Arboretum & Botan-**

ical Gardens ④. You could spend an afternoon here, but to sample just a bit of this fine facility take the first right after the bookstore. Follow the path as it winds north and west. Take your second right and you'll see signs for the Fragrance and Biblical gardens.

Backtrack from the gardens to the path you started on and make a right. As the path continues to wind north and west, you'll see a large fountain off to the left. Just before you get to the fountain, make a right and head toward the duck pond. A wooden footbridge on the pond's left side crosses the water. Signs on the other side identify the mallards, geese, American coots, mews, and other fowl in the pond. Stay to the right on the path, heading toward the exit gate. Just before the gate, continue to the right to the Primitive Garden. Take the looped boardwalk past ferns, gingko, cycads, conifers, moss, and other plants. At the end of the loop, make a left and then a right, exiting via the Eugene L. Friend gate. Go straight ahead on the crosswalk to the blacktop path on the other side. Make a right, walk about 100 ft, and make a left on Tea Garden Drive. A few hundred feet east of here is the entrance to the **Japanese Tea Garden** ⑤.

Tour the Japanese Tea Garden, exiting near the gate you entered. Make a left, and you'll soon pass the former Asian Art Museum and the M. H. de Young Memorial Museum; both buildings are closed for construction. A crosswalk leads south to the Music Concourse, with its gnarled trees, century-old fountains and sculptures, and the Golden Gate Bandshell. Turn left at the closest of the fountains and head east toward the bronze sculpture of Francis Scott Key.

Turn left at the statue and proceed north through two underpasses. At the end of the second underpass, you'll have traveled about 2 mi. If you're ready to leave the park, take the short staircase to the left of the blue-and-green playground equipment. At the top of the staircase is the 10th Avenue and Fulton Street stop for Bus 5–Fulton heading back downtown. If you're game for walking ½ mi more, make an immediate left as you exit the second underpass, cross 10th Avenue, and make a right on John F. Kennedy Drive. After approximately ¼ mi you'll see the Rose Garden on your right. Continue west to the first stop sign. To the left is a sign for **Stow Lake** ⑥. Follow the road past the log cabin to the boathouse.

From Stow Lake it's the equivalent of 30 long blocks on John F. Kennedy Drive to the western end of the park and the ocean. If you walk, you'll pass meadows, the Portals of the Past, the buffalo paddock, and a nine-hole golf course. You can skip most of this walk by proceeding west on John F. Kennedy Drive from the stop sign mentioned above, making the first right after you walk underneath Cross-Over Drive, and following the road as it winds left toward 25th Avenue and Fulton. On the northwest corner of Fulton Street and 25th Avenue, catch Bus 5–Fulton heading west, get off at 46th Avenue, walk one block west to 47th Avenue, and make a left. Make a right on John F. Kennedy Drive.

By foot or vehicle, your goal is the **Dutch Windmill** ⑦ and adjoining garden. A block to the south, wind up with a microbrew at the **Beach Chalet** ⑧.

TIMING

You can easily spend a whole day in Golden Gate Park, especially if you walk the whole distance. Set aside at least an hour for the Academy of Sciences. Even if you plan to explore just the eastern end of the park (up to Stow Lake), allot at least two hours.

Sights to See

❽ Beach Chalet. This Spanish colonial–style structure, architect Willis Polk's
last design, was built in 1925 after his death. A wraparound Federal
Works Project mural by Lucien Labaudt depicts San Francisco in the
1930s; the labels describing the various panels add up to a minihis-
tory of depression-era life in the city. A three-dimensional model of
Golden Gate Park, artifacts from the 1894 Mid-Winter Exposition and
other park events, a visitor center, and a gift shop that sells street signs
and other city paraphernalia are on the first floor as well. On a clear
day, the brewpub-restaurant upstairs (notice the carved banister on the
way up) has views past Ocean Beach to the Farallon Islands, about 30
mi offshore. ⊠ *1000 Great Hwy., at west end of John F. Kennedy Dr.,
Golden Gate Park,* WEB *www.beachchalet.com.*

★ ☝ ❸ **California Academy of Sciences.** A three-in-one attraction, the nationally renowned academy houses an aquarium, numerous science and
natural-history exhibits, and a planetarium. Leopard sharks, silver
salmon, sea bass, and other fish loop around the mesmerizing Fish
Roundabout, the big draw at **Steinhart Aquarium.** Feeding time is
1:30 PM. Elsewhere at Steinhart swim dolphins, sea turtles, piranhas,
manatees, and other sea life. There are also tide pool, tropical reef, rep-
tile and amphibian displays. Always amusing to watch, the penguins
dine at 11:30 AM and 4 PM. The multimedia earthquake exhibit in the
Earth and Space Hall at the **Natural History Museum** simulates quakes,
complete with special effects. Videos and displays in the Wild California
Hall describe the state's wildlife, and there's a re-creation of the environment of the rocky Farallon Islands. Other exhibits include the
African wildlife, fossils, the gem and mineral hall, an insect room, Far
Side of Science cartoons by Gary Larson, and an open play and learning space for small children. There is an additional charge ($2.50) for
Morrison Planetarium shows (☎ 415/750–7141 schedule), which you
enter through the Natural History Museum. Daily multimedia shows
present the night sky through the ages under a 55-ft dome, complete
with special effects and music. ⊠ *Music Concourse Dr. off South Dr.,
Golden Gate Park,* ☎ *415/750–7145,* WEB *www.calacademy.org.* 🖼
$8.50 ($2.50 discount with Muni transfer), free 1st Wed. of month.
🕙 *Memorial Day–Labor Day, daily 9–6; Labor Day–Memorial Day,
daily 10–5; 1st Wed. of month closes at 8:45 PM.*

❶ **Conservatory of Flowers.** The last remaining wood-frame Victorian conservatory in the country, the Conservatory, which was built in the late
1870s, is a copy of the one in the Royal Botanical Gardens in Kew,
England. Heavily damaged during a 1995 storm, the whitewashed facility is closed indefinitely but its architecture and gardens make it a
worthy stop nonetheless. The gardens in front of the Conservatory are
planted seasonally, with the flowers often fashioned like billboards—
depicting the Golden Gate Bridge or other city sights. On the east side
of the Conservatory (to the right as you face the building), cypress, pine,
and redwood trees surround the **Fuchsia Garden,** which blooms in summer and fall. To the west several hundred feet on John F. Kennedy Drive
is the **Rhododendron Dell.** The dell contains the most varieties—850
in all—of any garden in the country. It's especially beautiful in March,
when many of the flowers bloom, and is a favorite spot of locals for
Mother's Day picnics. ⊠ *John F. Kennedy Dr. at Conservatory Dr.,
Golden Gate Park.*

❼ **Dutch Windmill.** Two windmills anchor the western end of the park.
The restored 1902 Dutch Windmill once pumped 20,000 gallons of
well water per hour to the reservoir on Strawberry Hill. With its heavy
cement bottom and wood-shingled arms and upper section the wind-

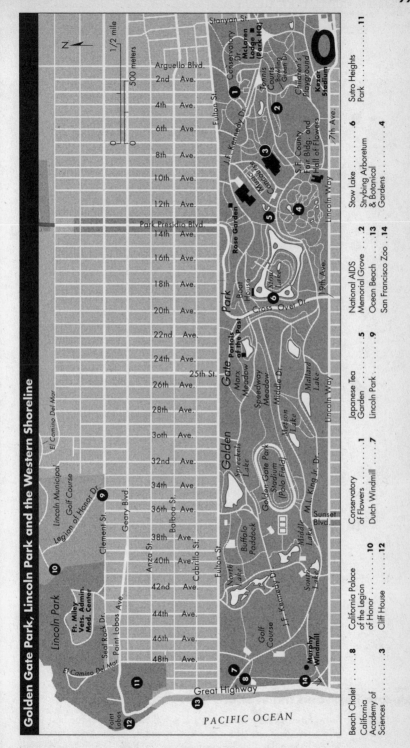

Golden Gate Park, Lincoln Park and the Western Shoreline

PACIFIC OCEAN

mill cuts quite the sturdy figure. It overlooks the equally photogenic **Queen Wilhelmina Tulip Garden,** which bursts into full bloom in early spring and late summer. The **Murphy Windmill,** on Martin Luther King Jr. Drive near the Great Highway, was the world's largest windmill when it was built in 1905. Now in disrepair, its wings clipped, the Murphy Windmill also pumped water to the Strawberry Hill reservoir. ⊠ *Between 47th Ave. and the Great Hwy., Golden Gate Park.*

★ ❺ **Japanese Tea Garden.** A serene 4-acre landscape of small ponds, streams, waterfalls, stone bridges, Japanese sculptures, *mumsai* (planted bonsai) trees, perfect miniature pagodas, and some nearly vertical wooden "humpback" bridges, the tea garden was created for the 1894 Mid-Winter Exposition. Go in the spring if you can (March is particularly beautiful), when the cherry blossoms are in bloom. ⊠ *Tea Garden Dr. off John F. Kennedy Dr., Golden Gate Park,* ☎ *415/752–4227 or 415/752–1171.* 🖾 *$3.50.* ☉ *Mar.–Sept., daily 9–6; Oct.–Feb., daily 8:30–5.*

❷ **National AIDS Memorial Grove.** San Francisco has lost many residents, gay and straight, to AIDS. This 15-acre grove, started in the early 1990s by people with AIDS and their families and friends, was conceived as a living memorial to those the disease has claimed. In 1996 Congress passed a bill granting the grove status as a national memorial. Coast live oaks, Monterey pines, coast redwoods, and other trees flank the grove, which is anchored at its east end by the stone Circle of Friends (of donors, people who have died of AIDS, and those who loved them). ⊠ *Middle Dr. E, west of tennis courts, Golden Gate Park,* WEB *www.aidsmemorial.org.*

❻ **Stow Lake.** One of the most picturesque spots in Golden Gate Park, this placid body of water surrounds Strawberry Hill. A couple of bridges allow you to cross over and ascend the hill. A waterfall cascades down from the top of the hill, and panoramic views make it worth the short hike up here. Down below, rent a boat, surrey, or bicycle or stroll around the perimeter. Just to the left of the waterfall sits the elaborate Chinese Pavilion, a gift from the city of Taipei. It was shipped in 6,000 pieces and assembled on the shore of Strawberry Hill Island in 1981. ⊠ *Off John F. Kennedy Dr., ½ mi west of 10th Ave., Golden Gate Park,* ☎ *415/752–0347.*

❹ **Strybing Arboretum & Botanical Gardens.** The 55-acre arboretum specializes in plants from areas with climates similar to that of the Bay Area, such as the west coast of Australia, South Africa, and the Mediterranean; more than 8,000 plant and tree varieties bloom in gardens throughout the grounds. Among the highlights are the Biblical, Fragrance, California Native Plants, Succulents, and Primitive Plant gardens, the new- and old-world cloud forests, and the duck pond. Maps are available at the main and Eugene L. Friend entrances. ⊠ *9th Ave. at Lincoln Way, Golden Gate Park,* ☎ *415/661–1316,* WEB *www.strybing.org.* 🖾 *Free.* ☉ *Weekdays 8–4:30, weekends 10–5. Tours from bookstore weekdays at 1:30, weekends at 10:20 and 1:30; tours from Friend Gate Wed., Fri., and Sun. at 2.*

Lincoln Park and the Western Shoreline

From Land's End in Lincoln Park you'll have some of the best views of the Golden Gate (the name was originally given to the opening of San Francisco Bay, long before the bridge was built) and the Marin Headlands. From the historic Cliff House south to the sprawling San Francisco Zoo, the Great Highway and Ocean Beach run along the western edge of the city. The wind is often strong along the shoreline, summer fog can blanket the ocean beaches, and the water is cold and usually too rough for swimming. Carry a jacket and bring binoculars.

A Good Drive

A car is useful out here. There are plenty of hiking trails, and buses travel to all the sights mentioned, but the sights are far apart. Start at **Lincoln Park** ⑨. The park entrance is at 34th Avenue and Clement Street. Those without a car can take Bus 38–Geary—get off at 33rd Avenue and walk north (to the right) one block on 34th Avenue to the entrance. At the end of 34th Avenue (labeled on some maps as Legion of Honor Drive within Lincoln Park) is the **California Palace of the Legion of Honor** ⑩, a splendid art museum. From the museum, head back out to Clement Street and follow it west. At 45th Avenue, Clement turns into Seal Rock Drive. When Seal Rock dead-ends at 48th Avenue, turn left on El Camino del Mar and right on Point Lobos Avenue. After a few hundred yards, you'll see parking lots for **Sutro Heights Park** ⑪ and the **Cliff House** ⑫. (To get from the Legion of Honor to Point Lobos Avenue by public transit, take Bus 18 from the Legion of Honor parking lot west to the corner of 48th and Point Lobos avenues.) Two large concrete lions near the southeast corner of 48th and Point Lobos guard the entrance to Sutro Heights Park. After taking a quick spin through the park, exit past the lions, cross Point Lobos, make a left, and walk down to the Cliff House. From the Cliff House it's a short walk farther downhill to **Ocean Beach** ⑬.

The **San Francisco Zoo** ⑭ is a couple of miles south, at the intersection of the Great Highway and Sloat Boulevard. If you're driving, follow the Great Highway (heading south from the Cliff House, Point Lobos Avenue becomes the Great Highway), turn left on Sloat Boulevard, and park in the zoo's lot on Sloat. The hike along Ocean Beach from the Cliff House to the zoo is a flat but scenic 3 mi. To take public transportation from the Cliff House, reboard Bus 18, which continues south to the zoo.

TIMING

Set aside at least three hours for this tour—more if you don't have a car. You can easily spend an hour in the Palace of the Legion of Honor and 1½ hours at the zoo.

Sights to See

★ ⑩ **California Palace of the Legion of Honor.** Spectacularly situated on cliffs overlooking the ocean, the Golden Gate Bridge, and the Marin Headlands, this landmark building is a fine repository of European art. The lower-level galleries exhibit prints and drawings, English and European porcelain, and ancient Assyrian, Greek, Roman, and Egyptian art. The 20-plus galleries on the upper level display the permanent collection of European art (paintings, sculpture, decorative arts, tapestries) from the 14th century to the present day. The noteworthy Rodin collection includes two galleries devoted to the master and a third with works by Rodin and other 19th-century sculptors. An original cast of Rodin's *The Thinker* resides in the courtyard. North of the museum (across Camino del Mar) is George Segal's *The Holocaust*, a sculpture that evokes life in concentration camps during World War II. ⊠ *34th Ave. at Clement St., Lincoln Park,* ☎ *415/863–3330 information,* WEB *www.thinker.org.* ⊡ *$8 ($2 off with Muni transfer); free 2nd Wed. of month.* ☉ *Tues.–Sun. 9:30–5.*

⑫ **Cliff House.** The original Cliff House, built in 1863, hosted several U.S. presidents and wealthy locals who would drive their carriages out to Ocean Beach; it was destroyed by fire on Christmas Day 1894. The second Cliff House, the most beloved and resplendent of the three, was built in 1896; it rose eight stories with an observation tower 200 ft above sea level, but it burned down in 1907. The current building dates from 1909. The complex, which includes restaurants, a pub, and a gift shop, remains open while undergoing a gradual renovation to restore its early 20th-century look. Below the Cliff House is the splendid **Musée Mécanique** (☎ 415/386–1170), a time-warped arcade with antique mechanical contrivances, including peep shows and nick-elodeons. At press time, the Musée was scheduled to close in early 2003 due to the renovations of Cliff House, and a temporary location had not yet been determined. Call for more details. The **Golden Gate National Recreation Area Visitors' Center** (☎ 415/556–8642, WEB www.nps.gov/goga), which contains historical photographs of the Cliff House and the glass-roof Sutro Baths. Eccentric onetime San Francisco mayor and Cliff House owner Adolf Sutro built the bath complex in 1896—including a train out to the site—so that everyday folks could enjoy the benefits of swimming. You can explore the ruins of the baths, which closed in the 1950s, on your own (they look a bit like water-storage receptacles) or take ranger-led walks on weekends. The visitor center, open daily from 10 to 5, provides information about these and other trails. ⊠ *1090 Point Lobos Ave., Lincoln Park,* ☎ *415/386–3330, www.cliffhouse.com and* WEB *www.nps.gov/goga/clho.* ☺ *Weekdays 8 AM–10:30 PM, weekends 8 AM–11 PM; cocktails served nightly until 2 AM.*

⑨ Lincoln Park. Large Monterey cypresses line the fairways at Lincoln Park's 18-hole golf course. There are scenic walks throughout the 275-acre park, with postcard-perfect views from many spots. The trail out to **Land's End** starts outside the Palace of the Legion of Honor, at the end of El Camino del Mar. Be careful if you hike here; landslides are frequent. ⊠ *Entrance at 34th Ave. at Clement St., Lincoln Park.*

⑬ Ocean Beach. Stretching 3 mi along the western side of the city, this is a good beach for walking, running, or lying in the sun—but not for swimming. Surfers here wear wet suits year-round, as the water is extremely cold. Riptides are also very dangerous here. Paths on both sides of the Great Highway lead from Lincoln Way to Sloat Boulevard (near the zoo); the beachside path winds through landscaped sand dunes, and the paved path across the highway is good for biking and in-line skating. ⊠ *Along the Great Hwy. from the Cliff House to Sloat Blvd. and beyond.*

☝ ⑭ San Francisco Zoo. More than 1,000 birds and animals—220 species altogether—reside at the zoo. Among the more than 130 endangered species are the snow leopard, Sumatran tiger, jaguar, and Asian elephant. African Kikuyu grass carpets the circular outer area of **Gorilla World,** one of the largest and most natural gorilla habitats of any zoo in the world. Trees and shrubs create communal play areas. Fifteen species of rare monkeys—including colobus monkeys, white ruffed lemurs, and macaques—live and play at the two-tier **Primate Discovery Center,** which contains 23 interactive learning exhibits on the ground level. The **Feline Conservation Center,** a natural setting for rare cats, plays a key role in the zoo's efforts to encourage breeding among endangered felines. The **children's zoo** has a population of about 300 mammals, birds, and reptiles, plus an insect zoo, a meerkat and prairie dog exhibit, a nature trail, a nature theater, and a restored 1921 Dentzel carousel. A ride astride one of the 52 hand-carved menagerie animals costs $2. ⊠ *Sloat Blvd. and 45th Ave., Sunset (Muni L–Taraval streetcar from downtown),* ☎ *415/753–7080,* WEB *www.sfzoo.org.* ⊡ *$10 ($1 off with Muni transfer), free 1st Wed. of month.* ☺ *Daily 10–5; children's zoo weekdays 11–4, weekends 10:30–4:30.*

⓫ **Sutro Heights Park.** Crows and other large birds battle the heady breezes at this cliff-top park on what were the grounds of the home of eccentric mining engineer and former San Francisco mayor Adolph Sutro. Monterey cypresses and Canary Island palms dot the park, and photos on placards depict what you would have seen before the house burned down in 1896. All that remains of the main house is its foundation. Climb up for a sweeping view of the Pacific Ocean and the Cliff House below. ⊠ *Point Lobos and 48th Aves., Lincoln Park.*

Mission District

The sunny Mission District wins out in San Francisco's system of microclimates—it's always the last to succumb to fog. Italian and Irish in the early 20th century, the Mission became heavily Latino in the late 1960s, when immigrants from Mexico and Central America began arriving. Despite its distinctive Latino flavor, in the 1980s and early 1990s the Mission saw an influx of Chinese, Vietnamese, Arabic, and other immigrants, along with a young bohemian crowd enticed by cheap rents and the burgeoning arts-and-entertainment scene. In the late 1990s gentrification led to skyrocketing rents, causing clashes between the longtime residents forced out and the wealthy yuppies moving in. The Mission, still a bit scruffy in patches, lacks some of the glamour of other neighborhoods, but a walk through it provides the opportunity to mix with a heady cross section of San Franciscans.

A Good Walk

The spiritual heart of the old Mission lies within the thick, white adobe walls of **Mission Dolores** ①, where Dolores Street intersects with 16th Street. From the mission, cross Dolores Street and head east on 16th Street. Tattooed and pierced hipsters abound a block from Mission Dolores, but the eclectic area still has room for a place like Creativity Explored, where people with developmental disabilities work on art and other projects. At the intersection of 16th and Valencia streets, head south (to the right). At 18th Street walk a half block west (right) to view the mural adorning the Women's Building.

Head south on Valencia Street and make a left on 24th Street. The atmosphere becomes distinctly Latin American. Record stores sell the latest Spanish-language hits, family groceries sell Latin-American ingredients and delicacies, shops proffer religious goods, and restaurants serve authentic dishes from several nations. A half block east of Folsom Street, mural-lined **Balmy Alley** ② runs south from 24th Street to 25th Street. View the murals and then head back up Balmy to 24th and continue east a few steps to the **Precita Eyes Mural Arts and Visitors Center** ③. From the center continue east past St. Peter's Church, where Isías Mata's mural *500 Years of Resistance,* on the exterior of the rectory, reflects on the struggles and survival of Latin-American cultures. At 24th and Bryant streets is the **Galería de la Raza/Studio 24** ④ art space.

Diagonally across from the Galería, on Bryant at the northeast corner near 24th Street, you can catch Bus 27–Bryant to downtown.

TIMING
The above walk takes about two hours, including brief stops at the various sights listed. If you plan to go on a mural walk with Precita Eyes or if you're a browser who tends to linger, add at least another hour.

Sights to See

② **Balmy Alley.** Mission District artists have transformed the walls of their neighborhood with paintings, and Balmy Alley is one of the best-exe-

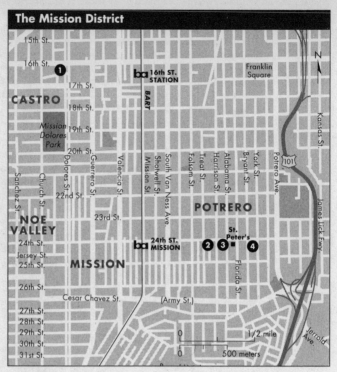

The Mission District

cuted examples. The entire one-block alley is filled with murals. Local children working with adults started the project in 1971. Since then dozens of artists have steadily added to it, with the aim of promoting peace in Central America, as well as community spirit and AIDS awareness. (Be careful here: the other end of the street adjoins a somewhat dangerous area.) ⊠ *24th St. between and parallel to Harrison and Treat Sts. (alley runs south to 25th St.), Mission.*

❹ **Galería de la Raza/Studio 24.** San Francisco's premiere showcase for Latino art, the gallery exhibits the works of local and international artists. Next door is the nonprofit Studio 24, which sells prints and paintings by Chicano artists, as well as folk art, mainly from Mexico. In early November the studio brims with art objects paying tribute to *Día de los Muertos* (Day of the Dead). In Mexican tradition death is not feared but seen as a part of life—thus the many colorful skeleton figurines doing everyday things like housework or playing sports. ⊠ *2857 24th St., at Bryant St., Mission,* ☎ *415/826–8009.* ☉ *Wed.–Sun. noon–6.*

❶ **Mission Dolores.** Mission Dolores encompasses two churches standing side by side. Completed in 1791, the small adobe building known as Mission San Francisco de Asís is the oldest standing structure in San Francisco and the sixth of the 21 California missions founded by Father Junípero Serra in the 18th and early 19th centuries. Its ceiling depicts original Ohlone Indian basket designs, executed in vegetable dyes. The tiny chapel includes frescoes and a hand-painted wooden altar; some artifacts were brought from Mexico by mule in the late 18th century. There is a small museum, and the pretty little mission cemetery (made famous by a scene in Alfred Hitchcock's *Vertigo*) maintains the graves of mid-19th-century European immigrants. (The remains of an estimated 5,000 Native Americans lie in unmarked graves.) ⊠ *Dolores* *and 16th Sts., Mission,* ☎ *415/621–8203.* 🖾 *Free (donations welcome), audio tour $7.* ☉ *Daily 9–4. www.sfmuseum.org/hist5/misdolor.html or* WEB *www.missiondolores.citysearch.com.*

❸ **Precita Eyes Mural Arts and Visitors Center.** This nonprofit arts organization sponsors guided walks of the Mission District's murals. Most tours start with a 45-minute slide presentation. The bike and walking trips, which take between one and three hours, pass by several dozen murals. You can pick up a map of 24th Street's murals at the center and buy art supplies, T-shirts, postcards, and other mural-related items. 🖂 *2981 24th St., Mission,* ☎ *415/285–2287,* WEB *www.precitaeyes.org.* 🖾 *Center free, tours $8–$12.* ☉ *Center weekdays 10–5, Sat. 10–4, Sun. noon–4; walks weekends at 11 and 1:30 or by appointment; bike tours 2nd Sun. of month at 11.*

The Castro and the Haight

The Castro district—the social, cultural and political center of the gay and lesbian community in San Francisco—is one of the liveliest and most welcoming neighborhoods in the city, especially on weekends. Come Saturday and Sunday, the streets teem with folks out shopping, pushing political causes, heading to art films, and lingering in bars and cafés. Cutting-edge clothing stores and gift shops predominate, and pairs of all genders and sexual persuasions (even heterosexual) hold hands.

Once an enclave of large middle-class families of European immigrants, the Haight began to change during the late 1950s and early 1960s. Families were fleeing to the suburbs, and the big old Victorians were deteriorating or being chopped up into cheap housing. Young people found the neighborhood an affordable spot in which they could live according to new precepts. By 1966 the Haight had become a hot spot for rock bands like the Grateful Dead—whose members moved into a big Victorian near the corner of Haight and Ashbury streets—and Jefferson Airplane, whose grand mansion was north of the district at 2400 Fulton Street.

A Good Walk

Begin in the Castro at **Harvey Milk Plaza** ① on the southwest corner of 17th and Market streets; it's outside the south entrance to the Castro Street Muni station (K, L, and M streetcars stop here). Across Castro Street from the plaza is the neighborhood's landmark, the **Castro Theatre** ②. Many shops line Castro Street between 17th and 19th streets, 18th between Sanchez and Eureka streets, and Market Street heading east toward downtown. After exploring the shops on 18th and Castro streets, get ready for a strenuous walk. For an unforgettable vista, continue north on Castro Street two blocks to 16th Street, turn left, and head up the steep hill to Flint Street. Turn right on Flint and follow the trail on the left (just past the tennis courts) up the hill. The beige buildings on the left contain the **Randall Museum** ③ for children. Turn right up the dirt path, which soon loops back up Corona Heights. At the top you'll be treated to an all-encompassing view of the city.

Now continue north to walk the Haight Street tour. Follow the trail down the other side of Corona Heights to a grassy field. The gate to the field is at the intersection of Roosevelt Way and Museum Way. Turn right on Roosevelt (head down the hill) and cross Roosevelt at Park Hill Terrace. Walk up Park Hill to Buena Vista Avenue, turn left, and follow the road as it loops west and south around Buena Vista Park to Central Avenue. Head down Central two blocks to Haight Street, and make a left.

Continue west to the fabled **Haight-Ashbury intersection** ④. Despite the franchise operations, you won't need to close your eyes to conjure the 1960s. A motley contingent of folks attired in retro fashions and often sporting hippie-long hair hangs here. One block south of Haight and Ashbury is the **Grateful Dead house** ⑤, the pad that Jerry Garcia and band inhabited in the 1960s. The stores along Haight Street up to Shrader Street are worth checking out despite the many panhandlers. At Clayton Street, you can stop in at the meditative Peace Arts Center on the ground floor of the Red Victorian Peace Center Bed & Breakfast.

TIMING

Allot an hour to an hour and a half to visit the Castro district. Set aside an extra hour to hike Corona Heights and visit the Randall Museum. The distance covered in the Haight is only several blocks, and although there are shops aplenty and other amusements, an hour or so should be enough. Don't linger in Buena Vista Park after nightfall.

Sights to See

★ ❷ **Castro Theatre.** The neon marquee is the neighborhood's great landmark, and the 1,500-seat theater, which opened in 1922, is the grandest of San Francisco's few remaining movie palaces. The Castro's elaborate Spanish baroque interior is fairly well preserved. Before many shows the theater's pipe organ rises from the orchestra pit and an organist plays pop and movie tunes, usually ending with the Jeanette McDonald standard "San Francisco" (go ahead, sing along). The crowd can be enthusiastic and vocal, talking back to the screen as loudly as it talks to them. ⊠ *429 Castro St., Castro,* ☎ *415/621–6120.*

❺ **Grateful Dead house.** Nothing unusual marks the house of legend. On the outside, it's just one more well-kept Victorian on a street that's full of them—but true fans of the Dead may find some inspiration here. The three-story house (closed to the public) is tastefully painted in sedate mauves, tans, and teals (no bright tie-dye colors). ⊠ *710 Ashbury St., just past Waller St., Haight.*

❹ **Haight-Ashbury intersection.** On October 6, 1967, hippies took over the intersection of Haight and Ashbury streets to proclaim the "Death of Hip." If they thought hip was dead then, they'd find absolute confirmation of it today, what with the Gap holding court on one quadrant of the famed corner. Among the folks who hung out in or near the Haight during the late 1960s were writers Richard Brautigan, Allen Ginsberg, Ken Kesey, and Gary Snyder; anarchist Abbie Hoffman; rock performers Marty Balin, Jerry Garcia, Janis Joplin, and Grace Slick; LSD champion Timothy Leary; and filmmaker Kenneth Anger.

❶ **Harvey Milk Plaza.** An 18-ft-long rainbow flag, a gay icon, flies above this plaza named for the man who electrified the city in 1977 by being elected to its Board of Supervisors as an openly gay candidate. The liberal Milk hadn't served a full year of his term before he and Mayor George Moscone, also a liberal, were shot in November 1978 at City Hall. Milk's assassination shocked the gay community, which became enraged when the famous "Twinkie defense"—that junk food had led to diminished mental capacity—resulted in a manslaughter verdict for the killer. During the so-called White Night Riot of May 21, 1979, gays and their sympathizers stormed City Hall, torching its lobby and several police cars. Milk's legacy is the high visibility of gay people throughout city government. A plaque at the base of the flagpole lists the names of past and present openly gay and lesbian state and local officials. ⊠ *Southwest corner of Castro and Market Sts., Castro.*

☝ ❸ **Randall Museum.** The highlight of this facility is the educational animal room, popular with children, where you can observe birds, lizards,

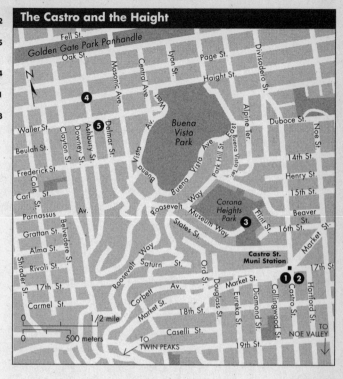

snakes, spiders, and other creatures that cannot be released to the wild because of injury or other problems. Also here are a greenhouse, wood-working and ceramics studios, and a theater. The Randall sits on 16 acres of public land; the hill that overlooks the museum is variously known as Red Rock, Museum Hill, and, correctly, Corona Heights. ✉ *199 Museum Way, off Roosevelt Way, Castro,* ☎ *415/554–9600,* WEB *www.randallmuseum.org.* ✉ *Free.* ☼ *Tues.–Sat. 10–5.*

DINING

By Sharon
Silva

San Francisco has more restaurants per capita than any other city in the United States, and nearly every ethnic cuisine is represented, from Afghan to Indian to Vietnamese. Whether it's the best tapas this side of Barcelona or the silkiest seared foie gras this side of Paris, San Francisco has it all—most often within convenient walking distance.

CATEGORY	COST*
$$$$	over $30
$$$	$22–$30
$$	$15–$21
$	under $15

* per person for a main course at dinner, exluding 8¼% tax.

Union Square

Contemporary

$$$–$$$$ ✗ **Postrio.** There's always a chance to catch a glimpse of some celebrity at this legendary eatery, including Postrio's owner, superchef Wolfgang Puck, who periodically commutes here from Los Angeles. A stunning three-level bar and dining area is highlighted by palm trees and mu-

108

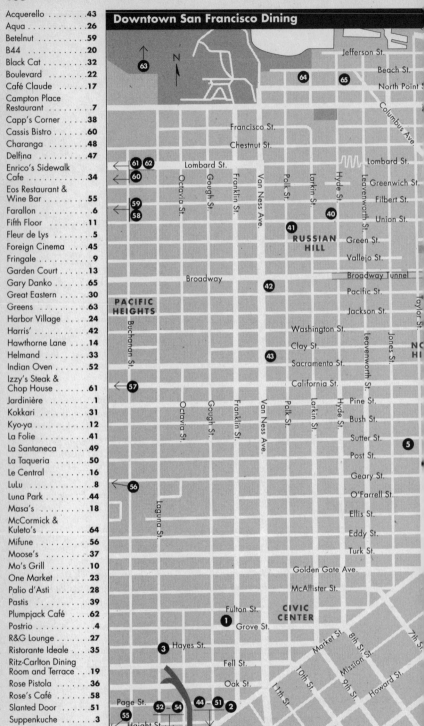

Downtown San Francisco Dining

seum-quality contemporary paintings. The lunch and dinner menus are Californian with Mediterranean and Asian overtones. ⊠ *545 Post St., Union Square,* ☎ *415/776–7825. Reservations essential. AE, D, DC, MC, V. No lunch Sun.*

French

$$$$ ✕ **Fleur de Lys.** The creative cooking of French chef-partner Hubert Keller has brought every conceivable culinary award to this romantic spot. The menu changes constantly, but such dishes as sea bass with ratatouille crust and quail stuffed with wild mushrooms are among the possibilities in the elaborately canopied dining room. Perfectly smooth service adds to the overall enjoyment of eating here. ⊠ *777 Sutter St., Union Square,* ☎ *415/673–7779. Reservations essential. Jacket required. AE, DC, MC, V. Closed Sun. No lunch.*

$$$–$$$$ ✕ **Campton Place Restaurant.** This elegant, ultrasophisticated small hotel helped put new American cooking on the local culinary map in the 1980s. Today, the kitchen is in the talented hands of Gascony-born Laurent Manrique, who prepares a fine southern French menu that puts foie gras at center stage but still keeps a homespun *poule au pot* (poached chicken) as an option. ⊠ *340 Stockton St., Union Square,* ☎ *415/955–5555. Reservations essential. AE, D, DC, MC, V.*

Seafood

$$$–$$$$ ✕ **Farallon.** Outfitted with sculpted jellyfish lamps, kelp-covered
★   columns, and sea urchin chandeliers, this swanky Pat Kuleto–designed restaurant is loaded with style *and* customers. Chef Mark Franz cooks up exquisite seafood that draws serious diners from coast to coast. When the restaurant opened, Franz whipped up very rich—and quite delicious—sauces for much of his food, but he has since tempered his enthusiasm for butter, to the delight of anyone watching his or her diet. ⊠ *450 Post St., Union Square,* ☎ *415/956–6969. AE, D, DC, MC, V. No lunch Sun. and Mon.*

South of Market (SoMa) and Embarcadero

American

$$$$ ✕ **Garden Court.** This quintessential Old San Francisco restaurant is in the Palace Hotel. During the daytime, light splashes through the dining room's beautiful stained-glass ceiling and against the towering Ionic columns and crystal chandeliers. The draw here is not the dinner menu, but rather the truly extravagant Sunday buffet brunch, one of the city's great traditions. If you can't make it to the Palace for breakfast, try the Saturday-afternoon high tea. ⊠ *Market and New Montgomery Sts., South of Market,* ☎ *415/546–5011. Reservations essential. AE, D, DC, MC, V. No lunch weekends. No dinner Sun.–Tues.*

$ ✕ **Mo's Grill.** The term "burger" takes on new meaning at Mo's. This eatery is devoted to what is arguably America's favorite food, and it dresses it up in lots of ways: with Monterey Jack and avocado; with cheese and chilies; and more. But beef burgers are not the only story here. Salmon, lamb, and turkey burgers are among the other choices also cooked over the volcanic-rock grill, and sides of fries or onion rings fill out the plates deliciously. ⊠ *772 Folsom St., South of Market,* ☎ *415/957–3779. MC, V.*

Chinese

$–$$$ ✕ **Harbor Village.** At lunchtime, businesspeople looking to impress their clients fill the dining room of this outpost of upmarket Cantonese cooking, all of them enjoying the extraordinary selection of dim sum. At dinnertime, fresh seafood from the restaurant's own tanks, crisp Peking duck, and various exotica—bird's nest, crab roe, shark fin—are among the most popular requests in this opulent 400-seat branch of a Hong

Kong establishment. There's validated parking at the Embarcadero Center Garage. ⊠ *4 Embarcadero Center, Embarcadero,* ☎ *415/781–8833. AE, DC, MC, V.*

Contemporary

$$$$ ✕ **Fifth Floor.** Chef Laurent Gras prepares elegant, sophisticated, visually stunning plates—and the crowds keep coming. The 75-seat room, done in dark wood and zebra-stripe carpeting, is where such exquisite dishes as venison saddle with cherry marmalade are served. There's even ice cream made to order—the machine churns out a creamy, cool, rich serving for one. ⊠ *Palomar Hotel, 12 4th St., South of Market,* ☎ *415/348–1555. Reservations essential. AE, DC, MC, V. Closed Sun. No lunch.*

$$$–$$$$ ✕ **Boulevard.** Two of San Francisco's top restaurant talents—chef Nancy Oakes and designer Pat Kuleto—are responsible for this high-profile eatery in the magnificent 1889 Audiffred Building, a Parisian look-alike that was one of the few downtown structures to survive the 1906 earthquake. Oakes's menu is seasonally in flux, but you can always count on her signature juxtaposition of delicacies such as foie gras with homey comfort foods like wood oven–roasted pork loin. ⊠ *1 Mission St., Embarcadero,* ☎ *415/543–6084. Reservations essential. AE, D, DC, MC, V. No lunch weekends.*

$$$–$$$$ ✕ **Hawthorne Lane.** This stylish restaurant draws a crowd to a quiet alley not far from the Yerba Buena Center. At the bar, you can order a selection of irresistible small plates—tuna tartare with nori chips, tempura green beans with mustard sauce—plus anything on the full menu. Patrons in the formal, light-flooded dining room engage in more serious eating. The bread basket, full of such house-made delights as biscuits, bread sticks, rye, and rolls, is the best in town. ⊠ *22 Hawthorne St., South of Market,* ☎ *415/777–9779. D, DC, MC, V. No lunch weekends.*

$$–$$$$ ✕ **One Market.** This huge, bustling brasserie across from the Ferry Building is chef Bradley Ogden's popular San Francisco outpost. The two-tier dining room, done in mustard tones, seats 170, and a spacious bar-café serves snacks, including addictive wire-thin onion rings, beginning at noon. Fine—and homey—preparations include rabbit in mustard, cinnamon-glazed pork shank, and caramel pecan tart with bourbon ice cream. ⊠ *1 Market St., Embarcadero,* ☎ *415/777–5577. AE, DC, MC, V. Closed Sun. No lunch Sat.*

French

$$–$$$ ✕ **Pastis.** At lunchtime the sunny cement bar and sleek wooden banquettes in this exposed-brick dining room are crowded with workers from nearby offices; they come to fuel up on such plates as grilled prawns marinated in pastis (anise-flavor liqueur). The evening menu may include buttery boned oxtails with *ravigote* sauce (with capers, onions, and herbs) and a thick veal chop with shallot sauce. ⊠ *1015 Battery St., Embarcadero,* ☎ *415/391–2555. AE, MC, V. Closed Sun. No lunch Sat.*

$$ ★ ✕ **Fringale.** The bright yellow paint on this small, dazzling bistro stands out like a beacon on an otherwise ordinary street. The well-dressed clientele comes for the French-Basque–inspired creations of Biarritz-born chef Gerald Hirigoyen, whose classic *frisées aux lardons* (curly salad greens with crisp bacon cubes and a poached egg), duck confit with tiny French lentils, and almond torte filled with custard cream are hallmarks of the regularly changing menu. ⊠ *570 4th St., South of Market,* ☎ *415/543–0573. Reservations essential. AE, MC, V. Closed Sun. No lunch Sat.*

Japanese

$$-$$$ ✕ **Kyo-ya.** Rarely replicated outside Japan, the refined experience of dining in a fine Japanese restaurant has been introduced with extraordinary authenticity at this showplace within the Palace Hotel. In Japan a *kyo-ya* is a nonspecialized restaurant that serves a wide range of food. Here, the range is spectacular, encompassing tempuras, one-pot dishes, deep-fried and grilled meats, and three dozen sushi selections. ✉ *Palace Hotel, 2 New Montgomery St., South of Market,* ☎ *415/546–5000. AE, D, DC, MC, V. Closed Sun. No lunch Mon. or Sat.*

Mediterranean

$-$$ ✕ **LuLu.** The food here, prepared under the watchful eye of executive
★ chef Jody Denton, is satisfyingly uncomplicated and delectable. Beneath a high barrel-vaulted ceiling, you can feast on mussels roasted in an iron skillet, wood-roasted poultry, meats, and shellfish. Each day a different main course prepared on the rotisserie is featured, such as the truly succulent suckling pig on Friday. ✉ *816 Folsom St., South of Market,* ☎ *415/495–5775. AE, D, DC, MC, V.*

Financial District

Chinese

$ ✕ **Yank Sing.** The city's oldest teahouse, Yank Sing prepares 100 varieties of dim sum on a rotating basis, serving some 60 varieties daily. The Spear Street location is large and upmarket, while the older Stevenson Street site is far smaller, a cozy refuge for neighborhood office workers who fuel up on steamed buns and parchment chicken at lunchtime. Take-out counters in both establishments make a meal on the run a delicious compromise. ✉ *49 Stevenson St., Financial District,* ☎ *415/541–4949;* ✉ *One Rincon Center, 101 Spear St., Financial District,* ☎ *415/957–9300. AE, DC, MC, V. No dinner.*

French

$-$$ ✕ **Le Central.** This venerable institution is the quintessential French brasserie: noisy and crowded, with tasty but not so subtly cooked classics, such as garlicky pâtés, leeks vinaigrette, steak au poivre, cassoulet, and grilled blood sausage with crisp french fries. Local power brokers, even an occasional rock star such as Mick Jagger, snag noontime tables. Staff from the nearby French consulate dine here as well, giving the place an air of authenticity. ✉ *453 Bush St., Financial District,* ☎ *415/391–2233. MC, V. Closed Sun.*

$ ✕ **Café Claude.** This standout French bistro, in an alley near the French consulate, has a true Parisian interior, with a zinc bar, old-fashioned banquettes, and cinema posters that once actually outfitted a bar in the City of Light's 11th arrondissement. Order an *assiette de charcuterie* (plate of assorted meats), *croque monsieur* (grilled cheese sandwich), or duck breast with braised endives from the French-speaking staff, and you might forget what country you're in. ✉ *7 Claude La., Financial District,* ☎ *415/392–3505. AE, DC, MC, V. Closed Sun.*

Greek

$$-$$$$ ✕ **Kokkari.** Inside this handsome taverna, complete with an outsize fireplace and a lively bar, folks sit down to a full menu of Aegean plates. Most savvy diners start off with a trio of dips—eggplant, yogurt and cucumber, *taramasalata* (fish roe pureed with olive oil and bread crumbs)—and then move on to such Athenian standards as moussaka, octopus salad, lemon chicken, braised lamb shank, and grilled whole bass. ✉ *200 Jackson St., Financial District,* ☎ *415/981–0983. AE, DC, MC, V. Closed Sun. No lunch Sat.*

Italian

$$–$$$ ✗ **Palio d'Asti.** Restaurateur Gianni Fassio draws a lively crowd to this authentic spot serving dishes from Tuscany and the Piedmont. The kitchen's freshly baked breads, exquisite pastas, and carefully constructed sauces are legendary. Colorful flags decorate the elegant restaurant, each representing a neighborhood that participates in the famed Palio, a horse race that's been held annually since medieval times in Fassio's hometown of Asti. ⊠ *640 Sacramento St., Financial District,* ☎ *415/395–9800. AE, D, MC, V. Closed weekends.*

Seafood

$$$–$$$$ ✗ **Aqua.** This quietly elegant and ultrafashionable spot, heavily mirrored and populated by a society crowd, is among the city's most lauded seafood restaurants—and among the most expensive. Chef-owner Michael Mina creates contemporary versions of French, Italian, and American classics. Service is as smooth as silk, desserts are showy, and the wine list is as high class as the crowd. ⊠ *252 California St., Financial District,* ☎ *415/956–9662. Reservations essential. Jacket and tie. AE, DC, MC, V. No lunch weekends.*

$–$$$ ✗ **Tadich Grill.** Owners and locations have changed many times since this old-timer opened during the gold-rush era, but the 19th-century atmosphere remains. Simple sautés are the best choices, or cioppino during crab season, petrale sole during sole season, and an old-fashioned house-made tartar sauce anytime. The crusty, white-coated waiters are a reminder of good, old-fashioned service. ⊠ *240 California St., Financial District,* ☎ *415/391–2373. Reservations not accepted. MC, V. Closed Sun.*

Spanish

$$ ✗ **B44.** Belden Place is a restaurant gold mine, with a cluster of won-
★ derful European eateries. This spare, modern Spanish addition, with its open kitchen, draws locals who love the menu of Catalan tapas and paellas. Among the small plates are white anchovies with pears and Idiazábal cheese, sherry-scented fish cheeks, warm octopus with tiny potatoes, and blood sausage with white beans. ⊠ *44 Belden Pl., Financial District,* ☎ *415/986–6287. AE, MC, V. Closed Sun. No lunch Sat.*

Chinatown

Chinese

$–$$$ ✗ **Great Eastern.** Cantonese chefs are known for their expertise with seafood, and the kitchen at Great Eastern continues that venerable tradition. In the busy dining room, tanks are filled with Dungeness crabs, black bass, abalone, catfish, shrimp, and other creatures of the sea, and a wall-hung menu in both Chinese and English specifies the cost of selecting what can be pricey indulgences. ⊠ *649 Jackson St., Chinatown,* ☎ *415/986–2550. AE, MC, V.*

$–$$$ ✗ **R&G Lounge.** The name conjures up an image of a dark bar with a cigarette-smoking piano player, but the restaurant, on two floors, is actually as bright as a new penny. Downstairs (entrance on Kearny Street) is a no-tablecloth dining room that is always packed at lunch and dinner. The classier upstairs space (entrance on Commercial Street) is a favorite stop for Chinese businessmen on expense accounts and anyone else seeking Cantonese banquet fare. ⊠ *631 Kearny St., Chinatown,* ☎ *415/982–7877 or 415/982–3811. AE, DC, MC, V.*

North Beach

Afghan

$ ✗ **Helmand.** Don't be put off by Helmand's location on a rather scruffy block of Broadway—inside you'll find authentic Afghan cooking, elegant surroundings with white table linens and Afghan carpets, and amazingly low prices. Highlights include *aushak* (leek-filled ravioli served with yogurt and ground beef), pumpkin with a yogurt and garlic sauce, and any of the lamb dishes. ✉ *430 Broadway, North Beach,* ☎ *415/362–0641. AE, MC, V. Closed Mon. No lunch.*

Contemporary

$$–$$$ ✕ **Enrico's Sidewalk Café.** For years this historic North Beach hangout was more a drinking spot than a dining destination, but a steadier kitchen has changed all that. Diners regularly tuck into thin-crust pizzas, steamed mussels, thick and juicy burgers, and grilled fish while gently swaying to first-rate live music. An outdoor patio is outfitted with heat lamps to keep the serious people-watchers warm until closing. ✉ *504 Broadway, North Beach,* ☎ *415/982–6223. AE, MC, V.*

$–$$$ ✕ **Moose's.** Ed Moose and his wife, Mary Etta, are well known in San Francisco and beyond, so local and national politicians and media types typically turn up at their restaurant. The menu is a sophisticated take on familiar preparations, such as grilled calamari salad, rosemary-braised lamb shank, and butterscotch pot-de-crème. The surroundings are classic and comfortable, with views of Washington Square and live music at night. ✉ *1652 Stockton St., North Beach,* ☎ *415/989–7800. Reservations essential. AE, D, DC, MC, V. No lunch Sat.–Wed.*

French

$$–$$$ ✕ **Black Cat.** A combination restaurant and lounge—the latter called the Blue Bar—Black Cat takes its name from a famous San Francisco café-bar that was a hangout for everyone from artists to trade unionists in the 1930s through the 1960s. Today's Black Cat is a fine French brasserie, complete with zinc bar, alfresco seating, and raw-seafood platters. The ambience is a spirited one, with live jazz and a bar menu served up until the wee hours in the seriously blue lounge. ✉ *501 Broadway, North Beach,* ☎ *415/981–2233. AE, DC, MC, V. Closed Sun. No lunch.*

Italian

$–$$$ ✕ **Rose Pistola.** Chef-owner Reed Hearon's busy 130-seat spot draws
★ huge crowds. The name honors one of North Beach's most revered barkeeps, and the food celebrates the neighborhood's Ligurian roots. An assortment of antipasti—roasted peppers, house-cured fish, fava beans dusted with pecorino shards—and pizzas from the wood-burning oven are favorites, as are the cioppino and fresh fish of the day served in various ways. ✉ *532 Columbus Ave., North Beach,* ☎ *415/399–0499. AE, DC, MC, V.*

$$ ✕ **Capp's Corner.** This is one of North Beach's last family-style trattorias, a pleasantly down-home spot where the men at the bar still roll dice for drinks and diners sit elbow to elbow at long oilcloth-covered tables. The fare is bountiful, well-prepared five-course dinners—not award winning, but a meal here will mean you'll still be able to send your children to college. ✉ *1600 Powell St., North Beach,* ☎ *415/989–2589. AE, D, DC, MC, V.*

$$ ✕ **Ristorante Ideale.** The food here is what you might sit down to in a Roman trattoria—grilled vegetables, fettuccine with porcini, ravioli filled with ricotta and spinach, pork marsala, *pesce misto* (mixed seafood for two), and tiramisu. The red tile floors, rows of wine racks, and friendly, although sometimes frazzled, staff make this one of the nicest spots in the neighborhood, a place where you appreciate just how *simpatico* North Beach can be. ✉ *1309 Grant Ave., North Beach,* ☎ *415/391–4129. DC, MC, V. Closed Mon. No lunch.*

Nob Hill and Russian Hill

French

$$$$ ✕ **La Folie.** Long a favorite of dedicated Francophiles, this small, *très*
★ Parisian establishment is a jewel. The surroundings are lovely, but the
food is the star here, especially the five-course "discovery menu" that
offers a treasure trove of rarified mouthfuls, from foie gras to truffles.
Much of the food is edible art--whimsical presentations in the form
of savory terrines and napoleons—or such elegant accompaniments as
bone-marrow flan. ⊠ *2316 Polk St., Russian Hill,* ☎ *415/776–5577.*
Reservations essential. AE, D, DC, MC, V. No lunch.

$$$$ ✕ **Masa's.** Chef Ron Siegel, famous for besting Japan's Iron Chef, is
at the helm of Masa's, one of the country's most celebrated food temples, and his efforts have pleased the fussiest restaurant critics. Dinners are prix-fixe with two menus offered, a four-course menu du jour
and a five-course menu, both laced with truffles and foie gras and both
priced at a king's ransom. ⊠ *648 Bush St., Nob Hill,* ☎ *415/989–7154.*
Reservations essential. Jacket required. AE, D, DC, MC, V. Closed Sun.
and Mon. No lunch.

$$$$ ✕ **Ritz-Carlton Dining Room and Terrace.** There are two distinctly different places to eat in this neoclassic Nob Hill showplace. The Dining
Room is formal and elegant and serves only three- to five-course
French seasonal dinners. The Terrace, a cheerful, informal spot with
a large garden patio for outdoor dining, serves breakfast, lunch, dinner, and a Sunday jazz brunch. In both cases, executive chef Sylvain
Portay, previously chef de cuisine at New York's Le Cirque, oversees
the superb menus. ⊠ *600 Stockton St., Nob Hill,* ☎ *415/296–7465.*
AE, D, DC, MC, V. Closed Sun. No lunch.

Spanish

$ ✕ **Zarzuela.** The small, crowded storefront serves nearly 40 different
hot and cold tapas plus some dozen main courses. There is a tapa to
suit every palate, from poached octopus atop new potatoes and hot
garlic-flecked shrimp to slabs of manchego cheese with paper-thin
slices of serrano ham. Hop a cable car to get here, as parking is night-
marish. ⊠ *2000 Hyde St., Russian Hill,* ☎ *415/346–0800. D, MC, V.*
No lunch.

Steak

$$–$$$$ ✕ **Harris'.** Ann Harris knows her beef. She grew up on a Texas cattle
ranch and was married to the late Jack Harris of Harris Ranch fame.
In her own large, New York–style restaurant she serves some of the
best dry-aged steaks in town, including some truly pricey Japanese beef.
If you're a martini drinker, take this opportunity to enjoy an artful ex-
ample of the cocktail. ⊠ *2100 Van Ness Ave., Russian Hill,* ☎ *415/*
673–1888. AE, D, DC, MC, V. No lunch.

Pacific Heights and Japantown

Italian

$$$–$$$$ ✕ **Acquerello.** This elegant restaurant—white linens, fresh flowers,
exquisite china—is one of the most romantic spots in town. Both the
service and the food are exemplary, and the menu covers the full range
of Italian cuisine. The gnocchi, especially pumpkin gnocchi with sage
and truffles, and green onion fettuccine with crab and wine are mem-
orable, as are the fish dishes. ⊠ *1722 Sacramento St., Van Ness/Polk,*
☎ *415/567–5432. AE, D, MC, V. Closed Sun. and Mon. No lunch.*

$–$$ ✕ **Vivande Porta Via.** Tucked in among the boutiques on upper Fillmore Street, this pricey Italian delicatessen-restaurant, operated by well-
known chef and cookbook author Carlo Middione, draws a crowd at
lunch and dinner for both its take-out and sit-down fare. Glass cases

holding dozens of prepared delicacies span one wall. The rest of the room is given over to seating and to shelves laden with wines, olives, and other gourmet goods. ⊠ *2125 Fillmore St., Lower Pacific Heights,* ☎ *415/346–4430. AE, MC, V.*

Japanese

$ ✕ **Mifune.** Thin, brown soba and thick, white udon are the specialties at this North American outpost of an Osaka-based noodle empire. A line often snakes out the door, but the house-made noodles, served both hot and cold and with more than a score of toppings, are worth the wait. ⊠ *Japan Center, Kintetsu Bldg., 1737 Post St., Japantown,* ☎ *415/922–0337. Reservations not accepted. AE, D, DC, MC, V.*

Civic Center

Contemporary

$$$–$$$$ ✕ **Jardinière.** One of the city's most talked-about restaurants since its
★ opening in the late 1990s, Jardinière continues to be *the* place to dine before a performance at the nearby Opera House or any time you have something to celebrate. The chef-owner is Traci Des Jardins, and the sophisticated interior, with its eye-catching oval atrium and curving staircase, is the work of designer Pat Kuleto. The menu is a match for the decor, from a foie gras first course to a superb monkfish main to a berry-rich shortcake for dessert. ⊠ *300 Grove St., Hayes Valley,* ☎ *415/861–5555. Reservations essential. AE, DC, MC, V. No lunch.*

German

$–$$ ✕ **Suppenkuche.** Bratwurst and braised red cabbage accompany a long list of German beers at this lively, hip outpost of simple German cooking in the trendy Hayes Valley corridor. Strangers sit down together at unfinished pine tables when the room gets crowded, which it regularly does. The food—potato pancakes with homemade applesauce, sauerbraten, cheese spaetzle, schnitzel, apple strudel—is tasty and easy on the pocketbook, and the brews are first-rate. ⊠ *601 Hayes St., Hayes Valley,* ☎ *415/252–9289. AE, MC, V. No lunch.*

Mediterranean

$$–$$$ ✕ **Zuni Café & Grill.** Zuni's Italian-Mediterranean menu, created by nationally known chef Judy Rodgers, packs in an eclectic crowd. A balcony dining area overlooks the large zinc bar, where a first-rate oyster selection and drinks are dispensed. The menu changes daily, but the superb whole roast chicken and Tuscan bread salad for two is always on it. Even the hamburgers (served until 5:30 and after 10:30) have an Italian accent—they're topped with Gorgonzola and served on focaccia. ⊠ *1658 Market St., Hayes Valley,* ☎ *415/552–2522. Reservations essential. AE, MC, V. Closed Mon.*

The Northern Waterfront

French

$$$$ ✕ **Gary Danko.** At his eponymous restaurant, chef Gary Danko de-
★ livers the same fine food that won him a 1995 James Beard best chef award during his stint at the city's Ritz-Carlton. The plates run the gamut from horseradish-crusted salmon to quail with morels to a truly decadent chocolate soufflé with two sauces. The wine list is the size of a small-town phone book, and the look of the banquette-lined room is as high class as the food. ⊠ *800 N. Point St., Northern Waterfront,* ☎ *415/749–2060. Reservations essential. AE, D, DC, MC, V. No lunch.*

Seafood

$–$$$ ✕ **McCormick & Kuleto's.** This seafood emporium in Ghirardelli Square is a visitor's dream come true: a fabulous view of the bay from every seat in the house; an Old San Francisco atmosphere; and dozens of varieties of fish and shellfish prepared in scores of international ways. The food has its ups and downs—stick with the simplest preparations— but even on foggy days you can count on the view. Validated parking is available in the Ghirardelli Square garage. ✉ *Ghirardelli Sq. at Beach and Larkin Sts., Northern Waterfront,* ☎ *415/929–1730. AE, D, DC, MC, V.*

Marina and the Presidio

French

$ ✕ **Cassis Bistro.** Take a seat at the tiny bar and enjoy a glass of wine while you wait for a free table in this sunny yellow, postage stamp– size operation, which recalls the small bistros tucked away on side streets in French seaside towns. The servers have Gallic accents; the food— onion tart, veal ragout, braised rabbit, tarte Tatin—is comfortingly home style; and the prices are geared toward the penurious. ✉ *2120 Greenwich St., Cow Hollow,* ☎ *415/292–0770. No credit cards. Closed Sun. and Mon. No lunch.*

Italian

$ ✕ **Rose's Café.** Breakfast, lunch, and dinner can be taken in the dining room or outside on a heater-equipped patio at this more casual kin of the famed Rose Pistola. In the morning, folks line up for seductive breads and even breakfast pizzas with ham and eggs. Midday is the time for a hot hero sandwich, a grilled-chicken salad, or a pizza topped with arugula and prosciutto. Evening hours find customers working their way through hanger steak or plump mussels roasted in the pizza oven. ✉ *2298 Union St., Cow Hollow,* ☎ *415/775–2200. AE, MC, V.*

Mediterranean

$$–$$$ ✕ **PlumpJack Café.** This clubby dining room, with its smartly attired clientele of bankers and brokers, socialites and society scions, takes its name from an opera composed by oil tycoon and music lover Gordon Getty, whose sons are two of the partners here. The regularly changing menu spans the Mediterranean; possible dishes include lamb sirloin with squash risotto and beef fillet with green peppercorn sauce. ✉ *3127 Fillmore St., Cow Hollow,* ☎ *415/463–4755. AE, MC, V. Closed Sun. No lunch Sat.*

Pan-Asian

$–$$ ✕ **Betelnut.** A pan-Asian menu and an adventurous drinks list—with everything from house-brewed rice beer to martinis—draw a steady stream of hip diners to this Union Street landmark. Lacquered walls, bamboo ceiling fans, and period posters create a comfortably exotic mood in keeping with the unusual but accessible food. ✉ *2030 Union St., Cow Hollow,* ☎ *415/929–8855. D, DC, MC, V.*

Steak

$–$$ ✕ **Izzy's Steak & Chop House.** Izzy Gomez was a legendary San Francisco saloon keeper, and his namesake eatery carries on the tradition. In this old-fashioned, clamorous spot, you'll find terrific steaks—especially dry-aged sirloins—chops, and seafood, plus all the trimmings, from cheesy scalloped potatoes to creamed spinach. A collection of Izzy memorabilia and antique advertising art covers almost every inch of wall space. ✉ *3345 Steiner St., Marina,* ☎ *415/563–0487. AE, DC, MC, V. No lunch.*

Vegetarian

$–$$ ✕ Greens. This beautiful restaurant with expansive bay views is owned and operated by the Green Gulch Zen Buddhist Center of Marin County. Creative meatless dishes are served, such as Thai-style vegetable curries, thin-crust pizzas, house-made pastas, and desserts like apricot and blueberry cobbler with vanilla ice cream. Dinners are à la carte on weeknights, but only a four-course prix-fixe dinner is served on Saturday. ✉ *Bldg. A, Fort Mason (enter across Marina Blvd. from Safeway), Marina,* ☎ *415/771–6222. D, MC, V. No lunch Mon., no dinner Sun.*

Mission District

Contemporary

$ ✕ Luna Park. Anytime after 6:30, it's a tight and noisy fit in this wildly popular bistro in the busy North Mission. The crowd is here to sip *mojitos* and eat steamed mussels served with a paper cone crammed with french fries; poke salad (Hawaiian raw tuna partnered with won-ton chips); or grilled flatiron steak. For dessert, an order of s'mores includes cups of melted chocolate and marshmallows and a handful of house-made graham crackers for constructing your own campfire classic. ✉ *694 Valencia St., Mission,* ☎ *415/553–8584. MC, V. No lunch weekends.*

French

$–$$ ✕ Foreign Cinema. The Bay Area is home to many of the country's most respected independent filmmakers, making this innovative spot a sure-fire hit with cinemaphiles. In the hip, loftlike space not only can you sit down to orders of crab cakes and duck confit, but you can also watch such foreign classics as Fellini's *La Dolce Vita,* plus a passel of current indie features, projected in the large courtyard. ✉ *2534 Mission St., Mission,* ☎ *415/648–7600. MC, V. Closed Mon. No lunch.*

$ ✕ Ti Couz. Big, thin buckwheat crepes just like you find in Brittany are the specialty here, filled with everything from ham and Gruyère cheese to Nutella and banana ice cream. The blue-and-white European-style dining room is always crowded, and diners too hungry to wait for a seat can try for one next door, where the same owners operate a seafood bar. Although there is a full bar serving mixed drinks, the best beverage to sip in this Gallic spot is French hard cider served in pottery bowls. ✉ *3108 16th St., Mission,* ☎ *415/252–7373. MC, V. Reservations not accepted.*

Italian

$–$$ ✕ Delfina. Delfina is always hopping. Chef-owner Craig Stoll serves
★ simple yet exquisite Italian fare from a daily changing menu: grilled fresh sardines; orecchiette with broccoli rabe and chickpeas; halibut riding atop olives and braised fennel. If calories are no concern, try the profiteroles packed with coffee ice cream and dressed with a lava-like chocolate sauce. ✉ *3621 18th St., Mission,* ☎ *415/552–4055. MC, V. No lunch.*

Latin

$–$$ ✕ Charanga. Cozy and lively, this neighborhood tapas restaurant, named for a Cuban salsa style that relies on flute and violins, serves an eclectic mix of small plates, from mushrooms cooked with garlic and sherry to *patatas bravas* (twice-fried potatoes with a roasted-tomato sauce). The small dining room, with its walls of exposed brick and soothing green, is a friendly place, so order a pitcher of sangria and enjoy yourself. ✉ *2351 Mission St., Mission,* ☎ *415/282–1813. Reservations not accepted. MC, V. Closed Sun. and Mon. No lunch.*

$ ✕ **La Santaneca.** Lots of El Salvadorans live in the Mission, and here they can find *pupusa,* a stuffed cornmeal round that is more or less the hamburger of their homeland. It usually comes filled with cheese, meat, or both and is eaten along with seasoned shredded cabbage. This plain-Jane, home-cooking place also turns out fried plantains, tamales filled with pork and potatoes, and *chicharrones* (fried pork skins) and yucca as well as other dishes popular in Central America. ✉ *3781 Mission St., Mission,* ☎ *415/648–1034. No credit cards.*

Mexican

$ ✕ **La Taqueria.** Although there are many taquerías in the Mission, this attractive spot, with its arched exterior and modest interior, is one of the oldest and finest. The tacos are superb: two warm corn tortillas topped with your choice of meat—*carne asada* (grilled steak) and *carnitas* (slowly cooked pork) are favorites—and a spoonful of perfectly fresh salsa. Chase your meal with an *agua fresca* (fresh fruit cooler). ✉ *2889 Mission St., Mission,* ☎ *415/285–7117. No credit cards.*

Vietnamese

$$–$$$ ✕ **Slanted Door.** Behind the canted facade of this highly popular North Mission restaurant, you'll find upmarket Vietnamese food with a thick Western accent. There are fresh spring rolls packed with rice noodles, pork, shrimp, and pungent mint leaves, and fried vegetarian imperial rolls concealing bean thread noodles, cabbage, and taro. The menu changes regularly, but crowd pleasers are never abandoned. ✉ *584 Valencia St., North Mission,* ☎ *415/861–8032. MC, V. Closed Mon.*

The Castro and the Haight

Contemporary

$$–$$$ ✕ **Eos Restaurant & Wine Bar.** The culinary marriage of California cuisine and the Asian pantry is the specialty of chef-owner Arnold Wong, who serves an impressive East-West menu at this popular spot. Grilled lamb chops are marinated in a red Thai curry and served with mashed potatoes; skirt steak is treated to a Korean marinade before it is slapped on the grill; and a tea-smoked duck breast replaces the usual whole bird. ✉ *901 Cole St., Haight,* ☎ *415/566–3063. Reservations essential. AE, MC, V. No lunch.*

$–$$ ✕ **2223.** Opened in the mid-1990s, the smart, sophisticated 2223—the address became the name when the principals couldn't come up with a better one—was an instant success and has continued to attract a loyal clientele. That means you'll need strong lungs, however, as the restaurant's popularity makes conversation difficult. Thin-crust pizzas, dim sum dumplings, and superthick pork chops are among the kitchen's popular dishes. ✉ *2223 Market St., Castro,* ☎ *415/431–0692. AE, DC, MC, V. No lunch Mon.–Sat.*

Indian

$–$$ ✕ **Indian Oven.** One of the Lower Haight's most popular restaurants, this cozy Victorian storefront never lacks for customers. Many of them come here to order the tandoori specialties—chicken, lamb, breads—but the *sag paneer* (spinach with Indian cheese) and *aloo gobhi* (potatoes and cauliflower with black mustard seeds and other spices) are also excellent. ✉ *223 Fillmore St., Lower Haight,* ☎ *415/626–1628. AE, D, DC, MC, V. No lunch.*

Thai

$–$$ ✕ **Thep Phanom.** The fine Thai food and the lovely interior at this Lower
★ Haight institution keep local food critics and restaurant goers singing its praises. Duck is deliciously prepared in several ways—in a fragrant curry, minced for salad, resting atop a bed of spinach. Other special-

ties are seafood in various guises, stuffed chicken wings, fried quail, and addictive Thai curries. ⊠ *400 Waller St., Lower Haight,* ☎ *415/431–2526. AE, D, DC, MC, V. No lunch.*

LODGING

Revised by
Andy Moore

Few cities in the United States can rival San Francisco's variety in lodging. San Francisco hotel prices, however, may come as a not-so-pleasant surprise. Weekend rates for double rooms start at about $75 but average about $165 per night citywide (slightly less on weekdays and off-season).

CATEGORY	COST*
$$$$	over $225
$$$	$160–$225
$$	$100–$159
$	under $100

All prices are for a standard double room, excluding 14% tax.

Union Square

$$$$ 🏨 **Campton Place.** Highly attentive service is the hallmark of this small, top-tier hotel behind a simple brownstone facade. The pampering—from unpacking assistance to nightly turndown—begins the moment the uniformed doormen greet you outside the marble lobby. Although many rooms are smallish, all are elegant in a contemporary Italian style, with light earth tones and handsome pearwood panelling and cabinetry. The large modern baths have deep soaking tubs, and double-paned windows keep city noises out (a plus in this active neighborhood). ⊠ *340 Stockton St., Union Square 94108,* ☎ *415/781–5555 or 800/235–4300,* FAX *415/955–5536,* WEB *www.camptonplace.com. 101 rooms, 9 suites. Restaurant, room service, in-room data ports, in-room safes, minibars, some microwaves, gym, bar, lobby lounge, dry cleaning, laundry service, concierge, business services, meeting room, parking (fee), some pets allowed (fee), no-smoking floors. AE, DC, MC, V.*

$$$$ 🏨 **Hotel Monaco.** A cheery yellow 1910 beaux-arts facade and snap-
★   pily dressed doormen welcome you into the Monaco's plush lobby, with its grand marble staircase, French inglenook fireplace, and a high vaulted ceiling with murals of WWI planes and hot-air balloons. The hotel hosts a complimentary evening wine and appetizer hour in this delightful space. Guest rooms, with Chinese-inspired armoires, canopy beds, and high-back upholstered chairs, are full of flair with vivid stripes and colors. In the outer rooms, bay-window seats overlook the bustling theater district. There are special amenities for pets, and if you didn't bring a pet, ask for one of the "companion goldfishes" available. ⊠ *501 Geary St., Union Square 94102,* ☎ *415/292–0100 or 800/214–4220,* FAX *415/292–0111,* WEB *www.monaco-sf.com. 181 rooms, 20 suites. Restaurant, room service, in-room data ports, in-room fax, in-room safes, some in-room hot tubs, minibars, some in-room VCRs, gym, massage, sauna, spa, steam room, bar, dry cleaning, laundry service, business services, Internet, parking (fee), some pets allowed, no-smoking floors. AE, D, DC, MC, V.*

$$$$ 🏨 **Hotel Nikko.** The vast marble lobby of this Japan Airlines–owned hotel is airy and serene, and its rooms are some of the most handsome in the city. They have inlaid cherrywood furniture with clean, elegant lines; gold drapes; wheat-color wall coverings; and ingenious window shades which screen the sun while allowing views of the city. Service throughout the hotel is attentive and sincere, and the staff is multilingual. Don't miss the excellent fifth-floor fitness facility ($6 fee), which

has traditional *ofuros* (Japanese soaking tubs), a *kamaburo* (Japanese sauna), and a glass-enclosed swimming pool and whirlpool. ⊠ *222 Mason St., Union Square 94102,* ☏ *415/394–1111 or 800/645–5687,* FAX *415/421–0455,* WEB *www.nikkohotels.com. 510 rooms, 22 suites. Restaurant, room service, in-room data ports, some in-room hot tubs, some kitchenettes, some microwaves, minibars, indoor pool, gym, hair salon, Japanese baths, massage, sauna, bar, dry cleaning, laundry service, concierge, concierge floor, business services, meeting rooms, car rental, parking (fee), some pets allowed, no-smoking floors. AE, D, DC, MC, V.*

$$$$ ▦ **Prescott Hotel.** Although not as famous as many hotels in the area, the Prescott has several advantages: the relatively small size means personalized service, and its relationship with Postrio, the Wolfgang Puck restaurant attached to its lobby, means you get preferred reservations. Rooms are traditional, with a rich hunter-green theme. Bathrooms have marble-top sinks and gold and pewter fixtures. Complimentary coffee service and evening wine receptions are held by the fireplace in the hunting lodge–style living room. ⊠ *545 Post St., Union Square 94102,* ☏ *415/563–0303 or 800/283–7322,* FAX *415/563–6831,* WEB *www. prescotthotel.com. 155 rooms, 9 suites. Restaurant, room service, in-room data ports, some in-room hot tubs, minibars, some in-room VCRs, gym, bar, lobby lounge, concierge, concierge floor, business services, meeting room, parking (fee), some pets allowed, no-smoking floors. AE, D, DC, MC, V.*

$$$–$$$$ ▦ **Hotel Rex.** Literary and artistic creativity are celebrated at the stylish Hotel Rex, where thousands of books, largely antiquarian, line the 1920s-style lobby. Original artwork adorns the walls, and the proprietors even host book readings and round-table discussions in the common areas. Upstairs, quotations from works by California writers are painted on the terra-cotta–color walls near the elevator landings. Good-size rooms have writing desks and lamps with whimsically hand-painted shades. Muted check bedspreads, striped carpets, and restored period furnishings upholstered in deep, rich hues may evoke the spirit of 1920s salon society, but the rooms also have modern amenities like voice mail and CD players. ⊠ *562 Sutter St., Union Square 94102,* ☏ *415/433–4434 or 800/433–4434,* FAX *415/433–3695,* WEB *thehotelrex.com. 92 rooms, 2 suites. Room service, in-room data ports, minibars, bar, lobby lounge, dry cleaning, laundry service, concierge, Internet, business services, meeting room, parking (fee), no-smoking floors. AE, D, DC, MC, V.*

$$$ ▦ **Chancellor Hotel on Union Square.** Built for the 1915 Panama Pacific International Exposition, the Chancellor was the tallest building in San Francisco when it opened. Although not as grand as some of its new neighbors, this busy hotel is one of the best buys on Union Square for comfort without extravagance. Floor-to-ceiling windows in the modest lobby overlook cable cars on Powell Street en route to Union Square or Fisherman's Wharf. The moderate-size Edwardian-style rooms have high ceilings and blue, cream, and rose color schemes, and connecting rooms are available for families. Bathrooms are small but modern; deep bathtubs are a treat, and a rubber ducky is provided. ⊠ *433 Powell St., Union Square 94102,* ☏ *415/362–2004 or 800/428–4748,* FAX *415/362–1403,* WEB *www.chancellorhotel.com. 135 rooms, 2 suites. Restaurant, room service, fans, in-room safes, bar, laundry service, concierge, meeting room, car rental, parking (fee); no air-conditioning, no smoking. AE, D, DC, MC, V.*

$$$ ▦ **White Swan Inn.** A library with book-lined walls and a crackling fire is the heartbeat of the White Swan. Wine, cheese, and afternoon tea are served in the lounge, where comfortable chairs and sofas encourage lingering. Each of the good-size rooms in this warm and invit-

Downtown San Francisco Lodging

Chestnut St.

Lombard St.

Octavia St.

Gough St.

Franklin St.

Van Ness Ave.

Polk St.

Larkin St.

Hyde St.

Leavenworth St.

RUSSIAN HILL

Green St.

Vallejo St.

Broadway

Broadway Tunne

Pacific St.

Jackson St.

PACIFIC HEIGHTS

Alta Plaza

Lafayette Park

Washington St.

Clay St.

Sacramento St.

California St.

Leavenworth St.

Jones St.

Scott St.

Pierce St.

Steiner St.

Fillmore St.

Webster St.

Buchanan St.

Laguna St.

Octavia St.

Gough St.

Franklin St.

Van Ness Ave.

Polk St.

Larkin St.

Pine St.

Bush St.

Sutter St.

Hyde St.

Post St.

JAPANTOWN

Geary St.

O'Farrell St.

Ellis St.

Eddy St.

Turk St.

Golden Gate Ave.

McAllister St.

Alamo Square

Fulton St.

CIVIC CENTER

Grove St.

Market St.

8th St.

Hayes St.

Abigail Howard
Johnson Hotel **6**
The Andrews **19**
The Archbishop's
Mansion **5**
Bijou **30**
Campton Place **25**
Chancellor Hotel on
Union Square **24**
Commodore
International **18**
The Fairmont **11**

Galleria Park **26**
Golden Gate
Hotel **22**
Grant Plaza
Hotel **17**
Harbor Court **16**
Hotel Bohème **10**
Hotel Del Sol **1**
Hotel Monaco **28**
Hotel Nikko **29**
Hotel Palomar **31**
Hotel Rex **21**

Hyatt Regency **15**
Hyatt Regency San
Francisco Airport . . .**32**
King George **27**
La Quinta
Motor Inn **33**
Mandarin
Oriental **14**
Phoenix Hotel **7**
Prescott Hotel **23**

Radisson Hotel
at Fisherman's
Wharf **8**
Ritz–Carlton,
San Francisco **13**
San Francisco
Residence Club **12**
San Remo **9**
Sherman House **4**
Town House Motel . . .**2**
Union Street Inn **3**
White Swan Inn . . .**20**

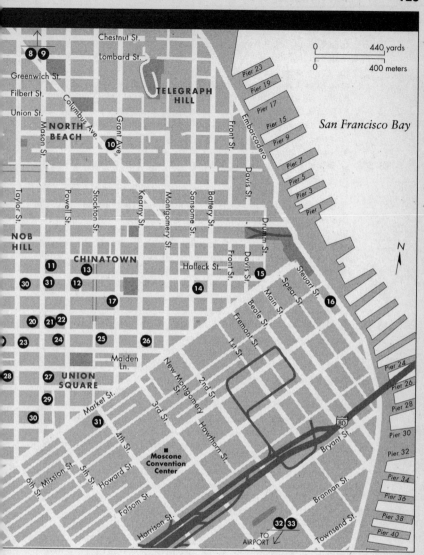

ing inn has a gas fireplace with interesting old books on the mantle, private bath, refrigerator, and reproduction Edwardian furniture. Bedspreads and upholstery are in plaids of deep reds and greens; the carpeting and wallpaper are vibrantly floral. The breakfasts (included in the room rate) are famous, and you can buy the inn's cookbook and take a crack at crab-and-cheese soufflé toasts or artichoke pesto puffs. ⊠ *845 Bush St., Union Square 94108,* ☎ *415/775–1755 or 800/999–9570,* FAX *415/775–5717,* WEB *www.foursisters.com. 23 rooms, 3 suites. Fans, in-room data ports, refrigerators, some in-room VCRs, gym, dry cleaning, laundry service, concierge, meeting room, parking (fee); no air-conditioning, no smoking. AE, MC, V. BP.*

$$–$$$ 🛏 **Bijou.** This hotel is a nostalgic tribute to 1930s cinema. The lobby's tiny theater, Le Petit Theatre Bijou, treats you to screenings from the hotel's collection of 65 San Francisco–theme films—from *The Maltese Falcon* to *What's Up Doc?* The smallish but cheerful rooms are decorated with black-and-white movie stills. For those who want to be in pictures, the hand-crafted chrome ticket booth in the lobby has a hot line with information on current San Francisco film shoots seeking extras. Complimentary coffee and pastries are served mornings in the lobby. ⊠ *111 Mason St., at Eddy St., Union Square 94102,* ☎ *415/771–1200 or 800/771–1022,* FAX *415/346–3196,* WEB *www.hotelbijou.com. 65 rooms. Laundry service, concierge, meeting rooms, parking (fee), no-smoking floor; no air-conditioning. AE, D, DC, MC, V. CP.*

$$–$$$ 🛏 **Commodore International.** Entering the fanciful and colorful lobby through the Commodore's big glass double doors is like stepping onto the main deck of an ocean liner of yore: neo-Deco chairs look like the backdrop for a film about transatlantic crossings; steps away is the Titanic Café, where goldfish bowls and bathysphere-inspired lights add to the maritime mood. The fairly large rooms with monster closets are painted in soft yellows and golds and display photographs of San Francisco landmarks. If red is your color, you may find yourself glued to a seat in the hotel's Red Room, a startlingly scarlet cocktail lounge filled with well-dressed hipsters bathed in crimson. ⊠ *825 Sutter St., Union Square 94109,* ☎ *415/923–6800 or 800/338–6848,* FAX *415/923–6804,* WEB *thecommodorehotel.com. 112 rooms, 1 suite. Restaurant, in-room data ports, nightclub, dry cleaning, laundry service, concierge, parking (fee), no-smoking floors; no air-conditioning. AE, D, MC, V.*

$$–$$$ 🛏 **King George.** The staff at the King George has prided itself on service and hospitality since the hotel's opening in 1914, when guest rooms started at $1 a night. Prices are still relatively low compared to other hotels in the neighborhood, and local and toll-free calls are free. The front desk and concierge staff are adept at catering to your every whim: they'll book anything from a Fisherman's Wharf tour to a dinner reservation. Rooms are compact but nicely furnished in classic English style, with walnut furniture and a crimson and green color scheme. High tea or a glass of ale in the mezzanine pub is an authentic English treat. ⊠ *334 Mason St., Union Square 94102,* ☎ *415/781–5050 or 800/288–6005,* FAX *415/391–6976,* WEB *www.kinggeorge.com. 141 rooms, 1 suite. Tea shop/wine bar, room service, fans, in-room data ports, in-room safes, 1 kitchenette, dry cleaning, laundry service, concierge, Internet, business services, meeting room, parking (fee), no smoking floors; no air-conditioning in some rooms. AE, D, DC, MC, V.*

$$ 🛏 **The Andrews.** Two blocks west of Union Square, this Queen Anne–style abode with a gold-and-buff facade and a huge Elliott grandfather clock in the lobby began its life in 1905 as the Sultan Turkish Baths. Today Victorian antique reproductions, old-fashioned flower curtains with lace sheers, iron bedsteads, ceiling fans, and large closets more than make up for the diminutive size of guest rooms (the scrupulously clean bathrooms—most with showers only—are even smaller). Com-

plimentary wine is served each evening in the lobby. ⊠ *624 Post St., Union Square 94109,* ☎ *415/563–6877 or 800/926–3739,* FAX *415/928– 6919,* WEB *www.andrewshotel.com. 48 rooms. Restaurant, fans, some in-room VCRs, concierge, parking (fee); no smoking. AE, DC, MC, V. CP.*

$–$$ 🖬 **Golden Gate Hotel.** Captain Nemo, a 25-pound cat who must live very well indeed, serves as the unofficial doorman for this homey, family-run B&B. Built in 1913 as a hotel, the four-story Edwardian has a yellow-and-cream facade with black trim, and bay windows front and back. The original "birdcage" elevator lifts you to hallways lined with historical photographs and guest rooms individually decorated with antiques, wicker pieces, and Laura Ashley bedding and curtains. Fourteen rooms have private baths, some with claw-foot tubs. Continental breakfast and afternoon tea and cookies are served in the cozy parlor by a fire. ⊠ *775 Bush St., Union Square 94108,* ☎ *415/392–3702 or 800/835–1118,* FAX *415/392–6202,* WEB *www. goldengatehotel.com. 25 rooms, 14 with bath. Parking (fee); no smoking. AE, DC, MC, V. CP.*

South of Market (SoMa) and Embarcadero

$$$$ 🖬 **Harbor Court.** Overlooking the Embarcadero and within shouting distance of the Bay Bridge, this cozy hotel, formerly an Army/Navy YMCA, is noted for the exemplary service of its friendly staff. Some guest rooms, with double sets of soundproof windows, overlook the bay. Rooms are smallish but have fancy touches like partially canopied, plushly upholstered beds; tastefully faux-textured walls; and fine reproductions of late-19th-century nautical and nature prints. In the evening complimentary wine is served in the lounge, sometimes accompanied by live guitar music, and coffee and tea are served in the morning. There is free access to adjacent YMCA facilities and limousine service to the Financial District. ⊠ *165 Steuart St., Embarcadero 94105,* ☎ *415/882–1300 or 800/346–0555,* FAX *415/882–1313,* WEB *www.harborcourthotel.com. 130 rooms, 1 suite. Room service, in-room data ports, minibars, dry cleaning, laundry service, Internet, business services, parking (fee), some pets allowed, no-smoking floors. AE, D, DC, MC, V.*

$$$$ 🖬 **Hotel Palomar.** The top five floors of the green-tiled and turreted 1908 Pacific Place Building have been transformed by Bill Klimpton into an urbane and luxurious oasis above the busiest part of the city. A dimly lit lounge area with plush sofas gives way to restaurant Fifth Floor where modern French cuisine is served. Rooms have muted leopard-pattern carpeting and bold navy and cream striped drapes. The sleek furniture echoes a 1930s moderne sensibility. In the sparkling baths, a "tub menu" (with various herbal and botanical infusions) tempts adventurous bathers. In-room spa services such as massage, manicures, and body wraps are arranged through Hotel Monaco's Spa Equilibrium. ⊠ *12 Fourth St., South of Market 94103,* ☎ *415/348–1111 or 877/294–9711,* FAX *415/348–0302,* WEB *www.hotelpalomar.com. 182 rooms, 16 suites. Restaurant, bar, lobby lounge, room service, in-room data ports, in-room fax, some in-room hot tubs, minibars, some in- room VCRs, gym, massage, dry cleaning, laundry service, concierge, Internet, business services, meeting room, parking (fee), some pets allowed (fee), no-smoking floors. AE, D, DC, MC, V.*

$$$$ 🖬 **Hyatt Regency.** The 20-story gray concrete Hyatt, at the foot of Market Street, is the focal point of the Embarcadero Center, where more than 100 shops and restaurants cater to the Financial District. The spectacular 17-story atrium lobby (the world's largest) is a wonder of sprawling trees, a running stream, and a huge fountain. Glass eleva-

tors whisk you up to the Equinox restaurant, the city's only revolving rooftop restaurant. Rooms, some with bay-view balconies and all with city or bay views, have a handsome, contemporary look with blond-wood furniture and a grayish yellow-green color scheme. Ergonomic desk chairs are a relief for the hard-working businessperson. ⊠ *5 Embarcadero Center, Embarcadero 94111,* ☎ *415/788–1234 or 800/233–1234,* FAX *415/398–2567,* WEB *www.hyatt.com. 760 rooms, 45 suites. 2 restaurants, bar, lobby lounge, in-room data ports, in-room safes, some in-room hot tubs, some in-room VCRs, room service, gym, concierge, business services, meeting rooms, parking (fee), no-smoking floors. AE, D, DC, MC, V.*

The Financial District

$$$$ 🏨 **Galleria Park.** Two blocks east of Union Square in the Financial District, this hotel with a black-marble facade is close to the Chinatown Gate and Crocker Galleria, one of San Francisco's most elegant shopping complexes. Guest rooms are comfortable, and each one has a floral bedspread, cream-colored striped wallpaper, and blond-wood furniture including a large writing desk. In the lobby, dominated by a massive hand-sculpted Art Nouveau fireplace and brightened by a restored 1911 skylight, complimentary coffee and tea are served in the mornings, wine in the evenings. The third-floor rooftop Cityscape Park has an outdoor jogging track. ⊠ *191 Sutter St., Financial District 94104,* ☎ *415/781–3060; 800/792–9639; 800/792–9855 in CA;* FAX *415/433–4409,* WEB *www.galleriapark.com. 169 rooms, 8 suites. Room service, air conditioning, in-room data ports, in-room fax, 1 in-room hot tub, minibars, gym, dry cleaning, laundry service, concierge, Internet, business services, meeting room, parking (fee), no-smoking floors. AE, D, DC, MC, V.*

$$$$ 🏨 **Mandarin Oriental.** Since the Mandarin comprises the top 11 floors of San Francisco's third-tallest building, all rooms provide panoramic vistas of the city and beyond. The glass-enclosed sky bridges connecting the two towers are almost as striking as the views. And the windows in the rooms actually open, unlike in many modern buildings, so you can hear the "ding ding" of the cable cars 48 floors below as you peer into the distant horizon (the hotel provides binoculars). Bowls of fruit and shoe-shine are complimentary for all, and those staying in the Mandarin Rooms can enjoy a decadent bathing experience in the extra deep bathtubs right next to picture windows. ⊠ *222 Sansome St., Financial District 94104,* ☎ *415/276–9888 or 800/622–0404,* FAX *415/433–0289,* WEB *www.mandarinoriental.com. 154 rooms, 4 suites. Restaurant, lobby lounge, room service, in-room data ports, in-room safes, minibars, some in-room VCRs, gym, dry cleaning, laundry service, concierge, Internet, business services, meeting room, parking (fee), some pets allowed (fee), no-smoking floors. AE, D, DC, MC, V.*

Chinatown

$ 🏨 **Grant Plaza Hotel.** Amazingly low room rates for this part of town
★   make the Grant Plaza a find for budget travelers wanting to look out their window at the striking architecture and fascinating street life of Chinatown. The small rooms, all with private baths, are very clean and modern. Rooms on the top floor are newer, slightly brighter, and a bit more expensive; for a quieter stay ask for one in the back. The two large, beautiful stained-glass windows near the top-floor elevator area are worth a look. ⊠ *465 Grant Ave., Chinatown 94108,* ☎ *415/434–3883 or 800/472–6899,* FAX *415/434–3886,* WEB *www.grantplaza.com. 71 rooms, 1 suite. Some in-room VCRs, concierge, business services, parking (fee); no air-conditioning. AE, DC, MC, V.*

North Beach

$$ ⊞ **Hotel Bohème.** The Bohème, in the middle of historic North Beach and near many Italian restaurants and cafés, takes you back in time with coral-color walls, bistro tables, and memorabilia recalling the Beat generation. Allen Ginsberg, who stayed here many times, could in his later years be seen sitting in a window tapping away on his laptop computer. Screenwriters from Francis Ford Coppola's nearby American Zoetrope studio stay here often, as do poets and other artists. Beds have unnecessary but fun mosquito netting and baths have cheerful yellow tiles. Rooms in the rear are quieter. Complimentary sherry is served in the lobby. ⊠ *444 Columbus Ave., North Beach 94133,* ☎ *415/433–9111,* ℻ *415/362–6292,* WEB *www.hotelboheme.com. 16 rooms. In-room data ports, Internet; no air-conditioning, no smoking. AE, D, DC, MC, V.*

$ ⊞ **San Remo.** This three-story 1906 Italianate Victorian just a few blocks
★ from Fisherman's Wharf was once home to longshoremen and Beats. A narrow stairway from the street leads to the front desk, and labyrinthine hallways to the small but charming rooms with lace curtains, forest-green wooden floors, brass beds, and other antique furnishings. The upper floors are brighter, being closer to the skylights that provide sunshine to the many potted plants in the brass-banistered hallways. About a third of the rooms have sinks; all rooms, except a charming penthouse cottage, share scrupulously clean black-and-white tile shower and toilet facilities with pull-chain toilets. ⊠ *2237 Mason St., North Beach 94133,* ☎ *415/776–8688 or 800/352–7366,* ℻ *415/776–2811,* WEB *www.sanremohotel.com. 62 rooms, 1 suite. Laundry facilities, Internet, parking (fee); no room phones, no room TVs, no smoking. AE, DC, MC, V.*

Nob Hill and Russian Hill

$$$$ ⊞ **The Fairmont.** Commanding the top of Nob Hill like a European palace, the Fairmont has experienced plenty of drama including its triumph over the 1906 earthquake and the creation of the United Nations Charter here in 1945. Architect Julia Morgan's 1907 lobby design includes alabaster walls and gilt-embellished ceilings supported by Corinthian columns. Gracious guest rooms, in pale color schemes, all have high ceilings, fine dark-wood furniture and colorful Chinese porcelain lamps. Rooms in the Tower are generally larger and have better views; all rooms have handsome marble baths. An array of amenities and services (including free chicken soup if you're under the weather) keep loyal (and royal) guests coming back. ⊠ *950 Mason St., Nob Hill 94108,* ☎ *415/772–5000 or 800/527–4727,* ℻ *415/837–0587,* WEB *www.fairmont.com. 531 rooms, 65 suites. 2 restaurants, 2 bars, room service, in-room data ports, in-room fax, minibars, health club, hair salon, nightclub, baby-sitting, dry cleaning, laundry service, concierge, business services, meeting room, car rental, parking (fee), some pets allowed (fee), no-smoking floors. AE, D, DC, MC, V.*

$$$$ ⊞ **Ritz-Carlton, San Francisco.** This world-class hotel is a stunning tribute to beauty and warm, sincere service. Beyond the 17 Ionic columns of the neoclassic facade, crystal chandeliers in the lobby illuminate Georgian antiques and museum-quality 18th- and 19th-century paintings. The fitness center is a destination in its own right, with an indoor swimming pool, steam baths, saunas, and a whirlpool. All rooms have feather beds with 300-count Egyptian cotton sheets and down comforters. Club Level rooms include use of the Club Lounge with its dedicated concierge and several elaborate complimentary food presentations daily. Afternoon tea in the Lobby Lounge—overlooking the beautifully landscaped garden courtyard—is a San Francisco institution. ✉ *600 Stockton St., at California St., Nob Hill 94108, ☎ 415/296–7465 or 800/241–3333, ℻ 415/986–1268, WEB www. ritzcarlton.com. 294 rooms, 42 suites. 2 restaurants, 3 bars, lobby lounge, in-room data ports, some in-room VCRs, indoor pool, health club, hot tub, sauna, dry cleaning, laundry service, concierge, concierge floor, Internet, business services, meeting room, parking (fee), no-smoking floors. AE, D, DC, MC, V.*

$–$$ 🖼 **San Francisco Residence Club.** In contrast to the neighboring show-place hotels, the S. F. Residence Club is a humble guest house with million-dollar views, a money-saving meal plan, and a pleasant garden patio. The building has seen better days, and most of the modest rooms share baths, but many have sweeping bay views. The international clientele ranges from leisure travelers and business professionals to longer-term residents who take advantage of the full American breakfast *and* dinner included in the daily, weekly, or monthly room rate. A $100 advance deposit via check is required. ✉ *851 California St., Nob Hill 94108, ☎ 415/421–2220, ℻ 415/421–2335. 84 rooms. Dining room, some refrigerators, laundry facilities; no TV in some rooms. No credit cards. MAP.*

Pacific Heights and Japantown

$$$$ 🖼 **Sherman House.** This magnificent Italianate mansion at the foot of
★   residential Pacific Heights is San Francisco's most luxurious small hotel. Rooms are individually decorated with Biedermeier, English Jacobean, or French Second Empire antiques. The decadent mood is enhanced by tapestry-like canopies over four-poster feather beds, wood-burning fireplaces with marble mantels, and sumptuous bathrooms, all with whirlpool baths. The six romantic suites attract honeymooners from around the world, and the elegant in-house dining room serves superb French-inspired cuisine. Room rates include valet parking, a full breakfast, and evening wine and hors d'oeuvres in the Gallery, an upstairs sitting room. ✉ *2160 Green St., Pacific Heights 94123, ☎ 415/563–3600 or 800/424–5777, ℻ 415/563–1882, WEB www.theshermanhouse.com. 8 rooms, 6 suites. Dining room, room service, in-room VCRs, piano, concierge, Internet, 1 meeting room, free parking; no air-conditioning, no smoking. AE, D, DC, MC, V. BP.*

Civic Center

$$$$ 🖼 **The Archbishop's Mansion.** Everything here is extravagantly romantic, starting with the cavernous common areas, where a chandelier used in the movie *Gone with the Wind* hangs above a 1904 Bechstein grand piano once owned by Noël Coward. The 15 guest rooms, each named for a famous opera, are individually decorated with intricately carved antiques; many have whirlpool tubs or fireplaces (there are 16 fireplaces in the mansion). Though not within easy walking distance of many restaurants or attractions, its perch on the corner of Alamo Square near the Painted Ladies—San Francisco's famous Victorian homes—makes for a scenic, relaxed stay. ✉ *1000 Fulton St., Western Addition 94117, ☎ 415/563–7872 or 800/543–5820, ℻ 415/885–3193, WEB www.thearchbishopsmansion.com. 10 rooms, 5 suites. Some fans, in-room data ports, some in-room hot tubs, in-room VCRs, piano, meeting room, free parking, no-smoking rooms; no air-conditioning. AE, MC, V. CP.*

$$–$$$ 🖼 **Phoenix Hotel.** From the piped-in, poolside jungle music to the aquatic-theme, ultrahip Backflip restaurant and lounge immersed in shimmering hues of blue and green, the Phoenix evokes the tropics—or at least a fun, kitschy version of it. Although probably not the place for a traveling executive seeking peace and quiet—or anyone put off

by its location on the fringes of the seedy Tenderloin District—celebrities, including such big-name bands as R.E.M. and Pearl Jam have stayed here. Rooms are simple, with handmade bamboo furniture, tropical-print bedspreads, and original art by local artists. All rooms face the courtyard pool and sculpture garden. A hairstylist is on call if you want to look like a rock star. ⊠ *601 Eddy St., Civic Center 94109,* ☎ *415/776–1380 or 800/248–9466,* ℻ *415/885–3109,* ⅦⅢ *www. thephoenixhotel.com. 41 rooms, 3 suites. Restaurant, bar, room service, pool, massage, nightclub, laundry service, free parking; no air-conditioning. AE, D, DC, MC, V. CP.*

$–$$ ⛳ **Abigail Howard Johnson Hotel.** This hotel, built in 1926 and a former B&B, retains its Art Deco–tiled lobby floor, faux-marble front desk, vintage gated elevator, and old-fashioned telephone booth in the lobby. Smallish rooms have hissing steam radiators and antiques. Room 211—the hotel's only suite—is the most elegant and spacious. The hotel caters to artists performing at nearby theaters. Complimentary Continental breakfast is served. Millennium Restaurant, right off the lobby, serves food so delicious it's hard to believe it's vegan (no meat or dairy). ⊠ *246 McAllister St., Civic Center 94102,* ☎ *415/626–6500,* ℻ *415/ 626–6580. 60 rooms, 1 suite. Restaurant, fans, dry cleaning, business services, laundry service, parking (fee), no-smoking floors; no air-conditioning. AE, D, DC, MC, V.*

The Northern Waterfront

$$$–$$$$ ⛳ **Radisson Hotel at Fisherman's Wharf.** Occupying an entire city block, and part of a complex including 25 shops and restaurants, this is the only bayfront hotel at Fisherman's Wharf and the nearest to Pier 39 and the bay cruise docks. The medium-size lobby has plenty of comfortable couches and chairs. Eighty percent of the rooms have views of the bay and overlook a landscaped courtyard and pool. Rooms are contemporary, cleanly designed and bright, with tan carpeting, black-and-tan striped drapes, and cherrywood furniture. ⊠ *250 Beach St., Northern Waterfront 94133,* ☎ *415/392–6700 or 800/333–3333,* ℻ *415/986–7853,* ⅦⅢ *www.radisson.com. 355 rooms. 3 restaurants, in-room data ports, some refrigerators, pool, gym, concierge, parking (fee), no-smoking rooms. AE, D, DC, MC, V.*

Marina and the Presidio

$$$–$$$$ ⛳ **Union Street Inn.** With the help of many precious family antiques
★ and unique artwork, the innkeepers—Jane Bertorelli and David Coyle, who was once a chef for the Duke and Duchess of Bedford—made this green and cream colored 1902 Edwardian a delightful B&B inn. Equipped with candles, fresh flowers, and wineglasses, rooms are popular with honeymooners and romantics. The Carriage House, with its own hot tub, is set off from the main house by an old-fashioned English garden with lemon trees. An elaborate breakfast is included, as are afternoon tea and evening hors d'oeuvres. ⊠ *2229 Union St., Cow Hollow 94123,* ☎ *415/346–0424,* ℻ *415/922–8046,* ⅦⅢ *www. unionstreetinn.com. 6 rooms. Parking (fee); no smoking. AE, MC, V. BP.*

$$–$$$ ⛳ **Hotel Del Sol.** Once a typical '50s-style motor court, the Del Sol is
★ now an anything-but-typical artistic statement. The sunny yellow and blue, three-story building and courtyard are a riot of stripes and bold colors. Rooms open onto the courtyard's heated pool and hammock under towering palm trees, and evoke a beach-house mood with plantation shutters, tropical-stripe bedspreads, and rattan chairs; some have brick fireplaces. The baths are small with bright-yellow tiling. Family suites have child-friendly furnishings and games for the kiddies, and the hotel maintains a "pillow library" with about 15 different kinds.

⊠ *3100 Webster St., Cow Hollow 94123,* ☎ *415/921–5520 or 877/433–5765,* FAX *415/931–4137,* WEB *www.thehoteldelsol.com. 47 rooms, 10 suites. In-room data ports, in-room safes, some kitchenettes, pool, sauna, laundry service, concierge, free parking, no-smoking rooms. AE, D, DC, MC, V.*

$–$$ 🖫 **Town House Motel.** What this family-oriented motel lacks in luxury and atmosphere, it makes up for in value. The simple rooms, in blue tones with contemporary lacquered-wood furniture, all have refrigerators, irons and ironing boards, and hair dryers. Plantation shutters cover the windows. A light Continental breakfast in the lobby is complimentary. ⊠ *1650 Lombard St., Cow Hollow 94123,* ☎ *415/885–5163 or 800/255–1516,* FAX *415/771–9889,* WEB *www.sftownhousemotel.com. 24 rooms. Some microwaves, refrigerators, free parking, no-smoking rooms; no air-conditioning. AE, D, DC, MC, V. CP.*

Near the Airport

$$–$$$$ 🖫 **Hyatt Regency San Francisco Airport.** A spectacular 10-story lobby atrium encompasses 29,000 square ft of this dramatic hotel 2 mi south of the airport. This is the largest airport convention hotel in northern California, and almost every service and amenity you could think of is here, including athletic facilities and several dining and entertainment options. Rooms, in warm earth tones with traditional dark-wood furniture and floral bedspreads, are modern and well equipped. ⊠ *1333 Bayshore Hwy., Burlingame 94010,* ☎ *650/347–1234,* FAX *650/696–2669,* WEB *www.sanfrancisco.hyatt.com. 767 rooms, 26 suites. Restaurant, snack bar, café, lobby lounge, piano bar, sports bar, room service, in-room data ports, some in-room faxes, pool, gym, outdoor hot tub, dry cleaning, laundry service, concierge, Internet, business services, convention center, meeting room, airport shuttle, car rental, parking (fee), no-smoking floors. AE, D, DC, MC, V.*

$$ 🖫 **La Quinta Motor Inn.** Literally a stone's throw from U.S. 101, this motel with weathered-wood balconies and a red-tile roof provides quiet, well-insulated accommodations. Baths are bright and sparkling. A complimentary Continental breakfast, which includes a juice bar, is served in the lobby until 10 daily; there's also a restaurant next door. ⊠ *20 Airport Blvd., South San Francisco 94080,* ☎ *650/583–2223,* FAX *650/589–6770,* WEB *www.laquinta.com. 169 rooms, 3 suites. In-room data ports, some microwaves, some refrigerators, pool, gym, hot tub, dry cleaning, laundry service, laundry facilities, airport shuttle, some pets allowed, no-smoking floors. AE, D, DC, MC, V. CP.*

NIGHTLIFE AND THE ARTS

The Arts

Updated by
Sharron Wood

Half-price, same-day tickets to many local and touring stage shows go on sale (cash only) at 11 AM from Tuesday through Saturday at the **TIX Bay Area** (☎ 415/433–7827) booth, inside the Geary Street entrance of the Union Square Garage, between Stockton and Powell streets. The city's charge-by-phone ticket service is **Tickets.com** (☎ 415/776–1999 or 510/762–2277). **City Box Office** (⊠ 180 Redwood St., Suite 100, Civic Center, ☎ 415/392–4400) has a charge-by-phone service for many concerts and lectures.

Dance

The **San Francisco Ballet** (⊠ 301 Van Ness Ave., Civic Center, ☎ 415/865–2000) has regained much of its luster under artistic director Helgi

Tomasson, and both classical and contemporary works have won admiring reviews. Tickets and information are available at the **War Memorial Opera House** (⊠ 301 Van Ness Ave., Civic Center).

Film

The **Castro Theatre** (⊠ 429 Castro St., Castro, ☎ 415/621–6120), designed by Art Deco master Timothy Pfleuger, is worth visiting for its appearance alone. It hosts revivals as well as foreign and independent engagements. Across the bay, the spectacular Art Deco **Paramount Theatre** (⊠ 2025 Broadway, near 19th St. BART station, Oakland, ☎ 510/465–6400) occasionally screens vintage flicks when it's not occupied by live music performances or the Oakland Ballet. The avant-garde **Red Vic Movie House** (⊠ 1727 Haight St., Haight, ☎ 415/668–3994) screens an adventurous lineup of contemporary and classic American and foreign titles in a funky setting.

Music

San Francisco Opera. Founded in 1923, this world-renowned company has resided in the Civic Center's War Memorial Opera House since it was built in 1932. Over its season, the opera presents approximately 70 performances of 10 to 12 operas from September through January and June through July. ⊠ *301 Van Ness Ave., Civic Center,* ☎ *415/ 864–3330.*

San Francisco Symphony. The symphony performs from September through May, with additional summer performances of light classical musical and show tunes. ⊠ *Davies Symphony Hall, 201 Van Ness Ave., Civic Center,* ☎ *415/864–6000.*

Theater

The city's major nonprofit theater company is the **American Conservatory Theater (ACT),** which was founded in the mid-1960s and quickly became one of the nation's leading regional theaters. The ACT ticket office is at 405 Geary Street (☎ 415/749–2228). The leading producer of new plays is the **Magic Theatre** (⊠ Fort Mason Center, Bldg. D, Laguna St. at Marina Blvd., Northern Waterfront, ☎ 415/441–8822). Once Sam Shepard's favorite showcase, the Magic presents works by the latest rising American playwrights, such as Matthew Wells, Karen Hartman, and Claire Chafee.

Nightlife

For information on who is performing where, check out the *San Francisco Chronicle*'s pink "Datebook" insert—or consult the *San Francisco Bay Guardian,* free and available in racks around the city, listing neighborhood, avant-garde, and budget-priced events. The *SF Weekly* is also free and packed with information on arts events around town. Another handy reference is the weekly magazine *Where,* offered free in most major hotel lobbies and at Hallidie Plaza (Market and Powell Sts.)

Bars of Note

Backflip (⊠ 601 Eddy St., Civic Center, ☎ 415/771–3547), attached to the hipster Phoenix Hotel near the sketchy Tenderloin, is a clubhouse for a space-age rat pack—a combination of aqua-tiled retro and Jetsons-attired waitresses and bartenders. The **Beach Chalet** (⊠ 1000 Great Hwy., near Martin Luther King Jr. Dr., Golden Gate Park, ☎ 415/386–8439), in a historic building filled with Works Project Administration murals, has a stunning view overlooking the Pacific Ocean. **Buena Vista Café** (⊠ 2765 Hyde St., Northern Waterfront, ☎ 415/474–5044), the wharf area's most popular bar, introduced Irish coffee to the New World—or so it says.

Carnelian Room (✉ 555 California St., Financial District, ☎ 415/433–7500), on the 52nd floor of the Bank of America Building, has, at 779 ft, what is perhaps the loftiest view of San Francisco's magnificent skyline. **Harry Denton's Starlight Room** (✉ 450 Powell St., Union Square, ☎ 415/395–8595), on the 21st floor of the Sir Francis Drake Hotel, re-creates the 1950s high life with rose-velvet booths and romantic lighting. Attached to the restaurant Foreign Cinema, **Laszlo** (✉ 2532 Mission St., Mission, ☎ 415/401–0810), with its bilevel design, dim lighting, and candles on each table, is a great spot for a romantic tête-à-téte over a classy cocktail or single malt whisky.

The venerable **Redwood Room** (✉ 495 Geary St., Union Square, ☎ 415/929–2372) underwent extensive renovations by über-hip designer Philippe Starck. Bizarre video installations, sleek seating, a lush monochromatic look, and a host of glamorous patrons in the arts and entertainment mean it's tough to get in many nights. **Specs'** (✉ 12 Saroyan Pl., North Beach, ☎ 415/421–4112), a hidden hangout for artists, poets, and other heavy drinkers, is worth looking for. The **Tonga Room** (✉ 950 Mason St., Nob Hill, ☎ 415/772–5278), on the Fairmont hotel's terrace level, has given San Francisco a taste of high Polynesian kitsch for more than 50 years.

Top of the Mark (✉ 999 California St., Nob Hill, ☎ 415/616–6916), in the Mark Hopkins Inter-Continental, was immortalized by a famous magazine photograph as a hot spot for World War II servicemen on leave or about to ship out. **Tosca Café** (✉ 242 Columbus Ave., North Beach, ☎ 415/391–1244) has an Italian flavor, with opera, big band, and Italian standards on the jukebox, plus an antique espresso machine that's nothing less than a work of art. **Vesuvio Café** (✉ 255 Columbus Ave., North Beach, ☎ 415/362–3370), near the legendary City Lights Bookstore, has a second-floor balcony that is a fine vantage point for watching the colorful Broadway-Columbus intersection.

Cabaret
At **asiaSF** (✉ 201 9th St., South of Market, ☎ 415/255–2742), the entertainment, as well as gracious food service, is provided by "gender illusionists." These gorgeous men don daring dresses and strut in impossibly high heels on top of the bar, which serves as a catwalk. **Club Fugazi** (✉ 678 Green St., North Beach, ☎ 415/421–4222) is famous for *Beach Blanket Babylon,* a wacky musical revue that pokes fun at San Francisco moods and mores. Order tickets as far in advance as possible.

Dance Clubs
El Rio (✉ 3158 Mission St., Mission, ☎ 415/282–3325) is a casual spot with a range of acts, from an open mike Tuesday to Arab dance music on Thursday and a packed world music dance party on Friday. Live bands play on Saturday. No matter what day you attend, expect to find a diverse crowd. **Roccapulco** (✉ 3140 Mission St., Mission, ☎ 415/648–6611), a cavernous dance hall and restaurant that brings in crowds, has live music and salsa dancing on Friday and Saturday. Look for salsa lessons on Wednesday, gay and lesbian dancing on Thursday. **330 Ritch Street** (✉ 330 Ritch St., South of Market, ☎ 415/541–9574), a popular nightclub with a stylish modern look, has an extensive tapas menu, a dance floor, and extremely varied music lineup; soul, R&B, salsa, and Brit pop music are only some of the styles you'll hear here. The club is closed on Monday and Tuesday nights.

Gay and Lesbian
MEN
Café Flore (✉ 2298 Market St., Castro, ☎ 415/621–8579), more of a daytime destination, attracts a mixed crowd including poets, punks,

and poseurs. The **Cinch** (✉ 1723 Polk St., Van Ness/Polk, ☎ 415/776–4162), a Wild West–theme neighborhood bar with pinball machines and pool tables, is one of several hosts of the gay San Francisco Pool Association's weekly matches. **Divas** (✉ 1002 Post St., Tenderloin, ☎ 415/928–6006), around the corner from the Polk Street bars in the rough-and-tumble Tenderloin, is *the* place for transvestites, transsexuals, and their admirers, with frequent stage performances.

Eagle Tavern (✉ 398 12th St., South of Market, ☎ 415/626–0880) is one of the few SoMa bars that remain from the days before AIDS and gentrification. Bikers are courted with endless drink specials. **Martuni's** (✉ 4 Valencia St., Mission, ☎ 415/241–0205), an elegant, low-key bar draws a mixed crowd that enjoys cocktails in a refined environment; variations on the martini are a specialty. **Midnight Sun** (✉ 4067 18th St., Castro, ☎ 415/861–4186), one of the Castro's longest-standing and most popular bars, has riotously programmed giant video screens, showing a mix of old sitcoms, *Will and Grace* episodes, and musicals and show tunes. The **Stud** (✉ 399 9th St., South of Market, ☎ 415/252–7883) is still going strong seven days a week more than 35 years after its opening. Each night's music is different—from funk, soul, and hip-hop to '80s tunes to favorites from the glory days of disco.

WOMEN

Hollywood Billiards (✉ 61 Golden Gate Ave., Tenderloin, ☎ 415/252–9643), a macho pool hall six nights a week, has become the unlikely host of a smoldering lesbian scene every Wednesday during its ladies' night. **Girl Spot** (✉ 401 6th St., South of Market, ☎ 415/337–4962), at SoMa's End Up club, is held the third Saturday of every month. The **Lexington Club** (✉ 3464 19th St., Mission, ☎ 415/863–2052) is where, according to its slogan, "Every night is ladies' night." This all-girl club is geared toward the younger lesbian set.

Jazz

Blue Bar (✉ 501 Broadway, North Beach, ☎ 415/981–2233), tucked beneath the restaurant Black Cat, finds thirty- and fortysomethings lounging in funky aqua armchairs around Formica tables. Live jazz bands play nightly. **Cafe du Nord** (✉ 2170 Market St., Castro, ☎ 415/861–5016) hosts some of the coolest local jazz, blues, rock, and alternative sounds in town. The basement poolroom bar is "speakeasy hip." **Enrico's** (✉ 504 Broadway, North Beach, ☎ 415/982–6223) was the city's hippest North Beach hangout after its 1958 opening. Today it's hip once again, with an indoor-outdoor café, a fine menu (tapas and Italian), and mellow nightly jazz combos.

Jazz at Pearl's (✉ 256 Columbus Ave., North Beach, ☎ 415/291–8255) is one of the few reminders of North Beach's heady beatnik days. With mostly straight-ahead jazz acts and dim lighting, this club has a mellow feel. **Moose's** (✉ 1652 Stockton St., North Beach, ☎ 415/989–7800), a popular restaurant, also has great music in its small but stylish bar area. Combos play classic jazz nightly from 8 PM, as well as during Sunday brunch. **Yoshi's** (✉ 510 Embarcadero St., Oakland, ☎ 510/238–9200) is one of the area's best jazz venues. Dr. John and Charlie Hunter are just a few of the musicians who play here when they're in town.

Piano Bars

The **Big Four Bar** (✉ 1075 California St., Nob Hill, ☎ 415/474–5400), on the ground floor of the Huntington Hotel, is a quietly opulent spot for piano music daily from 5:30 PM to around 11:30. The elegant, dimly lit spot has polished wood and brass, green leather chairs, and a carved ceiling. **Ovation** (⌧ 333 Fulton St., Hayes Valley, ☎ 415/553–8100), in the Inn at the Opera hotel, is a popular spot for a romantic rendezvous, especially weekends, when the pianist is playing.

The **Ritz-Carlton** (⌧ 600 Stockton St., Nob Hill, ☎ 415/296–7465) has a tastefully appointed lobby lounge where a harpist plays during high tea (roughly 3–4:30) and a jazz trio or a pianist plays Thursday to Sunday evenings. **Seasons Bar** (⌧ 757 Market St., Financial District, ☎ 415/633–3000) echoes the muted tones and elegant furnishings of the coolly minimalist Four Season Hotel. Discreet staff in dark suits serve cocktails and salty nibbles like olives, while a piano player entertains, usually Tuesday through Sunday evenings.

Rock, Pop, Folk, World, and Blues

Bimbo's 365 Club (⌧ 1025 Columbus Ave., North Beach, ☎ 415/474–0365), in the same location since 1951, has a plush main room and an adjacent lounge that retain a retro vibe perfect for the "Cocktail Nation" programming that keeps the crowds hopping. **Boom Boom Room** (⌧ 1601 Fillmore St., Japantown, ☎ 415/673–8000) continues to attract old-timers and hipsters alike with top-notch blues acts. The **Fillmore** (⌧ 1805 Geary Blvd., Western Addition, ☎ 415/346–6000), San Francisco's most famous rock music hall, serves up a varied menu of national and local acts: rock, reggae, grunge, jazz, folk, acid house, and more.

Freight and Salvage Coffee House (⌧ 1111 Addison St., Berkeley, ☎ 510/548–1761), one of the finest folk houses in the country, is worth a trip across the bay. Some of the most talented practitioners of folk, blues, Cajun, and bluegrass perform in this alcohol-free space. **Great American Music Hall** (⌧ 859 O'Farrell St., Tenderloin, ☎ 415/885–0750) has top-drawer entertainment, with acts running the gamut from the best in blues, folk, and jazz to alternative rock. **Paradise Lounge** (⌧ 1501 Folsom St., South of Market, ☎ 415/621–1912), a quirky lounge with three stages for eclectic live music, DJ events, and dancing, also has beyond-the-fringe performances at the adjoining Transmission Theatre.

The **Saloon** (⌧ 1232 Grant Ave., North Beach, ☎ 415/989–7666) is a favorite blues and rock spot among North Beach locals in the know. **Slim's** (⌧ 333 11th St., South of Market, ☎ 415/522–0333), one of SoMa's most popular nightclubs, specializes in national touring acts—mostly classic rock, blues, jazz, and world music.

OUTDOOR ACTIVITIES AND SPORTS

Beaches

San Francisco

Updated by John Andrew Vlahides

Nestled in a quiet cove between the lush hills adjoining Fort Mason, Ghirardelli Square, and the crowds at Fisherman's Wharf, **Aquatic Park** has a tiny, ¼-mi-long sandy beach with gentle water. There are no grills, but you will find rest rooms and showers. **Baker Beach** has gorgeous views of the Golden Gate Bridge and the Marin Headlands, but the pounding surf makes swimming a dangerous prospect. Picnic tables, grills, rest rooms, and drinking water are available. One of the city's safest swimming beaches, **China Beach** is a 600-ft strip of sand, just south of the Presidio, with gentle waters as well as changing rooms, rest rooms, and showers. You'll also find grills, drinking water, and picnic tables. South of the Cliff House, **Ocean Beach** is certainly not the city's cleanest shore, but its wide, sandy expanse stretches for miles, making it ideal for long walks and runs. Because of extremely dangerous currents, swimming is not recommended. Rest rooms are available.

Marin County

The beaches at the Marin Headlands are not safe for swimming. The giant cliffs are steep and unstable, and hiking down them can be dangerous. Farther north along the Marin coast, however, Muir and Stinson beaches beckon picnickers and sunbathers. Tucked in a rocky cove, **Muir Beach** is a tiny, picturesque beach usually filled with kids, dogs, families, and cuddling couples. Swimming is recommended only at the wide, flat expanse of **Stinson Beach,** and only from early May through September, when lifeguards are on duty, as shark sightings here—although not frequent—are not unusual.

Participant Sports

Bicycling

San Francisco has a number of scenic routes of varied terrain. The *San Francisco Biking/Walking Guide* ($3), sold in select bookstores, indicates street grades and delineates biking routes that avoid major hills and heavy traffic.

Golden Gate Park is a beautiful maze of roads and hidden bike paths and, ultimately, a spectacular view of the Pacific Ocean. On Sundays, John F. Kennedy Drive is closed to motor vehicles, making it a popular and crowded route for those on people-powered wheels. Rent a bike for about $40 per day at **Golden Gate Cyclery** (⊠ 672 Stanyan St., Haight, ☎ 415/379–3870) and join the throng. The **Marina Green** is a picturesque lawn stretching along Marina Boulevard, adjacent to Fort Mason. It's also the starting point of a well-trod route to the Golden Gate Bridge and beyond. Rent a bike ($5 per hour or $19 per day) at **Holiday Adventure Sales and Rentals** (⊠ 1937 Lombard St., Marina, ☎ 415/567–1192).

Fishing

San Franciscans cast lines from the Municipal Pier, Fisherman's Wharf, Baker Beach, and Aquatic Park. One-day licenses, good for ocean fishing only, are available for $7 on charters, or you can pick up a California State Fishing License at the Lake Merced facility. Trout fishing is possible at San Francisco's **Lake Merced.** You can rent rods and boats, purchase permits and licenses (up to $5 for a permit and $11 for a two-day license), and buy bait at the **Lake Merced Boating & Fishing Company** (⊠ 1 Harding Rd., Lake Merced, ☎ 415/681–3310). **Lovely Martha's Sportfishing** (⊠ Fisherman's Wharf, Berth 3, Northern Waterfront, ☎ 650/871–1691) offers salmon-fishing excursions as well as bay cruises. **Wacky Jacky** (⊠ Fisherman's Wharf, Pier 45, Northern Waterfront, ☎ 415/586–9800) will take you salmon fishing in a sleek, fast, and comfortable 50-ft boat.

Golf

Call the automated **golf information line** (☎ 415/750–4653) to get detailed directions to the city's public golf courses or to reserve a tee time ($1 reservation fee per player) up to seven days in advance. **Glen Eagles Golf Course** (⊠ 2100 Sunnydale Ave., Excelsior/Visitacion Valley, ☎ 415/587–2425) is a challenging 9-hole, par-36 course in McLaren Park. **Harding Park Golf Course** (⊠ Harding Rd. and Skyline Blvd., Lake Merced, ☎ 415/661–1865) has an 18-hole, par-72 course. Inside the second 9 is the par-32 Jack Fleming Golf Course, with all the characteristics of a championship course, only this one is designed to be less difficult. The **Presidio Golf Course** (⊠ 300 Finley Rd., at Arguello Blvd., Presidio, ☎ 415/561–4661) is an 18-hole, par-72 course managed by Arnold Palmer's company.

In-line and Roller-skating

Golden Gate Park is one of the country's best places for in-line skating, with smooth surfaces, manageable hills, and lush scenery. John F. Kennedy Drive, which extends almost to the ocean, is closed to traffic on Sunday. **Skates on Haight** (✉ 1818 Haight St., Haight, ☎ 415/752–8375), near the Stanyan Street entrance to the park, offers free lessons (with rentals) on Sunday morning at 9 AM and rents recreational in-line or roller skates for $6 per hour and $24 overnight. For beginners, the path along the **Marina** offers a 1½-mi (round-trip) easy route on a flat, well-paved surface, with glorious views of San Francisco Bay.

Sailing

San Francisco Bay offers year-round sailing, but tricky currents and strong winds make the bay hazardous for inexperienced navigators. **A Day on the Bay** (☎ 415/922–0227) is in San Francisco's small-craft marina, just minutes from the Golden Gate Bridge and open waters. **Cass' Marina** (✉ 1702 Bridgeway, at Napa St., ☎ 415/332–6789), in Sausalito, will rent you 22- to 35-ft sailboats, as long as there's a qualified sailor in your group.

Tennis

The San Francisco Recreation and Park Department maintains 132 public tennis courts throughout the city. All courts are free, except those in Golden Gate Park. The 21 courts in **Golden Gate Park** (☎ 415/753–7001) are the only public ones for which you can make advance reservations. Fees range from $5 to $10, but kids and seniors play for free. Popular with Marina locals, the four lighted courts at the **Moscone Recreation Center** (✉ 1800 Chestnut St., at Buchanan St., Marina, ☎ 415/292–2006) are free, but sometimes require a wait of one set or 30 to 40 minutes. Let the players know you're next and follow the posted etiquette rules. In the southeast corner of the beautiful Presidio, **Julius Kahn Playground** (✉ W. Pacific Ave., between Spruce and Locust Sts., Presidio, ☎ 415/753–7001) has four free courts.

Spectator Sports

Baseball

You can usually buy same-day tickets for major league baseball games at the stadiums, but advance purchase is recommended. Call the **Tickets.com Baseball Line** (☎ 510/762–2255). There's a per-call processing charge of $2.50, and per-ticket handling fees may also apply. The **San Francisco Giants** play at the downtown bay-front stadium, Pacific Bell Park (✉ 24 Willie Mays Plaza, China Basin, ☎ 415/972–2000 or 800/734–4268). The **Oakland A's** are across the bay at the Network Associates Coliseum (✉ 7000 Coliseum Way, off I–880, north of Hegenberger Rd., Oakland, ☎ 510/638–0500).

Basketball

The **Golden State Warriors** play NBA basketball at the Oakland Arena (✉ 7000 Coliseum Way, off I–880, north of Hegenberger Rd., Oakland, ☎ 510/986–2200) from November through April. Tickets are available through Tickets.com (☎ 510/762–2277).

Football

The NFC West's **San Francisco 49ers** play at 3Com Park (✉ 3Com Park at Candlestick Point, Jamestown Ave. and Harney Way, Candlestick Point, ☎ 415/656–4900). Tickets are almost always sold out far in advance. The AFC West's **Oakland Raiders** play at the Network As-

sociates Coliseum (✉ 7000 Coliseum Way, off I–880, north of Hegenberger Rd., Oakland). Except for high-profile games, tickets, sold
through **Tickets.com** (☎ 510/762–2277), are usually available.

SHOPPING

Shopping Neighborhoods

Updated by
Sharron Wood

The **Castro,** often called the gay capital of the world, is also a major
shopping destination for nongay travelers. The Castro is filled with men's
clothing boutiques, home accessory stores, and various specialty stores.

The intersection of Grant Avenue and Bush Street marks the gateway
to **Chinatown**—24 blocks of shops, restaurants, and markets. Domi-
nating the exotic cityscape are the sights and smells of food: crates of
bok choy, tanks of live crabs, and hanging whole chickens. Racks of
Chinese silks, toy trinkets, colorful pottery, baskets, and carved figurines
are displayed chockablock on the sidewalks, alongside fragrant herb
shops.

A constant throng of sightseers crowds **Fisherman's Wharf,** and with
good reason: Pier 39, the Anchorage, Ghirardelli Square, and the Cannery are all here, each with shops and restaurants, as well as outdoor
entertainment—musicians, mimes, and magicians. Best of all are the
wharf's view of the bay and its proximity to cable car lines, which can
shuttle shoppers directly to Union Square.

Haight Street is a perennial attraction for visitors, if only to see the sign
at Haight and Ashbury streets—the geographic center of the Flower
Power movement during the 1960s. These days chain stores like the
Gap and Ben and Jerry's have taken over large storefronts near the famous intersection, but it's still possible to find high-quality vintage clothing, funky jewelry, folk art from around the world, and used records
and CDs galore in this always-busy neighborhood.

Elegant **Jackson Square,** in the Financial District, is home to a dozen
or so of San Francisco's finest retail antiques dealers, many of which
occupy Victorian-era buildings.

Sometimes compared to New York City's Greenwich Village, **North
Beach** is only a fraction of the size, clustered tightly around Washington Square and Columbus Avenue. Most of its businesses are small eateries, cafés, and shops selling clothing, antiques, and vintage wares.

Pacific Heights residents seeking fine items for their luxurious homes
head straight for Fillmore Street between Post Street and Pacific Avenue, and Sacramento Street between Lyon and Maple streets, where
private residences alternate with fine clothing and gift shops and housewares stores.

High San Francisco rents mean that there aren't many discount outlets in the city, but a few do exist in the semi-industrial zone known
as **South of Market.** At the other end of the spectrum is the gift shop
of the San Francisco Museum of Modern Art, which sells books, handmade ceramics, art-related games, and other great gift items.

Serious shoppers head straight to **Union Square,** San Francisco's main
shopping area and the site of most department stores, as well as the
Virgin Megastore, F.A.O. Schwarz, and the Disney Store. Nearby are
the pricey international boutiques of Alfred Dunhill, Cartier, Empo-
rio Armani, Gucci, Hermès of Paris, Louis Vuitton, and Versace.

Malls and Department Stores

At Post and Kearny streets, the **Crocker Galleria** (✉ 50 Post St., Financial District, ☎ 415/393–1505) is a complex of 40 or so mostly upscale shops and restaurants housed beneath a glass dome.

Five modern towers of shops, restaurants, offices, and a popular movie theater—plus the Hyatt Regency hotel—make up the **Embarcadero Center** (✉ Clay and Sacramento Sts., between Battery and Drumm Sts., Financial District, ☎ 415/772–0734). Most of the stores are branches of upscale national chains, like Ann Taylor, Banana Republic, and housewares giant Pottery Barn. It's one of the few major shopping centers with an underground parking garage.

Japan Center (✉ Laguna and Fillmore Sts., between Geary Blvd. and Post St., Japantown) is a three-block complex that includes an 800-car public garage and three shops-filled buildings. Especially worthwhile are the Kintetsu and Kinokuniya buildings, where shops and showrooms sell electronics, tapes and records, jewelry, antique kimonos, *tansu* chests, paintings, colorful glazed dinnerware and teapots, and more.

Gump's (✉ 135 Post St., Union Square, ☎ 415/982–1616) sometimes looks more like a museum than a department store, stocked as it is with large decorative vases, ornate Asian-inspired furniture, and extravagant jewelry. Luxurious bed linens are tucked away upstairs.

Macy's (✉ Stockton and O'Farrell Sts., Union Square, ☎ 415/397–3333) two downtown locations are behemoths. One branch—with entrances on Geary, Stockton, and O'Farrell streets—houses the women's, children's, furniture, and housewares departments. The men's department occupies its own building across Stockton Street.

Neiman Marcus (✉ 150 Stockton St., at Geary Blvd., Union Square, ☎ 415/362–3900), with its Philip Johnson–designed checkerboard facade, gilded atrium, and stained-glass skylight, is one of the city's most luxurious shopping experiences.

Nordstrom (✉ 865 Market St., Union Square, ☎ 415/243–8500), the store that's known for service, is housed in a stunning building with spiral escalators circling a four-story atrium. Designer fashions, accessories, cosmetics, and most notably shoes are specialties.

The **San Francisco Shopping Centre** (✉ 865 Market St., Union Square, ☎ 415/495–5656), across from the cable car turnaround at Powell and Market streets, is distinguished by spiral escalators that wind up through the sunlit atrium. Inside are more than 35 retailers, including Nordstrom and Godiva.

Saks Fifth Avenue (✉ 384 Post St., Union Square, ☎ 415/986–4300) feels like an exclusive multilevel mall, with a central escalator ascending past a series of designer boutiques.

SIDE TRIPS FROM SAN FRANCISCO

Updated by
Marty
Olmstead

One of San Francisco's best assets is its surroundings. To the north is Marin County, where the lively waterfront town of Sausalito has charming homes that hug narrow, winding streets. To the east are Berkeley and Oakland—one a colorful university town and the other a multifaceted port. Explore a bit beyond the city limits, and you're bound to discover what makes the Bay Area such a coveted place to live.

Sausalito

Like much of San Francisco, Sausalito had a raffish reputation before it went upscale. The town served as a port for whaling ships during the 19th century. By the mid-1800s wealthy San Franciscans were making Sausalito their getaway across the bay. They built lavish Victorian summer homes in the hills, many of which still stand today. In 1875 the railroad from the north connected with ferryboats to San Francisco, bringing the merchant and working classes with it. This influx polarized the town into "hill snobs" and "wharf rats," and the waterfront area grew thick with saloons, gambling dens, and bordellos.

Sausalito developed its bohemian flair in the 1950s and '60s, when a group of artists established a houseboat community here. Since then Sausalito has also become a major yachting center. The town remains friendly and casual, although summer traffic jams can fray nerves. If possible, visit on a weekday—and take the ferry.

The U.S. Army Corps of Engineers uses the **Bay Model,** a 400-square-ft replica of the entire San Francisco Bay and the San Joaquin–Sacramento River delta, to reproduce the rise and fall of tides, the flow of currents, and the other physical forces at work on the bay. ⊠ *2100 Bridgeway, at Marinship Way,* ☎ *415/332–3871.* ☜ *Free.* ☉ *Labor Day–Memorial Day, Tues.–Sat. 9–4; Memorial Day–Labor Day, Tues.– Fri. 9–4, weekends 10–5.*

Some of the more than 450 **houseboats** that make up Sausalito's floating-homes community line the shore of Richardson Bay. For a close-up view of the houseboats, head north on Bridgeway from downtown, turn right on Gate 6 Road, and park where it dead-ends at the public shore.

ↂ The **Bay Area Discovery Museum** fills five former military buildings with entertaining and enlightening hands-on exhibits related to science and the arts. Kids and their families can fish from a boat at the indoor wharf, explore the skeleton of a house, and make multitrack recordings. From San Francisco take the Alexander Avenue exit from U.S. 101 and follow signs to East Fort Baker. ⊠ *557 McReynolds Rd., at East Fort Baker,* ☎ *415/487–4398.* ☜ *$7.* ☉ *Tues.–Fri. 9–4; weekends 10–5.*

Dining and Lodging

$$$ ✗ **Ondine.** Jutting out into the bay with clear views of San Francisco and Angel Island, this second-story restaurant is extremely romantic for dinner or Sunday brunch. However, some diners never look up from the dazzling displays on their plates. Star dishes include sautéed halibut cheeks, seared scallops, and roast lamb with figs and fingerling potatoes. ⊠ *558 Bridgeway Ave.,* ☎ *415/331–1133. Reservations essential. AE, DC, MC, V. No lunch.*

$$–$$$ ✗ **Christophe.** Small and very French, this charming dining room is one of the few bargains in town. The early bird dinners, which change seasonally, are a penny-pincher's delight. Prices rise reasonably as the night goes on. ⊠ *1919 Bridgeway,* ☎ *415/332–9244. MC, V. Closed Mon. No lunch Sun.*

$ ✗ **Bayside Cafe.** Just a few steps from the bay, this dependable coffee shop is regularly patronized by members of the nearby houseboat community. Dozens of egg dishes, waffles, pancakes, and combos are on the long breakfast menu; all kinds of sandwiches, salads, pastas, and burgers constitute the lunch listings, available until 4 PM. ⊠ *1 Gate Six Rd.,* ☎ *415/331–2313. AE, D, DC, MC, V. No dinner.*

$$$$ ⊞ **Casa Madrona.** What began as a small inn with a handful of historic accommodations in a 19th-century landmark house has expanded over the decades to incorporate five cottages and a variety of accommodations that cascade down the hill from Bulkley Avenue to Bridgeway. The design in these rooms and suites ranges from the cutesiness of the Artist's Loft to elegant Mediterranean and Asian-inspired motifs. ⊠ *801 Bridgeway, 94965,* ☎ *415/332–0502 or 800/567–9524,* FAX *415/332–2537,* WEB *casamadrona.com. 34 rooms. Restaurant, hot tub, spa. AE, D, DC, MC, V. CP.*

$$–$$$$ ⊞ **Hotel Sausalito.** Soft yellow, green, and orange tones create a warm, Mediterranean feel at this well-run inn with handmade furniture and tasteful original art and reproductions. The rooms, some of which have harbor or park views, range from small ones that are good for budget-minded travelers to commodious suites. Continental breakfast is included. ⊠ *16 El Portal, 94965,* ☎ *415/332–0700 or 888/442–0700,* FAX *415/332–8788,* WEB *www.hotelsausalito.com. 14 rooms, 2 suites. In-room data ports, concierge, no-smoking room. 2-night minimum weekends. AE, DC, MC, V. CB.*

Berkeley

Although the University of California dominates Berkeley's history and contemporary life, the university and the town are not synonymous. The city of 100,000 facing San Francisco across the bay has other interesting attributes. Berkeley is culturally diverse and politically adventurous, a breeding ground for social trends, a continuing bastion of the counterculture, and an important center for Bay Area writers, artists, and musicians.

Numbers in the text correspond to numbers in the margin and on the Berkeley map.

❶ The **Berkeley Visitor Information Center** (⊠ University Hall, Room 101, 2200 University Ave., at Oxford St., ☎ 510/642–5215) is the starting point for weekday 1½-hour student-guided tours of the campus starting at 10. The tours leave from Sather Tower at 10 on Saturday and 1 on Sunday.

❷ The **U.C. Berkeley Art Museum** houses a surprisingly interesting collection of works spanning five centuries, with an emphasis on contemporary art. Changing exhibits line the spiral ramps and balcony galleries. Don't miss the series of vibrant paintings by abstract expressionist Hans Hofmann. ⊠ *2626 Bancroft Way,* ☎ *510/642–0808; 510/642–1124 film-program information.* ▦ *$6.* ☉ *Wed. and Fri.–Sun. 11–5, Thurs. 11–9.*

More than 13,500 species of plants from all over the world flourish ❸ in the 34-acre **U.C. Botanical Garden**—thanks to Berkeley's temperate climate. Informative tours of the garden are given weekends at 1:30. Benches and shady picnic tables make this a relaxing alternative to the busy main campus. ⊠ *Centennial Dr.,* ☎ *510/642–3343.* ▦ *$3.* ☉ *Daily 9–5. Closed first Tues. of each month.*

☾ ❹ The fortresslike **Lawrence Hall of Science,** a dazzling hands-on science center, lets kids look at insects under microscopes, solve crimes using chemical forensics, and explore the physics of baseball. ⊠ *Centennial Dr., near Grizzly Peak Blvd.,* ☎ *510/642–5132,* WEB *www.lawrencehallofscience.org.* ▦ *$7.* ☉ *Daily 10–5.*

Dining and Lodging

$$$$ ✕ **Chez Panisse Café & Restaurant.** The downstairs portion of Alice ★ Waters's legendary eatery is noted for its formality and personal ser-

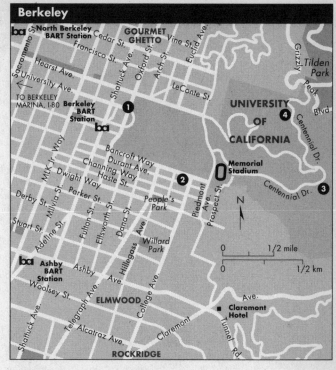

vice. Here, the daily-changing multi-course dinners are prix-fixe and pricey—although the cost is lower on weekdays. Upstairs, in the informal café, the crowd livelier, the prices lower, and the ever-changing menu à la carte. The food is simpler, too: penne with new potatoes, arugula, and sheep's-milk cheese; fresh figs with Parmigiano-Reggiano cheese and arugula; and grilled tuna with savoy cabbage. ⊠ *1517 Shattuck Ave., north of University Ave.,* ☎ *510/548–5525 restaurant; 510/ 548–5049 café. Reservations essential. AE, D, DC, MC, V. Closed Sun.*

$–$$$ ✕ **Café Rouge.** You can recover from shopping in this spacious two-story bistro, complete with zinc bar, skylights, and festive lanterns. The short, seasonal menu runs the gamut from the sophisticated—rack of lamb, juniper berry-cured pork chops—to the homey—spit-roasted chicken or pork loin or a hamburger topped with cheddar. ⊠ *1782 4th St.,* ☎ *510/525–1440. AE, MC, V. No dinner Mon.*

$$–$$$ ✕ **Lalime's.** In this charming, flower-covered house, the cuisine reflects the entire Mediterranean region. Prix-fixe and à la carte menus are offered, both of them in constant flux. Choices can range from grilled ahi tuna to creamy Italian risotto to seared duck foie gras. The dining room, on two levels, is done in light colors, creating a cheerful mood that makes this the perfect spot for any special occasion. ⊠ *1329 Gilman St.,* ☎ *510/527–9838. Reservations essential. AE, DC, MC, V. No lunch.*

$$ ✕ **Mazzini.** Simple, unpretentious food is what you'll find in this trattoria outfitted with marble-topped tables and trompe l'oeil murals of Tuscan landscapes. The lunch menu has straightforward dishes such as *orecchiette* (ear-shape pasta) with rapini and chili. At dinnertime, the menu expands to include authentic trattoria dishes such as steak tagliata and a Tuscan seafood stew. ⊠ *2826 Telegraph Ave., near Ashby Ave.,* ☎ *510/848–5599. AE, MC, V.*

$-$$ ✕ **Rivoli.** Italian-inspired dishes using fresh, mostly organic California ingredients star on a menu that changes frequently. Typical meals include fresh line-caught fish, pastas, and inventive dishes such as its trademark Portobello mushroom fritters with aioli and Parmesan with arugula. Attentive service adds to the overall appeal, and the lovely garden is cheerful. ⊠ *1539 Solano Ave.,* ☎ *510/526–2542. Reservations essential. AE, D, DC, MC, V. No lunch.*

$ ✕ **Bette's Oceanview Diner.** Buttermilk pancakes that you'll never forget are just one of the specialties at this 1930s-inspired diner, complete with checkered floors and burgundy booths. The wait for a seat can be long. If you're starving, Bette's to Go, next door, offers takeout. ⊠ *1807 4th St.,* ☎ *510/644–3230. MC, V. No dinner.*

$$$–$$$$ 🏨 **Hotel Durant.** Long the mainstay of parents visiting their children at U.C. Berkeley, the Hotel Durant is a good option for those who want to be a short walk from campus and from the restaurants and shops of Telegraph Avenue. Rooms, accented with dark woods set against neutral shades of green and mauve, are small without feeling cramped. The hotel's bar, Henry's, is *the* place for U.C. Berkeley sports fans to congregate after football games. ⊠ *2600 Durant Ave., 94704,* ☎ *510/ 845–8981,* 𝖥𝖠𝖷 *510/486–8336,* 𝖶𝖤𝖡 *www.hoteldurant.com. 135 rooms, 5 suites. Restaurant, bar, room service, dry cleaning, laundry service, business services, meeting room, parking (fee), no-smoking room. AE, D, DC, MC, V.*

$–$$ 🏨 **French Hotel.** The only hotel in north Berkeley, this three-story brick structure has a certain *pensione* feel. Its 18 rooms have pastel or brick walls and modern touches such as white wire baskets in lieu of actual dressers. Balconies make the rooms seem larger than their modest dimensions. A ground-floor café buzzes day and night with students and other denizens of the Gourmet Ghetto; Chez Panisse is across the street. ⊠ *1538 Shattuck Ave., 94709,* ☎ *510/548–9930,* 𝖥𝖠𝖷 *510/548– 9930. 18 rooms. Room service, concierge; no air-conditioning. AE, D, DC, MC, V.*

Oakland

Often overshadowed by San Francisco's beauty and Berkeley's offbeat antics, Oakland's allure lies in its amazing diversity. Here you can find a Nigerian clothing store, a beautifully renovated Victorian home, a Buddhist meditation center, and a lively salsa club, all within the same block. Oakland is a mosaic of its past. The affluent have once again flocked to the city's hillside homes as a warmer and more spacious alternative to San Francisco, while a constant flow of new residents— many from Central America and Asia—ensures continued diversity, vitality, and growing pains. Many neighborhoods to the west and south of downtown remain run-down and unsafe, but a renovated downtown area and the thriving Jack London Square have injected new life into the city.

Numbers in the text correspond to numbers in the margin and on the Oakland map.

★ ❶ One of Oakland's top attractions, the **Oakland Museum of California,** is an inviting series of landscaped buildings that display the state's art, history, and natural wonders. The museum is the best possible introduction to a tour of California, and its detailed exhibits can help fill the gaps on a brief visit. The museum's rambling Cowell Hall of California History includes everything from Spanish-era armor to a gleaming fire engine that battled the flames in San Francisco in 1906. ⊠ *1000 Oak St., at 10th St.,* ☎ *510/238–2200,* 𝖶𝖤𝖡 *www.museumca.org.* 🎟 *$6.* ☉ *Tues.–Thurs. and Sat. 10–5, Fri. 10–9, Sun. noon–5.*

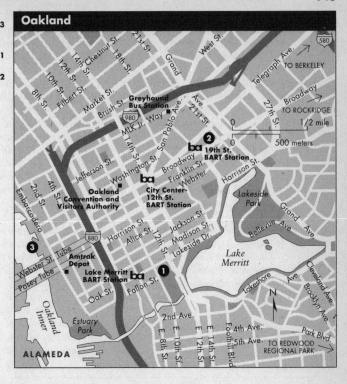

Oakland

★ ❷ The **Paramount Theatre** (✉ 2025 Broadway, ☎ 510/465–6400), perhaps the most glorious example of Art Deco architecture in the city if not all the Bay Area, operates as a venue for concerts and performances of all kinds.

❸ When the author Jack London lived in Oakland, he spent many a day boozing and brawling in the waterfront area now called **Jack London Square** (✉ Embarcadero at Broadway, ☎ 510/814–6000). Lined with shops, restaurants, small museums, and historic sites, the square contains a bronze bust of London, author of *The Call of the Wild, The Sea Wolf, Martin Eden,* and other books. The tiny, wonderful **Heinold's First and Last Chance Saloon** (✉ 56 Jack London Sq., ☎ 510/839–6761), one of Jack London's old haunts, has been serving since 1883, although it's a little worse for the wear since the 1906 earthquake.

Dining and Lodging

$$–$$$ ✕ **Oliveto.** This locally renowned restaurant, with respected chef Paul Bertolli at its helm, combines a first-class dining room and casual café. Upstairs, in a sea of subtle Mediterranean tones, you're treated to imaginative yet restrained Italian cuisine from a menu that changes daily. Downstairs, in the terra-cotta-walled café, everything from an espresso to a pizza to a full-blown Italian meal can be enjoyed at one of the small tables or at the bar. ✉ *5655 College Ave.,* ☎ *510/547–5356 restaurant; 510/547–4382 café. AE, DC, MC, V. No lunch in restaurant weekends.*

$–$$ ✕ **Autumn Moon Café.** Home-style American café food is served in this friendly spot in a century-old house. Enjoy such tantalizing items as roast chicken hash with poached eggs for breakfast; salmon teriyaki with rice and fresh vegetables for lunch; and pan-seared halibut with griddled corn polenta and roasted wild mushrooms for dinner. A root beer float makes for a delightful finish. ✉ *3909 Grand Ave.,* ☎ *510/595–3200. AE, MC, V. No lunch Mon. and Tues.*

$ ✕ **Le Cheval Restaurant.** A longtime favorite among the city's many Vietnamese restaurants, Le Cheval is known for big parties and family-style dining. Try the *pho* (Hanoi-style beef noodle soup fragrant with star anise). At midday, everyone seems to be downing bowls of noodles topped with marinated grilled meats and chili-laced fish sauce. ✉ *1007 Clay St.,* ☎ *510/763–8495. AE, D, DC, MC, V. No lunch Sun.*

$$$$ 🏨 **Claremont Resort and Spa.** Straddling the Oakland-Berkeley border, the Claremont Hotel beckons like a gleaming white castle in the
★ hills. Traveling executives come for the business amenities, while leisure travelers are drawn by luxurious suites, therapeutic massages, and personalized yoga workouts at the on-site spa. ✉ *41 Tunnel Rd., at Ashby and Domingo Aves., 94705,* ☎ *510/843–3000 or 800/323–7500,* FAX *510/843–6629.* WEB *www.claremontresort.com. 282 rooms. 3 restaurants, 2 bars, in-room data ports, tennis courts, 2 pools, spa, dry cleaning, concierge, meeting rooms, parking (fee), no-smoking floor. AE, D, DC, MC, V.*

$$$–$$$$ 🏨 **Waterfront Plaza Hotel.** The waterfront views and Jack London
★ Square's vibrant collection of shops and restaurants make the neighborhood one of the most appealing in Oakland. Despite its large size, the ever-friendly staff and management put immense effort into making your stay comfortable—perks include VCRs, hair dryers, twice-daily housekeeping, and ironing essentials in every room. ✉ *10 Washington St., in Jack London Square, 94607,* ☎ *510/836–3800 or 800/729–3638,* FAX *510/832–5695,* WEB *www.waterfrontplaza.com. 144 rooms. Restaurant, room service, in-room data ports, in-room VCRs, pool, gym, dry cleaning, laundry service, concierge, business services, meeting room, parking (fee), no-smoking room. AE, D, DC, MC, V.*

SAN FRANCISCO A TO Z

To research prices, get advice from other travelers, and book travel arrangements, visit www.fodors.com.

AIR TRAVEL
Heavy fog is infamous for causing chronic delays in and out of San Francisco. If you're heading to the East Bay make every effort to fly into Oakland. The Oakland airport, which is easy to navigate and is accessible by public transit, is a good alternative to San Francisco's airport.

Alaska, America West, American, Continental, Delta, Southwest, United, and US Airways fly into both San Francisco and Oakland. Northwest flies into San Francisco only. *See* Air Travel *in* Smart Travel Tips A to Z for airline phone numbers.

AIRPORTS AND TRANSFERS
The major gateway to San Francisco is San Francisco International Airport (SFO), just south of the city, off U.S. 101. Several domestic airlines serve Oakland Airport (OAK), which is across the Bay but not much farther away from downtown San Francisco (via I–880 and I–80), although rush-hour traffic on the Bay Bridge may make travel times longer.

➤ AIRPORT INFORMATION: **San Francisco International Airport** (☎ 650/761–0800). **Oakland International Airport** (☎ 510/577–4000).

AIRPORT TRANSFERS

From San Francisco International Airport: A taxi ride from SFO to downtown costs about $30. Airport shuttles are inexpensive and efficient. The SFO Airporter ($12) picks up passengers at baggage claim (lower level) and serves selected downtown hotels. SuperShuttle stops at the upper-level traffic islands and takes you from the airport to anywhere within the city limits of San Francisco. It costs from $12 to $17 depending on your destination. Inexpensive shuttles to the East Bay (among them Bayporter Express) also depart from SFO's upper-level traffic islands; expect to pay around $30. The cheapest way to get from the airport to San Francisco is via SamTrans Bus 292 (55 minutes; $2.20) and KX (35 minutes; $3; only one small carry-on bag permitted) to San Francisco or Bus BX to the Colma BART train station. Board the SamTrans buses at the north end of the lower level. A new BART extension will connect SFO to downtown San Francisco directly. When the line is completed, which is scheduled to happen in 2003, the trip from the new International Terminal at SFO to downtown will take just 29 minutes. Check at airport information kiosks, or the SFO website, for the latest information.

From Oakland International Airport: A taxi from Oakland's airport to downtown San Francisco costs between $30 and $35. America's Shuttle, Bayporter Express, and other shuttles serve major hotels and provide door-to-door service to the East Bay and San Francisco. Marin Door to Door serves Marin County for a flat $50 fee. The best way to get to San Francisco via public transit is to take the AIR BART bus ($2) to the Coliseum/Oakland International Airport BART station (BART fares vary depending on where you're going; the ride to downtown San Francisco costs $2.75).

➤ TAXIS AND SHUTTLES: **American Airporter** (☎ 415/202–0733). **Bayporter Express** (☎ 415/467–1800). **East Bay Express Airporter** (☎ 510/547–0404). **Marin Door to Door** (☎ 415/457–2717). **SamTrans** (☎ 800/660–4287). **SFO Airporter** (☎ 800/532–8405). **SuperShuttle** (☎ 415/558–8500 or 800/258–3826).

BOAT AND FERRY TRAVEL

Blue & Gold Fleet ferries depart daily for Sausalito from Pier 41 at Fisherman's Wharf. Golden Gate Ferry crosses the bay to Sausalito from the south wing of the Ferry Building at Market Street and the Embarcadero. The trip to Sausalito takes 30 minutes. The Oakland/Alameda Ferry runs several times daily between San Francisco's Ferry Building, Alameda, and the Clay Street dock near Jack London Square. Purchase tickets on board.

➤ FERRY LINES: **Blue & Gold Fleet** (☎ 415/705–5555, WEB www.tele-sails.com).**Golden Gate Ferry** (☎ 415/923–2000). **Oakland/Alameda Ferry** (☎ 510/522–3300, WEB www.eastbayferry.com).

BUS TRAVEL TO AND FROM SAN FRANCISCO

Greyhound, the only long-distance bus company in San Francisco, operates buses to and from most major cities in the country. Golden Gate Transit buses travel to Sausalito from 1st and Mission streets and from other points in San Francisco.

➤ BUS INFORMATION: **Golden Gate Transit** (☎ 415/923–2000).**Greyhound** (✉ 425 Mission St., ☎ 415/495–1569 or 800/231–2222, WEB www.greyhound.com).

BUS AND TRAIN TRAVEL WITHIN SAN FRANCISCO

BART: You can use Bay Area Rapid Transit (BART) trains to reach Oakland, Berkeley, Concord, Richmond, Fremont, Martinez, and Dublin/Pleasanton. Trains also travel south from San Francisco as far as Daly City and Colma. The BART-SFO Extension Project, which at press time was scheduled for completion in 2003, will connect downtown San Francisco to the San Francisco International Airport. Fares range from $1.10 to $4.70; trains run until midnight.

CalTrain: CalTrain connects San Francisco to Palo Alto, San Jose, Santa Clara, and many smaller cities en route. In San Francisco, trains leave from the main depot at 4th and King streets, and a rail-side stop at 22nd St. and Pennsylvania streets. One-way fares run $1.25–$6.75. Trips last 1–1½ hours.

Muni: The San Francisco Municipal Railway, or Muni, operates light-rail vehicles, the historic streetcar line along Fisherman's Wharf and Market Street, trolley buses, and the world-famous cable cars. On buses and streetcars, the fare is $1. Exact change is required, and dollar bills are accepted in the fare boxes. For all Muni vehicles other than cable cars, 90-minute transfers are issued free upon request at the time the fare is paid. Transfers are valid for two additional transfers in any direction. Cable cars cost $2 and include no transfers. Muni provides 24-hour service on selected lines to all areas of the city.

➤ BUS AND TRAIN INFORMATION: **Bay Area Rapid Transit** (☎ 650/992–2278, WEB www.bart.gov). **CalTrain** (☎ 800/660–4287, WEB www.caltrain.com). **San Francisco Municipal Railway System (Muni)** (☎ 415/673–6864, WEB www.sfmuni.com).

CAR RENTAL

All of the national car-rental companies have offices at the San Francisco and Oakland airports. *See* Car Rental *in* Smart Travel Tips A to Z for national rental agency phone numbers.

CAR TRAVEL

Driving in San Francisco is a challenge because of the hills, one-way streets, traffic, and limited parking. Use public transportation or cab it whenever possible. Although "rush hour" is 7 to 10 in the morning and 4 to 7 in the evening, you can hit gridlock on any day at any time, especially over the Bay Bridge, and leaving and/or entering the city from the south. Sunday afternoon traffic can be heavy as well, especially over the bridges.

PARKING

Remember to curb your wheels when parking on hills (turn wheels away from the curb when facing uphill, toward the curb when facing downhill). On certain streets, parking is forbidden during rush hours. Look for the warning signs; illegally parked cars are towed. Downtown parking lots are often full and most are expensive. Larger hotels often have parking available, but it doesn't come cheap; many charge as much as $30 a day for the privilege.

EMERGENCIES

In an emergency dial 911.

➤ DOCTORS AND DENTISTS: **California Pacific Center Physician Referral Service** (☎ 415/565–6333). **San Francisco Dental Society Referral Service** (☎ 415/421–1435).

➤ 24-HOUR PHARMACIES: **Walgreens Drug Store** (✉ 498 Castro, ☎ 415/861–3136; ✉ 3201 Divisadero St., ☎ 415/931–6417).

LODGING

The San Francisco Convention and Visitors Bureau publishes a free lodging guide with a map and listings of San Francisco and Bay Area hotels; call them to reserve a room at more than 60 visitors bureau–recommended hotels in the city or near the airport. San Francisco Reservations handles advance reservations at more than 300 Bay Area hotels, often at special discounted rates.

➤ CONTACTS: **San Francisco Convention and Visitors Bureau** (☎ 415/283–0177 or 888/782–9673, WEB www.sfvisitor.org). **San Francisco Reservations** (☎ 800/677–1500, WEB www.hotelres.com).

TAXIS

Taxi service is notoriously bad in San Francisco, and hailing a cab can be frustratingly difficult in some parts of the city, especially on the weekends. In a pinch, hotel taxi stands are an option, as is calling ahead for a pick-up. But be forewarned: taxi companies frequently don't answer the phone in peak periods.

Taxis in San Francisco charge $2.50 for the first ⅙ of a mile, $1.80 for each additional mile, and 40¢ per minute in stalled traffic. There is no charge for additional passengers, there is no surcharge for luggage.

➤ TAXI COMPANIES: **City Wide Cab** (☎ 415/920–0700; San Francisco). **DeSoto Cab** (☎ 415/970–1300; San Francisco). **Veteran's Taxicab** (☎ 415/552–1300; San Francisco). **Yellow Cab** (☎ 415/626–2345; San Francisco).

TOURS

ORIENTATION TOURS

In addition to bus and van tours of the city, most tour companies run excursions to various Bay Area and Northern California destinations such as Marin County. City tours generally last 3½ hours and cost $28–$32. Golden Gate Tours offers bay cruises ($38) as well as standard city bus tours. In addition to bay cruises, Gray Line offers city tours in motor coaches and motorized cable cars ($15–$37); Great Pacific Tours conducts the city tours (starting at $37).

➤ TOUR COMPANIES: **Golden Gate Tours** (☎ 415/788–5775). **Gray Line Tours** (☎ 415/558–9400, WEB www.graylinesanfrancisco.com). **Great Pacific Tour** (☎ 415/626–4499, WEB www.greatpacifictour.com). **Tower Tours** (☎ 415/434–8687, WEB www.towertours.com).

WALKING TOURS

One of the best ways to experience San Francisco is to walk its neighborhoods. Tours of various San Francisco neighborhoods generally cost $15–$40. Some tours explore culinary themes, such as Chinese food or coffeehouses: lunch and snacks are often included. Others focus on architecture or history.

➤ ARCHITECTURE TOURS: **"Victorian Home Walk"** (☎ 415/252–9485, WEB www.victorianwalk.com).

➤ CULINARY TOURS: **"Chinatown with the Wok Wiz"** (☎ 415/981–8989, WEB www.wokwiz.com). **"Javawalk"** (☎ 415/673–9255, WEB www.javawalk.com).

➤ GENERAL INTEREST TOURS: **San Francisco Convention and Visitors Bureau's Visitor Information Center** (☎ 415/974–6900, WEB www.sfcvb.org). **City Guides** (☎ 415/557–4266, WEB www.sfcityguides.org).

➤ HISTORIC TOURS: **Chinese Culture Center** (☎ 415/986–1822, WEB www.c-c-c.org). **Trevor Hailey's "Cruising the Castro"** (☎ 415/550–8110, WEB www.webcastro.com/castrotour).

TRAIN TRAVEL TO AND FROM SAN FRANCISCO

Amtrak trains travel to San Francisco and the Bay Area from different cities in California and the United States. The *Coast Starlight* travels north from Los Angeles to Seattle, passing the Bay Area along the way. Amtrak also has several inland routes between San Jose, Oakland, and Sacramento. The *California Zephyr* route travels from Chicago to the Bay Area. There is no Amtrak station in San Francisco. Instead, there is one Amtrak station in Emeryville, just over the Bay Bridge, and one in Oakland. A free shuttle operates between these two stations and the Ferry Building and CalTrain station in San Francisco.

➤ TRAIN INFORMATION: **Amtrak** (☎ 800/872–7245, WEB www.amtrak.com).

VISITOR INFORMATION

➤ TOURIST INFORMATION: **Berkeley Convention and Visitors Bureau** (✉ 2015 Center St., 94704, ☎ 510/549–8710, WEB www.berkeleycvb.com). **Oakland Convention and Visitors Bureau** (✉ 475 14th St., Suite 120, 94612, ☎ 510/839–9000, WEB www.oaklandcvb.com). **San Francisco Convention and Visitors Bureau's Visitor Information Center** (✉ Box 429097, San Francisco 94142-9097, or ✉ lower level of Hallidie Plaza, ☎ 415/391–2000 or 415/974–6900, WEB www.sfvisitor.org). **Sausalito Visitor Center** (✉ 780 Bridgeway, 94965, ☎ 415/332–0505).

5 THE WINE COUNTRY

You don't have to be a wine enthusiast to
appreciate the mellow beauty of Napa and
Sonoma counties, whose hills and verdant
vineyards resemble those of Tuscany and
Provence. Here, among state-of-the-art
wineries, fabulous restaurants, and luxury
hotels where aromatherapy and massage
are daily rituals, you just might discover that
life need have no nobler purpose than
enjoying the fruits of the earth.

Updated by
Marty
Olmstead

IN 1862, AFTER AN EXTENSIVE TOUR of the wine-producing areas of Europe, Count Agoston Haraszthy de Mokcsa reported a promising prognosis about his adopted California: "Of all the countries through which I passed, not one possessed the same advantages that are to be found in California. . . . California can produce as noble and generous a wine as any in Europe; more in quantity to the acre, and without repeated failures through frosts, summer rains, hailstorms, or other causes."

The "dormant resources" that the father of California's viticulture saw in the balmy days and cool nights of the temperate Napa and Sonoma valleys have come to fruition today. The wines produced here are praised and savored by connoisseurs throughout the world. The area also continues to be a proving ground for the latest techniques of grape growing and wine making.

In 1975 Napa Valley had no more than 20 wineries; today there are more than 240. In Sonoma County, where the web of vineyards is looser, there are well over 150 wineries, and development is now claiming the cool Carneros region, at the head of the San Francisco Bay, deemed ideal for growing the chardonnay grape. Within these combined regions of the Wine Country, at least 120 wineries have opened in the last eight years alone. Nowadays many individual grape growers produce their own wines instead of selling their grapes to larger wineries. As a result, smaller "boutique" wineries harvest excellent, reasonably priced wines that have caught the attention of connoisseurs and critics, while the larger wineries consolidate land and expand their varietals.

This state-of-the-art viticulture has also given rise to a gastronomic renaissance. Inspired by the creative spirit that produces the region's great wines, esteemed chefs are opening restaurants in record numbers, making culinary history in the process.

Pleasures and Pastimes

Dining

Many star chefs from urban areas throughout the United States have migrated to the Wine Country, drawn by the area's renowned produce and world-class wines—the products of fertile soil and near-perpetual sun during the growing season. As a result of this marriage of imported talent and indigenous bounty, food now rivals wine as the principal attraction of the region.

With few exceptions (which are noted in individual restaurant listings), dress is informal. Where reservations are indicated as essential, you may need to reserve a week or more ahead. During the summer and early fall harvest seasons you may need to book several months ahead.

CATEGORY	COST*
$$$$	over $30
$$$	$22–$30
$$	$15–$21
$	under $15

* per person for a main course at dinner, excluding 7½% tax

Hot-Air Ballooning

Day after day, colorful balloons fill the morning sky high above the Wine Country's valleys. To aficionados, peering down at vineyards from the vantage point of the clouds is the ultimate California experience.

Balloon flights take place soon after sunrise, when the calmest, coolest conditions offer maximum lift and soft landings. Prices depend on the duration of the flight, number of passengers, and services. Some companies provide such extras as pickup at your lodging or champagne brunch after the flight.

Lodging

In a region where first-class restaurants and wineries attract connoisseurs from afar, it's no surprise that elegant lodgings have sprung up. Most local bed-and-breakfasts have historic Victorian and Spanish architecture and serve a full breakfast highlighting local produce. The newer hotels and spas include state-of-the-art buildings offering such comforts as massage treatments or spring water–fed pools.

All of this luxury does come with a hefty price tag. Since Santa Rosa is the largest population center in the area, it has the widest selection of moderately priced rooms. Try there if you've failed to reserve in advance or have a limited budget. Many B&Bs are fully booked long in advance of the summer and fall seasons, and small children are often discouraged as guests. For all accommodations in the area, rates are lower on weeknights and about 20% less in the winter.

CATEGORY	COST*
$$$$	over $225
$$$	$160–$225
$$	$100–$159
$	under $100

All prices are for a standard double room, excluding 14% tax.

Spas and Mud Baths

Mineral water soaks, mud baths, and massage are rejuvenating local traditions. Calistoga, known worldwide as the Hot Springs of the West, is famous for its warm, spring water–fed mineral tubs and mud baths full of volcanic ash. Sonoma, St. Helena, and other towns also have full-service spas.

Wine Tasting

For those new to the wine tasting game, Robert Mondavi and Korbel Champagne Cellars give general tours geared toward teaching novices the basics on how wine and champagne are made and what to look for when tasting.

There are more than 400 wineries in Sonoma and Napa, so it pays to be selective when planning your visit. Better to mix up the wineries with other sights and diversions—a picnic, trips to local museums, a ride in a hot-air balloon—than attempt to visit too many in one day. Unless otherwise noted, the wineries in this chapter are open daily year-round and charge no fee for admission, tours, or tastings.

Exploring the Wine Country

Numbers in the text correspond to numbers in the margin and on the Wine Country map.

Great Itineraries

The Wine Country is composed of two main areas: the Napa Valley and the Sonoma Valley. Five major paths cut through both valleys: U.S. 101 and Routes 12 and 121 through Sonoma County, and Route 29 north from Napa. The 25-mi Silverado Trail, which runs parallel to Route 29 north from Napa to Calistoga, is a more scenic, less crowded route with a number of distinguished wineries. Because the Wine Country is expansive, it's best to plan smaller, separate trips over the course of several days.

152

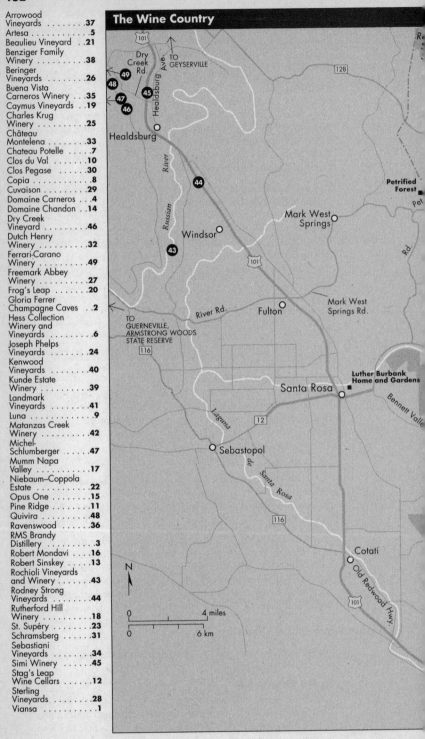

The Wine Country

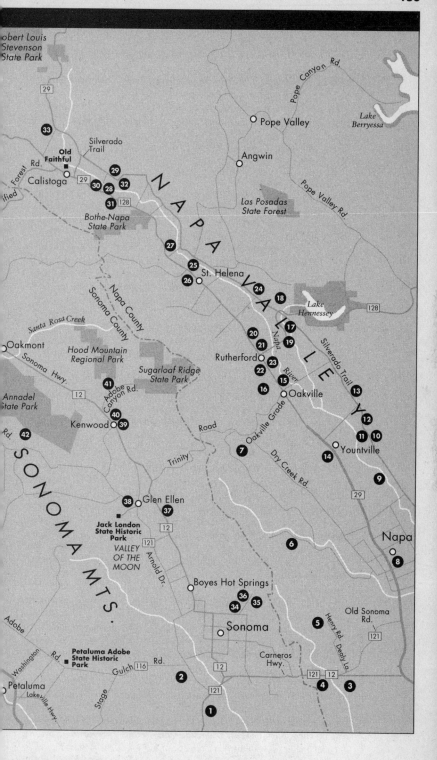

IF YOU HAVE 2 DAYS

Start at the circa-1857 **Buena Vista Carneros Winery** ㉟ just outside of Sonoma. From there, take Route 12 north to the Trinity Road/Oakville Grade. Drive east over the Mayacamas Mountains, taking time to admire the views as you descend into the Napa Valley. Take Route 29 north into historic ⊡ **St. Helena** for lunch. After lunch in St. Helena, take the 30-minute tour of **Beringer Vineyards** ㉖. The next day continue up 29 North to **Calistoga** for an early morning balloon ride, an afternoon trip to the mud baths, and a visit to **Clos Pegase** ㉚ before heading back to St. Helena for dinner at Greystone—the Culinary Institute of America's beautiful West Coast campus and highly acclaimed restaurant.

IF YOU HAVE 4 DAYS

Concentrate on the Napa Valley, starting at Yountville and traveling north to Calistoga. Make your first stop in **Oakville,** where the circa-1880s Oakville Grocery—once a Wells Fargo Pony Express stop—is indisputably the most popular place for picnic supplies. Enjoy the picnic grounds at **Robert Mondavi** ⑯ before touring the winery and tasting the wine. If time permits, spend the night in the town of ⊡ **Rutherford** and visit either **Rutherford Hill Winery** ⑱ or the **Niebaum–Coppola Estate** ㉒, or continue north to ⊡ **St. Helena.** Take a look at the Silverado Museum and visit the shopping complex surrounding the **Freemark Abbey Winery** ㉗. On the third day drive to ⊡ **Calistoga** for a balloon ride before heading north to Old Faithful Geyser of California; then continue on to Robert Louis Stevenson State Park, which encompasses the summit of Mount St. Helena. On the fourth day take Route 29 just north of Calistoga proper, head west on Petrified Forest Road, and then go south on Calistoga Road, which runs into Route 12. Follow Route 12 southeast to **Glen Ellen** for a taste of the Sonoma Valley. Visit Jack London State Historic Park, and then loop back north on Bennett Valley Road to beautiful **Matanzas Creek Winery** ㊷ in Santa Rosa.

IF YOU HAVE 7 DAYS

Begin in the town of **Sonoma,** whose colorful plaza and mission evoke early California's Spanish past. Afterward, head north to ⊡ **Glen Ellen** and the Valley of the Moon. Picnic and explore the grounds at Jack London State Historic Park. Next morning visit **Kenwood Vineyards** ㊵ before heading north to ⊡ **Healdsburg** in Dry Creek Valley via Santa Rosa and U.S. 101. In this less-trafficked haven of northern Sonoma County, a host of "hidden" wineries—including **Ferrari-Carano Winery** ㊾—lie nestled in the woods along the roads. Spend the night in ⊡ **Healdsburg.** On the third day cross over into Napa Valley—take Mark Springs Road east off U.S. 101's River Road exit and follow the signs on Porter Creek Road to Petrified Forest Road to Route 29. Spend the day (and the night) in the quaint western-style town of ⊡ **Calistoga,** noted for its mud baths and mineral springs. Wake up early on the fourth day for a balloon ride. If you're feeling energetic, take to the Silverado Trail for a bike ride with stops at **Cuvaison** ㉙, **Stag's Leap Wine Cellars** ⑫, and **Clos du Val** ⑩. On day five, visit the galleries, shops, and eateries of St. Helena before heading to Oakville for the Oakville Grocery, a must-see (and must-taste) landmark. Spend the night and visit the wineries in ⊡ **Rutherford.** On day six, explore nearby **Yountville,** stopping for lunch at one of its many acclaimed restaurants before heading up the hill to the **Hess Collection Winery and Vineyards** ⑥, on Mt. Veeder, where a brilliant art collection and excellent wines may keep you occupied for hours. Splurge on dinner at Domaine Chandon. On your last day return to the town of Sonoma via the Carneros Highway, stopping for a look at how brandies are made at the **RMS Brandy**

Distillery ③, then moving on to the landmark **Buena Vista Carneros Winery** ㉟, or **Gloria Ferrer Champagne Caves** ②.

When to Tour the Wine Country

"Crush," the term used to indicate the season when grapes are picked and crushed, usually takes place in September or October, depending on the weather. From September until December the entire Wine Country celebrates its bounty with street fairs and festivals. The Sonoma County Harvest Fair, with its famous grape stomp, is held the first weekend in October. The Napa Valley Wine Festival takes place the first weekend in November.

In season (April–October), Napa Valley draws crowds of tourists, and traffic along Route 29 from St. Helena to Calistoga is often backed up on weekends. The Sonoma Valley, Santa Rosa, and Healdsburg are less crowded. In season and over holiday weekends it's best to book lodging, restaurant, and winery reservations well in advance. Many wineries give tours at specified times and require appointments.

To avoid crowds, visit the Wine Country during the week and get an early start (most wineries open around 10). Pack a sun hat, since summer is usually hot and dry and autumn can be even hotter.

CARNEROS REGION

One of the most important viticultural areas in the Wine Country straddles southern Sonoma and Napa counties. The Carneros region has a long, cool growing season tempered by maritime breezes and lingering fogs off the San Pablo Bay—optimum slow-growing conditions for pinot noir and chardonnay grapes.

Southern Sonoma County

36 mi from San Francisco, north on U.S. 101, east on Rte. 37, and north on Rte. 121.

❶ Sam Sebastiani, of the famous Sebastiani family, and his wife, Vicki, established their own hilltop winery, **Viansa.** Reminiscent of a Tuscan villa, the winery's ocher-color building is surrounded by olive trees and overlooks the valley. The varietals produced here depart from the traditionally Californian and include muscat canelli and nebbiolo. The adjacent Wine Country Visitor Center has brochures and information. ✉ *25200 Arnold Dr., Sonoma County,* ☎ *707/935–4700,* WEB *www.viansa.com.* ☉ *Daily 10–5. Tours by appointment.*

❷ The sparkling and still wines at **Gloria Ferrer Champagne Caves** originated with a 700-year-old stock of Ferrer grapes. The method here is to age the wines in a "cava," or cellar, where several feet of earth maintain a constant temperature. ✉ *23555 Carneros (Rte. 121),* ☎ *707/ 996–7256,* WEB *www.gloriaferrer.com.* ▦ *Tasting fees vary.* ☉ *Daily 10:30–5:30. Tours daily between 11 and 4.*

Southern Napa County

7 mi east of Rte. 121/116 junction on Rte. 121/12.

❸ Learn the history and folklore of rare alembic brandy at the **RMS Brandy Distillery.** Tours include an explanation of the double-distillation process, which eliminates all but the finest spirits for aging; a view of the French-built alembic distillation pots that resemble Aladdin's lamp; a trip to the atmospheric oak barrel house, where taped chants create an otherworldly mood; and a sensory evaluation of vintage brandies (no tasting allowed, by law). ✉ *1250 Cuttings Wharf Rd.,*

Napa (from Domaine Carneros, head 1 mi east on Carneros Hwy.), ☎ 707/253–9055, FAX 707/253–0116, WEB *www.rmsbrandy.com.* ◷ *Apr.– Oct., daily 10–5; Nov.–Mar., daily 10:30–4:30. Tours every hr.*

❹ Domaine Carneros occupies a 138-acre estate dominated by a classic château inspired by Champagne Taittinger's historic Château de la Marquetterie in France. Carved into the hillside beneath the winery, Domaine Carneros's cellars produce sparkling wines reminiscent of the Taittinger style and using only Carneros grapes. ✉ *1240 Duhig Rd., Napa,* ☎ 707/ 257–0101, FAX 707/257–3020, WEB *www.domainecarneros.com.* 🍷 *Tasting fees vary.* ◷ *Daily 10:30–6:30. Tours daily at 11, noon, 1, 2, 3, and 4, Apr.–Nov.; Mon.–Thurs. at 11, 1, and 3 and Fri.–Sun. hourly 11–4, Dec.–Mar.*

❺ Artesa is bunkered into a scenic Carneros hilltop, formerly the site of Codorniu Napa. The Spanish owners are now producing primarily still wines under the talented wine maker Don Van Staaveren (formerly of Chateau St. Jean). ✉ *1345 Henry Rd., north off Old Sonoma Rd. and Dealy La.,* ☎ 707/224–1668, FAX 707/224–1672, WEB *www. artesawinery.com.* 🍷 *Tasting fees vary.* ◷ *Daily 10–5. Tours daily; times vary.*

THE NAPA VALLEY

The Napa Valley is the undisputed capital of American wine production, with more than 240 wineries. Famed for its unrivaled climate and neat rows of vineyards, the area is made up of small, quirky towns whose Victorian Gothic architecture—narrow, gingerbread facades and pointed arches—is reminiscent of a distant world. Calistoga feels like an Old West frontier town, with wooden-plank storefronts and people in cowboy hats. St. Helena is posh, with tony shops and elegant restaurants. Yountville is compact and redolent of American history, yet fast becoming an up-to-the-minute culinary hub.

Napa

46 mi from San Francisco, east and north on I–80 to Rte. 37 west to Rte. 29 north.

The city of Napa is undergoing quite a metamorphosis, especially since the opening of Copia: The American Center for Wine, Food and the Arts. New restaurants and inns also opened at about the same time, and the Napa Valley Opera House is also being renovated. The oldest town in the Napa Valley—established in 1848—it also claims an advantageous location. Most destinations in both the Napa and Sonoma valleys are easily accessible from here. For those seeking an affordable alternative to the hotels and B&Bs in the heart of the Wine Country, Napa is a good option.

★ **❻** The **Hess Collection Winery and Vineyards** is a delightful discovery on a hilltop 9 mi northwest of Napa (don't give up; the road leading to the winery is long and winding). Within the simple, rustic limestone structure, circa 1903, you'll find Swiss owner Donald Hess's personal art collection. Cabernet sauvignon is the real strength here, though Hess also produces some fine chardonnays. ✉ *4411 Redwood Rd., west off Rte. 29,* ☎ 707/255–1144, FAX 707/253–1682, WEB *www.hesscollection.com.* 🍷 *Tasting fee $3.* ◷ *Daily 10–4.*

❼ Chateau Potelle, on the slopes of Mt. Veeder, produces acclaimed estate zinfandel, chardonnay, and cabernet sauvignon, all of which thrive in the poor soil at nearly 2,000 ft above the valley floor. It's a quiet, out-of-the-way spot for a picnic. ✉ *3875 Mt. Veeder Rd. (5 mi west* *of Rte. 29 off the Oakville Grade),* ☎ *707/255–9440,* WEB *www.chateaupotelle.com.* ⊘ *Thurs.–Mon. 11–5.*

⑧ Copia: The American Center for Wine, Food and the Arts is a two-story complex that celebrates American cultural contributions to wine and food and offers related exhibitions, demonstrations and classes, as well as dining at Julia's Kitchen, named for the legendary Julia Child. Tours of seasonal gardens are also available. ⊠ *2921 Silverado Trail,* ☎ *707/ 259–1600,* WEB *www.copia.org.* ⊡ *Tasting fee: $7* ⊘ *Daily 10–5. Tours by appointment.*

⑨ Luna, the southernmost winery on the Silverado Trail, was established in 1996 by three veterans of the Napa wine industry intent on making less-conventional wines, particularly Italian varieties. They've planted pinot gris on the historic property and also make sangiovese and merlot. ⊠ *2921 Silverado Trail,* ☎ *707/255–5862,* WEB *www. lunavineyards.com.* ⊡ *Tasting fee: $7.* ⊘ *Daily 10–5. Tours by appointment.*

⑩ Clos du Val, founded by French owner Bernard Portet, produces a celebrated reserve cabernet. It also makes zinfandel, pinot noir, merlot, sangiovese, and chardonnay. Although the winery itself is austere, the French-style wines age beautifully. ⊠ *5330 Silverado Trail,* ☎ *707/259– 2200,* WEB *www.closduval.com.* ⊡ *Tasting fee $5.* ⊘ *Daily 10–5. Tours by appointment.*

⑪ Small **Pine Ridge** makes estate-bottled wines, including chardonnay, cabernet, and merlot, as well as a first-rate chenin blanc. Tours include barrel tastings in the winery's caves. ⊠ *5901 Silverado Trail,* ☎ *707/ 253–7500,* FAX *707/253–1493,* WEB *www.pineridgewinery.com.* ⊡ *Tasting fees vary.* ⊘ *Daily 10:30–4:30. Tours by appointment at 10:15, 1, and 3.*

Dining and Lodging

$$–$$$ ✕ **Bistro Don Giovanni.** Even in winter, the valley views from the covered patio are extraordinary. The wine list at the restaurant of Giovanni and Donna Scala is as locally representative as the menu is eclectic. Don't miss the individual pizzas cooked in a wood-burning oven, the handmade pastas, or the focaccia sandwiches encasing grilled vegetables. ⊠ *4110 St. Helena Hwy. (Rte. 29),* ☎ *707/224–3300. AE, D, DC, MC, V.*

$$–$$$ ✕ **Foothill Cafe.** On the less glamorous side of Route 29, this low-key restaurant is a big favorite with locals, who may or may not know that the chef is an alumnus of Masa's in San Francisco. ⊠ *2766 Old Sonoma Rd.,* ☎ *707/252–6178. MC, V. No lunch. Closed Mon.–Tues.*

$–$$ ✕ **Celadon.** Dishes like flash-fried calamari with a chipotle chili and ginger glaze and small tasting plates such as a large crab cake laced with whole-seed mustard sauce make this an ideal place to sample contemporary cuisine accompanied by any of a dozen wines available by the glass. ⊠ *1040 Main St.,* ☎ *707/254–9690. AE, MC, V. Closed Sun. No lunch Sat.*

$ ✕ **ZuZu.** Spanish glass lamps, a carved-wood Latin American goddess and hammered-tin ceiling panels set the tone for a menu composed almost entirely of tapas. White anchovies with endive, ratatouille, grilled tuna, and lamb sausage are typical fare. ⊠ *829 Main St.,* ☎ *707/224– 8555. AE, D, DC, MC, V. No lunch weekends.*

$$$–$$$$ ✕▣ **Silverado Country Club and Resort.** This luxurious if somewhat staid 1,200-acre property in the hills east of Napa has cottages, kitchen apartments, and one- to three-bedroom condominiums, many with fireplaces. With multiple golf courses, pools, and tennis courts, it's a place for serious sports enthusiasts and anyone who enjoys the conveniences of a

full-scale resort. There are also two restaurants of note on the grounds. The elegant Vintner's Court has California–Pacific Rim cuisine ($$$–$$$$), and Royal Oak ($$–$$$$) serves steak and seafood nightly. ⊠ *1600 Atlas Peak Rd. (6 mi east of Napa via Rte. 121), 94558, ☎ 707/257–0200 or 800/532–0500, FAX 707/257–2867, WEB www.silveradoresort. com. 277 condo units. 3 restaurants, bar, kitchenettes, 2 18-hole golf courses, 23 tennis courts, 9 pools, bicycles. AE, D, DC, MC, V.*

$$$$ 🏨 **Milliken Creek Inn.** This lavishly landscaped inn is on the banks of the Napa River. The understated interiors have pale green walls, rattan furniture, water views, and lots of palm and elephant motifs. ⊠ *1815 Silverado Trail, 94558, ☎ 707/255–1197, 888/622–5775, WEB www.millikencreekinn.com. 277 condo units. Massage, Internet. AE, D, DC, MC, V.*

$$–$$$ 🏨 **Chateau Hotel.** Despite the name, this is a pretty simple motel with only the barest nod to France. Clean rooms, its location at the entrance to the Napa Valley, Continental breakfast, and discounts for senior citizens make up for its lack of charm. ⊠ *4195 Solano Ave. (west of Rte. 29, exit at Trower Ave.), 94558, ☎ 707/253–9300; 800/253–6272 in CA, FAX 707/253–0906, WEB www.napavalleychateauhotel.com. 115 rooms. Refrigerators, pool, hot tub. AE, D, DC, MC, V.*

Outdoor Activities and Sports

GOLF

The 18-hole **Chardonnay Club** (⊠ 2555 Jameson Canyon Rd., ☎ 707/257–8950) course is a favorite among Bay Area golfers. The greens fee, $55 weekdays and $70 weekends, includes a cart. Within the vicinity of the Silverado Trail, the **Silverado Country Club** (⊠ 1600 Atlas Peak Rd., ☎ 707/257–0200) has two challenging 18-hole courses with a beautiful view at every hole. The greens fee for hotel guests is $130, including a cart; the reciprocal rate for members of other clubs is $150.

Yountville

13 mi north of the town of Napa on Rte. 29.

Yountville has become the valley's boomtown. No other small town in the entire Wine Country has as many inns, restaurants, or shops—and new ones seem to open every few months. A popular Yountville attraction is **Vintage 1870** (⊠ 6525 Washington St., ☎ 707/944–2451), a 26-acre complex of boutiques, restaurants, and gourmet stores. The vine-covered brick buildings were built in 1870 and housed a winery, livery stable, and distillery. The original mansion of the property is now the popular Mexican-style **Compadres Bar and Grill.** Nearby is the **Pacific Blues Café,** housed in the train depot Samuel Brannan built in 1868 for his privately owned Napa Valley Railroad. At **Yountville Park** there's a picnic area with tables, barbecue pits, and a view of grapevines.

At the intersection of Madison and Washington streets is Yountville's **Washington Square.** It is now a complex of boutiques and restaurants. **Pioneer Cemetery,** the final resting place of the town's founder, George Yount, is nearby, on the far side of Washington Street.

⑫ In 1995, the World Wine Championships gave **Stag's Leap Wine Cellars** a platinum award for its 1990 reserve chardonnay, designating it the highest-ranked premium chardonnay in the world. But it was the 1973 cabernet sauvignon that put the winery—and the California wine industry—on the map by placing first in the famous Paris tasting of 1976. ⊠ *5766 Silverado Trail, ☎ 707/944–2020, WEB www.cask23.com. 🍷 Tasting fee $5. ☉ Daily 10–4:30. Tours by appointment.*

⑬ **Robert Sinskey** makes estate-bottled wines, including chardonnay, cabernet, and merlot, but is best known for its pinot noir. ✉ *6320 Silverado Trail,* ☎ *707/944–9090,* FAX *707/994–9092,* WEB *www. robertsinskey.com.* ✉ *Tasting fees vary.* ⊙ *Daily 10–4:30. Tours by appointment.*

⑭ French-owned **Domaine Chandon** claims one of Yountville's prime pieces of real estate, on a knoll west of downtown. Tours of the sleek, modern facilities on the beautifully maintained property include sample flutes of the méthode champenoise sparkling wine. ✉ *California Dr., west of Rte. 29,* ☎ *707/944–2280,* WEB *www.chandon.com.* ⊙ *Daily 10–6; closed Mon.–Tues. Dec.–Mar. Tours on the hr 11–5.*

Dining and Lodging

$$$$ ✕ **French Laundry.** Napa Valley's most acclaimed restaurant can be found
★ inside an old converted stone building on a residential street corner. The prix-fixe menus, one of which is vegetarian, include five or nine courses and usually have two or three additional surprises—little bitefuls such as a tiny ice cream cone filled with salmon tartare. Reservations are hard won and not accepted more than two months in advance, but lunch is a little easier to come by. ✉ *6640 Washington St.,* ☎ *707/ 944–2380. Reservations essential. AE, MC, V. Closed 1st 2 wks in Jan. No lunch Mon.–Thurs.*

$$–$$$$ ✕ **Brix.** This spacious dining room has artisan glass, fine woods, and an entire wall of west-facing windows that overlooks vineyards and the Mayacamas Mountains. Mains include tamari-glazed Atlantic salmon, spicy ahi on a futomaki roll, as well as New York strip with a goat cheese–potato gratin. Desserts receive an Asian accent as well, with a ginger crème brûlée among the offerings. ✉ *7377 St. Helena Hwy. (Rte. 29),* ☎ *707/944–2749. AE, D, DC, MC, V.*

$$–$$$ ✕ **Bistro Jeanty.** Philippe Jeanty's restaurant has a menu inspired by the cooking of his French childhood. His traditional cassoulet will warm those nostalgic for bistro cooking, while classic coq au vin rises above the ordinary with the infusion of a spicy red wine sauce. The scene here is Gallic through and through with a small bar and a handful of tables in a crowded room. ✉ *6510 Washington St.,* ☎ *707/944–0103. MC, V.*

$$–$$$ ✕ **Livefire.** Fred Halpert's rustic restaurant opened in 1998 on
★ Yountville's expanding restaurant row. This is a cozy spot warmed with earthy colors like mustard and terra-cotta. Fish, ribs, and poultry come piping hot out of a French rotisserie or a Chinese smoker. Service is top-notch. ✉ *5518 Washington St., 1 mi north of Yountville,* ☎ *707/944–1500. AE, D, DC, MC, V.*

$$–$$$ ✕ **Mustards Grill.** Everyone's favorite Napa Valley restaurant attracts
★ wine makers and other locals as well as hungry tourists. Grilled fish, steak, local fresh produce, and an impressive wine list are the trademarks of this boisterous bistro with a black-and-white marble floor and upbeat artwork. The thin, crisp, golden onion rings are addictive. ✉ *7399 St. Helena Hwy. (Rte. 29), 1 mi north of Yountville,* ☎ *707/ 944–2424. Reservations essential. D, DC, MC, V.*

$–$$$ ✕ **Bouchon.** The team that brought the French Laundry to its current pinnacle opened a second restaurant nearby in 1998. French country fare—*steak frites,* leg of lamb, and sole meunière—is served amid elegant antique chandeliers and a snazzy zinc bar. Late-night diners are pleased it's open until at least 1 AM. ✉ *6534 Washington St.,* ☎ *707/ 944–8037. AE, MC, V.*

$$$$ 🏠 **Napa Valley Lodge.** The balconies, covered walkways, and red-tile roof are reminiscent of a hacienda. The large pool area is landscaped with lots of greenery. Many spacious second-floor rooms have vineyard views, and five suites are available. Fresh brewed coffee, Conti-

nental breakfast, and the morning paper are complimentary. ✉ *2230 Madison St., at Rte. 29,* ☎ *707/944–2468 or 800/368–2468,* ℻ *707/ 944–9362,* WEB *www.woodsidehotels.com/napa. 55 rooms. Refrigerators, pool, gym, hot tub, sauna. AE, D, DC, MC, V. CP.*

$$$$ 🏨 **Vintage Inn.** Accommodations in this luxurious inn are arranged in two-story villas throughout the 3½-acre property. All the spacious rooms were revamped in 2001, adding French fabrics and 19th-century antiques as well as whirlpools to all the bathrooms. Some private patios have vineyard views. You're treated to a bottle of wine, Continental breakfast with champagne, and afternoon tea. ✉ *6541 Washington St., 94599,* ☎ *707/944–1112 or 800/351–1133,* ℻ *707/ 944–1617,* WEB *www.vintageinn.com. 80 rooms. Refrigerators, tennis court, pool, hot tub, bicycles. AE, DC, MC, V. CP.*

$$$–$$$$ 🏨 **La Résidence.** Romantically secluded in extensive landscaping, these deluxe accommodations are in two buildings: the Mansion, a renovated 1870s Gothic Revival manor house built by a riverboat captain from New Orleans; and the French Barn. The spacious rooms have period antiques, fireplaces, and double French doors opening onto verandas or patios. ✉ *4066 St. Helena Hwy. (Rte. 29, 4 mi south of Yountville),* ☎ *707/253–0337,* ℻ *707/253–0382,* WEB *www.laresidence.com. 20 rooms. Dining room, pool, hot tub, business services. AE, D, DC, MC, V. BP.*

$$$ 🏨 **Petit Logis Inn.** In 1997 Jay and Judith Caldwell remodeled a row of shops into a small, charming one-story inn. Murals and 11-ft ceilings infuse each unique room with a European elegance. Breakfast, included in the room rate, is offered at one of two nearby restaurants. ✉ *6527 Yount St., 94599,* ☎ *707/944–2332,* WEB *www.petitlogis.com. 5 rooms. Refrigerators, hot tubs. AE, MC, V. CP.*

Outdoor Activities and Sports

HOT-AIR BALLOONING

Balloons Above the Valley (✉ Box 3838, Napa 94558, ☎ 707/253–2222; 800/464–6824 in CA) is a reliable organization; rides are $185 per person. **Napa Valley Balloons** (✉ Box 2860, Yountville 94599, ☎ 707/944–0228; 800/253–2224 in CA) charges $175 per person.

Oakville

2 mi west of Yountville on Rte. 29.

There are three reasons to visit the town of Oakville: its grocery store, its scenic mountain road, and its magnificent, highly exclusive winery. The **Oakville Grocery** (✉ 7856 St. Helena Hwy. [Rte. 29]), built in the late 1880s to serve as a grocery store and Wells Fargo Pony Express stop, carries gourmet foods and difficult-to-find wines. Custom-packed picnic baskets are a specialty. Along the mountain range that divides Napa and Sonoma, the **Oakville Grade** is a twisting half-hour route with breathtaking views of both valleys. Though the surface of the road is good, it can be difficult to negotiate at night, and trucks are advised not to attempt it at any time.

🔟 **Opus One,** the combined venture of California wine maker Robert Mondavi and French baron Philippe Rothschild, is famed for its vast, semicircular cellar modeled on the Château Mouton Rothschild winery in France. The state-of-the-art facilities produce about 20,000 cases of ultrapremium Bordeaux-style red wine. ✉ *7900 St. Helena Hwy. (Rte. 29),* ☎ *707/963–1979,* ℻ *707/944–1753,* WEB *www.opusonewinery. com.* 🍷 *Tasting fee $25.* ☉ *Daily 10–3:30. Tasting and tours by appointment.*

⑯ At **Robert Mondavi,** the most famous winery in the nation, you're encouraged to take the 60-minute production tour with complimentary tasting, before trying the reserve reds ($1–$5 per glass). In-depth three- to four-hour tours and gourmet lunch tours are also popular. ✉ *7801 St. Helena Hwy. (Rte. 29),* ☎ *707/259–9463,* WEB *www.robertmondavi.com.* ☉ *Daily 9–5. Tours by appointment.*

Rutherford

1 mi northwest of Oakville on Rte. 29.

From a fast-moving car, Rutherford is a quick blur of dark forest, a rustic barn or two, and maybe a country store. But don't speed by this tiny hamlet. With its singular microclimate and soil, this is an important viticultural center.

⑰ **Mumm Napa Valley** is considered one of California's premier sparkling-wine producers. Its Napa Brut Prestige and ultrapremium Vintage Reserve are the best known. The excellent tour and comfortable tasting room are two more good reasons to visit. ✉ *8445 Silverado Trail,* ☎ *707/942–3434,* WEB *www.mummnapavalley.com.* ✉ *Tasting fees vary.* ☉ *Daily 10–5. Tours daily on the hour 10–3.*

⑱ The wine at **Rutherford Hill Winery** is aged in French oak barrels stacked in more than 44,000 square ft of caves—one of the largest such facilities in the nation. Tours of the caves can be followed by a picnic in oak, olive, or madrone orchards. ✉ *200 Rutherford Hill Rd., off the Silverado Trail,* ☎ *707/963–7194,* WEB *www.rutherfordhill.com.* ✉ *Tasting fees vary.* ☉ *Daily 10–5. Tours 11:30, 1:30, and 3:30.*

A 100% cabernet sauvignon special selection is the claim to fame at ⑲ **Caymus Vineyards.** Caymus also turns out a superior white, the Conundrum Proprietary, made of an unusual blend of grapes—sauvignon blanc, semillon, chardonnay, muscat canelli, and viognier. ✉ *8700 Conn Creek Rd.,* ☎ *707/963–4204.* ☉ *Daily 10–4. Tours and complimentary sit-down tastings by appointment.*

⑳ **Frog's Leap** is the perfect place for wine novices to begin their education. Owners John and Julie Williams maintain a sense of humor and a humble attitude that translates into an informative and satisfying experience. They also happen to produce some of the finest zinfandel, cabernet sauvignon, and sauvignon blanc in the Wine Country. ✉ *8815 Conn Creek Rd.,* ☎ *707/963–4704,* FAX *707/963–0242,* WEB *www.frogsleap.com.* ☉ *Tours and tasting by appointment.*

㉑ **Beaulieu Vineyard** utilizes the same wine-making process, from crush to bottle, as it did the day it opened in 1900. The winery's cabernet is a benchmark of the Napa Valley. The Georges du Latour Private Reserve consistently garners high marks from major wine publications. ✉ *1960 St. Helena Hwy. (Rte. 29),* ☎ *707/963–2411,* WEB *www.bvwines.com.* ✉ *Tasting fee $5, $25 in Reserve Room.* ☉ *Daily 10–5. Tours daily at 11, 1, 2, 3, and 4, and on Sat. on the half-hr.*

In the 1970s, filmmaker Francis Ford Coppola bought the old Niebaum estate, a part of the world-famous Inglenook estate. He resurrected an early Inglenook-like quality red with his first bottle of Rubicon, released ㉒ in 1985. Since then, **Niebaum–Coppola Estate** has consistently received high ratings. When you're through touring the winery, take a look at the Coppola movie memorabilia, which includes Don Corleone's desk and chair from *The Godfather.* ✉ *1991 St. Helena Hwy. (Rte. 29),* ☎ *707/963–9099,* WEB *www.niebaum-coppola.com.* ✉ *Tasting fee $7.50.* ☉ *Daily 10–5. Tours daily at 10:30 and 2:30.*

㉓ **St. Supéry** makes such excellent sauvignon blanc that it often sells out, but you can usually sample that variety as well as chardonnay, several red wines, and two kosher wines in the tasting room. This winery's unique discovery center allows you to inhale distinct wine aromas and match them with actual black pepper, cherry, citrus, and the like. ⊠ *8440 St. Helena Hwy. S (Rte. 29),* ☎ *707/963–4507,* WEB *www. stsupery.com.* ⊡ *Tasting fee $5 (lifetime).* ☉ *Daily 10–5. Tours at 11, 1, and 3.*

Dining and Lodging

$$$$ ✕ **La Toque.** Chef-owner Ken Frank specializes in intense flavors in his
★ changing prix-fixe menu that may include braised chanterelles, ravioli with chestnuts and rabbit, and cannellini-cranberry ragout. His cheese courses and desserts are worth saving some room for. ⊠ *1140 Rutherford Rd.,* ☎ *707/963–9770. Reservations essential. AE, MC, V. Closed Mon.–Tues. and first 2 wks in Jan. No dinner Sun.*

$$$$ ✕⊡ **Auberge du Soleil.** This stunning property, terraced on a hill stud-
★ ded by olive trees, has some of the valley's best views. The hotel's renowned restaurant is reclaiming its original glory with an award-winning wine list and dishes like raw yellowfin tuna with baby beets and Florida red snapper with pureed cauliflower, and the moderately priced bar menu is almost as good. Guest rooms are decorated with a nod to the spare side of southwestern style. ⊠ *180 Rutherford Hill Rd., off Silverado Trail just north of Rte. 128, 94573,* ☎ *707/963–1211 or 800/ 348–5406,* FAX *707/963–8764,* WEB *www.aubergedusoleil.com. 50 rooms. Restaurant, 3 tennis courts, pool, gym, hot tub, massage, steam room. AE, D, DC, MC, V. EP.*

$$$–$$$$ ⊡ **Rancho Caymus Inn.** California-Spanish in style, this cozy inn has well-maintained gardens and large suites with kitchens and whirlpool baths. Well-chosen details include beehive fireplaces, tile murals, stoneware basins, and Ecuadorean llama-hair blankets. ⊠ *1140 Rutherford Rd., junction of Rtes. 29 and 128, 94573,* ☎ *707/963–1777 or 800/845–1777,* FAX *707/963–5387,* WEB *www.ranchocaymus.com. 26 rooms. Restaurant, some kitchenettes, refrigerators. AE, DC, MC, V. 2-night minimum on weekends. CP.*

St. Helena

2 mi northwest of Oakville on Rte. 29.

By the time pioneer winemaker Charles Krug planted grapes in St. Helena around 1860, quite a few vineyards already existed. Today the town greets you with its abundant selection of wineries—many of which lie along the route from Yountville to St. Helena—and restaurants, including Greystone on the West Coast campus of the Culinary Institute of America.

Bordeaux blends, Rhône varietals, and a cabernet sauvignon are the
㉔ house specialties at **Joseph Phelps Vineyards.** One of Napa's top wineries, it first hit the mark with Johannisberg riesling. ⊠ *200 Taplin Rd.,* ☎ *707/963–2745,* WEB *www.jpvwines.com.* ⊡ *Tasting fee $5.* ☉ *Mon.–Sat. 9–5, Sun. 10–4. Tours and tastings by appointment only.*

㉕ **Charles Krug Winery** opened in 1861 when Count Haraszthy loaned Krug a small cider press. Today, it is run by the Peter Mondavi family. The gift shop stocks everything from gourmet food baskets with grape-shape pasta to books about the region and its wines. ⊠ *2800 N. Main St.,* ☎ *707/963–5057.* ☉ *Daily 10:30–5:30. Tours at 11:30, 1:30, and 3:30.*

Arguably the most beautiful winery in the Napa Valley, the 1876
㉖ **Beringer Vineyards** is also the oldest continuously operating one. In

1883 the Beringer brothers, Frederick and Jacob, built the Rhine House Mansion, where tastings are now held among Belgian Art Nouveau hand-carved oak and walnut furniture and stained-glass windows. ✉ *2000 Main St. (Rte. 29),* ☎ *707/963–4812,* WEB *www.beringerblass.com.* 🍷 *Tasting fees vary.* ◔ *Daily 9:30–4. Tours daily.*

㉗ **Freemark Abbey Winery** was originally called the Tychson Winery after Josephine Tychson, the first woman to establish a winery in California. It has long been known for its cabernets, whose grapes come from the fertile Rutherford Bench. ✉ *3022 St. Helena Hwy. N (Rte. 29),* ☎ *707/963–9694,* WEB *www.freemarkabbey.com.* ◔ *Daily 10–4:30. Tour daily at 2.*

Grape-seed mud wraps and Ayurvedic-inspired massages performed by two attendants are among the trademarks of the upscale **Health Spa Napa Valley** (✉ 1030 Main St., ☎ 707/967–8800), which has a pool and a health club. Should your treatments leave you too limp to operate your car, you can walk to Tra Vigne and other St. Helena restaurants.

The **Culinary Institute of America,** the country's leading school for chefs, set up its West Coast headquarters in the Greystone Winery, the former site of the Christian Brothers Winery and a national historic landmark. The CIA campus consists of 30 acres of herb and vegetable gardens, a 15-acre merlot vineyard, and a Mediterranean-inspired restaurant, which is open to the public. ✉ *2555 Main St.,* ☎ *707/967–2600 or 800/333–9242,* FAX *707/967–1113,* WEB *www.ciachef.edu.*

Dining and Lodging

$$–$$$$ **✕ Tra Vigne.** This fieldstone building has been transformed into a
★ striking trattoria with a huge wood bar, high ceilings, and plush banquettes. Homemade mozzarella, olive oil, and vinegar, and house-cured pancetta and prosciutto contribute to a mouthwatering tour of Tuscan cuisine. The outdoor courtyard in summer and fall is a sun-splashed Mediterranean vision of striped umbrellas and awnings, crowded café tables, and rustic pots overflowing with flowers. ✉ *1050 Charter Oak Ave., off Rte. 29,* ☎ *707/963–4444. Reservations essential. D, DC, MC, V.*

$$–$$$ **✕ Terra.** A romantic restaurant housed in an 1888 stone foundry, Terra is especially known for its exquisite Mediterranean-inspired dishes, many with Asian touches. The sweetbreads ragout, grilled squab, and sake-marinated Chilean sea bass are memorable. ✉ *1345 Railroad Ave.,* ☎ *707/963–8931. Reservations essential. DC, MC, V. Closed Tues. No lunch.*

$$–$$$ **✕ Wine Spectator Greystone Restaurant.** This restaurant, housed in the handsome old Christian Brothers' winery, is run by the Culinary Institute of America. Century-old stone walls house a large and bustling restaurant, with cooking, baking, and grilling stations in full view. The menu has a Mediterranean spirit and emphasizes such small plates as bruschetta topped with wild mushrooms and *muhammara* (a spread of roasted red peppers and walnuts). ✉ *2555 Main St.,* ☎ *707/967–1010. AE, DC, MC, V.*

$$$$ **✕▥ Meadowood Resort.** Secluded at the end of a semiprivate road, this 256-acre resort has accommodations in a rambling country lodge and several bungalows. The elegant dining room specializes in California Wine Country cooking. The Grill, a less formal, less expensive restaurant, serves a lighter menu of pizzas and spa food for breakfast and lunch (and early dinners on Friday and Saturday). ✉ *900 Meadowood La., 94574,* ☎ *707/963–3646 or 800/458–8080,* FAX *707/963–5863,* WEB *www.meadowood.com. 40 rooms, 45 suites. 2 restaurants, bar, room service, 9-hole golf course, 7 tennis courts, 2 pools,* *health club, hot tub, massage, sauna, steam room, croquet. AE, D, DC, MC, V.*

$$$$ ▦ **Harvest Inn.** Many of the larger-than-average rooms in this Tudor-esque inn on lushly landscaped grounds were renovated and brightened in 2000. Most rooms have wet bars, antique furnishings, and fireplaces. Pets are allowed in certain rooms for a fee. Complimentary breakfast is served in the breakfast room and on the patio overlooking the vineyards. ⊠ *1 Main St., 94574,* ☎ *707/963–9463 or 800/950–8466,* ℻ *707/963–4402,* ᴡᴇʙ *www.harvestinn.com. 55 rooms. Room service, refrigerators, 2 pools, 2 hot tubs. AE, D, DC, MC, V. CP.*

$$$–$$$$ ▦ **Wine Country Inn.** Surrounded by a pastoral landscape of hills, old
★ barns, and stone bridges, this is a peaceful New England–style retreat. Rural antiques fill all the rooms, most of which overlook the vineyards with either a balcony, patio, or deck. Most rooms have fireplaces, and some have private hot tubs. A hearty country breakfast is served buffet style in the sun-splashed common room. ⊠ *1152 Lodi La. (off Rte. 29), 94574,* ☎ *707/963–7077,* ℻ *707/963–9018,* ᴡᴇʙ *www. winecountryinn.com. 24 rooms. Pool, hot tub. MC, V. BP.*

$$$–$$$$ ▦ **El Bonita Motel.** This cute motel with such pleasant touches as window boxes and landscaped grounds has relatively elegant furnishings with muted pastel walls and floral upholstery. Some rooms have whirlpool spas. ⊠ *195 Main St. (Rte. 29), 94574,* ☎ *707/963–3216 or 800/ 541–3284,* ℻ *707/963–8838,* ᴡᴇʙ *www.elbonita.com. 41 rooms. Pool. AE, MC, V. 2-night minimum weekends.*

Shopping

Handcrafted candles made on the premises are for sale at the **Hurd Beeswax Candle Factory** (⊠ 3020 St. Helena Hwy. N (Rte. 29), ☎ 707/963–7211). At **I. Wolk Gallery** (⊠ 1235 Main St., ☎ 707/963–8800) you'll find works by established and emerging artists from New York, Chicago, Los Angeles, and Santa Fe—everything from abstract and contemporary realist paintings to high-quality works on paper and sculpture. **Vanderbilt & Company** (⊠ 1429 Main St., ☎ 707/963–1010), the prettiest store in town, is filled with Italian ceramics, tabletop decor, and other high-quality home accessories.

Calistoga

3 mi northwest of St. Helena on Rte. 29.

In addition to its wineries, Calistoga is noted for its mineral water, hot mineral springs, mud baths, steam baths, and massages. The Calistoga Hot Springs Resort was founded in 1859 by maverick entrepreneur Sam Brannan, whose ambition was to found "the Saratoga of California." He tripped up the pronunciation of the phrase at a formal banquet—it came out "Calistoga"—and the name stuck.

The **Sharpsteen Museum** has a magnificent diorama of the Calistoga Hot Springs Resort in its heyday. Other exhibits document Robert Louis Stevenson's time in the area and the career of museum founder Ben Sharpsteen, an animator at the Walt Disney studio. ⊠ *1311 Washington St.,* ☎ *707/942–5911.* ☛ *$3 donation.* ☉ *Daily 11–4.*

Indian Springs, an old-time spa, has been pumping out 212°F water from its three geysers since the late 1800s. The place offers some of the best bargains on mud bathing and short massages and has a large mineral-water pool. ⊠ *1712 Lincoln Ave.,* ☎ *707/942–4913.* ☉ *Daily 9–7. Reservations recommended for spa treatments.*

㉘ **Sterling Vineyards** sits on a hilltop 1 mi south of Calistoga, its pristine white Mediterranean-style buildings reached by an aerial tramway from the valley floor. The view from the tasting room is superb, and the gift shop is one of the best in the valley. ⊠ *1111 Dunaweal La.,* ☎ *707/942–3300,* WEB *www.sterlingvineyards.com.* ⊠ *Tram $6.* ☉ *Daily 10:30–4:30.*

㉙ Cuvaison specializes in chardonnay, merlot, and cabernet sauvignon for the export market. Two small picnic areas on the grounds look out over Napa Valley. ⊠ *4550 Silverado Trail,* ☎ *707/942–6266,* WEB *www.cuvaison.com.* ⊠ *Tasting fees vary.* ☉ *Daily 10–5. Tours at 10:30 and by appointment.*

★ **㉚** Designed by postmodern architect Michael Graves, **Clos Pegase** is a one-of-a-kind structure packed with unusual art objects from the collection of art-book publisher and owner Jan Shrem. Works of art even appear in the underground wine tunnels. ⊠ *1060 Dunaweal La.,* ☎ *707/942–4981,* WEB *www.clospegase.com.* ☉ *Daily 10:30–5. Tours at 11 and 2.*

㉛ Schramsberg, perched on a wooded knoll on the southeast side of Route 29, is one of Napa's most historic wineries, with caves that were dug by Chinese laborers in 1880. The winery makes sparkling wines in several styles, in several price ranges. ⊠ *1400 Schramsberg Rd.,* ☎ *707/ 942–4558,* WEB *www.schramsberg.com.* ⊠ *Tasting and tour $7.50.* ☉ *Daily 10–4. Tours by appointment only.*

㉜ It's worth taking a slight detour off the main artery to find **Dutch Henry Winery,** a small winery whose wines are available only on-site or through mail order. Free tastings are held in a working winery, where winemakers also explain the winemaking process. This is a good place to try sauvignon blanc and syrah. ⊠ *4310 Silverado Trail,* ☎ *707/942– 5771,* WEB *www.dutchhenry.com.* ☉ *Daily 10–4:30. Tours by appointment only.*

㉝ Château Montelena is a vine-covered stone French château constructed circa 1882 and set amid Chinese-inspired gardens, complete with a manmade lake with gliding swans and islands crowned by Chinese pavilions. Château Montelena produces chardonnays and cabernet sauvignons. ⊠ *1429 Tubbs La.,* ☎ *707/942–5105,* WEB *www. montelena.com.* ⊠ *Tasting fees vary: $10.* ☉ *Daily 10–4. Tours by appointment at 11 and 2.*

☾ Many families bring children to Calistoga to see **Old Faithful Geyser of California** blast its 60-ft tower of steam and vapor about every 40 minutes (the pattern is disrupted during heavy rains or if there's an earthquake in the offing). The spout usually lasts three minutes. Picnic facilities are available. ⊠ *1299 Tubbs La. (1 mi north of Calistoga),* ☎ *707/942–6463,* WEB *www.oldfaithfulgeyser.com.* ⊠ *$6.* ☉ *Apr.–Sept., daily 9–6; Oct.–Mar., daily 9–5.*

☾ The **Petrified Forest** contains the remains of the volcanic eruptions of Mount St. Helena 3.4 million years ago. The force of the explosion uprooted the gigantic redwoods, covered them with volcanic ash, and infiltrated the trees with silica and minerals, causing petrifaction. ⊠ *4100 Petrified Forest Rd. (5 mi west of Calistoga),* ☎ *707/942–6667.* ⊠ *$5.* ☉ *Late Apr.–early Sept., daily 10–6; early Sept.–late Apr., daily 10–5.*

☾ **Robert Louis Stevenson State Park,** on Route 29, 3 mi northeast of Calistoga, encompasses the summit of Mount St. Helena. It was here, in the summer of 1880, in an abandoned bunkhouse of the Silverado Mine, that Stevenson and his bride, Fanny Osbourne, spent their honeymoon. The stay inspired Stevenson's "The Silverado Squatters," and Spyglass Hill in *Treasure Island* is thought to be a portrait of Mount St. Helena. The park's approximately 3,600 acres are mostly undeveloped except for a fire trail leading to the site of the bunkhouse—which is marked with a marble tablet—and to the summit beyond.

Dining and Lodging

$$–$$$ ✕ **Catahoula Restaurant and Saloon.** Using a large wood-burning
★ oven, chef Jan Birnbaum turns out such dishes as spicy gumbo with rooster and pork porterhouse. The large barroom opposite the dining room has its own menu of small plates, which are ideal for sampling Birnbaum's kitchen wizardry. ⊠ *Mount View Hotel, 1457 Lincoln Ave.,* ☎ *707/942–2275. Reservations essential. MC, V. Closed Tues. and Jan.*

$$ ✕ **All Seasons Café.** Bistro cuisine takes a California spin in this sun-filled space with marble tables and a black-and-white checkerboard floor. The seasonal menu includes organic greens, wild mushrooms, local game birds, and house-smoked beef, as well as homemade breads, desserts, and freshly made ice cream. ⊠ *1400 Lincoln Ave.,* ☎ *707/ 942–9111. D, DC, MC, V. No lunch Mon.–Wed.*

$$ ✕ **Calistoga Inn.** Grilled meat and fish for dinner and soups, salads, and sandwiches for lunch are prepared with flair at this microbrewery with a tree-shaded outdoor patio. ⊠ *1250 Lincoln Ave.,* ☎ *707/ 942–4101. AE, MC, V.*

$–$$ ✕ **Wappo Bar Bistro.** This colorful restaurant is an adventure in international dining with a menu ranging from Asian noodles and Thai shrimp curry to chiles rellenos to Turkish meze. ⊠ *1226 S. Washington St.,* ☎ *707/942–4712. AE, MC, V. Closed Tues. and first 2 wks. in Dec.*

$ ✕ **Pacifico.** Technicolor ceramics and subtropical plants adorn this Mexican restaurant, which serves Oaxacan and other fare. Fajitas and moles are among the specialties. ⊠ *1237 Lincoln Ave.,* ☎ *707/942– 4400. MC, V.*

$$$$ 🏨 **Cottage Grove Inn.** Sixteen elegant and contemporary cottages are shaded by elm trees. Rooms have skylights and plush furnishings. Fireplaces, CD players, two-person hot tubs, and porches with wicker rocking chairs add to the coziness. Rates include Continental breakfast and afternoon wine and cheese. ⊠ *1711 Lincoln Ave., 94515,* ☎ *707/942– 8400 or 800/799–2284,* FAX *707/942–2653,* WEB *www.cottagegrove.com. 16 rooms. Refrigerators, in-room VCRs. AE, D, DC, MC, V. 2-night minimum weekends. CP.*

$$$–$$$$ 🏨 **Meadowlark Country House.** Decidedly laid-back and sophisticated, this inn is surrounded by 20 hillside acres just north of downtown Calistoga. The main house, built in 1886, and a newer building, added in the 1990s, hold unfussy but country-stylish rooms. Rates include a full breakfast. ⊠ *601 Petrified Forest Rd., 94515,* ☎ *707/942–5651 or 800/ 942–5651,* FAX *707/942–5023,* WEB *www.meadowlarkinn.com. 7 rooms. Pool, hot tub, sauna. AE, MC, V. BP.*

$$$–$$$$ 🏨 **Mount View Hotel.** Listed on the National Register of Historic Places, the Mount View is the largest Napa Valley hotel north of St. Helena. A full-service European spa provides state-of-the-art pampering, and three cottages are each equipped with a private redwood deck, Jacuzzi, and wet bar. ⊠ *1457 Lincoln Ave., 94515,* ☎ *707/942– 6877,* FAX *707/942–6904,* WEB *www.mountviewhotel.com. 32 rooms. Restaurant, pool, spa. AE, D, MC, V.*

$$–$$$ 🏨 **Brannan Cottage Inn.** This pristine Victorian cottage with lacy white fretwork, large windows, and a shady porch is the only one of Sam Brannan's 1860 resort cottages still standing on its original site. Rooms have private entrances, and elegant stenciled friezes of stylized wildflowers cover the walls. A full breakfast is included. ⊠ *109 Wapoo Ave., 94515,* ☎ *707/942–4200,* WEB *www.brannancottageinn.com. 6 rooms. MC, V. CP.*

$$ 🏠 **Calistoga Spa Hot Springs.** No-nonsense motel-style rooms have kitch-enettes stocked with utensils and coffeemakers, which makes them pop-ular with families and travelers on a budget. (There's a supermarket a block away.) The on-premises spa includes mineral baths, mud baths, swimming pools, and a hot tub. ⊠ *1006 Washington St., 94515,* ☎ *707/942–6269,* FAX *707/942–4214,* WEB *www.calistogaspa.com. 57 rooms. Snack bar, kitchenettes, 2 pools, wading pool, hot tub, spa, meet-ing room. MC, V. 2-night minimum weekends, 3-night minimum hol-iday weekends.*

Outdoor Activities and Sports

BIKING

Getaway Adventures and Bike Shop (⊠ 1117 Lincoln Ave., ☎ 707/942–0332 or 800/499–2453) rents bikes and conducts winery and other bike tours. It's closed Wednesday.

GLIDING, HOT-AIR BALLOONING

The **Calistoga Ballooning** (☎ 707/944–2822) charters early morning flights (exact times vary) out of Calistoga or, depending on weather conditions, St. Helena, Oakville, or Rutherford. Pilots are well versed in Napa Valley lore.

THE SONOMA VALLEY

Unlike its upscale neighbor, Sonoma Valley is rustic and unpretentious. Its name is Miwok Indian for "many moons," but Jack London's nick-name for the region—Valley of the Moon—is more fitting. The scenic valley, bounded by the Mayacamas Mountains on the east and Sonoma Mountain on the west, extends north from San Pablo Bay nearly 20 mi to the eastern outskirts of Santa Rosa. The varied terrain, soils, and climate (cooler in the south because of the bay influence and hotter towards the north) allow grape growers to raise cool-weather varietals such as chardonnay and pinot noir as well as merlot, cabernet sauvi-gnon, and other heat-seeking vines.

Sonoma

14 mi west of Napa on Rte. 12; 45 mi from San Francisco, north on U.S. 101, east on Rte. 37, and north on Rte. 121/12.

Sonoma is the oldest town in the Wine Country. Its historic town plaza is the site of the last and the northernmost of the 21 missions es-tablished by the Franciscan order of Father Junípero Serra. The **Mis-sion San Francisco Solano,** whose chapel and school were used to bring Christianity to the Native Americans, is now a museum with a fine collection of 19th-century watercolors. ⊠ *114 Spain St. E,* ☎ *707/938–9560.* 🎫 *$1 (includes same-day admission to Sonoma Barracks on the central plaza and General Vallejo's home, Lachryma Montis).* ☉ *Daily 10–5.* Sonoma's central plaza also includes the largest group of old adobes north of Monterey.

Originally planted by Franciscans of the Sonoma Mission in 1825, the
34 **Sebastiani Vineyards** were bought by Samuele Sebastiani in 1904. Red wine is king here. ⊠ *483 4th St. E,* ☎ *707/938–5532.* ☉ *Daily 10–5. Tours 10:30–4.*

35 **Buena Vista Carneros Winery** is the oldest continually operating win-ery in California. It was here, in 1857, that Count Agoston Haraszthy de Mokcsa laid the basis for modern California wine making, bucking the conventional wisdom that vines should be planted on well-watered ground by instead planting on well-drained hillsides. Chinese laborers dug tunnels 100 ft into the hillside, and the limestone they extracted was used to build the main house. The winery, which is surrounded by redwood and eucalyptus trees, has a specialty food shop, an art gallery, and picnic areas. ⊠ *18000 Old Winery Rd., off Napa Rd. (follow signs from the plaza),* ☎ *707/938–1266 or 800/678–8504,* WEB *www. buenavistawinery.com.* ✆ *Daily 10:30–4:30. Tour daily at 2.*

❸❻ Ravenswood, literally dug into the mountains like a bunker, is famous for its zinfandel. The merlot should be tasted as well. ⊠ *18701 Gehricke Rd., off E. Spain St.,* ☎ *707/938–1960,* WEB *www.ravenswood-wine.com.* ✆ *Tasting fee: $4.* ✆ *Daily 10–4:30. Tours by appointment at 10:30.*

A tree-lined driveway leads to **Lachryma Montis,** which General Mariano G. Vallejo, the last Mexican governor of California, built for his large family in 1851; the state purchased the home in 1933. The Victorian Gothic house is secluded in the midst of beautiful gardens. ⊠ *W. Spain St., near 3rd St. E,* ☎ *707/938–9559.* ✆ *$1.* ✆ *Daily 10–5. Tours by appointment.*

Dining and Lodging

$$–$$$ ✗ **The Girl and the Fig.** This popular Glen Ellen restaurant revitalized the historic barroom in the Sonoma Hotel with cozy banquettes and an inventive cuisine. A seasonally changing menu may include something with figs, a fillet of turbot on beet risotto, steak frites, or cassoulet. ⊠ *110 W. Spain St., Sonoma Plaza,* ☎ *707/938–3634. AE, D, DC, MC, V.*

$–$$$ ✗ **Cafe La Haye.** In a postage-stamp-size kitchen, skillful chefs turn out a half dozen main courses that star on a small but worthwhile menu. Chicken, beef, pasta, fish, and risotto get a deluxe treatment without fuss or fanfare. This offbeat café turns out some of the best food in the Wine Country. ⊠ *140 E. Napa St.,* ☎ *707/935–5994. MC, V. Closed Mon. No dinner Sun. No lunch.*

$–$$$ ✗ **Meritage.** A fortuitous blend of southern French and northern Italian cuisine is the backbone of this restaurant, where chef Carlo Cavalli works wonders with house-made pastas, particularly *gemelli.* An oyster bar augments extensive seafood choices and breakfast is available Wednesday through Sunday. ⊠ *522 Broadway,* ☎ *707/938–9430. AE, MC, V.*

$$ ✗ **La Salette.** Chef-owner Manny Azevedo, born in the Azores and raised in Sonoma, found culinary inspiration in his travels. The flavors of his dishes, such as Mozambique prawns with tomatoes and grilled plantains and salt cod baked with white onions, stand strong while complementing each other. ⊠ *18625 Rte. 12, Boyes Hot Springs,* ☎ *707/ 938–1927. MC, V. Closed Mon.–Tues.*

$–$$ ✗ **The Big 3 Diner.** Overstuffed booths, ceiling fans, and an open kitchen give this corner bistro an informal feel. Country breakfasts, pizza from the wood-burning oven, and mostly straightforward American fare are the specialties. ⊠ *Sonoma Mission Inn, 18140 Sonoma Hwy. (2 mi north of Sonoma on Rte. 12 at Boyes Blvd.), Boyes Hot Springs,* ☎ *707/938–9000. AE, DC, MC, V.*

$–$$ ✗ **Della Santina.** This longstanding favorite is a world unto itself, with the most authentic Italian food in town and a charming enclosed brick patio in back. Of special note are the gnocchi and, when available, petrale sole and sand dabs. ⊠ *133 E. Napa St.,* ☎ *707/935–0576. AE, D, MC, V.*

$$$$ ✗▥ **Sonoma Mission Inn & Spa.** This beautifully landscaped Mission-style property has an Olympic-size pool supplied, as are the spa facilities, by warm mineral water pumped up from wells beneath the property. Gourmet and classic spa food is served at the Sante restaurant. Thirty suites in a secluded, tree-shaded area have verandas or patios, whirlpools, and fireplaces. ⊠ *18140 Rte. 12 (2 mi north of*

Sonoma at Boyes Blvd.), Box 1447, Boyes Hot Springs 95476, ☎ *707/
938–5358,* FAX *707/996–5358. 168 rooms, 60 suites. 2 restaurants, coffee shop, 2 bars, 2 pools, hot tub, spa. AE, DC, MC, V.*

$$$$ 🖬 **El Dorado Hotel.** A modern hotel in a remodeled old building, this
★ place has unusually spare and simple accommodations. Rooms reflect
Sonoma's Mission era, with Mexican-tile floors and white walls. The
best rooms are Nos. 3 and 4, which have larger balconies that overlook the Sonoma Plaza. ⊠ *405 1st St. W, 95476,* ☎ *707/996–3030 or
800/289–3031,* FAX *707/996–3148,* WEB *www.hoteleldorado.com. 27
rooms. Restaurant, pool. AE, MC, V.*

$$–$$$$ 🖬 **Thistle Dew Inn.** The public rooms of this turn-of-the-20th-century
Victorian home are filled with collector's-quality Arts and Crafts fur-
nishings. Four of the six rooms have private entrances and decks, and
all have queen-size beds with antique quilts, private baths, and air-con-
ditioning. Welcome bonuses include a hot tub and free use of the inn's
bicycles. ⊠ *171 W. Spain St., 95476,* ☎ *707/938–2909; 800/382–7895
in CA,* FAX *707/996–8413,* WEB *www.thistledew.com. 6 rooms. Hot tub,
bicycles. AE, MC, V. BP.*

$–$$$ 🖬 **Vineyard Inn.** Built as a roadside motor court in 1941, this B&B
inn with red-tile roofs brings a touch of Mexican village charm to an
otherwise lackluster and somewhat noisy location at the junction of
two main highways. It's across from two vineyards and is the closest
lodging to Sears Point Raceway. ⊠ *23000 Arnold Dr., at junction of
Rte. 116 and 121, 95476,* ☎ *707/938–2350 or 800/359–4667,* FAX *707/
938–2353,* WEB *www.sonomavineyardinn.com. 17 rooms, 7 suites. AE,
MC, V. CP.*

Shopping

Several shops in the four-block **Sonoma Plaza** attract food lovers from
miles around. The **Sonoma Cheese Factory** (⊠ Sonoma Plaza, 2 Spain
St., ☎ 707/996–1000), run by the same family for four generations,
makes Sonoma Jack cheese and the tangy Sonoma Teleme. Great
swirling baths of milk and curds are visible through the windows, along
with flat-pressed wheels of cheese.

Glen Ellen

7 mi north of Sonoma on Rte. 12.

Jack London lived in the Sonoma Valley for many years. The craggy,
quirky, and creek-bisected town of Glen Ellen commemorates him
with place-names and nostalgic establishments. In the hills above Glen
Ellen lies **Jack London State Historic Park.** London's collection of South
Seas and other artifacts are on view at the House of Happy Walls, a
museum of London's effects. ⊠ *2400 London Ranch Rd.,* ☎ *707/938–
5216.* 🚗 *Parking $3.* ☉ *Park daily 9:30–5, museum daily 10–5.*

㊲ **Arrowood Vineyards** is neither as old nor as famous as some of its neighbors, but wine makers and critics are quite familiar with the excellent
handcrafted wines produced here. The winery's harmonious architecture overlooking the Valley of the Moon earned it an award from the
Sonoma Historic Preservation League, and the wine-making equipment
is state-of-the-art. ⊠ *14347 Sonoma Hwy.,* ☎ *707/938–5170,* WEB
www.robertmondavi.com. 🚗 *Tasting fees vary.* ☉ *Daily 10–4:30.
Tours by appointment.*

㊳ One of the best-known wineries along Route 12 is **Benziger Family Winery,** which specializes in premium estate and Sonoma County wines.
Among the first wineries to identify certain vineyard blocks for particularly desirable flavors, Benziger is noted for its merlot, pinot blanc,
chardonnay, and fumé blanc. ⊠ *1883 London Ranch Rd.,* ☎ *707/935–*

3000, WEB *www.benziger.com.* ⬛ *Tasting fees for reserve wines vary.* ☉ *Daily 10–4:30. Tours every ½ hr Mar.–Sept. 9:30–5, Oct.–Feb. 9:30–4.*

Lodging

$$$$ 🏠 **Gaige House Inn.** This glamorous country inn blends the comfort of a 19th-century residence with contemporary, uncluttered furnishings accented with Asian details such as prints and bamboo and rattan woods. A large pool surrounded by a green lawn, striped awnings, white umbrellas, and magnolias conjures a manicured Hamptons-like glamour in the midst of rustic Glen Ellen. ⊠ *13540 Arnold Dr., 95442,* ☎ *707/935–0237 or 800/935–0237,* FAX *707/935–6411,* WEB *www. gaige.com. 15 rooms. Pool, outdoor hot tub. AE, D, MC, V. BP.*

$$–$$$ 🏠 **Beltane Ranch.** On a slope of the Mayacamas range on the eastern side of the Sonoma Valley lies this 100-year-old house built by a retired San Francisco madam. The Wood family have stocked the comfortable living room with dozens of books on the area. The rooms, furnished with antiques, open onto the building's wraparound porch. ⊠ *11775 Sonoma Hwy. (Rte. 12), 95442,* ☎ *707/996–6501.* WEB *www.beltaneranch.com. 6 rooms. Tennis court, hiking. No credit cards. BP.*

$$–$$$$ 🏠 **Glenelly Inn.** On the outskirts of Glen Ellen, this sunny little establishment, built as an inn in 1916, offers all the comforts of home—plus a hot tub in the garden. Innkeeper Kristi Hallamore serves breakfast in front of the common room's cobblestone fireplace and provides local delicacies in the afternoon. ⊠ *5131 Warm Springs Rd., 95442,* ☎ *707/ 996–6720,* FAX *707/996–5227,* WEB *www.glenelly.com. 8 rooms. Outdoor hot tub. MC, V. BP.*

Kenwood

3 mi north of Glen Ellen on Rte. 12.

Kenwood has a historic train depot and several restaurants and shops that specialize in locally produced goods. Its inns, restaurants, and winding roads nestle in soothing bucolic landscapes.

❸❾ **Kunde Estate Winery** is managed by the fourth generation of Kunde family grapegrowers and winemakers. The standard tour of the grounds includes its extensive caves. A tasting and dining room lies 175 ft below a chardonnay vineyard. Tastings usually include viognier, chardonnay, cabernet sauvignon, and zinfandel. ⊠ *10155 Rte. 12,,* ☎ *707/833–5501.* WEB *www.kunde.com.* ☉ *Daily 10:30–4:30. Tours 11– 3 Apr.–Dec., Fri.–Mon.; Jan.–Mar., Fri.–Sun.*

❹⓪ The beautifully rustic grounds at **Kenwood Vineyards** complement the attractive tasting room and artistic bottle labels. Although Kenwood produces all premium varietals, the winery is best known for its Jack London Vineyard reds—pinot noir, zinfandel, merlot, and a unique Artist Series cabernet. ⊠ *9592 Sonoma Hwy.,* ☎ *707/833–5891,* WEB *www. kenwoodvineyards.com.* ☉ *Daily 10–4:30. No tours.*

❹❶ **Landmark Vineyards.** The landscaping and design of this winery, established by the heirs of John Deere, are as classical as its wine-making methods. Landmark's Damaris Reserve and Overlook chardonnays have been particularly well received, as has the winery's Grand Detour pinot noir. ⊠ *101 Adobe Canyon Rd., off Sonoma Hwy.,* ☎ *707/833– 1144 or 800/452–6365,* WEB *www.landmarkwine.com.* ☉ *Daily 10–4:30. Horse-drawn carriage vineyard tours Sat. 11:30–3:30 Apr.–Sept.*

Dining

$$–$$$ ✕ **Kenwood Restaurant & Bar.** One of the enduring favorites in an area known for fine dining, this is where Napa and Sonoma chefs eat on

their nights off. You can indulge in California country cuisine in the sunny, South of France–style dining room or head through the French doors to the patio for a memorable view of the vineyards. ⊠ *9900 Rte. 12,* ☏ *707/833–6326. MC, V. Closed Mon.*

$–$$ ✕ **Café Citti.** The aroma of garlic envelops the neighborhood whenever the Italian chef-owner is roasting chickens at this homey roadside café. Deli items, hot pastas, and soups makes this an excellent budget stop. ⊠ *9049 Rte. 12,* ☏ *707/833–2690. MC, V.*

ELSEWHERE IN SONOMA COUNTY

At nearly 1,598 square mi, Sonoma is far too large a county to cover in one or two days. The land mass extends from San Pablo Bay south to Mendocino County and from the Mayacamas Mountains on the Napa side west to the Pacific Ocean. Wineries can be found from the cool flatlands of the south to the hot interior valleys to the foggy coastal regions. Sonoma, though less famous than Napa, in fact has more award-winning wines.

Santa Rosa

8 mi northwest of Kenwood on Rte. 12.

Santa Rosa is the Wine Country's largest city and a good bet for moderately priced hotel rooms, especially for those who have not reserved in advance.

★ ㊷ **Matanzas Creek Winery** specializes in three varietals—sauvignon blanc, merlot, and chardonnay—and makes a hard-to-find sparkling wine. Huge windows in the visitor center overlook a field of 3,100 tiered and fragrant lavender plants. Acres and acres of gardens planted with unusual grasses and plants from all over the world have caught the attention of horticulturists. ⊠ *6097 Bennett Valley Rd.,* ☏ *707/528–6464 or 800/590–6464,* WEB *www.matanzascreek.com.* ⊑ *Tasting fees vary.* ☼ *Daily 10–4:30, Apr.–Dec. Tours weekdays at 10:30 and 3, weekends at 10:30.*

Dining and Lodging

$$–$$$ ✕ **John Ash & Co.** The first Wine Country restaurant to tout locally grown ingredients in the 1980s, John Ash has maintained its status despite the departure of its namesake chef in 1991. With patio seating outside and a cozy fireplace indoors, the slightly formal restaurant looks like a villa amid the vineyards. ⊠ *4330 Barnes Rd. (River Rd. exit west from U.S. 101),* ☏ *707/527–7687. Reservations essential. AE, DC, MC, V. No lunch Mon.*

$–$$$ ✕ **Café Lolo.** This casual but sophisticated spot is the territory of chef and co-owner Michael Quigley, who has single-handedly made downtown Santa Rosa a culinary destination. His dishes stress fresh ingredients and an eye to presentation. Don't pass up the chocolate kiss, an individual cake with a wonderfully soft, rich center. ⊠ *620 5th St.,* ☏ *707/576–7822. AE, MC, V. Closed Sun. No lunch Sat.*

$–$$$ ✕ **Mixx.** Great service and an eclectic mix of dishes made with locally grown ingredients define this small restaurant with large windows, high ceilings, and Italian blown-glass chandeliers. House-made ravioli, grilled Cajun prawns, and grilled leg of lamb are among the favorites of the many regulars. ⊠ *135 4th St., at Davis St. (behind the mall on Railroad Sq.),* ☏ *707/573–1344. AE, D, MC, V. Closed Sun. No lunch Sat.*

$–$$ ✕ **Sassafras.** The focus is on regional American cuisine, with a largely North American wine list. Dishes that sound familiar get a contemporary twist, as in a pizza with Creole-style ingredients, a meatloaf-with-ketchup that's really a venison-and-pork terrine with cranberry sauce, or a pecan pie served with a lavender custard. ⊠ *1229 N. Dutton Ave.,* ☎ *707/578–7600. AE, D, DC, MC, V. No lunch weekends.*

$$$–$$$$ 🏨 **Fountaingrove Inn.** A redwood sculpture and a wall of cascading
★   water distinguish the lobby at this elegant, comfortable hotel and conference center. A buffet breakfast is complimentary, and, for an additional fee, you'll have access to a nearby 18-hole golf course, a tennis court, and a health club. ⊠ *101 Fountaingrove Pkwy., near U.S. 101, 95403,* ☎ *707/578–6101 or 800/222–6101,* FAX *707/544–3126,* WEB *www.fountaingroveinn.com. 124 rooms, 6 suites. Restaurant, room service, in-room data ports, pool, hot tub, meeting room. AE, D, DC, MC, V. CP.*

$$$–$$$$ 🏨 **Vintner's Inn.** Set on 50 acres of vineyards, this French provincial inn has large rooms, many with wood-burning fireplaces, and a trellised sundeck. Breakfast is complimentary, and discount passes to an affiliated health club are available. ⊠ *4350 Barnes Rd., River Rd. exit west from U.S. 101, 95403,* ☎ *707/575–7350 or 800/421–2584,* FAX *707/575–1426,* WEB *www.vintnersinn.com. 44 rooms. Restaurant, hot tub. AE, DC, MC, V. CP.*

$–$$ 🏨 **Los Robles Lodge.** This pleasant, relaxed motel overlooks a pool that's set into a grassy landscape. Pets are allowed, except in executive rooms. Some rooms have whirlpools. ⊠ *1985 Cleveland Ave., Steele La. exit west from U.S. 101, 95401,* ☎ *707/545–6330 or 800/255–6330,* FAX *707/575–5826. 100 rooms. Restaurant, coffee shop, pool, outdoor hot tub, lounge, laundry facilities. AE, DC, MC, V.*

Outdoor Activities and Sports

GOLF

The **Fountaingrove Country Club** (⊠ 1525 Fountaingrove Pkwy., ☎ 707/579–4653) has an 18-hole course. **Oakmont Golf Club** (⊠ west course: 7025 Oakmont Dr., ☎ 707/539–0415; ⊠ east course: 565 Oak Vista Court, ☎ 707/538–2454) has two 18-hole courses.

HOT-AIR BALLOONING

For views of the ocean coast, the Russian River, and San Francisco on a clear day, **Above the Wine Country** (☎ 707/829–9850 or 888/238–6359) operates out of Santa Rosa, although many flights actually originate outside Healdsburg.

Russian River Valley

5 mi northwest of Santa Rosa.

The Russian River flows all the way from Mendocino to the Pacific Ocean, but in terms of winemaking, the Russian River Valley is centered on a triangle with points at Healdsburg, Guerneville, and Sebastopol. Tall redwoods shade many of the two-lane roads that access this scenic area where, thanks to the cooling marine influence, pinot noir and chardonnay are the king and queen of grapes. For a free map of the area, contact **Russian River Wine Road** (⊠ Box 46, Healdsburg 95448, ☎ 707/433–6782, WEB www.wineroad.com).

Rustic woods and a homey tasting room await you at **Topolos at Russian River Vineyards,** an unusual winery in a hop kiln-style building. Michael Topolos, a leader in biodynamic farming, will gladly talk about environmental-friendly practices over a taste of port, alicante bouschet, or other unusual varieties. ⊠ *5700 Gravenstein Hwy. N (Hwy. 116),* ☎ *707/887–1575,* WEB *www.topolos.com.* ☉ *11–5:30.*

Tucked into Green Valley, **Iron Horse** is equally as successful at making still wine as the sparkling type. You should allow time to meander around the gardens, which are planted to bloom practically all year round, thanks to the winery's proximity (12 mi) to the ocean. ⊠ *9786*

Ross Station Rd. (near Sebastopol), ☏ *707/433–2305,* WEB *www. ironhorsevineyards.com.* ⊙ *Feb.–Nov., daily 10–5; Dec.–Jan., daily 11–4.*

㊸ **Rochioli Vineyards and Winery** claims one of the prettiest picnic sites in the area, with tables overlooking vineyards. The winery makes one of the county's best chardonnays, but is particularly known for its pinot noir and sauvignon blanc. ✉ *6192 Westside Rd.,* ☏ *707/433–2305.* ⊙ *Feb.–Nov., daily 10–5; Dec.–Jan., daily 11–4.*

You can easily spot the triple towers of **Hop Kiln,** a California state historical landmark. One of the friendliest wineries in the Russian River area, Hop Kiln has a vast tasting room just steps away from a duck pond where you can picnic. ✉ *6050 Westside Rd.,* ☏ *707/433–6491,* WEB *www.hopkilnwinery.com.* ⊙ *Daily 10–5.*

Old Vine zinfandel, along with chardonnay and pinot noir, is top of **㊹** the line at **Rodney Strong Vineyards.** Picnic areas overlook the vineyards. ✉ *11455 Old Redwood Hwy.,* ☏ *707/433–6511,* WEB *www. rodneystrong.com.* ⊙ *Daily 10–5. Tours daily 11 and 3.*

OFF THE
BEATEN PATH

KORBEL CHAMPAGNE CELLARS – In order to be called champagne, a wine must be made in the French region of Champagne or it's just sparkling wine. But despite the objections of the French, champagne has entered the lexicon of California wine makers, and many refer to their sparkling wines as champagne. Whatever you call it, Korbel produces a tasty, reasonably priced wine as well as its own beer, which is available at a brewpub on the premises. The winery's 19th-century buildings and gorgeous rose gardens are a delight in their own right. ✉ *13250 River Rd., Guerneville,* ☏ *707/824–7000,* WEB *www.korbel.com.* FAX *707/869–2981.* ⊙ *Oct.– Apr., daily 9–4:30; May–Sept., daily 9–5. Tours on the hr 10–3.*

Dining and Lodging

$–$$ ✕ **Chez Marie.** It took a New Orleans chef to turn this tiny restaurant into a California auberge. Forestville is light on places to eat, so the place fills up with locals familiar with the jambalaya and gumbos and sprinkling of French specialties. ✉ *6675 Front St., Forestville,* ☏ *707/ 887–7503. Closed Mon.–Wed. No lunch.*

$$–$$$$ ✕🛏 **The Farmhouse Inn.** Members of a longtime Guerneville family bought this property in 2001, reconfigured the restaurant and lobby in the 1873 farmhouse and upgraded the adjacent guest cottages. These deluxe accommodations have feather beds, wood-burning fireplaces, and private saunas. The restaurant, open for dinner Thursday–Sunday, relies largely on seasonal local products and fresh seafood. ✉ *7871 River Rd., Forestville 95436,* ☏ *707/887–3300 or 800/464–6642,* WEB *www.farmhouseinn.com. 8 rooms. Restaurant, refrigerators, pool, massage, saunas. AE, MC, V.*

$$–$$$$ 🛏 **Applewood Inn.** On a knoll in the shelter of towering redwoods, ★ this hybrid inn has two distinct types of accommodations. Those in the original Belden House are comfortable but modest in scale. Most of the 10 accommodations in the newer buildings, both salmon-pink stucco, are larger and airier, particularly the second-floor rooms and the penthouse minisuite. ✉ *13555 Rte. 116, Guerneville 95421,* ☏ *707/869–9093,* FAX *707/869–9170,* WEB *www.applewoodinn.com. 19 rooms. Restaurant, pool, outdoor hot tub. AE, MC, V.*

Healdsburg

17 mi north of Santa Rosa on U.S. 101.

Healdsburg itself is centered on a fragrant plaza surrounded by shady trees, appealing antiques shops, and restaurants. A whitewashed bandstand is the venue for free summer concerts, where the music ranges from jazz to bluegrass.

Dining and Lodging

\$\$–\$\$\$ ✕ **Bistro Ralph.** In a town where good restaurants rarely seem to last, Ralph Tingle has sustained success with his California home-style cuisine, serving up a small menu that changes weekly. The stark industrial space includes a stunning wine rack of graceful curves fashioned in metal and wood. ✉ *109 Plaza St., off Healdsburg Ave.,* ☎ *707/433–1380. Reservations essential. MC, V. No lunch weekends.*

\$\$\$\$ ⊡ **Hotel Healdsburg.** Healdsburg's first luxury downtown hotel rises three stories, but its green facade blends in nicely with the plaza across the street. The attention to detail is striking, from the sleek decor to the wide, uncarpeted hallways, not to mention lots of "HH" motifs, a la Gucci. ✉ *25 Matheson St., 95448,* ☎ *707/431–2800 or 800/889–7188,* ℻ *707/431–0414,* 🌐 *www.hotelhealdsburg.com. 49 rooms, 6 suites. Restaurant, bar, room service, refrigerator, pool, spa, Internet. AE, D, DC, MC, V.*

\$\$\$\$ ⊡ **Madrona Manor.** The oldest continuously operating inn in the area, this 1881 Victorian mansion, surrounded by eight acres of wooded and landscaped grounds, is straight out of a storybook. Sleep in the splendid three-story mansion, the carriage house, or one of two separate cottages. ✉ *1001 Westside Rd. (take central Healdsburg exit from U.S. 101, turn left on Mill St.), Box 818, 95448,* ☎ *707/433–4231 or 800/258–4003,* ℻ *707/433–0703,* 🌐 *www.madronamanor.com. 22 rooms. Restaurant, pool. MC, V.*

\$\$\$–\$\$\$\$ ⊡ **Healdsburg Inn on the Plaza.** This 1900 brick building on the town plaza has a bright solarium and a roof garden. The rooms, most with fireplaces, are spacious, with quilts and pillows piled high on antique beds. In the bathrooms claw-foot tubs are outfitted with rubber ducks; six rooms have whirlpool baths. Full champagne breakfast, afternoon coffee and cookies, and early evening wine and hors d'oeuvres are included. ✉ *110 Matheson St., Box 1196, 95448* ☎ *707/433–6991,* ℻ *707/433–9513,* 🌐 *www.healdsburginn.com. 11 rooms. D, MC, V. CP.*

\$\$\$–\$\$\$\$ ⊡ **The Honor Mansion.** This photogenic 1883 Italianate Victorian has won rave reviews for its interior design. Antiques, feather beds, and fancy water bottles are luxurious touches found in the rooms in the main house. Full breakfast is included. ✉ *14891 Grove St., 95448,* ☎ *707/433–4277 or 800/554–4667,* ℻ *707/431–7173,* 🌐 *www. honormansion.com. 7 rooms. Pool, hot tub. D, MC, V. BP.*

Shopping

Oakville Grocery (✉ 124 Matheson St., ☎ 707/433–3200) has a bustling Healdsburg branch filled with wine, produce, condiments, and deli items. For a good novel, children's literature, and books on interior design and gardening, head to **Levin & Company** (✉ 306 Center St., ☎ 707/433–1118), which also stocks a lot of CDs and tapes. Every Saturday morning from early May through October, Healdsburg locals gather at the open-air **Farmers' Market** (✉ North Plaza parking lot, North and Vine Sts., ☎ 707/431–1956) to pick up supplies from local producers of vegetables, fruits, flowers, cheeses, and olive oils.

Dry Creek and Alexander Valleys

On the west side of Hwy. 101, Dry Creek Valley remains one of the least developed appellations in Sonoma. The valley made its name on the zinfandel grapes that flourish on the benchlands, while the gravelly, well-drained soil of the valley floor is better known for chardonnay and, in the north, sauvignon blanc.

The Alexander Valley, which lies east of Healdsburg, has a number of family-owned wineries. Most can be found right on Hwy. 28, which runs through this scenic, diverse appellation where zinfandel and chardonnay grow particularly well.

45 **Simi Winery.** Giuseppe and Pietro Simi, two brothers from Italy, began growing grapes in Sonoma in 1876. Though their winery's operations are strictly high-tech these days, its tree-studded entrance area and stone buildings recall a more genteel era. ⊠ *16275 Healdsburg Ave. (take Dry Creek Rd. exit off U.S. 101), Alexander Valley,* ☎ *707/433–6981,* WEB *www.simiwinery.com.* ☉ *Tours Mar.–Dec., daily 11, 1, and 3; Jan.–Feb., daily 11 and 2.*

46 **Dry Creek Vineyard,** whose fumé blanc is an industry benchmark, is also earning notice for its reds, especially zinfandels and cabernets. Picnic beneath the flowering magnolias and soaring redwoods. ⊠ *3770 Lambert Bridge Rd., Dry Creek Valley,* ☎ *707/433–1000,* WEB *www.drycreekvineyard.com.* ☉ *Daily 10:30–4:30. Tours by appointment.*

47 Housed in a California Mission–style complex off the main drag, **Michel-Schlumberger** produces ultrapremium wines including chardonnay, merlot, pinot blanc, and syrah, but its reputation is based on the exquisite cabernet sauvignon. ⊠ *4155 Wine Creek Rd., Dry Creek Valley,* ☎ *707/ 433–7427 or 800/447–3060,* WEB *www.michelschlumberger.com.* ☉ *Tastings and tours at 11 and 2 by appointment.*

48 An unassuming winery in a wood and cinder-block barn, **Quivira** produces some of the most interesting wines in Dry Creek Valley. Though it is known for its exquisitely balanced and fruity zinfandel, it also makes a superb blend of red varietals called Dry Creek Cuvée. ⊠ *4900 W. Dry Creek Rd., Dry Creek Valley,* ☎ *707/431–8333,* WEB *www.quivirawine.com.* ☉ *Daily 10–4:30. Tours by appointment.*

49 Noted for its beautiful Italian villa–style winery and visitor center (the breezy courtyard is covered with just about every kind of flower imaginable), **Ferrari-Carano Winery** produces chardonnays, fumé blancs, and merlots. ⊠ *8761 Dry Creek Rd., Dry Creek Valley,* ☎ *707/433–6700,* WEB *www.ferrari-carano.com.* ▦ *Tasting fee $2.50.* ☉ *Daily 10–5. Tours by appointment.*

OFF THE BEATEN PATH **CLOS DU BOIS –** Five miles north of Healdsburg on Route 116, these vineyards produce the fine estate chardonnays of the Alexander and Dry Creek valleys that have been mistaken for great French wines. ⊠ *19410 Geyserville Ave., Geyserville,* ☎ *707/857–3100 or 800/222–3189,* WEB *www.closdubois.com.* ☉ *Daily 10–4:30. No tours.*

Lodging

$$ ⊞ **Best Western Dry Creek Inn.** Continental breakfast and a bottle of wine are complimentary at this three-story Spanish Mission–style motel. Midweek discounts are available. A coffee shop is next door. ⊠ *198 Dry Creek Rd., 95448,* ☎ *707/433–0300 or 800/222–5784,* FAX *707/433–1129. 102 rooms. Pool, hot tub, laundry facilities. AE, D, DC, MC, V. CP.*

WINE COUNTRY A TO Z

To research prices, get advice from other travelers, and book travel arrangements, visit www.fodors.com.

AIR TRAVEL

The major gateway to Wine Country is **San Francisco International Airport (SFO)**, just south of the city, off U.S. 101. Several domestic airlines serve **Oakland Airport (OAK)**, which is in the East Bay and gives easy access to Wine Country via I–80.

➤ AIRPORT INFORMATION: **Oakland International Airport** (☎ 510/577–4000).**San Francisco International Airport** (☎ 650/761–0800).

BUS TRAVEL

Greyhounds runs buses from the Transbay Terminal at 1st and Mission streets in San Francisco to Sonoma and Santa Rosa. There is also some bus service available within the Wine Country. Valley Intracity Neighborhood Express provides bus service within the city of Napa and between other Napa Valley towns, and Sonoma County Area Transit offers daily bus service to points all over the county

➤ BUS LINES: **Greyhound** (☎ 800/231–2222). **Sonoma County Area Transit** (☎ 707/585–7516 or 800/345–7433). **VINE** (Valley Intracity Neighborhood Express; ☎ 707/255–7631).

CAR RENTAL

Rentals are available at the airports and in San Francisco, Oakland, Sonoma, Santa Rosa, and Napa. *See* Car Rental *in* Smart Travel Tips A to Z for national rental agency phone numbers.

CAR TRAVEL

From San Francisco, cross the Golden Gate Bridge, go north on U.S. 101, east on Route 37, and north and east on Route 121. For Sonoma wineries, head north at Route 12; for Napa, turn left (to the northwest) when Route 121 runs into Route 29.

From Berkeley and other East Bay towns, take Interstate 80 north to Route 37 west to Route 29 north, which will take you directly up the middle of the Napa Valley. To reach Sonoma county, take Route 121 west off Route 29 south of the city of Napa. From points north of the Wine Country, take U.S. 101 south to Geyserville and take Route 128 southeast to Calistoga and Route 29. Most Sonoma County wine regions are clearly marked and accessible off U.S. 101; to reach the Sonoma Valley, take Route 12 east from Santa Rosa.

EMERGENCIES

In an emergency dial 911.

➤ HOSPITAL: **Santa Rosa Memorial Hospital** (✉ 1165 Montgomery Dr., Santa Rosa, ☎ 707/546–3210).

LODGING

A number of outfits can help you find a room at a Wine Country B&B.

➤ RESERVATIONS SERVICES: **The Bed & Breakfast Association of Sonoma Valley** (✉ 3250 Trinity Rd., Glen Ellen 95442, ☎ 707/938–9513 or 800/969–4667, WEB www.sonomabb.com). **Bed & Breakfast Exchange** (✉ 15 Angwin Plaza, Box 762, Angwin 94508, ☎ 707/965–3400, WEB www.apollotravel.net). **The Wine Country Inns of Sonoma County** (☎ 707/433–4667; 800/354–4743 brochure). **Wine Country Reservations** (☎ 707/257–7757).

TOURS

Full-day guided tours of the Wine Country usually include lunch and cost about $60 per person. The guides, some of whom are winery owners themselves, know the area well and may show you some lesser-known cellars. Reservations are usually required.Several companies offer bus tours of the Wine Country, with services ranging from full-size tour bus groups to customized tours for smaller parties ranging from six to 14 people. The Napa Valley Wine Train allows you to enjoy lunch, dinner, or weekend brunch on one of several restored 1915 Pullman railroad cars that run between Napa and St. Helena.

➤ Bus Tours: **Gray Line** (✉ 350 8th St., San Francisco 94103, ☎ 415/558–9400). **Great Pacific Tour Co.** (✉ 518 Octavia St., Civic Center, San Francisco 94102, ☎ 415/626–4499, WEB www.greatpacifictour.com). **HMS Travel Group** (✉ 707 4th St., Santa Rosa 95404, ☎ 707/526–2922 or 800/367–5348).

➤ Rail Tours: **Napa Valley Wine Train** (✉ 1275 McKinstry St., Napa 94559, ☎ 707/253–2111 or 800/427–4124, WEB www.winetrain.com).

VISITOR INFORMATION

➤ Tourist Information: **Napa Valley Conference and Visitors Bureau** (✉ 1310 Napa Town Center, Napa 94559, ☎ 707/226–7459, WEB www.napavalley.com). The **North Coast Visitors Bureau** (✉ The Cannery, 2801 Leavenworth St., 2nd floor, Fisherman's Wharf, San Francisco 94133, ☎ 415/394–5991). **Sonoma County Tourism Program** (✉ 520 Mendocino Ave., Suite 210, Santa Rosa 95401, ☎ 707/565–5383 or 800/576–6662, WEB www.sonomacounty.com). **Sonoma Valley Visitors Bureau** (✉ 453 1st St. E, Sonoma 95476, ☎ 707/996–1090, WEB www.sonomavalley.com).

6 SACRAMENTO AND THE GOLD COUNTRY

HIGHWAY 49 FROM NEVADA CITY TO MARIPOSA

The gold-mining region of the Sierra Nevada foothills is a less expensive, if less sophisticated, region of California, but it's not without its pleasures, natural and cultural. Spring brings wildflowers, and in fall the hills are colored by bright red berries and changing leaves. The hills are golden in the summer—and hot. The Gold Country has a mix of indoor and outdoor activities, one of the many reasons it's a great place to take the kids.

A NEW ERA DAWNED FOR CALIFORNIA when James Marshall turned up a gold nugget in the tailrace of a sawmill he was constructing along the American River. Before January 24, 1848, Mexico and the United States were still wrestling for ownership of what would become the Golden State. With Marshall's discovery the United States tightened its grip on the region, and prospectors from all over the world came to seek their fortunes in the Mother Lode.

Updated by
Reed Parsell

As gold fever seized the nation, California's population of 15,000 swelled to 265,000 within three years. The mostly young, mostly male adventurers who arrived in search of gold—the '49ers—became part of a culture that discarded many of the conventions of the eastern states. It was also a violent time. Yankee prospectors chased Mexican miners off their claims, and California's leaders initiated a plan to exterminate the local Native American population. Bounties were paid and private militias hired to wipe out the Native Americans or sell them into slavery. California was now to be dominated by the Anglo.

The boom brought on by the gold rush lasted scarcely 20 years, but it changed California forever. It produced 546 mining towns, of which fewer than 250 remain. The hills of the Gold Country were alive, not only with prospecting and mining but also with business, the arts, gambling, and a fair share of crime. Opera houses went up alongside brothels, and the California state capitol, in Sacramento, was built with the gold dug out of the hills. A lot of important history was made in Sacramento, the key center of commerce during this period. Pony Express riders ended their nearly 2,000-mi journeys in the city in the 1860s. The transcontinental railroad, completed in 1869, was conceived here.

By the 1960s the scars that mining had inflicted on the landscape had largely healed. To promote tourism, locals began restoring vintage structures, historians developed museums, and the state established parks and recreation areas to preserve this extraordinary episode in American history. Today you can come to Nevada City, Auburn, Coloma, Sutter Creek, and Columbia not only to relive the past but also to explore art galleries and to stay at inns full of character.

Pleasures and Pastimes

Adventuring
Scenic and challenging Gold Country rivers, particularly the American and Tuolumne, lure white-water enthusiasts each spring and summer. Early morning hot-air balloon excursions float above treetops in deep canyons of the American River. Throughout the region weekend prospectors pan for gold, turning up nuggets frequently enough to inspire others to participate.

Dining
American, Italian, and Mexican fare are common in the Gold Country, but chefs also prepare ambitious Continental, French, and California cuisine. It's not difficult to find the makings for a good picnic in most towns.

CATEGORY	COST*
$$$$	over $30
$$$	$22–$30
$$	$15–$21
$	under $15

*per person for a main course at dinner, excluding tip and 7¼% tax

Lodging

Full-service hotels, budget motels, small inns, and even a fine hostel can all be found in Sacramento. The main accommodations in the larger towns along Highway 49—among them Placerville, Nevada City, Auburn, and Mariposa—are chain motels and inns. Many Gold Country B&Bs occupy former mansions, miners' cabins, and other historic buildings.

CATEGORY	COST*
$$$$	over $225
$$$	$160–$225
$$	$100–$159
$	under $100

All prices are for a standard double room, excluding 7¼% tax (12% in Sacramento).

Shopping

Shoppers visit the Gold Country in search of antiques, collectibles, art, quilts, toys, tools, decorative items, and furnishings. Handmade quilts and crafts can be found in Sutter Creek, Jackson, and Amador City. Auburn and Nevada City support many gift boutiques.

Exploring Sacramento and the Gold Country

Visiting Old Sacramento's museums is a good way to steep yourself in history, but the Gold Country's heart lies along Highway 49, which winds the 325-mi north–south length of the historic mining area. The highway, often a twisting, hilly two-lane road, begs for a convertible with the top down.

Numbers in the text correspond to numbers in the margin and on the Gold Country and Sacramento maps.

Great Itineraries

IF YOU HAVE 1 DAY

Drive east from Sacramento on I–80 to **Auburn** ㉑ for a tour of the **Placer County Courthouse** and its museum. Travel south on Highway 49 to the **Marshall Gold Discovery State Historic Park**, at **Coloma** ㉒. Head back to Sacramento for a drink at the bar on the *Delta King* and an evening stroll and dinner along the waterfront in **Old Sacramento** ④– ⑧. The historical attractions will be closed, but you'll still get a feel for life here during the last half of the 19th century.

IF YOU HAVE 3 DAYS

Begin your tour on Highway 49 north of I–80. Walk deep into the recesses of the **Empire Mine**, near **Grass Valley** ⑳, and then drive 4 mi north on Highway 49 for a visit to the **Miners Foundry** in **Nevada City** ⑲. After lunch travel south to ⊞ **Auburn** ㉑, where you can take in the **Placer County Courthouse** and museum, have dinner, and spend the night. Early the next morning head south to tour **Marshall Gold Discovery State Historic Park**, in **Coloma** ㉒. Continue south to ⊞ **Sutter Creek** ㉕ and spend the afternoon exploring the boutiques and antiques stores. If exploring a good vintage is more your game, take a detour to the **Shenandoah Valley** ㉔, southeast of **Placerville** ㉓, and taste some wine. Either way, spend the night in Sutter Creek. Return early the next day to **Sacramento** to visit the **California State Railroad Museum** ① and **Sutter's Fort** ⑮.

IF YOU HAVE 5 DAYS

Visit the **Empire Mine, Nevada City** ⑲, and ⊞ **Auburn** ㉑ on day one. See **Coloma's** ㉒ **Marshall Gold Discovery State Historic Park** on the second day, and then continue on to ⊞ **Sutter Creek** ㉕. On your third morn-

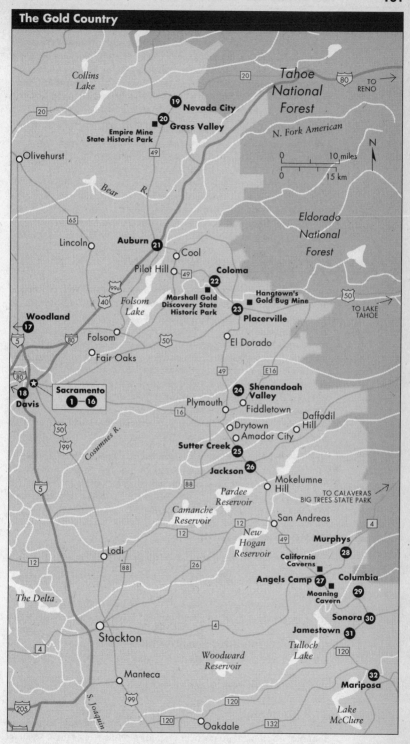

The Gold Country

Collins Lake

Tahoe National Forest

20

80 TO RENO

N. Fork American

19 Nevada City

20 Grass Valley

Empire Mine State Historic Park

20

49

Olivehurst

Bear R.

65

Eldorado National Forest

50

TO LAKE TAHOE

N

0 _____ 10 miles
0 _____ 15 km

Lincoln

Auburn **21**

Cool

Pilot Hill

49

Coloma

22

Marshall Gold Discovery State Historic Park

Hangtown's Gold Bug Mine

23 Placerville

TO LAKE TAHOE

99a

40

Folsom Lake

Woodland

17

80

Folsom

Fair Oaks

50

El Dorado

5

18 **Davis**

★

Sacramento

1 **16**

50

99

16

Plymouth

49

E16

24 Shenandoah Valley

Fiddletown

Daffodil Hill

Cosumnes R.

Drytown

Amador City

Sutter Creek **25**

Jackson **26**

Mokelumne Hill

TO CALAVERAS BIG TREES STATE PARK

88

Pardee Reservoir

Camanche Reservoir

12

New Hogan Reservoir

San Andreas

4

Lodi

12

88

26

49

California Caverns

Murphys

28

5

Angels Camp **27**

Moaning Cavern

Columbia

29

Stockton

4

4

Woodward Reservoir

Tulloch Lake

120

Sonora **30**

Jamestown **31**

The Delta

Manteca

99

120

32

Mariposa

205

S. Joaquin

120

Oakdale

132

Lake McClure

ing visit the **Amador County Museum,** in **Jackson** ㉖, before heading south on Highway 49 and east on Highway 4 for lunch in **Murphys** ㉘. Back on Highway 49 farther south is ☷ **Columbia State Historic Park,** in ☷ **Columbia** ㉙. You can relive the 1800s by dining and spending the night at the City Hotel. If you've been itching to pan for gold, do that in the morning in the state park, and then head back to ☷ **Sacramento** (Highway 49 north to Highway 16 west) for a riverboat cruise. Visit the **California State Railroad Museum** ① and **Sutter's Fort** ⑮ on day five.

When to Tour the Gold Country

The Gold Country is the most pleasant in the spring, when the wildflowers are in bloom, and in the fall. Summers are beautiful but hot: temperatures near or above 100°F are common. Sacramento winters tend to be cold and foggy. Throughout the year Gold Country towns stage community and ethnic celebrations. In December many towns deck themselves out for Christmas. Sacramento hosts the annual Jazz Jubilee over Memorial Day weekend and the California State Fair in August and early September. Flowers bloom on Daffodil Hill in March.

SACRAMENTO AND VICINITY

The gateway to the Gold Country, the seat of state government, and an agricultural hub, the city of Sacramento plays many important contemporary roles. Nearly 2 million people live in the metropolitan area, and the continuing influx of newcomers seeking opportunity, sunshine, and lower housing costs than in coastal California has made it one of the nation's fastest-growing regions. The central "midtown" area contains most of the city's culture and much of its charm, though pedestrians-only K Street Mall is not quite as clean and vibrant as city planners would have hoped when the downtown-revitalization project was conceived. Ten miles west is the college town of Davis, which like nearby Woodland is beginning to feel more suburban than agricultural because many Sacramento workers are settling there.

Sacramento contains more than 2,000 acres of natural and developed parkland. Grand old evergreens, deciduous and fruit-bearing trees (some streets are littered with oranges in springtime), and even giant palms give it a shady, lush quality. Genteel Victorian edifices sit side by side with art deco and postmodern skyscrapers.

Old Sacramento and Downtown

87 mi northeast of San Francisco, I–80 to Hwy. 99 or I–5 north.

Wooden sidewalks and horse-drawn carriages on cobblestone streets lend a 19th-century feel to Old Sacramento, a 28-acre district along the Sacramento River waterfront. The museums at the north end hold artifacts of state and national significance. Historic buildings house shops and restaurants. River cruises and train rides bring gold-rush history to life. Call the **Old Sacramento Events Hotline** (☎ 916/558–3912) for information about living-history re-creations and merchant hours. An entertaining audio tour of Old Sacramento can be found at kiosks placed throughout the historic district, which, when fed with special tokens or 50¢ in quarters, activate the voice of "Mark Twain" telling tales of the gold-rush days. A water taxi run by **River Otter Taxi Co.** (☎ 916/446–7704) serves the Old Sacramento waterfront during spring and summer, stopping at points near restaurants and other sights. **Channel Star Excursions** (✉ 110 L St., ☎ 916/552–2933 or 800/433–0263) operates the *Spirit of Sacramento,* a paddle-wheel riverboat, which takes passengers on happy-hour, dinner, luncheon, and champagne-brunch cruises in addition to one-hour narrated river tours.

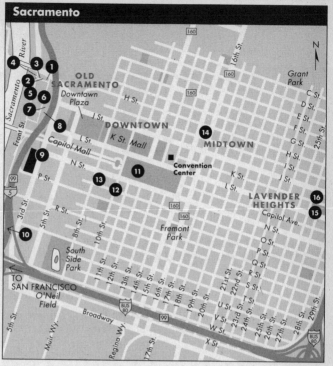

A Good Tour

Old Sacramento, the capitol and park surrounding it, and Sutter's Fort lie on an east–west axis that begins in the west at the Sacramento River. The walk from Old Sacramento to the state's capitol is easy, passing through the Downtown Plaza shopping mall and down K Street. This area becomes quite festive during an outdoor market held on Thursday evening. A DASH (Downtown Area Shuttle) bus and the No. 30 city bus both link Old Sacramento, the K Street Mall, the convention center, downtown, midtown, and Sutter's Fort in a loop that travels eastward on J Street and westward on L Street. The fare is 50¢ within this area, and buses run every 15 minutes weekdays, every 20 minutes Saturday, and every 30 minutes Sunday.

Park your car in the municipal garage under I–5 at 2nd Street (enter on I Street between 2nd and 3rd streets), and head to the superb **California State Railroad Museum** ①; then browse through the hardware and household items at the **Huntington, Hopkins & Co.** ② store. Next door are the hands-on exhibits of the **Discovery Museum** ③.

To learn more about Sacramento's role in rail history, walk a few paces south to the **Central Pacific Passenger Depot** ④. The **Central Pacific Freight Depot,** next to the passenger depot, houses a **public market** (closed Monday), whose merchants sell food and gift items. Across Front Street is the historic **Eagle Theater** ⑤. The foot of K Street (at Front Street) is a great spot for viewing the Sacramento River wharf area and the restored stern-wheeler the *Delta King*.

At the corner of 2nd and J streets is the historic **B. F. Hastings Building** ⑥. The **Old Sacramento Visitor Information Center** ⑦ is on 2nd Street in the same block as the **California Military Museum** ⑧. A must-see a few blocks south of Old Sacramento is the **Crocker Art Museum** ⑨, the oldest art museum in the American West. From here walk south on

Front Street to the **Towe Auto Museum** ⑩. If you'd rather skip the automotive museum, walk up 3rd Street to the Capitol Mall, which leads to the **capitol** ⑪. If you're still going strong, explore the **Golden State Museum** ⑫, at O and 10th streets, one block south of the capitol, and the **Leland Stanford Mansion** ⑬, a block west of that. Or walk north to H Street and then east to the **Governor's Mansion** ⑭. Otherwise, walk back to your car via J Street.

A bit more than a mile to the east, accessible via a ride on the DASH or No. 30 city bus, is **Sutter's Fort** ⑮. It was Sacramento's earliest Euro-American settlement; evocative exhibits bring that era back to life. North of the fort is the **State Indian Museum** ⑯.

TIMING

This tour makes for a leisurely day. Most of the attractions are open daily, except for the Military Museum, the Eagle Theater, the Crocker Art Museum, and the Golden State Museum, which are closed on Monday.

Sights to See

❻ B. F. Hastings Building. A reconstruction of the first chambers of the California Supreme Court occupies the second floor of this 1853 building. On the first floor there are a Wells Fargo History Museum and an ATM. ⊠ *1000 2nd St.,* ☎ *916/440–4263.* ☉ *Daily 10–5.*

❽ California Military Museum. A storefront entrance leads to three floors containing more than 30,000 artifacts—uniforms, weapons, photographs, documents, medals, and flags of all kinds—that trace Californians' roles in military and militia activities throughout U.S. history. An interesting display outlines military life for African-Americans. ⊠ *1119 2nd St.,* ☎ *916/442–2883.* 🎫 *$3.* ☉ *Tues.–Sun. 10–4.*

★ ✋ ❶ California State Railroad Museum. Near what was once the terminus of the transcontinental and Sacramento Valley railroads (the actual terminus was at Front and K streets), this 100,000-square-ft museum has 21 locomotives and railroad cars on display and 46 exhibits. You can walk through a post-office car and peer into cubbyholes and canvas bags of mail, enter a sleeping car that simulates the swaying on the roadbed and the flashing lights of a passing town at night, or glimpse the inside of the first-class dining car on the *Super Chief.* Allow at least two hours to enjoy the museum. ⊠ *125 I St.,* ☎ *916/445–6645,* WEB *www.csrmf.org.* 🎫 *$3.* ☉ *Daily 10–5.*

★ ⑪ Capitol. The Golden State's capitol was built in 1869. The lacy plasterwork of the 120-ft-high rotunda has the complexity and color of a Fabergé egg. Underneath the gilded dome are marble floors, glittering chandeliers, monumental staircases, original artwork, replicas of 19th-century state offices, and legislative chambers decorated in the style of the 1890s. Guides conduct tours of the building and the 40-acre Capitol Park, which contains a rose garden, an impressive display of camellias (Sacramento's city flower), and the California Vietnam Veterans Memorial. ⊠ *Capitol Mall and 10th St.,* ☎ *916/324–0333.* 🎫 *Free.* ☉ *Daily 9–5; tours hourly 9–4.*

✋ ❹ Central Pacific Passenger Depot. At this reconstructed 1876 station there's rolling stock to admire, a typical waiting room, and a small restaurant. Rides on a steam-powered train depart from the freight depot, south of the passenger depot. The train makes a 40-minute loop along the Sacramento riverfront. ⊠ *930 Front St.,* ☎ *916/445–6645.* 🎫 *$3 (free with same-day ticket from California State Railroad Museum); train ride $5 additional.* ☉ *Depot daily 10–5. Train Apr.–Sept. every weekend, Oct.–Dec 1st weekend of the month.*

⑨ Crocker Art Museum. The oldest art museum in the American West has a collection of art from Europe, Asia, and California, including *Sunday Morning in the Mines* (1872), a large canvas by Charles Christian Nahl depicting the mining industry of the 1850s, and the magnificent *The Great Canyon of the Sierra, Yosemite* (1871), by Thomas Hill. The museum's lobby and ballroom retain the original 1870s woodwork, plaster moldings, and imported English tiles. ⊠ *216 O St.,* ☎ *916/264–5423,* WEB *www.crockerartmuseum.org.* 🎫 *$6.* ☉ *Tues.–Wed. and Fri.–Sun. 10–5, Thurs. 10–9.*

③ Discovery Museum. The building that holds this child-oriented museum is a replica of the 1854 city hall and waterworks. The emphasis is on interactive exhibits that combine history, science, and technology to examine the evolution of everyday life in the Sacramento area. You can sift for gold, examine a Native American thatch hut, or experience the goings-on in the print shop of the old *Sacramento Bee* newspaper. The Gold Gallery displays nuggets and veins. ⊠ *101 I St.,* ☎ *916/264–7057.* 🎫 *$5.* ☉ *June–Aug., daily 10–5; Sept.–May, Tues.–Sun. 10–5.*

⑤ Eagle Theater. When the Eagle opened in 1849, audiences paid between $3 and $5 in gold coin or -dust to sit on rough boards and watch professional actors. This replica was constructed with the tentlike canvas and ship's-timber walls of olden times, though now there's insulation, and the bench seats are cushioned. The theater hosts programs that range from a 13-minute slide show called *City of the Plains* to puppet shows and juggling acts. ⊠ *925 Front St.,* ☎ *916/323–6343.* 🎫 *Fees vary depending on program.* ☉ *Tues.–Fri. 10–4.*

⑫ Golden State Museum. Drawing from the vast collections of the California State Archives, this state-of-the-art museum vividly portrays the story of California's land, people, and politics. Exhibits utilize modern technology, but there are also scores of archival drawers that you can pull out to see the real artifacts of history and culture—from the California State Constitution to surfing magazines. Board a 1949 cross-country bus to view a video on immigration, visit a Chinese herb shop inhabited by a holographic proprietor, or stand on a gubernatorial balcony overlooking a sea of cameras and banners. Admission includes the use of an innovative personal audio guide—choose an adult or children's program and the level of detail you desire for each exhibit. There's also a café where you can take a break from the fun. ⊠ *1020 O St., at 10th St.,* ☎ *916/653–7524,* WEB *www.goldenstatemuseum.org.* 🎫 *$5.* ☉ *Tues.–Sat. 10–5, Sun. noon–5.*

⑭ Governor's Mansion. This 15-room house was built in 1877 and used by the state's chief executives from the early 1900s until 1967, when Ronald Reagan vacated it in favor of a newly built home in the more upscale suburbs. Many of the Italianate mansion's interior decorative details were ordered from the Huntington, Hopkins & Co. hardware store, one of whose partners, Albert Gallatin, was the original occupant. Each of the seven marble fireplaces has a petticoat mirror that ladies strolled past to see if their slips were showing. The mansion is said to have been one of the first homes in California to have an indoor bathroom. ⊠ *1526 H St.,* ☎ *916/323–3047.* 🎫 *$1.* ☉ *Daily 10–4; tours hourly.*

② Huntington, Hopkins & Co. Store. This museum is a replica of the 1855 hardware store opened by Collis Huntington and Mark Hopkins, two of the Big Four businessmen who established the Central Pacific Railroad. Picks, shovels, gold pans, and other paraphernalia used by miners during the gold rush are on display, along with typical household hardware and appliances from the 1880s. Some items, such as blue enamelware, wooden toys, and oil lamps, are for sale. ⊠ *113 I St.,* ☎ *916/323–7234.* ⊙ *Hrs vary.*

⑬ Leland Stanford Mansion. The home of Leland Stanford, a railroad baron, California governor, and U.S. senator, was built in 1856, with additions in 1862 and the early 1870s. This once-grand edifice is currently undergoing major renovations. Some floors of the mansion, which will operate as a museum and a site for official state receptions, will be featured in tours that museum officials say might not be launched for another year or two, but meanwhile it is interesting to view the exterior transformation as it progresses. ⊠ *802 N St.,* ☎ *916/324–0575.*

❼ Old Sacramento Visitor Information Center. Obtain brochures about nearby attractions, check local restaurant menus, and get advice from the helpful staff here. ⊠ *1101 2nd St., at K St.,* ☎ *916/442–7644,* ᴡᴇʙ *www.oldsacramento.com.* ⊙ *Daily 10–5.*

⑯ State Indian Museum. Among the interesting displays at this well-organized museum is one devoted to Ishi, the last Yahi Indian to emerge from the mountains, in 1911. Ishi provided scientists with insight into the traditions and culture of this group of Native Americans. Arts-and-crafts exhibits, a demonstration village, and an evocative 10-minute video bring to life the multifaceted past and present of California's native peoples. ⊠ *2618 K St.,* ☎ *916/324–0971,* ᴡᴇʙ *www.parks.ca.gov.* ⊠ *$1.* ⊙ *Daily 10–5.*

★ ⊙ **⑮ Sutter's Fort.** Sacramento's earliest Euro-American settlement was founded by German-born Swiss immigrant John Augustus Sutter in 1839. Audio speakers at each stop along a self-guided tour explain exhibits that include a blacksmith's shop, a bakery, a prison, living quarters, and livestock areas. Costumed docents sometimes reenact fort life, demonstrating crafts, food preparation, and firearms maintenance. ⊠ *2701 L St.,* ☎ *916/445–4422,* ᴡᴇʙ *www.parks.ca.gov.* ⊠ *$1.* ⊙ *Daily 10–5.*

⊙ **❿ Towe Auto Museum.** With more than 150 vintage automobiles on display, and exhibits ranging from the Hall of Technology to Dreams of Speed and Dreams of Cool, this museum explores automotive history and car culture. Docents provide information about specific models, including a 1931 Chrysler, a 1960 Lotus, and a luxurious and sleek 1927 Hispano-Suiza. A 1920s roadside café and garage exhibit re-creates the early days of motoring. A gift shop sells vintage-car magazines, model kits, and other car-related items. ⊠ *2200 Front St., 1 block off Broadway,* ☎ *916/442–6802,* ᴡᴇʙ *www.toweautomuseum.org.* ⊠ *$6.* ⊙ *Daily 10–6.*

Dining

$$–$$$ ✕ **Biba.** Owner Biba Caggiano is an authority on Italian cuisine, author of several cookbooks, and the star of a national TV show on cook-
★   ing. The capitol crowd flocks here for homemade ravioli, osso buco, grilled pork loin, and veal and rabbit specials. ⊠ *2801 Capitol Ave.,* ☎ *916/455–2422. AE, DC, MC, V. Closed Sun. No lunch Sat.*

$$–$$$ ✕ **The Firehouse.** The menu includes rich and well-presented meals such as seared foie gras and pan-roasted elk with a blueberry-and-chestnut chutney in such formal surroundings that gentlemen might feel out of place without a tuxedo. The Firehouse consistently is rated by local publications as among the city's top 10 restaurants. ⊠ *1112 2nd St.,* ☎ *916/442–4772. AE, MC, V. Closed Sun. No lunch Sat.*

$$–$$$ ✕ **Twenty Eight.** An intimate space with smoked mirrors, a golden crushed-satin ceiling, richly upholstered furniture, and artful lighting, Twenty Eight further charms with genteel and attentive service. The food—appetizers such as roasted butternut squash soup and main courses that include sesame-crusted ahi tuna with crispy noodles and Colorado lamb chops with artichoke risotto and black olive sauce— is as refined as the room. ⊠ *2730 N. St.,* ☎ *916/456–2800. AE, D, DC, MC, V. Closed Sun. No lunch.*

$–$$$ ✕ **Rio City Café.** Eclectic lunch and dinner menus and huge floor-to-ceiling windows with views of an Old Sacramento wharf are the dual attractions of this bright restaurant. Rio City serves both light and hearty fare: calamari salad, New York steak with wild mushroom demiglace, mesquite-grilled salmon on garlic mashed potatoes, and duck breast with ginger-apple marmalade over couscous. ⊠ *1110 Front St.,* ☎ *916/ 442–8226. AE, D, DC, MC, V.*

$–$$ ✕ **Centro.** The motorcycle with a skeleton rider in the front window denotes the vibrant wackiness that spices up this popular midtown Mexican eatery. Bright yellow booths and salsa music make a contribution here, but the tasty food—well outside the taco-burrito realm—is the real attraction. Dishes include citrus-marinated rotisserie chicken with plantains and pork slow-roasted in banana leaves. The bar carries more than 60 Mexican tequilas, but it's easy to lose count after the first two. ⊠ *2730 J St.,* ☎ *916/442–2552. AE, DC, MC, V. No lunch weekends.*

$–$$ ✕ **Frank Fat's.** A longtime favorite of lawmakers and lobbyists, Frank Fat's is renowned more as a watering hole than as a restaurant. The menu of so-so Chinese food emphasizes Cantonese cuisine, but there are items from other regions as well. Signature dishes include brandy-fried chicken, honey-glazed walnut prawns, plus a couple of American items: New York steak and banana cream pie. ⊠ *806 L St.,* ☎ *916/442–7092. AE, MC, V. No lunch weekends.*

$–$$ ✕ **Paragary's Bar and Oven.** Pastas and brick-oven pizzas are the specialties of this casual spot. You won't go hungry here—portions are enormous. A waterfall flows near the back patio, which holds hundreds of plants. ⊠ *1401 28th St.,* ☎ *916/457–5737. AE, D, DC, MC, V. No lunch weekends.*

$–$$ ✕ **Tapa the World.** As defined at this midtown hot spot, tapas are bite-size portions of meats, seafood, chicken, and veggies shared at the table. One of Sacramento's liveliest night spots (it's open till midnight), Tapa presents Flamenco and Spanish classical music performers nightly. ⊠ *2125 J St.,* ☎ *916/442–4353. AE, D, DC, MC, V.*

$–$$ ✕ **The Waterboy.** Rural French and California cooking are the culi★ nary treasures at this increasingly popular midtown restaurant. Patrons always seem to be in a good mood, enjoying each other and such distinctive dishes as chicken potpie, veal sweetbreads, and beet salad. ⊠ *2000 Capitol Ave.,* ☎ *916/498–9891. AE, D, DC, MC, V. Closed Mon. No lunch weekends.*

Lodging

$$$–$$$$ 🏠 **Amber House Bed & Breakfast Inn.** This B&B near the capitol en★ compasses three separate homes. The original house, the Poet's Refuge, is a craftsman-style home with five bedrooms named for famous writers. Next door the 1913 Mediterranean-style Artist's Retreat has a French impressionist motif. The third, an 1897 Dutch colonial-revival home named Musician's Manor, has gardens where weddings occasionally take place. All rooms have private baths tiled with Italian marble. Several rooms have fireplaces and bathrooms with skylights and two-person hot tubs. ⊠ *1315 22nd St., 95816,* ☎ *916/444–8085 or 800/755– 6526,* ℻ *916/552–6529,* ᴡᴇʙ *www.amberhouse.com. 14 rooms. Some in-room hot tubs; no-smoking room. AE, D, DC, MC, V. BP.*

$$$–$$$$ 🏠 **Hyatt Regency at Capitol Park.** With a marble-and-glass lobby and ★ luxurious rooms, this hotel across from the capitol and adjacent to the convention center is arguably Sacramento's finest. The best rooms have Capitol Park views. The service and attention to detail are outstanding. ✉ *1209 L St., 95814,* ☎ *916/443–1234,* FAX *916/321–3799,* WEB *www.hyatt.com. 500 rooms, 24 suites. 2 restaurants, pool, gym, hot tub, bar, dry cleaning, laundry service, concierge, business services, meeting room, car rental, parking (fee). AE, D, DC, MC, V.*

$$$ 🏨 **Hartley House.** Innkeeper Randy Hartley's great-grandfather built Hartley House in 1906. The quiet midtown inn prides itself on having the feel of a small European hotel. All the antiques-filled rooms, which are named after British cities, have stereos and cable TV. Breakfast is cooked to order, and horse-and-carriage rides are available. ✉ *700 22nd St., 95816,* ☎ *916/447–7829 or 800/831–5806,* FAX *916/447–1820,* WEB *www.hartleyhouse.com. 5 rooms. Dining room, in-room data ports. AE, D, DC, MC, V. BP.*

$$$ 🏨 **The Sterling Hotel.** This gleaming white Victorian mansion just three blocks from the capitol has been transformed into a small luxury hotel. Rose-hue guest rooms have handsome furniture including four-poster or canopy beds. The bathrooms are tiled in Italian marble and have Jacuzzi tubs. Cookies or pastries baked on the premises are delivered to guests' rooms each evening. Restaurant Chanterelle ($15–$20) serves contemporary Continental cuisine in its candlelighted dining room and pleasant patio area. ✉ *1300 H St., 95814,* ☎ *916/448–1300 or 800/365–7660,* FAX *916/448–8066,* WEB *www.sterlinghotel.com. 17 rooms, 2 suites. Restaurant, bar, room service, in-room data ports, dry cleaning, business services, meeting room, parking (fee); no-smoking rooms. AE, D, DC, MC, V.*

$$–$$$ 🏨 **Delta King.** This grand old riverboat, now permanently moored on Old Sacramento's waterfront, once transported passengers between Sacramento and San Francisco. Among many notable design elements are its main staircase, mahogany paneling, and brass fittings. The best of the 43 staterooms are on the river side toward the back of the boat. ✉ *1000 Front St., 95814,* ☎ *916/444–5464 or 800/825–5464,* FAX *916/447–5959,* WEB *www.deltaking.com. 44 rooms. Restaurant, lounge, meeting room, parking (fee). AE, D, DC, MC, V. CP.*

$$ 🏨 **Holiday Inn Capitol Plaza.** Despite its decided lack of charm, this hotel has modern rooms and the best location for visiting Old Sacramento and the Downtown Plaza. It's also within walking distance of the capitol. ✉ *300 J St., 95814,* ☎ *916/446–0100,* FAX *916/446–7371,* WEB *www.holiday-inn.com. 362 rooms, 4 suites. Restaurant, bar, pool, convention center. AE, DC, MC, V.*

$$ 🏨 **Best Western Sutter House.** Many of the pleasant, modern rooms in this downtown hotel open onto a courtyard surrounding a pool. The stylish restaurant, Grape's, serves contemporary cuisine. ✉ *1100 H St., 95814,* ☎ *916/441–1314; 800/830–1314 in CA,* FAX *916/441–5961,* WEB *www.thesutterhouse.com. 97 rooms, 1 suite. Restaurant, pool, lounge, laundry service, free parking; no-smoking floor. AE, D, DC, MC, V. CP.*

$–$$ 🏨 **Radisson Hotel Sacramento.** Mediterranean-style two-story buildings clustered around a large artificial lake on an 18-acre landscaped site contain good-size rooms, with art deco appointments and furnishings. Many have patios or balconies. More of a resort than other Sacramento-area hotels, the Radisson presents summer jazz concerts in a lakeside amphitheater and holds barbecues on warm evenings. ✉ *500 Leisure La., 95815,* ☎ *916/922–2020 or 800/333–3333,* FAX *916/649–9463,* WEB *www.radisson.com/sacramentoca. 307 rooms, 22 suites. 2 restaurants, bar, room service, pool, gym, outdoor hot tub, boating, bicycles, meeting room. AE, D, DC, MC, V.*

$ 🏨 **Sacramento International Hostel.** This landmark 1885 Victorian mansion has a grand mahogany staircase, a stained-glass atrium, frescoed ceilings, and carved and tiled fireplaces. Dormitory rooms and bedrooms suitable for singles, couples, and families are available, as is a communal kitchen. ⊠ *900 H St., 95814,* ☎ *916/443–1691 or 800/ 909–4776 Ext. 40,* FAX *916/443–4763,* WEB *www.norcalhostels.org. 70 beds. Kitchen. MC, V.*

Nightlife and the Arts

Downtown Events Line (☎ 916/442–2500) has recorded information about seasonal events in the downtown area.

The **Blue Cue** (⊠ 1004 28th St., ☎ 916/442–7208), upstairs from Centro restaurant, is an eclectic billiard lounge known for its very large selection of single-malt scotches. The **Fox and Goose** (⊠ 1001 R St., ☎ 916/443–8825) is a casual pub with live music (including open-mike Monday). Traditional pub food (fish-and-chips, Cornish pasties) is served on weekday evenings from 5:30 to 9:30. **Harlow's** (⊠ 2708 J St., ☎ 916/441–4693) draws a young crowd to its art deco bar-nightclub for live music after 9. **Streets of London Pub** (⊠ 1804 J St., ☎ 916/498–1388) is popular among Anglophiles and stays open until 2 AM every night except Sunday, when it closes an hour earlier.

Sacramento Community Center Theater (⊠ 13th and L Sts., ☎ 916/264–5181) hosts concerts, opera, and ballet. The **Sacramento Light Opera Association** (⊠ 1419 H St., ☎ 916/557–1999) presents Broadway shows at the Sacramento Community Center Theater and in the huge Music Circus tent during summer. If you want the really *big* picture, the historic **Esquire Theater** (☎ 916/446–2333), at 13th Street on the K Street Mall, screens IMAX movies.

Outdoor Activities and Sports

The basement-level **California Family Health & Fitness** (⊠ 428 J St., at 5th St., ☎ 916/442–9090) has a workout area, weight machines, and a sauna. The fee for nonmembers is $10. **Jedediah Smith Memorial Bicycle Trail** runs for 23 mi from Old Sacramento to Beals Point in Folsom, mostly along the American River. The **Sacramento Kings** of the National Basketball Association play at the Arco Arena (⊠ 1 Sports Pkwy., ☎ 916/928–6900). The minor-league **Sacramento River Cats** baseball team is a major hit, playing before mostly sold-out crowds its first two seasons at West Sacramento's Raley Field (⊠ 400 Ballpark Dr., ☎ 916/371–4487).

Shopping

Top local artists and craftspeople exhibit their works at **Artists' Collaborative Gallery** (⊠ 1007 2nd St., ☎ 916/444–3764). The **Elder Craftsman** (⊠ 130 J St., ☎ 916/264–7762) specializes in items made by local senior citizens. **Gallery of the American West** (⊠ 121 K St., ☎ 916/446–6662) has a large selection of Native American arts and crafts.

Arden Fair Mall, northeast of downtown off I–80 in the north area, is Sacramento's largest shopping center. **Downtown Plaza,** comprising the K Street Mall along with many neighboring shops and restaurants, has shopping and entertainment. There's a Thursday-night market in the summer and an outdoor ice-skating rink in winter. **Pavilions Mall** (⊠ Fair Oaks Blvd. and Howe Ave.) has many boutiques.

Woodland

⑰ *20 mi northwest of Sacramento on I–5.*

Woodland's downtown core, 20 min north of Sacramento, lies frozen in a quaint and genteel past. In its heyday it was one of the wealthiest cities in California, established in 1861 by gold seekers and entrepreneurs. Once the boom was over, attention turned to the rich surrounding land, and the area became an agricultural gold mine. The legacy of the old land barons lives on in the Victorian homes that line Woodland's wide streets. Many of the houses have been restored and are surrounded by lavish gardens.

More than 300 touring companies, including Frank Kirk, the Acrobatic Tramp, and John Philip Sousa's marching band, appeared at **The Woodland Opera House,** built in 1885 (and rebuilt after it burned in 1892). Now restored, the building hosts a season of musical theater from September through July every year in addition to concerts. Weekly guided tours reveal old-fashioned stage technology. ⊠ *Main and 2nd Sts.* ☎ *530/666–9617,* WEB *for performance schedules, www.wohtheatre.org.* 🎫 *Tours free.* ◷ *Mon. and Tues. 10–2, weekends 2–4; tours Tues. noon–4.*

The former 10-room Classic Revival home of settler William Byas Gibson was purchased by volunteers and restored as the **Yolo Country Historical Museum.** You can see collections of furnishings and artifacts from the 1850s to 1930s. Old trees and established lawn cover the 2-acre site off Highway 113. ⊠ *512 Gibson Rd.,* ☎ *530/666–1045.* 🎫 *$2.* ◷ *Mon.–Tues. 10–4, weekends noon–4.*

Ancient trucks and farm machinery seem to rumble to life within this shedlike **Heidrick Ag History Center.** You can see the world's largest collection of antique agricultural equipment, plus interactive exhibits, a food court, gift shop, and a kids' play area. ⊠ *1962 Hays La.,* ☎ *530/666–9700,* FAX *530/666–9712,* WEB *www.aghistory.org.* 🎫 *$6.* ◷ *Weekdays 10–5, Sat. 10–6, Sun. 10–4.*

Dining and Lodging

$–$$$ ✕ **Morrison's Upstairs.** A Victorian building registered as a State Historic Landmark houses this restaurant. Downstairs is a bar, deli, and patio. The top floor, once the attic, is full of nooks and alcoves where you can have your meal. It's furnished throughout with polished wood tables that suit the style of the house. The menu lists burgers and sandwiches, scampi, Chinese chicken salad, pasta, and prime rib, with some vegetarian choices. ⊠ *428½ 1st St.,* ☎ *530/666–6176. AE, D, DC, MC, V.*

$ ✕ **Ludy's Main Street BBQ.** Here's a big, casual restaurant next door to the Opera House that looks like something out of the *Beverly Hillbillies.* You can tuck into huge portions of ribs, beef, chicken, or fish-and-chips, or have a half-pound burger slathered in red sauce. On the patio water misters cool you in summer and heaters keep you toasty in winter. There is a kids' menu. ⊠ *667 Main St.,* ☎ *530/666–4400. AE, MC, V.*

$ 🏨 **Best Western Shadow Inn.** Palm trees wave over the landscaped pool area at this two-story hotel. Some rooms have wet bars and kitchenettes, and a complimentary Continental breakfast is served. ⊠ *584 N. East St.,* ☎ *530/666–1251,* FAX *530/662–2804,* WEB *www.bestwestern.com. 120 rooms. Cable TV, pool, hot tub, laundry facilities, business services. AE, D, DC, MC, V. CP.*

$ 🏨 **Cinderella Motel Woodland.** The basic rooms at this two-story motel have combination or shower baths. ⊠ *99 W. Main St.,* ☎ *530/662–1091,* FAX *530/662–2804. Refrigerators, cable TV, in-room VCRs (and movies), pool, hot tub, some pets allowed (fee); no smoking. 30 rooms. AE, D, DC, MC, V.*

$ 🏨 **Valley Oaks Inn.** Rooms in this two-story motel have basic furnishings and amenities. ⊠ *600 N. East St.,* ☎ *530/666–5511. 62 rooms. Refrigerators, cable TV, pool. AE, D, DC, MC, V.*

Davis

18 *10 mi west of Sacramento; take I–80 to I–5.*

Though it began as and still is a rich agricultural area, Davis doesn't feel like a cow town. It's home to the University of California at Davis, whose students hang at the cafés and bookstores in the central business district, making the city feel a little more cosmopolitan. Davis is also known for its energy conservation programs and projects, including an entire solar village. In addition, it is a leading institution for wine education and has one of the top veterinary programs on the West Coast.

The center of action in town is the **Davis Campus of the University of California,** which ranks among the top 25 research universities in the United States. You can take tours of the campus, which depart from Buehler Alumni and Visitors Center. ✉ *1 Shields Ave.,* ☎ *530/752–8111,* WEB *www.ucdavis.edu.* ⊙ *Tours weekends at 11:30 and 1:30, weekdays by appointment.*

The work by northern California craftspeople displayed at the **Artery** (✉ 207 G St., ☎ 530/758–8330, www.arteryart.com), an artists' cooperative, includes decorative and functional ceramics, glass, wood, jewelry, fiber arts, painting, sculpture, drawing, and photography. ✉ *207 G St.,* ☎ *530/758–8330,* WEB *www.arteryart.com.* ⊙ *Mon.–Thurs. and Sat. 10–6, Fri. 10–9, Sun. noon–5.*

Dining and Lodging

$$$–$$$$ ✕ **Soga's.** Watercolors by local artists hang on the walls of this elegant restaurant. The California-style menu features variations on salmon fillet, swordfish, and veal and also offers vegetable plates. You can eat on the long, covered patio in good weather. ✉ *217 E St.,* ☎ *530/757–1733. Reservations essential. No lunch weekends. AE, D, MC, V.*

$–$$ ✕ **Café California.** The locals who gather at this downtown Davis eatery favor such dishes as a salad of prawns and baby greens with avocado-tarragon vinaigrette, Cajun-style prime rib with chili onion rings, and roast chicken with garlic mashed potatoes, served in a contemporary dining room set with white linens. ✉ *808 2nd St., 95616,* ☎ *530/757–2766,* FAX *530/758–5236. AE, MC, V.*

$–$$ 🛏 **Aggie Inn.** Named for the University of California at Davis Aggies, this hotel is less than a block from the campus. ✉ *245 First St., 95616,* ☎ *530/756–0352,* FAX *530/753–5738,* WEB *www.stayanight.com. Kitchenettes (some), in-room hot tubs (some), outdoor hot tub, sauna, laundry service. 25 rooms, 9 suites. AE, D, DC, MC, V.*

$–$$ 🛏 **Hallmark Inn.** Two buildings make up this inn, which is five blocks from the University of California campus and is next door to a restaurant. ✉ *110 F St.,* ☎ *800/753–0035,* WEB *www.hallmarkinn.com. 135 rooms. Restaurant, refrigerators (some), pool, free parking. AE, D, DC, MC, V.*

$ 🛏 **Best Western University Lodge.** This three-story lodge is a good place to stop if you have business at the university, which is one block away. ✉ *123 B St.,* ☎ *530/756–7890,* FAX *530/756–0245,* WEB *www.bestwestern.com. 53 rooms. Kitchenettes (some), microwaves, refrigerators, cable TV, spa, exercise equipment, some pets allowed. AE, D, DC, MC, V.*

THE GOLD COUNTRY

Highway 49 from Nevada City to Mariposa

Highway 49 winds the length of the gold-mining area, linking the towns of Nevada City, Grass Valley, Auburn, Placerville, Sutter Creek, Sonora, and Mariposa. Most are gentrified versions of once-rowdy mining camps, vestiges of which remain in roadside museums, old mining structures, and historic inns.

Nevada City

⑲ *62 mi north of Sacramento; take I–80 to Hwy. 49.*

Nevada City, once known as the Queen City of the Northern Mines, is the most appealing of the northern Mother Lode towns. The iron-shutter brick buildings that line the narrow downtown streets contain antiques shops, galleries, bookstores, boutiques, B&Bs, restaurants, and a winery. Horse-drawn carriage tours add to the romance, as do gas streetlamps. At one point in the 1850s Nevada City had a population of nearly 10,000, enough to support much cultural activity.

With its gingerbread-trim bell tower, **Firehouse No. 1** is one of the Gold Country's most photographed buildings. A museum, it houses gold-rush artifacts and a Chinese joss house (temple). Also on display are relics of the ill-fated Donner Party, a group of 19th-century travelers who, trapped in the Sierra Nevada by winter snows, were forced to cannibalize their dead in order to survive. ⊠ *214 Main St.,* ☎ *530/265–5468.* 🖼 *Donation requested.* ⊙ *Apr.–Nov., daily 11–4; Dec.–Mar., Thurs.–Sun. 11:30–4.*

The redbrick **Nevada Theatre,** constructed in 1865, is California's oldest theater building in continuous use. Mark Twain, Emma Nevada, and many other notable persons of bygone times appeared on its stage. Housed in the Nevada Theatre, the **Foothill Theater Company** (☎ *530/ 265–8587* or *888/730–8587*) screens films and hosts theatrical and musical events. ⊠ *401 Broad St.,* ☎ *530/265–6161; 530/274–3456 for film show times.*

The **Miners Foundry,** erected in 1856, produced machines for gold mining and logging. The Pelton Water Wheel, a source of power for the mines (the wheel also jump-started the hydroelectric power industry), was invented here. A cavernous building, the foundry hosts plays, concerts, an antiques show, weddings, receptions, and other events. ⊠ *325 Spring St.,* ☎ *530/265–5040.*

You can watch while you sip at the **Nevada City Winery,** where the tasting room overlooks the production area. ⊠ *Miners Foundry Garage, 321 Spring St.,* ☎ *530/265–9463* or *800/203–9463,* ᴡᴇʙ *www. ncwinery.com.* ⊙ *Tastings daily noon–5.*

Dining and Lodging

$$–$$$$ ✕ **Country Rose Café.** The lengthy country-French menu at this antiques-laden café includes seafood, beef, lamb, chicken, and ratatouille. If you crave seafood, try the swordfish Oscar, topped with crab, shrimp, and béarnaise sauce. In the summer there is outdoor service on a verdant patio. ⊠ *300 Commercial St.,* ☎ *530/265–6248. AE, D, DC, MC, V.*

$$–$$$ ✕ **Friar Tuck's.** A guitar player performs (and patrons sing along) at this vaguely retro-1960s gathering spot, which feels like a wine cellar. Rack of lamb, roast duck, fondue, Iowa beef, and Hawaiian fish specials are on the menu. There's an extensive wine and beer list as well as a full bar. ⊠ *111 N. Pine St.,* ☎ *530/265–9093. AE, MC, V. No lunch.*

$$–$$$ ✕ **Kirby's Creekside Restaurant & Bar.** This two-level restaurant-bar complex perches over the quieter side of Deer Creek. You can dine on the large outdoor deck in warm weather or sit by the fireplace on chilly days. Among the inventive Continental preparations is the pork loin stuffed with roasted peppers. If you choose the Chef's Culinary Ad-

venture, the chef will design a 3- to 6-course meal for you based on your food preferences. ⊠ *101 Broad St.,* ☎ *530/265–3445. AE, D, MC, V.*

$–$$ ✕ **Cirino's.** American-Italian dishes—seafood, pasta, and veal—are served at this informal bar and grill. The restaurant's handsome Brunswick bar is of gold-rush vintage. ⊠ *309 Broad St.,* ☎ *530/265– 2246. AE, D, MC, V.*

$$–$$$ ▥ **Deer Creek Inn.** The main veranda of this 1860 Queen Anne Victorian overlooks a huge lawn that rolls past a rose-covered arbor to the creek below. You can play croquet on the lawn or pan for gold in the creek. All rooms have king- or queen-size beds. Some rooms have two-person tubs. Wine service and a full breakfast are included. ⊠ *116 Nevada St., 95959,* ☎ *530/265–0363 or 800/655–0363,* ℻ *530/265– 0980,* ⓦⓔⓑ *www.deercreekinn.com. 5 rooms. AE, MC, V. BP.*

$$–$$$ ▥ **Flume's End.** This charming inn was built in 1860 at the end of a large flume that once brought water into Nevada City's mines. The soothing sound of the waterfall now lulls you to sleep. Lovely hardwood floors and antiques add an air of elegance. Two guest rooms have hot tubs, and most, including a small cottage, have creek views. ⊠ *317 S. Pine St., 95959,* ☎ *530/265–9665 or 800/991–8118,* ⓦⓔⓑ *www. flumesend.com. 6 rooms. MC, V. BP.*

$$–$$$ ▥ **Red Castle Historic Lodgings.** A state landmark, this 1857 Gothic-
★ revival mansion stands on a forested hillside overlooking Nevada City. Its brick exterior is trimmed with white-icicle woodwork. A steep private pathway leads down through the terraced gardens into town. Handsome antique furnishings and Oriental rugs decorate the rooms. Home-cooked dishes are featured at the opulent afternoon tea and morning breakfast buffet. ⊠ *109 Prospect St., 95959,* ☎ *530/265–5135 or 800/761–4766,* ⓦⓔⓑ *www.historic-lodgings.com. 4 rooms, 3 suites. MC, V. BP.*

$–$$ ▥ **Northern Queen Inn.** Most accommodations at this bright creek-side inn are typical motel units, but there are eight two-story chalets and eight rustic cottages with efficiency kitchens and gas-log fireplaces in a secluded wooded area. If you stay here, you can ride free on the hotel's narrow-gauge railroad, which offers excursions through Maidu Indian homelands and a Chinese cemetery from gold-rush days. ⊠ *400 Railroad Ave. (Sacramento St. exit off Hwy. 49), 95959,* ☎ *530/265–5824 or 800/226–3090,* ℻ *530/265–3720,* ⓦⓔⓑ *www.northernqueeninn.com. 70 rooms, 16 suites. Restaurant, kitchenettes (some), refrigerators, pool, hot tub, convention center. AE, D, DC, MC, V.*

Grass Valley

㉑ *4 mi south of Nevada City on Hwy. 49.*

More than half of California's total gold production was extracted from mines around Grass Valley. Unlike in neighboring Nevada City, urban sprawl surrounds Grass Valley's historic downtown. The Empire Mine and the North Star Power House are among the Gold Country's most fascinating exhibits.

In the center of town, on the site of the original, stands a reproduction of the **Lola Montez House,** home of the notorious dancer. Montez, who arrived in Grass Valley in the early 1850s, was no great talent—her popularity among miners derived from her suggestive spider dance—but her loves, who reportedly included composer Franz Liszt, were legendary. According to one account, she arrived in California after having been "permanently retired from her job as Bavarian king Ludwig's mistress," literary muse, and political adviser. She seems to have pushed too hard for democracy, which contributed to his overthrow and her banishment as a witch—or so the story goes. The memory of licentious Lola lingers in Grass Valley, as does her bathtub (on the front porch of the house). The Grass Valley/Nevada County Chamber of Commerce is headquartered here. ⊠ *248 Mill St.,* ☎ *530/273–4667 or 800/655–4667.*

The landmark **Holbrooke Hotel,** built in 1851, hosted Lola Montez, Mark Twain, and Ulysses S. Grant and a stream of other U.S. presidents. Its restaurant-saloon is one of the oldest still operating west of the Mississippi. ⊠ *212 W. Main St.,* ☎ *530/273–1353 or 800/933–7077.*

★   The hard-rock gold mine at **Empire Mine State Historic Park** was one of California's richest. An estimated 5.8 million ounces were extracted from its 367 mi of underground passages between 1850 and 1956. On the 50-minute tours you can walk into a mine shaft, peer into the mine's deeper recesses, and view the owner's "cottage," which has exquisite woodwork. The visitor center has mining exhibits, and a picnic area is nearby. ⊠ *10791 E. Empire St. (exit south from Hwy. 49),* ☎ *530/273–8522,* WEB *www.parks.ca.gov.* ⊠ *$1.* ☼ *May–Aug., daily 9–6; Sept.–Apr., daily 10–5; tours May–Aug., daily on the hr 11–4; Sept.–Apr., weekends at 1 (cottage only) and 2 (mine yard only), weather permitting.*

☾   Housed in the former North Star powerhouse, the **North Star Mining Museum** displays a 32-ft-high enclosed Pelton waterwheel said to be the largest ever built. It was used to power mining operations and was a forerunner of the modern turbines that generate hydroelectricity. Hands-on displays are geared to children. There's a picnic area nearby. ⊠ *Empire and McCourtney Sts. (Empire St. exit north from Hwy. 49),* ☎ *530/273–4255.* ⊠ *Donation requested.* ☼ *May–mid-Oct., daily 10–5.*

Lodging

$ 🛏 **Holiday Lodge.** This modest hotel is close to many of the town's main attractions and offers gold-panning excursions from mid-May through mid-October ($20 per person), in addition to year-round historical tours. There is a complimentary Continental breakfast. ⊠ *1221 E. Main St., 95945,* ☎ *530/273–4406 or 800/742–7125. 35 rooms. Pool, sauna. AE, MC, V. CP.*

Auburn

㉑   *24 mi south of Grass Valley on Hwy. 49, 34 mi northeast of Sacramento on I–80.*

Auburn is the Gold Country town most accessible to travelers on the interstate. An important transportation center during the gold rush, Auburn has a small Old Town district with narrow climbing streets, cobblestone lanes, wooden sidewalks, and many original buildings. Fresh produce, flowers, baked goods, and gifts are for sale at the farmers' market, held Saturday morning year-round.

A $1 **trolley** operated by the Placer County Visitor Information Center (☎ *530/887–2111 or 800/427–6463*) loops through downtown and Old Town, with stops at some hotels and inns.

Auburn's standout structure is the **Placer County Courthouse.** The classic gold-dome building houses the Placer County Museum, which documents the area's history—Native American, railroad, agricultural, and mining—from the early 1700s to 1900. ⊠ *101 Maple St.,* ☎ *530/889–6500.* ⊠ *Free.* ☼ *Tues.–Sun. 10–4.*

The **Bernhard Museum Complex,** whose centerpiece is the former Traveler's Rest Hotel, was built in 1851. A residence and adjacent winery buildings reflect family life in the late Victorian era. The carriage house contains period conveyances. ⊠ *291 Auburn-Folsom Rd.,* ☏ *530/889–6500.* ⌨ *$1 (includes entry to Gold Country Museum).* ☉ *Tues.–Fri. 10:30–3, weekends noon–4.*

The **Gold Country Museum** surveys life in the mines. Exhibits include a walk-through mine tunnel, a gold-panning stream, and a replica saloon. ⊠ *1273 High St., off Auburn-Folsom Rd.,* ☏ *530/889–6500.* ⌨ *$1 (includes entry to Bernhard Museum Complex).* ☉ *Tues.–Fri. 10–3:30, weekends 11–4.*

Dining and Lodging

$$–$$$ ✕ **Latitudes.** Delicious multicultural cuisine is served up in an 1870 Victorian. The menu (with monthly specials from diverse geographical regions) includes seafood, chicken, beef, and turkey entrées prepared with Mexican spices, curries, cheeses, or teriyaki sauce. Sunday brunch is deservedly popular, as are evenings at the bar downstairs, where mellow live music is performed Friday and Saturday. ⊠ *130 Maple St.,* ☏ *530/885–9535. AE, D, MC, V. No lunch Sat., no dinner Mon.–Tues.*
★

$–$$ ✕ **Le Bilig French Café.** Simple and elegant cuisine is the goal of the chefs at this country-French café on the outskirts of Auburn. Escargots, coq au vin, and quiche are standard offerings; specials might include salmon in parchment paper. ⊠ *11750 Atwood Rd., off Hwy. 49 near the Bel Air Mall,* ☏ *530/888–1491. MC, V. Closed Mon.–Tues. No lunch.*

$ ✕ **Awful Annie's.** Big patio umbrellas (and outdoor heaters when necessary) allow patrons to take in the view of the Old Town from this popular spot for breakfast—one specialty is a chili omelet—or lunch. ⊠ *160 Sacramento St.,* ☏ *530/888–9857. AE, MC, V. No dinner.*

$–$$$ ⌂ **Powers Mansion Inn.** This inn hints at the lavish lifestyle enjoyed by the gold-rush gentry. Two light-filled parlors have gleaming oak floors, Asian antiques, and ornate Victorian chairs and settees. A second-floor maze of narrow corridors leads to the guest rooms, which have brass and pencil-post beds. The honeymoon suite has a fireplace and heart-shape hot tub. ⊠ *164 Cleveland Ave., 95603,* ☏ *530/885–1166,* ℻ *530/885–1386,* ᴡᴇʙ *www.vfr.net/~powerinn. 10 rooms, 3 suites. AE, MC, V. BP.*

$$ ⌂ **Holiday Inn.** On a hill above the freeway across from Old Auburn, the hotel has an imposing columned entrance but a welcoming lobby. Rooms are chain-standard but attractively furnished. All have work areas and coffeemakers. Those nearest the parking lot can be noisy. ⊠ *120 Grass Valley Hwy., 95603,* ☏ *530/887–8787 or 800/814–8787,* ℻ *530/887–9824,* ᴡᴇʙ *www.6c.com. 96 rooms, 6 suites. Restaurant, room service, in-room data ports, pool, gym, spa, bar, business services, convention center. AE, D, DC, MC, V.*

$ ⌂ **Best Inns and Suites.** The contemporary-style rooms at this well-maintained property are softened with teal and pastel colors. Though a short distance from the freeway, the inn is fairly quiet. The expanded Continental breakfast includes many choices of baked goods, cereals, fruits, and juices. ⊠ *1875 Auburn Ravine Rd. (Forest Hill exit north from I–80), 95603,* ☏ *530/885–1800 or 800/626–1900,* ℻ *530/888–6424. 77 rooms, 2 suites. Pool, spa, exercise room, laundry facilities, meeting room; no-smoking floor. AE, D, DC, MC, V. CP.*

Coloma

㉒ *18 mi south of Auburn on Hwy. 49.*

The California gold rush started in Coloma. "My eye was caught with the glimpse of something shining in the bottom of the ditch," James

Marshall recalled. Marshall himself never found any more "color," as gold came to be called.

★ Most of Coloma lies within **Marshall Gold Discovery State Historic Park.** Though crowded with tourists in summer, Coloma hardly resembles the mob scene it was in 1849, when 2,000 prospectors staked out claims along the streambed. The town's population grew to 4,000, supporting seven hotels, three banks, and many stores and businesses. But when reserves of the precious metal dwindled, prospectors left as quickly as they had come. A working replica of an 1840s mill lies near the spot where James Marshall first saw gold. A trail leads to a monument marking Marshall's discovery. The museum is not as interesting as the outdoor exhibits. ⊠ *Hwy. 49,* ☎ *530/622–3470,* WEB *www.parks.ca.gov.* ☞ *$2 per vehicle (day use).* ☉ *Park daily 8 AM–sunset. Museum Memorial Day–Labor Day, daily 10–5; Labor Day–Memorial Day, daily 10–4:30.*

Lodging

$$ ⛫ **Coloma Country Inn.** Five of the rooms at this B&B on 5 acres in the state historic park are inside a restored 1852 Victorian. Two suites, one with a kitchenette, are in the carriage house. Appointments include antique double and queen-size beds, handmade quilts, stenciled friezes, and fresh flowers. Hot-air ballooning and rafting excursion packages are available. ⊠ *345 High St., 95613,* ☎ *530/622–6919,* FAX *530/622–1795,* WEB *www.colomacountryinn.com. 5 rooms, 3 with bath; 2 suites. Kitchenette. No credit cards. BP.*

Placerville

㉓ *10 mi south of Coloma on Hwy. 49, 44 mi east of Sacramento on Rte. 50.*

It's hard to imagine now, but in 1849 about 4,000 miners staked out every gully and hillside in Placerville, turning the town into a rip-roaring camp of log cabins, tents, and clapboard houses. The area was then known as Hangtown, a graphic allusion to the nature of frontier justice. It took on the name Placerville in 1854 and became an important supply center for the miners. Mark Hopkins, Philip Armour, and John Studebaker were among the industrialists who got their starts here.

★ ♺ **Hangtown's Gold Bug Mine,** owned by the City of Placerville, centers around a fully lighted mine shaft open for self-guided touring. A shaded stream runs through the park, and there are picnic facilities. ⊠ *1 mi off Rte. 50, north on Bedford Ave.,* ☎ *530/642–5207,* WEB *www.goldbugpark.org.* ☞ *$3.* ☉ *Tours mid-Apr.–Oct., daily 10–4; Nov.–mid-Apr., weekends 10–4. Gift shop Mar.–Nov., daily 10–4.*

OFF THE BEATEN PATH **APPLE HILL –** Roadside stands sell fresh produce from more than 50 family farms in this area. During the fall harvest season (from September through December) members of the Apple Hill Growers Association open their orchards and vineyards for apple and berry picking, picnicking, and wine- and cider tasting. Many sell baked items and picnic food. ⊠ *About 5 mi east of Hwy. 49; take Camino exit from Rte. 50,* ☎ *530/644–7692.*

Dining and Lodging

$$–$$$ ✕ **Café Luna.** Tucked into the back of the Creekside Place shopping complex is a small restaurant with about 30 seats inside, plus outdoor tables overlooking a creek. The menu, which changes weekly, encompasses many ethnic foods, including Indian, Russian, and Thai. ⊠ *451 Main St.,* ☎ *530/642–8669. AE, D, MC, V. Closed Sun. No dinner Mon.–Tues.*

$$-$$$ ✕ **Zachary Jacques.** It's not easy to locate, so call for directions, be-
★ cause finding this country-French restaurant is worth the effort. Appetizers on the seasonal menu might include escargots or mushrooms
prepared in several ways, roasted garlic with olive oil served on toast,
or spicy lamb sausage. Entrées such as roast rack of lamb, beef stew,
and scallops and prawns in lime butter receive traditional preparation.
The attached wine bar, open during the daytime, sells box lunches to
go. ✉ *1821 Pleasant Valley Rd. (3 mi east of Diamond Springs),* ☎
530/626–8045. AE, MC, V. Closed Mon.–Tues. No lunch.

$–$$ ✕ **Lil' Mama D. Carlo's Italian Kitchen.** This comfortable Italian restau-
rant with a pleasant staff serves large portions of homemade pasta,
chicken, and some vegetarian dishes, heavy on the garlic. A wine bar,
featuring local varieties, opened in 2001. ✉ *482 Main St.,* ☎ *530/626–
1612. AE, MC, V. Closed Mon.–Tues. No lunch.*

$$–$$$ 🏠 **Shadowridge Ranch and Lodge.** In the wooded hills outside Plac-
erville, you'll find a beautifully restored rustic lodge complex. The im-
maculate hand-hewn log-and-stone cottages, most with wood-burning
stoves, are filled with interesting artifacts of ranch and lodge life—including some dramatic stuffed specimens—and modern amenities.
Each unit has its own patio. In the afternoon complimentary local wines
and a huge appetizer platter are laid out. ✉ *3700 Fort Jim Rd., 95667,*
☎ *530/295–1000 or 800/644–3498,* FAX *530/626–5613,* WEB *www.
shadowridgeranch.com. 4 suites. Minibars, refrigerators, hiking; no-
smoking room. AE, MC, V. Closed Jan.–Mar. BP.*

$$ 🏠 **The Seasons Bed & Breakfast.** A 10-minute walk from downtown,
one of Placerville's oldest historic homes has been transformed into a
lovely and relaxing oasis. The main house, two cottages, and the gar-
dens are filled with original artwork. Privacy is treasured here. A suite
with a sitting room and stained-glass windows fills the main house's
top floor. One cottage has a little white picket fence around its own
minigarden; the other has a two-person shower. ✉ *2934 Bedford Ave.,
95667,* ☎ *530/626–4420,* WEB *www.theseasons.net. 3 rooms, 1 suite.
No-smoking room. MC, V. BP.*

$ 🏠 **Best Western Placerville Inn.** This motel's serviceable rooms are done
in the chain's trademark pastels. The pool comes in handy during the
hot summer months. ✉ *6850 Greenleaf Dr., near Missouri Flats exit
of Rte. 50, 95667,* ☎ *530/622–9100 or 800/854–9100,* FAX *530/622–
9376,* WEB *www.bestwestern.com. 105 rooms. Restaurant, pool, out-
door hot tub. AE, D, DC, MC, V.*

Shenandoah Valley

㉔ *20 mi south of Placerville on Shenandoah Rd., east of Hwy. 49.*

The most concentrated Gold Country wine-touring area lies in the hills
of the Shenandoah Valley, east of Plymouth. Robust zinfandel is the
primary grape grown here, but vineyards also produce cabernet sauvi-
gnon, sauvignon blanc, and other varietals. Most wineries are open on
weekend afternoons; several have shaded picnic areas, gift shops, and
galleries or museums.

Sobon Estate (✉ 14430 Shenandoah Rd., ☎ 209/245–6554) operates
the Shenandoah Valley Museum, illustrating pioneer life and wine mak-
ing in the valley. It's open daily from 9:30 to 5. **Charles Spinetta
Winery** (✉ 12557 Steiner Rd., ☎ 209/245–3384, WEB www.
charlesspinettawinery.com), where you can see a wildlife art gallery
in addition to tasting the wine, is open daily between 9 and 4. The
gallery at **Shenandoah Vineyards** (✉ 12300 Steiner Rd., ☎ 209/
245–4455), open daily from 10 to 5, displays contemporary art.

Lodging

$$–$$$ 🏨 **Indian Creek Bed & Breakfast.** This log-and-stone lodge near Plymouth is a western movie buff's *and* a nature lover's dream. Built in 1932 by a Hollywood producer who hosted parties for stars such as John Wayne, the house emphasizes a Hollywood version of the West. The two-story great room is dominated by a 28-ft-high stone fireplace, while the dining room (where breakfast is served) is dominated by a 14-ft oak table. The 10-acre spread includes a creek and frog pond and is a haven for birds of all kinds. All rooms now have fireplaces. ⊠ *21950 Hwy. 49, 95669,* ☎ *209/245–4648,* FAX *209/245–3230,* WEB *www. indiancreek.com. 4 rooms. Dining room, pool, outdoor hot tub. D, MC, V. BP.*

$$ 🏨 **Amador Harvest Inn.** This B&B adjacent to Deaver Vineyards occupies a bucolic lakeside spot in the Shenandoah Valley. A contemporary Cape Cod–style structure has homey guest rooms with private baths. Public areas include a living room with fireplace and a music room with a view of the lake. ⊠ *12455 Steiner Rd., 95669,* ☎ *209/245–5512 or 800/217–2304,* FAX *209/245–5250,* WEB *www.amadorharvestinn.com. 4 rooms. AE, MC, V. BP.*

Amador City

6 mi south of Plymouth on Hwy. 49.

The history of tiny Amador City mirrors the boom-bust-boom cycle of many Gold Country towns. With an output of $42 million in gold, its Keystone Mine was one of the most productive in the Mother Lode. After all the gold was extracted, the miners cleared out, and the area suffered. Amador City now derives its wealth from tourists, who come to browse through its antiques and specialty shops, many of them on or off Highway 49.

Dining and Lodging

$–$$ ✕🏨 **Imperial Hotel.** The whimsically decorated mock-Victorian rooms
★ at this 1879 hotel give a modern twist to the excesses of the era. Antique furnishings include iron and brass beds, gingerbread flourishes, and, in one room, art deco appointments. The two front rooms, which can be noisy, have balconies. The hotel's fine dinner-only restaurant (closed Mon.), whose menu changes quarterly, serves meals in a bright dining room and on the patio. The cuisine ranges from vegetarian to country hearty to contemporary eclectic. There is a 2-night minimum stay on weekends. ⊠ *Hwy. 49, 95601,* ☎ *209/267–9172 or 800/242–5594,* FAX *209/267–9249,* WEB *www.imperialamador.com. 6 rooms. Restaurant, bar. AE, D, DC, MC, V. BP.*

Sutter Creek

★ ㉕ *2 mi south of Amador City on Hwy. 49.*

Sutter Creek is a charming conglomeration of balconied buildings, Victorian homes, and neo–New England structures. The stores along Highway 49 (called Main Street in the town proper) are worth visiting for works by the many local artists and craftspeople. Seek out the **J. Monteverde General Store** (⊠ 3 Randolph St.; closed Jan.), a typical turn-of-the-20th-century emporium with vintage goods on display (but not for sale), an elaborate antique scale, and a chair-encircled pot-bellied stove in the corner. The museum is open weekends 10–3. You can also stop by the **Sutter Creek Visitor Center** (11A Randolph St., ☎ 209/267–1344 or 800/400–0305).

OFF THE
BEATEN PATH

DAFFODIL HILL – Each spring a 4-acre hillside east of Sutter Creek erupts in a riot of yellow and gold as 300,000 daffodils burst into bloom. The garden is the work of members of the McLaughlin family, which has owned this site since 1887. Daffodil plantings began in the 1930s. The display usually takes place between mid-March and mid-April. ⊠ *From Main St. (Hwy. 49) in Sutter Creek take Shake Ridge Rd. east 13 mi,* ☎ *209/223–0350,* WEB *www.amadorcountychamber.com.* 🎟 *Free.* ☉ *Mid-Mar.–mid-Apr., daily 9–5.*

Dining and Lodging

$$–$$$ ✕ **Zinfandel's.** Black-bean chili in an edible bread tureen and smoked mussels and bay shrimp with roasted garlic cloves are among the appetizers at this casual restaurant with an adventurous menu. A favorite entrée is rack of lamb marinated in red wine, rosemary, and garlic on garlic smashed potatoes with mushroom port sauce. There's also a cozy wine-and-espresso bar with a fireplace, open Friday and Saturday nights. ⊠ *51 Hanford St.,* ☎ *209/267–5008. AE, D, MC, V. Closed Mon.–Wed. No lunch.*

$–$$$ ✕ **Chatterbox Café.** This classic 1940s luncheonette has only five tables and 14 counter stools. Read a vintage newspaper or examine the jazz instruments and Disney memorabilia on the shelves while you wait for your chicken-fried steak, burger, homemade pie, or hot-fudge sundae. The menu is as big as the Chatterbox is small. Beer and wine are available. Dinner, a five-course prix-fixe affair served on Tuesday night only, is fancier and more expensive ($$$), with such offerings as prime rib and shrimp scampi. ⊠ *39 Main St.,* ☎ *209/267–5935. AE, D, MC, V. No dinner Wed.–Mon.*

$ ✕ **Back Roads Coffee House.** Airy and spacious, Back Roads is roughly in the middle of a frenzied four-block stretch of Highway 49 where traffic crawls and sidewalks bulge. Muffins, pastries, and coffee seem to be the biggest draws here, though hot, simple breakfasts are available. The lunch menu includes soups and salads. All the tables have a small stack of Trivial Pursuit cards, which should amuse baby boomers. ⊠ *74 Main St.,* ☎ *209/267–0440. D, MC, V. No dinner.*

$$–$$$ ★ 🛏 **The Foxes Bed & Breakfast.** The rooms in this 1857 white-clapboard house are handsome, with high ceilings, antique beds, and armoires. All have queen-size beds; five have wood-burning fireplaces or cable TV with VCRs. Breakfast is cooked to order and delivered on a silver service to your room or to the gazebo in the garden. Innkeepers Min and Pete Fox have pampered guests here since 1980, and they are full of local lore. ⊠ *77 Main St., 95685,* ☎ *209/267–5882 or 800/987–3344,* FAX *209/267–0712,* WEB *www.foxesinn.com. 5 rooms, 2 suites. No-smoking room. D, MC, V. BP.*

$$–$$$ 🛏 **Grey Gables Inn.** Charming yet modern, this inn brings a touch of the English countryside to the Gold Country. The rooms, named after British literary figures, have gas-log fireplaces. Afternoon tea and evening refreshments are served in the parlor. Birds flit about the wisteria in the terraced garden. ⊠ *161 Hanford St., 95685,* ☎ *209/267–1039 or 800/473–9422,* FAX *209/267–0998,* WEB *www.greygables.com. 8 rooms. MC, V. BP.*

$$ 🛏 **Eureka Street Inn.** Original redwood paneling, wainscoting, beams, and cabinets as well as lead- and stained-glass windows lend the Eureka Street Inn—formerly the Picture Rock Inn—a certain coziness. The craftsman-style bungalow was built in 1914 as a family home. Most rooms have gas-log fireplaces. ⊠ *55 Eureka St., 95685,* ☎ *209/267–5500 or 800/399–2389,* WEB *www.eurekastreetinn.com. 4 rooms. AE, D, MC, V. BP.*

$ ⊡ **Aparicio's Hotel.** If you're touring the Gold Country on a budget, this hotel is a good choice. The rooms contain two queen-size beds, and three rooms are wheelchair accessible. ⊠ *271 Hanford St., 95685,* ☎ *209/267–9177,* FAX *209/267–5303. 52 rooms. D, MC, V.*

Jackson

❷❻ *8 mi south of Sutter Creek on Hwy. 49.*

Jackson wasn't the Gold Country's rowdiest town, but the party lasted longer here than most anywhere else: "Girls' dormitories" (brothels) and nickel slot machines flourished until the mid-1950s. Jackson also had the world's deepest and richest gold mines, the Kennedy and the Argonaut, which together produced $70 million in gold. These were deep-rock mines with tunnels extending as much as a mile underground. Most of the miners who worked the lode were of Serbian or Italian origin, and they gave the town a European character that persists to this day. Jackson has aboveground pioneer cemeteries whose headstones tell the stories of local Serbian and Italian families. The terraced cemetery on the grounds of the handsome **St. Sava Serbian Orthodox Church** (⊠ 724 N. Main St.) is the most impressive of the town's burial grounds.

The heart of Jackson's historic section is the **National Hotel** (⊠ 2 Water St.), which operates an old-time saloon in the lobby. The hotel is especially active on weekends, when people come from miles around to participate in the Saturday-night sing-alongs.

The **Amador County Museum,** built in the late 1850s as a private home, provides a colorful take on gold-rush life. Displays include a kitchen with a woodstove, the Amador County bicentennial quilt, and a classroom. A time line recounts the county's checkered past. The museum conducts hourly tours of large-scale working models of the nearby Kennedy Mine. ⊠ *225 Church St.,* ☎ *209/223–6386.* ⊡ *Museum free; building with mine $1.* ☉ *Wed.–Sun. 10–4.*

Dining and Lodging

$$–$$$ ✕ **Upstairs Restaurant.** Chef Layne McCollum takes a creative approach to contemporary American cuisine in his 12-table restaurant with a menu that changes weekly. The baked-Brie and roast-garlic appetizer and homemade soups are specialties. Local wines are reasonably priced. Downstairs there's a street-side bistro and wine bar. ⊠ *164 Main St.,* ☎ *209/223–3342. AE, D, MC, V. Closed Mon.–Tues.*

$ ✕ **Rosebud's Classic Café.** Art deco accents and music from the 1930s and 1940s set the mood at this homey café. Among the classic American dishes served are hot roast beef, turkey, and meat loaf with mashed potatoes smothered in gravy. Charbroiled burgers, freshly baked pies, and espresso coffees round out the lunch menu. Omelets, hotcakes, and many other items are served for breakfast. ⊠ *26 Main St.,* ☎ *209/223–1035. MC, V. No dinner.*

$$–$$$ ⊡ **Court Street Inn.** This Victorian has tin ceilings and a redwood staircase. The cozy first-floor Burgundy Court Room has a fireplace; the Champagne Court Room has a large whirlpool and a Wedgwood stove. The Indian House, a two-bedroom cottage, has a large bathroom, a 61-inch TV with VCR, and a stereo. A third building, Vintage Court, is decorated in wine colors and contains two guest rooms that share a parlor and deck. ⊠ *215 Court St., 95642,* ☎ *209/223–0416 or 800/200–0416,* FAX *209/223–5429,* WEB *www.courtstreetinn.com. 5 rooms, 2 suites. In-room VCRs (some), outdoor hot tub. AE, D, MC, V. BP.*

$ ⊞ **Best Western Amador Inn.** Convenience and price are the main attractions of this two-story motel right on the highway. Many rooms have gas fireplaces. ⊠ *200 S. Hwy. 49, 95642,* ☎ *209/223–0211 or 800/543–5221,* FAX *209/223–4836,* WEB *www.bestwestern.com. 118 rooms. Restaurant, pool, laundry service. AE, D, DC, MC, V.*

Angels Camp

㉗ *20 mi south of Jackson on Hwy. 49.*

Angels Camp is famed chiefly for its May jumping-frog contest, based on Mark Twain's "The Jumping Frog of Calaveras County." The writer reputedly heard the story of the jumping frog from Ross Coon, proprietor of Angels Hotel, which has been in operation since 1856.

Angels Camp Museum has gold-rush relics—photos, rocks, petrified wood, old mining equipment, and a horse-drawn hearse. The carriage house out back holds 25 carriages and an impressive display of mineral specimens. ⊠ *753 S. Main St.,* ☎ *209/736–2963.* ⌑ *$2.* ☉ *Jan.– Feb., weekends 10–3; Mar.–Nov., daily 10–3.*

OFF THE BEATEN PATH

CALIFORNIA CAVERNS AND MOANING CAVERN – A ½-mi subterranean trail at the California Caverns winds through large chambers and past underground streams and lakes. There aren't many steps to climb, but it's a hefty walk, with some narrow passageways and steep spots. The caverns, at a constant 53°F, contain crystalline formations not found elsewhere; the 80-minute guided tour explains local history and geology. A 235-step spiral staircase leads into the vast Moaning Cavern. More adventurous sorts can rappel into the chamber—ropes and instruction are provided. Otherwise, the only way inside is via the 45-minute tour, during which you'll see giant (and still growing) stalactites and stalagmites and an archaeological site that holds some of the oldest human remains yet found in America (an unlucky person has fallen into the cavern about once every 130 years for the last 13,000 years). ⊠ *California Caverns: 9 mi east of San Andreas on Mountain Ranch Rd., then about 3 mi on Cave City Rd. (follow signs),* ☎ *209/736–2708.* ⌑ *$9.* ☉ *Usually May–Dec., but call ahead.* ⊠ *Moaning Cavern: Parrots Ferry Rd., 2 mi south of town of Vallecito, off Hwy. 4 east of Angels Camp,* ☎ *209/736–2708,* WEB *www.caverntours.com.* ⌑ *$8.75.* ☉ *May–Oct., daily 9–6; Nov.–Apr., weekdays 10–5, weekends 9–5.*

Murphys

㉘ *10 mi east of Angels Camp on Hwy. 4.*

Murphys is a well-preserved town of white picket fences, Victorian houses, and interesting shops. Horatio Alger and Ulysses S. Grant are among the guests who have signed the register at **Murphys Historic Hotel and Lodge.** The men were among the 19th-century visitors to the giant sequoia groves in nearby Calaveras Big Trees State Park.

The **Kautz Ironstone Winery and Caverns** is worth a visit even if you don't drink wine. Tours take you into underground tunnels cooled by a waterfall from a natural spring; they include a performance on a massive automated pipe organ. The winery schedules concerts during spring and summer in its huge outdoor amphitheater, plus art shows and other events on weekends. On display is a 44-pound specimen of crystalline gold. A deli offers lunch items. ⊠ *1894 Six Mile Rd.,* ☎ *209/728–1251.* ☉ *Daily 11–5.*

OFF THE
BEATEN PATH

CALAVERAS BIG TREES STATE PARK – This state park protects hundreds of the largest and rarest living things on the planet—magnificent giant sequoia redwood trees. Some are nearly 3,000 years old, 90 ft around at the base, and 250 ft tall. The park's self-guided walks range from a 200-yard trail to 1-mi and 5-mi (closed in winter) loops through the groves. There are campgrounds and picnic areas; swimming, wading, fishing, and sunbathing on the Stanislaus River are popular in summer. ⊠ *Off Hwy. 4, 15 mi northeast of Murphys (4 mi northeast of Arnold),* ☎ *209/795-2334.* ⊠ *$2 per vehicle (day use); campsites $12.* ☉ *Park daily sunrise–sunset (day use). Visitor center May–Oct., daily 10– 4; Nov.–Apr., weekends 11–3.*

Dining and Lodging

$–$$ ✕ **Grounds.** Light Italian entrées, grilled vegetables, chicken, seafood, and steak are the specialties at this bistro and coffee shop. Sandwiches, salads, and homemade soups are served for lunch. The crowd is friendly and the service attentive. ⊠ *402 Main St.,* ☎ *209/728-8663. MC, V. Closed Tues. No dinner Mon.*

$–$$ ✕⌂ **Murphys Historic Hotel & Lodge.** This 1855 stone hotel, whose register has seen the signatures of Mark Twain and the bandit Black Bart, figured in Bret Harte's short story "A Night at Wingdam." Accommodations are in the hotel and a modern motel-style addition. The older rooms are furnished with antiques, many of them large and hand-carved. The hotel has a convivial old-time saloon, which can be noisy into the wee hours. ⊠ *457 Main St., 95247,* ☎ *209/728-3444 or 800/532-7684,* ℻ *209/728-1590,* ⓦⒺⒷ *www.murphyshotel.com. 29 rooms, 20 with bath. Restaurant, bar, meeting room. AE, D, DC, MC, V.*

$$$–$$$$ ⌂ **Dunbar House 1880.** The oversize rooms in this elaborate Italianate-style home have brass beds, down comforters, gas-burning stoves, and claw-foot tubs. Broad wraparound verandas encourage lounging, as do the colorful gardens and large elm trees. The Cedar Room's sunporch has a two-person whirlpool tub; in the Sequoia Room you can gaze at the garden while soaking in a bubble bath. In the afternoon you are treated to trays of appetizers and wine in your room. ⊠ *271 Jones St., 95247,* ☎ *209/728-2897 or 800/692-6006,* ℻ *209/728-1451,* ⓦⒺⒷ *www.dunbarhouse.com. 3 rooms, 2 suites. Refrigerators, in-room VCRs. AE, MC, V. BP.*

$–$$$$ ⌂ **Redbud Inn.** Some rooms at this inn have double-sided fireplaces, cathedral ceilings, garden balconies, or claw-foot tubs. A room with brass beds and a tin ceiling replicates a miner's cabin. Wine and snacks are served in the parlor each evening. ⊠ *402 Main St., Unit H, 95247,* ☎ *209/728-8533 or 877/473-3283,* ℻ *209/728-8123,* ⓦⒺⒷ *www. redbudinn.com. 12 rooms, 2 suites. D, MC, V. BP.*

Columbia

㉙ *14 mi south of Angels Camp, Hwy. 49 to Parrots Ferry Rd.*

Columbia is the gateway for Columbia State Historic Park, which is one of the Gold Country's most visited tourist sites.

★ ♺ **Columbia State Historic Park,** known as the Gem of the Southern Mines, comes as close to a gold-rush town in its heyday as any site in the Gold Country. You can ride a stagecoach, pan for gold, and watch a blacksmith working at an anvil. Street musicians perform in summer. Restored or reconstructed buildings include a Wells Fargo Express office, a Masonic temple, stores, saloons, two hotels, a firehouse, churches, a school, and a newspaper office. All are staffed to simulate a working 1850s town. The park also includes the **Historic Fallon House**

Theater, where a full schedule of entertainment is presented.☎ 209/ 532–0150, WEB *www.parks.ca.gov.* ⬜ *Free.* ☉ *Daily 9–5.*

Dining and Lodging

$$ ✕🏠 **City Hotel.** The rooms in this restored 1856 hostelry are furnished with period antiques. Two have balconies overlooking Main Street, and six rooms open onto a second-floor parlor. All the accommodations have private half-baths with showers nearby; robes and slippers are provided. The restaurant ($–$$; closed Monday), one of the Gold Country's best, serves French-accented California cuisine complemented by a large selection of California wines. The What Cheer Saloon is right out of a western movie. The hotel offers combined lodging, dinner, and theater packages. ✉ *22768 Main St., Columbia 95310,* ☎ *209/532–1479 or 800/532–1479,* FAX *209/532–7027,* WEB *www. cityhotel.com. 10 rooms. Restaurant, bar. AE, D, MC, V. CP.*

$–$$ 🏠 **Fallon Hotel.** The state of California restored this 1857 hotel. All rooms have antiques and a private half-bath; there are separate men's and women's showers. If you occupy one of the five balcony rooms, you can sit outside with your morning coffee and watch the town wake up. ✉ *11175 Washington St., Columbia 95310,* ☎ *209/532–1470,* FAX *209/532–7027,* WEB *www.cityhotel.com. 14 rooms. AE, D, MC, V. CP.*

Nightlife and the Arts

Sierra Repertory Theater Company (☎ 209/532–4644), a local professional company, presents a full season of plays, comedies, and musicals at the Historic Fallon House Theater and another venue in East Sonora.

Sonora

③⓪ *4 mi south of Columbia, Parrots Ferry Rd. to Hwy. 49.*

Miners from Mexico founded Sonora and made it the biggest town in the Mother Lode. Following a period of racial and ethnic strife, the Mexican settlers moved on. Yankees built the commercial city that is visible today. Sonora's historic downtown section sits atop the Big Bonanza Mine, one of the richest in the state. Another mine, on the site of nearby Sonora High School, yielded 990 pounds of gold in a single week in 1879. Reminders of the gold rush are everywhere in Sonora, in prim Victorian houses, typical Sierra-stone storefronts, and awning-shaded sidewalks. Reality intrudes beyond the town's historic heart, with strip malls, shopping centers, and modern motels. If the countryside surrounding Sonora seems familiar, that's because it has been the backdrop for many movies over the years. Scenes from *High Noon, For Whom the Bell Tolls, The Virginian, Back to the Future III,* and *Unforgiven* were filmed here.

The **Tuolumne County Museum and History Center** occupies a building that served as a jail until 1951. Restored to an earlier period, it houses a jail museum, vintage firearms and paraphernalia, a case with gold nuggets, a cute exhibit on soapbox derby racing in hilly Sonora, and the libraries of a historical society and a genealogical society. ✉ *158 W. Bradford St.,* ☎ *209/532–1317.* ⬜ *Free.* ☉ *Sun.–Fri. 10–4, Sat. 10–3:30.*

Dining and Lodging

$–$$ ✕ **Banny's Cafe.** Its pleasant environment and hearty yet refined dishes make Banny's a quiet alternative to Sonora's noisier eateries. Try the grilled salmon fillet with scallion rice and ginger-wasabi-soy aioli. ✉ *83 S. Stewart St.,* ☎ *209/533–4709. D, MC, V.*

$-$$ ✕ **Josephine's California Trattoria.** Seared ahi tuna, duckling with polenta, crayfish risotto, and angel-hair pasta with fresh seafood are among the dishes you might find on the seasonal menu. Single-portion pizzas are a staple. The reasonably priced wine list showcases Sierra foothill and Italian vintages. Musicians perform on some nights. ⊠ *Gunn House Hotel, 286 S. Washington St.,* ☎ *209/533–4111. AE, D, MC, V. Closed Mon. No lunch.*

$ ✕ **Garcia's Taqueria.** This casual, inexpensive eatery serves Mexican and southwestern fare with an emphasis on seafood dishes. Murals of Yosemite and other California landscapes adorn the walls. The spicy roasted-garlic soup is popular. ⊠ *145 S. Washington St.,* ☎ *209/588–1915. No credit cards. Closed Sun.*

$ 🏨 **Best Western Sonora Oaks Motor Hotel.** The standard motel-issue rooms at this East Sonora establishment are clean and roomy. The larger ones have outdoor sitting areas. Suites have fireplaces, whirlpool tubs, and tranquil hillside views. Because the motel is right off Highway 108, the front rooms can sometimes be noisy. ⊠ *19551 Hess Ave., 95370,* ☎ *209/533–4400 or 800/532–1944,* FAX *209/532–1964,* WEB *www.bestwestern.com. 96 rooms, 4 suites. Restaurant, pool, outdoor hot tub, lounge, meeting room. AE, D, DC, MC, V.*

Jamestown

③① *4 mi south of Sonora on Hwy. 49.*

Compact Jamestown supplies a touristy, superficial view of gold-rush-era life. Shops in brightly colored buildings along Main Street sell antiques and gift items.

The California State Railroad Museum operates **Railtown 1897** at what were the headquarters and general shops of the Sierra Railway from 1897 to 1955. The railroad has appeared in more than 200 movies and television productions, including *Petticoat Junction, The Virginian, High Noon,* and *Unforgiven.* You can view the roundhouse, an air-operated 60-ft turntable, shop rooms, and old locomotives and coaches. Six-mile, 40-minute steam train rides through the countryside operate on weekends during part of the year. ⊠ *5th Ave. and Reservoir Rd., off Hwy. 49,* ☎ *209/984–3953,* WEB *www.csrmf.org.* 🚂 *Roundhouse tour $2; train ride $6.* ☉ *Daily 9:30–4:30. Train rides Apr.–Oct., weekends 11–3; Nov., Sat. 11–3.*

Dining and Lodging

$-$$ ✕🏨 **National Hotel.** The National has been in business since 1859, and the furnishings here are authentic—brass beds, patchwork quilts, and lace curtains—but not overly embellished. Some rooms have no phone. The saloon, which still has its original 19th-century redwood bar, is a great place to linger. The popular restaurant ($–$$$) serves big lunches: hamburgers and fries, salads, and Italian entrées. More upscale Continental cuisine is prepared for dinner (reservations essential). ⊠ *18183 Main St., 95327,* ☎ *209/984–3446; 800/894–3446 in CA,* FAX *209/984–5620,* WEB *www.national-hotel.com. 9 rooms. Restaurant, bar. AE, D, DC, MC, V. CP.*

Mariposa

③② *50 mi south of Jamestown on Hwy. 49.*

Mariposa marks the southern end of the Mother Lode. Much of the land in this area was part of a 44,000-acre land grant Colonel John C. Fremont acquired from Mexico before gold was discovered and California became a state.

At the **California State Mining and Mineral Museum** a glittering 13-pound chunk of crystallized gold makes it clear what the rush was about. Displays include a replica of a typical tunnel dug by hard-rock miners, a miniature stamp mill, and a panning and sluicing exhibit. ⊠ *Mariposa County Fairgrounds, Hwy. 49,* ☎ *209/742–7625.* ⊡ *$1.* ☉ *May–Sept., daily 10–6; Oct.–Apr., Wed.–Mon. 10–4.*

Dining and Lodging

$$ ✕ **Ocean Sierra Restaurant.** Deep in the woods about 14 mi southeast of Mariposa is this comfortable spot for seafood, meat, pasta, and vegetarian dishes. The owner-chef grows many of her fresh ingredients, including the delicate crystallized rose petals atop some of the desserts. ⊠ *3292 E. Westfall Rd. (from Hwy. 49 take Triangle Rd. 2 mi northeast),* ☎ *209/742–7050. D, MC, V. Closed Mon.–Tues. May–Sept. and Mon.–Thurs. Oct.–Apr. No lunch.*

$–$$ ✕ **Castillo's Mexican Food.** Tasty tacos, enchiladas, *chiles rellenos,* and burrito combinations plus chimichangas, fajitas, steak, and seafood are served in a casual storefront. ⊠ *4995 5th St.,* ☎ *209/742–4413. MC, V.*

$$ ⌂ **Little Valley Inn.** Pine paneling, historical photos, and old mining tools recall Mariposa's heritage at this modern B&B with six bungalows. A suite that sleeps five people includes a full kitchen. All rooms have private entrances, baths, and decks. The large grounds include a creek where you can pan for gold. The enthusiastic innkeepers will also take you to their off-site claim for prospecting. ⊠ *3483 Brooks Rd., off Hwy. 49, 95338,* ☎ *209/742–6204 or 800/889–5444,* FAX *209/742–5099,* WEB *www.littlevalley.com. Private cabin, 4 rooms, 2 suites. Refrigerators, in-room VCRs, horseshoes. AE, MC, V. BP.*

$ ⌂ **Comfort Inn of Mariposa.** This white three-story building with a broad veranda sits on a hill above Mariposa. Some of the comfortable rooms have sitting areas. An expanded Continental breakfast is included. ⊠ *4994 Bouillon St., 95338,* ☎ *209/966–4344,* FAX *209/966–4655. 59 rooms, 2 suites. Pool, outdoor hot tub; no-smoking rooms. AE, D, DC, MC, V. CP.*

SACRAMENTO AND THE GOLD COUNTRY A TO Z

To research prices, get advice from other travelers, and book travel arrangements, visit www.fodors.com.

AIR TRAVEL

Sacramento International Airport is served by Alaska, America West, American, Delta, Frontier, Horizon Air, Northwest, Southwest, TWA, US Airways, and United airlines. *See* Air Travel *in* Smart Travel Tips A to Z for airline phone numbers.

➤ AIRPORT INFORMATION: **Sacramento International Airport** (⊠ 6900 Airport Blvd., 12 mi northwest of downtown off I–5, ☎ 916/874–0700, WEB www.sacairports.org).

BUS TRAVEL

Getting to and from SIA can be accomplished via taxi, the Super Shuttle service, or by Yolo County Public Bus 42, which operates a circular service around SIA, downtown Sacramento, West Sacramento, Davis, and Woodland.

Greyhound serves Sacramento, Davis, Auburn, and Placerville. It's a two-hour trip from San Francisco's Transbay Terminal, at 1st and Mission streets, to the Sacramento station, at 7th and L streets.

Sacramento Regional Transit buses and light-rail vehicles transport passengers in Sacramento. Most buses run from 6 AM to 10 PM, most trains from 5 AM to midnight. A DASH (Downtown Area Shuttle) bus and the No. 30 city bus both link Old Sacramento, midtown, and Sutter's Fort in a loop that travels eastward on J Street and westward on L Street. The fare is 50¢ within this area.

➤ BUS INFORMATION: **Greyhound** (☎ 800/231–2222, WEB www. greyhound.com). **Sacramento Regional Transit** (☎ 916/321–2877, WEB www.sacrt.com). **Super Shuttle** (☎ 800/258–3826). **Yolo County Bus** (WEB www.yolobus.com).

CAR RENTAL

You can rent a car from any of the major national chains at Sacramento International Airport. *See* Car Rental *in* Smart Travel Tips A to Z for national rental agency phone numbers.

CAR TRAVEL

Traveling by car is the most convenient way to see the Gold Country. From Sacramento three highways fan out toward the east, all intersecting with Highway 49: I–80 heads 30 mi northeast to Auburn; Route 50 goes east 40 mi to Placerville; and Highway 16 angles southeast 45 mi to Plymouth. Highway 49 is an excellent two-lane road that winds and climbs through the foothills and valleys, linking the principal Gold Country towns.

Sacramento lies at the junction of I–5 and I–80, about 90 mi northeast of San Francisco. The 406-mi drive north on I–5 from Los Angeles takes 7–8 hours. I–80 continues northeast through the Gold Country toward Reno, about 163 mi (three hours or so) from Sacramento.

EMERGENCIES

In an emergency dial 911.

➤ HOSPITALS: **Mercy Hospital of Sacramento** (✉ 4001 J St., Sacramento, ☎ 916/453–4424). **Sutter General Hospital** (✉ 2801 L St., Sacramento, ☎ 916/733–8900). **Sutter Memorial Hospital** (✉ 52nd and F Sts., Sacramento, ☎ 916/733–1000).

LODGING

A number of regional lodging organizations can supply information about area B and Bs and other accommodations.

➤ LODGING ASSOCIATIONS: **Amador County Innkeepers Association** (☎ 209/267–1710 or 800/726–4667). **Gold Country Inns of Tuolumne County** (☎ 209/533–1845). **Historic Bed & Breakfast Inns of Grass Valley & Nevada City** (☎ 530/477–6634 or 800/250–5808).

TOURS

Gold Prospecting Adventures, LLC, based in Jamestown, arranges gold-panning trips. Gray Line/Frontier Tours operates city tours for groups of 10 or more.

➤ CONTACTS: **Gold Prospecting Adventures, LLC** (☎ 209/984–4653 or 800/596–0009, WEB www.goldpanning.com). **Gray Line/Frontier Tours** (☎ 916/564–8687 or 800/356–9838).

TRAIN TRAVEL

Several trains operated by Amtrak stop in Sacramento and Davis. Trains making the 2½-hour trip from Jack London Square, in Oakland, stop in Emeryville (across the bay from San Francisco), Richmond, Martinez, and Davis before reaching Sacramento; some stop in Berkeley and Suisun-Fairfield as well.

➤ TRAIN INFORMATION: **Amtrak** (☎ 800/872–7245, WEB www. amtrak.com).

VISITOR INFORMATION

➤ CONTACTS: **Amador County Chamber of Commerce** (✉ 125 Peek St., Jackson 95642, ☎ 209/223–0350, WEB www.amadorcountychamber. com). **Davis Chamber of Commerce** (✉ 130 G St., Davis 95616, ☎ 530/ 756–5160, WEB www.davischamber.com). **El Dorado County Chamber of Commerce** (✉ 542 Main St., Placerville 95667, ☎ 530/621–5885 or 800/457–6279, WEB www.eldoradocounty.org). **Grass Valley/Nevada County Chamber of Commerce** (✉ 248 Mill St., Grass Valley 95945, ☎ 530/273–4667 or 800/655–4667, WEB www.ncgold.com/chamber). **Mariposa County Visitors Bureau** (✉ 5158 Hwy. 140, Mariposa 95338, ☎ 209/966–7081 or 800/208–2434, WEB mariposa.yosemite.net/ visitor). **Nevada City Chamber of Commerce** (✉ 132 Main St., ☎ 530/ 265–2692). **Placer County Tourism Authority** (✉ 13411 Lincoln Way, Auburn 95603, ☎ 530/887–2111 or 800/427–6463). **Sacramento Convention and Visitors Bureau** (✉ 1303 J St., Suite 600, Sacramento 95814, ☎ 916/264–7777, WEB www.sacramentocvb.org). **San Joaquin Convention & Visitors Bureau** (✉ 46 W. Freemont St., Stockton 95202, ☎ 209/943–1987, WEB www.ssjcvb.org). **Tuolumne County Visitors Bureau** (✉ 542 Stockton St., Sonora 95370, ☎ 209/533–4420 or 800/446–1333, WEB www.thegreatunfenced.com). **Woodland Chamber of Commerce** (✉ 307 1st St., Woodland 95695, ☎ 530/662–7327 or 888/843–2636, WEB www.woodlandchamber.org).

7 LAKE TAHOE

THE CALIFORNIA AND NEVADA SHORES

The largest alpine lake in North America is famous for its clarity, deep blue water, and snowcapped peaks. Though Lake Tahoe possesses abundant natural beauty and accessible wilderness, nearby towns are highly developed, and roads around the lake are often congested with traffic. Summertime is generally cooler here than in the Sierra Nevada foothills, and the clean mountain air is bracingly crisp. When it gets hot, the plentiful beaches and brisk water are only minutes away.

Revised by
Deke
Castleman

S TRADDLING THE STATE LINE between California and Nevada, Lake Tahoe lies 6,225 ft above sea level in the Sierra Nevada. The border gives this popular resort region a split personality. About half its visitors are intent on low-key sightseeing, hiking, fishing, camping, and boating. The rest head directly for the Nevada side, where bargain dining, big-name entertainment, and the lure of a jackpot draw them into the glittering casinos. Tahoe is also a popular wedding and honeymoon destination: couples can get married with no waiting period or blood tests at chapels all around the lake. On Valentine's Day the chapels become veritable assembly lines—up to four times as many ceremonies take place on that day than on any other. Incidentally, the legal marrying age in California and Nevada is 18 years, but you must be 21 to gamble or drink.

Summer's cool temperatures provide respite from the heat in the surrounding desert and valleys. Swimming in Lake Tahoe is always brisk—except for small, shallow, and sheltered coves—and the lake's beaches are generally crowded at this time of year. Those who prefer solitude can escape to the many state parks, national forests, and protected tracts of wilderness that ring the 22-mi-long, 12-mi-wide lake. From midautumn to late spring multitudes of skiers and winter-sports enthusiasts are attracted to Tahoe's downhill resorts and cross-country centers, North America's largest concentration of skiing facilities. Ski resorts try to open by Thanksgiving, if only with machine-made snow, and can operate through May or later. Most accommodations, restaurants, and even a handful of parks are open year-round.

The first white explorer to gaze upon this spectacular region was Captain John C. Fremont, in 1844, guided by the famous scout Kit Carson. Not long afterward, silver was discovered in Nevada's Comstock Lode, at Virginia City. As the mines grew larger and deeper, the Tahoe Basin's forests were leveled to provide lumber for subterranean support. By the early 1900s wealthy Californians were building lakeside estates here, some of which still stand. Improved roads brought the less affluent in the 1920s and 1930s, when modest bungalows began to appear. The first casinos opened in the 1940s. Ski resorts inspired another development boom in the 1950s and 1960s, turning the lake into a year-round destination.

During some summer weekends it seems that absolutely every tourist—100,000 at peak periods—is in a car on the main road that circles the 72-mi shoreline. The crowds and congestion increase as the day wears on. But at a vantage point overlooking Emerald Bay early in the morning, on a trail in the national forests that ring the basin, or on a sunset cruise on the lake itself, you can forget the hordes and the commercial development. You can even pretend that you're Mark Twain, who found "not fifteen other human beings throughout its wide circumference" when he visited the lake in 1861 and wrote that "the eye never tired of gazing, night or day, calm or storm."

Pleasures and Pastimes

Camping

Campgrounds abound in the Tahoe area, operated by both states' park departments, the U.S. Forest Service, city utility districts, and private operators. Sites range from primitive and rustic to upscale and luxurious. Make reservations far ahead in summer, when sites are in high demand.

Dining

On weekends and in high season expect a long wait in the more popular restaurants. During slower periods some places may close temporarily or limit their hours, so call ahead to make sure your choice is open.

Casinos use their restaurants to attract gaming customers. Marquees often tout "$5.99 prime rib dinners" or "$1.99 breakfast specials." Some of these meal deals, usually found in the coffee shops and buffets, may not be top quality, but at those prices, who cares? The finer restaurants in casinos, however, generally deliver good food, service, and atmosphere.

Unless otherwise noted, even the most expensive Tahoe-area restaurants welcome customers in casual clothes—not surprising in this year-round vacation spot—but don't expect to be served in most places if you're barefoot, shirtless, or wearing a skimpy bathing suit.

CATEGORY	COST*
$$$$	over $30
$$$	$22–$30
$$	$15–$21
$	under $15

per person for a main course at dinner, excluding tip and 7%–7¼% tax

Gambling

Nevada's major casinos share garish neon and noise, but high-tech ventilation and no-smoking areas have eliminated the hazy pall of the past. Six casinos are clustered on a strip of Route 50 in Stateline—Caesars, Harrah's, Harvey's, Horizon, and Lakeside, plus Bill's, a lower-stakes "junior" casino (no lodging) that appeals to frugal gamblers. Five other casinos operate on the north shore: the Hyatt Regency, Cal-Neva, Tahoe Biltmore, Crystal Bay Club, and Jim Kelley's Nugget. And, of course, in Reno there are upward of a dozen major and another dozen minor casinos. Open 24 hours a day, 365 days a year, these gambling halls have table games (craps, blackjack, roulette, baccarat, poker, keno, pai gow poker, bingo, and big six), race and sports books, and thousands of slot and video poker machines—for instance, 1,610 at Harrah's alone. There is no charge to enter, and there is no dress code; as long as you're wearing money, you'll be welcome. Along with the casinos come full-service hotels and resorts. They offer discounted lodging packages throughout the year.

Golf

The Tahoe area is nearly as popular with golfers as it is with skiers. A half-dozen superb courses dot the mountains around the lake, with magnificent views, thick pines, fresh cool air, and lush fairways and greens. Encountering wildlife is not uncommon if you have to search for your ball out-of-bounds.

Hiking

There are five national forests in the Tahoe Basin and a half-dozen state parks. The main areas for hiking include the Tahoe Rim Trail, a 150-mi path along the ridgelines that now completely rings the lake; Desolation Wilderness, a vast 63,473-acre preserve of granite peaks, glacial valleys, subalpine forests, the Rubicon River, and more than 50 lakes; and the trail systems in D. L. Bliss, Emerald Bay, Sugar Pine Point, and Lake Tahoe–Nevada state parks and near Lake Tahoe Visitor Center.

Lodging

Quiet inns on the water, motels near the casino area, rooms at the casinos themselves, lodges close to ski runs, and condos everywhere else are among the Tahoe options. During summer and ski season the lake is crowded; reserve space as far ahead as possible. Spring and fall give you a little more leeway and lower—sometimes significantly lower—rates. The price categories listed below reflect high-season rates.

CATEGORY	COST*
$$$$	over $225
$$$	$160–$225
$$	$100–$159
$	under $100

All prices are for a standard double room, excluding 9%–10% tax.

Skiing

The Lake Tahoe area is a great destination for Nordic skiers. You can even cross-country ski on fresh snow right on the lakeshore beaches. Skinny skiing (slang for cross-country) at the resorts can be costly, but you get the benefits of machine grooming and trail preparation. If it's bargain Nordic you're after, take advantage of thousands of acres of public forest and parkland trails.

The mountains around Lake Tahoe are bombarded by blizzards throughout most winters (some are wetter than others) and sometimes in the fall and spring; 10- to 12-ft bases are not uncommon. The profusion of downhill resorts guarantees an ample selection of different terrains, conditions, and challenges. To save money, look for packages offered by lodges and resorts; some include interchangeable lift tickets that allow you to try different slopes. Midweek packages are usually cheaper, and most resorts offer family discounts. Free shuttle-bus service is available between most ski resorts and nearby lodgings.

Exploring Lake Tahoe

The typical way to explore the Lake Tahoe area is to drive the 72-mi road that follows the shore through wooded flatlands and past beaches, climbing to vistas on the rugged southwest side of the lake and passing through the busiest commercial developments and casinos on its northeastern and southeastern edges. Undeveloped Lake Tahoe–Nevada State Park occupies more than half of the Nevada side of Lake Tahoe, stretching along the shore from just north of Zephyr Cove to just south of the upscale community of Incline Village. The California side, particularly South Lake Tahoe, is more developed, though much wilderness remains.

Great Itineraries

Although, or perhaps because, the distance around Lake Tahoe is relatively short, the desire to experience the whole area can be overwhelming. It takes only one day "to see it"—drive around the lake, stretch your legs at a few overlooks, take a nature walk, and wander among the casinos at Stateline. If you have more time, you can laze on a beach and swim, venture onto the lake or into the mountains, and sample Tahoe's finer restaurants. If you have five days, you may become so attached to Tahoe that you begin visiting real-estate agents.

Numbers in the text correspond to numbers in the margin and on the Lake Tahoe map.

IF YOU HAVE 3 DAYS

On your first day stop in **South Lake Tahoe** ① and pick up provisions for a picnic lunch. Start with some morning beach fun at the **Pope-Baldwin Recreation Area** ② and check out the area's Tallac Historic Site. Head west on Highway 89, stopping at the **Lake Tahoe Visitor Center** and the **Emerald Bay State Park** ③ lookout. Have lunch at the look-

Lake Tahoe

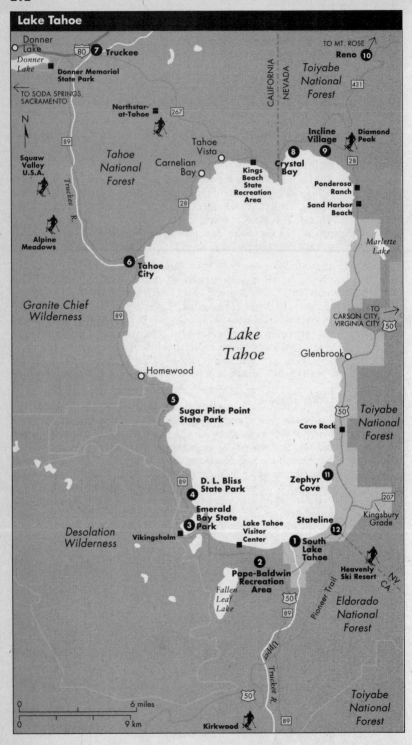

Donner Lake
80 **7** Truckee
Donner Memorial State Park
TO SODA SPRINGS, SACRAMENTO
N
89

Tahoe National Forest

Northstar-at-Tahoe
267
Tahoe Vista
Carnelian Bay
Squaw Valley U.S.A.
Truckee R.
Alpine Meadows

TO MT. ROSE
Reno **10**
Toiyabe National Forest
431
CALIFORNIA | NEVADA

Incline Village **9**
8 Crystal Bay
Diamond Peak
28
Ponderosa Ranch
Sand Harbor Beach

Kings Beach State Recreation Area

Marlette Lake

6 Tahoe City

Granite Chief Wilderness
89

Lake Tahoe

TO CARSON CITY, VIRGINIA CITY
50

Glenbrook

Homewood

5
Sugar Pine Point State Park

Toiyabe National Forest
50
Cave Rock

D. L. Bliss State Park
89
4

11 Zephyr Cove
207
Kingsbury Grade

Emerald Bay State Park
3
Vikingsholm

Desolation Wilderness

Lake Tahoe Visitor Center
Stateline
12
1 South Lake Tahoe

2
Pope-Baldwin Recreation Area
Fallen Leaf Lake
50
89

Heavenly Ski Resort
NV CA
Pioneer Trail

Eldorado National Forest

Upper Truckee R.

0 —— 6 miles
0 —— 9 km
50
89
Kirkwood

Toiyabe National Forest

out, or hike down to Vikingsholm, a Viking castle replica. In the late afternoon explore the trails and mansions at **Sugar Pine Point State Park** ⑤; then backtrack on Highway 89 and Route 50 for dinner in ☎ **Stateline** ⑫. On your second day cruise on the *Hornblower's Tahoe Queen* glass-bottom stern-wheeler out of South Lake Tahoe or the MS *Dixie II* stern-wheeler out of **Zephyr Cove** ⑪ in the morning, then ride the **Heavenly Tram** at Heavenly Ski Resort in South Lake Tahoe. Have lunch high above the lake and (except in snow season) take a walk on one of Heavenly's nature trails. You'll have an hour or two to try your luck at the Stateline casinos before it's time for dinner. Start your third day by heading north on Route 50, stopping at **Cave Rock** and (after turning north on Highway 28) at **Sand Harbor Beach.** If *Bonanza* looms large in your memory, drop by **Ponderosa Ranch,** just south of **Incline Village** ⑨, or continue on to **Crystal Bay** ⑧ to hike the State-line Lookout Trail. If you have time, drive to **Tahoe City** ⑥ to see its Gatekeeper's Log Cabin Museum, or make the 45-minute drive down to ☎ **Reno** ⑩ for dinner and some nightlife.

IF YOU HAVE 5 DAYS

On your first day, have a picnic at **Pope-Baldwin Recreation Area** ②. Then head west to **Lake Tahoe Visitor Center** and the **Emerald Bay State Park** ③ lookout. Hike to Vikingsholm, or if that seems too strenuous, proceed directly to **Sugar Pine Point State Park** ⑤. Have dinner in ☎ **South Lake Tahoe** ①. On your second day cruise on *Hornblower's Tahoe Queen* or MS *Dixie II* in the morning, then ride the **Heavenly Tram,** have lunch, and possibly take a hike. Spend the late afternoon or early evening at one of the ☎ **Stateline** ⑫ casinos. On the third day visit **Cave Rock** and the **Ponderosa Ranch,** just south of **Incline Village** ⑨, and hike the Stateline Lookout Trail, above **Crystal Bay** ⑧. Have lunch in Crystal Bay and spend the afternoon at the nearby **Kings Beach State Recreation Area.** That evening would be a good time to drive down to ☎ **Reno** ⑩ for dinner and entertainment. On the fourth day hang out at **Sand Harbor Beach.** On day five rent a bike and ride from **D. L. Bliss State Park** ④ to **Tahoe City** ⑥ and explore the Gatekeeper's Log Cabin Museum.

When to Tour Lake Tahoe

Unless you want to ski, you'll find that Tahoe is most fun during the summer. The best strategy for avoiding crowds is to do as much as you can early in the day. The parking lots of the Lake Tahoe Visitor Center, Vikingsholm, and Gatekeeper's Log Cabin Museum can be jammed at any time. Weekends are the most congested, but weekdays are busy as well.

September and October, when the throngs have dispersed but the weather is still pleasant, are among the most satisfying months to visit Lake Tahoe. During the winter ski season Tahoe's population swells on the weekends. If you're able to come midweek, you'll have the re-sorts and neighboring towns almost to yourself. Most visitor centers, mansions, state parks, and beaches are closed from November through May.

CALIFORNIA SIDE

Two states share Lake Tahoe. The California side is the more devel-oped, both with commercial enterprises—restaurants, motels, lodges, resorts, residential subdivisions—and public-access facilities, such as historic sites, parks, campgrounds, marinas, and beaches.

South Lake Tahoe

❶ *50 mi south of Reno on Rte. 395 and Rte. 50, 198 mi northeast of San Francisco on I–80 and Rte. 50.*

South Lake Tahoe's raison d'être is tourism. The lake region's largest community feeds the casinos at Stateline; the ski slopes at Heavenly Valley; the beaches, docks, bike trails, and campgrounds of the south shore; and the backcountry of Eldorado National Forest and Desolation Wilderness. Motels, lodges, and restaurants line Route 50 heading northeast into town, but if you go northwest on Highway 89, which follows the lakefront, commercial development gives way to national forests and state parks.

★ ☺ Whether you ski or not, you'll appreciate the impressive view of Lake Tahoe from the 50-passenger **Heavenly Tram,** which runs 2,000 ft up the slopes of Heavenly Ski Resort to 8,200 ft (carrying skiers during the season and groups only from June through October). ⊠ *Head north on Ski Run Blvd. off Rte. 50 and follow signs to parking lot,* ☎ *775/ 586–7000,* WEB *www.skiheavenly.com.* ⊠ *$15.*

The **Heavenly Gondola** has 138 eight-passenger cars traveling the 2½ mi up the mountain in 11 minutes. When the weather's fine, you can take one of three (successively more difficult) hikes around the mountaintop. Monument Peak Restaurant, open daily during gondola hours, serves both cafeteria-style food and fancier fare for lunch and Sunday brunch in summer, lunch in winter. ⊠ *Gondola leaves from downtown South Lake Tahoe,* ☎ *775/586–7000,* WEB *www.skiheavenly.com.* ⊠ *$18.* ☉ *Winter, daily 9–4, summer, daily 9–9.*

The 500-passenger **Hornblower's Tahoe Queen** (⊠ Ski Run Marina, off Rte. 50, ☎ 530/541–3364 or 800/238–2463), a glass-bottom paddle-wheeler, makes 2¼-hour sightseeing cruises and three-hour dinner-dance cruises year-round from South Lake Tahoe. Fares range from $22 to $49. In winter the boat becomes the only waterborne ski shuttle in the world: $87 covers hotel transfers, breakfast, transportation across the lake to Squaw Valley, and a lift ticket; $107 includes dinner.

Dining and Lodging

$$–$$$ ✕ **Swiss Chalet.** The Swiss theme is carried out with great consistency at this Tahoe institution. The steep sloping roof, wrought-iron grill-work, Swiss clocks, and cowbells may make you feel as if you've been transported to the Alps. The Continental menu includes schnitzel, sauerbraten, excellent stroganoff, fondue, steaks, and homemade pastries. ⊠ *2544 Rte. 50,* ☎ *530/544–3304. AE, MC, V. Closed late Nov.– early Dec. No lunch.*

$–$$ ✕ **Nepheles.** A chalet on the road to Heavenly Ski Resort houses this ★ cozy restaurant, which has been serving creative contemporary cuisine since 1977. Entrées range from Chilean sea bass with a hot mustard glaze to broiled tenderloin of elk with a sauce made from black currants and merlot. Appetizers include escargots, swordfish egg rolls, and Cajun calamari. You can also soak in private-room hot tubs here. ⊠ *1169 Ski Run Blvd.,* ☎ *530/544–8130. AE, D, DC, MC, V. No lunch.*

$–$$ ✕ **Scusa!** This intimate Italian restaurant on the road to the Heavenly Ski Resort occupies a smart, modern room. Capellini, linguine, fettuccine, and penne are on the menu, along with steak, chicken, and fresh fish. The panfried calamari with red peppers and capers shouldn't be missed. And don't pass up the rosemary-flavor flat bread, baked fresh daily. ⊠ *1142 Ski Run Blvd.,* ☎ *530/542–0100. AE, MC, V. No lunch.*

$ ✕ **Red Hut Café.** A vintage Tahoe diner (from 1959), all chrome and red plastic, the Red Hut is a tiny place with a dozen counter stools and a dozen booths. It's a traditional breakfast spot for those in the know, all of whom appreciate the huge omelets; the banana, pecan, and co-conut waffles; and other tasty vittles. ✉ 2749 Rte. 50, ☎ 530/541–9024. *Reservations not accepted. No credit cards. No dinner.*

$–$$$ ✕⊞ **Christiania Inn.** An antiques-filled bed-and-breakfast across the street from the base of the Heavenly Tram, the Christiania has long been a local favorite. The American-Continental menu ($–$$) emphasizes prime beef, duck, and wild game. Upstairs at the inn, two rooms and four suites come with king- or queen-size beds and private baths. Three of the suites are two-story affairs, with woodburning fireplaces and wet bars; two have saunas, and one has a whirlpool tub. ✉ 3819 Saddle Rd., 96151, ☎ 530/544–7337, FAX 530/544–5342, WEB www.christianiainn.com. 6 rooms. Restaurant, minibars (some), bar. MC, V. CP.

$$$–$$$$ ⊞ **Embassy Suites.** In this opulent all-suites hotel, decorated Sierra-
★ lodge style, fountains and waterwheels splash in the nine-story atrium, where complimentary breakfasts and evening cocktails are served daily. Glass elevators rise to guest suites, each with a living room, dining area, and separate bedroom. ✉ 4130 Lake Tahoe Blvd., 96150, ☎ 530/544–5400 or 800/362–2779, FAX 530/544–4900, WEB www.embassysuites.com. 400 suites. 4 restaurants, cable TV with movies, microwaves, indoor pool, gym, hot tub, sauna, nightclub, meeting rooms. AE, D, DC, MC, V. BP.

$$–$$$$ ⊞ **Inn by the Lake.** Across the road from a beach, this luxury motel
★ has spacious rooms and suites furnished in contemporary style. All have balconies; some have lake views, wet bars, and kitchens. You can sum-mon the casino shuttles from a direct-dial phone in the lobby. ✉ 3300 Lake Tahoe Blvd., 96150, ☎ 530/542–0330 or 800/877–1466, FAX 530/541–6596, WEB www.innbythelake.com. 87 rooms, 12 suites. Kitchenettes (some), minibars (some), pool, hot tub, sauna, bicycles, laundry facil-ities, TVs with movies and video games. AE, D, DC, MC, V. CP.

$$–$$$$ ⊞ **Tahoe Seasons Resort.** Most rooms at this resort, which is set in the alpine forest within walking distance of the Heavenly Ski Resort, are outfitted with fireplaces. Every room has a whirlpool and a small kitchen. The earth tones of the contemporary rooms reflect the natu-ral surroundings. ✉ 3901 Saddle Rd., 96157, ☎ 530/541–6700 or 800/540–4874, FAX 530/541–0653, WEB www.tahoeseasons.com. 183 suites. Restaurant, kitchenettes, refrigerators, microwaves, 2 tennis courts, pool, hot tub, volleyball, cable TV with VCR, video game room, meeting rooms. AE, DC, MC, V.

$–$$$$ ⊞ **Best Western Station House Inn.** This inn has won design awards
★ for its exterior and interior. The rooms have king- and queen-size beds and double-vanity bathrooms. The location is ideal, one block from a private beach, two blocks from the casinos, and three blocks from the Heavenly gondola. ✉ 901 Park Ave., 96150, ☎ 530/542–1101 or 800/822–5953, FAX 530/542–1714, WEB www.stationhouseinn.com. 100 rooms, 2 suites. Restaurant, pool, hot tub. AE, D, DC, MC, V.

$–$$$ ⊞ **Lakeland Village Beach and Mountain Resort.** This complex with a quarter mile of private beach has several types of accommodations: studios, suites, and town houses, all with kitchens, fireplaces, and pri-vate decks or balconies. Ask about ski packages. ✉ 3535 Lake Tahoe Blvd., 96150, ☎ 530/544–1685 or 800/822–5969, FAX 530/544–0193, WEB www.lakeland-village.com. 210 units. Kitchenettes, 2 tennis courts, 2 pools, wading pool, hot tub, sauna, beach, boating, fishing, laundry facilities, TVs with VCRs, some pets allowed. AE, MC, V.

$$ ⊞ **Forest Inn Suites.** The location is excellent—5½ acres bordering a forest, a half block from Harrah's and Harvey's, and adjacent to a su-permarket, cinema, and shops. Rooms are condo style, among the largest at the lake, with six classes of suites. Ski rentals are available, and free shuttles to Heavenly and Kirkwood ski areas stop here. ✉ 1 Lake Pkwy., 96150, ☎ 530/541–6655 or 800/822–5950, FAX 530/544–3135, WEB www.forestinn.com. 17 rooms, 101 suites. Kitchenettes, 5 putting *greens, 2 pools, health club, 2 hot tubs, sauna, bicycles, volleyball, laundry facilities, video game room, meeting rooms, some pets allowed. AE, D, DC, MC, V.*

$–$$ ⊡ **Royal Valhalla Motor Lodge.** Two- and three-bedroom suites with complete kitchens make this motel attractive to families. Some of the simple, modern rooms have private balconies with views of the lake. ⊠ *4104 Lakeshore Blvd., 96150,* ☎ *530/544–2233 or 800/999–4104,* FAX *530/544–1436,* WEB *www.tahoedigital.com/royalvalhalla. 80 suites. Kitchenettes, pool, hot tub, laundry facilities. AE, DC, MC, V. CP.*

$ ⊡ **Best Tahoe West Inn.** The Tahoe West is three blocks from the beach and casinos. The exterior is rustic, rooms are neatly furnished, and beds are queen size. Twelve rooms have kitchenettes. The inn offers every possible kind of discount; ask and ye might receive. ⊠ *4107 Pine Blvd., 96150,* ☎ *530/544–6455 or 800/522–1021,* FAX *530/544–0508,* WEB *www.besttahoe.com. 60 rooms. Kitchenettes (some), pool, hot tub, sauna, TVs with movies. AE, D, DC, MC, V.*

$ ⊡ **Travelodge.** There are three branches of this national chain in South Lake Tahoe. All are convenient to casinos, shopping, and recreation and have some no-smoking rooms. The Bijou Center property has a restaurant. Free local calls and in-room coffee add to the budget appeal. ⊠ *3489 Rte. 50, at Bijou Center, 96150,* ☎ *530/544–5266 or 800/982–1466,* FAX *530/544–6985.* WEB *www.travelodge.com. 59 rooms. Cable TV, pool; no-smoking rooms. AE, D, DC, MC, V;* ⊠ *4011 Rte. 50, 96150,* ☎ *530/544–6000 or 800/982–3466,* FAX *530/544–6869 50 rooms;* ⊠ *4003 Rte. 50, 96150,* ☎ *530/541–5000 or 800/982–2466,* FAX *530/544–6910. 66 rooms.*

Outdoor Activities and Sports

CROSS-COUNTRY SKIING

For the ultimate in groomed conditions head to the nation's largest cross-country ski resort, **Royal Gorge** (⊠ follow signs from Soda Springs–Norden exit off I–80, Box 1100, Soda Springs 95728, ☎ 530/426–3871), which has 197 mi of 18-ft-wide track for all abilities, 88 trails on 9,172 acres, two ski schools, and 10 warming huts. Four cafés, two hotels, and a hot tub and sauna are among the facilities. **Kirkwood Ski Resort** has 58 mi of groomed-track skiing, with skating lanes, instruction, and rentals.

DOWNHILL SKIING

Heavenly Ski Resort. When first seen from the California side, Heavenly's mogul-choked slopes look impossibly difficult. But this vast resort—composed of nine peaks, two valleys, and three base-lodge areas and boasting the largest snowmaking equipment in the western United States—has something for every skier. Beginners can choose wide, well-groomed trails accessed via the Heavenly Tram and the gondola from downtown South Lake Tahoe or short and gentle runs in the Enchanted Forest area. The Sky Express high-speed quad chair whisks intermediate and advanced skiers to the summit for wide cruisers or steep tree skiing. Mott and Killebrew canyons draw expert skiers to the Nevada side for the steep chutes and thick-timber slopes. For snowboarders there's the Airport Park near the Olympic lift. The ski school, like everything else at Heavenly, is large and offers everything from learn-to-ski packages for novices to canyon adventure tours for advanced skiers. Skiing lessons and day care are available for children age four and up. ⊠ *Ski Run Blvd. off Hwy. 89/Rte. 50 (mailing address: Box 2180, Stateline, NV 89449),* ☎ *775/586–7000; 800/243–2836; 530/541–7544 snow phone. 82 trails on 4,800 acres, rated 20% beginner, 45% intermediate, 35% expert. Longest run 5½ mi, base 6,540′,* *summit 10,040'. Lifts: 29, including 2 aerial trams, 1 high-speed 6-passenger lift, and 5 high-speed quads.*

Kirkwood Ski Resort. Thirty-six miles south of Lake Tahoe, Kirkwood is a destination resort with 135 condominiums and several shops and restaurants. Most of the runs off the top are rated expert-only, but intermediate and beginning skiers have their own vast bowl, where they can ski through trees or on wide, open trails. Snowboarding is permitted on all runs and in an exclusive terrain park. Skiing and snowboarding lessons and equipment rentals and sales are available. The children's ski school has programs for ages 4–12, and day care is available for children ages 2–6. Arrangements for younger children must be made in advance. ⊠ *Hwy. 88 off Hwy. 89 (mailing address: Box 1, Kirkwood, CA 95646),* ☎ *209/258–6000; 209/258–7000 for lodging information; 209/258–3000 snow phone. 72 trails on 2,300 acres, rated 15% beginner, 50% intermediate, 20% advanced, 15% expert. Longest run 2½ mi, base 7,800', summit 9,800'. Lifts: 14.*

FISHING

Tahoe Sports Fishing, in business for 48 years, is one of the largest and oldest fishing-charter services on the lake. It runs several charters (morning, afternoon, and all-day). Trips include all necessary gear and bait, and the crew cleans and packages your catch. ⊠ *Ski Run Marina, South Lake Tahoe,* ☎ *530/541–5448; 800/696–7797 in CA.*

KAYAKING

For more than a decade **Kayak Tahoe** has been in the business of teaching people to kayak on Lake Tahoe and the Truckee River. Lessons and excursions (Emerald Bay, Cave Rock, Zephyr Cove) are offered June through September. You can also take your pick of kayaks to rent and paddle off on your own. ⊠ *Timber Cove Marina at Tahoe Paradise,* ☎ *530/544–2011.*

Pope-Baldwin Recreation Area

❷ *5 mi west of South Lake Tahoe on Hwy. 89.*

George S. Pope, who made his money in shipping and lumber, hosted the business and cultural elite of 1920s America at his home, the **Pope House.** The magnificently restored 1894 mansion and two other estates—those of entrepreneur "Lucky" Baldwin (which houses a museum of Baldwin memorabilia and Washoe Indian artifacts) and Walter Heller (the Valhalla, used for community events)—form the heart of the Pope-Baldwin Recreation Area's **Tallac Historic Site.** The lakeside site, a pleasant place to take a stroll or have a picnic, hosts cultural activities (including a Renaissance festival) throughout the summer. Docents conduct tours of the Pope House during summer. ☎ *530/541–5227.* ▣ *Pope House tour $2.* ☉ *Tallac Historic Site grounds daily dawn–sunset; house and museum hrs vary.*

The U.S. Forest Service operates the **Lake Tahoe Visitor Center,** on Taylor Creek. You can visit the site of a Washoe Indian settlement; walk self-guided trails through meadow, marsh, and forest; and inspect the Stream Profile Chamber, an underground underwater display with windows that afford views right into Taylor Creek (in the fall you may see spawning kokanee salmon digging their nests). In summer U.S. Forest Service naturalists organize discovery walks and nighttime campfires with singing and marshmallow roasts. ⊠ *Hwy. 89,* ☎ *530/573–2674 (in season only).* ☉ *June–Sept., daily 8–5:30; Oct., weekends 8–5:30.*

Emerald Bay State Park

★ **3** *4 mi west of Pope-Baldwin Recreation Area on Hwy. 89.*

Emerald Bay, a 3-mi-long and 1-mi-wide fjordlike bay, was carved by a massive glacier millions of years ago. Famed for its jewel-like shape and colors, it surrounds Fannette, Tahoe's only island. Highway 89 curves high above the lake through Emerald Bay State Park; from the Emerald Bay lookout, the centerpiece of the park, you can survey the whole scene.

A steep 1-mi-long trail from the lookout leads down to **Vikingsholm,** a 38-room estate completed in 1929. The original owner, Lora Knight, had this precise replica of a 1,200-year-old Viking castle built out of materials native to the area. She furnished it with Scandinavian antiques and hired artisans to custom-build period reproductions. The sod roof sprouts wildflowers each spring. There are picnic tables nearby and a gray-sand beach for strolling. The hike back up is hard (especially if you're not yet acclimated to the elevation), but there are benches and stone culverts to rest on. At the 150-ft peak of Fannette Island are the remnants of a stone structure known as the Tea House, built in 1928 so that guests of Lora Knight could have a place to enjoy afternoon refreshments after a motorboat ride. The island is off-limits from February through June to protect nesting Canada geese. The rest of the year it's open for day use only. ☎ 530/525–7277. ⌸ *$2.* ☉ *Memorial Day–Labor Day, daily 10–4.*

D. L. Bliss State Park

4 *3 mi north of Emerald Bay State Park on Hwy. 89.*

D. L. Bliss State Park takes its name from Duane LeRoy Bliss, a 19th-century lumber magnate. At one time Bliss owned nearly 75% of Tahoe's lakefront, along with local steamboats, railroads, and banks. The Bliss family donated these 1,200 acres to the state in the 1930s. The park now shares 6 mi of shoreline with Emerald Bay State Park. At the north end of Bliss is Rubicon Point, which overlooks one of the lake's deepest spots. Short trails lead to an old lighthouse and Balancing Rock, which weighs in at 250,000 pounds and balances on a fist of granite. A longer trail leads all the way to Vikingsholm. Two white-sand beaches front some of Tahoe's warmest water. ☎ 530/525–7277. ⌸ *$2 per vehicle (day use).* ☉ *Memorial Day–Sept., daily sunrise–sunset.*

Camping

⌂ **D. L. Bliss State Park Campground.** Quiet, wooded hills make for blissful family camping near the lake. None of the sites has hookups. You're allowed to make reservations up to seven months in advance. *Flush toilets, drinking water, showers bear boxes, fire pits, grills, picnic tables, public telephone, swimming.* ✉ *Off Hwy. 89, 17 mi south of Tahoe City on lake side,* ☎ *800/444–7275. 168 sites.* ☉ *Memorial Day–Sept.*

Sugar Pine Point State Park

★ **5** *8 mi north of D. L. Bliss State Park on Hwy. 89.*

The main attraction at Sugar Pine Point State Park is Ehrman Mansion, a 1903 stone-and-shingle summer home furnished in period style. In its day it was the height of modernity, with a refrigerator, an elevator, and an electric stove. Also in the park are a trapper's log cabin from the mid-19th century, a nature preserve with wildlife exhibits, a lighthouse, the start of the 10-mi-long biking trail to Tahoe City, and an extensive system of hiking and cross-country trails. ☎ 530/525–7232

year-round; 530/525–7982 in season. ✉ *$2 per vehicle (day use).* ☉
Memorial Day–Labor Day, daily 11–4.

Camping

⚠ **General Creek Campground.** This homey campground on the
mountain side of Highway 89 is one of the few public ones to remain
open in winter, when it is popular with cross-country skiers. There are
no hookups here, and the showers operate Memorial Day–Labor Day
only. *Flush toilets, drinking water, showers, bear boxes, fire pits, grills,
public telephone, swimming.* ✉ *Hwy. 89, 1 mi south of Tahoma,* ☎
800/444–7275. 175 sites. ☉ *Year-round.*

Tahoe City

❻ *10 mi north of Sugar Pine Point State Park on Hwy. 89, 14 mi south
of Truckee on Hwy. 89.*

Tahoe City's many stores and restaurants lie within a compact area,
all within walking distance of the Outlet Gates, where in very wet years
water is spilled into the Upper Truckee River to control the surface level
of the lake. Giant trout are commonly seen in the river from Fanny
Bridge, so called for the views of the backsides of sightseers leaning
over the railing. Here, Highway 89 turns north from the lake and leads
to Squaw Valley, Donner Lake, and Truckee, and Highway 28 continues
northeast around the lake toward Kings Beach and Nevada.

★ The **Gatekeeper's Cabin Museum,** in Tahoe City, preserves a little-known
part of the region's history. Between 1910 and 1968 the gatekeeper
who lived on this site was responsible for monitoring the level of the
lake, using a hand-turned winch system to keep the water at the correct level. That winch system is still used today. ✉ *130 W. Lake Blvd.,*
☎ *530/583–1762.* ✉ *Free.* ☉ *May 15–Sept., daily 11–5.*

The **Watson Cabin Living Museum,** a 1909 log cabin built by Robert
M. Watson and his son and filled with century-old furnishings, is in
the middle of Tahoe City. Costumed docents act out the daily life of a
typical pioneer family. ✉ *560 N. Lake Blvd.,* ☎ *530/583–8717 or 530/
583–1762.* ✉ *Free.* ☉ *June 15–Labor Day, daily noon–4.*

Dining and Lodging

$$–$$$ ✕ **Christy Hill.** Panoramic lake views and fireside dining distinguish this
restaurant, which serves seasonal California cuisine including fresh
seafood (such as smoked salmon marinated in cilantro and lime and
Malpeque Bay oysters), beef, Australian lamb loin, and pasta. ✉ *Lake-
house Mall, 115 Grove St.,* ☎ *530/583–8551. AE, MC, V. Closed Mon.
Labor Day–Thanksgiving and Apr.–May. No lunch.*

$$–$$$ ✕ **Jake's on the Lake.** Overlooking the waterfront, soothingly hand-
★ some rooms of oak and glass are the backdrop for contemporary cuisine. The varied dinner menu includes beef (New York steak, tournedos)
and New Zealand rack of lamb but emphasizes fresh fish, such as crispy
herb-crusted catch of the day and seafood pasta Provençale. The
seafood bar here is extensive. ✉ *Boatworks Mall, 780 N. Lake Blvd.,*
☎ *530/583–0188. AE, MC, V.*

$$–$$$ ✕ **Sierra Vista.** The smell of garlic warms you as soon as you enter
this northern Italian restaurant, as does the fire in the wide, double-
side fireplace. Hearty pasta dishes and pizzas are on the menu, but the
stars are the baked goat-cheese salad, filet mignon, and vegetable
tower. Surround your entrée with a duck-leg confit salad dressed with
a raspberry vinaigrette and the classic southern bread pudding. ✉
Roundhouse Mall, 700 N. Lake Blvd., ☎ *530/583–0233. AE, D, DC,
MC, V.*

$$–$$$ ✕ **Wolfdale's.** An intimate restaurant inside the oldest building in
★ Tahoe City (1889), Wolfdale's food has Japanese and California overtones. The menu, which changes weekly, showcases several imaginative entrées, such as sea bass tempura, Asian braised duck leg and breast,
and coconut crepe stuffed with stir-fried vegetables. ⌧ *640 N. Lake
Blvd.,* ☎ *530/583–5700. MC, V. No lunch.*

$–$$$ ✕⌐ **Sunnyside Restaurant and Lodge.** This impressive lodge has a ma-
★ rina and an expansive lakefront deck with steps down to a narrow gravel
beach. Prints of boats hanging on the pinstripe wall coverings and sea
chests acting as coffee tables give the rooms a crisp nautical style. Each
room has its own deck with a lake or mountain view. Seafood is the
specialty of the unique alpine-lodge dining room ($–$$). ⌧ *1850 W.
Lake Blvd., Box 5969, 96145,* ☎ *530/583–7200 or 800/822–2754,*
FAX *530/583–2551. 18 rooms, 5 suites. Restaurant, room service, beach.
AE, MC, V. CP.*

$$$$ ⌐ **Resort at Squaw Creek.** Nearly half the rooms are suites at this complex with a main lodge, an outdoor arcade of shops and boutiques,
and a 403-room hotel. Some units have fireplaces and full kitchens,
and all have original art, custom furnishings, and good views. Outside
the hotel entrance is a triple chairlift to Squaw Valley's slopes. Dining
options range from haute cuisine to pastries and coffee. ⌧ *400 Squaw
Creek Rd., Olympic Valley 96146,* ☎ *530/583–6300 or 800/327–3353,*
FAX *530/581–5407,* WEB *www.squawcreek.com. 203 rooms, 200 suites.
5 restaurants, bar, 18-hole golf course, 2 tennis courts, 3 pools, health
club, 4 hot tubs, sauna, spa, ice-skating. AE, D, DC, MC, V.*

$$$–$$$$ ⌐ **Chinquapin Resort.** A deluxe development on 95 acres of forested
★ land and a mile of lakefront 3 mi northeast of Tahoe City contains one-
to four-bedroom town houses and condos with great views of the lake
and the mountains. Each unit has a fireplace, a fully equipped kitchen,
and a washer and dryer. A one-week minimum stay is required in late
December and over Presidents' Week in February; two- and three-night
minimums apply the rest of the year. ⌧ *3600 N. Lake Blvd., 96145,*
☎ *530/583–6991 or 800/732–6721,* FAX *530/583–0937,* WEB *www.
chinquapin.com. 172 town houses and condos. Kitchenettes, TVs with
cable, 7 tennis courts, pool, sauna, 2 beaches, hiking, horseshoes. AE,
D, MC, V.*

$–$$ ⌐ **Peppertree Inn.** This skinny seven-story tower is within easy walking distance of the beaches, marina, shops, and restaurants of Tahoe
City. Rooms are clean and comfortable, if not luxurious, and have great
lake views. ⌧ *645 N. Lake Blvd., 96145,* ☎ *530/583–3711 or 800/
624–8590,* FAX *530/583–6938,* WEB *www.peppertreetahoe.com. 45
rooms, 5 suites. TVs with cable and movies, pool, hot tub. AE, D, DC,
MC, V.*

Outdoor Activities and Sports

BIKING

Cyclepaths Mountain Bike Adventures (⌧ 1785 W. Lake Blvd., Tahoe
City, ☎ 530/581–1171, 800/780–2453) is a combination full-service
bike shop and bike-adventure outfitter. It offers instruction in mountain biking, guided tours (from half-day to weeklong excursions), tips
for self-guided bike touring, bike repairs, and books and maps on the
area.

DOWNHILL SKIING

Alpine Meadows Ski Area. The two peaks here are well suited to intermediate skiers. For snowboarders there's a terrain park with a half-
pipe. The ski area has some of Tahoe's most reliable conditions; this
is usually one of the first areas to open in November and one of the
last to close in May. There is a ski school for adults and children of all
skill levels and for skiers with disabilities. There's also an area for

overnight RV parking. ⊠ *6 mi northwest of Tahoe City off Hwy. 89,
13 mi south of I–80 (mailing address: Box 5279, 96145),* ☎ *530/583–
4232; 530/581–8374 for snow phone; 800/441–4423 for information.
100 trails on 2,000 acres, rated 25% easier, 40% more difficult, 35%
most difficult. Longest run 2½ mi, base 6,835′, summit 8,637′. Lifts:
12, including 1 high-speed 6-passenger lift and 1 high-speed quad.*

Squaw Valley USA. Known for some of the toughest skiing in the
Tahoe area, Squaw was the site of the 1960 Olympics. Although the
immense resort has changed significantly since then, the skiing is still
world class, with steep chutes and cornices on six peaks. Expert skiers
often head directly to the untamed terrain of the infamous KT-22 face,
which has bumps, cliffs, and gulp-and-go chutes. Plenty of wide,
groomed trails start near the beginner-designated High Camp lift and
around the more challenging Snow King Peak. Snowboarders have the
run of two terrain parks. You can ski until 9 PM, and lift tickets for
skiers under 12 are only $10. Nonskiing recreational opportunities—
bungee jumping, rock climbing, and ice-skating—abound. The Village
Mall has shops, eateries, and accommodations. ⊠ *Hwy. 89, 5 mi
northwest of Tahoe City (mailing address: Box 2007, Olympic Valley
96146),* ☎ *530/583–6985; 800/545–4350 for reservations; 530/583–
6955 for snow phone. 100 trails on 4,300 acres, rated 25% beginner,
45% intermediate, 30% advanced. Longest run 3 mi, base 6,200′, summit 9,050′. Lifts: 29, including a gondola, a cable car, and 5 high-speed
quads.*

GOLF

Resort at Squaw Creek Golf Course (⊠ 400 Squaw Creek Rd., Olympic
Valley, ☎ 530/583–6300), an 18-hole championship course, was designed by Robert Trent Jones, Jr. The $90–$120 greens fee includes the
use of a cart. Golfers use pull carts or caddies at the historic (1917) 9-
hole **Tahoe City Golf Course** (⊠ Hwy. 28, Tahoe City, ☎ 530/583–1516).
The greens fees are $22–$33 for 9 holes, $40–$55 for 18; a power cart
is $10–$12 additional.

Carnelian Bay to Kings Beach

5–10 mi northeast of Tahoe City on Hwy. 28.

The small lakeside commercial districts of Carnelian Bay and Tahoe
Vista service the thousand or so locals who live in the area year-round
and the thousands more who have summer residences or launch their
boats here. Kings Beach, the last town heading east on Highway 28
before the Nevada border, is to Crystal Bay what South Lake Tahoe is
to Stateline: a bustling California village full of motels and rental condos, restaurants and shops, used by the hordes of hopefuls who pass
through on their way to the casinos.

The 28-acre **Kings Beach State Recreation Area,** one of the largest such
areas on the lake, is open year-round. The long beach becomes crowded
with people swimming, sunbathing, jet-skiing, riding in paddleboats,
spiking volleyballs, and tossing Frisbees. There's a good playground
here. ⊠ *N. Lake Blvd., Kings Beach,* ☎ *530/546–7248.* ☜ *Free.*

Dining

$$–$$$ ✕ **Captain Jon's.** On chilly evenings a fireplace with a brick hearth warms
diners at this cozy establishment. The lengthy dinner menu is country
French with an emphasis on fish and hearty salads. There are also a
dozen daily specials. The restaurant's lounge, which serves light meals,
has a pier where hungry boaters can come ashore. ⊠ *7220 N. Lake
Blvd., Tahoe Vista,* ☎ *530/546–4819 or 775/831–4176. AE, DC,
MC, V. No lunch during ski season.*

$$–$$$ ✕ **Gar Woods Grill and Pier.** Boating photographs on the walls remind diners of the area's past at this stylish but casual restaurant. A river-rock fireplace keeps out the chill, floor-to-ceiling picture windows overlook the lake, and there's a heated deck for alfresco dining. The menu includes dishes such as prime rib, fillet and scampi, free-range chicken, and pan-seared ahi. There's an extensive wine list, and Sunday brunch is served. ⌧ *5000 N. Lake Blvd., Carnelian Bay,* ☎ *530/546–3366. AE, MC, V.*

$ ✕ **Log Cabin Caffe.** Almost always hopping, this Kings Beach eatery specializes in healthful, hearty breakfast and lunch entrées—five kinds of eggs Benedict, Mexican and smoked salmon scrambles, omelets, pancakes, waffles, freshly baked pastries, and sandwiches. It's a good place on the north shore for an espresso or cappuccino. Get here early on weekends for the popular brunch. ⌧ *8692 N. Lake Blvd., Kings Beach,* ☎ *530/546–7109. MC, V.*

Outdoor Activities and Sports

SNOWMOBILING

Snowmobiling Unlimited (⌧ Hwys. 267 and 28, Kings Beach, ☎ 530/583–7192) is the oldest snowmobiling concession on the lake. It conducts 1½-, 2-, and 3-hour guided cross-country tours, mostly along the trails in the nearby national forest. You can rent everything from snowmobiles to mittens.

SWIMMING

The **North Tahoe Beach Center** has a 26-ft hot tub and a beach with an enclosed swimming area and four sand volleyball courts. The complex includes a barbecue and picnic area, a fitness center, windsurfing and nonmotorized boat rentals, a snack bar, and a clubhouse with games. ⌧ *7860 N. Lake Blvd., Kings Beach,* ☎ *530/546–2566.* ⌑ *$8.*

Truckee

❼   *13 mi northwest of Kings Beach on Hwy. 267, 14 mi north of Tahoe City on Hwy. 89.*

Old West facades line the main street of Truckee, a favorite stopover for people traveling from the San Francisco Bay area to the north shore of Lake Tahoe. Galleries and boutiques are plentiful, but you will also find low-key diners, discount skiwear, and an old-fashioned five-and-dime store. Six miles south of Truckee on Hwy. 267 lies Northstar-at-Tahoe, a major ski resort. Stop by the **information booth** in the Amtrak depot (⌧ Railroad St. at Commercial Rd.) for a walking-tour map of historic Truckee.

Donner Memorial State Park commemorates the Donner Party, a group of 89 westward-bound pioneers who were trapped in the Sierra in the winter of 1846–47 in snow 22 ft deep. Only 47 survived, some by resorting to cannibalism and others by eating animal hides. The Immigrant Museum's hourly slide show details the Donner Party's plight. Other displays relate the history of other settlers and of railroad development through the Sierra. ⌧ *Off I–80, 2 mi west of Truckee,* ☎ *530/582–7892.* ⌑ *$2.* ☉ *Daily 9–4.*

Dining and Lodging

$$$–$$$$ ✕⌷ **Northstar-at-Tahoe Resort.** The center of action at the Truckee area's most complete destination resort is the Village Mall, a concentration of restaurants, shops, recreation facilities, and accommodations. The many sports activities—from golf and tennis to skiing and snowmobiling—make the resort especially popular with families. Lodgings range from hotel rooms to condos to private houses. Summer rates are lower than winter rates. Guests receive free lift tickets and shuttle

transportation, and have complimentary access to the Swim and Racquet Club's swimming pools, outdoor hot tubs, fitness center, and teen center. ⊠ *Hwy. 267, 6 mi southeast of Truckee (mailing address: Box 129, Truckee 96160),* ☎ *530/562–1010 or 800/466–6784,* FAX *530/562–2215,* WEB *www.skinorthstar.com. 230 units. 4 restaurants, kitchenettes (some), microwaves (some), in-room VCRs, 18-hole golf course, 12 tennis courts, bicycles, horseback riding, downhill skiing, sleigh rides, snowmobiling, recreation room, baby-sitting, children's programs (ages 2–6), laundry facilities. AE, D, MC, V.*

Outdoor Activities and Sports

CROSS-COUNTRY AND DOWNHILL SKIING

At **Northstar-at-Tahoe Resort,** two northeast-facing, wind-protected bowls provide some of the best powder skiing in the area, including steep chutes and long cruising runs. Top-to-bottom snowmaking and intense grooming assure good conditions on the 40 mi of trails. There are a wide skating lane for Nordic skiers and a terrain park and trails with dragon tails and magic moguls for snowboarders. The school offers programs for skiers ages five and up, and day care is available for children older than two. ⊠ *Hwy. 267 6 mi southeast of Truckee,* ☎ *530/562–1010; 530/562–1330 for snow phone,* FAX *530/562–2215. 66 trails on 1,800 acres, rated 25% beginner, 50% intermediate, 25% advanced. Longest run 2.9 mi, base 6,400′, summit 8,600′. Lifts: 13 lifts, including a gondola and 4 high-speed quads.*

HORSEBACK RIDING

Northstar Stables is the place for horseback riding in summer. With stables for three dozen horses, Northstar offers guided 45-minute, half-day, and full-day (for experienced riders only) rides. Instruction is provided, ponies are available for tots, and you can even board your own horse here. ⊠ *Northstar access road,* ☎ *530/562–2480.*

NEVADA SIDE

You don't need a roadside sign to know when you've crossed from California into Nevada. The lake's water and the pine trees may be identical, but the flashing lights and elaborate marquees of casinos announce legal gambling in garish hues.

Crystal Bay

❽ *1 mi east of Kings Beach on Hwy. 28; 30 mi north of South Lake Tahoe via Rte. 50 to Hwy. 28.*

Right at the Nevada border, Crystal Bay holds a cluster of casinos. The **Cal-Neva Lodge** (⊠ 2 Stateline Rd., ☎ 775/832–4000) is bisected by the state line. This joint opened in 1927 and has weathered nearly as many scandals—the largest involving former owner Frank Sinatra (he lost his gaming license in the 1960s for alleged mob connections)—as it has blizzards. The **Tahoe Biltmore** (⊠ Hwy. 28 at Stateline Rd., ☎ 775/ 831–0660) serves its popular $1.99 breakfast special 24 hours a day. **Jim Kelley's Nugget** (⊠ Hwy. 28 at Stateline Rd., ☎ 775/831–0455) serves 101 kinds of beers.

Dining and Lodging

$–$$$ ✕ **Soule Domain.** Some of Lake Tahoe's most creative and delicious
★ dinners are served in this romantic 1927 pine-log cabin. Chef-owner Charles Edward Soule IV's specialties include curried cashew chicken, smoked rabbit ravioli, rock shrimp with sea scallops, and a vegan sauté. Reservations are essential on weekends. ⊠ *Cove St. across from Tahoe Biltmore,* ☎ *530/546–7529. AE, DC, MC, V. No lunch.*

$–$$$ 🖼 **Cal-Neva Lodge.** All the rooms in this hotel-casino have views of Lake Tahoe and the mountains. The hotel also rents out seven two-bedroom chalets and 12 cabins with living rooms. There is an arcade with video games for children and cabaret entertainment for grown-ups. ✉ *2 Stateline Rd., Box 368, 89402,* ☎ *775/832–4000 or 800/225–6382,* 🅵🅰🆇 *775/831–9007,* 🆆🅴🅱 *www.calnevaresort.com. 220 rooms, 20 suites, 19 cabins. Restaurant, TVs with movies, video game room, some pets allowed, coffee shop, tennis court, pool, hot tub, sauna, casino. AE, D, DC, MC, V.*

Incline Village

9   *3 mi east of Crystal Bay on Hwy. 28.*

Incline Village, Nevada's only privately owned town, dates to the early 1960s, when an Oklahoma developer bought 10,000 acres north of Lake Tahoe. His idea was to sketch out a plan for a town without a central commercial district, hoping to prevent congestion and to preserve the area's natural beauty. One-acre lakeshore lots originally fetched $12,000–$15,000; today you couldn't touch even the land for less than several million. Check out **Lakeshore Drive,** along which you'll see some of the most expensive real estate in Nevada. Incline Village's **recreation center** (✉ 980 Incline Way, ☎ 775/832–1300) has an eight-lane swimming pool and a fitness area, basketball court, game room, and snack bar.

OFF THE BEATEN PATH   **MOUNT ROSE –** If you want to ski some of the highest slopes in the Lake Tahoe region, take Highway 431 north out of Incline Village to Mt. Rose. Reno is another 30 mi farther. On the way is Tahoe Meadows, the most popular area near North Lake for noncommercial sledding, tubing, snowshoeing, cross-country skiing, and snowmobiling. ☎ *775/849–0704.*

☾   The 1960s television western *Bonanza* inspired the **Ponderosa Ranch** theme park. Attractions include the Cartwrights' ranch house, a western town complete with museums, shops, snack bars, gunfight and stunt show, roping demonstrations, petting zoo, and a big saloon. There are a self-guided nature trail, free pony rides for children, and if you're here from 8 to 9:30, a breakfast hayride. ✉ *Hwy. 28, 2 mi south of Incline Village,* ☎ *775/831–0691.* 🎟 *$9.50, breakfast $2 extra.* ☉ *Mid-Apr.–Oct., daily 9:30–5.*

The *Sierra Cloud* (☎ 775/831–1111), a large trimaran, cruises the north-shore area morning and afternoon May through October from the Hyatt Regency Hotel in Incline Village. Fares run between $50 and $60.

Dining and Lodging

$–$$ ✕ **Azzara's.** An Italian trattoria with a light, inviting dining room, Azzara's serves a dozen pasta dishes and many pizzas, as well as chicken, lamb, veal, shrimp, and beef. Dinners include soup or salad, a vegetable, and olive-oil garlic bread. ✉ *Incline Center Mall, 930 Tahoe Blvd.,* ☎ *775/831–0346. MC, V. Closed Mon.*

$–$$ ✕ **Stanley's Restaurant and Lounge.** With its intimate bar and venerable dining room (1958), this local favorite is a good bet any time for American fare on the hearty side, such as barbecued pork ribs. Lighter bites, such as a fresh snapper taco, are also available. Ample breakfasts featuring eggs Benedict and green-goddess omelets are served weekends. Stanley's has a huge lakefront deck for outdoor dining in summer. ✉ *941 Tahoe Blvd.,* ☎ *775/831–9944. AE, D, MC, V.*

$$–$$$$ ✕⌷ **Hyatt Lake Tahoe Resort Hotel/Casino.** All the rooms, suites, and cottages in this luxurious hotel on the lake are top-notch, and many have fireplaces. The restaurants are the Lone Eagle Grille (fairly good Continental food—steak, seafood, pasta, and rotisserie dishes; $$–$$$), Ciao Mein Trattoria (Asian-Italian), and the Sierra Café (open 24 hours; $–$$). ⌷ *Lakeshore and Country Club Drs., 89450,* ☎ *775/ 831–1111 or 800/233–1234,* FAX *775/831–7508,* WEB *www. hyatt-tahoe.com. 432 rooms, 28 suites. 4 restaurants, coffee shop, room service, TVs with cable and movies, pool, health club, 2 saunas, spa, beach, bicycles, lobby lounge, casino, children's programs (ages 18 months–16 years), laundry service. AE, D, DC, MC, V.*

Outdoor Activities and Sports

CROSS-COUNTRY AND DOWNHILL SKIING

Diamond Peak. A fun family mood prevails at Diamond Peak, which has many special programs and affordable rates. Snowmaking covers 80% of the mountain, and runs are groomed nightly. The ride up the 1-mi Crystal chair rewards you with the best views of the lake from any ski area. Diamond Peak is less crowded than some of the larger areas and provides free shuttles to nearby lodging. A first timer's package, which includes rentals, a lesson, and a lift ticket, is $42. A parent-and-child ski package is $50, with each additional child's lift ticket $8. There is a half-pipe for snowboarders. **Diamond Peak Cross-Country** (⌷ off Hwy. 431, ☎ 775/832–1177) has 22 mi of groomed track with skating lanes. The trail system rises from 7,400 ft to 9,100 ft, with endless wilderness to explore. ⌷ *1210 Ski Way, off Hwy. 28 to Country Club Dr., Incline Village, NV 89450,* ☎ *775/832–1177 or 800/468– 2463. 29 trails on 655 acres, rated 18% beginner, 46% intermediate, 36% advanced. Longest run 2½ mi, base 6,700′, summit 8,540′. Lifts: 6, including 2 high-speed quads.*

GOLF

Incline Championship (⌷ 955 Fairway Blvd., ☎ 775/832–1144) is an 18-hole, par-72 course with a driving range. The greens fee is $125. **Incline Mountain** (⌷ 690 Wilson Way, ☎ 775/832–1150) is an easy 18-holer; par is 58. The greens fee starts at $50; optional power carts at both courses cost $15.

Reno

➓ *45 mi northeast of Crystal Bay on I–80*

Reno, once the gambling and divorce capital of the country, is smaller, less crowded, friendlier, and prettier than Las Vegas. Established in 1859 as a trading station at a bridge over the Truckee River, Reno grew along with the silver mines of nearby Virginia City (starting in 1860), the railroad (railroad officials named the town in 1868), and gambling (legalized in 1931). Temperatures year-round are warmer than Tahoe's, though the summer thermometer is always cooler than Sacramento and the Central Valley's, making strolling around town a pleasure. The city's focal point is the famous Reno Arch, a sign over the upper end of Virginia Street proclaiming it THE BIGGEST LITTLE CITY IN THE WORLD. As in Stateline, gambling is a favorite pastime, and most of the casinos are crowded into five square blocks downtown. Besides the casino-hotels, Reno has a number of cultural and family-friendly attractions.

Circus Circus (⌷ 500 N. Sierra St., ☎ 775/329–0711 or 800/648–5010, WEB www.circusreno.com), marked by a neon clown sucking a lollipop, is the best stop for families with children. Complete with clowns, games, fun-house mirrors, and circus acts, the midway on the mezzanine above the casino floor is open from 10 AM to midnight. **Eldorado**

(⊠ 345 N. Virginia St., ☎ 775/786–5700 or 800/648–5966, WEB www.eldoradoreno.com) is action packed, with tons of slots, good bar-top video poker, and great coffee shop and food-court fare. **Harrah's** (⊠ 219 N. Center St., ☎ 775/786–3232 or 800/648–3773, WEB www.harrahsreno.com) debuted in 1937 as the Tango Club and now occupies two city blocks, with a sprawling casino, a race-and-sports book, and an outdoor promenade; it also has a 29-story Hampton Inn annex. Minimums are low, and service is friendly. **Silver Legacy** (⊠ 407 N. Virginia St., ☎ 775/329–4777 or 800/687–7833, WEB www.silverlegacyresort.com) is a classy, Victorian-themed casino with a 120-ft-tall mining rig that mints silver-dollar tokens.

The always-festive **Downtown River Walk** (⊠ S. Virginia St. and the river, ☎ 775/334–2077) often hosts special events featuring street performers, musicians, dancers, food, art exhibits, and games. On the University of Nevada campus, the sleekly designed **Fleischmann Planetarium** (⊠ 1600 N. Virginia St., ☎ 775/784–4811, WEB www.planetarium.unr.nevada.edu; ⊡ free) has films and astronomy shows. The **Nevada Museum of Art** (⊠ 160 W. Liberty St., ☎ 775/329–3333, WEB www.nevadaart.org; ⊡ $3), the state's largest art museum, has changing exhibits. More than 220 antique and classic automobiles, including an Elvis Presley Cadillac, are on display at the **National Automobile Museum** (⊠ Mill and Lake Sts., ☎ 775/333–9300, WEB www.automuseum.org; ⊡ $7.50). **Victorian Square** (⊠ Victorian Ave. between Rock and Pyramid in downtown Sparks, Reno's sister city to the east) is fringed by restored turn-of-the-20th-century houses and Victorian-dressed casinos and storefronts; its bandstand is the focal point of the many festivals held here.

OFF THE
BEATEN PATH

CARSON CITY AND VIRGINIA CITY – Nevada's capital, Carson City, is a 30-minute drive from Stateline. At Spooner Junction, about 10 mi north of Stateline, head east on Route 50. In 10 mi you reach Route 395, where you go 1 mi north to Carson City. Most of its historic buildings and other attractions, including the Nevada State Museum and the Nevada Railroad Museum, are along Route 395, the main street through town. About a 30-minute drive up Highway 342 northeast of Carson City is the fabled mining town of Virginia City, one of the largest and most authentic historical mining towns in the West. It's chock full of mine tours, mansions, museums, saloons, and, of course, dozens of shops selling everything from amethysts to yucca. For information on the area contact the **Carson City Chamber of Commerce** (⊠ 1900 S. Carson St., Carson City, ☎ 775/882–1565, WEB www.carsoncitychamber.com).

Dining and Lodging

$$$–$$$$ ✕ **White Orchid.** The fanciest and some say best restaurant in northern Nevada, this cozy room at the Peppermill hosts a menu of contemporary cuisine that changes regularly according to what's fresh. The selection of wine by the glass is extensive. ⊠ 2707 S. Virginia St., ☎ 775/689-7300. *D, MC, V. No lunch.*

$$–$$$ ✕ **Harrah's Steak House.** This casino-hotel's dark and romantic restaurant has been serving prime beef and fresh seafood since 1967. ⊠ 219 N. Center St., ☎ 775/786–3232. *AE, D, DC, MC, V.*

$–$$ ✕ **Café de Thai.** The soups, salads, stir-fries, and curries are expertly prepared by a Thai national trained at the Culinary Institute; the new location, in a stand-alone building, is a major improvement over the old shopping center storefront. ⊠ 7499 Longley La., ☎ 775/829–8424. *MC, V.*

$–$$ ✕ **Louis' Basque Corner.** Basque shepherds once populated northern Nevada; sample their heritage at this family-style restaurant, which specializes in oxtail, lamb, and tongue. ⊠ *301 E. 4th St.,* ☎ *775/323–7203. AE, DC, MC, V.*

$ ✕ **Bertha Miranda's Mexican Restaurant.** Begun as a hole-in-the-wall, this has grown into a highly successful establishment. The food is made fresh by Bertha's family, and the salsa is the best in town. ⊠ *336 Mill St.,* ☎ *775/786–9697. MC, V.*

$ ✕ **John A's Oyster Bar.** Entirely nautical in theme, John A's restaurant and bar serves the best steamers, pan roasts, cioppino, chowder, shrimp Louie, and cocktails this side of Fisherman's Wharf. ⊠ *1100 Nugget Ave., Sparks,* ☎ *775/356–3300. AE, D, DC, MC, V.*

$ ✕ **Nugget Diner.** Think classic Americana diner: seating is on stools at front and back counters. The Awful Awful Burger is renowned, as is the prime rib. ⊠ *Nugget Casino, 233 N. Virginia St.,* ☎ *775/323–0716. MC, V.*

$–$$$$ 🏨 **Eldorado.** Owned by fourth-generation locals, the Eldorado is known for its fine food and attention to detail. Rooms, including an all-suite tower, overlook the mountains or downtown. ⊠ *345 N. Virginia St., 89501,* ☎ *775/786–5700 or 800/648–5966,* 𝖥𝖠𝖷 *702/322–7124,* 𝖶𝖤𝖡 *www.eldoradoreno.com. 836 rooms. 8 restaurants, meeting rooms, pool, cable TV with movies. AE, D, DC, MC, V.*

$–$$$ 🏨 **Harrah's.** This is one of the most luxurious hotels in downtown Reno. Large guest rooms decorated in blues and mauves overlook downtown and the entire mountain-ringed valley. ⊠ *219 N. Center St., 89501,* ☎ *775/786–3232 or 800/648–3773,* 𝖶𝖤𝖡 *www.harrahsreno.com. 565 rooms. 6 restaurants, pool, health club, cable TV with movies, video game room. AE, D, MC, V.*

$–$$$ 🏨 **Peppermill.** Three miles from downtown, the Peppermill has Reno's most colorful casino. It has eight room sizes (and styles) to choose from; their photos are on display in the lobby. ⊠ *2707 S. Virginia St., 89502,* ☎ *775/826–2121 or 800/648–6992,* 𝖥𝖠𝖷 *775/826–5205,* 𝖶𝖤𝖡 *www.peppermillcasinos.com. 1,070 rooms. 5 restaurants, pool, health club, meeting rooms, cable TV with movies, video game room. AE, D, DC, MC, V.*

$–$$$ 🏨 **Reno Hilton.** This 27-story hotel near the airport is Nevada's largest hotel north of Las Vegas. In fact, almost everything here is the area's largest: the buffet, race and sports books, showroom, convention facilities, bowling alley, arcade, wedding chapel, driving range, and RV park. ⊠ *2500 E. 2nd St., 89595,* ☎ *775/789–2000 or 800/648–5080,* 𝖥𝖠𝖷 *775/789–2418,* 𝖶𝖤𝖡 *www.renohilton.com. 6 restaurants, pool, health club, meeting rooms, video game room, cable TV with movies. AE, D, DC, MC, V.*

$–$$$ 🏨 **Silver Legacy.** This two-tower megaresort centers on a 120-ft-tall mining machine that coins dollar tokens. Skywalks connect it to Circus Circus and the Eldorado. The rooms are still the newest in Reno. ⊠ *407 N. Virginia St., 89501,* ☎ *775/329–4777 or 800/687–8733,* 𝖶𝖤𝖡 *www.silverlegacy.com. 1,700 rooms. 5 restaurants, cable TVs with movies. AE, D, DC, MC, V.*

$ 🏨 **Boomtown.** Ten miles west of Reno on I–80, this is the first hotel-casino on the way into Nevada from California. It has comfortable newer rooms and suites, a large RV park, a good bargain buffet, and the largest family fun center in northern Nevada. ⊠ *I–80 Exit 4, Verdi 89431,* ☎ *775/345–6000 or 877/726–6686,* 𝖥𝖠𝖷 *775/345–8550,* 𝖶𝖤𝖡 *www.boomtowncasinos.com. 347 rooms. 3 restaurants, pool, meeting rooms, cable TV. AE, D, DC, MC, V.*

$ 🏨 **Circus Circus.** This smaller version of the giant Las Vegas hotel has ♻ the same family-oriented theme, including circus midway games. The rooms, though small and garish, are good values—when you can get one. ⊠ *500 N. Sierra St., 89503,* ☎ *775/329–0711 or 800/648–5010,* FAX *775/329–0599,* WEB *www.circusreno.com. 1,625 rooms. 3 restaurants, meeting rooms, cable TV. AE, DC, MC, V.*

Lake Tahoe–Nevada State Park

Hwy. 28, between Incline Village and Zephyr Cove.

Protecting much of the lake's eastern shore from development, Lake Tahoe–Nevada State Park comprises several units. Beaches and trails provide access to a wilder side of the lake, whether you are into cross-country skiing, hiking, or just relaxing at a picnic.

★ Ⓒ **Sand Harbor Beach** is sometimes filled to capacity by 11 AM on summer weekends. Stroll the boardwalk and read the information signs to get a good lesson in the local ecology. A **pop-music festival** (☎ 775/832–1606 or 800/468–2463) is held at the beach in July, and a **Shakespeare festival** (☎ 775/832–1616) is held every August. ⊠ *Hwy. 28, 4 mi south of Incline Village,* ☎ *775/831–0494.*

★ **Cave Rock,** 25 yards of solid stone at the southern end of Lake Tahoe–Nevada State Park, is the throat of an extinct volcano. Tahoe Tessie, the lake's version of the Loch Ness monster, is reputed to live in a cavern below the impressive outcropping. For the Washoe Indians this area is a sacred burial site. Cave Rock towers over a parking lot, a lakefront picnic ground, and a boat launch. The rest area provides the best vantage point of this cliff. ⊠ *Rte. 50, 13 mi south of Sand Harbor Beach,* ☎ *775/831–0494.*

Zephyr Cove

⑪ *Rte. 50, 22 mi south of Incline Village.*

The largest settlement between Incline Village and Stateline is Zephyr Cove, a tiny resort. It has a beach, marina, campground, picnic area, coffee shop in a historic log lodge, rustic cabins, and nearby riding stables. The 550-passenger **MS *Dixie II*** (☎ 775/588–3508), a stern-wheeler, sails year-round from Zephyr Cove Marina to Emerald Bay on lunch and dinner cruises. Fares range from $24 to $49. The ***Woodwind*** (☎ 775/588–3000), a glass-bottom trimaran, sails on regular and champagne cruises April through October from Zephyr Cove Resort. Fares range from $24 to $30. In winter you can rent snowmobiles and snowshoes.

OFF THE BEATEN PATH **KINGSBURY GRADE –** This road, also known as Highway 207, is one of three roads that access Tahoe from the east. Originally a toll road used by wagon trains to get over the crest of the Sierra, it has sweeping views of the Carson Valley. Off Highway 206, which intersects Highway 207, is Genoa, the oldest settlement in Nevada. Along Main Street are a museum in Nevada's oldest courthouse, a small state park, and the state's longest-standing saloon.

Camping

⚠ **Zephyr Cove Resort.** This sprawling campground on the mountain side of Route 50 is one of the largest on the lake and remains open all winter long. It's mostly for RVers but has drive-in and walk-in tenting sites. Across the highway are 28 lakefront cabins, a marina with boat rentals, and horseback riding and snowmobiling facilities. Be careful crossing the road! *Flush toilets, full hookups, partial hookups, dump station, drinking water, laundry facilities, showers, fire pits, grills, picnic tables, restaurant, snack bar, general store, playground, swim-*

ming. ⊠ *Rte. 50, 5 mi north of Stateline,* ☎ *775-589-4981. 175 sites.* ⊙ *Year-round.*

Stateline

⑫ *5 mi south of Zephyr Cove on Rte. 50.*

Stateline is a great border town in the Nevada tradition. Its four high-rise casinos are as vertical and contained as the commercial district of South Lake Tahoe, on the California side, is horizontal and sprawling. And Stateline is as relentlessly indoors oriented as the rest of the lake is focused on the outdoors. This strip is where you'll find the most concentrated action at Lake Tahoe: restaurants (including typical casino buffets), showrooms with famous headliners and razzle-dazzle revues, luxury rooms and suites, and 24-hour casino gambling.

Dining and Lodging

$–$$$ ✕ **Chart House.** It's worth the drive up the steep grade to see the view from here. Try to arrive for sunset. The American menu of steak and seafood is complemented by an abundant salad bar. The restaurant has a children's menu. ⊠ *329 Kingsbury Grade,* ☎ *775/588–6276. AE, D, DC, MC, V. No lunch.*

$–$$$ ✕ **Llewellyn's Restaurant.** Elegantly decorated in blond wood and
★ pastels, the restaurant atop Harvey's casino merits special mention. Almost every table has superb views of Lake Tahoe. Dinner entrées—seafood, meat, and poultry—are served with unusual accompaniments, such as smoked duck with orange-chili plum sauce, lobster tails with Thai red-curry sauce, and wild boar tenderloin with a dried cherry and fig compote. Lunches are reasonably priced, with high-end selections as well as hamburgers. ⊠ *Harvey's Resort, Rte. 50,* ☎ *775/588–2411 or 800/553–1022. AE, D, DC, MC, V.*

$$–$$$$ ✕🏨 **Harvey's Resort Hotel/Casino.** Harvey's, which started as a cabin
★ in 1944, is now the largest resort in Tahoe. Rooms have custom furnishings, oversize marble baths, and minibars. Use of the health club, spa, and pool is free to guests—a rarity for this area. ⊠ *Rte. 50, Box 128, 89449,* ☎ *775/588–2411 or 800/648–3361,* FAX *775/782–4889,* WEB *www.harveys-tahoe.com. 705 rooms, 38 suites. 8 restaurants, minibars, cable TV with movies, meeting rooms, pool, hair salon, health club, hot tub, spa, casino. AE, D, DC, MC, V.*

$–$$$ 🏨 **Caesars Tahoe.** Most rooms and suites at Caesars have oversize tubs, king-size beds, two telephones, and a view of Lake Tahoe or the encircling mountains. Top-name entertainers perform in the 1,600-seat Circus Maximus. Planet Hollywood is here, plus Chinese, Italian, and American restaurants; a 24-hour coffee shop with a buffet; and a frozen-yogurt emporium. ⊠ *55 Rte. 50, Box 5800, 89449,* ☎ *775/588–3515; 800/648–3353 for reservations and show information,* FAX *775/586–2068,* WEB *www.caesars.com. 328 rooms, 112 suites. 5 restaurants, coffee shop, meeting rooms, cable TV with movies, 4 tennis courts, indoor pool, health club, hot tub, sauna, spa, showroom. AE, D, DC, MC, V.*

$$–$$$$ ✕🏨 **Harrah's Tahoe Hotel/Casino.** Luxurious guest rooms here have two full bathrooms, each with a television and telephone. All rooms have views of the lake and the mountains. Top-name entertainment is presented in the South Shore Room. Among the restaurants, the romantic 16th-floor Summit is a standout; the buffet is also on the 16th floor. A tunnel runs under Route 50 to Harvey's, which Harrah's now owns. ⊠ *Rte. 50, Box 8, 89449,* ☎ *775/588–6611 or 800/427–7247,* FAX *775/588–6607,* WEB *www.harrahstahoe.com. 470 rooms, 62 suites. 7 restaurants, room service, cable TV with movies, meeting rooms, indoor pool, hair salon, health club, hot tub, casino, laundry service, kennel. AE, D, DC, MC, V.*

\$-\$\$\$\$ 🏨 **Horizon Casino Resort.** Many guest rooms at this hotel-casino have lake views. The casino has a beaux arts look, brightened by pale molded wood and mirrors. The Grande Lake Theatre, Golden Cabaret, and Aspen Lounge present shows, as well as up-and-coming and name entertainers. Le Grande Buffet has a nightly prime-rib special. ✉ *Rte. 50, Box C, 89449,* ☎ *775/588–6211 or 800/322–7723,* FAX *775/588–1344,* WEB *www.horizoncasino.com. 516 rooms, 23 suites. 3 restaurants, cable TV with movies, meeting rooms, pool, gym, 3 hot tubs, casino, meeting room. AE, D, DC, MC, V.*

\$-\$\$ 🏨 **Lakeside Inn and Casino.** The smallest of the Stateline casinos, the Lakeside has a rustic look. Guest rooms are in two-story motel-style buildings away from the casino area. ✉ *Rte. 50 at Kingsbury Grade, Box 5640, 89449,* ☎ *775/588–7777 or 800/624–7980,* FAX *775/588–4092,* WEB *www.lakesideinn.com. 115 rooms, 9 suites. Restaurant, pool, casino. AE, D, DC, MC, V.*

Nightlife

The top entertainment venues are the **Circus Maximus,** at Caesars Tahoe; the Emerald Theater, at Harvey's; the **South Shore Room,** at Harrah's; and Horizon's **Grand Lake Theatre.** Comedy fans might laugh with Jay Leno, while illusion lovers could catch David Copperfield. For Las Vegas–style production shows—fast-paced dancing, singing, and novelty acts—try Harrah's or the Horizon. The big showrooms occasionally present performances of musicals by touring Broadway companies. Reservations are almost always required for superstar shows. Depending on the act, cocktail shows usually cost from \$15 to \$60. Smaller casino cabarets sometimes have a cover charge or drink minimum.

Bars around the lake present pop and country-western singers and musicians, and in winter the ski resorts do the same. Summer alternatives are outdoor music events, from chamber quartets to rock performers, at **Sand Harbor** and the **Lake Tahoe Visitor Center amphitheater.**

Outdoor Activities and Sports

GOLF

Edgewood Tahoe (✉ Rte. 50 and Lake Pkwy., behind Horizon Casino, Stateline, ☎ 775/588–3566), right on the lake, is an 18-hole, par-72 course with a driving range. The \$200 greens fee includes a cart (though you can walk if you wish); the course is open from 7 AM to 4 PM from May through October. The 18-hole, par-70 **Lake Tahoe Golf Course** (✉ Rte. 50, between Lake Tahoe Airport and Meyers, ☎ 530/577–0788) has a driving range. The greens fee starts at \$45 midweek; a cart (mandatory from Friday through Sunday) costs \$20.

SCUBA DIVING

Sun Sports (✉ 3564 Lake Tahoe Blvd., South Lake Tahoe, ☎ 530/541–6000) is a full-service PADI dive center with rentals and instruction.

LAKE TAHOE A TO Z

To research prices, get advice from other travelers, and book travel arrangements, visit www.fodors.com.

AIR TRAVEL

Reno–Tahoe International Airport, in Reno, 35 mi northeast of the closest point on the lake, is served by Alaska, American, America West, Continental, Delta, Northwest, Skywest, Southwest, and United airlines. (*See* Air Travel *in* Smart Travel Tips A to Z for airline phone numbers.)

➤ AIRPORT INFORMATION: **Reno–Tahoe International Airport** (✉ Rte. 395, Exit 65B, Reno, NV, ☎ 775/328–6400). **Tahoe Casino Express**

(☎ 775/785–2424 or 800/446–6128). **Lake Tahoe Airport** (☎ 530/542–6180).

BUS TRAVEL

Greyhound stops in Sacramento, Truckee, and Reno, Nevada.

South Tahoe Area Ground Express runs along Route 50 and through the neighborhoods of South Lake Tahoe daily from 6 AM to 12:15 AM. Tahoe Area Regional Transit (TART) operates buses along Lake Tahoe's northern and western shores between Tahoma (from Meeks Bay in summer) and Incline Village daily from 6:30 to 6:30. Free shuttle buses run among the casinos, major ski resorts, and motels of South Lake Tahoe. Tahoe Casino Express runs upward of 14 daily buses between Reno-Tahoe Airport and hotels in Stateline.

➤ BUS INFORMATION: **Greyhound** (☎ 800/231–2222). **South Tahoe Area Ground Express** (STAGE; ☎ 530/573–2080). **Tahoe Area Rapid Transit** (TART; ☎ 530/581–6365 or 800/736–6365). **Tahoe Casino Express** (☎ 775/785–2424).

CAR RENTAL

The major car-rental agencies—Hertz, Avis, Budget, National, Thrifty, Enterprise, and Dollar—all have counters at Reno-Tahoe International Airport. Enterprise has an outlet at the South Lake Tahoe Airport; Avis has one at Harrah's Stateline; and Dollar has counters at the Reno Hilton, Circus Circus, and Caesars Tahoe. *See* Car Rental *in* Smart Travel Tips A to Z for national rental agency phone numbers.

CAR TRAVEL

Lake Tahoe is 198 mi northeast of San Francisco, a drive of less than four hours when traffic and the weather cooperate. Try to avoid the heavy traffic leaving the San Francisco area for Tahoe on Friday afternoon and returning on Sunday afternoon. The major route is I–80, which cuts through the Sierra Nevada about 14 mi north of the lake. From there Highway 89 and Highway 267 reach the west and north shores, respectively. Route 50 is the more direct route to the south shore, taking about 2½ hours from Sacramento. From Reno you can get to the north shore by heading west on Highway 431 (a total of 35 mi). For the south shore, head south on Route 395 through Carson City, and then turn west on Route 50 (50 mi total).

The scenic 72-mi highway around the lake is marked Highway 89 on the southwest and west shores, Highway 28 on the north and northeast shores, and Route 50 on the east and southeast. Sections of Highway 89 sometimes close during winter, making it impossible to complete the circular drive. Interstate 80, Route 50, and Route 395 are all-weather highways, but there may be delays as snow is cleared during major storms. Carry tire chains from October through May (car-rental agencies provide them with their vehicles).

➤ CONTACTS: **California Highway Patrol** (☎ 530/587–3510). **Nevada Highway Patrol** (☎ 775/687–5300).

EMERGENCIES

In an emergency dial 911.

➤ HOSPITALS: **Barton Memorial Hospital** (✉ 2170 South Ave., South Lake Tahoe, ☎ 530/541–3420). **Tahoe Forest Hospital** (✉ 10121 Pine Ave., Truckee, ☎ 530/587–6011.)

LODGING

The Lake Tahoe Visitors Authority provides information on south-shore lodging, while the North Lake Tahoe Resort Association does the same for the north shore. For campgrounds in California state parks, contact Park.net. Contact the Reno-Sparks Convention and Visitors Authority for lodging in the Reno metropolitan area.

➤ LOCAL AGENTS: **Lake Tahoe Visitors Authority** (☎ 800/288–2463, www.virtualtahoe.com). **North Lake Tahoe Resort Association** (☎ 800/ 824–6348, www.tahoefun.org). **Park.net** (☎ 800/444–7275, www. reserveamerica.com). **Reno-Sparks Convention and Visitors Authority** (☎ 775/827–7647, www.renolaketahoe.com).

TOURS

Hornblower's Tahoe Queen (South Lake Tahoe), the *Sierra Cloud* (Incline Village), and the MS *Dixie II* and the *Woodwind* (both Zephyr Cove) all operate guided boat tours. See the listings under each town for more information.

Gray Line/Frontier Tours runs daily tours to South Lake Tahoe, Carson City, and Virginia City. Lake Tahoe Adventures operates a summer trek skirting the Desolation Wilderness on the Rubicon Trail in four-wheel-drive all-terrain vehicles; in winter they head across Carson Valley to the Pine Nut Mountains for two-hour excursions on ATVs and snowmobiles.

Lake Tahoe Balloons conducts excursions year-round over the lake or over the Carson Valley for $129 per person for half-hour flights and $195 for hour-long flights (champagne brunch included).

CalVada Seaplanes Inc. provides rides over the lake for $60–$100 per person, depending on the length of the trip. High Country Soaring glider rides over the lake and valley depart from the Douglas County Airport, Gardnerville.

➤ CONTACTS: **CalVada Seaplane** (☎ 530/544–1221 or 530/546–3984). **Gray Line/Frontier Tours** (☎ 775/331–8687 or 800/831–2877). **Lake Tahoe Adventures** (☎ 530/577–2940). **Lake Tahoe Balloons** (☎ 530/ 544–1221 or 800/872–9294).

TRAIN TRAVEL

Amtrak's cross-country rail service makes stops in Reno. The *California Zephyr* stops in the heart of downtown Reno once eastbound (Salt Lake, Denver, and Chicago) and once westbound (Truckee, Sacramento, and Oakland) daily, blocking traffic for 5–10 minutes. Amtrak also operates several buses daily between Reno and Sacramento to connect with the *Coast Starlight,* which runs south to southern California and north to Oregon and Washington.

➤ CONTACT: **Amtrak** (✉ 135 E. Commercial Row, ☎ 775/329–8638 or 800/872–7245).

VISITOR INFORMATION

➤ CONTACTS: **California State Department of Parks and Recreation** (☎ 916/324–4442, WEB www.cal-parks.ca.gov). **Lake Tahoe Hotline** (☎ 530/ 542–4636 for south-shore events; 530/546–5253 for north-shore events; 775/831–6677 for Nevada events, WEB www.laketahoehotline.com). **Lake Tahoe Visitors Authority** (✉ 1156 Ski Run Blvd., South Lake Tahoe, CA 96150, ☎ 530/544–5050 or 800/288–2463, WEB www.virtualtahoe. com). **North Lake Tahoe Resort Association** (✉ Box 5578, Tahoe City, CA 96145, ☎ 530/583–3494 or 800/824–6348, FAX 530/581–4081, WEB www.tahoefun.org). **Reno-Sparks Convention and Visitors Authority** (✉ 4590 S. Virginia St., Reno 89502, ☎ 775/827–7600 or 800/367– 7366; WEB www.renolaketahoe.com). **Ski Report Hotline** (☎ 415/864– 6440). **U.S. Forest Service** backcountry recording (☎ 530/587–2158).

8 THE PENINSULA AND SOUTH BAY

SOUTH OF SAN FRANCISCO TO SAN JOSE

South of San Francisco lie two parallel worlds. On the fog-shrouded coast, rural towns perch between the mountains and the beach. A few miles to the east the suburban Peninsula pulses with prosperity and draws innovative inspiration from Stanford University. The South Bay contains old-fashioned neighborhoods, abundant green hills, and the corporate corridors of Silicon Valley—all within minutes of each other. To the surprise of many visitors, San Francisco's backyard is wonderfully multifaceted, with some of the Bay Area's finest restaurants and shops as well as hiking and whale-watching.

By Marty
Olmstead and
John A.
Vlahides

ONLY A FEW MILES FROM SAN FRANCISCO, the San Mateo County coast's undeveloped hills, rugged coastline, and quaint towns and inns are worlds away from both the city to the north and the suburbs to the east and south. Most towns that dot the coast are no more than a few blocks long, with just enough room for a couple of B&Bs, restaurants, and boutiques or galleries. As you wind your way from town to town, past Christmas tree farms, pumpkin patches, and stunning beaches, you'll find that the pace of life is slower here than in the rest of the Bay Area.

Over the Santa Cruz Mountains from the coast, the Inland Peninsula is often slighted by visitors to the Bay Area, many of whom associate the area with traffic congestion and urban sprawl. Indeed, much of the area from Santa Clara County to San Francisco is clogged with office complexes and strip-mall shopping centers. But the Peninsula also has lovely hills and redwood forests. Former country estates built by the mining and transportation "bonanza kings" of the 19th century are hidden away, waiting to be discovered by those who care to look.

Farther south is the heart of Silicon Valley, the birthplace of the tiny electronic chips and circuits that support the information superhighway. Look beyond what seems to be an endless sprawl of office parks, intertwined highways, shopping centers, and high-rises, and you'll find such diverse towns as Santa Clara, with its 200-year-old mission; Saratoga, with its fine antiques stores and French restaurants; Campbell, whose old town center boasts a finely renovated historic mansion and a classic melodrama theater; and San Jose—the third-largest city both in California and on the West Coast—with its burgeoning core, its many microneighborhoods, and a growing ribbon of urban green connecting the city from north to south. Take a weekend, rent a car, open the windows or fold down the top, and head south.

Pleasures and Pastimes

Beaches
The main draw of coastal San Mateo County is its beaches. From Montara to Pescadero the strands accessible from Route 1 are surprisingly uncrowded. Fog and cool weather may keep many people out of the water for large portions of the year, but the unspoiled beauty and wildlife make these beaches a treasure of the Bay Area.

Dining
It used to be that for a really world-class dining experience, Peninsula and South Bay food lovers would head to San Francisco. No longer. Today some of the country's greatest chefs recognize the area's appeal and have opened trendy bistros and eateries, especially in San Jose's revitalized downtown. Dining might be a notch more casual than in San Francisco—and a notch less expensive, too—but that doesn't mean you won't need reservations. Along the coast, however, restaurants are strictly casual, and unless otherwise noted, you can generally walk in without a wait for a table.

CATEGORY	COST*
$$$$	over $30
$$$	$22–$30
$$	$15–$21
$	under $15

per person for a main course at dinner, excluding tip and 8¼% tax

Lodging

Plan ahead because during the week many hotels in the region are heavily booked by business travelers up to two weeks in advance. Conversely, many business- and convention-oriented hotels can be nearly empty on weekends, when rates plummet and package deals abound. If you have a car, also consider smaller hotels in such outlying areas as Campbell, along the Alameda in Santa Clara, or on Stevens Creek Boulevard in San Jose or Santa Clara. Along the coast distinctive inns and B&Bs are the norm.

CATEGORY	COST*
$$$$	over $225
$$$	$160–$225
$$	$100–$159
$	under $100

All prices are for a standard double room, excluding 10% tax.

Historic Homesteads

The communities of the Peninsula and South Bay—once known not for computers but for their blossoming fruit orchards and vineyards—work hard to preserve their parklands and turn-of-the-20th-century homesteads. In Woodside, Filoli stands as one of the great California country houses that remain intact. The Winchester Mystery House, in San Jose, may be the best-known site, but look beyond the tales of ghosts to see the sprawling farmhouse it once was. You can also visit former vineyards and historic homes in the Santa Cruz Mountains, notably Villa Montalvo and the Mountain Winery in Saratoga.

Exploring the Peninsula and South Bay

You'll need a car to get around. The Inland Peninsula and South Bay is a tangle of freeways, especially in the area around San Jose, so avoid driving in rush hour if you can avoid it. Once you get over the coastal hills and onto Highway 1 along the coast, you'll feel a world away from the Silicon Valley.

Numbers in the text correspond to numbers in the margin and on the San Mateo County and the South Bay and Downtown San Jose maps.

Great Itineraries

IF YOU HAVE 1 DAY

Spend your morning in **Palo Alto** ⑤, taking a look around town and a tour of **Stanford University.** In the afternoon head for ⊞ **San Jose** ⑨–⑳ and the **Tech Museum of Innovation** ⑬, the **Rosicrucian Egyptian Museum** ⑰, and the **Winchester Mystery House** ⑲. Depending on your taste, have a raucous evening at **Big Lil's Barbary Coast Dinner Theater** or an evening of symphony, ballet, or theater at San Jose's **Center for Performing Arts.**

IF YOU HAVE 3 DAYS

Spend your first day on the coast, noodling around ⊞ **Half Moon Bay** ①, **Pescadero State Beach,** and **Año Nuevo State Reserve** ③. After overnighting in a Half Moon Bay B&B, drive Route 92 through the countryside to I–280 and head south to **Woodside** ④, where you can tour **Filoli.** Drive south on I–280 to the Sand Hill Road exit and take that route to the central campus of **Stanford University.** Take an afternoon tour of the university and its **Iris and B. Gerald Cantor Center for Visual Arts,** then have dinner at one of the fine restaurants in ⊞ **Palo Alto** ⑤. For an unusual evening outing visit the **Hewlett-Packard garage** before retiring to your hotel. On your third day stop in **Santa Clara** ⑥ to see **Mission Santa Clara de Asis,** or if you have kids in tow, you might want to treat them to a morning at **Paramount's Great Amer-**

Peninsula and South Bay

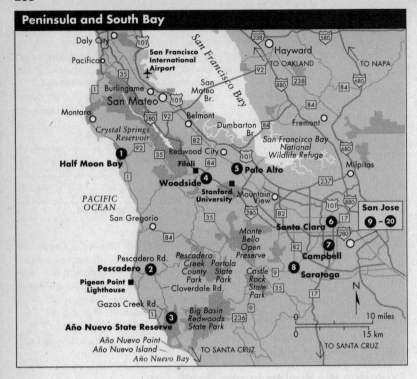

ica. Devote your afternoon to 🏙 **San Jose** ⑨–⑳ and its attractions, then take a sunset drive to **Saratoga** ⑧.

When to Visit the Peninsula and South Bay

The hills that separate the Santa Clara Valley from the coastal peninsula block summertime fog from blowing into the Inland Peninsula and South Bay. Thus, there can be drastic variations in temperatures between the coast and inland from April through October. In July you can expect sunny days in inland regions, with temperatures in the mid-80s, but along the coastline, plan on foggy weather and temperatures only in the mid-60s. The rainy season runs from about November through March, and temperatures are generally constant across the region; expect daytime highs in the 50s and 60s.

THE COASTAL PENINSULA

From Half Moon Bay to Año Nuevo

The towns along the coast below San Francisco were founded in the late 18th century, when Spanish explorer Gaspar de Portola arrived. After the Mexican government gained control, the land was used for agriculture by ranchers who provided food to San Francisco's Mission Dolores. Soon, lighthouses and ships were being built to facilitate the transport of goods to San Francisco. You can still visit the short, squat Point Montara Lighthouse, in Montara, 8 mi north of Half Moon Bay, or the 115-ft Pigeon Point Lighthouse, one of the tallest on the West Coast, 7 mi south of Pescadero. Set out from San Francisco down scenic Route 1, hugging the twists and turns of the coast, or venture 11 mi west from I–280 near San Mateo over hilly Route 92.

Half Moon Bay

❶ *27 mi south of San Francisco on Rte. 1.*

The largest and most visited of the coastal communities, Half Moon Bay is nevertheless a tiny town with a population of fewer than 10,000. The town's hub, Main Street, is lined with five blocks of small crafts shops, art galleries, and outdoor cafés, many housed in renovated 19th-century structures. Half Moon Bay comes to life on the third weekend in October, when 300,000 people gather for the **Half Moon Bay Art and Pumpkin Festival** (☎ 650/726–9652).

The 4-mi stretch of **Half Moon Bay State Beach** (✉ Rte. 1, west of Main St., ☎ 650/726–8819) is perfect for long walks, kite flying, and picnic lunches, though the 50°F water and dangerous currents discourage swimming.

Built in 1928 after two horrible shipwrecks on the point, the **Point Montara Lighthouse** still has its original light keeper's quarters from the late 1800s. Gray whales pass this point during their migration from November through April, so bring your binoculars. The lighthouse is also a hostel known for its outdoor hot tub at the ocean's edge. ✉ *16th St. at Rte. 1, Montara,* ☎ *650/728–7177. Call for hrs, tours, and lodging rates.*

Dining and Lodging

$$ ✕ **Pasta Moon.** The sight of the wood-burning oven tips you off to the thin-crust pizzas that are served in this small restaurant. The kitchen also turns out handmade pastas, a wonderful crisp-skinned roast chicken, grilled quail, and marinated flank steak. ✉ *315 Main St.,* ☎ *650/726–5125. AE, D, DC, MC, V.*

$$ ✕ **San Benito House.** Tucked inside a historic inn in the heart of Half Moon Bay, this ground-floor restaurant serves a limited dinner menu that changes weekly and often includes bouillabaisse, roasted quail, sea bass or other fresh fish, a vegetarian meal, and house-made ravioli or other pastas. By day the kitchen prepares memorable sandwiches with bread baked in the restaurant's oven and sells them, deli style, for a picnic by the sea. ✉ *356 Main St.,* ☎ *650/726–3425. AE, DC, MC, V. No dinner Mon.–Wed.*

$$$$ 🛏 **Mill Rose Inn.** Pampering touches include in-room fireplaces, brass beds stacked high with down comforters, decanters of sherry and brandy on the tables, in-room coffee and cocoa, and baskets of fruit and candies. The lush gardens are planted extensively with roses and climbing sweet peas. Room rates include a lavish champagne breakfast and afternoon snacks. ✉ *615 Mill St., 94019,* ☎ *650/726–8750 or 800/900–7673,* FAX *650/726–3031,* WEB *www.millroseinn.com. 4 rooms, 2 suites. Refrigerators, in-room VCRs; no smoking. AE, D, DC, MC, V. BP.*

$$–$$$$ 🛏 **Old Thyme Inn.** Rooms in this charming 1898 Princess Anne Victorian are named for herbs, such as mint, and are decorated accordingly. The more expensive rooms have fireplaces and whirlpool tubs. Antiques, fresh-flower bouquets, a homemade breakfast, complimentary sherry, and afternoon snacks make this a lovely place to spend a relaxing weekend. ✉ *779 Main St., 94019,* ☎ *650/726–1616 or 800/720–4277,* FAX *650/726–6394,* WEB *www.oldthymeinn.com. 7 rooms. In-room data ports; no-smoking rooms. AE, D, MC, V. BP.*

Outdoor Activities and Sports

The **Bicyclery** (✉ 101 Main St., ☎ 650/726–6000) rents out bikes and can provide information on organized rides up and down the coast. If you prefer to go it alone, try the 3-mi bike trail that leads from Kelly Avenue in Half Moon Bay to Mirada Road in Miramar.

En Route   In addition to beautiful scenery and expansive state beaches, on your way from Half Moon Bay to Pescadero you will pass the town of San Gregorio and its idiosyncratic **San Gregorio General Store** (⊠ Rte. 84 at Stage Rd., 1 mi east of Rte. 1, ☎ 650/726–0565). Part old-time saloon, part hardware store, part grocery, the place has been a fixture in town since the late 1800s. The current Spanish-style structure replaced the original wooden building when it burned down in 1930. Come to browse through the hodgepodge items—camp stoves, books, and boots, to name just a few—or to listen to Irish music and bluegrass on weekend afternoons.

Pescadero

❷ *16 mi south of Half Moon Bay on Rte. 1.*

As you walk down Stage Road, Pescadero's main street, it's hard to believe you're only 30 minutes from Silicon Valley. The few short blocks of the downtown area could almost serve as the backdrop for a western movie, with Duarte's Tavern serving as the centerpiece. In fact, Pescadero was larger in the late 19th century than it is today. This is a good place to stop for a bite or to browse for antiques. The town's real attractions, though, are spectacular beaches and hiking.

If a quarantine is not in effect (watch for signs), from November through April you can look for mussels at **Pescadero State Beach** amid sandy expanses, tidal pools, and rocky outcroppings. Barbecue pits and picnic tables attract many families. Across U.S. 101, at the **Pescadero Marsh Natural Preserve**, hikers can spy on birds and other wildlife by following the trails that crisscross 600 acres of marshland. Early spring and fall are the best times to visit. ☎ 650/879–2170. ⊠ *Free, parking $5.* ☉ *Daily 8–sunset.*

If you prefer mountain trails to sand dunes, head for **Pescadero Creek County Park,** a 7,500-acre expanse of shady, old-growth redwood forests, grasslands, and mountain streams. The park is actually composed of three smaller ones: Heritage Grove Redwood Preserve, Sam McDonald Park, and San Mateo Memorial County Park. The Old Haul Road Trail, 6½ mi long, runs the length of the park. Campsites cost $15 per night. ☎ 650/879–0238. ⊠ *$4 per vehicle.*

Dining

$–$$ ✕ **Duarte's Tavern.** This 19th-century roadhouse serves simple American fare, with locally grown vegetables and fresh fish as standard items. If you really want a treat, order the abalone, for $45. Don't pass up the famed house artichoke soup or the old-fashioned berry pie à la mode. Breakfasts, of eggs, bacon, sausage, and hotcakes, are hearty here. ⊠ *202 Stage Rd.,* ☎ *650/879–0464. AE, MC, V.*

En Route   About 6 mi south of Pescadero State Beach stands the 115-ft **Pigeon Point Lighthouse,** one of the tallest on the West Coast. Built in 1872, it has been used as a backdrop in numerous TV shows and commercials. The light from the 8,000-pound Fresnel lens can be seen 20 mi at sea. The former coast guard quarters now serves as a youth hostel. ⊠ *Pigeon Point Rd. and Rte. 1,* ☎ *650/879–2120.* ⊠ *$2.* ☉ *Weekends 11–4, guided tours 10:30–3.*

Año Nuevo State Reserve

❸ *12 mi south of Pescadaro on Rte. 1.*

At the most southerly point of the San Mateo County Coast, Año Nuevo is the world's only approachable mainland rookery for elephant seals. If you know you'll be in the area between mid-December and March, make reservations early for a 2½-hour guided walking tour to view the huge (up to 3 tons), fat, furry elephant seals mating or birthing, depending on the time of year. Tours proceed rain or shine, so dress for anything. From April through November there's less excitement, but you can still watch the seals lounging on the beach. The visitor center has a fascinating film and exhibits, and there are plenty of hiking trails in the area. ⊠ *Rte. 1,* ☎ *650/879–0227; 800/444–4445 for tour reservations.* ☞ *$4, parking $5.* ☉ *Tours leave every 15 mins 8:45–3.*

THE INLAND PENINSULA

Much of your first impression of the Inland Peninsula will depend on where and when you enter. Take the 30-mi stretch of U.S. 101 from San Francisco along the eastern side of the Peninsula, and you'll see office complex after shopping center after corporate tower—and you'll likely get caught in horrific morning and evening commuter traffic. On the west side, however, the less crowded I–280 takes you past soul-soothing hills, lakes, and reservoirs.

Woodside

④ *31 mi south of San Francisco via I–280.*

West of Palo Alto, Woodside is a tiny, rustic town where weekend warriors stock up on espresso and picnic fare before charging off on their mountain bikes. Blink once, and you're past the town center. The main draw here is the wealth of surrounding lush parks and preserves.

★ One of the few great country houses in California that remains intact is **Filoli.** Built 1915–1917 for wealthy San Franciscan William B. Bourn II, it was designed by Willis Polk in a Georgian-revival style, with red-brick walls and a tile roof. The name is Bourn's acronym for "fight, love, live." As interesting as the house are the 16 acres of formal gardens, which encompass a sunken garden and a teahouse in the Italian Renaissance style. From June through September Filoli hosts a series of Sunday-afternoon jazz concerts. Bring a picnic or buy a box lunch; Filoli provides tables, sodas, wine, fruit, and popcorn. In December the mansion is festively decorated for a series of holiday events: brunches, afternoon teas, Christmas concerts, and more. ⊠ *Cañada Rd. near Edgewood Rd.,* ☎ *650/364–2880,* WEB *www.filoli.org.* ☞ *$10.* ☉ *Mid-Feb.–Oct., Tues.–Sat. 10–3. Reservations are essential for guided tours.*

One Peninsula oddity unknown even to most residents is the **Pulgas Water Temple,** where exquisitely groomed grounds surround a Romanesque temple and a reflecting pool. The temple commemorates the massive underground pipeline project of the early 1930s that channeled water from Hetch Hetchy, near Yosemite, to the Crystal Springs Reservoir, on the Peninsula. Walk up the steps of the columned circular temple to feel the power of the water as it thunders under your feet. ⊠ *Cañada Rd., 1½ mi north of Edgewood Rd.,* ☎ *650/872–5900.* ☞ *Free.* ☉ *Weekdays 9:30–4.*

Dining

$$ ✕ **Bucks in Woodside.** Giant plastic alligators, Elvis paintings, a human-size Statue of Liberty reproduction, and framed computer chips on the walls make the aesthetic statement at this casual restaurant. The menu is a grab bag of crowd pleasers: soups, sandwiches, burgers, and salads. For breakfast there's a "U-do-it" omelet in addition to standard choices. ⊠ *3062 Woodside Rd.,* ☎ *650/851–8010. AE, D, MC, V.*

$-$$ ✕ **Woodside Bakery and Café.** Stop by the bakery section for a cup of hot cocoa and a fresh-baked pastry, or sit in the café for a glass of wine and a light meal. Everything is fresh and well presented. The menu tends toward light seasonal dishes such as fresh pastas and salads. But you'll also find more substantial entrées like oven-braised lamb shank and baked Dijon chicken. ✉ *3052 Woodside Rd.,* ☎ *650/851–0812. AE, MC, V.*

Palo Alto

⑤ *34 mi south of San Francisco via I–280 or U.S. 101.*

Palo Alto's main attraction is the bucolic campus of Stanford University, 8,200 acres of grassy hills. Downtown Palo Alto is a hotbed of restaurants, shops, and attractions catering to high-income Peninsula residents as well as the university crowd. Wander up and down University Avenue and the surrounding side streets, and you'll discover the historic Stanford Theatre, a 1920s-style movie palace, and a Barbie Hall of Fame.

Stanford University was former California governor Leland Stanford's horse-breeding farm, and it is still known as the Farm. Founded in 1885 and opened in 1891 the university occupies a campus designed by Frederick Law Olmsted. Its unique California mission–Romanesque sandstone buildings, joined by arcades and topped by red-tile roofs, are mixed with newer buildings in variations on Olmstead's style. Lined with majestic palm trees, the main campus entrance, Palm Drive (an extension of University Avenue from Palo Alto) leads directly to the main quadrangle. The quadrangle, a group of 12 original classroom buildings, is the center of the university. There, the facade and interior walls of Memorial Church are covered with mosaics of biblical scenes. Students lounge or rush around the quadrangle and near the Clock Tower and White Plaza in a constant stream of bicycles and in-line skates. The 285-ft Hoover Tower is a landmark and a tourist attraction; an elevator ($2) leads to an observation deck that provides sweeping views of the area. Free one-hour **walking tours** of the Stanford campus leave daily at 11 and 3:15 from the visitor center in front of Memorial Hall (✉ Serra St., opposite Hoover Tower, ☎ 650/723–2560 or 650/723–2053). ✉ *Galvez St. at Serra St.,* ☎ *650/ 723–2300,* ⓦⒺⒷ *www.stanford.edu.*

★   **Iris and B. Gerald Cantor Center for Visual Arts,** one of the most comprehensive and varied art collections in the Bay Area, spans the centuries as well as the globe, from pre-Columbian to modern. Included is the world's largest collection—180 pieces—of Rodin sculptures outside Paris, many of them displayed in the outdoor sculpture garden. Other highlights include a bronze Buddha from the Ming dynasty, wooden masks and carved figurines from 18th- and 19th-century Africa, paintings by Georgia O'Keeffe, and sculpture by Willem de Kooning and Bay Area artist Robert Arneson. ✉ *328 Lomita Dr. and Museum Way, off Palm Dr. at Stanford University,* ☎ *650/723–4177,* ⓦⒺⒷ *www.stanford.edu/dept/ccva.* ▱ *Free.* ☉ *Wed. and Fri.–Sun. 11–5, Thurs. 11–8. Rodin Sculpture Garden tours Sat. at 11, Sun. at 3.*

Tucked into a small, heavily wooded plot of land is the **Papua New Guinea Sculpture Garden.** The inconspicuous garden is filled with tall, ornately carved wooden poles, drums, and carved stones—all created on location by 10 artists from Papua New Guinea who spent six months here in 1994. A Stanford anthropology professor proposed the idea for the garden. Detailed plaques explain the concept and the works themselves. ✉ *Santa Teresa St. and Lomita Dr., at Stanford University.* ▱ *Free.*

Though it doesn't look like much, the **Hewlett-Packard garage** is a good place to get a sense of the humble origins of one of the world's largest technology companies. It all started in this one-car garage, where former Stanford freshman roommates William Hewlett and David Packard put their heads together back in the 1930s. The rest is history. Today the Hewlett-Packard garage is a California State Landmark. ⊠ *Behind 367 Addison Ave.*

Two-hour tours of the **Stanford Linear Accelerator Center (SLAC)** reveal the workings of the 2-mi-long electron accelerator, which is used by Stanford University scientists for research into elementary particles. Call for times and reservations. ⊠ *Sand Hill Rd., 2 mi west of the central campus,* ☎ *650/926–2204.*

OFF THE BEATEN PATH	**PALO ALTO BAYLANDS NATURE PRESERVE** – East of downtown Palo Alto is a wetlands area of creeks, sloughs, mudflats, and freshwater and salt-water marshland. The area supports abundant bird life (more than 150 species) and is an important stopover on the Pacific Flyway. You can walk the Bay Trail through the middle of the preserve and visit the Lucy Evans Nature Interpretive Center to learn about the wildlife of the Baylands. ⊠ *East end of Embarcadero Rd.,* ☎ *650/329–2506,* WEB *www.city.palo-alto.ca.us.* ⊡ *Free.* ☉ *Tues.–Wed. 10–5, Thurs.–Fri. 2–5, weekends 1–5.*

Dining and Lodging

$$–$$$$ ✕ **Evvia.** An innovative Greek menu and a stunning interior ensure that
★   Evvia always packs in a crowd. A large fireplace, hand-painted pottery, and a big bar area with colorful backlighted glassware make this one of Palo Alto's most inviting restaurants. Though the menu is written out in Greek (with English translations), there's an unmistakable California influence in dishes like wild-mushroom risotto and *psari sta karvouna* (mesquite-grilled striped bass with herbs and braised greens). ⊠ *420 Emerson St.,* ☎ *650/326–0983. Reservations essential. AE, D, DC, MC, V. No lunch weekends.*

$$–$$$ ✕ **L'Amie Donia.** Chef-owner Donia Bijan, who made a name for herself at San Francisco's Sherman House and Brasserie Savoy, has decorated her utterly charming French bistro in sunny yellow and soothing blue. Her menus, which reflect the seasons, focus on the rustic, flavorful fare that one might find in the French countryside: roast beets with warm goat cheese and walnuts, rabbit with mustard sauce, or pan-roasted veal chop with an almond crust. ⊠ *530 Bryant St.,* ☎ *650/323–7614. Reservations essential. AE, D, MC, V. Closed Sun.–Mon. and late Dec.–mid-Jan. No lunch.*

$–$$$ ✕ **Zibibbo.** This lively restaurant's eclectic menu includes selections from
★   an oak-fired oven, rotisserie, grill, and oyster bar. Large platters are placed in the center of the table so you can share dishes like skillet-roasted mussels, Swiss chard tart with goat cheese and currants, leg of lamb with chickpea-tomato *tagine,* and more. The menu changes seasonally in this two-story Victorian, where you can sit in a garden, a glassed-in atrium, or an upstairs loft or cozy up to the exhibition kitchen counter or high-ceilinged bar. ⊠ *430 Kipling St.,* ☎ *650/328–6722. AE, DC, MC, V.*

$ ✕ **Pluto's.** The space-age name and design have nothing to do with the earthly pleasures of this loud and lively restaurant's fresh, custom-made salads, sandwiches, and hot meals. Service is quasi–buffet style. Grab a menu and make your choices from any of the food stations, and the server will determine how much you owe. Choose greens with a choice of eight fixings such as grilled fennel or roasted peppers, or build your own sandwich with a base of marinated flank steak or grilled eggplant, and add extras like caramelized onions or garlic mayo. ✉ *482 University Ave.,* ☎ *650/853–1556. MC, V.*

$$$$ 🏨 **Garden Court Hotel.** From the outside this boutique hotel looks like
★ an Italian villa, complete with columns and arches, a dormer roof, and balconies dressed up with bougainvillea. The inside is even more appealing, with tasteful, sunlight-filled rooms outfitted with a two- or four-poster bed with comforter. Some rooms overlook a lush central courtyard; all suites have private terraces. Ground-floor shops and restaurants include Il Fornaio. ✉ *520 Cowper St., 94301,* ☎ *650/322–9000 or 800/824–9028,* FAX *650/324–3609,* WEB *www.gardencourt.com. 50 rooms, 12 suites. Restaurant, bar, room service, in-room data ports, room TVs with movies, gym, laundry service, concierge, business services. AE, D, DC, MC, V.*

$–$$ 🏨 **Cowper Inn.** In a quiet residential neighborhood five minutes from downtown Palo Alto, this former Victorian home is one of the least expensive lodging options in the area, and it's charming to boot. The cozy parlor has a brick fireplace, piano, and a big window looking out on tree-lined Cowper Street. Breakfast includes homemade muffins and granola and fresh-squeezed orange juice. ✉ *705 Cowper St., 94301,* ☎ *650/327–4475,* FAX *650/329–1703,* WEB *www.cowperinn.com. 14 rooms, 12 with bath. Piano. AE, MC, V. CP.*

Shopping

The **Stanford Shopping Center** has an excellent selection of upscale stores such as Ralph Lauren, Smith & Hawken, Crate & Barrel, and Bloomingdale's. You will also find some irresistible eateries here. ✉ *180 El Camino Real, take Sand Hill Rd. east off I–280 or Embarcadero Rd. west off U.S. 101,* ☎ *650/617–8585.*

SOUTH BAY

West of San Jose

To many the South Bay is synonymous with Silicon Valley, the center of high-tech research and the corporate headquarters of such giants as Apple, Sun Microsystems, Oracle, and Hewlett-Packard. But Silicon Valley is more a state of mind than a place—it is an attitude held by the legions of software engineers, programmers, and computerphiles who call the area home. And that home is increasingly visitor-friendly. Within the sprawl are towns with individual personalities, history that stretches back to the Spanish, thriving arts scenes, and shops and restaurants to satisfy the most discerning wallet.

Santa Clara

❻ *40 mi south of San Francisco on Rte. 101.*

Santa Clara's offerings include two major attractions at opposite ends of the sightseeing spectrum: Mission Santa Clara de Asis, founded in 1777, and Paramount's Great America, northern California's answer to Disneyland. Although many visitors head straight to the amusement park, Santa Clara has plenty of history and is worthy of a brief visit—despite the sprawling shopping malls and sterile business parks.

Santa Clara University, founded in 1851 by Jesuits, was California's first college. The campus's **de Saisset Art Gallery and Museum** has a permanent collection that includes California mission artifacts and a full calendar of temporary exhibits. ✉ *500 El Camino Real,* ☎ *408/554–4528,* WEB *www.scu.edu/desaisset.* 🎟 *Free.* ☉ *Tues.–Sun. 11–4.*

In the center of Santa Clara University's campus is the **Mission Santa Clara de Asis,** the eighth of 21 California missions founded under the direction of Father Junípero Serra and the first to honor a woman. The mission's present site was the fifth chosen, after the first four were flooded by the Guadalupe River and destroyed by earthquakes. In 1926 the permanent mission chapel was destroyed by fire. Roof tiles of the current building, a replica of the original, were salvaged from earlier structures, which dated from the 1790s and 1820s. Early adobe walls and a spectacular rose garden with 4,500 roses—many classified as antiques—remain as well. Part of the wooden Memorial Cross, from 1777, is set in front of the church. ⊠ *500 El Camino Real,* ☎ *408/554–4023,* WEB *www.scu.edu/visitors/mission.* ⊠ *Free.* ☉ *Daily 1–sundown for self-guided tours.*

🖑 At **Paramount's Great America** 100-acre theme park, on the edge of San Francisco Bay, each section recalls a familiar part of North America: Hometown Square, Yukon Territory, Yankee Harbor, or County Fair. Popular attractions include the Drop Zone Stunt Tower, the tallest free-fall ride in North America; the Vortex, a stand-up roller coaster; a *Top Gun* movie–theme roller coaster, whose cars travel along the outside of a 360-degree loop track; Xtreme Skyflyer, which lifts you by harness more than 17 stories high and drops you back to earth at 60 mph; and Nickelodeon Splat City, 3 acres of obstacle courses apparently designed for kids who love to get wet and dirty. The park is served by Santa Clara County Transit and the Fremont BART station. ⊠ *Great America Pkwy. between U.S. 101 and Rte. 237, 6 mi north of San Jose,* ☎ *408/988–1776,* WEB *www.pgathrills.com.* ⊠ *$43.99, parking $6.* ☉ *Apr.–May and Sept.–Oct., weekends; June–Aug., daily; opens 10 AM, closing times vary. AE, D, MC, V.*

At the **Intel Museum** you can learn how computer chips are made and follow the development of Intel Corporation's microprocessor, memory, and systems product lines. Guided tours are available by reservation. ⊠ *Robert Noyce Bldg., 2200 Mission College Blvd.,* ☎ *408/765–0503,* WEB *www.intel.com/intel/intelis/museum.* ⊠ *Free.* ☉ *Weekdays 9–6, Sat. 10–5.*

The **Carmelite Monastery** is a fine example of Spanish ecclesiastical architecture. Built in 1917, it's on the grounds of a historic ranch crossed by shady walkways and dotted with benches perfect for quiet contemplation. ⊠ *1000 Lincoln St.,* ☎ *408/296–8412,* WEB *members.aol.com/santaclaracarmel.* ⊠ *Free.* ☉ *Grounds open Mon.–Sat. 6:30–5, Sun. 8–5.*

In the Civic Center Park, a **statue of St. Clare,** patron saint of the city of Santa Clara, rises out of a fountain. The sculpture was cast in Italy in 1965 by Anne Van Kleeck, who used an ancient wax process. It was then shipped around Cape Horn and dedicated on this site in 1985. ⊠ *Civic Center Park, Lincoln St. at El Camino Real.*

Skylights cast natural light for viewing the exhibitions in the **Triton Museum of Art.** A permanent collection of 19th- and 20th-century sculpture by artists from the Bay Area is displayed in the garden, which you can see through a curved-glass wall at the rear of the building. Inside there are rotating exhibits of contemporary works in a variety of media and a permanent collection of 19th- and 20th-century American artists, many from California. There is also a very good Native American collection. ⊠ *1505 Warburton Ave.,* ☎ *408/247–3754,* WEB *www.tritonmuseum.org.* ⊠ *$2 suggested donation.* ☉ *Mon.–Tues. 10–5, Thurs. 10–9, Fri.–Sun. 10–5.*

Open only on Sunday afternoon, the tiny **Santa Clara Historic Museum** exhibits artifacts and photos that trace the history of the region. ⊠ *1509 Warburton Ave.,* ☎ *408/248–2787.* 🎟 *Free.* ☉ *Sun. 1–4.*

Walk over to the grounds of city hall to see noted San Francisco sculptor Benny Bufano's primitive **Universal Child,** facing the Santa Clara Historic Museum. The 85-ft statue depicts the children of the world standing as one. ⊠ *1500 Warburton Ave.* 🎟 *Free.*

The **Harris-Lass Historic Museum** is built on Santa Clara's last farmstead. A restored house, summer kitchen, and barn convey a sense of life on the farm from the early 1900s through the 1930s. Guided tours take place every half hour until 3:30. ⊠ *1889 Market St.,* ☎ *408/249–7905.* 🎟 *$3.* ☉ *Weekends noon–4.*

Dining and Lodging

$$–$$$ ✕ **Birk's.** Silicon Valley's businesspeople come to this sophisticated American grill to unwind. High-tech sensibilities will appreciate the modern, open kitchen and streamlined, multilevel dining area—yet the menu is traditional, strong on steaks and chops. An oyster bar adds a lighter element. Try the smoked prime rib, served with garlic mashed potatoes and creamed spinach. ⊠ *3955 Freedom Circle, at Rte. 101 and Great America Pkwy.,* ☎ *408/980–6400. AE, D, DC, MC, V. No lunch weekends.*

$$ ✕ **Mio Vicino.** Mio's is a small, bare-bones, checkered-tablecloth Italian bistro in Old Santa Clara. The menu includes a long list of classic and contemporary pastas—and if you don't see it on the menu, just ask. The house specialties are shellfish pasta and chicken cannelloni. ⊠ *1290 Benton St.,* ☎ *408/241–9414;* ⊠ *384 E. Campbell Ave., Campbell,* ☎ *408/378–0335. MC, V. No lunch weekends.*

$$$$ 🏨 **Embassy Suites.** This upper-end chain hotel is ideal for Silicon Valley business travelers and families bound for Paramount's Great America. Every room is a two-room suite. Guests receive complimentary cooked-to-order breakfasts and evening beverages. ⊠ *2885 Lakeside Dr., 95054,* ☎ *408/496–6400 or 800/362–2779,* FAX *408/988–7529,* WEB *www.embassy-suites.com. 257 suites. Restaurant, lounge, room service, in-room data ports, refrigerators, cable TV with movies, pool, gym, hot tub, sauna, meeting room, Internet, business services, airport shuttle, free parking; no-smoking rooms. AE, D, DC, MC, V. BP.*

$–$$ 🏨 **Madison Street Inn.** At this Queen Anne Victorian, a complimentary full breakfast and afternoon refreshments are served on a brick garden patio with a bougainvillea-draped trellis. The inn has the distinct look of a private home, with a green-and-red-trim facade. ⊠ *1390 Madison St., Santa Clara 95050,* ☎ *408/249–5541 or 800/491–5541,* FAX *408/249–6676,* WEB *www.madisonstreetinn.com. 6 rooms, 4 with bath. Fans (some), in-room data ports, refrigerators (some), microwaves (some), cable TV, no TV in some rooms, pool, bicycles, hot tub, Internet, laundry services, meeting room, some pets allowed; no air-conditioning in some rooms, no smoking. AE, D, DC, MC, V. BP.*

Nightlife and the Arts
ComedySportz (⊠ 3428 El Camino Real, ☎ 408/985–5233) offers evenings of good-natured comedy appropriate for all ages. Book in advance or pay $7–$14 at the door.

Campbell

❼ *6 mi southwest of Santa Clara on Hwy. 17.*

Buried in the heart of metropolitan Santa Clara County 10 minutes south of San Jose on Highway 17, the town of Campbell has a small-town center with a friendly neighborhood mood. Within a couple of blocks are the city hall, an old fruit cannery that now houses offices, and a handful of galleries, boutiques, and restaurants.

On Campbell's Civic Center Plaza, the historic Tudor-revival **Ainsley House** gives a glimpse of South Bay life in the 1920s and '30s. The structure was moved in one piece from its previous location a half mile away, after descendants of the owners, the valley's founding canner, donated it to the city for preservation. Admission to the house includes admission to the Campbell Historical Museum down the street. ⊠ *300 Grant St.,* ☎ *408/866–2119.* ⌨ *$6 for Ainsley House; $8 includes admission to Campbell Historical Museum.* ⊘ *Guided tours Thurs.–Sun. noon–4; gardens daily sunrise–sunset.*

Committed to exploring themes in Americana, the **Campbell Historical Museum** presents exhibits on life in the Silicon Valley in the age before computers. ⊠ *51 N. Central Ave.,* ☎ *408/866–2119.* ⌨ *$4 for museum; $8 includes admission to Ainsley House.* ⊘ *Thurs.–Sun. noon–4.*

Dining and Lodging

$ ✕ **Chez Sovan.** This Cambodian jewel, with a pleasant setting and satisfying food, is a wonderful addition to the South Bay dining scene. The spring rolls are delectable, as are the noodle dishes, grilled meats, and flavorful curries. ⊠ *2425 S. Bascom Ave.,* ☎ *408/371–7711. AE, MC, V.*

$ ✕ **Orchard Valley Coffee.** At this favorite local hangout, the large-pane front windows open wide on spring and summer days. It's also an Internet café where you can rent computer time and check your E-mail. The café keeps its cozy feel with well-worn pillows and benches you're comfortable putting your feet up on. The menu includes light meals, salads, soups, and pastries. ⊠ *349 E. Campbell Ave.,* ☎ *408/374–2115. D, MC, V.*

$$$$ ▥ **Campbell Inn.** There are plenty of reasons to stay 10 minutes from downtown San Jose at this creek-side inn in Campbell. You can play tennis, swim in the pool, ride one of the inn's bicycles on a nearby trail, or simply relax in the lobby, which has large, comfortable chairs and a fireplace. Suites have whirlpool tubs and saunas, and all room rates include a complimentary breakfast buffet. ⊠ *675 E. Campbell Ave., Campbell 95008,* ☎ *408/374–4300 or 800/582–4449,* ℻ *408/379–0695,* WEB *www.campbell-inn.com. 85 rooms, 10 suites. In-room data ports, in-room hot tubs (some), cable TV with movies, in-room VCRs, refrigerators, pool, outdoor hot tub, tennis court, bicycles, airport shuttle; no-smoking rooms. AE, D, DC, MC, V. BP.*

Outdoor Activities and Sports

The paved 9-plus-mi **Los Gatos Creek Trail** spans San Jose, Campbell, and Los Gatos, with one staging area with parking and rest rooms on Gilman Street and Campbell Avenue.

Saratoga

❽ *6 mi west of Campbell on Hwy. 85.*

A 10-mi detour southwest from San Jose's urban core puts you in the heart of Saratoga, at the foot of the Santa Cruz Mountains. Once an artists' colony, the town is now home to many Silicon Valley CEOs, whose mansions dot the hillsides. Spend a slow-paced afternoon exploring Big Basin Way, the ½-mi main drag of the Village, as the downtown area is locally known. Here you'll find antiques stores, galleries, spas, and a handful of worthwhile restaurants.

Built in 1912 by former governor James Phelan, **Villa Montalvo** is a striking white mansion presiding over an expansive lawn. Inside there's an art gallery with changing exhibits by local artists and artists-in-residence (call ahead to make sure an exhibit is on). You can picnic and lounge on the lawn. Additional draws are a gift shop and 175-acre park with several hiking trails, as well as a first-rate summer concert series. ⊠ *15400 Montalvo Rd.,* ☎ *408/961–5800,* WEB *www.villamontalvo.org.* ⌘ *Free.* ☉ *Park Oct.–Mar., daily 9–5; Apr.–Sept., daily 9–7; call for gallery hours and concert information.*

One of the most peaceful and meditative attractions in the area is the Zen-style **Hakone Gardens,** nestled on a steep hillside just south of downtown. Designed in 1918 by Aihara Naoharu, who had been an imperial gardener in Japan, the gardens have been carefully maintained, with koi (carp) ponds and sculptured shrubs. Formal tea ceremonies, which cost $5 per person, are held from 1 to 4 on the first Thursday of the month; call for reservations. ⊠ *21000 Big Basin Way,* ☎ *408/741–4994,* WEB *www.hakone.com.* ⌘ *Free; parking $5, free 1st Tues. of month.* ☉ *Weekdays 10–5, weekends 11–5.*

For a quick driving tour of the hills with their sweeping valley views, drive south out of Saratoga on Big Basin Way, which is **Scenic Highway 9.** The road leads into the Santa Cruz Mountains, all the way to the coast at the city of Santa Cruz. But you can take in some great views about 1½ mi out of town by taking a right on Pierce Road toward the **Mountain Winery.** Built by Paul Masson in 1905 and now listed on the National Register of Historic Places, it is constructed of masonry and oak to resemble a French-country chateau. No longer serving its original purpose, Mountain Winery is now a venue for private events; it also presents a summer concert series.

Dining and Lodging

$$$–$$$$ ✕ **Sent Sovi.** At this small, flower-draped restaurant, housed in a
★ quaint cottage on Saratoga's quiet main street, chef and co-owner David Kinch offers a small, regularly changing menu of refined European fare. You might find potato-wrapped sea bass with wild mushrooms and red-wine broth, spice-glazed roast quail stuffed with gingerbread, or napoleon of lobster salad with toasted cumin crackers. Desserts are equally tantalizing. A five-course tasting menu will let you sample more widely from Kinch's remarkable repertoire. ⊠ *14583 Big Basin Way,* ☎ *408/867–3110. Reservations essential. AE, MC, V. Closed Mon. No lunch.*

$ ✕ **Willow Street Wood-Fired Pizza.** What began as a quaint "secret" pizzeria in the Willow Glen neighborhood just south of downtown has become one of the best and trendiest spots in the South Bay. Order an individual wood-fired pizza with classic cheese or try something less mundane, such as chicken Brie or artichoke and goat cheese. During lunch you can order from a quick and downsized version of the dinner menu. Reservations are accepted only for parties of eight or more, but smaller parties can call ahead to secure a spot on the waiting list. ⊠ *1072 Willow St.,* ☎ *408/971–7080. AE, MC, V.*

$$$–$$$$ 🏨 **Inn at Saratoga.** Though this five-story European-style inn is only 10 minutes from San Jose, its aura of calm makes it feel far from busy Silicon Valley. All rooms are decorated in soft earth tones and include secluded sitting alcoves overlooking a peaceful creek. A complimentary Continental breakfast is served in the morning; in the evening wine and hors d'oeuvres are set out in the cozy lobby. Modern business conveniences are available but discreetly hidden. The entire hotel is smoke-free. ⊠ *20645 4th St., 95070,* ☎ *408/867–5020; 800/543–5020 in CA,* FAX *408/741–0981,* WEB *www.innatsaratoga.com. 42 rooms, 3 suites. In-*

room data ports, refrigerators, cable TV, in-room VCRs, exercise equipment, laundry service, Internet, business services, meeting room; no smoking. AE, DC, MC, V. CP.

$$–$$$ ☷ **Saratoga Oaks Lodge.** This small and cozy place occupies a historic site that was once the tollgate to a private road heading over the Santa Cruz Mountains. Several rooms have fireplaces and steam baths, and a complimentary Continental breakfast is served. ⊠ *14626 Big Basin Way, 95070,* ☎ *408/867–3307,* FAX *408/867–6765,* WEB *www.saratogaoakslodge.com. 15 rooms, 5 suites. In-room data ports, microwaves, refrigerators, cable TV; no smoking. AE, D, MC, V. CP.*

Nightlife and the Arts

Summer concerts at **Villa Montalvo** (⊠ 15400 Montalvo Rd., ☎ 408/961–5858 tickets) are performed on an intimate outdoor stage where seats give you a sweeping view of the valley—particularly spectacular at sunset. There's also a carriage house where concerts are performed throughout the rest of the year.

Outdoor Activities and Sports

Garrod Farms Stables (⊠ 22600 Mount Eden Rd., ☎ 408/867–9527) provides horse rentals and free weekend tastings of wines made on the premises.

Shopping

Stock up on dishes, linens, home accessories, and gifts at the **Butter Paddle** (⊠ 14510 Big Basin Way, ☎ 408/867–1678), where all profits are donated to the local Eastfield Ming Quong Foundation for abused and troubled children.

SAN JOSE

San Jose has its own ballet, symphony, repertory theater, nationally recognized museums, downtown nightlife, and exclusive hotels. Downtown can be easily explored by foot, and Guadalupe River Park, a 3-mi belt of trees and gardens, connects downtown with the Children's Discovery Museum, to the south. By 2004 the trail will extend to San Jose International Airport, to the north, and will include even more parks and playgrounds. A 21-mi urban light-rail system links downtown to the business district and to Paramount's Great America, to the north, and to various suburbs and malls to the south. You will still need a car to get to outlying communities and such sights as the Egyptian Museum and the Winchester Mystery House.

A historical walking tour of downtown San Jose is detailed in a brochure available from the Convention and Visitors Bureau. The self-guided walk leads you past the 14 historic buildings described in the brochure. Vintage trolleys operate in downtown San Jose from 10:30 to 5:30 in summer and on some holidays throughout the year. Buy tickets for the trolleys at vending machines in any transit station.

Downtown San Jose and Vicinity

4 mi east of Santa Clara on Hwy. 82, 55 mi south of San Francisco on Rte. 101 or I–280.

A Good Tour

Much of downtown San Jose can be toured easily on foot. Start at the **Children's Discovery Museum** ⑨ and be sure to wander around the outside of this outrageously purple building. Crossing through the surrounding park, take a stroll through the "herd" of larger-than-life animal sculptures facing San Carlos Street. The nearby steps lead down to Guadalupe Creek and a parallel walking path; a good detour leads

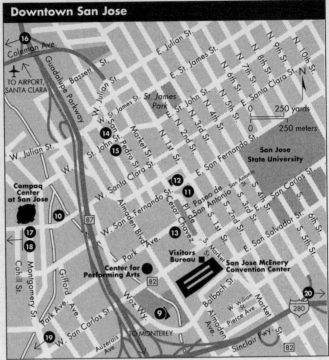

Downtown San Jose

north to the San Jose Arena and the **Guadalupe River Park** ⑩, with a carousel and children's playground.

Back at the sculpture park, continue east on San Carlos Street into the heart of downtown San Jose. Immediately on the left is the Center for the Performing Arts, home to the city's ballet and symphony. San Jose's McEnery Convention Center and the visitor center are catercorner across the road. In front of the center an outdoor skating rink (open daily) is set up from mid-November to mid-January.

Continue down San Carlos Street and turn left on Market Street; ahead is Plaza de Cesar Chavez. On the square's northeast corner are the must-see **San Jose Museum of Art** ⑪ and adjacent **Cathedral Basilica of St. Joseph** ⑫. On the square's western edge at Park Avenue is the **Tech Museum of Innovation** ⑬, with its children-friendly hands-on exhibits.

Follow Market Street north from the plaza and turn left on Santa Clara Street. For a glimpse of the historic Hotel De Anza, walk four blocks ahead to the corner of North Almaden Boulevard. Otherwise, walk one block, turn right on San Pedro Street, and continue two blocks—past the sidewalk cafés and restaurants—to St. John Street and turn left. The **Fallon House** ⑭ will be on your right, the **Peralta Adobe** ⑮ on your left. At this point you can turn around and go east three blocks on St. John Street and board the light rail to return to your starting point.

Pick up your car and drive northwest from the center of town on Coleman Avenue. At Taylor Street take a right to reach **Heritage Rose Garden** ⑯. After you've strolled the grounds, head southwest on Taylor Street, which turns into Naglee Avenue at the Alameda, Naglee will take you to the **Rosicrucian Egyptian Museum** ⑰ and, across the street, the **Municipal Rose Garden** ⑱. When you're done there, continue southwest on Naglee until it turns into Forest Avenue, which intersects Winchester Boulevard. Turn left onto Winchester Boulevard to reach **Winchester Mystery House** ⑲. Finally, take I–280 east to Highway 82 (Monterey Road) south and turn left on Phelan Avenue. At Kelley Park you can visit **History San Jose** ⑳. To return to downtown, backtrack to Monterey Road and turn right to drive north.

TIMING

The walking portion of this tour can easily be completed in about two hours. However, if you decide to spend time in the museums or at a café along San Pedro Street, give yourself at least four hours. The length of the driving tour depends on how long you spend at each sight. Plan on anywhere from three to six hours.

Sights to See

⑫ **Cathedral Basilica of St. Joseph.** The Renaissance-style cathedral, built in 1877, is completely restored and has extraordinary stained-glass windows and murals. The multidome cathedral occupies the site where a small adobe church served the first residents of the Pueblo of San Jose in 1803. ⊠ *90 S. Market St.,* ☎ *408/283–8100,* WEB *www.stjosephcathedral.org.*

🐾 ⑨ **Children's Discovery Museum of San Jose.** An angular purple building across the creek from the convention center at the rear of Discovery Meadow Park, the museum exhibits interactive installations on science, the humanities, and the arts. Children can dress up in period costumes, create art from recycled materials, or play on a real fire truck. The park is also a favorite site for school and family picnics, and kids can crawl all over the oversize animal sculptures, nicknamed the Parade of Animals. ⊠ *180 Woz Way, at Auzerais St.,* ☎ *408/298–5437,* WEB *www.cdm.org.* ⓢ *$7.* ☉ *Tues.–Sat. 10–5, Sun. noon–5.*

⑭ **Fallon House.** San Jose's seventh mayor, Thomas Fallon, built this Victorian mansion in 1855. The house's period-decorated rooms can be viewed on a 90-minute tour that includes the Peralta Adobe and a screening of a video about the two houses. ⊠ *175 W. St. John St.,* ☎ *408/993–8182,* WEB *www.historysanjose.org.* ⓢ *$6 (includes admission to Peralta Adobe).* ☉ *Guided tours weekends noon–5.*

🐾 ⑩ **Guadalupe River Park.** This downtown park includes the Arena Green, next to the sports arena, with a carousel, children's playground, and artwork honoring five champion figure skaters from the area. The River Park path, which stretches for 3 mi, starts at the Children's Discovery Museum and runs north, ending at the Arena Green. ⊠ *345 W. Santa Clara St.,* ☎ *408/277–5904,* WEB *www.grpg.org.* ⓢ *Free.*

⑯ **Heritage Rose Garden.** The newer of the city's two rose gardens has won national acclaim for its 5,000 rosebushes and trees on 4 acres. A quiet retreat, the garden has benches perfect for a break or a picnic and is alongside the still-developing Historic Orchard, which houses fruit trees indigenous to the Santa Clara Valley. The garden is northwest of Downtown, near the airport. ⊠ *Taylor and Spring Sts.,* ☎ *408/298–7657.* ⓢ *Free.* ☉ *Daily dawn–dusk.*

⑳ **History San Jose.** Southeast of the city center, occupying 25 acres of Kelley Park, this outdoor "museum" highlights the history of San Jose and the Santa Clara Valley. You can see 28 historic and reconstructed buildings, hop a historic trolley, observe letterpress printing, and buy ice cream and candy at O'Brien's. ⊠ *1650 Senter Rd., at Phelan Ave.,* ☎ *408/287–2290,* WEB *www.historysanjose.org.* ⓢ *$6.* ☉ *Tues.–Fri. noon–5, weekends noon–5; call for weekend tour times.*

18 Municipal Rose Garden. Installed in 1931, the Municipal Rose Garden is one of several outstanding green spaces in the city's urban core. West of Downtown San Jose you'll find 5½ acres of roses with 4,000 shrubs and trees in 189 well-labeled beds, as well as marvelous walkways, fountains, and trellises. Some of the neighboring homes in the Rose Garden district date to the city's founding fathers. ⊠ *Naglee and Dana Aves.,* ☎ *408/277–4191,* WEB *www.ci.san-jose.ca.us/cae/parks/rg.* 🎟 *Free.* ⊙ *Daily 8 AM–sunset.*

15 Peralta Adobe. California pepper trees shade the last remaining structure (circa 1797) from the pueblo that was once San Jose. The whitewashed two-room home has been furnished to interpret life in the first Spanish civil settlement in California and during the Mexican rancho era. ⊠ *184 W. St. John St.,* ☎ *408/993–8182,* WEB *www.historysanjose.org.* 🎟 *$6 (includes admission to Fallon House).* ⊙ *Guided tours weekends noon–5.*

★ **17 Rosicrucian Egyptian Museum.** Owned by the Rosecrucian Order, the museum exhibits the West Coast's largest collection of Egyptian and Babylonian antiquities, including mummies and an underground replica of a rock tomb. The museum's entrance is a reproduction of the Avenue of Ram Sphinxes from the Temple at Karnak in Egypt. The complex, 3 mi from downtown, is surrounded by a garden filled with palms, papyrus, and other plants recalling ancient Egypt. ⊠ *1342 Naglee Ave., at Park Ave.,* ☎ *408/947–3636,* WEB *www.rosicrucian.org.* 🎟 *$7 museum.* ⊙ *Tues.–Fri. 10–5, weekends 11–6.*

11 San Jose Museum of Art. Housed partly in a former post office building, the museum has a permanent collection that includes paintings, large-scale multimedia installations, photographs, and sculptures by local and nationally known artists. ⊠ *110 S. Market St.,* ☎ *408/294–2787 or 408/271–6840,* WEB *www.sjmusart.org.* 🎟 *Free.* ⊙ *Tues.–Thurs. and weekends 11–5; Fri. 11–10.*

★ ☝ **13 Tech Museum of Innovation.** Designed by renowned architect Ricardo Legorreta of Mexico City, San Jose's nationally recognized museum of technology presents high-tech and hands-on exhibits that allow you to discover and demystify such disciplines as multimedia, communications, biotechnology, robotics, and space exploration. Another worthwhile attraction is the 299-seat Hackworth IMAX Dome Theater. The Tech Café, with street-side and indoor seating, is a perfect stop for coffee or a light meal. ⊠ *201 S. Market St., at Park Ave.,* ☎ *408/294–8324,* WEB *www.thetech.org.* 🎟 *Museum $9, IMAX $9, combination ticket $16.* ⊙ *Tues.–Sun. 10–5; open some Mon., call in advance.*

☝ **19 Winchester Mystery House.** Perhaps San Jose's best-known site, the Mystery House, which is on the National Register of Historic Places, is 3 mi west of downtown. Convinced that spirits would harm her if construction ever stopped, firearms heiress and house owner Sarah Winchester constantly added to her house. For 38 years, beginning in 1884, she kept hundreds of carpenters working around the clock, creating a bizarre 160-room Victorian labyrinth with stairs going nowhere and doors that open into walls. The brightly painted house is a favorite family attraction, and though the grounds are no longer dark and overgrown, the place retains an air of mystery. Explore the house on the 65-minute estate tour and the 50-minute behind-the-scenes tour, or come on a Friday the 13th for an evening flashlight tour. Tours usually depart every 20–30 minutes. ⊠ *525 S. Winchester Blvd., between Stevens Creek Blvd. and I–280,* ☎ *408/247–2101,* WEB *www.winchestermysteryhouse.com.* 🎟 *Estate tour $16.95, behind-the-scenes tour $13.95, combination ticket $23.95.* ⊙ *Daily 9–5:30 (last admission at 5).*

Dining and Lodging

$$$–$$$$ ✕ **A. P. Stump's.** With its tin ceilings, dramatic lighting, and gold- and copper-tone walls, this restaurant's extravagant interior is well matched to the food. Chef-partner Jim Stump offers creative dishes on his frequently changing menu, which may include sesame ahi with bok choy and soba noodle cake, molasses-glazed pork chop with huckleberry sauce, or one of his signature dishes like lobster corn pudding. If you plan to come during spring or summer, ask about the program of outdoor live-music performances. ⊠ *163 W. Santa Clara St.,* ☎ *408/292–9928. AE, D, DC, MC, V. No lunch weekends.*

$$$–$$$$ ✕ **Emile's Restaurant.** Swiss chef and owner Emile Mooser's menu is
★ a blend of classical European and contemporary California influences. Specialties include house-cured gravlax, rack of lamb, fresh game, and Grand Marnier soufflé. Mooser is an expert at matching food and wine. He'll gladly make a selection from his restaurant's extensive list for you. The interior is distinguished by romantic lighting, stunning floral displays, and an unusual leaf sculpture on the ceiling. ⊠ *545 S. 2nd St.,* ☎ *408/289–1960. AE, D, DC, MC, V. Closed Sun. and Mon. No lunch Tues.–Thurs. and Sat.*

$$–$$$$ ✕ **Blake's Steakhouse and Bar.** Blake's fully satisfies the carnivore while managing not to neglect even the staunchest non–beef eater. Uncluttered and tranquil for a steak house, the restaurant has intimate high-back booths, some with a view of bustling San Pedro Square. Order any cut of beef you fancy, as well as roasted fowl and charbroiled fish. ⊠ *17 N. San Pedro Sq.,* ☎ *408/298–9221. AE, D, DC, MC, V.*

$$–$$$$ ✕ **Paolo's.** A longtime meeting ground for South Bay notables, Paolo has a sponge-painted interior that is as contemporary as any in San Jose. Duck and delicate handmade pastas are among the appealing, up-to-the-moment dishes. At lunchtime the dining room is a sea of suits, with bankers and brokers entertaining clients. ⊠ *333 W. San Carlos St.,* ☎ *408/294–2558. AE, D, DC, MC, V. Closed Sun. No lunch Sat.*

$$–$$$ ✕ **Menara Moroccan Restaurant.** The delicious cumin- and coriander-spiced food is only part of the reason to come here for a leisurely meal. Arched entryways, lazily spinning ceiling fans, and a tile fountain all lend to the faraway feel. Sit on jewel-tone cushions around low tables while feasting on lamb with honey, delicately spiced chicken kebabs, or hare with paprika. You can choose from five multicourse dinners—all include couscous, salad, dessert, and sweet mint tea. A nightly belly dancing performance completes the experience. ⊠ *41 E. Gish Rd.,* ☎ *408/453–1983. AE, D, MC, V. No lunch.*

$–$$$ ✕ **71 Saint Peter.** This could easily be the best restaurant in San Jose.
★ The selection is somewhat small, but each dish is prepared with care, from the seafood linguine (a mix of clams, shrimp, and scallops in a basil-tomato broth) to the roasted duck prepared in a raspberry–black pepper demiglace. The ceramic-tile floors and wood-beam ceiling add rustic touches to the warm, elegant atmosphere. You can watch chef-owner Mark Tabak at work in the glass-wall kitchen. ⊠ *71 N. San Pedro St.,* ☎ *408/971–8523. AE, D, DC, MC, V. Closed Sun. No lunch Sat.*

$–$$ ✕ **Bella Mia.** Locals love this restaurant for its elegant interior and good Italian food. There are plenty of fresh pastas to choose from, like salmon ravioli in tomato dill sauce and pasta carbonara, as well as flatbread pizzas. You can also choose from a number of grilled entrées, like spit-roasted chicken and citrus-grilled pork chops. On some nights during spring and summer jazz is performed on the patio. ⊠ *58 S. 1st St.,* ☎ *408/280–1993. AE, D, DC, MC, V.*

$ ✕ **Lou's Living Donut Museum.** If you want a real taste of San Jose, do like the locals and stop for a sweet breakfast or afternoon snack at Lou's, just two blocks from the Children's Discovery Museum. Lou's serves a variety of handmade doughnuts—from pumpkin to old-fashioned chocolate—and lets you watch the bakers in action. This family-run shop has been around since 1955; the owners are glad to talk to you about the history of the shop and of San Jose. ⊠ *387 Delmas Ave.,* ☎ *408/295–5887. No credit cards. Closed Sun. No dinner.*

$ ✕ **Señora Emma's.** This *taquería* serves up large and tasty portions of nachos, tacos, burritos, and quesadillas as well as full meals. You can help yourself to several kinds of salsas, limes, and jalapeños at the salsa bar and get a margarita at the full bar. The restaurant's interior may be nothing special to look at, but there's a great sidewalk patio that affords terrific people-watching opportunities. ⊠ *177 N. Santa Clara St.,* ☎ *408/279–3662 or 408/261–8448. AE, MC, V. No dinner Mon.–Wed. No lunch Sun.*

$ ✕ **White Lotus.** The Southeast Asian–influenced meatless dishes at this slightly worn restaurant are deliciously prepared using fresh ingredients. Choose from an extensive menu of vegetable and meat-substitute dishes, like soft, chewy panfried rice noodles with tofu and crisp vegetables; curry "chicken"; or spicy garlic eggplant. Start your meal with an order of crunchy imperial rolls or the Thai sweet-and-sour soup. ⊠ *80 N. Market St.,* ☎ *408/977–0540. MC, V. Closed Sun.*

$$$$ ▥ **Hotel De Anza.** This lushly appointed art deco hotel has hand-painted ceilings, a warm coral-and-green color scheme, and an enclosed terrace with towering palms and dramatic fountains. Business travelers will appreciate the many amenities, including a full-service business center and personal voice-mail services. ⊠ *233 W. Santa Clara St., 95113,* ☎ *408/286–1000 or 800/843–3700,* FAX *408/286–0500,* WEB *www.hoteldeanza.com. 91 rooms, 9 suites. Restaurant, bar, in-room data ports, in-room hot tubs (some), minibars, refrigerators, cable TV with movies, in-room VCRs, gym, laundry services, business services, concierge, Internet; no-smoking rooms. AE, D, DC, MC, V.*

$$$$ ▥ **Hyatt Sainte Claire.** The first American hotel to utilize an earthquake-protective roller system when it was built in 1926, the Sainte Claire has survived decades of quakes without a whimper. Its high ceilings, classic chandeliers, and courtyard lined in Spanish tiles, as well as the superb painted ceiling in the Palm Room parlor, are magnificent. Each room is unique, and many have a colorful night-sky theme. ⊠ *302 S. Market St., 95113,* ☎ *408/885–1234 or 800/233–1234,* FAX *408/977–0403,* WEB *www.hyatt.com. 170 rooms, 17 suites. Restaurant, café, bar, in-room data ports, in-room fax (some), in-room safes, in-room hot tubs, minibars, cable TV with movies, pool, exercise equipment, concierge, Internet, business services, laundry services, meeting rooms; no-smoking rooms. AE, D, DC, MC, V.*

$$$–$$$$ ▥ **The Fairmont.** Affiliated with the famous San Francisco hotel of the
★ same name, this downtown gem offers the local utmost in luxury and sophistication. Get lost in the lavish lobby sofas under dazzling chandeliers or dip your feet in the fourth-floor pool, making rings in the exotic palms mirrored in the water. Rooms have every imaginable comfort, from down pillows and custom-designed comforters to oversize bath towels changed twice a day. ⊠ *170 S. Market St., at Fairmont Pl., 95113,* ☎ *408/998–1900 or 800/866–5577,* FAX *408/287–1648,* WEB *www.fairmont.com. 541 rooms. 3 restaurants, lobby lounge, room service, in-room data ports, in-room fax (some), in-room safes, in-room hot tubs (some), minibars, refrigerators (some), cable TV with movies and video games, pool, health club, steam room, massage, laundry services, concierge, Internet, business services, meeting rooms; no-smoking floor; no-smoking rooms. AE, D, DC, MC, V.*

$$–$$$$ ▥ **The Hensley House.** This is the only B&B in downtown San Jose,
★ with rooms in neighboring Victorian and craftsman-style houses. The antiques-decorated rooms have thoughtful touches like robes, feather

mattresses, and down comforters and pillows. Some rooms have full kitchens. Breakfast frequently includes chorizo and eggs or quiche and homemade bread; dine in the tranquil breakfast room or on the patio. ✉ *456 N. 3rd St., 95112,* ☎ *408/298–3537 or 800/498–3537,* FAX *408/ 298–4676,* WEB *www.hensleyhouse.com. 11 rooms, 4 suites. In-room data ports, in-room hot tubs (some), minibars, refrigerators, cable TV, in-room VCRs, kitchenettes (some), outdoor hot tub, laundry services, concierge, Internet, business services; no smoking. AE, D, DC, MC, V. BP.*

$$–$$$ 🛏 **Briar Rose Bed & Breakfast Inn.** This charming bed-and-breakfast in a restored 1875 Victorian farmhouse sits on nearly half an acre of gardens. There are plenty of thoughtful touches in the rooms, like antique furniture and feather mattresses, and a lovely front parlor with a marble fireplace. The complimentary breakfast often includes quiche, pancakes, waffles, and omelets. Groups of five or more can enjoy afternoon tea in the garden or back parlor with advance reservations. ✉ *897 E. Jackson St., 95112,* ☎ *408/279–5999,* FAX *408/279–4534,* WEB *www.briar-rose.com. 5 rooms, 1 cottage. In-room data ports, refrigerators (some), cable TV, in-room VCRs; no smoking. AE, D, DC, MC, V. BP.*

$ 🛏 **Days Inn.** There's nothing fancy about these motel-style accommodations, but there's an Olympic-size pool on the premises and a coffeemaker in every room. The hotel is about 5 mi from downtown. ✉ *4170 Monterey Rd., 95111,* ☎ *408/224–4122 or 800/329–7466,* FAX *408/224–4177,* WEB *www.daysinn.com. 34 rooms. Refrigerators, microwaves, pool, hot tub; no-smoking rooms. AE, D, DC, MC, V. CP.*

Nightlife and the Arts

NIGHTLIFE

Try **Big Lil's Barbary Coast Dinner Theater** (✉ 157 W. San Fernando St., ☎ 408/295–7469) for an evening of turn-of-the-20th-century melodrama, vaudeville, and audience participation (lots of popcorn throwing) on Friday and Saturday evenings; there are also comedy and live music on Thursday. Just west of downtown, the **Garden City Lounge** (✉ 360 S. Saratoga Ave, ☎ 408/244–3333) has free jazz nightly. **Agenda** (✉ 399 S. 1st St., ☎ 408/287–3991) is one of the most popular nightspots downtown, with a restaurant on the main floor, a bar upstairs, and a nightclub on the bottom floor. Pick up a pool cue at trendy **South First Billiards** (✉ 420 S. 1st St., ☎ 408/294–7800), amid the burgeoning cluster of small clubs in an area called SoFA—South of First Area—along 1st and 2nd streets south of San Carlos Avenue.

THE ARTS

The **Center for Performing Arts** (✉ 255 Almaden Blvd., ☎ 408/277–3900) is the city's main performance venue. The **American Musical Theatre of San Jose** (☎ 408/453–7108) presents four musicals per year. The **San Jose Symphony** (☎ 408/288–2828) performs in the fall, winter, and spring. The **Ballet San Jose Silicon Valley** (☎ 408/288–2800) performs from October through May. The **San Jose Repertory Theatre** (✉ 101 Paseo de San Antonio, ☎ 408/291–2255) occupies a contemporary four-story, 528-seat theater, dubbed the Blue Box because of its angular blue exterior.

City Lights Theater Co. (☎ 408/295–4200) presents a variety of progressive and traditional pieces in an intimate 99-seat theater.

Outdoor Activities and Sports

GOLF

The **San Jose Municipal Golf Course** (✉ 1560 Oakland Rd., ☎ 408/441–4653) is an 18-hole course. The **Cinnabar Hills Golf Club** (✉ 23600 McKean Rd., ☎ 408/323–5200) is a 27-hole course.

Known to area sports fans as the Shark Tank or, simply, the Tank, the 17,483-seat **Compaq Center at San Jose** (⊠ Santa Clara St. at Autumn St., ☎ 408/287–9200; 408/998–2277 for tickets), formerly the San Jose Arena, looks like a giant hothouse, with its glass entrance, shining metal armor, and skylight ceiling. The arena hosts various sporting and other events and is the home of the National Hockey League's **San Jose Sharks.** In **Spartan Stadium** (⊠ 7th St. between E. Alma Ave. and E. Humboldt St.) the **San Jose Earthquakes** (formerly the San Jose Clash) play major league soccer. At other times of the year the stadium hosts qualifying games for international soccer competitions. The only venue of its type in northern California, the **Hellyer Velodrome** (⊠ 985 Hellyer Ave., ☎ 408/226–9716) attracts national-class cyclists and Olympians in training to bicycle races from May through August.

Shopping

It originally opened in 1960 with only 20 sellers, but today the **San Jose Flea Market** (⊠ 1590 Berryessa Rd., between I–680 and Rte. 101, ☎ 408/453–1110) is part Mexican *mercado* (market), part carnival, and part garage sale. Some 2,700 vendors spread over 120 acres sell handicrafts, leather, jewelry, furniture, produce, and more. Be sure to examine merchandise before buying. The flea market operates Wednesday–Sunday dawn–dusk; parking is $1 weekdays and $5 weekends. With more than 150 retail outlets and an ice rink, **Eastridge Mall** (⊠ Capitol Expressway and Tully Rd., ☎ 408/274–0360), is one of the state's largest.

THE PENINSULA AND SOUTH BAY A TO Z

To research prices, get advice from other travelers, and book travel arrangements, visit www.fodors.com.

AIR TRAVEL

All the major airlines serve San Francisco International Airport, and most of them fly into San Jose International Airport. South & East Bay Airport Shuttle can transport you between the airport and Saratoga, Palo Alto, Campbell, and other destinations. *See* Air Travel *in* Smart Travel Tips A to Z for airline phone numbers.

➤ AIRPORT INFORMATION: **San Francisco International Airport** (⊠ Off U.S. 101, 15 mi south of downtown, ☎ 650/761–0800). **San Jose International Airport** (⊠ 1661 Airport Blvd., off Hwy. 87, ☎ 408/277–4759, WEB www.sjc.org). **South & East Bay Airport Shuttle** (☎ 408/559–9477).

BUS TRAVEL

SamTrans buses travel to Half Moon Bay from the Daly City BART station. Another bus connects Half Moon Bay with Pescadero. Each trip takes approximately one hour. Call for schedules, because departures are infrequent. The Valley Transportation Authority (VTA) shuttle links downtown San Jose to the CalTrain station, across from the Arena, every 20 minutes during morning and evening commute hours.
➤ CONTACTS: **SamTrans** (☎ 800/660–4287). **VTA Shuttle** (☎ 408/321–2300).

CAR RENTAL

You can rent a car at the San Jose airport from any of the many major agencies that operate there. Specialty Rentals offers standard cars and luxury vehicles; it has an office in Palo Alto and will deliver a car to you anywhere on the Peninsula or at the airport. *See* Car Rental *in* Smart

Travel Tips A to Z for national rental agency phone numbers.
➤ RENTAL AGENCIES: **Specialty Rentals** (☎ 800/400–8412).

CAR TRAVEL

Public transportation to coastal areas is limited, so it's best to drive.
To get to Half Moon Bay, take Route 1, also known as the Coast Highway, south along the length of the San Mateo coast. A quicker route
is via I–280, the Junipero Serra Freeway; follow it south as far as Route
92, where you can turn west toward the coast. To get to Pescadero,
drive south 16 mi on Route 1 from Half Moon Bay. For Año Nuevo
continue south on Route 1 another 12 mi.

By car the most pleasant route down the Inland Peninsula to Palo Alto,
Woodside, Santa Clara, and San Jose is I–280, the Junipero Serra Freeway, which passes along Crystal Springs Reservoir. U.S. 101, also
known as the Bayshore Freeway, is more direct but also more congested.
To avoid the often-heavy commuter traffic on Route 101, use I–280
during rush hours.

To reach Saratoga, take I–280 south to Highway 85 and follow Highway 85 south toward Gilroy. Exit on Saratoga–Sunnyvale Road, go
south, and follow the signs to the Village—about 2½ mi. Signs will also
direct you to Hakone Gardens and Villa Montalvo.

EMERGENCIES

In an emergency dial 911.
➤ HOSPITALS: **San Jose Medical Center** (✉ 675 E. Santa Clara St., San
Jose, ☎ 408/998–3212). **Stanford Hospital** (✉ 300 Pasteur Dr., Palo
Alto, ☎ 650/723–5111).

LODGING

Lodging in the Inland Peninsula and South Bay areas targets business
travelers and run to chain motels and hotels, though a number of
B&Bs have popped up. Along the coast the lodgings tend to have
more character and cater to weekending San Franciscans and tourists.
Local visitor bureaus or chambers of commerce can help you find a
room in the town you plan to visit.

TRAIN TRAVEL

CalTrain runs from 4th and Townsend streets in San Francisco to Palo
Alto ($4 each way); from there take the free Marguerite shuttle bus to
the Stanford campus and the Palo Alto area. Buses run about every 15
minutes 6 AM–7:45 PM and are timed to connect with trains and public transit buses.

CalTrain service continues south of Palo Alto to Santa Clara's Railroad and Franklin streets stop, near Santa Clara University ($4.75 one-
way), and to San Jose's Rod Diridon station ($5.25 one-way). The trip
to Santa Clara takes approximately 1¼ hours; the trip to San Jose takes
about 1½ hours.

Valley Transportation Authority buses run efficiently throughout the
Santa Clara Valley, although not as frequently as you might like. Operators can help you plan routes.

In San Jose light-rail trains run 24 hours a day and serve most major
attractions, shopping malls, historic sites, and downtown. Trains run
every 10 minutes weekdays from 6 AM to 8 PM and vary during weekends and late-night hours from every 15 minutes to once an hour. Tickets are valid for two hours; they cost $1.25 one-way or $3 for a day
pass. Buy tickets at vending machines in any transit station. For more
information call or visit the Downtown Customer Service Center.

➤ CONTACTS: **CalTrain** (☏ 800/660–4287). **Downtown Customer Service Center** (Light Rail; ✉ 2 N. 1st St., San Jose, ☏ 408/321–2300). **Marguerite Shuttle** (☏ 650/723–9362). **Valley Transportation Authority** (☏ 408/321–2300 or 800/894–9908).

VISITOR INFORMATION

➤ TOURIST INFORMATION: **California State Parks Bay Area District Office** (✉ 250 Executive Park Blvd., Suite 4900, San Francisco, 94134, ☏ 415/330–6300). **Half Moon Bay Chamber of Commerce** (✉ 520 Kelly Ave., 94019, ☏ 650/726–8380, WEB www.halfmoonbaychamber. org). **Palo Alto Chamber of Commerce** (✉ 325 Forest Ave., 94301, ☏ 650/324–3121). **San Jose Convention and Visitors Bureau** (✉ 125 South Market St., 3rd floor, 95113, ☏ 800/726–5673, 408/295–2265, or 408/295–9600, WEB www.sanjose.org). **Santa Clara Chamber of Commerce and Convention and Visitors Bureau** (✉ 1850 Warburton Ave., 95050, ☏ 408/244–8244, WEB www.santaclara.org). **Saratoga Chamber of Commerce** (✉ 20460 Saratoga–Los Gatos Rd., 95070, ☏ 408/867–0753, WEB www.saratogachamber.org). **Woodside Town Hall** (✉ 2955 Woodside Rd., 94062, ☏ 650/851–6790).

9 THE CENTRAL VALLEY

HIGHWAY 99 FROM LODI TO BAKERSFIELD

The Central Valley, one of the world's most fertile working landscapes, is California's heartland. This sunbaked region contains a wealth of rivers, lakes, and waterways that host a tremendous diversity of wildlife. Humans, in turn, have created a profusion of vineyards, dairy farms, orchards, and pastures that stretch to the horizon. You'll find the area possesses myriad attractions, beginning with the warmth of its land and people.

Updated by
Lisa M.
Hamilton

L USH FIELDS AND ORCHARDS crisscrossed by miles of back roads define the landscape of California's Central Valley. Nearly every telephone post is crowned by a hawk or kestrel hunting the land below. In the towns, myriad museums and historical societies display artifacts of the valley's eccentric past, and restored theaters host a vibrant contemporary cultural life. From the back roads to the main streets the people are not only friendly but proud to help outsiders see that the Central Valley is anything but the nowhere it's made out to be.

The well-populated Central Valley remains California's Great Touristic Unknown, and it does appear, at first glance, to be a traveler's void. However, that's not because there's nothing here; rather, it's because most folks never get off the highway (and, at that, they drive boring old I–5 instead of busy Highway 99). The valley's history of being passed over dates back hundreds of years. Until the mid-19th century the area was a desert. Gold discoveries, starting in the 1850s, sparked the birth of some towns; the railroads' arrival in following decades spurred the development of others. But it was the coming of simple water, courtesy of private dams and, in the 1930s, the Central Valley Project, that transformed this land into the country's most vital agricultural region.

As soon as irrigation gave potential to the valley's open acres, the area became a magnet for farmers, ranchers, developers, World War II refugees, and immigrants from places as diverse as Portugal, China, Armenia, and Laos. More recently, refugees from the state's big cities have arrived in search of cheaper real estate, safer neighborhoods, and more space. With development has come unsightly sprawl, traffic jams, air pollution, and pressure on crucial water supplies, all of which threaten to overwhelm the valley's traditional charms. It is this image that keeps most tourists away. But the region's cultural diversity and agricultural roots have woven a textured social fabric that has been chronicled by some of the country's finest writers, including Fresno native William Saroyan, Stockton native Maxine Hong Kingston, and *Grapes of Wrath* author John Steinbeck.

Just as these authors found inspiration in a place you cannot view while speeding down the highway, you must invest time and footwork to appreciate the Central Valley. In turn, the rewards can be surprising, relaxing, thrilling. . . even poetic.

Pleasures and Pastimes

Dining

Fast-food places and chain restaurants dominate valley highways and major intersections, but why deprive your taste buds in the midst of this agricultural cornucopia? A sprinkling of cutting-edge bistros and fine restaurants revels in the availability of fresh local produce and meats, the cornerstone of California cuisine. Even simple restaurants manage to produce hearty, tasty fare, which often reflects the valley's ethnic mix. In addition to the more numerous Mexican, Chinese, and Italian eateries, look out for Armenian kitchens, Vietnamese eateries, and traditional Basque restaurants, which serve massive, many-course meals.

CATEGORY	COST*
$$$$	over $30
$$$	$22–$30
$$	$15–$21
$	under $15

*per person for a main course at dinner, excluding tip and 7¼% tax

Festivals, Tours, and Tastings

The Central Valley is a great destination for anyone who likes to taste produce fresh from the fields. As billboards announce, fruit and nut orchards and cheese and chocolate factories offer educational tours that include tastings. Better yet, there are farmers' markets in virtually every town and roadside stands in between. Good places to find produce stands are Highway 198 between Visalia and Hanford, Herndon Avenue in Clovis, and Highway 12 in Lodi. Prime season for farmers' markets is May through October, though many larger ones are open year-round, including those held every Saturday in Bakersfield, Fresno, Merced, Stockton, and Visalia. Especially in fall check with the local chamber of commerce for festivals celebrating everything from the asparagus and raisin crops to residents' Chinese, Greek, Swedish, and Tahitian roots.

Lodging

Chain motels and hotels are the norm in the Central Valley. Most are utilitarian but perfectly clean and comfortable, and prices tend to be considerably lower than those in more heavily traveled areas. The few Victorian-style bed-and-breakfasts around here are a good bet, not only because they are cheaper than in more touristy destinations but because they offer a taste of local life.

CATEGORY	COST*
$$$$	over $225
$$$	$160–$225
$$	$100–$159
$	under $100

*All prices are for a standard double room, excluding 8% tax.

Outdoor Activities and Sports

Several cities and towns serve as convenient starting points for whitewater rafting trips on the Stanislaus, Merced, Kings, and Kern rivers. Fishing in the rivers and lakes is another favored activity; the lakes are also prime spots for boating and windsurfing. Stockton is a popular rental area for houseboating on the Sacramento River delta, and Bakersfield is a center for NASCAR racing. Wildlife refuges are world-class sites for watching birds, especially migrating waterfowl.

Exploring the Central Valley

The 225-mi Central Valley cuts through San Joaquin, Stanislaus, Merced, Madera, Fresno, Kings, Tulare, and Kern counties and is bounded on the east by the mighty Sierra Nevada and on the west by the smaller coastal ranges. I–5 runs north–south through the valley, as does Highway 99.

Numbers in the text correspond to numbers in the margin and on the Central Valley and Fresno Area maps.

Great Itineraries

IF YOU HAVE 1 DAY

Touring the **Fresno** area is a good strategy if you only have a day to spend in the valley. **Roeding Park** ⑧ has a striking tropical rain forest within **Chaffee Zoological Gardens**; the park's **Playland** and **Storyland** are great stops if you have children. Don't miss the **Forestiere Underground Gardens** ⑦, on Shaw Avenue. In springtime take the self-guided **Blossom Trail** driving tour through orchards, vineyards, and fields. Along the trail in Reedley is the **Mennonite Quilt Center.** Depending on your mood and the weather, you can spend part of the afternoon at **Wild Water Adventures** or visit the **Fresno Metropolitan Museum** ⑪, whose highlights include an exhibit about author William Saroyan.

The Central Valley

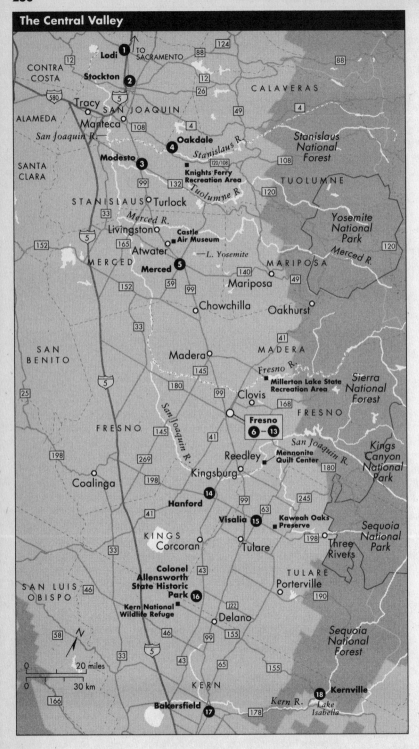

CONTRA
COSTA
12
Lodi ①
TO
SACRAMENTO
124
88
88

Stockton ②
CALAVERAS
580
Tracy
SAN JOAQUIN
12
26
ALAMEDA
Manteca
108
49
4
San Joaquin R.
Oakdale ④
Stanislaus R.
Stanislaus
National
Forest
SANTA
CLARA
Modesto ③
Knights Ferry
Recreation Area
120/108
108
TUOLUMNE
99
132
STANISLAUS
Turlock
120
Merced R.
Yosemite
National
Park
120
33
152
Livingston
165
Castle
Air Museum
Merced R.
5
Atwater
L. Yosemite
MERCED
Merced ⑤
MARIPOSA
49
152
59
140
49
Mariposa
Oakhurst
33
Chowchilla
41
MADERA
SAN
BENITO
Madera
145
Fresno R.
Sierra
National
Forest
25
180
Millerton Lake State
Recreation Area
99
Clovis
168
5
FRESNO
145
Fresno
⑥ – ⑬
FRESNO
41
San Joaquin R.
Kings
Canyon
National
Park
198
269
Reedley
Mennonite
Quilt Center
180
Kingsburg
Coalinga
198
⑭
245
41
Hanford
99
63
Sequoia
National
Park
Visalia ⑮
Kaweah Oaks
Preserve
KINGS
Corcoran
198
Three
Rivers
33
Tulare
Colonel
Allensworth
State Historic
Park
TULARE
43
Porterville
190
SAN LUIS
OBISPO
46
⑯
122
58
Kern National
Wildlife Refuge
Delano
46
99
155
Sequoia
National
Forest
33
5
43
65
155
KERN
166
⑱ Kernville
Bakersfield ⑰
178
Kern R.
Lake
Isabella

0   20 miles
0   30 km
N

IF YOU HAVE 3 DAYS

On your first morning visit **Micke Grove Park and Zoo,** in ① **Lodi.** That afternoon head for ② ⊞ **Stockton** and wander around the **Haggin Museum.** The next morning stop off at the **Castle Air Museum,** north of **Merced** ⑤ in Atwater, or proceed directly to ⊞ **Fresno** ⑥–⑬. In the evening take in a show at **Roger Rocka's** or the **Tower Theatre,** both in Fresno's Tower District. On the third morning drive to **Hanford** ⑭ via Highways 99 and 43 and stroll around **Courthouse Square** and **China Alley.** After lunch continue south on Highway 43 to **Colonel Allensworth State Historic Park** ⑯, which is on the site of a now-deserted town founded by African-Americans in 1908. Head south on Highway 43 and east on Highway 46 to return to Highway 99, which continues south to ⊞ **Bakersfield** ⑰. If you arrive before it closes, stop in for a quick visit to the **Kern County Museum.**

When to Visit the Central Valley

Spring, when wildflowers are in bloom and the scent of fruit blossoms is in the air, and fall, when leaves turn red and gold, are the prettiest times to visit. Many of the valley's biggest festivals take place during these seasons. Summer, when temperatures often top 100°F, can be oppressive. Many attractions close in winter, which can get cold and raw. Thick, ground-hugging fog, called tule fog by locals, is a common driving hazard that time of year.

NORTH CENTRAL VALLEY

From Lodi to Merced

The northern section of the valley cuts through San Joaquin, Stanislaus, and Merced counties, from the edges of the Sacramento River delta and the fringes of the Gold Country south to the flat, almost featureless terrain between Modesto and Merced. If you're heading to Yosemite National Park from northern California, chances are you'll pass through (or very near) at least one of these gateway cities.

Lodi

❶ *25 mi south of Sacramento on Hwy. 99.*

Founded on agriculture, Lodi was once the watermelon capital of the country, and today it is surrounded by fields of asparagus, pumpkins, beans, almonds, safflowers, sunflowers, kiwis, melons, squashes, peaches, and cherries. It has also become a wine grape capital of sorts, as it produces more zinfandel, merlot, cabernet sauvignon, chardonnay, and sauvignon blanc grapes than anywhere else in the state. For years, California wineries have built their reputations for fine wine on the juice of grapes grown around Lodi. Now the area that includes Lodi, Lockeford, and Woodbridge is turning itself into an independent wine destination, but Lodi still retains some of its old rural charm. You can stroll downtown and visit wildlife refuges, all the while benefiting from a Sacramento River delta breeze that keeps this microclimate cooler in summer than anyplace else in the area. With a short, mild winter and a long, rain-free summer, Lodi is ideal for outdoor recreation.

☾ The 65-acre **Micke Grove Park and Zoo,** an oak-shaded county park off I–5, includes a Japanese garden, picnic areas, a golf course, and an agricultural museum with a collection of 94 tractors. Ringtail lemurs and other endangered primates found only on the African island of Madagascar inhabit *An Island Lost in Time,* an exhibit at the **Micke Grove Zoo** (☎ 209/953–8840, WEB www.mgzoo.com). Mountain lions have the run of *Paseo Pantera,* another highlight of this compact facility. Admission is $2. The rides and other diversions at Micke Grove's **Funderwoods** (☎ 209/369–5437), a family-oriented amusement park, are geared to children under 10. Ride tickets cost $1. ⊠ *11793 N. Micke Grove Rd.,* ☎ *209/331–7400.* ☞ *Parking $2 weekdays, $4 weekends.* ⊙ *Daily 10–5.*

Stop by the **Lodi Wine & Visitor's Center** (⊠ 2545 W. Turner Rd., ☎ 209/365–0621) to see exhibits on Lodi's viticultural history. Here you can pick up a map of area wineries, as well as buy wine. The stand-
★ out winery in the Lodi area is **Jessie's Grove** (⊠ 1973 W. Turner Rd., ☎ 209/368–0880), a wooded horse ranch and vineyard that has been in the same family for 150 years. In addition to producing outstanding old-vine zinfandels, it presents blues concerts on the second Saturday of the month April through October. If you taste at **Peirano Estate Vineyards** (⊠ 21831 N. Hwy. 12, Acampo, ☎ 209/369–9463), bring a lunch and have a picnic on the grass between the grapevines. At its homey facility kid-friendly **Phillips Farms** (⊠ 4580 W. Hwy. 12, ☎ 209/368–7384) offers tastings from its affordable Michael-David and premium Phillips Winery labels (the latter famed for its syrah). You can also cut flowers from the garden, pet the animals, eat breakfast and lunch at the café, and buy Phillips's produce. **Vino Piazza** (⊠ 12470 Locke Rd., Lockeford, ☎ 209/727–9770) is a sort of wine co-op housed in the old Lockeford Winery building, where 13 vineyards now make their wine and operate tasting rooms. At the expense of not seeing the vineyards themselves, this is a good way to sample the area's many wines in a short time.

Dining and Lodging

$–$$$ ✕ **Rosewood Bar & Grill.** In downtown Lodi, Rosewood offers fine dining without formal dress. Operated by the folks at Wine and Roses inn, the lower-key spot serves globally influenced American food such as pork chops with chipotle and jack cheese polenta. There's a large bar with its own menu, plus live jazz nightly. ⊠ *28 S. School St.,* ☎ *209/369–0470. MC, V. Closed Sun.–Mon.*

$ ✕ **Avenue Grill.** This family-style grill with an open cooking pit is a best bet for burgers and steaks. ⊠ *506 W. Lodi Ave.,* ☎ *209/333–8006. No credit cards.*

$ ✕ **Habanero Hots.** If your mouth can handle the heat promised by the restaurant's name, try the tamales. If you want to take it easy on your taste buds, stick with the rest of the menu. ⊠ *1024 E. Victor Rd.,* ☎ *209/369–3791. AE, D, MC, V.*

$$–$$$$ ✕▦ **Wine and Roses Country Inn.** This inn and restaurant is leading
★ the Lodi renaissance, cultivating a sense of refinement typically associated with Napa or Carmel. Some rooms are country style, some newly remodeled, but all have balconies that look onto the commons, a tapestry of informal gardens and exotic trees. Some rooms have fireplaces, and all have coffeemakers, irons, and hair dryers; there are TVs in some bathrooms. The eponymous restaurant is *the* place to eat in Lodi—locals make a special occasion of it, and for good reason: served in the light and airy dining room, the lunches are decadent, dinners sumptuous, and buffet champagne brunch unparalleled this side of the Bay Area. ⊠ *2505 W. Turner Rd., 95242,* ☎ *209/334–6988,* ☎☎ *209/ 334–6570,* ☷☷ *www.winerose.com. 32 rooms, 6 suites. Restaurant, room service, in-room data ports, refrigerators, cable TV, bar, laundry service; no-smoking rooms. AE, D, DC, MC, V.*

$$–$$$ ▦ **The Inn at Locke House.** Built in 1862, this B&B was a pioneer family's home and is now on the National Register of Historic Places. Its blend of old and new makes it special: each bedroom has an armoire built during the Civil War alongside stereos and gas-powered "wood"

stoves; the spectacular brick barn (also on the National Register) is capped with solar panels. The Watertower Room is especially dreamy: nestled in the house's white-brick tower, its private sitting room has a view of the Sierras out one window and of the sunset out the other. In the oak-paneled parlor you'll find books, games, historical artifacts, and an old pump organ. Refreshments welcome you on arrival. ⊠ *19960 N. Elliott Rd., Lockeford 95237,* ☎ *209/727–5715,* ℻ *209/727–0873,* ⒲ *www. theinnatlockehouse.com. 4 rooms, 1 suite. Library; no room phones, no TV in some rooms, no-smoking rooms. AE, D, DC, MC, V. BP.*

$-$$ 🏨 **Lodi Comfort Inn.** This Spanish-style downtown motel accented with palm trees has quiet rooms with contemporary furnishings. Doughnuts brought in from a chain bakery and coffee make up the complimentary breakfast. ⊠ *118 N. Cherokee La.,* ☎ *209/367–4848,* ℻ *209/367–4898. 35 rooms. Refrigerators, cable TV, pool, hot tub, baby-sitting, laundry facilities, laundry service. AE, D, MC, V. CP.*

Outdoor Activities and Sports

Even locals need respite from the heat of Central Valley summers, and **Lodi Lake Park** (⊠ Turner Rd. at Holly Dr., ☎ 209/333–6742) is where they find it. The banks, shaded by grand old elms and oaks, are much cooler than other spots in town. Swimming, bird-watching, and picnicking are possibilities, as is renting a kayak, canoe, pedal boat, or aqua cycle ($2–$4 per half hour, Tuesday–Sunday).

Stockton

❷ *13 mi south of Lodi on Hwy. 99.*

California's first inland port—connected since 1933 to San Francisco via a 60-mi-long deepwater channel—is wedged between I–5 and Highway 99, on the eastern end of the great Sacramento River delta. Stockton, founded during the gold rush as a way station for miners traveling from San Francisco to the Mother Lode and now a city of 250,000, helps distribute the valley's agricultural products to the world. If you're here in late April, don't miss the **Stockton Asparagus Festival** (☎ 800/350–1987), in Oak Grove Park.

★   The **Haggin Museum,** in pretty Victory Park, has one of the Central Valley's finest art collections. Highlights include landscapes by Albert Bierstadt and Thomas Moran, a still life by Paul Gauguin, a Native American gallery, and an Egyptian mummy. ⊠ *1201 N. Pershing Ave.,* ☎ *209/940–6300.* 🎟 *$5.* ☉ *Tues.–Sun. 1:30–5.*

Dining and Lodging

$$-$$$$ ✕ **Le Bistro.** The dishes at one of the valley's most upscale restaurants are fairly standard Continental fare—lamb tenderloin, fillet of sole, sautéed prawns, soufflé Grand Marnier—but you can count on high-quality ingredients and presentation with a flourish. ⊠ *Marina Center Mall, 3121 W. Benjamin Holt Dr. (off I–5, behind Lyon's),* ☎ *209/ 951–0885. AE, D, DC, MC, V. No lunch Sat.*

$ ✕ **On Lock Sam.** Run by the same family since 1898, this Stockton landmark is in a modern pagoda-style building, with framed Chinese prints on the walls, a garden outside one window, and a sparkling bar area. One touch of old-time Chinatown remains: a few booths have curtains that can be drawn for complete privacy. The Cantonese food would be considered ho-hum in San Francisco, but it's among the valley's best. ⊠ *333 S. Sutter St.,* ☎ *209/466–4561. AE, D, MC, V.*

$-$$ 🏨 **Best Western Stockton Inn.** Four miles from downtown, this good-size motel has a convenient location off Highway 99. The large central courtyard with a pool and lounge chairs is a big plus on hot days.

Most rooms are spacious; free in-room movies are provided by satellite. ✉ *4219 Waterloo Rd., 95215,* ☎ *209/931–3131, 877/293–8697,* FAX *209/931–0423,* WEB *www.bestwesterncalifornia.com. 141 rooms. Restaurant, pool, wading pool, hot tub, bar, laundry service, meeting room; no-smoking rooms. AE, D, DC, MC, V.*

$ ⚑ **La Quinta Inn.** Close to downtown and near many upscale restaurants, this is a good choice for business and pleasure travelers alike. The spacious and quiet rooms have large desks and televisions with access to first-run movies. ✉ *2710 W. March La., 95219,* ☎ *209/952–7800,* FAX *209/472–0732,* WEB *www.laquinta.com. 158 rooms. In-room data ports, pool, exercise room, laundry service, meeting room; no-smoking rooms. AE, D, DC, MC, V.*

Outdoor Activities and Sports

There are several companies that rent houseboats (of various sizes, usually for three, four, or seven days) on the Sacramento River delta waterways near Stockton: **Delta Rental Houseboat Hotline** (☎ 209/477–1840), **Forever Resorts** (✉ 115830 W. 8 Mile Rd., ☎ 800/676–4841), **Herman & Helen's** (✉ Venice Island Ferry, ☎ 209/951–4634), and **Paradise Point Marina** (✉ 8095 Rio Blanco Rd., ☎ 209/952–1000).

En Route The top attraction in Manteca, the largest town between Stockton and Modesto, is **Manteca Waterslides.** Kids will head to the wild Thunder Falls, which has three 3-story slides. ✉ *874 E. Woodward Ave., between I–5 and Hwy. 99,* ☎ *209/249–2520, 877/625–9663.* 🎟 *$21.* ☉ *Memorial Day–Labor Day, weekdays 10–5, weekends 10–7.*

Modesto

❸ *29 mi south of Stockton on Hwy. 99.*

Modesto, a gateway to Yosemite and the southern reaches of the Gold Country, was founded in 1870 to serve the Central Pacific Railroad. The frontier town was originally to be named Ralston, after a railroad baron, but as the story goes, he modestly declined—thus the name Modesto. The Stanislaus County seat, a tree-lined city of 190,000, is perhaps best known as the site of the annual Modesto Invitational Track Meet and Relays and birthplace of film producer-director George Lucas, creator of *Star Wars* and *American Graffiti.*

The **Modesto Arch** (✉ 9th and I Sts.) bears the city's motto: WATER, WEALTH, CONTENTMENT, HEALTH. The prosperity that water brought to Modesto has attracted people from all over the world. The city holds a well-attended **International Festival** (☎ 209/521–3852) in early October that celebrates the cultures, crafts, and cuisines of many nationalities. You can witness the everyday abundance of the Modesto area at the **Blue Diamond Growers Store** (✉ 4800 Sisk Rd., ☎ 209/545–6229), which offers free samples, shows a film about almond-growing, and sells nuts in many flavors.

★ A wheat farmer and banker built the 1883 **McHenry Mansion,** the city's sole surviving original Victorian home. The Italianate-style mansion has been decorated to reflect Modesto life in the late 19th century. Oaks, elms, magnolias, redwoods, and palms shade the grounds. ✉ *15th and I Sts.,* ☎ *209/577–5341,* WEB *www.mchenrymuseum.org.* 🎟 *Free.* ☉ *Dec.–mid-Nov., Sun.–Thurs. 1–4, Fri. noon–3.*

The **McHenry Museum of Arts** is a jumbled repository of early Modesto and Stanislaus County memorabilia, including re-creations of an old-time barbershop, a doctor's office, a blacksmith's shop, and a general store stocked with period goods such as hair crimpers and corsets. ✉ *1402 I St.,* ☎ *209/577–5366.* 🎟 *Free.* ☉ *Tues.–Sun. noon–4.*

Dining and Lodging

$$–$$$$ ✕ **Early Dawn Cattlemen's Steakhouse and Saloon.** The parking lots overflow at this local hangout, and so do the platters bearing barbecued steaks that weigh 2 pounds or more. The whiskey-marinated saloon steak, cooked over Santa Maria red oak, is a house specialty; chicken and seafood are among the lighter choices. ⊠ *1000 Kansas Ave.,* ☎ *209/577–5833. AE, D, MC, V. No lunch Sat.*

$$–$$$$ ✕ **Hazel's Elegant Dining.** Hazel's is *the* special-occasion restaurant in Modesto. The seven-course dinners include Continental entrées served with soup, salad, pasta, dessert, and beverage. Members of the Gallo family, which owns much vineyard land in the Central Valley, eat here often, perhaps because the wine cellar is so comprehensive. ⊠ *431 12th St.,* ☎ *209/578–3463. AE, D, DC, MC, V. Closed Sun.–Mon. No lunch Sat.*

$–$$ ✕ **Tresetti's World Café.** This bright restaurant, one of the newer ones in downtown Modesto, is part wine shop, part restaurant. For a small fee the staff will uncork any wine you select from the shop. The menu changes seasonally, but the smoked chicken quesadilla is outstanding, as are the Cajun-style crab cakes. ⊠ *927 11th St.,* ☎ *209/572–2990. Reservations not accepted. AE, DC, MC, V. Closed Sun.*

$ ✕ **St. Stan's.** Modesto's renowned microbrewery makes St. Stan's beers. The 14 on tap include the delicious Whistle Stop pale ale and Red Sky ale. The restaurant is casual and serves up good corned beef sandwiches loaded with sauerkraut as well as a tasty beer-sausage nibbler. ⊠ *821 L St.,* ☎ *209/524–2337. AE, D, MC, V.*

$$ ☷ **Doubletree Hotel.** Modesto's largest lodging towers 15 stories over downtown. Each room has a coffeemaker, iron, desk, and three phones. The convention center is adjacent, and a good brewpub, St. Stan's, is across the street. ⊠ *1150 9th St., 95354,* ☎ *209/526–6000,* FAX *209/526–6096. 258 rooms. Restaurant, café, room service, pool, gym, hot tub, sauna, bar, nightclub, laundry service, meeting room, airport shuttle; no-smoking rooms. AE, D, DC, MC, V.*

$–$$ ☷ **Best Western Mallard's Inn.** The duck theme is, thankfully, unobtrusive at this nicely landscaped motel off Highway 99. The comfortably furnished rooms are large, and all have coffeemakers. Some rooms have microwaves and refrigerators stocked with milk and cookies. ⊠ *1720 Sisk Rd., 95350,* ☎ *209/577–3825 or 800/294–4040,* FAX *209/577–1717. 126 rooms. Restaurant, room service, pool, gym, hot tub, laundry service, business services, meeting room; no-smoking rooms. AE, D, DC, MC, V.*

En Route Heading south on Highway 99 from Modesto, stop at the outdoor ℭ **Castle Air Museum,** adjacent to the former Castle Air Force Base (now Castle Aviation, an industrial park). You can stroll among fighter planes and other historic military aircraft. The 44 restored vintage war birds include the B-25 Mitchell medium-range bomber (best known for the Jimmy Doolittle raid on Tokyo following the attack on Pearl Harbor) and the speedy SR-71 Blackbird, used for reconnaissance over Vietnam and Libya. ⊠ *Santa Fe Dr. and Buhach Rd. (6 mi north of Merced, take the Buhach Rd. exit off Hwy. 99 in Atwater and follow signs), Atwater,* ☎ *209/723–2178.* ☷ *$7.* ☉ *May–Sept., daily 9–5; Oct.–Apr., daily 10–4.*

Oakdale

❹ *15 mi east of Modesto on Hwy. 108.*

Oakdale, a bit off the beaten path from Modesto, has two year-round ℭ attractions of great interest to children. The **Hershey Chocolate Fac-**

tory in Oakdale is the only one in the country that allows the public to tour its production facilities. After the half-hour guided tours—which cover the chocolate-making process from cocoa bean to candy bar—everyone gets a sample. ⊠ *120 S. Sierra Ave.,* ☎ *209/848–8126.* ☒ *Free.* ☉ *Tours weekdays 8:30–3, visitor center weekdays 8:30–5.*

★ ☺ The featured attraction at the **Knights Ferry Recreation Area** is the 355-ft-long Knights Ferry covered bridge. The beautiful and haunting structure, built in 1863, crosses the Stanislaus River near the ruins of an old gristmill. The park has picnic and barbecue areas along the riverbanks, as well as three environmental campgrounds, accessible only by boat, bicycle, or foot. Among the activities here are fishing, hiking, canoeing, and rafting on 4 mi of rapids. ⊠ *Corps of Engineers Park, 18020 Sonora Rd., Knights Ferry, 12 mi east of Oakdale via Hwy. 108,* ☎ *209/881–3517.* ☒ *Free.* ☉ *Daily dawn–dusk.*

You can sample the wares at **Oakdale Cheese & Specialties** (⊠ 10040 Hwy. 120, ☎ 209/848–3139), which has tastings (try the aged Gouda) and cheese-making tours. There's a picnic area next to a pond and a petting zoo.

If you're in Oakdale the third weekend in May, check out the **Oakdale Chocolate Festival** (☎ 209/847–2244), which attracts 40,000–50,000 people to this small town. Festivities include music, arts and crafts, and Chocolate Avenue, where vendors proffer cakes, cookies, ice cream, fudge, truffles, and cheesecake.

Outdoor Activities and Sports

Rafting on the Stanislaus River is a popular activity near Oakdale. **River Journey** (⊠ 14842 Orange Blossom Rd., ☎ 209/847–4671 or 800/292–2938) will take you out for a few hours of fun. To satisfy your whitewater or flat-water cravings, contact **Sunshine River Adventures** (⊠ Box 1445, 95361, ☎ 209/848–4800 or 800/829–7238) about its trips on the Stanislaus.

Merced

⑤ *38 mi south of Modesto on Hwy. 99; 53 mi from Oakdale, west and then south on Hwy. 108 and south on Hwy. 99.*

Thanks to a soon-to-open branch of the University of California and an aggressive community redevelopment plan, the downtown of county seat Merced is coming back to life. The transformation is not yet complete, but there are promising signs: a brewpub, several boutiques, the restoration of numerous historic buildings, and foot traffic won back from outlying strip malls.

Even if you don't go inside, be sure to swing by the **Merced County Courthouse Museum.** The three-story former courthouse, built in 1875, is a striking example of the Victorian Italianate style. The upper two floors are now a museum of early Merced history. Highlights include an ornate restored courtroom and an 1870 Chinese temple with carved redwood altars. ⊠ *21st and N Sts., Merced,* ☎ *209/723–2401.* ☒ *Free.* ☉ *Wed.–Sun. 1–4.*

The **Merced Multicultural Arts Center** displays paintings, sculpture, and photography. Threads, a festival that celebrates the area's ethnic diversity, is held here on a mid-October weekend. ⊠ *645 W. Main St., Merced,* ☎ *209/388–1090.* ☒ *Free.* ☉ *Weekdays 9–5, Sat. 10–2.*

OFF THE
BEATEN PATH
MILLERTON LAKE STATE RECREATION AREA – This lake at the top of Friant Dam is a great place for boating and fishing but is otherwise unspectacular—until you look up. The lake and its surrounding hills are popular

wintering grounds for bald eagles, and if you are patient, you can almost surely spot them here between December and February. The park offers guided boat rides (on weekends in December and January, daily in February) on which rangers help you find the magnificent birds. ⊠ *5290 Millerton Rd., 20 mi northeast of Fresno via Hwy. 41 and Hwy. 145, Friant,* ☎ *209/822–2332.* ☷ *Free.* ☉ *Daily sunrise–sunset.*

Dining and Lodging

$$–$$$$ ✕ **DeAngelo's.** Not only the best restaurant in Merced, it's one of the
★ best in the entire Central Valley. Chef Vincent DeAngelo, a graduate of the Culinary Institute of America, brings his considerable skill to everything from basic ravioli to Portobello mushrooms in brandied peppercorn sauce. The delicious crusty bread, from the Golden Sheath in Watsonville, is a meal in itself. Note: because locals know all this, reservations are a good idea on weekends. ⊠ *350 W. Main St., Merced,* ☎ *209/383–3020. AE, D, DC, MC, V. Closed Sun. Mar.–Nov.*

$ ✕ **Main Street Café.** This bright downtown café dishes up soups, pizza, salads, sandwiches, pastries, ice cream, and espresso. Sandwiches (try the chicken breast with pesto mayonnaise on Francesi bread) are served with tasty side salads. ⊠ *460 W. Main St., Merced,* ☎ *209/725–1702. AE, MC, V. Closed Sun. No dinner.*

$–$$ ⊡ **Hooper House Bear Creek Inn.** This 1931 neocolonial home is so gorgeously unlike anything else in Merced, you'll be surprised to find it standing regally at the corner of M Street. The 1½ acres of tightly clipped grounds host fruit trees and grapevines, while the house itself offers a sunroom, well-chosen antiques, and big, soft beds. Breakfast is hearty and imaginative, featuring locally grown foods such as fried sweet potatoes and sweet black walnuts. ⊠ *575 N. Bear Creek Dr., at M St., 95340,* ☎ *209/723–3991,* ⒻⒶⓍ *209/723–7123,* ⒲ⒺⒷ *www. hooperhouse.com. 2 rooms, 1 suite, 1 cottage. In-room data ports; no-smoking rooms. AE, MC, V. BP.*

Outdoor Activities and Sports

At **Lake Yosemite Regional Park** (⊠ N. Lake Rd. off Yosemite Ave., 5 mi northeast of Merced, ☎ 209/385–7426), you can boat, swim, windsurf, waterski, and fish on a 387-acre reservoir. Boat rentals and picnic areas are available.

MID-CENTRAL VALLEY
From Fresno to Visalia

The Mid–Central Valley extends over three counties—Fresno, Kings, and Tulare. From Fresno Highway 41 leads north 95 mi to Yosemite and Highway 180 snakes east 55 mi to Kings Canyon (Sequoia National Park is 30 mi farther). From Visalia Highway 198 winds east 35 mi to Generals Highway, which leads into Sequoia and Kings Canyon. Historic Hanford and bustling Visalia are unadvertised but wonderful discoveries.

Fresno

50 mi south of Merced on Hwy. 99.

Sprawling Fresno, with more than 400,000 people, is the center of the richest agricultural county in America; grapes, cotton, oranges, and turkeys are among the major products. The city's most famous native, Pulitzer Prize–winning playwright and novelist William Saroyan (*The Time of Your Life, The Human Comedy*), was born here in 1908. Today the seemingly endless parade of strip malls and fast-food joints can be

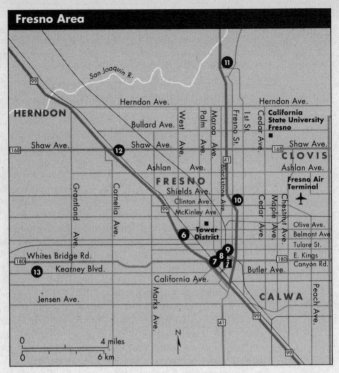

Fresno Area

depressing, but local character does lurk beneath the commercializa-tion. Approximately 75 ethnic communities (from Armenian to Viet-namese) call Fresno home, and there is a burgeoning arts scene and several public parks. There is even a hipster scene, centered in the Tower District, where chic restaurants, coffeehouses, and boutiques defy Fresno's stereotype as a place from which young people flee.

★ ☺ ❻ You can cool off in tree-shaded **Roeding Park,** which has picnic areas, playgrounds, tennis courts, horseshoe pits, and a zoo. The most strik-ing exhibit at **Chaffee Zoological Gardens** (☎ 559/498–2671, WEB www.chaffeezoo.org), in Roeding Park, is the tropical rain forest, where you are likely to encounter exotic birds along the paths and bridges. Elsewhere you'll find tigers, grizzly bears, sea lions, tule elk, camels, elephants, and hooting siamangs. Also here are a high-tech rep-tile house and a petting zoo. Open year-round, the zoo charges $6 ad-mission. A miniature train, a Ferris wheel, a small roller coaster, and a merry-go-round are among the amusements that operate February–November at **Playland** (☎ 559/486–2124). Children can explore at-tractions with fairy-tale themes and attend puppet shows at Roeding Park's **Storyland** (☎ 559/264–2235), which is open February–Novem-ber. Admission to Storyland is $3. ✉ *Olive and Belmont Aves.,* ☎ *559/ 498–4239.* 🅿 *Parking $1.* ☉ *Mar.–Oct., daily 7 AM–10 PM; Nov.–Feb., daily 7–7.*

☺ ❼ The **Fresno Metropolitan Museum** mounts art, history, and hands-on science exhibits, many of them quite innovative. The William Saroyan History Gallery presents a riveting introduction in words and pictures to the author's life and times. ✉ *1515 Van Ness Ave.,* ☎ *559/441–1444,* WEB *www.fresnomet.org.* 🅿 *$6.* ☉ *Tues.–Wed. and Fri.–Sun. 11–5, Thurs. 11–8.*

❽ The **Legion of Valor Museum** is a real find for military history buffs of all ages. It has German bayonets and daggers, a Japanese Namby pistol, a full-size Gatling gun, and an extensive collection of Japanese, German, and American uniforms. The staff is extremely enthusiastic. ✉ *2425 Fresno St.,* ☎ *559/498–0510,* WEB *www.legionofvalor.com/museum.htm.* 🎟 *Free.* ⊙ *Mon.–Sat. 10–3.*

❾ Inside a restored 1888 Victorian, the **Meux Home Museum**displays furnishings typical of early Fresno. Guided tours lead from the front parlor to the backyard carriage house. ✉ *Tulare and R Sts.,* ☎ *559/233–8007,* WEB *www.meux.mus.ca.us.* 🎟 *$5.* ⊙ *Feb.–Dec., Fri.–Sun. noon–3:30.*

❿ The **Fresno Art Museum** exhibits American, Mexican, and French art; highlights of the permanent collection include pre-Columbian works and graphic art from the Postimpressionist period. The 152-seat Bonner Auditorium hosts lectures, films, and concerts. ✉ *Radio Park, 2233 N. 1st St.,* ☎ *559/441–4221,* WEB *www.fresnoartmuseum.com.* 🎟 *$4; free Tues.* ⊙ *Sept.–mid-Aug., Tues.–Fri. 10–5, weekends noon–5.*

⓫ **Woodward Park,** 300 acres of jogging trails, picnic areas, and playgrounds in the northern reaches of the city, is especially pretty in the spring, when plum and cherry trees, magnolias, and camellias bloom. Big-band concerts take place in summer. Well worth a look is the **Shin Zen Japanese Friendship Garden,** which has a teahouse, a koi pond, arched bridges, a waterfall, and lakes. ✉ *Audubon Dr. and Friant Rd.,* ☎ *559/498–1551.* 🎟 *$1; parking $2.* ⊙ *Mar.–Oct., daily 7 AM–10 PM; Nov.–Dec., daily 7–5; Jan.–Feb., daily 7–7.*

★ ☙ **⓬** Sicilian immigrant Baldasare Forestiere spent four decades (1906–46) carving out the **Forestiere Underground Gardens,** a subterranean realm of rooms, tunnels, grottoes, alcoves, and arched passageways that extends for more than 10 acres beneath busy, mall-pocked Shaw Avenue. Only a fraction of Forestiere's prodigious output is on view, but you can tour his underground living quarters, including bedrooms (one with a fireplace), the kitchen, the living room, the bath, a fish pond, and an aquarium. Skylights allow exotic full-grown fruit trees—including one that bears seven kinds of citrus as a result of of grafting—to flourish at more than 20 ft below ground. You have to make reservations for the tour. ✉ *5021 W. Shaw Ave., 2 blocks east of Hwy. 99,* ☎ *559/271–0734.* 🎟 *$6.* ⊙ *Memorial Day–Labor Day, Wed.–Sun. 10–4 (tours at 10, noon, 2, and 4); Easter–Memorial Day and Labor Day–Thanksgiving (weather permitting; tour hrs vary), weekends noon–3.*

⓭ The drive along palm-lined Kearney Boulevard is one of the best reasons to visit the **Kearney Mansion Museum,** which stands in shaded 225-acre **Kearney Park,** 7 mi west of town. The century-old home of M. Theo Kearney, Fresno's onetime "raisin king," is accessible only by taking a guided 45-minute tour. ✉ *7160 W. Kearney Blvd.,* ☎ *559/441–0862.* 🎟 *$4 (park entrance $3, waived for museum visitors).* ⊙ *Museum tours Fri.–Sun. at 1, 2, and 3.*

OFF THE **BLOSSOM TRAIL** – This 62-mi self-guided driving tour takes in Fresno-area
BEATEN PATH orchards, citrus groves, and vineyards during spring blossom season. Pick up a route map at the **Fresno Convention & Visitors Bureau** (✉ 848 M St., 3rd floor, ☎ 559/233–0836 or 800/788–0836). The route passes through several small towns and past rivers, lakes, and canals. The most colorful and aromatic time to go is from late February to mid-March, when almond, plum, apple, orange, lemon, apricot, and peach blossoms shower the landscape with shades of white, pink, and

red. Directional and crop identification signs mark the trail. Allow at least 2–3 hours for the tour.

Along the Blossom Trail, roughly halfway between Fresno and Visalia, the colorful handiwork of local Mennonite quilters is on display at the **Mennonite Quilt Center** (⊠ 1012 G St. [take Manning Ave. exit off Hwy. 99 and head east 12 mi], Reedley, ☎ 559/638–3560). The center is open weekdays 9:30–4:30 and Saturday 10–2, but try to visit on Monday (except holidays) between 8 and 3, when two dozen or so quilters come in to stitch, patch, and chat over coffee. Prime viewing time—with the largest number of quilts—is in February and March, right before the center holds its early April auction. Ask a docent to take you to the locked upstairs room, where most of the quilts hang; she'll explain the fine points of patterns such as the Log Cabin Romance, the Dahlia, and the Snowball-Star. Admission is free.

Dining and Lodging

$$$ ✕ **Echo.** This Tower District restaurant would seem to belong in San Francisco, with its well-appointed dining room and chic sensibility. Its tantalizing menu draws largely on food grown locally (or at least in northern California), much of it organic, with exquisite results: grilled quail marinated in Dijon, garlic and herbs, organic range beef with red wine and yellowfoot mushrooms, and Meyer lemon pudding cake, to name a few. This is *the* place for a fine meal in Fresno. ⊠ 609 E. Olive Ave., ☎ 559/442–3246. AE, D, MC, V. Closed Sun.– Mon.

$$–$$$ ✕ **Giulia's Italian Trattoria.** The look here is light and airy, but the Abruzzi cuisine (from Italy's Adriatic coast) is hearty and intensely flavored. Bruschetta, steamed mussels, and polenta with grilled sausage are top choices. The adjoining Oyster Bar & Grill serves sandwiches and seafood appetizers; many patrons have cocktails there before dining at Giulia's. ⊠ *Winepress Shopping Center, 3050 W. Shaw Ave.,* ☎ *559/ 276–3573. AE, D, DC, MC, V. Closed Sun. No lunch weekends.*

$–$$ ✕ **Armenian Cuisine.** Local Armenians flock to this small restaurant for tasty lamb, beef, and chicken kebabs, which come with pita bread, eggplant salad, and stuffed grape leaves. ⊠ *742 W. Bullard Ave.,* ☎ *559/435–4892. AE, DC, MC, V. Closed Sun.*

$–$$ ✕ **Kim's Vietnamese Restaurant.** Specialties here include hot beef salad, sizzling chicken, and sautéed seafood with ginger. Complete lunches or dinners—from soup to dessert and tea, with salad, entrée, and rice in-between—cost as little as $10. ⊠ *5048 N. Maroa St.,* ☎ *559/225–0406. MC, V. Closed Sun.*

$–$$$ ☷ **Piccadilly Inn Shaw.** This two-story property is attractively landscaped, with a big central swimming pool on 7½ acres. The sizable rooms have king- and queen-size beds, full-size robes, ironing boards, fresh cookies, and coffeemakers; some rooms have refrigerators, microwaves, and fireplaces. ⊠ 2305 W. Shaw Ave., 93711, ☎ 559/226–3850, FAX 559/ 226–2448, WEB www.piccadilly-inn.com/shaw.html. 188 rooms, 6 suites. Pool, gym, hot tub, laundry facilities, laundry service, business services, meeting room; a no-smoking rooms. AE, D, DC, MC, V.

$ ☷ **La Quinta Inn.** Rooms are of good size at this basic but decent three-story motel near downtown. Some rooms have king-size beds, microwaves, and refrigerators. ⊠ 2926 Tulare St., 93721, ☎ 559/442–1110, FAX 559/237–0415. 130 rooms. Refrigerators (some), pool; no-smoking rooms. AE, D, DC, MC, V. CP.

Nightlife and the Arts

The **Fresno Philharmonic Orchestra** (☎ 559/261–0600) performs classical concerts (sometimes pops) on weekends, usually at the William Saroyan Theatre (⊠ 700 M St.), from September through June. **Roger Rocka's Music Hall** (⊠ 1226 N. Wishon Ave., ☎ 559/266–9494 or 800/

371–4747), a dinner theater in the Tower District, stages six Broadway-style musicals or comedies a year. The **Tower Theatre for the Performing Arts** (⊠ 815 E. Olive Ave., ☎ 559/485–9050), a restored 1930s art deco movie house that has given its name to the trendy Tower District of theaters, clubs, restaurants, and cafés, presents theatrical, ballet, classical, jazz, and other cultural events from spring to fall.

Outdoor Activities and Sports

Kings River Expeditions (⊠ 211 N. Van Ness Ave., ☎ 559/233–4881 or 800/846–3674) arranges white-water rafting trips on the Kings River. **Wild Water Adventures** (⊠ 11413 E. Shaw Ave., Clovis, ☎ 559/299–9453 or 800/564–9453), a 50-acre water theme park about 10 mi east of Fresno, is open from late May to early September.

Shopping

Old Town Clovis (⊠ Upper Clovis Ave., Clovis) is an area of restored brick buildings and brick sidewalks, with numerous antiques shops and art galleries (along with restaurants and saloons). Be warned, though: not much here is open on Sunday. Head east on Fresno's Shaw Avenue about 10 mi to get to Clovis.

Hanford

★ ⑭ *35 mi from Fresno, south on Hwy. 99 and Hwy. 43.*

Founded in 1877 as a Southern Pacific Railroad stop, Hanford had one of California's largest Chinatowns—the Chinese came to help build the railroads and stayed to farm and open restaurants. You can take a self-guided walking tour or sign up in advance for guided tours ($2.50) arranged by the **Hanford Visitor Agency** (☎ 559/582–5024). One tour explores the restored historic buildings of Courthouse Square. Another heads to narrow China Alley, with stops at the town's Taoist Temple and other sights.

The **Hanford Carnegie Museum,** inside the former Carnegie Library, a Romanesque building dating from 1905, displays fashions, furnishings, toys, and military artifacts. ⊠ 109 E. 8th St., ☎ 559/584–1367. ☒ $1. ☉ *Tues.–Fri. noon–3, Sat. noon–4.*

A first-floor museum in the 1893 **Taoist Temple** displays photos, furnishings, and kitchenware from Hanford's once-bustling Chinatown. The second-floor temple, largely unchanged for a century, contains altars, carvings, and ceremonial staves. You can visit as part of a guided walking tour or by calling the temple directly and making an appointment two weeks in advance. ⊠ 12 China Alley, ☎ 559/582–4508. ☒ *Free; donations welcome.*

Dining and Lodging

$$–$$$ ✕ **Imperial Dynasty.** Despite its name and elegant teak-and-porcelains Chinese accents, Imperial Dynasty serves primarily French cuisine. Its heyday was in the 1970s and '80s, but this spot is still one of the better restaurants in the valley. For a memorable meal start with the garlicky escargots and continue with the veal sweetbreads or rack of lamb. The extensive wine list contains many prized vintages. ⊠ *China Alley (corner of 7th and Green Sts.),* ☎ *559/582–0196. AE, MC, V. Closed Mon. No lunch.*

$ ✕ **La Fiesta.** Mexican-American families, farmworkers, and farmers all eat here, polishing off traditional Mexican dishes such as enchiladas and tacos. The Fiesta Special—for two or more—includes nachos, garlic shrimp, deviled-style shrimp, clams, and two pieces of top sirloin. ⊠ *106 N. Green St.,* ☎ *559/583–8775. AE, D, DC, MC, V.*

$-$$ ⊡ **Irwin Street Inn.** This inn is one of the few lodgings in the valley
★   that warrant a detour. Four tree-shaded, restored Victorian homes
have been converted into spacious, comfortable rooms and suites.
Most have antique armoires, dark-wood detailing, lead-glass windows, and four-poster beds; bathrooms have old-fashioned tubs, brass
fixtures, and marble basins. ⊠ *522 N. Irwin St., 93230,* ☎ *559/583–
8000 or 866/583–7378,* FAX *559/583–8793,* WEB *www.irwinsteetinn.com.
27 rooms. Restaurant, pool. AE, D, DC, MC, V. CP.*

Nightlife and the Arts

The restored 1,000-seat Moorish-Castilian–style **Hanford Fox Theater**
(⊠ 326 N. Irwin St., ☎ 559/584–7423), built as a movie palace in 1929,
now periodically hosts country-and-western bands and other live performances.

Visalia

⓯   *16 mi from Hanford, east on Hwy. 198; 40 mi from Fresno, south on
Hwy. 99 and east on Hwy. 198.*

Visalia's combination of a reliable agricultural economy and immense
civic pride has yielded perhaps the most vibrant downtown in the
Central Valley. A clear day's view of the Sierra from Main Street is spectacular; and even Sunday night finds the streets busy with pedestrians,
many coming from Bakersfield and Fresno for the excellent restaurants
that abound here. Founded in 1852, the town contains a number of
historic homes; ask for a free guide at the **visitor center** (⊠ 720 W. Mineral King Ave., 93921, ☎ 559/734–5876).

The **Chinese Cultural Center,** housed in a pagoda-style building, mounts
exhibits about Asian art and culture. ⊠ *500 Akers Rd., at Hwy. 198,*
☎ *559/625–4545.* ⊡ *Free.* ⊙ *Wed.–Sun. 11–6.*

☺ In oak-shaded **Mooney Grove Park** you can picnic alongside duck ponds,
rent a boat in a lagoon, and view a replica of the famous *End of the Trail*
statue. The original, designed by James Earl Fraser for the 1915 Panama-
Pacific International Exposition, is now in the Cowboy Hall of Fame in
Oklahoma. ⊠ *27000 S. Mooney Blvd., 5 mi south of downtown,* ☎
559/733–6616. ⊡ *$5 per vehicle, Mar.–Oct.* ⊙ *Daily 8 AM–sunset.*

The indoor-outdoor **Tulare County Museum** contains several re-created
environments from the pioneer era. On display are Yokuts tribal artifacts (basketry, arrowheads, clamshell-necklace currency) as well as sad-
dles and guns, Victorian-era dolls, and quilts and gowns. ⊠ *Mooney
Grove Park, 27000 S. Mooney Blvd., 5 mi south of downtown,* ☎ *559/
733–6616.* ⊡ *Free.* ⊙ *June–Aug., Mon. and Wed.–Fri. 10–4, weekends 10–5; Sept.–Oct., Thurs.–Mon. 10–4; Nov.–Feb., Mon. and
Thurs.–Fri. 10–4, weekends 1–4; Mar.–May, Thurs.–Mon. 10–4.*

Trails at the 300-acre **Kaweah Oaks Preserve,** a wildlife sanctuary off
the main road to Sequoia National Park and accessible only to hikers,
lead past oak, sycamore, cottonwood, and willow trees. Among the
125 bird species you might spot are hawks, hummingbirds, and great
blue herons. Lizards, coyotes, and cottontails also live here. ⊠ *Follow
Hwy. 198 for 7 mi east of Visalia, turn north on Rd. 182, and proceed
½ mi to gate on left-hand side of road,* ☎ *559/738–0211,* WEB
www.kaweahoaks.com. ⊡ *Free.* ⊙ *Daily sunrise–sunset.*

Dining and Lodging

$$–$$$$ ✗ **The Vintage Press.** Built in 1966, the Vintage Press is the best restau-
★   rant in the Central Valley. Cut-glass doors and bar fixtures decorate
the artfully designed rooms. The California-Continental cuisine includes
dishes such as baby abalone in a champagne-butter sauce, wild mush-

rooms in puff pastry, and sturgeon in caviar butter. The chocolate Grand Marnier cake is a standout among the many wonderful homemade desserts and ice creams. The wine list has more than 900 selections. ⊠ *216 N. Willis St.,* ☎ *559/733–3033. AE, DC, MC, V.*

$–$$ ✕ **Café 225.** This downtown favorite combines high ceilings and warm yellow walls with soft chatter and butcher-papered tables to create an elegance that's relaxed enough for kids. The basic menu of pastas and grilled items is highlighted with unusual treats—Gorgonzola amandine and oak-rotisserie chicken, the house specialty. ⊠ *225 W. Main St.,* ☎ *559/733–2967. AE, D, DC, MC, V. Closed Sun.*

$–$$ ⊡ **Ben Maddox House.** Housed in a building dating to 1876, this homey B&B offers the best of both worlds: plush beds, a cool swimming pool, and excellent service remind you you're on vacation, while private porches, bathrooms, and dining tables on the sunny porch make you feel as if you were at home. With its two bedrooms, living room, and full kitchen, the cottage is a good option for families. ⊠ *601 N. Encina St., 93291,* ☎ *559/739–0721, 800/401–9800,* FAX *559/ 625–0420,* WEB *www.benmaddoxhouse.com. 6 rooms, 1 cottage. In-room data ports, cable TV, pool. MC, V. BP.*

$ ⊡ **The Spalding House.** This restored colonial-revival B&B—decked out with antiques, Oriental rugs, handcrafted woodwork, and glass doors—is one of several historic homes in the vicinity. The house, built in 1901, has three guest suites that each have a separate sitting room and private bath but no phone or TV. The historical neighborhood that hosts this and the nearby Ben Maddox House offers a pleasure that is simple but rare in the Central Valley: evening walks on quiet tree-lined streets. ⊠ *631 N. Encina St., 93291,* ☎ *559/739–7877,* FAX *559/625–0902. 3 suites. No-smoking room. MC, V. BP.*

Colonel Allensworth State Historic Park

★ ⑯ *40 mi from Visalia, south on Hwy. 99, west on J22 (at town of Earlimart), and south on Hwy. 43.*

A former slave who rose to become the country's highest-ranking black military officer of his time founded Allensworth—the only California town settled, governed, and financed by African-Americans—in 1908. After enjoying early prosperity, Allensworth was plagued by hardships and was eventually deserted. Its buildings have been rebuilt or restored to reflect the era when it thrived. Each October three days of festivities mark the town's rededication. ⊠ *4129 Palmer Ave.,* ☎ *661/849–3433,* WEB *www.cal-parks.ca.gov.* ⊠ *$3 per car.* ☉ *Daily 10–4:30.*

OFF THE BEATEN PATH

KERN NATIONAL WILDLIFE REFUGE – Dozens of types of ducks, snowy egrets, peregrine falcons, warblers, and other birds inhabit the marshes and wetlands here from November through April. Follow the 6½-mi loop drive (pick up maps at the entrance) to find good viewing spots, but beware that waterfowl hunting is allowed October through January. ⊠ *10811 Corcoran Rd., 19 mi west of Delano on Hwy. 155 (Garces Hwy.); from Allensworth take Hwy. 43 south to Hwy. 155 west,* ☎ *661/725–2767,* WEB *www.natureali.com/KNWR.htm.* ⊠ *Free.* ☉ *Daily sunrise–sunset.*

SOUTHERN CENTRAL VALLEY
Bakersfield and Kernville

When gold was discovered in Kern County in the 1860s, settlers flocked to the southern end of the Central Valley. Black gold—oil—is now the area's most valuable commodity, but Kern is also the country's third-most-productive agricultural county. From the flat plains around Bakersfield the landscape grows gently hilly and then graduates to mountains as it climbs east to Kernville, which lies in the Kern River valley.

Bakersfield

⑰ *80 mi from Visalia, west on Hwy. 198, south on Hwy. 99.*

Bakersfield's founder, Colonel Thomas Baker, arrived with the discovery of gold in the nearby Kern River valley in 1851. Now Kern County's biggest city (population 212,000, including the largest community of Basque people in the United States), Bakersfield probably is best known as Nashville West, a country-music haven and hometown of performers Buck Owens and Merle Haggard. It also has its own symphony orchestra and two good museums.

★ ⓒ The **Kern County Museum and Lori Brock Children's Discovery Center** form one of the Central Valley's top museum complexes. The indoor-outdoor Kern County Museum is set up as an open-air walk-through historic village with more than 50 restored or re-created buildings dating from the 1860s–1940s. The indoor part of the museum holds exhibits about Native Americans and the "Bakersfield sound" in country music. The adjacent Children's Discovery Center has permanent and changing hands-on displays and activities. ⊠ *3801 Chester Ave.,* ☎ *661/861-2132,* WEB *www.kcmuseum.org.* ⊡ *$6.* ☼ *Weekdays 8–5, Sat. 10–5, Sun. noon–5.*

★ ⓒ At the **California Living Museum,** a combination zoo, botanical garden, and natural-history museum, the emphasis is on zoo. All animal and plant species displayed are native to the state. Within the reptile house lives every species of rattlesnake found in California. The landscaped grounds—in the hills about a 20-minute drive northeast of Bakersfield—also shelter captive bald eagles, tortoises, coyotes, mountain lions, black bears, and foxes. ⊠ *10500 Alfred Harrell Hwy. (Hwy. 178 east, then 3½ mi northwest on Alfred Harrell Hwy.),* ☎ *661/872-2256,* WEB *www.calmzoo.org.* ⊡ *$4.50.* ☼ *Tues.–Sun. 9–5.*

Dining and Lodging

$–$$ ✕ **Uricchio's Trattoria.** This downtown restaurant draws everyone from office workers to oil barons—all attracted by the tasty food, open kitchen, and indoor and outdoor seating. *Panini* (Italian sandwiches, served at lunch only), pasta, and Italian-style chicken dishes dominate the menu; the chicken *piccata* outsells all other offerings. ⊠ *1400 17th St.,* ☎ *661/326-8870. AE, D, DC, MC, V. Closed Sun. No lunch Sat.*

$ ✕ **Jake's Original Tex-Mex Cafe.** Don't let the cafeteria-style service fool you; this is probably the best lunch place in Bakersfield. The chicken burritos and the chili fries (with meaty chili ladled on top) are worth a visit. For dessert try the Texas sheet cake or the homemade chocolate-chip cookies. It's open for dinner, too. ⊠ *1710 Oak St.,* ☎ *661/322-6380. Reservations not accepted. AE, DC, MC, V. Closed Sun.*

$ ✕ **Noriega Hotel.** Established in 1893, this Basque restaurant is part of the oldest boardinghouse in California, which put up generations of sheepherders. The restaurant is known for its thick and tender lamb chops, oxtail stew, prime rib, soup, pink beans, hors d'oeuvres, vegetables, and potatoes—all served family style. Lunch is served promptly at noon and dinner at 7, so don't dawdle. ⊠ *525 Sumner St.,* ☎ *661/322-8419. No credit cards. Closed Mon.*

$$–$$$$ ☷ **Four Points Hotel.** The grounds of this hotel, voted the best in the Sheraton chain in 1999, are lush and green. A mile west of Highway

99, this hotel has room amenities such as coffeemakers, irons and ironing boards, and hair dryers. There's also a free airport shuttle. ☒ *5101 California Ave., 93309,* ☎ *661/325–9700,* FAX *661/323–3508,* WEB *www.fourpoints.com. 197 rooms, 8 suites. In-room data ports, pool, gym, hot tub, airport shuttle; no-smoking rooms. AE, D, DC, MC, V.*

$–$$ ⊡ **Quality Inn.** Near downtown in a relatively quiet location off Highway 99, this two-story motel offers good value. Most rooms have king- or queen-size beds, and all have HBO. Some have refrigerators and a patio or a balcony looking out on the heated pool. Complimentary coffee and doughnuts are served. ☒ *1011 Oak St., 93304,* ☎ *661/325–0772,* FAX *661/325–4646,* WEB *www.qualityinn.com. 90 rooms. Refrigerators (some), pool, gym, indoor hot tub, laundry facilities. AE, D, DC, MC, V.*

Nightlife and the Arts

The **Bakersfield Symphony Orchestra** (☎ 661/323–7928) performs classical music concerts at the Convention Center (☒ 1001 Truxton Ave.) from October through May.

Buck Owens' Crystal Palace (☒ 2800 Buck Owens Blvd., ☎ 661/328–7560) is a combination nightclub, restaurant, and showcase of country-music memorabilia. Country-and-western singers—owner Buck Owens among them—perform. Buck Owens and the Buckaroos perform Friday and Saturday. A dance floor beckons customers who can still twirl after sampling the menu of steaks, burgers, nachos, and gooey desserts. Entertainment is free on most weeknights; Friday and Saturday nights bring a $6 cover charge, and some big-name acts require tickets.

Outdoor Activities and Sports

CAR RACING

At **Bakersfield Speedway** (☒ 5001 N. Chester Extension, ☎ 661/393–3373), stock and sprint cars race around a ⅓-mi clay oval track. **Mesa Marin Raceway** (☒ 11000 Kern Canyon Rd., ☎ 661/366–5711) presents high-speed stock-car, supertruck, and NASCAR racing on a ½-mi paved oval course.

SKATING

If you have children who can't get enough of in-line skating or skateboarding, Bakersfield has two great skate parks. The **Vans Skate Park** (☒ 3737 Rosedale Hwy., off Hwy. 99, ☎ 661/327–1794) is a 30,000-square-ft facility with ramps, rails, and half-pipes. Two-hour sessions are $9–$11. The free skate park at **Beach Park** (☒ corner of Oak and 21st Sts.) has good street skating as well as a relaxing grassy area for parents.

Shopping

Many antiques shops are on 18th and 19th streets between H and R streets and on H Street between Brundage Lane and California Avenue. **Central Park Antique Mall** (☒ 701 19th St., ☎ 661/633–1143) has a huge selection. The **Great American Antique Mall** (☒ 625 19th St., ☎ 661/322–1776) is full of treasures.

Dewar's Candy Shop (☒ 1120 Eye St., ☎ 661/322–0933) was founded in 1909 and has been owned by the Dewar family since. Try the hand-dipped chocolate cherries and the Dewar's Chews, a mouthwatering taffy concoction available in peanut butter, peppermint, caramel, and almond flavors. There's also an old-fashioned soda fountain.

Kernville

⓲ *50 mi from Bakersfield, northeast on Hwy. 178 and north on Hwy. 155.*

The wild and scenic Kern River, which flows through Kernville en route from Mount Whitney to Bakersfield, delivers some of the most exciting white-water rafting in the state. Kernville (population 1,200) rests in a mountain valley on both banks of the river and also at the northern tip of Lake Isabella (a dammed portion of the river used as a reservoir and for recreation). A center for rafting outfitters, Kernville has lodgings, restaurants, and antiques shops. The main streets are lined with Old West–style buildings, reflecting Kernville's heritage as a rough-and-tumble gold-mining town known as Whiskey Flat. (Present-day Kernville dates from the 1950s, when it was moved upriver to make room for Lake Isabella.) The scenic road from Bakersfield winds between the rushing river on one side and sheer granite cliffs on the other.

Dining and Lodging

$ ✕ **All Seasons Family Restaurant.** This down-home restaurant serves up some of the best food in town. The hamburgers and fried chicken are the stars of the show—along with the colorful talk from the locals, who drop in for biscuits and gravy or meat loaf. Don't miss the freshly baked pastries, pies, and cobblers. ✉ *13423 Sierra Way,* ☏ *760/376–4663. DC, MC, V.*

$ ✕ **That's Italian.** For northern Italian cuisine in a typical trattoria, this is the spot. Try the chicken marsala stuffed with prosciutto and mozzarella or the pasta with clams, mussels, calamari, and whitefish in a red or white clam sauce. ✉ *9 Big Blue Rd.,* ☏ *760/376–6020. AE, D, MC, V. No lunch Nov.–Apr.*

$$–$$$ ⌂ **Whispering Pines Lodge.** Perched on the banks of the Kern River, this inn gives you a choice of rustic cottages and bungalows. Some accommodations have full kitchens, fireplaces, and whirlpool tubs; all have refrigerators, coffeemakers, and cable TV. ✉ *13745 Sierra Way, 93238,* ☏ *760/376–3733 or 877/241–4100,* FAX *760/376–6513,* WEB *www.kernvalley.com/whisperingpines. 17 rooms. Kitchenettes (some), pool. AE, D, MC, V. BP.*

$ ⌂ **River View Lodge.** This rustic motel has knotty-pine walls and compact but clean rooms, some with microwaves and VCRs. And, yes, many units do have river views. Picnic and barbecue facilities are in the tree-shaded yard. ✉ *2 Sirretta St., off Kernville Rd., 93238,* ☏ *760/376–6019,* FAX *760/376–4147. 10 rooms. Refrigerators; no-smoking rooms. AE, DC, MC, V. CP.*

Outdoor Activities and Sports

BOATING, FISHING, AND WINDSURFING

The Lower Kern River, which extends from Lake Isabella to Bakersfield and beyond, is open for fishing year-round. Catches include rainbow trout, catfish, smallmouth bass, crappie, and bluegill. Lake Isabella is popular with anglers, water-skiers, sailors, and windsurfers. Its shoreline marinas have boats for rent, bait and tackle, and moorings year-round; try: **Dean's North Fork Marina** (☏ 760/376–1812), **French Gulch Marina** (☏ 760/379–8774), or **Red's Kern Valley Marina** (☏ 760/379–1634 or 800/553–7337).

WHITE-WATER RAFTING

The three sections of the Kern River—known as the Lower Kern, Upper Kern, and the Forks—add up to nearly 50 mi of white water, ranging from Class I (easy) to Class V (expert). The Lower and Upper Kern are the most popular and accessible sections. Organized trips can last from one hour (for as little as $15) to two days and more. Rafting season generally runs from late spring until the end of summer. Outfitters include **Chuck Richards Whitewater** (☎ 760/379–4444), **Kern River Tours** (☎ 800/844–7238), **Mountain & River Adventures** (☎ 760/376–6553 or 800/861–6553), and **Sierra South** (☎ 760/376–3745 or 800/457–2082).

THE CENTRAL VALLEY A TO Z

To research prices, get advice from other travelers, and book travel arrangements, visit www.fodors.com.

AIR TRAVEL

Fresno Yosemite International Airport is serviced by America West, Alaska, Allegiant, American and American Eagle, Continental, Delta, Hawaiian, Horizon, Northwest, Skywest, and United. Kern County Airport, at Meadows Field, is serviced by American and American Eagle, America West Express, Skywest-Delta, and United Express. United Express flies from San Francisco to Modesto City Airport and Visalia Municipal Airport. *See* Air Travel *in* Smart Travel Tips A to Z for airline phone numbers.

➤ AIRPORT INFORMATION: **Fresno Yosemite International Airport** (⌂ 4995 E. Clinton Way, ☎ 559/498–4700). **Kern County Airport at Meadows Field** (⌂ 1401 Skyway Dr., Bakersfield, ☎ 661/393–7990). **Modesto City Airport** (⌂ 617 Airport Way, ☎ 209/577–5318). **Visalia Municipal Airport** (⌂ 9501 W. Airport Dr., ☎ 559/713–4201).

BUS TRAVEL

Greyhound provides service between major valley cities. Orange Belt Stages provides bus service, including Amtrak connections, to many valley locations, including Stockton, Merced, Madera, Fresno, Hanford, and Bakersfield.

➤ BUS INFORMATION: **Greyhound** (☎ 800/231–2222). **Orange Belt Stages** (☎ 888/299–7433, WEB www.orangebelt.com).

CAR RENTAL

Avis, Budget, Dollar, Hertz, and National rent cars at Fresno Yosemite International Airport. Avis, Budget, Hertz, and National rent cars at Kern County Airport, at Meadows Field. Avis, Enterprise, and Hertz rent cars at Modesto City Airport. Hertz and Enterprise rent cars at Visalia Municipal Airport. *See* Car Rental *in* Smart Travel Tips A to Z for national rental-agency phone numbers.

CAR TRAVEL

To drive to the Central Valley from San Francisco, take I–80 east to I–580 and then I–580 east to I–5, which leads south into the valley (several roads from I–5 head east to Highway 99); or continue east on I–580 to I–205, which leads to I–5 north to Stockton or (via Highway 120) east to Highway 99 at Manteca. To reach the valley from Los Angeles, follow I–5 north; Highway 99 veers north about 15 mi after entering the valley.

Highway 99 is the main route between the valley's major cities and towns. Interstate 5 runs roughly parallel to it to the west but misses the major population centers; its main use is for quick access from San Francisco or Los Angeles. Major roads that connect I–5 with Highway 99 are Highways 120 (to Manteca), 132 (to Modesto), 140 (to Merced), 152 (to Chowchilla, via Los Baños), 198 (to Hanford and Visalia), and 58 (to Bakersfield). For road conditions call the California Department of Transportation hot line.

➤ CONTACTS: **California Department of Transportation** (☎ 800/427–7623 or 916/445–1534).

EMERGENCIES

In an emergency dial 911.

➤ HOSPITALS: **Bakersfield Memorial Hospital** (✉ 420 34th St., Bakersfield, ☎ 805/327–1792). **St. Joseph's Medical Center** (✉ 1800 North California St., Stockton, ☎ 209/943–2000). **University Medical Center** (✉ 445 S. Cedar Ave., Fresno, ☎ 559/459–4000).

TOURS

Central Valley Tours provides general and customized tours of the Fresno area and the valley.

➤ CONTACTS: **Central Valley Tours** (✉ 1869 E. Everglade Ave., Fresno 93720, ☎ 559/323–5552).

TRAIN TRAVEL

Amtrak's daily *San Joaquin* travels between San Jose, Oakland, and Bakersfield, stopping in Stockton, Riverbank (near Modesto), Merced, Fresno, and Hanford. Amtrak Thruway bus service connects Bakersfield with Los Angeles.

➤ TRAIN INFORMATION: **Amtrak** (☎ 800/872–7245).

VISITOR INFORMATION

➤ CONTACTS: **Fresno City & County Convention and Visitors Bureau** (✉ 848 M St., 93721, ☎ 559/233–0836 or 800/788–0836). **Greater Bakersfield Convention & Visitors Bureau** (✉ 1325 P St., 93301, ☎ 661/325–5051 or 800/325–6001). **Hanford Visitor Agency** (✉ 200 Santa Fe Ave., Suite D, 93230, ☎ 800/722–1114). **Kern County Board of Trade** (✉ 2101 Oak St., Bakersfield 93302, ☎ 661/861–2367 or 800/500–5376). **Lodi Conference and Visitors Bureau** (✉ 2545 W. Turner Dr., 95242, ☎ 209/365–1195 or 800/798–1810). **Merced Conference and Visitors Bureau** (✉ 690 W. 16th St., 95340, ☎ 209/384–7092 or 800/446–5353). **Modesto Convention and Visitors Bureau** (✉ 1114 J St., 95353, ☎ 800/266–4282). **Stockton/San Joaquin Convention and Visitors Bureau** (✉ 46 W. Fremont St., Stockton 95202, ☎ 209/943–1987 or 800/350–1987). **Visalia Convention and Visitors Bureau** (✉ 720 W. Mineral King Ave., 93291, ☎ 559/734–5876).

10 THE SOUTHERN SIERRA

WITH YOSEMITE, SEQUOIA, AND KINGS CANYON NATIONAL PARKS

For many travelers to California a visit to the southern portion of the Sierra Nevada, famous for its national parks, is the highlight of their trip. All three of the national parks here protect groves of giant sequoia (*Sequoiadendron giganteum*) trees, nature's largest living things. In Yosemite, the state's most famous national park, the staggering U-shape valleys carved by glaciers during the Ice Age are indeed sublime. Also endowed with glacial valleys, Kings Canyon and Sequoia national parks are adjacent to each other and easy to visit together. Outside the parks, pristine lakes, spectacular ski resorts, and small towns complete the picture of the southern Sierra.

Updated by
John A.
Vlahides

VAST GRANITE PEAKS AND GIANT SEQUIOAS are among the mind-boggling natural wonders of the southern Sierra, many of which are protected in three national parks. Yosemite, Sequoia, and Kings Canyon national parks should without a doubt be on your "don't miss" California vacation list. Unfortunately, they're on everyone else's as well, so lodging reservations are essential when you visit this spectacular region of the state. Try visiting in winter, when the skiing at Mammoth rocks, or in early spring, when the towering waterfalls are at their most intense and you can see it all without tripping over throngs of tourists.

Pleasures and Pastimes

Camping

Camping in the Sierra Nevada means awakening to the sights of nearby meadows and streams and, in the distance, the unforgettable landscape of giant granite. Camping here also means gazing up at an awe-inspiring collection of constellations and spying a shooting star in the night sky.

The Sierra Nevada is home to thousands of bears, and if you plan on camping, you should take all necessary precautions to keep yourself—and the bears—safe. Bears that acquire a taste for human food can become very aggressive and destructive and often must be destroyed. The national parks' campgrounds and some campgrounds outside the parks provide food-storage boxes that can keep bears from pilfering your edibles (portable canisters for backpackers can be rented in most park stores). It is imperative that you move all food, coolers, and items with a scent (including toiletries and air fresheners) from your car to the storage box at your campsite. If you don't, a bear may break into your car, ransack your tent, or worse.

In the absence of storage boxes, you'll have to hang your food from a tree, at least 20 ft off the ground and 10 ft out from the main trunk, on a branch no greater than 3 inches in diameter at the place it joins the trunk and no greater than 1 inch at the spot from which you plan to hang the food. (Bears won't climb on branches that they know will snap under their weight, so make sure you choose a branch that narrows as it extends out from the tree.) Place your food in a ditty bag or in a heavy plastic garbage bag. Tie a rock to the end of a long rope and throw it over the limb. Then tie the food to the end of the rope, hoist it into the air, and tie the loose end securely around an adjacent tree or to the trunk of the same tree.

Dining

Towns in the Sierra Nevada are small, but they usually have at least one diner or restaurant. In the national parks, snack bars, coffee shops, and cafeterias are not expensive. The three fanciest lodgings within Yosemite National Park are prime dining spots, with a heftier price tag to match. With few exceptions, which are noted, dress is casual at the restaurants listed in this chapter.

When you're traveling in the area, you can expect to spend a lot of time in the car, so pick up snacks and drinks to keep with you—especially in winter, when roads can unexpectedly close due to inclement weather. Stopping at a grocery store and filling the ice chest ahead of time will also allow you to explore the national parks without having to search for food—with picnic supplies on hand you can enjoy a meal under giant trees. Just be certain to clean up after yourself and leave no food or trash behind. It's not just polite—human food is bad for wildlife and can cause health and behavioral problems.

CATEGORY	COST*
$$$$	over $30
$$$	$22–$30
$$	$15–$21
$	under $15

per person for a main course at dinner, excluding tip and 7%–7¼% tax

Hiking

Hiking is the primary outdoor activity in the Sierra Nevada. Whether you walk the paved loops that pass by major attractions in the national parks or head off the beaten path into the backcountry, a hike through groves and meadows or alongside streams and waterfalls will allow you to see, smell, and feel nature up close. Some of the most popular trails are described briefly in this chapter; stop by the visitor centers for maps and advice from park rangers.

Lodging

Towns are few and far between in the southern Sierra. Whenever possible, book lodging reservations in advance—especially in summer—or plan to camp out. If you don't, you may find yourself driving long distances to find a place to sleep.

Most accommodations inside Yosemite, Kings Canyon, and Sequoia national parks can best be described as "no frills"—many have no electricity or indoor plumbing. Other than the Ahwahnee and Wawona hotels in Yosemite, lodgings tend to be basic motels or rustic cabins. Except during the off-peak season, from November through March, rates in Yosemite are pricey, given the general quality of the lodging. In Sequoia and Kings Canyon lodging rates are are not seasonal, remaining the same throughout the year. In winter only some lodgings in Grant Grove remain open.

CATEGORY	COST*
$$$$	over $225
$$$	$160–$225
$$	$100–$159
$	under $100

All prices are for a standard double room, excluding 9%–10% tax.

Exploring the Southern Sierra

For the full Sierra experience, explore the national forests as well as the national parks. Stop at any of the ranger stations near the forests' borders and pick up information on lesser-known sights and attractions. Spend a few nights in the small towns outside the parks. If, however, you're tight on time and want to focus on the attractions that make the region famous, then stay in the parks themselves instead of the "gateway cities" in the foothills or the Central Valley; you won't want to lose time shuttling back and forth.

Yosemite Valley is the primary destination for many visitors. Because the valley is only 7 mi long and averages less than 1 mi wide, you can visit its attractions in whatever order you choose and return to your favorites at different times of the day. Famous for hiking trails and giant sequoias, Kings Canyon and Sequoia provide a truer wilderness experience, less tainted by civilization and crowds.

Numbers in the text correspond to numbers in the margin and on the Yosemite, the Southern Sierra, and the Kings Canyon and Sequoia national parks maps.

Great Itineraries

IF YOU HAVE 3 DAYS

If your time is limited, choose ⊞ **Yosemite National Park** to explore. Enter the park via the Big Oak Flat entrance, and head east on Big Oak Flat Road. As you enter the valley, traffic is diverted onto a one-way road. Continue east, following the signs to **Yosemite Village** ① and the **Valley Visitor Center.** Loop back west for a short hike near **Yosemite Falls** ③, the highest waterfall in North America. Continue west for a valley view of the famous **El Capitan** ⑧ peak. This area is a good place for a picnic. Backtrack onto Southside Drive, stopping at misty **Bridalveil Fall** ④; then follow Highway 41/Wawona Road south 14 mi to the Chinquapin junction and make a left turn onto Glacier Point Road. From **Glacier Point** ⑩ (road closed in winter) you'll get a phenomenal bird's-eye view of the entire valley, including **Half Dome** ⑨, **Vernal Fall** ⑥, and **Nevada Fall** ⑦. If you want to avoid the busloads of tourists at Glacier Point, stop at **Sentinel Dome** ⑪ instead. After a mildly strenuous 1-mi hike you get a view similar to that from Glacier Point. Head south on Highway 41 to the **Wawona Hotel** (closed weekdays much of the winter), where you can have a relaxing drink on the veranda or in the cozy lobby bar and listen to pianist Tom Bopp play folk songs.

On day two visit the **Mariposa Grove of Big Trees** ⑬ and return to Wawona to tour the **Pioneer Yosemite History Center** ⑫. Head back to Yosemite Valley on Wawona Road for an early evening beverage at the **Ahwahnee Hotel**'s bar (try out the patio in good weather), and view the lobby's paintings of Native American leaders. On the third day have breakfast near the Valley Visitor Center before hiking to Vernal Fall or Nevada Fall.

IF YOU HAVE 5 DAYS

Spend your first day exploring the ⊞ **Yosemite Valley** ①–⑪ area. On the second day pack some food and drive to **Hetch Hetchy Reservoir** (closed in winter) via Big Oak Flat Road and Highway 120. Then continue east on Tioga Road to **Tuolumne Meadows,** the largest subalpine meadow in the Sierra. Time permitting, head east through 9,900-ft Tioga Pass to ⊞ **Lee Vining** ⑮ for a look at **Mono Lake** and, possibly, **Bodie Ghost Town** ⑭. (Tioga Road closes for several months after the first snow; if the road isn't open, on day two you can instead take a hike to **Vernal Fall** ⑥ or **Nevada Fall** ⑦.) Wake up early on day three and spend the morning visiting Wawona's **Pioneer Yosemite History Center** ⑫ and wandering beneath the giant sequoias at the nearby **Mariposa Grove of Big Trees** ⑬. Then head south to ⊞ **Kings Canyon National Park** (about a three- to four-hour drive), entering on Highway 180 at the Big Stump Entrance. Stop to see the sequoias at **Grant Grove** ⑲. If you're camping, you'll need to get situated before sunset; if you're staying at one of the park's lodges, check in and have dinner. On the fifth day pass briefly through **Lodgepole** ㉖, in **Sequoia National Park,** and pick up tickets to **Crystal Cave** ㉙. Visit the **Giant Forest** ㉗ before stopping at the cave.

When to Tour the Southern Sierra

Summer brings crowds to the Sierra Nevada. Because much of the range is covered by very deep snow in winter, trails in the backcountry and in wilderness areas aren't accessible until late spring. As you rise in elevation, you'll see "spring" wildflowers blooming late in summer.

Summer is also the most crowded season for all the parks, though things never get as hectic at Kings Canyon and Sequoia as they do at Yosemite. During extremely busy periods—when snow closes high-country roads in late spring or on crowded summer weekends—Yosemite Valley may be closed to all vehicles unless their drivers have overnight reservations.

Avoid these restrictions by visiting from mid-April through Memorial Day and from Labor Day to mid-October, when the parks are less busy and the weather is usually hospitable.

The falls at Yosemite are at their most spectacular in May and June. By the end of summer some will have dried up. They begin flowing again in late fall with the first storms, and during winter they may be hung with ice, a dramatic sight. Snow on the floor of Yosemite Valley is never deep, so you can camp there even in winter (January highs are in the mid-40s, lows in the mid-20s). Tioga Road is usually closed from late October through May; unless you ski or snowshoe in, you can't see Tuolumne Meadows then. The road to Glacier Point beyond the turnoff for Badger Pass is not cleared in winter, but it is groomed for cross-country skiing.

YOSEMITE NATIONAL PARK

Yosemite, with 1,169 square mi of parkland, is 94.5% undeveloped wilderness, most of it accessible only on foot or horseback. The western boundary dips as low as 2,000 ft in the chaparral-covered foothills; the eastern boundary rises to 13,000 ft at points along the Sierra crest.

Yosemite is so large you can think of it as five different parks. Yosemite Valley, famous for waterfalls and cliffs, and Wawona, where the giant sequoias stand, are open all year. Hetch Hetchy, home of less-used backcountry trails, closes after the first big snow and reopens in May or June. The subalpine high country, Tuolumne Meadows, is open for summer hiking and camping; in winter it's accessible only by cross-country skis or snowshoes. Badger Pass Ski Area is open in winter only. The fee to visit Yosemite National Park (good for seven days) is $20 per car, $10 per person if you don't arrive in a car.

From early May to late September and during some holiday periods, actor Lee Stetson portrays naturalist John Muir, bringing to life Muir's wit, wisdom, and storytelling skill. You can also join park rangers on free 60- to 90-minute nature walks focusing on geology, wildlife, waterfalls, forest ecology, and other topics. Locations and times for both are listed in the *Yosemite Guide*, the newspaper that you receive on entering the park.

Yosemite Valley

214 mi east of San Francisco, I–80 to I–580 to I–205 to Hwy. 120; 330 mi northeast of Los Angeles, I–5 to Hwy. 99 to Hwy. 41.

Yosemite Valley has been so extravagantly praised (John Muir described it as "a revelation in landscape affairs that enriches one's life forever") and so beautifully photographed (by Ansel Adams, who said, "I knew my destiny when I first experienced Yosemite") that you may wonder if the reality can possibly measure up. For almost everyone it does. It's a true reminder of what "breathtaking" really means. The Miwok people, the last of several Native American tribes who inhabited the Yosemite area, named the valley "Ahwahnee," which is thought to mean "the place of the gaping mouth." Members of the tribe, who were forced out of the area by gold miners in 1851, called themselves the Ahwahneechee. The roads at the eastern fringes of the valley are closed to private cars, but a free shuttle bus runs frequently from the village (between 7 AM and 10 PM May–September, between 9 AM and 10 PM the rest of the year).

❶ The center of activity in Yosemite Valley is **Yosemite Village,** which contains restaurants, stores, a post office, the Ahwahnee Hotel, Yosemite

Lodge, and a medical clinic. You can get your bearings, pick up maps, and obtain information from park rangers at the village's **Valley Visitor Center.** At the **Wilderness Center** you can find out everything you need to know about backcountry activities like hiking and camping. A 1-mi paved loop from the visitor center, called **A Changing Yosemite,** traces the park's natural evolution and includes a couple of interesting stops. The **Yosemite Museum** has an Indian cultural exhibit, with displays about the Miwok and Paiute people who lived in the region; there's a re-created Ahwahneechee village behind it. The **Ansel Adams Gallery** shows works of the master Yosemite photographer. ⊠ *Off Northside Dr.,* ☎ 209/372–0200. ☼ *Visitor center fall–spring, daily 9–5; summer, daily 9–6.*

Yosemite Concession Services Corporation (☎ 209/372–1240, WEB www.yosemitepark.com) operates daily guided bus tours of the Yosemite Valley floor year-round, plus seasonal tours of Glacier Point and the Mariposa Grove of Big Trees. The company's Grand Tour ($55), offered between Memorial Day and October 29, weather permitting, covers the park's highlights.

As you venture through the valley amid Yosemite's natural wonders, ❷ stop at **Happy Isles Nature Center,** about half a mile east of Curry Village, to see ecology exhibits and books especially geared to children. ☼ *May–Oct., daily 9–5.*

★ ❸ Yosemite Valley is famed for its waterfalls, and the mightiest of them all is **Yosemite Falls,** the highest waterfall in North America and the fifth highest in the world. The upper fall (1,430 ft), the middle cascades (675 ft), and the lower fall (320 ft) combine for a total drop of 2,425 ft. When viewed from the valley the three sections appear as a single waterfall. A ¼-mi trail leads from the parking lot to the base of the falls. The Upper Yosemite Fall Trail, a strenuous 3½-mi climb rising 2,700 ft, takes you above the top of the falls. It starts at Camp 4, formerly known as Sunnyside Campground.

★ ❹ **Bridalveil Fall,** a filmy fall of 620 ft that is often diverted as much as 20 ft one way or the other by the breeze, is the first view of Yosemite Valley for those who arrive via Wawona Road. Native Americans called the fall Pohono (spirit of the puffing wind). A ¼-mi trail leads from the parking lot off Wawona Road to the base of the fall.

❺ At 1,612 ft **Ribbon Fall** is the highest single fall in North America. It is also the first waterfall in the valley to dry up; the rainwater and melted snow that create the slender fall evaporate quickly at this height.

❻ Fern-covered black rocks frame **Vernal Fall** (317 ft), and rainbows play in the spray at its base. The hike on a paved trail from the Happy Isles Nature Center to the bridge at the base of Vernal Fall is only moderately strenuous and less than 1 mi long. It's another steep (and often wet) ¾ mi up the Mist Trail—which is open only from late spring to early fall—to the top of Vernal Fall. Allow 2–4 hours for the 3-mi round-trip hike.

❼ **Nevada Fall** (594 ft) is the first major fall as the Merced River plunges out of the high country toward the eastern end of Yosemite Valley. A strenuous 2-mi section of the Mist Trail leads from Vernal Fall to the top of Nevada Fall. Allow 6–8 hours for the full 7-mi round-trip hike.

★ ❽ Yosemite Valley's waterfalls tumble past magnificent geological scenery. **El Capitan,** rising 3,593 ft above the valley, is the largest exposed granite monolith in the world, almost twice the height of the Rock of Gibraltar.

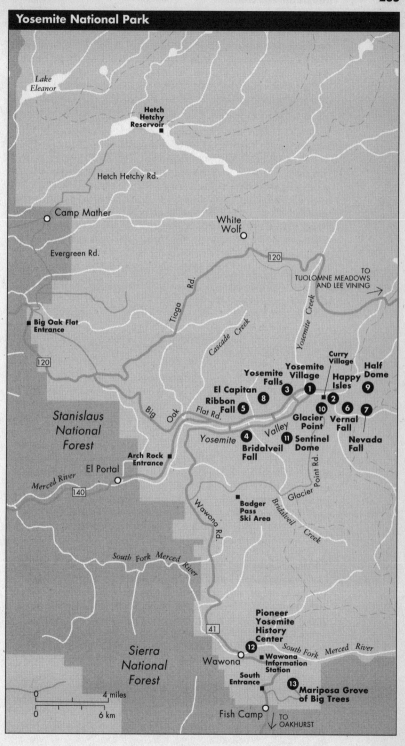

Yosemite National Park

Lake Eleanor

Hetch Hetchy Reservoir ■

Hetch Hetchy Rd.

○ Camp Mather

White Wolf ○

Evergreen Rd.

120

TO
TUOLOMNE MEADOWS
AND LEE VINING →

■ Big Oak Flat Entrance

120

Tioga Rd.

Cascade Creek

Yosemite Creek

Stanislaus National Forest

Big Oak

Flat Rd.

Curry Village

Yosemite Falls | **Yosemite Village** ③ ①

Half Dome ⑨

Happy Isles

El Capitan ⑧

Ribbon Fall ⑤

② ⑩ ⑥ ⑦

Glacier Point

Vernal Fall

④ **Bridalveil Fall**

Yosemite

Valley

⑪ **Sentinel Dome**

Nevada Fall

Arch Rock Entrance ■

○ El Portal

Merced River

140

Point Rd.

Glacier

■ **Badger Pass Ski Area**

Wawona Rd.

Bridalveil Creek

South Fork Merced River

41

Sierra National Forest

Pioneer Yosemite History Center

⑫

Wawona ○

South Fork Merced River

■ **Wawona Information Station**

South Entrance ■

⑬ **Mariposa Grove of Big Trees**

○ Fish Camp

↓ TO OAKHURST

0 —— 4 miles
0 —— 6 km

★ **9** Astounding **Half Dome** rises 4,733 ft from the valley floor to a height 8,842 ft above sea level. The west side of the dome is fractured vertically and cut away to form a 2,000-ft cliff. The highly strenuous **John Muir Trail** (which incorporates the Mist Trail) leads from Yosemite Valley to the top of Half Dome. Allow 10–12 hours round-trip for the 16¼-mi round-trip hike; start early in the morning and beware of afternoon thunderstorms.

★ **10** **Glacier Point** yields what may be the most spectacular vistas of the valley and the High Sierra that you can get without hiking, especially at sunset. Glacier Point Road splits off from Wawona Road (Highway 41) about 23 mi southwest of the valley; then it's a 16-mi drive, with fine views into higher country. From the parking area walk a few hundred yards, and you'll be able to see Nevada, Vernal, and Yosemite Falls as well as Half Dome and other peaks. You can hike to the valley floor (3,214 ft below) via the Panorama or Four-Mile Trails. To avoid a grueling round-trip, catch a ride to Glacier Point on one of the three daily hikers' buses ($10.50 one-way, $20.50 round-trip), which run from late spring through October (☎ 209/372–1240 for reservations). The road to Glacier Point is closed beyond the turnoff for the Badger Pass Ski Area in winter.

11 The view from **Sentinel Dome** is similar to that from Glacier Point, except you can't see the valley floor. A 1.1-mi path begins at a parking lot on Glacier Point Road a few miles below Glacier Point. The trail is long and steep enough to keep the crowds and tour buses away, but not overly rugged.

OFF THE BEATEN PATH

HETCH HETCHY RESERVOIR AND TUOLUMNE MEADOWS – Hetch Hetchy Reservoir, which supplies water and hydroelectric power to San Francisco, is about 40 mi from Yosemite Valley via Big Oak Flat Road to Highway 120 to Evergreen Road to Hetch Hetchy Road. Some say John Muir died of heartbreak when this valley was dammed and flooded beneath 300 ft of water in 1913. Tioga Road (Highway 120) stays open until the first big snow of the year, usually about mid-October. The road is the scenic route to Tuolumne Meadows, altitude 8,575 ft, which is 55 mi from Yosemite Valley. The largest subalpine meadow in the Sierra and the trailhead for many backpack trips into the High Sierra, the area contains campgrounds, a gas station, a store (with limited and expensive provisions), stables, a lodge, and a visitor center that is open from late June until Labor Day from 8 AM to 7:30 PM.

Dining, Lodging, and Camping

$$–$$$ ✕ **Mountain Room Restaurant.** The food becomes secondary when you see Yosemite Falls through this dining room's wall of windows. Almost every patron has a view of the falls. Gulf shrimp stuffed with crabmeat, grilled halibut, steak, pasta, and several children's dishes are on the menu. ⊠ *Yosemite Lodge, off Northside Dr.,* ☎ *209/372–1281. AE, D, DC, MC, V. Closed weekdays Thanksgiving–Easter except for holiday periods. No lunch.*

$$$$ ✕⛺ **Ahwahnee Hotel & Dining Room.** This grand 1920s-era mountain ★ lodge, designated a National Historical Landmark, is constructed of rocks and sugar-pine logs. In the Ahwahnee's comfortable rooms you'll enjoy some of the amenities found in a luxury hotel, including turndown service and guest bathrobes. The Ahwahnee Dining Room, with its 34-ft-tall trestle-beam ceiling, full-length windows, and wrought-iron chandeliers, is by far the most impressive eating establishment in the park. Specialties include poached salmon, roasted duckling, and prime rib. Jackets are required, and reservations are essential. ⊠ *Ahwahnee Rd. north of Northside Dr., 95389, Yosemite Reservations, 5410*

E. Home Ave., Fresno, 93727, ☎ 559/252–4848 for lodging reservations; 209/372–1489 for restaurant, WEB www.yosemitepark.com. 99 rooms, 4 suites, 24 cottages. Restaurant, refrigerators, in-room data ports, tennis court, pool, lounge, concierge; no air-conditioning in cottages, no-smoking rooms. AE, D, DC, MC, V.

$$ ✕🏨 **Yosemite Lodge.** This lodge near Yosemite Falls, which dates from 1915, once housed the U.S. army cavalry. Typical motel-style rooms have two double beds, while the larger lodge rooms also have dressing areas and balconies. Of the lodge's three eating places, the Mountain Room Restaurant is the most formal. The cafeteria-style Food Court serves three meals a day and offers salads, soups, sandwiches, pastas, and hot meats. ✉ Off Northside Dr., 95389, Yosemite Reservations, 5410 E. Home Ave., Fresno, 93727, ☎ 559/252–4848, FAX 559/456–0542, WEB www.yosemitepark.com. 239 rooms. Restaurant, cafeteria, fans, in-room data ports, pool, bicycles, bar; no air-conditioning, no-smoking rooms. AE, D, DC, MC, V.

$–$$ 🏨 **Curry Village.** Opened in 1899 as a place where travelers could enjoy the beauty of Yosemite for a modest price, Curry Village offers plain accommodations: standard motel rooms, cabins, and tent cabins, which have rough wood frames and canvas walls and roofs. It's a step up from camping, as linens, blankets, and maid service are provided, although many cabins have shared shower and toilet facilities. ✉ South side of Southside Dr., 95389, Yosemite Reservations, 5410 E. Home Ave., Fresno, 93727, ☎ 209/372–8333; 559/252–4848 for reservations, FAX 559/456–0542, WEB www.yosemitepark.com. 19 rooms; 182 cabins, 102 with bath; 427 tent cabins. Cafeteria, pizzeria, pool, bicycles, ice-skating; no air-conditioning, no in-room phones, no room TVs, no-smoking rooms. AE, D, DC, MC, V.

$ 🏨 **Housekeeping Camp.** These rustic three-sided concrete units with canvas roofs, set on a beach along the Merced River, are difficult to come by; reserving a year in advance is advised. You can cook here on gas stoves rented from the front desk, or you can use the fire pits. Toilets and showers are in a central building, and there is a camp store for provisions. ✉ North side of Southside Dr. near Curry Village, 95389, Yosemite Reservations, 5410 E. Home Ave., Fresno, 93727, ☎ 209/372–8338; 559/252–4848 for reservations, FAX 559/456–0542, WEB www.yosemitepark.com. 226 units. Picnic area, beach, laundry facilities; no air-conditioning, no room phones, no room TVs. AE, D, DC, MC, V. Closed early Oct.–late Apr.

△ **Camp 4.** Formerly known as Sunnyside Walk-In, this is the only valley campground available on a first-come, first-served basis and the only one west of Yosemite Lodge. It is a favorite for rock climbers and solo campers, so it fills quickly and is typically sold out by 9 AM every day from spring through fall. Flush toilets, drinking water, hot showers, bear boxes, fire grates, picnic tables, public telephone, ranger station. 35 sites. ✉ At base of Yosemite Falls Trail, near Yosemite Lodge, ☎ 209/372–0265, FAX 209/372–0371. Reservations not accepted. No credit cards. ☉ Year-round.

△ **Tuolumne Meadows.** The campground is in a wooded area at 8,600 ft, just south of a subalpine meadow, and it affords easy access to high peaks with spectacular views. Campers here can use the hot showers at the Tuolumne Meadows Lodge (only at certain strictly regulated times). Half the sites are first-come, first-served, but arrive very early if you hope to get one. Because of the beautiful scenery, this is one of the most sought-after campgrounds in Yosemite. Flush toilets, drinking water, dump station, bear boxes, fire grates, picnic tables, public telephone, ranger station, general store. 314 sites (tent or RV). ✉ Rte. 120, 46 mi east of Big Oak Flat entrance station, ☎ 800/436–7275 or 209/

372–0265, FAX *209/372–0371,* WEB *reservations.nps.gov. Reservations essential. D, MC, V. ☉ June–Sept.*

🏕 **Upper Pines.** This is the valley's largest campground and is closest to the trailheads. Expect large crowds in the summer—and little privacy. *Flush toilets, dump station, drinking water, hot showers, bear boxes, fire grates, picnic tables, public telephone, ranger station, swimming (river). 238 sites (tent or RV). ⊠ At east end of valley, ☎ 800/436–7275,* WEB *reservations.nps.gov. Reservations essential. D, MC, V. ☉ Year-round.*

Outdoor Activities and Sports

BICYCLING

For those who wish to explore the 8 mi of bike paths in eastern Yosemite Valley, **Yosemite Lodge** (☎ 209/372–1208) rents bicycles all year. Bikes are $5.50 an hour or $21 per day. You can ride on 196 mi of paved park roads in Yosemite; rental bikes are available at **Curry Village** (☎ 209/372–8319) April through October. Baby jogger strollers and bikes with child trailers are also available.

HIKING

Yosemite's 840 mi of hiking trails range from short strolls to rugged multiday treks. The park's visitor centers have trail maps and information. Rangers will recommend easy trails to get you acclimated to the altitude. Overnight backpackers need wilderness permits, which can be obtained during the off-season at permit stations within the park. The staff at the **Wilderness Center** in Yosemite Village provides trail-use reservations (strongly advised for popular trailheads from May through September and on weekends), permits ($5), maps, and advice to hikers heading into the backcountry. ⊠ *Yosemite Village near Ansel Adams Gallery (Box 545, Yosemite 95389),* ☎ *209/372–0740.*

HORSEBACK RIDING

Tuolumne Meadows Stables (☎ 209/372–8427) offers day trips from $35 to $80 and High Sierra four- to six-day camping treks on mules beginning at $617. **Wawona Stables** (☎ 209/375–6502) offers several rides, starting at $40. You can tour the backcountry on two-hour, four-hour, and all-day rides at **Yosemite Valley Stables** (☎ 209/372–8348).

ROCK CLIMBING

Yosemite Mountaineering School (☎ 209/372–8344) conducts rock-climbing, backpacking, cross-country skiing, and skate-skiing classes. It also offers guided hiking trips or can design a customized hike for you.

WINTER SPORTS

Badger Pass Ski Area, off Yosemite's Glacier Point Road, has nine downhill runs, 90 mi of groomed cross-country trails, and two excellent ski schools. Free shuttle buses from Yosemite Valley to Badger Pass operate in ski season. The gentle slopes of Badger Pass make **Yosemite Ski School** (☎ 209/372–8430) an ideal spot for children and beginners. The highlight of Yosemite's cross-country skiing center is a 21-mi loop from Badger Pass to Glacier Point. You can rent cross-country skis for $16 per day at the **Cross-Country Ski School** (☎ 209/372–8444). ⊠ *Badger Pass Rd. off Glacier Point Rd., approximately 18 mi from Yosemite Valley,* ☎ *209/372–8430.* 🎟 *Lift tickets, $31; downhill equipment rental, $22; cross-country equipment rental, $16. ☉ Dec.–early Apr., weather permitting.*

The outdoor **ice-skating rink** at Curry Village in Yosemite Valley is open from Thanksgiving Day through April. The cost is $7 and includes skates. ⊠ *South side of Southside Dr.,* ☎ *209/372–8341.*

Wawona

25 mi south of Yosemite Valley on Hwy. 41, 16 mi north of Fish Camp on Hwy. 41.

⑫ The historic buildings in **Pioneer Yosemite History Center** were moved to Wawona from their original sites in the park. From Wednesday through Sunday in summer costumed park employees re-create life in 19th-century Yosemite in a blacksmith's shop, a Wells Fargo office, a jail, and other structures. Ranger-led walks leave from the covered bridge on Saturday at 10. Near the center are a post office, a general store, and a gas station. ⊠ *Rte. 41 near south entrance gate, Wawona,* ☎ *209/379–2646.* ▣ *Free.* ⊙ *Daily year-round; building interiors accessible mid-June–Labor Day, Wed.–Sun. 9–1, Mon.–Tues. 2–5.*

⑬ **Mariposa Grove of Big Trees,** Yosemite's largest grove of giant sequoias, can be visited on foot—trails all lead uphill—or, during the summer, on one-hour tram rides (reservations essential). The Grizzly Giant, the oldest tree here, is estimated to be 2,700 years old. A free shuttle connects Wawona to the Mariposa Grove of Big Trees in summer only from 9 to 4:30. The last return shuttle from the grove departs at 5. If the road to the grove is closed (which happens when Yosemite is crowded), park in Wawona and take the free shuttle; passengers are picked up near the gas station. The access road to the grove may also be closed by snow for extended periods from November to mid-May. You can still usually walk, snowshoe, or ski in. ⊠ *Off Hwy. 41, 2 mi north of south entrance gate.* ▣ *Free; tram $11.* ⊙ *Tram May–Oct., daily 9–4; shuttle Memorial Day–Labor Day, daily 9–5.*

Dining, Lodging, and Camping

$–$$ ✕▦ **Wawona Hotel and Dining Room.** This 1879 National Historic Landmark sits at the southern end of Yosemite National Park, near the Mariposa Grove of Big Trees. It's an old-fashioned New England–style estate of whitewashed buildings with wraparound verandas. The hotel has small but pleasant rooms decorated with period pieces. Dine in the romantic, candlelighted dining room ($–$$; reservations essential), which dates from the late 1800s. The smoky corn trout soup hits the spot on cold winter nights. ⊠ *Hwy. 41, 95389, Yosemite Reservations, 5410 E. Home Ave., Fresno, 93727,* ☎ *559/252–4848 for lodging reservations; 209/375–1425 for dining reservations,* ℻ *559/456–0542,* ⓌⒺⒷ *www.yosemitepark.com. 104 rooms, 52 with bath. Restaurant, bar, 9-hole golf course, putting green, tennis court, pool, horseback riding; no in-room phones, no in-room TVs, no smoking. AE, D, DC, MC, V. Closed weekdays Nov.–Easter except holidays.*
△ **Wawona.** Near the Mariposa Grove, just downstream from a good fishing spot, this campground has larger, less closely packed sites than campgrounds in the valley. The downside is that it's an hour's drive to the major attractions of the valley. *Flush toilets, drinking water, fire grates, bear boxes, picnic tables, ranger station, general store nearby, swimming (river). 93 sites (tent or RV).* ⊠ *Rte. 41, 1 mi north of village of Wawonam,* ☎ *800/436–7275 or 209/372–0265,* ℻ *209/372–0371,* ⓌⒺⒷ *www.reservations.nps.gov. Reservations essential. D, MC, V.* ⊙ *Year-round.*

EAST OF YOSEMITE NATIONAL PARK
From Bridgeport to Lee Vining

The area to the north and east of Yosemite National Park includes some ruggedly handsome terrain, most notably around Mono Lake. Bodie State Historic Park is north of the lake. The area is best visited by car.

The Southern Sierra

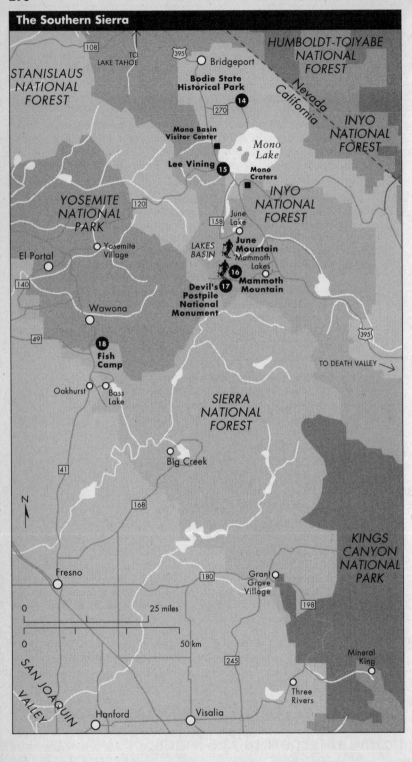

STANISLAUS NATIONAL FOREST

HUMBOLDT-TOIYABE NATIONAL FOREST

108

TO LAKE TAHOE

395

Bridgeport

Bodie State Historical Park

270

14

Nevada
California

INYO NATIONAL FOREST

Mono Basin Visitor Center

Mono Lake

Lee Vining **15**

Mono Craters

YOSEMITE NATIONAL PARK

120

June Lake

158

INYO NATIONAL FOREST

El Portal

Yosemite Village

LAKES BASIN

June Mountain

Mammoth Lakes

140

16

17

Devil's Postpile National Monument

Mammoth Mountain

Wawona

49

18

395

TO DEATH VALLEY

Fish Camp

Oakhurst

Bass Lake

SIERRA NATIONAL FOREST

41

Big Creek

168

N

KINGS CANYON NATIONAL PARK

Fresno

0   25 miles

0   50 km

180

Grant Grove Village

198

245

Mineral King

SAN JOAQUIN VALLEY

Hanford

Visalia

Three Rivers

Route 395, the main north–south road on the eastern side of the Sierra Nevada, passes through Bridgeport and Lee Vining and by the west edge of Mono Lake and west of Bodie.

Bridgeport

25 mi north of Lee Vining on Rte. 395; 55 mi north of Mammoth Lakes on Rte. 395.

Historic Bridgeport lies within striking distance of a myriad alpine lakes and streams and both forks of the Walker River, making it a prime spot for fishing. It is also the gateway to Bodie Ghost Town.

Dining and Lodging

$$–$$$ ✕ **Bridgeport Inn.** Tables spread with white linen grace the dining room of this clapboard Victorian inn, built in 1877. The prime rib and Alaskan crab legs are complemented by homemade soups, pastas, and a large wine list. Victorian-appointed rooms are also available. ⊠ *205 Main St.,* ☎ *760/932–7380. Closed Dec.–Feb. MC, V.*

$$–$$$ ✕ **Restaurant 1881.** Everything is made in-house at one of the east-
★ ern Sierra's only haute-cuisine restaurants. Specialties include marinated chateaûbriand with a black-truffle butter and cabernet glaze, rack of lamb with a pistachio crust, and stuffed bacon-wrapped trout with a chive-leek sauce. ⊠ *362 Main St.,* ☎ *760/932–1918. Reservations essential. AE, D, MC, V. Closed Jan.–mid-Feb. and Mon.–Weds. between Nov. 15 and Apr. 15.*

$–$$ ⛺ **Cain House.** This old home has been refurbished as a B&B in an elegant country style. Afternoon wine-and-cheese service is offered daily, and all beds have down comforters. ⊠ *340 Main St., 93517,* ☎ *760/ 932–7040,* ℻ *760/932–7419,* ⓦ *www.cainhouse.com. 7 rooms. Refrigerators (some), microwaves (some), cable TV, tennis; no smoking. AE, D, MC, V. Closed Nov.–Mar. BP.*

$–$$ ⛺ **Walker River Lodge.** Right in the center of Bridgeport, this hotel's lobby doubles as an antiques shop. Many rooms overlook the East Walker River. ⊠ *100 Main St., 93517,* ☎ *760/932–7021,* ℻ *760/932–7914,* ⓦ *www.walkerriverlodge.com. 36 rooms. Refrigerators, microwaves (some), cable TV, VCRs (some), pool, some pets allowed; no-smoking rooms. AE, D, DC, MC, V.*

$ ⛺ **Silver Maple Inn.** Next to the Mono County Courthouse (1880), this inn is in central Bridgeport, on attractive wooded grounds with views of the nearby Sierra. Built in the 1940s, the motel provides fish cleaning and freezing facilities and barbecue pits in which to cook your catch. ⊠ *310 Main St., 93517,* ☎ *760/932–7383,* ℻ *760/932–7419,* ⓦ *www.silvermapleinn.com. 20 rooms. Fans, refrigerators, cable TV, tennis (nearby), some pets allowed; no air-conditioning, no-smoking rooms. AE, D, MC, V. Closed Nov.–Mar.*

Bodie State Historic Park

⑭ *23 mi from Lee Vining, north on Rte. 395, east on Hwy. 270 (last 3 mi are unpaved). Snow may close Hwy. 270 in winter and early spring, but park stays open.*

Old shacks and shops, abandoned mine shafts, a Methodist church, the mining village of Rattlesnake Gulch, and the remains of a small
★ ☾ Chinatown are among the sights at fascinating **Bodie Ghost Town.** The town, at an elevation of 8,200 ft, boomed from about 1878 to 1881 as gold prospectors, having worked the best of the western Sierra mines, headed to the high desert on the eastern slopes. Bodie was a mean place—the booze flowed freely, shootings were commonplace, and licentiousness reigned. The big strikes were made during the boom

years, and though some mining continued into the 1930s, the town had long since begun its decline. By the late 1940s all its residents had departed. A state park was established in 1962, with a mandate to preserve but not restore the town. Evidence of Bodie's wild past survives at an excellent museum, and you can tour an old stamp mill (where ore was stamped into fine powder to extract gold and silver) and a ridge that contains many mine sites. No food, drink, or lodging is available in Bodie, and the nearest picnic area is a half mile away. ⊠ *Museum: Main and Green Sts.,* ☎ *760/647–6445.* ⊑ *Park $2; museum $1.* ☉ *Park: Memorial Day–Labor Day, daily 8–7; Labor Day–Memorial Day, daily 8–4. Museum: Memorial Day–Labor Day, daily 9–6; Sept.–May, hrs vary.*

Lee Vining

⑮ *20 mi east of Tuolumne Meadows, Hwy. 120 to Rte. 395; 30 mi north of Mammoth Lakes on Rte. 395*

Lee Vining is mostly known as an eastern gateway to Yosemite National Park and the location of Mono Lake. Pick up supplies or stop for lunch before or after the drive through the high country.

★ Eerie tufa towers—calcium carbonate formations that often resemble castle turrets—rise from impressive **Mono Lake.** Since the 1940s the city of Los Angeles has diverted water from streams that feed the lake, lowering its water level and exposing the tufa. Court victories by environmentalists in the 1990s forced a reduction of the diversions, and the lake has since risen about 9 ft. April through August millions of migratory birds nest in and around Mono Lake. The best place to view the tufa is at the south end of the lake along the mile-long **South Tufa Trail.** To reach it, drive 5 mi south from Lee Vining on Route 395, then 5 mi east on Highway 120. There is a $3 fee. You can swim (or float) in the highly salty water at Navy Beach near the South Tufa Trail or take a kayak or canoe trip for close-up views of the tufa (check with rangers for boating restrictions during bird-nesting season). The **Scenic Area Visitor Center** (⊠ Rte. 395, ☎ 760/647–3044) is open daily from April through October, 9–5:30, and the rest of the year Friday through Sunday 9–4. Rangers and naturalists lead walking tours of the tufa daily in summer and on weekends only (sometimes on cross-country skis) in winter.

Dining and Lodging

$ ✕ **Nicely's.** Plants and pictures of local attractions decorate this eatery that has been around since 1965. Try the blueberry pancakes and homemade sausages at breakfast. For lunch or dinner try the chicken-fried steak or the fiesta salad. There's also a kids' menu. ⊠ *Rte. 395 and 4th St.,* ☎ *760/647–6477. MC, V. Closed Wed. in winter.*

$–$$ 🛏 **Tioga Lodge.** Just 2½ mi north of Yosemite's eastern gateway, this 19th-century building has been by turns a store, a saloon, a tollbooth, and a boarding house. Now restored and expanded, it's a popular lodge that's close to local ski areas and fishing spots. ⊠ *Rte. 395, Box 580, 93541,* ☎ *760/647–6423 or 888/647–6423,* ℻ *760/647–6074. 13 rooms. Restaurant; no air-conditioning, no room phones, no room TVs, no smoking. AE, D, MC, V.*

En Route   Heading south from Lee Vining, Route 395 intersects the **June Lake Loop** (⊠ Hwy. 158 west). This wonderfully scenic 17-mi drive follows an old glacial canyon past Grant, June, Gull, and other lakes before reconnecting with Route 395 on its way to Mammoth Lakes. The loop is especially colorful in fall.

MAMMOTH AREA

A jewel in the eastern Sierra Nevada, the Mammoth Lakes area provides California's finest skiing and snowboarding south of Lake Tahoe. Skiers hit the slopes at 11,053-ft-high Mammoth Mountain as late as June or even July. As soon as snows melt, Mammoth transforms itself into a warm-weather playground—fishing, mountain biking, hiking, and horseback riding are among the activities. Nine deep-blue lakes are spread through the Mammoth Lakes Basin, and another 100 lakes dot the surrounding countryside. Crater-pocked Mammoth Mountain hasn't had a major eruption for 50,000 years, but the region is alive with hot springs, mud pots, fumaroles, and steam vents.

Mammoth Lakes

30 mi south of Mono Lake on Rte. 395.

Much of the architecture in the hub town of Mammoth Lakes (elevation 7,800 ft) is in the faux-alpine category. You'll find basic services here, plus plenty of dining and lodging. Highway 203 heads west from U.S. 395, becoming Main Street as it passes through the town of Mammoth Lakes and later Minaret Road (which makes a right turn) as it continues west to the Mammoth Mountain ski area and Devils Postpile National Monument.

The lakes of the **Mammoth Lakes Basin,** reached by Lake Mary Road off Highway 203 southwest of town, are popular for fishing and boating in summer. First comes Twin Lakes, at the far end of which is Twin Falls, where water cascades 300 ft over a shelf of volcanic rock. Also popular are Lake Mary, the largest lake in the basin, Lake Mamie, and Lake George. Horseshoe Lake is the only lake in which you can swim.

The glacial-carved sawtooth spires of the Minarets, the remains of an ancient lava flow, are best viewed from the **Minaret Vista,** off Highway 203 west of Mammoth Lakes.

Even if you don't ski, you'll want to see the aptly named landmass that gives Mammoth Lakes its name—**Mammoth Mountain.** Gondolas serve skiers in winter and mountain bikers and sightseers in summer. The high-speed eight-passenger *Panorama Gondola* whisks you from the chalet to the summit. The boarding area for the lower gondola is at the main lodge of the ski area. ⊠ *Off Hwy. 203, Mammoth Lakes,* ☎ *760/934–2571 Ext. 3850.* ☑ *$10.* ☉ *July 4–Oct., daily 9:30–5; Nov.– July 3, daily 8:30–4.*

An easy 10-minute walk from the ranger station at **Devils Postpile National Monument** takes you to a geologic formation of smooth, vertical basalt columns sculpted by volcanic and glacial forces. A short but steep trail winds to the top of the 60-ft-high rocky cliff for a bird's-eye view of the columns. A 2-mi hike past the Postpile leads to the monument's second scenic wonder, **Rainbow Falls,** where a branch of the San Joaquin River plunges more than 100 ft over a lava ledge. When the water hits the pool below, sunlight turns the resulting mist into a spray of color. Walk down a bit from the top of the falls for the best viewing.

During summer Devils Postpile National Monument is accessible only via a shuttle bus ($9) that begins operation as soon as the road is cleared of snow—usually in June, but sometimes as late as July. The shuttle departs from Mammoth Mountain Inn every 20 minutes from 7:30 to 5:30. The shuttle stops running after Labor Day, but you can drive to the falls until the snows come again, usually around the beginning of

November. Scenic picnic spots dot the bank of the San Joaquin River. ⊠ *Hwy. 203, 13 mi west of Mammoth Lakes,* ☎ *760/934–2289; 760/ 934–0606 for shuttle bus information.* ⛱ *Free.* ☉ *Late June–late Oct., daily, weather permitting.*

OFF THE BEATEN PATH **HOT CREEK GEOLOGIC SITE/HOT CREEK FISH HATCHERY –** Forged by an ancient volcanic eruption, the Hot Creek Geologic Site is a landscape of boiling hot springs, fumaroles, and occasional geysers about 10 mi southeast of the town of Mammoth Lakes. You can soak (at your own risk) in hot springs or walk along boardwalks through the canyon to view the steaming volcanic features. Fly-fishing for trout is popular up-stream from the springs. En route to the geologic site is the Hot Creek Fish Hatchery, the breeding ponds for most of the fish (3–5 million annu-ally) with which the state stocks eastern Sierra lakes and rivers. ⊠ *Hot Creek Hatchery Rd. east of Rte. 395,* ☎ *760/924–5500 for geologic site; 760/934–2664 for hatchery.* ⛱ *Free.* ☉ *Site daily sunrise–sunset; hatchery June–Oct., daily 8–4, depending on snowfall.*

Dining and Lodging

$$–$$$ ✕ **Nevados.** In a restaurant scene known mostly for meat, potatoes, and pizza, this bistro serves contemporary cuisine. The menu changes frequently but always includes creative soups and salads, fresh seafood, and grilled meats. Eggplant lasagna, sesame-crusted ahi tuna, and orange-scented duckling are popular entrées. ⊠ *Main St. and Minaret Rd.,* ☎ *760/934–4466. Reservations essential. AE, D, DC, MC, V. No lunch.*

$$–$$$ ✕ **The Restaurant at Convict Lake.** Tucked in a grove of aspens, ten ★ minutes south of town in the middle of nowhere, is one of the best restau-rants in the eastern Sierra. Sit beside the fire under a knotty-pine cathe-dral ceiling at one of the well-spaced tables or booths, and sup on impeccable cuisine such as sautéed venison medallions, pan-seared local trout, and beef Wellington. This is a haven for wine aficionados, with an extensive selection of reasonably priced European and Cali-fornia varietals. The service is as good as the food. ⊠ *2 mi off U.S. 395, 4 mi south of Mammoth Lakes,* ☎ *760/934–3803. Reservations essential. No lunch Labor Day–July 4th. AE, D, MC, V.*

$$–$$$ ✕ **Skadi.** Named for the Viking goddess of skiing and hunting, Skadi draws inspiration from Scandinavian and alpine cooking. Its sophis-ticated menu is diverse, with specialties including game meats and fish. The dining room has spectacular views of the surrounding moun-tains. ⊠ *587 Old Mammoth Rd.,* ☎ *760/934–3902. Reservations es-sential. AE, MC, V. Closed Mon.–Tues. No lunch.*

$–$$ ✕ **Berger's.** Don't even think about coming to this bustling pine-panel restaurant unless you're hungry. Berger's is known, appropriately enough, for burgers and generously sized sandwiches. Everything comes in mountainous portions. For dinner try the beef ribs or the buf-falo steak. ⊠ *Minaret Rd. near Canyon Blvd.,* ☎ *760/934–6622. MC, V. Closed 2 wks May and 4–6 wks Oct.–Nov.*

$–$$ ✕ **The Mogul.** This longtime steak house is friendly and relaxed. The charbroiled shrimp and the grilled beef or chicken come with a baked potato or rice pilaf and soup or salad. A children's menu is available. ⊠ *Mammoth Tavern Rd. off Old Mammoth Rd.,* ☎ *760/934–3039. AE, D, MC, V. No lunch.*

$ ✕ **Blondie's Kitchen and Waffle Shop.** A good place to stoke up be-fore a morning on the slopes or trails (it opens at 6 AM), this comic-strip-theme diner serves up waffles, pancakes, omelets, and Dagwood "pig-out" plates. ⊠ *Main and Lupin Sts.,* ☎ *760/934–4048. AE, D, DC, MC, V. No dinner.*

$ ✕ **Giovanni's Pizza.** Children love this casual restaurant. It serves
☾ standard Italian dinners, but your best bet is to stick to the delicious
pizza. Don't come here for quiet conversation—it's a high-decibel
joint. ✉ *Minaret Village Mall, Old Mammoth Rd. and Meridian St.,*
☎ *760/934–7563. AE, MC, V. No lunch Sun.*

$$–$$$ ✕🏠 **Tamarack Lodge Resort.** Nordic skiers (and, in summer, nature
★ lovers) favor this lodge, which overlooks Twin Lakes, about 3 mi west
of town. The main building is surrounded by quiet woods, and cross-
country ski trails loop past the cabins. In warm months fishing, canoeing, hiking, and mountain biking are close by. The cozy cabins are
modern, neat, and clean, with knotty-pine kitchens and private baths;
some have fireplaces or wood-burning stoves. The romantic Lakefront
Restaurant ($$; reservations essential, no lunch) serves outstanding
contemporary French-inspired cuisine, with an emphasis on game. ✉
Box 69 (take Lake Mary Rd. off Hwy. 203), 93546, ☎ *760/934–2442
or 800/626–6684,* FAX *760/934–2281,* WEB *www.tamaracklodge.com.
11 rooms, 25 cabins. Restaurant, fans, kitchenettes (some), cross-coun-
try skiing, ski shop; no air-conditioning, no room TVs, no smoking.
AE, MC, V.*

$$$–$$$$ 🏠 **Juniper Springs Lodge.** Opened in 2002, this is Mammoth Moun-
tain's first luxury property. Accommodations are in a four-story stone-
and-timber building directly adjacent to one of the ski lifts. All rooms
are condominium-style units, with full kitchens and ski-in, ski-out ac-
cess to the mountain. Amenities include stone fireplaces, balconies, and
stereos with CD players. The heated outdoor pool—surrounded by a
heated deck—is open year-round. ✉ *4000 Meridian Blvd., Box 2129,
93546,* ☎ *760/924–1102 for front desk; 800/626–6684 for reserva-
tions,* FAX *760/924–8152,* WEB *www.mammothmountain.com. 10 stu-
dios, 99 1-bedrooms, 92 2-bedrooms, 5 3-bedrooms. Restaurant, café,
bar, room service, fans, in-room data ports, kitchens, microwaves, re-
frigerators, cable TV, in-room VCRs, 18-hole golf course, pool, 2 hot
tubs, exercise equipment, mountain bikes, downhill skiing, ski stor-
age, ski shop, laundry service, concierge, meeting rooms; no air-con-
ditioning, no smoking. AE, MC, V.*

$$–$$$$ 🏠 **Mammoth Mountain Inn.** If you want to be within walking distance
of the Mammoth Mountain ski area, this is the place to stay. You can
check your skis with the concierge after a day on the slopes and pick
them up in the morning and head directly to the lifts. The staff keeps
you apprised of snow conditions. The accommodations, some of which
are cramped, include standard hotel rooms and condo units; the latter have kitchenettes, and many have lofts. The inn has licensed on-
site child care. ✉ *Minaret Rd., Box 353 (4 mi west of Mammoth Lakes),
93546,* ☎ *760/934–2581 or 800/626–6684,* FAX *760/934–0701,* WEB
*www.mammothmountain.com. 124 rooms, 91 condos. 2 restaurants,
fans, in-room data ports (some), microwaves (some), refrigerators
(some), kitchenettes (some), cable TV, video game room, hot tub, bar,
baby-sitting, playground, meeting room; no air-conditioning, no-smoking rooms. AE, MC, V.*

$$–$$$$ 🏠 **Snowcreek Resort.** In a valley surrounded by mountain peaks, this
355-acre condominium community on the outskirts of Mammoth
Lakes contains one- to four-bedroom units. All have kitchens, living
and dining rooms, and fireplaces; some have washers and dryers. You
will have free use of the well-supplied athletic club. ✉ *Old Mammoth
Rd., Box 1647, 93546,* ☎ *760/934–3333 or 800/544–6007,* FAX *760/
934–1619,* WEB *www.snowcreekresort.com. 195 condos. Cable TV, in-
room data ports, kitchens, refrigerators, microwaves, 9-hole golf
course, 9 tennis courts, 2 pools, health club, hot tub, sauna, racquet-
ball, meeting room; no air-conditioning, no smoking. AE, D, MC, V.*

$-$$ ⊡ **Alpenhof Lodge.** You can walk to restaurants and shops from this Swiss-style family-owned motel. Accommodations are simple, rates reasonable, and the service good. Some rooms have fireplaces. ⊠ *6080 Minaret Rd., Box 1157, 93546,* ☎ *760/934–6330 or 800/828–0371,* FAX *760/934–7614,* WEB *www.alpenhof-lodge.com. 54 rooms, 3 cabins. Restaurant, bar, kitchens (some), refrigerators (some), microwaves (some), cable TV, pool, hot tub, recreation room, laundry facilities; no air-conditioning, no smoking. AE, D, MC, V.*

$-$$ ⊡ **Convict Lake Resort.** This resort stands beside a lake named for an 1871 gunfight between local vigalantes and an escaped posse of six prisoners. You can camp here, right on the lake, or in the meadow nearby, or stay in one of the cabins. Everything you need is waiting in your cabin, including a fully equipped kitchen (with coffeemaker and premium coffee). Large luxury homes ($$$$) can sleep up to 35 people. ⊠ *2 mi off U.S. 395, 35 mi north of Bishop,* ☎ *760/934–3800 or 800/992–2260,* WEB *www.convictlakeresort.com. 88 campsites; 23 cabins. Restaurant, kitchens, microwaves (some), lake, boating, fishing, bicycles, horseback riding, shop, Internet, some pets allowed (fee); no room phones, no air-conditioning. AE, MC, V.*

$-$$ ⊡ **Sierra Lodge.** This modern motel on Main Street has spacious rooms. A covered parking garage with ski lockers is helpful in winter. Free shuttles take skiers to Mammoth Mountain. ⊠ *3540 Main St., 93546,* ☎ *760/934–8881; 800/356–5711 in CA,* FAX *760/934–7231,* WEB *www.sierralodge.com. 35 rooms. Fans, in-room data ports, kitchenettes, microwaves, refrigerators, cable TV, hot tub, Internet, ski storage, some pets (fee); no air-conditioning, no smoking. AE, D, MC, V. CP.*

$ ⊡ **Swiss Chalet.** One of the most reasonably priced motels in town, the Swiss Chalet has great views of the mountains. Among the amenities are a fish-cleaning area and a freezer to keep your summer catch fresh. In winter the shuttle to Mammoth Mountain stops out front. ⊠ *3776 Viewpoint Rd., Box 16, 93546,* ☎ *760/934–2403 or 800/937–9477,* FAX *760/934–2403,* WEB *www.mammoth-swisschalet.com. 20 rooms. Refrigerators, microwaves (some), kitchenettes, cable TV, hot tub, sauna, some pets (fee); no air-conditioning, no smoking. AE, D, MC, V.*

⚠ **Lake Mary Campground.** You can catch trout in Lake Mary, the biggest of the lakes in the region. The camp is set on its shores at 8,900 ft, and though it is popular (and hence busy), there are few sites as beautiful as this. If it's full, try the adjacent Coldwater campground. There is a general store nearby. *Flush toilets, drinking water, fire grates, picnic tables. 48 sites (tent or RV).* ⊠ *Rte. 203 west to Lake Mary Loop Dr. (turn left and go ¼ mi),* ☎ *760/924–5500,* FAX *760/924–5537. No credit cards.* ☉ *June–Sept.*

⚠ **Minaret Falls Campground.** At 7,700 ft, this is one of several campgrounds along Minaret Rd. past the entrance gate to Devils Postpile National Monument. It's close to many trails in the high country above Mammoth Lakes, including the Pacific Crest Trail. *Pit toilets, drinking water, grills, picnic tables. 27 sites (tent or RV).* ⊠ *Off Minaret Rd. (Rte. 203), 6 mi beyond the Devils Postpile entrance,* ☎ *760/924–5500,* FAX *760/924–5537. No credit cards.* ☉ *June–Sept.*

Nightlife and the Arts

The summertime **Mammoth Lakes Jazz Jubilee** is hosted by the local group Temple of Folly Jazz Band and takes place in 10 venues, most with dance floors (☎ 760/934–2478 or 800/367–6572, WEB www.mammothjazz.org). For one long weekend every summer, Mammoth Lakes hosts **Bluesapalooza,** a blues and beer festival—with emphasis on the beer tasting (☎ 760/934–0606 or 800/367–6572, WEB www.mammothconcert.com). Ongoing concerts occur throughout the year on Mammoth Mountain; call **Mammoth Mountain Music** for current listings (☎ 760/934–0606, www.mammothconcert.com or WEB www. visitmammoth.com).

Rock, country, and blues acts perform at **La Sierra's** (⊠ Main St. near Minaret Rd., ☎ 760/934–8083), which has Mammoth's largest dance floor. On Tuesday and Saturday evenings, you can sing karaoke at **Shogun** (⊠ 452 Old Mammoth Rd., ☎ 760/934–3970), Mammoth's only Japanese restaurant. The bar at **Whiskey Creek** (⊠ Main St. and Minaret Rd., ☎ 760/934–2555) hosts musicians on weekends year-round and on most nights in winter.

Outdoor Activities and Sports

For information on winter conditions around Mammoth, call the **Snow Report** (☎ 760/934–7669 or 888/766–9778). The **U.S. Forest Service ranger station** (☎ 760/924–5500) can provide information year-round.

BICYCLING

Mammoth Mountain Bike Park (☎ 760/934–0706), at the ski area, opens when the snows melt, usually by July, with 70-plus mi of single-track trails—from mellow to superchallenging. Chairlifts and shuttles provide trail access, and rentals are available.

DOGSLEDDING

Dog Sled Adventures (☎ 760/934–6270) operates 25-minute rides through the forest on dogsleds pulled by teams of 10 dogs.

FISHING

Crowley Lake is the top trout-fishing spot in the area; Convict Lake, June Lake, and the lakes of the Mammoth Basin are other prime spots. One of the best trout rivers is the San Joaquin, near Devils Postpile. Hot Creek, a designated Wild Trout Stream, is renowned for fly-fishing (catch and release only). The fishing season runs from the last Saturday in April until the end of October. **Kittredge Sports** (⊠ Main St. and Forest Trail, ☎ 760/934–7566) rents rods and reels and conducts guided trips.

GOLFING

Because it's nestled right up against the forest, you might see deer and bears on the fairways at the 18-hole **Sierra Star Golf Course** (⊠ 2001 Sierra Star Pkwy., 93546, ☎ 760/924–2200).

HIKING

Trails wind around the Lakes Basin and through pristine alpine scenery. Stop at the **U.S. Forest Service ranger station** (⊠ On right-hand side of Hwy. 203, just before town of Mammoth Lakes, ☎ 760/924–5500) for a Mammoth area trail map and permits for backpacking in wilderness areas.

HORSEBACK RIDING

Stables around Mammoth are typically open from June through September. There are several outfitters available. Call or write **Mammoth Lakes Pack Outfit** (⊠ Box 61, along Lake Mary Rd., 93546, ☎ 760/934–2434) to find out about their horseback trips. **McGee Creek Pack Station** (⊠ Box 162, Rte. 1, 93546, ☎ 760/935–4324 or 800/854–7407) can set you up with horses and gear. **Sierra Meadows Ranch** (⊠ Sherwin Creek Rd., ☎ 760/934–6161) outfits rides in the area.

HOT-AIR BALLOONING

The balloons of **Mammoth Balloon Adventures** (☎ 760/937–8787) glide over the countryside in the morning from spring until fall, weather permitting.

June Mountain Ski Area. This low-key resort 20 mi north of Mammoth Mountain is a favorite of snowboarders, who have a half-pipe all to themselves, and there are three free-style terrain areas for both skiers and boarders. Seven lifts service the area, which has a 2,664-ft vertical drop; the skiing ranges from beginner to expert. There's rarely a line for the lifts, and the area is better protected than Mammoth from wind and storms. You can use your lift ticket at either resort. A rental and repair shop, a ski school, and a sport shop are all on the premises. ⊠ *Box 146, off June Lake Loop (Hwy. 158) north of Mammoth Lakes, June Lake 93529,* ☎ *760/648–7733 or 888/586–3686. 35 trails on 500 acres, rated 35% beginner, 45% intermediate, 20% expert. Longest run 2½ mi, base 7,510′, summit, 10,174′. Lifts: 7.*

Mammoth Mountain Ski Area. With 28 lifts (nine high-speed) and more than 3,500 acres of skiable terrain, Mammoth is one of the West's largest ski areas. The base elevation is 7,953 ft. When it's not too windy, you can ski off the top of the mountain (11,053 ft), for a 3,100-ft vertical drop. The terrain includes beginning-to-expert runs. Snowboarders are welcome on all slopes; the Unbound Snowboard Arena has a half-pipe and two freestyle terrain parks. Mammoth's season begins in November and often lingers until June or beyond. Lessons and rental equipment are available, and there's a children's ski and snowboard school. Mammoth Mountain runs four free **shuttle bus** routes around town to and from the ski area. Buses run from 7 to 5:30 daily in snow season, with limited service in the evenings until midnight (☎ 760/934–0687 or 760/934–2571). ⊠ *Minaret Rd. west of Mammoth Lakes, Box 24, 93546,* ☎ *760/934–2571 or 800/626–6684. 150 trails on 3,500 acres, rated 30% beginner, 40% intermediate, 30% expert. Longest run 3 mi, base 7,953′, summit 11,053′. Lifts: 28.*

Trails at **Tamarack Cross Country Ski Center** (⊠ Lake Mary Rd. off Hwy. 203, ☎ 760/934–2442), adjacent to Tamarack Lodge, meander around several lakes. Rentals are available.

Mammoth Sporting Goods (⊠ 1 Sierra Center Mall, Old Mammoth Rd., ☎ 760/934–3239) rents skis and sells equipment, clothing, and accessories.

Mammoth Snowmobile Adventures, at the Main Lodge at the Mammoth Mountain Ski Area (☎ 760/934–9645), conducts guided tours along wooded trails.

SOUTH OF YOSEMITE NATIONAL PARK
From El Portal to Bass Lake

Several gateway towns to the south and west of Yosemite National Park, most within an hour's drive of Yosemite Valley, have food, lodging, and other services. Highway 140 heads east from the San Joaquin Valley to El Portal. Highway 41 heads north from Fresno to Oakhurst and Fish Camp; Bass Lake is off Highway 41.

El Portal

14 mi west of Yosemite Valley on Hwy. 140.

The market in town is a good place to pick up provisions before you get to Yosemite. There is also a post office, but no place to buy gas.

Lodging

$$ ⊞ **Cedar Lodge.** The lobby of this rustic lodge in the pines is filled with teddy bears. Rooms range from suites with kitchenettes to family units to romantic accommodations with whirlpool tubs for two. ⊠ *9966 Hwy. 140, 95318,* ☎ *209/379–2612,* ℻ *209/379–2712. 188 rooms, 22 suites, 2 apartments, 1 house. Restaurant, cable TV, kitchenettes (some), 2 pools, hot tub; no-smoking rooms. AE, MC, V.*

$$ ⊞ **Yosemite View Lodge.** Many rooms with balconies overlook the boul-
Ⓒ der-strewn Merced River and majestic pines. Also in view is a picnic patio with hot tubs and heated pools. The pleasant facility is on the public bus route to Yosemite National Park and near fishing and river rafting. Many rooms have spa baths, fireplaces, and kitchenettes. ⊠ *11136 Hwy. 140, 95318,* ☎ *209/379–2681,* ℻ *209/379–2704. 276 rooms. Restaurant, pizzeria, bar, cable TV, kitchenettes (some), pool, indoor pool, 5 hot tubs, laundry facilities, meeting room, some pets (fee); no-smoking rooms. MC, V.*

Fish Camp

⑱ *37 mi south of Yosemite Valley floor on Hwy. 41, 4 mi south of Yosemite National Park's South Entrance on Hwy. 41.*

In the small town of Fish Camp there are a post office and a general
Ⓒ store. The **Yosemite Mountain Sugar Pine Railroad** has a narrow-gauge steam engine that chugs through the forest. It follows 4 mi of the route the Madera Sugar Pine Lumber Company cut through the forest in 1899 in order to harvest timber. Saturday evening's Moonlight Special excursion (reservations essential) includes dinner and music by the Sugar Pine Trio. ⊠ *56001 Hwy. 41,* ☎ *559/683–7273.* 🎫 *$12; Moonlight Special $35.* ☉ *Mar.–Oct., daily.*

Dining and Lodging

$$–$$$$ ✕⊞ **Tenaya Lodge.** One of the region's largest hotels, the Tenaya Lodge is ideal for people who enjoy wilderness treks by day but prefer luxury at night. A southwestern motif prevails in the ample regular rooms. The deluxe rooms have minibars and other extras, and the suites have balconies. The cozy Sierra Restaurant ($–$$$) offers Continental cuisine; the fare at the lodge's casual Jackalopes Bar and Grill includes burgers, salads, and sandwiches. ⊠ *1122 Hwy. 41, Box 159, 93623,* ☎ *559/683–6555 or 888/514–2167,* ℻ *559/683–0249,* 🕸 *www.tenayalodge.com. 244 rooms, 6 1-bedroom suites. 2 restaurants, snack bar, bar, room service, in-room data ports, cable TV with movies and video games, minibars (some), indoor pool, pool, health club, hot tub, mountain bikes, hiking, cross-country skiing, children's programs (ages 5–12), playground, laundry service, meeting room, concierge, business services; no smoking. AE, D, DC, MC, V.*

$$ ✕⊞ **Narrow Gauge Inn.** This motel-style property is comfortably furnished with old-fashioned accents and railroad memorabilia. The inn's restaurant ($–$$), which serves standard American fare, is festooned with moose, bison, and other wildlife trophies. ⊠ *48571 Hwy. 41, 93623,* ☎ *559/683–7720 or 888/644–9050,* ℻ *559/683–2139. 25 rooms, 1 suite. Restaurant, bar, no air-conditioning in some rooms, in-room data ports, some VCRs, cable TV, pool, hot tub, some pets (fee); no smoking. D, MC, V.*

Oakhurst

50 mi south of Yosemite Valley on Hwy. 41, 23 mi south of Yosemite National Park's South Entrance on Hwy. 41.

Motels and restaurants line both sides of Highway 41 as it cuts through the town of Oakhurst. You can stock up on provisions at the grocery and general stores.

Dining and Lodging

$$$$ ✕ **Erna's Elderberry House.** The restaurant, operated by Vienna-born
★   Erna Kubin, owner of Château du Sureau, is an expression of her passion for beauty, charm, and impeccable service. Red walls and dark beams accent the dining room's high ceilings, and arched windows reflect the glow of many candles. A seasonal six-course prix-fixe dinner is elegantly paced and accompanied by superb wines. The moment the waitstaff places all the plates on the table in perfect synchronicity, you know this will be a meal to remember. ⊠ *48688 Victoria La.*, ☎ *559/683–6800. AE, MC, V. Reservations essential. Closed 1st 3 wks in Jan. No lunch.*

$$$$ ⊟ **Château du Sureau.** This romantic inn, adjacent to Erna's Elder-
★   berry House, is out of a children's book. From the moment you drive through the wrought-iron gates and up to the fairy-tale castle, you will be pampered. You'll fall asleep in the glow of a crackling fire amid goose-down pillows and a fluffy comforter. In the morning, after a hearty European breakfast in the dining room, relax in the piano room, which has an exquisite ceiling mural. ⊠ *48688 Victoria La., Box 577, 93644,* ☎ *559/683–6860,* FAX *559/683–0800,* WEB *www.elderberryhouse.com. 10 rooms, 1 villa. Restaurant, in-room data ports, dining room, pool; no room TVs, no smoking. AE, D, MC, V. BP.*

$$–$$$ ⊟ **The Homestead Cottages.** Serenity is the order of the day at this secluded getaway in Ahwahnee, 6 mi west of Oakhurst. On 160 acres that once held a Miwok village, these cottages have fireplaces, living rooms, fully equipped kitchens, and queen-size beds. The cottages, built by hand by the owners, are stocked with soft green robes, oversize towels, and a good supply of paperback books. ⊠ *41110 Rd. 600, 2½ mi off Hwy. 49, Ahwahnee 93601,* ☎ *559/683–0495,* FAX *559/683–8165,* WEB *www.homesteadcottages.com. 4 cottages, 1 loft. Microwaves, cable TV, kitchenettes; no room phones, no smoking. AE, D, MC, V.*

$$ ⊟ **Shilo Inn.** Rooms at this upscale multistory motel are spacious and sunny and offer extra amenities, such as in-room coffeemakers, irons, and hair dryers. ⊠ *40644 Hwy. 41, Oakhurst 93644,* ☎ *559/683–3555 or 800/222–2244,* FAX *559/683–3386,* WEB *www.shiloinns.com. 80 rooms, 1 suite. Cable TV with movies, refrigerators, microwaves, pool, gym, hot tub, sauna, steam room, laundry facilities; no-smoking rooms. AE, D, DC, MC, V. CP.*

Bass Lake

18 mi south of Yosemite National Park's south entrance; take Hwy. 41 to Bass Valley Rd.

For the most part surrounded by the Sierra National Forest, Bass Lake is a warm water lake whose waters can reach 80° in summer. Created by a dam on a tributary of the San Joaquin River, the lake is owned by Pacific Gas and Electric Company and is used to generate electricity as well as for recreation.

Dining

$$–$$$$ ✕ **Ducey's on the Lake.** With elaborate chandeliers sculpted from deer antlers, the lodge-style restaurant at Ducey's (part of the larger Pines Resort complex) attracts boaters, locals, and tourists with its lake views and standard lamb, beef, seafood, and pasta dishes. Burgers, salads, tacos, and sandwiches are served at the upstairs Ducey's Bar & Grill. ⊠ *54432 Rd. 432,* ☎ *559/642–3121. AE, D, DC, MC, V.*

Outdoor Activities and Sports

Pines Marina (⊠ Bass Lake Reservoir, ☎ 559/642–3565), open from April through October, rents ski boats, houseboats, and fishing boats.

KINGS CANYON AND SEQUOIA NATIONAL PARKS

Though they're overshadowed by Yosemite today, naturalist John Muir thought no less of Kings Canyon and Sequoia national parks in the early 20th century. He declared that the beauty of Kings Canyon rivaled that of Yosemite and described the sequoia trees as "the most beautiful and majestic on Earth." *Sequoiadendron giganteum* trees are not as tall as the coast redwoods (*Sequoia sempervirens*), but on average they are older and more massive. Exhibits at the visitor centers explain the special relationship between these trees and fire (their thick, fibrous bark helps protect them from fire and insects) and why they can live so long and grow so big.

A little more than 1.5 million people visit Kings Canyon and Sequoia annually, wandering trails through groves and meadows or tackling the rugged backcountry. The topography of the two parks runs the gamut from chaparral, at an elevation of 1,500 ft, to the giant sequoia belt, at 5,000–7,000 ft, to the towering peaks of the Great Western Divide and the Sierra Crest. Mt. Whitney, the highest point in the contiguous United States, at 14,494 ft, is the crown jewel of the less crowded eastern side (the border between Sequoia National Park and John Muir Wilderness, to the east, runs right through the summit of Mt. Whitney). You cannot access Mt. Whitney from Sequoia's western side; you must circumnavigate the Sierra range via a 10-hour, nearly 400-mi drive outside the park (*see* Chapter 11, Death Valley and the Mojave Desert, *for* Mt. Whitney).

Kings Canyon and Sequoia national parks share their administration and a main highway, called the Generals Highway, which connects Highway 180 in Kings Canyon to Highway 198 in Sequoia. The entrance fee to Kings Canyon and Sequoia (good for admission to both on seven consecutive days) is $10 per vehicle, $5 for those who don't arrive by car. An information-packed quarterly newspaper and a map are handed out at the parks' entrances.

Grant Grove and Cedar Grove

100 mi southeast of Oakhurst, Hwy. 41 to Hwy. 180.

⑲ Grant Grove, Kings Canyon's most highly developed area, was designated General Grant National Park (the forerunner of Kings Canyon National Park) in 1890. A walk along 1-mi **Big Stump Trail,** which starts near the park entrance, graphically demonstrates the toll heavy logging takes on wilderness. An alternative ⅓-mi trail is fairly accessible to travelers with disabilities; there are some rough spots, and rain can muddy up the trail. The **General Grant Tree Trail,** a paved ⅓-mi path through Grant Grove, winds past the General Grant, an enormous, 2,000-year-old sequoia, the world's third largest, which has been designated "the nation's Christmas tree." The **Gamlin Cabin,** an 1867 structure listed on the National Register of Historic Places, is a pioneer cabin. Also within Grant Grove is the **Centennial Stump,** the remains of a huge sequoia cut for display at the 1876 Philadelphia Centennial Exhibition. **Grant Grove Village** has a visitor center, a grocery store, a gift shop, campgrounds, a restaurant that has family dining, overnight lodging, and a post office. The visitor center has exhibits on the sequoias and

Kings Canyon and Sequoia National Parks

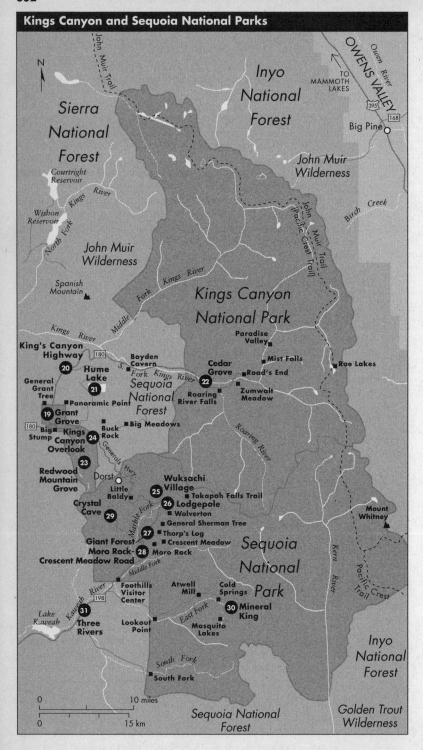

N

Sierra National Forest

John Muir Trail

Courtright Reservoir

Wishon Reservoir

Kings River

North Fork

John Muir Wilderness

Spanish Mountain ▲

Middle Fork

Inyo National Forest

OWENS VALLEY

Owen River

TO MAMMOTH LAKES

395

Big Pine

168

John Muir Wilderness

Birch Creek

John Muir Trail (Pacific Crest Trail)

Kings River

South Fork Kings River

Kings Canyon National Park

Paradise Valley

Mist Falls

Rae Lakes ■

King's Canyon Highway
20

Hume Lake
21

180

General Grant Tree ■

Boyden Cavern ■

South Fork Kings River

Cedar Grove ●
22

Road's End ■

Roaring River Falls ■

Zumwalt Meadow ■

Roaring River

Grant Grove
19

Panoramic Point ■

Sequoia National Forest

Big Stump ■

180

Kings Canyon Overlook
24

Buck Rock ■

■ Big Meadows

Generals Hwy.

23

Redwood Mountain Grove

Dorst ○

Little Baldy ■

Crystal Cave
29

Marble Fork

Wuksachi Village
25

■ Tokapah Falls Trail

26 **Lodgepole**
■ Wolverton

■ General Sherman Tree

27 ■ Thorp's Log
■ Crescent Meadow

Giant Forest
Moro Rock-
28 ■ Moro Rock
Crescent Meadow Road

Middle Fork

Mount Whitney ▲

Sequoia National Park

Kern River

Pacific Crest Trail

Kaweah River

Three Rivers
31

198

Foothills Visitor Center ■

Lookout Point ■

Atwell Mill ■

Cold Springs ■

East Fork

30 **Mineral King** ■

Mosquito Lakes ■

Lake Kaweah

Inyo National Forest

South Fork

■ South Fork

0 ———— 10 miles

0 ———— 15 km

Sequoia National Forest

Golden Trout Wilderness

the area. ⊠ *Kings Canyon Hwy./Hwy. 180, 1 mi from Big Stump Entrance,* ☎ *559/565–4307.*

★ ⓴ A spectacular 30-mi descent along **Kings Canyon Highway** takes about an hour from Grant Grove to the end of the road, where you can hike, camp, or turn right around for the drive back up. Built by convict labor in the 1930s, the road (usually closed from mid-October through April) clings to some dramatic cliffs along the way: watch out for falling rocks. The highway passes the scars where large groves of sequoias were felled at the beginning of the 20th century. It runs along the south fork and through dry hills covered with yuccas that bloom in the summer. There are amazing views into the deepest gorge in the United States (deeper even than the Grand Canyon), at the confluence of the two forks, and up the canyons to the High Sierra.

⓴ **Hume Lake,** a reservoir built in the early 1900s by loggers, is now the site of several church-affiliated camps, a gas station, and a public campground. This small lake off King's Canyon Highway outside Kings Canyon's borders has views of high mountains in the distance. ⊠ *Hwy. 180 northeast 8 mi from Grant Grove off Hume Lake Rd.*

⓴ **Cedar Grove,** in a valley that snakes along the south fork of the Kings River, was named for the incense cedars that grow in the area. At **Cedar Grove Village** (☎ 559/565–3793) you can rent horses, a good way to continue your explorations. Campgrounds, lodgings, a small visitor center, a snack bar, a cafeteria, a convenience market, and a gift shop round out the facilities. ⊠ *At end of Hwy. 180 east.*

About 4½ mi southeast of Cedar Grove Village are the short trails that circle **Zumwalt Meadow.** The trails from Zumwalt Meadow lead to the base of **Roaring River Falls.** Hikers can self-register for wilderness permits at **Road's End,** 6 mi east of Cedar Grove Village. Permits are free and are given out on a first-come, first-served basis from mid-May to late September. You can also pay $10 for a reservation if you make it more than 21 days in advance. ☎ *559/565–3766.*

Dining, Lodging, and Camping

$ ✕⊡ **Cedar Grove Lodge.** Although accommodations are close to the road, Cedar Grove manages to deliver peace and quiet. Book far in advance—the lodge has only 21 rooms. Each room has two queen-size beds, and three have kitchenettes. You can order trout, hamburgers, hot dogs, and sandwiches at the snack bar ($–$$) and take them to one of the picnic tables along the river's edge. ⊠ *Kings Canyon Hwy., 31 mi east of Grant Grove Village, Sequoia Kings Canyon Park Services Co., 5755 E. Kings Canyon Rd., Suite 101, Fresno, 93727,* ☎ *559/335–5500,* 𝔽𝔸𝕏 *559/335–5507,* 𝖶𝖤𝖡 *www.sequoia-kingscanyon.com. 18 rooms. Kitchenettes (some), snack bar; no room phones, no room TVs. AE, D, DC, MC, V. Closed mid-Oct.–mid-May.*

$ ✕⊡ **Grant Grove Cabins.** Some of the wood-panel cabins here have heaters, electric lights, and private baths, but most have woodstoves, battery lamps, and shared baths. Those who don't mind roughing it might opt for the tents. The Grant Grove Restaurant ($–$$), a family-style coffee shop, serves American standards for breakfast, lunch, and dinner. ⊠ *Kings Canyon Hwy. in Grant Grove Village, Sequoia Kings Canyon Park Services Co., 5755 E. Kings Canyon Rd., Suite 101, Fresno, 93727,* ☎ *559/335–5500,* 𝔽𝔸𝕏 *559/335–5507,* 𝖶𝖤𝖡 *www. sequoia-kingscanyon.com. 36 cabins, 9 with bath; 19 tents. Coffee shop. AE, D, DC, MC, V. Closed mid-Oct.–mid-May.*

$$–$$$ ⊡ **John Muir Lodge.** This modern timber-sided lodge is nestled in a wooded area near Grant Grove Village. The 30 rooms and six suites all have queen beds and private baths. There's a comfortable lobby with

a stone fireplace, but no restaurant. ⊠ *Kings Canyon Hwy., ¼ mi north of Grant Grove Village, Sequoia Kings Canyon Park Services Co., 5755 E. Kings Canyon Rd., Suite 101, Fresno, 93727,* ☎ *559/335–5500,* FAX *559/335–5507,* WEB *www.sequoia-kingscanyon.com. 24 rooms, 6 suites. Meeting room; no air-conditioning, no room TVs. AE, D, DC, MC, V.*

$–$$ ⊡ **Montecito-Sequoia Lodge.** In Sequoia National Forest just south of Kings Canyon National Park, this family-oriented resort specializes in all-inclusive holidays that include all meals and activities. It offers everything from skiing and snowboarding in winter to sailing and horseback riding in summer. ⊠ *Generals Hwy., 11 mi south of Grant Grove,* ☎ *559/565–3388 or 800/227–9900,* FAX *650/967–0540,* WEB *www.montecitosequoia.com. 32 rooms, 13 cabins. Dining room, snack bar, tennis court, pool, lake, bicycles, volleyball, boating, waterskiing, fishing, archery, hiking, horseback riding, cross-country skiing, sledding, children's programs (seasonal; ages 2–18); no air-conditioning, no room phones, no room TVs. AE, D, MC, V.*

⚠ **Azalea Campground.** One of three campgrounds in the Grant Grove area (the other two are Sunset and Crystal Springs, both open May–September only), Azalea is open year-round. It sits at 6,500 ft amid giant sequoias yet is close to restaurants, stores, and other facilities. Some sites at Azalea are wheelchair accessible. The campground can accommodate RVs up to 30 ft. *Flush toilets, dump station (nearby), drinking water, showers (nearby), bear boxes, fire grates, picnic tables, public telephone. 113 sites (tent or RV).* ⊠ *Kings Canyon Hwy., ¼ mi north of Grant Grove Village,* ☎ *559/565–3341.* ▨ *$14. Reservations not accepted. No credit cards.* ۞ *Year-round.*

⚠ **Sentinel Campground.** Of the three campgrounds in the Cedar Grove area (the other two are Sheep Creek and Moraine, both open June–September only), Sentinel is open the longest. At 4,600 ft and within walking distance of Cedar Grove Village, it fills up fast in the summer. Some sites are wheelchair accessible, and the campground can accommodate RVs up to 30 ft. Nearby, there are laundry facilities, a restaurant, a general store, and a ranger station. ⊠ *Flush toilets, dump station, drinking water, showers, bear boxes, fire grates, picnic tables, public telephone. 82 sites (tent or RV).* ⊠ *Kings Canyon Hwy., ¼ mi west of Cedar Grove Village,* ☎ *559/565–3341.* ▨ *$14. Reservations not accepted. No credit cards.* ۞ *Apr.–Oct.*

Outdoor Activities and Sports

The primary activity in Kings Canyon is hiking. Bicycling is discouraged, because the only paved roads outside village areas are the Kings Canyon and Generals highways, both winding mountain roads with heavy traffic. Horseback riding is an enjoyable alternative in summer. Winter snows turn the park into a playground for cross-country skiers and snowshoers, and there are dedicated areas for sledding. Check with the visitors center for current conditions and trail maps.

HORSEBACK RIDING

For horseback rides in the wilderness, head to **Cedar Grove Pack Station** (☎ 559/565–3464 in summer; 559/337–2314 in winter). **Grant Grove Stables** (☎ 559/335–9292 or 559/335–9292 in summer; 559/564–3839 in winter) organizes rides of various lengths.

WINTER SPORTS

Pick up ski and snowshoe rentals (sleds are for sale only) at **Grant Grove Village Market** (☎ 559/565–5500 Ext 1611).

Along Generals Highway

Generals Highway begins south of Grant Grove, continuing through the lower portion of Kings Canyon National Park and through a section of the Sequoia National Forest before entering Sequoia National Park.

★ ❷ The **Redwood Mountain Grove** is the largest grove of sequoias in the world. As you exit Kings Canyon on the Generals Highway, several paved turnouts allow you to look out over the grove (and into the smog of the Central Valley). The grove itself is accessible only on foot or horseback.

❷ **Kings Canyon Overlook,** a large turnout on the north side of the Generals Highway less than 2 mi from Redwood Mountain Grove, has views across the canyon of mountain peaks and the backcountry. If you drive east on Highway 180 to Cedar Grove along the south fork, you will see these canyons at much closer range.

Lodging

$ 🏨 **Stony Creek.** Sitting at 6,800 ft among the peaceful pines, Stony Creek is on national forest land between Grant Grove and Giant Forest. Rooms are plain but are carpeted and have private showers. A pizza parlor is adjacent to the lodge. ✉ *Generals Hwy., between Sequoia and Kings Canyon parks, Sequoia National Forest, Sequoia Kings Canyon Park Services Co., 5755 E. Kings Canyon Rd., Suite 101, Fresno, 93727,* ☎ *559/565–3909,* FAX *559/565–3913,* WEB *www.sequoia-kingscanyon.com. 11 rooms. Pizzeria; no air-conditioning, no room phones, no room TVs. AE, D, DC, MC, V.*

Wuksachi Village to Giant Forest

21 mi south of Grant Grove on Generals Hwy.

❷ **Wuksachi Village** is the northern gateway to Sequoia National Park. The dining and lodging facilities here have replaced the antiquated facilities of the old Giant Forest Village, most of which has been demolished. There's also a gift shop. ✉ *Generals Hwy., 21 mi south of Grant Grove.*

❷ **Lodgepole** sits in a canyon on the Marble Fork of the Kaweah River. Lodgepole pines, rather than sequoias, grow here because the U-shape canyon funnels in air from the high country that is too cold for the big trees. This area has a campground, a market and deli, a public laundry, a gift shop, and a post office. A pizza stand, an ice cream parlor, and showers are open in the summer only. The **Lodgepole Visitor Center** has the most extensive exhibits in Sequoia or Kings Canyon, a small theater that shows films about the parks, and a first-aid center. You can buy tickets for the Crystal Cave, get advice from park rangers, purchase maps and books, and pick up wilderness permits (except during summer, when they're available from 7 to 4 at the permit office next door). The **Tokopah Falls Trail** is an easy and rewarding 3½-mi round-trip hike from the Lodgepole Campground up the Marble Fork of the Kaweah River. The walk to the 1,200-ft falls, which flow down granite cliffs, is the closest you can get to the high country without substantial wear and tear on your hiking boots. Trail maps are available at the Lodgepole Visitor Center. Bring insect repellent during the summer; the mosquitoes can be ferocious. ✉ *Generals Hwy., 5 mi south of Wuksachi Village,* ☎ *559/565–3782.* ☉ *Mid-June–Labor Day, daily 8–6; Labor Day–mid-June, Fri.–Mon. 9–4:30.*

★ The most famous sequoia in the Giant Forest area is the **General Sherman Tree,** off the Generals Highway 3 mi south of Lodgepole and about 1 mi north of the Giant Forest. Benches allow you to sit and contemplate the tree's immensity: weighing in at 2.7 million pounds, it has the greatest volume of any living thing in the world. The first major branch is 130 ft above the ground. The paved **Congress Trail,** a very popular 2-mi hike, starts at the General Sherman Tree and loops through the heart of the Giant Forest. In the 1–2 hours it takes to complete the loop you will pass groups of trees known as the House and Senate and individual trees called the President and McKinley.

🔴27 **Giant Forest** is known for its trails through a series of sequoia groves. You can get the best views of the big trees from the park's meadows, where flowers are in full bloom by June or July. The outstanding ex-
★ hibits at the **Giant Forest Museum,** opened in 2002, trace the ecology of the giant sequoia. Though the museum is housed in a historic building, it is entirely wheelchair accessible. The **Big Trees Trail,** a ⅓-mi wheelchair-accessible paved trail, is easy to reach from the Giant Forest Museum. ⊠ *4 mi south of Lodgepole on Generals Hwy.*

🔴28 The **Moro Rock–Crescent Meadow Road** is a 3-mi spur road (closed in winter) that begins just south of the old Giant Forest Village and leads to Crescent and Log Meadows, passing several landmarks along the way. The Auto Log is a wide fallen tree that you can drive onto; it's a great place to pose for photographs. The road also passes through the Tunnel Log, which is exactly that. If your vehicle is too tall—7 ft 9 inches or more—a bypass is provided. John Muir called **Crescent Meadow** the "gem of the Sierra"—brilliant wildflowers bloom here by midsummer; a nearly 2-mi trail loops around the meadow. A 1½-mi round-trip trail that begins at Crescent Meadow leads to **Tharp's Log,** named for Hale Tharp, who built a pioneer cabin (still standing) out of a fire-
★ hollowed sequoia. **Moro Rock,** an immense granite monolith, stands along Moro Rock–Crescent Meadow Road, rising 6,725 ft from the edge of the Giant Forest. Four hundred steps lead to the top; the trail often climbs along narrow ledges over steep drops. The view from the top is striking. To the southwest you look down the Kaweah River to Three Rivers, Lake Kaweah, and—on clear days—the Central Valley and the Coast Range. To the northeast are views of the High Sierra. Thousands of feet below lies the middle fork of the Kaweah River.

★ ✋ 🔴29 Discovered in 1918 by two park employees, **Crystal Cave** is the best known of Sequoia's many caverns. Its interior, which was formed from limestone that metamorphosed into marble, is decorated with stalactites and stalagmites of various shapes, sizes, and colors. To visit the cave, you must first stop at the Lodgepole Visitor Center or the Foothills Visitor Center at Ash Mountain (on the Generals Highway, 1 mi inside Sequoia National Park) to buy tickets; *tickets are not sold at the cave.* Drive to the end of a narrow, twisting 7-mi road off the Generals Highway, 2.2 mi south of the old Giant Forest Village. From the parking area it's a 15-minute hike down a steep path to the cave's entrance. It's cool inside—48°F—so bring a sweater. ⊠ *Crystal Cave Rd. off Generals Hwy.,* ☎ *559/565–3759,* 🌐 *www.sequoiahistory.org.* 🔲 *$8.* ⊙ *Call for tour times.*

Dining, Lodging, and Camping

$–$$ ✗ **Wuksachi Village Dining Room.** In the high-ceiling dining room at
★ Sequoia's only white-tablecloth restaurant, huge windows run the length of the room so you can look out on the trees. The southwestern menu borrows elements from Asian cooking, and although some items are a bit too ambitious, this is the best place to eat in either park.

⊠ *Wuksachi Village,* ☎ *559/565–4070. Reservations essential. AE, D, DC, MC, V.*

$$–$$$ 🏨 **Wuksachi Village.** Three cedar-and-stone lodge buildings house
★ comfortable rooms with modern amenities. Set at 7,200 ft above sea
level, many of them have spectacular views of the surrounding mountains. ⊠ *Wuksachi Village,* ☎ *559/253–2199 or 888/252–5757,* FAX
559/456–0542, WEB *www.visitsequoia.com. 102 rooms. Restaurant, bar,
in-room data ports, refrigerators, hiking, cross-country skiing, meeting room; no air-conditioning, no room TVs. AE, D, DC, MC, V.*

⚠ **Buckeye Flat Campground.** This tents-only campground at the
southern end of Sequoia National Park is smaller—and consequently
quieter—than the larger campgrounds elsewhere in the park. *Flush toilets, drinking water, bear boxes, fire grates, picnic tables. 28 sites.* ⊠
Generals Hwy., 6 mi north of Foothills Visitor Center, ☎ *559/565–
3341. Reservations not accepted. No credit cards.* ☯ *Apr.–Labor Day.*

⚠ **Lodgepole Campground.** The largest of the campgrounds in the
Lodgepole area is also the noisiest, though things do quiet down at night.
Rest rooms are nearby. Lodgepole and Dorst (a mile or so to the west)
are the two campgrounds within Sequoia that accept reservations (up
to five months in advance for stays between mid-May and mid-October). *Flush toilets, dump station, drinking water, laundry facilities, showers, bear boxes, fire grates, picnic tables, public telephone, general store.
214 sites (tent and RV).* ⊠ *Off Generals Hwy. beyond Lodgepole Village,* ☎ *559/565–3341 Ext. 2 for information; 800/365–2267 for
reservations,* WEB *www.reservations.nps.gov. Reservations essential. D,
MC, V.* ☯ *Year-round.*

⚠ **Potwisha Campground.** On the Marble Fork of the Kaweah River,
this mid-size campground with attractive surroundings sits at 2,100
ft. Some sites are wheelchair accessible, and RVs up to 30 ft long can
camp here. *Flush toilets, dump station, drinking water, bear boxes, fire
grates, picnic tables, public telephone. 42 sites (tent and RV).* ⊠ *Generals Hwy., 4 mi north of Foothills Visitor Center,* ☎ *559/565–3341.
Reservations not accepted. No credit cards.* ☯ *Year-round.*

Outdoor Activities and Sports

As in Kings Canyon, hiking is the number one outdoor activity in Sequoia National Park. In winter you can ski, snowshoe, and sled, and
in summer mule rides are available. The visitor center always has information on trail conditions.

MULE RIDES

The **Wolverton Pack Station** (⊠ Off Generals Hwy., between General
Sherman Tree and Lodgepole Village, ☎ 559/565–3039 or 520/855–
5885, WEB www.muleriding.com) is the starting point for mule rides
through the park.

WINTER SPORTS

You can rent winter sports equipment at **Wuksachi Village Market** (☎
559/565–3435).

Mineral King

③⓪ *52 mi south of Lodgepole on Generals Hwy. and Mineral King Rd.*

The Mineral King area was incorporated into Sequoia National Park
in 1978. It is accessible from Memorial Day weekend through October (weather permitting) by a narrow, twisting, steep road (trailers and
RVs are prohibited) off Highway 198 several miles outside the park
entrance. This is a tough but exciting 25-mi drive (budget 90 minutes

each way) to an alpine valley. There are two campgrounds and a ranger station here. Facilities are limited, but some supplies are available. Many backpackers use this as a trailhead. Fine day-hiking trails lead from here as well.

Lodging and Camping

$–$$$$ 🏨 **Silver City Resort.** High on the Mineral King Road, this resort offers an alternative to staying at one of the more crowded properties at lower elevations of the park. Lodgings range from modern Swiss-style chalets to rustic traditional alpine cabins. There are a small general store and restaurant on site ($-$$), though the latter serves Thursday through Monday only. Some cabins share a central shower and bath. The beach is creek-side. ⊠ *Mineral King Rd., 20 mi east of Rte. 198, 93271,* ☎ *559/561–3223 or 805/528–2730,* 🅵🅰🆇 *805/528–8039,* 🆆🅴🅱 *www. silvercityresort.com. 13 cabins. Restaurant, in-room data ports (some), kitchenettes (some), beach, hiking; no air-conditioning, no room TVs, no phones in some rooms. MC, V. Closed Nov.–May.*

🏕 **Atwell Mill Campground.** Set at 6,650 ft, this tents-only campground is just south of the Western Divide. There are telephones and a general store at the nearby Silver City Resort. *Pit toilets, drinking water, bear boxes, fire grates, picnic tables. 21 sites.* ⊠ *Mineral King Rd., 20 mi east of Rte. 198,* ☎ *559/565–3341. Reservations not accepted. No credit cards.* ⊙ *May–Sept.*

🏕 **Cold Springs Campground.** At the end of Mineral King Road, this tents-only campground sits up high at 7,500 ft. You can hike to the spectacular high country from here. *Pit toilets, drinking water, cold showers, bear boxes, picnic tables, public phones, general store, ranger station. 40 sites.* ⊠ *At end of Mineral King Rd.,* ☎ *559/565–3341. Reservations not accepted. No credit cards.* ⊙ *May–Sept.*

Three Rivers

③① *8 mi south of Ash Mountain/Foothills entrance to Sequoia National Park on Hwy. 198.*

In the foothills of the Sierra along the Kaweah River, Three Rivers is a leafy hamlet whose livelihood depends largely on tourism from Sequoia and Kings Canyon national parks. The parks' main gateway town is a good spot to find a room when park lodgings are full.

Dining and Lodging

$$–$$$ ✕ **Gateway Restaurant and Lodge.** The patio of this local favorite overlooks the Kaweah River. Dishes include a half rack of baby-back ribs and a large portion of eggplant parmigiana. Reservations are essential on weekends. ⊠ *45978 Sierra Dr.,* ☎ *559/561–4133. AE, D, MC, V. No breakfast Tues.–Wed.*

$–$$ ✕ **Noisy Water.** The name of this restaurant comes from the Kaweah River, which flows within view of the many windows. You can try eggs, pancakes, or French toast for breakfast; a grilled burger on sourdough for lunch; and a 16-ounce T-bone for dinner. Items geared toward vegetarians and health-conscious diners are available as well. Stunning views of the river can be had from the glass-enclosed patio. ⊠ *41775 Sierra Dr.,* ☎ *559/561–4517. AE, MC, V. Closed Wed.*

$$–$$$ 🏨 **Cinnamon Creek Ranch.** Rooms have mountain views at this 10-acre ranch with resident donkeys. One room has a private terrace overlooking the river. ⊠ *Box 54, 93271,* ☎ *559/561–1107,* 🆆🅴🅱 *www. cinnamoncreek.com. 2 rooms, 2 cabins. Kitchenettes (some), in-room VCRs, hot tub, hiking; no smoking. AE, MC, V. CP.*

$–$$$ 🏨 **Lazy J Ranch Motel.** In the foothills of the Sierra Nevada alongside the Kaweah River lies this single-story motel. Some rooms have fireplaces. ✉ *39625 Sierra Dr., 93271,* ☎ *559/561–4449 or 800/341–8000,* FAX *559/561–4889,* WEB *www.bestvalueinn.com/Lodges/W031.htm. 11 rooms, 7 cottages. Picnic area, kitchenettes (some), refrigerators, cable TV, in-room VCRs, pool, fishing, playground, laundry facilities, some pets allowed; no smoking. AE, D, DC, MC, V. CP.*

\$–\$\$ 🖥 **Sierra Lodge.** Hundred-year-old oak trees surround this property, which is near the entrance to Sequoia National Park and Lake Kaweah. The lodge has mountain views and a small library. Some rooms have fireplaces. ✉ *43175 Sierra Dr. (Rte. 198), 93271,* ☎ *559/561–3681 or 800/367–8879,* FAX *559/561–3264,* WEB *www.sierra-lodge.com. 22 rooms, 5 suites. Picnic area, kitchenettes (some), refrigerators, pool, some pets (fee). AE, D, DC, MC, V. CP.*

\$ 🖥 **Best Western Holiday Lodge.** This two-story stucco lodge is 8 mi from Sequoia National Park and 4 mi from Lake Kaweah. The lobby has a stone fireplace and Navajo-print fabrics. ✉ *40105 Sierra Dr., 93271,* ☎ *559/561–4119,* FAX *559/561–3427,* WEB *www. bestwesterncalifornia.com. 54 rooms. Refrigerators, cable TV, pool, hot tub, playground, some pets allowed (fee). AE, D, MC, V. CP.*

Outdoor Activities and Sports

Contact the **Sequoia Natural History Association** (HCR 89, Box 10, 93271 ☎ 559/565–3759, WEB www.sequoiahistory.org) for information on bird-watching in the southern Sierra.

THE SOUTHERN SIERRA A TO Z

To research prices, get advice from other travelers, and book travel arrangements, visit www.fodors.com.

AIR TRAVEL

Fresno Yosemite International Airport is the nearest airport to Kings Canyon and Sequoia national parks. Alaska, American, America West, Allegiance, Continental, Delta, Northwest, Horizon, United Express, US Airways, and several regional carriers. *See* Air Travel *in* Smart Travel Tips A to Z for airline phone numbers.

➤ AIRPORT INFORMATION: **Fresno Yosemite International Airport** (✉ 5175 E. Clinton Ave., ☎ 559/498–4095).

BUS TRAVEL

Greyhound serves Fresno, Merced, and Visalia from many California cities. VIA Adventures runs three daily buses from Merced to Yosemite Valley; buses also depart daily from Mariposa. The 2½- to 4½-hour trip from Merced costs \$38 per person round-trip, which includes admission to the park.

➤ BUS INFORMATION: **Greyhound** (☎ 800/231–2222). **VIA Adventures** (✉ 710 W. 16th St., Merced, ☎ 209/384–1315 or 800/369–7275).

CAMPING

In the national parks you can camp only in designated areas, but in the national forests you can pitch a tent anywhere you want, so long as there are no signs specifically prohibiting camping in that area. Always know and obey fire regulations; you can find out what they are in your area by checking with Forest Service rangers, either by telephone or at any of the ranger stations just inside park boundaries.

Most of Yosemite's 14 campgrounds are in Yosemite Valley and along the Tioga Road. Glacier Point and Wawona have one each. Several campgrounds operate on a first-come, first-served basis year-round (some 400 of the park's sites remain open year-round), while some take reservations in high season; during summer reservations are strongly recommended. It's sometimes possible to get a campsite on arrival by stopping at the campground reservations office in Yosemite Valley, but this is a risky strategy. Yosemite Campground Reservations handles all bookings for the reservable campgrounds within the park. During the last two weeks of each month, beginning on the 15th, you can reserve a site up to five months in advance. Yosemite Concession Services Corporation handles reservations for the tent-cabin and other sites at Curry Village and for the camping shelters at Housekeeping Camp.

Except for Lodgepole and Dorst in Sequoia, all sites at the campgrounds near each of the major tourist centers in Kings Canyon and Sequoia parks are assigned on a first-come, first-served basis; on weekends in July and August they are often filled by Friday afternoon. Lodgepole, Potwisha, and Azalea campsites stay open all year, but Lodgepole is not plowed, and camping is limited to snow-tenting or recreational vehicles in plowed parking lots. Other campgrounds in Sequoia and Kings Canyon are open from whenever the snow melts until late September or early October.

RVs and trailers are permitted in most national park campgrounds, though space is scarce at some. The length limit is 40 ft for RVs and 35 ft for trailers, but the park service recommends that trailers be no longer than 22 ft. Disposal stations are available in most of the main camping areas.

➤ CONTACTS: **Inyo National Forest** (☎ 760/873–2400, FAX 760/873–2458, WEB www.r5.fs.fed.us/inyo). **Lodgepole/Dorst campgrounds** (☎ 559/565–3774 or 800/365–2267). **Sequoia Campgrounds** (☎ 559/565–3341). **Sequoia National Forest** (☎ 559/784–1500, FAX 559/781–4744, WEB www.r5.fs.fed.us/sequoia). **Yosemite Campground Reservations** (☎ 800/436–7275, WEB reservations.nps.gov). **Yosemite Concession Services Corporation** (☎ 559/252–4848, WEB www.yosemitepark.com).

CAR RENTAL

The car-rental outlets closest to the southern Sierra are at Fresno Yosemite International Airport, where the national chains have outlets. *See* Car Rental *in* Smart Travel Tips A to Z for national rental agency phone numbers.

CAR TRAVEL

From San Francisco I–80 and I–580 are the fastest routes toward the Sierra Nevada. Through the Central Valley, I–5 and Highway 99 are the fastest north–south routes. To get to Yosemite, plan on driving 4–5 hours. Enter the park either on Highway 140, which is the best route in inclement weather, or on Highway 120, which is the fastest route when the roads are clear. To get to Kings Canyon, plan on a six-hour drive. Two major routes, Highways 180 and 198, intersect with Highway 99 (Highway 180 is closed east of Grant Grove in winter). To get to Mammoth Lakes in summer and early fall (or whenever snows aren't blocking Tioga Road), you can travel via Highway 120 (to Route 395 south) through the Yosemite high country; the quickest route in winter is I–80 to Route 50 to Highway 207 (Kingsbury Grade) to Route 395 south; either route takes 6–7 hours.

Keep your tank full, especially in winter. Distances between gas stations can be long, and there is no fuel available in Yosemite Valley, Kings Canyon, or Sequoia. If you're traveling from October through April, rain on the coast can mean heavy snow in the mountains. Carry tire chains, and know how to put them on (on I–80 and Route 50 you can pay a chain installer $20 to do it for you, but on other routes you'll have to do it yourself). Always check road conditions before you leave.

Traffic in national parks in summer can be heavy, and there are sometimes travel restrictions.

➤ CONTACTS: **Northern California Road Conditions** (☎ 800/427–7623). **Sequoia–Kings Canyon Road and Weather Information** (☎ 559/565–3341). **Yosemite Area Road and Weather Conditions** (☎ 209/372–0200).

EMERGENCIES

In an emergency dial 911.

➤ EMERGENCY SERVICES: **Mammoth Hospital** (✉ 185 Sierra Park Rd., Mammoth Lakes, ☎ 760-934-3311). **Yosemite Medical Clinic** (✉ Ahwahnee Rd. north of Northside Dr., ☎ 209/372–4637).

LODGING

Most lodgings in the southern Sierra are simple and basic. A number of agencies can help you find a room.

➤ RESERVATION SERVICES:: **Kings Canyon Lodging** (☎ 559/335–5500). **Mammoth Lakes Visitors Bureau Lodging Referral** (☎ 760/934–2712 or 888/466–2666). **Mammoth Reservations** (☎ 760/934–5571 or 800/223–3032). **Sequoia Lodging** (☎ 559/561–3314 or 888/252–5757). **Three Rivers Reservation Center** (☎ 559/561–0410). **Yosemite Concession Services Corporation** (☎ 559/252–4848, WEB www.yosemitepark.com).

TOURS

California Parlor Car Tours, in San Francisco, serves Yosemite. Lodging and some meals are included with the rail fare. VIA Adventures runs bus tours from Merced to Yosemite Valley. For $63 you get transportation, lunch, park admission, and a two-hour tour.

➤ CONTACTS: **California Parlor Car Tours** (☎ 415/474–7500 or 800/227–4250, WEB www.calpartours.com). **VIA Adventures** (✉ 710 W. 16th St., Merced, ☎ 209/384–1315 or 800/369–7275).

VISITOR INFORMATION

➤ CONTACTS: **Bridgeport Chamber of Commerce** (✉ Box 541, Bridgeport 93517, ☎ 760/932–7500, WEB www.ca-biz.com/bridgeportchamber). **Lee Vining Chamber of Commerce** (✉ Box 29, Lee Vining, 93541, ☎ 760/647–6595, WEB www.monolake.org/chamber). **Mammoth Lakes Visitors Bureau** (✉ Box 48, along Hwy. 203 [Main St.], near Sawmill Cutoff Rd., 93546, ☎ 760/934–2712 or 888/466–2666). **Mono Lake** (✉ Box 49, Lee Vining 93541, ☎ 760/647–3044, WEB www.monolake.org). **National Park Service** (✉ Three Rivers, 93271, ☎ 559/565–3341 or 559/565–3134, WEB www.nps.gov/seki). **Yosemite Concession Services Corporation** (☎ 209/372–1000, WEB www.yosemitepark.com). **Yosemite National Park** (✉ Information Office, Box 577, Yosemite National Park, 95389, ☎ 209/372–0200 or 209/372–0264, WEB www.nps.gov/yose). **Yosemite Sierra Visitors Bureau** (✉ 40637 Hwy. 41, Box 1998, Oakhurst 93644, ☎ 559/683–4636, WEB www.yosemite-sierra.org).

11 DEATH VALLEY AND THE MOJAVE DESERT

WITH THE OWENS VALLEY

When most people assemble their must-see list of California attractions, the desert isn't often among the top contenders. With its heat and vast, sparsely populated tracts of land, the desert is no Disneyland. But that's precisely why it deserves a closer look. The natural riches here are overwhelming: rolling waves of sand dunes, black cinder cones thrusting up hundreds of feet from blistered desert floors, riotous sheets of wildflowers, and an abundant silence that is both dramatic and startling. A single car speeding down an empty road can sound as loud as a low-flying airplane.

Revised by
Veronica Hill
and Susan D.
Lawson

D UST AND DESOLATION, tumbleweeds and rattlesnakes—mention the word *desert*, and most people envision a bleak and barren landscape. True, all these things do exist east of the Sierra Nevada, where the land quickly flattens out and where rain seldom falls. But the desert is much more. Death Valley, an area of low desert, drops to almost 300 ft below sea level and contains the lowest spot on land in the western hemisphere. To the south of Death Valley lies the Mojave Desert, which stretches from the base of the San Bernardino Mountains, northeast of Los Angeles, all the way to the Colorado River. The Mojave, with elevations ranging from 3,000 ft to 5,000 ft above sea level, is known as high desert. These remote regions hold a unique beauty found nowhere else in California. From vast open spaces populated with spiky Joshua trees to faulted mountains and mysterious moving rocks, the desert deserves a closer look. The Owens Valley is where the desert meets the mountains, its 80-mi width separating the depths of Death Valley from Mt. Whitney, the highest mountain in the continental United States. You can explore the wonders of Death Valley in the morning and head to the Sierra to cool off in the heat of the day.

Believe everything you've ever heard about desert heat: it can be brutal. Bring sunglasses, sunblock, a hat, and sufficient clothing to block the sun's rays and the wind. Because of the vast size of this region—it's about as big as Ohio—and the frequently extreme weather, plan your travel here carefully. Conveniences and facilities such as gas stations and supermarkets are few, so be sure to fill your gas tank whenever you can and check your vehicle's fluids and tire pressure frequently. At the start of each day load the car with 3 gallons of water per person, plus additional radiator water. Keep a cooler in your car, stocked with extra food. Reliable maps are a must, as signage is often limited or, in some places, nonexistent. Other important accessories include a compass and a cellular phone (though the signal may fade in remote areas). Shut off your car's air-conditioning on steep grades to avoid engine overheating. A pair of binoculars can come in handy, and don't forget your camera— you're likely to see things you've never seen before.

Pleasures and Pastimes

Camping
There's nothing like sleeping under a starry desert sky or amid a Sierra forest, but wherever you choose to pitch your tent, be prepared for weather extremes. Make sure your equipment can handle (and protect you from) the Mojave's hot sun or the sometimes freezing temperatures and sudden storms of the eastern Sierra. Campgrounds throughout the region are inexpensive or free, and sites tend to be primitive.

Dining
Throughout the desert and the eastern Sierra, dining is a fairly simple affair. The Owens Valley is home to many mom-and-pop eateries, as well as a few fast-food chains. The restaurants in Death Valley range from coffee shop to upscale Continental. In the Mojave there are chain establishments in Ridgecrest, Victorville, and Barstow, as well as some ethnic eateries.

CATEGORY	COST*
$$$$	over $30
$$$	$22–$30
$$	$15–$21
$	under $15

*per person for a main course at dinner, excluding tip and 7¼% tax

Hiking

Hiking trails are abundant throughout the desert and along the eastern base of the Sierra, meandering toward sights that you can't see from the road. Some of the best trails are unmarked; ask locals for directions. Whether at elevation or in the desert, wear sunblock and protective clothing such as a hat. Plan your desert walks for before or after the noonday sun and be wary of tarantulas, black widows, scorpions, snakes, and other potentially hazardous creatures (if you wear closed shoes and watch where you're walking, these shouldn't be a problem). Paths through canyons are sometimes partially shielded from the sun and not as hot, so if your time is limited, save these for midday.

Lodging

For a true American experience, visit one of the many historic Route 66 motels along the Mother Road, which travels through the heart of the Mojave Desert along I–40 and I–15. If you want to be pampered, stop at the nicest resort in the entire desert: the Furnace Creek Inn, at Death Valley.

CATEGORY	COST*
$$$$	over $225
$$$	$160–$225
$$	$100–$159
$	under $100

All prices are for a standard double room, excluding 7¼% tax.

Exploring Death Valley and the Mojave Desert

If your visit begins in Bishop, be sure to plan a day in the wilderness, as the eastern Sierra is famous for its trout fishing and hiking. Likewise, a visit to the Mojave Desert wouldn't be complete without a stop in Death Valley National Park, the hottest spot in the western hemisphere. To the south you can visit the Edwards Air Force Base Air Flight Test Center Museum, in Palmdale, to learn about the birthplace of supersonic flight. For a change of scenery, head to the mountain community of Wrightwood, which lies at the highest point along the San Andreas Fault. Back on the desert floor is the Mojave National Preserve, 1.4 million acres of sand dunes, volcanic cinder cones, rock-strewn mountains, and mile after mile of scrub brush. The eastern Mojave stretches to the Arizona border at the Colorado River, popular with water-sports enthusiasts.

Note: You may spot fossils at some of the archaeological sites in the desert. If you do, leave them where they are; it's against the law to remove fossils.

Numbers in the text correspond to numbers in the margin and on the Owens Valley and Death Valley map and the Mojave Desert map.

Great Itineraries

IF YOU HAVE 3 DAYS

Start in the eastern Sierra, taking a hike or casting a line near **Bishop** ①and paying a visit to the craggy trees of **Ancient Bristlecone Pine Forest.** Overnight in 🏨 **Independence** ②; then stop at the spooky **Manzanar National Historic Site** ③ and catch a glimpse of majestic **Mt. Whitney** on your way to **Death Valley National Park** ⑤–⑱. Stop for lunch at **Stovepipe Wells Village** ⑥; then spend the rest of the afternoon at **Scotty's Castle** ⑧ and **Ubehebe Crater** ⑨. Stay the night in 🏨 **Furnace Creek Village** ⑬ and explore the southern half of the park on day three. Be sure not to miss the vivid desert colors of **Artists Palette** ⑭, the western hemisphere's lowest spot, at **Badwater** ⑯, or the stunning panorama from **Dante's View** ⑱.

Spend two days exploring the many wonders of ▣ **Death Valley National Park** ⑤–⑱. On your third day head out of the park to ▣ **Ridgecrest** ㉑ for a hike through **Red Rock Canyon, Fossil Falls,** or **Trona Pinnacles Natural National Landmark.** If you're visiting on a spring or fall weekend, make advance arrangements at the Maturango Museum to tour **Petroglyph Canyons.** The next morning continue south to **Lancaster** ㉓ to see **Antelope Valley Poppy Reserve,** where poppies cover the hillsides as far as the eye can see. Move on to **Palmdale** ㉔ and its **Antelope Valley Indian Museum,** then drive to **Pearblossom** to pick up some ceramic tiles at **St. Andrew's Abbey.** Head for the mountains for a quiet evening strolling the village streets of ▣ **Wrightwood** ㉕. On the morning of day five, after a stop at **Big Pines Visitor Center,** at the highest point on the San Andreas Fault, venture north on I–15 into Route 66 country. In **Victorville** ㉖, the **California Route 66 Museum** tells the story of one of America's most famous roads and the **Roy Rogers–Dale Evans Museum** of one of America's most beloved celebrity couples. Heading for ▣ **Barstow** ㉗, get another hit of Route 66 nostalgia at **Casa del Desierto Harvey House,** site of the **Route 66 Mother Road Museum and Gift Shop.** Explore the Barstow area, including **Desert Discovery Center, Calico Ghost Town,** and **Rainbow Basin National Natural Landmark,** on day six. The next morning drive to **Mojave National Preserve** ㉙ to see **Kelso Dunes** and to tour **Mitchell Caverns,** in **Providence Mountains State Recreation Area.** If time and road conditions permit, drive through **Afton Canyon** on your way back to Barstow.

When to Tour Death Valley and the Mojave Desert

Spring and fall are the best seasons to tour the desert and Owens Valley. Winters are generally mild, but summers can be cruel. If you're on a budget, keep in mind that room rates drop as the temperatures rise. Early morning is the best time to visit sights and avoid crowds, but some museums and visitor centers don't open until 10. If you schedule your town arrivals for late afternoon, you can drop by the visitor centers just before closing hours to line up an itinerary for the next day. Plan indoor activities for midday during hotter months. Because relatively few people visit the desert, many attractions have limited hours of access: for instance, Petroglyph Canyon tours are given only on weekends in fall and spring, and the Calico Early Man Archeological Site does not offer tours Monday and Tuesday. Summer is best time to visit the Ancient Bristlecone Pine Forest, near Big Pine. During the winter snowpack may prohibit vehicles from entering the area.

OWENS VALLEY

Along U.S. 395 East of the Sierra Nevada

Lying in the shadow of the eastern Sierra Nevada, the Owens Valley stretches along U.S. 395 from the Mono/Inyo county line, in the north, to the town of Olancha, in the south. This stretch of highway is dotted with tiny towns, some with no more than a minimart and a gas station. If you are traveling from Yosemite National Park to Death Valley National Park or are headed from Lake Tahoe or Mammoth to the desert, U.S. 395 is your corridor.

Bishop

❶ *U.S. 395, 44 mi south of Mammoth Lakes.*

One of the biggest towns along U.S. 395, Bishop has views of the Sierra Nevada, and the White and Inyo mountains. First settled by the North-

Owens Valley and Death Valley

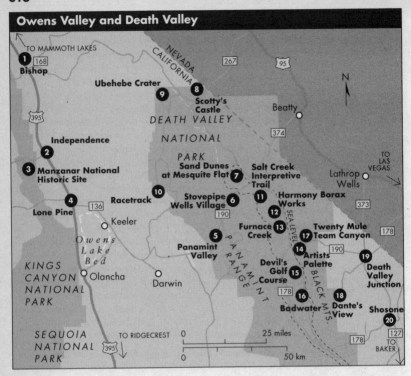

ern Paiute Indian tribe, the area was named in 1861 for cattle rancher Samuel Bishop, who established a camp here. The Paiute and Shoshone people still reside on four reservations in the area.

One of Bishop's biggest draws is its **Mule Days Celebration** each Memorial Day weekend. More than 40,000 tourists and RVers pack into this lazy town for the longest nonmotorized parade in the world, mule races, a rodeo, and good old-fashioned country-and-western concerts. ☎ 760/872–4263, WEB *www.muledays.org.*

🖑 ★ Train buffs are bound to enjoy the **Laws Railroad Museum**, a complex of historic buildings and train cars from the Carson and Colorado Railroad Company, which set up a narrow-gauge railroad yard here in 1883. Among the exhibits are a self-propelled car from the Death Valley Railroad and a full village of rescued buildings, including a post office, an 1883 train depot, the 1909 North Inyo Schoolhouse, and a restored 1900 ranch house. ⊠ *Rte. 6, 3 mi north of U.S. 395,* ☎ *760/873–5950,* WEB *www. mam-biz.com/lawsmuseum.* 🖼 *Donation requested.* ☉ *Daily 10–4.*

To learn about life in the Bishop region before white settlers arrived, visit the **Paiute-Shoshone Indian Cultural Center,** a museum on the Bishop Paiute Indian Reservation. Here you can see exhibits of early clothing, shelters, tools and basketry used by these tribes. ⊠ *2300 W. Line Rd.,* ☎ *760/873–4478,* WEB *www.paiute.com.* 🖼 *Donation requested.* ☉ *Daily 9–4.*

For those in the mood for some gambling, the Paiute tribe runs the **Paiute Palace Casino** on the reservation. ⊠ *2742 N. Sierra Hwy.,* ☎ *888/3–PAIUTE or 760/873–4150,* WEB *www.paiutepalace.com.*

Dining and Lodging

$–$$ ✕ **Whiskey Creek.** This Wild West–style saloon, restaurant, and gift shop has been serving up crisp salads, warm soups, and juicy barbecued steaks since 1924, making it a favorite spot for locals and tourists. On a warm day sit out on the shaded deck and enjoy one of their many microbrews. ⊠ *524 N. Main St.,* ☎ *760/873–7174. AE, MC, V.*

$ ✕ **Erick Schat's Bakery.** A popular stop for motorists traveling to and from Mammoth Lakes, this shop is chock-full of delicious pastries, cookies, rolls, and other baked goods. But the real reason to stop here is for the sheepherder bread, a hand-shaped and stone-hearth-baked sourdough introduced during the gold rush by immigrant Basque sheepherders—it's been baked here since 1907. In addition to the bakery, Schat's also has a gift shop and a sandwich bar. ⊠ *763 N. Main St.,* ☎ *760/873–7156. AE, MC, V.*

$–$$ ⊞ **Best Western Creekside Inn.** One of the nicest spots to stay in Bishop, this clean and comfortable mountain-style hotel is a good base from which to explore the town or go skiing and trout fishing nearby. In summer you can sit on the patio near a babbling creek. ⊠ *725 N. Main St.,* ☎ *760/872–3044 or 800/273–3550,* WEB *www.thesierraweb.com/ lodging/creeksideinn. 89 rooms. Cable TV, pool, hot tub, kitchenettes (some). AE, MC, V.*

Outdoor Activities and Sports

Sierra Mountain Center (⊠ 174 W. Line St., ☎ 760/873–8526, WEB www.sierramountaincenter.com) offers instruction and guided hiking, skiing, rock-climbing, and mountain-biking trips for all levels of experience. Some guided hiking trips explore the John Muir Trail. The horse-packing outfit **Rock Creek Pack Station** (⊠ Box 248, 93516, ☎ 760/935–4493 in summer; 760/872–8331 in winter, WEB www. rockcreekpackstation.com) runs 3- to 24-day trips in the High Sierra, including Mt. Whitney, Yosemite National Park, and other parts of the John Muir Wilderness. One expedition tracks wild mustangs through Inyo National Forest, another is an old-fashioned horse drive between the Owens Valley and the High Sierra.

The Owens Valley is trout country, its glistening alpine lakes and streams brimming with feisty rainbow, brown, brook, and golden trout. You can fish in Bishop year-round. Popular spots include Owens River, the Owens River gorge, and Pleasant Valley Reservoir. Some fishing is catch-and-release. Bishop hosts several fishing derbies throughout the year, including the very popular Blake Jones Blind Bogey Trout Derby, in March. Whether you want to take a fly-fishing class or a guided wade trip, **Brock's Flyfishing Specialists and Tackle Experts** (⊠ 100 N. Main St., ☎ 760/872–3581 or 888/619–3581, WEB www.brocksflyfish. com) is a valuable resource. **Osprey Lure** (⊠ 287 Academy Ave. #C, ☎ 760/873–0014, WEB www.ospreylure.com) will make you the fly you need to catch the big one.

En Route Traveling south from Bishop on U.S. 395, turn onto Route 168 and follow the signs 31 mi to the **Ancient Bristlecone Pine Forest** Here you can see some of the oldest living trees on earth, some of which date back more than 40 centuries. These rare, gnarled pines in the White Mountains can only grow in harsh, arcticlike conditions above 9,000 ft. At the **Schulman Grove Visitor Center** (⊠ ☎ 760/873–2500, WEB www.r5.fs.fed.us/inyo), open weekdays 8–4:30, you can learn about the bristlecone and take a walk to the 4,723-year-old Methuselah tree. Admission to the forest is free, but a donation is requested for the trail map.

Independence

➋ *U.S. 395, 43 mi south of Bishop.*

Named for a military outpost that was established near here in 1862, Independence is small and sleepy. But the town is certainly worth a stop and a little exploration on your way from the Sierra Nevada to Death Valley.

☺ As you approach Independence from the north, you pass the **Mt. Whitney Fish Hatchery,** a delightful place for a family picnic. Bring some dimes as there are machines filled with fish food, and the hatchery's lakes are full of hefty breeder trout looking for a handout. Built in 1915, the hatchery was one of the first trout farms in California, and today it produces fish to stock many of the lakes throughout the state. ⊠ *Fish Hatchery Rd., 1 mi north of Independence,* ☎ *760/878–2272.* ☒ *Free.* ◔ *Daily 8–5.*

The **Eastern California Museum** preserves the history of Inyo County. Highlights include a fine collection of Paiute and Shoshone Indian basketry and a yard full of agricultural implements used by early area miners and farmers. ⊠ *155 N. Grant St.,* ☎ *760/878–0364,* WEB *www.independence-ca.com.* ☒ *Donations accepted.* ◔ *Wed.–Mon. 10–4.*

OFF THE BEATEN PATH	**ONION VALLEY –** Thirteen miles west of Independence on Onion Valley Road, Onion Valley (so called because wild onions grow here) is one of the main access points to the eastern slope of the Sierra Nevada. At 9,600 ft, where the valley enters the John Muir Wilderness, a trailhead leads to popular Kearsarge Pass. The trail takes you through mountain valleys where glacial lakes team with trout, eventually reaching Kings Canyon National Park. If you make reservations, you can camp in Onion Valley. ⊠ *Off U.S. 395.*

Lodging

$ 🏨 **Winnedumah Hotel Bed & Breakfast.** Built in 1927, this B&B qualifies as the best digs in town. Celebrities such as Roy Rogers, John Wayne, and Bing Crosby have stayed here while filming movies nearby. Outfitted in a eclectic mix of Wild West chic and modern bric-a-brac, the rooms are simple yet comfortable. The Winnedumah also has hostel rooms, and breakfast is usually a hearty affair of bacon, eggs, waffles, and fresh fruit. ⊠ *211 N. Edwards St.,* ☎ *760/878–2040,* FAX *760/878–2833,* WEB *www.av.qnet.com. 24 rooms, 14 with bath. AE, D, DC, MC, V. BP.*

Manzanar National Historic Site

❸ *U.S. 395, 5 mi south of Independence.*

A reminder of an ugly episode in U.S. history, the remnants of the Manzanar War Relocation Center have been designated **Manzanar National Historic Site.** This is where some 10,000 Japanese-Americans were confined behind barbed-wire fences between 1942 and 1945. Manzanar was the first of 10 such internment camps erected by the federal government following Japan's attack on Pearl Harbor in 1941. In the name of national security, American citizens of Japanese descent were forcibly relocated to these camps, many of them losing their homes and businesses, and most of their possessions in the process. Today not much remains of Manzanar but for a guard post, the auditorium, and some concrete foundations. Stop at the entrance station to pick up a brochure, and drive the one-way dirt road past the ruins to a small cemetery where a monument stands as a reminder of what took place here. Signs mark where structures such as the barracks, hospital, school, and fire station once stood. Work is underway to restore the camp and create an interpretive center. ⊠ *Manzanar Information, c/o Superintendent: Death Valley National Park, Death Valley 92398,* ☎ *760/878–0062,* WEB *www.nps.gov/manz.* ☒ *Free.*

Lone Pine

4 *U.S. 395, 11 mi south of Manzanar National Historic Site.*

Named for a single pine tree found at the bottom of the canyon of the same name, Lone Pine supplied nearby gold- and silver-mining outposts in the 1860s. More than 300 movies and many TV shows and commercials have been filmed in and around the tiny community, making the nearby Alabama Hills a Hollywood icon. The Lone Pine Film Festival now takes place here every October. Lone Pine is where you'll find towering, majestic Mt. Whitney.

Drop by the Lone Pine Visitor Center for a map of the **Alabama Hills** and take a drive up Whitney Portal Road (turn west at the light) to this wonderland of granite boulders. Erosion has worn the rock smooth; some have been chiseled to leave arches and other formations. The hills have become a popular location for rock climbing. There are three campgrounds among the rocks, each with a stream for fishing. ⊠ *Whitney Portal Rd., 4½ mi west of Lone Pine.*

★ Straddling the border of Sequoia National Park and Inyo National Forest/John Muir Wilderness, **Mt. Whitney** (14,496 ft) is the highest mountain in the continental United States. A favorite game for travelers passing through Lone Pine is trying to guess which peak is Mt. Whitney. Almost no one gets it right because Mt. Whitney is hidden behind other peaks. There is no road that ascends the peak, but you can catch a glimpse of the mountain by driving curvy Whitney Portal Road west from Lone Pine into the mountains. The pavement ends at the trailhead to the top of the mountain, which is also the start of the 211-mi John Muir Trail from Mt. Whitney to Yosemite National Park. At the portal there are a restaurant (known for its pancakes) and a small store that mostly cater to hikers and campers staying at Whitney Portal Campground. You can see a waterfall from the parking lot and go fishing in a small trout pond. The portal area is closed mid-October–early May; the road closes when snow conditions require.

Climbers from around the world come to Mt. Whitney to tackle its slopes. The hike of 6,000 vertical ft and 11 mi is for experienced backcountry hikers only. If you want to climb Mt. Whitney, note that trailhead reservations are difficult to obtain. Permits are available through the **U.S. Forest Service** (⊠ 873 N. Main St., Bishop 93514, ☎ 760/873–2400, WEB www.r5.fs.fed.us/inyo) by a lottery held each February. In May a few permits become available if other hikers have canceled. ⊠ *Whitney Portal Rd., 13 mi west of Lone Pine,* ☎ *909/734–7726 or 760/876–0030,* WEB *www.whitneyportalstore.com.*

Dining, Lodging, and Camping

$$ ✕ **Seasons Restaurant.** This spot dishes up beef, veal, lamb, pasta, and fresh seafood in a number of preparations. ⊠ *206 S. Main St.,* ☎ *760/876–8927. AE, D, MC, V. No lunch.*

$ ✕ **Mt. Whitney Restaurant.** The best hamburgers in town aren't just your plain old beef burger—choices include ostrich, venison, and buffalo. There's also a gift shop on the premises. ⊠ *227 S. Main St.,* ☎ *760/876–5751. D, MC, V.*

$–$$ 🏨 **Best Western Frontier.** You're only minutes from the base of Mt. Whitney when you stay at this single-level property. Some rooms have views of the nearby Sierra Nevada, and all have in-room coffee and ironing boards. Continental breakfast is included in the price. ⊠ *1008 S. Main St.,* ☎ *760/876–5571,* FAX *760/876–5357,* WEB *www.bestwesterncalifornia.com. 73 rooms. In-room data ports, refrigerators, cable TV, pool, pets allowed. AE, D, DC, MC, V. CP.*

$–$$ 🏨 **Dow Villa Motel and Hotel.** John Wayne slept here, and you can, too. Built in 1923 to cater to the film industry, Dow Villa is in the center of Lone Pine. Some rooms have views of the mountains; both buildings are within walking distance of just about everything in town. There are in-room coffee and whirlpool tubs, though some of the hotel rooms share bathrooms. Pets are allowed only in smoking rooms. ✉ *310 S. Main St.,* ☎ *760/876–5521,* FAX *760/876–5643,* WEB *www.dowvillamotel.com. 91 rooms. In-room data ports, refrigerators, in-room VCRs, heated pool, hot tub, whirlpool tubs in deluxe rooms, no-smoking rooms. AE, D, DC, MC, V.*

🏕 **Boulder Creek RV Resort.** Near the base of Mt. Whitney, this campground has a hot tub, a playground, a small petting zoo, fishing, and hiking. The hookups include cable TV and Web TV. *Showers, flush toilets, full hookups, laundry facilities, fire pits, grills, pool. 53 RV sites, 10 tent sites.* ✉ *2550 U.S. 395,* ☎ *760/876–4243,* WEB *boulder-creekrv@webtv.net. AE, D, DC, MC, V.*

🏕 **Whitney Portal.** The campsites here are spread out beneath towering pines, adjacent to a small pond. The campground can accommodate tents or RVs up to 16 ft. The spot is popular with hikers, so it's best to call ahead. Whitney Portal also has a store and café that are open in summer. *Flush toilets, drinking water, showers (nearby), fire grates, picnic tables, public telephone (nearby), general store (nearby). 43 sites.* ✉ *Whitney Portal Rd., 13 mi west of Lone Pine,* ☎ *877/444–6777 or 760/867–6200,* FAX *760/876–6202,* WEB *www.reserveusa.com. Reservations essential. AE, D, MC, V.* ☉ *Early May–mid-Oct.*

En Route   As you drive Route 136 toward Death Valley, you will pass **Keeler** about 13 mi out of Lone Pine. Now a semi–ghost town, Keeler had a population of 300 in the 1880s and was the dumping site for silver, lead, and zinc gathered from the mine at Cerro Gordo, one of the greatest silver mines in California. A handful of people still live here, and many of the town's early structures still stand, including the old train station and remnants of the mill site that once processed the ore.

DEATH VALLEY

Anglo-Americans first learned of the existence of Death Valley in 1849, when wayward travelers looking for a shortcut to the California goldfields stumbled into the area and were temporarily stranded. By 1873 borax, the so-called white gold of the desert, was found in the valley, and 20-mule teams hauled borax out from 1883 to 1889.

The topography of Death Valley is a lesson in geology. Two hundred million years ago seas covered the area, depositing layers of sediment and fossils. Between 35 million and 5 million years ago faults in the earth's crust and volcanic activity pushed and folded the ground, causing mountain ranges to rise and the valley floor to drop. The valley was then filled periodically by lakes, which eroded the surrounding rocks into fantastic formations and deposited the salts that now cover the floor of the basin. The area has 14 square mi of sand dunes, 200 square mi of crusty salt flats, and hills, mountains, and canyons of many colors. If you have a four-wheel-drive vehicle, bring it, for many of Death Valley's most spectacular canyons are only reachable in a four-by-four.

There are more than 1,000 species of plants and trees here, 21 of which are unique to the valley, such as the yellow Panamint daisy and the blue-flowered Death Valley sage. Many annual plants lie dormant as seeds for all but a few months of the year, when spring rains trigger a bloom. At higher elevations you will find piñon, juniper, and bristlecone pine. Wildlife such as the bighorn sheep spend most of their time in rugged, secluded canyons and upper ridges. You may see coyotes lazing in the shade at lower elevations, and the smaller desert fox is a regular sight among the sand dunes.

Death Valley National Park

105 mi west of Lone Pine on Rtes. 136 and 190 (to Furnace Creek).

With more than 3.3 million acres (5,200 square mi), Death Valley National Park is America's largest national park outside Alaska. The Panamint Range parallels Death Valley, to the west; the Amargosa Range, to the east. Minerals and ores in the rugged, barren mountains turn them shades that range from green and yellow to brown, white, and black. Of course, Death Valley is hot: the park's record high temperature (and the record high for the entire United States), recorded in 1913, was 134°F. Seeing nature at its most extreme is precisely what attracts many people, especially Europeans. There are more visitors to Death Valley in July and August than in December and January. Despite its popularity, Death Valley is still an empty and lonely place. Distances here can be deceiving: some sights appear in clusters, but others require extensive travel. The 54-mi trip from Furnace Creek to Scotty's Castle, for example, can take two hours or more.

The park entrance fee is $10 per vehicle and $5 for those entering on foot, bus, bike, or motorcycle. Admission, valid for seven consecutive days, is collected at the park's entrance stations and at the visitor center at Furnace Creek. For information on Death Valley National Park, contact the National Park Service. ✉ *Box 579, Death Valley 92328,* ☎ *760/786–3200,* FAX *760/786–3283,* WEB *www.nps.gov/deva.*

⑤ The **Panamint Valley,** west of the forbidding Panamint Range, is a great place to stop if you are arriving late in the day and don't want to drive over the winding mountain roads into Death Valley after dark. The views here are spectacular. From Route 178 south of Route 190, turn north on Wildrose Canyon Road and east onto the dirt track leading to the **Charcoal Kilns** (✉ 9 mi east of Rte. 178). The drive will take about half an hour, but it's worth it. Ten stone kilns, each 30 ft high and 25 ft wide, stand as if on parade in a line up a mountain. The kilns, built by Chinese laborers in 1879, were used to burn wood from piñon pines to turn it into charcoal. The charcoal was then transported over the mountains into Death Valley, where it was used to extract lead and silver from the ore mined there. If you hike nearby Wildrose Peak, you will be rewarded with terrific views of the kilns, with Death Valley's phenomenal colors as a backdrop. ✉ *51 mi southeast of Lone Pine on Rte. 190.*

⑥ **Stovepipe Wells Village** was the first resort in Death Valley. The tiny town, which dates to 1926, takes its name from the stovepipe that an early prospector left to indicate where he found water. The area contains a motel, a restaurant, a grocery store, campgrounds, and a landing strip. The multicolor walls of **Mosaic Canyon** (✉ off Rte. 190, on a 3-mi gravel road immediately southwest of Stovepipe Wells Village) are extremely close together in spots. A reasonably easy ¼-mi hike will give you a good sense of the area. If weather permits, it's rewarding to continue into the canyon for a few more miles. Be prepared to clamber over larger boulders. ✉ *77 mi east of Lone Pine on Rte. 190.*

⑦ Made up of minute pieces of quartz and other rock, the **Sand Dunes at Mesquite Flat** are ever-changing products of the wind—rippled hills with curving crests and a sun-bleached hue. The dunes are the most photographed destination in the park, and you can see them at their best at sunrise and sunset. There are no trails; you can roam where you please. Keep your eyes open for animal tracks—you may even spot a fox or coyote roaming the dunes. Bring plenty of water, and remember where you parked your car: it's easy to become disoriented in this ocean of sand. If you lose your bearings, simply climb to the top of a dune and scan the horizon for the parking lot. ⊠ *Rte. 190, between Stovepipe Wells Village and Furnace Creek.*

❽   **Scotty's Castle** is an odd apparition rising out of a canyon. This Moorish mansion, begun in 1924 and never completed, takes its name from Walter Scott, better known as Death Valley Scotty. An ex-cowboy, prospector, and performer in Buffalo Bill's Wild West Show, Scotty always told people the castle was his, financed by gold from a secret mine. In reality, there was no mine, and the house belonged to a Chicago millionaire named Albert Johnson (advised by doctors to spend time in a warm, dry climate), whom Scott had finagled into investing in the fictitious mine. The house functioned for a while as a hotel—guests included Bette Davis and Norman Rockwell—and still contains works of art, imported carpets, handmade European furniture, and a tremendous pipe organ. Costumed rangers re-create life at the castle circa 1939. Try to arrive for the first tour of the day to avoid a wait. ⊠ *Scotty's Castle Rd., 33 mi north of Sand Dune Junction,* ☎ 760/786–2392, 🕸 *www.nationalparks.com.* 💳 *$8.* ☉ *Daily 8–6; tours daily 9–5.*

❾   The impressive **Ubehebe Crater,** 500 ft deep and ½ mi across, is the result of underground steam and gas explosions about 3,000 years ago. Its volcanic ash spreads out over most of the area, and the cinders lie as deep as 150 ft, near the crater's rim. You'll get some superb views of the valley from here, and you can take a fairly easy hike around the west side of the rim to Little Hebe Crater, one of a smaller cluster of craters to the south and west. It's always windy here, so hold on to your hat. ⊠ *8 mi northwest of Scotty's Castle on N. Death Valley Hwy.*

★ **❿**   Although reaching the **Racetrack** involves a 27-mi journey over rough and almost nonexistent dirt road, the trip is well worth the reward. Where else in the world do rocks move on their own? This phenomenon has baffled scientists for years. Is it some sort of magnetic field? No one has actually seen the rocks in motion, but theory has it that when it rains, the hard-packed lake bed becomes slippery enough that gusty winds push the rocks along—sometimes for several hundred yards. When the mud dries, it leaves a telltale trail. The trek to the Racetrack can be made in a passenger vehicle, but high-clearance is suggested. ⊠ *From Ubehebe Crater, west 27 mi on the dirt road.*

On Route 190, south of its junction with Scotty's Castle Road and 14 mi north of the town of Furnace Creek, is a 1-mi gravel road that leads
⓫   to the **Salt Creek Interpretive Trail.** The trail, a ½-mi boardwalk circuit, loops through a spring-fed wash. The nearby hills are brown and gray, but the floor of the wash is alive with aquatic plants such as pickerelweed and salt grass. The stream and ponds here are among the few places in the park to see the rare pupfish, the only native fish species in Death Valley. The tiny fish are shy and hard to see, so you'll have to be a little sneaky or stand quietly and wait for them to appear. Animals such as birds, bobcats, fox, coyote and snakes visit the spring, and you might see ravens, common snipes, killdeer, or great blue herons. ⊠ *Off Rte. 190, 14 mi north of Furnace Creek.*

⓬   From the **Harmony Borax Works,** Death Valley's mule teams hauled borax to the railroad town of Mojave, 165 mi away. Those teams were a sight to behold: 20 mules hitched to two massive wagons, each carrying a load of 10 tons of borax through the burning desert. The teams plied the route between 1884 and 1907, when the railroad finally arrived in

Zabriskie. Constructed in 1883, one of the oldest buildings in Death Valley houses the **Borax Museum** (⊠ Rte. 190, 2 mi south of the borax works; 🎫 free). Originally a miners' bunkhouse, the building once stood in Twenty Mule Team Canyon. Now it displays mining machinery and historical exhibits. The adjacent structure is the original mule-team barn. ⊠ *Harmony Borax Works Rd., west of Rte. 190.*

⑬ Furnace Creek Village is a center of activity amid the sprawling quiet of Death Valley. Covered with tropical landscaping, it has jogging and bicycle paths, golf, tennis, a general store, and—rare for these parts—a few dining options. The exhibits and artifacts at **Death Valley Visitors Center** (⊠ ☎ 760/786–2331, WEB www.nps.gov/deva) provide a broad overview of how Death Valley formed; you can pick up maps at the bookstore run by the Death Valley Natural History Association. Furnace Creek Ranch conducts guided horseback, carriage, and hayrides that traverse trails with views of the surrounding mountains, where multicolor volcanic rock and alluvial fans make a dramatic backdrop for date palms and other vegetation. ⊠ *54 mi south of Scotty's Castle, 25 mi southeast of Stovepipe Wells Village on Rte. 190.*

★ ⑭ Artists Palette, so called for the brilliant colors of its volcanic deposits, is one of the most magnificent sights in Death Valley. Artists Drive, the approach to the area, is one-way heading north off Badwater Road, so if you're visiting Badwater, it saves time to come here on the way back. The drive winds through foothills of sedimentary and volcanic rocks. Within the palette, the huge expanses of Death Valley are replaced by intimate, small-scale natural beauty. It's a quiet, lonely drive. ⊠ *11 mi south of Furnace Creek off Badwater Rd.*

⑮ At **Devil's Golf Course** thousands of miniature salt pinnacles carved into surreal shapes by the desert wind dot the landscape. In places perfectly round holes descend into the ground through the minerals. The salt was pushed up to the earth's surface by pressure created as underground salt- and water-bearing gravel crystallized. Nothing grows in this barren landscape. ⊠ *Badwater Rd., 13 mi south of Furnace Creek. Turn right onto dirt road and drive 1 mi.*

⑯ Reaching **Badwater,** you'll see a shallow pool containing mostly sodium chloride—the pool is saltier than the sea—in an expanse of desolate salt flats. It's a sharp contrast to the expansive canyons and elevations not too far away. At 282 ft below sea level, Badwater is the lowest spot on land in the western hemisphere—and also one of the hottest. The legend of its name is that an early surveyor noticed his mule wouldn't drink from the pool and wrote "badwater" on his map. ⊠ *Badwater Rd., 19 mi south of Furnace Creek.*

⑰ A drive in colorful **Twenty Mule Team Canyon** delivers its share of thrills. At times along the loop road off Route 190 the soft rock walls reach high on both sides, making it seem like you're on an amusement-park ride. Remains of prospectors' tunnels are visible here, along with some brilliant rock formations. You can park and walk in places. ⊠ *Twenty Mule Team Rd. off Rte. 190, 4 mi south of Furnace Creek. Trailers not permitted.*

★ ⑱ Dante's View is more than 5,000 ft up in the Black Mountains. In the dry desert air you can see across most of 110-mi-wide Death Valley. The views up and down are equally astounding, as you can spot the highest and lowest points in the contiguous United States. The tiny blackish patch far below is Badwater, at 282 ft below sea level; on the western horizon is Mt. Whitney, which rises to 14,496 ft. It's one of the most extraordinary sights anywhere in California. ⊠ *Dante's View Rd. off Rte. 190, 20 mi south of Twenty Mule Team Canyon.*

Dining, Lodging, and Camping

$$$–$$$$ ✕ **Furnace Creek Inn Dining Room.** Fireplaces, beamed ceilings, and spectacular views provide a visual feast to match the inn's ambitious menu. Dishes may include desert-theme items such as rattlesnake empanadas and crispy cactus, as well as less exotic fare such as cumin-lime shrimp, lamb, and New York strip steak. An evening dress code (no jeans, T-shirts, or shorts) is enforced. Lunch is served October–May only, but you can always have afternoon tea, an inn tradition since 1927. Breakfast and Sunday brunch are also served. ✉ *Furnace Creek Village,* ☎ *760/786–2345,* WEB *www.furnacecreekresort.com. Reservations essential. AE, D, DC, MC, V.*

$ ✕ **The 19th Hole.** Overlooking the world's lowest golf course (214 ft below sea level), this open-air spot serves hamburgers, hot dogs, chicken, and sandwiches. There is drive-through service for golfers in carts. ✉ *Furnace Creek Golf Club, Furnace Creek Village,* ☎ *760/786–2345,* WEB *www.furnacecreekresort.com. AE, D, DC, MC, V. No dinner.*

$$$–$$$$ ✕🏠 **Furnace Creek Inn.** Built in 1927, this adobe-brick-and-stone
     ★   lodge nestles in one of the greenest oases in the park. A warm mineral stream gurgles throughout the property, and the pool is fed by a warm spring with waters at a constant 85°. All the rooms here have views, and some have balconies. The rooms are decorated in earth tones, with a refined air reminiscent of the inn's early days. Certain amenities, such as room service and massage, are only available October–May. ✉ *Furnace Creek Village, Hwy. 190, 92328,* ☎ *760/786–2361,* FAX *760/786–2514,* WEB *www.furnacecreekresort.com. 66 rooms. Restaurant, bar, room service, in-room data ports, cable TV with video games, pool, hot tubs, sauna, massage, 4 tennis courts, shop, meeting rooms. AE, D, DC, MC, V.*

$$ ✕🏠 **Furnace Creek Ranch.** Originally crew headquarters for the Pacific Coast Borax Company, the four two-story buildings here have motel-type rooms that are good for families. The best rooms overlook the green lawns of the resort, with the mountains soaring in the background. Adjacent to a golf course with its own team of pros, the ranch has a general store and a campground. The family-style Wrangler Steak House and 49er Café serve American fare in simple surroundings. ✉ *Furnace Creek Village, 92328,* ☎ *760/786–2345,* FAX *760/786–9945,* WEB *www.furnacecreekresort.com. 224 rooms. Restaurant, coffee shop, bar, grocery, pool, golf course, 4 tennis courts, horseback riding, shop, playground, laundry facilities, Internet; no pets. AE, D, DC, MC, V.*

$ ✕🏠 **Stovepipe Wells Village.** If you prefer quiet nights and an unfettered view of the night sky and nearby sand dunes, this property will no doubt suit you. No telephones break the silence here, and only the deluxe rooms have televisions. Rooms are simple yet comfortable and offer views of the wide-open desert. The Toll Road Restaurant serves American breakfast, lunch, and dinner favorites, from omelets and sandwiches to burgers and steaks. RV campsites with full hookups are available on a first-come, first-served basis. ✉ *Stovepipe Wells Village, Hwy. 190, 92328,* ☎ *760/786–2387,* FAX *760/786–2389,* WEB *www.stovepipewells.com. 83 rooms. Restaurant, bar, pool, gift shop, airstrip. AE, D, MC, V.*

    ⚑ **Mesquite Springs.** Some of the tent and RV spaces at the only campground on the north end of the park are shaded. Its remote location attracts younger campers intent on getting away from the crowds. No generators are allowed. *Flush toilets, dump station, drinking water, fire grates, picnic tables. 30 sites.* ✉ *Access road 2 mi south of Scotty's Castle,* ☎ *800/365–2267. Reservations not accepted.*

    ⚑ **Sunset Campground.** This campground is a gravel-and-asphalt RV city. Hookups are not available, but you can walk across the street to the showers, laundry facilities, and swimming pool at Furnace Creek Ranch. Many of Sunset's denizens are senior citizens who migrate to Death Valley each winter to play golf and tennis or just to enjoy the mild, dry climate. *Flush toilets, dump station, drinking water, public telephones, ranger station, playground. 1,000 sites.* ⊠ *1 mi north of Furnace Creek Village,* ☎ *800/365–2267. Reservations not accepted. No credit cards.* ⊙ *Mid-Oct.–mid-Apr.*

Outdoor Activities and Sports

BIRD-WATCHING

Approximately 250 bird species have been identified in Death Valley. The best spot to peep at the park's birds is along the Salt Creek Interpretive Trail, where you might see ravens, common snipes, spotted sandpipers, killdeer, and great blue herons. Along the fairways at Furnace Creek Golf Club (stay off the greens), look for kingfishers, peregrine falcons, hawks, Canada geese, yellow warblers, and an occasional golden eagle. Scotty's Castle is another good place to catch a glimpse of some birds.

GOLF

At **Furnace Creek Golf Club,** the lowest golf course in the world, you can opt to play 9 or 18 holes. The club rents clubs and carts, and greens fees are reduced if you're a guest of Furnace Creek Ranch or Furnace Creek Inn. Special rates for 2–20 weeks of play are available. In winter reservations are essential. ⊠ *Furnace Creek Village,* ☎ *760/786–2301.* 🎟 *$10–$50.* ⊙ *Tee times daily sunrise–sundown; pro shop daily 7–5.*

HIKING

Hiking trails and routes abound throughout Death Valley National Park, though few are maintained by the Park Service. Try the 2-mi round-trip Keane Wonder Mine Trail, with spectacular views of the valley; the winding 4-mi round-trip Mosaic Canyon Trail, between smoothly polished walls of a narrow canyon; or Natural Bridge Canyon trail, an easy half-mi round-trip to a bridge formation. Plan to take your walks before or after the noonday sun. Be sure to carry plenty of water, wear protective clothing, and be wary of tarantulas, black widows, scorpions, snakes, and other potentially dangerous creatures. Some of the best trails are unmarked; ask locals for directions.

Death Valley Junction

⑲ *29 mi south of Furnace Creek Village on Rte. 190.*

With the exception of the Opera House and hotel, Death Valley Junction has little to offer, but it is a fine place to stop and stretch your legs. There are no services here.

Marta Becket's Amargosa Opera House is an unexpected novelty in the desert. An artist and dancer from New York, Becket first visited the former railway town of Amargosa while on tour in 1964. Three years later she returned to town and bought a boarded-up theater that sat amid a group of run-down mock–Spanish colonial buildings. To compensate for the sparse audiences in the early days, Becket painted a Renaissance-era Spanish crowd on the walls and ceiling, turning the theater into a trompe l'oeil masterpiece. Now in her late seventies, Becket performs her blend of ballet, mime, and 19th-century melodrama to sellout crowds. After the show you can meet her in the adjacent gallery, where she sells her paintings and autographs her books. There are no performances May through September. ⊠ *Rte. 127,* ☎ *760/852–4441,* FAX *760/852–4138,* WEB *www.amargosa–opera–house.com.* 🎟 *$15.* ⊙ *Nov. and Feb.–Apr., Mon. and Sat. 8:15; Oct. and Dec.–Jan., Sat. 8:15.*

Lodging

$ 🏨 **Opera House Hotel.** The Pacific Coast Borax Company built this hotel in 1923 to serve railroad passengers. After closing down in 1985, the adobe bungalow, a neighbor of the Amargosa Opera House, was renovated and reopened in 1990. Listed on the National Register of Historic Places, it offers rooms with one or two double beds, furnished with antiques and adorned with hand-painted murals. It's nothing fancy, but if you are planning a winter visit, make your reservations at least two months in advance. ⊠ *Rte. 127,* ☎ *760/852–4441,* FAX *760/852–4138,* WEB *www.amargosa-opera-house.com. 14 rooms. No room phones, no room TVs. AE, MC, V.*

Shoshone

⓴ *30 mi south of Death Valley Junction on Rte. 127.*

Unincorporated Shoshone started out as a mining town where prospectors lived in small caves dynamited out of the rock. One miner who struck it rich was so attached to his hillside dwelling that he hollowed out another cave as a garage for his new automobile. Shoshone is now a hot spot for paleontologists, who have discovered fossilized saber-tooth tiger and camel footprints here.

Visit the **Shoshone Museum** to see a complete woolly mammoth skeleton excavated nearby. The museum also houses a unique collection of antiques, minerals, and other items related to the history of Death Valley. ⊠ *Rte. 127,* ☎ *760/852–4524,* WEB *www.shoshone.org.* 🎟 *Free.* ☉ *Daily 8–4.*

Dining and Lodging

$–$$ ✕ **Crowbar Café & Saloon.** Housed in an old wooden building with antique photos adorning the walls and mining equipment standing in the corners, this establishment serves surprisingly good food in enormous helpings. Fare ranges from steaks to taco salads. Home-baked fruit pies make fine desserts, and frosty beers are surefire thirst quenchers. ⊠ *Rte. 127,* ☎ *760/852–4224. AE, D, MC, V.*

$–$$ 🏨 **Shoshone Inn.** Built in 1956, the rustic Shoshone Inn is the only motel in town. Rooms are simple and cozy, but the big draw here is the warm spring-fed swimming pool built into the foothills. A market, café, gas station, and museum are all within walking distance. ⊠ *Rte. 127,* ☎ *760/852–4335,* FAX *760/852–4250,* WEB *www.shoshonevillage.com. 16 rooms. Kitchenettes (some), cable TV, laundry facilities, pets allowed; no smoking. AE, D, MC, V.*

THE WESTERN MOJAVE

Stretching from the town of Ridgecrest to the base of the San Gabriel Mountains, the western Mojave is a varied landscape of ancient Native American petroglyphs, tufa towers, and hillsides covered in bright-orange poppies.

Ridgecrest

㉑ *77 mi south of Lone Pine via U.S. 395.*

A military town that serves the U.S. Naval Weapons Center, to its north, Ridgecrest has dozens of stores, restaurants, and hotels. It is a good base for exploring the northwestern Mojave.

The **Maturango Museum,** which also serves as a visitor information center, has pamphlets and books about the region. Small but informative exhibits detail the natural and cultural history of the northern Mojave.

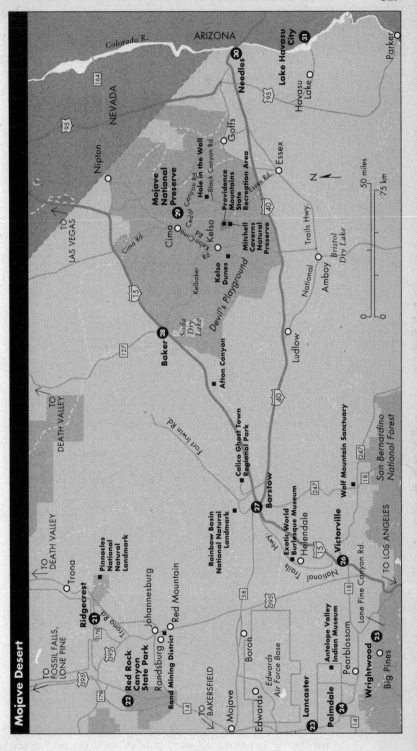

Mojave Desert

The museum runs wildflower tours in March and April. ⊠ *100 E. Las Flores Ave.,* ☎ *760/375–6900,* FAX *760/375–0479,* WEB *www. maturango.org.* ⊠ *$2.* ☉ *Daily 10–5.*

★ Guided tours conducted by the Maturango Museum are the only way to see **Petroglyph Canyons,** among the desert's most amazing spectacles. The two canyons, commonly called Big Petroglyph and Little Petroglyph, are in the Coso Mountain range on the million-acre U.S. Naval Weapons Center at China Lake. Each of the canyons holds a superlative concentration of ancient rock art, the largest of its kind in the northern hemisphere. Thousands of well-preserved images of animals and humans are scratched or pecked into dark basaltic rocks. The tour takes you as far as 3 mi through sandy washes and over boulders, so wear comfortable walking shoes. At an elevation of 5,000 ft weather conditions can be quite extreme, so dress in layers and bring plenty of drinking water (none is available at the site) and snacks. Children under 10 are not allowed on the tour. The military requires everyone to produce a valid driver's license, Social Security number, and vehicle registration prior to the trip (nondrivers must provide a birth certificate). At press time the area was closed to tourists; call ahead to confirm accessibility. ⊠ *Tours depart from Maturango Museum,* ☎ *760/ 375–6900,* WEB *www.maturango.org.* ⊠ *$25.* ☉ *Tours Mar.–June and Sept.– or Oct.–early Dec.; call for tour times.*

Ⓒ Rounded up by the Bureau of Land Management on public lands throughout the Southwest, the animals at the **Wild Horse and Burro Corrals** are up for adoption. You can bring along an apple or carrot to feed the horses, but the burros are usually too wild to approach. ⊠ *Off Rte. 178, 3 mi east of Ridgecrest,* ☎ *760/384–5765 or 1-866-4-MUS-TANGS,* WEB *www.adoptahorse.blm.gov.* ⊠ *Free.* ☉ *Weekdays 7–4.*

It's worth the effort (especially for sci-fi buffs, who will recognize the landscape from the film *Star Trek V*) to seek out **Trona Pinnacles National Natural Landmark.** These fantastic-looking formations of calcium carbonate, known as tufa, were formed underwater along fault lines in the bed of what is now Searles Dry Lake. A ½-mi trail winds around this surreal landscape of more than 500 spires, some of which stand as tall as 140 ft. Wear sturdy shoes—tufa cuts like coral. The best road to the area can be impassable after a rainstorm. ⊠ *5 mi south of Rte. 178, 18 mi east of Ridgecrest,* ☎ *760/384–5400 (Ridgecrest BLM office),* WEB *www.ca.blm.gov/ridgecrest.*

OFF THE BEATEN PATH   **FOSSIL FALLS –** About 30 mi northwest of Ridgecrest via U.S. 395, a stark area of dark basalt rocks is evidence of volcanic eruptions 20,000 years ago. You'll find neither fossils nor waterfalls here, but the name given to this tumble of solidified lava is apt. A short hike to the bottom of the formation leads to a spot where Native Americans once camped. South of the falls the Owens River cut the huge valley between the Sierra Nevada range, to the west, and the Coso range, to the east. There's a very primitive campsite amid the boulders. ⊠ *Cinder Cone Rd., ½ mi east of U.S. 395.*

Dining and Lodging

$$–$$$$ ✕ **Santa Fe Grill.** Locals say this is the best of Ridgecrest's numerous
★   restaurants. Unexpectedly hip and health-conscious, the menu includes New Mexico–style dishes. Hot tortillas, made on the premises, come to the table with a wonderful salsa, its distinctive smoky taste derived from fire-grilled chilies. Beans (not refried) and sweet-corn cake accompany most entrées. ⊠ *901 N. Heritage Dr.,* ☎ *760/446–5404. AE, D, MC, V.*

$–$$ ✕▦ **Carriage Inn.** Large and well-kept, this hotel has large and taste-fully decorated rooms. You can also stay in poolside cabanas that are a bit homier. A mister cools off sunbathers during the hot summer months. Café Potpourri serves a mix of American, Italian, and south-western specials. ✉ *901 N. China Lake Blvd.,* ☎ *760/446–7910 or 800/772–8527,* ℻ *760/446–6408,* WEB *www.carriageinn.biz. 152 rooms, 8 suites, 2 cabanas. Restaurant, café, bar, pool, gym, hot tub, sauna, meeting room. AE, D, DC, MC, V.*

$–$$ ✕▦ **Heritage Inn.** This well-appointed though somewhat bland es-tablishment is geared toward business travelers, but the staff is equally attentive to tourists' concerns. A nearby sister property is an all-suites hotel. The Farris Restaurant, with an American/casual menu, is a favorite fine-dining spot for locals. ✉ *1050 N. Norma St.,* ☎ *760/446–6543 or 800/843–0693,* ℻ *760/446–2884,* WEB *www.greatwesternhotels.com. 125 rooms. Restaurant, bar, mi-crowaves, refrigerators, pool, gym, hot tub, laundry facilities, busi-ness services, meeting room. AE, D, DC, MC, V.*

En Route The towns of Randsburg, Red Mountain, and Johannesburg make up the **Rand Mining District** (✉ U.S. 395, 20 mi south of Ridgecrest), which first boomed with the discovery of gold in the Rand Mountains in 1895. Rich tungsten ore, used in World War I to make steel alloy, was dis-covered in 1907, and silver was found in 1919. The boom has gone bust, but the area still has a few residents, a dozen antiques shops, and plenty of character. Johannesburg is overlooked by an archetypal Old West cemetery in the hills above town. Randsburg's tiny city jail is among the original buildings still standing; its White House Saloon is one of the Wild West's few surviving saloons, swinging wooden doors and all. **The Randsburg General Store** (✉ 35 Butte Ave., Randsburg, ☎ 760/374–2418) serves as the area's informal visitor center, selling maps, rock-hounding guides, and a terrific selection of books on the gold rush and the California desert. With a century-old soda fountain, it's also a good place to stop to quench your thirst. The small **Desert Museum** (✉ 161 Butte Ave., Randsburg, ☎ no phone) exhibits old min-ing paraphernalia and historic photos.

Red Rock Canyon State Park

㉒ *17 mi west of U.S. 395 via Red Rock–Randsburg Rd., or 28 mi south-west of Ridgecrest via Rte. 14.*

A geological feast for the eyes with its layers of pink, white, red, and brown rock, Red Rock Canyon State Park is also a region of fascinating biological diversity—the ecosystems of the Sierra Nevada, the Mojave Desert, and the Basin Range all converge here. Entering the park from the south on Red Rock–Randsburg Road, you pass through a steep-walled gorge to a wide bowl tinted pink by volcanic ash. Native Amer-icans known as the Old People lived here 20,000 years ago or longer; later, Mojave Indians roamed the land for centuries. Gold-rush fever hit the region in the mid-1800s, and you can still see remains of min-ing operations in the park. In the 20th century Hollywood invaded the canyon, shooting westerns, TV shows, commercials, music videos, and movies such as *Jurassic Park* here. On Route 14, check out the Red Cliffs Preserve, across the highway from the entrance to the Red Rock campground. ✉ *Ranger station: Abbott Dr. off Rte. 14,* ☎ *661/ 942–0662,* WEB *www.calparksmojave.com.* 🎫 *$2.* ☉ *Visitor center, week-ends and occasional weekdays.*

Camping

⚠ **Red Rock Canyon State Park.** Open year-round, the park's camp-ground is in the colorful cliff region of the southern El Paso Mountains, where there are lots of hiking trails. *Pit toilets, drinking water, fire pits, picnic tables. 50 sites. ⊠ Off Rte. 14, 30 mi southwest of Ridgecrest, ☏ 661/942–0662. Reservations not accepted.*

Lancaster

㉓ *Rte. 14, 48 mi south of Red Rock Canyon State Park.*

Lancaster was founded in 1876, when the Southern Pacific Railroad arrived. Before that it was inhabited by Native American tribes: Kawarisu, Kitanemuk, Serrano, Tataviam, and Chemehuevi. Today descendants of some of these tribes still live in the surrounding mountains. Points of interest around Lancaster are far from the downtown area, some in neighboring communities.

California's state flower, the California poppy, can be spotted just about anywhere in the state, but the densest concentration is in the

★ **Antelope Valley Poppy Reserve.** Seven miles of trails lead you through 1,745 acres of hills carpeted with poppies and other wildflowers as far as the eye can see. Peak blooming time is usually March through May. The visitor center has books and information about the reserve and other desert areas. Many trails are wheelchair- and stroller accessible. ⊠ *Avenue I between 110th and 170th Sts. W, ☏ 661/724–1180 or 661/942–0662, WEB www.calparksmojave.com. ☑ $2 per vehicle. ☉ Visitor center mid-Mar.–mid-May, weekdays 9–4, weekends 9–5.*

Thirteen species of wild cats, from the weasel-size jaguarundi to leop-
🐾 ards, tigers, and jaguars, inhabit the **Exotic Feline Breeding Compound & Feline Conservation Center.** You can see the cats in the parklike public zoo and research center, behind fence-and-concrete barriers. The center's biggest accolade is for the successful breeding of the rare Amur leopard, whose native habitat is remote border areas between Russia and China. ⊠ *Off Mojave-Tropico Rd., Rosamond, 4½ mi west of Rte. 14 via Rosamond Blvd. (10 mi north of Lancaster), ☏ 661/256–3793; 61/256–3332 for recorded information, WEB www.cathouse-fcc.org. ☑ $3. ☉ Thurs.–Tues. 10–4.*

If you love aviation history, you'll no doubt enjoy a visit to the **Air Flight Test Center Museum at Edwards Air Force Base.** Considered the birthplace of supersonic flight, Edwards Air Force Base has been the world's premiere flight-testing and flight research center since the World War II era. It was here the sound barrier was broken on October 14, 1947. The museum displays the rich history of the base and of USAF flight testing and has a dozen airplanes on exhibit, from the first F-16B to the giant B-52D bomber. To visit, you must call in advance to arrange an approximate time of arrival and to supply your vehicle information. On arrival you must show a valid driver's license, vehicle registration, and proof of insurance (nondrivers must produce a birth certificate). If you are coming from abroad, you must give the museum three weeks' prior notice of your visit and provide your full name, date of birth, city and country of birth, and passport alien identification number. At press time the base and museum were closed to tourists; call ahead to confirm accessibility and to get driving directions. ⊠ *Edwards Air Force Base, Edwards, ☏ 661/277–8050, WEB www.edwards.af.mil/museum. ☑ Free. ☉ Tues.–Sat. 9–5.*

Dining and Lodging

$–$$ ✕🏨 **Desert Inn.** Year after year this 1950s hotel remains a local favorite for dining and lodging. The rooms are basic, in tones of plum and mauve, with wood accents. On the premises are the D.I. Cafe and the fancier Granada Room, where you can dine on American-French cuisine such as breaded, baked chicken breast stuffed with cream cheese and walnuts or beef tenderloin stuffed with a medley of shrimp, mushrooms, and Swiss cheese. The well-kept parklike grounds are a half mile from downtown Lancaster. ⊠ *44219 N. Sierra Hwy., 93534,* ☎ *661/942–8401 or 800/942–8401,* FAX *661/942–8950,* WEB *www.desert-inn.com. 144 rooms. 2 restaurants, bar, room service. In-room data ports, in-room hot tubs (some), kitchenettes (some), microwaves, refrigerators, cable TV, 2 pools, wading pool, exercise equipment, hot tub, massage, steam room, racquetball. AE, D, DC, MC, V.*

Palmdale

㉔ *Rte. 14 8 mi south of Lancaster.*

Calling itself the aerospace capital of the world, the desert community of Palmdale is 60 mi from downtown Los Angeles.

★ Notable for its one-of-a-kind American Indian artifacts, **Antelope Valley Indian Museum** has more than 2,500 artifacts on display, including pieces from California, southwestern, and Great Basin Indian tribes. The unusual Swiss chalet–style building, built in 1928 by homesteader Howard Arden Edwards, clings to the rocky hillside of Piute Butte and is listed on the National Register of Historic Places. ⊠ *Ave. M between 150th and 170th Sts. E, 17 mi east of Antelope Valley Freeway (Rte. 14),* ☎ *661/942–0662,* WEB *www.avim.av.org.* ☞ *$1.* ◷ *Mid-Sept.–mid-June, weekends 11– 4 (tours available Tues.–Thurs. by appointment).*

Just a mile from the San Andreas fault, the centerpiece of the **Devil's Punchbowl Natural Area** is a natural bowl-shape depression in the earth, framed by 300-ft rock walls. At the bottom is a stream, which you can reach via a 1-mi hike; at the top an interpretive center has displays of native flora and fauna, including live animals such as snakes, lizards, and several birds of prey. ⊠ *28000 Devil's Punchbowl Rd. (south of Rte. 138), Pearblossom,* ☎ *661/944–2743.* ☞ *Free.* ◷ *Daily 8–4.*

★ ☺ The Benedictine monastery **St. Andrew's Abbey** stands on 760 acres of lush greenery and natural springs. What makes this monastery unique is its ceramics studio, established in 1969. St. Andrew's Ceramics sells handmade tiles designed by Father Maur van Doorslaer, a monk from Sint Adre Zevenkerken, the Bruges, Belgium, monastery that founded St. Andrew's. Don't miss the abbey's fall festival, where you can sample tasty dishes and enjoy live entertainment that includes singing nuns. ⊠ *31101 N. Valyermo Rd. (south of Rte. 138), Valyermo,* ☎ *661/944–2178 for general information; 661/944–1047 for ceramic studio,* WEB *www.SaintsandAngels.org.* ☞ *Free.* ◷ *Weekdays 9:30–11:45 and 1:30–4, weekends 9:30–11:45 and 1:30–4:30.*

Lodging

$ ▦ **Best Western John Jay Inn & Suites.** At this full-service property the accommodations are conservatively done up with Empire-style furnishings. All rooms have a coffeemaker, a hair dryer, an iron and ironing board, and a large desk with ergonomic chair. The two-line speakerphones in each room are equipped with voice mail. Suites are decked out with balconies, fireplaces, wet bars, and Jacuzzis. Buffet breakfast and a *USA Today* newspaper is included with your room rate. ⊠ *600 W. Palmdale Blvd., 93551,* ☎ *661/575–9322,* FAX *661/575–9495,* WEB *www.bwjohnjaypalmdale.com. 45 rooms. 18 suites. In-room data ports, microwaves, refrigerators, cable TV with movies, pool, gym, sauna, laundry service, business services, meeting room; no-smoking rooms. AE, D, DC, MC, V. CP.*

$$ ▦ **Residence Inn Palmdale.** Accommodations here range from studios to 1-bedroom suites, all with a full kitchen and a sitting area with a sleeper sofa. Some suites have fireplaces, and each has an iron and ironing board, a hair dryer, and a two-line phone with voice mail. Sip your complimentary in-room coffee while reading the free newspaper that's delivered to your room weekdays. There is a complimentary hot breakfast daily, and you can have dinner delivered from several local restaurants. The staff will also do your grocery shopping for you. ✉ *514 W. Avenue P, 93551,* ☎ *661/947–4204,* WEB *www.residenceinn.com. 90 suites. In-room data ports, kitchens, refrigerators, cable TV, tennis court, indoor pool, hot tub, gym, dry cleaning, laundry facilities, laundry service, concierge, business services, meeting room, car rental. AE, D, DC, MC, V. BP.*

En Route   For a bit of a thrill, leave Route 138 a few miles west of U.S. 395 and drive up **Lone Pine Canyon Road** toward Wrightwood. The road follows a stretch of the San Andreas Fault but does not have too many twists, turns, or drop-offs. Along the way, you'll get a breathtaking view of the Mormon Rocks, tilted sandstone boulders displaced by the fault (a popular spot for rock climbing), and pass the old Clyde Ranch, where a small wooden cabin that was once the home of Wyatt and Virgil Earp still stands near the apple orchards.

Wrightwood

㉕   *Rte. 2 (Angeles Crest Hwy.) 5 mi west of Rte. 138 (42 mi southeast of Palmdale), or 14 mi northwest of Cajon on Lone Pine Canyon Rd.*

With about 3,500 full-time residents, Wrightwood prides itself on having no stoplights, fast-food restaurants, or chain stores. You'll just find old-fashioned candy shops, antiques shops, and mountain crafts boutiques.

At the **Old Firehouse Museum** you can see exhibits on the area's mining heritage and natural history. Upstairs, step back in time into the village's first fire fighters' quarters. ✉ *6000 Cedar St.,* ☎ *760/249–4650.* 🎟 *Free.* ☉ *Sat. 10–2 or by appointment.*

The **Four Seasons Gallery** shows local art ranging from landscape paintings to Native American sculptures and crafts. The gallery regularly hosts artist showcase parties and chocolate-tasting parties. ✉ *6013 Park Dr.,* ☎ *760/249–3712.* 🎟 *Free.* ☉ *Wed.–Sun. 10–5.*

An old stone tower at **Big Pines Visitors Center,** part of Angeles National Forest, marks the highest spot (6,862 ft) along the San Andreas Fault, the unstable crack in the earth's crust that has caused so many California earthquakes. At the center you can get information on camping, fishing, and hiking in the forest and purchase the Forest Adventure passes ($5 per day) that allow you access to the forest. A small shop sells key chains, postcards, T-shirts, and toys. ✉ *Rte. 2, 3 mi west of Wrightwood,* ☎ *760/249–3504.* ☉ *Fri.–Sun. 8:30–4:30, Tues.–Thurs. 7:30–3:30.*

Dining, Lodging, and Camping

$–$$ ✕ **Blue Ridge Inn.** This rustic lodge, in business since 1948, plays the
★   woodsy card, from the bar with a huge fireplace to the cozy wood-paneled dining room with flickering lanterns, 19th-century clocks, and friendly waitstaff. The food—surf-and-turf specialties such as grilled Malaysian shrimp and prime rib—is probably the best you'll find in Wrightwood. ✉ *6060 Park Dr.,* ☎ *760/249–3440. AE, MC, V. Closed Mon. No lunch.*

$$ 🏠 **The Golden Acorn.** Surrounded by a lush English garden and bubbling fountain, this large mountain estate wraps you in splendor, from the winding staircase, roaring fire, and decorative moldings to the

four-poster beds and oval soaking tubs in each room. The Honeymoon Suite has a floor-to-ceiling canopy bed with a fireplace that opens onto the bath as well as the bedroom. Afternoon tea is served on request. ⊠ *5487 Morningstar Ct.,* ☎ *760/249–6252,* WEB *www.thegoldenacorn.com. 2 rooms. Cable TV; no smoking. MC, V. BP.*

⚠ **Table Mountain.** Scenic views of the desert from 7,000 ft make this park a popular spot for weddings. The campground stands next to Big Pines Visitor Center. You can buy firewood at the campground and there is a restaurant nearby. *Pit toilets, portable toilets, drinking water, bear boxes, fire pits, grills, picnic tables, public telephone, ranger station. 118 tent/RV sites.* ⊠ *22223 Big Pines Hwy. AE, D, MC, V.* ☉ *May–Nov.*

Outdoor Activities and Sports

HIKING

Wrightwood is a major stopping point for hikers traveling the **Pacific Crest Trail** (⊠ Big Pines Visitors Center, Rte. 2, 3 mi west of Wrightwood, ☎ 760/249–3504), which runs 2,600 mi from Mexico to Canada. There is a trailhead near Inspiration Point on Rte. 2, 5 mi west of Wrightwood.

SKIING

In addition to a vertical peak of 8,200 ft, two mountains, and 220 skiable acres, **Mountain High** (⊠ 24510 Rte. 2, ☎ 760/249–5808, WEB www.mthigh.com) has more than 47 trails for skiing and snowshoeing. Boarders flock here for Faultline Terrain Park. There is regular bus service between the mountains. At **Ski Sunrise** (⊠ 24501 Rte. 2, ☎ 760/249–6150), runs like Devil's Dive and Purgatory pack quite a wallop. The skiing suffers when there's no fresh snow, but after a storm it's a local favorite. April through October the resort specializes in disk golf, with 27 holes.

THE EASTERN MOJAVE

In sharp contrast to Death Valley, the eastern Mojave has substantial vegetation and regular stretches of cool weather. Like the western Mojave, the east has plenty of flat, open land dotted with Joshua trees and rock-strewn mountains. Much of this area is uninhabited, so be cautious when driving the back roads, where towns and services are few and far between.

Victorville

㉖ *34 mi southwest of Barstow on I–15.*

the southwest corner of the Mojave is the sprawling town of Victorville, an area rich in Route 66 heritage. Fans of the Mother Road

★ can visit the **California Route 66 Museum,** whose exhibits chronicle the history of America's most famous highway. At the museum you can pick up a book that details a self-guided tour of the old Sagebrush Route from Oro Grande to Helendale. The road passes Route 66 icons such as Potapov's Gas and Service Station (where the words BILL'S SERVICE are still legible) and the once-rowdy Sagebrush Inn, now a private residence. ⊠ *16825 D Street (Rte. 66),* ☎ *760/951–0436,* WEB *www.califrt66museum.org.* 🎫 *Free.* ☉ *Thurs.–Mon. 10–4.*

★ The **Roy Rogers–Dale Evans Museum** draws old-timers and cowboy kitsch fans who come to see the personal and professional memorabilia. Everything from glittering costumes and custom cars to cereal-box promotions demonstrates just how famous the museum's namesakes and their friends on the western film circuit once were. Animal-rights activists will probably want to stay away, as exhibits include safari trophies—stuffed exotic cats and other animals shot by Roy and sometimes Dale. Even Trigger and Buttermilk have been preserved, though they died of natural causes. ⊠ *15650 Seneca Rd.,* ☎ *760/243–4547,* WEB *www.royrogers.com.* ☞ *$8.* ☉ *Daily 9–5.*

Ⓒ The California high desert's only zoo, the small-scale **Cinema Safari** houses all kinds of creatures. You can see wild animals such as a lion, a tiger, and a baboon up close, take a guided tour, and see a performing animal show. The animals here are either retired from or still working in the entertainment industry. The only way to visit Cinema Safari is on a regularly scheduled tour, or by appointment. ⊠ *19038 Willow St., Hesperia,* ☎ *760/948–9430.* ☞ *$6.* ☉ *Tours weekends 11 and 2.*

OFF THE   **WOLF MOUNTAIN SANCTUARY** – Apache Indian Tonya "Littlewolf" Car-
BEATEN PATH loni founded this desert sanctuary in 1980. Today it is a refuge for a
        Ⓒ dozen injured or abused wolves, including the rare buffalo wolf, the
            white arctic tundra wolf, and the Alaskan timber wolf. The most famous
            resident is Apache Moon, a McKenzie timber-wolf "ambassador" who
            visits local schools. ⊠ 7520 Fairlane, Lucerne Valley, ☎ 760/248–
            7818, WEB www.wolfmountain.com. ☞ $10. ☉ By appointment.

Dining, Lodging, and Camping

$ ✕ **Emma Jean's Hollandburger Cafe.** This circa-1940s diner sits right on U.S. Historic Route 66 and is favored by locals for its generous portions and old-fashioned home cooking. Try the biscuits and gravy, chicken-fried steak, or the famous Trucker's Sandwich, chock-full of roast beef, bacon, chilies, and cheese. ⊠ *17143 D St.,* ☎ *760/243–9938. AE, MC, V. Closed Sun. No dinner.*

$ ✕ **Summit Inn.** Elvis is one of many famous customers who have passed through this kitschy diner perched atop the Cajon Pass. You can't go wrong with a date shake and a Hillbilly Burger, or with ostrich burgers or ostrich-egg omelets fresh from a nearby ostrich farm. Open since 1951, the restaurant is filled with Route 66 novelty items, a gift shop, and vintage jukebox, which still plays oldies from the 1960s. ⊠ *6000 Mariposa Rd., Oak Hills,* ☎ *760/949–8688. MC, V.*

$ ⊡ **Best Western Green Tree Inn.** This no-nonsense property stands off I–15 a few blocks from the Roy Rogers–Dale Evans Museum. Many of the rooms are suite-size, making the inn a good choice for families. ⊠ *14173 Green Tree Blvd., 92392,* ☎ *760/245–3461 or 800/528–1234,* FAX *760/245–7745,* WEB *www.bestwestern.com. 168 rooms. Restaurant, coffee shop, bar, microwaves (some), refrigerators (some), pool, hot tub, shuffleboard, meeting room. AE, D, DC, MC, V.*

   ⚠ **Mojave Narrows Regional Park.** In one of the few spots where the Mojave River flows above ground, this park has two lakes surrounded by cottonwoods and cattails. You'll find fishing, rowboat rentals, a bait shop, equestrian paths, and a trail for people with disabilities. The campsites cluster by the lake amid grass and trees. *Flush toilets, full hookups, dump station, drinking water, showers, fire pits, grills, picnic tables, snack bar, electricity, public telephone. Playground. 87 sites, 37 with hookups.* ⊠ *18000 Yates Rd.,* ☎ *760/245–2226,* WEB *www.co.san-bernardino.ca.us/parks/mojavenarrows.*

En Route Along National Trails Highway in Helendale, about halfway between Victorville and Barstow, 1950s burlesque beauty Dixie Evans runs the entertaining and bawdy **Exotic World Burlesque Museum** (⊠ 29053 Wild Rd., ☎ 760/243–5261, WEB www.exoticworld.org; ☞ Donation). The place is filled with naughty burlesque costumes, jewelry, and photos dating to the 18th century. In June the museum hosts the annual Exotic World Contest, which draws big-bosomed women from around the globe.

Barstow

㉗ *32 mi northeast of Victorville on I–15.*

In 1886, when a subsidiary of the Atchison, Topeka, and Santa Fe Railway began construction of a depot and hotel here, Barstow was born. Today outlet stores, chain restaurants, and motels define the landscape, though old-time neon signs light up the city's main street. The **California Welcome Center** has exhibits about desert ecology, wildflowers, and wildlife, as well as general visitor information for the state of California. ✉ *2796 Tanger Way,* ☏ *760/253–4782,* WEB *www. barstowca.com.* ⊙ *Daily 9–6.*

✧ Stop by the **Desert Discovery Center** to see exhibits of fossils, plants, and local animals. The main attraction here is Old Woman, the second-largest iron meteorite ever found in the United States. It was discovered in 1976 about 50 mi from Barstow in the Old Woman Mountains. The center also has visitor information for the Mojave Desert. ✉ *831 Barstow Rd.,* ☏ *760/252–6060,* WEB *www.ca.blm.gov/barstow.* ▣ *Free.* ⊙ *Tues.–Sat. 11–4.*

Its name a Spanish phrase meaning "house of the desert," the **Casa Del Desierto Harvey House** was one of many hotel and restaurant depots opened by Santa Fe railroad guru Fred Harvey in the early 20th century. The location where Judy Garland's film *The Harvey Girls* was shot, the building is now completely restored. Inside Casa Del Desierto you will find the **Route 66 Mother Road Museum and Gift Shop.** ✉ *681 N. 1st Ave.,* ☏ *760/255–1890,* WEB *barstow66museum.itgo.com.* ▣ *Free.* ⊙ *Fri.–Sun. 11–4. Guided tours by appointment.*

✧ ★ What's now **Calico Ghost Town** was once a wild and wealthy mining town. Prospectors found a rich deposit of silver around 1881, and the boom lasted until 1886, when the price of silver fell. By that time more than $85 million worth of silver, gold, and other precious metals had been harvested from the hills, but the town slipped into decline. Frank "Borax" Smith started a second boom in 1889, when he started mining the unglamorous but profitable mineral borax, but that boom went bust by the dawn of the 20th century. Many buildings here are authentic, but the restoration has created a theme-park version of the 1880s. You can stroll the wooden sidewalks of Main Street, browse shops filled with western goods, roam the tunnels of Maggie's Mine, and take a ride on the Calico–Odessa Railroad. Festivals in March, May, October, and November celebrate Calico's Wild West theme. ✉ *Ghost Town Rd., 3 mi north of I–15, 5 mi east of Barstow,* ☏ *760/254–2122,* WEB *www.calicotown.com.* ▣ *$6.* ⊙ *Daily 9–5.*

★ So many science-fiction movies set on Mars have been filmed at **Rainbow Basin National Natural Landmark** that this site, 8 mi north of Barstow, may remind you of the red planet. Huge slabs of red, orange, white, and green stone tilt at crazy angles like ships about to capsize. Hike the many washes, and you'll probably see the fossilized remains of creatures—mastodons, camels, rhinos, dog-bears, birds, and insects—that roamed the basin from 16 million to 12 million years ago. You can camp here, at Owl Canyon Campground, on the east side of Rainbow Basin. Part of the drive to the basin is on dirt roads. ✉ *Fossil Bed Rd., 3 mi west of Fort Irwin Rd.,* ☏ *760/252–6000.*

North of Barstow in the Black Mountains, **Inscription Canyon** is rich with nearly 10,000 petroglyphs and pictographs of bighorn sheep and other Mojave wildlife. This is one of the world's largest natural Native American art galleries. ✉ *EF373, off Copper City Rd. 10 mi west of Fort Irwin Rd.,* ☏ *760/252–6000.*

★ The earliest-known Americans fashioned the artifacts buried in the walls and floors of the pits at **Calico Early Man Archeological Site.** Nearly 12,000 tool-like stones—scrapers, cutting tools, choppers, handpicks, stone saws, and the like—have been excavated here. The apparent age of some of these items—perhaps as much as 200,000 years old—contradicts the dominant theory among archaeologists that humans populated North America only 13,000 years ago. Louis Leakey, the noted archaeologist, was so impressed with the Calico findings that he became project director in 1963 and served in that capacity until his death in 1972. His old camp is now a visitor center and museum. The only way into the site itself is by guided tour (call ahead, as scheduled tours sometimes don't take place). ⊠ *Off I–15 (Minneola Rd. exit), 15 mi northeast of Barstow,* ☎ *760/252–6000,* WEB *www.ca.blm.gov/ barstow/calico.* ☞ *$5 for 1 or 2 adults, each additional person $2.50.* ☉ *Visitor center Wed. 12:30–4:30, Thurs.–Sun. 9–4:30; tours Wed. 1:30 and 3:30, Thurs.–Sun. 9:30, 11:30, 1:30, and 3:30.*

Dining, Lodging, and Camping

$$ ✕ **Idle Spurs Steakhouse.** Since the 1950s this roadside ranch has been a Barstow dining staple, with a menu of choice cuts of meat, ribs, and lobster and a great microbrew list. Covered in cacti outside and Christmas lights inside, it's a colorful and nostalgic place with a big wooden bar. ⊠ *690 Rte. 58,* ☎ *760/256–8888. AE, D, MC, V.*

$ ✕ **Bagdad Cafe.** Tourists from all over the world flock to the site where the 1988 film of the same name was shot. Built in the 1940s, this Route 66 eatery offers up a home-style menu of burgers, chicken fried steak, and seafood. An old Airstream trailer from the movie sits outside the café. ⊠ *46548 National Trails Hwy., Newberry Springs,* ☎ *760/257–3101. AE, MC, V.*

$ ☷ **Ramada Inn.** This large property has more amenities than the other hotels that line Main Street, so it tends to attract business travelers. It's slightly more expensive than the others but worth it if you want the highest level of comfort Barstow has to offer. ⊠ *1511 E. Main St.,* ☎ *760/256–5673,* FAX *760/256–5917,* WEB *www.ramada.com. 148 rooms. Restaurant, pool, hot tub, laundry service, meeting room. AE, D, DC, MC, V.*

⚵ **Calico Ghost Town Regional Park.** This dusty, flat campsite with views of the ghost town provides a real Wild West atmosphere. In addition to the campsites there are six cabins ($28) and bunkhouse accommodations ($5 per person, with a 12-person minimum). There is a two-night minimum during Calico Ghost Town festival weekends. *Flush toilets, full hookups, partial hookups, dump stations, drinking water, showers, fire pits, grills, picnic tables, restaurant, electricity, public telephone, general store. 250 sites, 104 with hookups.* ⊠ *Ghost Town Rd., 3 mi north of I–15, 5 mi east of Barstow,* ☎ *760/254–2122; 800/ 862–2542 for reservations,* WEB *www.calicotown.com.* ☞ *$18–$22. D, MC, V.*

En Route Because of its colorful, steep walls, **Afton Canyon** (⊠ off Afton Canyon Rd., 36 mi northeast of Barstow via I–15) is often called the Grand Canyon of the Mojave. Afton was carved over many thousands of years by the rushing waters of the Mojave River, which makes one of its few aboveground appearances here. Where you find water in the desert you'll also find trees, grasses, and wildlife, so the canyon has attracted people for a long time: Native Americans and, later, white settlers following the Mojave Trail from the Colorado River to the Pacific Ocean, set up camp here. Now you also can camp here, at a 22-site campground amid high-desert cliffs and a mesquite thicket. The dirt road that leads to the canyon is ungraded in spots, so you are best off driving it in an all-terrain vehicle. Check with the Mojave Desert Information Center (☎

760/733–4040, WEB www.nps.gov/moja), in Baker, regarding road conditions before you head in.

Baker

㉘ *63 mi northeast of Barstow on I–15; 84 mi south of Death Valley Junction via Rte. 127.*

The small town of Baker is the gateway to the western Mojave from Death Valley, to the north. There are several gas stations and restaurants (most of them fast-food outlets) here, a few motels, and one general store, which has the distinction of selling the most winning Lotto tickets in California. You can't help but notice Baker's 134-ft-tall **thermometer** (⊠ 72157 Baker Blvd.), whose height in feet pays homage to the record-high U.S. temperature: 134°F, recorded in Death Valley on July 10, 1913. The Baker thermometer marks the location of the National Park Service's **Mojave Desert Information Center** (☎ 760/733–4040, WEB www.nps.gov/moja), where you can browse the bookstore, pick up maps, and buy souvenir posters and postcards. The center also has visitor information for Mojave National Preserve, Death Valley, and other Mojave attractions.

Dining and Lodging

$ ✕ **The Mad Greek.** Oozing with over-the-top atmosphere, this place has somehow fused Athens, Los Angeles, and the Mojave Desert. Deep-blue ceramic tiles adorn the walls, and neoclassical statues pose amid the tables. The food ranges from traditional Greek (gyros, kebabs, strong coffee) to classic American (hot dogs and ice cream sundaes). ⊠ *I–15 at Baker Blvd.,* ☎ *760/733–4354. AE, D, DC, MC, V.*

$ ⌂ **Wills Fargo Motel.** Two of Baker's three motels have the same owner and they're just down the road from each other, so there's little difference in rates or amenities. This one, however, has rooms with marginally more character, as well as a pool and a small grassy lawn out front. ⊠ *72252 Baker Blvd., 92309,* ☎ *760/733–4477,* FAX *760/733–4680. 30 rooms. Cable TV, pool. AE, D, DC, MC, V.*

Mojave National Preserve

㉙ *Between I–15 and I–40, roughly east of Baker and Ludlow to the California/Nevada border.*

The 1.4 million acres of the Mojave National Preserve don't conform to the stereotypical image of the desert, as they hold a surprising abundance of plant and animal life at elevations to nearly 8,000 ft. There are traces of human history here as well, including abandoned army posts and vestiges of mining and ranching towns. The town of Cima still has a small functioning store.

As you enter the preserve from the south, you'll pass miles of open scrub brush, Joshua trees, and beautiful red-black cinder cones before en-
★ countering the **Kelso Dunes** (⊠ Kelbaker Rd., 90 mi east of I–15 and 14 mi north of I–40, ☎ 760/255–8801 or 760/733–4040, WEB www.nps.gov/moja). These perfect, pristine slopes of gold-white sand cover 70 square mi, often reaching heights of 500–600 ft. You can reach them via an easy ½-mi walk from the main parking area. When you reach the top of a dune, kick a little bit of sand down the lee side and listen to the sand "sing." North of the dunes in the town of Kelso, a mission revival–style train depot dating from 1925 is one of the few of its kind still standing. Primitive campsites are available at no charge near the dunes' main parking area.

The National Park Service administers most of the Mojave preserve, but **Providence Mountains State Recreation Area** is under the jurisdiction of the California Department of Parks. The visitor center (☉ May–Sept., Fri.–Sat. 9–4) has views of mountain peaks, dunes, buttes, crags, and desert valleys. At **Mitchell Caverns Natural Preserve** (🎫 $3) you have a rare opportxunity to see all three types of cave formations—dripstone, flowstone, and erratics—in one place. The year-round 65°F temperature provides a break from the desert heat. Tours are given weekdays at 1:30 and weekends at 10, 1:30, and 3. Arrive a half hour before tour time to secure a slot on the tour. Between Memorial Day and Labor Day, tours are given only on weekends and holidays at 1:30. ✉ *Essex Rd., 16 mi north of I–40,* ☎ *760/928–2586,* WEB *www.calparksmojave.com.* 🎫 *$3.*

Created millions of years ago by volcanic activity, **Hole in the Wall** formed when gases were trapped between layers of deposited ash, rock, and lava; the gas bubbles left holes in the solidified material. The area was named by Bob Hollimon, a member of the Butch Cassidy gang, because it reminded him of his former hideout in Wyoming. To hike the canyon, you first must make your way down Rings Trail, a narrow 200-ft vertical chute. To make the descent you must grasp a series of metal rings embedded in the rock; smaller or larger people may find the route unmanageable. The trail drops you into Banshee Canyon, where you are surrounded by steep, pock-marked walls and small caverns. You can explore the length of the canyon, but climbing the walls is not recommended as the rock is soft and crumbles easily. Keep your eyes open for native lizards such as the chuckwalla. The Hole in the Wall ranger station has docents that can answer questions about the area. ✉ *Black Canyon Rd., 9 mi north of Mitchell Caverns,* ☎ *760/255–8801, 769/928–2572 or 760/733–4040,* WEB *www.nps.gov/moja.* ☉ *Winter, Wed.–Sun. 9–3; summer, Fri.–Sat. 9–3.*

OFF THE
BEATEN PATH

AMBOY – South of Mojave National Preserve, about midway between Barstow and Needles, lies tiny Amboy, a privately owned desert town. Here 250-ft-high Amboy Crater, an 8,000-year-old volcanic cinder cone, is surrounded by a lava field. During the winter experienced hikers can take the marked trail to the top and back, a round-trip of about three hours. While you're in Amboy, don't miss Roy's Cafe, Gas and Motel (✉ 6666 Old National Trails Hwy., ☎ 760/733–4263, WEB www.rt66roys.com), which founder Buster Burris called "the crustiest, dustiest gas stop in all of Route 66." Built in 1938, the joint is still preserved in its original condition. The restaurant offers greasy-spoon grub such as burgers, homemade chili, and tart home-style lemonade. ✉ *Old National Trails Hwy., 28 mi east of Ludlow and 47 mi west of Fenner.*

Camping

🏕 **Hole-in-the-Wall Campground.** At a cool 4,500 ft above sea level, backed by volcanic rock formations, this is a fine place to spend a quiet night and use as a base for hiking. The campground is near the Hole in the Wall ranger station. *Pit toilets, dump station, drinking water, fire pits, picnic tables. 35 RV/trailer sites, 2 walk-in tent sites.* ✉ *Black Canyon Rd. north of Essex,* ☎ *760/255–8801 or 760/733–4040,* WEB *www.nps.gov/moja. No credit cards. Reservations not accepted.*

Needles

③⓪ *I–40, 150 mi east of Barstow.*

On Route 66 and the Colorado River, Needles is a fine base for exploring a wealth of desert attractions, including Mojave National Preserve. In town don't miss the historic 1908 **El Garces Hotel and Depot** (⊠ 900 Front St., ☎ 760/326–5678), one of the many restaurant/boarding houses built by the Fred Harvey company. **Mystic Maze** (⊠ Park Moabi Rd., off I–40 11 miles southeast of Needles, ☎ 760/326–5678) is an unexplained geological site of spiritual significance to Pipa Aha Macav (Fort Mojave) Indians. The maze consists of several rows of rocks and mounds of dirt in different patterns.

★ In 1941, after the construction of Parker Dam, President Franklin D. Roosevelt set aside **Havasu National Wildlife Refuge,** a 24-mi stretch of land along the Colorado River between Needles and Lake Havasu City. Best seen by boat, this beautiful waterway is punctuated with isolated coves, sandy beaches, and Topock Marsh, a favorite nesting site of herons, egrets, and other water birds. You can see wonderful petroglyphs on the rocky red canyon cliffs of Topock Gorge. The park has 11 access points, including boat launches at Catfish Paradise, Five Mile Landing, and Pintail Slough. There is camping below Castle Rock. ⊠ *3 mi southeast of Needles off U.S. 95, Topock Marsh I–40 Arizona exit 1 to Rte. 66 north,* ☎ *760/326–3853,* WEB *southwest.fws. gov/refuges/arizona/havasu.htm.*

Moabi Regional Park, on the banks of the Colorado River, is a good place for swimming, boating, picnicking, and horseback riding, among other activities. Bass, bluegill, and trout are plentiful in the river. There are 600 campsites with full amenities, including RV hookups, laundry and showers, and grills. ⊠ *11 mi southeast of Needles on Park Moabi Rd.,* ☎ *760/326–3831,* WEB *www.moabi.com.* ⊞ *$6 day use, $12–$20 camping.*

Dining, Lodging, and Camping

$–$$ ✕ **Hungry Bear Restaurant.** If you've got a big appetite, head to this family diner for chicken-fried steak or top sirloin. You can also get breakfast. ⊠ *1906 Needles Hwy.,* ☎ *760/326–2988. AE, DC, V, MC.*

$–$$ 🏨 **Best Western Colorado River Inn.** Each room at this property off I–40 has a hair dryer; deluxe rooms also have coffeemakers. Local phone calls are free, and there is complimentary coffee in the lobby every morning. Microwaves and refrigerators are available. ⊠ *2371 Needles Hwy., 92363,* ☎ *760/326–4552,* FAX *760/326–4562,* WEB *www. bestwestern.com. 63 rooms. Cable TV with movies, indoor pool, hot tub, sauna, laundry facilities, some pets allowed; no-smoking rooms. AE, DC, MC, V.*

🛶 **Havasu Landing Resort & Casino.** This full-service RV resort in Havasu Lake is about as close as you'll get on the California side to Lake Havasu City, which is 3 mi away by ferry. There is casual lakeshore dining at the restaurant and a small casino with slot machines and some card games. A passenger ferry ($1) travels to and from London Bridge every hour, from 6 AM to midnight. *Flush toilets, full hookups, drinking water, laundry, showers, picnic tables, restaurant, snack bar, electricity, public telephone, general store, service station. 183 sites.* ⊠ *Havasu Lake Rd., 17 mi east of U.S. 95, 39 mi south of Needles, Havasu Lake 92363,* ☎ *800/307–3610 or 760/858–4593,* WEB *www.havasulanding.com. AE, D, MC, V.*

🛶 **Needles Marina Park.** Easily accessible from I–40, this luxury campground sits alongside the glassy waters of the Colorado River and is just a 30-minute boat ride from Topock Gorge or a 1½-hour ride to London Bridge on Lake Havasu. A recreation room, Jacuzzi, and 18-hole golf course are at your disposal. The resort has its own boat ramp and slips. *Flush toilets, full hookups, drinking water, laundry facilities, showers, grills, picnic tables, electricity, public telephone, general store,* *playground, pool. 194 sites with hookups. ⊠ River Rd. off Broadway,* ☏ *760/326–2197,* WEB *www.needlesmarina.com. MC, V.*

Lake Havasu City, AZ

③ *AZ Rte. 95, 43 mi southeast of Needles in Arizona.*

Every summer Los Angelenos head to Lake Havasu, a wide spot in the Colorado River backed up behind Parker Dam, for some wet-and-wild fun. Access to the lake is from its eastern shore, in Arizona. Here you can zip around on a personal watercraft, paddle a kayak, cast a fishing line, or go boating under the London Bridge, one of the oddest sights in the desert. During sunset the views are breathtaking.

✋ ★ A trip to Lake Havasu would not be complete without a visit to **London Bridge.** Robert P. McCulloch, founder of Lake Havasu City, had the bridge shipped over from England and meticulously reconstructed, piece by piece, between 1968 and 1971. Today the bridge has become the center of town, with numerous restaurants, hotels, RV parks, and a reconstructed English village surrounding it. ☏ *520/453–3444,* WEB *www.golakehavasu.com.* 🎟 *Free.* ⊘ *Daily 24 hrs.*

Dining and Lodging

$ ✕ **Frigate Restaurant and Lounge.** A Neptune's bounty of seafood and steaks awaits you at this nautical-theme spot. Locals rave about the sweet baby-back ribs. ⊠ *350 London Bridge Rd.,* ☏ *928/453–9907. AE, MC, V.*

$$–$$$ ✕🏨 **Nautical Inn.** The only beachfront property in Arizona, completely remodeled in 2002, has views of Lake Havasu and the nearby mountain ranges. Large water-view rooms are beautifully appointed and have oversize patios or balconies. You can rent water-sports equipment, and dock your boat outside the hotel. There's an 18-hole golf course next door, and the hotel offers golf packages with three local courses. The hotel's two restaurants, Captain's Table and the Tiki Terrace, offer waterfront dining on American fare such as London broil and grilled halibut. ⊠ *1000 McCullough Blvd., 86403,* ☏ *800/892–2141 or 928/855–2141,* WEB *www.nauticalinn.com. 64 rooms, 56 suites. 2 restaurants, kitchenettes (some), microwaves, cable TV, pool, lake, beach, jet skiing, marina, parasailing, hiking, lounge, meeting rooms. AE, D, MC, V.*

Nightlife

One of the hottest dance clubs on Lake Havasu is **Kokomo's on the Channel** (⊠ 1477 Queen's Bay, ☏ 928/855–0888), an island-style watering hole with a full selection of drinks and a killer view of the river.

Outdoor Activities and Sports

Located right at the London Bridge, **Kon-Tiki Tour Boat** (☏ 928/855–0888 or 928/453–6776, WEB www.londonbridgeresort.com) conducts daily narrated pontoon boat tours to the river's wild and beautiful party spots—Copper Canyon and Topock Gorge. Reservations are required for the Topock Gorge trip. **London Bridge Watercraft Tours & Rentals** (⊠ 141 Swanson Ave., ☏ 928/453–8883, WEB www.londonbridgewatercraft.com) is the place to rent a personal watercraft for a day or to join a 50-mi personal-watercraft adventure through Topock Gorge.

DEATH VALLEY AND THE MOJAVE DESERT A TO Z

To research prices, get advice from other travelers, and book travel arrangements, visit www.fodors.com.

AIR TRAVEL

Inyokern Airport, near Ridgecrest, is served by United Express from Los Angeles. McCarran International Airport, in Las Vegas, Nevada, served by dozens of major airlines, is about as close to Furnace Creek, in Death Valley National Park, as is Inyokern Airport. *See* Air Travel *in* Smart Travel Tips A to Z for airline phone numbers.

➤ AIRPORT INFORMATION: **Inyokern Airport** (✉ Inyokern Rd. (Rte. 178), 9 mi west of Ridgecrest, ☎ 760/377–5844). **McCarran International Airport** (☎ 702/261–5733). **Needles Airport** (✉ 711 Airport Road, ☎ 760/326–5263).

BUS TRAVEL

Greyhound serves Baker, Barstow, Ridgecrest, and Victorville, but traveling by bus to the Mojave Desert is neither convenient nor cheap. There is no scheduled bus service to Death Valley National Park or within Owens Valley.

➤ BUS INFORMATION: **Greyhound** (☎ 800/231–2222, WEB www.greyhound.com). **Barstow Greyhound station** (✉ 681 N. 1st Ave., ☎ 760/256–8757). **Baker Greyhound Station** (✉ 72097 Baker Blvd., ☎ 760/733–4205). **Lancaster Greyhound station** (✉ 44812 N. Sierra Hwy., ☎ 661/949–2827). **Needles Greyhound station** (✉ 1109 Broadway, ☎ 760/326–5066). **Victorville Greyhound station** (✉ 16838 D St., ☎ 760/245–2041).

CAR RENTAL

In the Owens Valley reliable regional car-rental agencies include Eastern Sierra Motors and U-Save Auto Rentals. The major national agencies serve the larger cities of the Mojave Desert: Barstow has Hertz and Avis offices, while Victorville has Avis, Budget, and Enterprise offices. *See* Car Rental *in* Smart Travel Tips A to Z for national rental agency phone numbers.

➤ RENTAL AGENCIES: **Eastern Sierra Motors** (✉ 1440 N. Hwy. 6, Bishop, ☎ 760/873–4291 or 877/503–6257). **U-Save Auto Rentals** (✉ 1075 Main St., Bishop, ☎ 800/207–2681, WEB www.usavemammothbishop.com).

CAR TRAVEL

Much of the desert can be seen from the comfort of an air-conditioned car, though you need not despair if you are without air-conditioning—just avoid driving in the middle of the day and in the middle of summer. You can approach Death Valley from the west or the southeast. Whether you've come south from Bishop or north from Ridgecrest, head east from U.S. 395 on Route 190 or Route 178. To enter Death Valley from the southeast, take Route 127 north from I–15 in Baker and link up with Route 178, which travels west into the valley and then cuts north toward Route 190 at Furnace Creek.

The Mojave is shaped like a giant L, with one leg jutting north toward the Owens Valley and the other extending east toward California's borders with Nevada and Arizona. The major north–south route through the western Mojave is U.S. 395, which intersects with I–15 between Cajon Pass and Victorville. U.S. 395 travels north into the Owens Valley, passing such little dusty stops as Lone Pine, Independence, Big Pine, and Bishop. Farther west, Route 14 runs north–south between Inyokern (near Ridgecrest) and Palmdale. Two major east–west routes travel through the Mojave: to the north, I–15 between Barstow and Las Vegas, Nevada; to the south, I–40 between Barstow and Needles. At the intersection of the two interstates, in Barstow, I–15 veers south toward Victorville and Los Angeles, and I–40 gives way to Route 58 toward Bakersfield.

➤ CONTACTS: **California Highway Patrol 24-hour road info** (☏ 800/ 427–7623, WEB www.dot.ca.gov/hq/roadinfo).

EMERGENCIES

In an emergency dial 911.

Of course, it's best to avoid emergencies, which can arise easily in the desert. You can protect yourself by being prepared and taking a few simple safety precautions: Never travel alone. Always take a companion, especially if you are not familiar with the area. Let someone know your trip route, destination, and estimated time and date of return. Before setting out, make sure your vehicle is in good condition. Carry a jack, tools, and tow rope or chain. Fill up your tank whenever you see a gas pump—it can be miles between service stations. Stay on main roads: if you drive even a few feet off the pavement, you could get you stuck in sand. Plus, venturing off-road is illegal in many areas. When driving, watch out for wild burros, horses, and range cattle. They roam free throughout much of the desert and have the right-of-way.

Drink at least a gallon of water a day (three gallons if you are hiking or otherwise exerting yourself), even if you don't feel thirsty. Dress in layered clothing and wear comfortable, sturdy shoes and a hat. Keep snacks, sunscreen, and a first-aid kit on hand. If you suddenly have a headache or feel dizzy or nauseous, you could be suffering from dehydration. Get out of the sun immediately and drink plenty of water. Dampen your clothing to lower your body temperature.

Do not enter mine tunnels or shafts. The structure may be unstable, and there may be hidden dangers such as pockets of bad air. Avoid canyons during rainstorms. Floodwaters can quickly fill up dry riverbeds and cover or wash away roads. Never place your hands or feet where you can't see. Rattlesnakes, scorpions, and black widow spiders may be hiding there.

➤ CONTACTS: **BLM Rangers** (☏ 760/255–8700). **Community Hospital** (✉ Barstow, ☏ 760/256–1761). **Northern Inyo Hospital** (✉ 150 Pioneer Ln., Bishop, ☏ 760/873–5811). **San Bernardino County Sheriff** (☏ 760/256–1796 in Barstow; 760/733–4448 in Baker).

TOURS

Old West Tours operates luxury bus tours of some of the most breathtaking Mojave Desert and eastern Sierra sights, from majestic Red Rock Canyon and Mt. Whitney to the dusty ghost towns of Bodie and Cerro Gordo. Lodging, snacks, and most meals are included. Tours depart from locations in Lancaster, Palmdale, and Rosamond. The Mojave Group of the Sierra Club regularly organizes field trips to interesting spots such as Red Mountain, Silverwood Lake, and the San Gabriel Mountains. The San Gorgonio Sierra Club chapter also conducts desert excursions. Call WSC chair Ralph Salisbury at 909/686–4141.

➤ CONTACTS: **Old West Tours** (✉ Box 2240, Rosamond 93560, ☏ 800/ 868–7777, WEB www.oldwesttours.com). **Sierra Club** (✉ 3345 Wilshire Blvd., Suite 508, Los Angeles 90010, ☏ 213/387–4287; 909/686– 6112 for San Gorgonio chapter, www.sierraclub.com).

TRAIN TRAVEL

Amtrak makes stops in Victorville, Barstow, and Needles, but the stations are not staffed and do not have phone numbers, so you have to purchase your tickets in advance and handle your baggage yourself. You can travel west to connect with the *Coast Starlight* in Los Angeles or the *San Diegan* in Fullerton. The *Southwest Chief* stops twice a day at the above cities on its route from Los Angeles to Chicago and back. The Barstow station is served daily by Amtrak California motor coaches that travel between San Joaquin, Bakersfield, and Las Vegas. ➤ TRAIN INFORMATION: **Amtrak** (☎ 800/872–7245, WEB www. amtrak.com). **Barstow Amtrak station** (✉ 658 N. 1st Ave.). **Needles Amtrak station, at El Garces Harvey House** (✉ 900 E. Front St.). **Victorville Amtrak station** (✉ 16858 E St.).

VISITOR INFORMATION

➤ TOURIST INFORMATION: **Big Pine Chamber of Commerce** (✉ Box 23, 93513, ☎ 760/938–2114). **Bishop Chamber of Commerce** (✉ 690 N. Main St., 93514, ☎ 760/873–8405, WEB www.bishopvisitor.com). **Bureau of Land Management** (✉ California Desert District Office, 6221 Box Springs Blvd., Riverside 92507, ☎ 909/697–5200, WEB www.ca.blm.gov). **California Welcome Center** (✉ 2796 Tanger Way, Barstow 92311, ☎ 760/253–4782, WEB www.barstowca.com). **Death Valley Chamber of Commerce** (✉ Box 157, 92384, ☎ 760/852–4524, WEB www.deathvalleychamber.org). **Death Valley National Park** (✉ Visitor Center at Furnace Creek, 92328, ☎ 760/786–2331, WEB www.nps.gov/deva). **Death Valley Natural History Association** (✉ Box 188, Death Valley 92328, ☎ 800/478–8564). **Desert Discovery Center** (✉ 831 Barstow Rd., Barstow 92311, ☎ 760/252–6060). **Independence Chamber of Commerce** (✉ Box 435, 93526, ☎ 760/878–0084, WEB www.independencechamber.com). **Lone Pine Chamber of Commerce** (✉ 126 S. Main St., 93545, ☎ 760/876–4444 or 877/253–8981, WEB www.lonepinechamber.org). **Needles Chamber of Commerce** (✉ P.O. Box 705, Needles, 92363, ☎ 760/326–2050, WEB www.needleschamber.com). **Ridgecrest Area Convention and Visitors Bureau** (✉ 100 W. California Ave., 93555, ☎ 760/375–8202 or 800/847–4830, WEB www.visitdeserts.com). **San Bernardino County Regional Parks Department** (✉ 777 E. Rialto Ave., San Bernardino 92415, ☎ 909/387–2594, WEB www.co.san-bernardino.ca.us/parks). **Wrightwood Chamber of Commerce** (✉ Box 416, 92397, ☎ 760/249–4320; 760/249–6822 for recorded information, WEB www.wrightwoodcalifornia.com). **Victorville Chamber of Commerce** (✉ 14174 Green Tree Blvd., 92393, ☎ 760/245–6506, WEB www.vvchamber.com).

12 MONTEREY BAY

FROM SANTA CRUZ TO CARMEL VALLEY

Famed for its scenic beauty, the Monterey Peninsula is also steeped in history. The town of Monterey was California's first capital, the Carmel Mission headquarters for California's mission system. John Steinbeck's novels immortalized the area in *Cannery Row,* and Robert Louis Stevenson strolled its streets, gathering inspiration for *Treasure Island.* The present is equally illustrious. Blessed with a natural splendor undiminished by time or commerce, the bay accommodates both high-tech marine habitats and luxurious resorts.

MARITIME BOUNTY AND CULTURAL DIVERSITY have made the Monterey Bay area what it is today. Set along a 90-mi crescent of coastline like jewels in a tiara, the towns of Monterey Bay combine the somewhat funky, beachcomber aspects of California's culture with the state's more refined tendencies. Past and present merge gracefully here.

Revised by
John A.
Vlahides

About 2,500 years ago, the Ohlone Indians recognized the region's potential and became its first settlers. Europeans followed in 1542, when the white-sand beaches, pine forests, and rugged coastline captivated explorer Juan Rodríguez Cabrillo, who claimed the Monterey Peninsula for Spain. Spanish missionaries, Mexican rulers, and land developers have come and gone throughout the centuries since then, yet the area's natural assets and historic sites remain remarkably untarnished.

In 1770 Monterey became the capital of the Spanish territory of Alta California. Commander Don Gaspar de Portola established the first of California's four Spanish presidios here, and Father Junípero Serra founded the second of 21 Franciscan missions (he later moved it to Carmel). Mexico revolted against Spain in 1822 and claimed Alta California as its own, but by the mid-1840s Monterey grew into a lively seaport that attracted many Yankee sea traders. On July 7, 1846, Commodore John Sloat raised the flag of the United States over the Custom House. For Anglos, being governed by the United States proved far more profitable than being aligned with Mexico. But for the Ohlone Indians, the transition to American rule was disastrous: state and federal laws passed in the late 1800s took away rights and property that had been granted them by Spain and Mexico.

California's constitution was framed in Monterey's Colton Hall, but the town was all but forgotten once gold was discovered at Sutter's Mill on the American River. After the gold rush the state capital moved to Sacramento, while in Monterey the whaling industry boomed until the early 1900s. Tourists began to arrive at the turn of the 20th century with the opening of the Del Monte Hotel, the most palatial resort the West Coast had ever seen. Writers and artists such as John Steinbeck, Henry Miller, Robinson Jeffers, and Ansel Adams also discovered Monterey Bay, adding their legacy to the region while capturing its magic on canvas, paper, and film. In the 1920s and 1930s Cannery Row's sardine industry took off, but by the late 1940s and early 1950s the fish disappeared. The causes are still in dispute, though overfishing, water contamination, and a change in ocean currents were the likely culprits.

Today the Monterey Peninsula's diverse cultural and maritime heritage is evident in the town's 19th-century buildings and busy harbor. Cannery Row has been reborn as a tourist attraction, with shops, restaurants, hotels, and the Monterey Bay Aquarium. The bay itself is protected by the Monterey Bay National Marine Sanctuary, the nation's largest undersea canyon, bigger and deeper than the Grand Canyon. The preserve supports a rich brew of marine life, from fat barking sea lions to tiny plantlike anemones. Indeed, nature is still at its best around Monterey Bay, as the view from almost anywhere along Route 1 will tell you.

Pleasures and Pastimes

Dining

Between San Francisco and Los Angeles, the finest dining is to be found around Monterey Bay—with the possible exception of Santa Barbara. The surrounding waters abound with fish, wild game roams the foothills, and the inland valleys are the vegetable basket of California; nearby Castroville dubs itself the "artichoke capital of the world." Except at beachside stands and inexpensive eateries, where anything goes, casual but neat resort wear is the norm. The few places where more formal attire is required are noted.

CATEGORY	COST*
$$$$	over $30
$$$	$22–$30
$$	$15–$21
$	under $15

per person for a main course at dinner, excluding tip and 7¼%–8¼% tax

Golf

Since the opening of the Del Monte Golf Course in 1897, golf has been an integral part of the Monterey Peninsula's social and recreational scene. Pebble Beach's championship courses host prestigious tournaments, and though the greens fees at these courses can run well over $200, elsewhere on the peninsula you'll find less expensive—but still challenging and scenic—options. Many hotels will help with golf reservations or have golf packages; inquire when you book your room.

Lodging

Monterey-area accommodations range from no-frills motels to luxurious resorts. Some of the area's small inns and B&Bs pamper the individual traveler in grand style, serving not only full breakfasts but afternoon or early evening wine and hors d'oeuvres. Pacific Grove has quietly turned itself into the region's B&B capital; Carmel also has fine B&Bs. Truly lavish resorts, with everything from featherbeds to heated floors, cluster in exclusive Pebble Beach and pastoral Carmel Valley. Many of these accommodations are not suitable for children, so if you're traveling with kids, be sure to ask before you book.

Around Monterey Bay high season runs April through October. Rates during winter, especially at the larger hotels, may drop by 50% or more, and B&Bs often offer midweek specials in the off-season. However, even the simplest of the area's lodgings are expensive, and most properties require a two-night stay on weekends.

CATEGORY	COST*
$$$$	over $225
$$$	$160–$225
$$	$100–$159
$	under $100

All prices are for a standard double room, excluding 10%–10½% tax.

Whale-Watching

On their annual migration between the Bering Sea and Baja California, thousands of gray whales pass not far off the Monterey coast. They are sometimes visible through binoculars from shore, but a whale-watching cruise is the best way to get a close look at these magnificent mammals. The migration south takes place from December through March. January is prime viewing time. The migration north occurs from March through June. In addition, some 2,000 blue whales and 600 humpbacks pass the coast and are easily spotted in late summer and early fall. Smaller numbers of minke whales, orcas, sperm whales, and fin whales have been sighted in mid-August. Even if no whales surface, bay cruises almost always encounter some unforgettable marine life, including sea otters, sea lions, and porpoises.

Exploring Monterey Bay

The individual charms of its towns complement Monterey Bay's natural beauty. Santa Cruz sits at the northern tip of the crescent formed by Monterey Bay; the Monterey Peninsula, including Monterey, Pacific Grove, and Carmel, occupies the southern end. In between, Route 1 cruises along the coastline, passing windswept beaches piled high with sand dunes. Along the route are artichoke fields and the towns of Watsonville and Castroville.

Numbers in the text correspond to numbers in the margin and on the Monterey Bay and Monterey maps.

Great Itineraries

Although it is compact, the Monterey Peninsula is packed with diversions. If you have an interest in California history and historic preservation, the place to start is Monterey, with its adobe buildings along the downtown Path of History. Fans of Victorian architecture will want to search out the many fine examples in Pacific Grove. In Carmel you can shop 'til you drop, and when summer and weekend hordes overwhelm the town's clothing boutiques, art galleries, housewares outlets, and gift shops, you can slip off to enjoy the coast.

IF YOU HAVE 3 DAYS

Start in ⊞ **Monterey** ④–⑲, spending your first day along **Cannery Row** and **Fisherman's Wharf** ⑯. Be sure not to miss the **Monterey Bay Aquarium** ⑲ or **Steinbeck's Spirit of Monterey Wax Museum** ⑱. Catch the sunset from the bustling wharf or slip into the serene bar at the Monterey Plaza Hotel and Spa. On the following day visit a few of the historic buildings of **Monterey State Historic Park** in the morning and motor down **17-Mile Drive** ㉑ in the afternoon. Linger for sunset views along the drive or at nearby **Point Lobos State Reserve.** On day three head for **Carmel** ㉒ to visit **Carmel Mission** and **Tor House** if it's open. Leave yourself plenty of time to browse the shops of **Ocean Avenue,** then stroll over to **Scenic Road** and spend time on **Carmel Beach** before dinner.

IF YOU HAVE 5 DAYS

If you are coming from the north, stop in **San Juan Bautista** ②, a classic mission village, on your way to ⊞ **Monterey** ④–⑲. Fill the rest of day one with a glimpse of the city's fascinating past at **Monterey State Historic Park.** The next morning get up-close and personal with Monterey Bay marine life by boarding a whale-watching or other cruise vessel at **Fisherman's Wharf** ⑯. Spend the afternoon on the wharf and along **Cannery Row.** Start day three at the **Monterey Bay Aquarium** ⑲ and enjoy the afternoon either relaxing on the Monterey waterfront or tasting wine at **Ventana Vineyards,** on the Monterey–Salinas Highway. On your fourth day drive to **Carmel** ㉒ to see its sights and explore its shops. Take a late-afternoon spin on **17-Mile Drive** ㉑ and catch the sunset there or at **Point Lobos State Reserve.** Take day five to explore the shoreline and Victorian houses of **Pacific Grove** ⑳.

When to Tour Monterey Bay

Summer is peak season, with crowds everywhere and generally mild weather. A sweater or windbreaker is nearly always necessary along the coast, where a cool breeze usually blows and fog is on the way in or out. Inland, temperatures in Salinas or Carmel Valley can be a good 15 or 20 degrees warmer than those in Carmel and Monterey. Off-season, from November through April, fewer people visit, and the mood is mellower. Rainfall is heaviest in January and February.

Monterey Bay

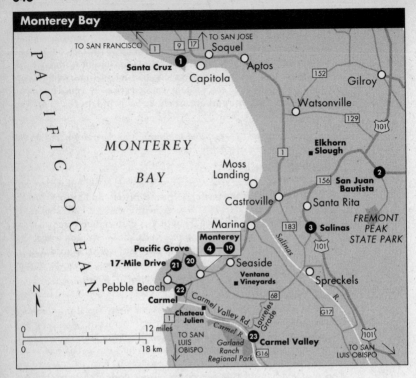

SANTA CRUZ COUNTY

Less manicured than its upmarket Monterey Peninsula neighbors to the south, Santa Cruz is the big city on its stretch of the California coast. A haven for those opting out of the rat race and a bastion of 1960s-style counterculture values, Santa Cruz has been at the forefront of such quintessential "left coast" trends as health food, recycling, and environmentalism. Between Santa Cruz and the Monterey Peninsula, the agricultural towns of Capitola, Soquel, and Aptos have their own quality restaurants, small inns, resorts, and antiques shops.

Santa Cruz

❶ *74 mi south of San Francisco, I–280 to Rte. 17 to Rte. 1; 48 mi north of Monterey on Rte. 1.*

The surrounding mountains shelter the beach town of Santa Cruz from the coastal fog and from the smoggy skies of the San Francisco Bay Area and Silicon Valley. The climate here is mild, and it is usually warmer and sunnier than elsewhere along the coast this far north. The heart of downtown Santa Cruz is along Pacific Avenue south of Water St., where you'll find shops, restaurants, and other establishments in the outdoor **Pacific Garden Mall.**

Santa Cruz gets some of its youthful spirit from the nearby **University of California at Santa Cruz.** The school's harmonious redwood buildings are perched on the forested hills above the town, and the campus is tailor-made for the contemplative life, with a juxtaposition of sylvan settings and sweeping vistas over open meadows onto the bay. ⊠ *Bay and High Sts.,* ☎ *831/459–0111,* WEB *www.ucsc.edu.*

Santa Cruz has been a seaside resort since the mid-19th century. The Looff carousel and classic wooden Giant Dipper roller coaster at the **Santa Cruz Beach Boardwalk** date from the early 1900s. Elsewhere along the boardwalk, the Casino Fun Center has its share of video-game technology. But this is still primarily a place for good old-fashioned fun for toddlers, teens, and adults. Take a break from the rides with boardwalk favorites such as corn dogs or chowder fries. ⊠ *Along Beach St. west from San Lorenzo River,* ☎ *831/423–5590 or 831/426–7433,* WEB *www.beachboardwalk.com.* ⌷ *$23.95 (day pass for unlimited rides).* ☉ *Memorial Day–Labor Day, daily; Labor Day–Memorial Day, weekends, weather permitting (call for hrs).*

The **Santa Cruz Municipal Wharf** (☎ 831/420–5270, WEB www. santacruzwharf.com), just up the beach from the boardwalk, is lined with restaurants, shops, and seafood takeout windows. The barking of sea lions that lounge in heaps under the wharf's pilings enliven the area.

Drive southwest from the municipal wharf on West Cliff Drive about ¾ mi to the promontory at **Seal Rock,** where you can watch pinnipeds hang out, sunbathe, and occasionally frolic. The **Mark Abbott Memorial Lighthouse,** adjacent to the promontory, has a surfing museum with artifacts that include the remains of a board that a shark munched on. ⊠ *W. Cliff Dr.,* ☎ *831/420–6289.* ⌷ *Free.* ☉ *Wed. –Mon. noon–4 (summer); Thurs.–Mon. noon–4 (winter).*

About 1¾ mi west of the lighthouse is secluded **Natural Bridges State Beach,** a stretch of soft sand with tidal pools and a natural rock bridge nearby. From October to early March a colony of monarch butterflies resides here. ⊠ *2531 W. Cliff Dr.,* ☎ *831/423–4609,* WEB *www.cruzio.com/lae/natbr.* ⌷ *Parking $3.* ☉ *Park daily 8 AM–sunset. Visitor center Oct.–Feb., daily 10–4; Mar.–Sept., weekends 10–4.*

Dining and Lodging

$$$ ✕ **Theo's.** Set in a residential neighborhood on a quiet side street, ★ Theo's is one of the area's top destinations for California cuisine. Seasonal standouts include duck with garden vegetables and currants as well as rack of lamb with ratatouille. Much of the produce used in the kitchen comes from the ¼-acre organic garden behind the restaurant, where diners can stroll between courses. Service is gracious and attentive, and the wine list is outstanding. ⊠ *3101 N. Main St., Soquel,* ☎ *831/ 462–3657. Reservations essential. AE, DC, MC, V. Closed Sun.–Mon. No lunch.*

$$–$$$ ✕ **Bittersweet Bistro.** A large old tavern with cathedral ceilings houses ★ the popular bistro of chef-owner Thomas Vinolus, who draws his culinary inspiration from the Mediterranean. The menu changes seasonally, but look for Maui onion soup gratinée, made with 15-year-old Madeira, or duck foie gras to start, and then move on to one of the outstandingly fresh fish specials, a grilled vegetable platter, a seafood *puttanesca* (with tomatoes, garlic, olives, and anchovies), or grilled lamb tenderloins. Finish with any of the chocolate desserts. ⊠ *787 Rio Del Mar Blvd., off Rte. 1, Aptos,* ☎ *831/662–9799. AE, MC, V. No lunch.*

$$–$$$ ✕ **Oswald's.** Intimate and stylish, this tiny courtyard bistro serves a sophisticated yet unpretentious, seasonally changing, perfectly prepared menu of European-inspired California cooking, such as sherry-steamed mussels, and sautéed veal livers. ⊠ *1547 Pacific Ave.,* ☎ *831/423–7427. Reservations essential. AE, DC, MC, V. Closed Mon. No lunch.*

$$–$$$ ✕ **Pearl Alley Bistro.** Popular with locals and oenophiles, this bustling bistro changes its menu monthly to focus on a particular country's cuisine. Book a table in advance or sit at the marble-top bar and meet the bon vivants of Santa Cruz. ⊠ *110 Pearl Alley, off Walnut Ave.,* ☎ *831/ 429–8070. Reservations essential. AE, MC, V.*

$$ ✕ **Gabriella Café.** In a small brown stucco building, this café is intimate without being stuffy. The seasonal Italian menu highlights local organic produce. Watch for such dishes as steamed mussels, braised lamb shank, and grilled Portobello mushrooms. ✉ *910 Cedar St.,* ☎ *831/457–1677. AE, DC, MC, V.*

$–$$ ✕ **El Palomar.** The restaurant of the Palomar Hotel has well-preserved Spanish architecture with vaulted ceilings, wood beams, and an atrium that opens up in warm weather. Among the best dishes are seviche tostadas, chili *verde*, and fish tacos. The attractive taco bar, off to one side, is open all day. You can book a table during the week, but expect long waits on Friday and Saturday, when reservations are not accepted. ✉ *1336 Pacific Ave.,* ☎ *831/425–7575. AE, D, DC, MC, V.*

$–$$ ✕ **O'mei.** Don't let its plain shopping-center location fool you; this unpretentious provincial Chinese restaurant serves outstanding seasonal dishes with fresh and dynamic flavors. ✉ *2316 Mission St.,* ☎ *831/ 425–8458. Reservations essential. AE, MC, V. No lunch weekends.*

$–$$ ✕ **Paradise Beach Grille.** Sit under the vaulted ceiling in the casual dining room or outside on the deck overlooking the sea at Capitola's liveliest eatery. The contemporary menu is diverse—including salads, pastas, seafood, and meats—and the portions are huge. ✉ *215 Esplanade, Capitola,* ☎ *831/476–4900. Reservations essential. AE, MC, V.*

$ ✕ **Seabright Brewery.** Great burgers, seafood, and stellar house-made
☺ microbrews make this a perfect stop after a day at the beach. Sit outside on the large patio or inside at one of the comfortable, spacious booths, and watch the locals at one of their favorite hangouts. ✉ *519 Seabright Ave.,* ☎ *831/426–2739. AE, MC, V.*

$ ✕ **Zachary's.** With its mostly young clientele, this noisy café defines the funky essence of Santa Cruz. It also dishes up great breakfasts: omelets, sourdough pancakes, artichoke frittatas, and "Mike's Mess"— eggs scrambled with bacon, mushrooms, and home fries, then topped with sour cream, melted cheese, and fresh tomatoes. ✉ *819 Pacific Ave.,* ☎ *831/427–0646. Reservations not accepted. MC, V. Closed Mon. No dinner.*

$$$$ ▦ **Inn at Depot Hill.** This inventively designed B&B in a former rail depot sees itself as a link to the era of luxury train travel. Each double room or suite, complete with fireplace and feather beds, is inspired by a different destination—Italy's Portofino, France's Côte d'Azur, Japan's Kyoto. One suite is decorated like a Pullman car for a railroad baron. Some accommodations have private patios with hot tubs. This is a great place for an adults-only weekend. ✉ *250 Monterey Ave. (Box 1934), Capitola-by-the-Sea 95010,* ☎ *831/462–3376 or 800/572– 2632,* 🖷 *831/462–3697,* 🖳 *www.innatdepothill.com. 6 rooms, 6 suites. Fans, in-room data ports, cable TV, in-room VCRs, hot tub; no air-conditioning, no smoking. AE, D, MC, V. BP.*

$$$$ ▦ **Pleasure Point Inn.** Tucked in a residential neighborhood at the east end of town, this modern Mediterranean-style B&B sits right across the street from the ocean and a popular surfing beach. The immaculately clean rooms are handsomely appointed with high-quality furnishings and perfectly outfitted with several deluxe amenities, including heated tiles on the bathroom floors, dimmer switches, and fireplaces in some of the rooms. You have use of the large roof-top sun deck and hot tub overlooking the Pacific. Since this is a place for a romantic getaway, it's not a good place for kids. ✉ *2–3665 E. Cliff Dr., Santa Cruz 95062,* ☎ *831/469–6161 or 877/557–2567,* 🖷 *831/479–1347,* 🖳 *www.pleasurepointinn.com. 4 rooms. Fans, in-room data ports, in-room safes, in-room hot tubs (some), minibars, refrigerators, cable TV, hot tub, beach; no air-conditioning, no smoking. MC, V. CP.*

$$$$ 🏨 **Seascape Resort.** On a bluff overlooking Monterey Bay, Seascape
ⓒ   is a place to unwind. The spacious all-suite units sleep from two to six
       people, and each has a kitchenette, a fireplace, and an ocean-view patio
       with a barbecue grill. The resort is about 9 mi south of Santa Cruz. ✉
       1 Seascape Resort Dr., Aptos 95003, ☎ *831/688–6800 or 800/929–
       7727,* FAX *831/685–2753,* WEB *www.seascaperesort.com. 285 suites.
       Restaurant, room service, fans, in-room data ports, kitchens (some),
       kitchenettes (some), cable TV with movies and video games, golf priv-
       ileges, 3 pools, health club, 3 hot tubs, sauna, spa, beach, children's
       programs (ages 5–10), laundry service, Internet, business services, con-
       vention center, meeting room; no air-conditioning, no smoking. AE,
       D, DC, MC, V.*

$$$$ 🏨 **WestCoast Santa Cruz Hotel.** Within a short stroll of the boardwalk
       and wharf, this resort opens right onto Cowell Beach. Though the hotel
       is a monolithic concrete structure, all rooms have private balconies or
       patios overlooking the Pacific. If it's too cold to swim in the ocean,
       you can head for the heated swimming pool and tub. ✉ *175 W. Cliff
       Dr., Santa Cruz 95060,* ☎ *831/426–4330 or 800/426–0670,* FAX *831/
       427–2025,* WEB *www.westcoastsantacruz.com. 147 rooms, 16 suites.
       Restaurant, bar, room service, refrigerators, cable TV, pool, 2 hot
       tubs, laundry service; no-smoking rooms. AE, D, DC, MC, V.*

$$$–$$$$ 🏨 **Babbling Brook Inn.** Though smack in the middle of Santa Cruz,
       the lush gardens, running stream, and tall trees of this B&B make you
       feel as though you are in a secluded wood. Most rooms have fireplaces
       (though a few are electric) and private patios. Complimentary wine,
       cheese, and fresh-baked cookies are available in the afternoon. ✉
       1025 Laurel St., 95060, ☎ *831/427–2456 or 800/866–1131,* FAX *831/
       427–2457,* WEB *www.babblingbrookinn.com. 13 rooms. In-room hot
       tubs (some), cable TV, in-room VCRs; no air-conditioning, no smok-
       ing. AE, DC, MC, V. BP.*

$$$–$$$$ 🏨 **Historic Sand Rock Farm.** On the site of a former winery, this cen-
★   tury-old Arts and Crafts–inspired farmhouse has been lovingly re-
       stored and modernized. You are pampered with comfortable, spacious
       accommodations and a sumptuous chef-prepared breakfast. Most
       rooms have oversize Jacuzzi tubs; the others share a large outdoor red-
       wood hot tub. ✉ *6901 Freedom Blvd., Aptos 95003,* ☎ *831/688–8005,*
       FAX *831/688–8025,* WEB *www.sandrockfarm.com. 5 rooms. Fans, in-room
       data ports, in-room hot tubs (some), cable TV, in-room VCRs, out-
       door hot tub, Internet; no air-conditioning. AE, MC, V. BP.*

$$–$$$ 🏨 **Ocean Pacific Lodge.** By staying a few blocks from the beach, you
       can save money at this modern, multistory motel with a heated pool
       and two hot tubs. ✉ *120 Washington St., 95060,* ☎ *831/457–1234
       or 800/995–0289,* FAX *831/457–0861. 44 rooms, 13 suites. Refrigera-
       tors, cable TV, in-room VCRs, pool, gym, 2 hot tubs, some pets al-
       lowed. AE, D, DC, MC, V. CP.*

Nightlife and the Arts

Shakespeare Santa Cruz (✉ Performing Arts Complex, University
of California at Santa Cruz, ☎ 831/459–2121, WEB www.
shakespearesantacruz.org) stages a six-week Shakespeare festival
in July and August that also may include one modern work. Most
performances are outdoors in the striking Redwood Glen. There is
also a program around the holidays in December.

Outdoor Activities and Sports

BICYCLING

Rent a a bike at **Bike Shop Santa Cruz** (✉ 1325 Mission St., ☎ 831/
454–0909).

BOATS AND CHARTERS

Chardonnay Sailing Charters (☎ 831/423–1213) accommodates 49 passengers for year-round cruises on Monterey Bay aboard the 70-ft *Chardonnay II,* leaving from the yacht harbor in Santa Cruz. Reservations are essential. **Original Stagnaro Fishing Trips** (✉ center of Santa Cruz Municipal Wharf, ☎ 831/427–2334) operates salmon- and rock-cod-fishing expeditions; the fees ($40–$50) include bait. The company also runs whale-watching cruises ($25) from December through April.

SURFING

Manresa State Beach (✉ Manresa Dr., La Selva Beach, ☎ 831/761–1795), south of Santa Cruz, has premium surfing conditions, but the currents can be treacherous; campsites are available. The surf at **New Brighton State Beach** (✉ 1500 State Park Dr., Capitola, ☎ 831/464–6330) is challenging; campsites are available. Surfers gather for the spectacular waves and sunsets at **Pleasure Point** (✉ E. Cliff and Pleasure Point Drs.). **Steamer's Lane,** near the lighthouse on West Cliff Drive, has a decent break. The area plays host to several competitions in the summer.

Cowell's Beach 'n' Bikini Surf Shop (✉ 30 Front St., ☎ 831/427–2355) rents surfboards and wet suits.

En Route About halfway between Santa Cruz and Monterey, east of the tiny harbor town of Moss Landing, is one of only two federal research reserves in California, the **Elkhorn Slough at the National Estuarine Research Reserve** (✉ 1700 Elkhorn Rd., Watsonville, ☎ 831/728–2822, WEB www.elkhornslough.org). Its 1,400 acres of tidal flats and salt marshes form a complex environment that supports more than 300 species of birds. A walk along the meandering waterways and wetlands can reveal hawks, white-tailed kites, owls, herons, and egrets. Wednesday through Sunday 9–5 you can wander at your leisure, or take a guided walk (10 and 1) to the heron rookery on weekends. There is an admission charge of $2.50.

San Juan Bautista

❷ *Rte. 156, 19 mi east of Rte. 1, 34 mi south of Santa Cruz.*

Sleepy San Juan Bautista has been protected from development since 1933, when much of the town became a state park. This is about as close to early 19th-century California as you can get. Small antiques shops and art galleries line the side streets.

The centerpiece of **San Juan Bautista State Historic Park** is a wide green plaza ringed by historic buildings: a restored blacksmith shop, a stable, a pioneer cabin, and a jailhouse. The **Castro-Breen Adobe,** furnished with Spanish colonial antiques, presents a view of mid-19th-century domestic life in the village. Running along one side of the town square is **Mission San Juan Bautista** (✉ 408 S. 2nd St., ☎ 831/623–2127), a long, low, colonnaded structure, founded by Father Fermin Lasuen in 1797. Adjoining it is Mission Cemetery, where more than 4,300 Native Americans who converted to Christianity are buried in unmarked graves. You must pay $2 to enter the mission building, which is open daily 9:30–5.

After the mission era San Juan Bautista became an important crossroads for stagecoach travel. The principal stop in town was the **Plaza Hotel,** a collection of adobe buildings with furnishings from the 1860s. ★ On **Living History Day,** which takes place on the first Saturday of each month, costumed volunteers engage in quilting bees, tortilla making, butter churning, and other frontier activities. ⊠ *2nd and Franklin Sts., off Rte. 156,* ☎ *831/623–4881 or 831/623–4526,* WEB *www. cal-parks.ca.gov.* ⊡ *$1.* ⊘ *Daily 10–4:30.*

Salinas

❸ *U.S. 101, 20 mi south of San Juan Bautista; 17 mi east of Monterey via Rte. 68.*

Salinas is the population center of a rich agricultural valley where fertile soil, an ideal climate, and a good water supply produce optimum growing conditions for crops such as lettuce, broccoli, tomatoes, strawberries, flowers, and wine grapes. This unpretentious town may lack the sophistication and scenic splendors of the coast, but it will interest literary and architectural buffs. Turn-of-the-20th-century buildings have been the focus of ongoing renovation, much of it centered on the original downtown area of South Main Street, with its handsome stone storefronts. The memory and literary legacy of Salinas native (and winner of Pulitzer and Nobel prizes) John Steinbeck are well honored here.

The **National Steinbeck Center** is a museum and archive dedicated to the life and works of John Steinbeck. Many exhibits are interactive, bringing to life Steinbeck worlds such as Cannery Row, Hooverville (from *The Grapes of Wrath*), and the Mexican Plaza (from *The Pearl*). The library and archives contain Steinbeck first editions, notebooks, photographs, and audiotapes. Access to the archives is by appointment only. The center has information about Salinas's annual Steinbeck Festival, in August, and about tours of area landmarks mentioned in his novels. ⊠ *1 Main St.,* ☎ *831/796–3833,* WEB *www.steinbeck.org.* ⊡ *$8.* ⊘ *Daily 10–5.*

The **Jose Eusebio Boronda Adobe** contains furniture and artifacts depicting the lifestyle of Spanish California in the 1840s. Call for directions. ⊠ *333 Boronda Rd.,* ☎ *831/757–8085.* ⊡ *Free (donation requested).* ⊘ *Weekdays 10–2; call for weekend hrs.*

Dining

$–$$ ✕ **Spado's.** Spado's brings Monterey-style culinary sophistication to the valley. For lunch visit the antipasto bar for fresh salads and Mediterranean morsels; the *panini* (Italian-style sandwiches) are also excellent. For dinner try the pizza with chicken and sun-dried-tomato pesto, the angel-hair pasta and prawns, or the risotto of the day. ⊠ *66 W. Alisal St.,* ☎ *831/424–4139. AE, D, DC, MC, V. Closed Mon. No lunch weekends.*

$ ✕ **Steinbeck House.** John Steinbeck's birthplace, a Victorian frame house, has been converted into a lunch-only (11:30–2) eatery run by the volunteer Valley Guild. The restaurant displays some Steinbeck memorabilia. The set menu, which includes such dishes as zucchini lasagna and spinach crepes, incorporates locally grown produce. ⊠ *132 Central Ave.,* ☎ *831/424–2735. MC, V. Closed Sun. and 3 wks in late Dec. and early Jan.*

Outdoor Activities and Sports

The **California Rodeo** (☎ *831/775–3100,* WEB www.carodeo.com), one of the oldest and most famous rodeos in the West, takes place in Salinas in mid-July.

MONTEREY

Early in the 20th century Carmel Martin, the first mayor of the city of Monterey, saw a bright future for his town: "Monterey Bay is the one place where people can live without being disturbed by manufacturing and big factories. I am certain that the day is coming when this will be the most desirable place in the whole state of California." It seems that Mayor Martin was not far off the mark.

Historic Monterey

48 mi south of Santa Cruz on Rte. 1; 19 mi west of Salinas Rte. 68.

A Good Tour

You can glimpse Monterey's early history in the well-preserved adobe buildings at **Monterey State Historic Park.** Far from being a hermetic period museum, the park facilities are an integral part of the day-to-day business life of the town—within some of the buildings are a store, a theater, and government offices. Some of the historic houses are graced with gardens that are worthy sights in and of themselves. Free guided tours of Casa Soberanes, Larkin House, Cooper-Molera Adobe, and Stevenson House are given daily. Spend the first day of your Monterey visit exploring the historic park, starting at **Stanton Center** ④, which also houses the **Maritime Museum of Monterey** ⑤. Take the guided 90-minute tour of the park (call for times), after which you can tour the historic adobes and their gardens. Start next door to the Maritime Museum at **Pacific House** ⑦ and cross the plaza to the **Custom House** ⑥. It's a short walk up Scott St. to **California's First Theatre** ⑧, then one block down Pacific to **Casa Soberanes** ⑨. Afterward, see the **Stevenson House** ⑭, **Cooper-Molera Adobe** ⑬, **Larkin House** ⑩, and **Colton Hall** ⑪. Stop in at the **Monterey Museum of Art** ⑫ and finish the day at **La Mirada** ⑮.

Start day two on **Fisherman's Wharf** ⑯, then head for the **Presidio of Monterey Museum** ⑰. You'll spend the rest of the day on **Cannery Row,** which has undergone several transformations since it was immortalized in John Steinbeck's 1945 novel of the same name. The street that Steinbeck described was crowded with sardine canneries processing, at their peak, nearly 200,000 tons of the smelly silver fish a year. During the mid-1940s, however, the sardines disappeared from the bay, causing the canneries to close. Through the years the old tin-roof canneries have been converted into restaurants, art galleries, and malls with shops selling T-shirts, fudge, and plastic sea otters. Recent tourist development along the row has been more tasteful, however, and includes several stylish inns and hotels. The **Monterey Plaza Hotel and Spa,** on the site of a historic estate at 400 Cannery Row, is a great place to relax over a drink and watch for sea otters. Wisps of the neighborhood's colorful past appear at **651 Cannery Row,** whose tile Chinese dragon roof dates to 1929.

Poke around in **Steinbeck's Spirit of Monterey Wax Museum** ⑱ before heading for a weathered wooden building at 800 Cannery Row. This was the site of **Pacific Biological Laboratories,** where Edward F. Ricketts, the inspiration for Doc in *Cannery Row,* did much of his marine research. The **Wing Chong Building,** at 835 Cannery Row, is the former Wing Chong Market that Steinbeck called Lee Chong's Heavenly Flower Grocery in *Cannery Row.* Step back into the present at the spectacular **Monterey Bay Aquarium** ⑲ and commune with the marine life.

TIMING

Depending on how quickly you tour (it's easy to spend a couple of hours at both the maritime museum and the art museum), day one will be a long one, but all of the historic park sites are in a small area. Monterey Museum of Art and La Mirada are a short drive or taxi ride from the historic park. Day two will also be full; it's easy to linger for hours at Fisherman's Wharf and the aquarium.

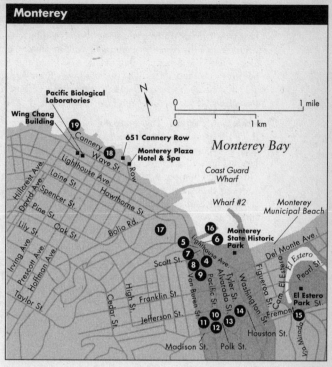

Monterey

Sights to See

8 **California's First Theatre.** Closed for renovations, the theater is due to reopen in 2003. The theater was constructed in the 1840s as a saloon with adjoining apartments by Jack Swan, an English sailor who settled in Monterey. Soldiers from the New York Volunteers who were on assignment in Monterey put on plays in the building. Melodramas and other theatrical performances are still staged here. ⊠ *Monterey State Historic Park, Scott and Pacific Sts.,* ☎ *831/375–4916.*

9 **Casa Soberanes.** A classic low-ceilinged adobe structure built in 1842, this was once a Custom House guard's residence. Exhibits at the house survey life in Monterey from the era of Mexican rule to the present. There's a peaceful garden in back. ⊠ *Monterey State Historic Park, 336 Pacific St.,* ☎ *831/649–7118.*

11 **Colton Hall.** A convention of delegates met in 1849 to draft the first state constitution at California's equivalent of Independence Hall. The stone building, which has served as a school, a courthouse, and the county seat, is a museum furnished as it was during the constitutional convention. The extensive grounds outside the hall surround the Old Monterey Jail. The museum closes each day from noon to 1. ⊠ *Monterey State Historic Park, 500 block of Pacific St., between Madison and Jefferson Sts.,* ☎ *831/646–5640.*

13 **Cooper-Molera Adobe.** The restored 2-acre complex includes a house dating from the 1820s, a visitor center, a bookstore, and a large garden enclosed by a high adobe wall. The mostly Victorian-era antiques and memorabilia that fill the house provide a glimpse into the life of a prosperous pioneer family. ⊠ *Monterey State Historic Park, Polk and Munras Sts.,* ☎ *831/649–7118.*

❻ Custom House. This adobe structure built by the Mexican government in 1827—now California's oldest standing public building—was the first stop for sea traders whose goods were subject to duties. At the beginning of the Mexican-American War, in 1846, Commodore John Sloat raised the American flag over the building and claimed California for the United States. The house's lower floor displays cargo from a 19th-century trading ship. ✉ *Monterey State Historic Park, 1 Custom House Plaza, across from Fisherman's Wharf,* ☎ *831/649–2909.*

❶❻ Fisherman's Wharf. The mournful barking of sea lions is the soundtrack for Monterey's waterfront. The whiskered marine mammals are best enjoyed while walking along this aging pier across from Custom House Plaza. Most of the commercial fishermen have moved to Wharf No. 2, a five-minute walk away, and Fisherman's Wharf is lined with souvenir shops, fish markets, seafood restaurants, and popcorn stands. It's a lively and entertaining place to bring children and is the departure point for fishing, diving, and whale-watching trips. ✉ *At the end of Calle Principal,* ☎ *831/373–0600,* WEB *www.montereywharf.com.*

❶❺ La Mirada. Asian and European antiques fill this 19th-century adobe house. A newer 10,000-square-ft gallery space, designed by Charles Moore, houses Asian and California regional art. Outdoors are magnificent rose and rhododendron gardens. The entrance fee for La Mirada includes admission to Monterey Museum of Art. ✉ *720 Via Mirada, at Fremont St.,* ☎ *831/372–3689.* ✇ *$5.* ☉ *Wed.–Sat. 11–5, Sun. 1–4.*

....

NEED A
BREAK?

El Estero Park's **Dennis the Menace Playground** (✉ Pearl St. and Camino El Estero, ☎ 831/646–3866) is an imaginative play area designed by local resident and cartoonist Hank Ketcham. The equipment is on a grand scale and made for daredevils; there are a roller slide, a clanking suspension bridge, and a real Southern Pacific steam locomotive. You can rent a rowboat or a paddleboat to cruise about U-shape Lake El Estero, populated with an assortment of ducks, mud hens, and geese. The park is closed Mondays except for holidays.

For a little down time, kick off your shoes at **Monterey Municipal Beach,** (✉ North of Del Monte, east of Wharf No. 2), where the shallow waters are usually warm and calm enough for wading.

....

❶⓪ Larkin House. A veranda encircles the second floor of this architecturally significant two-story adobe built in 1835, whose design bears witness to the Mexican and New England influences on the Monterey style. The rooms are furnished with period antiques, many of them brought from New Hampshire by the Larkin family. ✉ *Monterey State Historic Park, 510 Calle Principal, between Jefferson and Pacific Sts.,* ☎ *831/649–7118.*

❺ Maritime Museum of Monterey. This collection of maritime artifacts belonged to Allen Knight, who was Carmel's mayor from 1950 to 1952. Among the exhibits of ship models, scrimshaw items, and nautical prints, the highlight is the enormous multifaceted Fresnel lens from the Point Sur Light Station. ✉ *Monterey State Historic Park, 5 Custom House Plaza,* ☎ *831/375–2553.* ✇ *$5. Closed Mon.*

★ ❶❾ Monterey Bay Aquarium. The Outer Bay wing of this institution contains a million-gallon indoor ocean—observed through the largest window on Earth—that re-creates the sunlighted blue water where Monterey Bay meets the open sea. In this habitat soupfin sharks, barracuda, pelagic stingrays, ocean sunfish (which can weigh several hundred pounds), green sea turtles, and schools of fast-moving tuna swim together. The Outer Bay wing also houses a mesmerizing collection (the largest in the nation) of jellyfish. Expect long lines and sizable crowds at the aquarium on weekends, especially during the summer, but it's worth it. Don't miss the original wing's three-story Kelp Forest exhibit, the only one of its kind in the world, or the display of the sea creatures and vegetation found in Monterey Bay. Among other standouts are a bat-ray petting pool where you can touch their velvetlike skin; a 55,000-gallon sea-otter tank; an enormous outdoor artificial tidal pool that supports anemones, crabs, sea stars, and other colorful creatures; and Splash Zone, a hands-on activity center geared especially to families with small children. ⊠ *886 Cannery Row,* ☎ *831/648–4888; 800/756–3737 in CA for advance tickets,* WEB *www.montereybayaquarium.org.* ⊠ *$17.95.* ☉ *Memorial Day–Labor Day, daily 9:30–6; Labor Day–Memorial Day, daily 10–6.*

⑫ Monterey Museum of Art. Here you can see the works of photographers Ansel Adams and Edward Weston and of other artists who have spent time on the Peninsula. Another focus is international folk art; the colorful collection ranges from Kentucky hearth brooms to Tibetan prayer wheels. The entrance fee for the Monterey Museum of Art includes admission to La Mirada. ⊠ *559 Pacific St., across from Colton Hall,* ☎ *831/372–7591,* WEB *www.montereyart.org.* ⊠ *$5.* ☉ *Wed.–Sat. 11–5, Sun. 1–4.*

❼ Pacific House. Once a hotel and saloon, this park visitor center and museum surveys life in early California with gold-rush relics and photographs of old Monterey. The upper floor displays Native American artifacts. ⊠ *Monterey State Historic Park, 10 Custom House Plaza,* ☎ *831/649–7118.*

⑰ Presidio of Monterey Museum. Learn about the cultural and military history of Monterey, from the 17th century to the present. Exhibits highlight the period between the two world wars. ⊠ *Corporal Ewing Rd., lower Presidio Park, Monterey Presidio,* ☎ *831/646–3456,* WEB *www. monterey.org/museum/pom.* ⊠ *Free.* ☉ *Thurs.–Sat. 10–4, Sun. 1–4.*

★ ❹ Stanton Center. View a free 20-minute film about Monterey State Historic Park and gather maps and information. Then take the 90-minute walking tour along the 2-mi Path of History, marked by round gold tiles set into the sidewalk. The tour passes several landmark buildings and details the history and significance of the park's sites. You can do the walk on your own, or join a guided tour of the park. Admission to most sites along the walk is free, and most sites are open daily. ⊠ *Monterey State Historic Park, 5 Custom House Plaza,* ☎ *831/649–7118,* WEB *www.mbay.net/~mshp.* ⊠ *Free; park tours $5. Thurs.–Sat. 10–4, Sun. 1–4.*

⑱ Steinbeck's Spirit of Monterey Wax Museum. Characters from the novel *Cannery Row* are depicted in the displays here. An easy-to-digest 25-minute nutshell of 400 years of Monterey history is narrated by an actor playing John Steinbeck. ⊠ *700 Cannery Row,* ☎ *831/375–3770,* WEB *www.wax-museum.com.* ⊠ *$4.95.* ☉ *Memorial Day–Labor Day, Sun.–Fri. 10:30–7, Sat. 10:30–8; Labor Day–Memorial Day, daily noon–8.*

⑭ Stevenson House. Closed for renovations until early 2003, this house was named in honor of author Robert Louis Stevenson, who boarded here briefly in a tiny upstairs room. Items from his family's estate furnish Stevenson's room. Period-decorated chambers elsewhere in the house include a gallery of the author's memorabilia and a children's nursery stocked with Victorian toys and games. ⊠ *Monterey State Historic Park, 530 Houston St.,* ☎ *831/649–7118.*

OFF THE
BEATEN PATH

VENTANA VINEYARDS – A short drive from downtown Monterey leads to this winery known for chardonnays and Rieslings. Ventana's knowledge-able and hospitable owners, Doug and LuAnn Meador, invite you to bring a lunch to eat while tasting wines on a patio. ⊠ *2999 Monterey–Salinas Hwy. (Rte. 68),* ☎ *831/372–7415,* WEB *www.ventanavineyards.com.* ☉ *Daily 11–5.*

Dining and Lodging

$$$–$$$$
★

✕ **Fresh Cream.** The views of the bay are as superb as the imaginative French cuisine at this outstanding restaurant in Heritage Harbor. The menu, which changes weekly, might include rack of lamb Dijonnaise, roast boned duck in black-currant sauce, or blackened ahi tuna with pineapple rum-butter sauce. Service is formal, and though there is no requirement for dress, gentlemen will feel more comfortable in a jacket. ⊠ *99 Pacific St., Suite 100C,* ☎ *831/375–9798. Reservations essential. AE, D, DC, MC, V. No lunch.*

$$$–$$$$

✕ **Whaling Station Prime Steaks and Seafood.** A modern room with a lively crowd makes this restaurant above Cannery Row a festive yet comfortable place to enjoy real USDA prime beef and fresh seafood. ⊠ *763 Wave St.,* ☎ *831/373–3778. Reservations essential. AE, D, DC, MC, V. No lunch.*

$$$

✕ **Duck Club.** The elegant and romantic dining room of the Monterey Plaza Hotel and Spa is built over the waterfront on Cannery Row. The dinner menu highlights inventive dishes such as seared scallops with artichoke-potato mash and air-dried, wood-roasted duck and includes seafood, meat, and house-made pasta. It also serves breakfast. ⊠ *400 Cannery Row,* ☎ *831/646–1706. AE, D, DC, MC, V. No lunch.*

$$–$$$

✕ **Cafe Fina.** Mesquite-grilled fish dishes and linguine in clam sauce with baby shrimp and tomatoes are among the highlights at this un-derstated Italian restaurant on the wharf. The wine list is extensive. ⊠ *47 Fisherman's Wharf,* ☎ *831/372–5200. AE, D, DC, MC, V.*

$$–$$$

✕ **Domenico's.** Italian seafood preparations, mesquite-grilled meats, and homemade pastas are the specialties at Domenico's. The nautical theme keeps the place comfortably casual; white drapery lends an air of elegance other wharf restaurants lack. ⊠ *50 Fisherman's Wharf,* ☎ *831/372–3655. AE, D, DC, MC, V.*

$$–$$$

✕ **Mike's Seafood Restaurant.** A large, open brass fireplace and ex-cellent water views make this a cozy and inviting spot for lunch or din-ner on the wharf. Though standard seafood preparations are the focus, the chef also highlights some unusual Italian- and Japanese-inspired dishes. ⊠ *25 Fisherman's Wharf No. 1,* ☎ *831/372–6153. Reserva-tions essential. AE, D, DC, MC, V.*

$$–$$$

✕ **Monterey's Fish House.** Casual yet stylish and away from the hub-bub of the wharf, this always-packed seafood restaurant attracts lo-cals and frequent travelers to the city. If the dining room is full, you can wait at the bar with deliciously plump oysters on the half shell. The bartenders and waitstaff will gladly advise you on the perfect wine to go with your poached, blackened, or oak-grilled seafood. ⊠ *2114 Del Monte Ave.,* ☎ *831/373–4647. Reservations essential. AE, D, DC, MC, V. No lunch weekends.*

$$–$$$
★

✕ **Montrio Bistro.** Style reigns at this trendy, eclectic downtown restau-rant, which was formerly Monterey's firehouse. Wrought-iron trellises, metal sculpture, and rawhide complement the artful presentations of California cuisine. Clean, strong flavors typify the cooking here. Grilled Portobello mushrooms with polenta and rotisserie chicken with gar-lic mashed potatoes are two of the menu highlights. ⊠ *414 Calle Prin-cipal,* ☎ *831/648–8880. Reservations essential. AE, D, MC, V.*

$$–$$$ ✕ **Paradiso Trattoria and Oyster Bar.** Follow the aroma of marinating olives, roasted garlic, and platters of focaccia to this bright Cannery Row establishment. Mediterranean specialties and pizzas from a wood-burning oven are the luncheon fare. Seafood is a good choice for dinner, served in a dining room overlooking a lighted beachfront. ⊠ *654 Cannery Row,* ☎ *831/375–4155. AE, D, DC, MC, V.*

$$–$$$ ✕ **Stokes Restaurant & Bar.** Chef Brandon Miller's restaurant, set in-
★ side an 1833 adobe, seamlessly balances innovative cooking and traditional design. Miller specializes in the cuisines of Provence, northern Italy, and Catalan Spain, turning out imaginative pasta, seafood, and vegetarian dishes that change with the seasons. His creations have included slow-roasted duck breast on squash-chestnut risotto, rustic pasta tubes with fennel sausage and Manila clams, and a vegetable napoleon of crepes and house-made ricotta with smoked tomato sauce. ⊠ *500 Hartnell St.,* ☎ *831/373–1110. Reservations essential. AE, DC, MC, V. No lunch Sun.*

$–$$$ ✕ **Tarpy's Roadhouse.** Fun, dressed-down roadhouse lunch and dinner are served in this renovated farmhouse from the early 1900s. The kitchen cooks everything Mom used to make, only better. Eat indoors by a fireplace or outdoors in the courtyard. ⊠ *2999 Monterey–Salinas Hwy. (Rte. 68), at Canyon Del Rey Rd.,* ☎ *831/647–1444. Reservations essential. AE, D, MC, V.*

$–$$ ✕ **Thai Bistro.** In a former residence on one of Monterey's main drags, this airy and bright mom-and-pop restaurant serves excellent, authentic Thai cuisine from family recipes. Though technically just over the city line in Pacific Grove, it is within walking distance of Cannery Row and the Monterey Aquarium. ⊠ *159 Central Ave., Pacific Grove,* ☎ *831/372–8700. AE, D, MC, V.*

$ ✕ **Old Monterey Cafe.** Breakfast here, which is served until closing time (2:30 PM), might include fresh-baked muffins and eggs Benedict. Soups, salads, and sandwiches appear on the lunch menu. This is also a good place to relax with a cappuccino after touring Monterey's historic adobes. ⊠ *489 Alvarado St.,* ☎ *831/646–1021. Reservations not accepted. D, MC, V. No dinner.*

$$$$ 🏨 **Hotel Pacific.** All the rooms at this modern adobe-style hotel are junior suites, handsomely appointed with featherbeds, hardwood floors, fireplaces, and balconies or patios. The rates include Continental breakfast and afternoon snacks. ⊠ *300 Pacific St., 93940,* ☎ *831/373–5700 or 800/554–5542,* FAX *831/373–6921,* WEB *www.hotelpacific.com. 105 rooms. Fans, in-room data ports, refrigerators, cable TV, in-room VCRs, 2 hot tubs, meeting room; no air-conditioning, no smoking. AE, D, DC, MC, V. CP.*

$$$$ 🏨 **Old Monterey Inn.** One of just two residential-area B&Bs in Mon-
★ terey, the three-story English Tudor country manor, completed in 1929, is replete with hand-carved window frames, balustrades, and Gothic archways. Loving restoration by proprietors Gene and Ann Swett included a rose garden surrounded by giant holly trees, gnarled oaks, and majestic redwoods. The inn is legendary for its 20 different bathroom amenities, featherbeds with down comforters, sumptuous breakfast, and solicitous service. Because of the very expensive and fragile furnishings, this is not a suitable place to bring children of any age. ⊠ *500 Martin St., 93940,* ☎ *831/375–8284 or 800/350–2344,* FAX *831/ 375–6730,* WEB *www.oldmontereyinn.com. 8 rooms, 2 suites, 1 cottage. In-room data ports, cable TV, in-room VCRs, concierge; no air-conditioning, no smoking. MC, V. BP.*

$$$$ 🏨 **Spindrift Inn.** This boutique hotel on Cannery Row, under the same management as the Hotel Pacific and the Monterey Bay Inn, has beach access and a rooftop garden that overlooks the water. Spacious rooms with sitting areas, hardwood floors, fireplaces, and down comforters are among the indoor pleasures. This is a place for adults; families would not be comfortable here. ✉ *652 Cannery Row, 93940,* ☎ *831/646–8900 or 800/841–1879,* FAX *831/646–5342,* WEB *www.spindriftinn.com. 42 rooms. In-room data ports, refrigerators, cable TV, in-room VCRs, concierge; no air-conditioning, no smoking. AE, D, DC, MC, V. CP.*

$$$–$$$$ ☷ **Embassy Suites.** As you drive into Monterey from the north on Route 1, you can't miss this high-rise property, which towers over the town of Seaside just before the Monterey line. Two blocks from the beach, it has views of Laguna Grande Lake and Monterey Bay. All accommodations here are smallish two-room suites with microwaves, refrigerators, and coffeemakers. Complimentary cocktails are available each evening. ✉ *1441 Canyon Del Rey, Seaside 93955,* ☎ *831/393–1115,* FAX *831/393–1113,* WEB *www.embassymonterey.com. 225 suites. Restaurant, bar, in-room data ports, kitchenettes, cable TV with movies and video games, indoor pool, gym, hot tub, sauna, video game room, business services, meeting rooms; no-smoking rooms. AE, D, DC, MC, V. BP.*

$$$–$$$$ ☷ **Hyatt Regency Monterey.** Although its rooms and overall vibe are less glamorous than those at some other resorts in the region, the facilities here are very good. ✉ *1 Old Golf Course Rd., 93940,* ☎ *831/372–1234; 800/824–2196 in CA,* FAX *831/372–4277,* WEB *www.montereyhyatt.com. 535 rooms, 40 suites. Restaurant, café, fans, refrigerators (some), cable TV with movies, 18-hole golf course, 5 tennis courts, 2 pools, gym, 2 hot tubs, massage, bicycles, recreation room, bar, concierge, business services, Internet, laundry services, meeting room, some pets allowed (fee); no-smoking rooms, no air-conditioning. AE, D, DC, MC, V.*

$$$–$$$$ ☷ **Monterey Bay Inn.** On Cannery Row, this hotel takes full advantage of its location on the water, providing binoculars for viewing marine life. Rooms have private balconies. ✉ *242 Cannery Row, 93940,* ☎ *831/373–6242 or 800/424–6242,* FAX *831/373–7603,* WEB *www.montereybayinn.com. 47 rooms. In-room data ports, refrigerators, cable TV, in-room VCRs, exercise equipment, 2 hot tubs, sauna, meeting room; no air-conditioning, no smoking. AE, D, DC, MC, V. CP.*

$$$–$$$$ ☷ **Monterey Plaza Hotel and Spa.** This full-service hotel commands a ★ waterfront location on Cannery Row, where frolicking sea otters can be observed from the wide outdoor patio and many room balconies. The architecture and design blend early California and Mediterranean styles and retain elements of the old cannery design. The property is meticulously maintained and offers accommodations from simple to luxurious. You have use of a state-of-the-art full-service rooftop spa facility. ✉ *400 Cannery Row, 93940,* ☎ *831/646–1700; 800/631–1339; 800/334–3999 in CA,* FAX *831/646–0285,* WEB *www.montereyplazahotel.com. 285 rooms, 3 suites. 2 restaurants, room service, fans, in-room data ports, minibars, cable TV with movies, health club, spa, laundry service, business services, concierge, Internet, meeting rooms; no air-conditioning, no smoking. AE, D, DC, MC, V.*

$$$ ☷ **The Beach Resort.** The rooms here may be nondescript, but this Best Western hotel has a great waterfront location about 2 mi north of town that affords views of the bay and the city skyline. The grounds are pleasantly landscaped, and there's a large pool with a sunbathing area. ✉ *2600 Sand Dunes Dr., 93940,* ☎ *831/394–3321 or 800/242–8627,* FAX *831/393–1912,* WEB *www.montereybeachhotel.com. 196 rooms. Restaurant, fans (some), in-room data ports, refrigerators, cable TV with movies, pool, exercise equipment, hot tub, business services, lounge, some pets allowed (fee); no air-conditioning, no smoking. AE, D, DC, MC, V.*

$$–$$$$ ☷ **Holiday Inn Express Monterey.** Rooms are clean and comfortable at this modest hotel, well situated above Cannery Row. Complimentary wine and cheese are served in the evening. ✉ *443 Wave St., 93940,* ☎ *831/372–1800,* FAX *831/372–1969,* WEB *www.hiexpress.com/*

montereyca. 42 rooms. Cable TV, hot tub; no smoking. AE, D, DC, MC, V. CP.

$$$ 🖼 **Merritt House.** Built around a historic adobe house and garden, this inn provides simple yet attractive accommodations within walking distance of Fisherman's Wharf. All rooms have gas fireplaces and re-frigerators, and upstairs rooms have vaulted ceilings. Suites are in the adobe. ⊠ *386 Pacific Ave., 93940,* ☎ *831/646–9686,* FAX *831/646– 5392,* WEB *www.merritthouseinn.com. 22 rooms, 3 suites. Room ser-vice, in-room data ports (some), refrigerators, cable TV, Internet, laun-dry service; no air-conditioning, no smoking. AE, D, MC, V. CP.*

$$–$$$ 🖼 **Monterey Hotel.** Standard rooms in this restored Victorian are small but contain well-chosen reproduction antique furniture. The master suites have fireplaces and oval bathtubs. ⊠ *406 Alvarado St., 93940,* ☎ *831/375–3184 or 800/727–0960,* FAX *831/373–2899,* WEB *www. montereyhotel.com. 39 rooms, 6 suites. Fans, in-room data ports, cable TV, refrigerators (some); no air-conditioning, no smoking. AE, D, DC, MC, V. CP.*

$$ 🖼 **Monterey Bay Lodge.** Its location on the edge of Monterey's El Es-
🐾 tero Park gives this motel an edge over those along the busy Munras Avenue motel row. Indoor plants and a secluded courtyard with a heated pool are other pluses. ⊠ *55 Camino Aguajito Rd., 93940,* ☎ *831/372–8057 or 800/558–1900,* FAX *831/655–2933,* WEB *www. montereybaylodge.com. 45 rooms. Restaurant, in-room data ports, cable TV, in-room VCRs, pool, some pets allowed (fee); no air-condi-tioning in some rooms, no-smoking rooms. AE, D, DC, MC, V.*

$ 🖼 **Quality Inn Monterey.** This attractive motel has a friendly, country-inn feeling. Rooms are light and airy, and some have fireplaces. Con-tinental breakfast is served in a blue-wallpapered lobby. ⊠ *1058 Munras Ave., 93940,* ☎ *831/372–3381,* FAX *831/372–4687,* WEB *www.montereyqualityinn.com. 55 rooms. In-room data ports, mi-crowaves, refrigerators, cable TV, in-room VCRs, indoor pool, hot tub; no smoking. AE, D, DC, MC, V. CP.*

Nightlife and the Arts

BARS AND CLUBS

Bluefin (⊠ 685 Cannery Row, ☎ 831/375–7000) offers live music, danc-ing, and 19 pool tables. **Planet Gemini** (⊠ 625 Cannery Row, ☎ 831/ 373–1449) presents comedy shows on weekends and dancing to a DJ or live music. **Sly McFlys** (⊠ 700-A Cannery Row, ☎ 831/649–8050) has live jazz and blues every night.

MUSIC FESTIVALS

Dixieland Monterey (⊠ 177 Webster St., Suite A-206, ☎ 831/443–5260 or 888/349–6879, WEB www.dixieland-monterey.com), held on the first full weekend of March, presents Dixieland jazz bands in cabarets, restaurants, and hotel lounges on the Monterey waterfront. The **Mon-terey Bay Blues Festival** (☎ 831/394–2652, WEB www.montereyblues.com) draws blues fans to the Monterey Fairgrounds over a June weekend. The **Monterey Jazz Festival,** the world's oldest (☎ 831/373–3366, WEB www.montereyjazzfestival.org), attracts jazz and blues greats from around the world to the Monterey Fairgrounds on the third full week-end of September.

THEATER

The **Barbary Coast Theatre** performs comedy melodramas near Can-nery Row (⊠ 324 Hoffman, ☎ 831/655–4992). **Monterey Bay The-atrefest** (☎ 831/622–0700) presents free outdoor performances at Custom House Plaza on weekend afternoons and evenings from late June to mid-July. The **Wharf Theater** (⊠ Fisherman's Wharf, ☎ 831/ 649–2332) focuses on American musicals past and present.

Outdoor Activities and Sports

BICYCLING

For bicycle rentals try **Bay Bikes** (⊠ 640 Wave St., ☎ 831/646–9090). **Adventures by the Sea Inc.** (⊠ 299 Cannery Row, ☎ 831/372–1807) rents tandem and standard bicycles.

CAR RACING

Five major races take place each year on the 2.2-mi, 11-turn **Laguna Seca Raceway** (⊠ 1021 Monterey–Salinas Hwy. (Rte. 68), ☎ 831/648–5100 or 800/327–7322).

FISHING

Monterey Sport Fishing (⊠ 96 Fisherman's Wharf, ☎ 831/372–2203 or 800/200–2203) has one of the largest boats afloat and can accommodate up to 100 people for half- or full-day fishing trips. **Randy's Fishing Trips** (⊠ 66 Fisherman's Wharf, ☎ 831/372–7440 or 800/251–7440) has been operating under the same skippers continuously since 1958. **Sam's Fishing Fleet** (⊠ 84 Fisherman's Wharf, ☎ 831/372–0577 or 800/427–2675) has been fishing the Monterey Bay since 1914.

GOLF

The greens fee at the 18-hole **Del Monte Golf Course** (⊠ 1300 Sylvan Rd., ☎ 831/373–2700) is $90, plus $18 per person for an optional cart. The $20 twilight special (plus cart rental) begins two hours before sunset.

KAYAKING

Monterey Bay Kayaks (⊠ 693 Del Monte Ave., ☎ 831/373–5357; 800/649–5357 in CA) rents equipment and conducts classes and natural-history tours.

ROLLER-SKATING AND IN-LINE SKATING

Del Monte Gardens (⊠ 2020 Del Monte Ave., ☎ 831/375–3202) is an old-fashioned rink for roller-skating and in-line skating.

SCUBA DIVING

The staff at **Aquarius Dive Shops** (⊠ 2040 Del Monte Ave., ☎ 831/375–1933; ⊠ 32 Cannery Row, ☎ 831/375–6605) gives diving lessons and tours and rents equipment. The **scuba-diving conditions information line** (☎ 831/657–1020) is updated regularly.

WALKING

From Custom House Plaza, you can walk along the coast in either direction on the 29-mi long **Monterey Bay Coastal Trail** (☎ 831/372–3196, WEB www.mprpd.org/parks/coastaltrail.html) for spectacular views of the sea. It runs all the way from north of Monterey to Pacific Grove, with sections continuing around Pebble Beach.

WHALE-WATCHING

Monterey Sport Fishing (⊠ 96 Fisherman's Wharf, ☎ 831/372–2203 or 800/200–2203) offers trips throughout the migration season in boats large enough to carry 100 people. **Randy's Fishing Trips** (⊠ 66 Fisherman's Wharf, ☎ 831/372–7440 or 800/251–7440) has been operating under the same two skippers since 1958. **Sam's Fishing Fleet** (⊠ 84 Fisherman's Wharf, ☎ 831/372–0577 or 800/427–2675) has been in operation since 1914.

Shopping

Antiques and reproductions of merchandise popular in Monterey in the 1850s are available at **The Boston Store** (⊠ Monterey State Historic Park, 1 Custom House Plaza, across from Fisherman's Wharf, ☎ 831/649–3364). You can sometimes find little treasures at the **Cannery Row Antique Mall** (⊠ 471 Wave St., ☎ 831/655–0264), which houses a number of local vendors under one roof. **The Cooper Store** (⊠ Polk and Munras Streets, in the Cooper-Molera Adobe, ☎ 831/649–7111) is an 1800s-themed shop that is dedicated to the preservation of antiquities in the Monterey State Historic Park. **Old Monterey Book Co.** (⊠ 136 Bonifacio Pl., off Alvarado St., ☎ 831/372–3111) specializes in antiquarian books and prints. Historical Society–operated, **The Pickett Fence** (⊠ Monterey State Historic Park, 1 Custom House Plaza, across from Fisherman's Wharf, ☎ 831/649–3364) sells high-end garden accessories and furnishings.

MONTEREY PENINSULA

Pacific Grove to Carmel Valley

If after the relative hubbub of Monterey you want to see smaller towns and spectacular vistas, be sure to visit Pacific Grove, Pebble Beach, Carmel-by-the-Sea, and Carmel Valley. Each is very different from the next, and you'll see everything from thatch-roofed cottages to palatial estates, rolling hills to craggy cliffs.

Pacific Grove

⑳ *3 mi from Monterey south on Rte. 1 and west on Rte. 68; from Cannery Row, Wave St. heading west becomes Ocean View Blvd. at Monterey–Pacific Grove border.*

If not for the dramatic strip of coastline in its backyard, Pacific Grove could easily pass for a typical small town in the heartland. The town, which began as a summer retreat for church groups more than a century ago, recalls its prim and proper Victorian heritage in its host of tiny board-and-batten cottages and stately mansions.

Even before the church groups flocked here, Pacific Grove had been receiving thousands of annual pilgrims in the form of bright orange-and-black monarch butterflies. Known as Butterfly Town USA, Pacific Grove is the winter home of monarchs that migrate south from Canada and the Pacific Northwest to take residence in pine and eucalyptus groves from October through March. The sight of a mass of butterflies hanging from the branches like a long, fluttering veil is unforgettable.

A prime way to enjoy Pacific Grove is to walk or bicycle along its 3 mi of city-owned shoreline, a cliff-top area following Ocean View Boulevard that is landscaped with native plants and has benches on which to sit and gaze at the sea. You can spot many types of birds here, including colonies of web-footed cormorants drawn to the massive rocks rising out of the surf.

Among the Victorians of note is the **Pryor House** (⊠ 429 Ocean View Blvd.), a massive shingled private residence with a leaded- and beveled-glass doorway. **Green Gables** (⊠ 5th St. and Ocean View Blvd., ☎ 831/375–2095), a romantic Swiss Gothic–style mansion with steeply peaked gables and stained-glass windows, is a B&B.

Ⓒ The view of the coast is gorgeous from **Lovers Point Park** (☎ 831/649–2954), on Ocean View Boulevard midway along the waterfront. The park's sheltered beach has a children's pool and picnic area. Glass-bottom boat rides, which provide views of the plant and sea life below,
Ⓒ are offered in summer. At the 1855-vintage **Point Piños Lighthouse,** the oldest continuously operating lighthouse on the West Coast, you can learn about the lighting and foghorn operations and wander through a small museum containing U.S. Coast Guard memorabilia. ⊠ *Light-*

house Ave. off Asilomar Blvd., ☎ *831/648–3116,* WEB *www. pgmuseum.org.* ⌦ *Free.* ☉ *Thurs.–Sun. 1–4.*

Monarchs sometimes vary their nesting sites from year to year, but the **Monarch Grove Sanctuary** (✉ 1073 Lighthouse Ave., at Ridge Rd., WEB www.pacificgrove.com/butterflies/index.html) is a fairly reliable spot for viewing the butterflies. If you are in Pacific Grove when the monarch butterflies aren't, you can view the well-crafted butterfly tree exhibit at the **Pacific Grove Museum of Natural History.** The museum also displays 400 mounted birds and has a Touch Gallery for children. ✉ *165 Forest Ave.,* ☎ *831/648–3116,* WEB *www.pgmuseum.org.* ⌦ *Free.* ☉ *Tues.–Sun. 10–5.*

Asilomar State Beach (☎ 831/372–4076), a beautiful coastal area, is on Sunset Drive between Point Piños and the Del Monte Forest in Pacific Grove. The 100 acres of dunes, tidal pools, and pocket-size beaches form one of the region's richest areas for marine life.

Dining and Lodging

$$$–$$$$ ✕ **Old Bath House.** A romantic, nostalgic air permeates this converted bathhouse overlooking the water at Lovers Point. The classic regional menu makes the most of local produce and seafood (such as Monterey Bay prawns) and specializes in game meats. The restaurant has a less expensive menu for late-afternoon diners. ✉ *620 Ocean View Blvd.,* ☎ *831/375–5195. AE, D, DC, MC, V. No lunch.*

$$–$$$ ✕ **Taste Café and Bistro.** A favorite of locals, Taste serves hearty European-inspired California cuisine in a casual, airy room with high ceilings and an open kitchen. Meats are excellent here, particularly the marinated lamb fillets and the filet mignon. ✉ *1199 Forest Ave.,* ☎ *831/655–0324. Reservations essential. AE, MC, V. Closed Mon.*

$–$$$ ✕ **Fandango.** With its stone walls and country furniture, Fandango has the earthy feel of a southern European farmhouse. Complementing the appointments are the robust flavors of cuisine from the Mediterranean, including paella, cannelloni, and couscous. ✉ *223 17th St.,* ☎ *831/ 372–3456. AE, D, DC, MC, V.*

$$ ✕ **Fifi's Café.** Despite its location at the edge of a strip mall a few blocks from downtown, this French bistro is intimate, cozy, and popular with locals, many of whom come for the $19 three-course prix-fixe dinner. Try the roast duck with huckleberry sauce. The extensive wine list is reasonably priced, and there are a number of fine choices by the glass. ✉ *1188 Forest Ave.,* ☎ *831/372–5325. Reservations essential. AE, D, DC, MC, V. No lunch Wed.*

$$ ✕ **Joe Rombi's.** Pastas, fish, and veal are the specialties at this modern trattoria, which is the best in town for Italian food. The mood is convivial and welcoming. Try the sautéed veal with red-wine reduction, mozzarella, and herbs. ✉ *208 17th St.,* ☎ *831/373–2416. AE, MC, V. Closed Mon.–Tues.*

$–$$ ✕ **Passion Fish.** South American artwork and artifacts decorate the room, but both Latin and Asian flavors permeate many of the adventurous dishes. Try the crispy squid with spicy orange-cilantro vinaigrette. Fresh fish is paired with creative sauces. Wines are an exceptional value here. ✉ *701 Lighthouse Ave.,* ☎ *831/655–3311. AE, D, MC, V. Closed Tues. No lunch.*

$ ✕ **Fishwife.** Fresh fish with a Latin accent makes this a favorite of locals for lunch or a casual dinner. ✉ *1996½ Sunset Dr., at Asilomar Blvd.,* ☎ *831/375–7107. AE, D, MC, V.*

$ ✕ **Peppers Mexicali Cafe.** This cheerful white-walled restaurant serves fresh seafood and traditional dishes from Mexico and Latin America. The red and green salsas are excellent. ✉ *170 Forest Ave.,* ☎ *831/373– 6892. AE, D, DC, MC, V. Closed Tues. No lunch Sun.*

$ ✕ **Toasties Cafe.** Three-egg omelets, burritos, pancakes, waffles, French toast, and other breakfast items are served at this crowded café until 3 PM. The lunch selections include burgers and other sandwiches. Toasties also serves dinner—fish-and-chips, seafood pasta—but it's best to stick to daytime meals. ✉ *702 Lighthouse Ave.,* ☎ *831/373–7543. AE, D, MC, V.*

$$$–$$$$ 🏠 **Centrella Hotel.** A handsome century-old Victorian mansion two blocks from Lovers Point Beach, the Centrella fills its guest rooms and cottages with wicker and brass furnishings and claw-foot bathtubs. A buffet breakfast is served each morning, and a sideboard in the large parlor is laden with cookies and hors d'oeuvres in the afternoon. Because sound can easily travel in a Victorian building, families are asked to stay in the cottages. ✉ *612 Central Ave., 93950,* ☎ *831/372–3372 or 800/233–3372,* FAX *831/372–2036,* WEB *www.centrellainn.com. 17 rooms, 4 suites, 5 cottages. Fans (some), in-room data ports, minibars (some), refrigerators (some), cable TV in some rooms, concierge; no air-conditioning, no smoking. AE, D, MC, V. BP.*

$$$–$$$$ 🏠 **Martine Inn.** In a pink-stucco Mediterranean-style villa overlook-
★ ing the water, the glassed-in parlor and several rooms have stunning ocean views. The many antiques include a mahogany suite exhibited at the 1893 Chicago World's Fair, movie costume designer Edith Head's bedroom suite, and an 1860 Chippendale Revival four-poster bed. Lavish breakfasts are served on lace-clad tables set with china, crystal, and silver. Because of the fragility of the many antiques, the inn is not suitable for children. ✉ *255 Ocean View Blvd., 93950,* ☎ *831/373–3388 or 800/852–5588,* FAX *831/373–3896,* WEB *www.martineinn.com. 25 rooms, 1 suite. Fans (some), microwaves, refrigerators, in-room data ports, hot tub; no air-conditioning, no room TVs, no smoking. AE, D, MC, V. BP.*

$$$–$$$$ 🏠 **Seven Gables Inn.** An elegant Victorian mansion and four smaller buildings share a corner lot and a great view of the ocean. The main house was built in 1886, the others between 1910 and 1940. European antiques of various periods—gold-leaf mirrors, crystal chandeliers, and marble statues—create a genteel formality. The gracious innkeeper, Susan Flatley, grew up in the house and shares her knowledge about it and the area. Families would not be comfortable here, as there are many irreplaceable, breakable items in the house. ✉ *555 Ocean View Blvd., 93950,* ☎ *831/372–4341,* FAX *831/372–2544,* WEB *www.pginns.com. 10 rooms, 4 cottages. Fans; no air-conditioning, no room phones, no room TVs, no smoking. MC, V. BP.*

$$–$$$$ 🏠 **Green Gables Inn.** Stained-glass windows framing an ornate fire-
★ place and other interior details compete with the spectacular ocean views at this Queen Anne–style mansion built by a businessman for his mistress in 1888. Rooms in a carriage house perched on a hill out back are larger, have more modern amenities, and afford more privacy, but rooms in the main house have more charm. ✉ *301 Oceanview Blvd., 93950,* ☎ *831/375–2095 or 800/722–1774,* FAX *831/375–5437,* WEB *www.foursisters.com. 10 rooms, 6 with bath; 1 suite. Fans (some), in-room data ports, in-room hot tubs (some), cable TV, in-room VCRs (some), bicycles; no air-conditioning, no smoking. AE, MC, V. BP.*

$$–$$$$ 🏠 **The Inn at 213 Seventeen Mile Drive.** Set in a residential area just past town, this carefully restored 1920s craftsman-style home and cottage has spacious, well-appointed rooms. The affable innkeepers offer complimentary wine and hors d'oeuvres in the evening and tea and snacks throughout the day. Redwood, cypress, and eucalyptus trees tower over the garden and outdoor spa. ✉ *213 17-Mile Dr., 93950,* ☎ *831/642–9514 or 800/526–5666,* FAX *831/642–9546,* WEB *www.innat17.com. 14 rooms. Fans (some), in-room data ports, cable TV, hot tub; no air-conditioning, no smoking. AE, MC, V. BP.*

$$–$$$ ⊞ **Gosby House Inn.** Though in the town center, this turreted yellow Queen Anne Victorian has an informal country air. The two most private rooms are in the rear carriage house; they have fireplaces, balconies, and whirlpool tubs. Buffet breakfast is served in the parlor or garden. ⊠ *643 Lighthouse Ave., 93950,* ☎ *831/375–1287 or 800/527–8828,* FAX *831/655–9621,* WEB *www.foursisters.com. 22 rooms, 20 with bath. In-room data ports, refrigerators (some), in-room hot tubs (some); no air-conditioning, no TVs in some rooms, no smoking. AE, DC, MC, V. BP.*

$$ ⊞ **Asilomar Conference Center.** A summer-camp congeniality prevails at this assortment of 28 rustic but comfortable lodges in the middle of a woodsy 105-acre state park near the beach. Rooms are available when they're not booked for conferences. ⊠ *800 Asilomar Blvd., Box 537, 93950,* ☎ *831/372–8016,* FAX *831/372–7227,* WEB *www.visitasilomar. com. 314 rooms. Cafeteria, refrigerators (some), business services, pool; no air-conditioning, no room phones, no room TVs, no smoking. AE, MC, V. BP.*

$–$$ ⊞ **Lighthouse Lodge and Suites.** Near the tip of the peninsula, this complex straddles Lighthouse Avenue—the lodge is on one side, the all-suites facility on the other. It's a woodsy alternative to downtown Pacific Grove's B&B scene. The suites have fireplaces and whirlpool tubs. The rooms are simple, but they're decent in size and much less expensive. ⊠ *1150 and 1249 Lighthouse Ave., 93950,* ☎ *831/655–2111 or 800/ 858–1249,* FAX *831/655–4922,* WEB *www.lhls.com. 64 rooms, 31 suites. Fans, kitchenettes (some), microwaves, refrigerators, in-room data ports, cable TV with movies, pool, hot tub, some pets allowed (fee); no air-conditioning, no smoking. AE, D, DC, MC, V. BP.*

Outdoor Activities and Sports

GOLF

The greens fee at the 18-hole **Pacific Grove Municipal Golf Links** (⊠ 77 Asilomar Blvd., ☎ 831/648–5777) runs between $32 and $38 (you can play 9 holes for between $18 and $20), with an 18-hole twilight rate of $20. Optional carts cost $28. The course has spectacular ocean views on its back 9. Tee times may be reserved up to seven days in advance.

TENNIS

The **Pacific Grove Municipal Courts** (⊠ 515 Junipero St., ☎ 831/648–5729) are available for public play.

Shopping

American Tin Cannery Outlet Center (⊠ 125 Ocean View Blvd., ☎ 831/ 372–3071) carries designer clothing, jewelry, accessories, and home decorating items at discounts between 25% and 65%. **Wooden Nickel** (⊠ Central and Fountain Aves., ☎ 831/646–8050) sells accent pieces for the home.

17-Mile Drive

㉑ *Off Sunset Dr. in Pacific Grove or off N. San Antonio Rd. in Carmel.*

Primordial nature resides in quiet harmony with palatial late-20th-century estates along 17-Mile Drive, which winds through an 8,400-acre microcosm of the Monterey coastal landscape. Dotting the drive are rare Monterey cypresses, trees so gnarled and twisted that Robert Louis Stevenson once described them as "ghosts fleeing before the wind." Some sightseers balk at the $8-per-car fee collected at the gates—this is the only private toll road west of the Mississippi—but most find the drive well worth the price. An alternative is to grab a bike: cyclists tour for free, as do those with confirmed lunch or dinner reservations at one of the hotels.

Bird Rock, the largest of several islands at the southern end of the Monterey Country Club's golf course, teems with harbor seals, sea lions, cormorants, and pelicans. Sea creatures and birds also make use of **Seal Rock,** the larger of a group of islands south of Bird Rock. The most photographed tree along 17-Mile Drive is the weather-sculpted **Lone Cypress,** which grows out of a precipitous outcropping above the waves about 2 mi south of Seal Rock. You can stop for a view of the Lone Cypress at a parking area, but you can't walk out to the tree.

Many of the stately homes along 17-Mile Drive reflect the classic Monterey or Spanish mission style typical of the region. A standout is the **Crocker Marble Palace** about a mile south of the Lone Cypress; it's a private waterfront estate inspired by a Byzantine castle. This mansion is easily identifiable by its dozens of marble arches.

You can take in views of the impeccable greens at **Pebble Beach Golf Links** (⊠ 17-Mile Dr. near the Lodge at Pebble Beach, ☎ 800/654–9300, WEB www.pebblebeach.com) over a drink or lunch at the Lodge at Pebble Beach. The ocean plays a major role in the 18th hole of the famed golf course. Each winter the course is the main site of the AT&T Pebble Beach Pro-Am (formerly the Bing Crosby Pro-Am), where show business celebrities and pros team up for one of the nation's most glamorous golf tournaments.

Dining and Lodging

$$$$ ✕🏨 **Inn at Spanish Bay.** This resort sprawls across a breathtaking stretch of shoreline. Under the same management as the Lodge at Pebble Beach, the inn has a slightly more casual feel, though its 600-square-ft rooms are no less luxurious. The inn has its own tennis courts and golf course, but you also have privileges at the Lodge. Peppoli's restaurant ($–$$), which serves Tuscan cuisine, overlooks the coast and the golf links. Try Roy's Restaurant ($–$$) for more casual and innovative Euro-Asian fare. ⊠ 2700 17-Mile Dr., Box 1418, Pebble Beach 93953, ☎ 831/647–7500 or 800/654–9300, FAX 831/644–7960. 252 rooms, 17 suites. 3 restaurants, lobby lounge, bar, room service, in-room data ports, minibars, refrigerators, cable TV with movies and video games, in-room VCRs, 18-hole golf course, 8 tennis courts, pro shop, pool, aerobics, health club, massage, sauna, steam room, beach, bicycles, hiking, laundry service, concierge, Internet, business services, meeting rooms; no smoking. AE, D, DC, MC, V.

$$$$ ✕🏨 **Lodge at Pebble Beach.** Luxurious rooms with fireplaces and
★ wonderful views set the tone at this resort that was built in 1919. The golf course, tennis club, and equestrian center are highly regarded; you also have privileges at the Inn at Spanish Bay. Overlooking the 18th green, the very fine Club XIX restaurant ($$$–$$$$; jackets recommended) is an intimate, clublike dining room serving expertly prepared French cuisine. ⊠ 1700 17-Mile Dr., Box 1128, Pebble Beach 93953, ☎ 831/624–3811 or 800/654–9300, FAX 831/644–7960, WEB www.pebblebeach.com. 142 rooms, 19 suites. 3 restaurants, coffee shop, lobby lounge, 2 bars, in-room data ports, in-room hot tubs (some), minibars, refrigerators, cable TV with movies and video games, in-room VCRs, 18-hole golf course, 12 tennis courts, pro shop, pool, gym, health club, massage, sauna, spa, beach, bicycles, horseback riding, laundry services, concierge, Internet, business services, meeting rooms, some pets allowed; no air-conditioning, no smoking. AE, D, DC, MC, V.

$$$$ 🏨 **Casa Palmero.** This exclusive spa resort captures the essence of a
★ Mediterranean villa. The rooms are decorated with sumptuous fabrics and fine art, each has a wood-burning fireplace and heated floor, and some have a private outdoor patio with in-ground Jacuzzi. Complimentary cocktail service is offered each evening in the main hall and

library. The spa is state-of-the-art, and you have use of all facilities at the Lodge at Pebble Beach and the Inn at Spanish Bay. ⊠ *1518 Cypress Dr., 93953,* ☎ *831/622–6650 or 800/654–9300,* FAX *831/622–6655,* WEB *www.pebblebeach.com. 21 rooms, 3 suites. Room service, in-room data ports, in-room hot tubs (some), minibars, refrigerators, cable TV with movies and video games, in-room VCRs, golf privileges, pool, health club, spa, bicycles, billiards, lounge, library, laundry service, concierge, meeting rooms; no air-conditioning, no smoking. AE, D, DC, MC, V.*

Outdoor Activities and Sports

GOLF

The **Links at Spanish Bay** (⊠ 17-Mile Dr., north end, ☎ 831/624–3811, 831/624–6611, or 800/654–9300), which hugs a choice stretch of shoreline, is designed in the rugged manner of a traditional Scottish course, with sand dunes and coastal marshes interspersed among the greens. The greens fee is $210, plus $25 for cart rental ($210 for resort guests, including cart); nonguests can reserve tee times two months in advance.

Pebble Beach Golf Links (⊠ 17-Mile Dr. near the Lodge at Pebble Beach, ☎ 831/624–3811, 831/624–6611, or 800/654–9300) attracts golfers from around the world, despite a greens fee of $350, plus $25 for an optional cart ($350 with a complimentary cart for guests of the Pebble Beach and Spanish Bay resorts). Nonguests can reserve a tee time only one day in advance on a space-available basis (up to a year for groups); resort guests can reserve up to 18 months in advance.

Peter Hay (⊠ 17-Mile Dr., ☎ 831/625–8518 or 831/624–6611), a 9-hole, par-3 course, charges $20 per person, no reservations necessary. **Poppy Hills** (⊠ 3200 Lopez Rd., at 17-Mile Dr., ☎ 831/625–2035), a splendid 18-hole course designed in 1986 by Robert Trent Jones Jr. has a greens fee of $125–$150; an optional cart costs $30. Individuals may reserve up to one month in advance, groups up to a year.

Spyglass Hill (⊠ Stevenson Dr. and Spyglass Hill Rd., ☎ 831/624–3811, 831/624–6611, or 800/654–9300) is among the most challenging Pebble Beach courses. With the first 5 holes bordering on the Pacific and the rest of the 18 reaching deep into the Del Monte Forest, the views offer some consolation. The greens fee is $250; an optional cart costs $25 (the cart is complimentary for resort guests). Reservations are essential and may be made up to one month in advance (18 months for guests).

HORSEBACK RIDING

The **Pebble Beach Equestrian Center** (⊠ Portola Rd. and Alva La., ☎ 831/624–2756) offers guided trail rides along the beach and through 26 mi of bridle trails in the Del Monte Forest.

Carmel

❷ *5 mi south of Monterey on Rte. 1 (or via 17-Mile Drive's Carmel Gate).*

Although the community has grown quickly through the years and its population quadruples with tourists on weekends and during the summer, Carmel retains its identity as a quaint village. Self-consciously charming, the town is populated by many former celebrities, major and minor, and it has a lot of quirky ordinances. For instance, women wearing high heels do not have the right to pursue legal action if they trip and fall on the cobblestone streets; drivers who hit a tree and leave the scene are charged with hit-and-run; live music is banned in local watering holes; and ice cream parlors are not allowed to sell cones—only cups—because children might drop them, leaving unsightly puddles on the pretty streets. Buildings still have no street numbers—and consequently no mail delivery (if you really want to see the locals, go to the post office). Artists started this community, and their legacy is evident in the numerous galleries. Wander the side streets off Ocean Avenue, poking into hidden courtyards and stopping at cafés to recharge on tea and crumpets.

Downtown Carmel's chief lure is shopping, especially along its main street, **Ocean Avenue,** between Junipero Avenue and Camino Real; the architecture here is a mishmash of ersatz Tudor, Mediterranean, and other styles. **Carmel Plaza** (⊠ Ocean and Junipero Aves., ☎ 831/624–0137), in the east end of the village proper, holds more than 50 shops and restaurants.

Long before it became a shopping and browsing destination, Carmel was an important religious center during the establishment of Spanish California. That heritage is preserved in the Mission San Carlos

★ Borromeo del Rio Carmelo, more commonly known as the **Carmel Mission.** Founded in 1770, it served as headquarters for the mission system in California under Father Junípero Serra. Adjoining the stone church is a tranquil garden planted with California poppies. Museum rooms at the mission include an early kitchen, Serra's spartan sleeping quarters, and the oldest college library in California. ⊠ *3080 Rio Rd. (at Lasuen Dr.)*, ☎ *831/624–3600*, WEB *www.carmelmission.org.* *$2.* ☼ *Sept.–May, Mon.–Sat. 9:30–4:30, Sun. 10:30–4:30; June–Aug., Mon.–Sat. 9:30–7:30, Sun. 10:30–7:30.*

Scattered throughout the pines in Carmel are the houses and cottages that were built for the writers, artists, and photographers who discovered the area decades ago. Among the most impressive dwellings is **Tor House,** a stone cottage built in 1919 by poet Robinson Jeffers on a craggy knoll overlooking the sea. Portraits, books, and unusual art objects fill the low-ceiling rooms. The highlight of the small estate is Hawk Tower, a detached edifice set with stones from the Carmel coastline as well as one from the Great Wall of China. The docents who lead tours (six persons maximum) are well informed about the poet's work and life. ⊠ *26304 Ocean View Ave.*, ☎ *831/624–1813 or 831/624–1840,* WEB *www.torhouse.org.* *$7. No children under 12.* ☼ *Tours Fri.–Sat. 10–3; reservations recommended.*

Carmel's greatest beauty is its rugged coastline, with pine and cypress forests and countless inlets. **Carmel Beach** (⊠ End of Ocean Ave.), an easy walk from downtown shops, has sparkling white sands and magnificent sunsets. **Carmel River State Beach** stretches for 106 acres along Carmel Bay. On sunny days the waters appear nearly as turquoise as those of the Caribbean. The sugar-white beach is adjacent to a bird sanctuary, where you might spot pelicans, kingfishers, hawks, and sandpipers. ⊠ *Off Scenic Rd., south of Carmel Beach,* ☎ *831/624–4909 or 831/649–2836,* WEB *http://cal-parks.ca.gov.* *Free.* ☼ *Daily 9 AM–sunset.*

★ **Point Lobos State Reserve,** a 350-acre headland harboring a wealth of marine life, lies a few miles south of Carmel. The best way to explore the reserve is to walk along one of its many trails. The Cypress Grove Trail leads through a forest of Monterey cypress (one of only two natural groves remaining) clinging to the rocks above an emerald-green cove. Sea Lion Point Trail is a good place to view sea lions. From those and other trails you may also spot otters, harbor seals, and (during winter and spring) migrating whales. An additional 750 acres of the reserve is an undersea marine park open to qualified scuba divers. Arrive early (or in late afternoon) to avoid crowds; the parking lots fill up. No pets are allowed. ⊠ *Rte. 1,* ☎ *831/624–4909; 831/624–8413 for scuba-diving reservations,* ⓦⓔⓑ *www.pointlobos.org.* ⊠ *$3 per vehicle.* ⊙ *Apr.–Oct., daily 9–7; Nov.–Mar., daily 9–5.*

Dining and Lodging

$$$–$$$$ ✕ **Casanova.** Southern French and northern Italian cuisine come to-
★   gether at Casanova, one of the most romantic restaurants in Carmel. A heated outdoor garden and the more than 1,000 domestic and imported vintages from the hand-dug wine cellar enhance the dining experience. The menu, which changes monthly, includes such delights as *cotelette de veau aux morilles* (grilled veal chop with sautéed morel mushrooms). All entrées come with an antipasto plate and choice of appetizers. ⊠ *5th Ave. between San Carlos and Mission Sts.,* ☎ *831/ 625–0501. Reservations essential. MC, V.*

$$$–$$$$ ✕ **Kurt's Carmel Chop House.** USDA-prime steaks and chops are cooked over almond and oak woods at this stylish steak house, which serves up an abundance of seafood and inventive appetizers. ⊠ *5th Ave. and San Carlos,* ☎ *831/625–1199. Reservations essential. AE, MC, V. No lunch.*

$$$–$$$$ ✕ **Robert's Bistro.** Chef-owner Robert Kincaid is a master culinarian.
★   At his French bistro, dried sage and lavender hanging from exposed ceiling beams, painted floors, and ocher-washed walls will make you feel as if you've stepped into an old farmhouse in Provence. The menu stresses seasonal ingredients; cassoulet made with white beans, duck confit, rabbit sausage, and garlic prawns is always on the stove. Leave room for dessert, particularly the soufflé with lemon and orange zest or the chocolate bag with chocolate shake, a masterful invention. ⊠ *Crossroads Center, 217 Crossroads Blvd.,* ☎ *831/624–9626. Reservations essential. AE, D, DC, MC, V. No lunch.*

$$$ ✕ **Anton and Michel.** Expect superb European cuisine at this elegant restaurant in Carmel's shopping district. The tender lamb dishes are fantastic and well complemented by the wines. The ultimate treats, however, are the flaming desserts. You can dine in the outdoor courtyard in summer. ⊠ *Mission St. and 7th Ave.,* ☎ *831/624–2406. Reservations essential. AE, D, DC, MC, V.*

$$$ ✕ **La Bohème.** The chefs at campy La Bohème prepare one entrée each night, accompanied by soup and salad. You may find yourself bumping elbows with your neighbor in the faux-European-village courtyard, but the predominantly French cuisine is very good, and the mood is convivial. ⊠ *Dolores St. and 7th Ave.,* ☎ *831/624–7500. Reservations not accepted. MC, V. No lunch.*

$$–$$$ ✕ **Flying Fish.** This Japanese-California seafood restaurant is simple in appearance yet bold with its flavors. It has quickly established itself as one of Carmel's most inventive eateries. Among the best entrées is the almond-crusted sea bass with Chinese cabbage and rock shrimp stir-fry. ⊠ *Mission St. between Ocean and 7th Aves.,* ☎ *831/625–1962. AE, D, MC, V. Closed Tues. No lunch.*

$$–$$$ ✕ **French Poodle.** Specialties on the traditional French menu at this intimate restaurant include the duck breast in port and the abalone. The floating island—a meringue-and-custard combo—is a delicious dessert. ⊠ *Junipero and 5th Aves.,* ☎ *831/624–8643. Reservations essential. AE, DC, MC, V. Closed Sun. No lunch.*

$$–$$$ ✕ **Grasing's Coastal Cuisine.** Chef Kurt Grasing's contemporary adaptations of American and European provincial cooking include a roast rack of lamb marinated in pomegranate juice, and medallions of pork with shiitake mushrooms, bacon, peas, and polenta. A casually elegant room, gracious service, and an extensive wine list make this one of

Carmel's top restaurants. ⊠ *6th Ave. and Mission St.,* ☎ *831/624–6562. Reservations essential. AE, MC, V.*

$$–$$$ ✕ **Loutas on Mission.** Great care and attention go into every plate at this cozy, romantic, unpretentious, and understated classic French restaurant. Menu highlights include a caramelized onion and goat cheese tart, bouillabaisse, and beef Wellington. Service is warm and attentive. ⊠ *Mission St. between 4th and 5th Aves.,* ☎ *831/620–1942. Reservations essential. AE, DC, MC, V. No lunch.*

$–$$$ ✕ **The Forge in the Forest.** This former blacksmith's shop houses a lively bar and restaurant suited to all ages and tastes. The menu has excellent prime steaks, sandwiches, and pizzas. You can sit under the trees outside by a fireplace on cool evenings. ⊠ *5th Ave. and Junipero Ave.,* ☎ *831/624–2233. AE, D, MC, V.*

$–$$$ ✕ **Lugano Swiss Bistro.** Fondue is the centerpiece here. The house specialty is a version made with Gruyère, Emmentaler, and Appenzeller. Rosemary chicken, plum-basted duck, and fennel pork loin rotate on the rotisserie. Ask for a table in the back room, which contains a hand-painted street scene of Lugano. ⊠ *The Barnyard, Rte. 1 and Carmel Valley Rd.,* ☎ *831/626–3779. AE, DC, MC, V. Closed Mon.*

$–$$$ ✕ **Rio Grill.** The best bets in this lively Santa Fe–style roadhouse are the meat and seafood cooked over an oak-wood grill. The fire-roasted artichoke and the Monterey Bay squid are exceptional starters. ⊠ *Crossroads Center, 101 Crossroads Blvd., Rte. 1 and Rio Rd.,* ☎ *831/625–5436. Reservations essential. AE, D, MC, V.*

$–$$ ✕ **Bahama Billy's.** The energy is electric at always-bustling Bahama Billy's. An excellent and diverse menu of Caribbean food combined with the colorful and lively action in the dining room make this a prime spot for fun and good eating in Carmel. Because it's outside the area covered by the town's strict zoning laws, there is often live music in the bar. ⊠ *Barnyard Shopping Center,* ☎ *831/626–0430. Reservations essential. AE, D, MC, V.*

$–$$ ✕ **Caffé Napoli.** Redolent of garlic and olive oil, this small, atmospheric Italian restaurant is a favorite of locals, who come for the crisp-crusted pizzas, house-made pastas, and fresh seafood. Specialties include grilled artichokes, fresh salmon and grilled vegetable risotto, and fisherman's pasta. There's a good Italian wine list. ⊠ *Ocean Ave. and Lincoln St.,* ☎ *831/625–4033. Reservations essential. MC, V.*

$–$$ ✕ **Jack London's.** If anyone's awake after dinner in Carmel, he's at Jack London's. This publike spot is the only Carmel restaurant to serve food until 12:30 AM, and it's where the locals eat and drink. The menu includes everything from snacks to steaks. ⊠ *Su Vecino Court on Dolores St., between 5th and 6th Aves.,* ☎ *831/624–2336 or 831/625–6765. AE, D, DC, MC, V.*

$ ✕ **The Cottage Restaurant.** The best breakfast in Carmel is served here. This local favorite offers six different preparations of eggs Benedict, sweet and savory crepes, and sandwiches and homemade soups at lunch. Good dinners are served on weekends, but the best meals here are served in the daytime. ⊠ *Lincoln St. between Ocean and 7th Aves.,* ☎ *831/625–6260. MC, V. No dinner Sun.–Wed.*

$$$$ ✕⚬ **Highlands Inn.** High on a hill overlooking the Pacific, this place
★ has superb views. Accommodations are in spa suites (with a Jacuzzi) and condominium-style units, a number with full kitchens, fireplaces, and decks overlooking the ocean. The excellent prix-fixe menus at the inn's Pacific's Edge restaurant ($$$$; jackets recommended) blend French technique and California cooking; the sommelier pairs the perfect wines. ⊠ *120 Highlands Dr., 93921,* ☎ *831/624–3801; 800/682–4811; 831/622–5445 for restaurant,* FAX *831/626–1574,* WEB *www.hyatt.com. 105 suites, 37 rooms. 2 restaurants, room service, kitchenettes (some), refrigerators, in-room data ports, in-room safes, cable*

TV with movies, in-room VCRs (some), in-room hot tubs (some), pool, 3 hot tubs, bicycles, exercise equipment, lounge, piano, baby-sitting, laundry service, business services, concierge, Internet, meeting rooms, some pets allowed (fee); no air-conditioning, no-smoking rooms. AE, D, DC, MC, V.

\$\$\$\$ ⊞ **Carriage House Inn.** This small inn with a wood-shingle exterior has spacious rooms with beam ceilings, fireplaces, down comforters, and, in most, whirlpool baths. Afternoon wine and hors d'oeuvres are included. ⊠ *Junipero Ave. between 7th and 8th Aves., Box 1900, 93921,* ☎ *831/625–2585 or 800/422–4732,* FAX *831/624–0974,* WEB *www. innsbythesea.com. 11 rooms, 2 suites. In-room hot tubs (some), in-room safes, minibars, refrigerators, cable TV, in-room VCRs; no smoking. AE, D, MC, V. CP.*

\$\$\$\$ ⊞ **Tickle Pink Inn.** Atop a towering cliff, this inn has views of the Big Sur coastline, which you can contemplate from your private balcony. Fall asleep to the sound of surf crashing below and wake up to Continental breakfast and the morning paper in bed. If you prefer the company of fellow travelers, breakfast is also served buffet style in the lounge, as are complimentary wine and cheese in the afternoon. Many rooms have wood-burning fireplaces, and there are six luxurious spa suites. ⊠ *155 Highlands Dr., 93923,* ☎ *831/624–1244 or 800/635–4774,* FAX *831/626–9516,* WEB *www.ticklepink.com. 24 rooms, 11 suites. Fans, in-room data ports, in-room hot tubs (some), refrigerators, in-room VCRs, outdoor hot tub, concierge; no air-conditioning, no smoking. AE, MC, V. CP.*

\$\$–\$\$\$\$ ⊞ **The Briarwood.** This ivy-covered B&B offers comfortable accommodations within steps of Carmel's shops and galleries. Most rooms have fireplaces and flower-lined verandas. An expanded Continental breakfast is available in your room or in the common area. ⊠ *San Carlos between 4th and 5th Aves., Box 5245, 93921,* ☎ *831/626–9056 or 800/999–8788,* FAX *831/626–8900,* WEB *www.briarwood-inn-carmel.com. 12 rooms. Fans, refrigerators, cable TV, in-room VCRs; no air-conditioning, no smoking. AE, MC, V. CP.*

\$\$–\$\$\$\$ ⊞ **Carmel River Inn.** Besides attracting those looking for a relative bargain in pricey Carmel, this half-century-old inn appeals to travelers who enjoy a bit of distance from the madding crowd—downtown Carmel in July, for instance. Yet the area's beaches are only 1½ mi away. The blue-and-white motel at the front of the property contains units with cable TV, small refrigerators, and coffeemakers. Cabins out back sleep up to six; some have fireplaces and kitchens. ⊠ *Rte. 1 at Carmel River Bridge, Box 221609, 93922,* ☎ *831/624–1575 or 800/882–8142,* FAX *831/624–0290,* WEB *www.carmelriverinn.com. 19 rooms, 24 cabins. Microwaves (some), refrigerators, cable TV, pool, Internet, some pets allowed (fee); no-smoking rooms, no air-conditioning. MC, V.*

\$\$–\$\$\$\$ ⊞ **Cobblestone Inn.** Thick quilts and country antiques, stone fireplaces
★ in guest rooms and the sitting-room area, a complimentary breakfast buffet, and afternoon wine and hors d'oeuvres contribute to the homey feel at this English-style inn. ⊠ *8th and Junipero Aves., Box 3185, 93921,* ☎ *831/625–5222 or 800/833–8836,* FAX *831/625–0478,* WEB *www. foursisters.com. 22 rooms, 2 suites. In-room data ports, refrigerators, cable TV; no air-conditioning, no smoking. AE, DC, MC, V. BP.*

\$\$–\$\$\$\$ ⊞ **Cypress Inn.** When Doris Day became part owner of this inn in 1988,
★ she added her own touches, such as posters from her many movies and photo albums of her favorite canines (pets are welcome in most rooms here). In nice weather you can enjoy your Continental breakfast in a garden surrounded by bougainvillea. ⊠ *Lincoln St. and 7th Ave., Box Y, 93921,* ☎ *831/624–3871 or 800/443–7443,* FAX *831/624–8216,* WEB *www.cypress-inn.com. 33 rooms, 1 suite. Bar, fans, in-room data ports, in-room hot tubs (some), cable TV, laundry service, concierge,*

some pets allowed (fee); no air-conditioning in some rooms, no smoking. AE, MC, V. CP.

$$–$$$$ ⊡ **La Playa Hotel.** Norwegian artist Christopher Jorgensen built the original structure in 1902 for his bride, a member of the Ghirardelli chocolate clan. The property has since undergone many additions and now resembles a Mediterranean estate. Though some of the rooms are small and could use a few modern amenities, the history and location more than compensate. You can also opt for a cottage; most have full kitchens and wood-burning fireplaces, and all have a patio or a terrace. ⊠ *Camino Real at 8th Ave., Box 900, 93921,* ☎ *831/624–6476 or 800/582–8900,* ℻ *831/624–7966,* Ⓦ *www.laplayacarmel.com. 75 rooms, 5 cottages. Restaurant, bar, refrigerators, cable TV, kitchenettes (some), pool, laundry service; no air conditioning, no smoking. AE, DC, MC, V.*

$$–$$$$ ⊡ **Mission Ranch.** Sheep graze in the ocean-side pasture near the 19th-century farmhouse at Mission Ranch. The six rooms in the main house are set around a Victorian parlor; other options include cottages, a hayloft, and a bunkhouse. Handmade quilts and carved wooden beds complement the country location. ⊠ *26270 Dolores St., 93923,* ☎ *831/624–6436 or 800/538–8221,* ℻ *831/626–4163. 31 rooms. Restaurant, piano bar, fans, in-room data ports, in-room hot tubs (some), refrigerators (some), cable TV, 6 tennis courts, pro shop, gym; no air-conditioning, no smoking. AE, MC, V.*

$$–$$$$ ⊡ **Tally Ho Inn.** This small hotel with an English garden courtyard is one of the few in Carmel's center with good views of the ocean. The penthouse units have fireplaces. ⊠ *Monte Verde St. and 6th Ave., Box 3726, 93921,* ☎ *831/624–2232 or 877/482–5594,* ℻ *831/624–2661,* Ⓦ *www.tallyho-inn.com. 12 rooms, 2 suites. Fans (some), in-room data ports (some), cable TV, laundry service; no air-conditioning, no smoking. AE, D, DC, MC, V. CP.*

$$–$$$ ⊡ **Pine Inn.** A favorite with generations of Carmel visitors, the Pine Inn has red-and-black Victorian style, complete with grandfather clock, padded fabric wall panels, antique tapestries, and marble-top furnishings. Only four blocks from the beach, the complex includes a brick courtyard of specialty shops and a modern Italian restaurant. ⊠ *Ocean Ave. and Lincoln St., Box 250, 93921,* ☎ *831/624–3851 or 800/228–3851,* ℻ *831/624–3030,* Ⓦ *www.pine-inn.com. 43 rooms, 6 suites. Restaurant, fans, in-room data ports (some), refrigerators (some), cable TV, laundry service, meeting room; no air-conditioning, no smoking. AE, D, DC, MC, V.*

$$–$$$ ⊡ **Sea View Inn.** In a residential area a few hundred feet from the beach, this restored 1905 home has a double parlor with two fireplaces, Oriental rugs, canopy beds, and a spacious front porch. Afternoon tea and evening wine and cheese are offered daily. Because of the fragile furnishings and quiet atmosphere, families would be more comfortable elsewhere. ⊠ *Camino Real between 11th and 12th Aves., Box 4138, 93921,* ☎ *831/624–8778,* ℻ *831/625–5901,* Ⓦ *www.seaviewinncarmel.com. 8 rooms. No air-conditioning, no room phones, no room TVs, no smoking. AE, MC, V. CP.*

$–$$$ ⊡ **Best Western Carmel Mission Inn.** This motel on the edge of Carmel Valley has a lushly landscaped pool and hot tub area and is close to the Barnyard and Crossroads shopping centers. Rooms vary in size; request a large one. ⊠ *3665 Rio Rd., at Rte. 1, 93923,* ☎ *831/624–1841 or 800/348–9090,* ℻ *831/624–8684,* Ⓦ *www.bestwestern.com. 163 rooms, 2 suites. Restaurant, bar, in-room data ports, refrigerators, cable TV, pool, 2 hot tubs, exercise equipment, business services, some pets allowed (fee); no-smoking rooms. AE, D, DC, MC, V.*

$$ ⊞ **Lobos Lodge.** The white-stucco motel units here are set amid cypress, oaks, and pines on the edge of the business district. All accommodations have fireplaces, and some have private patios. ⊠ *Monte Verde St. and Ocean Ave., Box L-1, 93921,* ☎ *831/624–3874,* ℻ *831/624– 0135. 28 rooms, 2 suites. Fans, in-room data ports, refrigerators, cable TV no air-conditioning, no-smoking rooms. AE, MC, V. CP.*

Nightlife and the Arts

MUSIC

Carmel Bach Festival (☎ 831/624–2046, WEB www.bachfestival.org) has presented the works of Johann Sebastian Bach and his contemporaries in concerts and recitals since 1935. The festival runs for three weeks, starting in mid-July. **Monterey County Symphony** (☎ 831/624–8511, WEB www.montereysymphony.org) performs classical concerts from October through May. Because of renovations to its home in Carmel, the symphony will perform in Salinas this year.

THEATER

The **Pacific Repertory Theater** (☎ 831/622–0700, WEB www.pacrep.org) puts on the Carmel Shakespeare Festival from August through October and performs contemporary dramas and comedies from February through July. **Sunset Community Cultural Center** (⊠ San Carlos St. between 8th and 10th Aves., ☎ 831/624–3996), which presents concerts, lectures, and headline performers, is the Monterey Bay area's top venue for the performing arts, though the theater is undergoing renovations until early 2004.

Shopping

ART GALLERIES

Carmel Art Association (⊠ Dolores St. between 5th and 6th Aves., ☎ 831/624–6176, WEB www.carmelart.org) exhibits the paintings, sculpture, and prints of local artists. **Galerie Pleine Aire** (⊠ Dolores St. between 5th and 6th Aves., ☎ 831/625–5686) showcases oil paintings by a group of seven local artists. **Highlands Sculpture Gallery** (⊠ Dolores St. between 5th and 6th Aves., ☎ 831/624–0535) is devoted to contemporary indoor and outdoor sculpture, primarily works done in stone, bronze, wood, metal, and glass. **Masterpiece Gallery** (⊠ Dolores St. and 6th Ave., ☎ 831/624–2163) shows early California impressionist art. **Photography West Gallery** (⊠ Ocean Ave. and Dolores St., ☎ 831/625–1587) exhibits photography by Ansel Adams and other 20th-century artists.

SPECIALTY SHOPS

Madrigal (⊠ Carmel Plaza and Mission St., ☎ 831/624–3477) carries sportswear, sweaters, and accessories for women. **Mischievous Rabbit** (⊠ Lincoln Ave. between 7th and Ocean Aves., ☎ 831/624–6854) sells toys, nursery accessories, books, music boxes, china, and children's clothing, with a specialty in Beatrix Potter items. **Pat Areias Sterling** (⊠ Lincoln Ave. between Ocean and 7th Aves., ☎ 831/626–8668) puts a respectfully modern spin on the Mexican tradition of silversmithing with its line of sterling silver belt buckles, jewelry, and accessories. **Shop in the Garden** (⊠ Lincoln Ave. between Ocean and 7th Aves., ☎ 831/624–6047) is an indoor-outdoor sculpture garden where you can buy fountains or garden accoutrements. You'll hear the tinkle of its wind chimes before you see the courtyard establishment.

Carmel Valley

㉓   *5–10 mi east of Carmel, Rte. 1 to Carmel Valley Rd.*

Carmel Valley Road, which turns inland at Route 1 south of Carmel, is the main thoroughfare through the town of Carmel Valley, a secluded enclave of horse ranchers and other well-heeled residents who prefer the area's sunny climate to the fog and wind on the coast. Tiny Carmel Valley village holds several crafts shops and art galleries. You'll find stunning one-of-a-kind provincial French antiques, such as 18th-century stone mantelpieces, at **Jan de Luz** (⊠ 4 E. Carmel Valley Rd., ☎ 831/659–7966). They also carry a line of high-end linens.

Garland Ranch Regional Park (⊠ Carmel Valley Rd., 9 mi east of Carmel, ☎ 831/659–4488, WEB www.mprpd.org/parks/garland.html) has hiking trails and picnic tables. The beautiful **Château Julien** winery, recognized internationally for its chardonnays and merlots, gives tours on weekdays at 10:30 and 2:30 and weekends at 12:30 and 2:30, all by appointment. The tasting room is open daily. ⊠ 8940 Carmel Valley Rd., ☎ 831/624–2600, WEB www.chateaujulien.com. ☉ Weekdays 8–5, weekends 11–5.

Dining and Lodging

$–$$ ✕ **Café Rustica.** Italian-inspired country cooking is the focus at this lively roadhouse. Specialties include roasted meats, pastas, and pizzas from the wood-fired oven. Because of the tile floors, it can get quite noisy inside; opt for a table outside for a quieter meal. ⊠ 10 Delfino Pl., ☎ 831/659–4444. Reservations essential. MC, V. Closed Wed.

$ ✕ **Wagon Wheel Coffee Shop.** Grab a seat at the counter or wait for a table at this local hangout decorated with wood-beam ceilings, hanging wagon wheels, cowboy hats, and lassos. Then chow down on substantial breakfasts of huevos rancheros, Italian sausage and eggs, or trout and eggs; this is also the place to stoke up on biscuits and gravy. For lunch choose among a dozen types of burgers and other sandwiches. ⊠ Valley Hill Center, Carmel Valley Rd. next to Quail Lodge, ☎ 831/624–8878. No credit cards. No dinner.

$$$$ ✕🏠 **Bernardus Lodge.** A first-rate spa and outstanding cuisine are the ★ focus at this luxury resort, where services are geared to oenophiles and gourmands. The spacious rooms have vaulted ceilings, featherbeds, fireplaces, patios, complimentary minibars, and double-size bathtubs. Marinus, the intimate formal dining room ($$$–$$$$; jacket recommended), emphasizes modern French technique. Chef Cal Stamenov is one of the area's few master culinarians; he changes the menu daily to reflect availability of local game and produce. ⊠ 415 Carmel Valley Rd., 93924, ☎ 831/659–3131 or 888/648–9463, FAX 831/659–3529, WEB www.bernardus.com. 57 rooms. 2 restaurants, bar, lobby lounge, room service, in-room data ports, minibars, refrigerators, cable TV with movies, in-room VCRs (some), tennis court, pool, hair salon, hot tub, sauna, spa, gym, steam room, croquet, hiking, lawn bowling, laundry service, Internet, concierge, meeting room; no smoking. AE, D, DC, MC, V.

$$$$ ✕🏠 **Quail Lodge.** At this resort on the grounds of a private country ★ club you have access to golf, tennis, and an 850-acre wildlife preserve frequented by deer and migratory fowl. Modern rooms with European styling are clustered in several low-rise buildings. Each room has a private deck or patio overlooking the golf course, gardens, or a lake. The Covey at Quail Lodge ($$–$$$$; jacket recommended) serves European cuisine in a romantic lakeside dining room. Standouts include rack of lamb, mustard-crusted salmon, and mousseline of sole. ⊠ 8205 Valley Greens Dr., 93923, ☎ 831/624–1581 or 800/538–9516, FAX 831/624–3726, WEB www.quaillodge.com. 83 rooms, 14 suites. 2 restaurants, 2 bars, room service, fans (some), in-room data ports, in-room hot tubs (some), in-room faxes (some), in-room safes (some), minibars, refrigerators, cable TV with movies and video games, 18-hole golf course, putting green, 4 tennis courts, pro shop, 2 pools, hot tub, spa, sauna, steam room, gym, bicycles, croquet, hiking, baby-sitting, laundry services, concierge, Internet, business services, meeting rooms, some pets allowed (fee); no air-conditioning in some rooms, no-smoking rooms. AE, DC, MC, V.

$$$$ ★ 🏨 **Carmel Valley Ranch Resort.** This all-suites resort, well off Carmel Valley Road on a hill overlooking the valley, is typical of contemporary California architecture. Standard amenities include wood-burning fireplaces and watercolors by local artists. Rooms have cathedral ceilings, fully stocked wet bars, and large decks. If you're staying here, the greens fee at the resort's 18-hole golf course is $150, including cart rental; special golf packages can reduce this rate considerably. ⊠ 1 Old Ranch Rd., 93923, ☎ 831/625–9500 or 800/422–7635, FAX 831/624–2858, WEB www.wyndham.com. 144 suites. 2 restaurants, 2 bars, in-room data ports, in-room hot tubs (some), in-room safes, microwaves (some), minibars, refrigerators, cable TV with movies and video games, in-room VCRs (some), 18-hole golf course, 13 tennis courts, 2 pools, 2 hot tubs, 2 saunas, steam room, laundry services, concierge, Internet, business services, meeting rooms; no smoking. AE, D, DC, MC, V.

$$$$ ★ 🏨 **Stonepine Estate Resort.** The former estate of the Crocker banking family on 330 pastoral acres has been converted to an ultradeluxe inn. The oak-paneled, antiques-laden main château holds eight elegantly furnished rooms and suites and a dining room for guests, though with advance reservations it is possible for others to dine here. The property's romantic cottages include one that is straight out of *Hansel and Gretel*. An equestrian center offers riding lessons. This is a quiet property, best suited to couples traveling without children. ⊠ 150 E. Carmel Valley Rd., Box 1543, 93924, ☎ 831/659–2245, FAX 831/659–5160, WEB www.stonepinecalifornia.com. 8 rooms, 4 suites, 3 cottages. Dining room, room service, fans, in-room data ports, in-room hot tubs (some), in-room safes (some), minibars, cable TV, in-room VCRs, 5-hole golf course, 2 tennis courts, 2 pools, horseback riding, gym, massage, mountain bikes, archery, hiking, horseback riding, recreation room, library, piano, laundry services, concierge, Internet; no air-conditioning, no smoking. AE, MC, V. BP.

$$$ 🏨 **Carmel Valley Lodge.** This small inn has rooms surrounding a garden patio and separate one- and two-bedroom cottages with fireplaces and full kitchens. ⊠ 8 Ford Rd., at Carmel Valley Rd., Box 93, 93924, ☎ 831/659–2261 or 800/641–4646, FAX 831/659–4558, WEB www.valleylodge.com. 19 rooms, 4 suites, 8 cottages. Kitchenettes, refrigerators, cable TV, in-rooms VCRs, pool, hot tub, sauna, exercise equipment, horseshoes, ping pong, Internet, some pets allowed (fee); no-smoking rooms. AE, MC, V. CP.

Nightlife and the Arts

The **Magic Circle Center** (⊠ 8 El Caminito, ☎ 831/659–1108) presents three comedies, two dramas, and a music series annually in an intimate 60-seat theater.

Outdoor Activities and Sports

Golf Club at Quail Lodge (⊠ 8000 Valley Greens Dr., ☎ 831/624–2770) incorporates several lakes into its course. Depending on the season and day of the week, greens fees range from $115 to $140 for guests and $125 to 175 for nonguests, including cart rental. **Rancho Cañada Golf Club** (⊠ 4860 Carmel Valley Rd., 1 mi east of Rte. 1, ☎ 831/624–0111) is a public course with 36 holes, some of them overlooking the Carmel River. Fees range from $$35 to $80, plus $34 for cart rental, depending on course and tee time.

MONTEREY BAY A TO Z

To research prices, get advice from other travelers, and book travel arrangements, visit www.fodors.com.

AIR TRAVEL

Monterey Peninsula Airport is 3 mi east of downtown Monterey on Route 68 to Olmsted Road. It is served by American Eagle, Skywest-Delta, United, United Express, and US Airways Express. *See* Air Travel *in* Smart Travel Tips A to Z for airline phone numbers.

➤ AIRPORT INFORMATION: **Monterey Peninsula Airport** (⊠ 200 Fred Kane Dr., ☎ 831/648–7000, WEB www.montereyairport.com).

BUS TRAVEL

Greyhound serves Monterey from San Francisco three times daily. The trip takes about 4½ hours. Monterey-Salinas Transit provides frequent service between the peninsula's towns and many major sightseeing spots and shopping areas. The base fare is $1.75, with an additional $1.75 for each zone you travel into. A day pass costs $3.50–$7, depending on how many zones you'll be traveling through. Monterey-Salinas Transit also runs the WAVE shuttle, which links major attractions on the Monterey waterfront. The free shuttle operates Memorial Day through Labor Day, daily 9–6:30.

➤ BUS INFORMATION: **Greyhound** (☎ 800/231–2222, WEB www.greyhound.com). **Monterey-Salinas Transit** (☎ 831/424–7695, WEB www.mst.org).

CAR RENTAL

Most of the major agencies have locations in downtown Santa Cruz and at the Monterey Airport. *See* Car Rental *in* Smart Travel Tips A to Z for national car-rental agency phone numbers.

CAR TRAVEL

Parking is especially difficult in Carmel and in the heavily touristed areas of Monterey.

Two-lane Route 1 runs north–south along the coast, linking the towns of Santa Cruz, Monterey, and Carmel. Route 68 runs northeast from Pacific Grove toward Salinas at U.S. 101. North of Salinas, the freeway (U.S. 101) links up with Route 156 to San Juan Bautista. The drive south from San Francisco to Monterey can be made comfortably in three hours or less. The most scenic way is to follow Route 1 down the coast past flower, pumpkin, and artichoke fields and the seaside communities of Pacifica, Half Moon Bay, and Santa Cruz. Unless you drive on sunny weekends when locals are heading for the beach, the two-lane coast highway may take no longer than the freeway.

A sometimes faster route is I–280 south from San Francisco to Route 17, south of San Jose. Route 17 crosses the redwood-filled Santa Cruz Mountains between San Jose and Santa Cruz, where it intersects with Route 1. The traffic can crawl to a standstill, however, heading into Santa Cruz. Another option is to follow U.S. 101 south through San Jose to Prunedale and then take Route 156 west to Route 1 south into Monterey.

From Los Angeles the drive to Monterey can be made in 5–6 hours by heading north on U.S. 101 to Salinas and then west on Route 68. The spectacular but slow alternative is to take U.S. 101 to San Luis Obispo and then follow the hairpin turns of Route 1 up the coast. Allow about three extra hours if you take this route.

EMERGENCIES

In the event of an emergency, dial 911. Monterey Bay Dental Society provides dentist referrals and Monterey County Medical Society can refer you to a doctor. The Surf 'n' Sand pharmacy in Carmel is open on weekdays from 9 to 6, Saturday from 9 to 1. There is a 24-hour Walgreen's pharmacy in Seaside, about 4 mi northeast of Monterey via Route 1.

➤ MEDICAL ASSISTANCE: **Community Hospital of Monterey Peninsula** (✉ 23625 Holman Hwy., Monterey, ☎ 831/624–5311). **Monterey Bay Dental Society** (☎ 831/658–0168). **Monterey County Medical Society** (☎ 831/655–1019). **Surf 'n' Sand** (✉ 6th and Junipero Aves., Carmel, ☎ 831/624–1543).**Walgreen's** (✉ 1055 Fremont Blvd., Seaside, ☎ 831/393–9231).

LODGING

The Monterey County Conventions and Visitors Bureau Visitor Services operates a lodging referral line and publishes an informational brochure with discount coupons that are good at restaurants, attractions, and shops. Monterey Peninsula Reservations will assist you in booking lodgings. Bed and Breakfast Innkeepers of Santa Cruz County is an association of innkeepers that can help you find a B&B.

➤ RESERVATION SERVICES: **Monterey County Conventions and Visitors Bureau Visitor Services** (☎ 800/555–9283, WEB www.gomonterey.org). **Monterey Peninsula Reservations** (☎ 888/655–3424, WEB www.monterey-reservations.com). **Bed and Breakfast Innkeepers of Santa Cruz County** (☎ 831/425–8212 or 831/335–4011, WEB www.bnbinns-santacruzca.org).

TOURS

California Parlor Car Tours operates motor-coach tours from San Francisco to Los Angeles that include the Monterey Peninsula.

➤ CONTACTS: **California Parlor Car Tours** (☎ 415/474–7500 or 800/227–4250, WEB www.calpartours.com).

TRAIN TRAVEL

Amtrak's *Coast Starlight,* which runs between Los Angeles, Oakland, and Seattle, stops in Salinas. Connecting Amtrak Thruway buses serve Monterey and Carmel.

➤ TRAIN INFORMATION: **Amtrak** (✉ 11 Station Pl., Salinas, ☎ 800/872–7245, WEB www.amtrak.com).

VISITOR INFORMATION

➤ CONTACTS: **Monterey County Vintners and Growers Association** (Box 1793, Monterey, 93942-1793, ☎ 831/375–9400, WEB www.montereywines.org). **Monterey Peninsula Visitors and Convention Bureau** (✉ 380 Alvarado St., Monterey 93942, ☎ 831/649–1770, WEB www.monterey.com). **Salinas Valley Chamber of Commerce** (✉ 119 E. Alisal St., Salinas 93901, ☎ 831/424–7611, WEB www.salinaschamber.com). **Santa Cruz County Conference and Visitors Council** (✉ 1211 Ocean St., Santa Cruz 95060, ☎ 831/425–1234 or 800/833–3494, WEB www.scccvc.org). **Santa Cruz Mountain Winegrowers Association** (7605-A Old Dominion Ct., Aptos 95003, ☎ 831/479–9463, WEB www.scmwa.com).

13 THE CENTRAL COAST

FROM BIG SUR TO SANTA BARBARA

Route 1 between Big Sur and Santa
Barbara is a spectacular stretch of terrain.
The curving road demands an unhurried
pace, but even if it didn't, you'd find
yourself stopping often to take in the
scenery. Don't expect much in the way of
dining, lodging, or even history until you
arrive at Hearst San Simeon State Historical
Monument, which preserves for posterity
publisher William Randolph Hearst's
testament to his own fabulousness. Sunny,
well-scrubbed Santa Barbara's Spanish-
Mexican heritage is reflected in the
architectural style of its courthouse and
mission.

Revised by
Cheryl
Crabtree

T HE COASTLINE BETWEEN CARMEL AND SANTA BARBARA, a distance of about 200 mi, is one of the most popular drives in California. Except for a few smallish cities—Ventura and Santa Barbara, in the south, and San Luis Obispo, in the north—the area is sparsely populated. The countryside's few inhabitants relish their isolation at the sharp edge of land and sea. Around Big Sur the Santa Lucia Mountains drop down to the Pacific with dizzying grandeur, but as you move south, the shoreline gradually flattens into hills dotted with cattle and the long, sandy beaches of Santa Barbara, Ventura, and Oxnard.

Inland from the Pacific a burgeoning Central Coast wine region stretches 100 mi from Paso Robles, about 20 mi east of Cambria, south to Santa Ynez. The 150-plus wineries have earned reputations for quality vintages that rival those of northern California. Visual artists create and sell their works in such towns as Cambria and Ojai. The Danish town of Solvang is an amusing stopover for hearty Scandinavian fare and an architectural change of pace. Santa Barbara, only 95 mi north of Los Angeles, is your introduction to the unhurried hospitality and easy living of southern California.

Pleasures and Pastimes

Dining

The Central Coast, from Big Sur to Solvang, is far enough off the interstate to ensure that nearly every restaurant or café has its own personality—from chic to down-home and funky. There aren't many restaurants between Big Sur and Hearst San Simeon State Historical Monument. Cambria's cooks, true to the town's British-Welsh origins, craft English dishes complete with peas and Yorkshire pudding but also serve Continental and contemporary fare.

The dishes of Santa Barbara's chefs rival those of their counterparts in the state's larger centers. Fresh seafood is plentiful, prepared old-style American in longtime wharf-side hangouts or with trendier accents at newer eateries. If you're after good, cheap food with an international flavor, follow the locals to Milpas Street on the eastern edge of Santa Barbara's downtown. Dining attire on the Central Coast is generally casual, though slightly dressy casual wear is the custom at pricier restaurants.

CATEGORY	COST*
$$$$	over $30
$$$	$22–$30
$$	$15–$21
$	under $15

*per person for a main course at dinner, excluding taxes of 7¼–7¾%.

Lodging

Big Sur has only a few lodgings, but even its budget accommodations have character. Many moderately priced hotels and motels—some nicer than others, but most of them basic places to hang your hat—can be found between San Simeon and San Luis Obispo. Keep in mind that air-conditioning is a rarity at coastal lodgings from Big Sur to Cambria, because the sea breeze cools the air. Santa Barbara's numerous hotels and B&Bs—despite rates that range from pricy to downright shocking—attract thousands of patrons year-round. Budget-conscious travelers often find more affordable options in Carpinteria, Ventura, and Oxnard, just a short drive south along the coast. Many Central

Coast lodgings offer reduced rates and promotional packages during the slower winter season (October through March) and mid-week. Wherever you stay, make reservations for the summer and holiday weekends well ahead of time.

CATEGORY	COST*
$$$$	over $225
$$$	$160–$225
$$	$100–$159
$	under $100

All prices are for a standard double room, excluding taxes of 9–10%.

Missions

Five important California missions established by Franciscan friars are within the Central Coast region. San Miguel is one of California's best-preserved missions. La Purisima is the most fully restored, Mission Santa Barbara is perhaps the most beautiful of the state's 21 missions, and Mission San Luis Obispo de Tolosa has a fine museum with many Chumash Indian artifacts. Mission San Buenaventura has 250-year-old paintings and historic statuary.

Wineries

Hundreds of vineyards and wineries dot the hillsides from Paso Robles to San Luis Obispo, through the scenic Edna Valley and continuing south to Santa Maria and Santa Ynez in northern Santa Barbara County. The wineries offer much of the variety, but little of the glitz or crowds of northern California's Napa and Sonoma valleys. Since the early 1980s the region has steadily increased production and developed an international reputation for quality wines, most notably pinot noir, chardonnay, and zinfandel. Today there are more than 150 wineries. They tend to be small, but most have tasting rooms (some have tours), and you'll often meet the winemakers themselves. There are maps and brochures at the visitor centers in Solvang, San Luis Obispo, and Santa Barbara, or you can contact the wine associations of Paso Robles, Edna Valley–Arroyo Grande, and Santa Barbara. Many tasting rooms, hotels, and motels also keep a supply of wine touring maps for visitors.

Exploring the Central Coast

Driving is the easiest way to experience the Central Coast, which encompasses a vast area from the Big Sur coastline in the north to Ventura county in the south. A car gives you the flexibility to stop at scenic vista points along Highway 1, take detours through wine country and drive to rural lakes and mountains. In the summertime and on foggy days the traffic on windy, two-lane Highway 1 can seem to move at a snail's pace from Big Sur to Cambria. You'll want to take your time anyway, to enjoy the stop-in-your-tracks views. Especially in the summertime, make reservations for a visit to Hearst San Simeon State Historical Monument well before you depart for the coast. Traveling south from San Luis Obispo through Ventura County, feast your eyes on pastoral scenes of rolling hills, peaceful valleys, and rugged mountains that stretch for miles along the Santa Barbara/Ventura shores.

Numbers in the text correspond to numbers in the margin and on the Central Coast and Santa Barbara maps.

Great Itineraries

IF YOU HAVE 3 DAYS

From the Monterey Peninsula drive down the **Big Sur coastline.** Have lunch at **Nepenthe** and continue south to ⌂ **Cambria** ⑤. The next day take a morning tour of **Hearst San Simeon State Historical Monument** in **San Simeon** ④ and spend some time viewing the exhibits at the visitor center. Drive through **Morro Bay** ⑦ to 🏨 **San Luis Obispo** ⑧, pausing north of town to poke your head into the kitschy **Madonna Inn.** Then visit **Mission San Luis Obispo de Tolosa** and the nearby **County Historical Museum.** On day three continue on to 🏨 **Santa Barbara** ⑰–㉛, where you can tour the **Santa Barbara County Courthouse** ㉔ and **Mission Santa Barbara** ㉗. In the afternoon explore **Stearns Wharf** ⑳ and other waterfront sights, and stroll **State Street** if you like to shop, or have some fun at the **Santa Barbara Zoo** ㉚.

IF YOU HAVE 7 DAYS

Make 🏨 **Big Sur** your destination for the first day and most of the second. If you're in the area on a weekend, tour the **Point Sur State Historic Park.** Watch the waves break on **Pfeiffer Beach,** one of the few places where you can actually set foot on the shore. Observe the glories of **Los Padres National Forest** up close by hiking one of the many trails in the **Ventana Wilderness,** or stay along the shore and hunt for jade at **Jade Cove.** Plan to reach 🏨 **Cambria** ⑤ by the evening of day two for dinner and a little shopping. On day three tour **Hearst San Simeon State Historical Monument,** in **San Simeon** ④; have a beachfront lunch in **Morro Bay** ⑦; and take U.S. 101 south to Route 246 west to get to **La Purisima Mission State Historic Park,** in **Lompoc** ⑩. Loop back east on Route 246 to U.S. 101 and head south to 🏨 **Santa Barbara** ⑰–㉛. On day four visit **Stearns Wharf** ⑳ and walk or bike to **East Beach** and the **Andree Clark Bird Refuge** ㉛. Have dinner on **State Street** and check out the area's shops and clubs. On your fifth day get a feel for the city's architecture, history, and vegetation at the **Santa Barbara County Courthouse** ㉔, **Mission Santa Barbara** ㉗, and the **Santa Barbara Botanic Garden** ㉙. Have dinner in **Montecito** ⑯ and explore the Coast Village Road shopping district. It's a short walk south from here to the shore to catch the sunset before or after you eat. On your sixth day experience the area's marine life on a cruise to the **Channel Islands National Park** ㉝. Stay in 🏨 **Ventura** ㉜ overnight, then take Route 33 east to reach 🏨 **Ojai** ㉞.

When to Tour the Central Coast

The Central Coast is hospitable most of the year. Fog often rolls in north of Pismo Beach during the summer; you'll need a jacket, especially after sunset, close to the shore. The rains usually come from December through March. Santa Barbara and Ventura are pleasant year-round. Hotel rooms fill up in the summer, but from April to early June and in the early fall the weather is almost as fine and the pace is less hectic. Most hotels offer considerable discounts during the winter.

BIG SUR COASTLINE

Long a retreat of artists and writers, the Big Sur area contains ancient forests and a rugged coastline that residents have protected from overdevelopment. Much of the region lies within several state parks and the more than 165,000-acre Ventana Wilderness, itself part of the Los Padres National Forest.

Big Sur

❶ *Rte. 1, 26 mi south of Carmel.*

The counterculture spirit of the town of Big Sur is evident today in the tie-dyed clothing some locals wear and in the presence of the Esalen Institute, a center of the human-potential movement. Established in 1910 as a spa with curative baths, Esalen exploded in the 1960s as a place to explore consciousness, environmental issues, and nude bathing.

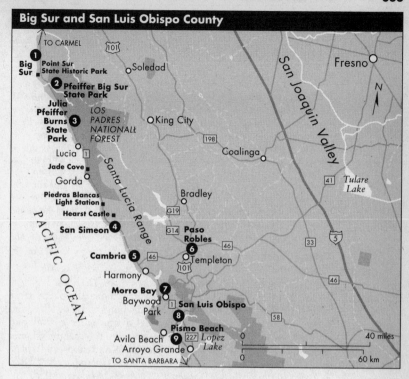

Big Sur and San Luis Obispo County

TO CARMEL

Big Sur ①

Point Sur State Historic Park

Soledad

Pfeiffer Big Sur State Park ②

Julia Pfeiffer Burns State Park ③

LOS PADRES NATIONAL FOREST

King City

Lucia

Jade Cove

Gorda

Piedras Blancas Light Station

Hearst Castle

San Simeon ④

Santa Lucia Range

Coalinga

Bradley

G19

G14 **Paso Robles** ⑥

Cambria ⑤ 46

Templeton

Harmony

Morro Bay ⑦

Baywood Park

① **San Luis Obispo** ⑧

Pismo Beach

Avila Beach ⑨ 227 *Lopez Lake*

Arroyo Grande

TO SANTA BARBARA

San Joaquin Valley

Fresno

N

198

41 *Tulare Lake*

33 5

46

58

PACIFIC OCEAN

0 ———— 40 miles

0 ———— 60 km

The graceful arc of **Bixby Creek Bridge** (⊠ Rte. 1, 13 mi south of Carmel) is a photographer's dream. From the parking area on the north side you can admire the view or walk across the 550-ft span. **Point Sur State Historic Park,** a century-old lighthouse, still stands watch from atop a large volcanic rock. Four lighthouse keepers lived here with their families until 1974, when the light station was automated. Their homes and working spaces are open to the public on 2½- to 3-hour ranger-led tours. Considerable walking, including up two stairways, is involved. Strollers are not allowed; you'll have to carry small children in a backpack. ⊠ *Rte. 1, 19 mi south of Carmel,* ☎ *831/625–4419,* WEB *www.cal-parks.ca.gov.* ⊡ *$5.* ☉ *Tours generally Nov.–Mar., Sat. 10 and 2, Sun. 10; Apr.–Oct., Wed. 10 and 2, Sat. 10 and 2, Sun. 10; call ahead to confirm.*

Dining and Lodging

$$–$$$ ✕⚏ **Big Sur River Inn.** The Big Sur River flows past the forested grounds of this old wooden structure. You can sip afternoon drinks on the river's banks in the summer. Some rooms are merely functional, but others are quite nice. Ask for one of the upper-floor rooms, all paneled in gnarled redwood. When there's a chill in the air, a fire roars in the stone fireplace in the inn's huge dining room ($–$$), which serves fresh fish and specials such as pasta Castroville (with artichokes and chicken in a pesto cream sauce). ⊠ *Hwy. 1, 2 mi north of the Pfeiffer Big Sur State Park entrance, 93920,* ☎ *831/667–2700,* FAX *831/667–2743,* WEB *www.bigsurriverinn.com. 14 rooms, 6 suites. Restaurant, bar, pool; no room phones, no room TVs, no smoking. AE, MC, V.*

$–$$ ⚏ **Glen Oaks Motel.** At this simple lodging in the heart of Big Sur you can choose between comfortable motel-style rooms and cottages in the woods that combine Laura Ashley flourishes with frontier style. ⊠ *Rte. 1, 1 mi north of the Pfeiffer Big Sur State Park entrance, 93920,* ☎ *831/667–2105,* FAX *831/667–1105,* WEB *www.glenoaksbigsur.com. 15* *rooms, 2 cottages. No room phones, no room TVs, no-smoking rooms. No credit cards.*

Pfeiffer Big Sur State Park

❷ *Rte. 1, 8½ mi south of Big Sur.*

A short hiking trail at Pfeiffer Big Sur State Park ($3 per vehicle for day use) leads through a redwood-filled valley to a waterfall. You can double back or continue on the more difficult trail along the valley wall for views of the tops of the trees you were just walking among. Stop in at the **Big Sur Station** visitor center, off Hwy. 1 less than 1/2 mi south of the park entrance, for information about the entire area. ✉ *47225 Hwy. 1,* ☎ *831/667–2315,* WEB *www.cal-parks.ca.gov.* ☉ *Daily 8–4:30.*

Through a hole in one of the big rocks at secluded **Pfeiffer Beach** you can watch the waves break first on the sea side and then on the beach side. The 2-mi road from the highway to the beach descends sharply. ✉ *Off Rte. 1, ½ mi south of Big Sur Station.* ☎ *$5 per vehicle (day use).*

Dining, Lodging, and Camping

$$–$$$ ✕ **Nepenthe.** You won't find a grander coastal view between San Francisco and Los Angeles than the one from here. The house was once owned by Orson Welles and Rita Hayworth, though they reportedly spent little time here. The lunchtime food—burgers, sandwiches, and salads—is overpriced but tasty. For real drama order a drink and watch the sun slip into the Pacific Ocean at sunset. Nepenthe's dinner menu focuses on fresh fish, hormone-free steaks and chops, and a huge wine list. The outdoor Café Kevah serves breakfast and lunch. ✉ *Rte. 1, 2½ mi south of Big Sur Station,* ☎ *831/667–2345. AE, MC, V.*

$$$$ ✕▥ **Post Ranch Inn.** This luxurious retreat, designed exclusively for
★ adult getaways, is the ultimate in environmentally conscious architecture. The redwood guest houses, all with views of the ocean or the mountains, blend into a wooded cliff 1,200 ft above the ocean. Each unit has its own fireplace, stereo, private deck, and massage table. On-site activities include everything from guided hikes to tarot-card readings. The inn's restaurant serves a stellar four-course prix fixe ($$$$) menu of cutting-edge American food. ✉ *Rte. 1, 1½ mi south of the Pfeiffer Big Sur State Park entrance, Box 219, 93920,* ☎ *831/667–2200 or 800/ 527–2200,* FAX *831/667–2824,* WEB *www.postranchinn.com. 30 units. Restaurant, bar, in-room hot tubs, refrigerators, 2 pools, gym, spa, library; no room TVs, no smoking. AE, MC, V. CP.*

$$$$ ✕▥ **Ventana Inn & Spa.** Hundreds of celebrities, from Oprah Winfrey
★ to Sir Anthony Hopkins, have escaped to Ventana, a romantic resort on 243 tranquil acres 1,200 ft above the Pacific. The activities here are purposely limited. Sunbathe (there is a clothing-optional deck and pool), walk or ride horses in the nearby hills, or pamper yourself with mind-and-body treatments in the Allegria Spa or your own private quarters. All rooms have natural-wood walls and cool tile floors, while some also have private hot tubs on their patios. The inn's Cielo restaurant ($$$$) showcases fine California foods and wines. ✉ *Rte. 1, ⅕ mi south of Pfeiffer Big Sur State Park, 93920,* ☎ *831/667–2331 or 800/628–6500,* FAX *831/667–2419,* WEB *www.ventanainn.com. 29 rooms, 31 suites, 3 houses. Restaurant, bar, in-room VCRs, 2 pools, gym, 2 Japanese baths, sauna, spa, library; no smoking. AE, D, DC, MC, V. 2-night minimum stay on weekends and holidays; children allowed only in houses. CP.*

$$–$$$ ✕▥ **Deetjen's Big Sur Inn.** This scene amid the redwoods has rustic charm, especially if you're not too attached to creature comforts. The room doors lock only from the inside, half the rooms have only wood-burning stoves to supply heat, and your neighbor can often be heard through the walls. Still, Deetjen's is a special place. The restaurant ($$–

$$$, reservations essential) in the main house serves stylish food that includes roasted duck, steak, and rack of lamb for dinner and wonderfully light and flavorful pancakes for breakfast. ⊠ *Rte. 1, 3½ mi south of the Pfeiffer Big Sur State Park entrance, 93920,* ☎ *831/667–2377 inn; 831/667–2378 restaurant,* WEB *www.deetjensbigsurinn.com. 20 rooms. Restaurant; no room phones, no room TVs, no smoking. MC, V.*

$$–$$$ 🔟 **Big Sur Lodge.** The motel-style cottages of this property in Pfeiffer Big Sur State Park make it a good choice for families. The lodging area sits in a meadow surrounded by redwood and oak trees. Some accommodations have fireplaces, and some have kitchens. ⊠ *47225 Rte. 1 (Pfeiffer Big Sur State Park entrance), 93920,* ☎ *831/667–3100 or 800/424–4787,* FAX *831/667–3110,* WEB *www.bigsurlodge.com. 61 rooms. Restaurant, no room phones, no room TVs, grocery, kitchenettes (some), pool, meeting rooms; no smoking. AE, MC, V.*

🔺 **Pfeiffer Big Sur State Park.** Redwood trees tower over this large campground. It's often crowded in summer, so reserve a site as far ahead as possible. There are no hook-ups. *Flush toilets. Dump station. Drinking water, laundry facilities, showers. Fire grates, fire pits, picnic tables, restaurant. Public telephone. General store, ranger station. Swimming (river). 218 sites.* ⊠ *Rte. 1, 8½ mi south of Point Sur State Historic Park,* ☎ *800/444–7275 for reservations,* WEB *www. cal-parks.ca.gov.* 🎫 *$12.*

Julia Pfeiffer Burns State Park

❸ *Rte. 1, 11 mi south of Pfeiffer Big Sur State Park.*

Julia Pfeiffer Burns State Park offers some fine hiking, from an easy half-mile stroll with marvelous coastal views to a strenuous 6-mi trek through the redwoods. Summer crowds lessen the appeal of the big attraction here, an 80-ft waterfall that drops into the ocean, but you'll still get an idea why the park's namesake, the daughter of one of the area's first white settlers, liked to sit here and contemplate nature. Migrating whales, not to mention harbor seals and sea lions, can sometimes be spotted not far from shore. ⊠ *Big Sur Station #1, 93920,* ☎ *831/667–2315,* WEB *www.cal-parks.ca.gov.* 🎫 *Free.* ☉ *Daily sunrise–sunset.*

Dining

$$–$$$ ✕ **Ragged Point Inn.** A good place to brunch or lunch near the area's parks, this restaurant, perched over the southernmost end of Big Sur, is not as fancy as the places farther north. But neither are the prices, and the food—sandwiches, salads, pastas, and fish and meat dishes—is tasty. It also serves dinner. ⊠ *Rte. 1, about 35 mi south of Julia Pfeiffer Burns State Park,* ☎ *805/927–5708. AE, D, MC, V.*

En Route   Route 1 snakes south along the coast from Big Sur toward San Simeon. Ten miles south of the town of Lucia is **Jade Cove** (⊠ *Hwy. 1, 21 mi south of Julia Pfeiffer Burns State Park.* ☎ *831/667–2315,* WEB www. cal-parks.ca.gov), a well-known jade-hunting spot. Rock hunting is allowed on the beach, but you may not remove anything from the walls of the cliffs.

SAN LUIS OBISPO COUNTY
From San Simeon to Pismo Beach

San Luis Obispo County's pristine landscapes and abundant wildlife areas, especially those around Morro Bay and Montaña de Oro State Park, have long attracted people seeking back-to-nature experiences. Inland, an up-and-coming wine region stretches from Paso Robles in the north through the Edna and Arroyo Grande Valleys in the south.

With historic attractions, a booming cultural scene, and eclectic restaurants, the college town of San Luis Obispo is at the heart of the county. In the south, Pismo Beach and other coastal towns give access to the beach and all its pleasures.

San Simeon

❹ *57 mi south of Big Sur on Rte. 1.*

Whalers founded San Simeon in the 1850s but had virtually abandoned the town by the time Senator George Hearst reestablished it 20 years later. Hearst bought up most of the surrounding ranch land, built a 1,000-ft wharf, and turned San Simeon into a bustling port. His son, William Randolph Hearst, further developed the area during the construction of Hearst Castle®. Today the town, which is 3 mi east of the road leading to the castle, is basically a row of gift shops, restaurants, and motels along Route 1.

★ ♺ A large and growing colony (at last count 5,000–7,000 members) of elephant seals gathers every year at **Piedras Blancas Elephant Seal Rook,** on the beaches near Piedras Blancas Lighthouse. The huge males with pendulous noses typically begin appearing on shore in late November, and the females start to arrive in December to give birth—most babies are born in the last two weeks of January. The newborn pups spend about four weeks nursing before the mothers head out to sea, leaving the young ones on their own. You can witness nature in action from the bluffs just a few feet above the beach. Park at the vista point just south of Piedras Blancas Lighthouse (4½ mi north of Hearst San Simeon State Historical Monument) and follow the signs. Docents are often on hand to give background information and statistics. ⊠ *Friends of the Elephant Seals, 250 San Simeon Ave., 93452,* ☎ *805/924–1628,* WEB *www.elephantseal.org.* ☑ *Free.* ☼ *Daily.*

★ At **Hearst San Simeon State Historical Monument,** Hearst Castle® sits in solitary splendor atop La Cuesta Encantada (the Enchanted Hill). Its buildings and gardens are spread over the 127 acres that were the heart of newspaper magnate William Randolph Hearst's 250,000-acre ranch. Hearst devoted nearly 30 years and about $10 million to building this elaborate estate. He commissioned renowned architect Julia Morgan—who was also responsible for buildings at the University of California at Berkeley—but he was very much involved with the final product, a hodgepodge of Italian, Spanish, Moorish, and French styles. The 115-room main building and three huge "cottages" are connected by terraces and staircases and surrounded by pools, gardens, and statuary. In its heyday the castle was a playground for Hearst, Hollywood celebrities, and the rich and powerful from around the world. Construction began in 1919 and was never officially completed. Work was halted in 1947 when Hearst had to leave San Simeon due to failing health. The Hearst family presented the property to the state of California in 1958.

Buses from the visitor center zigzag up the hillside to the neoclassical extravaganza above. Guides conduct four different daytime tours and (part of the year) one evening tour of various parts of the main house and grounds. Tour No. 1, the most basic, is recommended for newcomers. Daytime tours take about two hours. Docents in period costume portray Hearst's guests and staff for the slightly longer evening tour, which begins at sunset. All tours include a half-mile walk and between 150 and 400 stairs. A 40-minute film shown at a giant-screen theater gives a sanitized version of Hearst's life and of the construction of the castle. Reservations for the tours, which can be made up to eight weeks in advance, are necessary. ⊠ *San Simeon State Park,*

750 Hearst Castle Rd., ☎ 805/927–2020 or 800/444–4445, WEB www.hearst-castle.org. ⊠ Daytime tours $10 (tour plus movie $14), evening tours $20. ⊙ Tours daily 8:20–3:20 (later in summer); additional tours take place most Fri. and Sat. evenings Mar.–May and Sept.–Dec. MC, V.

Dining and Lodging

$$–$$$ ✕🏨 **Best Western Cavalier Oceanfront Resort.** Reasonable rates, an oceanfront location, evening bonfires, and well-equipped rooms—some with wood-burning fireplaces and private patios—make this motel a good choice. If you've just finished a tour of Hearst San Simeon State Historical Monument and want to eat lunch or dinner right away, stop at the Cavalier Restaurant ($–$$$, 805/927–3276) for grilled steak or seafood. ⊠ *9415 Hearst Dr., 93452, ☎ 805/927–4688 or 800/826–8168, FAX 805/927–6472, WEB www.cavalierresort.com. 90 rooms. 2 restaurants, in-room data ports, refrigerators, cable TV, in-room VCRs, 2 pools, gym, hot tub, laundry facilities, meeting rooms, some pets allowed; no-smoking rooms. AE, D, DC, MC, V.*

Cambria

⑤ *9 mi south of San Simeon on Rte. 1.*

Cambria, an artists' colony with many late-Victorian homes, is divided into the newer West Village and the original East Village. Each section has B&Bs, restaurants, art galleries, and shops. In the local architecture, the street names and the name of the town itself you can still detect the legacy of the Welsh miners who settled in Cambria in the 1890s. Motels line Moonstone Beach Drive, which runs along the coast. **Leffingwell's Landing** (⊠ north end of Moonstone Beach Dr., ☎ 805/927–2070), a state picnic ground, is a good place for examining tidal pools and watching otters as they frolic in the surf. Footpaths wind along the beach side of the drive.

Dining and Lodging

$$$–$$$$ ✕ **The Sea Chest.** By far the best seafood restaurant in town, this clifftop inn serves all kinds of fish from local waters and around the world. The oyster bar is highly recommended. Come early to catch the sunset. ⊠ *6216 Moonstone Beach Dr., ☎ 805/927–4514. Reservations not accepted. No credit cards. Closed Tues. Sept.–May. No lunch.*

$$–$$$ ✕ **Hamlet Restaurant at Moonstone Gardens.** Set amid 3 acres of lux-
★ uriant gardens, the Hamlet, open for lunch and dinner daily, has an enchanting patio that's perfect for relaxing. The ocean views from the upstairs dining room and full bar attract a steady stream of locals and tourists year-round. Entrées range from hamburgers to rack of lamb. ⊠ *Exotic Gardens Rd., Rte. 1 at Moonstone Beach Dr., ☎ 805/927–3535. AE, MC, V.*

$$ ✕ **Cambria Pines Lodge Restaurant.** Ribs, filet mignon, and large top sirloin steaks lure diners to the restaurant attached to the Cambria Pines Lodge. Bands in the lounge play light rock, jazz, and other music. ⊠ *2905 Burton Dr., ☎ 805/927–4200. AE, D, DC, MC, V.*

$–$$ ✕ **Robin's.** Multiethnic only begins to describe the dining at this antiques-filled restaurant. Tandoori prawns, quesadillas, a Thai red curry, numerous salads (more for lunch than dinner), numerous vegetarian entrées, hamburgers for the kids, and some truly fine desserts are all on Robin's eclectic menu, which emphasizes fresh fish and produce from local markets. ⊠ *4095 Burton Dr., ☎ 805/927–5007. MC, V.*

$$$$ 🏨 **Cypress Cove Inn.** Like many hotels on the beach, this romantic getaway was designed in the Welsh style, with outside walls made of old stone and rooms on the upper floors crisscrossed by wood beams. Many rooms face the Pacific; all rooms have fireplaces. ⊠ *6348 Moonstone*

Beach Dr., 93428, ☎ 805/927–2600 or 800/568–8517, WEB *www. cypresscoveinn.com. 21 rooms, 1 suite. Some fans, microwaves, refrigerators, in-room VCRs, hot tub; no smoking. AE, D, DC, MC, V. BP.*

$$$$ ⌂ **Pelican Suites.** This beachfront abode offers great views and extremely comfortable rooms. The storied king-size beds, complete with steps leading up to the mattress, the large fireplaces, and the hot tubs in some rooms make this a good romantic getaway. Ask for an ocean view. ✉ *6316 Moonstone Beach Dr., 93428, ☎ 805/927–1500 or 800/ 222–9160, FAX 805/927–0218, WEB www.moonstonehotels.com. 24 rooms. Microwaves, refrigerators, in-room VCRs, pool, massage. AE, D, MC, V. BP.*

$$$–$$$$ ⌂ **Blue Dolphin Inn.** The luxurious beachfront rooms here look like they've been transported straight out of a middle-class home in Surrey circa 1910. Heavy on frills, pinks, and pastels, they have fireplaces and superb ocean views. Five rooms have whirlpool tubs. ✉ *6470 Moonstone Beach Dr., 93428, ☎ 805/927–3300 or 800/222–9157, FAX 805/ 927–7311, WEB www.moonstonehotels.com. 18 rooms. Refrigerators, cable TV, in-room VCRs; no smoking. AE, D, DC, MC, V. BP.*

$$$–$$$$ ⌂ **Fog Catcher Inn.** The landscaped gardens and 10 thatch-roof buildings resemble an English country village. Most rooms (among them 10 minisuites) have ocean views. All have fireplaces and are done in floral chintz with light-wood furniture. ✉ *6400 Moonstone Beach Dr., 93428, ☎ 805/927–1400 or 800/425–4121, FAX 805/927–0204, WEB www.fogcatcherinn.com. 50 rooms, 10 suites. Minibars, refrigerators, cable TV, pool, hot tub, some pets allowed; no smoking. AE, D, DC, MC, V. CP.*

$$–$$$ ⌂ **Squibb House.** Owner Bruce Black restored this 1877 Gothic revival–Italianate structure, and craftsmen built many of the pine furnishings. The rooms contain antiques but have modern conveniences such as reading lamps with ample light and showers with sufficient water pressure. ✉ *4063 Burton Dr., 93428, ☎ 805/927–9600, FAX 805/927–9606, WEB www.squibbhouse.com. 5 rooms. No room phones, no room TVs, no smoking. AE, MC, V. CP.*

$–$$ ⌂ **San Simeon Pines Seaside Resort.** Amid 9 acres of pines and cypress, this motel-style resort has its own golf course and is directly across from Leffingwell's Landing. The accommodations include cottages with landscaped backyards. Parts of the complex are for adults only; others are reserved for families. ✉ *7200 Moonstone Beach Dr. (mailing address: Box 117, San Simeon 93452), ☎ 805/927–4648, WEB www.sspines.com. 58 rooms. Cable TV, 9-hole golf course, pool, croquet, shuffleboard, playground, meeting rooms; no smoking. AE, MC, V.*

Nightlife

Cambria doesn't have much nightlife, but if you're looking for a bar with music, cruise up Main Street until you hear some sounds that suit your fancy. A crowd of all ages hangs out at **Camozzi's Saloon** (✉ 2262 Main St., ☎ 805/927–8941), where vibe is old-time cowboy but the music is rock and R&B.

En Route   Seven miles south of Cambria on Route 1 is the town of **Harmony,** population 18. The **Harmony Pottery Studio Gallery** (✉ Rte. 1, ☎ 805/ 927–4293) shows some fine work amid the largest selection of pottery on the Central Coast.

Paso Robles

❻ *28 mi east of Cambria on Rte. 46; 30 mi north of San Luis Obispo on U.S. 101.*

Spanish explorers named this area El Paso de Robles, or "pass of oaks," presumably for the oak trees that dominated the countryside.

The Salinan Indians and Franciscan fathers also called it Agua Caliente for the many natural underground springs. In the 1860s tourists began flocking to Paso Robles to "take the cure" in the hot springs and mud baths. Other folks came to establish cattle and agricultural businesses. Even Jesse James came to hang out with the relatives while evading the law. Today Paso Robles is considered a major player in the wine industry, with more than 50 wineries and 200 vineyards. (You can pick up a regional wine-touring map at most hotels, wineries, and attractions in the area.) The wineries and vineyards of the area are primarily known for robust red wines—particularly zinfandels, cabernets, and merlots.

Paso Robles maintains its dual identities—cowboy town and booming winery hub with an upscale clientele—surprisingly well. Small-town friendliness prevails at the fanciest of restaurants, and wineries tend to treat visitors like neighbors. Seated at a tasting room bar, you can easily find yourself chatting with a rancher about trail rides in the hills while the owner/winemaker points out the merits of his latest vintages. At least for the time being, Paso Robles is a low-key town where you can still get a sense of 19th-century life in the Old West.

Much of Paso Robles life centers around **City Park** (✉ Spring St. between 11th and 12th streets), the historic town square in the heart of downtown. Folks gather around the fountain, gazebo, and horseshoe pits while kids romp in the playground. Restaurants, wine bars, antiques stores, and specialty shops line the perimeter. For a glimpse of old-time Paso Robles life, take a horse-drawn carriage ride around the square. Built by philanthropist Andrew Carnegie, the early 1900s **Carnegie Library** (✉ 800 12th St., ☎ 805/238–4996), which sits in the middle of City Park, houses exhibits on natural history, along with books and archival material; downstairs is the Western Art Museum. It's open Wednesday–Sunday 1–4.

★ **Mission San Miguel Archangel,** founded in 1797, stands as one of California's best-preserved missions. Many of the original decorations, including ornate murals on the walls and ceilings, are still intact, and the compound looks much as it did when the padres and conquistadores stayed there. A self-guided tour takes you to a mission model room, mission kitchen, padre's bedroom, church, and cemetery. ✉ 775 *Mission St. (off U.S. 101, 7 mi north of Paso Robles), San Miguel 93451,* ☎ *805/467–3256,* WEB *www.missionsanmiguel.org.* ✉ *Donation.* ☉ *Daily 9:30–4:30.*

The lakeside **Paso Robles Hot Springs & Spa,** a day spa on 240 hilly acres near the U.S. 101/Rte. 46E intersection, is a great place to relax before and after wine tasting. Soak in a private indoor or outdoor hot tub fed by natural mineral springs or indulge in a massage or facial (reserve treatments in advance). ✉ *3725 Buena Vista Dr.,* ☎ *805/238–4600,* WEB *www.pasohotsprings.com.* ✉ *Hot tubs $10 per person per hr.* ☉ *Daily.*

Waterski, fish for bass, trout, and bluegill, or lounge on the 165 mi of shoreline at **Lake Nacimiento Resort,** 16 mi northwest of downtown Paso Robles. There are campsites, family lodges, a full-service marina with boat and equipment rentals, a restaurant, a general store, horseshoe pits, volleyball, and basketball. In the summer you can swim in the pool for a fee. ✉ *10625 Nacimiento Lake Dr., Bradley 93426,* ☎ *805/238–3256 or 800/323–3839,* WEB *www.nacimientoresort.com.* ✉ *$10 day use (for up to 2 people, $3 for each additional person).* ☉ *Daily.*

Even if you don't drink wine, stop at **Eberle Winery** (✉ North side of Rte. 46E, 3½ mi east of U.S. 101, ☎ 805/238–9607, WEB www.

eberlewinery.com) for a tour of the 16,000 square ft of underground wine caves. The winery is known for premium handcrafted wines produced in limited quantities. You can't miss **EOS Estate Winery** (⊠ South side of Rte. 46E, about 5 mi east of U.S. 101, ☎ 805/239–2562, WEB www.eosvintage.com)—the huge Romanesque facility looms over Route 46. Pause here to visit one of the grandest visitor centers in the area, with rose gardens, a massive gift shop, and Indy 500 race car exhibit. The Old West–style tasting room filled with loud country music at **Tobin James Cellars** (⊠ 8950 Union Rd. (on the south side of Rte. 46E, 11 mi east of U.S. 101), ☎ 805/239–2204, WEB www. tobinjames.com) is probably the wildest in town. Jesse James reputedly drank at the 130-year-old mahogany wine bar, which was shipped out from Missouri in the early 1900s. The wine pourers' good-natured banter keeps you laughing taste after taste. Small but swank **Justin Vineyards & Winery** (⊠ 11680 Chimney Rock Rd., ☎ 805/238–6932, 800/726–0049, WEB www.justinwine.com) lies at the far-western reaches of Paso Robles wine country. It's well worth the 15-mi drive along quiet country roads through the hills, as the impeccable facility is widely acclaimed for its Bordeaux-style blends. They also run a tiny wine-themed restaurant and three-room luxury inn.

Dining and Lodging

$$–$$$$ ✕ **AJ Spurs Saloon & Dining Hall.** Laid-back and family-friendly, this dining hall dishes up gigantic meals. Entrées range from 35-oz. steaks and fresh fish grilled in the oak barbecue pit to pasta and cajun-style dishes. All dinners include soup, salsa, beans, rice, salad, breads, and an old-fashioned root beer float or after-dinner liqueur. ⊠ *508 Main St., Templeton,* ☎ *805/434–2700. AE, D, MC, V. No lunch.*

$$–$$$ ✕ **Bistro Laurent.** Owner chef Laurent Grangien has devised a winning menu at this authentic, unpretentious French bistro in an 1890s brick building across from City Park. He included traditional dishes like osso buco, cassoulet, rack of lamb, vichyssoise, and onion soup, plus contemporary specials and an international wine list. The bistro also prepares picnic baskets with advance notice. ⊠ *1202 Pine St. (at 12th St.),* ☎ *805/226–8191; 805/226–9750 (Le Petit Marcel). MC, V. Closed Sun.*

$$–$$$ ✕ **McPhee's Grill.** The grain silos across the street and the floral oil-
★   cloth on the tables belie the culinary delights within this casual eatery in an 1860s building in tiny Templeton, south of Paso Robles. Locals rave about the eclectic, contemporary cuisine, which takes traditional western fare (steaks, chops, fowl, and fish) and adds unusual accents like ancho chili apricot glaze. Reservations are recommended. ⊠ *416 Main St., Templeton,* ☎ *805/434–3204. AE, D, MC, V.*

$$$–$$$$ 🏨 **Summerwood Inn.** Built in 1995, this wine-themed B&B is next to the Summerwood Winery, 1 mi west of U.S. 101 at Rte. 46W and Arbor Road. Each individually decorated room is given a wine theme, such as Merlot and Bordeaux. All rooms have gas fireplaces and balconies overlooking the estate vineyards. For ultimate decadence, stay in the Cabernet Suite, with private deck and ultraluxurious bath. Lodgings include a full cooked-to-order breakfast. ⊠ *2130 Arbor Rd., 93446,* ☎ *805/227–1111, FAX 805/227–1112, WEB www.summerwoodinn.com. 9 rooms. Cable TV, no smoking. BP. AE, MC, V.*

$$ 🏨 **Paso Robles Inn.** In the 1890s, the Paso Robles Inn provided luxurious accommodations in the heart of town for tourists who came to rejuvenate themselves in the hot springs. In 1940 a fire destroyed all but the west wing of the original hotel. This restored historic wing is the centerpiece of today's inn, with oversized fireplace rooms that pipe the famed hot spring water into private spa tubs. The Monterey-style lodgings in other wings range from spacious fireplace and spa rooms to standard rooms with just the basics. Many of them overlook the

oak-studded gardens, streams, and waterfalls. A free-standing spa facility is scheduled for completion by early 2003. ⊠ *1103 Spring St.,*
93446, ☎ *805/238–2660, 800/676–1713,* FAX *805/238–4707,* WEB
www.pasoroblesinn.com. 88 rooms. Restaurant, coffee shop, mi-
crowaves (some), refrigerators (some), cable TV, pool, hot tub, gym,
lounge, meeting rooms; no-smoking rooms. AE, D, DC, MC, V.

$ ⊡ **Adelaide Inn.** Family owned and managed, the Adelaide Inn gives
you hotel amenities for motel prices. It's a clean, friendly oasis behind
a conglomerate of gas stations and fast-food outlets just west of the
U.S. 101 and Rte. 46E interchange. ⊠ *1215 Ysabel Ave., 93446,* ☎
805/238–2770, 800/549–7276, FAX *805/238–3497,* WEB *www.*
adelaideinn.com. In-room data ports, refrigerators, cable TV with
movies, miniature golf, putting green, pool, hot tub, laundry facilities,
laundry service, business services; no-smoking rooms. AE, D, MC, V.

Morro Bay

❼ *20 mi south of Cambria on Rte. 1.*

Fishermen in the town of Morro Bay slog around the harbor in ga-
loshes, and old-style ships teeter in its protected waters. Chumash Indians were the area's main inhabitants when Portuguese explorer Juan
Rodríguez Cabrillo dropped anchor in 1542. The Spanish claimed the
region in 1587, but Morro Bay remained a relatively quiet place until
the second half of the 19th century, when an enterprising farmer built
the town's wharf. Fishing was the main industry in the early 20th century, and it remains a vital part of the economy.

★ Locals are proud of the 576-ft-high **Morro Rock** (⊠ At the northern
end of the Embarcadero), one of nine such small volcanic peaks, or
"morros," in the area. A short walk leads to a breakwater, with the
harbor on one side and the crashing waves of the Pacific on the other.
Morro Bay is a wildlife preserve where endangered falcons and other
birds nest. You can't climb on Morro Rock, but even from its base you'll
be able to divine that the peak is alive with birds. The center of the action on land is the **Embarcadero** (⊠ On the waterfront, from Beach
St. to Tidelands Park), which holds lodgings and the restaurants that
make up the area's au courant dining scene. The town's well-designed
aquarium is here, as is the outdoor Giant Chessboard, made up of nearly
life-size hand-carved pieces.

Dining and Lodging

$$$–$$$$ ✕ **Windows on the Water.** Morro Bay's most notable restaurant com-
plements great views of Morro Bay from every table with first-rate con-
temporary California/American cuisine. The menu changes with the
season but always focuses on fresh fish and quality local ingredients.
They only serve lunch on busy high-season weekends. ⊠ *699 Embar-*
cadero, ☎ *805/772–0677. AE, D, DC, MC, V. Closed Mon.*

$$–$$$ ✕ **Dorn's.** This seafood café, which overlooks the harbor, resembles a
Cape Cod cottage. It's open for breakfast, lunch, and dinner. Excel-
lent fish and calamari steaks are on the dinner menu. ⊠ *801 Market*
Ave., ☎ *805/772–4415. D, MC, V.*

$$$$ ⊡ **Ascot Suites.** A hop and a skip from the Embarcadero, this hotel
★ has all the high-end conveniences. There are large hot tubs in most bath-
rooms, well-stocked wet bars, and gas fireplaces. A complimentary break-
fast basket arrives at your door in the morning. ⊠ *260 Morro Bay Blvd.,*
93442, ☎ *805/772–4437 or 800/887–6454,* FAX *805/772–8860,* WEB
www.ascotinn.com. 32 units. Minibars, refrigerators, cable TV, in-
room VCRs, pool, hot tub, massage, concierge, meeting room. AE, D,
DC, MC, V. CP.

$$$–$$$$ 🖫 **The Inn at Morro Bay.** This upscale hotel complex has romantic contemporary-style rooms with CD players and featherbeds. Many have fireplaces, private decks with spa tubs, and bay views; others look out at extensive gardens. There's an on-site wellness center with spa and massage treatments, a golf course across the road, and a heron rookery nearby (even bird lovers shouldn't book a room near the nesting grounds, as the morning din can be overwhelming). ⊠ *60 State Park Rd., 93442,* ☎ *805/772–5651 or 800/321–9566,* FAX *805/772–4779,* WEB *www.innatmorrobay.com. 97 rooms, 1 cottage. Restaurant, bar, cable TV with movies, room service, pool, massage, mountain bikes, meeting room; no smoking. AE, D, DC, MC, V.*

$–$$$ 🖫 **Adventure Inn.** Nautical murals decorate this small motel facing Morro Rock. Rooms are plain but comfortable. Amenities include coffeemakers and free HBO and local calls. ⊠ *1150 Embarcadero, 93442,* ☎ *805/772–5607; 800/799–5607 in CA,* WEB *www.adventureinn.net. 16 rooms. Restaurant, fans, cable TV with movies, refrigerators, pool, hot tub; no-smoking rooms. AE, D, MC, V. CP.*

$–$$$ 🖫 **Embarcadero Inn.** A drab metallic-color wooden exterior hides a more welcoming interior with sparkling clean rooms, all with old maritime photographs on the walls and balconies that face the sea. ⊠ *456 Embarcadero, 93442,* ☎ *805/772–2700 or 800/292–7625,* FAX *805/772–1060,* WEB *www.embarcaderoinn.com. 29 rooms, 3 suites. Microwaves, refrigerators, cable TV, in-room VCRs, 2 hot tubs; no-smoking rooms. AE, D, DC, MC, V. CP.*

$$ 🖫 **Grays Inn and Gallery.** With only three rooms, this beachfront property books up quickly, so you may have trouble getting a reservation. But make an effort because the place is a hidden treasure, its cozy rooms facing the sea. ⊠ *561 Embarcadero, 93442,* ☎ *805/772–3911,* WEB *www.hometown.aol.com/graysinn. 3 rooms. Kitchenettes. AE, MC, V.*

Outdoor Activities and Sports

Kayak Horizons (⊠ 551 Embarcadero, ☎ 805/772–6444) rents kayaks and gives lessons and guided tours. **Sub-Sea Tours** (⊠ 699 Embarcadero, ☎ 805/772–9463) operates glass-bottom boats and has kayak and canoe rentals and lessons. **Virg's Sport Fishing** (⊠ 1215 Embarcadero, ☎ 805/772–1222 or 800/762–5263) conducts deep-sea fishing and whale-watching trips.

En Route   From Morro Bay you can reach San Luis Obispo by continuing east on Route 1 or by hugging the coastline along South Bay Boulevard 10 mi to the quaint residential villages of **Los Osos and Baywood Park.** Check out the tide pools, watch the waves roll into the bluffs, and picnic in the eucalyptus groves at **Montaña de Oro State Park** (⊠ 7 mi south of Los Osos on Pecho Rd., ☎ 805/528–0513 or 805/772–7434, WEB www.cal-parks.ca.gov). The park has miles of nature trails along rocky shoreline, sandy beaches, and hills overlooking the some of California's most spectacular scenery.

San Luis Obispo

❽   *14 mi south of Morro Bay on Rte. 1, 230 mi south of San Francisco on I–280 to U.S. 101, 112 mi north of Santa Barbara on U.S. 101.*

About halfway between San Francisco and Los Angeles, San Luis Obispo is an appealing urban center set among gentle hills and extinct volcanoes. California Polytechnic State University, known as Cal Poly, gives the town collegiate energy. San Luis Obispo has restored its old railroad depot as well as several Victorian-era homes. On Thursday from 6 PM to 9 PM a four-block-long farmers' market lines Higuera Street.

San Luis Obispo is the commercial center of Edna Valley/Arroyo Grande Valley wine country, whose appellations stretch east–west from San Luis Obispo and Arroyo Grande near the coast toward Lake Lopez in the inland mountains. Many of the wineries line Route 227 and connecting roads. The region is best known for chardonnay and pinot noir, although many wineries experiment with other varietals and blends. Wine-touring maps are readily available at attractions and lodgings throughout San Luis Obispo County.

★ **Mission San Luis Obispo de Tolosa,** established in 1772, overlooks San Luis Obispo Creek. A museum exhibits artifacts of the Chumash Indians and early Spanish settlers. ⊠ *751 Palm St.,* ☎ *805/543–6850,* WEB *www.thegrid.net/slomission.* ⊡ *$2 suggested donation.* ⊙ *Late May–Dec., daily 9–5; Jan.–late May, daily 9–4.*

★ ⊙ **San Luis Obispo County Museum and History Center** presents revolving exhibits on various aspects of county history—Native American life, California ranchos, or how railroads affected the region. A separate kids' room captivates the younger set with themed activities and the chance to earn prizes. ⊠ *696 Monterey St.,* ☎ *805/543–0638.* ⊡ *Free.* ⊙ *Wed.–Sun. 10–4.*

For sweeping views of the Edna Valley and the unusual volcanic morros that pop up from the valley floor, go to the upscale tasting bar at **Edna Valley Vineyard** (⊠ 2585 Biddle Ranch Rd., ☎ 805/544–5855, WEB www.ednavalley.com). A refurbished century-old schoolhouse serves as tasting room for **Seven Peaks** (⊠ 5828 Orcutt Rd., ☎ 805/781–0777, WEB www.sevenpeaks.com).

Dining and Lodging

$$–$$$ ✕ **Buona Tavola.** Homemade *agnolotti* pasta with scampi in a creamy saffron sauce and porcini mushroom risotto are among the northern Italian dishes served at this local favorite. Daily fresh fish and salad specials and an impressive wine list attract a steady stream of regulars. In good weather you can dine on the flower-filled patio. ⊠ *1037 Monterey St.,* ☎ *805/545–8000. AE, D, MC, V. No lunch weekends.*

$–$$ ✕ **Cafe Roma.** Authentic northern Italian cuisine is the specialty of this restaurant on Railroad Square. Under a large mural of Tuscany, you can dine on squash-filled ravioli with a sage-and-butter sauce or filet mignon glistening with port and Gorgonzola. ⊠ *1020 Railroad Ave.,* ☎ *805/541–6800. AE, D, DC, MC, V. Closed Sun. No lunch Sat.*

$–$$ ✕ **Le Fandango Bistro.** Spicy Basque-country flavors take classic French cuisine to new heights at this intimate San Sebastian–style restaurant with an open kitchen. In the evening dine on traditional rabbit stew, escargot, foie gras, duck, seafood, and lamb dishes, or choose from among eight daily specials. Casual bistro-style dishes dominate the lunch menu. ⊠ *717 Higuera St.,* ☎ *805/544–5515. AE, D, MC, V. No lunch Sun. and Mon.*

$ ★ ✕ **Big Sky Café.** The menu here roams the world—the Mediterranean, North Africa, and the Southwest—but many of the ingredients are local, including organic fruits and vegetables, and chicken is hormone free. Big Sky is a hip gathering spot for breakfast, lunch, and dinner. ⊠ *1121 Broad St.,* ☎ *805/545–5401. Reservations not accepted. AE, MC, V.*

$$–$$$$ ★ ▥ **Apple Farm.** Decorated to the hilt with floral bedspreads and watercolors by local artists, this is the most comfortable place to stay in town. Each room in the country-style hotel has a gas fireplace; some have canopy beds and cozy window seats. There's a working gristmill in the courtyard; within the inn are an American restaurant and a cluttered gift shop. ⊠ *2015 Monterey St., 93401,* ☎ *805/544–2040; 800/374–3705 in CA; 800/255–2040 from other states,* FAX *805/546–9495,*

WEB *www.applefarm.com. 104 rooms. Restaurant, in-room data ports, cable TV, pool, hot tub, meeting rooms; no smoking. AE, D, MC, V.*

$$–$$$ 🏨 **Madonna Inn.** From its rococo bathrooms to its pink-on-pink froufrou dining areas, the Madonna Inn is the ultimate in kitsch. Each room is unique, to say the least: Rock Bottom is all stone; the Safari Room is decked out in animal skins. Humor value aside, the Madonna is pretty much a gussied-up motel, so don't expect much in the way of luxury. ⊠ *100 Madonna Rd., 93405,* ☎ *805/543–3000 or 800/543–9666,* FAX *805/543–1800,* WEB *www.madonnainn.com. 87 rooms, 22 suites. Restaurant, café, dining room, bar, cable TV with movies, massage, spa, meeting rooms; no air-conditioning in some rooms, no-smoking rooms. MC, V.*

$–$$ 🏨 **Adobe Inn.** The friendly owners of this establishment of cheerful motel-style rooms serve excellent breakfasts. They'll also help you plan your stay in the area. ⊠ *1473 Monterey St., 93401,* ☎ *805/549–0321 or 800/676–1588,* FAX *805/549–0383,* WEB *www.adobeinns.com. 15 rooms. Kitchenettes (some), cable TV, meeting room; no air-conditioning in some rooms, no smoking. AE, D, DC, MC, V. BP.*

$–$$ 🏨 **La Cuesta Inn.** The interiors of this adobe-style motel on the northern edge of town are understated, almost to the point of being generic. This is a good bet if you can forgo elegance; it's also great for families, especially because kids 12 and under stay free. VCR and movie rentals are available. ⊠ *2074 Monterey St., 93401,* ☎ *805/543–2777 or 800/543–2777,* FAX *805/544–0696,* WEB *www.lacuestainn.com. 72 rooms. Refrigerators, cable TV with movies, pool, hot tub; no smoking. AE, D, DC, MC, V. CP.*

Nightlife and the Arts

The **Performing Arts Center** (⊠ 1 Grand Ave., ☎ 805/756–7222 for information; 805/756–2787 for tickets outside CA; 888/233–2787 for tickets in CA) at Cal Poly hosts concerts and recitals. The **San Luis Obispo Mozart Festival** (☎ 805/781–3008) takes place in late July and early August. Not all the music is Mozart; you'll also hear Haydn and other composers.

The club scene in this college town is centered on Higuera Street off Monterey Street. The **Frog and Peach** (⊠ 728 Higuera St., ☎ 805/595–3764) is a decent spot to nurse a beer and listen to music. **Linnaea's Cafe** (⊠ 1110 Garden St., ☎ 805/541–5888), a mellow java joint, sometimes hosts poetry readings; blues, jazz, and folk music performances; and other diversions. The **San Luis Obispo Brewing Company** (⊠ 1119 Garden St., ☎ 805/543–1843), popular with pool players, serves several tasty ales and frequently hosts rock bands in the upstairs restaurant.

En Route From San Luis Obispo take U.S. 101 south 10 mi to **Avila Beach and Port San Luis.** Both are funky old fishing villages facing southward onto a cove and thus escaping the fog that rolls in off the ocean. In 2001 Avila Beach completed a lengthy restoration of its promenade; it's a fantastic spot for beachfront strolls and views of the hilly coastline and port. Port San Luis is still functioning, with a vibrant fish market lining the pier. The **Olde Port Inn** (⊠ Third Pier, Port San Luis, ☎ 805/595–2515) has been serving fresh seafood—mostly from its own boats right on the dock—from its end-of-the-pier perch since 1971.

Pismo Beach

❾ *Rte. 1, 15 mi south of San Luis Obispo.*

About 20 mi of sandy southern California–style shoreline begins at the town of Pismo Beach, optimistically nicknamed the "Bakersfield Riviera." The southern end of town runs along sand dunes, some of which are open to cars and other vehicles. The northern section sits perched above chalky cliffs.

For a town with a population of less than 10,000, Pismo Beach has quite a slew of hotels and restaurants. Despite the neon signs announcing all accommodations and dining spots, the area doesn't feel inundated by tourists. Most of the best hotels and restaurants provide great views of the Pacific Ocean. Good beachfront walks, top-quality clam chowder, a growing Dixieland jazz festival in February, and a colony of Monarch butterflies in the town's eucalyptus grove are some of the attractions.

East of Pismo Beach, get a little taste of Central Coast wine country in Arroyo Grande, at an ecofriendly winery built from straw bales. **Claiborne & Churchill** (✉ 2649 Carpenter Canyon Rd., Arroyo Grande, ☎ 805/544–4066, WEB www.claibornechurchill.com) makes small lots of specialty wines like dry Riesling and muscat.

Dining and Lodging

$$–$$$ ✕ **F. McLintocks.** A cross between a truck stop and a cowboy saloon, this place prides itself on enormous portions of hearty food. Before you even order your meal, you'll find a large bowl of onion rings in front of you. Every cut of steak you can imagine is here, along with piles of ribs, lobsters, and much more. ✉ *750 Mattie Rd.,* ☎ *805/773–1892. AE, D, MC, V. No lunch.*

$$–$$$ ✕ **Shore Cliff.** With probably the best seafood and clam chowder in town, this restaurant also has spectacular cliff-top views. The interior is airy, with large windows that let in lots of light. ✉ *2555 Price St.,* ☎ *805/773–4671. AE, D, MC, V.*

$–$$ ✕ **Giuseppe's.** Classic tastes of the Pugliese region of southern Italy are presented in a cheery, rustic dining room with booths in downtown Pismo Beach. Most recipes originate from Bari, a seaport on the Adriatic. Feast on breads and pizzas baked from scratch in the wood-burning oven, hearty dishes like osso buco and lamb, and homemade or imported pastas. The restaurant grows its own organic tomatoes, basil, peppers, and herbs. ✉ *891 Price St.,* ☎ *805/773–2870. Reservations not accepted. AE, D, MC, V. No lunch weekends.*

$$$$ ⌂ **Casa de Colores.** Innkeeper Sue Hutchison's upscale custom home and three private haciendas celebrate color in every way, from an amazing collection of world folk art to exotic gardens. It sits on seven hilltop acres overlooking Arroyo Grande Valley wine country, 5 mi east of downtown on the road to Lake Lopez. Sue cooks up scrumptious, eclectic dishes for evening appetizers and a massive breakfast. Each hacienda has a fireplace, refrigerator, fresh flowers and fruit, and patio. Designed for adult getaways, the inn is inappropriate for children. ✉ *2655 Lopez Dr., Arroyo Grande 93420,* ☎ *805/481–8895,* WEB *www.casadecolores.com. 3 haciendas. Refrigerators, pool, bicycles; no room phones, no room TVs, no smoking. No credit cards. BP.*

$$$–$$$$ ⌂ **The Cliffs at Shell Beach.** With a Spanish-modern exterior surrounded by manicured palm trees, this spot offers everything you would expect in a beachfront resort. Many of the modern rooms have fine ocean views (make sure your room faces the beach). Suites have huge marble bathrooms and hot tubs. ✉ *2757 Shell Beach Rd., 93449,* ☎ *805/773–5000 or 800/826–7827,* FAX *805/773–0764,* WEB *www.cliffsresort.com. 142 rooms, 23 suites. Restaurant, bar, pool, spa, meeting room. AE, D, DC, MC, V.*

$$$–$$$$ ⌂ **Sea Venture Resort.** Fireplaces and featherbeds create a cheery mood in each room. Those with an ocean view are perched over a beautiful stretch of sand. The best amenities are the private hot tubs on most balconies and a deluxe breakfast basket delivered to your room in the

morning. ✉ *100 Ocean View Ave., 93449,* ☎ *805/773–4994 or 800/ 662–5545,* FAX *805/773–0924,* WEB *www.seaventure.com. 50 rooms. Restaurant, fans, in-room data ports, in-room VCRs, minibars, refrigerators, pool, hot tubs, bicycles, meeting rooms; no air-conditioning, no smoking. AE, D, DC, MC, V. CP.*

En Route The spectacular **Guadalupe-Nipomo Dunes Preserve** stretches 18 mi along the coast between Oceano and Guadalupe. It's the largest and most ecologically diverse dune system in the state, habitat of more than 200 species of birds as well as sea otters, black bears, bobcats, coyotes, and deer. The 500-ft Mussel Rock is the highest beach dune in the western states. More than six major movies were filmed here, including Cecil B. DeMille's *Ten Commandments.* The entrance to the dunes is about 13 mi south of Pismo Beach on Route 1, then 3 mi west on Oso Flaco Road. Try to stop by the **Dunes Center** (✉ 1055 Guadalupe St., 1 mi north of Rte. 166W, ☎ 805/343–2455, WEB www. dunescenter.org), where you can get all sorts of dune and wildlife information and view an exhibit about *The Ten Commandments* movie set, which is buried near Guadalupe Beach. The center is open Friday–Sunday noon–4. Parking is $3 per vehicle.

SANTA BARBARA COUNTY
Including Solvang

Northern Santa Barbara County used to be known for its sprawling ranches and strawberry and broccoli fields. Today its 60-plus wineries and 18,000 acres of vineyards dominate the landscape from Santa Maria, in the north, down through the Santa Ynez Valley. The Santa Ynez Mountains divide the county geographically; U.S. 101 passes through a mountain tunnel leading to the ocean. Residents refer to the glorious 30-mi stretch of coastline as the South Coast. In this area are the cities of Goleta and Santa Barbara and the ritzy town of Montecito.

Lompoc

⑩ *Rte. 1, about 40 mi south of Pismo Beach.*

Known as the Flower-Seed Capital of the World, Lompoc is blanketed with vast fields of brightly colored flowers that bloom from May through August. For five days around the last weekend of June, the **Lompoc Valley Flower Festival** (☎ 805/735–8511, WEB www.flowerfestival.org) brings a parade, carnival, and crafts show to town.

★ ☾ At **La Purisima Mission State Historic Park** you can see Mission La Purisima Concepción, the most fully restored mission in the state. Founded in 1787, it stands in a stark and still remote location and powerfully evokes the lives of California's Spanish settlers. Docents lead tours twice daily, and displays illustrate the secular and religious activities at the mission. From March through October the mission hosts various special events, including crafts demonstrations by costumed docents. A corral near the parking area holds farm animals, including sheep that represent the original mission breeds. ✉ *2295 Purisima Rd., off Mission Gate Rd.,* ☎ *805/733–3713,* WEB *www.lapurisimamission.org.* ✉ *$2 per vehicle.* ☉ *Daily 9–5; tours at 11 and 2.*

Buellton

⑪ *17 mi east of Lompoc on Rte. 246.*

A small but busy town at the intersection of U.S. 101 and Rte. 246, Buellton serves as a commercial gateway to the Santa Ynez Valley. Restau-

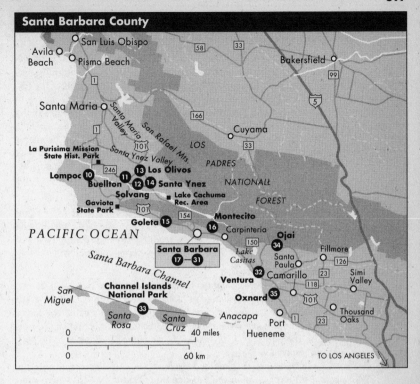

rants, shops, and hotels dominate the center of town, which is surrounded by scenic country roads, horse ranches, wineries, and residential tracts.

Sanford Winery (✉ 7250 Santa Rosa Rd., ☎ 805/688–3300) helped put Santa Barbara County on the international wine map with a 1989 pinot noir. Today Sanford has one of the most environmentally sensitive tasting rooms and picnic areas in the valley. All their vineyards are certified organic, and the pinot noirs and chardonnays are exceptional. It's about 5 mi west of town.

Dining and Lodging

$$–$$$ ✕ **The Hitching Post.** You'll find everything from grilled artichokes to ostrich at this casual eatery, but most people come for what is said to be the best Santa Maria–style barbecue in the state. The oak used in the barbecue imparts a wonderfully smoky taste. ✉ 406 E. Rte. 246, ☎ 805/688–0676. AE, MC, V. No lunch.

$–$$$ 🏨 **Rancho Santa Barbara Marriott.** Don't be misled by the name of this resort; the contemporary, Spanish-Mediterranean complex is actually 40 mi north of Santa Barbara. Its location near the intersection of U.S. 101 and Route 246 makes it a good choice if you're short on time while traveling the state. ✉ 555 McMurray Rd., 93427, ☎ 805/688–1000 or 800/638–8882, ℻ 805/688–0380, 🕸 www.marriott.com. 122 rooms, 27 suites. 2 restaurants, bar, in-room data ports, cable TV, tennis court, pool, gym, spa, billiards, Ping-Pong, racquetball, squash, meeting rooms; no-smoking rooms. AE, D, DC, MC, V.

En Route If you head from Buellton straight to Santa Barbara via U.S. 101, without detouring to the Solvang/Santa Ynez area, you will drive past some good beaches. In succession from west to east are **Gaviota, Refugio, and El Capitan state beaches,** each with campsites, picnic tables, and fire rings.

Solvang

☕ ⑫ *On Rte. 246, 3 mi east of U.S. 101.*

You'll know when you've reached the Danish town of Solvang: the architecture suddenly turns to half-timber buildings and windmills. The town has a genuine Danish heritage—more than two-thirds of the residents are of Danish descent. A good way to get your bearings is to browse in a few of the 300 or so shops that sell Danish goods; many are along Copenhagen Drive and Alisal Road. As an alternative, take a guided tour on a horse-drawn streetcar that leaves from the visitor center, at 2nd Street and Copenhagen Drive, every half hour. If Solvang seems too serene and orderly to be true, rent a copy of William Castle's 1961 film *Homicidal,* which used the town as the backdrop for gender-bending murder and mayhem.

Housed in an 1884 adobe, the **Rideau Vineyard** (✉ 1562 Alamo Pintado Rd., ☎ 805/688–0717, ⓦⒺⒷ www.rideauvineyard.com) tasting room provides simultaneous blasts from the area's ranching past and from its hand-harvested Rhone varietal winemaking present.

Dining and Lodging

$$ ✕ **River Grill.** Overlooking the fairways of the River Course at the Alisal, this casual spot is where the locals take visiting friends for fresh contemporary California cuisine and to-die-for views of the Santa Ynez mountains and river. Have Sunday brunch by the fireplace or outside on the patio. ✉ *150 Alisal Rd.,* ☎ *805/688–7784. AE, D, MC, V. No dinner Sun.–Mon.*

$–$$ ✕ **Bit O' Denmark.** Perhaps the most authentic Danish eatery in Solvang, this restaurant is in an old beamed building that was a church until 1929. The dishes have such names as *Frikadeller* (meatballs with pickled red cabbage, potatoes, and thick brown gravy) and *Medisterpolse* (Danish beef and pork sausage with cabbage). ✉ *473 Alisal Rd.,* ☎ *805/688–5426. AE, D, MC, V.*

$$$$ ⊡ **Alisal Guest Ranch and Resort.** Since 1946 celebrities and plain folk alike have headed to the 10,000-acre Alisal Ranch for the same reason: the easygoing atmosphere and resort activities. You can ride horses in the hills, fish or sail in the 100-acre spring-fed lake, play a round of golf, or just lounge by the pool. The California ranch-style rooms and suites come with garden views, covered porches, high-beamed ceilings and wood-burning fireplaces, with touches of Spanish tile and fine western art. Rates include breakfast and dinner every day (jacket required for dinner). ✉ *1054 Alisal Rd., 93463,* ☎ *805/ 688–6411 or 800/425–4725,* ⒻⒶⓍ *805/688–2510,* ⓦⒺⒷ *www.alisal.com. 36 rooms, 37 suites. Restaurant, bar, refrigerators, 2 18-hole golf courses, 7 tennis courts, pool, bicycles, billiards, croquet, hiking, horseback riding, Ping-Pong, shuffleboard, volleyball, baby-sitting, children's programs (ages 6 and up). AE, DC, MC, V. AP.*

$$$ ⊡ **Petersen Village Inn.** As with most of the buildings in Solvang, this ★ B&B-style property, heavy on the wood, is reminiscent of a European village. The overall effect is along the lines of a fine hunting lodge. The canopy beds here are plush, the bathrooms small but sparkling. ✉ *1576 Mission Dr., 93463,* ☎ *805/688–3121 or 800/321–8985,* ⒻⒶⓍ *805/ 688–5732,* ⓦⒺⒷ *www.peterseninn.comn. 39 rooms, 1 suite. Café, in-room data ports, cable TV, bar; no smoking. AE, MC, V. BP.*

$$–$$$ ⊡ **Story Book Inn.** Someone in Solvang had to do it: all the rooms at this B&B are named after Hans Christian Andersen stories. Some rooms are on the small side, but others are large and luxurious. All have a light, airy feel. The suites have four-poster beds and roomy whirlpool tubs. The inn caters to adults and is inappropriate for children under 12. ✉ *409 1st St., 93463,* ☎ *805/688–1703 or 800/786–*

7925, FAX 805/688–0953, WEB *www.solvangstorybook.com. 7 rooms, 2 suites. Cable TV, VCRs (some); no room phones, no smoking. D, MC, V. BP.*

$$ ⊞ **Royal Scandinavian Inn.** Just a half block from the outlet mall and across the street from Solvang's main drag, this tasteful, country-themed motel has lots of family-friendly amenities. ⊠ *400 Alisal Rd., 93463,* ☎ *805/688–8000, 800/624–5572,* FAX *805/688–0761,* WEB *www.royalscandinavianinn.com. 133 rooms and suites. Restaurant, in-room data ports, cable TV with movies, pool, gym, hot tub, lounge; no-smoking rooms. AE, D, DC, MC, V.*

Nightlife and the Arts

PCPA Theaterfest (☎ 805/922–8313, WEB www.pcpa.org), the Pacific Conservatory of the Performing Arts, presents contemporary and classic plays as well as musicals in theaters in Solvang and Santa Maria. Summer events in Solvang are held in the open-air Festival Theatre, on 2nd Street off Copenhagen Drive.

Outdoor Activities and Sports

Quadricycles, four-wheel carriages, and bicycles are available at **Surrey Cycle Rental** (⊠ 475 1st St., ☎ 805/688–0091).

Los Olivos

⑬ *5 mi north of Solvang on Alamo Pintado Rd.*

This pretty village in the Santa Ynez Valley was once on the Spanish-built El Camino Real and later a stop on major stagecoach and rail routes. It's so sleepy today, though, that TV's *Return to Mayberry* was filmed here. A row of tasting rooms, art galleries, antiques stores, and country markets lines Grand Avenue. At **Los Olivos Tasting Room & Wine Shop** (⊠ 2905 Grand Ave., ☎ 805/688–7406, WEB www.losolivoswines.com) you can sample locally produced wines and pick up winery maps. **Los Olivos Wine & Spirits Emporium** (⊠ 2531 Grand Ave., ☎ 805/688–4409, 888/SB-WINES, WEB www.sbwines.com) is in a 1920s cabin set back in a field about a half mile south of the Los Olivos flagpole. It serves as the main tasting room for a number of small but well-known wineries, such as Lane Tanner, Qupé, and Fiddlehead.

Sansone Gallery (⊠ 2948 Nojoqui Ave., ☎ 805/693–9769) showcases the best artwork in town. **Firestone Vineyard** (⊠ 5000 Zaca Station Rd., ☎ 805/688–3940, WEB www.firestonewine.com) has been around since 1972. They have daily tours, grassy picnic areas, and hiking trails in the hills overlooking the valley; the views are fantastic.

Dining and Lodging

$$$$ ✕⊞ **Fess Parker's Wine Country Inn and Spa.** The rooms at this luxury inn are in a lawn-fronted house and an equally attractive residence across the street with a pool and a hot tub. The spacious accommodations have fireplaces, seating areas, and wet bars; three also have private hot tubs. At the Vintage Room ($$$–$$$$) well-selected local wines complement entrées such as oven-roasted salmon and grilled lamb T-bone. ⊠ *2860 Grand Ave., 93441,* ☎ *805/688–7788 or 800/446–2455,* FAX *805/688–1942,* WEB *www.fessparker.com. 20 rooms, 1 suite. Restaurant, cable TV, pool, hot tub, spa, some pets allowed; no smoking. AE, MC, V.*

$$$–$$$$ ✕⊞ **The Ballard Inn.** This inn is a good choice for an elegant wine-country escape among orchards and vineyards in the tiny town of Ballard, 2 mi south of Los Olivos. The rooms are furnished with antiques and original art. Seven rooms have wood-burning fireplaces; TVs are available on request. A full breakfast is included. The on-site Café Chardonnay restaurant ($$$) is open to the public for dinner Wednesday–Sunday. ✉ *2436 Baseline Ave., Ballard 93463,* ☎ *805/688–7770 or 800/638–2466,* FAX *805/688–9560,* WEB *www. ballardinn.com. 15 rooms. Restaurant, bicycles, no room phones, no room TVs. AE, MC, V. BP.*

Santa Ynez

❶❹ *Rte. 246, 4 mi east of Solvang.*

Founded in 1882, the tiny, historic town of Santa Ynez still has many of its original frontier buildings. You can walk through the three-block downtown area in just a few minutes, shop for antiques, and hang around the old-time saloon. At some of the valley's best restaurants, you just might bump into one of the many celebrities who own nearby ranches.

OFF THE BEATEN PATH **SAN MARCOS PASS –** A former stagecoach route, Route 154 winds its spectacular way southeast from Santa Ynez through the Los Padres National Forest. Eight miles from Santa Ynez, **Cachuma Lake Recreation Area** (✉ Rte. 154, ☎ 805/686–5054, WEB www.sbparks.com) centers around a jewel of an artificial lake. Hiking, fishing, and boating are popular here, and there are eagle- and wildlife-watching excursions aboard the *Osprey,* a 48-ft cruiser. The lively, one-of-a-kind **Cold Spring Tavern** (✉ 5995 Stagecoach Rd., off Rte. 154, ☎ 805/967–0066), near Cachuma Lake, has been serving travelers since stagecoach days. Part biker hangout and part romantic country hideaway, the tavern specializes in game dishes—rabbit, venison, quail—along with American standards such as ribs, steak, and a great chili. The tavern serves lunch and dinner daily, plus breakfast on weekends.

Dining and Lodging

$–$$ ✕ **Grappolo.** Authentic Italian fare, an open kitchen, and festive, family-style seating make this upscale trattoria one the most popular dining spots in the Santa Ynez Valley. Banter with the friendly hosts and watch the chefs prepare thin-crusted pizza in the wood-burning oven. Italian favorites on the extensive menu range from homemade ravioli, risottos, and seafood linguine to grilled lamb chops in red-wine sauce. The noise level tends to rise in the evening hours, so come here for entertainment rather than a romantic getaway. ✉ *3687-C Sagunto St.,* ☎ *805/688–6899. MC, V.*

$$$$ 🏠 **Santa Ynez Inn.** It looks like a historic B&B, but this posh two-story Victorian inn in downtown Santa Ynez was built from scratch in 2000. The owners, who also have an antiques store, furnished all the rooms with handpicked, themed antiques. The inn caters to a discerning crowd with the finest amenities—Frette linens, thermostatically controlled heat and air-conditioning, DVD/CD entertainment systems, and custom-made bathrobes. Most rooms have gas fireplaces, double steam showers, and whirlpool tubs. Rates include a phenomenal evening wine and hors d'oeuvres hour and a full breakfast. For lunch or dinner you can walk just a few yards to a number of popular valley restaurants. ✉ *3627 Sagunto St., Box 628, 93460,* ☎ *805/688–5588,* FAX *805/686–4294,* WEB *www.santaynezinn.com. 14 rooms. Hot tub, gym, massages, laundry services, library, bicycles, laundry service, concierge, meeting rooms; no-smoking rooms. AE, D, MC, V.*

Outdoor Activities and Sports

The scenic rides operated by **Windhaven Glider** (✉ Santa Ynez Airport, Rte. 246, ☎ 805/688–2517) cost between $75 and $150 and last up to 40 minutes.

Goleta

⑮ *34 mi south of Buellton on U.S. 101; 31 mi south of Santa Ynez via Rte. 154.*

A sprawling, primarily residential community about 12 mi west of Santa Barbara, Goleta attained official cityhood in 2001. Its primary attractions include the University of California at Santa Barbara campus, discount warehouse stores, and the Santa Barbara Airport. **Goleta Beach Park** (✉ Ward Memorial Hwy.) is a favorite with college students from the nearby University of California campus.

Dining and Lodging

$$$$ ✕⌺ **Bacara Resort & Spa.** The ultraluxe Bacara touts itself as the
★ most exclusive full-service resort in the region. If you can't garner an invitation to stay at a Montecito estate, this place can help you live the illusion. The Spanish colonial–style buildings and manicured gardens sprawl across 78 hillside acres next to a rugged stretch of beach 15 mi north of downtown Santa Barbara. Bacara services run the gamut, from a 42,000-square-ft spa facility to horseback riding on the beach. For a special occasion treat yourself to a first-class California-French dinner at the elegant Miró restaurant ($$$–$$$$). ✉ *8301 Hollister Ave., 93117,* ☎ *805/968–0100 or 877/422–4245,* ⨳ *805/968–1800,* ⛏ *www.bacararesort.com. 311 rooms, 49 suites. 3 restaurants, bar, lobby lounge, room service, minibars, cable TV, in-room VCRs, 2 18-hole golf courses, 4 tennis courts, 3 pools, hair salon, health club, spa, hiking, horseback riding, baby-sitting, children's programs (ages 5–12), playground, concierge, business services, meeting rooms; no-smoking rooms. AE, D, DC, MC, V.*

Outdoor Activities and Sports

The **Circle Bar B Guest Ranch** (✉ 1800 Refugio Rd., ☎ 805/968–1113) operates trail rides from Goleta. **Sandpiper Golf Course** (✉ 7925 Hollister Ave., ☎ 805/968–1541) is a challenging 18-hole, par-72 course. The greens fee ranges from $118 to $130; an optional cart costs $12 per person.

Montecito

⑯ *3 mi east of Santa Barbara on U.S. 101.*

Since the late 1800s Montecito's tree-studded hills and valleys have attracted the rich and famous from around the world. Today's residents include Oprah Winfrey, John Cleese, and a host of other film actors, directors, and business tycoons. Shady roads wind through the community, which consists mostly of private gated estates. Swank boutiques line Coast Village Road, where members of the landed gentry pick up truffle oil, picture frames, and designer sweats. Residents also hang out in the Upper Village, a chic shopping area with restaurants and cafés at the intersection of San Ysidro and East Valley roads.

The 37-acre estate called **Lotusland** once belonged to Polish opera singer Ganna Walska. Many of the exotic trees and other subtropical flora were planted in 1882 by horticulturist R. Kinton Stevens. Among the highlights are an outdoor theater, a topiary garden, a huge collection of rare cycads, and a lotus pond. The only way to visit is to take a two-hour docent-led group walking tour. Advance reservations are required; call as early as possible, as tours fill up quickly. Children under 10 are not allowed, except on family tours, offered twice a month. ✉ *Ganna Walska Lotusland, 695 Ashley Rd.,* ☎ *805/969–9990,* ⛏ *www.lotusland.org.* ⛃ *$15.* ☉ *Tours mid-Feb.–mid-Nov., Wed.–Sat. at 10 and 1:30.*

Dining and Lodging

$$$–$$$$ ✕ **The Stonehouse.** This elegantly rustic restaurant in a century-old granite farmhouse is part of the San Ysidro Ranch resort. The contemporary fare includes prime fillet of beef with a peppercorn-cognac sauce, seared ahi tuna with wasabi mashed potatoes, and excellent vegetarian options. Even better than the generally wonderful food are the pastoral surroundings. Have breakfast or lunch—salads, pastas, and sandwiches—on the tree-house-like outdoor patio. At night the candlelighted interior is seriously romantic. ⊠ *900 San Ysidro La.,* ☎ *805/969–4100. Reservations essential. AE, DC, MC, V.*

$–$$ ✕ **Montecito Café.** This upscale yet casual restaurant serves contemporary cuisine—fresh fish, grilled chicken, steak, and pasta. The salads and lamb dishes are particularly inventive. ⊠ *1295 Coast Village Rd.,* ☎ *805/969–3392. AE, MC, V.*

$$$$ ✕⌷ **Four Seasons Biltmore Hotel.** Surrounded by lush (and always
★   perfectly manicured) gardens, Santa Barbara's grande dame has long been the favored spot for the town's high society and the visiting rich and famous to indulge in quiet California-style luxury. Dining is indoors and formal at the hotel's La Marina Restaurant ($$$–$$$$), where the California-Continental menu changes monthly; outdoors and more casual at the Patio ($–$$). ⊠ *1260 Channel Dr., 93108,* ☎ *805/969–2261 or 800/332–3442,* 𝖥𝖠𝖷 *805/565–8329,* 𝖶𝖤𝖡 *www.fourseasons.com. 196 rooms and 17 suites. 2 restaurants, bar, minibars, cable TV, in-room VCRs, putting green, 3 tennis courts, pool, health club, hot tub, spa, croquet, shuffleboard, baby-sitting, children's programs (ages 5–12), concierge, business services, meeting rooms; no-smoking rooms; some pets allowed (fee). AE, D, DC, MC, V.*

$$$$ ✕⌷ **San Ysidro Ranch.** You can feel equally at home in jeans and cow-
★   boy boots or designer jackets at this romantic hideaway, where John and Jackie Kennedy spent their honeymoon. Guest cottages, all with down comforters and wood-burning stoves or fireplaces, are scattered among 14 acres of orange trees and flower beds. Many cottages have private outdoor spas, and one has its own pool. Hiking trails crisscross 500 acres of open space surrounding the property. The Stonehouse Restaurant and Plow & Angel Bistro are Santa Barbara institutions. ⊠ *900 San Ysidro La., 93108,* ☎ *805/969–5046 or 800/368–6788,* 𝖥𝖠𝖷 *805/565–1995,* 𝖶𝖤𝖡 *www.sanysidroranch.com. 38 units. 2 restaurants, bar, room service, refrigerators, cable TVs, in-room VCRs, 2 tennis courts, pool, gym, massage, billiards, boccie, horseshoes, playground, some pets allowed (fee); no smoking. AE, DC, MC, V. 2-day minimum stay on weekends, 3 days on holiday weekends.*

$$$ ⌷ **Montecito Inn.** Every room at this late-1920s marble palace is adorned with original posters from the films of Charlie Chaplin. The glass doors to the conference room are etched with the great man's image, and the video library contains his entire oeuvre. The rooms on the second floor lead onto a cloisterlike arched colonnade. The bathrooms are fairly basic, although some suites have large marble whirlpool tubs. The suites also have vast Romanesque-style marble fireplaces. ⊠ *1295 Coast Village Rd., 93108,* ☎ *805/969–7854 or 800/843–2017,* 𝖥𝖠𝖷 *805/969–0623,* 𝖶𝖤𝖡 *www.montecitoinn.com. 53 rooms, 7 suites. Restaurant, bar, refrigerators, cable TV, in-room VCRs, pool, gym, hot tub, bicycles, meeting room; no air-conditioning in some rooms, no-smoking rooms. AE, D, DC, MC, V. CP.*

Nightlife and the Arts

The **Music Academy of the West** (⊠ 1070 Fairway Rd., ☎ 805/969–4726) showcases orchestral, chamber, and operatic works. The **Plow & Angel** (⊠ San Ysidro Ranch, 900 San Ysidro La., ☎ 805/969–

5046) books mellow jazz performers. The bar is perfect for those seeking quiet conversation, even romance.

SANTA BARBARA

45 mi south of Solvang and 9 mi east of Goleta on U.S. 101.

Santa Barbara has long been an oasis for Los Angeles residents in need of rest and recuperation. The attractions begin at the ocean and end in the foothills of the Santa Ynez Mountains. A few miles farther up the coast, but still very much a part of the city, is the exclusive residential district of Hope Ranch. Santa Barbara is on a jog in the coastline, so the ocean is actually to the south. Directions can be confusing. "Up" the coast toward San Francisco is west, "down" toward Los Angeles is east, and the mountains are north. A car is handy but not essential if you're planning to stay in town. The beaches and downtown are easily explored by bicycle or on foot, or you can take the local buses. A motorized San Francisco–style cable car operated by **Santa Barbara Trolley Co.** (☎ 805/965–0353, WEB www.sboldtowntrolley.com) makes 90-minute runs from 10 to 4 past major hotels, shopping areas, and attractions. Get off when you wish to, and pick up another trolley when you're ready to move on. The trolley departs from and returns to Stearns Wharf. The fare is $12 for the day.

From the Ocean to the Mountains

You'll hear locals refer to the waterfront as "the ocean," but by any name it's a beautiful area, with palm-studded promenades and plenty of sand. In the few miles between the beaches and the hills are downtown, the old mission, and the botanic gardens. For maps and visitor information, drop by the **Santa Barbara Chamber of Commerce Visitor Information Center** (⊠ 1 Garden St., at Cabrillo Blvd., ☎ 805/965–3021, WEB www.sbchamber.org).

A Good Tour

Start your tour at the west end of Cabrillo Boulevard, with a stroll around **Santa Barbara Harbor.** You can take a half-mile walk along the breakwater that protects the harbor. Check out the tackle and bait shops, or hire a boat. At the base of the breakwater stop in at the **Outdoors Santa Barbara Visitor Center** ⑰ and the **Santa Barbara Maritime Museum** ⑱; they're in the same building. For a cultural interlude walk three blocks up Castillo Street from the harbor to the **Carriage and Western Art Museum** ⑲. Return to Cabrillo Boulevard, the main harborfront drag, and stroll east along **West Beach** to **Stearns Wharf** ⑳, where the **Sea Center** ㉑ is a major attraction.

To explore downtown, walk up **State Street** (it starts at Stearns Wharf) from the harbor and turn left on Montecito Street, then walk one block to the corner of Chapala Street for a look at the **Moreton Bay Fig Tree.** Planted in 1874 and transplanted to its present location in 1877, this tree is so huge it reputedly can provide shade for 1,000 people. Return to State Street and continue northwest (away from the harbor) past **El Paseo,** a handsome shopping arcade built around an old adobe home. Make a right at East Cañon Perdido Street to reach **El Presidio State Historic Park** ㉒. From here turn right on Santa Barbara Street and right onto De La Guerra Street to reach the entrance of the **Santa Barbara Historical Museum** ㉓. Now make a right onto Anacapa Street and walk three blocks to the **Santa Barbara County Courthouse** ㉔, at Anapamu Street. On the next block of Anapamu Street stands the **Santa Barbara Museum of Art** ㉕, and one block farther is the **Karpeles Manuscript Library** ㉖.

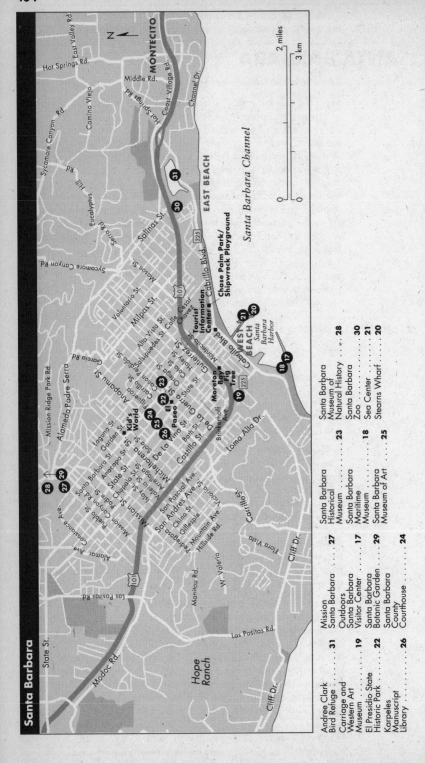

Santa Barbara

N

MONTECITO

Hot Springs Rd.
East Valley Rd.
Middle Rd.
Camino Viejo
Sycamore Canyon Rd.
Hill Rd.
Eucalyptus Rd.
Serra Rd.
Hot Springs Rd.
Coast Village Rd.
Channel Dr.

Santa Barbara Channel

EAST BEACH

Chase Palm Park/
Shipwreck Playground
Cabrillo Blvd.
225
Salinas St.
Voluntario St.
Milpas St.
Alto Vista St.
Salsipuedes St. Calle Cesar Chavez
Tourist
Information
Center
Montecito St.
Gutierrez St.
Haley St.
Cook St.
Ortega St.
Cota St.
Figueroa St.
Canon Perdido St.
Anapamu St.
De La Guerra St.
State St.
Moreton
Bay
Fig
Tree
225
Santa
Barbara
Harbor
WEST
BEACH
Cabrillo Blvd.
20
21
18 17
19
Garcia Rd.
Mission Ridge Park Rd.
Alameda Padre Serra
Laguna St.
Garden St.
Santa Barbara St.
Anacapa St.
Chapala St.
Bath St.
Castillo St.
Kid's
World
El
Paseo
22
23
24
25
26
Micheltorena St.
Sola St.
Arrellaga St.
Valerio St.
Mission St.
Pedregosa St.
Constance Ave.
Alamar Ave.
Pueblo St.
San Pascual Ave.
San Andres Ave.
Chino St.
Gillespie
Victoria St.
Mountain Ave.
Hillside Rd.
Bath St.
Padre St.
De La Vina St.
Loma Alta Dr.
Brinkerhoff Ave.
Bath St.
Cliff Dr.
27 29
28
101
101
Las Positas Rd.
Modoc Rd.
Manitou Rd.
W. Valerio St.
Carrillo St.
Flora Vista
Cliff Dr.
Hope
Ranch
Las Positas Rd.
30
31
2 miles
3 km

Andree Clark
Bird Refuge **31**

Carriage and
Western Art
Museum **19**

El Presidio State
Historic Park **22**

Karpeles
Manuscript
Library **26**

Mission
Santa Barbara **27**

Outdoors
Santa Barbara
Visitor Center **17**

Santa Barbara
Botanic Garden **29**

Santa Barbara
County
Courthouse **24**

Santa Barbara
Historical
Museum **23**

Santa Barbara
Maritime
Museum **18**

Santa Barbara
Museum of Art **25**

Santa Barbara
Museum of
Natural History **28**

Santa Barbara
Zoo **30**

Santa Barbara
Sea Center **21**

Stearns Wharf **20**

To see the sights of the foothills, hop into your car and take State Street northwest (away from the water) to Los Olivos Street. Turn right, and you'll soon see **Mission Santa Barbara** ㉗. From the mission you can walk the block north to the **Santa Barbara Museum of Natural History** ㉘. You'll probably want to drive the 1½ mi north (via Mission Canyon Road) to the **Santa Barbara Botanic Garden** ㉙. Continue in a natural vein by heading back toward the ocean via Alameda Padre Serra and Salinas Street to the **Santa Barbara Zoo** ㉚. More creatures await at the **Andree Clark Bird Refuge** ㉛, which is adjacent to the zoo.

TIMING

You could spend an entire day on the harbor front alone, or devote only two or three hours to it if you drive and only stop briefly at the various attractions. Set aside an hour each for the art and natural-history museums and for the botanic gardens. A spin through the zoo takes about an hour. Add plenty of time if you're a shopper—the stores and galleries around State Street may sidetrack you for hours.

Sights to See

㉛ **Andree Clark Bird Refuge.** This peaceful lagoon and gardens sits north of East Beach. Bike trails and footpaths, punctuated by signs identifying native and migratory birds, skirt the lagoon. ⊠ *1400 E. Cabrillo Blvd.* ☞ *Free.*

⑲ **Carriage and Western Art Museum.** The country's largest collection of old horse-drawn vehicles—painstakingly restored—is exhibited here. Everything from polished hearses to police buggies to old stagecoaches and circus vehicles is on display. In August the Old Spanish Days Fiesta borrows many of the vehicles for a jaunt about town. This is one of the city's true hidden gems, a wonderful place to help history come alive for the children. ⊠ *129 Castillo St.,* ☎ *805/962–2353,* WEB *www.carriagemuseum.org.* ☞ *Free.* ☉ *Weekdays 7:30–3:30, Sun. 1–4.*

㉒ **El Presidio State Historic Park.** Founded in 1782, El Presidio was one of four military strongholds established by the Spanish along the coast of California. El Cuartel, the adobe guardhouse, is the oldest building in Santa Barbara and the second oldest in California. ⊠ *123 E. Cañon Perdido St.,* ☎ *805/965–0093,* WEB *www.sbthp.org.* ☞ *Free (donation suggested).* ☉ *Daily 10:30–4:30.*

㉖ **Karpeles Manuscript Library.** Ancient political tracts and old Disney cartoons are among the varied holdings of this facility, which also houses one of the world's largest privately owned collections of rare manuscripts. Fifty cases contain a sampling of the archive's million-plus documents. ⊠ *21 W. Anapamu St.,* ☎ *805/962–5322,* WEB *www.karpeles.com.* ☞ *Free.* ☉ *Daily 10–4.*

★ ㉗ **Mission Santa Barbara.** The architecture and layout of this mission, established in 1786, evolved from adobe-brick buildings with thatch roofs to more permanent edifices as its population burgeoned. An earthquake in 1812 destroyed the third church built on the site. Its replacement, the present structure, is still a Catholic church, though during the postmission era it also served as a boys' school and a seminary. Cacti, palms, and other succulents grow beside the mission. ⊠ *2201 Laguna St.,* ☎ *805/682–4713,* WEB *www.sbmission.org.* ☞ *$4.* ☉ *Daily 9–5.*

⑰ **Outdoors Santa Barbara Visitor Center.** The small office provides maps and other information about Channel Islands National Park (*see* Ventura County, *below*), Channel Islands National Marine Sanctuary, and Los Padres National Forest. The same building houses the Santa Barbara Maritime Museum. ⊠ *113 Harbor Way,* ☎ *805/884–1475.* ☞ *Free.* ☉ *Daily 11–5, in summer extended hours on Sat. 11–7.*

★ ㉙ **Santa Barbara Botanic Garden.** More than 5 mi of trails meander through the garden's 65 acres of native plants. The Mission Dam, built in 1806, stands just beyond the redwood grove and above the partially uncovered aqueduct that once carried water to Mission Santa Barbara. An ethnobotanical display contains replicas of the plants used by the Chumash Indians. ✉ *1212 Mission Canyon Rd.,* ☎ *805/682–4726,* WEB *www.sbbg.org.* ⌸ *$5.* ☉ *Mar.–Oct., weekdays 9–5, weekends 9–6; Nov.–Feb., weekdays 9–4, weekends 9–5. Guided tours daily at 2; additional tour at 10:30 Thurs. and weekends.*

★ ㉔ **Santa Barbara County Courthouse.** Hand-painted tiles and a spiral staircase infuse the courthouse with the grandeur of a Moorish palace. This magnificent building was completed in 1929, part of a rebuilding process after a 1925 earthquake destroyed many downtown structures. At the time Santa Barbara was also in the midst of a cultural awakening, and the trend was toward an architecture appropriate to the area's climate and history. The result is the harmonious Mediterranean-Spanish look of much of the downtown area, especially the municipal buildings. An elevator rises to an arched observation area in the courthouse tower that provides a panoramic view of the city. The murals in the ceremonial chambers on the courthouse's second floor were painted by an artist who did backdrops for some of Cecil B. DeMille's films. Stop by at night to see the courthouse lighted by spotlights. ✉ *1100 block of Anacapa St.,* ☎ *805/962–6464,* WEB *www.santabarbaracourthouse.org.* ☉ *Weekdays 8:30–4:45, weekends 10–4:45. Free guided tours Mon., Tues., and Fri. at 10:30, Mon.–Sat. at 2.*

NEED A BREAK? | Children and adults enjoy **Kids' World** (✉ Santa Barbara St. near Micheltorena St.), a public playground with complex maze of fantasy ☝ climbing structures, turrets, slides, and tunnels built by Santa Barbara parents.

㉓ **Santa Barbara Historical Museum.** The historical society's museum exhibits decorative and fine arts, furniture, costumes, and documents from the town's past. Adjacent to it is the Gledhill Library, a collection of books, photographs, maps, and manuscripts. ✉ *136 E. De La Guerra St.,, ☎ 805/966–1601. ⌸ Museum by donation; library $2–$5 per hr for research. ☉ Museum Tues.–Sat. 10–5, Sun. noon–5; library Tues.–Fri. 10–4, 1st Sat. of month 10–1:30. Free guided tours Wed. and weekends at 1:30.*

☝ ⑱ **Santa Barbara Maritime Museum.** California's seafaring history is the focus of this museum. High-tech, hands-on exhibits, such as a sportfishing activity that lets you catch a "big one," make this a fun stop for children and adults. ✉ *113 Harbor Way,* ☎ *805/962–8404,* WEB *www.sbmm.org.* ⌸ *$5.* ☉ *June–Oct., Thurs.–Tues. 11–5; Nov.–May, Thurs.–Mon. 11–5.*

㉕ **Santa Barbara Museum of Art.** The highlights of this museum's fine permanent collection include ancient sculpture, Asian art, impressionist paintings, and American works in several media. ✉ *1130 State St.,* ☎ *805/963–4364,* WEB *www.sbmuseart.org.* ⌸ *$6; free Thurs. and 1st Sun. of month.* ☉ *Tues.–Thurs. and Sat. 11–5, Fri. 11–9, Sun. noon–5. Guided tours Tues.–Sun. at 1.*

☝ ㉘ **Santa Barbara Museum of Natural History.** The gigantic skeleton of a blue whale greets you at the entrance of this complex. The major draws include the planetarium and space lab. A room of dioramas illustrates Chumash Indian history and culture. Startlingly lifelike stuffed specimens, complete with nests and eggs, roost in the bird diversity room. Many exhibits have interactive components. Outdoors you can stroll on nature trails that wind through the serene oak-studded grounds. ✉ *2559 Puesta del Sol Rd.,* ☎ *805/682–4711,* WEB *www.sbnature.org.* 🖃 *$6.* ⊙ *Daily 9–5. Closed major holidays.*

Ⓒ ㉚ **Santa Barbara Zoo.** The natural settings of the zoo shelter elephants, gorillas, exotic birds, and big cats such as the rare amur leopard, a thick-furred high-altitude dweller from Asia. For the children there's a scenic railroad and barnyard petting zoo. ✉ *500 Niños Dr.,* ☎ *805/962–5339,* WEB *www.santabarbarazoo.org.* 🖃 *$8.* ⊙ *Daily 10–5.*

Ⓒ ㉑ **Sea Center.** A branch of the Santa Barbara Museum of Natural History, the Sea Center specializes in Santa Barbara Channel marine life and conservation. In December 2001 it closed temporarily to begin construction of a new, $6.5 million facility that is expected to open in summer 2003. When completed, the new Sea Center will be a fascinating, hands-on marine science laboratory that lets you participate in experiments, projects, and exhibits, including touch tanks. ✉ *211 Stearns Wharf,* ☎ *805/962–0885,* WEB *www.sbnature.org. Call for information on reopening date, hrs, and admission.*

NEED A BREAK?	The antique carousel, large playground with a nautical theme, picnic areas, and snack bar make the scenic waterfront **Chase Palm Park and** Ⓒ **Shipwreck Playground** (✉ Cabrillo Blvd. between Garden St. and Calle Cesar Chavez) a favorite destination for kids and parents.

㉚ **Stearns Wharf.** Built in 1872, historic Stearns Wharf is Santa Barbara's most visited landmark. Expansive views of the mountains, cityscape, and harbor unfold from every vantage point on the three-block-long pier. Although it's a nice walk from the Cabrillo Boulevard parking areas, you can also drive out and park on the pier and then wander through the shops or stop for a meal at one of the wharf's restaurants or the snack bar. ✉ *Cabrillo Blvd. at the foot of State St.,* ☎ *805/897–2683 or 805/564–5531.*

Dining and Lodging

$$$–$$$$ ✕ **Bouchon.** This upscale restaurant exists as a showcase for fine local wines and produce as well as regional foods, from swordfish to organic veal chops. The mood is intimate and the wine selection huge. ✉ *9 W. Victoria St.,* ☎ *805/730–1160. AE, DC, MC, V. No lunch.*

$$$–$$$$ ✕ **Citronelle.** At this offspring of chef Michel Richard's Citrus in Los ★ Angeles, intriguing flavors animate dishes such as the braised lamb shank with white beans and garlic sauce and the Chilean sea bass crusted with black trumpet mushroom powder. The desserts are stupendous. The dining room's picture windows yield splendid sweeping views of the sunset and East Beach. ✉ *901 E. Cabrillo Blvd.,* ☎ *805/963–0111. Reservations essential. AE, D, DC, MC, V.*

$$$–$$$$ ✕ **Wine Cask.** Seared peppercorn ahi tuna and potato-crusted white-★ fish, each prepared with a wine-based sauce, are among the most popular entrées at this slick restaurant with a beautiful wooden interior and Santa Barbara's most extensive wine list. In fine weather couples seek out the romantic outdoor patio. ✉ *813 Anacapa St.,* ☎ *805/966–9463. Reservations essential. AE, DC, MC, V.*

$$–$$$$ ✕ **Harbor Restaurant.** From this sparkling spot on the pier you can take in panoramic views of the city and ocean while dining on standard American food. The nautical-theme bar and grill upstairs serves sandwiches, large salads, and many appetizers; on a sunny day the terrace is a glorious spot for a sandwich or a beer. Downstairs you can dine on seafood, prime rib, and steaks. ✉ *210 Stearns Wharf,* ☎ *805/963–3311. AE, MC, V.*

$$–$$$ ✕ **Café Buenos Aires.** Salads, sandwiches, pastas, and traditional Argentine empanadas (small turnovers filled with chicken, beef, or vegetables) are on the lunch menu at this elegant café. Dinner can be fashioned from tapas such as potato omelets, shrimp brochettes, and octopus stewed with tomato and onion. Pastas, fish, and grilled steaks (imported from Argentina) are among the entrées. ✉ *1316 State St.,* ☎ *805/963–0242. Reservations essential. AE, DC, MC, V.*

$$–$$$ ✕ **Emilio's.** Starters on the seasonal northern Italian menu at this harborside restaurant might include white bean–garlic ravioli with shrimp and arugula. The main courses of paella and spaghettini with crisp salmon are standouts. During the week a vegetarian tasting menu is available, as are two prix-fixe wine-tasting menus. ✉ *324 W. Cabrillo Blvd.,* ☎ *805/966–4426. AE, D, MC, V. No lunch.*

$$–$$$ ✕ **Olio e Limone.** A half block from State Street near the Arlington Theatre, sophisticated Olio e Limone serves up delectable Italian fare with an accent on Sicily. Surprises abound here; be sure to try unusual dishes like ribbon pasta with quail and sausage in a mushroom ragout, duck ravioli, or swordfish with Sicilian ratatouille. ✉ *17 W. Victoria St.,* ☎ *805/899–2699. AE, D, DC, MC, V.*

$$–$$$ ✕ **Palace Grill.** The Palace has won acclaim for Cajun and creole dishes such as blackened redfish and jambalaya with dirty rice. Caribbean fare here includes delicious coconut shrimp. If you're spicephobic, you can choose a pasta, soft-shell crab, or filet mignon. Be prepared to wait as long as 45 minutes for a table on Friday and Saturday nights, when reservations are taken for a 5:30 seating only. ✉ *8 E. Cota St.,* ☎ *805/963–5000. AE, MC, V.*

$$–$$$ ✕ **Palazzio.** The only reservations are for 5:30, and then the waiting list begins at this casual, spirited Italian restaurant. The portions of tasty pasta dishes are family style, the staff is great, and the garlic rolls are legendary. Choose between two locations: downtown Santa Barbara and Montecito. ✉ *1026 State St., Santa Barbara,* ☎ *805/564–1985;* ✉ *1151 Coast Village Rd., Montecito,* ☎ *805/969–8565. AE, MC, V.*

$–$$$ ✕ **Arigato Sushi.** Sushi fans will appreciate the fresh seafood served in this Japanese restaurant and sushi bar. Innovation reigns, with creations such as sushi pizza on seaweed and Hawaiian sashimi salad. ✉ *1225 State St.,* ☎ *805/965–6074. Reservations not accepted. AE, MC, V. No lunch.*

$$ ✕ **Roy.** Owner-chef Leroy Gandy serves a $17.50 fixed-price dinner— a real bargain—that includes a small salad, fresh soup, and a selection from a rotating roster of nouveau American main courses. Half a block from State Street in the heart of downtown, Roy is a favorite spot for late-night dining (it's open until midnight and has a full bar). Expect a wait at this quirky storefront on weekends. ✉ *7 W. Carrillo St.,* ☎ *805/966–5636. AE, D, DC, MC, V.*

$–$$ ✕ **Brigitte's.** This lively State Street café serves California cuisine and local wines at reasonable prices. The individual pizzas are always worth trying, as are the pastas, grilled fish, and roast lamb. ✉ *1325– 1327 State St.,* ☎ *805/966–9676. AE, D, MC, V. No lunch Sun.*

$–$$ ✕ **Brophy Bros.** The outdoor tables at this casual restaurant in the harbor have perfect views of the marina and mountains. A fine place for lunch and dinner, Brophy's serves enormous, exceptionally fresh fish dishes. Try the seafood salad. ✉ *119 Harbor Way,* ☎ *805/966–4418. AE, MC, V.*

$–$$ ✕ **Your Place.** Tasty seafood (try the sea scallops garnished with crispy basil), curries, and vegetarian dishes keep this small restaurant packed for lunch and dinner. Locals consistently name Your Place the best Thai restaurant in town. ✉ *22 N. Milpas St.,* ☎ *805/966–5151. AE, MC, V. Closed Mon.*

$ ✕ **La Super-Rica.** Praised by Julia Child, this food stand with a patio
★ on the east side of town serves some of the spiciest Mexican dishes between Los Angeles and San Francisco. Fans drive for miles to fill up
on the soft tacos and incredible beans. ⊠ *622 N. Milpas St., at Alphonse
St.,* ☎ *805/963–4940. No credit cards.*

$$$$ ⌂ **El Encanto Hotel.** Actress Hedy Lamarr and President Franklin D.
Roosevelt are among those who have unwound at this woodsy property near Mission Santa Barbara. Mediterranean-style villas and craftsman-style cottages dot the lush 10-acre grounds. A major remodel to
update and restore the property is pending city approval. ⊠ *1900 Lasuen Rd., 93103,* ☎ *805/687–5000 or 800/346–7039,* FAX *805/687–
3903,* WEB *www.elencantohotel.com. 84 rooms. Restaurant, bar, room
service, minibars, cable TV, tennis court, pool, concierge, meeting
room; no air-conditioning, no-smoking rooms. AE, D, MC, V.*

$$$–$$$$ ⌂ **Simpson House Inn.** Traditional B&B fans will enjoy the beautifully
★ appointed Victorian main house of this inn on an acre of lush gardens
in the heart of town. Those seeking total privacy and sybaritic com-
fort should choose one of the elegant cottages or a room in the cen-
tury-old barn, each with a wood-burning fireplace, luxurious bedding,
and state-of-the-art electronics. Several have whirlpool baths. In-room
spa services such as massage and body wraps are available. ⊠ *121 E.
Arrellaga St., 93101,* ☎ *805/963–7067 or 800/676–1280,* FAX *805/564–
4811,* WEB *www.simpsonhouseinn.com. 11 rooms, 4 cottages. Refrig-
erators (some), cable TV, in-room VCRs; no smoking. AE, D, MC, V.
2-night minimum stay on weekends. BP.*

$$–$$$$ ⌂ **Cheshire Cat Inn.** A five-minute walk from downtown, this B&B with
an *Alice in Wonderland* motif is accessible yet quiet. The largest rooms
hold king-size beds and sunken whirlpool tubs. The smaller rooms come
with low-slung armchairs and have a quaint Edwardian look. Children
are welcome in the cottages. ⊠ *36 W. Valerio St., 93101,* ☎ *805/569–
1610,* FAX *805/682–1876,* WEB *www.cheshirecat.com. 21 rooms, 3 cottages. Refrigerators (some), cable TV in some rooms, some in-room
VCRs, microwaves (some), meeting rooms; no smoking. AE, D, MC,
V. 2-night minimum stay on weekends. BP.*

$$–$$$$ ⌂ **The Upham.** This restored Victorian hotel set in an acre of gardens
in the historic downtown area was established in 1871. Period furnishings
and antiques adorn the rooms and cottages, some of which have fire-
places and private patios. The rooms vary from small to quite spacious.
⊠ *1404 De la Vina St., 93101,* ☎ *805/962–0058 or 800/727–0876,*
FAX *805/963–2825,* WEB *www.uphamhotel.com. 46 rooms, 4 suites.
Restaurant, cable TV, Internet, meeting rooms; no air-conditioning in
some rooms, no-smoking rooms. AE, DC, MC, V. 2-night minimum
stay on weekends. CP.*

$$–$$$$ ⌂ **Villa Rosa.** The rooms and intimate lobby of this Spanish-style
stucco-and-wood hotel a half block from the beach are decorated in
an informal southwestern style. Children 14 and older are welcome.
⊠ *15 Chapala St., 93101,* ☎ *805/966–0851,* FAX *805/962–7159,* WEB
*www.villarosainn.net. 18 rooms. In-room data ports, pool, hot tub,
meeting rooms; no air-conditioning, no room TVs, no smoking. AE,
MC, V. 2-night minimum stay on weekends, 3-night minimum on holidays. CP.*

$$–$$$ ⌂ **Hotel Santa Barbara.** The central location of this hotel makes it one
of the best bargains in town. You won't get all the luxuries of Santa
Barbara's pricier accommodations, but the rooms are clean and modern, if a tad charmless. ⊠ *533 State St., 93101,* ☎ *805/957–9300 or
888/259–7700,* FAX *805/962–2412,* WEB *www.hotelsantabarbara.com.
75 rooms. In-room data ports, cable TV, concierge, meeting rooms;
no smoking. AE, D, DC, MC, V. CP.*

Nightlife and the Arts

Most major hotels present entertainment nightly during the summer season and on weekends all year. Much of the town's bar, club, and live music scene centers around lower State Street (300 to 800 blocks). The thriving arts district, with theaters, restaurants, and cafés, starts around the 900 block of State Street and continues north to the Arlington Theatre, in the 1300 block. Santa Barbara supports a professional symphony and a chamber orchestra. The proximity to the University of California at Santa Barbara assures an endless stream of visiting artists and performers. To see what's scheduled around town, pick up a copy of the free weekly *Santa Barbara Independent* newspaper.

BARS AND CLUBS

Rich leather couches, a crackling fire in chilly weather, a cigar balcony, and pool tables draw a fancy Gen-X crowd to **Blue Agave** (⊠ 20 E. Cota St., ☎ 805/899–4694) for good food and designer martinis. All types of people hang out at **Darghan's** (⊠ 18 E. Ortega St., ☎ 805/568–0702), a lively, traditional Irish Pub with four pool tables, a great selection of draught beer and Irish whiskeys, and a full menu of traditional Irish dishes. A chic after-theater crowd heads to **Epiphany** (⊠ 21 W. Victoria St., ☎ 805/564–7100) to hang out at the sleek wine bar and order upper-crust bar menu. The **James Joyce** (⊠ 513 State St., ☎ 805/962–2688), which sometimes hosts folk and rock performers, is a good place to while away an evening, beer in hand.

Joe's Cafe (⊠ 536 State St., ☎ 805/966–4638), where steins of beer accompany hearty bar food, is a fun, if occasionally rowdy, collegiate scene. The bartenders at **Left at Albuquerque** (⊠ 803 State St., ☎ 805/564–5040) pour 141 types of tequila, making the southwestern-style bar one of your less sedate nightspots. Smooth martinis, and balconies overlooking State Street, attract a crowd of varying ages to **Rocks** (⊠ 801 State St., ☎ 805/884–1190). **SOhO** (⊠ 1221 State St., ☎ 805/962–7776), a hip restaurant and bar, presents weeknight jazz music; on weekends the mood livens with good blues and rock.

PERFORMING ARTS

Arlington Theater (⊠ 1317 State St., ☎ 805/963–4408), a Moorish-style auditorium, is the home of the Santa Barbara Symphony. **Center Stage Theatre** (⊠ 700 block of State St., 2nd floor of Paseo Nuevo, ☎ 805/963–0408) presents plays and readings. **Ensemble Theatre Company** (⊠ 914 Santa Barbara St., ☎ 805/962–8606) stages plays by authors ranging from Priestley to Mamet. The **Granada Theatre** (⊠ 1216 State St., ☎ 805/966–2324), a restored movie palace, is headquarters of the Music Theater of Santa Barbara. The **Lobero Theatre** (⊠ 33 E. Canon Perdido St., ☎ 805/963–0761), a state landmark, hosts community theater groups and touring professionals.

Outdoor Activities and Sports

BEACHES

Santa Barbara's beaches don't have the big surf of the shoreline farther south, but they also don't have the crowds. You can usually find a solitary spot. Fog often hugs the coast until about noon in June and July. The wide swath of sand at the east end of Cabrillo Boulevard on the harbor front is a great spot for people-watching. **East Beach** (⊠ 1118 Cabrillo Blvd., ☎ 805/897–2680) has sand volleyball courts, summertime lifeguard and sports competitions, and arts-and-crafts shows on Sunday and holidays. Showers (no towels), lockers, and beach rentals—also a weight room—are provided at the Cabrillo Bathhouse. Next to the boathouse, there's an elaborate jungle-gym play area for children. The usually gentle surf at **Arroyo Burro County Beach** (⊠ Cliff Dr. at Las Positas Rd.) makes it ideal for families with young children.

BICYCLING

The level two-lane, 3-mi **Cabrillo Bike Lane** passes the Santa Barbara Zoo, the Andree Clark Bird Refuge, beaches, and the harbor. There are restaurants along the way, and you can stop for a picnic along the palm-lined path looking out on the Pacific. **Beach Rentals** (⊠ 22 State St., ☎ 805/966–6733) has bikes, quadricycles, and skates. **Cycles 4 Rent** (⊠ Fess Parker's Doubletree Resort, 633 E. Cabrillo Blvd., ☎ 805/564–4333 Ext. 444; ⊠ 101 State St., ☎ 805/966–3804) has bikes and quadricycles.

BOATS AND CHARTERS

Adventors Outdoor Excursions (☎ 805/898–9569) arranges everything from kayak to mountain-bike excursions. **Santa Barbara Sailing Center** (⊠ Santa Barbara Harbor launching ramp, ☎ 805/962–2826 or 800/350–9090) offers sailing instruction, rents and charters sailboats, and organizes dinner and sunset champagne cruises, island excursions, and whale-watching trips. **Sea Landing** (⊠ Cabrillo Blvd. at Bath St. and the breakwater, ☎ 805/963–3564) operates surface and deep-sea fishing charters year-round. From Sea Landing, the **Condor Express** (☎ 805/963–3564), a 75-ft high-speed catamaran, whisks up to 149 passengers toward the Channel Islands on dinner cruises, whale-watching excursions, and pelagic bird trips. **Truth Aquatics** (☎ 805/962–1127) departs from the Santa Barbara Harbor to ferry passengers to Channel Islands National Park.

GOLF

Robert Trent Jones, Jr. designed the stunning par-71 **Rancho San Marcos Golf Course** (⊠ 12½ mi north of Santa Barbara on Rte. 154, ☎ 805/683–6334). Greens fees range from $119 to $139 and include a golf cart and driving range time. **Santa Barbara Golf Club** (⊠ Las Positas Rd. and McCaw Ave., ☎ 805/687–7087) has an 18-hole, par-70 course. The greens fee is $27–$36; an optional cart costs $12 per person.

TENNIS

Many hotels in Santa Barbara have courts. Day permits ($3) can be purchased for excellent public courts. Buy your permit at the courts or call the number listed. **Las Positas Municipal Courts** (⊠ 1002 Las Positas Rd., ☎ 805/564–5418) has six lighted hard courts open daily (lighted play until 9 PM weekdays). The 12 hard courts at the **Municipal Tennis Center** (⊠ 1414 Park Pl., near Salinas St. and U.S. 101, ☎ 805/564–5418) include an enclosed stadium court and three lighted courts open daily (lighted play until 9 PM weekdays). **Pershing Park** (⊠ 100 Castillo St., near Cabrillo Blvd., ☎ 805/564–5418) has eight lighted courts available for public play after 5 PM weekdays and all day on weekends and Santa Barbara City College holidays (lighted play until 9 PM weekdays).

Shopping

SHOPPING AREAS

State Street, roughly between Cabrillo Boulevard and Sola Street, is the commercial hub of Santa Barbara and a joy to shop. Chic malls, quirky storefronts, antiques emporia, elegant boutiques, and funky thrift shops are on or near the street. Open-air **Paseo Nuevo** (⊠ 700 and 800 blocks of State St.), anchored by chains such as Nordstrom and Macy's, also contains a few local institutions like the children's clothier This Little Piggy. You can do your shopping on foot or by a battery-powered trolley (25¢) that runs between the waterfront and the 1300 block.

Shops, art galleries, and studios share the courtyard and gardens of **El Paseo** (⊠ Canon Perdido St. between State and Anacapa Sts.), an arcade rich in history. Lunch on the outdoor patio is a nice break during a downtown tour. Antiques and gift shops are clustered in restored Victorian buildings on **Brinkerhoff Avenue** (⊠ 2 blocks west of State St. at West Cota St.). Serious antiques hunters head a few miles south of Santa Barbara to the beach town of **Summerland,** which is rife with shops and markets.

BOOKS

Barnes & Noble Booksellers (⊠ 829 State St., ☎ 805/962–8509) lures bibliophiles in from the adjacent Paseo Nuevo mall. The **Book Den** (⊠ 11 E. Anapamu St., ☎ 805/962–3321) has the town's largest selection of used books. **Borders Books, Music & Cafe** (⊠ 900 State St., ☎ 805/899–3668) holds court in the heart of the State Street shopping district. **Chaucer's Bookstore** (⊠ Loreto Plaza, 3321 State St., ☎ 805/682–6787) is a well-stocked independent—the favorite bookstore of many local residents. **Sullivan Goss Books & Prints Ltd.** (⊠ 7 E. Anapamu St., ☎ 805/730–1460) stocks books on California history and art.

CLOTHING

The complete line of **Big Dog Sportswear** (⊠ 6 E. Yanonali St., ☎ 805/963–8728) is sold at the Santa Barbara–based company's flagship store. **Channel Islands Surfboards** (⊠ 29 State St., ☎ 805/966–7213) stocks the latest in California beachwear, sandals, and accessories. **Territory Ahead** (⊠ main store: 515 State St.; outlet store: 400 State St., ☎ 805/962–5558), a high-quality outdoorsy catalog company, sells fashionably rugged clothing for men and women. **Tienda Ho** (⊠ 1105 State St., ☎ 805/962–3643) is a bohemian bazaar combining Indian, Moroccan, and Indonesian influences.

En Route   About 12 mi east of Santa Barbara on U.S. 101 is sheltered, sunny, often crowded **Carpinteria State Beach** (☎ 805/684–2811 or 805/968–3294). From the mile-long strand you can sometimes see seals, sea lions, and gray whales in winter and spring.

VENTURA COUNTY
With Channel Islands National Park

Ventura County was first settled by the Chumash Indians, an agricultural society. Spanish missionaries were the first Europeans to arrive, followed by Americans and other Europeans, who established bustling towns, intensive agricultural operations, and transportation networks. Since the 1920s nonfarm industries like oil—and now tourism—have replaced agriculture as the area's main businesses.

Ventura

❸❷   *30 mi southeast of Santa Barbara on U.S. 101.*

The city of Ventura enjoys gorgeous weather and beaches like LA's, without the smog and congestion. Mile upon mile of beautiful, uncrowded beaches, with picnic areas, barbecues, rest rooms, snack shops, and umbrella rentals await you here. The beaches are a favorite destination for all types of athletes, who pursue everything from body surfing and boogie boarding to walking and biking. Ventura is also a magnet for antiques buffs, who come to browse the dozens of shops in the downtown area. You can pick up an antiques guide downtown at the **visitor center** (⊠ 89 S. California St., #C, ☎ 805/648–2075, WEB www.ventura-usa. com) run by the Ventura Visitors and Convention Bureau.

You can follow the course of more than three millennia of human history in the Ventura region through the archaeological exhibits on display at the small **Albinger Archaeological Museum.** The relics on display date back to 1600 BC. ⊠ *113 E. Main St.,* ☎ *805/648–5823.* ✆ *Free.* ⊙ *June–Aug., Wed.–Sun. 10–4; Sept.–May, Wed.–Fri. 10–2, weekends 10–4.*

Lunker largemouth bass, rainbow trout, crappie, red-ears, and channel catfish live in the waters at **Lake Casitas Recreation Area,** an impoundment of the Ventura River. The lake is one of the country's best bass-fishing areas, and anglers come from all over the United States to test their luck. Nestling below the Santa Ynez Mountains' Laguna Ridge, the park is very scenic as well. You can row or motor across the reservoir, cast a line, pitch a tent, or have a picnic. A water playground entertains children during the summer months. The park is 13 mi northwest of Ventura. ⊠ *Rte. 33,* ☎ *805/649–2233; 805/649–1122 for campground reservations,* WEB *www.ojai.org/casitas.htm.* ✆ *$6.50 per vehicle, $12.50 per boat.* ⊙ *Daily.*

The ninth of the 21 California missions, **Mission San Buenaventura** burned to the ground in the 1790s. It was rebuilt and rededicated in 1809. A self-guided tour takes you through a small museum, a quiet courtyard, and a chapel with 250-year-old paintings. ⊠ *211 E. Main St.,* ☎ *805/643–4318,* WEB *www.anacapa.net/~mission.* ✆ *1$.* ⊙ *Mon.– Sat. 10–5, Sun. 10–4.*

OFF THE
BEATEN PATH

SANTA PAULA – Eighteen miles northeast of Ventura on Route 126, past the orange, lemon, and avocado orchards of Heritage Valley, lies Santa Paula. Here, Queen Anne– and Victorian-style homes, antiques stores, and galleries line the streets. Visit the **California Oil Museum** (⊠ 1001 E. Main St., ☎ 805/933–0076, WEB www.oilmuseum.net), in the 1890 Union Oil Building, to learn about the history and huge impact of the oil industry in the region. It's open Wednesday–Sunday 10–4, and admission is $2.

FILLMORE – The tiny, well-preserved downtown area of Fillmore, 8 mi east of Santa Paula on Route 126, is a snapshot of turn-of-the-20th-century California history. If you're here on a weekend, hop aboard the **Fillmore & Western Railway** (⊠ 351 Santa Clara Ave., ☎ 805/524–2546 or 800/773–8724, WEB www.fwry.com). The vintage trains travel on century-old restored track to Santa Paula and back (the ride usually takes 2½ hours).

Dining and Lodging

$$–$$$ ✕ **Jonathan's at Peirano's.** The main dining room here has a gazebo where you can eat surrounded by plants and local artwork. The menu has dishes from Spain, Portugal, France, Italy, Greece, and Morocco. Standouts are the Moroccan-inspired chicken *penne checca* pasta and the halibut with almonds. ⊠ *204 E. Main St.,* ☎ *805/648–4853. AE, D, DC, MC, V. Closed Mon. No lunch Sun.*

$$–$$$ ✕ **71 Palm Restaurant.** In a 1910 house this refined restaurant has wooden floors and trim, lace curtains, and a fireplace. For an appetizer try the innovative potato caviar (boiled red potatoes hollowed out and filled with caviar); for dinner there are grilled salmon on a potato pancake or New Zealand rack of lamb Provençale. You can sit indoors or out. ⊠ *71 Palm Dr.,* ☎ *805/653–7222. AE, D, DC, MC, V. Closed Sun. No lunch Sat.*

$–$$ ✕ **Andria's Seafood.** Place your order at the counter, then sit at the large tables inside, or outside on a patio where you can overlook the harbor and marina. At this casual family-oriented restaurant the specialties are fish-and-chips (with angel shark) and homemade clam chowder. ⊠ *1449 Spinnaker Dr., Suite A,* ☎ *805/654–0546. No credit cards.*

$ ✕ **Christy's.** You can get breakfast all day—try the breakfast burrito—at this greasy spoon across the water from the Channel Islands. It also serves burgers, sandwiches, and soup. ⊠ *1559 Spinnaker Dr.,* ☎ *805/642–3116. AE, V.*

$$–$$$ 🏠 **Victorian Rose.** As you might guess from the 96-ft steeple, this inn was converted from an 1888 Victorian Gothic church. Carved beam ceilings reach dizzying heights and are adorned with elaborate stained-glass panels. The former sanctuary now holds several cozy rooms, each with a gas-burning fireplace and a well-appointed bath. ⊠ *896 E. Main St., 93001,* ☎ *805/641–1888,* ℻ *805/643–1335,* ᴡᴇʙ *www.victorian-rose.com. 5 rooms. Hot tub; no smoking. AE, MC, V. BP.*

$$ 🏠 **Best Western Inn of Ventura.** A block off U.S. 101 in the historic district, this hotel has large rooms with oversize beds. Some rooms have ocean views. Beaches, restaurants, and theaters are within walking distance. Local phone calls are free, as is a Continental breakfast. ⊠ *708 E. Thompson Blvd., 93001,* ☎ *805/648–3101 or 800/648–1508,* ℻ *805/648–4019,* ᴡᴇʙ *www.bestwestern.com. 75 rooms. In-room data ports, cable TV, pool, hot tub, some pets allowed (fee); no-smoking rooms. AE, D, DC, MC, V. CP.*

$$ 🏠 **Pierpont Inn & Racquet Club.** Back in 1910 Josephine Pierpont-Ginn built the original Pierpont Inn on a hill overlooking Ventura Beach. A 1999 renovation restored much of the hotel's original elegance. The wicker-filled lobby, lined with the warm woods of the arts and crafts style, showcases contemporary local art. Set amid gardens and gazebos, the English Tudor cottages have cozy fireplaces. Rates include guest privileges at the neighboring Pierpont Racquet Club, which has indoor and outdoor pools, 12 tennis courts, racquetball courts, spa services, aerobics, and childcare. The inn's restaurant has great views of the ocean and harbor; breakfast is included. ⊠ *550 Sanjon Rd., 93001,* ☎ *805/643–6144, 800/285–4667,* ℻ *805/643–9167,* ᴡᴇʙ *www.pierpontinn.com. 65 rooms, 9 suites, 2 cottages. Restaurant, bar, refrigerators (some), cable TV with movies, Internet, meeting rooms; no smoking; no air-conditioning in some rooms. AE, D, DC, MC, V. 2-night minimum on summer weekends. BP.*

$–$$ 🏠 **Clocktower Inn.** In the heart of downtown, this inn is next to Mission San Buenaventura, the Historical Museum, and the area's many boutique shops. Rooms are done up in soft southwestern colors, and many have private patios, fireplaces, carved headboards, desks, leather chairs, and armoires. Continental breakfast is complimentary. ⊠ *181 E. Santa Clara, 93001,* ☎ *805/652–0141 or 800/727–1027,* ℻ *805/643–1432,* ᴡᴇʙ *www.clocktowerinn.com. 50 rooms. Restaurant, room service, cable TV with movies, meeting room; no-smoking rooms. AE, D, DC, MC, V. CP.*

Outdoor Activities and Sports

Ventura is a great place for whale-watching. California gray whales migrate through the Santa Barbara Channel off the Ventura shore from late December through March; giant blue and humpback whales feed here mid-June through September. In fact, the channel is teeming with marine life year-round, so tours include more than just whale sightings. Cruise the Santa Barbara Channel with **Island Packers** (⊠ *1691 Spinnaker Dr.,* Ventura Harbor, ☎ *805/642–1393,* ᴡᴇʙ *www.islandpackers.com*) to spot whales and other marine life throughout the year.

Channel Islands National Park

③③   *In Santa Barbara Channel southwest of Ventura and Oxnard; accessible from Ventura, Santa Barbara, and Oxnard.*

Often referred to as America's Galapagos, this park includes five of the eight Channel Islands and 6 nautical mi of ocean. The Channel Islands range in size from 1-square-mi Santa Barbara to 96-square-mi Santa Cruz. Together they form a magnificent nature preserve, home of wildlife unique to the islands, such as the island scrub-jay, the island fox, and the Anacapa deer mouse. Plant species, such as the Santa Rosa Torrey pine and the island oak, have also evolved differently from their counterparts on the mainland. It all adds up to a living laboratory not unlike the one naturalist Charles Darwin discovered off the coast of Ecuador more than 150 years ago.

The channel waters are also teeming with life, including dolphins, whales, seals, sea lions, and thousands of sea birds. Sunrise over the water from Smuggler's Cove, an inlet on Santa Cruz Island, is spectacular. If you visit East Anacapa, you'll walk through a nesting area of western gulls. If you're lucky enough to get to windswept San Miguel, you might have a chance to see as many as 30,000 pinnipeds (seals and sea lions) camped out on the beach. Kayakers have an opportunity to paddle with the seals, while snorkelers and divers will move through some of the world's richest kelp forests. Even traveling on an excursion boat will give you a chance to visit the sea lions, spot a brown pelican, or watch a whale spout.

★ You can get a good taste of Channel Islands without even leaving the mainland, and if you plan to visit one or more of the islands, you should definitely stop by the **Channel Islands Visitor Center.** Here you can obtain a detailed trip-planning packet including a map and schedule of visitor center programs. The center has a museum, a bookstore, a three-story observation tower with telescopes, and island exhibits. In a small tide pool you can watch brilliant orange garibaldis cruise around, blood starfish cling to rocks, and anemones spread their colorful spiny tentacles. You'll see exhibits on the region's natural history, including a full-size replica of the pygmy mammoth skeleton fossil that was unearthed on Santa Rosa in 1994. You can view a 25-minute movie shown throughout the day in the auditorium. On weekends and holidays at 11 and 3, rangers lead various free public programs about park resources. ⊠ *1901 Spinnaker Dr., Ventura,* ☎ *805/658–5730,* WEB *www.nps.gov.chis.* ◻ *Free.* ☉ *Daily 8:30–5.*

You can get to the Channel Islands from Santa Barbara with **Island Packers** (⊠ 1867 Spinnaker Dr., Ventura, ☎ 805/642–1393, WEB www.islandpackers.com), which sails from Ventura and Oxnard. A 64-ft high-speed catamaran, the *Islander,* zips over to Santa Cruz Island, with stops at Anacapa Island, almost daily. Various boats in the fleet travel to Anacapa daily in the summer, less frequently the rest of the year. Island Packers also visits the other islands three or four times a month and provides transportation for campers. **Channel Islands Aviation** (⊠ 305 Durley Ave., Camarillo, ☎ 805/987–1301, WEB www.flycia.com) provides charter flights from Camarillo Airport, about 10 mi east of Oxnard, to an airstrip on Santa Rosa. It will also pick up groups of six or more at Santa Barbara Airport. Day trips are usually from 9:30 to 4.

Although most people think of it as an island, **Anacapa** comprises three narrow islets. The tips of these volcanic formations nearly touch, but they are inaccessible from each other except by boat. Here you'll find towering cliffs, isolated sea caves, and natural bridges such as Arch Rock, one of the best-known symbols of Channel Islands National Park. Wildlife viewing is the reason most people come to Anacapa, particularly in summer when the seagull chicks are crying for food and sea lions and seals are lounging on the beaches. Almost everyone who comes here heads to East Anacapa, the park's most popular destination. A limited number of boats travel to Frenchy's Cove, on West Anacapa, where there's a pristine tide pool. The rest of West Anacapa is closed to protect nesting brown pelicans. Middle Anacapa, a seabird nesting area, can be accessed only by ranger-led hikes. Displaying the original crystal-and-brass lens from the nearby lighthouse and other interesting items, the compact **museum** on East Anacapa tells the history of the island. If you come in summer, you can also learn about the nearby kelp forest from rangers.

Five miles west of Anacapa, 96-square-mi **Santa Cruz** is the largest of the Channel Islands. The National Park Service manages the easternmost 25% of the island; the rest is owned by the Nature Conservancy, which requires a permit to land. When your boat drops you off on the 70 mi of craggy coastline, you'll find two rugged mountain ranges with peaks soaring to 2,000 ft and deep canyons traversed by steams. This varied environment is the habitat of a remarkable variety of flora and fauna—more than 600 types of plants, 140 kinds of land birds, 11 mammal species, five varieties of reptiles, and three amphibian species. Bird-watchers will want to look for the endemic scrub-jay, found nowhere else in the world. Although the Chumash lived here from around 8,000 BC, the first European to visit was Gaspar Portola, in 1769.

The largest and deepest known sea cave in the world, **Painted Cave** lies along the northwest coastline of Santa Cruz Island. Named for the colorful lichen and algae that cover its walls, Painted Cave is nearly a quarter mile long and 100 ft wide. In spring a waterfall cascades over the entrance. Kayakers may encounter seals or sea lions cruising alongside their boats inside the cave. Remnants of a dozen Chumash villages can be seen here. The largest of these villages, at the eastern end of the island, occupied the area now called **Scorpion Ranch.** The Chumash mined extensive chert deposits on the island for tools to produce shell-bead money, which they traded with people on the mainland. Remnants of the ranching era can also be seen in the massive adobe ovens that produced bread for the entire island.

Between Santa Cruz and San Miguel islands, **Santa Rosa** is the second largest of the Channel Islands. The island has a relatively low profile, broken by a central mountain range rising to 1,589 ft. The coastal areas range from broad sandy beaches to sheer cliffs. The island is the home of about 500 species of plants, including the rare Torrey pine. Three unusual mammals—the endemic island fox, spotted skunk, and deer mouse—are among those that make their home here. They hardly compare to the mammoths that once roamed the island; a nearly complete skeleton of a 6-ft-tall pygmy mammoth was unearthed here in 1994. On Santa Rosa island once stood the historic **Vickers and Vail Ranch,** which raised cattle on the island for 160 years. You can see what the operation was like by viewing the historic ranch buildings, barns, equipment, and the wooden pier from which cattle were brought onto the island.

The westernmost of the Channel Islands, **San Miguel** is frequently battered by storms sweeping across the North Pacific. The 15-square-mi island's wild, windswept landscape is lush with vegetation. Point Bennett, at the western tip of the island, offers one of the world's most spectacular wildlife displays when more than 30,000 pinnipeds hit the beach. Explorer Juan Rodriguez Cabrillo was the first European to visit this island; he claimed it for Spain in 1542. Legend holds that Cabrillo died on the island; no one knows where he's buried, but there's a memorial to him on a bluff above Cuyler Harbor.

At about 1 square mi, **Santa Barbara** is the smallest of the Channel Islands. It's also the southernmost island in the chain, separated from the others by nearly 40 mi. Roughly triangular in shape, its steep cliffs are topped by twin peaks. The island was visited in 1602 by explorer Sebastian Vizcaino, who named it in honor of St. Barbara. Come in spring to see a brilliant display of yellow coreopsis. The cliffs here offer a perfect nesting spot for the Xantus' murrelet, a rare seabird. With exhibits on the region's natural history, the small Santa Barbara Island **museum** is a great place to learn about the wildlife on and around the Channel Islands.

Camping

Camping is the best way to experience the natural beauty and isolation of Channel Islands National Park. Unrestricted by tour schedules, you'll have plenty of time to explore mountain trails, snorkel in the kelp forests, or kayak into sea caves. Campsites are primitive, with no water (except on Santa Rosa and Santa Cruz) or electricity; enclosed camp stoves must be used. You must carry all your gear and pack out all trash. Campers must arrange transportation to the islands prior to reserving a campsite. You can reserve a campsite by contacting **Channel Islands National Park** (☎ 800/365–2267, WEB www.reservations.nps.gov) up to three months in advance.

🏕 **East Anacapa Campground.** You'll have to walk a half mile and ascend more than 150 steps to reach this open, treeless camping area above Cathedral Cove. *Pit toilets, picnic tables, ranger station. 7 sites.* ✉ *East Anacapa landing.*

🏕 **Santa Cruz Campground.** In a grove of eucalyptus trees, this campground is near the historic buildings of Scorpion Ranch. You can access it via an easy, flat half-mile trail from Scorpion Beach landing. *Pit toilets, drinking water, picnic tables. 40 sites.* ✉ *Scorpion Beach landing.*

Outdoor Activities and Sports

Because private vehicles are not allowed on the islands, hiking is the only way to explore their natural beauty. Terrain on most islands ranges from flat to moderately hilly. Santa Cruz has the most options, from a half-mile stroll to the historic ranch to a strenuous 8-mi off-trail hike to a climb up an 1,808-ft peak. Naturalist-led day trips and overnight camping trips are available year-round through the two official park concessionaires: Island Packers (*above*) and Truth Aquatics. A number of other outfits also arrange sailing, diving, hiking, and kayak excursions; contact the Channel Islands visitor center for more information. There are no services (including public phones) on the islands—you have to bring all your own food, water, and supplies.

Truth Aquatics (✉ 301 Cabrillo Blvd., Santa Barbara, ☎ 805/962–1127, WEB www.truthaquatics.com) departs from the Santa Barbara Harbor for single- and multiday hiking, scuba, and camping excursions to Santa Cruz, Santa Rosa, and San Miguel islands.

Ojai

③④ *40 mi southeast of Santa Barbara, U.S. 101 to Rte. 150 to Rte. 33.*

The acres of orange and avocado groves in and around rural Ojai look like the postcard images of agricultural southern California from decades ago. Recent years have seen an influx of artists, showbiz types, and others who have opted for life out of the fast lane. The Ojai Valley, which director Frank Capra used as a backdrop for his 1936 film *Lost Horizon,* sizzles in the summer, when temperatures routinely reach 90°F. Compact Ojai can be easily explored on foot, or you can hop on the **Ojai Valley Trolley** (25¢) which takes riders on a one-hour loop (between 7:40 and 5:40 on weekdays, 9 and 5 on weekends). Tell the driver you're a visitor, and you'll get an informal guided tour. Stop in at the **visitor center** (✉ 150 W. Ojai Ave., ☎ 805/646–8126, WEB www.the-ojai.org) for maps and tourist information. It's open daily.

You can see the work of local artists in the Spanish-style shopping arcade along Ojai Avenue (Route 150). Organic and specialty growers sell their produce on Sunday from 10 to 2 (9 to 1 in summer) at the farmers' market behind the arcade. The **Art Center** (✉ 113 S. Montgomery, ☎ 805/646–0117) exhibits artwork and presents theater and dance performances. Visit the **Ojai Valley Museum** (✉ 130 W. Ojai Ave., ☎ 805/640–1390) to learn about the valley's history and examine Native American artifacts. The 18-mi **Ojai Valley Trail** (✉ parallel to Rte. 33, from Soule Park in Ojai to the ocean in Ventura, ☎ 805/654–3951, WEB www.the-ojai.org) is open to pedestrians, bikers, joggers, equestrians, and nonmotorized vehicles. You can access it anywhere along its route.

Dining and Lodging

$$–$$$ ✕ **L'Auberge.** Tasty French-Belgian food is served in a lovely garden setting. When the weather's fine, reserve an early table on the patio, so you can accompany your rack of lamb with a glorious sunset. ✉ *314 El Paseo Rd.,* ☎ *805/646–2288. AE, MC, V. No lunch weekdays.*

$$–$$$ ✕ **The Ranch House.** The town's best eatery serves rich pâté appetizers and main dishes such as chicken soaked in vermouth and salmon poached in white wine. The verdant patio is a delight, especially for Sunday brunch. ✉ *S. Lomita Ave.,* ☎ *805/646–2360. AE, D, DC, MC, V. Closed Mon.–Tues. No lunch.*

$$–$$$ ✕ **Suzanne's Cuisine.** Peppered filet mignon, linguine with steamed clams, and salmon with sauerkraut in a dill beurre blanc are among the offerings at this European-style restaurant. Game, seafood, and vegetarian dishes dominate the dinner menu, and salads and soups star at lunchtime. Most of the bread and all the desserts are made on the premises. ✉ *502 W. Ojai Ave.,* ☎ *805/640–1961. MC, V. Closed Tues. and first 2 wks in Jan.*

$–$$ ✕ **Sea Fresh.** Fresh seafood—much of it caught from the restaurant's own boat—a lively crowd, and friendly service ensure a packed dining room practically every day of the week. The family-run enterprise also includes a sushi bar and fish market. ✉ *533 E. Ojai Ave.,* ☎ *805/646–7747. AE, D, MC, V.*

$$–$$$$ ✕🏨 **Oaks at Ojai.** Focus on rejuvenation at this comfortable, cell-phone-free spa. The fitness package includes lodging, use of the spa facilities, 18 fitness classes, and three nutritionally balanced low-calorie meals. Children age 16 and older are welcome. ✉ *122 E. Ojai Ave., 93023,* ☎ *805/646–5573 or 800/753–6257,* FAX *805/640–1504,* WEB *www.oaksspa.com. 46 rooms. Dining room, pool, gym, hair salon, hot tub, massage, sauna, spa; no smoking. D, MC, V. 2-day minimum stay.*

$$$$ 🏨 **Ojai Valley Inn & Spa.** This outdoorsy, golf-oriented resort with a full-
★   service spa facility is set on beautifully landscaped grounds, with hillside views in nearly all directions. Nearby is the inn's 800-acre ranch, where you can take riding lessons and go on guided trail rides. Some of the nicest rooms are in the original adobe building. The two restaurants tout "Ojai regional cuisine," which incorporates locally grown produce and locally made foods. ✉ *905 Country Club Rd., 93023,* ☎ *805/646–5511 or 800/422–6524,* FAX *805/646–7969,* WEB *www.ojairesort.com. 209 units. 2 restaurants, 2 bars, in-room data ports, minibars, cable TV with movies, 18-hole golf course, 8 tennis courts, 3 pools, spa, hiking, horseback riding, children's programs (ages 3–12), meeting rooms, some pets allowed (fee); no-smoking rooms. AE, D, DC, MC, V.*

$–$$$ 🏨 **The Blue Iguana Inn & Cottages.** Local artists run this southwestern-style hotel. The small, cozy main inn is about 2 mi west of downtown. The Emerald Iguana Inn consists of eight more art nouveau cottages close to downtown Ojai. The works of the artist-owners decorate the rooms and are for sale. The suites have kitchenettes. ✉ *11794 N. Ventura Ave. (Rte. 33), 93023,* ☎ *805/646–5277,* WEB *www.blueiguanainn.com. 4 rooms, 7 suites, 8 cottages. Refrigerators, pool, hot tub, massage, some pets allowed (fee); no smoking. AE, D, DC, MC, V.*

The Arts

On Wednesday evening in summer the free all-American music played by the Ojai Band draws crowds to **Libbey Park** (✉ Ojai Ave., ☎ 805/646–2560) in downtown Ojai. For more than five decades the **Ojai Music Festival** (☎ 805/646–2094, WEB www.ojaifestival.org) has attracted internationally known progressive and traditional musicians for outdoor concerts in Libbey Park on the weekend after Memorial Day.

Oxnard

35 *1 mi south of Ventura off Rte. 101.*

Oxnard has a reputation as a drowsy agricultural burg (a broccoli and lettuce capital), but lately it's promoting its charms as an undiscovered beach town. Its 7 mi of less trammeled beaches are great for folks who just want to feel the sand between their toes. With a busy harbor and unbusy beaches, this community of 170,000 offers myriad water and outdoor activities, ranging from beachcombing to sailboard surfing.

Take a stroll along **Heritage Square** to see more than a dozen late-19th-century homes and other structures, many trimmed with manicured gardens and courtyards. Some of the buildings were brought here from outlying ranchlands. Docent-led tours take you inside to see the gracious interiors. ✉ *715 S. A St.,* ☎ *805/483–7960,* WEB *www.ci.oxnard.ca.us/ heritagesquare.html.* ✉ *$2.* ⊙ *Guided tours Sat. 10–2.*

Housed in a 1906 neoclassical building, the permanent collection of the **Carnegie Art Museum** focuses on contemporary California painters. There are also changing exhibits of works by Ventura County artists as well as photography and decorative arts. ✉ *424 S. C St.,* ☎ *805/385–8157,* WEB *www.vcnet.com/carnart.* ✉ *$3.* ⊙ *Thurs.–Sat. 10–5, Sun. 1–5.*

More than 2,600 boats are moored at **Channel Islands Harbor,** a classic southern California–style seaside harbor. Concerts, boat shows, fireworks displays, arts festivals, and other events take place here year-round. At the **Ventura County Maritime Museum** (☎ 805/984–6260), you can learn everything you ever wanted to know about shipping and whaling in, and the maritime history of, the Channel Islands. Rent bikes, paddleboats, or even an electric boat to tour the harbor area. The harbor's visitor center, in a two-story building on the corner of Channel Islands Boulevard and Victoria Avenue, will help you get oriented. ✉ *3810 W. Channel Islands Blvd., Suite E,* ☎ *805/985–4852,* WEB *www.channelislandsharbor.org.* ✉ *Free.*

Kids explore fantasy worlds in the hands-on exhibits of the ocean-inspired **Ventura County Gull Wings Children's Museum.** Activities include a stage complete with costumes and videotape equipment, a puppet theater, a roomful of optical illusions, and a computer room. ✉ *418 W. 4th St.,* ☎ *805/483–3005,* WEB *www.gullwingsmuseum4kids.com.* ✉ *$4.* ⊙ *Tues.–Sun. 10–5.*

The warehouse-size collection of naval memorabilia at the **CEC/Seabee Museum** includes uniforms, photos, and weapons used by the Seabees in World War II and the Korean and Vietnam wars. The Seabees built the landing strips, airports, housing, roads, and facilities used by troops in combat. ✉ *4111 San Pedro St.,* ☎ *805/982–5163 or 805/982–5167,* WEB *www.cbcph.navy.mil/museum.* ✉ *Free.* ⊙ *Tues.–Sat. 9–4.*

Dining and Lodging

$$–$$$ ✕ **Port Royal.** You practically dine on the water at this popular eatery in Channel Islands Harbor. Sit in front of the fireplace for steak, fresh seafood, or pasta. Kids order from their own special menu. ⊠ *3900 Bluefin Circle,* ☎ *805/382–7678. AE, D, DC, MC, V.*

$ ✕ **Sal's Mexican Food.** Oxnard's Mexican-American community gathers at this friendly spot a mile south of downtown for south-of-the-border fare. The red-splashed room is casual and cheery. Try the *carne asada* (marinated strips of beef) or one of the large combination plates. ⊠ *1450 S. Oxnard Blvd.,* ☎ *805/483–9015. AE, D, DC, MC, V.*

$$$–$$$$ ✕🏨 **Embassy Suites Mandalay Beach Resort.** On 8-acres along a
★ white-sand beach north of Channel Islands Harbor, this nine-building complex houses two- and three-room suites with marble baths; cooked-to-order breakfasts are complimentary. Small waterfalls dress up the landscaped grounds and sprawling pool area. Capistrano's ($$–$$$) restaurant serves California cuisine in a garden courtyard and Polynesian-inspired dining rooms. You can dance to live music on Friday and Saturday nights or splurge on Sunday brunch. ⊠ *2101 Mandalay Beach Rd., 93035,* ☎ *805/984–2500,* 𝖥𝖠𝖷 *805/984–8339,* 𝖂𝖤𝖡 *www.embassymandalay.com. 248 suites. Restaurant, bar, in-room data ports, microwaves, refrigerators, cable TV, tennis courts, pool, exercise equipment, hot tub, spa, bicycles, children's programs, business services, airport shuttle, parking (fee); no-smoking rooms. AE, D, DC, MC, V. BP.*

$$ 🏨 **Radisson Hotel Oxnard.** This six-story hotel's expansive grounds and various resort-type amenities attract business travelers and vacationers alike. Five miles west of downtown, it has a landscaped courtyard and a pool complex. ⊠ *600 Esplanade Dr., 93030,* ☎ *805/485–9666 or 800/ 333–3333,* 𝖥𝖠𝖷 *805/485–2061,* 𝖂𝖤𝖡 *www.radisson.com. 161 rooms and 2 suites. Restaurant, bar, in-room data ports, refrigerators (some), cable TV with movies, pool, hot tub, Internet, business services, meeting rooms, some pets allowed (fee); no-smoking rooms. AE, D, DC, MC, V.*

$ 🏨 **Best Western Oxnard Inn.** This chain offers lots of services, making it an easy stop for families or business travelers. If you're not in the mood for a dip in the pool, consider a jaunt to Point Heuneme Beach, 4 mi northwest. ⊠ *1156 S. Oxnard Blvd., 93030,* ☎ *805/483–9581 or 800/ 469–6273,* 𝖥𝖠𝖷 *805/483–4072,* 𝖂𝖤𝖡 *www.bestwestern.com. 99 rooms, 3 suites. In-room data ports, microwaves, cable TV, VCRs, pool, hot tub, spa, exercise equipment, laundry facilities, business services, meeting room, some pets allowed; no-smoking rooms. AE, D, DC, MC, V. CP.*

$ 🏨 **Casa Sirena Resort.** This modest motor inn is 6 mi from downtown on the Channel Islands Harbor, with views of the marina from many rooms. The four Spanish-style wood buildings were constructed in 1962. The grounds are landscaped, and a park is next to the property. ⊠ *3605 Peninsula Rd, 93035,* ☎ *805/985–6311 or 800/447–3529,* 𝖥𝖠𝖷 *805/985– 4329,* 𝖂𝖤𝖡 *www.casasirenahotel.com. 261 rooms, 12 suites. Restaurant, bar, no air-conditioning in some rooms, in-room data ports, kitchenettes (some), refrigerators, cable TV, putting green, tennis courts, pool, gym, hair salon, hot tub, playground, business services, airport shuttle, some pets allowed; no-smoking rooms. AE, D, DC, MC, V.*

THE CENTRAL COAST A TO Z

To research prices, get advice from other travelers, and book travel arrangements, visit www.fodors.com.

AIR TRAVEL

America West Express, American/American Eagle, Delta/Skywest Connection, and United/United Express fly into Santa Barbara Municipal

Airport, 12 mi from downtown. *See* Air Travel *in* Smart Travel Tips A to Z for airline phone numbers.

Santa Barbara Airbus shuttles travelers between Santa Barbara and Los Angeles for $37 one-way and $69 round-trip (slight discount with 24-hour notice, larger discount for groups of two or more). The Santa Barbara Metropolitan Transit District Bus 11 runs every 30 minutes from the airport to the downtown transit center.

➤ AIRPORT INFORMATION: **Santa Barbara Municipal Airport** (✉ 500 Fowler Rd., ☎ 805/683–4011, WEB www.flysba.com). **Santa Barbara Airbus** (☎ 805/964–7759; 800/733–6354; 800/423–1618 in CA, WEB www.sbairbus.com). **Santa Barbara Metropolitan Transit District** (☎ 805/683–3702, WEB www.sbmtd.gov).

BUS TRAVEL

Greyhound provides service from San Francisco and Los Angeles to San Luis Obispo, Ventura, and Santa Barbara. From Monterey and Carmel, Monterey-Salinas Transit operates buses to Big Sur between May and mid-October. From San Luis Obispo Central Coast Transit runs buses around Santa Maria and out to the coast. Santa Barbara Metropolitan Transit District provides local service. The State Street and Waterfront shuttles cover their respective sections of Santa Barbara during the day. South Coast Area Transit buses serve the entire Ventura County region.

➤ BUS INFORMATION: **Central Coast Transit** (☎ 805/541–2228, WEB www.slorta.org). **Greyhound** (☎ 800/231–2222, WEB www.greyhound.com). **Monterey-Salinas Transit** (☎ 831/899–2555, WEB www.mst.org). **San Luis Obispo Transit** (☎ 805/541–2877, WEB www.slorta.org). **Santa Barbara Metropolitan Transit District** (☎ 805/683–3702 or 805/963–3364, WEB www.sbmtd.gov). **South Coast Area Transit** (for Oxnard and Ventura; ☎ 805/643–3158, WEB www.scat.org).

CAR RENTAL

Most major car-rental companies have offices in San Luis Obispo, Santa Barbara, and Ventura. *See* Car Rental *in* Smart Travel Tips A to Z for national rental agency phone numbers.

CAR TRAVEL

Route 1 and U.S. 101 run north–south and more or less parallel along the Central Coast, with Route 1 hugging the coast and U.S. 101 remaining inland. The best way to see the most dramatic section of the Central Coast, the 70 mi between Big Sur and San Simeon, is by heading south on Route 1—you'll be on the ocean side of the road and will get the best views. Don't expect to make good time along here: The road is narrow and twisting with a single lane in each direction, making it difficult to pass the many lumbering RVs. In fog or rain the drive can be downright nerve-racking. Once you start south from Carmel, there is no route east from Route 1 until Route 46 heads inland from Cambria to connect with U.S. 101. Along some stretches farther south, Route 1 and U.S. 101 join and run together for a while. At Morro Bay Route 1 moves inland for 13 mi and connects with U.S. 101 at San Luis Obispo. From here south to Pismo Beach the two highways run concurrently. South of Pismo Beach to Las Cruces the roads separate, then run together all the way to Oxnard. Along any stretch where they are separate, U.S. 101 is the quicker route.

U.S. 101 and Route 1 will get you to the Central Coast from Los Angeles and San Francisco. If you are coming from the east, you can take Route 46 west from I–5 in the Central Valley (near Bakersfield) to U.S. 101 at Paso Robles, where it becomes narrower as it continues to the coast, intersecting Route 1 a few miles south of Cambria. Route 33 heads south from I–5 at Bakersfield to Ojai. About 60 mi north of Ojai, Route 166 leaves Route 33, traveling due west through the Sierra Madre to Santa Maria at U.S. 101 and continuing west to Route 1 at Guadalupe. South of Carpinteria, Route 150 winds from Route 1/U.S. 101 through sparsely populated hills to Ojai. From Route 1/U.S. 101 at Ventura, Route 33 leads to Ojai and the Los Padres National Forest. South of Ventura Route 126 runs east from Route 1/U.S. 101 to I–5.

➤ ROAD CONDITIONS: **Caltrans** (☎ 800/427–7623, WEB www.dot. ca.gov/hq/roadinfo).

EMERGENCIES

In case of emergency dial 911.

➤ HOSPITALS: **Big Sur Health Center** (✉ Hwy. 1, 1/4 mi south of River Inn, Big Sur, ☎ 831/667–2580) is open weekdays 10–5. **Cottage Hospital** (✉ Pueblo St. at Bath St., Santa Barbara, ☎ 805/682–7111; 805/ 569–7210 for emergency). **Sierra Vista Regional Medical Center** (✉ 1010 Murray Ave., San Luis Obispo, ☎ 805/546–7600).

LODGING

Hot Spots provides room reservations and tourist information for destinations in Santa Barbara, Ventura, and San Luis Obispo counties.

➤ LOCAL AGENTS: **Hot Spots** (☎ 805/564–1637 or 800/793–7666, WEB www.hotspotsusa.com).

TOURS

Breakaway Tours and Event Planning can take you on a customized tour to wineries, Hearst Castle®, and other attractions in San Luis Obispo County and as far south as the Santa Ynez Valley. Vehicles range from a 14-passenger van to full-size motorcoaches; fares vary. Santa Barbara Wine Tours operates customized Santa Barbara County tours and narrated North County wine country tours in 27-passenger mini-coaches. Fares for the wine tours are $59–$69 per person and include visits to four wineries, tasting fees, a deli lunch, champagne, appetizers, and four souvenir wine glasses. Tours depart from Stearns Wharf daily at 9:40 AM; the coach also picks up passengers at major hotels. Spencer's Limousine & Tours offers a range of customized tours of the city of Santa Barbara and wine country via limousine, van, or minibus. Fares vary; a four-hour basic tour with at least four participants costs about $50 per person. Sultan's Limousine Service has a fleet of superstretches; each can take up to eight passengers on Paso Robles and Edna Valley–Arroyo Grande wine tours and tours of the San Luis Obispo County coast. Hiring a limo for a four-hour wine country tour typically costs $360 with tip. The Wine Affair runs daily 5½-hour bus tours through Paso Robles wine country. Fees are $32–$39 per person and include visits to five or six wineries and a packed lunch. The bus departs from Cypress Cove Inn in Cambria daily at 9:45 AM and picks up passengers at other hotels in the vicinity.

➤ TOUR OPERATORS: **Breakaway Tours and Event Planning** (✉ P.O. Box 535, Pismo Beach, 93448, ☎ 800/799–7657, 805/783–2929, WEB www.breakaway-tours.com). **Santa Barbara Wine Tours** (✉ Stearns Wharf, Santa Barbara, ☎ 805/965–0353, WEB www.sboldtowntrolley. com). **Spencer's Limousine & Tours** (✉ Santa Barbara, ☎ 805/884–9700, WEB www.spencerslimo.com). **Sultan's Limousine Service** (✉ Paso Robles, ☎ 805/466–3167, 805/543–3308, WEB www.sultanslimo.com). **The Wine Affair** (✉ Cypress Cove Inn, 6348 Moonstone Beach Dr., Cambria, ☎ 805/927–2600 or 800/568–8517).

TRAIN TRAVEL

The Amtrak *Coast Starlight,* which runs between Los Angeles, Oakland, and Seattle, stops in Paso Robles, San Luis Obispo, Santa Barbara, and Oxnard. Amtrak runs several *Pacific Surfliner* trains daily between San Luis Obispo, Santa Barbara, Los Angeles, and San Diego. Metrolink Regional Rail Service trains connect Ventura and Oxnard with Los Angeles and points between.

➤ TRAIN INFORMATION: **Amtrak** (☎ 800/872–7245; 805/963–1015 in Santa Barbara; 805/541–0505 in San Luis Obispo; WEB www.amtrakcalifornia.com). **Metrolink** (☎ 800/371–LINK [within service area]; 213/347–2800, WEB www.metrolinktrains.com).

VISITOR INFORMATION

Cambria Chamber of Commerce (✉ 767 Main St., West Village, Cambria 93428, ☎ 805/927–3624, WEB www.cambriachamber.org). **Central Coast Tourism Council** (✉ Box 14011, San Luis Obispo 93406, ☎ 805/544–0241, WEB www.centralcoast-tourism.com). **Ojai Valley Chamber of Commerce** (✉ Box 1134, 150 W. Ojai Ave., 93024, ☎ 805/646–8126, WEB www.the-ojai.org). **Oxnard Visitors Bureau** (✉ 200 W. 7th St., Oxnard 93030-7154, ☎ 805/385–7545, WEB www.oxnardtourism.com). **Paso Robles Chamber of Commerce** (✉ 1225 Park St., 93446, ☎ 805/238–0506, 800/406–4040, WEB www.pasorobleschamber.com). **Paso Robles Vintners and Growers Association** (✉ 1940 Spring St., Paso Robles 93446, ☎ 805/239–8463, WEB www.pasowine.com). **San Luis Obispo Chamber of Commerce** (✉ 1039 Chorro St., San Luis Obispo 93401, ☎ 805/781–2777). **San Luis Obispo County Visitors and Conference Bureau** (✉ 1037 Mill St., San Luis Obispo 93401, ☎ 800/634–1414, 805/541–8000, WEB www.sanluisobispocounty.com). **San Luis Obispo Vintners and Growers Association** (✉ 5828 Orcutt Rd., San Luis Obispo 93401, ☎ 805/541–5868, WEB www.sanluisobispowines.com). **Santa Barbara Conference and Visitors Bureau** (✉ 12 E. Carrillo St., 93101, ☎ 805/966–9222 or 800/927–4688, WEB www.santabarbaraCA.com). **Santa Barbara County Vintners' Association** (✉ Box 1558, Santa Ynez 93460, ☎ 805/688–0881 or 800/218–0881, WEB www.sbcountywines.com). **Solvang Conference & Visitors Bureau** (✉ 1511 Mission Dr., 93434, ☎ 805/688–6144 or 800/468–6765, WEB www.solvangusa.com). **Ventura Visitors and Convention Bureau** (✉ 89 S. California St., #C, Ventura 93001, ☎ 800/333–2989, 805/648–2075, WEB www.ventura-usa.com).

14 LOS ANGELES

Few cities in the world capture the imagination the way Los Angeles does—from the bronze stars in the sidewalk along Hollywood's Walk of Fame to the Spandex-clad in-line skaters zipping along the Venice Boardwalk. Visitors flock to Hollywood in search of film and television stars; to Beverly Hills and Malibu for a glimpse of glamour and privilege; and to the beaches all along the coast, where the sunny, laid-back California good life is alive for all to see.

DON'T BELIEVE EVERYTHING you've heard about Los Angeles. Chances are you've heard some exaggerated claim, good or bad. The truth lies, of course, somewhere in between. Few cities are as hard to categorize as L.A. It's just too big and too diverse. With 3.5 million people, L.A. sprawls across 467 square mi of desert, mountains, and beaches. Outside city limits, another 6 million people live in 80 incorporated cities within Los Angeles County. Beyond that, another 5 million reside within the economic shadow of Los Angeles, in the region's four other counties.

The largest population of Pacific Islanders in the nation lives in L.A., as well as the world's third-largest Hispanic population (after Mexico City and Guadalajara). People from 140 countries speaking 96 different languages call L.A. home. Signs in Spanish, Korean, Thai, Chinese, Japanese, Armenian, and Russian are as common in some areas of the city as English signs. What isn't so well known is that this kind of diversity dates back to L.A.'s beginnings: Native Americans, African Americans, mestizos, and Spaniards were among the 44 settlers who first arrived from the Mexican provinces of Sonora and Sinaloa in September 1781.

EXPLORING LOS ANGELES

Revised and updated by Bobbi Zane

Looking at a map of sprawling Los Angeles, first-time visitors are sometimes overwhelmed. Where to begin? What to see first? And what about all those freeways? Here's some advice: relax. There is no cookie-cutter version of Los Angeles; you get to dream up your own perfect visit. Begin by setting your priorities—movie and television fans should first head to Hollywood, Universal Studios, and a taping of a television show. Beach lovers and outdoorsy types might start out in Santa Monica or Venice or Malibu, or spend an afternoon in Griffith Park. Those with a cultural bent will probably make a beeline for the Getty Center in Brentwood, the Los Angeles County Museum of Art (LACMA), or the Norton Simon Museum. And urban explorers might begin with downtown Los Angeles.

Downtown Los Angeles

Most visitors to Los Angeles who aren't staying at one of the big convention hotels downtown never make it to this part of the city. But downtown is the heart of this great city, its financial core, as well as its historical and cultural soul.

A Good Tour
Numbers in the text correspond to numbers in the margin and on the Downtown Los Angeles map.

A convenient and inexpensive minibus service—DASH, or Downtown Area Short Hop—has several routes that travel past most of the sights on this tour, stopping every two blocks or so. Each ride costs 25¢, so you can hop on and off without spending a fortune. Special (limited) routes operate on weekends. Call **DASH** (☎ 808–2273 from all Los Angeles area codes) for routes and hours of operation.

Begin a downtown tour by heading north on Broadway from 8th or 9th Street. Around 3rd Street, look for parking and continue on foot. At the southeast corner of Broadway and 3rd, notice the Bradbury Building, a marvelous specimen of Victorian-era commercial architecture and the locale for many movies. Across the street is the Grand Central Market—once you've made to the other side of its tantalizing stalls, cross Hill Street and climb steps up a steep hill to Watercourt, a courtyard surrounding bubbling, cascading fountains. Here you can see the Angels Flight Railway, a now-closed 1901 funicular. Next, walk toward the glass pyramidal skylight topping the **Museum of Contemporary Art (MOCA)** ①, visible half a block north on Grand Avenue. Walk farther north on Grand past the Music Center to Temple Street for a look inside the Cathedral of Our Lady of the Angels, which opened in late 2001. Now walk two blocks south on Grand to 5th Street, where you'll find two of downtown's historical and architectural treasures: the Millennium Biltmore Hotel and the Central Library. Behind the library are the tranquil MacGuire Gardens. Across 5th Street are the Bunker Hill Steps, L.A.'s version of Rome's Spanish Steps.

Back in your car, continue north on Broadway to 1st Street. A right turn here will take you into Little Tokyo and the expanded **Japanese American National Museum** ②. The Geffen Contemporary art museum, an arm of MOCA, is just one block north on Central. From Little Tokyo, turn left (north) from 1st onto Alameda Street. As you pass over the freeway, you'll come to the next stop, Union Station, on the right. Street parking is limited, so your best bet is to park in the pay lot at Union Station (about $5). After a look inside this grand railway terminal, cross Alameda to **Olvera Street** ③.

From Union Station, turn right on Alameda and then immediately left on Cesar Chavez Avenue for three blocks. At Broadway, turn right to check out Chinatown. After Chintatown, reverse your route on Broadway, cross back over the freeway, and at Temple Street make a left. Look to the right as you drive down Temple to see the back of Los Angeles City Hall. Next, head out of downtown Los Angeles (take Los Angeles Street south to 11th Street, turn west on 11th to Figueroa, then south on Figueroa Street) past Staples Center with its flying saucer–esque roof to Exposition Park site of three fascinating museums: the **California Science Center** ④, the **Natural History Museum of Los Angeles County** ⑤, and the **California African-American Museum** ⑥. Adjacent to Exposition Park is the University of Southern California. Return to downtown at night for a performance at the Music Center or East West Players, and after the show take in the bright lights of the big city at BonaVista, the revolving rooftop lounge atop the Westin Bonaventure Hotel & Suites.

TIMING

Seeing everything mentioned on this tour would take at least a full day. Weekends are the best time to explore downtown: there's less traffic, street parking is easier to find, and cheaper day rates prevail in the lots. The **Los Angeles Conservancy** (☎ 213/623–2489) conducts Saturday morning walking tours of downtown architectural landmarks and districts. Tours begin at 10 AM, last about 2½ hours, and are offered rain or shine. Reservations are required. Call for a schedule and fees.

Sights to See

❻ **California African-American Museum.** Works by 20th-century African-American artists and contemporary works of the African diaspora are part of the permanent collection of this museum. The collection documents the African-American experience from Emancipation and Reconstruction through the 20th century, with an emphasis on that experience in the West and California. ⊠ *600 State Dr., Exposition Park,* ☎ *213/744–7432,* WEB *www.caam.ca.gov.* 🎫 *Free, parking $5.* ☉ *Tues.–Sun. 10–5.*

★ ✆ ❹ **California Science Center.** The science center has interactive exhibits that illustrate the relevance of science to everyday life. Tess, the 50-ft Animatronic star of the exhibit "Body Works," demonstrates how the body's organs work together to maintain balance. In other exhibits you

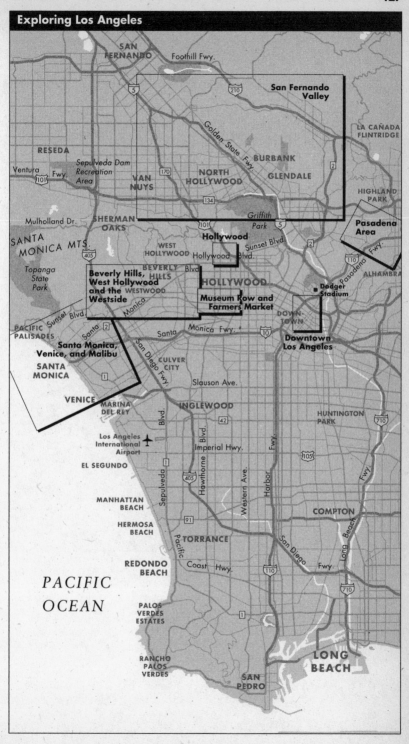

Exploring Los Angeles

SAN FERNANDO

Foothill Fwy.

San Fernando Valley

LA CAÑADA FLINTRIDGE

RESEDA

Golden State Fwy.

BURBANK

GLENDALE

Ventura Fwy.

Sepulveda Dam Recreation Area

VAN NUYS

NORTH HOLLYWOOD

HIGHLAND PARK

Mulholland Dr.

SHERMAN OAKS

Griffith Park

Pasadena Area

SANTA MONICA MTS.

Hollywood

Sunset Blvd.

ALHAMBRA

Topanga State Park

WEST HOLLYWOOD

Hollywood Blvd.

BEVERLY HILLS

HOLLYWOOD

Pasadena Fwy.

Beverly Hills, West Hollywood and the Westside

WESTWOOD

Blvd.

Museum Row and Farmers Market

Dodger Stadium

PACIFIC PALISADES

Sunset Blvd.

Santa Monica

DOWN-TOWN

Downtown Los Angeles

Santa Monica, Venice, and Malibu

Santa

Monica Fwy.

SANTA MONICA

San Diego Fwy.

CULVER CITY

VENICE

Slauson Ave.

MARINA DEL REY

INGLEWOOD

HUNTINGTON PARK

Los Angeles International Airport

Blvd.

Imperial Hwy.

Fwy.

EL SEGUNDO

Sepulveda

Hawthorne Blvd.

Western Ave.

Harbor

MANHATTAN BEACH

COMPTON

HERMOSA BEACH

TORRANCE

Pacific

San Diego

Long Beach

REDONDO BEACH

Coast Hwy.

Fwy.

PACIFIC OCEAN

PALOS VERDES ESTATES

RANCHO PALOS VERDES

SAN PEDRO

LONG BEACH

Downtown Los Angeles

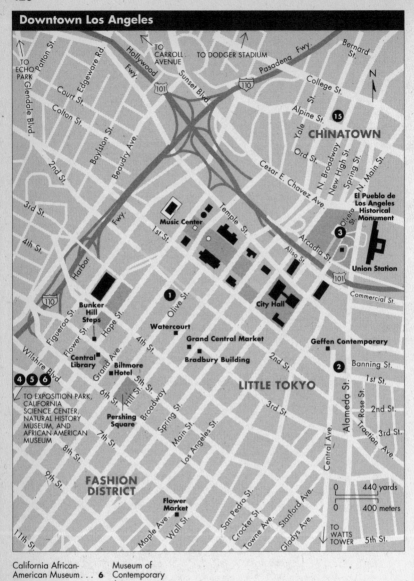

can build a structure to see how it stands up to an earthquake, or ride a high-wire bicycle to learn about gravity. The IMAX theater shows science-related films. ⊠ *700 State Dr., Exposition Park,* ☎ *323/724–3623; 213/744–2019 IMAX,* WEB *www.casciencectr.org.* ◻ *Free, except for IMAX (prices vary); parking $5.* ⊙ *Daily 10–5.*

★ ❷ **Japanese American National Museum.** What was it like to grow up on a coffee plantation in Hawaii? How difficult was life for Japanese Americans interned in concentration camps during World War II? These questions are addressed by changing exhibits at this museum in Little Tokyo. Insightful volunteer docents are on hand to share their own stories and experiences. The museum occupies an 85,000-square-ft adjacent pavilion as well as its original site in a renovated 1925 Buddhist temple. ⊠ *369 E. 1st St., at Central Ave., Downtown,* ☎ *213/625–0414,* WEB *www.janm.org.* ◻ *$6, free Thurs. 5 PM–7:30 PM and 3rd Thurs. of the month 10 AM–7:30 PM.* ⊙ *Tues., Wed., Fri., and weekends 10–5, Thurs. 10–8.*

★ ❶ **The Museum of Contemporary Art (MOCA).** The 5,000-piece permanent collection of MOCA (art from 1940 to the present, including works by Mark Rothko, Franz Kline, Susan Rothenberg, Diane Arbus, and Robert Frank) is split between **Geffen Contemporary** and the galleries at California Plaza in a red sandstone building designed by Japanese architect Arata Isozaki. MOCA also sponsors at least 20 exhibitions a year by both established and new artists in all visual media. ⊠ *250 S. Grand Ave., Downtown,* ☎ *213/626–6222,* WEB *www.moca.org.* ◻ *$8, free on same day with Geffen Contemporary admission, and also Thurs. 5–8.* ⊙ *Tues., Wed., Fri.–Sun. 11–5; Thurs. 11–8.*

★ ☝ ❺ **Natural History Museum of Los Angeles County.** With more than 3½ million specimens in its halls and galleries, this is the third-largest museum of its type in the United States after the Field Museum in Chicago and the American Museum of Natural History in New York. It has a rich collection of prehistoric fossils; and extensive bird, insect, and marine-life exhibits. A brilliant display of stones can be seen in the Gem and Mineral Hall. An elaborate taxidermy exhibit shows North American and African mammals in detailed replicas of their natural habitats. Exhibits typifying various cultural groups include pre-Columbian artifacts and a display of crafts from the South Pacific. The Ralph M. Parsons Discovery Center for children has hands-on exhibits. ⊠ *900 Exposition Blvd., Exposition Park,* ☎ *213/763–3466,* WEB *www.nhm.org.* ◻ *$8, free 1st Tues. of month.* ⊙ *Weekdays 9–5, weekends 10–5.*

★ ☝ ❸ **Olvera Street.** Lively, one-block Olvera Street tantalizes with tile walkways, piñatas, mariachis, and authentic Mexican food. Made into an open-air Mexican market in 1930, the street is the symbol of the city's beginnings when the original settlers—11 families of Indian, Spanish, Black, and mixed heritage—built earthen and willow huts near the river. Now that heritage is commemorated by the **El Pueblo de Los Angeles Historical Monument.**

The weekends that fall around two Mexican holidays, Cinco de Mayo (May 5) and Independence Day (September 16), draw huge crowds to the already lively and musical area. To see Olvera Street at its quietest and perhaps loveliest, visit late on a weekday afternoon, when long shadows heighten the romantic feeling of the passageway. For information, stop by the **Olvera Street Visitors Center,** in the Sepulveda House (⊠ *622 N. Main St.,* ☎ *213/628–1274,* WEB *www.olvera-street.com*), a Victorian built in 1887 as a hotel and boardinghouse. The center is open Monday–Saturday 10–3. Free 50-minute walking tours leave here at 10, 11, and noon Tuesday–Sunday.

Hollywood

Since the 1920s, Hollywood has lured us with its carefully manufactured images promising showbiz glitz and glamour. As visitors, we just want a glimpse of that sexy sophistication, a chance to come close enough to be able to say, "I was there!" Reality check: Hollywood is really a working town. Granted, some of the people who work in Hollywood—actors, directors, writers, composers—are among the highest paid and most celebrated workers in the world. But most of them face the same workaday grind as the rest of us, commuting daily to a factory—that is, a movie, television, or recording studio—and working long hours every day. For many years, the neighborhood slid into decay. But since 2000, Hollywood has undergone some serious revitalization, bringing back the glamor of the 1920s, '30s, and '40s. Restored 1920s facades beckon like doorways to a bygone era. Trendy restaurants and chic nightclubs have emerged, and perhaps most spectacular of all, the ritzy Hollywood & Highland complex opened with attractive new shops and theaters.

A Good Tour

Numbers in the text correspond to numbers in the margin and on the Hollywood map.

Start off by driving up into the Hollywood Hills on Beachwood Drive (off Franklin Avenue, just east of Gower Street) for an up-close look at one of the world's most familiar icons: the HOLLYWOOD sign ①. Follow the small sign pointing the way to the LAFD Helispot. Turn left onto Rodgerton Drive, which twists and turns higher into the hills. At Deronda Drive, turn right and drive to the end. The HOLLYWOOD sign looms off to the left. Turn around and retrace your route down the hill, back to Beachwood for the drive into Hollywood.

Make a right (west) at Franklin Avenue, and prepare to turn left at the next light at Gower Street. At Gower and Santa Monica Boulevard, look for the entrance to Hollywood Forever Cemetery, where numerous celebrities are buried. Abutting the cemetery's southern edge is Paramount Pictures, the last major studio in Hollywood. The famous gate Norma Desmond (Gloria Swanson in *Sunset Boulevard*) was driven through is no longer accessible to the public, but a replica marks the entrance on Melrose Avenue: turn left from Gower Street to reach the gate. Next, drive west (right off Gower) on Melrose for three blocks to Vine Street, turn right, and continue to the famous intersection of Hollywood and Vine. Across the street, the so-called "record stack" Capitol Records Tower resembles—to those who remember vinyl—a stack of 45s. A few steps east of the intersection on Hollywood Boulevard the ornate Pantages Theater, home of Academy Awards from 1949 to 1959, has been restored to its original elegance. A block west on Ivar Street are the former homes of literary giants William Faulkner and Nathanael West. Drive west along Hollywood Boulevard, stopping along the way for a look at the bronze stars that make up the **Hollywood Walk of Fame** ②, or to visit the Lingerie Museum at the purple Frederick's of Hollywood or the Hollywood Wax Museum—both shrines to Hollywood camp.

At Hollywood Boulevard and Las Palmas Avenue is the Egyptian Theatre. Continue west on Hollywood Boulevard two blocks until you see the giant, Babylonian-themed, hotel-retail-entertainment complex **Hollywood & Highland** ③, which includes the 3,300-seat Kodak Theatre, the new permanent home to the Academy Awards. Adjacent to Hollywood & Highland is **Mann's Chinese Theatre** ④, a genuine, if kitschy, monument to Hollywood history. The elaborate pagoda-style movie palace is still the biggest draw along Hollywood Boulevard. Also on the north side of the boulevard and west of the Chinese Theatre is the **Hollywood Entertainment Museum** ⑤. From the museum, cross Hollywood Boulevard and loop back east past the historic Hollywood Roosevelt Hotel, the site of the Cinegrill cabaret. In the next block, the Disney folks have impeccably restored the El Capitan Theatre's elaborate facade. Several blocks north of the boulevard on Highland Avenue is the Hollywood Bowl, where you can visit its interesting museum in the daytime or enjoy the outdoor concerts on summer evenings.

For a spectacular Cinemascope view of the glittering city lights, from Hollywood to the ocean, the **Griffith Observatory** perched on a promontory in Griffith Park is the place to take it all in.

TIMING

Plan to spend the better part of a morning or afternoon taking in Hollywood. Hollywood Boulevard attracts a sometimes-bizarre group of folks; if you've got children in tow, stick to a daytime walk. Later in the evening, you can return to Hollywood for a cabaret performance at the Cinegrill, a movie at the Chinese or the Egyptian, or a summertime concert at the Hollywood Bowl.

Sights to See

Griffith Observatory. High on a hillside overlooking the city, the Griffith Observatory is one of the most celebrated icons of Los Angeles, as much for the spectacular views as for academic astronomy shows in the planetarium, the free telescope viewings, and astronomy exhibits in the Hall of Science. Unfortunately, the building is closed through August 2004 for a major renovation. However, the grounds are open most of the time, so you can still take in the view. You might recognize the observatory and grounds from such movies as *Rebel Without a Cause* and *The Terminator*. ⊠ *2800 E. Observatory Rd., Griffith Park,* ☎ *323/664–1191,* WEB *www.griffithobservatory.org.*

★ ❸ **Hollywood & Highland.** This megamillion-dollar ($550 million and counting) hotel-retail-entertainment complex has finally brought back the glitz and attention Hollywood lacked for years. A grand staircase leads up to **Babylon Court,** a replica of the set used in the 1916 movie *Intolerance.* It's presided over by a pair of 33-ft-high elephants. An arch at the entrance frames the HOLLYWOOD sign, visible in the hills above. Surrounding Babylon Court are designer and chain stores, restaurants, concert halls, movie theaters, and a live-broadcast studio. Academy Awards attendees enter the gorgeous **Kodak Theatre** through a resplendent red-carpeted portal, designed to resemble a lineup of 1920s movie palaces. Abundant underground parking is accessible from Highland Avenue. There's also a Metro Red Line stop. ⊠ *Hollywood Blvd. and Highland Ave.,* WEB *www.hollywoodandhighland.com.* ▧ *Parking $10.*

❺ **Hollywood Entertainment Museum.** A multimedia presentation in the main rotunda and interactive exhibits along the 45-minute–one-hour guided tour track the evolution of Hollywood, from the low-tech silent era to today's hyper-tech world of special effects. Highlights are the detailed miniature model of 1936 Hollywood, and sets from television shows such as the original *Star Trek* and the bar from *Cheers,* into which the series' stars carved their names. Another exhibit displays the Max Factor makeup first used by movie stars. ⊠ *7021 Hollywood Blvd. , Hollywood,* ☎ *323/465–7900,* WEB *www.hollywoodmuseum.com.* ▧ *$8.75.* ⊙ *Mon., Tues., Thurs.–Sun. 11–6.*

★ ❶ **HOLLYWOOD Sign.** With letters 50 ft tall, Hollywood's trademark sign can be spotted from miles away. The sign, which originally spelled out "Hol-

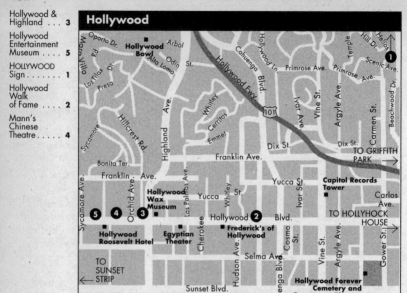

lywoodland," was erected on Mt. Lee in the Hollywood Hills in 1923 to promote a real-estate development. In 1949 the "land" portion of the sign was taken down. Over the years pranksters have altered it, albeit temporarily, to spell out "Hollyweed" (in the 1970s, to commemorate lenient marijuana laws), "Go Navy" (before a Rose Bowl game), and "Perotwood" (during the 1992 presidential election). In 1994, however, a fence and surveillance equipment were installed surrounding the sign to deter intruders.

★ ❷ **Hollywood Walk of Fame.** All along this mile-long stretch of Hollywood Boulevard sidewalk, entertainment legends' names are embossed in brass, each at the center of a pink star embedded in dark-gray terrazzo. Since then, more than 1,600 others have been immortalized. Here's a miniguide to a few of the more famous celebs' stars: Marlon Brando at 1765 Vine, Charlie Chaplin at 6751 Hollywood, W. C. Fields at 7004 Hollywood, Clark Gable at 1608 Vine, Marilyn Monroe at 6774 Hollywood (in front of McDonald's), Rudolph Valentino at 6164 Hollywood, Michael Jackson at 6927 Hollywood, and John Wayne at 1541 Vine. You can always contact the **Hollywood Chamber of Commerce** (✉ 7018 Hollywood Blvd., ☏ 323/469–8311, WEB www.hollywoodcoc.org) for celebrity-star locations and information on future star installations.

★ ❹ **Mann's Chinese Theatre.** The former "Grauman's Chinese," a fantasy of Chinese pagodas and temples, is a place only Hollywood could turn out. Although you have to buy a movie ticket to appreciate the interior trappings, the courtyard is open to the public. Here you'll see those oh-so-famous cement hand- and footprints. More than 160 celebrities have contributed imprints of their appendages for posterity, along with a few other oddball imprints, like the one of Jimmy Durante's nose. ✉ 6925 Hollywood Blvd. , Hollywood, ☏ 323/461–3331.

Museum Row and the Farmers Market

Just east of Fairfax Avenue in the Miracle Mile district is the three-block stretch of Wilshire Boulevard known as Museum Row, with five museums of widely varying themes and a prehistoric tar pit to boot. Only a few blocks away is the historic Farmers Market, a great place to start the day with coffee and pastries and people-watching. Finding parking along Wilshire Boulevard can present a challenge anytime of the day; you'll find advice on the information phone lines of most attractions.

A Good Tour

Numbers in the text correspond to numbers in the margin and on the Wilshire Boulevard, Museum Row, and Farmers Market map.

Start your day at the **Farmers Market** ①, a few blocks north of Wilshire Boulevard at 3rd Street and Fairfax Avenue. Then, drive south on Fairfax Avenue to the Miracle Mile district of Wilshire Boulevard, which streches between La Brea and Fairfax avenues. Turn left onto Wilshire and proceed to Ogden Drive or a block farther to Spaulding Avenue, where you can park the car and set out on foot to explore the museums.

The large complex of contemporary buildings surrounded by a park (on the corner of Wilshire and Ogden Drive) is the **Los Angeles County Museum of Art (LACMA)** ②. It's the largest art museum west of Chicago and houses works spanning the history of art from ancient times to the present. Also occupying the park are the prehistoric **La Brea Tar Pits** ③, where many of the fossils displayed at the adjacent Page Museum at the La Brea Tar Pits were found. Across Wilshire is the Craft and Folk Art Museum (CAFAM) and, back at the corner of Wilshire and Fairfax, the **Petersen Automotive Museum** ④ which surveys the history of the car in Los Angeles.

TIMING

The museums open between 10 and noon, so plan your tour around the opening time of the museum you wish to visit first. LACMA is open Monday but closed Wednesday, and has extended hours into the evening, closing at 8 (9 on Friday). The other museums are closed on Monday (except the Page). Set aside a good portion of a day to do this entire tour: an hour or two for the Farmers Market and four hours for the museums.

Sights to See

★ ❶ **Farmers Market.** In July 1934, two entrepreneurs envisioned a European-style open-air market, to be built near the corner of 3rd Street and Fairfax, where farmers would sell their produce to local housewives. The idea was an instant success: farmers agreed to pay the 50¢ daily parking fee; in exchange, they got to display their wares on the tailgates of their trucks. Today the market has more than 110 stalls and more than 20 restaurants, many with alfresco dining under umbrellas. Close to CBS Television Studios, the market is a major hub for stars and stargazers, tourists and locals—it's one of the few community gathering points in the sprawling city of L.A. An open-air shopping and entertainment center called the Grove has been constructed along the northern and eastern flanks of the Farmers Market. An electric, steel-wheeled "Red Car" trolley shuttles visitors back and forth between the Grove and the Farmers Market. Parking is free. ⊠ *6333 W. 3rd St., Fairfax District,* ☎ *323/933–9211,* WEB *www.farmersmarketla.com.* ☼ *May–Oct., Mon.–Sat. 9–7, Sun. 10–6; Nov–Apr., Mon.–Sat. 9–6:30, Sun. 10–5.*

434

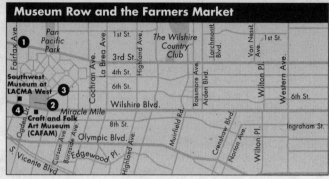

★ ❸ **La Brea Tar Pits.** About 40,000 years ago, deposits of oil rose to the Earth's surface, collected in shallow pools, and coagulated into sticky asphalt. In the early 20th century, geologists discovered that the sticky goo contained the largest collection of Pleistocene, or Ice Age, fossils ever found at one location: more than 600 species of birds, mammals, plants, reptiles, and insects. More than 100 tons of fossil bones have been removed in excavations over the last seven decades, making this one of the world's most famous fossil sites. Statues of a family of mammoths in the big pit near the corner of Wilshire and Curson suggest how many of them were entombed: edging down to a pond of water to drink, animals were caught in the tar and unable to extricate themselves. The **Page Museum at the La Brea Tar Pits** displays fossils from the tar pits. ✉ *Hancock Park, Miracle Mile,* WEB *www.tarpits.org.* 🎟 *Free.*

❷ **Los Angeles County Museum of Art (LACMA).** Since it opened in 1966, LACMA has assembled an encyclopedic collection of more than 150,000 works from around the world; its collection is widely considered the most comprehensive in the western United States. American, Latin American, Far Eastern, Islamic, and South and Southeast Asian works are especially well represented. The museum's five buildings also house fine collections of costumes and textiles, decorative arts, European paintings and sculpture, photography, drawings, and prints. Heavy on Mexican modern masters (Rivera, Tamayo, Orozco, Siquieros), the Bernard and Edith Lewin galleries also include the work of Cuban artist Wifredo Lam, Chilean Roberto Mata, Guatemalan Carlos Merida, the Uruguayan painter Pedro Figari. LACMA West also contains the Experimental Gallery that, with its high- and low-tech interactive technologies, reading room, and video stations, is geared primarily to schoolchildren and families. ✉ *5905 Wilshire Blvd., Miracle Mile,* ☎ *323/857–6000; 323/857–0098 TDD,* WEB *www.lacma.org.* 🎟 *$7, free 2nd Tues. of month.* ☉ *Mon., Tues., Thurs. noon–8; Fri. noon–9; weekends 11–8.*

★ ☺ ❹ **Petersen Automotive Museum.** More than just a building full of antique or unique cars, the Petersen proves highly entertaining and informative, thanks to the lifelike dioramas and street scenes that help establish a context for the history of the automobile and its influence on our lives. Rotating exhibits include Hollywood-celebrity and movie cars (for example, Fred's rockmobile from *The Flintstones* flick), "muscle" cars (like a 1969 Dodge Daytona 440 Magnum), motorcycles, and commemorative displays of the Ferrari. A children's interactive Discovery Center illustrates the mechanics of the automobile. ✉ *6060 Wilshire Blvd., Miracle Mile,* ☎ *323/930–2277,* WEB *www.petersen.org.* 🎟 *$7.* ☉ *Tues.–Sun. 10–6.*

Beverly Hills and West Hollywood

If you've got money to spend—lots of it—then come to Beverly Hills. Rodeo Drive is the platinum vein of its commercial district, a.k.a. the Golden Triangle. Beverly Hills means expensive boutiques; sky-high real estate prices; legendary hotels; high-powered restaurants; and—most of all—movie stars. Although nowadays stars are just as likely to be hiding out on a ranch in Montana, many stars still live in Beverly Hills, and each year the neighborhood draws armies of visitors on the lookout for a famous face and a glimpse of an opulent lifestyle most mortals are left only to imagine.

Northeast of and bordering Beverly Hills is West Hollywood, which isn't so much the place to "see" things like museums or movie studios as it is a place to "do" things—like go to a nightclub, party at a gay disco, eat at a world-famous restaurant, or attend an art gallery opening. Sunset Strip has been Hollywood's nighttime playground since the end of Prohibition, and today the Strip is still going strong. West Hollywood is also home to an important interior design and art gallery trade. And in the 1980s, a neighborhood coalition of seniors and gays and lesbians succeeded in gaining cityhood for West Hollywood. The city has emerged as one of the most progressive and gay-friendly cities in Southern California. The annual Gay Pride Parade is one of the largest in nation, drawing tens of thousands of participants each June.

A Good Tour

Numbers in the text correspond to numbers in the margin and on the Beverly Hills, West Hollywood, and the Westside map.

Begin a tour of Beverly Hills with a drive into the hills above Sunset Boulevard for a look at some of the enormous homes that make the neighborhood famous. Greystone Mansion, used in such films as *The Witches of Eastwick* and *Indecent Proposal* is on Loma Vista Drive. Less than a mile west on Sunset is the landmark Beverly Hills Hotel. Turn south here onto **Rodeo Drive** ① (pronounced ro-*day*-o). You'll pass through a residential neighborhood before hitting the shopping stretch of Rodeo south of Santa Monica Boulevard. This is where you'll want to get out of the car and walk around. At Rodeo Drive and Dayton Way, the Beverly Hills Trolley departs for 40- and 50-minute tours of the city (May–December). Across Wilshire, the Regent Beverly Wilshire Hotel serves as a temporary residence for the rich, famous, and cultured. The **Museum of Television & Radio** ② is a block east of Rodeo, on Beverly Drive at Little Santa Monica Boulevard.

After a visit to the museum and lunch on Beverly Drive, serious shoppers may want to detour to Century City, a few blocks southwest of Beverly Hills. Otherwise, head east on Wilshire Boulevard and then north on Robertson Boulevard to explore West Hollywood. The first sight you'll come to is the landmark **Pacific Design Center** ③. There's public parking available at the PDC, and you can get out and walk back a block to Santa Monica Boulevard or head west on Melrose Avenue. This walkable section of town is known as the **Avenues of Art and Design** ④, so designated because of the proliferation of design studios and art galleries. Next, drive up Robertson and go right on Santa Monica Boulevard,. This stretch of Santa Monica, until around La Ciénega Boulevard, is the commercial core of West Hollywood's large gay and lesbian community. At Crescent Heights Boulevard, turn left and head north to **Sunset Boulevard** ⑤. Turn left (west) on Sunset. Within the first block, look up the hill to the right for a glimpse of the famous hotel Chateau Marmont. About three blocks west of Chateau Marmont, you'll pass the landmark art deco masterpiece, the Argyle hotel, on the left. Next up are two famous nightclubs on the **Sunset Strip** ⑥: the Delta-inspired House of Blues on the left and the Comedy Store on the right. Sunset Plaza (the 8600 block of Sunset Boulevard, 2 blocks west of La Cienega Boulevard) is a good place to get out of the car and take a stroll, do some high-end window-shopping, or pass the time people-watching from a sidewalk café or restaurant. Look for parking in the lot behind the shops, off Sunset Plaza Drive. Have dinner and check out the nightlife along Sunset or Santa Monica boulevards.

TIMING

After a drive up into the hills for a look at the opulent homes, plan to arrive in the Golden Triangle of Beverly Hills mid-morning. Spend a couple of hours strolling along Rodeo Drive and having lunch. Skip either the Museum of Television and Radio or the Pacific Design Center if you want to take a leisurely walk around Sunset Plaza or Melrose Avenue. Keep in mind that traffic on Sunset, Santa Monica, and Wilshire boulevards is heavy most of the day, especially at night and on weekends. Special "no-cruising" regulations are in effect at certain times on certain streets. For street parking, bring plenty of quarters; parking on residential streets is by permit only.

Sights to See

❹ **Avenues of Art and Design.** A concentration of design studios and art and antique galleries along Melrose Avenue, San Vicente Boulevard, Robertson Boulevard, North Almont, and other streets around the Pacific Design Center has given rise to this catchy designation. The galleries are very high-end, but it doesn't cost anything to look (sometimes the window is as far as you can get; many of these studios are "to the trade only"). Periodically, usually on the first Saturday evening of the month, several of the galleries host group-opening receptions, or "Gallery Walks" to premiere new exhibits and artists. You can nibble on cheese and fruit and see some great art. Contact the **West Hollywood Convention and Visitors Bureau** (☎ 310/289–2525 or 800/368–6020, WEB www.visitwesthollywood.com) for information.

❷ **Museum of Television & Radio.** Revisit the great "Where's the beef?" commercial at this sleek stone-and-glass building, a sister to the Museum of Television & Radio in New York, entirely duplicating its collection of 100,000 programs spanning eight decades. Search for your favorite commercials and television and radio shows on easy-to-use computers, and then watch or listen to them in an adjacent room. There are special exhibits of television- and radio-related art and costumes, as well as frequent seminars with television and radio cast members. ✉ 465 N. Beverly Dr., Beverly Hills, ☎ 310/786–1000, WEB www.mtr.org. ✉ $6. ⊙ Wed. and Fri.–Sun. noon–5, Thurs. noon–9.

❸ **Pacific Design Center.** Cesar Pelli designed these two architecturally intriguing buildings, one sheathed in blue glass (the "Blue Whale"), the other in green (the "Green Whale"). Together, they house 150 design showrooms, making this the largest interior design complex in the western United States. The showrooms are open only to the trade, but you can have lunch or coffee at one of three cafés on the premises or visit the satellite **MOCA Gallery at Pacific Design Center** (☎ 213/626–6222, WEB www.moca.org; ✉ $3). Exhibits emphasize architecture and design. ✉ 8687 Melrose Ave., West Hollywood, ☎ 310/657–0800, WEB www.p-d-c.com. ⊙ Open weekdays 9–5.

★ ❶ **Rodeo Drive.** No longer an exclusive shopping street where a well-heeled clientele shops for $200 pairs of socks wrapped in gold leaf, Rodeo Drive is one of Southern California's bona fide tourist attractions. Just as if they were at Disneyland or in Hollywood, T-shirt-and-shorts-clad

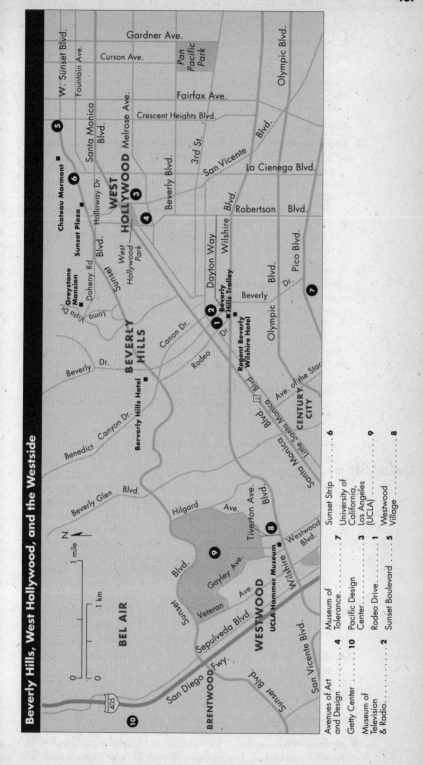

Beverly Hills, West Hollywood, and the Westside

437

Gardner Ave.

W. Sunset Blvd.

Fountain Ave.

Curson Ave.

Pan Pacific Park

Olympic Blvd.

Fairfax Ave.

Santa Monica Blvd.

Crescent Heights Blvd.

5

Melrose Ave.

3rd St.

Blvd.

Chateau Marmont

6

WEST HOLLYWOOD

Beverly Blvd.

Holloway Dr.

San Vicente

La Cienega Blvd.

Sunset Plaza

3

4

Robertson Blvd.

West Hollywood Park

Dayton Way

Wilshire

Doheny Rd.

Greystone Mansion

Sunset Blvd.

BEVERLY HILLS

Beverly Hills Trolley

Beverly

Dr. Pico Blvd.

7

Loma Vista Dr.

2

1

Regent Beverly Wilshire Hotel

Olympic

Canon Dr.

Rodeo

Beverly Hills Hotel

Beverly Dr.

Blvd.

Ave. of the Stars

CENTURY CITY

Canyon Dr.

Dr.

Benedict

Little Santa Monica Blvd.

Santa Monica Blvd.

Beverly Glen Blvd.

Hilgard Ave.

Tiverton Ave.

N

Westwood Blvd.

8

½ mile

Blvd.

Sunset

Gayley Ave.

WESTWOOD

9

UCLA Hammer Museum

Wilshire

1 km

Veteran Ave.

BEL AIR

Sepulveda Blvd.

San Diego Fwy.

San Vicente Blvd.

405

San Diego Fwy.

Sunset Blvd.

BRENTWOOD

10

Avenues of Art and Design **4**

Getty Center **10**

Museum of Television & Radio **2**

Museum of Tolerance **7**

Pacific Design Center **3**

Rodeo Drive **1**

Sunset Boulevard . . . **5**

Sunset Strip **6**

University of California, Los Angeles (UCLA) **9**

Westwood Village **8**

tourists wander along this tony stretch of avenue, window shopping at Tiffany & Co., Gucci, Armani, Hermes, Harry Winston, and Lladro. Fortunately the browsing is free, and strolling the section of Rodeo between Santa Monica and Wilshire boulevards is a fun way to spend the afternoon. Several nearby restaurants have patios where you can sip a drink while watching fashionable shoppers saunter by. At the southern end of Rodeo Drive (at Wilshire Boulevard) is **Via Rodeo**, a curvy cobblestone street designed to resemble a European shopping *via. Beverly Hills,* WEB *www.rodeodrive.com.*

❺ **Sunset Boulevard.** One of the most fabled avenues in the world, Sunset Boulevard began humbly enough in the 18th century as a route from El Pueblo de Los Angeles (today's downtown L.A.) to the ranches in the west and then to the Pacific Ocean. In West Hollywood, it turns into the sexy and seductive Sunset Strip, then slips quietly into the tony environs of Beverly Hills and Bel-Air, twisting and winding past gated estates. Continuing on past UCLA in Westwood, through Brentwood and Pacific Palisades, Sunset finally descends to the beach, the edge of the continent, and the setting sun.

❻ **Sunset Strip.** The 1¾-mi stretch of Sunset Boulevard between Crescent Heights Boulevard and Doheny Drive, known as the Sunset Strip, has been an L.A. nighttime hot spot for decades. In the 1930s and '40s, stars like Tyrone Power, Errol Flynn, and Rita Hayworth dressed up in tuxedos and fancy gowns for wild evenings of dancing and drinking at nightclubs like Trocadero, Ciro's, and Mocambo. By the '60s and '70s, the Strip had become the center of rock 'n' roll: Johnny Rivers, the Byrds, the Doors, Elton John, and Bruce Springsteen gave legendary performances on stages at clubs like the Whisky A Go-Go and Roxy. These days it's the **Viper Room** (✉ 8852 Sunset Blvd., West Hollywood, ☏ 310/358–1880), the **House of Blues** (✉ 8430 Sunset Blvd., West Hollywood, ☏ 323/848–5100, WEB www.hob.com), and **The Key Club** (✉ 9039 Sunset Blvd., West Hollywood, ☏ 310/274–5800, WEB www.keyclub.com) that keep young Hollywood busy after dark.

The Westside

Like the Mason-Dixon line marking the boundary between the North and the South, La Cienega Boulevard is the de facto demarcation between the east and west sides of Los Angeles. To the east of La Cienega, the city displays its more ethnic, heterogeneous side; to the west, consumerism is highly conspicuous, and looking good—and prosperous—is the name of the game. An informal and unscientific survey of Westside districts like West Los Angeles, Westwood, Bel-Air, Brentwood, and Pacific Palisades would probably reveal high concentrations of plastic surgeons and BMWs. The Westside, however, is also rich cultural territory, and the rewards of visiting UCLA's Westwood campus, the Museum of Tolerance, and the Getty Center in Brentwood are great, even if you just work out at the Y and drive a rented compact.

A Good Tour

Numbers in the text correspond to numbers in the margin and on the Beverly Hills and the Westside map.

The major sights on the Westside are spread out, so choosing a starting point is arbitrary; the best strategy is to select one of the major attractions as a destination and plan your visit accordingly. A visit to the **Museum of Tolerance** ⑦ in the morning, for example, can be easily followed with lunch and shopping in Beverly Hills or Century City. Afterward, you might drive through **Westwood Village** ⑧, home of the **UCLA** ⑨ campus and the Fowler Museum of Cultural History, stopping at the UCLA/Armand Hammer Museum of Art and Cultural Center. The vast **Getty Center** ⑩, fortresslike atop a hill in Brentwood, is currently L.A.'s most high-profile attraction.

TIMING

Advance reservations are not essential, but well-advised, for visits to the Museum of Tolerance, closed Saturday, and the Getty Center, closed Monday—so plan accordingly. Each museum merits at least a half day. In the evening and on weekends, Westwood Village and Brentwood's commercial district on San Vicente Boulevard come alive with a busy restaurant, café, and street scene. The afternoon rush hour is predictably congested along Wilshire and Sunset boulevards.

Sights to See

★ ⑩ **The Getty Center.** Atop a hill in Brentwood, the Getty Center occupies one of the most visible locations in Los Angeles, and its gardens and courtyards afford beautiful views of the city, reaching all the way out to the ocean and Catalina Island beyond. Many people go for the view but leave enriched by the cultural wealth and beauty of the center's museum, research institute gallery, libraries, and gorgeous gardens. The five, two-story pavilions containing the museum are the first stop for most people, and are well worth the hassle of getting into the museum. Parking reservations ($5) are required weekdays before 4 PM, for large groups, and for events. You can drive here without reservations on weekends, or take public transportation (MTA #561 or Santa Monica Big Blue Bus #14), but you'll still have to wait in line to reach the entrance. If you know when you want to go, reserve a few weeks ahead. Same-day reservations are sometimes possible.

J. Paul Getty, the billionaire oil magnate and art collector, began collecting Greek and Roman antiquities and French decorative arts in the 1930s. He opened the J. Paul Getty Museum at his Malibu estate in 1954, and in the 1970s, he built a re-creation of an ancient Roman village to house his initial collection. When Getty died in 1976, the museum received a endowment of $700 million that grew to a reported $4.2 billion. The Malibu villa, closed in 1997, is under renovation until further notice. The white city on a hill that is the Getty Center was designed by architect Richard Meier and unites the museum and its affiliated research, conservation, and philanthropic institutes. The permanent collections include European paintings, drawings, sculpture, illuminated manuscripts, furniture, and decorative arts, as well as American and European photographs. Notable among the paintings are Rembrandt's *The Abduction of Europa,* van Gogh's *Irises,* Monet's *Wheatstack, Snow Effects, Morning,* Cézanne's *Young Italian Woman Leaning on Her Elbow,* and James Ensor's *Christ's Entry Into Brussels.* ✉ *1200 Getty Center Dr., Brentwood,* ☎ *310/440–7300,* WEB *www.getty.edu.* ⚏ *Free, $5 parking.* ☉ *Tues.–Sun. 10–6.*

★ ❼ **Museum of Tolerance.** Using interactive technology, this important museum, (part of the Simon Weisenthal Center) challenges visitors to confront bigotry and racism. One of the most affecting sections covers the Holocaust, with film footage of deportation scenes and simulated sets of concentration camps. Anne Frank artifacts are part of the museum's permanent collection. Interactive exhibits include the "Millenium Machine," which engages visitors in finding solutions to human rights abuses around the world. To ensure a visit to this popular museum, make reservations in advance (especially for Fridays, Sundays, and holidays) and plan to spend at least three hours there. Testimony from Holocaust survivors is offered at specified times. ✉ *9786 W. Pico Blvd., south of Beverly Hills,* ☎ *310/553–8403,* WEB *www.wiesenthal.com/mot.* ⊠ *$9.* ⊙ *Sun. 11–5, Mon.–Thurs. 11:30–4, Fri. 11:30–1 (Fri. 11:30–3 Apr.–Oct.).*

❾ University of California, Los Angeles (UCLA). With spectacular buildings such as a Romanesque library, the parklike UCLA campus makes for a fine stroll. In the heart of the north campus, the **Franklin Murphy Sculpture Garden** contains more than 70 works of artists such as Henry Moore and Gaston Lachaise. The **Mildred Mathias Botanic Garden**, which contains some 5,000 species of plants from all over the world in a 7-acre outdoor garden, is in the southeast section of the campus and is accessible from Tiverton Avenue. West of the main campus bookstore, the **Morgan Center Hall of Fame** displays the sports memorabilia and trophies of the university's athletic departments. Many visitors head straight to the **UCLA Fowler Museum of Cultural History** (☎ 310/825–4361; ⊠ $5, free Thursday), which presents changing exhibits on the world's diverse cultures and visual arts, especially those of Africa, Asia, Oceania, and Native and Latin America. The eclectic permanent collection at the comparatively small **UCLA Hammer Museum** (☎ 310/443–7000; ⊠ $4.50, free Thursday, 3-hr parking $2.75 with validation) contains thousands of works by Old Masters, French Impressionists, and Postimpressionists, including some by Daumier, van Gogh, Gauguin, Degas, and Cassatt. Additionally, the museum houses the UCLA Grunwald Center for the Graphic Arts, a collection of more than 35,000 works of art on paper including prints; drawings by Michelangelo, Raphael, and Rembrandt; photographs; and artists' books from the Renaissance to the present.

Campus maps and information are available at drive-by kiosks at major entrances seven days a week, and free 90-minute walking tours of the campus are given on weekdays at 10:15 and 2:15, and Saturdays at 10:15. Call 310/825–8764 for reservations, which are required several days to two weeks in advance. The campus has indoor and outdoor cafés, plus bookstores selling UCLA Bruins paraphernalia. The main entrance gate is on Westwood Boulevard. Campus parking costs $6. ⊠ *Le Conte, Hilgard, and Gayley Aves. and Sunset Blvd. border the campus, in Westwood,* WEB *www.ucla.edu.*

❽ Westwood Village. Laid out in the 1930s as a master-planned shopping district next to the UCLA campus, Westwood Village is now one of the busiest places in the city on weekend evenings. A lively youth-oriented street scene that gets so busy during the summer that many streets are closed to car traffic and visitors must park at the Federal Building (Wilshire Blvd. and Veteran Ave.) and shuttle over. Besides having surpassed Hollywood as the city's moviegoing center, Westwood is the site of a cemetery, with one of the world's most famous graves. **Westwood Village Memorial Park** (⊠ 1218 Glendon Ave.) is tucked behind one of the office buildings on Wilshire Boulevard. Marilyn Monroe is buried in a simply marked crypt on the north wall. Also buried here are Truman Capote and Natalie Wood.

Santa Monica, Venice, and Malibu

In Los Angeles all roads lead, eventually, to the beach and Santa Monica, Venice, and Malibu. These coastal communities hug the Santa Monica Bay, in an arc of diversity, from the rich-as-can-be Malibu to the bohemian-seedy mix of Venice. What they have in common, however, is cleaner coastal air and an emphasis on being out in the sunshine, always within sight of the Pacific.

A Good Drive

*Numbers in the text correspond to numbers in the margin and on the
Santa Monica, Venice, and Malibu map.*

Look for the arched neon sign at the foot of Colorado Avenue marking the entrance to the **Santa Monica Pier** ①, the city's number-one landmark, built in 1906. Park on the pier and take a turn through Pacific
Park, a 2-acre amusement park. The wide swath of sand on the north
side of the pier is Santa Monica Beach, on hot summer weekends one
of the most crowded beaches in Southern California. From the pier,
walk to Ocean Avenue, where Palisades Park, a strip of lawn and
palms above the cliffs, provides panoramic ocean views. Three blocks
inland is the active **Third Street Promenade** ②. Next, retrieve the car
and drive two blocks inland on Colorado to Main Street. Turn right
and continue to Ocean Park Boulevard. On the southeast corner on
the side of a building is a colorful mural, and on the southwest corner
you'll find the California Heritage Museum. The next several blocks
south along Main Street are great for browsing.

Next stop: **Venice Boardwalk** ③. Walk up Main Street through the trendy
shopping district until you hit Rose Avenue. Ahead on the left you'll
spot an enormous pair of binoculars, the front of the Frank Gehry–
designed Chiat-Day Mojo building. Turn right toward the sea and the
boardwalk.

For the drive to Malibu, retrace your route along Main Street. At Pico
Boulevard, turn west, toward the ocean, and then right on Ocean Avenue. When you pass the pier, prepare to turn left down the California Incline (at the end of Palisades Park at Wilshire Boulevard) to the
Pacific Coast Highway (Highway 1). About 5 mi north, you'll pass the
J. Paul Getty Museum (not to be confused with the Getty Center in
Brentwood), closed for renovations. Another 6 mi or so will bring you
into Malibu proper. Malibu Pier is closed indefinitely due to storm damage and a lack of funds to repair it, but you can park in the adjacent
lot and take a walk on **Malibu Lagoon State Beach** ④, also known as
Surfrider Beach. On the highway side of the beach is the Moorish-Span-
ish Adamson House and Malibu Lagoon Museum, a tiled beauty with
a great Pacific view. From here, you can walk along the strand of beach
that fronts the famed Malibu Colony, the exclusive residential enclave
of celebrities.

TIMING
If you've got the time, break your coastal visit into two excursions:
Santa Monica and Venice in one, and Malibu in another. The best way
to "do" L.A.'s coastal communities is to park the car, rent a bike or a
pair of in-line skates in Santa Monica or Venice, and walk, cycle, or
skate along the 3-mi beachside bike path. Santa Monica Pier, Main Street,
and the Venice Boardwalk are interesting to observe as the day progresses. Only the boardwalk should be avoided at night, when the crowd
becomes unsavory. You can park on the Santa Monica Pier and in small
lots close to the beach in Venice (the smart thing to do, since break-
ins are common in the area) and Malibu. Main Street is a good place
to head for lunch and spend an hour or so shopping for gifts and souvenirs; Third Street Promenade is more interesting in the evening,
when cafés and restaurants are packed and strollers throng the promenade. Avoid driving to Malibu during rush hour, when traffic along
the PCH moves at a snail's pace—but do try to be there at sunset to
watch the sun dip into the Pacific.

Sights to See

④ Malibu Lagoon State Beach. Visitors are asked to stay on the boardwalks at this 5-acre haven for native and migratory birds so that the egrets, blue herons, avocets, and gulls can enjoy the marshy area. The signs listing opening and closing hours refer only to the parking lot; the lagoon itself is open 24 hours and is particularly enjoyable in the early morning and at sunset. Street-side parking is available at those times, but not at midday. ⊠ *23200 Pacific Coast Hwy., Malibu.*

OFF THE BEATEN PATH

MARINA DEL REY – A brilliant sight on a sunny day, this enormous man-made marina with moorings for 10,000 boats is just south of Venice. Stop by Burton Chace Park (at the foot of Mindanao Way) to watch the wind carry colorful sailboats out to sea. Small "Mother's Beach" (Marina Beach) has calm, protected waters ideal for young children. Call **Hornblower Dining Yachts** in Fisherman's Village (⊠ 13755 Fiji Way, Marina del Rey, ☎ 310/301–6000 or 310/301–9900, WEB www.hornblower.com) to arrange marina and dining cruises.

★ ☝ ① Santa Monica Pier. Eateries, souvenir shops, a psychic adviser, arcades, and **Pacific Park** are all part of this truncated pier at the foot of Colorado Boulevard below Palisades Park. The pier's trademark 46-horse Looff carousel, built in 1922, has appeared in many films, including *The Sting*. Free concerts are held on the pier in summer. ⊠ *Colorado Ave. and the ocean, Santa Monica,* ☎ 310/458–8900, WEB *www.santamonicapier.org.* 🎟 *Rides 25¢ and 50¢.* ☉ *Carousel: May–Sept., Tues.–Fri. 11–9, weekends 10–9; Oct.–Apr., Thurs.–Sun., hrs vary.*

② Third Street Promenade. Only foot traffic is allowed along a three-block stretch of 3rd Street, just a whiff away from the Pacific, lined with jacaranda trees, and accented with ivy-topiary dinosaur fountains. Outdoor cafés, street vendors, movie theaters, and a rich nightlife make this a main gathering spot. ⊠ *3rd St. between Wilshire Blvd. and Broadway, Santa Monica.*

★ ❸ **Venice Boardwalk.** "Boardwalk" may be something of a misnomer— it's really a paved walkway—but this L.A. must-see delivers year-round action: bicyclists zip along and bikini-clad roller and in-line skaters attract crowds as they put on impromptu demonstrations, vying for attention with magicians, fortune tellers, a chain-saw juggler, and street artists. A local bodybuilding club works out on the adjacent "Muscle Beach"—it's nearly impossible not to stop and ogle the strongmen's pecs. You can rent in-line skates, roller skates, and bicycles at the south end of the boardwalk.

The San Fernando Valley

There are other valleys in the Los Angeles area, but this is the one that people refer to simply as the Valley. Large portions of the Valley are bedroom communities of suburban tract homes and shopping centers, but most of the major film and television studios, such as Warner Bros., NBC, and CBS, have facilities here. Universal City is a one-industry town, and that industry is Universal Studios. The studio has been at this site since 1915.

A Good Drive

Numbers in the text correspond points of interest on the San Fernando Valley map.

On a clear day or evening, a trip along **Mulholland Drive** gives you a spectacular view of the sprawling San Fernando Valley below. Just over the hill from Hollywood via the Hollywood Freeway (U.S. 101, north) is Universal City, which has its own freeway off-ramp (Universal Center Drive). **Universal Studios Hollywood** ① is on a large hill overlooking the San Fernando Valley, a city-within-a-city. As you exit Universal, follow signs to Barham Boulevard. At Barham, turn left toward Burbank. After driving about a mile, the street curves around **Warner Bros. Studios** ②, whose outside wall is covered with billboards of current films and television shows. After the curve, you will be on West Olive Avenue. Keep to the right and look for the entrance to Gate No. 4 at Hollywood Way.

Just a minute away at the second big intersection, West Olive and Alameda avenues, is the main entrance to **NBC Television Studios** ③. Continue east on Alameda; on the next block to your right is Disney Studios, a very colorful bit of architecture. Drive south on Buena Vista and then turn left on Riverside to get a good look at the whimsical architecture.

TIMING

The Valley is surrounded by mountains and the major routes to and from it go through mountain passes. During rush hour, traffic jams on the Hollywood Freeway (U.S. 101/Highway 170), San Diego Freeway (I–405), and Ventura Freeway (U.S. 101/Highway 134) can be brutal, so avoid trips to or from the Valley at those times. Expect to spend a full day at Universal Studios Hollywood and CityWalk; studio tours at NBC and Warner Bros. last up to two hours.

Sights to See

Santa Monica Mountains National Recreation Area. The line that forms the boundary of the San Fernando Valley is one of the most famous thoroughfares in this vast metropolis and an urban playground. **Mulholland Drive** cuts through the Santa Monica Mountains National Recreation Area, a vast parkland that stretches along the top and west

San Fernando Valley

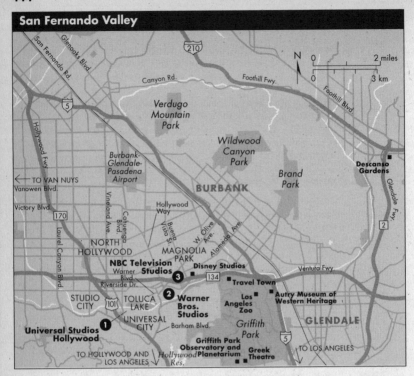

slopes of the Santa Monica Mountains from Hollywood to the Ventura County line. Driving the length of the hilltop road is slow and can be treacherous, but the rewards are sensational views of valley and city on each side and expensive homes along the way. From Hollywood reach Mulholland Drive via Outpost Drive off Franklin Avenue or Cahuenga Boulevard west via Highland Avenue north.

❸ NBC Television Studios. This major network's headquarters is in Burbank, as any regular viewer of *The Tonight Show* can't help knowing. For those who wish to be part of a live studio audience, free tickets are made available for tapings of the various NBC shows. ⊠ *3000 W. Alameda Ave., Burbank,* ☏ *818/840–3537.*

OFF THE
BEATEN PATH

SIX FLAGS MAGIC MOUNTAIN – If you're a true thrill-seeker looking for the "monster" rides and roller-coasters, this amusement park, less than an hour north of L.A., is where you'll find several of the biggest, fastest, and scariest in the entire world. In fact, Six Flags set a Guiness Book World record for most roller coasters (15) when it opened X in 2002. As at other theme parks, there are shows and parades, along with rides for younger kids, to fill out a long day. ⊠ *Magic Mountain Parkway, off I–5, 25 mi northwest of Universal Studios, Valencia,* ☏ *661/255–4100,* WEB *www.sixflags.com.* ⧉ *$43.* ☾ *Daily, except some winter weekdays; call for hrs.*

★ ☝ ❶ **Universal Studios Hollywood.** Though you probably won't see anything that actually has to do with making a real film, visiting the theme park is a sensational, even enlightening, introduction to the principles of special effects. Seated aboard a comfortable tram, which is equipped with state-of-the-art sound and LCD monitors, you can experience the parting of the Red Sea, an avalanche, a snowstorm, and a flood; meet a 30-ft-tall version of King Kong; be attacked by the ravenous killer shark of *Jaws* fame; survive an earthquake; and come face-to-face with an evil mummy. Narrated, hour-long tours traverse the 420-acre complex all day long.

Besides the tours, there are several entertainment attractions based on Universal films and television shows. The 20-minute *Spider-Man Rocks!* show, where you witness Peter Parker's transformation and watch breathtaking stunts, is one of the best. Aside from the park, **CityWalk** is a separate venue, where you'll find a slew of shops, restaurants, nightclubs, and movie theaters, including IMAX-3D. ⊠ *100 Universal City Plaza, Universal City,* ☎ *818/622–3801,* WEB *www.universalstudios.com.* ▭ *$45, parking $7.* ☉ *Mid-June–early Sept., daily 8–10; early Sept.– early June, daily 9–7.*

❷ **Warner Bros. Studios.** Two-hour tours at this major studio center in Burbank involve a lot of walking, so dress comfortably and casually. The tours are somewhat technically oriented and centered more on the actual filmmaking process than the ones at Universal. What you see varies day to day and usually has to do with what is going on at the lot (tapings of the Gilmore Girls TV show, various movies in production, etc.). Most tours take in the back-lot sets, prop construction department, and sound complex. A museum chronicles the studio's film and animation history. Reservations are required. Call at least one week in advance and ask about provisions for people with disabilities; children under 8 are not admitted. ⊠ *4000 Warner Blvd., Burbank,* ☎ *818/846–1403 or 818/954–1744,* WEB *www.wbsf.com.* ▭ *$32.* ☉ *Tours weekdays 9–3 on the half hr.*

Pasadena Area

Although now fully absorbed into the general Los Angeles sprawl, Pasadena is a separate and distinctly defined—and very refined—city. Its varied residential architecture, augmented by verdant landscaping, is among the most spectacular in Southern California. To reach Pasadena from downtown Los Angeles, drive north on the Pasadena Freeway (I–110). From Hollywood and the San Fernando Valley use the Ventura Freeway (Highway 134, east), which cuts through Glendale, skirting the foothills, before arriving in Pasadena.

A Good Tour
Numbers in the text correspond to numbers in the margin and on the Pasadena Area map.

A good place to start a short driving tour of Pasadena is on Orange Grove Boulevard, a.k.a. Millionaire's Row, where wealthy Easterners built grand mansions in the early 20th century. (One example is the Wrigley Mansion, an Italian Renaissance wedding-cake of a house with grounds and gardens reminiscent of the old neighborhood.) To get there, take the Orange Grove exit off the Ventura Freeway (Highway 134); turn right at Orange Grove and travel five blocks. From the Pasadena Freeway (Highway 110), stay on the freeway until it ends at Arroyo Parkway. From Arroyo Parkway turn left at California Boulevard and then right at Orange Grove.

Travel north on Orange Grove to Arroyo Terrace, where a left turn will take you into an architectural wonderland. Greene and Greene, the renowned Pasadena architects, designed all of the houses on Arroyo Terrace, as well as others in the area. To view their Craftsman masterpiece, the three-story, shingled **Gamble House** ①, turn right on Westmoreland Place. Also in this section is the Frank Lloyd Wright–designed Millard House ("La Miniatura") on Prospect Crescent (from Westmoreland, turn left onto Rosemont Avenue, right on Prospect Terrace, and right onto Prospect Crescent to No. 645). The famous **Rose Bowl** ② is nestled in a gully just to the west off Arroyo Boulevard. Leave this area via Rosemont Avenue, driving away from the hills to the south. From Rosemont, turn right onto Orange Grove Boulevard. Then, at Colorado Boulevard, turn left. Immediately on the left is the contemporary, austere **Norton Simon Museum** ③, a familiar backdrop to so many viewers of the annual New Year's Day Tournament of Roses Parade. West of the museum, paralleling the modern freeway bridge, Colorado crosses the historic concrete-arched Colorado Street Bridge, built in 1913, rising 160 ft above the Arroyo Seco gorge. East of the Norton Simon Museum, you'll enter **Old Town Pasadena** ④. You'll want to walk around this section of Pasadena, heading east. For a look at domed Pasadena City Hall, turn left on Fair Oaks Avenue, then right on Holly Street. Garfield Avenue will bring you back to Colorado.

A short drive south on El Molino will take you to California Boulevard, where a left turn will take you into San Marino and the **Huntington Library, Art Collections, and Botanical Gardens** ⑤ (follow the signs).

TIMING

You'll want to allow half a day for the entire driving tour. A stop at the Gamble House may take an hour, leaving plenty of time for an afternoon visit to the Norton Simon Museum. There's no need to stop at the Rose Bowl unless you happen by on the second Sunday of the month, when one of the country's largest flea markets (often called swap meets in California) is underway in the parking lot. Set aside an entire day for the Huntington Library, Art Collections, and Botanical Gardens—preferably on a sunny day, when the gardens are most pleasant.

Sights to See

★ ❶ **Gamble House.** Built by Charles and Henry Greene in 1908, this is a spectacular example of Craftsman-style bungalow architecture. The term "bungalow" can be misleading, since the Gamble House is a huge three-story home. To wealthy Easterners such as the Gambles (as in Procter & Gamble), this type of vacation home seemed informal compared with their mansions back home. What makes admirers swoon is the incredible amount of hand craftsmanship, including a teak staircase and cabinetry, Greene-designed furniture, and an Emil Lange glass door. The dark exterior has broad eaves, with sleeping porches on the second floor. If you want to see more Greene and Greene homes in the neighborhood, buy a self-guided tour map in the Gamble House's bookstore. ⌂ *4 Westmoreland Pl., Pasadena,* ☎ *626/793–3334,* WEB *www.gamblehouse.org.* ⌂ *$8.* ⊙ *Thurs.–Sun. noon–3 (tickets go on sale at 10), 1-hr tour every 20 mins.*

★ ❺ **Huntington Library, Art Collections, and Botanical Gardens.** If you have time for only one stop in the Pasadena area, it should be San Marino, where railroad tycoon Henry E. Huntington built his hilltop home in the early 1900s. The library contains more than 600,000 books and some 300 manuscripts, including such treasures as a Gutenberg Bible, the Ellesmere manuscript of Chaucer's *Canterbury Tales,* George Washington's genealogy in his own handwriting, and first editions by Ben Franklin and Shakespeare. The Huntington Gallery, housed in the original Georgian mansion built by Henry Huntington in 1911, holds a world-famous collection of British paintings, including the original *Blue Boy* by Gainsborough, *Pinkie,* a companion piece by Thomas Lawrence, and the monumental *Sarah Siddons as the Tragic Muse* by Joshua Reynolds. American paintings (Mary Cassat, Frederic Remington, and more) and decorative arts are housed in the Virginia Steele Scott Gallery of American Art. The 150-acre Huntington Gardens now in-

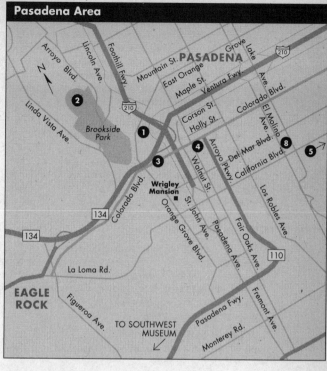

Pasadena Area

clude a Desert Garden, a Japanese Garden, a rose garden, a Shakespeare garden, and more. ✉ *1151 Oxford Rd., San Marino,* ☎ *626/405–2100; 626/405–2141 recorded information,* ⓦⒺⒷ *www.huntington.org.* ⓢ *$10, free 1st Thurs. of the month.* ☉ *Tues.–Fri. noon–4:30, weekends 10:30–4:30.*

★ ❸ **Norton Simon Museum.** Long familiar to television viewers of the New Year's Day Rose Parade, this sleek, modern building is more than just a stunning background for the passing floats. It's one of the finest small museums anywhere, with an excellent collection that spans more than 2,000 years of Western and Asian art. It all began in the 1950s when Norton Simon (Hunt-Wesson Foods, McCalls Corporation, and Canada Dry) started collecting the works of Degas, Renoir, Gauguin, and Cézanne. His collection grew to include Old Masters, Impressionists and modern work from Europe, and Indian and Southeast Asian art. After he retired, Simon reorganized the failing Pasadena Art Institute and continued to assemble one of the world's finest collections. Today the Norton Simon Museum is richest in works by Rembrandt, Goya, Picasso, and most of all, Degas. The museum's collections of Impressionist (van Gogh, Matisse, Cézanne, Monet, Renoir) and Cubist (Braque, Gris) work is extensive. Several Rodin sculptures are placed throughout the museum. From South Asia comes a sculpture collection that contains major examples from India, Nepal, Thailand, and Cambodia. The museum's remodeling was designed by architect Frank O. Gehry. Noted California landscape designer Nancy Goslee Power transformed the outdoor space into a new 79,000-square-ft sculpture garden inspired by Claude Monet's Giverny, with a natural pond at its center. ✉ *411 W. Colorado Blvd., Pasadena,* ☎ *626/449–6840,* ⓦⒺⒷ *www.nortonsimon.org.* ⓢ *$6.* ☉ *Wed.–Thurs. and Sat.–Mon. noon–6, Fri. noon–9.*

❹ Old Town Pasadena. Once the victim of decay, the area was revitalized in the 1990s as a blend of restored 19th-century brick buildings with a contemporary overlay. Cafés and restaurants are plentiful and varied. Old Town's shopping mall includes chain stores, boutiques, and speciality bookstores. In the evenings and on weekends, streets are packed with people and Old Town crackles with energy. The 12-block historic district is anchored along Colorado Boulevard, between Pasadena Avenue and Arroyo Parkway.

❹ Rose Bowl. With an enormous rose, the city of Pasadena's logo, tattooed onto its exterior, it's hard to miss this 100,000-seat stadium, host of many Super Bowls and home to the UCLA Bruins. The Rose Bowl Swap Meet, the granddaddy of West Coast flea markets, is held here the second Sunday of the month. ⊠ *Rose Bowl Drive at Rosemont Ave., Pasadena,* ☎ *626/577–3100.* ⊠ *$7–$20.* ☉ *Flea market, 2nd Sun. of month 7–3.*

Long Beach

Long Beach, wholly separate from the city of Los Angeles, began as a seaside resort in the 19th century. During the early part of the 20th century, an oil boom brought Midwesterners and Dust Bowlers in search of a better life. Bust followed boom and the city eventually took on a somewhat raw, neglected tone. A long-term redevelopment program begun in the 1970s has done much to brighten the city's image.

A Good Tour
Numbers in the text correspond to numbers in the margin and on the Long Beach Area map.

Long Beach's most famous attraction is the art deco ship, the **Queen Mary.** After a tour of it, take the Queens Way Bridge back across the bay to the **Long Beach Aquarium of the Pacific.** From here, stops along Shoreline Drive at Rainbow Harbor or the waterfront shopping center, Shoreline Village, afford the best views of the harbor and the Long Beach skyline. In the evening, head east along Ocean Boulevard to Alamitos Bay for a stroll through Naples, a picturesque enclave of canals and marinas.

TIMING
Guided tours of the *Queen Mary* last about an hour. The Long Beach Aquarium of the Pacific could occupy most of a morning or an afternoon.

Sights to See
★ ☺ **Long Beach Aquarium of the Pacific.** A full-scale model of a blue whale, the largest living creature on the planet, is suspended above the Great Hall, the entrance to this aquarium. Seventeen major exhibit tanks and 30 smaller focus tanks contain some 10,000 live marine animals. The exhibits focus on three regions of the Pacific Ocean: Southern California and Baja, the northern Pacific, and the tropical Pacific. ⊠ *100 Aquarium Way,* ☎ *562/590–3100,* WEB *www.aquariumofpacific.org.* ⊠ *$16.95.* ☉ *Daily 9–6.*

★ **Queen Mary.** The 80,000-ton *Queen Mary* was launched in 1934, a floating treasure of art deco splendor. The former first-class passenger quarters are now a hotel. Tours of the ship are available, and guests are invited to browse the 12 decks and walk around the bridge, staterooms, officers' quarters, and engine rooms. There are several restaurants and shops on board, a gallery of the ship's original art, and even a wedding chapel. ⊠ *Pier J,* ☎ *562/435–3511,* WEB *www.queenmary.com.* ⊠ *$19 for self-guided tours; $23 for guided first-class tours.* ☉ *Call for times and frequency of guided tours.*

DINING

By Bill Stern

L.A.'s restaurants reflect both the city's well-deserved reputation for culinary innovation and its rich ethnic cornucopia. It's the home ground not only of many of the country's best-known chefs—among them Wolfgang Puck, Joachim Splichal, Michael Richard—but also of many unheralded chefs who delight Angelenos daily with the cuisines of their native Shanghai, Oaxaca, Tuscany, and perhaps more of the world's other gastronomic regions than any other city. So whether you are looking for a traditionally elegant dinner, a culinary adventure, or just a really good burger, expect to find them all here—in spades.

CATEGORY	COST*
$$$$	over $30
$$$	$22–$30
$$	$15–$21
$	under $15

*per person for a main course at dinner, excluding 8.25% sales tax

Downtown

FRENCH

$$–$$$ ★ ✕ **Café Pinot.** Joachim and Christine Splichal, proprietors of Patina and a growing number of Pinot bistros, have earned great success with this warm, convivial restaurant housed in a contemporary pavilion in the garden of the Central Library. If the weather's fine, you can eat outside on the terrace under one of the old olive trees. The menu is rooted in traditional French bistro standards—steak frîtes, roast chicken with three mustards, and braised lamb shank. ⊠ 700 W. 5th St., ☎ 213/ 239–6500. Reservations essential. AE, D, DC, MC, V. No lunch weekends. Self and valet parking.

ITALIAN

$$–$$$ ✕ **Cicada.** Cicada occupies the ground floor of the 1928 art deco Oviatt Building. The glass doors are Lalique, carved wood interior columns rise two-stories, and from the balcony, a glamorous bar overlooks the spacious dining room. "Modern Italian" best describes the menu: marinated tuna with mint and white beans; smoked duck ravioli; sautéed sea bass with a roasted pepper beurre blanc, and grilled veal chop with braised endive. ⊠ 617 S. Olive St., ☎ 213/488–9488. Reservations essential. AE, DC, MC, V. Closed Sun. No lunch Sat.

LATIN

$$–$$$ ✕ **Ciudad.** The interior by architect Josh Schweitzer makes you feel as if you're lounging in Rio and not in a downtown office building, and the new wave, Latin American–inspired menu by Mary Sue Milliken and Susan Feniger continues the illusion. Among the starters, imagine the taste of *pasteles boriqua* (plantain tamales with pork, olives, and raisins). Entrées range from lamb shank with baby artichokes to chicken roasted Cuban-style with sweet garlic. ⊠ 445 S. Figueroa St., ☎ 213/486–5171. AE, MC, V. Valet and self parking.

Beverly Hills, Century City, Hollywood, and West Hollywood

Beverly Hills

CONTEMPORARY

$$$ ✕ **Spago Beverly Hills.** Wolfgang Puck, the chef who helped define California cuisine at his original, now closed, Spago on Sunset Strip, continues to wow celebrity circles, and everyone else, in his second location. The restaurant centers around an outdoor courtyard, from which you can glimpse the large open kitchen and, on occasion, Mr. Puck him-

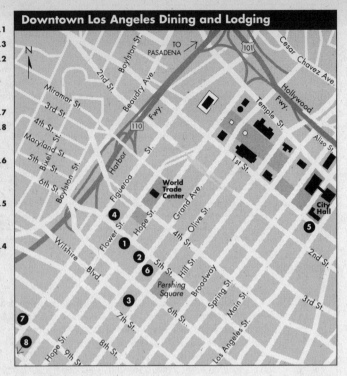

Downtown Los Angeles Dining and Lodging

self. The menu changes daily, offering such appetizers as white-bean and duck-confit soup, and such entrées as wild striped bass with celery-root puree. Also worth trying are Puck's renowned pizzas, with or without smoked salmon. ⊠ *176 N. Canon Dr.,* ☎ *310/385–0880. Reservations essential. AE, D, DC, MC, V. No lunch Sun.*

$$–$$$ ✕ **Café Blanc.** Chef-owner Tommy Harase's modern, warm, and unpretentious restaurant is an unexpected treat—especially when such lunchtime entrées as sautéed salmon with basil vinaigrette or poached Maine lobster top out at just $10. The five-course, prix-fixe dinner ($48) may include exquisite sautéed foie gras with corn chowder, seared jumbo scallops stuffed with black bean sauce, and roasted rack of lamb. Service is both gracious and unintrusive. ⊠ *9777 S. Little Santa Monica Blvd.,* ☎ *310/888–0108. Reservations essential. AE, D, MC, V. Closed Sun. and Mon.*

ITALIAN

$–$$ ✕ **Da Pasquale.** An affordable meal is hard to find here in the land of Gucci and Bijan, which is one reason to visit Da Pasquale. An even better reason is the pizza topped with ingredients like fresh tomato, garlic, and basil or three cheeses and prosciutto. The skillful kitchen staff also does a good job with such standards as pasta and roast chicken. Walls of glass face the street, giving the talent-agency regulars a chance to check out the scene. ⊠ *9749 S. Little Santa Monica Blvd.,* ☎ *310/859–3884. AE, MC, V. Closed Sun. No lunch Sat. Free parking after 6 PM.*

Century City

FRENCH

$$–$$$ ✕ **La Cachette.** Owner-chef Jean-François Meteigner developed a following while cooking at L'Orangerie and Cicada. At his own place (a *cachette* is a little, secret hiding place), he combines traditional French fare—Provençal bouillabaisse, rack of lamb with garlic-tarragon *jus*—with a lighter, more modern cuisine, including Alaskan butterfish with Cajun spices, and venison with cabernet-and-blueberry sauce. ⊠ *10506*

Beverly Hills, Century City, Hollywood, and West Hollywood Dining and Lodging

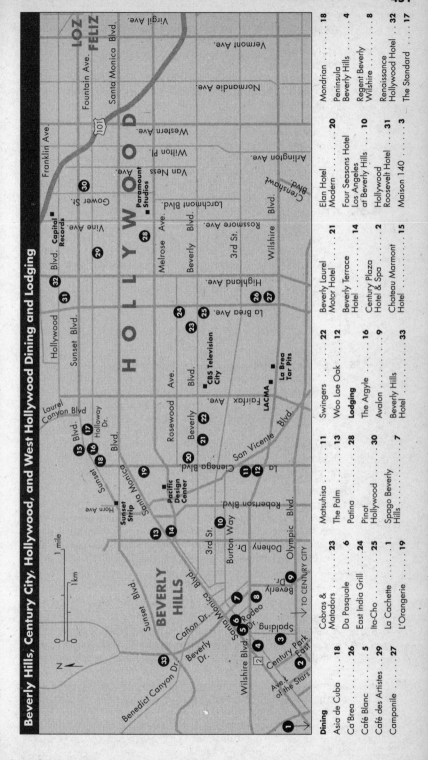

Dining

Asia de Cuba	18
Ca'Brea	26
Café Blanc	5
Café des Artistes	29
Campanile	27
Cobras & Matadors	23
Da Pasquale	6
East India Grill	24
Ita-Cho	25
La Cachette	1
L'Orangerie	19
Matsuhisa	11
The Palm	13
Patina	28
Pinot Hollywood	30
Spago Beverly Hills	7
Swingers	22
Woo Lae Oak	12

Lodging

The Argyle	16
Avalon	9
Beverly Hills Hotel	33
Beverly Laurel Motor Hotel	21
Beverly Terrace Hotel	14
Century Plaza Hotel & Spa	2
Chateau Marmont Hotel	15
Elan Hotel Modern	20
Four Seasons Hotel Los Angeles at Beverly Hills	10
Hollywood Roosevelt Hotel	31
Maison 140	3
Mondrian	18
Peninsula Beverly Hills	4
Regent Beverly Wilshire	8
Renaissance Hollywood Hotel	32
The Standard	17

S. Little Santa Monica Blvd., ☎ *310/470–4992. Reservations essential. AE, MC, V. No lunch weekends. Valet parking.*

Hollywood

CONTEMPORARY

$$$–$$$$ ✕ **Patina.** The exterior of Joachim Splichal's flagship restaurant is so understated that it's easy to miss, and the interior is a study in spare elegance. Generally considered one of the best restaurants in Los Angeles, this is the wellspring from which the various Pinot bistros have sprung. Among the mainstays are a corn blini filled with fennel-marinated salmon and crème fraîche, and scallops wrapped in potato slices with brown-butter vinaigrette. Specials might include grilled Arctic char with ginger–and–star anise french fries, and roasted salmon with oyster mushrooms. ⊠ *5955 Melrose Ave., Hollywood,* ☎ *323/467–1108. Reservations essential. AE, D, DC, MC, V. Closed Sun. No lunch Sat.–Thurs. Valet parking.*

$$–$$$ ✕ **Pinot Hollywood.** This link in the chain of Joachim "Patina" Splichal's bistros occupies a walled compound almost next door to Paramount Studios. With an outdoor terrace, martini bar, and lounge in addition to the main dining room, Pinot Hollywood is a comfortable venue for lunch, dinner, or late-night drinks. Lunch entrées include poached-salmon salad with tomato vinaigrette, and pappardelle with braised lamb. For dinner you might find grilled sardines à la Provençal, or parsnip gnocchi with lobster, and veal shank with caramelized root vegetables. ⊠ *1448 N. Gower St., Hollywood,* ☎ *323/461–8800. Reservations essential. AE, D, DC, MC, V. Closed Sun. No lunch Sat. Valet parking.*

FRENCH

$$ ✕ **Café des Artistes.** At its best, as here, new Hollywood is tasting a lot like old Paris. Behind a tall hedge, in the midst of film production companies, a California bungalow has been turned into a cozy bistro where you can have mussels Provençal, asparagus and fennel salad, monkfish *tagine* (a slow-cooked Moroccan stew) with olives and lemon confit, or even a major seafood platter (oysters, clams, crab, shrimp, periwinkles). Follow your meal with a cheese plate, brioche pudding, chocolate mousse, or lemon sorbet with vodka. ⊠ *1534 McCadden Pl., Hollywood,* ☎ *323/469–7300. AE, MC, V. No lunch weekends.*

INDIAN

$–$$ ✕ **East India Grill.** With its combination of high-tech sheet metal design and low-tech tandoori oven this popular café serves traditional, zesty Indian food with a California edge. Traditional dishes such as green-coconut and tomato-based curries and *sagwalas* (spinach dishes) are as well-prepared as the imaginative alternatives—tandoori chicken salad, mango ribs, and garlic-basil nan, to name just a few. You can eat indoors or on the patio. ⊠ *345 N. La Brea Ave., Beverly-La Brea,* ☎ *323/936–8844. AE, MC, V. Free garage parking.*

ITALIAN

$–$$$ ✕ **Ca'Brea.** Chef Antonio Tommasi turns out lamb chops with black-truffle and mustard sauce, whole boneless chicken marinated and grilled with herbs, and a very popular osso buco. Starters make the meal—try baked goat cheese wrapped in pancetta and served atop a Popeye-size mound of spinach. Daily specials include soup, salad, pasta, and fish dishes. Terra-cotta- or mustard-color walls combined with dark-wood paneling give the lively main room a warm Venetian look, and the cozy loft is ideal for those seeking privacy. ⊠ *346 S. La Brea Ave., Beverly-La Brea,* ☎ *323/938–2863. AE, D, DC, MC, V. Closed Sun. No lunch weekends.*

JAPANESE

$–$$$ ✕ **Ita-Cho.** In a large, new minimalist space, Ita-Cho is a chic destination for those in the know. Specializing in *koryori-ya* (Japanese pub cuisine), the small dining room also serves flawless sashimi (but no sushi). Also try the *tatsuta age*, the delicate Japanese take on fried chicken, and the grilled yellowtail collar, the succulent part of the fish just below the head. ⊠ *7311 Beverly Blvd., Beverly-La Brea,* ☎ *323/938–9009. Reservations essential. AE, MC, V. Dinner only. Closed Sun.–Mon. Valet parking.*

West Hollywood

AMERICAN/CASUAL

$ ✕ **Swingers.** Everyone from power-lunchers to Doc Martens–clad poseurs takes to this all-day, late-night coffee shop, so be prepared for a wait. Eat at sidewalk tables or inside the pseudo-diner on the ground floor of the no-frills Beverly Laurel Hotel. Loud alternative music plays to the Gen-X and Y crowd, and a casual menu—breakfast burritos, hamburgers, ostrich burgers, and chicken breast sandwiches on fresh French bread—goes easy on your pocketbook. ⊠ *8020 Beverly Blvd., West Hollywood,* ☎ *323/653–5858. AE, D, MC, V.*

CONTEMPORARY

$$$–$$$$ ✕ **Campanile.** In what was once Charlie Chaplin's office complex, Mark ★ Peel and Nancy Silverton—two of the finest modern American chefs— blend robust Mediterranean flavors with those of homey Americana. Appetizers may include celery-root soup with pesto, lobster risotto, and roasted black mussels. Among the entrées are bourride of snapper and Manila clams, and loin of venison with quince puree. You'll find some of the best desserts anywhere—try the light-as-a-feather bitter-almond *panna cotta.* Weekend brunch on the enclosed patio with a vintage fountain should not be missed. ⊠ *624 S. La Brea Ave., Miracle Mile,* ☎ *323/938–1447. Reservations essential. AE, D, DC, MC, V. No dinner Sun. Valet parking.*

$$$ ✕ **Asia de Cuba.** Can't get into Sky Bar? Well, you can watch those who can from this hot spot that shares the Mondrian hotel's city-view patio. Prices are high but portions are definitely large enough to share. Some, like the carpaccio, are mostly lettuce, but the tuna tartare and the roast-pork pancakes are more substantial. "Hacked" lime chicken and yucca-crusted mahimahi are a lot less peculiar than they sound. You'll also find here what are arguably the most beautiful people in town, and that's saying a lot for L.A. ⊠ *8440 W. Sunset Blvd., Sunset Strip,* ☎ *323/848–6000. Reservations essential. AE, MC, V.*

FRENCH

$$$$ ✕ **L'Orangerie.** Elegant French Mediterranean cuisine is served in this ★ rococo dining room, complete with white flower arrangements and oils depicting European castles. The elaborate setting and ultra-attentive service make this a place for special occasions—whether for an anniversary or closing the deal. Specialties include whole duck with coffee beans, John Dory with roasted figs, rack of lamb, coddled eggs served in the shell and topped with Sevruga caviar, and a rich apple tart accompanied by a jug of double cream. ⊠ *903 N. La Cienega Blvd., West Hollywood,* ☎ *310/652–9770. Reservations essential. AE, D, DC, MC, V. Closed Mon. No lunch. Valet parking.*

JAPANESE

$$–$$$$ ✕ **Matsuhisa.** Cutting-edge Pacific Rim cuisine is pushed to new lim- ★ its at this modest-looking yet high-profile Japanese bistro. Chef Nobu Matsuhisa creatively infuses his dishes with flavors encountered during his sojourn in Peru. Consider his caviar-capped tuna stuffed with black truffles, and the sea urchin wrapped in a *shiso* leaf. Tempuras are lighter than usual, and the sushi is fresh and authentic. There isn't another restaurant in the country like it—except Matsuhisa's own branches. ⊠ *129 N. La Cienega Blvd. Restaurant Row,* ☎ *310/659–9639. Reservations essential. AE, DC, MC, V. Valet parking.*

KOREAN

$$–$$$ ✕ **Woo Lae Oak.** This marble-clad, high-ceilinged restaurant has made Korean food more accessible to a wider audience. It's relatively pricey, but, as at many traditional Korean restaurants, you cook your own meats and seafood on your tabletop grill, which is great fun for a lively group. ⊠ *170 N. La Cienega Blvd., Restaurant Row,* ☎ *310/652–4187. AE, DC, MC, V. Valet parking.*

SPANISH

$–$$ ✕ **Cobras & Matadors.** An intimate space with an affordable, Mediterranean-leaning menu, Cobras & Matadors offers numerous tapa-like appetizers, among them traditional gazpacho, white anchovies with fried-garlic vinaigrette, and sautéed green lentils with serrano ham. Entrées include roast game hen with Catalan sweet-and-sour sauce, chorizo in red wine with white beans, and grilled prawns with cilantro sauce. There's no wine license, but you can buy a bottle from the owner's well-stocked wineshop next door; or bring your own for a modest corkage fee. ⊠ *7615 Beverly Blvd., south of West Hollywood,* ☎ *323/932–6178. MC, V. Closed Sun. Valet parking.*

STEAK

$$–$$$$ ✕ **The Palm.** All the New York elements are present at this West Coast replay of the famous Manhattan steak house—mahogany booths, tin ceilings, a boisterous atmosphere, and New York–style waiters rushing you through your cheesecake (flown in from the Bronx). This is where you'll find the biggest and best lobster, good steaks, prime rib, chops, great French-fried onion rings, and paper-thin potato slices. When writers sell a screenplay, they celebrate with a Palm lobster. ⊠ *9001 Santa Monica Blvd., West Hollywood,* ☎ *310/550–8811. AE, DC, MC, V. Reservations essential. No lunch weekends. Valet parking.*

Coastal and Western Los Angeles

Malibu

CONTEMPORARY

$$–$$$ ✕ **Granita.** Wolfgang Puck's famed Granita is a glamourous—some call
★ it garish—fantasy world of handmade tiles embedded with seashells, blown-glass lighting fixtures, and etched-glass panels with wavy edges (even the blasé Malibu film colony is impressed by its exotic koi pond and waterfall)—and its beachside location adds to the marine mood. Fitting, then, that chef Jennifer Naylor's menu favors seafood, including polenta crepes with Maine lobster and bigeye with spicy miso glaze. She has also prepared sautéed foie gras with spiced Asian pears, beef carpaccio with white truffles, and roasted Cantonese duck with a pomegranate-plum glaze. Brunch is served on weekends. ⊠ *23725 W. Malibu Rd., Malibu,* ☎ *310/456–0488. Reservations essential. D, DC, MC, V. Closed Mon. No lunch weekdays.*

Santa Monica

CONTEMPORARY

$$–$$$ ✕ **JiRaffe.** The gleaming, wood-paneled, two-story dining room with ceiling-high windows is as handsome as the menu is tasteful. Seasonal appetizers like goat cheese, leek, and roasted-tomato ravioli or a roasted-beet salad with caramelized walnuts and dried bing cherries, are an excellent way to kick off a main dish of roasted Chilean sea bass with a ragout of sweet corn, spring peas, and pearl onions. ⊠ *502 Santa Monica Blvd., Santa Monica,* ☎ *310/917–6671. Reservations essential. AE, DC, MC, V. No lunch weekends. Valet parking.*

Coastal Los Angeles Dining and Lodging

ITALIAN

$$–$$$ ✕ **Drago.** Celestino Drago's home-style fare is carefully prepared and
★ attentively served in stark designer surroundings. White walls and
white linen–covered tables line both sides of a floating service station
dressed up with a massive fresh-flower arrangement. Sample Drago's
pappardelle with pheasant ragout, squid-ink risotto, or ostrich breast
with red-cherry sauce. ⊠ *2628 Wilshire Blvd., Santa Monica,* ☎ *310/
828–1585. AE, DC, MC, V. No lunch weekends. Valet parking.*

Venice

CONTEMPORARY

$$–$$$ ✕ **Joe's Restaurant.** In what was originally a turn-of-the-20th-century
beach house Joe Miller has created a neighborhood restaurant so
definitive that it attracts diners from miles away. His French-influenced
California cooking is known for putting fresh ingredients to imaginative uses and his à la carte and prix-fixe dinners allow you to explore
his talent. Start with pistachio-crusted goat cheese with roasted pears,
and continue with lobster and black pasta with braised carrots. For
dessert, the strawberry granité is not to be missed. The wine list is well-
thought out and lunch is a bargain. ⊠ *1023 Abbott Kinney Blvd., Venice,*
☎ *310/399–5811. AE, MC, V. Closed Mon.*

FRENCH

$–$$ ✕ **Lilly's French Café & Bar.** Forget haute cuisine, Lilly's celebrates the
robust flavors of French regional and bistro cooking. Start with *flamiche*
(a northern French goat cheese and leek tart) or that bistro favorite,
escargots with garlic-herb butter. Then go on to duck breast with wild
cherry sauce or herbes-de-Provence-coated sea bass and finish with a
Paris-Brest puff pastry filled with hazelnut custard, or a true *tarte au
citron* (lemon tart). The chef in the kitchen of Lilly's converted beach
house is Catherine Dimanche, ex of 2424 Pico. The daily prix-fixe lunch

is a great value: soup or salad plus a glamorous sandwich or omelet for $10. ✉ *1031 Abbot Kinney Blvd., Venice,* ☎ *310/314–0004. AE, MC, V. Valet parking.*

LODGING

Revised and updated by Kathy A. McDonald

Whether you're going high-style or budget, consider location when selecting your hotel. Planning to hit the beach? Give some thought to Santa Monica. Want to enjoy L.A.'s legendary nightlife? Stay in West Hollywood or the Hollywood Boulevard area. For upscale and posh, you can't do better than Beverly Hills. The downtown area, though gaining ground in the tourist department, is still frequented mostly by conventioneers and business travelers. Because you will need a car no matter where you stay in Los Angeles, parking is an expense to consider: though a few hotels have free parking, most charge for the privilege—and some resorts have valet parking only.

CATEGORY	COST*
$$$$	over $300
$$$	$210–$300
$$	$120–$210
$	under $120

All prices are for a standard double room, excluding 9%–14% occupancy tax.

Downtown

$$–$$$$ 🏨 **Millennium Biltmore Hotel.** Built in 1923, this elegant landmark is a Beaux Arts masterpiece with a storied past; the lobby (formerly the Music Room) was the headquarters of JFK's democratic campaign, and the Biltmore Bowl ballroom hosted some of the earliest Academy Awards. Guest rooms are classicly decorated: canopied beds, shuttered windows, marble bathrooms, with high-tech updates such as CD players and cordless phones. ✉ *506 S. Grand Ave., 90071,* ☎ *213/624–1011 or 800/245–8673,* FAX *213/612–1545,* WEB *www.millenniumhotels.com. 683 rooms, 56 suites. 3 restaurants, 2 cafés, room service, some in-room data ports, in-room safes, minibars, cable TV with movies, indoor pool, health club, hot tub, massage, sauna, steam room, 3 bars, laundry service, concierge, concierge floor, Internet, business services, meeting rooms, car rental, parking (fee); no smoking. AE, D, DC, MC, V.*

$$$ 🏨 **New Otani Hotel and Garden.** "Japanese Experience" rooms at the
★   New Otani have tatami mats, futon beds, extra-deep bathtubs, and shoji screens on the windows. The American-style rooms are somewhat plain, but you can liven them up with a tea service and shiatsu massage. Two of the restaurants serve authentic Japanese cuisine, a third focuses on Continental fare. The hotel is on the edge of Little Tokyo, within walking distance of government buildings and the city's cultural center. For those who seek a contemplative moment or a scenic wedding spot, there's a ½-acre Japanese garden on the roof. ✉ *120 S. Los Angeles St., 90012,* ☎ *213/629–1200; 800/273–2294 in CA; 800/ 421–8795 elsewhere,* FAX *213/622–0980,* WEB *www.newotani.com. 434 rooms, 20 suites. 3 restaurants, room service, in-room safes, minibars, refrigerators, cable TV with movies, gym, massage, sauna, 3 bars, dry cleaning, laundry service, concierge, Internet, business services, meeting rooms, car rental, parking (fee); no smoking. AE, D, DC, MC, V.*

$$$ 🏨 **Westin Bonaventure Hotel & Suites.** You can't miss L.A.'s largest hotel: it has five towers, each one mirrored, cylindrical, and 35 stories tall. Inside is a futuristic lobby with fountains, an indoor lake, an indoor track, 12 glass elevators, and lots of activity. Navigating the hotel is a challenge; color-coded hotel floors and numerous signs help reduce mix-ups. Standard rooms are on the small side, while the suites and guest offices are expansive and come with practical extras. All rooms have floor-to-ceiling windows, many with terrific views. In addition to the revolving 34th-floor lounge and 35th-floor steak house, L.A. Prime, there are 16 eateries within the hotel. ☒ *404 S. Figueroa St., 90071,* ☎ *213/624–1000 or 800/937–8461,* FAX *213/612–4800,* WEB *www. westin.com. 1,354 rooms, 135 suites. 17 restaurants, room service, in-room data ports, in-room safe, minibars, cable TV with movies, pool, gym, hair salon, massage, sauna, spa, steam room, 5 bars, shops, children's programs, laundry service, concierge, Internet, business services, meeting rooms, airport shuttle, car rental, travel services, parking (fee); no smoking. AE, D, DC, MC, V.*

$$ ⊞ **Inn at 657.** Looking for the human touch? Proprietor Patsy Carter provides a homey atmosphere and then some at her intimate bed-and-breakfast–style inn near the University of Southern California, one mile south of downtown. Apartment-size suites and rooms have private entrances, down comforters, Oriental silks on the walls, and huge dining tables. You are welcome to frolic with the hummingbirds in the private garden. All rooms includes a hearty breakfast, homemade cookies, and local phone calls. ☒ *657 W. 23rd St., 90007,* ☎ *213/741–2200 or 800/347–7512,* WEB *www.patsysinn657.com. 11 rooms. Dining room, in-room data ports, some kitchenettes, some microwaves, refrigerators, cable TV, in-room VCRs, laundry service, business services, free parking; no smoking. MC, V.*

$$ ⊞ **Figueroa Hotel.** On the outside, it's Spanish Revival; on the inside, this 1926, 12-story hotel is a mix of Southwestern, Mexican, and Mediterranean styles, with earth tones, hand-painted furniture, and wrought-iron beds. The hotel's Music Room serves steak dinners, and the Lobby Café—notice the vaulted, painted ceiling—serves breakfast, lunch, and dinner. You can lounge around the pool and bubbling hot tub surrounded by tropical greenery under the shadow of downtown skyscrapers; a soothing beverage from the back patio bar will complete the L.A. experience. Since it's next to the convention center and Staples Center, this well-priced hotel books up months in advance of major events. ☒ *939 S. Figueroa St., 90015,* ☎ *213/627–8971 or 800/421–9092,* FAX *213/689–0305,* WEB *www.figueroahotel.com. 285 rooms, 2 suites. Restaurant, café, some fans, in-room data ports, refrigerators, cable TV, pool, outdoor hot tub, 2 bars, dry cleaning, laundry facilities, concierge, parking (fee); no smoking. AE, DC, MC, V.*

Beverly Hills, Century City, West Hollywood, and Hollywood

Beverly Hills

$$$$ ⊞ **Beverly Hills Hotel.** Since the Beverly Hills Hotel opened in 1912, ★ the "Pink Palace" has attracted generations of Hollywood legends. During awards season, the hotel hosts the American Film Institute's awards show and many celebrity guests, who favor the very private bungalows that come complete with *all* of life's little necessities. Bungalow 5 even has its own lap pool. Standard rooms are characteristically decadent, with original artwork, butler-service, Frette linens and duvets, CD players, walk-in closets, and huge marble bathrooms. Twelve acres of landscaped (and carpeted!) walkways make for prime strolling if you can bear to leave your room. The fabled Polo Lounge, with its banana-leaf wallpaper, remains a Hollywood meeting place and is a must-visit for wine lovers. Canine guests receive their own dog biscuits and bowl, and a dog-walking service is available 24-hours. ☒ *9641 Sunset Blvd., 90210,* ☎ *310/276–2251 or 800/283–8885,* FAX *310/887–2887,* WEB

www.beverlyhillshotel.com. 203 rooms, 21 bungalows. 4 restaurants, room service, in-room data ports, in-room fax, in-room safes, some kitchenettes, minibars, cable TV, in-room VCRs, 2 tennis courts, pool, gym, hair salon, hot tub, massage, bar, piano, shops, baby-sitting, dry cleaning, laundry service, concierge, Internet, parking (fee), some pets allowed (fee); no smoking. AE, DC, MC, V.

$$$$ ★ **Four Seasons Hotel Los Angeles at Beverly Hills.** High hedges and verdant patio gardens surround the Four Seasons, creating a secluded retreat even the hum of traffic can't permeate. Lavish flower arrangements fill the public spaces, including Windows Lounge, where film-industry executives, famous faces, and starlets socialize. Expect to be pampered here. The lavish guest rooms and suites have Frette-dressed beds that set the standard for comfort, soft robes and slippers, and French doors leading to balconies. The accommodating staff will take examplary care of you; extra touches include complimentary cellular phones at check-in (or your own cell phone linked to your hotel extension) and overnight shoe shine. ⊠ *300 S. Doheny Dr., 90048,* ☎ *310/273–2222 or 800/332–3442,* 𝖥𝖠𝖷 *310/385–4927,* 𝖶𝖤𝖡 *www.fourseasons.com/losangeles. 142 rooms, 143 suites. 2 restaurants, café, room service, in-room data ports, minibars, cable TV with movies and video games, pool, hot tub, sauna, spa, steam room, gym, bar, dry cleaning, laundry service, concierge, Internet, business services, meeting rooms, car rental, parking (fee); no smoking. AE, DC, MC, V.*

$$$$ ★ **Peninsula Beverly Hills.** This French Renaissance–style palace is a world removed from the bustle outside. Rooms overflow with antiques, artwork, marble, and high-tech room amenities controlled by a bedside panel. Whatever luxuries aren't on the standard bill of fare can be requested individually (monogrammed pillowcases, anyone?). For the full treatment, check in to one of the residential-style villas, which have private entrances, terraces, fireplaces, and Bose entertainment systems; some have kitchens and hot tubs. Soak up the sun alongside the fifth-floor pool or indulge at the full-service spa. Afternoon tea, hosted in the living room by a crackling fire and accompanied by a live harpist, is currently "in" for business and pleasure meetings. ⊠ *9882 Little Santa Monica Blvd., 90212,* ☎ *310/551–2888 or 800/462–7899,* 𝖥𝖠𝖷 *310/788–2319,* 𝖶𝖤𝖡 *www.peninsula.com. 196 rooms, 32 suites. 2 restaurants, room service, in-room data ports, in-room fax, in-room safes, minibars, cable TV with movies and video games, in-room VCRs, pool, outdoor hot tub, sauna, spa, steam room, gym, bar, shops, baby-sitting, dry cleaning, laundry service, concierge, business services, meeting rooms, parking (fee); no smoking. AE, D, DC, MC, V.*

$$$$ ★ **Regent Beverly Wilshire.** The moniker "grand dame" fits the landmark Regent Beverly Wilshire like a white kid glove. Opulent—an in-house florist looks after stunning seasonal arrangements—and completely devoted to the whims of its guests, the hotel has long been a home-away-from-home for visiting royalty, presidents, and heads of state. The Regent is also fondly known as the *Pretty Woman* hotel—a presidential suite was showcased in that film. Built in 1928, the Italian Renaissance–style Wilshire wing is replete with elegant details: crystal chandeliers, oak paneling, walnut doors, and crown moldings, pink marble. Added in 1971, the Beverly wing is more contemporary and equally luxurious. ⊠ *9500 Wilshire Blvd., 90212,* ☎ *310/275–5200; 800/427–4354 in CA; 800/421–4354 elsewhere,* 𝖥𝖠𝖷 *310/274–2851,* 𝖶𝖤𝖡 *www.regenthotels.com. 295 rooms, 120 suites. 2 restaurants, room service, in-room data ports, in-room safes, minibars, cable TV with movies and video games, pool, hair salon, outdoor hot tub, massage, sauna, spa, health club, bar, lobby lounge, piano, baby-sitting, dry cleaning, laundry service, concierge, business services, meeting room, travel services, parking (fee); no smoking. AE, DC, MC, V.*

$$$ ⊞ **Avalon.** Priced for the nonfamous crowd, Avalon is a boutique
★ hotel with Googie-era style and tech-savvy substance. Rooms at the three-building property are decorated with a bit of '50s retro and some classic pieces from Nelson, Eames, and Thonet; little luxuries like Frette linens, chenille throws, bathrobes, fax machines, Nintendo game consoles, and CD players are welcome. The downside may be the lack of a view. For extended stays, the Avalon offers stylish apartments and with all hotel services, including twice-daily housekeeping service. ⊠ *9400 W. Olympic Blvd., 90212,* ☎ *310/277–5221 or 800/535–4715,* FAX *310/277–4928,* WEB *www.avalon-hotel.com. 78 rooms, 10 suites. Restaurant, room service, in-room fax, in-room safes, minibars, refrigerators, cable TV with movies and video games, in-room VCRs, pool, gym, bar, dry cleaning, laundry facilities, laundry service, concierge, Internet, business services, meeting room, parking (fee), some pets allowed (fee); no smoking. AE, DC, MC, V.*

$$–$$$ ⊞ **Maison 140.** In a three-story, 1930s, colonial-style building, Beverly Hills' newest boutique hotel invites you into a French- and Far East–inspired world of gleaming antiques, textured wallpaper, and dazzling art. The dramatic visual treats compensate for the compact rooms and bathrooms. Little luxuries include down comforters and Frette linens and bathrobes. The ornate lounge, Bar Noir, is the setting for the complimentary Continental breakfast. Beverly Hills' golden triangle of shopping is within blocks. Take advantage of the pool and restaurant at sister property, the Avalon Hotel, 1 mi away. ⊠ *140 S. Lasky Dr., 90212,* ☎ *310/281–4000 or 800/432–5444,* FAX *310/281–4001,* WEB *www.maison140.com. 45 rooms. Room service, in-room data ports, in-room safes, minibars, cable TV with movies, gym, lobby lounge, dry cleaning, laundry service, concierge, parking (fee); no smoking. AE, DC, MC, V.*

$–$$ ⊞ **Beverly Terrace Hotel.** Rooms are basic (except for the leopard-print bedspreads), and bathrooms have shower stalls not tubs, but the price is right. On the corner of Santa Monica Boulevard and Doheny Drive, the hotel borders Beverly Hills and West Hollywood, close to the Sunset Strip. Complimentary Continental breakfast with La Brea Bakery breads is served outside by the pool. Trattoria Amici, the on-site Italian restaurant, is known to attract some of the neighborhood's high-profile clientele. ⊠ *469 N. Doheny Dr., Beverly Hills 90210,* ☎ *310/274–8141 or 800/842–6401,* FAX *310/385–1998* WEB *www.beverlyterracehotel.com. 39 rooms. Restaurant, some refrigerators, cable TV, pool, free parking, some pets allowed (fee); no smoking. AE, D, DC, MC, V.*

Century City

$$–$$$$ ⊞ **Century Plaza Hotel & Spa.** After a major renovation in 2001, the Century Plaza has become home to the largest hotel spa in Los Angeles, Spa Mystique. There's also a bright, spacious, two-story lobby lounge overlooking a swimming pool, reflective pools, landscaping, and cabanas. Breeze, the hotel restaurant, specializes in California cuisine. Guest-room improvements include expanded bathrooms, private hallways, and cherry-wood furniture. Stunning city views and balconies remain the same. The Century City Shopping Center is across the street. ⊠ *2025 Ave. of the Stars, 90067,* ☎ *310/277–2000 or 800/228–3000,* FAX *310/551–3355,* WEB *www.westin.com. 728 rooms, 14 suites. Restaurant, café, room service, in-room data ports, in-room safes, minibars, cable TV with movies, pool, hair salon, health club, outdoor hot tub, Japanese baths, massage, sauna, spa, steam room, bar, piano, dry cleaning, laundry service, concierge, Internet, business services, meeting rooms, car rental, parking (fee), some pets allowed; no smoking. AE, D, DC, MC, V.*

Hollywood

$$$ 🏨 **Renaissance Hollywood Hotel.** Part of the massive Hollywood & Highland entertainment complex, this 20-story Renaissance is at the center of the action. Contempory art, retro '60s furniture, terrazzo floors, and wood and aluminum accents greet you in the lobby. The rooms aren't huge, but they're well appointed, and in any case there are enough diversions, including many restaurants and shops, to keep you from spending a lot of time in your room. ⊠ *1755 N. Highland Ave., 90028,* ☎ *323/856–1200 or 800/468–3571,* FAX *323/856–1205,* WEB *www.renaissancehollywood.com. 604 rooms, 33 suites. 2 restaurants, room service, in-room data ports, minibars, cable TV with movies, pool, gym, 2 bars, shop, dry cleaning, concierge, Internet, business services, meeting rooms, parking (fee); no smoking. AE, D, DC, MC, V.*

$$$ 🏨 **Hollywood Roosevelt Hotel.** For its 75th anniversary in 2002, the Roosevelt underwent an extensive makeover in true Hollywood fashion. The painted ceilings and historic details in the Spanish Colonial Revival main building were dusted off and returned to their earlier luster. The hotel was the site of the first Academy Awards ceremony, and honoring that golden age are historic photos of Hollywood luminaries throughout, as well as a Gable-Lombard–themed penthouse suite. Sophisticated rooms have contemporary platform beds and fine linens. Cabana rooms face the landscaped pool area. The Cinegrill, also redone, presents live jazz and cabaret nightly. Hollywood & Highland is across the street. ⊠ *7000 Hollywood Blvd., 90028,* ☎ *323/466–7000 or 800/950–7667,* FAX *323/462–8056,* WEB *www.hollywoodroosevelt.com. 305 rooms, 48 suites. Restaurant, room service, in-room safes, minibars, cable TV with movies, pool, gym, outdoor hot tub, massage, bar, lobby lounge, cabaret, shops, dry cleaning, laundry service, concierge, concierge floor, Internet, business services, meeting rooms, parking (fee); no smoking. AE, D, DC, MC, V.*

West Hollywood

$$$$ 🏨 **Mondrian.** Ian Schrager, famed for his hipper-than-thou hotels—New ★   York City's Royalton, Miami Beach's Delano—is responsible for this all-white, high-rise, urban resort. Mod apartment-size accommodations have floor-to-ceiling windows, slip-covered sofas, and marble coffee tables; many have kitchens. Reservations are a must at Asia de Cuba, which fuses Asian cuisine and Latin flavors. Sip sake and sample the sushi at the Seabar for a lighter repast. The Skybar retains its mystique as the address for the powerful and beautiful people. ⊠ *8440 Sunset Blvd., Sunset Strip 90069,* ☎ *323/650–8999 or 800/525–8029,* FAX *323/ 650–9241,* WEB *www.mondrianhotel.com. 53 rooms, 185 suites. Restaurant, café, room service, in-room data ports, some kitchens, refrigerators, cable TV with movies, pool, gym, massage, sauna, spa, steam room, 2 bars, laundry service, concierge, Internet, business services, meeting room, parking (fee); no smoking. AE, D, DC, MC, V.*

$$$–$$$$ 🏨 **The Argyle.** You can't miss the gunmetal-gray, pink, and neon-lit ★   art deco facade. Inside, reproduction objets d'art and paintings fill the public spaces. Rooms are also deco. Though small, each has a separate living room with fantastic views over greater L.A. Bathrooms are done in black-and-white marble. Chef David Slatkin designs the California menu at the Fenix; ask for a table outside overlooking the city. Weekend nights, the hotel bar is packed with hipsters, actors, and models. ⊠ *8358 Sunset Blvd., West Hollywood 90069,* ☎ *323/654–7100 or 800/225–2637,* FAX *323/654–9287,* WEB *www.argylehotel.com. 20 rooms, 44 suites. Restaurant, room service, in-room data ports, in-room fax, in-room safes, minibars, cable TV, in-room VCRs, pool, gym, sauna, bar, laundry service, concierge, business services, meeting rooms, parking (fee); no smoking. AE, D, DC, MC, V.*

$$$–$$$$ ⊞ **Chateau Marmont Hotel.** You'll know this hotel, modeled after an actual chateau in Amboise, France, the minute you see it. Its decadent exterior reflects its lurid place in Hollywood history—locals remember it as the scene of John Belushi's fatal overdose in 1982. Actors like Johnny Depp and Keanu Reeves appreciate the hotel for its secluded cottages, bungalows, and understated suites and penthouses. The interior is 1920s-style though some of the decor looks dated rather than antique. Trendy Bar Marmont serves food until 1:30 AM—unusual in L.A. ⊠ *8221 Sunset Blvd., West Hollywood 90046,* ☏ *323/656–1010 or 800/242–8328,* ℻ *323/655–5311,* WEB *www.chateaumarmont.com. 11 rooms, 63 suites. Restaurant, room service, in-room data ports, in-room fax, in-room safes, minibars, cable TV with movies, in-room VCRs, pool, gym, massage, bar, laundry service, concierge, Internet, business services, parking (fee); no smoking. AE, DC, MC, V.*

$$ ⊞ **Élan Hotel Modern.** With progressive, high-tech amenities; swift, competent service; and a smooth, linear design to match, the Élan attracts young business people and those who appreciate a minimalist yet fully outfitted hotel. There's a Cyber Lounge where you can have coffee and breakfast (complimentary) while you navigate the Internet. Room decor is visually subdued and relaxing. The focus being the sense of touch, flashy colors are traded in for a creative mix of textures and fabrics, from mohair to chenille to down bedding. ⊠ *8435 Beverly Blvd., West Hollywood, 90048,* ☏ *323/658–6663 or 888/611–0398,* ℻ *323/ 658–6640,* WEB *www.elanhotel.com. 46 rooms, 4 suites. Restaurant, room service, in-room data ports, in-room safes, minibars, cable TV, in-room VCRs, gym, massage, bar, laundry service, concierge, Internet, airport shuttle, car rental, parking (fee); no smoking. AE, MC, V.*

$$ ⊞ **The Standard.** Hotelier André Balazs (also of the Chateau Marmont ★ and Manhattan's Mercer Hotel) has created an affordable, hip hotel in a chic neighborhood. With a wink to the '70s (shag carpets and ultrasuede sectionals in the lobby), the design spins off in a pop-arty and somewhat campy direction: inflatable sofas, beanbag chairs, surfboard tables, Warhol poppy-print curtains, and Blue AstroTurf poolside. The king-size beds are excellent, and the minibar essentials are anything but standard: patchouli-scented candles, sake, and Vaseline. Hollywood's beautiful people populate the space-age Standard lounge and the 24-hour coffeeshop. ⊠ *8300 Sunset Blvd., Sunset Strip 90069,* ☏ *323/650– 9090,* ℻ *323/650–2820,* WEB *www.standardhotel.com. 138 rooms, 8 suites. Coffee shop, room service, in-room data ports, minibars, in-room VCRs, pool, hair salon, lounge, shop, laundry service, concierge, Internet, meeting room, parking (fee); no smoking. AE, D, DC, MC, V.*

$ ⊞ **Beverly Laurel Motor Hotel.** A family-run operation for more than 40 years, the Beverly Laurel offers clean, spacious, brightly decorated rooms; a friendly front desk; and a '50s-era pool. The ground floor is home to Swingers coffee shop, very popular with actors, models, and musicians who also frequent the motel. Newcomers to Hollywood often reside in this hip motel before hitting the big time. Touring bands love the motel's funky atmosphere and reasonable rates. ⊠ *8018 Beverly Blvd., West Hollwyood 90048,* ☏ *323/651–2441; 800/962–3824 outside CA,* ℻ *323/651–5225. 52 rooms. Coffee shop, in-room data ports, some kitchenettes, microwaves, refrigerators, cable TV, pool, free parking, some pets allowed (fee); no smoking AE, D, MC, V.*

Coastal and Western Los Angeles

Bel-Air

$$$$ ⊞ **Hotel Bel-Air.** In a wooded canyon with lush gardens and a swan-★ filled lake, the Hotel Bel-Air's distincitve luxury and ultraprivacy have made it a discreet favorite of celebs (and royalty) for decades. Bungalow-style, country French rooms feel like fine homes with expensively upholstered furniture in silk or chenille. Most rooms have wood-burning fireplaces (the bell captain will build a fire for you). Eight suites have private outdoor hot tubs. Complimentary tea service greets you upon arrival and a pianist plays nightly in the bar. ⊠ *701 Stone Canyon Rd., Bel Air 90077*, ☎ *310/472–1211 or 800/648–4097*, FAX *310/476–5890*, WEB *www.hotelbelair.com. 52 rooms, 40 suites. Restaurant, room service, in-room data ports, in-room safes, minibars, cable TV with movies and video games, in-room VCRs, pool, health club, massage, shop, baby-sitting, dry cleaning, laundry service, concierge, Internet, business services, meeting rooms, parking (fee); no smoking. AE, DC, MC, V.*

Los Angeles International Airport

$$ 🏨 **Hilton Los Angeles Airport.** Sit in the well-hidden outdoor gardens at this enormous hotel, and you'll never know you're near the airport. The hotel has a multilingual staff, currency exchange, 24-hour restaurant, and an absurdly large health club (also open 24 hours). Stylish rooms are done in light woods and contemporary decor. Refrigerators can be provided for a nominal fee. Tower Level floors (with lots of extras) are a mere $25 extra. ⊠ *5711 West Century Blvd., LAX*, ☎ *310/410–4000 or 800/445–8667*, FAX *310/410-6250*, WEB *www.hilton.com. 1,234 rooms, 152 suites. 3 restaurants, room service, in-room data ports, minibars, cable TV with movies, pool, health club, 4 hot tubs, dry cleaning, laundry service, concierge, concierge floor, business services, meeting rooms, airport shuttle, travel services, parking (fee), some pets allowed (fee); no smoking. AE, D, DC, MC, V.*

Hermosa Beach

$$$ 🏨 **Beach House at Hermosa.** Although it opened in 1999, the Beach ★ House looks like a New England sea cottage from a century earlier. Gray shingles and overhanging white eaves decorate the exterior, but inside you'll find the best of contemporary amenities in split-level loft-like rooms. Ocean-front rooms facing the Strand have copasetic sunset views. All rooms have two TVs, four multiline phones, CD player, fireplace, wet bar, and extra sound-proofing. Spa services are available by appointment. Continental breakfast is complimentary ⊠ *1300 the Strand 90254*, ☎ *310/374–3001 or 88/895–4559*, FAX *310/372–2115*, WEB *www.beach-house.com. 96 suites. Dining room, room service, in-room data ports, kitchenettes, minibars, microwaves, cable TV, gym, outdoor hot tub, massage, dry cleaning, laundry service, concierge, business services, meeting rooms, parking (fee); no smoking. AE, D, DC, MC, V.*

Santa Monica

$$$$ 🏨 **Shutters on the Beach.** Set right on the sand, the gray-shingled inn ★ (think Martha's Vineyard) has become synonymous with opulent, in-town escape. A whirlpool tub, candles and dimmer switches, plush mattresses with Frette linens, a minibar stocked with splits of boutique California wines, and shutter doors (hence the hotel's name) all await you in your room. Shutters is a favorite of corporate executives who come for the personalized service, high-tech extras, and thoughtful homelike touches (books and scenic framed photographs bedside). Sit by the grand stone hearth at One Pico or watch the human parade on the boardwalk from the more casual Pedals Café. ⊠ *1 Pico Blvd., Santa Monica 90405*, ☎ *310/458–0030 or 800/334–9000*, FAX *310/458–4589*, WEB *www.shuttersonthebeach.com. 198 rooms, 12 suites. 2 restaurants, room service, in-room data ports, in-room safes, in-room hot tubs, minibars, cable TV, in-room VCRs, pool, gym, outdoor hot tub, sauna, spa, steam room, beach, mountain bikes, bar, lobby lounge, piano, shop, baby-*

sitting, dry cleaning, laundry service, concierge, Internet, business services, meeting rooms, parking (fee); no smoking. AE, D, DC, MC, V.

$$$–$$$$ 🏨 **Fairmont Miramar Hotel.** Former President Clinton's address of choice on his many visits to Southern California, the Fairmont Miramar presents luxury and professional service at land's end. Spread out over 5 landscaped acres are an 1889 mansion and lavish bungalows built between 1920 and 1946. Rooms in the 10-story towers have beautiful ocean views, marble entryways, alabaster light fixtures, carved wood armoires, Bose stereo systems, and down duvets. Extras include free shoeshine, an in-room wicker basket of office supplies, and Belgian chocolates at turndown. ✉ *101 Wilshire Blvd., Santa Monica 90401,* ☎ *310/576–7777 or 800/441–1414,* FAX *310/458–7912,* WEB *www.fairmont.com. 302 rooms, 55 suites, 32 bungalows. Restaurant, room service, in-room data ports, in-room safes, minibars, cable TV with movies and video games, pool, gym, hair salon, outdoor hot tub, massage, sauna, spa, steam room, bar, piano, baby-sitting, laundry service, concierge, Internet, business services, meeting room, car rental, travel services, parking (fee); no smoking. AE, D, DC, MC, V.*

$$$ 🏨 **The Georgian.** You can't miss the Georgian's distintive art deco exterior: it's aqua-colored with ornate bronze grillwork and a charming oceanfront veranda. Constructed in 1933, the hotel retains its historic character with cream-colored walls, marble floors accented with seafoam green and silver blue, and individually styled rooms with handsome cherry-wood furnishings and gold and silver accents. Gracious service and nostalgia of yesteryear are combined with the convenience of modern amenities, including Nintendo. The Speakeasy restaurant has always been a favorite of Hollywood celebrities. ✉ *1415 Ocean Ave., Santa Monica 90401,* ☎ *310/395–9945 or 800/538–8147,* FAX *310/656–0904,* WEB *www.georgianhotel.com. 56 rooms, 28 suites. Breakfast room, room service, in-room data ports, in-room safes, minibars, cable TV with movies, concierge, meeting room, parking (fee); no smoking. AE, D, DC, MC, V.*

$–$$ 🏨 **Bayside Hotel.** Room decor is modest, but you can't beat the location of this attractively landscaped hotel, just across the street from the beach and blocks from the Third Street Promenade and Santa Monica Pier. Some rooms have kitchens, and all have coffeemakers. If keeping cool is a must, request one of the seven rooms with air-conditioning or one of those with unobstructed ocean views and balconies. ✉ *2001 Ocean Ave., Santa Monica 90405,* ☎ *310/396–6000 or 800/525–4447,* FAX *310/396–1000.* WEB *www.baysidehotel.com. 45 rooms. Some fans, in-room data ports, some refrigerators, cable TV, free parking; no air-conditioning in some rooms. AE, D, MC, V.*

Westwood

$$$$ 🏨 **W Los Angeles.** Walk on water to enter the W—frosted glass stairs
★   over a fiber-optic-lit waterfall lead to the lobby. Sophisticated, luxurious surroundings are enhanced by the latest in cutting-edge technology. A beautiful garden terrace overlooks the pool. Cabanas wired for Internet access are perfect for lounging day or night. Business travelers will appreciate the "Cyber suites," complete with a combination printer-fax-scanner, a VCR, and three phone lines. The lobby bar and Mojo, the nuevo Latino restaurant, are local favorites. ✉ *930 Hilgard Ave., Westwood 90024,* ☎ *310/208–8765 or 888/946–8357,* FAX *310/ 824–0355,* WEB *www.whotels.com. 258 suites. 2 restaurants, café, room service, in-room data ports, minibars, refrigerators, cable TV with movies and video games, in-room VCRs, 2 pools, exercise equipment, spa, bar, lobby lounge, laundry service, concierge, Internet, business services, meeting rooms, car rental, parking (fee), some pets allowed (fee); no smoking. AE, D, DC, MC, V.*

$$ ⊡ **Century Wilshire Hotel.** This homey, English-style hotel is within walking distance of UCLA and Westwood Village. Quaint reminders of the hotel's former life as an apartment building abound, and many of the small, well-kept rooms have full kitchens and balconies. A daily Continental breakfast is included; it can be upgraded to a full breakfast for a nominal fee. ⊠ *10776 Wilshire Blvd., Westwood 90024,* ☎ *310/474–4506 or 800/421–7223,* ℻ *310/474–2535,* ⊞ *www.centurywilshirehotel.com. 41 rooms, 58 suites. Dining room, some kitchens, cable TV, pool, laundry service, travel services, car rental, free parking, some pets allowed (fee); no smoking. AE, D, DC, MC, V.*

Pasadena

$$$$ ⊡ **Ritz-Carlton, Huntington Hotel & Spa.** An azalea-filled Japanese gar-
★ den with walking paths and an unusual Picture Bridge decorated with murals that celebrate California's history make this hotel an especially scenic place to stay. The Mediterranean-style main building is surrounded by 23 acres of green lawns, blending seamlessly with the posh Pasadena neighborhood. Traditional guest rooms are handsome, if a bit small for the price. Suites and cottages, however, are as lavish as they come. Frette bed linens, feather beds, and thick bathrobes are standard. The Grill, serves modern American cuisine and earned a rare shining re- view from the *Los Angeles Times.* ⊠ *1401 S. Oak Knoll Ave., Pasadena 91106,* ☎ *626/568–3900 or 800/241–3333,* ℻ *626/585–1842,* ⊞ *www.ritzcarlton.com. 392 rooms, 31 suites. 2 restaurants, room ser- vice, in-room safes, in-room data ports, minibars, cable TV with movies, 3 tennis courts, pool, health club, hair salon, outdoor hot tub, sauna, spa, steam room, bar, shops, baby-sitting, children's programs (ages 7–12), dry cleaning, laundry service, concierge, concierege floor, business services, meeting rooms, car rental, travel services, parking (fee); no smoking. AE, D, DC, MC, V.*

NIGHTLIFE AND THE ARTS

Revised and updated by Lina Lecaro

Hollywood and West Hollywood are the chief focus of L.A. nightlife, where happening nightspots dot Sunset and Hollywood Boulevards. L.A. is one of the top cities for seeing soon-to-be-famous rockers as well as jazz, blues, and classical performers. Film emporia are natu- rally well represented here, but so are dance events, performance art, and an under-rated theater community that might just be L.A.'s best- kept secret.

For the most complete listing of weekly events, consult the current issue of *Los Angeles Magazine.* The Calendar section of the *Los An- geles Times* also lists a wide survey of Los Angeles arts events, espe- cially on Thursday and Sunday, as do the more alternative publications, the *LA Weekly* and the *New Times Los Angeles* (both free, and is- sued every Thursday). Call ahead to confirm that what you want to see is ongoing. A reliable source for times and tickets is the **Theatre League Alliance L.A.** (www.theatrela.org). Most tickets can be pur- chased by phone with a credit card. **Good Time Tickets** (☎ 323/464– 7383) tries to compete with Ticketmaster by acquiring harder-to-get tickets. Try **TeleCharge** (☎ 800/762–7666) for theater events. **Tick- etmaster** (☎ 213/480-3232 or 213/365–3500, fine arts ☎ 213/480- 3232 or 213/365–3500) is still the top dog. **Tickets L.A.** (☎ 323/655– 8587) brokers shows and cultural events, primarily at museums and smaller theaters.

The Arts

Concert Halls

Part of the Music Center, the 3,200-seat **Dorothy Chandler Pavilion** (✉ 135 N. Grand Ave., Downtown, ☎ 213/972–7211) is the home of the Los Angeles Philharmonic and the Los Angeles Master Chorale. The L.A. Opera presents classics from September through June.In Griffith Park, the open-air auditorium known as the **Greek Theater** (✉ 2700 N. Vermont Ave., Los Feliz, ☎ 323/665–1927), complete with Doric columns, presents big-name performers in its mainly pop-rock-jazz schedule from June through October.

Ever since it opened in 1920, in a park surrounded by mountains, trees, and gardens, the **Hollywood Bowl** (✉ 2301 Highland Ave., Hollywood, ☎ 323/850–2000, WEB www.hollywoodbowl.com) has been one of the world's largest and most atmospheric outdoor amphitheaters. Its season runs from early July through mid-September; the L.A. Philharmonic spends its summer season here. There are performances daily except Monday (and some Sundays); the program ranges from jazz to pop to classical. Concertgoers usually arrive early, bringing picnic suppers; there are plenty of picnic tables. Additionally, a moderately priced outdoor grill and a more upscale restaurant are among the dining options operated by the **Patina Group** (☎ 323/850-1885). Avoid the hassle of parking by taking one of the Park-and-Ride buses, which leave from various locations around town; call the Bowl for information.

The jewel in the crown of Hollywood & Highland is the **Kodak Theatre** (✉ 6801 Hollywood Blvd., Hollywood, ☎ 323-308-6363, WEB www.kodaktheatre.com). It was created to be the permanent host of the Academy Awards, but the lavish 3,500-seat theater also hosts music concerts and ballets. Booking a show here is worthwhile just to see the gorgeous, sparkling interior. The one-of-a-kind, 6,300-seat ersatz-Arabic **Shrine Auditorium** (✉ 665 W. Jefferson Blvd., Downtown, ☎ 213/749–5123), built in 1926 as Al Malaikah Temple, hosts touring companies from all over the world, assorted gospel and choral groups, and other musical acts, as well as high-profile televised awards shows such as the American Music Awards and the Grammys. It's used mainly for sporting events, but the **Staples Center** (✉ 1111 S. Figueroa St., Downtown, ☎ 213/742–7340, WEB www.staplescenter.com) also offers blockbuster concerts. Madonna and U2 both took their megabudget extravaganzas to this huge, state-of-the-art arena. Adjacent to Universal Studios, the 6,250-seat **Universal Amphitheater** (✉ 100 Universal City Plaza, Universal City, ☎ 818/622–4440) holds more than 100 performances a year, including the Radio City Christmas Spectacular, star-studded benefit concerts, and the full range of rock and pop performers.

Film

Spending two hours at a movie while visiting Los Angeles doesn't have to mean taking time out from sightseeing. Some of the country's most historic and beautiful theaters are found here, hosting both first-run and revival films. Admission to first-run movies is usually about $9, but it can be lower for discount matinees and theaters or even higher for specialty venues like IMAX theatres. Prices for senior citizens, students, and children are as low as $4.50.

ART AND REVIVAL HOUSES

The **American Cinematèque Independent Film Series** (✉ 6712 Hollywood Blvd., Hollywood, ☎ 323/466–3456) screens classics plus recent independent films, sometimes with question-and-answer sessions with the filmmakers. The venue is the Lloyd E. Rigler Theater, which is in the 1922 Egyptian Theater. The best of Hollywood classics and kitsch, foreign films, and documentaries are on tap at the **New Beverly Cinema** (✉ 7165 Beverly Blvd., Hollywood, ☎ 323/938–4038). **Nuart** (✉ 11272 Santa Monica Blvd., West L.A., ☎ 310/478–6379) is the best-kept of L.A.'s revival houses, with relatively new seats, an excellent screen, and special midnight shows. The **Silent Movie Theater** (✉ 611 N. Fairfax Ave., Fairfax District, ☎ 323/655–2520, WEB www.silentmovietheater.com) screens the cream of the pre-talkies era with live musical accompaniment, plus shorts before the films, Thursday through Sunday. **UCLA** has two fine film series. The program of the **Film and Television Archives at the James Bridges Theater** (✉ Hilgard Ave. near Sunset Blvd., Westwood, ☎ 310/206–3456 or 310/206–8013, WEB www.cinema.ucla.edu) runs the gamut from documentaries to children's films to the most sophisticated of foreign fare. The **School of Film & Television** (WEB www.tft.ucla.edu) also uses the Bridges Theater, but it has its own program of newer, avant-garde films.

MOVIE PALACES

You almost don't mind paying the extra bucks to see a flick at **The Bridge Cinema De Lux** (✉ 6081 Center Dr., in the Promenade at Howard Hughes Center, West L.A., ☎ 310-568-3375), with its super-wide screens, comfy leather recliners, and top-notch food and drink offerings. While you wait for your movie, you can enjoy a cappuccino in the lounge, a cocktail at the bar, or a meal (anything from burgers to pasta) at the restaurant, where you also can order to go and take your dinner into the theaters. **Mann's Chinese Theatre** (✉ 6925 Hollywood Blvd., Hollywood, ☎ 323/464–8111), open since 1927, is perhaps the world's best-known theater, with its cement walkway marked by movie stars' hand- and footprints and its traditional gala premieres. The futuristic, geodesic **Pacific Cinerama Dome** (✉ 6360 Sunset Blvd., Hollywood, ☎ 323/466–3401) was the first theater in the United States designed specifically for the enormous screen and magnificent sound system of Cinerama. **Pacific's El Capitan** (✉ 6838 Hollywood Blvd., Hollywood, ☎ 323/467–7674), a classic art deco masterpiece renovated by Disney, screens first-run movies and Disney revivals, often in conjunction with stage shows.

Television

Audiences Unlimited (✉ 100 Universal City Plaza, Bldg. 153, Universal City 91608, ☎ 818/506–0043, WEB www.tvtickets.com) helps fill seats for television programs (and sometimes for televised award shows). There's no charge, but tickets are distributed on a first-come, first-served basis. Shows that may be taping or filming include *Will and Grace, Everybody Loves Raymond,* and *The Drew Carey Show.* Tickets are received by mail or reserved over the Internet only. You must be 16 or older to attend a television taping. For a schedule, send a self-addressed, stamped envelope to Audiences Unlimited, a few weeks prior to your visit.

Theater

Many film and television actors like to work on the stage between "big" projects. **Now Playing** (WEB www.reviewplays.com) lists what's currently in L.A. theaters and what's coming up in the next couple of months. If you can go on-line during your stay, look into **Theatre League Alliance** (WEB www.theatrela.org), which also gives information on what's playing in Los Angeles (albeit with capsules that are either noncommittal or positively biased), plus listings of the nominees and winners of its annual Ovation awards. Best of all, it has WebTIX, a service that enables you to buy tickets online the day of the performance at half-price or less plus a small service charge.

MAJOR THEATERS

Jason Robards and Nick Nolte got their starts at **Geffen Playhouse** (⊠ 10886 Le Conte Ave., Westwood, ☎ 310/208–5454), an acoustically superior, 498-seat theater that showcases new plays in the summer—primarily musicals and comedies. Many of the productions here are on their way to or from Broadway. **James A. Doolittle Theatre** (⊠ 1615 N. Vine St., Hollywood, ☎ 323/462–6666) has an intimate feeling despite its 1,038-seat capacity. The home of the Academy Awards telecast from 1949 to 1959, the **Pantages Theatre** (⊠ 6233 Hollywood Blvd., Hollywood, ☎ 323/468–1770, WEB www.nederlander.com) is a massive (2,600-seat), splendid example of high-style Hollywood art deco, presenting large-scale Broadway musicals such as *The Producers*. There are three major theaters in the **Los Angeles Music Center** (⊠ 135 N. Grand Ave., Downtown, ☎ 213/972–7211, WEB www.musiccenter.org). The 1,900-seat, art deco **Wilshire Theater** (⊠ 8440 Wilshire Blvd., Beverly Hills, ☎ 323/468–1716, WEB www.nederlander.com) presents Broadway musicals like *Annie Get Your Gun* and occasional concerts.

SMALLER THEATERS

The founders of **Actor's Gang Theater** (⊠ 6209 Santa Monica Blvd., Hollywood, ☎ 323/465–0566, WEB www.theactorsgang.com) include film star Tim Robbins; the fare runs the gamut from Molière to Eric Bogosian to international works by traveling companies. The **Company of Angels** (at the Angels Theater, ⊠ 2106 Hyperion Ave., Silver Lake, ☎ 323/666–6789) bills itself as L.A.'s oldest repertory company, and it may well be, having been founded by Richard Chamberlain and others in 1960. Associated with it more recently have been the likes of Marion Ross and writer Wil Calhoun (*Friends*), and some of the best undiscovered talent in town, largely doing original or lesser-known contemporary plays. **The Coronet Theatre** (⊠ 366 N. La Cienega Blvd., between Beverly Blvd. and Melrose Ave., West Hollywood, ☎ 310/657–7377) proves good things come in small packages. It's actually three small theaters in one, with consistently funny comedy or one-person performance pieces (sometimes audience-interactive) running on all stages simultaneously. Four performance venues in one, **The Hudson Theatres** (⊠ 6539 Santa Monica Blvd., Hollywood, ☎ 310/856–4249) aren't in the most high-falutin' area of Hollywood, but they're popular with TV actors longing to tread the boards during their summer vacations. What's more, the resident company, the Hudson Guild, has a reputation for some of the finest traditional theater in town, with consistent raves for its reinterpretations of the likes of *Twelfth Night* and *Hedda Gabler*. Founded in 1962, the nonprofit theater co-op **Theatre West** (⊠ 3333 Cahuenga Blvd. W, near Universal Center Dr., North Hollywood, ☎ 323/851–7977 or 818/761–2203, WEB www.theatrewest.org) has produced a lauded body of work both in Los Angeles and on tour across America and even the British Isles. Its plays have gone on to Broadway (*Spoon River Anthology*) and been made into films (*A Bronx Tale*), and stars like Carroll O'Connor and Richard Dreyfuss have acted with the company. Its interactive **Storybook Theatre** (for 3–9-year-olds) is a long-running favorite.

Nightlife

Despite the high energy level of the L.A. nightlife crowd, don't expect to be partying until dawn—this is still an early-to-bed city. Liquor laws require that bars stop serving alcohol at 2 AM, and it's safe to say that by this time, with the exception of a few after-hours venues and coffeehouses, most jazz, rock, and disco clubs have closed for the night. Due to the smoking ban, most bars and clubs with a cover charge allow "in and outs," in which patrons may leave the premises and return (usually with a hand stamp or paper bracelet).

Bars of Note

Barfly (✉ 8730 W. Sunset Blvd., Sunset Strip, ☎ 310/360-9490) is one of those places where celebs are usually whisked in while mere mortals have to wait—on the weekends, that is. Weeknights the vibe is much more relaxed and welcoming with comedy nights and DJs spinning ambient and funk. Hang out at the bar, sit in a booth and nibble on model food (sushi, salads, etc.), or boogie on the smallish dance floor. Like so many nightspots in this neck of the woods, the popularity and clientele of **Bar Marmont** (✉ 8171 Sunset Blvd., near Crescent Heights Ave., Sunset Strip, ☎ 323/650–0575) bulged—and changed—after word got out it was a favorite of celebrities (Leonardo DiCaprio evidently blabbed that he loved it). The bar is adjacent to the inimitable hotel, Chateau Marmont. The **Beauty Bar** (✉ 1638 Cahuenga Blvd., Hollywood, ☎ 323-464-7676) offers manicures and makeovers with their perfect martinis, but the hotties who flock to this retro salon-bar (the little sister of the Beauty Bars in NYC and San Fran) don't really need the cosmetic care—this is where the edgier "beautiful people" hang.

Soccer fans say **Bestie's** (✉ 1332 Hermosa Ave., at 14th St., Hermosa Beach, ☎ 310/318–3818), a British pub named after English football legend George Best, is the top sports bar in the South Bay. If imported beers chased down by greasy food, plus darts, pool, live music (Thursdays and some Fridays), and 17 TVs sound like your style, this is the place. The **Chez Jay** (✉ 1657 Ocean Ave., Santa Monica, ☎ 310/395–1741) saloon near Santa Monica Pier has endured since 1959. With only 10 tables, checkered tablecloths, and sawdust on the floor, it's a charmingly "shabby-chic" setting for inventive seafood fare and regular celebrity sightings (Michelle Pfeiffer, Sean Penn, Al Pacino, et al.). A '40s-style bar that was rediscovered during the mid-'90s lounge craze and immortalized in the film *Swingers,* **Dresden Room** (✉ 1760 N. Vermont Ave., Loz Feliz ☎ 323/665–4294) is still a popular hangout with old-timers and Gen X lounge lizards alike.

The **Rainbow Bar & Grill** (✉ 9015 Sunset Blvd., Sunset Strip, ☎ 310/278–4232), in the heart of the Strip and next door to the legendary Roxy, is a landmark in its own right as *the* drinking spot of the '80s hair-metal scene—and it still attracts a music-industry crowd. Patrons, including many celebrities, must have a Mondrian room key, screen credit, or a spot on the guest list to enter **Skybar** (✉ 8440 Sunset Blvd., Sunset Strip, ☎ 323/650–8999), the poolside bar at the Hotel Mondrian. The view is as phenomenal as the clientele. Wouldn't you know, an old-age home in the happening part of Sunset Strip gets converted into a smart, brash-looking hotel, the **Standard** (✉ 8300 Sunset Blvd., at Sweetzer Ave., Sunset Strip, ☎ 323/650-9090), for the young, hip, and "connected." Its bar is all that, and popular with those in The Biz. Want women to come to your new hangout? Give 'em what they love. That's the premise behind **Star Shoes** (✉ 6364 Hollywood Blvd., Hollywood, ☎ 323/462–7827), the vintage-shoe store and bar from the people behind the equally kitschy and conceptual Beauty Bar. Of course, the place attracts both sexes with its stiff drinks and funky DJ music, but it's the cool shoe displays that make it a step above the rest.

Blues

Babe & Ricky's Inn (✉ 4339 Leimert Blvd., Leimert Park, ☎ 323/295–9112) is an old blues favorite. The great jukebox and photo/poster gallery and the barbecue and brew (or wine) will get you in the mood. Closed Tuesday; covers vary from $4 to $10, and for Monday night's jam, admission will also get you a fried-chicken dinner, served at 10 PM. Talk about all-day blues: Saturday and Sunday, the **Blue Café** (✉ 210 The Promenade, Long Beach, ☎ 562/983–7111) starts the music off at half past noon (on the patio), and it ends around midnight (in the main room). The rest of the week, there's "only" an early band (starting at 5:30) and a late band (9:30). Dress casual (but you knew that). **Café Booga-loo** (✉ 1238 Hermosa Ave., near Pier Ave., Hermosa Beach, ☎ 310/318–2324, WEB www.boogaloo.com) is a small, down-to-earth, Louisiana-flavored restaurant and bar; more than two-dozen microbrews are on tap. Live blues is also on tap nearly every night, the cover ranges from free up to $10. Youthful crowds pack **Harvelle's** (✉ 1432 4th St., Santa Monica, ☎ 310/395–1676) on the weekends, many of them regulars; come early or be prepared to stand in line. Watch from the back if you want, but down front, you'll be dancing.

Cabaret

The Cinegrill (✉ Hollywood Roosevelt Hotel, 7000 Hollywood Blvd., Hollywood, ☎ 323/466–7000) is well worth a visit, not only to hear top-tier cabaret and jazz vocalists, but also to admire the many Hollywood artifacts lining the lobby of the landmark hotel that houses it. Merv Griffin's **Coconut Club** takes over the Grand Ballroom of the Beverly Hilton Hotel (✉ 9876 Wilshire Blvd., Beverly Hills, ☎ 310/285–1358) on Friday and Saturday nights, with live music and a classic supper-club menu.

Coffeehouses

Bored with reading a paper over coffee? Try a board game at **Anastasia's Asylum** (✉ 1028 Wilshire Blvd., near 10th St., Santa Monica, ☎ 310/394–7113). Or recline on a comfy sofa. There's a full vegetarian menu and teas and juices as alternative libations. The free nightly entertainment (mostly low-volume singer-songwriters and jazzy stuff) starts around 8-ish (earlier on Sunday). **Highland Grounds** (✉ 742 N. Highland Ave., near Melrose Ave., Hollywood, ☎ 323/466–1507) is one of L.A.'s oldest coffeehouses and serves a tasty breakfast (and Sunday brunch), lunch, and dinner menu, plus it has a balcony and a patio, a beer selection as good as that of the coffee, and nightly entertainment of a mostly unplugged nature. Wednesday's open mic, called "Open Mind Night," always attracts crowds. **Newsroom Espresso Café** (✉ 530 Wilshire Blvd., near 5th St., Santa Monica, ☎ 310/319–9100) is a habitat for tightly wired media junkies: you can catch CNN updates while sipping Bolt soda, a mix of espresso and cola. There's also a more centrally located branch nestled between West Hollywood and Beverly Hills, the **Newsroom Café** (✉ 120 N. Robertson Blvd., south of Beverly Blvd., West Hollywood, ☎ 310/652–4444). A good place to take a break from the nonstop fun you've been having in L.A. and write about it in your journal is the **Un-urban Coffee House** (✉ 3301 Pico Blvd., at Urban Ave., Santa Monica, ☎ 310/315–0056). Enjoy a good stiff cup of coffee or some luscious chai tea, view the knickknacks from the past with which the walls are lovingly decorated, scarf the good but inexpensive breakfast or a sandwich, and hear the music or spoken word performances on Sunday during the day or on weekend evenings.

Comedy

In addition to the clubs below, a number of nightspots not specializing in comedy have a hot comedy night every week. Check the listings in the *LA Weekly*.

A nightly premier comedy showcase, **Comedy Store** (✉ 8433 Sunset Blvd., West Hollywood, ☎ 323/656–6225) has been going strong for more than two decades, with three stages (with covers ranging from free to $20) to supply the yuks. Famous comedians occasionally make unannounced appearances. **The Comedy Underground** (✉ 320 Wilshire Blvd., Santa Monica, ☎ 310/451–1800) nearly lives up to its name:

you have to use the alley off the Third Street Promenade just to find it. Straight stand-up takes a back seat to improv and sketch comedy here Thursday–Sunday. No alcohol.

More than a quarter-century old, **Groundling Theatre** (✉ 7307 Melrose Ave., Hollywood, ☎ 323/934–9700) has been a breeding ground for *Saturday Night Live* performers; early members included Phil Hartman, Paul (Pee-Wee Herman) Reubens, and Laraine Newman. The primarily sketch and improv comedy shows run Wednesday–Sunday, costing $12–$18.50.Richard Pryor got his start at the **Improvisation** (✉ 8162 Melrose Ave., West Hollywood, ☎ 323/651–2583), a renowned establishment showcasing stand-up comedy. Drew Carey's *Totally Improv* is Thursday nights. Reservations are recommended. Cover is $10–$15, and there's a two-drink minimum.Look for top stand-ups—and the frequent celeb residency, like Bob Saget; or unnannounced drop-ins, like Rodney Dangerfield—at **Laugh Factory** (✉ 8001 Sunset Blvd., Sunset Strip, ☎ 323/656–1336), open nightly, with shows at 8 PM, plus added shows at 10 and midnight on Friday and Saturday; cover is $10–$12.

Country Music
Rustin' up fun since the '70s, **Cowboy Palace Saloon** (✉ 21635 Devonshire Blvd., Chatsworth, ☎ 310/394–7113) might just be L.A.'s last honky-tonk; if you want to tie up your horse, you can use the hitching post out back. Dance lessons (Monday–Thursday), and music (around 9) nightly are free of charge. There's a weakly enforced two-drink minimum and a complimentary barbecue on Sundays. **Viva Cantina** (✉ 900 Riverside Dr., Burbank, ☎ 818/845–2425) is mainly a family-oriented Mexican restaurant, but the large, ranch-style bar area is more for grown-ups. That's where the country music happens every night, from the best of the locals to the occasional legendary old-timer like Red Simpson. Music starts at 7:30, and there's no cover.

Dance Clubs
Though the establishments listed below are predominantly dance clubs as opposed to live music venues, there is often some overlap. Also, a given club can vary wildly in genre from night to night, or even on the same night. Gay/lesbian and promoter-driven theme nights also tend to "float" from venue to venue. So: call ahead to make sure you don't end up looking for retro '60s music at an industrial bondage celebration (or vice versa).

As a bar, **Boardner's** (✉ 1652 N. Cherokee Ave., between Hollywood Blvd. and Selma Ave., Hollywood, ☎ 323/769–5001) has a multidecade history (in the '20s it was a speakeasy), but it's only become a cutting-edge disco in recent years. DJs spin music ranging from electronica to funk to goth depending on the night—the latter at the popular Saturday promotion "Bar Sinister," where the dress code is simply "black." The cover is anywhere from free to $10. With private party rooms, a scantily clad crowd, and some see-through walls, **Deep** (✉ 1707 N. Vine St., Hollywood ☎ 323-462-1144) is one of the sexiest clubs in Tinseltown. The exclusive dance club has DJs spinning everything from techno to old school to current dance hits, plus grindingly good go-go dancers. **Garden of Eden** (✉ 7080 Hollywood Blvd., at La Brea Ave., Hollywood, ☎ 323/465–3336) is an exotically decorated space hosting four nights of dancing (Wednesday–Saturday) for a dapper, youngish (21–35) crowd (and, yes, there's a dress code). Music leans toward house and funk or Euro-house and trip hop. Three bars, smoking patio, and valet parking; cover is generally $15. **Lush** (✉ 2020 Wilshire Blvd., Santa Monica, ☎ 310/829–1933) calls its Friday an Saturday dance nights "Disco Inferno" and "Saturday Night Fever"; need more be said? No, except that there's no cover, and you can recharge with food from the cantina. Live alternative rock plays three nights a week, too. **Lush Glendale** (✉ 617 S. Brand St., Glendale, ☎ 818/246–1717) is the younger sister to the Santa Monica club and it's got the same retro-y vibe with '70s cover bands and DJs spinning disco, '80s hits, and Latin grooves on different nights

Inside Hollywood & Highland, **One Seven** (✉ 6800 Hollywood Blvd., Hollywood, ☎ 323/462–4172) is a wholesome hang for the under-21 set. The high-tech venue boasts *Seventeen* magazine as a backer, so the music and vibe is suitably mainstream and the crowds look like Britney Spears and NSYNC wanna-bes. Dark and sequestered, **The Room** (✉ 1626 N. Cahuenga Blvd., Hollywood, ☎ 323/462–7196) promises some of the town's hottest DJs every night. The accent is on hip hop and the like, but Thursday–Saturday, *anything* is fair game. Enter on the alley. Come at 10, stay 'til 2, pay nothing (except for drinks).

The Sunset Room (✉ 1430 N. Cahuenga Blvd., Hollywood, ☎ 323/463–2004) is a high-class Hollywood restaurant, and in its club room Thursday–Saturday there's DJ-fueled dancing to Top 40 and hip hop. Often on Thursday there's also live music from bands led by actors such as Dennis Quaid and Jeff Goldblum. **The 360 Restaurant** (✉ 6290 Sunset Blvd., Hollywood, ☎ 323/871–2995) is named for its sensational view from atop a tower at Sunset and Vine. Beautiful people gather Tuesday nights for the esteemed, gay-friendly, house 'n' lounge party-down ("Beige"), and groovesters go for house on Thursday and soul/funk/pop on Friday. It's free, open 10–2, and has valet parking. With giant tiki heads, a waterfall, and swanky VIP rooms, **Voodoo** (✉ 4120 W. Olympic Blvd., southwest of Hancock Park, northwest of Mid-City, ☎ 323/930–9600) is a colorful, over-the-top nightspot in a surprisingly low-key, out-of-the-way neighborhood. Clubsters make the trek out of Hollywood for the well-known promoters who take over (usually on weekends) and stellar (techno, trance, house) DJ lineups they bring in.

Gay and Lesbian Clubs

It's worth pointing out that some of the most popular gay and lesbian "clubs" are weekly theme nights at various venues, á la "Beige" at 360, so in addition to these below, some perusal of the preceding list of clubs, and listings in the *LA Weekly* and *New Times*, as well as gay publications such as *Odyssey* and *Female FYI*, will provide a wider spectrum of choices.

An ethnically mixed gay and straight crowd flocks to **Circus Disco and Arena** (✉ 6655 Santa Monica Blvd., Hollywood, ☎ 323/462–1291 or 323/462–0714), two huge side-by-side discos with techno and rock music, as well as a full bar and patio, open Tuesday, Thursday, and Friday 9–2. Certain nights are gay themed and others not. Saturday "Spundae" is for everyone: top local and international DJs spin funk, house, trance, disco, and more until 4 AM. The cover may be $3–$20. **The Factory** (✉ 652 La Peer Dr., near Santa Monica Blvd., West Hollywood, ☎ 310/659–4551) churns out the dance music: Wednesday is the mixed flashback "That '80s Night"; Friday is the lesbian night "Girl Bar." Covers range from $5 to $15. **Jewel's Catch One** (✉ 4067 W. Pico Blvd., Mid-City, ☎ 323/734-8849) is a lively hangout for gays and lesbians featuring male and female exotic dance and lip-synching shows, karaoke, and DJs spinning everything from hip hop to disco. A straight contingent has started to discover the place, too, making for a ragin' mix. A long-running gay-gal fave, **The Palms** (✉ 8572 Santa Monica Blvd., West Hollywood, ☎ 310/652-6188) continues to thrive thanks to great DJs spinning dance tunes Wednesday–Sunday, plus an outdoor patio, pool tables, and occasional live performances.

Jazz

Powerhouse jazz and blues pleases crowds at the tiny **Baked Potato** (⊠ 3787 Cahuenga Blvd. W, North Hollywood, ☎ 818/980–1615). The featured item on the menu is, of course, the baked potato: they're jumbo and stuffed with everything from steak to vegetables. The music's on every night at 9:30 and 11, with a $10 cover. Or visit the larger, snazzier **Baked Potato Hollywood** (⊠ 6266½ Sunset Blvd., Hollywood, ☎ 323/461–6400, WEB www.bakedpotatojazz.com) for your fix of jazz 'n' spuds. The musical fare may vary a little more than at the original site, including some rock, and cover charges are $5–$30.

The menu's focus is on seafood, and the musical agenda is big-name acts at **Catalina Bar and Grill** (⊠ 1640 N. Cahuenga Blvd., Hollywood, ☎ 323/466–2210), which is tied with rival Jazz Bakery for the title of top jazz club in town. Shows start at 8:30 and 10:30 Tuesday–Saturday; Sunday shows are at 7:15 and 9:15. The cover ranges from $16–$20. L.A.'s most dapper swingsters put on the ritz at **The Derby** (⊠ 4500 Los Feliz Blvd., Los Feliz, ☎ 323/663–8979), a spacious, elegant club with a 360° brass-railed bar and plush-velvet curtained booths. There's live music nightly with the emphasis on swing and jazz. Free dance lessons are held every night at 8 PM, the music begins at 9:30 or 10, and the cover is $7–$10. Come to **Jazz Bakery** (⊠ 3233 Helms Ave., Culver City, ☎ 310/271–9039), for world-class jazz nightly at 8 and 9:30, in a quiet, respectful concertlike setting. The adjoining Cafe Cantata serves coffee, beer, wine, snacks, and desserts. The cover is $15–$25; parking is free.

Latin

There's no ideal label for it, but this section includes venues for samba as well as salsa, rhumba, *roc en español,* and even flamenco. A number of other venues offer such music one or more nights a week, and can be found in papers like the *LA Weekly.*

The **Conga Room** (⊠ 5364 Wilshire Blvd., Mid-Wilshire, ☎ 323/938–1696), which is co-owned by local celebs, including Jimmy Smits, presents Latin music (primarily salsa) and the odd rock or soul show. Regular admission is $10–$20; VIP treatment, $30–$40. There are dance lessons Wednesday and Thursday. The Cuban food at **El Floridita** (1253 N. Vine St., at Fountain Ave., Hollywood, ☎ 323/871–8612) is anywhere from good to great—and the music (Monday, Friday, and Saturday) is anywhere from very good to through the roof. A frequent guest is ex-New Yorker Johnny Polanco, backed by the sizzling Conjunto Amistad. Things get hot every Saturday and Thursday at **PaPaz Nightclub** (⊠ 1716 N. Cahuenga Blvd., Hollywood, ☎ 323/461–8190) where live bands and DJs play salsa, merengue, and cumbia. Friday *roc en español* shakes the place. Admission is free before 9; call and make reservations in advance.

Rock and Other Live Music

Seven days a week, at **Coconut Teaszer** (⊠ 8117 Sunset Blvd., at Crescent Heights Blvd., Sunset Strip, ☎ 323/654–4773), you can dance to raw, live rock, usually four bands a night. There are also pool tables; cover is free to $10. At the longtime music-industry hangout known as **Genghis Cohen Cantina** (⊠ 740 N. Fairfax Ave., Hollywood, ☎ 323/653–0640), you can hear hopefuls and veteran performers of the singer-songwriter sort, and sample the Kosher Chinese cuisine at the same time. The **House of Blues** (⊠ 8430 Sunset Blvd., Sunset Strip, ☎ 323/848–5100) is a club that functions like a concert venue, hosting popular jazz, rock, and blues performers such as Etta James, Lou Rawls, Joe Cocker, Cheap Trick, Pete Townshend, and the Commodores. Occasional shows are presented cabaret style and include dinner in the restaurant area upstairs; you can *sort of* see from some of it. Every Sunday there's a gospel brunch. Similarly, **House of Blues Anaheim** (✉ 1530 S. Disneyland Dr., Anaheim, ☎ 714/778–2583) hosts touring acts and locals inside its colorful, Cajun-inspired interior.

The Knitting Factory (✉ 7021 Hollywood Blvd., Hollywood, ☎ 323/463–0204) is the L.A. offshoot of the downtown N.Y.C. club of the same name. A modern, medium-size room seeming all the more spacious for its balcony-level seating and sizable stage, it's a great set-up for the arty, big-name performers it presents. There's live music almost every night in the main room and in the smaller Alter-Knit Lounge; there's a restaurant, a full bar and Web stations for surfing music sites. Covers are free to $40. Musician/producer Jon Brion (Fiona Apple, Aimee Mann, et al.) shows off his ability to play virtually any instrument and any song in the the rock lexicon—and beyond—as host of a popular evening of music every Friday at **Largo** (✉ 432 N. Fairfax Ave., Hollywood, ☎ 323/852–1073). Other nights, low-key rock and singer-songwriter fare is offered at this cozy supper club/bar. And when comedy comes in, about one night a week, it's usually one of the hippest comedy nights in town, featuring folks like Margaret Cho. Reservations are required for tables, but bar stools are open. **The Smell** (✉ 247 S. Main St., between 2nd and 3rd Sts., Downtown, ☎ 213/625–4325) may have bands only two or three nights a week (Wednesdays, Fridays, or Saturdays), but they're often choice—in the alternative fringe world, anyway; if they're not playing at the Knitting Factory or Spaceland, they just might be at the Smell. There's no liquor, the cover's usually $5, and there's also an art gallery. Enter via the back alley.

The hottest bands of tomorrow, surprises from yesteryear, and unclassifiable bands of today perform at **Spaceland** (✉ 1717 Silver Lake Blvd., Silver Lake, ☎ 213/833–2843), which has a bar, jukebox, and pool table. Mondays are usually free. Spaceland has a nice selection of beers, some food if you're hungry, street parking (if you really hunt for space), and a hip but relaxed interior. At the **Viper Room** (✉ 8852 Sunset Blvd., Sunset Strip, ☎ 310/358–1880), actor Johnny Depp's notorious hangout for musicians and movie stars (celebs mainly in the VIP room), the interior is tastefully deco, but the live music is loud and purely contemporary, decidedly eclectic (and occasionally featuring names normally too big to play a room like this), and with an alternative bent. **Whisky-A-Go-Go** (✉ 8901 Sunset Blvd., Sunset Strip, ☎ 310/652–4202) is the most famous rock 'n' roll club on the Strip, where back in the '60s, Johnny Rivers cut hit singles and the Doors, Love, and the Byrds cut their musical eyeteeth. It's still going strong, with up-and-coming alternative, hard rock, and punk bands. Mondays launch L.A.'s cutting-edge acts.

OUTDOOR ACTIVITIES AND SPORTS

Updated by
Jim Green

The weather in L.A. is often dazzling. A word to the wise, though: the atmosphere is dry, so bottled water and some lip balm are essential. Also, don't forget sunscreen; even on overcast days the sunburn index can be high. (Check the *L.A. Times*' weather page or local AM radio news stations like KFWB 980 and KNX 1070.)

Beaches

From downtown, the easiest way to hit the coast is by taking the Santa Monica Freeway (I–10) due west. Once you reach the end of the freeway, I–10 runs into the famous Highway 1, better known as the Pacific Coast Highway, or PCH, and continues up to Oregon. MTA buses run from downtown along Pico, Olympic, Santa Monica, Sunset, and Wilshire boulevards.

Los Angeles County beaches (and state beaches operated by the county) have lifeguards on duty year-round. Several beaches have improved their parking facilities, and both rest rooms and beach access have been brought up to ADA standards. Generally, the northernmost beaches are best for surfing, hiking, and fishing, and the wider and sandier southern beaches are better for tanning and relaxing. Almost all are great for swimming, but beware: pollution in Santa Monica Bay sometimes approaches dangerous levels, particularly after storms. Call ahead for **beach conditions** (☎ 310/457–9701 Malibu; 310/578–0478 Santa Monica; 310/379–8471 South Bay area). The following beaches are listed in north–south order:

Leo Carrillo State Beach. On the very edge of Ventura County, this narrow beach is better for exploring than swimming or sunning. On your own or with a ranger, venture down at low tide to examine the tide pools among the rocks. Sequit Point, a promontory dividing the east and west halves of the beach, creates secret coves, sea tunnels, and boulders on which you can perch and fish. Generally, fishermen stick to the west end of the beach; experienced surfers brave the rocks on the east end. Campgrounds are set back from the beach; call to reserve campsites in advance. ⊠ *35000 PCH, Malibu,* ☎ *818/880–0350; 800/444–7275 camping reservations. Parking, lifeguard (year-round, except only as needed in winter), rest rooms, showers, fire pits.*

Robert H. Meyer Memorial State Beach. Perhaps Malibu's most beautiful coastal area, this state beach is made up of three minibeaches: El Pescador, La Piedra, and El Matador—all with the same spectacular view. Scramble down the steps to the rocky coves where nude sunbathers like to gather. The huge, craggy boulders that make this beach private and lovely also make it somewhat dangerous: watch the tide and don't get trapped between the boulders when it comes in. ⊠ *32350, 32700, and 32900 PCH, Malibu,* ☎ *818/880–0350. Parking, 1 roving lifeguard unit, rest rooms.*

Zuma Beach Park. Zuma, 2 mi of white sand usually littered with tanning teenagers, has it all: from fishing and diving to swings for the kids to volleyball courts. Beachgoers looking for quiet or privacy should head elsewhere. The surf is rough and inconsistent. ⊠ *30050 PCH, Malibu,* ☎ *310/457–9891. Parking, lifeguard (year-round, except only as needed in winter), rest rooms, food concessions, playground, volleyball.*

Malibu Lagoon State Beach/Surfrider Beach. Steady 3- to 5-ft waves make this beach, just west of Malibu Pier, a popular surfing location. The International Surfing Contest is held here in September—the surf is best around that time. Water runoff from Malibu Canyon forms a natural lagoon that's a sanctuary for 250 species of birds. Unfortunately, the lagoon is often polluted and algae-filled, and the debris tends to spill over into the surf. If you're leery of going into the water, you can bird-watch, play volleyball, or take a walk on one of the nature trails, which are perfect for romantic sunset strolls. ⊠ *23200 PCH, Malibu,* ☎ *818/880–0350. Parking, lifeguard (year-round), rest rooms, picnicking, visitor center.*

Topanga State Beach. The beginning of miles of public beach, Topanga has good surfing at the western end (at the mouth of the canyon). Close to a busy section of the PCH and rather narrow, Topanga is not serene; hordes of teenagers zip over Topanga Canyon Boulevard from the Valley. Fishing and swings for children are available. ⊠ *18700 block of*

PCH, Malibu, ☎ *310/577–5700. Parking, lifeguard (year-round, except only as needed in winter), rest rooms, food concessions.*

Will Rogers State Beach. This clean, sandy, 3-mi beach, with a dozen volleyball nets, gymnastics equipment, and playground equipment for kids, is a favorite with families, couples, and singles, including a substantial gay and lesbian patronage. The surf is even and gentle for swimmers and beginning surfers, but the beach has the dubious distinction of being one of the area's most polluted—beware after a storm. Construction to improve access by foot and wheelchair, as well as lifeguard facilities, should be done by summer 2003. ✉ *15100 PCH, 2 mi north of Santa Monica pier, Pacific Palisades/Castellamare,* ☎ *310/577–5700. Parking, lifeguard (year-round, except only as needed in winter), rest rooms.*

Santa Monica State Beach. It's the first beach you'll hit after the Santa Monica Freeway (I–10) runs into the PCH, and it's one of L.A.'s best-known. Wide and sandy, it's *the* place for sunning and socializing: be prepared for a mob scene at the pier and on the beach on summer weekends, when parking becomes an expensive ordeal. If you don't mind a crowd during peak hours, swimming is fine (with the usual poststorm pollution caveat); for surfing, go elsewhere. For a memorable view, climb up the stairway over the PCH to Palisades Park, a grassy strip at the top of the bluffs. Summer-evening concerts are often held here. ✉ *1642 Promenade (PCH at California Incline), Santa Monica,* ☎ *310/577– 5700. Parking, lifeguard (year-round), rest rooms, showers.*

Venice City Beach. There's swimming, fishing, surfing, and courts for basketball (it's the site of some of L.A.'s most hotly contested pickup games), raquetball, handball, and shuffleboard. You can rent a bike or some in-line skates and hit the Strand. ✉ *West of Pacific Ave., Venice,* ☎ *310/577–5700. Parking, rest rooms, showers, food concessions.*

Manhattan Beach. A wide, sandy strip with good swimming and rows of volleyball courts, Manhattan Beach is the preferred destination of muscled, tanned young professionals and dedicated bikini-watchers. There's also a bike path, a playground, fishing equipment for rent, and a bait shop. ✉ *Manhattan Beach Blvd. and North Ocean Dr., Manhattan Beach,* ☎ *310/372–2166. Parking, lifeguard (year-round), rest rooms, showers, food concessions.*

Redondo Beach. The Redondo Beach Pier marks the starting point of this wide, sandy, busy beach, which continues south for about 2 mi along a heavily developed shoreline community. Restaurants and shops flourish along the pier, excursion boats and privately owned craft depart from launching ramps, and a reef formed by a sunken ship creates prime fishing and snorkeling conditions. A series of rock and jazz concerts takes place at the pier every summer. ✉ *Torrance Blvd. at Catalina Ave., Redondo Beach,* ☎ *310/372–2166. Parking, lifeguard, rest rooms, showers, food concessions, volleyball.*

Participant Sports

The **City of Los Angeles Department of Recreation and Parks** (✉ 200 N. Main St., Suite 1350, 90012, ☎ 888/527–2757, WEB www.cityofla.org/rap) has information on city parks. For information on county parks, such as Eaton Canyon and Vasquez Rocks, contact the **Los Angeles County Department of Parks and Recreation** (✉ 433 S. Vermont Ave., 90020, ☎ 213/738–2961, WEB http://parks.co.la.ca.us).

Bicycling

South of the Strand, following the brief and pathless "RAT" (Right After Torrance) beach, is a 23-mi loop from which to view winding hills and clear ocean views on the relatively untrammeled **Palos Verdes Peninsula.** The circumnavigation, which takes at least three hours, is best attempted on a temperate morning when fog isn't obscuring the ocean. The marked bike lanes come and go, so be careful. Griffith Park, Malibu Creek State Park, and Topanga State Park are all part of the **Santa Monica Mountains,** which have good mountain-biking paths.

For bike-route suggestions or a little company, you can get in touch with the **San Fernando Valley Bicycle Club** (☎ 818/347–6148, WEB www.sfvbc.org). Gay and lesbian folks can check in with **Different Spokes Bicycle Club** (WEB www.differentspokes.com) for info on recreational rides and events (they have a newsletter, too). Any L.A.-area yellow pages will yield a bunch of retail bicycle shops where you can rent wheels, pick the brain of an advice-laden salesperson or customer, or at least pick up the twice-yearly *Bicycling Event Guide* (see Bike rentals). **MyBikeSite.com** has extensive national information, including good coverage of Southern California.

Bikecology (✉ 9006 W. Pico Blvd., West L.A., ☎ 310/278-0915) has sister franchises in Santa Monica and Marina Del Rey. **Perry's** has three locations along the Strand: **Perry's Bike & Skate** (✉ 2600 Ocean Front Walk, Venice, ☎ 310/452–1507), **Perry's Beach Rentals** (✉ 2400 Ocean Front Walk, Venice, ☎ 310/452–7609), and **Perry's Cafe & Sports Rentals** (✉ 1200 The Promenade, Santa Monica, ☎ 310/485–3975). **Spokes 'N Stuff** has a rental shop behind the ranger station in Griffith Park (✉ 4400 Crystal Springs Dr., Los Feliz, ☎ 323/662–6573), and two rental places on the Strand (✉ 1700 Ocean Ave., Santa Monica, ☎ 310/395–4748; ✉ 4175 Admiralty Way, Marina Del Rey, ☎ 310/306–3332).

Boating, Kayaking, and Jet Skiing

Long Beach Windsurf & Kayak Center (✉ 3850 E. Ocean Blvd., near the Belmont Pier, Long Beach, ☎ 562/433–1014) rents windsurfing gear. For boat and jet ski rentals, call **Offshore Water Sports** (✉ 128 E. Shoreline Dr., Long Beach, Rainbow Harbor, ☎ 562/436–1996). **Marina Boat Rentals** (✉ 13719 Fiji Way, Marina del Rey, ☎ 310/574–2822), behind the El Torito eatery in Fisherman's Village, rents single and double kayaks as well as speed boats, cruisers, and sail boats, by the hour or half-day. **Malibu Ocean Sports** (✉ 22935 PCH, Malibu, across from the pier at Malibu Point, ☎ 310/456–6302) has kayak rentals, lessons, and organized cruises.

Diving and Snorkeling

Anyone who can swim can snorkel, but you'll have to show proof of certification to touch a scuba tank. Snorkeling and scuba diving require calm waters, and despite its misleading name, the Pacific Ocean does not quite fit the bill. However, there is good diving to be had if you know where to look. Try **Leo Carrillo Beach** in Malibu, **Palos Verdes,** or the **Underwater Dive Trail** at White's Point, just east of Royal Palms State Beach, which winds by rope through kelp beds, sulfurous hot springs, and underwater coves. Farther afield, there's **Catalina Island,** the **Channel Islands,** or go down the coast to **Laguna Beach.** Web sites like www.ladiver.com can give you guidance.

If you or your diving partner are injured in a diving-related accident, the 24-hour staff at the **U.S. National Diving Accident Network** (☎ 919/684-8111) can help you find a doctor trained to treat divers.

All the scuba equipment (and diving lessons) you'll need for your voyage beneath the waves can be obtained from the following shops. Most rent standard scuba gear packages for $35 and up. Most certification lesson packages include an open-water training trip to Catalina

Island. Some shops arrange diving charters to Catalina and the Channel Islands. You might use **Pacific Wilderness and Ocean Sports** (✉ 1719 S. Pacific Ave., near the Cabrillo Marina, San Pedro, ☎ 310/833–2422), if you're diving at White Point or Palos Verdes. **Divers Discount** (✉ 3575 Cahuenga Blvd., Universal City, ☎ 323/850–5050) guarantees the lowest gear-rental rates in the area. **Malibu Divers** (✉ 21231 Pacific Coast Hwy., at Rambla Pacifico, Malibu, ☎ 310/456–2396, WEB www.malibudivers.com) may well be on your way to the diving area at Leo Carrillo State Beach, but be warned: their certification classes are so popular that rental gear may be scarce on weekends. It's just a short hop—or stroll, even—from many area hotels to the **Reef Seekers Dive Company** (✉ 8612 Wilshire Blvd., Beverly Hills, ☎ 310/652–4990, WEB www.reefseekers.com).

Fishing

There's plenty of freshwater fishing, in numerous lakes dotting the city and in the Angeles National Forest. Requisite fishing licenses ($6.05 for one day, $10 for two days) are available from many sporting goods stores. The **Fish and Game Department** (☎ 562/342–7100 or 562/590–5020 for lake-stocking information) can answer questions about licenses and give advice. Shore fishing and surf casting are excellent on many of the beaches, and pier fishing is popular because no license is necessary to fish off public piers. The **Santa Monica** and **Redondo Beach piers** have bait-and-tackle shops with everything you'll need.

If you want to break away from the piers, sign up for a boat excursion with one of the local charters, most of which will sell you a fishing license and rent tackle. Most also offer whale-watching excursions. **Del Rey Sport Fishing** (✉ 13759 Fiji Way, Marina del Rey, ☎ 310/822–3625) runs excursions for $25 per half day and $35 per three-quarters of a day. **Redondo Sport Fishing Company** (✉ 233 N. Harbor Dr., Redondo Beach, ☎ 310/372–2111) has half-day charters starting at $25 per person. Sea bass, halibut, bonita, yellowtail, and barracuda are the usual catch.

Golf

The City Parks and Recreation Department lists seven public 18-hole courses in Los Angeles, and L.A. County runs some good ones, too. **Rancho Park Golf Course** (✉ 10460 W. Pico Blvd., West L.A., ☎ 310/838–7373) is one of the most heavily played links in the country. It's a beautifully designed course, but the towering pines present an obstacle for those who slice or hook.

The **Sepulveda Golf Complex** (✉ 16821 Burbank Blvd., Encino, ☎ 818/995–1170) has the Balboa course (par 70) and the longer Encino course (par 72), plus a driving range. If you want a scenic course, you've got it in spades at the county-run, par-71 **Los Verdes Golf Course** (7000 W. Los Verdes Dr., Rancho Palos Verdes, ☎ 310/377–7370). You get a cliff-top view of the ocean—time it right and you can watch the sun set behind Catalina Island—and it's one of California's best-run courses to boot.

Griffith Park has two splendid 18-hole courses along with a challenging 9-hole course. **Harding Municipal Golf Course** and **Wilson Municipal Golf Course** (✉ 4730 Crystal Springs Dr., Los Feliz, ☎ 323/663–2555) are about 1½ mi inside the park entrance at Riverside Drive and Los Feliz Boulevard. Bridle paths surround the outer fairways, and the San Gabriel Mountains make a scenic background. The 9-hole **Roosevelt Municipal Golf Course** (✉ 2650 N. Vermont Ave., Los Feliz, ☎ 323/665–2011) can be reached through the park's Vermont Avenue entrance. You may recall the 9-hole pitch 'n' putt **Los Feliz Municipal Golf**

Course (✉ 3207 Los Feliz Blvd., Los Feliz, ☎ 323/663–7758) from the movie *Swingers*.

Hiking

One of the best places to begin is **Griffith Park;** pick up a map from the ranger station (✉ 4730 Crystal Springs Dr., Los Feliz). Many of the paths in the park are not shaded and can be quite steep. A nice short hike from Canyon Drive, at the southwest end of the park, takes you to **Bronson Caves,** where the *Batman* television show was filmed. Begin at the Observatory for a 3-mi round-trip hike to the top of **Mt. Hollywood.**

Who knows how many of Will Rogers's famed witticisms came to him while he and his wife hiked or rode horses along well-marked **Inspiration Point Trail** from their Pacific Palisades ranch, now **Will Rogers State Historic Park** (✉ 1501 Will Rogers State Park Rd., at Sunset Blvd., Pacific Palisades, ☎ 310/454–8212). The 2-mi loop trail takes you gently to the highest point in West Los Angeles. If you're looking for a longer trip, the path meets up with the 65-mi **Backbone Trail**, which connects to Topanga State Park.

Malibu Creek State Park (✉ 1925 Las Virgenes Rd., Calabasas, ☎ 818/880-0367) has some of the best hiking in the area, and if you bring a swimsuit, you can take a dip in the rock pool. See the wild country that has doubled as Korea in the *M*A*S*H* TV show and assorted alien worlds in the original *Star Trek* series.For information on hiking locations and scheduled outings in Los Angeles, contact the **Sierra Club** (✉ 3435 Wilshire Blvd., Suite 320, Los Angeles, 90010, ☎ 213/387–4287, WEB www.sierraclub.org). Or, check out *Outdoors*, the quarterly calendar of events throughout the Santa Monica Mountains from the **Santa Monica Mountains National Recreation Area** (✉ 401 W. Hillcrest Dr., Thousand Oaks 93160, ☎ 805/370–2301, WEB www.nps.gov/samo).

Surfing and Windsurfing

If you're not a strong swimmer, you should start with a lesson from a company like **Malibu Ocean Sports** (✉ 22935 PCH, across from the pier at Malibu Point, ☎ 310/456–6302). **Long Beach Windsurf & Kayak Center** (✉ 3850 E. Ocean Blvd., near the Belmont Pier, Long Beach, ☎ 562/433–1014) provides windsurfing lessons for $115, including gear and wet suit, and rents equipment to certified windsurfers starting from $25 for half a day. At **Captain Kirk's** (✉ 525 N. Harbor Blvd., San Pedro, near Slip 93 of the L.A. Harbor, ☎ 310/833–3397), you can get a basic beginner's setup for $45 a day. More advanced gear will run you up to $60 a day, and beginner lessons start at $75, which includes equipment and two hours of instruction.

When you hit the surfing hot spots mentioned in the Beaches section, surf shops with rentals will be in long supply. Competition keeps prices comparable; most rent long, short, and miniboards from $18 per day, and wet suits from $8 per day (some give discounts for additional days).To catch the best waves, call the **L.A. County Lifeguards'** prerecorded surf conditions hot lines (☎ 310/457–9701 Malibu; 310/578–0478 Santa Monica; 310/379–8471 Manhattan, Redondo, and Hermosa beaches).

Volleyball

The casual beach volleyballer can find pickup games at the beaches the length of the coast; more serious players might want to concentrate on the **Santa Monica State Beach** nets, or at **Manhattan Beach** (which has about 200 nets). If you are truly obsessed, contact the **California Beach Volleyball Association** (☎ 800/350–2282) to see about amateur tournaments (grass-court play as well as beach); their California Cup State Championship tourney is held in late July and early August.

Spectator Sports

For tickets to all sporting events call **Ticketmaster** (☎ 213/480–3232).Some of the major sports venues in the area are: **L.A. Sports Arena** (✉ 3911 S. Figueroa St., Downtown, ☎ 213/748–6136) hosts track meets and USC men's and women's basketball. The 92,000-seat **L.A. Memorial Coliseum** (✉ 3939 S. Figueroa St., Downtown L.A., ☎ 213/748–6136), a State and Federal historic landmark, is the site of USC football and soccer games, concerts, and special events (like two Olympics). The fabulous **Rose Bowl** (✉ 1010 Rose Bowl Dr., Pasadena, ☎ 626/449–7673) is the site of UCLA football and the Rose Bowl Game, pro soccer, megaconcerts, and the world-famous Pasadena Flea Market. The 20,000-seat, $375 million **Staples Center** (✉ 1111 S. Figueroa St., Downtown, ☎ 213/742–7100; 213/742–7340 box office, WEB www.staplescenter.com) opened in 1999 and is now the home of pro-basketball's L.A. Lakers, Clippers, and Sparks, and hockey's L.A. Kings. Seats range from nosebleed ($10) to courtside ($1,500). Staples also hosts big-name concerts.

Baseball

You can watch the **Dodgers** take on their National League rivals while you munch on pizza, tacos, or a foot-long "Dodger dog" at one of the game's most comfortable ballparks, **Dodger Stadium** (✉ 1000 Elysian Park Ave., exit off I–110, Pasadena Freeway, Elysian Park, ☎ 323/224–1448 for ticket information, WEB www.dodgers.com).

Basketball

The **Los Angeles Lakers** (☎ 310/412–5000, WEB www.nba.com/lakers) have enjoyed great seasons since the arrivals of superstar center Shaquille O'Neal and young star Kobe Bryant in 1996. Exciting games attract celebrity fans like Jack Nicholson, Dyan Cannon, and Spike Lee. L.A.'s "other" team, the much-maligned but newly revitalized **Clippers** (☎ 213/748–8000, WEB www.nba.com/clippers), sells tickets that are generally cheaper and easier to get than those for Lakers' games. Relatively new to the pro basketball scene in L.A. is the all-female **Los Angeles Sparks** (☎ 310/426–6031 or call Ticketmaster, WEB www.lasparks.com). They won the 2001 WNBA title.

Golf

The hot golf ticket in town each February is the PGA **Nissan Open** (☎ 800/752–6736, WEB www.lanissanopen.com). The $3 million purse attracts the best golfers in the world to its week of competition at the Riviera Country Club in Pacific Palisades.

Hockey

The National Hockey League's **L.A. Kings** (☎ 310/673–6003, WEB www.lakings.com) are playoff contenders at the Staples Center.

Horse Racing and Shows

Santa Anita Race Track (✉ 285 W. Huntington Dr., at Colorado Pl., Arcadia, ☎ 626/574–7223; ✉ $5–$15), is a beautiful facility with the lovely San Gabriel Mountains for a backdrop. **Hollywood Park** (✉ 1050 S. Prairie Ave., at Century Blvd., Inglewood, ☎ 310/419–1500), next to the Forum, is another favorite thoroughbred-racing venue. Several grand-prix jumping competitions and western riding championships are held throughout the year at the **Los Angeles Equestrian Center** (✉ 480 Riverside Dr., Burbank, ☎ 818/563–3252; 818/840–9066 box office).

Volleyball

There are half a dozen or more **pro volleyball** tournaments (men's and women's) held at L.A.'s beaches in June, July, and August. The best way to keep posted is to check the Web sites of the **Beach Volleyball Association**, at www.bvatour.com, and the **Association of Volleyball Professionals**, at WEB www.avptour.com. At a lesser level, call the **California Beach Volleyball Association** (☏ 800/350–2282) for info on both beach and grass court tourneys.

SHOPPING

Updated by
Kristina Brooks

Most stores in Los Angeles are open 10–6, although many stay open until 9 or later, particularly those on Melrose Avenue and in Santa Monica. Shops along Melrose and in the Los Feliz vicinity don't usually get moving until 11 AM. In most areas, shops are open at least in the afternoon on Sunday. Most stores take credit cards; traveler's checks are also accepted with proper identification. Check the *Los Angeles Times* or *LA Weekly* for sales, and if you're curious about who's shopping where (after all, this is L.A.), take a peek at *In Style* or *Los Angeles* magazines.

Shopping Neighborhoods

Shopping in **Beverly Hills** centers mainly around the three-block stretch of **Rodeo Drive**, between Santa Monica and Wilshire boulevards and the streets surrounding it. While you may feel cowed by some of the astronomical prices, stores in the district have joined efforts to present a more friendly sales front to the public. You'll find department stores like Barneys, Neiman Marcus, Robinsons-May, and Saks along **Wilshire Boulevard.** Some smaller stores have limited access except by appointment. **Two Rodeo Drive**, aka Via Rodeo or simply "the V," is a private cobblestone street with a collection of glossy retail shops, outdoor cafés, and sculpted fountains.

Century City is L.A.'s errand central, where entertainment executives and industry types do their serious shopping. In general, it's more affordable than Beverly Hills. There are also plenty of restaurants and live theaters, as well as a 14-screen AMC movie complex.

Downtown is home to several huge shopping venues: the the **Fashion District** (roughly between I–10 and 7th Street and San Pedro and Main streets), the **Flower Mart** (742 Maple Avenue), and the **Jewelry District** (between Hill Street and Broadway, from 5th to 8th streets). In addition, ethnic shopping areas abound, from colorful **Olvera Street** offering a taste of Mexico to the nearby neighborhoods of **Chinatown, Koreatown,** and, a little farther south and west, **Leimert Park** (between Crenshaw and Leimert boulevards and 43rd Street and Vernon Avenue), a vibrant African-theme shopping area. A Rupert Murdoch- and Philip Anschutz–owned 27-acre entertainment complex is currently in the works.

In **Hollywood,** the shopping focus is on Hollywood & Highland. Outside the complex, on La Brea Avenue especially, you'll find plenty of trendy, quirky, and hip merchandise, from records to furniture and clothing.

Revitalized by an influx of young musicians and actors, the once down-and-out **Los Feliz** area north and east of Hollywood is now a buzzing destination. Offbeat stores and restaurants along Vermont and Hillhurst avenues reflect the tastes of new bohemian residents.

Although it suffered a decline in the late '90s, **Melrose Avenue** has risen like a phoenix and is once again a bohemian shopping district and a great people-watching venue. Teens in gothic black, multipierced slackers, and aspiring actors and musicians mingle among the vintage-clothing shops. The L.A. section, from North Highland to Sweetzer, is the place to pick up anything from inexpensive trinkets and used clothing to fetish wear and vintage shoes.

In **Pasadena,** the stretch of Colorado Boulevard between Pasadena Avenue and Arroyo Parkway, known as **Old Town,** is a popular pedestrian shopping mecca where fashionable chain stores such as A/X Armani Exchange and J.Crew share the street with trendy boutiques. A few blocks west on Colorado between Los Robles and Marengo avenues, the open-air "urban village" known as **Paseo Colorado** mixes residential, retail, dining, and entertainment spaces.

Less frenetic and status-conscious than Beverly Hills, **Santa Monica** is an ideal place for leisurely shopping; the cool ocean breezes along the boulevards may tempt you to stay for hours. Most shopping activity takes place at the **Third Street Promenade,** between Broadway and Wilshire Boulevard; **Main Street** between Pico Boulevard and Rose Avenue; and **Montana Avenue,** from 9th to 17th streets. Parking is next to impossible on Wednesday, when some streets are blocked off for the farmers market.

In the very popular shopping area of **West Hollywood,** you'll find record stores along Sunset Boulevard, pricey antiques stores and galleries on Melrose Place, and upscale boutiques on Robertson Boulevard and upper Melrose Avenue. The **Fairfax District,** along Fairfax below Melrose, encompasses the unusual, historic Farmers Market at Fairfax Avenue and 3rd Street and some excellent galleries around Museum Row at Fairfax and Wilshire Boulevard.

Malls and Markets

The sophisticated, neon-touched **Beverly Center** (⊠ 8500 Beverly Blvd., at Beverly, La Cienega, and San Vicente boulevards and 3rd St., West Hollywood, ☎ 310/854–0070), anchored by Macy's and Bloomingdale's, has chain and upscale stores on three levels. Check out the terrific view of the city from the eighth-floor terrace.

Century City Shopping Center & Marketplace (⊠ 10250 Santa Monica Blvd., Century City, ☎ 310/277–3898), set among gleaming, tall office buildings on what used to be Twentieth Century Fox film studios' back lot, is an open-air mall with an excellent roster of upscale shops, moored by Macy's and Bloomingdale's. Across from Bloomie's is the Marketplace of eateries and vendor carts.

The **Farmers Market** (⊠ 6333 W. 3rd St. at Fairfax, Fairfax District, ☎ 323/933–9211), next to the Grove shopping center, is the granddaddy of L.A. markets, dating back to 1935. This large square of clapboard stalls, eccentric regulars, and, oh yes, produce and wares, remains one of the only public spaces in L.A. that truly encourages community.

The Grove (⊠ 6333 W. 3rd St. Fairfax District, ☎ 888/315–8883), a 575,000-square-ft retail and entertainment complex adjacent to the Farmers Market, has chain stores, restaurants, and movie theaters. A fountain choreographed with lights and music entertains, while a "Red Car" trolley shuttles visitors between the Grove and Farmers Market.

Hollywood & Highland (⊠ Hollywood Blvd. and Highland Ave., Hollywood, ☎ 323/960–2331) houses around 60 retail outlets and a slew of eateries in a complex that tries to embody the glamour and fantasy of the movies. Wide and sweeping "Miss America" steps will lead you between floors of this open-air mall with branches of designer shops

(Ralph Lauren Polo, Versace) and chain stores (Banana Republic, Planet Funk).

The **Santa Monica Farmers Market** (⊠ Arizona and 3rd Sts., Santa Monica, ☎ 310/458–8712), filling four large blocks every Wednesday 9–2, is the biggest farmers market in L.A. A smaller market Saturday 8:30–1 is geared toward organic produce.

Westwood Village Farmers' Market (⊠ Weyburn Ave. at Westwood Blvd., Westwood, ☎ 310/208–6115) attracts the UCLA crowd with more than 70 vendors of organic produce, hot foods, and crafts. The market is held Thursday 1 PM–7 PM. On the last Thursday of the month, Westwood chefs offer cooking demonstrations and free samples 3–4:30.

SIDE TRIPS FROM LOS ANGELES

Lake Arrowhead and Big Bear Lake

Big Bear comes alive in winter with downhill ski and snowboard resorts, cross-country trails, lodges, and an active village. Summer draws crowds to Lake Arrowhead, known for its cool mountain air, trail-threaded woods, and brilliant lake. The magnificent Rim of the World Scenic Byway connects the two communities.

Numbers in the margin correspond to points of interest on the Lake Arrowhead and Big Bear Lake map.

Lake Arrowhead

90 mi from Los Angeles, I–10 east to I–215 north to Hwy. 30 east (mountain resorts turnoff) to Hwy. 18 (Waterman Ave.), then Hwy. 138 north to Hwy. 173 (Lake Arrowhead turnoff); follow signs from there.

❶ **Lake Arrowhead Village** is an alpine community with offices, shops, outlet stores, and eateries that descend the hill to the lake. With the exception of the Village, access to the lake and its beaches is limited to residents and their guests. You can take a scenic 45-minute cruise ($11) on the *Arrowhead Queen*, operated daily by **LeRoy Sports** (☎ 909/336–6992) from the waterfront marina.

❷ Just past the town of Rim Forest, follow Bear Springs Road 2 mi north to the fire lookout tower at **Strawberry Peak.** Brave the steep stairway to the tower, and you'll be treated to a magnificent view and a lesson on fire-spotting by the lookout staff. Call the Ranger Station (☎ 909/337–2444) to find out when staff is on hand.If you're up for

❸ an outdoor barbecue, visit **Baylis Park Picnic Ground,** farther west on Highway 18.

❹ **Lake Gregory,** at the ridge of Crestline, was formed by a dam constructed in 1938. Because the water temperature in summer is seldom very cold—as it can be in the other lakes at this altitude—this is the best swimming lake in the mountains. It's open in summer only, and there's a nominal charge to swim. Fishing is permitted, there are water slides, and you can rent rowboats at Lake Gregory Village. ⊠ *Lake Dr. off Rim of the World Hwy.*

Dining and Lodging

$$–$$$ ✕ **Casual Elegance.** This intimate house with a fireplace is just a couple of miles outside Arrowhead Village. The steaks and seafood are first-rate. ⊠ *26848 Hwy. 189, Aqua Fria, Blue Jay,* ☎ *909/337–8932. AE, D, DC, MC, V.*

Lake Arrowhead and Big Bear Lake

$$–$$$ 🏠 **Lake Arrowhead Resort.** This lakeside lodge has an old-world feeling reminiscent of the Alps. Most rooms have water or forest views. The Village Bay Club and Spa on the premises is at your service. ✉ *27984 Hwy. 189, Lake Arrowhead Village 92352,* ☎ *909/336–1511 or 800/ 800–6792,* FAX *909/336–1378,* WEB *www.lakearrowheadresort.com. 177 rooms, 4 suites, 3 condos. 2 restaurants, cable TV, pool, health club, beach, bar, children's programs; no-smoking rooms. AE, D, DC, MC, V.*

Big Bear Lake

110 mi from Los Angeles, I–10 east to I–215 north to Hwy. 30 east; Hwy. 330 north to Hwy. 18 east; chains are sometimes needed in winter.

⑤ You'll spot an occasional chaletlike building in **Big Bear Lake Village,** an alpine- and Western-mountain-style town on the lake's south shore. The paddle wheeler *Big Bear Queen* (☎ 909/866–3218) departs daily from Big Bear Marina, between May and October, for 90-minute scenic tours ($10) of the lake. **Big Bear City,** at the east end of Big Bear Lake, has restaurants, motels, and a small airport.

⑥ Southeast of Big Bear Village is **Snow Summit,** one of the area's top ski resorts. The 8,200-ft peak has more advanced runs than nearby ski resorts and usually has the best snow. Trails are open to mountain bikers in summer. ✉ *880 Summit Blvd., off Big Bear Blvd. Big Bear Lake,* ☎ *909/866–5766,* WEB *www.snowsummit.com.*

⑦ **Bear Mountain Ski Resort,** also southeast of Big Bear Lake Village is best for intermediate skiers. On busy winter weekends and holidays it's best to reserve tickets before heading to the mountain. ✉ *43101 Goldmine Dr., off Moonridge Rd., Big Bear Lake,* ☎ *909/585–2519; 800/232–7686 for snow reports,* WEB *www.bearmtn.com.*

Dining and Lodging

$$–$$$ ✗ **Madlon's.** Inside this gingerbread-style cottage you'll be treated to sophisticated home cooking: lamb chops with Gorgonzola butter, cream of jalapeño soup, or perhaps Asian black peppercorn filet mignon. ✉ *829 W. Big Bear Blvd., Big Bear City,* ☎ *909/585–3762. D, DC, MC, V. Closed Mon.*

$$–$$$ ✗ **The Iron Squirrel.** Veal Normandie (veal scallopini sautéed with apples, Calvados, and cream) and duck à l'orange are two specialties here but you'll also find a big selection of fresh fish, grilled meats, pastas, and salads. ✉ *646 Pine Knot Blvd., Big Bear Lake,* ☎ *909/866–9121. AE, MC, V.*

$$–$$$ 🏠 **Apples Bed & Breakfast Inn.** Despite its location on a busy road
★   to the ski lifts, the Apples Inn feels remote and peaceful, thanks to the surrounding pine trees. The colorful rooms have names like Golden Delicious, Royal Gala, and Sweet Bough; all have working

gas fireplaces, four have Jacuzzis. A common room has a wood-burn-ing stove, baby grand piano, game table, and library loft. ⊠ *42430 Moonridge Rd., Big Bear Lake 92315,* ☏ *909/866–0903,* WEB *www. applesbedandbreakfast.com. 12 rooms. Room TVs, in-room VCRs, outdoor hot tub, basketball, volleyball, paddle tennis, volleyball; no room phones, no smoking. AE, D, MC, V.*

$–$$$ ⊞ **Northwoods Resort.** Northwoods is a giant log cabin with all the ameni-ties of a resort. The lobby resembles a 1930s hunting lodge, with canoes, antlers, fishing poles, and a grand stone fireplace. Rooms are large but cozy; some have fireplaces and whirlpool tubs. Stillwells Restaurant, next to the lobby, serves hearty American fare. Ski packages are available. ⊠ *40650 Village Dr., Big Bear Lake 92315,* ☏ *909/866–3121 or 800/866–3121,* FAX *909/878–2122,* WEB *www.northwoodsresort.com. 138 rooms, 9 suites. 2 restaurants, room TVs, pool, gym, outdoor hot tub, sauna, bar; no-smoking rooms. AE, D, DC, MC, V.*

Lake Arrowhead and Big Bear Lake A to Z

To research prices, get advice from other travelers, and book travel ar-rangements, visit www.fodors.com.

VISITOR INFORMATION

Lake Arrowhead Communities Chamber of Commerce has informa-tion on camping and lodging. Big Bear Lake Resort Association will help with lodging arrangements.

➤ TOURIST INFORMATION: **Big Bear Lake Resort Association** (⊠ 630 Bartlett Rd., Big Bear Lake 92315, ☏ 909/866–7000, 800/424–4232, FAX 909/866–5671, WEB www.bigbearinfo.com). **Lake Arrowhead Com-munities Chamber of Commerce** (⊠ Box 219, 28200 Hwy. 189, Bldg. F, Suite 290, Lake Arrowhead 92352, ☏ 909/337–3715, FAX 909/336–1548, WEB www.lakearrowhead.com).

Catalina Island

Just 22 mi out to sea from the L.A. coastline, Catalina has virtually unspoiled mountains, canyons, coves, and beaches; best of all, it gives you a glimpse of what undeveloped Southern California once looked like. Summer, weekends, and holidays, Catalina crawls with thou-sands of L.A.-area boaters, who tie their vessels at moorings protected in Avalon and other coves. Although Catalina is not known for wide, sandy beaches, sunbathing and water sports are big draws; divers and snorkelers come for the exceptionally clear water surrounding the is-land. The main town of Avalon is a charming, old-fashioned beach com-munity, where palm trees shade the main street and yachts bob in the crescent-shape bay. White buildings dotting the semi-arid hillsides give it a Greek-island feel.

Although Catalina can be seen in a day, several inviting hotels make it worth extending your stay for one or more nights. A short itinerary might include breakfast along the boardwalk, a tour of the interior, a snorkeling excursion at Casino Point, and dinner in Avalon.

Avalon

1- to 2-hr ferry ride from Long Beach, Newport Beach, or San Pedro; 15-min helicopter ride from Long Beach or San Pedro.

Avalon, Catalina's only real town, extends from the shore of its natu-ral harbor to the surrounding hillsides. Most of the city's activity, however, is centered along the pedestrian mall of **Crescent Avenue,** and most sights are easily reached on foot. Private cars are restricted and rental cars aren't allowed, but taxis, trams, and shuttles can take you anywhere you need to go. Bicycles and golf carts can be rented from shops along Crescent Avenue. Requisite permits for hiking the interior of the island are available free from the Santa Catalina Island Conservancy.

On the northwest point of Avalon Bay (looking to your right from Green Pleasure Pier) is the majestic landmark **Casino.** This circular white structure is considered one of the finest examples of art deco architecture anywhere. Its Spanish-inspired floors and murals show off brilliant blue and green Catalina tiles. "Casino" is the Italian word for "gathering place" and in this case has nothing to do with gambling. Rather, Casino life revolves around the magnificent ballroom: the same big-band dances that made the Casino famous in the 1930s and '40s still take place on holiday weekends. The New Year's Eve dance (☎ 310/510–1520) is hugely popular and sells out well in advance. Santa Catalina Island Company leads tours of the Casino, lasting about 55 minutes, for $9. You can also visit the **Catalina Island Museum,** in the lower level of the Casino, which investigates 7,000 years of island history; or stop at the **Casino Art Gallery** to see works by local artists. First-run movies are screened on weekends at the **Avalon Theatre,** noteworthy for its classic 1929 theater pipe organ. ⌧ *1 Casino Way, Avalon,* ☎ *310/510–2414 for museum; 310/510–0808 for art gallery; 310/510–0179 for Avalon Theatre.* ⌧ *Museum $2, art gallery free.* ⊙ *Museum: daily 10–4; closed Thursdays, Jan.–March. Art gallery: daily 10:30–4; closed Mon. and Wed., Jan.–Mar. 15.*

In front of the Casino are the crystal-clear waters of the **Casino Point Underwater Park,** a marine preserve protected from boats and other watercraft where moray eels, bat rays, spiny lobsters, halibut, and other sea animals cruise around kelp forests and along the sandy bottom. It's a terrific site for scuba diving, with some shallow areas suitable for snorkeling. Scuba and snorkeling equipment can be rented on and near the pier. The shallow waters of **Lover's Cove,** east of the boat landing, are also good for snorkeling.

Dining and Lodging

$$–$$$ ✗ **Channel House.** A longtime Avalon family owns this restaurant, serv-
★ ing dishes such as Catalina swordfish, coq au vin, and pepper steak with a Continental flair. There's a patio facing the harbor, as well as a comfortable dining room and Irish bar. ⌧ *205 Crescent Ave., Avalon,* ☎ *310/510–1617. AE, D, MC, V. Closed Mon.*

$$$$ ⊞ **Inn on Mt. Ada.** In the mansion where William Wrigley, Jr., once lived, the island's most exclusive hotel has all the comforts of a millionaire's home—at millionaires' prices. The six guest rooms are traditional and elegant; some have fireplaces and all have water views. The hilltop view of the Pacific is spectacular. ⌧ *398 Wrigley Rd., Avalon 90704,* ☎ *310/510–2030 or 800/608–7669,* ℻ *310/510–2237,* ᴡᴇʙ *www.catalina.com/mtada. 6 rooms. Dining room, meeting rooms; no room phones, no room TVs, no-smoking rooms. MC, V.*

$$–$$$$ ⊞ **Hotel Metropole and Market Place.** This romantic hotel could easily be in the heart of New Orleans' French Quarter. Some guest rooms have balconies overlooking a flower-filled courtyard of restaurants and shops; others have ocean views. Adding to the romance are fireplaces and whirlpool tubs (in some rooms). For a stunning panorama, head for the rooftop deck. Continental breakfast is included. ⌧ *205 Crescent Ave., Avalon 90704,* ☎ *310/510–1884 or 800/541–8528,* ℻ *310/510–2534,* ᴡᴇʙ *www.hotel-metropole.com. 44 rooms, 4 suites. Some in-room hot tubs, some minibars, cable TV; no-smoking rooms. AE, MC, V.*

$–$$ ⛺ **Hermosa Hotel and Catalina Cottages.** You'll find tiny, sparse rooms with shared baths in this 1890s hotel; the separate cottages have kitchens and private baths. The beach is a half block away. ⊠ *131 Metropole St., Avalon 90704,* ☎ *310/510–1010 or 877/453–1313,* FAX *310/510–2830,* WEB *www.hermosahotel.com. 35 rooms without bath, 14 cottages. Some kitchens, cable TV; no room phones. AE, DC, MC, V.*

Two Harbors

45- to 60-min ferry ride (summer only) or 90-min bus ride from Avalon; 3-hr ferry ride (summer only) from Los Angeles.

This fairly primitive community toward the western end of the island has long been a summer boating destination. The area is named for its two harbors, which are separated by a ½-mi-wide isthmus. Once inhabited by pirates and smugglers, Two Harbors recalls the days before tourism became the island's major industry. This side of the island is less tame, with abundant wildlife. Activities here include swimming, diving, boating, hiking, mountain biking, beachcombing, kayaking, and sportfishing.

Lodging

Tiny Two Harbors has limited overnight accommodations, including a few campgrounds. All reservations are made through the **visitor services** office (⊠ Box 5086, Two Harbors 90704, ☎ 310/510–0303, FAX 310/510–0224 WEB www.catalina.com/twoharbors), which you'll see when you arrive.

Catalina Island A to Z

To research prices, get advice from other travelers, and book travel arrangements, visit www.fodors.com.

AIR TRAVEL

Island Express helicopters depart hourly from San Pedro and Long Beach (8 AM–sunset). The trip takes about 15 minutes and costs $73 one-way, $136 round-trip. Reservations are recommended a week in advance.
➤ AIRLINES AND CONTACTS: **Island Express** (☎ 310/510–2525, WEB www.islandexpress.com).

BOAT AND FERRY TRAVEL

Two companies offer ferry service to Catalina Island, for about $42 to $44. Reservations are advised in summer and on weekends for all trips.
➤ BOAT AND FERRY INFORMATION: **Catalina Express** (☎ 310/519–1212 or 800/995–4386, FAX 800/410–9159, WEB www.catalinaexpress.com). **Catalina Passenger Service** (☎ 949/673–5245 or 800/830–7744, FAX 949/673–8340, WEB www.catalinainfo.com).

BUS TRAVEL

Catalina Safari Shuttle Bus has regular bus service (in season) between Avalon, Two Harbors, and several campgrounds.
➤ BUS INFORMATION: **Catalina Safari Shuttle Bus** (☎ 310/510–0303 or 800/322–3434).

GOLF CARTS

Golf carts constitute the island's main form of transportation. You can rent them along Avalon's Crescent Avenue and Pebbly Beach Road for about $30 per hour (although you generally pay for two hours up-front). Try Island Rentals. No credit cards are accepted.
➤ LOCAL AGENCIES: **Island Rentals** (⊠ 125 Pebbly Beach Rd., Avalon, ☎ 310/510–1456).

TOURS

Santa Catalina Island Company runs several tours for costing $9 to $36. There are ticket booths on the Green Pleasure Pier, at the Casino, in the plaza, and at the boat landing. Catalina Adventure Tours, which has booths at the boat landing and on the pier, arranges similar excursions at comparable prices. The requisite free permits for hikes into Catalina Island's interior are available daily from 9 to 5 at Two Harbors Visitor Services on the pier. Horseback riders can wrangle four-legged transportation for scenic trail rides. Guided rides start at $30 at Catalina Stables.

➤ CONTACTS: **Catalina Adventure Tours** (☎ 310/510–2888, FAX 310/510–2797, WEB www.catalinaadventuretours.com). **Catalina Stables** (✉ 600 Avalon Canyon Rd. Avalon, ☎ 310/510–0478). **Santa Catalina Island Company**(☎ 310/510–8687 or 800/322–3434, WEB www.catalina.com/scico). **Santa Catalina Island Conservancy** (✉ 3rd and Claressa Sts., Avalon 90704, ☎ 310/510–2595, WEB www.catalinaconservancy.org). **Two Harbors Visitor Services** (✉ Box 5086, Two Harbors 90704, ☎ 310/510–0303).

VISITOR INFORMATION

The Catalina Island Visitor's Bureau, is a good place to get your bearings, check into special events, and plan your itinerary. The staff will help you find lodgings.

➤ TOURIST INFORMATION: The **Catalina Island Visitor's Bureau** (✉ Green Pleasure Pier, Box 217, Avalon 90704, ☎ 310/510–1520, FAX 310/510–7606 WEB www.catalina.com).

LOS ANGELES A TO Z

To research prices, get advice from other travelers, and book travel arrangements, visit www.fodors.com.

AIR TRAVEL

More than 85 major carriers serve Los Angeles International Airport (LAX), the third-largest airport in the world in terms of passenger traffic. The Burbank/Glendale/Pasadena Airport (BUR) is convenient to much of L.A. and domestic flights to it can be cheaper than flights to LAX. *See* Air Travel *in* Smart Travel Tips A to Z for airline phone numbers.

AIRPORTS AND TRANSFERS

➤ AIRPORT INFORMATION: **Burbank/Glendale/Pasadena Airport** (✉ 2627 N. Hollywood Way, Burbank, ☎ 818/840–8830 or 818/840–8847).**Los Angeles International Airport (LAX)** (☎ 310/646–5252, WEB www.lawa.org/lax/laxframe.html).

➤ SHUTTLES: **Prime Time** (☎ 800/733–8267). **SuperShuttle** (☎ 323/775–6600, 310/782–6600, or 800/258–3826, WEB www.supershuttle.com). **Xpress Shuttle**(☎ 800/427–7483, WEB www.expressshuttle.com).

BUS TRAVEL TO AND FROM LOS ANGELES

➤ BUS INFORMATION: **Greyhound** (✉ 1716 E. 7th St., Downtown, ☎ 800/231–2222 or 213/629–8405, WEB www.greyhound.com).

BUS TRAVEL WITHIN LOS ANGELES

Serving the whole city is the Metropolitan Transit Authority DASH (Downtown Area Short Hop) minibuses, with six different circular routes in Hollywood, Mid-Wilshire, and the downtown area. The Santa Monica Municipal Bus Line, also known as the Big Blue Bus, is a pleasant and inexpensive way to move around the Westside, where the MTA lines leave off. There's also an express bus to and from downtown L.A., and a shuttle bus, the *Tide Shuttle,* which runs between Main Street and the Third Street Promenade and stops at hotels along the way.

➤ BUS INFORMATION: **DASH** (☎ 213/626–4455 or 310/808–2273). **Metropolitan Transit Authority (MTA)** (☎ 213/626–4455 or 800/ COMMUTE, WEB www.mta.net). **Santa Monica Municipal Bus Line** (☎ 310/451–5444).

CAR RENTAL

Major-chain rates in L.A. begin at $29 a day and $125 a week, plus 8.25% sales tax. Luxury and sport utility vehicles start at $49 a day. *See* Car Rental *in* Smart Travel Tips A to Z for national rental agency phone numbers.

CAR TRAVEL

L.A. is sprawling and traffic-clogged, so buy a good map and try to avoid traveling during the rush hours (7 AM–10 AM and 3 PM–7 PM). That said, having your own car really is the best way to get around L.A. Keep in mind that most freeways are known by a name and a number; for example, the San Diego Freeway (I–405), the Hollywood (U.S. 101) or Ventura (a different stretch of U.S. 101) freeways, the Santa Monica Freeway (I–10), and the Harbor Freeway (I–110).

EMERGENCIES

In case of emergency dial 911.

➤ HOSPITALS: **Cedar-Sinai Medical Center** (✉ 8700 Beverly Blvd., ☎ 310/855–5000). **Century City Hospital** (✉ 2070 Century Park East near Pico Blvd., ☎ 310/553–6211). **Queen of Angels Hollywood Presbyterian Medical Center** (✉ 1300 N. Vermont Ave., ☎ 213/413–3000).

LODGING

➤ RESERVATIONS: **visit-Los-Angeles.com** (☎ 800/638–0006). **Los Angeles Hotel Finder** (☎ 888/649–6331, WEB www.losangeles-hotel-finder.com).

TOURS

BUS AND VAN TOURS

Casablanca Tours gives sightseeing tours all around L.A., but their specialty is an insider's look at Hollywood and Beverly Hills; it's available in two- and four-hour versions ($29–$79). L.A. Tours and Sightseeing has several tours ($42), by van and bus, covering various parts of the city, including downtown, Hollywood, and Beverly Hills. The company also operates tours to Disneyland, Universal Studios, Magic Mountain, beaches, and stars' homes. Starline Tours of Hollywood ($29–$75) picks up passengers from area hotels and from Mann's Chinese Theater. Sights such as Universal Studios, Sea World, Knott's Berry Farm, stars' homes, and Disneyland, are on this popular tour company's agenda.

➤ CONTACTS: **Casablanca Tours** (✉ Hollywood Roosevelt Hotel, 7000 Hollywood Blvd., Hollywood 90028, ☎ 323/461–0156 or 800/498–6871, WEB www.casablancatours.com). **L.A. Tours and Sightseeing** (✉ 1617 Gower, ☎ 323/937–3361 or 800/881–7715, WEB www.latours.net). **Starline Tours of Hollywood** (✉ 6541 Hollywood Blvd. and 6925 Hollywood Blvd., Hollywood 90028, ☎ 323/463–3333 or 800/959–3131, WEB www.starlinetours.com).

WALKING TOURS

A very pleasant self-guided walking tour of the Santa Monica mountains is detailed in a brochure available at the park's visitors center. The Los Angeles Conservancy offers walking tours (each about 2½ hours long), chiefly of the downtown area. Cost is $8 per person. Reservations are required.

➤ CONTACTS: The **Los Angeles Conservancy** (☎ 213/623–2489, WEB www.laconservahcy.org). **Santa Monica Visitors Center** (✉ 1400 Ocean Blvd., Santa Monica 90401, ☎ 310/393–7593).

TAXIS

Don't even try to hail a cab on the street in Los Angeles. Instead, phone a taxi company. The metered rate is $1.60 per mi, plus $1.90–$2.50 to start.

➤ TAXI COMPANY: **Yellow Cab/LA Taxi Co-Op** (☎ 800/200–1085 or 800/200–0011).

TRAIN TRAVEL

Amtrak serves downtown L.A.'s Union Station. A surface light rail line, Metro Rail Blue Line, and the underground Metro Rail Red Line run approximately 5 AM–11 PM. The Red Line has two segments, one running west from downtown to Wilshire and Western, one running northwest from downtown through Hollywood to Universal City and North Hollywood. The Blue Line runs from downtown south to Long Beach. The fare on both lines is $1.35 one-way. Metrolink is a commuter train serving towns in Los Angeles county.

➤ TRAIN INFORMATION: **Amtrak** (☎ 800/872–7245, WEB www. amtrak). **Metrolink** (☎ 800/371–5465 or 213/347–2800, WEB www. metrolinktrains.com). **Metropolitan Transit Authority (MTA)** (☎ 800/266–6883 or 213/626–4455, WEB www.mta.net).

VISITOR INFORMATION

➤ TOURIST INFORMATION: **Beverly Hills Conference and Visitors Bureau** (✉ 239 S. Beverly Dr., 90212, ☎ 310/248–1000 or 800/345–2210). **Hollywood Chamber of Commerce Info Center** (✉ 7018 Hollywood Blvd., 90028, ☎ 323/469–8311, WEB www.hollywoodcoc.org). **Los Angeles Visitors Information Center** (✉ 685 S. Figueroa St., ☎ 213/689–8822, WEB www.visitlanow.com). **Pasadena Convention and Visitors Bureau** (✉ 171 S. Los Robles Ave., 91101, ☎ 626/795–9311, WEB www.pasadenacal.com). **Santa Monica Convention and Visitors Bureau** (✉ 520 Broadway, Suite 250, 90401-2428, ☎ 310/319–6263 or 800/544–5319, WEB www.santamonica.com). **West Hollywood Convention and Visitors Bureau** (✉ 8687 Melrose Ave., Suite M25, 90069, ☎ 310/289–2525 or 800/368–6020, WEB www.visitwesthollywood.com).

15 ORANGE COUNTY

No place in Southern California evokes the stereotype of California's good life quite the way Orange County does: million-dollar mansions dot the coastline, lush golf courses line beaches and meander through inland hills, and tony convertibles glide down the Pacific Coast Highway. But, while visitors and residents are adept at lounging under swaying palm trees on the shore, the inland cities are alive with amusement parks, professional sporting events, and dozens of hotels and restaurants, all within minutes of each other.

F EW OF THE CITRUS GROVES that gave Orange County its name remain. This region south and east of Los Angeles is now a high-tech business hub where tourism is the number-one industry.

Updated by
Tina Carr

Anaheim's theme parks lure hordes of funseekers, and numerous festivals celebrate the county's culture and relatively brief history. With its tropical flowers and palm trees, the stretch of coast between Seal Beach and San Clemente is often called the "American Riviera." Exclusive Newport Beach, artsy Laguna, and the up-and-coming surf town of Huntington Beach are the stars, but lesser-known gems on the glistening coast—such as Corona del Mar—are also worth visiting.

Pleasures and Pastimes

Dining

Burger joints abound, but you'll also find Italian, French, Chinese, Thai, Scandinavian, Cuban, and other types of cuisine, in every type of setting—from the elegant Dining Room at the Ritz-Carlton, Laguna Niguel, to the rustic digs at down-home Memphis Soul, a Cajun café in Costa Mesa.

CATEGORY	COST*
$$$$	over $30
$$$	$22–$30
$$	$15–$21
$	under $15

per person for a main course at dinner, excluding 7¼% tax.

Lodging

In a uniquely SoCal way, accommodations here fulfill their patrons' paradoxical need for serenity and glamour. Limos speed in and out of hotel driveways, ferrying people hankering to be noticed. Still, a few nights at the Four Seasons Hotel in Newport Beach, or the Ritz-Carlton, Laguna Niguel in Dana Point make for a soothing contrast to the traffic-snarled city experience. The prices listed in this chapter are based on summer rates. Prices are often lower in winter, especially near Disneyland, unless there's a convention in Anaheim, and weekend rates are often rock-bottom at business hotels; it's worth calling around to search for bargains.

CATEGORY	COST*
$$$$	over $225
$$$	$160–$225
$$	$100–$159
$	under $100

All prices are for a standard double room, excluding 8%–15% tax.

Outdoor Activities and Sports

Predictably, water sports rule the coast of Orange County, but other sports don't lag far behind: the sight of people jogging, walking, biking, and blading is nearly inescapable.

Wave action along the coastline ranges from beginner to expert. Beginners can get a feel for the waves by riding a Boogie board at Seal Beach or at the Newport River Jetties. Surfing is permitted at most beaches year-round (check local newspapers or talk to lifeguards for conditions), and surfboard-rental stands line the coast. The best waves are usually at San Clemente, Newport Beach, and Huntington Beach.

From June through September the ocean temperature tops 70° and lifeguards patrol almost every beach. Keep a lookout for signs warning of dangerous conditions: undertow, strong currents, and big waves can all be hazardous. Never go in the water when flags with a black circle are flying, and avoid swimming near surfers. Many beaches close just after sunset.

Golf and tennis are two more reasons to visit Orange County, thanks to the area's great weather and dozens of facilities. A few public golf courses are listed in this chapter; for more information contact the Southern California Golf Association (☎ 818/980–3630) or the Southern California Public Links Golf Association (☎ 714/ 994–4747).

For those who wish to enjoy the coastline by bike or on foot, the Santa Ana Riverbed Trail hugs the Santa Ana River for 20½ mi between the Pacific Coast Highway (PCH) at Huntington State Beach and Imperial Highway in Yorba Linda. Joggers enjoy an uninterrupted path the entire way and don't have to run alongside cars. There are entrances, rest rooms, and drinking fountains at all crossings. A bike path winds south from Marina del Rey all the way to San Diego with only minor breaks. Most beaches have bike rental stands.

Exploring Orange County

Like Los Angeles, Orange County stretches over a large area, lacks a singular focal point, and has limited public transportation. You'll need a car and a sensible game plan to make the most of your visit. If you're headed to Disneyland, you'll probably want to stay in or near Anaheim, organize your activities around the inland-county attractions, and take excursions to the coast. If the mouse's kingdom is not part of your itinerary, try staying at a midpoint location such as Irvine or Costa Mesa, both equidistant from inland tourist attractions and the coast. These towns are less crowded than Anaheim and less expensive than the beach cities. Of course, if you can afford it, staying at the beach is always recommended.

Numbers in the text correspond to numbers in the margin and on the Orange County map.

Great Itineraries

IF YOU HAVE 1 DAY

You're going to **Disneyland** ①.

IF YOU HAVE 3 DAYS

You're still going to **Disneyland** ① (stay overnight in 🏨 **Anaheim**), and if it's up to the kids you could add **Disney's California Adventure** ① to the mix and easily devote all three days (not to mention a considerable amount of money) to the Disneyland Resort. If you'd prefer to escape from the Magic Kingdom, get up early on day two and head to **Laguna Beach,** before the crowds arrive. Breakfast alfresco, then take a walk on the sand. Afterward, stroll around the local streets adorned with great bookstores and art galleries. Don't miss the basketball court where *White Men Can't Jump* was filmed. Pick up a game if you like or hold out for an impromptu chess match with a local at one of the nearby tables surfside and plan to spend the night. On day three, visit **Dana Point** or **Huntington Beach,** then either hang out on the sand with a surfboard or head inland to **Costa Mesa,** where you can browse through **South Coast Plaza,** ⑬ one of the world's largest retail, entertainment, and dining complexes, or visit The Lab, the area's "anti-mall," a selection of renegade fashion, book, and music stores. Here, alternative types sip Chai teas, practicing the art of extemporaneous poetry, and appear hopelessly hip.

When to Tour Orange County

The sun shines year-round in Orange County. Beat the crowds and the heat by visiting in winter, spring, or fall. Smart parents give kids their Disney fix on weekdays or during the winter months.

INLAND ORANGE COUNTY

About a 35-minute drive from downtown Los Angeles on I–5 (also known as the Santa Ana Freeway) is Anaheim, Orange County's tourist hub, which centers around the big D.

Anaheim

26 mi southeast of Los Angeles on I–5.

The snowcapped Matterhorn, the centerpiece of the Magic Kingdom, dominates Anaheim's skyline, serving, along with the city's landscaped streets, as an enduring reminder of the role Disneyland has played in the urbanization and growth of Orange County. Since Walt Disney chose this once-quiet farming community for the site of his first amusement park in 1955, Disneyland has attracted more than 450 million visitors and thousands of workers, and Anaheim has been their host. To understand the symbiotic relationship between Disneyland and Anaheim, one need only look at the $4.2 billion spent in a combined effort by the Walt Disney Company and Anaheim, the latter to revitalize the city's tourist center and run-down areas, the former to expand and renovate the Disney properties into what is known now as **Disneyland Resort.** The resort is a sprawling complex that includes Disney's two amusement parks; three hotels; and Downtown Disney, a shopping, dining, and entertainment promenade. Anaheim's tourist center includes Edison International Field, home of the Anaheim Angels baseball team; Arrowhead Pond, where the Mighty Ducks hockey team plays; and the enormous Anaheim Convention Center.

★ ☾ ❶ One of the biggest misconceptions people have about **Disneyland** is that they've "been there, done that" if they've visited either the more mammoth Disney World or one of the two Disney parks overseas. But Disneyland, the only one of the four kingdoms overseen by Walt himself, has a genuine historic feel and occupies a unique place in the Disney legend. There's plenty here that you won't find anywhere else; for example, Storybook Land, with its miniature replicas of animated Disney scenes from classics such as *Pinocchio* and *Alice In Wonderland*; the Matterhorn Bobsleds; the Indiana Jones Adventure ride; and the Rocket Rods speed ride.

To give you an idea of Disneyland's geography, there are eight themed lands that comprise more than 60 major rides, 50 shops, and 30 restaurants. You enter the park through a recreated 19th-century railroad station. Start your visit with a stroll along **Main Street, U.S.A.** Walt's hometown of Marceline, Missouri was the inspiration behind this romanticized image of small-town America, circa 1900. Trolleys, double-decker buses, and horse-drawn wagons travel up and down the quaint thoroughfare, and the sidewalks are lined with rows of shops selling everything from Disney products to magic tricks, crystal ware, sports memorabilia, and photo supplies. If you want to save some of the walking for later, board the Disneyland Railroad at the park entrance; it tours all the lands.

Directly across from Main Street, Sleeping Beauty's Castle marks the entrance to **Fantasyland,** where you can fly on Peter Pan's Flight, take an aerial spin with Dumbo the Flying Elephant, bobsled through the

494

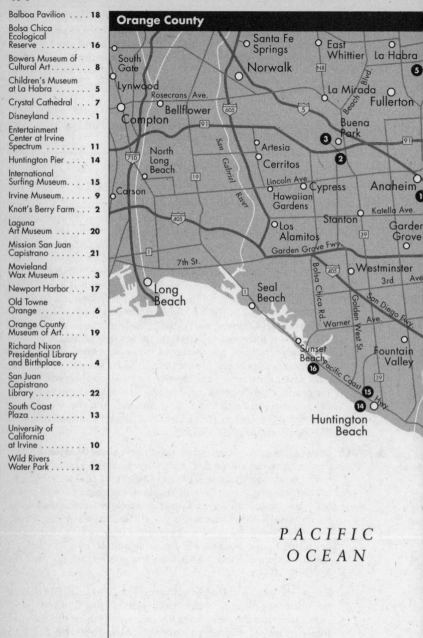

Orange County

PACIFIC
OCEAN

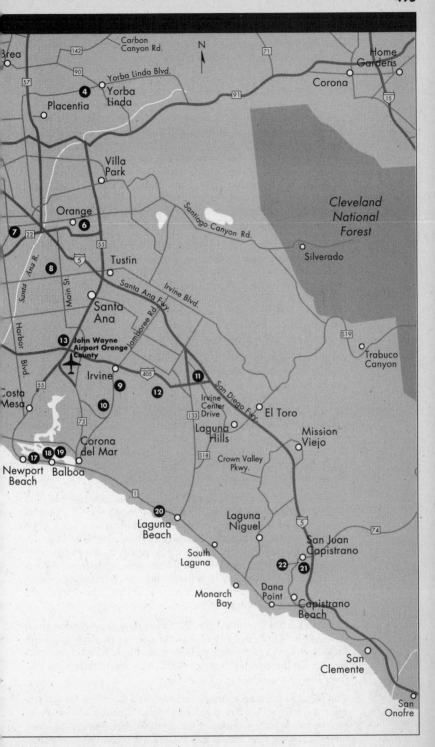

Matterhorn, and float through It's a Small World, singing and waving to children from 100 countries.The steamboat *Mark Twain* and the sailing ship *Columbia* both set sail from **Frontierland.** Here also, kids of all ages can raft to Tom Sawyer Island for an hour or so of climbing and exploring.

Inspired by some of the more exotic corners of the world, **Adventureland** is home to the popular Jungle Cruise and the Indiana Jones Adventure, which keeps you entertained in line with special effects and decipherable hieroglyphics. **Critter Country**, populated by animated bears, is where to find Splash Mountain, Disney's steepest, wettest adventure. In **Tomorrowland,** you can ride on the futuristic Astro Orbitor rockets, race through Space Mountain, tinker with the toys of tomorrow at Innoventions, and enjoy *Toy Story's* new Buzz Lightyear stage show at "Club Buzz." One note: kids love getting soaked in the Cosmic Wave. Either save this one for the end of the day, bring a change of clothes, or expect to shell out for dry (and pricey) T-shirts.

Stroll in the company of Dixieland musicians through the twisting streets of **New Orleans Square,** where you'll find theme shops selling everything from hats to gourmet foods. This is also where to catch the ever-popular Pirates of the Caribbean and Haunted Mansion rides. **Mickey's Toontown** is a land where kids feel like they're actually in a cartoon. They can climb up a rope ladder on the *Miss Daisy* (Donald Duck's boat), talk to a mailbox, walk through Mickey's House to meet the famous mouse, and take a spin on the Roger Rabbit Car Toon Spin.

Besides the eight lands, the daily live-action shows and parades are indelible crowd-pleasers. **Fantasmic!** is a musical, firework, and laser show in which Mickey and friends wage a spellbinding battle against Disneyland's darker characters; and the daytime and nighttime Parade of the Stars features just about every animated Disney character ever drawn. Arrive early to secure a good view; if there are two shows scheduled for the day, the second one tends to be less crowded. New in 2002, the "Believe.There's Magic in the Stars" fireworks display is showcased on Friday and Saturday evenings. Brochures with maps, available at the entrance, list show and parade times.

During the busy summer season, Disneyland is usually mobbed with visitors. The Fastpass system, which allows you to reserve a place in line at the park's more popular attractions (only one at a time), helps cut down on some of the waiting time. But if possible, visit on a mid-week day. In summer, try to avoid the hot midday hours; though most Disney attractions are indoors, you'll be standing in direct sunlight as you wait in lines. Also, try to arrive early if you're planning on purchasing tickets at the park; the box office opens a half hour before the park's scheduled opening time.

Characters appear for autographs and photos throughout the day; check with a Disneyland employee (or cast member, as they're called here) for information about designated character stops. You can also meet some of the animated icons at one of the character meals served at the three Disney hotels (open to the public).

Plan meals to avoid peak mealtime crowds and more long lines. If you want to eat at the **Blue Bayou** in New Orleans Square, it's best to make reservations in person as soon as you get to the park. For a quick lunch on the go, try the **Blue Ribbon Bakery,** which sells gourmet sandwiches.

You can store belongings in lockers just off Main Street; purchases can also be sent to the Package Pickup desk at the front of the park. Note that Main Street stays open an hour after the attractions close, so you may want to save your shopping for the end of your visit. If you plan to visit for more than a day, you can save money by buying three- and four-day Park Hopper tickets that grant same-day "hopping" privileges between Disneyland and Disney's California Adventure. ⊠ *1313 Harbor Blvd., Anaheim,* ☎ *714/781–4565,* WEB *www.disneyland.com.* 🎟 *$43.* ☼ *Daily, year-round, with longer hrs on weekends, holidays, and summers. Call for specific times.*

★ ☾ The 55-acre **Disney's California Adventure** opened in 2001 next to Disneyland and pays tribute to the Golden State with three theme areas: **Paradise Pier** re-creates the glory days of California's seaside piers. If you're looking for thrills, the California Screamin' roller coaster takes its riders from 0 to 55 mph in about four seconds and proceeds through scream tunnels, steeply angled drops, and a 360° loop. The Sun Wheel, a giant Ferris wheel, provides a good view of the grounds at a more leisurely pace.

Hollywood Pictures Backlot lets anyone who has ever dreamed of fame and glory indulge their fantasies for a while. You can imagine yourself as a movie star, character voice, or extra having lunch on a TV soap opera set. *Who Wants to Be a Millionaire—Play It!* is a replica of the set where the popular game show is filmed, and where you can play for prizes.

Golden State celebrates California's history and natural beauty with six regions, including the Bay Area, Pacific Wharf, and Condor Flats, where you can enjoy Soarin' Over California, a spectacular simulated hang-glider ride over California terrain. The film *Golden Dreams* is a sentimental super-fast run through California history with Whoopi Goldberg. There's also a working 1-acre farm and winery, a 40,000-square-ft animation exhibit, Broadway-style theater, nature trail, and tortilla factory. Like its sister park, California Adventure has a daily parade. Retail shops and restaurants—including McDonald's Burger Invasion; the usual Disney Asian, Italian, and grill options; and a Wolfgang Puck restaurant—will occupy some time. ⊠ *1313 Harbor Blvd., Anaheim,* ☎ *714/781–4565,* WEB *www.disneyland.com.* 🎟 *$43.* ☼ *Daily, year-round, with longer hrs on weekends, holidays, and summers. Call for specific times.*

Downtown Disney is a 20-acre, nongated, promenade of dining, shopping, and entertainment that connects the Disneyland Resort hotels and theme parks. Restaurant-nightclubs here include **Y Arriba! Y Arriba!,** with Latin dishes, dancing, and entertainment; **House of Blues,** offering Delta-inspired ribs and seafood along with a variety of music; **Ralph Brennan's Jazz Kitchen,** with New Orleans–style food and music; and **Rainforest Café,** specializing in Latin American and Caribbean food in a room full of animated jungle animals. Sports fans gravitate to **ESPN Zone,** a sports bar–restaurant–entertainment center with American grill food, interactive video games, and 175 video screens telecasting worldwide sports events. For movie goers, there is an **AMC** megaplex theater with stadium-style seating and 12 screens. Promenade shops sell everything from Disney goods to fine art. **Hoypoloi** showcases one-of-a-kind gifts made by artists from around the world; **Tin Pan Alley** sells magnets, lunch boxes, and other metal goods; and **Lego Imagination Center** appeals to kids. ⊠ *Disneyland Dr. between Ball Rd. and Katella Ave., Anaheim,* ☎ *714/300–7800,* WEB *www.disneyland.com.* 🎟 *Free.* ☼ *Daily 7 AM–2 AM; hrs at shops and restaurants vary.*

A 1908 Carnegie Library building houses the **Anaheim Museum,** which documents the history of Anaheim. Changing exhibits include art collections, women's history, and hobbies. A hands-on children's gallery keeps the kids entertained. ✉ *241 S. Anaheim Blvd., at Broadway North Anaheim,* ☎ *714/778–3301,* FAX *714/778–6740,* WEB *www. anaheimmuseum.net.* 🎫 *$2 donation.* ⊙ *Wed.–Fri. 10–4, Sat. noon–4, Sun.–Tues. by appointment only.*

Dining and Lodging

Most Anaheim hotels have complimentary shuttle service to a designated drop-off/pick-up area within the Disneyland Resort, though many hotels are within walking distance.

$$–$$$$ ✕ **JW's Steakhouse.** This subdued steak house inside the Anaheim Marriott specializes in aged beef but also serves seafood. It's great for business or romance. ✉ *700 W. Convention Way, Anaheim,* ☎ *714/750–8000. AE, D, DC, MC, V. No lunch. Valet parking.*

$$–$$$ ✕ **Anaheim White House.** Several small dining rooms are set with crisp linens and candles in this flower-filled 1909 mansion. The northern Italian menu includes pasta, rack of lamb, and a large selection of fresh seafood. A three-course prix-fixe lunch, served weekdays only, costs $16. ✉ *887 S. Anaheim Blvd., Anaheim,* ☎ *714/772–1381. AE, MC, V. No lunch weekends.*

$$–$$$ ✕ **Mr. Stox.** Intimate booths and linen tablecloths create an elegant setting at this family-owned restaurant. Prime rib, mesquite-grilled rack of lamb, and fresh fish specials are excellent; the pasta, bread, and pastries are homemade; and the wine list covers all the bases. ✉ *1105 E. Katella Ave., Anaheim,* ☎ *714/634–2994. AE, D, DC, MC, V. No lunch weekends. Valet parking.*

$$–$$$ ✕ **Yamabuki.** Part of Disney's Paradise Pier Hotel complex, this stylish Japanese restaurant serves traditional dishes and has a full sushi bar. The plum-wine ice cream is a treat. ✉ *1717 S. Disneyland Dr., Disneyland Resort,* ☎ *714/956–6755. AE, D, DC, MC, V. No lunch weekends.*

$–$$ ✕ **Catal Restaurant & Uva Bar.** This Mediterranean-style restaurant and bar in the heart of lively, pedestrian-oriented Downtown Disney offers two dining options: The Uva ("grape" in Spanish) bar on the ground level serves a selection of appetizer-sized tapas plus 40 wines by the glass, while Catal upstairs has a full menu that includes grilled seafood, rotisserie chicken, and salads. ✉ *1580 Disneyland Dr., Suite 103, Downtown Disney,* ☎ *714/774–4442. AE, D, DC, MC, V.*

$–$$ ✕ **Luigi's D'Italia.** Despite the simple surroundings—red vinyl booths and plastic checkered tablecloths—Luigi's serves outstanding Italian cuisine: spaghetti marinara, cioppino, and all the classics. Kids will feel right at home here; there's even a children's menu. ✉ *801 S. State College Blvd., Anaheim,* ☎ *714/490–0990. AE, MC, V.*

$$$$ 🏨 **Disneyland Hotel.** Not surprisingly, Disney's first hotel is the most Disney-themed of the resort's three properties, with memorabilia and Disney music almost everywhere you turn. Check out the Peter Pan–theme pool, with its wooden bridge, 100-ft water slide, and relaxing whirlpool. The cove pools' sandy shores are great for sunning and volleyball. East-facing rooms in the Sierra Tower have the best views of the park, while west-facing rooms in the Bonita Tower overlook the illuminated fountain of the Fantasy Waters. At Goofy's Kitchen, kids can dine with Disney characters. Room-and-ticket packages are available. ✉ *1150 Magic Way, Disneyland Resort 92802,* ☎ *714/778–6600,* FAX *714/956–6582,* WEB *www.disneyland.com. 990 rooms, 62 suites. 5 restaurants, café, room service, in-room data ports, in-room safes, minibars, cable TV, 3 pools, health club, hot tub, massage, sauna, spa, beach, 2 bars, video game room, children's programs, laundry service, concierge, business services, airport shuttle, car rental, parking (fee). AE, D, DC, MC, V.*

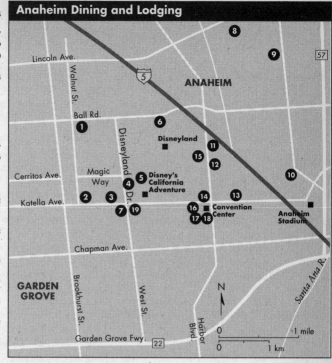

Anaheim Dining and Lodging

$$$$
★ 🏨 **Disney's Grand Californian.** The newest of Disney's Anaheim hotels, this Craftsman-style luxury property has guest rooms with views of the California Adventure and Downtown Disney. Restaurants include the Napa Rose dining room, Hearthstone Lounge, and Storytellers Cafe, where Disney characters entertain children at breakfast. Of the three pools, one just for kids is in the shape of Mickey Mouse, and there's an evening child activity center. Room-and-ticket packages are available. ⊠ *1600 S. Disneyland Dr., Disneyland Resort 92803,* ☎ *714/ 635–2300,* 𝔽𝔸𝕏 *714/300–7701,* 𝖶𝖤𝖡 *www.disneyland.com. 712 rooms, 38 suites. 2 restaurants, room service, in-room data ports, in-room safes, minibars, cable TV, pool, health club, hot tub, 2 lounges, video game room, shop, children's programs, dry cleaning, laundry service, concierge, Internet, business services, parking (fee); no smoking. AE, D, DC, MC, V.*

$$$$ 🏨 **Disney's Paradise Pier Hotel.** Formerly the Disneyland Pacific Hotel, the Paradise Pier has many of the same Disney touches as the Disneyland Hotel, but the atmosphere is a bit quieter and more ordinary. From here you can walk to Disneyland or pick up a shuttle or monorail. Start the day with the Minnie and Friends character breakfast, or visit with Mary Poppins in her parlor at the Practically Perfect Tea. Room-and-ticket packages are available. ⊠ *1717 S. Disneyland Dr., Disneyland Resort 92802,* ☎ *714/999–0990,* 𝔽𝔸𝕏 *714/776–5763,* 𝖶𝖤𝖡 *www.disneyland. com. 712 rooms, 38 suites. 3 restaurants, room service, in-room data ports, in-room safes, minibars, cable TV, pool, health club, 2 lounges, video game room, dry cleaning, laundry service, concierge, business services, parking (fee). AE, D, DC, MC, V.*

$$$$ 🏨 **Hilton Anaheim.** Next to the Anaheim Convention Center, this busy Hilton is the largest hotel in Southern California: it even has its own post office, as well as shops, restaurants, and cocktail lounges. Rooms are pleasingly bright, and a shuttle runs to Disneyland, or you can walk

the few blocks. Special summer children's programs include a "Vacation Station Lending Desk" with games, toys, and books, as well as children's menus. There's a $12 fee to use the health club. ✉ *777 Convention Way, Downtown Anaheim 92802,* ☎ *714/750–4321 or 800/445–8667,* ⨎ *714/740–4460,* ⟦WEB⟧ *www.hilton.com. 1,576 rooms, 95 suites. 4 restaurants, room service, cable TV with movies, pool, health club, hair salon, hot tub, massage, sauna, 2 lounges, piano, children's programs, laundry service, concierge, Internet, business services, meeting rooms, airport shuttle, car rental, travel services, parking (fee); no-smoking floor. AE, D, DC, MC, V.*

$$$ ✕⌂ **Anaheim Marriott.** Rooms at this busy convention hotel are well equipped for business travelers, with desks, two phones, and data ports. Some rooms have balconies, and accommodations on the north side have good views of Disneyland's summer fireworks shows. Discounted weekend and Disneyland packages are available. Two restaurants are on site: JW's Steakhouse and Cafe del Sol. ✉ *700 W. Convention Way, Downtown Anaheim 92802,* ☎ *714/750–8000 or 800/228–9290,* ⨎ *714/750–9100,* ⟦WEB⟧ *www.marriott.com. 1,033 rooms, 52 suites. 2 restaurants, room service, in-room data ports, in-room safes, cable TV with movies, 2 pools, health club, 2 hot tubs, lounge, piano, video game room, laundry facilities, laundry service, concierge, Internet, meeting rooms, car rental, parking (fee), some pets allowed (fee); no-smoking floors. AE, D, DC, MC, V.*

$$–$$$$ ⌂ **Sheraton Anaheim Hotel.** If you're hoping to escape from the com-
   ★   mercial atmosphere of the hotels near Disneyland, consider this sprawling replica of a Tudor castle. In the flowers-and-plants-filled lobby you're welcome to sit by the grand fireplace, watching fish swim around in a pond. "Smart Rooms" come equipped for business with copier-printer-fax gizmos, and include a daily Continental breakfast and evening hors d'oeuvres. Rooms are sizable; some first-floor rooms open onto interior gardens and a pool area. A shuttle to Disneyland is available. ✉ *1015 W. Ball Rd., Downtown Anaheim 92802,* ☎ *714/778–1700 or 800/325–3535,* ⨎ *714/535–3889,* ⟦WEB⟧ *www.sheraton.com/anaheim. 447 rooms, 42 suites. Restaurant, café, room service, in-room data ports, in-room safes, cable TV with movies and video games, pool, health club, outdoor hot tub, bar, video game room, laundry facilities, laundry services, concierge, meeting rooms, parking (fee); no-smoking rooms. AE, D, DC, MC, V.*

$$–$$$ ⌂ **West Coast Anaheim Hotel.** Service is extra helpful at this hotel near the convention center. Rooms have balconies, and those in the tower have good views of Disneyland's summer fireworks shows. You can also relax in the nicely landscaped outdoor area or take a dip in the Olympic-size pool. ✉ *1855 S. Harbor Blvd., Downtown Anaheim 92802,* ☎ *714/750–1811 or 800/426–0670,* ⨎ *714/971–3626. 498 rooms, 6 suites. Restaurant, coffee shop, room service, in-room data ports, refrigerators, cable TV with movies and video games, pool, outdoor hot tub, lounge, laundry service, meeting room, car rental, parking (fee); no-smoking floor. AE, D, DC, MC, V.*

$$ ⌂ **The Annabella.** This mission-style hotel, opened in 2001, is across from Disneyland Resort on the convention center campus. The hotel's "Oasis," with a pool and hot tub, is perfect for relaxing. The Tangerine Grill and Patio serves a fantastic tangerine cheesecake. ✉ *1030 W. Katella Ave., Downtown Anaheim 92802,* ☎ *714/905–1050 or 800/863–4888,* ⨎ *714/905–1054,* ⟦WEB⟧ *www.anabellahotel.com. 359 rooms, 12 suites. Restaurant, room service, in-room data ports, in-room safes, microwaves, refrigerators, cable TV with movies and video games, 2 pools, health club, outdoor hot tub, lounge, laundry facilities, laundry services, business services, free parking. AE, D, DC, MC, V.*

$–$$ 🏨 **Anaheim Fairfield Inn by Marriott.** A chain hotel with character, the Anaheim Fairfield provides friendly, detail-oriented service and spacious rooms, most with sleeper sofas as well as beds. Across the street from Disneyland, the hotel runs a free shuttle service to the park. Keep an eye out for the magician who roams the premises entertaining adults and kids alike. ⊠ *1460 S. Harbor Blvd., Downtown Anaheim 92802,* ☎ *714/772–6777 or 800/228–2800,* FAX *714/999–1727,* WEB *www.anaheimfairfieldinn.com. 467 rooms. Restaurant, room service, some microwaves, refrigerators, cable TV with movies, pool, outdoor hot tub, recreation room, video game room, travel services, free parking; no-smoking floor. AE, D, DC, MC, V.*

$–$$ 🏨 **Anaheim Holiday Inn.** Formerly the Conestoga Hotel, this Holiday Inn underwent renovation but kept the previous hotel's Old West theme. Pint-size cowboys love the swinging saloon doors and *Bonanza*-style lobby. There's a nice pool area for relaxing after a day in the saddle. The residential location makes for quiet evenings. A complimentary shuttle heads to Disneyland, one long block away, every hour. ⊠ *1240 S. Walnut Ave., Downtown Anaheim 92802,* ☎ *714/535–0300 or 800/ 824–5459,* FAX *714/491–8953,* WEB *www.holidayinn-anaheim.com. 229 rooms, 23 suites. Restaurant, room service, some microwaves, cable TV, pool, exercise equipment, outdoor hot tub, bar, video game room, laundry service, business services, meeting rooms, free parking; no-smoking rooms. AE, D, DC, MC, V.*

$–$$ 🏨 **Best Western Stovall's Inn.** Nice touches at this well-kept motel include a small topiary garden where the plants and shrubs are shaped like animals, a free shuttle to Disneyland, and Nintendo and movie rentals. Ask about discounts if you're staying several nights. ⊠ *1110 W. Katella Ave., Downtown Anaheim 92802,* ☎ *714/778–1880 or 800/ 854–8175,* FAX *714/778–3805,* WEB *www.bestwestern.com. 290 rooms. In-room data ports, 2 pools, cable TV, outdoor hot tub, video game room, bar, laundry service, laundry facilities, meeting rooms, free parking; no-smoking rooms. AE, D, DC, MC, V.*

$–$$ 🏨 **Candy Cane Inn.** One of the Disneyland area's first hotels (deeds
★ were executed Christmas Eve, hence the name), the Candy Cane has earned a reputation as one of Anaheim's most beautiful properties. Rooms are spacious but basic. The hotel is just steps from the Disneyland parking lot. A free Disneyland shuttle runs every half hour. ⊠ *1747 S. Harbor Blvd., Downtown Anaheim 92802,* ☎ *714/774–5284 or 800/ 345–7057,* FAX *714/772–5462,* WEB *www.candycaneinn.net. 172 rooms. Refrigerators, cable TV, pool, wading pool, outdoor hot tub, laundry facilities, laundry service, free parking; no-smoking rooms. AE, D, DC, MC, V.*

$ 🏨 **Castle Inn and Suites.** Faux-stone trim and towers, shield decor, and replica gas lamps dress up the Castle Inn. Suites have microwaves, and all rooms have refrigerators. Some rooms also have whirlpool tubs. Across the street from Disneyland, the hotel runs a complimentary shuttle to the park. ⊠ *1734 S. Harbor Blvd., Downtown Anaheim 92802,* ☎ *714/774–8111 or 800/521–5653,* FAX *714/956–4736,* WEB *www. castleinn.com. 150 rooms, 50 suites. Some microwaves, refrigerators, cable TV, pool, wading pool, outdoor hot tub, laundry facilities, laundry service, free parking; no-smoking rooms. AE, D, DC, MC, V.*

$ 🏨 **Desert Palm Inn and Suites.** This hotel midway between Disneyland and the convention center is a great value, with $129 one-bedroom suites that can accommodate the whole family. A light Continental breakfast is included. Book well in advance, especially when large conventions are in town. ⊠ *631 W. Katella Ave., Downtown Anaheim 92802,* ☎ *714/535–1133 or 800/635–5423,* FAX *714/491–7409,* WEB *www.anaheimdesertpalm.com. 50 rooms, 50 suites. In-room data ports, refrigerators, cable TV with movies, pool, outdoor hot tub, video*

*game room, laundry facilities, laundry service, Internet, free parking;
no smoking. AE, D, DC, MC, V.*

Outdoor Activities and Sports

Dad Miller Golf Course (⊠ 430 N. Gilbert St., Anaheim, ☎ 714/765–
4653), an 18-hole par-71 course, requires reservations seven days in
advance. Greens fees are $23–$32; optional cart rental is $24.

Pro baseball's **Anaheim Angels** play at Edison International Field (⊠
2000 Gene Autry Way, East Anaheim, ☎ 714/634–2000). The National
Hockey League's **Mighty Ducks of Anaheim** play at Arrowhead Pond
(⊠ 2695 E. Katella Ave., East Anaheim, ☎ 714/703–2545).

Buena Park

25 mi south of Los Angeles on I–5.

The land where the boysenberry was invented (by crossing red raspberry, blackberry, and loganberry bushes) is now occupied by Knott's
Berry Farm. You can see Buena Park in a day, but plan to start early
and finish fairly late. Traffic can be heavy so factor in time for delays.

★ ☺ ❷ **Knott's Berry Farm** got its start in 1934, when Cordelia Knott began
serving chicken dinners on her wedding china to supplement her family's income. Or so the story goes. The dinners and her boysenberry
pies proved more profitable than husband Walter's berry farm, so the
two moved first into the restaurant business and then into the entertainment business. Their park, ideal for young children too small to
fully enjoy the "other" Southern California park, is now a 150-acre
complex with 100-plus rides and new attractions designed to lure
older kids and teens. There are also 60 food concessions and restaurants and 60 unusual shops with everything from suede moccasins for
kids to collectible ceramics.

GhostRider is Orange County's first wooden roller coaster. Traveling
56 mph at its fastest and reaching 118 ft at its highest, the coaster is
riddled with sudden dips and curves, subjecting riders to G-forces
comparable to three times the force of the Earth's gravitational pull.
Your next stop might be **Ghost Town,** whose authentic old buildings
have been relocated from their original mining-town sites. You can stroll
down the street, stop and chat with the blacksmith, pan for gold,
crack open a geode, ride in an authentic 1880s passenger train, or take
the Gold Mine ride and descend into a replica of a working gold mine.
A real treasure here is the antique Dentzel carousel.

Smaller fry will want to head straight for **Camp Snoopy,** a miniature
High Sierra wonderland where the *Peanuts* gang hangs out. Nearby
is **Big Foot Rapids,** where you can ride white water in an inner tube
and commune with the native peoples of the Northwest coast in the
spooky Mystery Lodge. For more water thrills, check out the dol-
phin and sea lion shows in the Pacific Pavilion at the **Boardwalk,** where
you'll also find the **Boomerang** roller coaster and the **Perilous Plunge,**
billed as the world's tallest, steepest and—thanks to its big splash—
wettest thrill ride; **Kingdom of the Dinosaurs,** a *Jurassic Park*–like
thrill ride; and **Montezooma's Revenge,** a roller coaster that goes from
0 to 55 mph in less than five seconds. **Jaguar!** simulates the motions
of a cat stalking its prey, twisting, spiraling, and speeding up and slow-
ing down as it takes you on its stomach-dropping course. It's a good
idea to confirm the park's opening hours, which are subject to change.
⊠ *8039 Beach Blvd., Buena Park, between La Palma Ave. and Crescent St., 2 blocks south of Hwy. 91,* ☎ *714/220–5200,* WEB *www.
knotts.com.* ⊠ *$40.* ☉ *June–mid-Sept., daily 9 AM–midnight; mid-*

Sept.–May, weekdays 10–6, Sat. 10–10, Sun. 10–7; closed during inclement weather.

❸ More than 75 years of movie magic are immortalized at the **Movieland Wax Museum,** which holds several hundred wax sculptures of Hollywood's stars and American political figures, including Michael Jackson, John Wayne, Marilyn Monroe, Geena Davis, and George Burns. Likenesses ranging from the haunting to the comical are displayed in a maze of realistic sets from movies such as *Gone With The Wind, Star Trek, The Wizard of Oz,* and *Titanic.* President George W. Bush stands in the Oval Office. A combination ticket for $16.90 includes admission to the so-so Ripley's Believe It or Not!, across the street. ⊠ *7711 Beach Blvd., between La Palma and Orangethorpe Aves., Buena Park,* ☎ *714/522–1155,* WEB *www.movielandwaxmuseum.com.* ⌲ *$12.95.* ☉ *Weekdays 10–6, weekends 9–7.*

Dining and Lodging

$ ✕ **Mrs. Knott's Chicken Dinner Restaurant.** Cornelia Knott's fried-chicken and boysenberry pies drew crowds so big that Knott's Berry Farm was built to keep the hungry customers occupied while they waited. The restaurant's current incarnation at the park's entrance still serves all-American crispy fried chicken, along with tangy coleslaw and Mrs. Knott's signature chilled cherry-rhubarb compote. Long lines on weekends may not be worth your valuable time. ⊠ *Knott's Berry Farm, 8039 Beach Blvd., Buena Park,* ☎ *714/220–5080. AE, D, DC, MC, V.*

$$–$$$ 🏨 **The Radisson Resort Knott's Berry Farm.** The only hotel on Knott's Berry Farm grounds has family-oriented "camp rooms" that are decorated in the amusement park's Camp Snoopy motif. Shuttle service to Disneyland and nearby golf courses is available. Ask about packages that include entry to Knott's Berry Farm. ⊠ *7675 Crescent Ave., Buena Park 90620,* ☎ *714/995–1111,* FAX *714/828–8590,* WEB *www. radisson.com. 304 rooms, 16 suites. 2 restaurants, room service, cable TV with movies and video games, pool, hot tub, health club, tennis, bar, video game room, laundry facilities, concierge, Internet. AE, D, DC, MC, V.*

Nightlife

For $42 per person, the **Medieval Times Dinner and Tournament** (⊠ 7662 Beach Blvd., Buena Park, ☎ 714/521–4740 or 800/899–6600, WEB www.medievaltimes.com) brings back the days of yore, with medieval games, fighting, and jousting. Standard chicken-and-ribs dinners with plenty of sides are served just as they were in the Middle Ages: with, ugh, no utensils. **Wild Bill's Wild West Extravaganza** (⊠ 7600 Beach Blvd., Buena Park, ☎ 714/522–6414), a two-hour, action-packed Old West show ($40 per person), features foot-stomping musical numbers, cancan dancers, live bears, trick-rope artists, and sing-alongs. An all-you-can-eat chicken-and-ribs dinner is served by a chosen "grub-server" guest at each multigroup table during the show.

Fullerton

8 mi east of Buena Park, Hwy. 91.

Fullerton is an educational center in Orange County, with Cal State Fullerton, Western State University College of Law, and two other houses of higher learning. It's also an old railroading and citrus-processing town with a shop-lined brick pedestrian street running through its center.

Dining

$$–$$$ ✕ **The Cellar.** Choosing a vintage to pair with your classic panfried Dover sole with lemon-caper-butter sauce, or your veal Oscar with crab meat and asparagus, might prove a formidable task at this old-world din-

ing establishment. The stone-walled underground French restaurant has one of the finest wine collections in the West, with more than 1,400 vintages from 15 countries. ⊠ *305 N. Harbor Blvd., Fullerton,* ☎ *714/ 525–5682. AE, D, DC, MC, V. Closed Sun.–Mon. No lunch.*

$–$$ ✗ **Angelo's & Vinci's Cafe Ristorante.** Families with kids love this boisterous Italian café, where huge portions of Sicilian-style pizza and pasta are served in lively surroundings. You can't miss the display of giant knights in shining armor, tableaux of Italian street scenes, altar with old family photos and cherubs from Sicily, or the pair of aerial puppets and tightrope walker overhead. ⊠ *550 N. Harbor Blvd., Fullerton,* ☎ *714/879–4022. AE, MC, V.*

$–$$ ✗ **Mulberry Street Ristorante.** Resembling a turn-of-the-century New
★ York Italian–style eatery, Mulberry Street is a favorite among North Orange County hipsters. All the pasta is homemade, and the menu also includes chicken, veal, and daily fish specials. ⊠ *114 W. Wilshire Ave., Fullerton,* ☎ *714/525–1056. AE, D, DC, MC, V. No lunch Sun.*

Yorba Linda, La Habra, and Brea

7–12 mi north of Anaheim, on Hwy. 57.

Clustered together just north of Anaheim, Yorba Linda, La Habra, and Brea are quiet suburban towns characterized by lush parks and family-oriented shopping centers complete with megacinemas showing films for virtually every taste. The redevelopment of downtown Brea has brought shopping, dining, and entertainment to the Birch Street Promenade.

❹ Yorba Linda's main claim to fame is the **Richard Nixon Presidential Library and Birthplace,** final resting place of the 37th president and his wife, Pat. Exhibits illustrate the checkered career of Nixon, from heralded leader of the free world to beleaguered resignee. Visitors can listen to the so-called smoking-gun tape from the Watergate days, among other recorded material. Life-size sculptures of foreign world leaders, gifts Nixon received from international heads of state, and a large graffiti-covered section of the Berlin Wall are on display. In contrast to some of the high-tech displays here are Pat Nixon's tranquil rose garden and the small farmhouse where Richard Nixon was born in 1913. Don't miss the bookstore, selling everything from commemorative birdhouses to photos of Nixon with Elvis. ⊠ *18001 Yorba Linda Blvd., at Imperial Hwy., Yorba Linda,* ☎ *714/993–3393,* WEB *www.nixonlibrary.org.* ☞ *$5.95.* ☉ *Mon.–Sat. 10–5, Sun. 11–5.*

❺ The **Children's Museum at La Habra** is in a 1923-vintage Union Pacific railroad depot, with old railroad cars resting nearby. Children can climb behind the wheel of Buster the Bus, a retired transit bus, or "dig up" bones in the huge Dinosaur Dig sandbox. There's also an informative railroad safety exhibit. ⊠ *301 S. Euclid St., La Habra,* ☎ *562/ 905–9793,* WEB *www.lhcm.org.* ☞ *$4.* ☉ *Mon.–Sat. 10–5, Sun. 1–5.*

Dining

$$–$$$$ ✗ **La Vie en Rose.** It's worth the detour to Brea to sample the stylishly
★ presented traditional French cuisine served in this reproduction Norman farmhouse. There's seafood, lamb, veal, and for dessert, a silky crème brûlée and a Grand Marnier soufflé. ⊠ *240 S. State College Blvd., across from Brea mall, Brea,* ☎ *714/529–8333. AE, MC, V. Closed Sun.*

Garden Grove and Orange

South of Anaheim, I–5 to Hwy. 22.

Orange, like any well-rounded city, is a mix of old and new. **The Block at Orange,** a dining, shopping, and 30-screen AMC movie theater complex, is near the 5 and 22 freeways. The complex also has a Van's skate park for skateboarders. Around the intersection of Glassell Street and Chapman Avenue is Orange Plaza (or Orange Circle, as locals call it),

6 the heart of **Old Towne Orange.** The area was recently added to the National Register of Historic Places and is a must-stop for antiques browsers and architecture aficionados. Locals take great pride in their many California Craftsman–style cottages; Christmas is a particularly lovely time to visit, when many of the area's charming homes are festooned with tasteful yet elaborate decorations. If the town looks familiar to you, perhaps it's because many a film crew has popped in for shooting, including Robert De Niro and Rene Russo for *The Adventures of Rocky and Bullwinkle.*

7 In Garden Grove the main attraction is the **Crystal Cathedral,** the domain of television evangelist Robert Schuller. Designed by architect Philip Johnson, the sparkling glass structure resembles a four-pointed star, with more than 10,000 panes of glass covering a web-like steel truss to form transparent walls. Two annual pageants, "The Glory of Christmas" and "The Glory of Easter," feature live animals, flying angels, and other special effects. ⊠ *12141 Lewis St., take I–5 to Chapman Ave. W, Garden Grove,* ☎ *714/971–4000 or 714/971–4013,* WEB *www. crystalcathedral.org.* ⊡ *Tickets for the pageants $20–$30.* ☉ *Guided tours Mon.–Sat. 9–3:30; call for schedule. Sun. services at 9:30, 11, and 6.*

OFF THE BEATEN PATH
LITTLE SAIGON – Little Saigon, the largest Vietnamese community outside of Vietnam, encompasses much of the city of Westminster. But the heart of the action is around Brookhurst and Bolsa streets, where colorful Little Saigon Plaza tempts shoppers with jewelry and gift shops, Asian herbalists, and informal family restaurants. ⊠ *Bolsa St. between Bushard and Magnolia Sts., Westminster.*

Dining and Lodging

$$ ✕ **P.J.'s Abbey.** Locals come to this former abbey to enjoy American favorites such as pork chops with garlic-mashed potatoes, rack of lamb, and fresh-baked desserts. ⊠ *182 S. Orange St., Old Towne Orange,* ☎ *714/771–8556. AE, MC, V.*

$–$$$ ✕ **Citrus City Grill.** Innovative cuisine and a dining room that combines history with modernity characterize one of the best restaurants in the county. The citrus theme plays out in everything, including the art on the walls. Don't miss the ahi poke salad (tuna on wonton strips). The inviting half-moon bar is a surefire lively gathering place for martini aficionados. ⊠ *122 N. Glassell St., Old Towne Orange,* ☎ *714/639– 9600. AE, DC, MC, V. Closed Sun.*

$–$$ ⊡ **Doubletree Hotel Anaheim/Orange.** This contemporary 20-story hotel has a dramatic lobby of marble and granite, with waterfalls cascading down the walls. The hotel is near The Block, Anaheim Stadium, and the Anaheim Convention Center. ⊠ *100 The City Dr., downtown Orange, 92868,* ☎ *714/634–4500 or 800/222–8733,* FAX *714/978–3839,* WEB *www.doubletreehotels.com. 454 rooms, 11 suites. 2 restaurants, in-room data ports, cable TV with movies, pool, health club, bar, concierge floor, Internet, meeting rooms. AE, D, DC, MC, V.*

Santa Ana

12 mi south of Anaheim, I–5 to Hwy. 55.

8 The main attraction in the county seat is the **Bowers Museum of Cultural Art.** Permanent exhibits include Pacific Northwest wood carvings; dazzling beadwork of the Plains cultures; California basketry; and still-life paintings. The 11,000-square-ft **Bowers Kidseum** (⊠ 1802 N. Main St., Santa Ana) has interactive exhibits geared toward kids ages 6–12, in addition to classes, story-telling, and arts and crafts workshops. ⊠ *2002 N. Main St., off I–5, Santa Ana,* ☎ *714/567–3600,* WEB *www.bowers.org.* ⊡ *$4.* ⊙ *Tues.–Fri. 10–4, weekends 10–6.*

Dining

$$–$$$$ ╳ **Morton's of Chicago.** Hearty eaters flock to this wood-paneled quintessential steak house for huge portions of prime-aged beef and fresh seafood. The soft lighting bears sharp contrast to the noise level. ⊠ *South Coast Plaza Village, 1661 W. Sunflower Ave., Santa Ana,* ☎ *714/444–4834. AE, DC, MC, V. No lunch. Valet parking.*

$$–$$$ ╳ **Gustaf Anders.** At this cool, Scandinavian restaurant, you'll find top-
★   notch grilled gravlax, and a wonderful fillet of beef prepared with Stilton cheese, a red-wine sauce, and creamed morel mushrooms. Next door is the more casual, less expensive Back Pocket, with equally excellent food. Don't miss the flat breads, parsley salad, and Swedish beef casserole. ⊠ *South Coast Plaza Village, 3851 Bear St., Santa Ana,* ☎ *714/668–1737. AE, DC, MC, V. Closed Mon. No lunch Sun.*

$ ╳ **Tangata.** Inside the Bowers Museum, this eatery has a menu overseen by owner/executive chef Joachim Splichal. Choose among salads, pastas, soups, French-style roasted chicken, lamb shank over polenta, and tasty desserts. Dine on the patio; or, in the main dining room, watch the "chef theater." ⊠ *2002 N. Main St., Santa Ana,* ☎ *714/550–0906. AE, DC, MC, V. Closed Mon. No dinner.*

Irvine

6 mi south of Santa Ana, Hwy. 55 to I–405; 12 mi south of Anaheim, I–5.

Irvine—characterized by its impeccably designed neighborhoods, tree-lined streets, uniformly manicured lawns, and pristine parks—may feel surreal to urban visitors. Yet it's ranked in several national surveys as America's safest city. The master-planned community has top-notch schools, a university and a community college, plus dozens of shopping centers, and a network of well-lit walking and biking paths.

❾ Some of the Californian impressionist paintings on display at the small yet intriguing **Irvine Museum** depict the state's rural landscape in the years before massive freeways and sprawling housing developments. The paintings, which are displayed on the 12th floor of the cylindrical marble-and-glass Tower 17 building, were assembled by Joan Irvine Smith, granddaughter of James Irvine, who once owned one-quarter of what is now Orange County. ⊠ *18881 Von Karman Ave., at Martin St. north of the UC Irvine campus, Irvine,* ☎ *949/476–2565,* WEB *www.irvinemuseum.org.* ⊡ *Free.* ⊙ *Tues.–Sat. 11–5.*

❿ The **University of California at Irvine,** was established on 1,000 acres of rolling ranch land donated by the Irvine family in the mid-1950s. The campus contains more than 11,000 trees from around the world and features a stellar biological science department and creative writing program. The **Irvine Barclay Theater** (☎ 949/854–4646) presents an impressive roster of music, dance, and dramatic events, and there's not a bad seat in the house. The **Art Gallery at UC Irvine** (☎ 949/824–6206) sponsors exhibitions of student and professional art. It's free and open mid-September–mid-June, Tuesday–Sunday noon–5, until 8 Thursday. ⊠ *I–405 to Jamboree Rd., west to Campus Dr. S, Irvine,* ☎ *949/824–5011,* WEB *www.uci.edu.*

⓫ The mind-boggling 32-acre **Entertainment Center at Irvine Spectrum** contains a huge, 21-theater cinema complex (with a six-story IMAX

3-D theater), several lively restaurants (including Crazy Horse Steakhouse and Saloon, a local bastion of country music) and cafés, 150 shops, as well as a virtual-reality experience set inside the NASCAR Silicon Motor Speedway. Other highlights: Gameworks, a high-tech arcade for kids, and the Improvisation comedy club. ⊠ *Exit Irvine Center Dr. at intersection of I–405, I–5, and Hwy. 133, Irvine,* ☎ 949/450–4900 *for film listings,* WEB *www.irvinespectrum.com.*

⑫ **Wild Rivers Water Park** has more than 40 rides and attractions, including a wave pool, daring slides, and a river inner-tube ride, plus several cafés and shops. ⊠ *8770 Irvine Center Dr., off I–405, Irvine,* ☎ 949/768–9453, WEB *www.wildrivers.com.* ☜ *$24.* ☉ *Mid-May–Sept.; call for hrs.*

Dining and Lodging

$$–$$$ ✕ **Il Fornaio.** Two weeks a month, regional dishes from Tuscany or Puglia supplement the regular fare—duck lasagna, rotisserie chicken, pizza, succulent grilled eggplant with goat cheese—at this elegant Italian chain eatery. The local elite meet here for power lunches. ⊠ *18051 Von Karman Ave., Irvine, near the John Wayne/Orange County airport,* ☎ 949/261–1444. *AE, DC, MC, V. No lunch Sun. Valet parking.*

$–$$$ ✕ **Bistango.** A sleek, postmodern, art-filled bistro serves first-rate American cuisine with a European flair: salads, steak, seafood, pasta, and pizzas. Try the tuna grilled rare. An attractive group comes to savor the food, listen to live jazz, and mingle with their well-dressed peers (so book ahead). ⊠ *19100 Von Karman Ave. Irvine, near the John Wayne/Orange County airport,* ☎ 949/752–5222. *AE, D, DC, MC, V. No lunch weekends. Valet parking.*

$–$$$ ✕ **Prego.** Reminiscent of a Tuscan villa, this is a much larger version
★ of the Beverly Hills Prego, with soft lighting, golden walls, and an outdoor patio. Try the spit-roasted meats and chicken, charcoal-grilled fresh fish, or pizzas from the oak-burning oven. California and Italian wines are reasonably priced. ⊠ *18420 Von Karman Ave., Irvine, near the John Wayne/Orange County airport,* ☎ 949/553–1333. *AE, DC, MC, V. No lunch weekends. Valet parking.*

$–$$ ✕ **Kitima Thai Cuisine.** Tucked away on the ground floor of an office building, Orange County's best Thai restaurant is a favorite with the business-lunch crowd. The names may be gimmicky—Rock-and-Roll Shrimp Salad, Rambo Chicken (sautéed with green chilies and sweet basil), Four Musketeers (shrimp with asparagus, mushrooms, and spinach)—but fresh ingredients are used in every dish. ⊠ *2010 Main St., Suite 170, Irvine,* ☎ 949/261–2929. *AE, MC, V. Closed Sun.*

$$–$$$$ ⌂ **Hyatt Regency Irvine.** The sleek, ultramodern rooms here offer practical amenities such as coffeemakers, irons, and hair dryers. Special golf packages at nearby Oak Creek and Pelican Hills are available, and a complimentary shuttle runs to the airport. Rates are lower on weekends. ⊠ *17900 Jamboree Rd., Irvine, near the John Wayne/Orange County airport 92614,* ☎ 949/975–1234 *or* 800/233–1234, FAX 949/852–1574, WEB *www.hyatt.com. 536 rooms, 20 suites. 2 restaurants, cable TV with movies, 4 tennis courts, pool, health club, bicycles, 2 bars, concierge, Internet, business services. AE, D, DC, MC, V.*

$$–$$$$ ⌂ **Irvine Marriott John Wayne Airport.** Towering over Koll Business Center, the Marriott offers a convenient location and amenities designed to appeal to business travelers. Despite its size, the hotel has an intimate feel, due in part to the convivial lobby with love seats and evening entertainment. Weekend discounts and packages are available, and there's a courtesy van to South Coast Plaza and the airport. ⊠ *18000 Von Karman Ave., Irvine, 92612,* ☎ 949/553–0100 *or* 800/228–9290, FAX 949/261–7059, WEB *www.marriott.com. 484 rooms, 8 suites. 2 restaurants, cable TV with movies, 4 tennis courts, pool, health club, hot tub,*

Internet, business services, meeting rooms, airport shuttle, some pets allowed (fee). AE, D, DC, MC, V.

Nightlife

The Improvisation (✉ Irvine Spectrum, 71 Fortune Dr., Irvine, ☎ 949/854–5455) is a comedy club that's open nightly. The **Verizon Wireless Amphitheater** (✉ 8808 Irvine Center Dr., Irvine, ☎ 949/855–8095 or 949/855–6111), a 16,300-seat open-air venue, presents musical events from April through October.

Costa Mesa

> *6 mi northeast of Irvine, I–405 to Bristol St.*

Though it's probably best known for its top-notch shopping mall, Costa Mesa is also the performing-arts hub of Orange County, and a formidable local business center. Patrons of the domestic and international theater, opera, and dance productions fill area restaurants and nightspots. Cinema buffs have several theaters to choose from, too.

★ ⑬ Costa Mesa's most famous landmark, **South Coast Plaza** is an immense retail, entertainment, and dining complex consisting of two enclosed shopping areas—Jewel Court and the Crate & Barrel Wing—and an open-air collection of boutiques at South Coast Village. The Plaza rivals Rodeo Drive in its number of top international designers' shops—Gucci, Armani, Christian Dior, Hermès, Versace, and Prada, to name just a few—along with standard upscale shops such as J. Crew, Ralph Lauren, and FAO Schwarz. A pedestrian bridge, called the Bridge of Gardens, and a free shuttle transport the Plaza's 33 million annual visitors between sections. ✉ *3333 S. Bristol St., off I–405 north Costa Mesa, Costa Mesa,* ☎ *714/435–2000,* WEB *www.southcoastplaza.com.* ☉ *Weekdays 10–9, Sat. 10–7, Sun. 11–6:30.*

The **Orange County Performing Arts Center** (✉ 600 Town Center Dr., east of Bristol St., Costa Mesa, ☎ 714/556–2787, WEB www.ocpac.org) houses Sagerstrom Hall for opera, ballet, symphony, and musicals and the more intimate Founders Hall for chamber music. Richard Lippold's enormous *Firebird,* a triangular-shape sculpture of polished metal surfaces that resembles a bird taking flight, extends outward from the glass-enclosed lobby. Within walking distance of the center is the **California Scenario** (✉ 611 Anton Blvd., northern Costa Mesa), a 1½-acre sculpture garden designed by Isamu Noguchi.

The **Trinity Christian City International** (✉ 3150 Bear St., Costa Mesa 92626, ☎ 714/708–5405) is the cable television network's Southern California headquarters, complete with a frescoed ceiling in the lobby and a grandiose stairway. At Christmas, a light display attracts freeway drivers and onlookers who drive through the grounds for a peek. An extensive gift shop sells seasonal items, books, and videos. The facility offers daily self-guided tours and a virtual-reality theater shows one-hour presentations of three different movies about the life of Christ. Call for hours for the attraction you desire.

Dining and Lodging

$$–$$$ ✕ **Pinot Provence.** The county's hottest French dining spot showcases the innovative cuisine of chef Joachim Splichal (of L.A.'s Patina). Discover the wildly imaginative mix of fresh California ingredients and traditional Provençal cooking, which results in such innovative fare as pistou of milk-fed lamb ragout. The well-heeled meet in the main dining room amid 18th-century antiques to be seen (and unfortunately heard), so many prefer the more intimate patio. ✉ *686 Anton Blvd., Costa Mesa,* ☎ *714/444–5900. AE, D, DC, MC, V.*

$–$$ ✕ **Bangkok IV.** This restaurant's elegant interior, with striking flower
★ arrangements on every table, defies conventional mall dining. The
deep-fried catfish with a chile-garlic-lemongrass sauce is exceptional.
Or try the *kai pudd keng,* succulent ginger chicken with mushrooms
and garlic. ✉ *South Coast Plaza, 3333 Bear St., Costa Mesa,* ☎ *714/
540–7661. AE, D, DC, MC, V.*

$–$$ ✕ **Habana Restaurant and Bar.** With rustic candelabras and murals
in a candlelit former industrial space, Habana blends an old-world flavor with a hip modern flair. The Cuban and Caribbean specialties are
as flavorful as the setting is cool. Chocolate lovers can't miss the Café
Cubano—chocolate mousse topped with chocolate whipped cream
and rum sauce. With entertainment two nights a week (including flamenco on Wednesdays) this restaurant is a popular nightspot. ✉ *2930
Bristol St., Costa Mesa,* ☎ *714/556–0176. AE, D, MC, V.*

$–$$ ✕ **Memphis Soul Café and Bar.** The gumbo here is the best in the county,
★ bar none. The turkey sandwich with pesto is addicting, and the pork
chops are a work of art. The retro setting—it used to be a dive bar—
and Southern-influenced menu have made this one of the area's most
worthwhile (and affordable) eateries. ✉ *2920 Bristol St., Costa Mesa,*
☎ *714/432–7685. AE, D, DC, MC, V.*

$$–$$$$ ▥ **Westin South Coast Plaza.** This downtown high-rise adjoins the South
Coast Plaza complex, making it convenient for shoppers and busi-
nesspeople. The beds in these comfortably sized rooms come with
feather duvets. Park or city views are available. Tennis courts are
nearby. ✉ *686 Anton Blvd., Costa Mesa 92626,* ☎ *714/540–2500 or
888/627–7213,* ℻ *714/662–6695,* ⌨ *www.westin.com. 393 rooms,
3 suites. Restaurant, in-room data ports, cable TV with movies, pool,
Internet, business services, meeting rooms, some pets allowed (fee). AE,
D, DC, MC, V.*

$$ ▥ **Country Inn and Suites.** Here you'll get closer to the bed-and-breakfast experience with rooms and common areas that look more like
Mom's house than a hotel. The Queen Anne–style rooms are homey
and inviting, plus you can mingle with other guests when evening cocktails and hors d'oeuvres are served. ✉ *325 Bristol St., Costa Mesa
92626,* ☎ *714/549–0300 or 800/322–9992,* ℻ *714/662–0828,* ⌨
*www.countrysuites.com. 150 rooms, 150 suites. Restaurant, some mi-
crowaves, refrigerators, cable TV with movies and video games,
2 pools, gym, 2 hot tubs, bar, laundry facilities, meeting rooms. AE,
D, DC, MC, V.*

Nightlife and the Arts

The **Orange County Performing Arts Center** (✉ 600 Town Center Dr.,
Costa Mesa, ☎ 714/556–2787, ⌨ www.ocpac.org) presents major
touring companies, among them, the American Ballet Theater and the
Los Angeles Philharmonic Orchestra. Blockbuster opera, musical, and
theater productions attract patrons from greater L.A. and beyond. Free,
guided backstage tours are conducted Mondays, Wednesdays, and
Saturdays at 10:30 AM. The **South Coast Repertory Theater** (✉ 655 Town
Center Dr., Costa Mesa, ☎ 714/708–5555 ⌨ www.scr.org) is a Tony
award–winning theater presenting new and traditional works on two
stages.

Outdoor Activities and Sports

Costa Mesa Country Club (✉ 1701 Golf Course Dr., Costa Mesa, ☎
714/540–7500) has a pro shop, a driving range, and two 18-hole
courses (par 70 and 72). Greens fees range from $18 to $33; optional
cart rental is $22. Reservations are a must.

THE COAST

Running along the Orange County coastline is the scenic Pacific Coast Highway (Highway 1, known locally as PCH); it's well worth the effort to take this route instead of the freeways. Pull over on PCH and a public beach is often just steps away.

Huntington Beach

25 mi west of Anaheim, Hwy. 57 south to Hwy. 22 West to I–405; 40 mi southeast of Los Angeles, I–5 south to I–605 south to I–405 south to Beach Blvd.

Once a sleepy residential town with little more than a string of rugged surf shops, Huntington Beach is slowly transforming itself into a resort destination. The town's appeal is its broad white-sand beaches with often-towering waves, complemented by a lively pier, a large shopping pavilion on Main Street, and the luxurious Hilton Waterfront Beach Resort. This family-oriented town generally ranks in the top five of America's safest cities. A draw for sports fans: the U.S. Open professional surf competition takes place here every August.

⑭ **Huntington Pier** stretches 1,800 ft out to sea, well past the powerful waves that made Huntington Beach America's "Surf City." At the end of the pier sits **Ruby's** (☎ 714/969–7829), part of a California chain of 1940s-style burger joints. The **Pierside Pavilion** (⊠ PCH across from Huntington Pier), contains shops, restaurants, bars with live music, and a theater complex.

⑮ Just up Main Street from the pier, the **International Surfing Museum** pays tribute to the sport's greats with the Surfing Hall of Fame, which has an impressive collection of surfboards and related memorabilia. ⊠ *411 Olive Ave., Huntington Beach,* ☎ *714/960–3483,* WEB *www.surfingmuseum.org.* ⊡ *$2.* ☉ *June–Sept., daily noon–5; Oct.–May, Thurs.–Mon. noon–5.*

Huntington City Beach (☎ 714/536–5281) stretches for 3 mi from the pier area. The beach is most crowded around the pier; amateur and professional surfers brave the waves daily on its north side. Continuing north, **Huntington State Beach** (☎ 714/536–1454) parallels Pacific Coast Highway. On the state and city beaches there are changing rooms, concessions, lifeguards, and ample parking; the state beach also has barbecue pits. At the northern section of the city, **Bolsa Chica State Beach** (☎ 714/846–3460) has barbecue pits and RV campsites and is usually less crowded than its southern neighbors.

★ ⑯ **Bolsa Chica Ecological Reserve** beckons wildlife-lovers and bird-watchers with an 1,180-acre salt marsh that is home to 315 species of birds, including great blue herons, snowy and great egrets, and common loons. Throughout the reserve are trails for bird-watching, including a comfortable 1½-mi loop. Free guided tours depart from the walking bridge the first Saturday of each month at 9 AM. ⊠ *Entrance at Warner Ave. and PCH, opposite Bolsa Chica State Beach,* ☎ *714/840–1575.* ⊡ *Free.* ☉ *Daily dawn–sunset.*

Dining and Lodging

$$ ✕ Baci. Romantic or kitschy, depending on your style, Baci nevertheless serves dependable Italian food. The menu lists every kind of pasta-and-sauce combination imaginable and almost as many meat dishes (which include a side of pasta or vegetable). If there are two of you and you're feeling brave, try the Fondue alla Baci house special: thinly sliced beef cooked in veal broth and served with six different sauces and pasta. ✉ *18748 Beach Blvd., Huntington Beach,* ☎ *714/965–1194. AE, D, DC, MC, V. No lunch weekends.*

$ ✕ **Fred's Mexican Café.** This casual eatery serves up spicy Mexican seafood and 50 kinds of tequila. A large wraparound patio with two fire pits provides ample space for people-watching, and there are views of the ocean. ✉ *300 PCH, Huntington Beach,* ☎ *714/374–8226. AE, D, MC, V.*

$ ✕ **Wahoo's Fish Taco.** Mahimahi- and wahoo-filled tacos are the specialty of this casual, incredibly popular restaurant, part of a regional chain capitalizing on the trend toward healthful fast-food. Surf stickers cover the walls. Lines can be long at peak times. ✉ *120 Main St., Huntington Beach,* ☎ *714/536–2050. MC, V.*

$$$–$$$$ 🏨 **Hilton Waterfront Beach Resort.** Rising 12 stories above the surf, this Mediterranean-style hotel occupies a spot overlooking 8½ mi of white-sand beach. All guest rooms have private lanais, many with panoramic ocean views. With 21,000 square ft of meeting space (including two ocean-view meeting rooms), the Hilton is also a prime conference facility. ✉ *21100 PCH, Huntington Beach 92648,* ☎ *714/960–7873 or 800/822–7873,* ℻ *714/845–8425,* 🌐 *www.waterfrontbeachresort.hilton.com. 258 rooms, 32 suites. Restaurant, some microwaves, cable TV with movies, 3 tennis courts, pool, gym, hot tub, bar, children's programs, concierge floor, Internet, business services, meeting rooms, some pets allowed (fee). AE, D, DC, MC, V.*

Outdoor Activities and Sports

TENNIS

Edison Community Center (✉ 21377 Magnolia Ave., Huntington Beach, ☎ 714/960–8870) has four tennis courts available on a first-come, first-served basis in the daytime. Reservations are accepted for evening play, 5–10, for $2 per hour. **Murdy Community Center** (✉ 7000 Norma Dr., Huntington Beach, ☎ 714/960–8895) has four courts available; reservations are available only for evening ($2 an hour) play.

Newport Beach

6 mi south of Huntington Beach, PCH.

Newport Beach has two distinct personalities: there's the island-dotted yacht harbor, where the idle wealthy play. (Newport is said to have the highest per-capita number of Mercedes-Benz vehicles in the world.) And then there's inland Newport Beach, just southwest of John Wayne Airport, a business and commercial hub that's lined with high-rise office buildings, shopping centers, and hotels.

★ ⓱ **Newport Harbor,** which shelters nearly 10,000 small boats, may seduce even those who don't own a yacht. Exploring the charming avenues and surrounding alleys can be great fun. Within Newport Harbor are eight small islands, including Balboa and Lido. The houses lining the shore may seem modest, but this is some of the most expensive real estate in the world. Several grassy areas on Lido Isle have views of Newport Harbor but, evidence of the upper-crust Orange County mind-set, each is marked PRIVATE COMMUNITY PARK. To see Newport Harbor from the water, take a one-hour gondola cruise operated by the **Gondola Company of Newport** (✉ 3400 Via Oporto, Suite 102B, Newport Beach, ☎ 949/675–1212). It costs $75 for two and includes salami, cheese, bread, ice, glasses, blankets, music, and a Polaroid picture.

Newport Pier, which juts out into the ocean near 20th Street, is the heart of Newport's beach community and a popular fishing spot. Street parking is difficult at the pier, so grab the first space you find and be prepared to walk. A stroll along West Ocean Front reveals much of the town's character. On weekday mornings, head for the beach near the pier, where you're likely to encounter the dory fishermen hawking their predawn catches, as they've done for generations. On weekends the walk is alive with kids of all ages on Rollerblades, skateboards, and bikes dodging pedestrians and whizzing past fast-food joints, swimsuit shops, and bars.

Newport's best beaches are on **Balboa Peninsula,** whose many jetties pave the way to ideal swimming areas. The **Balboa Pavilion** (⊠ bay side of Balboa Peninsula, Newport Beach), was built in 1905 as a bath-and boathouse. Today it houses a restaurant and shops and is a departure point for harbor and whale-watching cruises. Look for it on Main Street, off Balboa Boulevard. Adjacent to the pavilion is the three-car ferry that connects the peninsula to Balboa Island. Several blocks surrounding the pavilion contain restaurants, beachside shops, and the small **Fun Zone**—a local kiddie hangout with a Ferris wheel, video games, rides, and arcades.

The **Orange County Museum of Art** has gathered an esteemed collection of Abstract Expressionist paintings and cutting-edge contemporary works by California artists. The museum also displays some of its collection at a gallery at South Coast Plaza, free of charge; it's open the same hours as the mall. ⊠ 850 San Clemente Dr., Newport Beach, ☎ 949/759–1122, WEB www.ocma.net. ⊠ $5. ⊙ Tues.–Sun. 11–5.

Dining and Lodging

$$$$ ✕ **Aubergine.** The husband-and-wife team who run this restaurant (he
  ★ runs the kitchen and she handles the dining room) have set new standards for fine cuisine in Orange County with their recently enlarged restaurant. The five- and nine-course prix-fixe menus (and an exceptional wine list) offer an unforgettable gastronomical experience. Classic French dishes are prepared with a modern flair, using only the freshest ingredients. A four-course prix-fixe brunch menu on Sundays is $39. ⊠ 508 29th St., Cannery Village, ☎ 949/723–4150. Reservations essential. AE, MC, V. Closed Mon. No lunch.

$$$–$$$$ ✕ **The Ritz.** Indeed, this is one of the ritziest restaurants in Southern California, complete with black-leather booths, etched-glass mirrors, polished-brass trim, and the requisite attitude. Don't pass up the "carousel" appetizer—a lavish spread of cured gravlax, prawns, Dungeness crab legs, Maine lobster tails, goose liver pâté, fillet of smoked trout, Parma prosciutto, filet mignon tartare, and marinated herring, all served on a lazy Susan. Dessert soufflés are also a specialty. ⊠ 880 Newport Center Dr., Newport Beach, ☎ 949/720–1800. Reservations essential. AE, DC, MC, V. No lunch weekends.

$–$$ ✕ **El Torito Grill.** You'll find Southwestern and south-of-the-border
  ★ specialties here: the tortilla soup is to die for, as is the carne asada. Just-baked tortillas with fresh salsa replace the usual chip basket. The bar serves margaritas and 80 brands of tequila. ⊠ 951 Newport Center Dr., Fashion Island, ☎ 949/640–2875. AE, D, DC, MC, V.

$ ✕ **P. F. Chang's China Bistro.** The tasty Cal-Chinese food at this trendy chain restaurant includes Mongolian spicy beef and Chang's chicken, stir-fried in a sweet-and-spicy Szechuan sauce. Almost every table has an ocean view, but many diners are too busy people-watching to notice. Food can also be ordered at the lively bar. ⊠ 1145 Newport Center Dr., near Fashion Island, ☎ 949/759–9007. Reservations not accepted. AE, MC, V.

$$$$ ▥ **Four Seasons Hotel.** A suitably stylish hotel in an ultrachic neigh-
  ★ borhood (it's across the street from the tony Fashion Island mall), the 20-story Four Seasons caters to luxury seekers by offering weekend golf packages (in conjunction with the nearby Pelican Hill golf course). Guest

rooms have outstanding views, private bars, and original art. Kids are given special treatment: balloons, cookies and milk, game books, video games, and more. ⊠ *690 Newport Center Dr., near Fashion Island 92660,* ☎ *949/759–0808 or 800/332–3442,* FAX *949/759–0568,* WEB *www.fourseasons.com. 295 rooms, 92 suites. 2 restaurants, room service, cable TV with movies and video games, 2 tennis courts, pool, health club, hair salon, massage, sauna, mountain bikes, bar, concierge, Internet, business services, some pets allowed (fee). AE, D, DC, MC, V.*

$$$ ⌷ **Newport Beach Marriott Hotel and Tennis Club.** Popular with the international set, this hotel overlooking Newport Harbor features a distinctive fountain surrounded by a plant-filled atrium. Rooms are in one of two towers; all have balconies or patios that look out onto lush gardens or the Pacific. ⊠ *900 Newport Center Dr., near Fashion Island, 92660,* ☎ *949/640–4000 or 800/228–9290,* FAX *949/640–5055,* WEB *www.marriott.com. 577 rooms, 6 suites. Restaurant, cable TV with movies, 8 tennis courts, 2 pools, health club, sauna, bar, concierge, Internet, business services, meeting rooms, some pets allowed (fee). AE, D, DC, MC, V.*

$$$ ⌷ **Sutton Place Hotel.** An eye-catching ziggurat design is the trademark of this ultramodern hotel in Koll Center. Despite its futuristic exterior, the inside reflects a traditional elegance with tasteful beige and burgundy accents. ⊠ *4500 MacArthur Blvd., Newport Beach, 92660,* ☎ *949/476–2001 or 800/243–4141,* FAX *949/476–0153,* WEB *www.suttonplace.com. 435 rooms, 29 suites. 2 restaurants, in-room data ports, minibars, cable TV with movies, 2 tennis courts, pool, health club, spa, bicycles, 2 bars, concierge, Internet, business services, airport shuttle. AE, D, DC, MC, V.*

Nightlife

Margaritaville (⊠ 2332 PCH, Newport Beach, ☎ 949/631–8220) has tasty margaritas and a mix of live entertainment that includes jazz, blues, soft rock, and reggae, daily until 12:30 AM.

Outdoor Activities and Sports

BOAT RENTAL

You can rent kayaks ($10 an hour), sailboats ($25 an hour), small motorboats ($40 an hour), cocktail boats ($50 an hour), and ocean boats ($75–$85 an hour) at **Balboa Boat Rentals** (⊠ 510 E. Edgewater Ave., Newport Beach, ☎ 949/673–7200). You must have a driver's license, and some knowledge of boating is helpful; rented boats are not allowed out of the bay.

BOAT TOURS

Catalina Passenger Service (⊠ 400 Main St., Newport Beach, ☎ 949/ 673–5245, WEB www.catalinainfo.com) at the Balboa Pavilion operates 90-minute sightseeing tours ($8) and daily round-trip passage to Catalina Island ($37). **Hornblower Cruises & Events** (⊠ 2431 W. Coast Hwy., Newport Beach, ☎ 949/646–0155 or 800/668–4322, WEB www.hornblower.com) books three-hour weekend dinner cruises with dancing for $60, Friday; $64 Saturday; two-hour Sunday brunch cruises are $40. Reservations are required.

FISHING

In addition to a complete tackle shop, **Davey's Locker** (⊠ Balboa Pavilion, 400 Main St., Newport Beach, ☎ 949/673–1434, WEB www.hornblower.com) operates sportfishing trips starting at $26, as well as private charters and, in winter, whale-watching trips.

GOLF

Newport Beach Golf Course (⊠ 3100 Irvine Ave., Newport Beach, ☎ 949/852–8681), an 18-hole, par-59 course, is lighted for nighttime play.

Greens fees range from $12 to $22 for 18-hole play; hand carts rent for $2. Reservations are accepted up to one week in advance, but walk-ups are accommodated when possible. **Pelican Hill Golf Club** (⊠ 22651 Pelican Hill Rd. S, Newport Beach, ☎ 949/960–0707) has two 18-hole courses (par 70 and 71) with canyon and ocean views. Greens fees range from $175 to $250 and include the mandatory cart.

RUNNING

The **Beach Trail** runs along the coast from Huntington Beach to Newport. Paths throughout **Newport Back Bay** wrap around a marshy area inhabited by lizards, rabbits, and waterfowl. For information on free walking tours in this ecological reserve, call ☎ 949/640–6746.

TENNIS

Call the **recreation department** (☎ 949/644–3151) for information about use of the courts in locations throughout Orange County where play is free and first-come, first-served. Reservations are required at the **Newport Beach Marriott Hotel and Tennis Club** (⊠ 900 Newport Center Dr., Newport Beach, ☎ 949/640–4000). The cost is $15 per person per hour for nonguests.

Shopping

Resplendent with Mediterranean tiles and dramatic arches, the ritzy outdoor **Fashion Island** offers stellar ocean views for alfresco shopping and dining at several restaurants and stores, including Bloomingdale's, Robinsons-May, Neiman-Marcus, and Macy's, as well as upscale boutiques. ⊠ *410 Newport Center Dr., between Jamboree and MacArthur Blvds., off PCH, Newport Beach*, ☎ 949/721–2000.

Corona del Mar

2 mi south of Newport Beach, Hwy. 1.

A small jewel on the Pacific Coast, Corona del Mar (known by locals as "CDM") has exceptional beaches that some say resemble their majestic northern California counterparts. The town stretches only a few blocks along Pacific Coast Highway, but some of the toniest stores in the county line the route.

Corona del Mar Beach (☎ 949/644–3151) is actually made up of two beaches, Little Corona and Big Corona, separated by a cliff. Facilities include fire pits, volleyball courts, food stands, rest rooms, and parking. Two colorful reefs (and the fact that it's off-limits to boats) make Corona del Mar great for snorkeling and for beachcombers who prefer privacy.

Midway between Corona del Mar and Laguna, stretching along both sides of Pacific Coast Highway, **Crystal Cove State Park** (☎ 949/494–3539) is a favorite of local beachgoers and wilderness trekkers. This hidden treasure encompasses a 3½-mi stretch of unspoiled beach and has some of the best tide-pooling in Southern California. Here you can see starfish, crabs, and other sea life on the rocks. The park's 2,400 acres of backcountry are ideal for hiking, horseback riding, and mountain biking, but stay on the trails to preserve the beauty. Docents lead nature walks on most weekend mornings. Parking costs $3 per car.

Sherman Library and Gardens, a botanical garden and library specializing in the history of the Pacific Southwest, provides a diversion from sun and sand. You can wander among cactus gardens, rose gardens, a wheelchair-height touch-and-smell garden, and a tropical conservatory. ⊠ *2647 PCH, Corona del Mar*, ☎ *949/673–2261.* ▨ *$3.* ☉ *Daily 10:30–4.*

Dining

$$–$$$$ ✕ **The Bungalow.** Specializing in prime steaks and seafood, this Craftsman-style restaurant is known for its lobster. The younger, local moneyed set packs the place. ⊠ *2441 E. Coast Hwy., Corona del Mar,* ☎ *949/673–6585. AE, MC, V. No lunch.*

$$–$$$ ✕ **Oysters.** This decidedly hip yet surprisingly convivial seafood restaurant, complete with a bustling bar and live music, caters to a late night
★ crowd. The eclectic menu runs the gamut, from fire-roasted artichokes to some of the best ahi tuna dishes in town. Outstanding desserts and a comprehensive assortment of cognacs and dessert wines make for an adventurous end to the meal. ⊠ *2515 E. Coast Hwy., Corona del Mar,* ☎ *949/675–7411. AE, DC, MC, V. No lunch.*

$ ✕ **C'est Si Bon.** This tiny French café serves delightful breakfasts and interesting sandwiches at lunch. For those not lucky enough to secure a table, there's take-out. ⊠ *149 Riverside Dr., Corona del Mar,* ☎ *949/ 645–0447. AE, MC, V. No dinner.*

Laguna Beach

★ *10 mi south of Newport Beach on Hwy. 1; 60 mi south of Los Angeles, I–5 south to Hwy. 133, which turns into Laguna Canyon Rd.*

The wealthy artist colony of Laguna Beach, compared by some with New York City's SoHo, is decidedly picturesque and serves as a getaway spot for inlanders. Traditionally a haven of conservative wealth, the town attracted the beat, hip, and far-out during the 1950s and '60s (along with what has grown to be Orange County's most visible gay community). Art galleries dot the village streets, which can be unbearably congested in the summer. The surrounding canyons and hills provide a beautiful backdrop to the beachfront village, which is also home to an annual arts festival. A 1993 fire, which destroyed more than 300 homes in the hillsides surrounding Laguna Beach, miraculously left the village untouched. The town's main street, the Pacific Coast Highway, is referred to as either South Coast or North Coast Highway, depending on the address. All along the highway and side streets, you'll find dozens of eclectic fine-art and crafts galleries, clothing boutiques, and jewelry shops.

At the **Pageant of the Masters** (☎ 949/494–1145 or 800/487–3378, WEB www.foapom.com), Laguna's most impressive event and part of the city's annual Festival of Arts, live models and carefully orchestrated backgrounds are arranged in striking mimicry of classical and contemporary paintings. The festival usually takes place in July and August.

20 The **Laguna Art Museum** displays American art, with an emphasis on California artists and works. Special exhibits change quarterly. Galleries throughout the area stay open late in coordination with the museum on the first Thursday of each month. Free shuttle service runs from the museum to galleries and studios along Laguna Canyon Road and Pacific Coast Highway's Gallery Row. ⊠ *307 Cliff Dr., Laguna Beach,* ☎ *949/494–6531.* ▣ *$5.* ☉ *Thurs.–Tues. 11–5.*

Laguna Beach's **Main Beach Park,** at the end of Broadway at South Coast Highway, has sand volleyball, two half-basketball courts, children's play equipment, picnic areas, rest rooms, showers, and street parking. The colorful crowd ranges from authentic hippies to beach volleyball champs to resident celebrities such as Bette Midler. **Aliso Beach County Park** (☎ 949/661–7013), in south Laguna, is a recreation area with a playground, fire pits, parking, food stands, and rest rooms. **Woods Cove,** off South Coast Highway at Diamond Street, is especially quiet during the week. Big rock formations hide lurking crabs. As you climb the steps to leave, you can see an English-style mansion that was once the home of Bette Davis.

Dining and Lodging

$$–$$$$ ✕ **Five Feet.** Others have attempted to mimic this restaurant's inno-
★ vative blend of Chinese and French cooking styles, but Five Feet remains the leader of the pack. Among the standout dishes is the house catfish. The setting is pure Laguna: exposed ceiling, open kitchen, high noise level, and brick walls hung with works by local artists. ✉ *328 Glenneyre St., Laguna Beach,* ☎ *949/497–4955. AE, D, DC, MC, V. No lunch.*

$$–$$$$ ✕ **French 75.** This bistro and champagne bar, inspired by a 1940s-style Paris-after-dark supper club, offers intimate dining in an opulent setting. Daring combinations such as duck in caramelized honey and tangerine sauce engage your taste buds. ✉ *1464 S. Coast Hwy., Laguna Beach,* ☎ *949/494–8444. AE, D, DC, MC, V. No lunch.*

$$ ✕ **Ti Amo.** A romantic setting and creative Mediterranean cuisine have earned this place acclaim. Try the seared ahi with a sesame-seed crust. All the nooks and crannies are charming, candlelit, and private, but to maximize romance, request a table in the enclosed garden in back. ✉ *31727 S. Coast Hwy., Laguna Beach,* ☎ *949/499–5350. AE, D, DC, MC, V. No lunch.*

$–$$$ ✕ **Javier's.** This lively restaurant offers a wide selection of Mexican dishes that owner Javier describes as homemade, but not necessarily traditional. Especially popular are the fresh lobster enchiladas, mole poblano, and *lomo* Azteca (pork loin medallions in chipotle cream sauce). The bar serves tequila and beer, and the two patios offer plenty of outdoor seating. ✉ *480 S. Coast Hwy., Laguna Beach,* ☎ *949/494–1239. AE, D, MC, V.*

$–$$$ ✕ **Mosun.** Fans of this restaurant-nightclub favor the Pacific Rim cuisine, fresh sushi, and large selection of sake. Among the entrées are teriyaki steak and pan-seared, five-spice duck breast. ✉ *680 S. Coast Hwy., Laguna Beach,* ☎ *949/497–5646. Reservations essential. AE, D, MC, V. No lunch.*

$ ✕ **Café Zinc.** Laguna Beach cognoscenti gather at the tiny counter and plant-filled patio of this vegetarian breakfast-and-lunch café. Oatmeal is sprinkled with berries in season, poached eggs are dusted with herbs, and the orange juice is fresh-squeezed. For lunch, try the spicy Thai pasta, asparagus salad with orange peel and capers, or one of the gourmet pizzettes. ✉ *350 Ocean Ave., Laguna Beach,* ☎ *949/494–6302. No credit cards. No dinner.*

$$$$ 🏨 **Surf and Sand Hotel.** Laguna's largest beachfront hotel has taste-
★ fully furnished rooms decorated with soft sand colors and bleached-wood shutters. Private balconies hover gently over the rolling waves. ✉ *1555 S. Coast Hwy., Laguna Beach 92651,* ☎ *949/497–4477 or 800/524–8621,* FAX *949/497–1092,* WEB *www.surfandsandresort.com. 165 rooms, 16 suites. Restaurant, cable TV with movies, pool, health club, beach, bar, concierge, meeting rooms; no air-conditioning. AE, D, DC, MC, V.*

$$$–$$$$ 🏨 **Inn at Laguna Beach.** On a bluff overlooking the ocean, the inn has a Mediterranean feel, with terra-cotta tiles and exotic flowers all over the grounds. Most guest rooms have views; those on the coastal level border Laguna's oceanfront cliffs. The inn is close to Main Beach, yet far enough away to feel secluded. ✉ *211 N. Coast Hwy., Laguna Beach 92651,* ☎ *949/497–9722 or 800/544–4479,* FAX *949/497–9972,* WEB *www.innatlagunabeach.com. 70 rooms. In-room data ports, mini-bars, some microwaves, refrigerators, cable TV, in-room VCRs, pool, meeting rooms. AE, D, DC, MC, V.*

$$–$$$
★
🛏 **Eiler's Inn.** A light-filled courtyard with a fountain is the focal point of this quaint, European-style bed-and-breakfast. Every room is unique, but all are full of antiques and travelers' journals for you to write in. Afternoon wine and cheese is served in the courtyard or in the cozy reading room, where you'll find the inn's only TV and phone. A sundeck in back has an ocean view. ⊠ *741 S. Coast Hwy., Laguna Beach 92651,* ☎ *949/494–3004,* FAX *949/497–2215. 12 rooms. No room phones, no room TVs. AE, D, MC, V.*

$$–$$$
🛏 **Hotel Laguna.** The oldest hotel in Laguna (opened in 1890) has manicured gardens, beach views and an ideal location downtown. Among the perks is access to the hotel's private beach, where guests are provided with lounges, umbrellas, towels and can order lunch or cocktails from the Beach Club menu. Complimentary wine and cheese are served in the afternoons. ⊠ *425 S. Coast Hwy., Laguna Beach 92651,* ☎ *949/494–1151 or 800/524–2927,* FAX *949/497–2163,* WEB *www.hotellaguna.com. 65 rooms. 2 restaurants, beach, bar, meeting rooms, parking (fee); no air-conditioning. AE, DC, MC, V. CP.*

Nightlife

The **Boom Boom Room** (⊠ Coast Inn, 1401 S. Coast Hwy., Laguna Beach, ☎ 949/494–7588) is the town's most popular gay club. The **Sandpiper** (⊠ 1183 S. Coast Hwy., Laguna Beach, ☎ 949/494–4694), a hole-in-the-wall dancing joint, attracts an eclectic crowd. **White House** (⊠ 340 S. Coast Hwy., Laguna Beach, ☎ 949/494–8088), a chic club on the main strip, has nightly entertainment and dancing.

Outdoor Activities and Sports

BICYCLING

Mountain bikes can be rented at **Rainbow Bicycles** (⊠ 485 N. Coast Hwy., Laguna Beach, ☎ 949/494–5806).

GOLF

Aliso Creek Golf Course (⊠ 31106 S. Coast Hwy., Laguna Beach, ☎ 949/499–1919) is a scenic 9-hole facility with a putting green. Greens fees are $19–$28; carts (optional) cost $2 for pullcarts and $9 for motorized. Reservations are taken up to a week in advance.

TENNIS

Six metered courts can be found at **Laguna Beach High School.** Two courts are available at the **Irvine Bowl.** Six courts are available at **Alta Laguna Park** on a first-come, first-served basis. **Moulton Meadows** has two courts. For information on public tennis courts, call the **City of Laguna Beach Recreation Department** (☎ 949/497–0716).

WATER SPORTS

Because its entire beach area is a marine preserve, Laguna Beach is ideal for snorkelers. Scuba divers should head to the Marine Life Refuge area, which runs from Seal Rock to Diver's Cove. Bodyboards are available for rent at **Hobie Sports** (⊠ 294 Forest Ave., Laguna Beach, ☎ 949/497–3304).

Shopping

Forest and Ocean avenues and Glenneyre Street are full of art galleries and fine jewelry and clothing boutiques. The **Tung & Groov** (⊠ 950 Glenneyre St., Laguna Beach, ☎ 949/494–0768) has an eclectic mix of handcrafted and decorator items like traditional umbrellas from Bali, brass elephant bells from India, and papier-mâché boxes. **Georgeo's Art Glass and Jewelry** (⊠ 269 Forest Ave., Laguna Beach, ☎ 949/497–0907) has a large selection of etched-glass bowls, vases, and fine jewelry. **Chicken Little's** (⊠ 574 S. Coast Hwy., Laguna Beach, ☎ 949/497–4818) has a variety of gifts for children and adults and a wide assortment of cards.

Dana Point

10 mi south of Laguna Beach, PCH.

Dana Point's claim to fame is its small-boat marina tucked into a dramatic natural harbor and surrounded by high bluffs. In late February, a whale festival features concerts, films, sports competitions, and a weekend street fair. **Dana Point Harbor** (☎ 949/496–1094, WEB www.danapointharbor.com) was first described more than 100 years ago by its namesake Richard Henry Dana in his book *Two Years Before the Mast.* At the marina are docks for small boats, marine-oriented shops, and some restaurants.

Inside Dana Point Harbor, **Swim Beach** has a fishing pier, barbecues, food stands, parking, rest rooms, and showers. At the south end of Dana Point, **Doheny State Park** (☎ 949/496–6171) is one of Southern California's top surfing destinations, but there's a lot more to do within this 63-acre area. Divers and anglers hang out at the beach's western end, and during low tide, the tidal pools beckon both young and old. Here you'll also find five indoor tanks and an interpretive center devoted to the wildlife of the Doheny Marine Refuge. There are also food stands and shops, picnic facilities, volleyball courts, and a pier for fishing. Camping is permitted, though there are no RV hook-ups.

Two indoor tanks at the **Ocean Institute** contain touchable sea creatures, as well as the complete skeleton of a gray whale. Anchored near the institute is *The Pilgrim,* a full-size replica of the square-rigged vessel on which Richard Henry Dana sailed. You can tour the boat daily from 10 to 2:30. Weekend cruises are also available. You can arrange to go on marine-mammal exploration cruises from January through March, or to explore regional tide pools year-round. ⊠ *24200 Dana Point Harbor Dr., Dana Point,* ☎ *949/496–2274,* WEB *www.ocean-institute.org.* ⌦ *Donation requested to tour ship, tide pool tour $4, cruises vary.* ☉ *Weekends 10–4:30.*

Dining and Lodging

$$–$$$$ ✕ **Chart House.** Set into a cliff overlooking Dana Point Harbor, this architecturally distinct chain restaurant prepares eight varieties of fish nightly, as well as steak and prime ribs. Also worthy of mention are the Chart House's signature salad bar and chocolate lava cake, served warm at your table. ⊠ *34442 Green Lantern St., Dana Point,* ☎ *949/ 493–1183. AE, D, DC, MC, V. No lunch.*

$–$$ ✕ **Luciana's.** This intimate Italian restaurant is a real find, especially for couples seeking a romantic evening. Dining rooms are small, warmed by two fireplaces inside and yet another fireplace on the patio. Try the linguine with clams, prawns, calamari, and green-lip mussels in a light tomato sauce; or grilled cured pork chops in a fennel-herb marinade. ⊠ *24312 Del Prado Ave., Dana Point,* ☎ *949/661–6500. AE, DC, MC, V. No lunch.*

$ ✕ **Proud Mary's.** On a terrace overlooking the fishing boats and pleasure craft in Dana Point Harbor, Proud Mary's serves the best burgers and sandwiches in southern Orange County. This "Cheers" on the water also serves steaks, chicken, and other American standards, and you can order breakfast all day. ⊠ *34689 Golden Lantern St., Dana Point,* ☎ *949/493–5853. AE, D, MC, V. No dinner.*

$$$$ ✕🖬 **Ritz-Carlton, Laguna Niguel.** An unrivaled setting on the edge of ★ the Pacific, combined with hallmark Ritz-Carlton service, have made this resort justly famous. Rooms have marble bathrooms and private balconies with ocean or pool views. Tea is served afternoons in the library. In the formal Dining Room (no lunch; reservations essential) chef

Yvon Goetz's French Continental prix-fixe menu includes items such as veal tournedos with cipollini (wild onions), walnut emulsion, port wine, and thyme cream. Subdued lighting, crystal chandeliers, and original paintings on the walls add to the dining experience. Two other restaurants here have à la carte menus. ⊠ *1 Ritz-Carlton Dr., Laguna Niguel, 92629,* ☎ *949/240–2000 or 800/241–3333,* FAX *949/240–0829,* WEB *www.ritzcarlton.com. 362 rooms, 31 suites. 3 restaurants, in-room data ports, cable TV with movies and video games, 2 tennis courts, 2 pools, health club, hair salon, massage, lobby lounge, concierge, Internet, business services, meeting rooms. AE, D, DC, MC, V.*

$$$$ ✕⊡ **St. Regis Monarch Beach Resort and Spa.** This Tuscan-style luxury resort occupies 172 acres. Rooms command views of either the coast or the lushly landscaped grounds, and beds are spread with goose down comforters. Guests have access to a private beach and tennis courts across the street. Michael Mina's acclaimed seafood dishes are served at the resort's Aqua, where unimpeded coastal views complement specialities like the ahi medallions in pinot noir sauce, and miso-glazed sea bass. The signature dessert is an old-fashioned root beer float with warm chocolate-chip cookies. ⊠ *1 Monarch Beach Resort, off Nigual Rd., Monarch Bay, 92629,* ☎ *949/234–3200 or 800/722–1543,* FAX *949/234–3201,* WEB *www.stregismonarchbeach.com. 400 rooms, 74 suites. 3 restaurants, in-room data ports, cable TV with movies and video games, 18-hole golf course, 3 pools, health club, hair salon, massage, spa, beach, bar, lobby lounge, laundry facilities, dry cleaning, concierge, Internet, business services, some pets allowed (free). AE, D, DC, MC, V.*

$$$–$$$$ ⊡ **Laguna Cliffs Marriott Resort.** Formerly known as the Dana Point Resort, this red and white hillside hotel looks like it's straight out of Cape Cod, except that its views are of the Pacific, not the Atlantic. ⊠ *25135 Park Lantern, Lantern Bay County Park, 92629,* ☎ *949/661–5000 or 800/533–9748,* FAX *949/661–5358,* WEB *www.marriott.com. 347 rooms, 13 suites. Restaurant, in-room data ports, cable TV with movies and video games, 2 pools, health club, 2 outdoor hot tubs, basketball, croquet, volleyball, bar, lobby lounge, concierge, Internet, business services, meeting rooms, some pets allowed (fee). AE, D, DC, MC, V.*

$$–$$$$ ⊡ **Blue Lantern Inn.** Combining New England–style architecture with
★ a Southern California setting, this white clapboard B&B rests on a bluff overlooking the harbor and ocean. A fire warms the intimate, inviting living area, where you may enjoy complimentary snacks and play backgammon every afternoon. The Nantucket–style guest rooms also have fireplaces and whirlpool tubs. The top-floor tower suite has a 180° ocean view. ⊠ *34343 St. of the Blue Lantern, Lantern Bay County Park, 92629,* ☎ *949/661–1304 or 800/950–1236,* FAX *949/496–1483,* WEB *www.foursisters.com. 29 rooms. In-room data ports, in-room VCRs, gym, concierge, meeting rooms; no smoking. AE, DC, MC, V.*

Outdoor Activities and Sports

Rental stands for surfboards, Windsurfers, small powerboats, and sailboats can be found near most of the piers. **Embarcadero Marina** (⊠ 34512 Embarcadero Pl., Dana Point, ☎ 949/496–6177) has small powerboats and sailboats for rent near the launching ramp at Dana Point Harbor. **Hobie Sports** (⊠ 24825 Del Prado, Dana Point, ☎ 949/496–2366) rents surfboards and Boogie boards. **Dana Wharf Sportfishing** (⊠ 34675 Golden Lantern St., Dana Point, ☎ 949/496–5794) runs charters and whale-watching excursions from early December to late March.

San Juan Capistrano

5 mi north of Dana Point, Hwy. 74; 60 mi north of San Diego, I–5.

Quaint San Juan Capistrano, one of the few noteworthy historical districts in Southern California, is best known for its mission. It is to the mission that the swallows are supposed traditionally to return, migrating each year from their winter haven in Argentina, but these days they are more likely to choose other local sites for nesting. St. Joseph's Day, March 19, launches a week of festivities. After summering in the arches of the old stone church, the swallows head home on St. John's Day, October 23.

If you arrive by train, you will be dropped off across from the mission at the San Juan Capistrano depot. With its appealing brick café and preserved Santa Fe cars, the depot retains much of the magic of early American railroads. If driving, park near Ortega and Camino Capistrano, the city's main streets, lined with colorful restaurants and charming boutiques.

★ ㉑ **Mission San Juan Capistrano,** founded in 1776 by Father Junípero Serra, was the major Roman Catholic outpost between Los Angeles and San Diego. Though the original Great Stone Church is permanently supported by scaffolding, many of the mission's adobe buildings have been preserved to illustrate mission life, with exhibits of an olive millstone, tallow ovens, tanning vats, metalworking furnaces, and padres' living quarters. The bougainvillea-covered Serra Chapel is believed to be the oldest building standing in California. Mass takes place daily at 7 AM in the chapel and 8:30 in the new church. ⊠ *Camino Capistrano and Ortega Hwy., San Juan Capistrano,* ☎ *949/234–1300,* WEB *http:// missionsjc.com.* ⊡ *$6.* ⊙ *Daily 8:30–5.*

㉒ Near Mission San Juan Capistrano is the **San Juan Capistrano Library,** a postmodern structure erected in 1983. Architect Michael Graves combined a classical design with the style of the mission to striking effect. Its courtyard has secluded places for reading. ⊠ *31495 El Camino Real, San Juan Capistrano,* ☎ *949/493–1752,* WEB *www.oc.ca.gov/ocpl/ sanjuan/sanjuan.htm.* ⊙ *Mon.–Wed. 10–8, Thurs. 10–6, Sat. 10–5, Sun. noon–5.*

Dining

$$–$$$ ✕ **L'Hirondelle.** Roast duck, rabbit, and Belgian dishes are the hallmark
★ of this French and Belgian restaurant, which also has an extensive wine list and impressive selection of Belgian beers. You can dine inside or out on the patio. ⊠ *31631 Camino Capistrano, San Juan Capistrano,* ☎ *949/661–0425. AE, MC, V. Closed Mon. No lunch Tues.*

$–$$$ ✕ **Cedar Creek Inn.** Equally suitable for family meals and romantic get-
★ away dinners, the inn has a children's menu as well as a secluded outdoor patio for couples dining alone. The contemporary American menu features crowd-pleasers like an ahi burger, rack of lamb, pecan chicken, and herb-crusted halibut. ⊠ *26860 Ortega Hwy., San Juan Capistrano,* ☎ *949/240–2229. AE, MC, V.*

$–$$ ✕ **El Adobe.** This early Mission–style eatery serves enormous portions of mildly seasoned Mexican food. Mariachi bands play Friday and Saturday nights and during Sunday brunch. ⊠ *31891 Camino Capistrano, San Juan Capistrano,* ☎ *949/830–8620. AE, D, DC, MC, V.*

Nightlife

Coach House (⊠ 33157 Camino Capistrano, San Juan Capistrano, ☎ 949/496–8930), a roomy, casual club with long tables and a dark-wood bar, draws crowds of varying ages for entertainment from hip new bands to mellow acoustic guitar to comedy acts.

OFF THE
BEATEN PATH

SAN CLEMENTE – Travelers who shun the throngs in favor of a low-key beach experience where pure sea air and steamed mussels are more appealing than celebrity sightings and goat cheese appetizers should drive 10 mi south of Dana Point on Pacific Coast Highway to San Clemente. There, 20 square mi of prime bicycling terrain await. Camp Pendleton, the country's largest Marine Corps base, welcomes cyclists to use some of its roads—just don't be surprised to see a troop helicopter taking off right beside you. Surfers favor **San Clemente State Beach** (☎ 949/492–3156), which has camping facilities, RV hook-ups, and fire rings. San Onofre State Beach, just south of San Clemente, is another surfing destination. Below the bluffs are 3½ mi of sandy beach, where you can swim, fish, and watch wildlife.

ORANGE COUNTY A TO Z

To research prices, get advice from other travelers, and book travel arrangements, visit www.fodors.com.

AIR TRAVEL

The county's main facility is John Wayne Airport Orange County, served by many major domestic airlines. Los Angeles International Airport (LAX) is only 35 mi west of Anaheim. Ontario International Airport is just northwest of Riverside, 30 mi north of Anaheim. Long Beach Airport is about 20 minutes by bus from Anaheim.

➤ AIRPORT INFORMATION: **John Wayne Airport Orange County** (✉ MacArthur Blvd. at I–405, Santa Ana, ☎ 949/252–5252, WEB www.ocair.com). **Long Beach Airport** (✉ 4100 Donald Douglas Dr., ☎ 562/570–2600). **Los Angeles International Airport (LAX)** (☎ 310/646-5252, WEB www.lawa.org/lax/laxframe.html). **Ontario International Airport** (✉ Airport Dr. and Vineyard Ave., ☎ 909/937–2700).

BUS TRAVEL

The Los Angeles MTA has limited service to Orange County. From downtown, Bus 460 goes to Knott's Berry Farm and Disneyland Resort. Greyhound serves Anaheim and Santa Ana. The Orange County Transportation Authority will take you virtually anywhere in the county, but it will take time; OCTA buses go from Knott's Berry Farm and Disneyland to Huntington Beach and Newport Beach. Bus 1 travels along the coast; there is also an express bus to Los Angeles.

➤ BUS INFORMATION: **Greyhound** (☎ 714/999–1256 or 800/231–2222, WEB www.greyhound.com). **Los Angeles MTA** (☎ 213/626–4455, WEB www.mta.net). The **Orange County Transportation Authority (OCTA)** (☎ 714/636–7433, WEB www.octa.net).

CAR RENTAL

All of the national car-rental companies have offices at Los Angeles International Airport and most of them are represented at John Wayne Airport Orange County. Ontario International Airport and Long Beach Airport each have outlets for several of the major companies. *See* Car Rental *in* Smart Travel Tips A to Z for national rental agency phone numbers.

CAR TRAVEL

The San Diego Freeway (I–405) and the Santa Ana Freeway (I–5) run north–south through Orange County. South of Laguna I–405 merges into I–5 (called the San Diego Freeway south from this point). Do your best to avoid freeways during rush hours (6–9 AM and 3:30–6 PM), when they literally can back up for miles.

Highways 55 and 91 head west to the ocean and east into the mountains. Take Highway 91 to Garden Grove and inland points (Buena Park, Anaheim). Highway 55 leads to Newport Beach. Pacific Coast Highway (Highway 1) allows easy access to beach communities and is the most scenic route.

EMERGENCIES
In an emergency dial 911.
➤ HOSPITALS: **Anaheim General Hospital**(⊠ 3350 W. Ball Rd., Anaheim, ☎ 714/827–6700).**UCI Medical Center**(⊠ 101 The City Dr. S., Orange, ☎ 714/456–7002).

LODGING
You can search for hotel rooms and make reservations online through the Web site of the Anaheim-Orange County Visitor and Convention Bureau.
➤ RESERVATIONS: **Anaheim-Orange County Visitor and Convention Bureau** (⊠ Anaheim Convention Center, 800 W. Katella Ave., 92802, ☎ 714/765–8888, WEB www.anaheimoc.org).

TOURS
Pacific Coast Gray Line Tours provides guided tours from Orange County hotels to Universal Studios Hollywood, Los Angeles/Hollywood, Six Flags Magic Mountain, the San Diego Zoo, SeaWorld, Catalina Island, and the Long Beach Aquarium.
➤ CONTACT: **Pacific Coast Gray Line Tours** (☎ 714/978–8855, WEB www.pacificcoastgrayline.com).

TRAIN TRAVEL
Amtrak makes stops in Orange County: at Fullerton, Anaheim, Santa Ana, Irvine, San Juan Capistrano, and San Clemente. Metrolink is a weekday commuter train that runs to and from Los Angeles and Orange County, starting as far south as Oceanside and stopping in Laguna Niguel, Tustin, San Juan Capistrano, San Clemente, Irvine, Santa Ana, Orange, Anaheim, and Fullerton.
➤ TRAIN INFORMATION: **Amtrak** (☎ 800/872–7245, WEB www.amtrak.com). **Metrolink** (☎ 800/371–5465, WEB www.metrolinktrains.com).

VISITOR INFORMATION
➤ CONTACTS: **Anaheim-Orange County Visitor and Convention Bureau** (⊠ Anaheim Convention Center, 800 W. Katella Ave., 92802, ☎ 714/765–8888, WEB www.anaheimoc.org). **Huntington Beach Conference and Visitors Bureau**(⊠ 417 Main St., 92648, ☎ 714/969–3492, WEB www.hbvisit.org). **Laguna Beach Visitors Bureau** (⊠ 252 Broadway, 92651, ☎ 949/376–0511, WEB www.lagunabeachinfo.org). **Newport Beach Conference and Visitors Bureau** (⊠ 3300 W. Coast Hwy., 92663, ☎ 800/942–6278, WEB www.newportbeach-cvb.com). **San Juan Capistrano Chamber of Commerce and Visitors Center** (⊠ 31781 Camino Capistrano, Suite 306, 92693, ☎ 949/493–4700, WEB www.sanjuanchamber.com). **Southern California Golf Association**(☎ 818/980–3630, WEB www.scga.org). **Southern California Public Links Golf Association**(☎ 714/994–4747, WEB www.plga.org).

16 SAN DIEGO

Exploring San Diego is an endless adventure. To newcomers the city and county may seem like a conglomeration of theme parks: Old Town and the Gaslamp Quarter, historically oriented; the wharf area, a maritime playground; La Jolla, a throwback to southern California elegance; Balboa Park, a convergence of the town's cerebral and action-oriented personae. There are, of course, real theme parks— SeaWorld and the San Diego Zoo—but the great outdoors, in the form of forests, landscaped urban areas, and sandy beaches, is the biggest of them all.

S AN DIEGO IS A BIG CITY, where locals take pride in its small-town feel. With more than 1 million people, San Diego is second only to Los Angeles in population among California cities. It also covers a lot of territory, roughly 400 square mi of land and sea. To the north and south of the city are 70 mi of beaches. Inland, a succession of chaparral-covered mesas are punctuated with deep-cut canyons that step up to savanna-like hills, separating the verdant coast from the arid Anza-Borrego Desert. Unusually clear skies make the inland countryside ideal for stargazing.

The San Diego area, the birthplace of California, was claimed for Spain by explorer Juan Rodríguez Cabrillo in 1542 and eventually came under Mexican rule. You'll find reminders of San Diego's Spanish and Mexican heritage throughout the region—in architecture and place-names, in distinctive Mexican cuisine, and in the historic buildings of Old Town.

In 1867 developer Alonzo Horton, who called the town's bay-front "the prettiest place for a city I ever saw," began building a hotel, a plaza, and prefab homes on 960 downtown acres. The city's fate was sealed in 1908, when President Theodore Roosevelt's Great White Fleet sailed into the bay. The U.S. Navy, impressed by the city's excellent harbor and temperate climate, decided to build a destroyer base on San Diego Bay in the 1920s. The newly devleoped aircraft industry soon followed (Chales Lindbergh's plane *Spirit of St. Louis* was built here.) The military, which operates many bases and installations throughout the county, continues to contribute to the local economy.

EXPLORING SAN DIEGO

Updated by
Rob Aikins

Although many attractions in San Diego are separated by some distance, the downtown area is delightfully urban and accessible. You can walk around the Gaslamp Quarter and the harbor, then catch a trolley or bus to the Balboa Park museums and zoo, the funky neighborhood of Hillcrest, the Old Town historic sites, and Mission Bay marine park and SeaWorld. After that, a car is the quickest way to get to the Coronado, Point Loma, and the beachside communities, though public transportation is available and reliable.

Great Itineraries

IF YOU HAVE 3 DAYS

Start with the San Diego Zoo in Balboa Park on the morning of Day One. It would be easy to spend your entire visit to the park here, but it would be a shame to miss El Prado and its rows interesting museums. Start Day Two downtown at Seaport Village. After browsing the shops catch a ferry from the Broadway Pier to Coronado, and board a bus going down Orange Avenue to see the Hotel Del Coronado. Back in San Diego after lunch, stroll north on the Embarcadero to Ash Street; if you have time, you can view the Maritime Museum or the San Diego Aircraft Carrier Museum. Spend the morning of Day Three, in La Jolla. Have lunch before heading back to the Gaslamp Quarter.

IF YOU HAVE 5 DAYS

Follow the three-day itinerary above, and begin Day Four with a morning visit to Cabrillo National Monument. Have lunch at one of the seafood restaurants on Scott Street, and then head over to Old Town (take Rosecrans Street north to San Diego Avenue). If the daily schedule lists low tide for the afternoon, reverse the order to catch the tide pools at Cabrillo. If you're traveling with young children, make

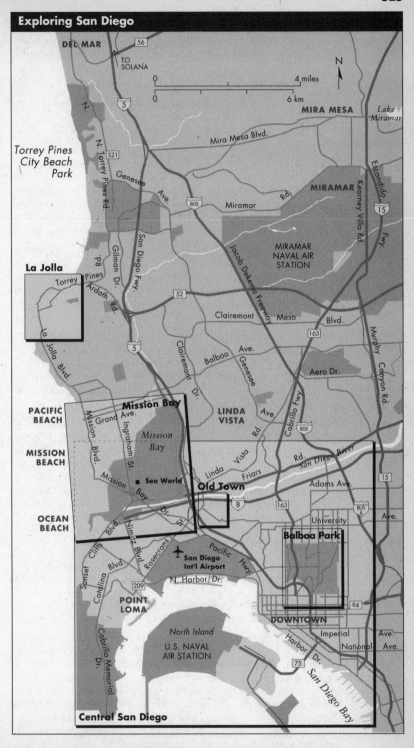

Legoland California in Carlsbad your main destination for Day Five. En route to North County stop off at Torrey Pines State Park. If you're not going to Legoland, take Interstate 5 north to Del Mar for lunch, shopping, and sea views. A visit to Mission San Luis Rey, slightly inland from Oceanside on Highway 76, will infuse some history and culture into the tour.

Numbers in the text correspond to numbers in the margin and on the Central San Diego and Mission Bay map.

Balboa Park

Overlooking downtown and the Pacific Ocean, 1,200-acre Balboa Park is the cultural heart of San Diego, where you'll find most of the city's museums and the San Diego Zoo. Cultivated and wild gardens are an integral part of Balboa Park, thanks to the "Mother of Balboa Park," Kate Sessions, who made sure the park was planted with thousands of palms, purple-blossoming jacaranda trees, and other trees.

Many of the park's Spanish colonial revival buildings were meant to be temporary exhibit halls for the Panama–California International Exposition of 1915, which celebrated the opening of the Panama Canal. Fortunately, city leader realized the value of the buildings and incoporated them into their plans for Balboa Park's acreage, which had been set aside by the city founders in 1868.

Parking near Balboa Park's museums is no small accomplishment. If you end up parking a bit far from your destination, consider the stroll back through the greenery part of the day's recreational activities. Alternatively, you can park at Inspiration Point on the east side of the park, off Presidents Way. Free trams run from there to the museums every 8 to 10 minutes, 9:30–5:30 daily.

Two Good Walks

It's impossible to cover all the park's museums in one day, so choose your focus before you head out. Enter via Cabrillo Bridge through the West Gate, which depicts the Panama Canal's linkage of the Atlantic and Pacific oceans. Park south of the **Alcazar Garden** ①. It's a short stretch north across El Prado to the landmark California Building, home to the San Diego Museum of Man. Next door are The Globe Theatres, which adjoin the sculpture garden of the **San Diego Museum of Art** ②, an ornate Plateresque-style structure built to resemble the 17th-century University of Salamanca in Spain.

Continuing east you'll come to the Botanical Building, the Timken Museum of Art, and the Spanish colonial revival–style Casa del Prado. At the end of the row is the San Diego Natural History Museum. If you were to continue north, you would come to the carousel, the miniature railroad, and, finally, the entrance to the **San Diego Zoo** ③.

Return to the Natural History Museum and cross the Plaza de Balboa— its large central fountain is a popular meeting spot—to reach the **Reuben H. Fleet Science Center** ④. On the south side of the Prado heading west, you'll next pass Casa de Balboa; inside are the model-railroad and photography museums and the historical society. Next door in the newly reconstructed House of Hospitality is the Balboa Park Visitors Center, where you can buy a reduced-price pass to the museums, and the Prado restaurant. Across the Plaza de Panama, the Franciscan mission–style House of Charm houses the Mingei International Museum and a gallery for San Diego artists. Your starting point, the Alcazar Garden, is west of the House of Charm.

Balboa Park

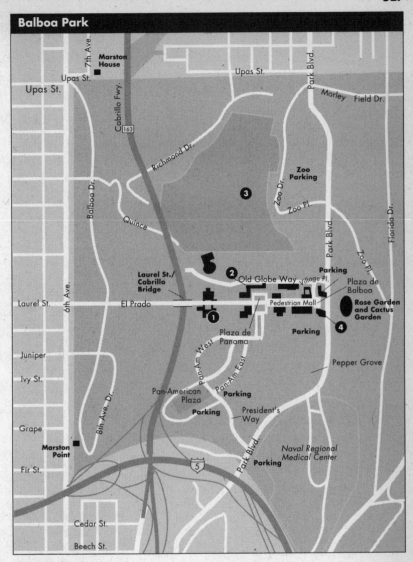

7th Ave.

Marston House

Upas St.

Upas St.

Upas St.

Park Blvd.

Morley Field Dr.

Cabrillo Fwy.

[163]

Richmond Dr.

Balboa Dr.

Quince

Zoo Parking

Zoo Dr.

Zoo Pl.

3

Florida Dr.

Zoo Pl.

6th Ave.

Parking

Village Pl.

2 Old Globe Way

Plaza de Balboa

Laurel St./ Cabrillo Bridge

Laurel St.

El Prado

Rose Garden and Cactus Garden

Pedestrian Mall

1

4

Plaza de Panama

Parking

Park Blvd.

Juniper

Pan-Am West

Pepper Grove

Ivy St.

Pan-Am East

8th Ave. Dr.

Pan-American Plaza

Parking

Parking

President's Way

Grape

Marston Point

[5]

Naval Regional Medical Center

Fir St.

Park Blvd.

Parking

Cedar St.

Beech St.

528

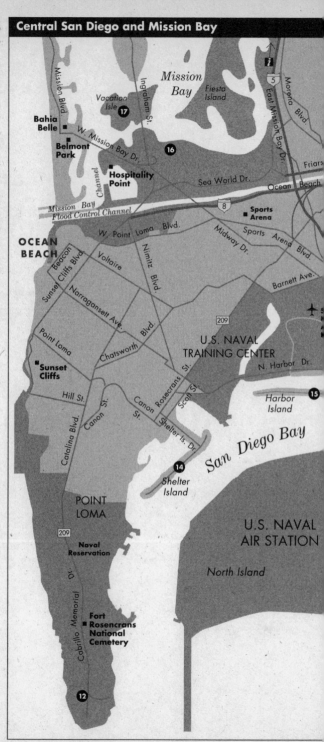

Central San Diego and Mission Bay

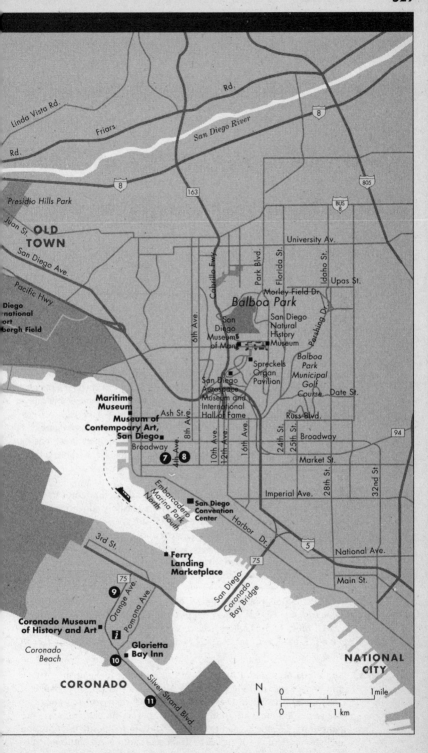

Linda Vista Rd.

Friars

Rd.

Rd.

San Diego River

8

8

163

805

BUS 8

Presidio Hills Park

Juan St.

OLD TOWN

San Diego Ave.

Pacific Hwy.

Diego national ort bergh Field

University Av.

Park Blvd.

Florida St.

Idaho St.

Upas St.

Cabrillo Fwy.

Morley Field Dr.

Balboa Park

6th Ave.

San Diego Museum of Man

San Diego Natural History Museum

Pershing Dr.

Balboa Park Municipal Golf Course

Spreckels Organ Pavilion

Date St.

San Diego Aerospace Museum and International Hall of Fame

Maritime Museum

Ash St.

Russ Blvd.

8th Ave.

94

Museum of Contempoary Art, San Diego

10th Ave.

12th Ave.

16th Ave.

24th St.

25th St.

Broadway

Broadway

4th Ave.

7 8

Market St.

28th St.

32nd St.

Embarcadero Marina Park North South

Imperial Ave.

San Diego Convention Center

Harbor Dr.

5

3rd St.

Ferry Landing Marketplace

75

National Ave.

75

San Diego-Coronado Bay Bridge

Main St.

9

Orange Ave.

Pomona Ave.

Coronado Museum of History and Art

Coronado Beach

i

Glorietta Bay Inn

NATIONAL CITY

10

CORONADO

Silver Strand Blvd.

11

N

0   1 mile

0   1 km

A second walk leads south from the Plaza de Panama to the ornate Spreckels Organ Pavilion, the San Diego Aerospace Museum and International Aerospace Hall of Fame, and the San Diego Halls of Champions.

TIMING

Unless you're pressed for time, you'll want to devote an entire day to the perpetually expanding zoo, and return another day to see the museums and gardens. The zoo is free for kids the entire month of October.

Though some of the park's museums are open on Monday, most are open Tuesday–Sunday 10–4; in summer many have extended hours—phone ahead to ask. On Tuesday the museums have free admission to their permanent exhibits on a rotating basis; call the Balboa Park Visitors Center for a schedule. Free architectural, historical, or nature tours depart from the visitor center every Saturday at 10, while park ranger–led tours start out from the visitor center at 1 PM every Wednesday and Sunday.

Sights to See

❶ **Alcazar Garden.** The colorful gardens surrounding the Alcazar Castle in Seville, Spain, inspired the landscaping here; you'll feel like royalty resting on the benches by the tiled fountains. It's next to the House of Charm and across from the Museum of Man. *off El Prado.*

OFF THE BEATEN PATH

HILLCREST – Northwest of Balboa Park, Hillcrest is San Diego's center for the gay community and artists of all types. University, 4th, and 5th avenues are filled with cafés, interesting boutiques, and several indie new and used bookstores. The self-contained residential-commercial Uptown District, on University Avenue at 8th Avenue, was built to resemble an inner-city neighborhood, with shops and restaurants within easy walking distance of high-price town houses. To the northeast, Adams Avenue, reached via Park Boulevard heading north off Washington Street, has many antiques stores. Adams Avenue leads east into Kensington, a handsome old neighborhood that overlooks Mission Valley.

★ ❹ **Reuben H. Fleet Science Center.** Children and adults alike enjoy the Fleet Center's clever interactive exhibits that are sneakily educational. You can reconfigure your face to have two left sides, or, by replaying an instant video clip, watch yourself coming and going at different speeds. The IMAX Dome Theater screens exhilarating nature and science films. The SciTours simulator is designed to take you on virtual voyages—stomach lurches and all. The Meteor Storm lets up to six players at a time have an interactive virtual-reality experience, this one sans motion sickness potential. ✉ *1875 El Prado,* ☎ *619/238–1233,* WEB *www.rhfleet.org.* *Gallery exhibits $6.75; Gallery exhibits and one IMAX film $11.50; Gallery exhibits and two IMAX films $15.* ⏲ *Mon.–Thurs. 9:30–5, Fri.–Sat. 9:30–8, Sun. 9:30–6 (hrs vary seasonally; call ahead).*

★ ❷ **San Diego Museum of Art.** Known primarily for its Spanish Baroque and Renaissance paintings, including works by El Greco, Goya, Rubens, and van Ruisdael, San Diego's most comprehensive art museum also has strong holdings of South Asian art, Indian miniatures, and contemporary California paintings. The Baldwin M. Baldwin collection includes more than 100 pieces by Toulouse-Lautrec. An outdoor Sculpture Garden exhibits both traditional and modern pieces. Free docent tours are offered throughout the day. ✉ *Casa de Balboa, 1450 El Prado,* ☎ *619/232–7931,* WEB *www.sdmart.org.* *$8 ($10–$12 for special exhibits).* ⏲ *Tues.–Sun. 10–6 (till 9 on Thurs.).*

★ **3** **San Diego Zoo.** Balboa Park's—and perhaps the city's—most famous attraction is its 100-acre zoo, and it deserves all the press it gets. Nearly 4,000 animals of some 800 diverse species roam in hospitable, expertly crafted habitats that replicate natural environments as closely as possible. Walkways wind over bridges and past waterfalls ringed with tropical ferns; elephants in a sandy plateau roam so close you're tempted to pet them.

Open-air trams can whisk you around 85% of the exhibits, but the zoo is at its best when you wander the paths, such as the one that climbs through the huge, enclosed **Scripps Aviary,** where brightly colored tropical birds swoop between branches just inches from your face, and into the neighboring **Gorilla Tropics,** among the zoo's latest ventures into bioclimatic zone exhibits. Here animals live in enclosed environments modeled on their native habitats. These zones may look natural, but they're helped a lot by modern technology: the sounds of the tropical rain forest emerge from a 144-speaker sound system that plays CDs recorded in Africa.

The zoo's simulated Asian rain forest, **Tiger River,** has 10 exhibits with more than 35 species of animals; tigers, Malayan tapirs, and Argus pheasants wander among the collection of exotic trees and plants. At the popular **Polar Bear Plunge,** where you can watch the featured animals take a chilly dive, Siberian reindeer, white foxes, and other Arctic creatures are separated from their predatory neighbors by a series of camouflaged moats. **Ituri Forest**—a 4-acre African rain forest at the base of Tiger River—lets you glimpse huge but surprisingly graceful hippos frolicking underwater, and buffalo cavorting with monkeys. ⊠ *2920 Zoo Dr.,* ☎ *619/231–1515; 888/697–2632 Giant panda hot line,* 🌐 *www.sandiegozoo.org.* ⊟ *$19.50 includes zoo, Children's Zoo, and animal shows; $32 includes above, plus 40-min guided bus tour and round-trip Skyfari ride; Kangaroo bus tour $12 additional (only $3 additional for purchasers of $32 deluxe package); zoo free for children under 12 in Oct. and for all on Founder's Day (1st Mon. in Oct.); $46.80 pass good for admission to zoo and San Diego Wild Animal Park within 5 days. AE, D, MC, V.* ☉ *May–Sept., daily 9–9; Sept.–May, daily 9–4; Children's Zoo and Skyfari ride close earlier.*

Downtown

Downtown is San Diego's Lazarus. Written off as moribund by the 1970s, when few people willingly stayed in the area after dark, downtown is now one of the city's prime draws for tourists and real estate agents. Massive redevelopment started in the late 1970s, giving rise to the Gaslamp Quarter Historic District, Horton Plaza shopping center, and San Diego Convention Center, which have spurred an upsurge of elegant hotels, upscale condominium complexes, and swank, trendy cafés and restaurants that have people lingering downtown well into the night—if not also waking up there the next morning.

Two Good Walks

Most people do a lot of parking-lot hopping when visiting downtown, but for the energetic, two distinct areas may be explored on foot.

To stay near the water, start a walk of the **Embarcadero** ⑤ at the foot of Ash Street on Harbor Drive, where the *Berkeley,* headquarters of the Maritime Museum, is moored. At Harbor Drive and Broadway, you can walk inland two long blocks to Kettner Boulevard to see the mosaic-domed Santa Fe Depot and, right next door, the downtown branch of the Museum of Contemporary Art, San Diego. Return to Harbor Drive and continue south past Tuna Harbor to **Seaport Village** ⑥.

A tour of the working heart of downtown can begin at the corner of 1st Avenue and Broadway, near Spreckels Theater, a grand old stage that presents pop concerts and touring plays. Two blocks east and across the street sits the historic U. S. Grant Hotel, built in 1910. If you cross Broadway, you'll be able to enter **Horton Plaza** ⑦, San Diego's favorite retail playland. Fourth Avenue, the eastern boundary of Horton Plaza, doubles as the western boundary of the 16-block **Gaslamp Quarter** ⑧. Head south to Island Avenue and Fourth Avenue to the William Heath Davis House, where you can get a touring map of the district. If you continue west on Island Avenue, you'll arrive at the Children's Museum/Museo de los Niños, which younger kids might prefer over a historical excursion.

TIMING

The above walks take about an hour each, though there's enough to do in downtown San Diego to keep you busy for at least two days. For a guided tour of the Gaslamp Quarter, plan to visit on Saturday. A boat trip on the harbor, or at least a hop over to Coronado on the ferry, is a must at any time of year, but during the gray whales' migration, from December through March, you should definitely consider booking a whale-watching excursion from the Broadway Pier.

Sights to See

⑤ **Embarcadero.** The bustle along Harbor Drive's waterfront walkway comes less these days from the activities of fishing folk than from the throngs of tourists, but it remains the nautical soul of San Diego. People here still make a living from the sea. Seafood restaurants line the piers, as do sea vessels of every variety—cruise ships, ferries, tour boats, houseboats, and naval destroyers.

On the north end of the Embarcadero, at Ash Street, you'll find the Maritime Museum. South of it, the **B Street Pier** is used by ships from major cruise lines as both a port of call and a departure point. Day-trippers getting ready to set sail gather at the **Broadway Pier,** also known as the excursion pier. Tickets for the harbor tours and whale-watching trips are sold here. The terminal for the Coronado Ferry lies just beyond the Broadway pier.

The USS *Midway* is slated to dock on the south side of Navy Pier in early 2003. It will house the much-anticipated **San Diego Aircraft Carrier Museum,** (☎ 619/702–7700, WEB www.midway.org), which will include five aircraft, a flight simulator, and interactive exhibits focusing on naval aviation. The U.S. Navy has control of the next few waterfront blocks to the south—**destroyers, submarines, and carriers** cruise in and out, some staying for weeks at a time. Unless the Navy is engaged in military maneuvers or activities, on weekends you can tour these floating cities. Check out the carrier USS *Constellation,* which docks across the harbor at North Island naval base when it's in port. (☎ Call 619/437–2735 for hours and types of ships; 619/545–1141 for aircraft carriers).The **San Diego Convention Center,** on Harbor Drive between 1st and 5th avenues, was designed by Arthur Erickson. The center often holds trade shows that are open to the public, and tours of the building are available.

⑧ **Gaslamp Quarter.** The 16-block national historic district between 4th and 5th avenues from Broadway to Market Street contains most of San Diego's Victorian-style commercial buildings. Businesses thrived in this area in the latter part of the 19th century, but at the turn of the century downtown's commercial district moved west toward Broadway, and many of San Diego's first buildings fell into disrepair. During the early 1900s the quarter became known as the Stingaree district.

Prostitutes picked up sailors in lively area taverns, and dance halls and crime flourished.

History buffs, developers, architects, and artists formed the Gaslamp Quarter Council in 1974. Bent on preserving the district, they gathered funds from the government and private benefactors and began cleaning up the quarter, restoring the finest old buildings, and attracting businesses and the public back to the heart of New Town. Their efforts have paid off. Former flophouses have become choice office buildings, and the area is dotted with shops and restaurants.

The **William Heath Davis House** (✉ 410 Island Ave., at 4th Ave., ☎ 619/233–4692), one of the first residences in town, now serves as the information center for the historic district. Davis was a San Franciscan whose ill-fated attempt to develop the waterfront area preceded the more successful one of Alonzo Horton. Two-hour walking tours ($8) of the historic district leave from the house on Saturday at 11. The museum also sells detailed self-guided tour maps ($2).

The majority of the quarter's landmark buildings are on 4th and 5th avenues, between Island Avenue and Broadway. Highlights on 5th Avenue include the Backesto Building (No. 614), the Mercantile Building (No. 822), the Louis Bank of Commerce (No. 835), and the Watts-Robinson Building (No. 903). The Tudor-style **Keating Building** (✉ 432 F St., at 5th Ave.,) was designed by the same firm that created the famous Hotel Del Coronado. The section of G Street between 6th and 9th avenues has become a haven for galleries; stop in one of them to pick up a map of the downtown arts district. For additional information about the historic area, call the **Gaslamp Quarter Association** (☎ 619/233–5227) or log on to their Web site (WEB www.gaslamp.org).

★ ❼ **Horton Plaza.** Downtown's centerpiece is the shopping, dining, and entertainment mall that fronts Broadway and G Street from 1st to 4th avenues, covering more than six city blocks. A collage of pastels with elaborate, colorful tile work on benches and stairways, banners waving in the air, and modern sculptures marking the entrances, Horton Plaza rises in uneven, staggered levels to six floors; great views of downtown from the harbor to Balboa Park and beyond can be had here. The complex's architecture has strongly affected the rest of downtown's development—new apartment and condominium complexes along G and Market streets mimic its brightly colored towers and cupolas.

Inside you'll find more than 150 stores, a movie complex, and restaurants and food shops. The respected San Diego Repertory Theatre has two stages below ground level. Most stores are open 10–9 weekdays, 10–6 Saturday, and 11–7 Sunday, but during the winter holidays and the summer many places stay open longer (619/238–1596 for up-to-the-minute information). The **International Visitors Information Center** is the best resource for information on San Diego. ✉ *Visitors center: 11 Horton Plaza, street level at corner of 1st Ave. and F St.,* ☎ *619/236–1212,* WEB *www.sandiego.org.* ☾ *Mon.–Sat. 8:30–5; June–Aug. also Sun. 11–5.*

★ ☚ ❻ **Seaport Village.** On a prime stretch of waterfront that spreads out across 14 acres, the village's three bustling shopping plazas are designed to reflect the architectural styles of early California, especially New England clapboard and Spanish mission. A ¼-mi wooden boardwalk that runs along the bay and 4 mi of paths lead to specialty shops, snack bars, and restaurants. Seaport Village's shops are open daily 10 to 9 (10 to 10 in summer). I. D. Looff crafted the hand-carved, hand-painted steeds on the **Broadway Flying Horses Carousel.** Strolling clowns, balloon sculptors, mimes, musicians, and magicians are also on hand throughout the village to entertain kids; those not impressed by such pretechnological displays can duck into the Time Out entertainment center near the carousel and play video games. ☎ *619/235–4014; 619/235–4013 for events hot line,* WEB *www.spvillage.com.*

Coronado

Although it's actually an isthmus, easily reached from the mainland if you head north from Imperial Beach, Coronado has always seemed like an island—and is often referred to as such. The streets of Coronado are wide, quiet, and friendly, with lots of neighborhood parks and grand Victorian homes. North Island Naval Air Station was established in 1911 on Coronado's north end, across from Point Loma, and was the site of Charles Lindbergh's departure on the transcontinental flight that preceded his famous transatlantic voyage.

Coronado is visible from downtown and Point Loma and accessible via the San Diego–Coronado Bridge. There is a $1 toll for crossing the bridge into Coronado, but cars carrying two or more passengers may enter through the free carpool lane. Until the bridge was completed in 1969, visitors and residents relied on the Coronado Ferry. San Diego's Metropolitan Transit System runs a shuttle bus, No. 904, around the island; you can pick it up where you disembark the ferry and ride it out as far as the Silver Strand State Beach. Buses start leaving from the ferry landing at 10:30 AM and run once an hour on the half hour until 6:30 PM.

You can board the ferry, operated by **San Diego Harbor Excursion** (☎ 619/234–4111; 800/442–7847 in CA), at downtown San Diego's Embarcadero from the excursion dock at Harbor Drive and Broadway; you'll arrive at the Ferry Landing Marketplace. Boats depart every hour on the hour from the Embarcadero and every hour on the half hour from Coronado, Sunday through Thursday 9–9, Friday and Saturday until 10; the fare is $2 each way, 50¢ extra for bicycles. San Diego Harbor Excursion also offers water taxi service from 10 to 10 between any two points in San Diego Bay. The fare is $5 per person for the North Bay, more for the South Bay. Call ☎ 619/235–8294 to book.

A Good Tour

Coronado is easy to navigate without a car. When you depart the ferry, you can explore the shops at the Ferry Landing Marketplace and from there rent a bicycle or catch the shuttle bus that runs down **Orange Avenue** ⑨, Coronado's main tourist drag. You might disembark the bus near the tourist information office, just off Orange, and pick up a map, return to Orange to stroll along the boutiques-filled promenade until you reach the **Hotel Del Coronado** ⑩ at the end of Orange Avenue. Right across the street from the Del is the Glorietta Bay Inn, another of the island's outstanding early structures. On Tuesday, Thursday, and Saturday mornings at 11, the Glorietta is the departure point for a fun and informative 1½-hour walking tour of a few of the area's 86 officially designated historical homes. If you've brought your swimsuit, you might continue on to **Silver Strand State Beach** ⑪—just past the Hotel Del, Orange Avenue turns into Silver Strand Boulevard, which soon resumes its original across-the-bridge role as Route 75.

TIMING

A leisurely stroll through Coronado takes an hour or so, more if you shop or walk along the beach. If you're a history buff, you might want to visit on Tuesday, Thursday, or Saturday, when you can combine the tour of Coronado's historic homes that departs from the Glorietta Bay

Inn at 11 AM with a visit to the Coronado Museum of History and Art, open Tuesday through Saturday.

Sights to See

★ ⑩ **Hotel Del Coronado.** The "Del" has a colorful history, integrally connected with that of Coronado itself. The hotel opened in 1888 as the brainchild of financiers Elisha Spurr Babcock Jr. and H. L. Story, who saw the potential of Coronado's virgin beaches and its view of San Diego's emerging harbor. The Del's distinctive red-tile peaks and Victorian gingerbread architecture has served as a set for many movies, political meetings, and extravagant social happenings. Fourteen presidents have been guests of the Del, and the film *Some Like It Hot*—starring Marilyn Monroe, Jack Lemmon, and Tony Curtis—was filmed here. The gift shop sells books that elaborate on the hotel's history and resident ghost. ⊠ *1500 Orange Ave., Coronado,* ☏ *619/435–6611,* WEB *www.hoteldel.com.*

⑨ **Orange Avenue.** It's easy to imagine you're on a street in Cape Cod when you stroll along this thoroughfare, Coronado's version of a downtown: the clapboard houses, small restaurants, and boutiques are in some ways more characteristic of New England than they are of California. Just off Orange Avenue, the **Coronado Visitors Bureau** (⊠ 1047 B Ave., Coronado, ☏ 619/437–8788, WEB www.coronadovisitors.com) is open weekdays 8–5, Saturday 10–5, and Sunday 11–4 year-round.

☾ ⑪ **Silver Strand State Beach.** The stretch of sand that runs along Silver Strand Boulevard from the Hotel Del Coronado to Imperial Beach is a perfect family gathering spot, with rest rooms and lifeguards. Don't be surprised if you see groups exercising in military style along the beach; this is a training area for the U.S. Navy's SEAL teams.

Harbor Island, Point Loma, and Shelter Island

Point Loma protects the center city from the Pacific's tides and waves. It's shared by military installations, funky motels and fast-food shacks, stately family homes, and private marinas packed with sailboats and yachts. Newer to the scene, Harbor and Shelter islands were created out of sand dredged from the San Diego Bay in the second half of the past century. They've become tourist hubs, their high-rise hotels, seafood restaurants, and boat-rental centers looking as solid as those anywhere else in the city.

A Good Tour

Take Catalina Boulevard all the way south to the tip of Point Loma to reach **Cabrillo National Monument** ⑫; you'll be retracing the steps of the earliest European explorers if you use this as a jumping-off point for a tour. North of the monument, as you head back into the neighborhoods of Point Loma, you'll see the white headstones of Fort Rosecrans National Cemetery, with its rows upon rows of white headstones. Continue north on Catalina Boulevard to Hill Street and turn left to reach the dramatic Sunset Cliffs, at the western side of Point Loma near Ocean Beach. The 60-ft high-bluffs are a perfect place to watch the sunset. Return to Catalina Boulevard and backtrack south for a few blocks to find Canon Street, which leads toward the peninsula's eastern (bay) side. Almost at the shore you'll see **Scott Street** ⑬, Point Loma's main commercial drag. Scott Street is bisected by Shelter Island Drive, which leads to **Shelter Island** ⑭. For another example of what can be done with tons of material dredged from a bay, go back up Shelter Island Drive, turn right on Rosecrans Street, and make another right on North Harbor Drive to reach **Harbor Island** ⑮.

TIMING

If you're interested in seeing the tide pools at Cabrillo National Monument, call ahead or check the weather page of the *Union-Tribune* to find out when low tide will occur. Scott Street, with its Point Loma Seafoods, is a good place to find yourself at lunchtime, and Sunset Cliffs Park is where to be at sunset. This drive takes about an hour if you stop briefly at each sight, but you'll want to devote at least an hour to Cabrillo National Monument.

Sights to See

★ ⑫ **Cabrillo National Monument.** This 144-acre preserve marks the site of the first European visit to San Diego, made by 16th-century explorer Juan Rodríguez Cabrillo (circa 1498–1543)—historians have never conclusively determined whether he was Spanish or Portuguese. Cabrillo came to this spot, which he called San Miguel, in 1542. Government grounds were set aside to commemorate his discovery in 1913, and today the site, with its rugged cliffs and shores and outstanding overlooks, is one of the most frequently visited of all the national monuments.

The **visitor center** presents films and lectures about Cabrillo's voyage, the sea-level tide pools, and migrating gray whales. **Interpretive stations** with recorded information have been installed along the walkways that edge the cliffs. The moderately steep 2-mi **Bayside Trail** (☉ 9–4) winds through coastal sage scrub, curving under the cliff-top lookouts and bringing you ever closer to the bay-front scenery. You cannot reach the beach from this trail and must stick to the path to protect the cliffs from erosion and yourself from thorny plants and snakes—including rattlers. The climb back is long but gradual, leading up to the old lighthouse **Old Point Loma Lighthouse** (☉ 9–5)

You can see sea creatures in the **tide pools** (☉ 9–4:30) at the foot of the monument's western cliffs. Drive north from the visitor center to the first road on the left, which winds down to the coast guard station and the shore. ⊠ *1800 Cabrillo Memorial Dr.,* ☎ *619/557–5450,* WEB *www.nps.gov/cabr.* ⊡ *$5 per car, $3 per person entering on foot or by bicycle (entrance pass allows unlimited admissions for one week from date of purchase); free for Golden Age, Golden Access, and Golden Eagle passport holders, and children under 17. ☉ Park daily 9–5:15 (call for later summer hrs, which vary).*

⑮ **Harbor Island.** This 1½-mi-long peninsula adjacent to San Diego International Airport was created in 1961 and today is lined with restaurants and high-rise hotels. The bay shore has pathways, gardens, and picnic spots. On the west point, Tom Ham's Lighthouse restaurant has a U.S. Coast Guard–approved beacon shining from its tower.

⑬ **Scott Street.** Running along Point Loma's waterfront from Shelter Island to the old Naval Training Center on Harbor Drive, this thoroughfare is lined with deep-sea fishing charters and whale-watching boats. It's a good spot from which to watch fishermen (and women) haul marlin, tuna, and puny mackerel off their boats.

⑭ **Shelter Island.** Shelter Island is the center of San Diego's yacht-building industry and home to the San Diego Yacht Club. Boats in every stage of construction are visible in the yacht yards. The peninsula also supports towering palms, a cluster of resorts, and restaurants. On the bay side, fishermen launch their boats or simply stand on shore and cast. Families relax at picnic tables along the grass, where there are fire rings and permanent barbecue grills.

Mission Bay and the Beaches

The 4,600-acre Mission Bay aquatic park is San Diego's monument to sports and fitness. Admission to its 27 mi of bay-shore beaches and 17 mi of ocean frontage is free.

A Good Tour

If you're coming from I–5, stop to pick up maps and information at the San Diego Visitor Information Center just about at the end of the Clairemont Drive–East Mission Bay Drive exit (you'll see the prominent sign). At the point where East Mission Bay Drive turns into Sea WorldDrive you can detour left to Fiesta Island, popular with jet skiers and speedboat racers. Continue around the curve to the west to reach **SeaWorld of California** ⑯, the area's best-known attraction.

You'll next come to Ingraham Street, the central north–south drag through the bay. If you take it north, you'll shortly spot Vacation Road, which leads into the focal point of this part of the bay, the waterskiing hub of **Vacation Isle** ⑰. At Ingraham, Sea World Drive turns into Sunset Cliffs Boulevard and intersects with West Mission Bay Drive. Past this intersection, Quivira Way leads west toward Hospitality Point, where there are nice, quiet places to have a picnic.

If you continue west on West Mission Bay Drive, just before it meets Mission Boulevard, you'll come to the Bahia Resort Hotel, where you can catch the *Bahia Belle* for a cruise around the bay. Ventura Cove, opposite the Bahia Hotel, is another good spot to unpack your cooler. Almost immediately south of where West Mission Bay Drive turns into Mission Boulevard is the resurrected Belmont Park amusement park, with it's 1925 roller coaster.

TIMING

It would take less than an hour to drive this tour. You may not find a visit to SeaWorld fulfilling unless you spend at least a half day; a full day is recommended. The park is open daily, but not all its attractions are open year-round.

Sights to See

⑯ **SeaWorld of California.** One of the world's largest marine-life amusement parks, SeaWorld is spread over 100 tropically landscaped bayfront acres—and it seems to be expanding into every square inch of available space with new exhibits, shows, and activities.

The majority of the exhibits are walk-through marine environments. Kids get a particular kick out of the **Shark Encounter,** where they come face-to-face with sandtiger, nurse, bonnethead, black-tipped, and white-tipped reef sharks by walking through a 57-ft clear acrylic tube that passes through the 280,000-gallon shark habitat. At **Wild Arctic,** a simulated helicopter ride takes you to a research post at the North Pole, where beluga whales, walruses, and polar bears are decked out like the wrecked hulls of 19th-century sailing ships. Various **freshwater and saltwater aquariums** hold underwater creatures from around the world.

SeaWorld's highlights are its four large-arena entertainments. You can arrive 10 or 15 minutes in advance to get front-row seats, and the stadiums are large enough for everyone to get a seat even at the busiest times. The traditional favorite is the **Shamu show,** with synchronized killer whales bringing down the house, but the less publicized **Fools With Tools** stars two California sea lions, Clyde and Seamore, as comic handymen whose best-laid plans are foiled by a supporting cast of Asian sea otters. Another favorite is the **Pirates 4-D** show, a hilarious tale of a hapless pirate crew and its wacky captain. More than a 3-D movie, Pirates 4-D introduces a "fourth dimension," namely special effects like sprays of water, blasts of air, and other wild surprises. **Shipwreck Rapids,** the park's first adventure ride, offers plenty of excitement—but you may end up getting soaked.

Since it's hard to come away from here without spending a lot of money on top of the hefty entrance fee and parking tab, consider the two-day entry option, only $4 more than a single-day admission. ⊠ *1720 South Shores Rd., near the west end of I–8,* ☎ *619/226–3815; 619/226– 3901 for recorded information,* WEB *www.seaworld.com.* ⌦ *$42.95, 2- day package $46.95; parking $7–$9; 90-min behind-the-scenes walking tours $10 additional. AE, D, MC, V.* ☉ *Daily 10–dusk; extended hrs in summer.*

⓱ **Vacation Isle.** Ingraham Street bisects the island, providing two distinct experiences for visitors. The west side is taken up by the San Diego Paradise Point Resort, but you don't have to be a guest to enjoy the hotel's lushly landscaped grounds and bay-front restaurants. The water-ski clubs congregate at **Ski Beach** on the east side of the island, where there's a parking lot as well as picnic areas and rest rooms. At a pond on the south side of the island children and young-at-heart adults take part year-round in motorized miniature boat races. ⊠ *Mission Bay.*

Old Town

San Diego's Spanish and Mexican history and heritage are most evident in Old Town, north of downtown at Juan Street, near the intersection of Interstates 5 and 8. Old Town is the first European settlement in southern California, but the pueblo's true beginnings took place overlooking Old Town from atop Presidio Park, where Father Junípero Serra established the first of California's missions, San Diego de Alcalá, in 1769. On San Diego Avenue, the district's main drag, art galleries and expensive gift shops are interspersed with tacky curios shops, restaurants, and open-air stands selling inexpensive Mexican pottery, jewelry, and blankets. The Old Town Esplanade on San Diego Avenue between Harney and Conde streets is the best of several mall-like affairs constructed in mock Mexican-plaza style. Shops and restaurants also line Juan and Congress streets.

Ten bus lines stop here, as do the San Diego Trolley and the Coaster commuter rail line. Two large parking lots linked to the park by an underground pedestrian walkway ease some of the parking congestion, and signage leading from I–8 to the Transit Center is easy to follow. If you're not familiar with the area, however, avoid the "Old Town" exit from I–5, which leaves you floundering near Mission Bay without further directions.

A Good Tour

It's possible to trek around Old Town and see all its sights in one day, but we recommend making this a walking-driving combination.

Visit the information center at Seeley Stable, just off Old Town Plaza, to orient yourself to the various sights in **Old Town San Diego State Historic Park** ⑱. When you've had enough history, cross north on the west side of the plaza to Bazaar del Mundo, where you can shop or enjoy some nachos on the terrace of a Mexican restaurant. Walk down San Diego Avenue, which flanks the south side of Old Town's historic plaza. If you have the time, detour on Harney Street to the Thomas Whaley Museum, or continue east 2½ blocks on San Diego Avenue to the El Campo Santo cemetery. Heritage Park, with a number of restored Victorian buildings, is perched on a hill above Juan Street, north of

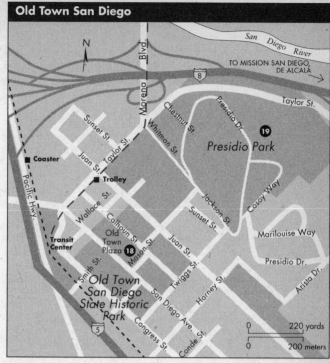

Old Town San Diego

the museum and cemetery. Drive west on Juan Street and north on Taylor Street to Presidio Drive, which will lead you up the hill on which **Presidio Park** ⑲ and the Junípero Serra Museum sit.

TIMING

Try to time your visit to coincide with the free daily tours of Old Town given at 11 AM and 2 PM by costumed park service employees at Seeley Stable. It takes about two hours to walk through Old Town. If you drive to Presidio Park, allot another hour to explore the grounds and museum.

Sights to See

★ ⑱ **Old Town San Diego State Historic Park.** The six square blocks on the site of San Diego's original pueblo are the heart of Old Town. Most of the 20 historic buildings preserved or re-created by the park cluster around **Old Town Plaza.** You can see the presidio from behind the cannon by the flagpole. San Diego Avenue is closed to vehicle traffic here. Worth exploring in the plaza area are the Casa de Bandini, Seeley Stable, Casa de Estudillo, Dental Museum, Mason Street School, Wells Fargo Museum, San Diego Courthouse, Commercial Kitchen Museum, and the Machade Stewart Adobe Museum. The **Robinson-Rose House** (☎ 619/220–5422) was the original commercial center of old San Diego, housing railroad offices, law offices, and the first newspaper press. In addition to serving as the park's visitor center and administrative center, it now hosts a model of Old Town as it looked in 1872, as well as various historic exhibits. Stop here for directions to other park sights.

⑲ **Presidio Park.** The hillsides of the 40-acre green space overlooking Old Town from the north end of Taylor Street are popular with picnickers. It's a nice walk to the summit from Old Town if you're in good shape and wearing the right shoes—it should take about half an hour.

You can also drive to the top of the park via Presidio Drive, off Taylor Street. Presidio Park has a private canyon surrounded by palms at the bottom of the hill, off Taylor Street before it intersects with I–8.

If you do decide to walk, look in at the Presidio Hills Golf Course on Mason Street, which has an unusual clubhouse: it incorporates the ruins of Casa de Carrillo, the town's oldest adobe, constructed in 1820. At the end of Mason Street, veer left on Jackson Street to reach the **Presidio Ruins**, where adobe walls and a bastion have been built above the foundations of the original fortress and chapel. Also on the site are the 28-ft-high Serra Cross, built in 1913 out of brick tiles found in the ruins, and a bronze statue of Father Serra. Before you do much poking around here, however, it's a good idea to get some historical perspective at the **Junípero Serra Museum** (2727 Presidio Dr., ☎ 619/297–3258; ⌷ $5) just to the east. It's open Friday through Sunday 10–4:30. Take Presidio Drive southeast of the museum and you'll come to the site of Fort Stockton, built to protect Old Town and abandoned by the United States in 1848.*1 block north of Old Town.*

La Jolla

La Jollans have long considered their village to be the Monte Carlo of California, and with good cause. Its coastline curves into natural coves backed by verdant hillsides covered with homes worth millions. Although La Jolla is considered part of San Diego, it has its own postal zone and a coveted sense of class; it's gotten far more plebeian these days, but old-monied residents still mingle here with visiting film stars.

The Native Americans called the site La Hoya, meaning "the cave," referring to the grottoes that dot the shoreline. The Spaniards changed the name to La Jolla (same pronunciation as La Hoya), "the jewel," and its residents have cherished the name and its allusions ever since.

To reach La Jolla from I–5, if you're traveling north, take the Ardath Road exit, which veers into Torrey Pines Road, and turn right onto Prospect Street. If you're heading south, get off at the La Jolla Village Drive exit, which will also lead into Torrey Pines Road. Traffic is virtually always congested in this popular area.For those who enjoy meandering, the best way to approach La Jolla from the south is to drive through Mission and Pacific beaches on Mission Boulevard, which becomes La Jolla Boulevard. You'll pass homes designed by such respected architects as Frank Lloyd Wright and Irving Gill. As you approach the village, La Jolla Boulevard turns into Prospect Street. Prospect Street and Girard Avenue, the village's main drags, are lined with expensive shops and office buildings. The La Jolla nightlife scene is an active one, with jazz clubs, piano bars, and watering holes for the well-heeled younger set.

Numbers in the text correspond to numbers in the margin and on the La Jolla map.

A Good Tour

At the intersection of La Jolla Boulevard and Nautilus Street, turn toward the sea to reach Windansea Beach, one of the best surfing spots in town. Mount Soledad, about 1½-mi east on Nautilus Street, is La Jolla's highest spot and a good place to see a view of San Diego on a clear day. Down in the village you'll find the town's cultural center, the **Museum of Contemporary Art, San Diego** ①, on the less trafficked southern end of Prospect. A bit farther north, at the intersection of Prospect Street and Girard Avenue, sits the pretty-in-pink La Valencia hotel. The hotel looks out onto the village's great natural attraction, **La Jolla Cove** ②, which can be accessed from Coast Boulevard, one block to the west.

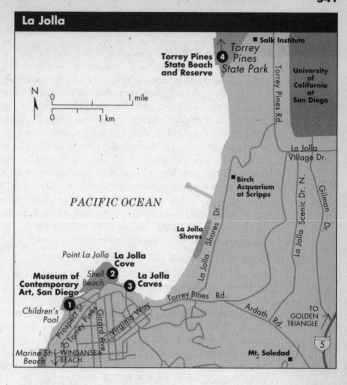

La Jolla

Past the far northern point of the cove, a trail leads down to **La Jolla Caves** ③. The beaches along La Jolla Shores Drive north of the caves are some of the finest in the San Diego area, with long stretches allotted to surfers or swimmers. Nearby is the campus of the Scripps Institution of Oceanography. The institution's Birch Aquarium at Scripps is inland a bit, off Torrey Pines Road, across from the campus of University of California at San Diego.

La Jolla Shores Drive eventually curves onto Torrey Pines Road, off which you'll soon glimpse the world-famous Salk Institute, designed by Louis I. Kahn. The same road that leads to the institute ends at the cliffs used as the Torrey Pines Glider Port. The hard-to-reach stretch of sand at the foot of the cliffs is officially named Torrey Pines City Park Beach, but locals call it Black's Beach. At the intersection of Torrey Pines Road and Genesee Avenue you'll come to the northern entrance of the huge campus of the University of California at San Diego and, a bit farther north, to the stretch of wilderness that marks the end of what most locals consider San Diego proper, **Torrey Pines State Beach and Reserve** ④.

TIMING

This tour makes for a leisurely day, although it can be driven in a couple of hours, including stops to take in the views and explore the village of La Jolla (though not to hit any of the beaches—or even a fraction of all the pricey boutiques). The Museum of Contemporary Art is closed Monday, and guided tours of the Salk Institute are given on weekdays only.

Sights to See

❸ **La Jolla Caves.** It's a walk down 145 sometimes slippery steps to Sunny Jim Cave, the largest of the grottoes in La Jolla Cove. The cave entrance is through the Cave Store, a throwback to the 1902 shop that served as the underground portal. ✉ *1325 Cave St.,* ☎ *858/459–0746.* ✍ *$2.* ☼ *Daily 9 until dark.*

★ ❷ **La Jolla Cove.** The wooded spread that looks out over a shimmering blue inlet is what first attracted everyone to La Jolla, from Native Americans to the glitterati; it is the village's enduring cachet. You'll find the cove beyond where Girard Avenue dead-ends into Coast Boulevard, marked by towering palms that line a promenade. An underwater preserve at the north end of La Jolla Cove makes the adjoining beach the most popular one in the area. On summer days, the beach and water seem to disappear under the mass of bodies swimming, snorkeling, or sunbathing. The **Children's Pool**, at the south end of the park, has a curving beach protected by a seawall from strong currents and waves. Due to an ever-growing population of sea lions, it's not open to swimmers, but it's the best place on the coast to view these engaging creatures. Walk through **Ellen Browning Scripps Park**, past the groves of twisted junipers to the cliff's edge. You can spread your picnic out on a table at one of the open-air shelters and enjoy the scenery.

★ ❶ **Museum of Contemporary Art, San Diego.** A patterned terrazzo floor leads to galleries where the museum's permanent collection of post-1950s art and rotating exhibits are on display. Works by Andy Warhol, Robert Rauschenberg, Frank Stella, Joseph Cornell, and Jenny Holzer, to name a few, get major competition from the setting: you can look out from the top of a grand stairway onto a landscaped garden that contains permanent and temporary sculpture exhibits as well as rare 100-year-old California plant specimens and, beyond that, to the Pacific Ocean. ✉ *700 Prospect St.,* ☎ *858/454–3541,* WEB *www.mcasandiego.org.* ✍ *$4; free 1st Sun. and 3rd Tues. of month.* ☼ *Thurs. 11–8, Fri.–Tues 11–5.*

❹ **Torrey Pines State Beach and Reserve.** *Pinus torreyana,* the rarest native pine tree in the United States, enjoys a 1,750-acre sanctuary at the northern edge of La Jolla. Hiking trails lead to the cliffs, 300 ft above the ocean; trail maps are available at the park station. Wildflowers grow profusely in the spring, and the ocean panoramas are always spectacular. When the tide is out, it's possible to walk south all the way past the lifeguard towers to Black's Beach over rocky promontories. **Los Peñasquitos Lagoon** at the north end of the reserve is a good place to watch shorebirds. Volunteers lead guided nature walks at 11:30 and 1:30 on most weekends. ✉ *N. Torrey Pines Rd. (also known as Old Hwy. 101). Exit I–5 onto Carmel Valley Rd. going west, then turn left (south) on Old Hwy. 101,* ☎ *858/755–2063.* ✍ *Parking $2 (2 large parking lots on both sides of Los Peñasquitos Lagoon; another up the hill by the park visitor center).* ☼ *Daily 8–sunset.*

DINING

By David Nelson

A stroll down 5th Avenue will provide ample evidence of San Diego's love affair with Italian cuisine, echoed in other parts of the city. But the cooking of Mexico, Spain, and France, as well as the various cuisines of South and Latin America, Asia, the Middle East—and even the United States—are also well-represented. Casual attire is the norm at most San Diego restaurants.

CATEGORY	COST*
$$$$	over $30
$$$	$22–$30
$$	$15–$21
$	under $15

*per person for a main course at dinner, excluding 7½% tax

Downtown

Contemporary

$$–$$$ ✕ **Chive.** Chive aims to capture the urban and urbane moods of London, New York, and San Francisco restaurants with an interior design of flat surfaces and monochromatic colors that seems hard-edged at first. On some evenings the crowd is determinedly under-30 and super trendy, on other nights the restaurant may be occupied by large groups of conventioneers. All sorts are drawn by a contemporary menu highlighted by clever treatments of Hudson Valley foie gras, lamb, and briny-fresh seafood. For dessert, the fluffy, doughnut-like beignets with pineapple custard sauce is recommended. ✉ *558 4th Ave., Gaslamp Quarter,* ☎ *619/232–4483. AE, D, MC, V. No lunch weekends.*

French

$$$–$$$$ ✕ **Bertrand at Mister A's.** Operated by noted restaurateur Bertrand Hug,
★ the sumptuous dining room perches on the 12th floor of a midtown office building overlooking a view that stretches from the mountains in the east to Mexico, San Diego Bay, and a sliver of the blue Pacific. At both lunch and dinner you can watch the aerial ballet of jets descending upon nearby Lindbergh Field. Bertrand at Mister A's serves luxurious seasonal dishes such as veal braised in white wine, pan-seared ocean perch with creamy celery root sauce, and Dover sole in lemon butter. The dessert list encompasses a galaxy of sweets; the caramelized peach tart is a favorite. ✉ *2550 5th Ave., Middletown,* ☎ *619/239–1377. Reservations essential. Jacket required. AE, DC, MC, V. No lunch weekends.*

Italian

$$–$$$ ✕ **Trattoria La Strada.** Perhaps the busiest Italian restaurant in the Gaslamp Quarter, La Strada offers comfortable seating on both a spacious terrace and in an airy dining room whose broad windows assure good views of the bustle outside. Carpaccio appetizers are a house specialty. Moving on, try the polenta dressed with rich, melted Fontina cheese and wild mushrooms, or any one of the excellent pastas: fusilli with shrimp and fresh artichokes is a favorite. The second-course selection stars grilled lamb chops with herb sauce and fillet mignon in a heady Chianti sauce. ✉ *702 5th Ave., Gaslamp Quarter,* ☎ *619/239–3400. AE, DC, MC.*

$ ✕ **Trattoria Fantastica.** The shady, very private courtyard at the rear of this laid-back establishment is no secret, so reserve ahead if you want to score a table. Sicilian flavors abound on the menu, which is highlighted by such offerings as a salad of tomatoes, red onions, olive oil, and oregano; and the pasta Palermitana, rigatoni with spicy sausage, olives, capers, and marinara sauce. Many pastas come with cargoes of fresh seafood, and the pizzas baked in the wood-burning oven are robust and beautifully seasoned. ✉ *1735 India St., Little Italy,* ☎ *619/234–1735. AE, DC, MC, V.*

Mexican

$$–$$$ ✕ **Candelas.** The scents and flavors of nouvelle Mexican cuisine permeate this handsome, romantic little hideaway in the shadow of San Diego's tallest residential towers. Candles glow everywhere around the small, comfortable dining room and the bar. There isn't a burrito or taco in sight at this haven of stylish, imaginative cooking, where such fine openers as cream of black bean and beer soup set the stage for local lobster stuffed with mushrooms, jalapeño peppers, and aged tequila; or tequila-flamed jumbo prawns over creamy, seasoned goat cheese. ✉ *416 3rd Ave., Gaslamp Quarter,* ☎ *619/702–4455. MC, V. Closed Sun. No lunch.*

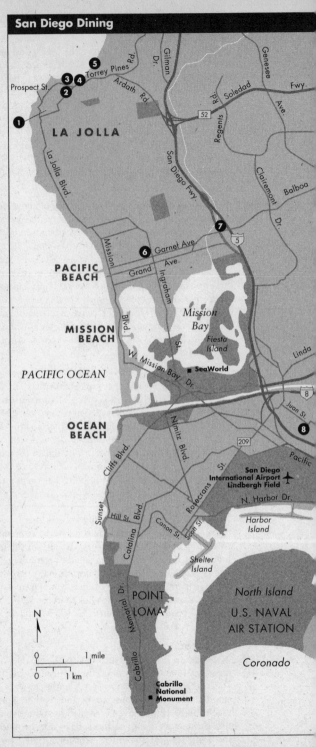

San Diego Dining

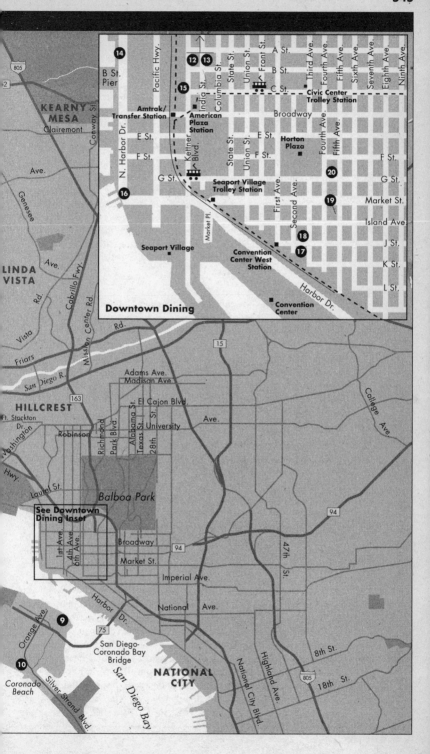

Downtown Dining

14

B St. Pier

12 13

15

Pacific Hwy.

A St.
B St.
C St.

Civic Center Trolley Station

KEARNY MESA

Clairemont

Ave.

Genesee

Ave.

LINDA VISTA

Coway St.

N. Harbor Dr.

Cabrillo Fwy.

Vista

Rd.

Friars

Road

San Diego R.

HILLCREST

Ft. Stockton Dr.

Washington

Hwy.

Robinson

Laurel St.

Amtrak/ Transfer Station

American Plaza Station

E St.
F St.

G St.

Kettner Blvd.

16

Market Pl.

Seaport Village

India St.

Columbia St.

State St.

Union St.

Front St.

State St.

Union St.

E St.
F St.

Broadway

Horton Plaza

Fourth Ave.

Fifth Ave.

20

19

18

17

Seaport Village Trolley Station

First Ave.

Second Ave.

Convention Center West Station

Convention Center

Third Ave.
Fourth Ave.
Fifth Ave.
Sixth Ave.
Eighth Ave.
Ninth Ave.

F St.

G St.

Market St.

Island Ave.

J St.

K St.

L St.

Harbor Dr.

Adams Ave.
Madison Ave.

El Cajon Blvd.

University

Ave.

College Ave.

Alabama St.
Texas St.
28th

Richmond
Park Blvd.

Balboa Park

See Downtown Dining Inset

1st Ave.
4th Ave.
6th Ave.

Broadway

Market St.

Imperial Ave.

National Ave.

47th St.

94

94

Harbor Dr.

9

75

San Diego- Coronado Bay Bridge

Orange Ave.

10

Coronado Beach

Silver Strand Blvd.

San Diego Bay

NATIONAL CITY

National City Blvd.

Highland Ave.

8th St.

18th St.

Seafood

$$$–$$$$ ✕ **Star of the Sea.** The flagship of the Anthony's chain of seafood restau-
★   rants ensconces its patrons in its most formal dining room, making it
an all-around favorite for location, cuisine, and design (although dress
is quite casual). The menu changes seasonally; you may find butter-
poached lobster tail with wild mushrooms or macadamia-crusted
swordfish in a yellow curry sauce. The baked-to-order soufflés are puffy,
fragrant, and lovely on the palate. The outdoor patio takes full advantage
of the choice waterfront location. ⊠ *1360 N. Harbor Dr., Downtown,*
☎ *619/232–7408. AE, D, DC, MC, V. No lunch.*

$–$$$ ✕ **Fish Market.** Fresh mesquite-grilled fish is the specialty at this in-
formal restaurant. There's also an excellent little sushi bar and good
steamed clams and mussels. The view is stunning: enormous plate-glass
windows look directly out onto the harbor. A more formal restaurant
upstairs, the Top of the Market ($$$–$$$$), is expensive but worth
the splurge, and is the place to find such rarities as true Dover sole,
which the kitchen delicately browns in butter and finishes with a
lemon-caper sauce. ⊠ *750 N. Harbor Dr., Downtown,* ☎ *619/232–
3474 for Fish Market; 619/234–4867 for Top of the Market. Reser-
vations not accepted.*

Southwestern

$$–$$$ ✕ **Indigo Grill.** A showcase for chef/partner Deborah Scott's contem-
porary Southwestern cuisine, Indigo Grill has both a stone interior and
a broad terrace whose cool breezes do nothing to moderate the chiles
that heat such one-of-a-kind offerings as oven clams and jalapeño-maize
pappardelle with prawns and smoked pineapple. Entrées like the wild
blueberry–lacquered venison chop make a big impression, as do such
desserts as a puff pastry confection dressed with pears, Stilton cheese,
and balsamic vinegar. ⊠ *1536 India St., Little Italy,* ☎ *619/234–
6802. AE, D, DC, MC, V. No lunch weekends.*

Steak Houses

$$$–$$$$ ✕ **Rainwater's on Kettner.** Downtown San Diego's premier homegrown
★   steak house also ranks as the longest running of the pack, not least be-
cause it has the luxurious look and mood of an old-fashioned Eastern
men's club. Settle back into the exceptionally deep banquettes and start
with Rainwater's signature black bean soup with Madeira. Continue
with the tender, expertly roasted prime rib. The menu branches out to
encompass superb calves' liver with onions and bacon, broiled free-range
chicken, fresh seafood, and even pastas, all served in vast portions with
plenty of hot-from-the-oven cornsticks on the side. The well-chosen wine
list offers pricey but superior selections. ⊠ *1202 Kettner Blvd., Down-
town,* ☎ *619/233–5757. AE, D, MC, V. No lunch weekends.*

$$–$$$$ ✕ **Morton's of Chicago.** Housed in the soaring Harbor Club towers near
★   both the San Diego Convention Center and the Gaslamp Quarter, Mor-
ton's often teems with conventioneers out for a night on the town. Servers
present the menu by wheeling up a cart laden with crimson prime steaks,
behemoth veal and lamb chops, thick cuts of swordfish, and huge Maine
lobsters that may wave their claws in alarm when they hear the prices
(based on the market, but always astronomical) quoted. Expect a treat,
since this restaurant knows how to put on a superb spread that takes the
concept of self-indulgence to new heights. ⊠ *The Harbor Club, 285
J St., Downtown,* ☎ *619/696–3369. AE, D, MC, V. No lunch.*

Coronado

Italian

$$–$$$ ✕ **Il Fornaio.** This handsome restaurant occupies an amazing waterfront
location, framing stellar views of downtown San Diego with windows

that stretch from floor to ceiling. The menu tends toward the creative side, and in deference to the restaurant's name, which means "The Oven," offers an abundance of baked specialties, including pizzas that arrive fragrant and bubbling from the wood-fired hearth. Other choices are lobster-stuffed ravioli and mesquite-grilled lamb chops flavored with thyme and garlic. ✉ *1333 1st Ave.,* ☎ *619/437–4911. AE, D, MC, V.*

Seafood

$$$ ✗ **Prince of Wales.** The romance of the 1930s lives on in the Hotel Del Coronado's restored Prince of Wales, which affords sweeping ocean views from an elegant indoor room and a breezy terrace. Consider such novelties as an "aerated" wild mushroom bisque; a parfait of layered warm potatoes, sour cream, and osetra caviar; and Hawaiian yellowfin tuna with sautéed foie gras and truffle sauce. Although seafood dominates the menu, you'll also find toothsome meat choices like roasted Sonoma County squab with Savoy cabbage and wild boar tenderloin in a peppery beet sauce. After all this, the red fruit consommé brings the evening to a tart conclusion. ✉ *Hotel Del Coronado, 1500 Orange Ave.,* ☎ *619/435–6611. AE, D, DC, MC, V. No lunch.*

Mission Bay and the Beaches

Italian

$–$$ ✗ **Caffe Bella Italia.** Contemporary Italian cooking as prepared in Italy—an important point in fusion-mad San Diego—is the rule at this simple restaurant near one of the principle intersections in Pacific Beach. The menu presents Neapolitan-style macaroni with sausage and artichoke hearts in spicy tomato sauce, *pappardelle* (wide ribbons of pasta) with a creamy Gorgonzola and walnut sauce, plus formal entrées like chicken breast sautéed with balsamic vinegar, and slices of rare filet mignon tossed with herbs then topped with arugula and shavings of Parmesan cheese. ✉ *1525 Garnet Ave., Pacific Beach,* ☎ *858/273–1224. MC, V. Closed Mon.*

Japanese

$ ✗ **Sushi Ota.** Wedged into a minimall between a convenience store and
★ a looming medical building, Sushi Ota initially seems less than prepossessing. But look closely at the expressions on customers' faces as they stream in and out of the doors, and you'll see eager anticipation and satisfied glows due to San Diego's best sushi. Besides the usual California roll and tuna and shrimp sushi, sample the sea urchin or surf clam sushi, and the soft-shell crab roll. Sushi Ota offers the cooked as well as the raw. There's additional parking behind the mall. ✉ *4529 Mission Bay Dr., Pacific Beach,* ☎ *619/270–5670. Reservations essential. AE, D, MC, V. No lunch Sat.–Mon.*

Old Town

Mexican

$–$$ ✗ **El Agave.** A charmer on the edge of historic Old Town, El Agave
★ promises caring service, a bar stocked with hundreds of tequilas (a collection that El Agave claims is unrivaled in the United States), and a delicious, truly unique Mexican menu. Make a meal of such appetizers as crisp chicken tacos covered with thick, tart cream and rolled taquitos stuffed with shredded pork. Or save room for entrées like chicken in spicy Don Julio mole sauce, and terrific, crisp-skinned roast leg of pork. ✉ *2304 San Diego Ave.,* ☎ *619/220–0692. MC, V.*

La Jolla

Contemporary

$$$–$$$$ ✕ **George's at the Cove.** Hollywood types and other visiting celebri-
 ★   ties can be spotted in the elegant main dining room, where a wall-length
          window overlooks La Jolla Cove. Renowned for fresh seafood specials
          and fine preparations of beef and lamb, this also is the place to taste
          seasonal produce from local specialty growers. When available, the sweet
          corn soup is a revelation of flavor. Next move on to the pancetta-wrapped
          salmon with garlic-lemon vinaigrette, or the rich, succulent free-range
          veal chop. Save room for the dark-chocolate soufflé cake served with
          fresh fruit compote. For more informal dining and a sweeping view of
          the coast try the rooftop Ocean Terrace ($–$$). ✉ *1250 Prospect St.,*
          ☎ *858/454–4244. Reservations essential. AE, D, DC, MC, V.*

$$$–$$$$ ✕ **Marine Room.** Diners can gaze at the ocean from this venerable La
          Jolla Shores mainstay and, if they're lucky, watch the grunion run or
          the waves race across the sand and beat against the glass. The Ma-
          rine Room offers genteel beachfront dining-and-dancing and creative
          (although some will think *too* creative) contemporary cuisine. Appe-
          tizers include an *étude*, or "study," of foie gras served two ways, and
          a basket of skillet-roasted forest mushrooms. A representative entrée
          would be New Zealand John Dory poached in almond broth. Sun-
          day brunch is lavish. ✉ *2000 Spindrift Dr.,* ☎ *858/459–7222. AE,*
          D, DC, MC, V.

$$–$$$ ✕ **Roppongi.** A hit from the moment it opened, Roppongi serves global
 ★   cuisine with strong Asian notes. The contemporary dining room has
          a row of comfortable booths lining a wall, and is accented with Asian
          statuary. It can get noisy when crowded; tables near the bar are gen-
          erally quieter. Order the imaginative Euro-Asian tapas as appetizers
          or combine them for a full meal. Try the chicken and porcini mush-
          room dumplings, Vietnamese chicken salad, and the high-rising Poly-
          nesian crab stack. Good entrées are East-meets-West noodle preparations
          and fresh seafood. ✉ *875 Prospect St.,* ☎ *858/551–5252. AE, D, DC,*
          MC, V.

French

$$–$$$ ✕ **Tapenade.** The celebrated restaurant Tapenade (named after the de-
 ★   licious Provençal black olive–and–anchovy paste that accompanies
          the bread) takes its inspiration from the south of France. In an un-
          pretentious, light, and airy room it serves cuisine to match. Very fresh
          ingredients, a delicate touch with sauces, and an emphasis on seafood
          characterize the menu. It changes frequently, but with good fortune may
          include old-fashioned cassoulet rich with sausage and other meats,
          porcini-stuffed rabbit, and roasted monkfish with eggplant. While the
          tables inside are a bit closely spaced, the terrace is pleasant and invit-
          ing. ✉ *7612 Fay Ave.,* ☎ *858/551–7500. AE, D, DC, MC, V.*

Italian

$–$$$ ✕ **Trattoria Acqua.** Reservations are a good idea for this Mediter-
          ranean-inspired bistro above La Jolla Cove. On the lower level of
          Coast Walk center, this romantic eatery has dining rooms that are semi-
          open to the weather and the view, yet sufficiently sheltered for com-
          fort. Trattoria Acqua is frequently packed with diners eager to sample
          the likes of stuffed, deep-fried zucchini blossoms, lobster-filled ravioli
          in a lobster-scented *beurre blanc* (white butter) sauce, and stuffed
          roasted quail flavored with bacon. The superb wine list earns kudos
          from aficionados. ✉ *1298 Prospect St.,* ☎ *858/454–0709. AE, DC,*
          MC, V.

LODGING

Updated by
Lenore Greiner

San Diego is spread out, so the first thing to consider when selecting lodging is location. If you choose a hotel with a waterfront location and extensive outdoor sports facilities, you may decide never to leave. But if you plan to sightsee, take into account a hotel's proximity to attractions. High season is summer, and rates are lowest in the fall. An ocean-view room will cost significantly more than a non–ocean-view room. If you are planning an extended stay or need lodgings for four or more people, consider an apartment rental. **Oakwood Apartments** (☎ 800/888–0808, WEB www.oakwood.com) rents comfortable furnished apartments in the Mission Valley, La Jolla Colony, and Coronado areas with maid service and linens. The **Bed and Breakfast Guild of San Diego** (☎ 619/523–1300, WEB www.bandbguildsandiego.org) lists a number of high-quality member inns. The **Bed & Breakfast Directory for San Diego** (✉ Box 3292, 92163, ☎ 619/297–3130 or 800/619–7666, WEB www.sandiegobandb.com) covers San Diego County. Most hostels require an international passport to check in.

CATEGORY	COST*
$$$$	over $225
$$$	$160–$225
$$	$100–$159
$	under $100

for a double room in high (summer) season, excluding 10.5% tax.

Downtown

The following downtown hotels are within walking distance of Seaport Village, the Embarcadero, the Gaslamp Quarter, theaters and nightspots, and the Horton Plaza shopping center.

$$$$ ★ 🏨 **Hyatt Regency San Diego.** This high-rise adjacent to Seaport Village combines old-world opulence with California airiness. Palm trees pose next to ornate tapestry couches in the light-filled lobby, and all of the British Regency–style guest rooms have views of the water. A trolley station is one block away. The 40th-floor lounge is one of the city's most romantic spots to watch the sun set. ✉ *1 Market Pl., Embarcadero 92101,* ☎ *619/232–1234 or 800/233–1234,* FAX *619/233–6464,* WEB *www.hyatt.com. 820 rooms, 56 suites. 3 restaurants, 2 bars, room service, in-room data ports, minibars, pool, 4 tennis courts, outdoor hot tub, sauna, steam room, health club, boating, bicycles, shops, dry cleaning, laundry service, concierge, concierge floor, business services, meeting rooms, airport shuttle, car rental, parking (fee); no smoking. AE, D, DC, MC, V.*

$$$$ 🏨 **San Diego Marriott Hotel and Marina.** This 25-story twin tower next to the San Diego Convention Center has everything a businessperson—or leisure traveler—could want. Lagoon-style pools nestled between cascading waterfalls are among the appealing on-site features. Seaport Village and a trolley station are nearby. The standard rooms are smallish, but pay a bit extra for a room with a balcony overlooking the bay and you'll have a serene, sparkling world spread out before you. ✉ *333 W. Harbor Dr., Embarcadero 92101,* ☎ *619/234–1500 or 800/228–9290,* FAX *619/234–8678,* WEB *www.marriotthotels.com/sandt. 1,300 rooms, 54 suites. 3 restaurants, 3 bars, in-room data ports, cable TV with movies, room service, 2 pools, hair salon, outdoor hot tub, massage, sauna, 6 tennis courts, aerobics, basketball, health club, boating, bicycles, recreation room, video game room, shops, laundry facilities, concierge, concierge floor, business services, convention*

550

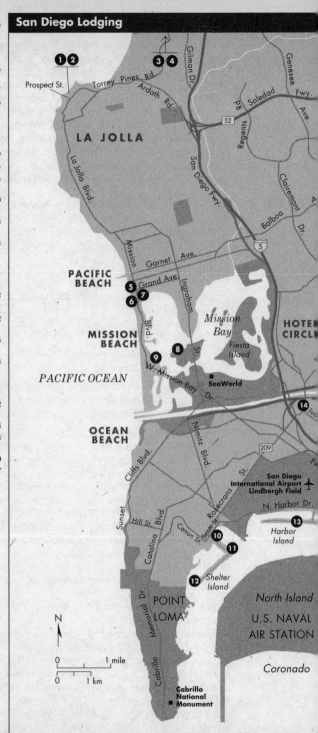

San Diego Lodging

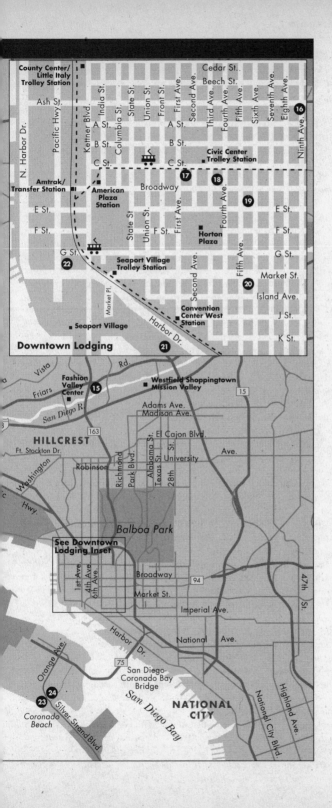

center, meeting rooms, airport shuttle, car rental, parking (fee); no smoking. AE, D, DC, MC, V.

$$$$ ★ ⊞ **Westgate Hotel.** A nondescript, modern high-rise across from Horton Plaza hides what must be the most opulent hotel in San Diego. The lobby, modeled after the anteroom at Versailles, has hand-cut Baccarat chandeliers; rooms are individually furnished with antiques, Italian marble counters, and bath fixtures with 24-karat-gold overlays. From the ninth floor up the views of the harbor and city are breathtaking. Afternoon high tea is served in the lobby to the accompaniment of piano music. ⊠ *1055 2nd Ave., Gaslamp Quarter 92101, ☎ 619/238–1818 or 800/221–3802; 800/522–1564 in CA, ⅺ 619/557–3737, ᴡᴇʙ www.westgatehotel.com. 223 rooms. 2 restaurants, bar, deli, room service, in-room data ports, cable TV with movies, health club, hair salon, spa, bicycles, concierge, business services, meeting rooms, airport shuttle, parking (fee); no smoking. AE, D, DC, MC, V.*

$$$$ ⊞ **U. S. Grant Hotel.** Across the street from Horton Plaza, this San Diego classic was built in 1910 by the grandson of President Ulysses S. Grant. Crystal chandeliers and polished marble floors in the lobby and Queen Anne–style mahogany furnishings in the stately rooms recall a more gracious era when such dignitaries as President Franklin D. Roosevelt and Charles Lindbergh stayed here. High-power business types still gather at the hotel's clubby Grant Grill, and English high tea is served in the lobby from 2 to 6. ⊠ *326 Broadway, Gaslamp Quarter, 92101, ☎ 619/ 232–3121 or 877/999–3223, ⅺ 619/232–3626, ᴡᴇʙ www.wyndham.com. 225 rooms, 60 suites. 2 restaurants, bar, café, room service, in-room data ports, cable TV with movies, gym, shops, Internet, concierge, business services, meeting rooms, airport shuttle, parking (fee); no smoking. AE, D, MC, V.*

$–$$$ ★ ⊞ **Gaslamp Plaza Suites.** On the National Registry of Historic Places, this 11-story structure a block from Horton Plaza was built in 1913 as one of San Diego's first "skyscrapers." Appealing public areas have old marble, brass, and mosaics. Although most rooms are rather small, they are well decorated with dark-wood furnishings that give the hotel an elegant flair. You can enjoy the view and a complimentary Continental breakfast on the rooftop terrace. Book ahead if you're visiting in summer. ⊠ *520 E St., Gaslamp Quarter 92101, ☎ 619/232–9500 or 800/874–8770, ⅺ 619/238–9945, ᴡᴇʙ www.gaslampplaza.com. 52 suites. Restaurant, no a/c, microwaves, refrigerators, hot tub, bar, nightclub, parking (fee). AE, D, DC, MC, V.*

$ ⊞ **Comfort Inn.** This three-story, stucco property surrounds a parking lot and courtyard. There's nothing fancy about the accommodations, but some rooms on the south side of the hotel have good views of the city skyline. It's close to downtown hot spots and Balboa Park. ⊠ *719 Ash St., Downtown 92101, ☎ 619/232–2525 or 800/404–6835, ⅺ 619/687– 3024, ᴡᴇʙ www.comfortinn.com. 45 rooms. In-room data ports, microwave, cable TV with movies, hot tub, car rental, business services, airport shuttle, free parking; no smoking. AE, D, DC, MC, V.*

$ ⊞ **HI–San Diego Downtown.** This two-story hostel has basic, modern furnishings and facilities. A special event—from pizza and movie parties to discussions on traveling in Mexico—is scheduled every evening. There are 150 beds, a large common kitchen, and a TV room. Most rooms are dorm style with four bunks each. There are a few doubles, coed dorms, and group rooms (with 10 beds). ⊠ *521 Market St., Gaslamp Quarter 92101, ☎ 619/525–1531 or 800/909–4776 ext. 43, ⅺ 619/338–0129. Bicycles, billiards, laundry facilities; no room phones, no room TVs, no smoking. MC, V.*

Coronado

Quiet, out-of-the-way Coronado feels like something out of an earlier, more gracious era. The isthmus is great for a getaway, but if you plan to do a lot of sightseeing in San Diego, you'll probably spend a lot of time commuting across the bridge or riding the ferry.

$$$$ ☆ 🏨 **Hotel Del Coronado.** Preserving the memory of seaside vacations long gone by, "The Del" stands as a social and historic landmark, its whimsical red turrets, white siding, and balconied walkways taking you as far back as 1888, the year it was built. U.S. presidents, European royalty, and movie stars have stayed in the Victorian-decorated rooms and suites, which have been fully renovated to include all the necessities of modern-day life. The hotel's public areas are always bustling with activity; for quieter quarters, consider staying in the contemporary, seven-story Ocean Towers building or one of the eight beachfront cottages. Rates are defined largely by room views. ⊠ *1500 Orange Ave. 92118,* ☏ *619/435–6611 or 800/468–3533,* FAX *619/522–8262,* WEB *www. hoteldel.com. 676 rooms. 2 restaurants, coffee shop, deli, room service, in-room data ports, cable TV with movies, 3 tennis courts, 2 pools, gym, hair salon, outdoor hot tub, massage, sauna, spa, steam room, beach, bicycles, 4 bars, piano bar, shops, children's programs, laundry service, concierge, business services, convention center, meeting rooms, parking (fee); no smoking. AE, D, DC, MC, V.*

$$–$$$$ 🏨 **Glorietta Bay Inn.** The main building of this property—adjacent to the Coronado harbor, and near many restaurants and shops—was built in 1908 for sugar baron John D. Spreckels, who once owned much of downtown San Diego. Rooms in this Edwardian-style mansion and in the newer motel-style buildings are attractively furnished. The inn is much smaller and quieter than the Hotel Del across the street. Tours ($8) of the island's historical buildings depart from the inn three mornings a week. Some rooms have patios or balconies. Ginger snaps and lemonade are served daily from 3 to 5. ⊠ *1630 Glorietta Blvd. 92118,* ☏ *619/435– 3101 or 800/283–9383,* FAX *619/435–6182,* WEB *www.gloriettabayinn.com. 100 rooms. Dining room, in-room data ports, some kitchenettes, refrigerators, cable TV with movies, pool, outdoor hot tub, bicycles, library, laundry service, concierge, business services, free parking; no smoking. AE, MC, V.*

Harbor Island, Point Loma, and Shelter Island

Harbor Island, Shelter Island, and Point Loma have grassy parks, views of the downtown skyline, and good restaurants.

$$$$ 🏨 **Sheraton San Diego Hotel & Marina.** Of this property's two highrises, the smaller, more intimate West Tower has larger rooms with separate areas suitable for business entertaining. The East Tower has better sports facilities. Rooms throughout are decorated with plush, contemporary furnishings. Views from the upper floors of both sections are superb, but because the West Tower is closer to the water it has fine outlooks from the lower floors, too. Continental breakfast is complimentary. ⊠ *1380 Harbor Island Dr., Harbor Island 92101,* ☏ *619/291– 2900 or 888/625–5144,* FAX *619/692–2337,* WEB *www.sheraton.com. 1,045 rooms, 50 suites. 3 restaurants, 2 bars, deli, patisserie, room service, in-room data ports, minibars, cable TV with movies, 4 tennis courts, 3 pools, wading pool, health club, 2 outdoor hot tubs, massage, sauna, beach, boating, marina, bicycles, shop, dry cleaning, laundry service, concierge, business services, meeting rooms, airport shuttle, free parking; no smoking. AE, D, DC, MC, V.*

$$$–$$$$ ⊞ **Humphrey's Half Moon Inn & Suites.** This sprawling South Seas–style resort has grassy open areas with palms and tiki torches. Rooms, some with kitchens and some with harbor or marine views, have modern furnishings. Locals throng to Humphrey's, the on-premises seafood restaurant, and to the jazz lounge; the hotel also hosts outdoor jazz and pop concerts from June through October. ⊠ *2303 Shelter Island Dr., Shelter Island 92106,* ☎ *619/224–3411 or 800/542–7400,* FAX *619/224–3478,* WEB *www.halfmooninn.com. 128 rooms, 54 suites. Restaurant, bar, room service, in-room data ports, kitchenettes, minibars, refrigerators, cable TV with movies, putting green, pool, pond, health club, hot tub, boating, bicycles, croquet, Ping-Pong, concert hall, laundry facilities, business services, meeting rooms, airport shuttle, free parking; no smoking. AE, D, DC, MC, V.*

$$–$$$ ⊞ **Shelter Pointe Hotel & Marina.** This 11-acre property has been refurbished in a mixture of Mexican and Mediterranean styles. The spacious and light-filled lobby, with its Mayan sculptures and terra-cotta tiles, opens onto a lush esplanade that overlooks the hotel's marina. The rooms are well appointed, if a bit small, and most look out onto either the marina or San Diego Bay. The attractive hotel is a hot spot for business meetings. ⊠ *1551 Shelter Island Dr., Shelter Island 92106,* ☎ *619/221–8000 or 800/566–2524,* FAX *619/221–5953,* WEB *www.shelterpointe.com. 206 rooms, 31 suites. Restaurant, bar, room service, kitchenettes, cable TV with movies with video games, 2 tennis courts, 2 pools, health club, 2 hot tubs, 2 saunas, beach, boating, marina, bicycles, volleyball, meeting rooms, airport shuttle, free parking; no smoking. AE, D, DC, MC, V.*

$ ⊞ **Vagabond Inn–Point Loma.** This two-story budget motel is safe, clean, and comfortable, close to the airport, yacht clubs, and Cabrillo National Monument—and the popular and excellent Point Loma Seafoods restaurant is next door. A daily newspaper and Continental breakfast are included. ⊠ *1325 Scott St., Point Loma 92106,* ☎ *619/224–3371,* FAX *619/223–0646,* WEB *www.vagabondinn.com. 40 rooms. Restaurant, bar, in-room safes, some kitchens, some refrigerators, cable TV with movies, pool, bar, airport shuttle, free parking; no smoking. AE, D, DC, MC, V.*

Mission Bay and the Beaches

Mission Bay Park, with its beaches, bike trails, boat-launching ramps, golf course, and grassy parks—not to mention SeaWorld—is a hotel haven. Mission Beach and Pacific Beach have many small hotels, motels, and hostels.

$$$$ ⊞ **Catamaran Resort Hotel.** Exotic birds often perch in the lush lobby
★   of this appealing hotel on Mission Bay. Tiki torches light the way through grounds thick with tropical foliage for guests staying at one of the six two-story buildings or the 14-story high-rise. The room design echoes the Hawaiian theme. The popular Cannibal Bar hosts rock bands; the Moray Bar hosts a classical or jazz pianist. The resort's many water-oriented activities include complimentary cruises on Mission Bay aboard a stern-wheeler. ⊠ *3999 Mission Blvd., Mission Beach 92109,* ☎ *858/488–1081 or 800/422–8386,* FAX *858/488–1387,* WEB *www.catamaranresort.com. 313 rooms. Restaurant, 2 bars, room service, in-room data ports, kitchenettes, refrigerators, cable TV with movies, pool, gym, outdoor hot tub, beach, boating, jet skiing, bicycles, volleyball, nightclub, shops, business services, meeting rooms, parking (fee); no smoking. AE, D, DC, MC, V.*

$$$$ ⊞ **San Diego Paradise Point Resort.** The landscape at this 44-acre resort on Vacation Isle is so beautiful that it's been the setting for a number of movies, and it provides a wide range of recreational activities as well as access to a marina. Bright fabrics and plush carpets make for a cheery ambience; unfortunately, the walls here are motel-thin. Take a walk through the botanical gardens with their ponds, waterfalls, footbridges, waterfowl, and more than 600 varieties of tropical plants. ⊠ *1404 W. Vacation Rd., Mission Bay 92109,* ☎ *858/274–4630 or 800/ 344–2626,* FAX *858/581–5929,* WEB *www.paradisepoint.com. 462 cottages. 3 restaurants, 2 bars, room service, in-room data ports, refrigerators, cable TV with movies, putting green, 6 tennis courts, 6 pools, pond, aerobics, gym, outdoor hot tub, massage, sauna, spa, beach, boating, jet skiing, bicycles, croquet, shuffleboard, volleyball, concierge, business services, meeting rooms, airport shuttle, free parking; no smoking. AE, D, DC, MC, V.*

$$$–$$$$ 🖼 **Bahia Resort Hotel.** This huge complex on a 14-acre peninsula in Mission Bay Park has furnished studios and suites with kitchens; many have wood-beam ceilings and a tropical theme. The hotel's *Bahia Belle* offers complimentary cruises on the bay at sunset and also has a Blues Cruise on Saturday night and live entertainment on Friday night. Rates are reasonable for a place so well located—within walking distance of the ocean—and with so many amenities, including use of the facilities at its sister hotel, the nearby Catamaran. ⊠ *998 W. Mission Bay Dr., Mission Bay 92109,* ☎ *858/488–0551 or 800/576–4229,* FAX *858/ 488–1387,* WEB *www.bahiahotel.com. 321 rooms. Restaurant, 2 bars, room service, in-room data ports, kitchenettes, cable TV with movies, 2 tennis courts, pool, gym, outdoor hot tub, boating, bicycles, shops, children's program, business services, meeting rooms, free parking; no smoking. AE, D, DC, MC, V.*

$$–$$$ 🖼 **Best Western Blue Sea Lodge.** All rooms in this low-rise have patios or balconies, and many have ocean views. Suites have kitchenettes, and many of them front the ocean. A shopping center with restaurants and boutiques is nearby. ⊠ *707 Pacific Beach Dr., Pacific Beach 92109,* ☎ *858/488–4700 or 800/258–3732,* FAX *858/488–7276,* WEB *www.bestwestern-bluesea.com. 52 rooms, 48 suites. In-room safes, cable TV with movies, pool, outdoor hot tub, fishing, bicycles, laundry service, concierge, travel services, parking (fee); no smoking. AE, D, DC, MC, V.*

$ 🖼 **Banana Bungalow San Diego.** Literally a few feet from the beach, this hostel's location is its greatest asset. However, dampness and sand take their toll, and some parts of the hostel are in need of repair. All dorm rooms are coed and there are a total of 70 beds. Keg and movie-night parties are held weekly, as are various organized events. Complimentary Continental breakfast is served on the sundeck. There are lockers and a small TV room. ⊠ *707 Reed Ave., Pacific Beach 92109,* ☎ *858/273–3060 or 800/546–7835,* FAX *858/273–1440,* WEB *www. bananabungalow.com. Beach, bicycles, volleyball, travel services, airport shuttle; no room phones, no room TVs, no smoking. MC, V.*

Old Town (with Mission Valley)

Old Town is quaint, moderately priced, and within a short drive of Balboa Park, downtown, and Mission Bay. Although not particularly scenic, Mission Valley hotels are near shopping, and it's an easy drive to the beaches and Mission Bay marine park.

$$–$$$ 🖼 **Heritage Park Inn.** The beautifully restored mansions in Heritage ★ Park include this romantic 1889 Queen Anne–style bed and breakfast. Rooms range from smallish to ample, and most are bright and cheery. A full breakfast and afternoon tea are included. There is a two-night minimum stay on weekends, and weekly and monthly rates are available. Some rooms share a bath. Classic vintage films are shown nightly in the parlor on a small film screen. Transportation is available to area

attractions, the airport, and the Amtrak station. ⊠ *2470 Heritage Park Row, Old Town 92110,* ☎ *619/299–6832 or 800/995–2470,* FAX *619/ 299–9465,* WEB *www.heritageparkinn.com. 10 rooms, 2 suites. Fans, in-room data ports, cable TV, in-room VCRs, library, meeting rooms, airport shuttle; no smoking. AE, MC, V.*

$$ 🏨 **Doubletree Hotel San Diego Mission Valley.** Near Fashion Valley Center and adjacent to the Hazard Center—which has a seven-screen movie theater, four major restaurants, a food pavilion, and more than 20 shops—the Doubletree is also convenient to Route 163 and I–8. A San Diego Trolley station is within walking distance. Public areas are bright and comfortable, well suited to this hotel's large business clientele. Spacious rooms decorated in pastels have ample desk space. ⊠ *7450 Hazard Center Dr., Mission Valley 92108,* ☎ *619/297–5466 or 800/222–8733,* FAX *619/297–5499,* WEB *www.doubletree.com. 294 rooms, 6 suites. Restaurant, 2 bars, room service, in-room data ports, minibars, cable TV with movies, 2 tennis courts, 2 pools, gym, outdoor hot tub, sauna, shops, laundry facilities, laundry service, concierge, business services, meeting rooms, airport shuttle, free parking; no smoking. AE, D, DC, MC, V.*

La Jolla

La Jolla Village, chockablock full of expensive boutiques, galleries, and restaurants, is a popular vacation spot for celebrities and CEOs. Fortunately for the non-elite, affordable lodging choices exist as well.

$$$$ 🏨 **Hilton La Jolla Torrey Pines.** The low-rise, high-class hotel blends
★   discreetly into the Torrey Pines cliff top, looking almost insignificant until you step inside the luxurious lobby and gaze through native and subtropical foliage at the Pacific Ocean and the 18th hole of the Torrey Pines Municipal Golf Course. Amenities include complimentary butler service and free town-car service to La Jolla and Del Mar. The oversize accommodations are simple but elegant; most have balconies or terraces. ⊠ *10950 N. Torrey Pines Rd. 92037,* ☎ *858/558–1500 or 800/ 774–1500,* FAX *858/450–4584,* WEB *www.hilton.com. 377 rooms, 17 suites. 3 restaurants, 3 bars, room service, in-room data ports, in-room safes, minibars, putting green, 3 tennis courts, pool, gym, outdoor hot tub, sauna, bicycles, baby-sitting, children's programs, laundry service, concierge, business services, meeting rooms, airport shuttle, car rental, parking (fee); no smoking. AE, D, DC, MC, V.*

$$$$ 🏨 **La Valencia.** This pink Spanish-Mediterranean confection drew
★   Hollywood film stars in the 1930s and '40s for its setting and views of La Jolla Cove. Many rooms have a genteel European look, with antique pieces and rich-color rugs. The personal attention provided by the staff, as well as the plush robes and grand bathrooms, make the stay even more pleasurable. All rooms have wet bars, coffeemakers, and video games. The hotel is near the shops and restaurants of La Jolla Village. Rates are lower if you're willing to look out on the village. Be sure to stroll around the tiered gardens in back. ⊠ *1132 Prospect St. 92037,* ☎ *858/454–0771 or 800/451–0772,* FAX *858/456–3921,* WEB *www.lavalencia.com. 117 rooms, 15 villas. 3 restaurants, bar, lounge, room service, in-room safes, minibars, cable TV with movies, in-room VCRs, pool, health club, outdoor hot tub, massage, sauna, beach, bicycles, Ping-Pong, shuffleboard, laundry facilities, concierge, business services, meeting rooms, airport shuttle, parking (fee); no smoking. AE, D, MC, V.*

$$$$ 🏨 **Lodge at Torrey Pines.** This beautiful Craftsman-style lodge sits on
★   a bluff between La Jolla and Del Mar, and commands a view of miles of coastline. You know you're in for different sort of experience when you see the Scottish kilted doorman. Rooms, though dim, are very roomy

and furnished with antiques and reproduction turn-of-the-20th-century pieces. The service is excellent and the restaurant, A. R. Valentin, serves fine California cuisine. Beyond the 6-acre grounds are the Torrey Pines Municipal Golf Course and scenic trails that lead to the Torrey Pines State Beach and Reserve. The village of La Jolla is a 10-minute drive away. ⊠ *11480 N. Torrey Pines Rd. 92037,* ☎ *858/453–4420 or 800/995–4507,* FAX *858/453–7464,* WEB *www.lodgetorreypines.com. 175 rooms. 2 restaurants, 2 bars, in-room data ports, in-room safes, kitchenettes, cable TV, 18-hole golf course, pool, gym, hot tub, massage, spa, Internet, meeting rooms, free parking; no smoking. AE, D, DC, MC, V.*

$$–$$$ 🏨 **La Jolla Inn.** One block from the beach and near some of the best shops and restaurants, this European-style inn with a delightful staff sits in a prime spot in La Jolla Village. Many rooms (some with kitchenettes) have sweeping ocean views from their balconies; one spectacular penthouse suite faces the ocean, another the village. An upstairs sundeck is a great spot to enjoy the delicious complimentary Continental breakfast. ⊠ *1110 Prospect St. 92037,* ☎ *858/454–0133 or 800/433–1609,* FAX *858/454–2056,* WEB *www.lajollainn.com. 21 rooms, 2 suites. Room service, in-room data ports, kitchenettes, some refrigerators, cable TV with movies, library, shop, dry cleaning, laundry facilities, concierge, business services, free parking; no smoking. AE, D, DC, MC, V.*

NIGHTLIFE AND THE ARTS

Check the *Reader,* San Diego's free alternative newsweekly; *San Diego* magazine's "Restaurant & Nightlife Guide"; or the *San Diego-Union Tribune* Thursday "Night and Day" insert for the full slate of after-dark possibilities.

The Arts

Book tickets well in advance, preferably at the same time you make hotel reservations. Half-price tickets to theater, music, and dance events may be available on the day of performance at **Times Arts Tix** (⊠ Horton Plaza, Gaslamp Quarter, ☎ 619/497–5000). Only cash is accepted. Advance full-price tickets are also sold. **Ticketmaster** (☎ 619/220–8497) sells tickets to many performances. Service charges vary according to the event, and most tickets are nonrefundable.

Dance

California Ballet Company (☎ 858/560–6741) performs high-quality contemporary and traditional works, from story ballets to Balanchine, September–May.

Film

The **Cove** (⊠ 7730 Girard Ave., La Jolla, ☎ 858/459–5404) is an older one-screen theater with a distinctive 1950s ambience. **Hillcrest Cinemas** (⊠ 3965 5th Ave., Hillcrest, ☎ 619/299–2100) is a posh multiplex uptown. **Ken Cinema** (⊠ 4061 Adams Ave., Kensington, ☎ 619/283–5909) playing art and revival films, is considered by many to be the last bastion of true avant-garde film in San Diego. It publishes its listings in the *Ken,* a small newspaper distributed in nearly every coffeehouse and music store in the county.

Music

San Diego Opera (⊠ Civic Theatre, 3rd Ave. and B St., Downtown, ☎ 619/232–7636) draws international artists. Its season runs January–

May. Past performances have included *The Magic Flute, Faust, Idomeneo,* and *Aida,* plus concerts by such talents as Luciano Pavarotti. **San Diego Symphony Orchestra** (⊠ 750 B St., Downtown, ☎ 619/235–0804) presents year-round special events including classics, and summer and winter pops. Concerts are held at Copley Symphony Hall, except the Summer Pops series at the Navy Pier, on North Harbor Drive downtown. **Spreckels Organ Pavilion** (⊠ Balboa Park, ☎ 619/702–8138) holds a giant outdoor pipe organ dedicated in 1915 by sugar magnates John and Adolph Spreckels. The beautiful Spanish Baroque pavilion hosts concerts by civic organist Carol Williams on most Sunday afternoons and on most Monday evenings in summer. Local military bands, gospel groups, and barbershop quartets also perform here. All shows are free. **Spreckels Theatre** (⊠ 121 Broadway, Downtown, ☎ 619/235–0494), a designated-landmark theater erected more than 80 years ago, hosts musical events—everything from mostly Mozart to small rock concerts. Ballets and theatrical productions are also held here. Its good acoustics and historical status make this a special venue.

Theater

La Jolla Playhouse (⊠ Mandell Weiss Center for the Performing Arts, University of California at San Diego, 2910 La Jolla Village Dr., La Jolla, ☎ 858/550–1010) crafts exciting productions, from May through November. Many Broadway shows, such as *Tommy* and *How to Succeed in Business Without Really Trying,* have previewed here before heading for the East Coast. **Lyceum Theatre** (⊠ 79 Horton Plaza, Gaslamp Quarter, ☎ 619/544–1000) is home to the San Diego Repertory Theatre and also presents productions from visiting theater companies **Old Globe Theatre** (⊠ Simon Edison Centre for the Performing Arts, 1363 Old Globe Way, Balboa Park, ☎ 619/239–2255) is the oldest professional theater in California, performing classics, contemporary dramas, and experimental works. It produces the famous summer Shakespeare Festival at the Old Globe and its sister theaters, the Cassius Carter Centre Stage and the Lowell Davies Festival Theatre. **Starlight Musical Theatre** (⊠ Starlight Bowl, 2005 Pan American Plaza, Balboa Park, ☎ 619/544–7827 during season), a summertime favorite, is a series of musicals performed in an outdoor amphitheater mid-June–early September. Because of the theater's proximity to the airport, actors often have to freeze mid-scene while a plane flies over.

Nightlife

Bars of Note

Bitter End (⊠ 770 5th Ave., Gaslamp Quarter, ☎ 619/338–9300) is a sophisticated martini bar and a hip dance club where you can kick up your feet. **Blind Melons** (⊠ 710 Garnet Ave., Pacific Beach, ☎ 858/483–7844), not named after the band, draws well-known local and national bands to play rock and blues tunes that will keep you groovin'. If you get bored, meander along the boardwalk. **'Canes Bar and Grill** (⊠ 3105 Ocean Front Walk, Mission Beach, ☎ 858/488–1780) lets you step outside for a walk on the beach where the sounds of the national rock, reggae, and hip-hop acts onstage create a cacophony with the crashing waves.

Karl Strauss' Old Columbia Brewery & Grill (⊠ 1157 Columbia St., Downtown, ☎ 619/234–2739; ⊠ 1044 Wall St., La Jolla, ☎ 858/551–2739), San Diego's first microbrewery, draws an after-work downtown crowd and later fills with beer connoisseurs from all walks of life; the newer La Jolla version draws a mix of locals and tourists. **Martini Ranch** (⊠ 528 F St., Gaslamp Quarter, ☎ 619/235–6100) mixes more than

30 varieties of its namesake. Actually two clubs in one, the original Martini Ranch hosts jazz groups on weekdays and a DJ spining an eclectic mix on Friday and Saturday. Next door in the larger Shaker Room, local and traveling DJs spin all-star dance beats.

Onyx Room (✉ 852 5th Ave., Gaslamp Quarter, ☎ 619/235–6699) is one of San Diego's hippest hangs. It's actually two bars in one. In front there's a mood-lit cocktail lounge, and in the next room acid jazz bands and DJs keep the crowds dancing on the tiny dance floor. **Pacific Beach Bar & Grill** (✉ 860 Garnet Ave., Pacific Beach, ☎ 858/272–4745) is a stumbling block away from the beach. The popular nightspot has a huge outdoor patio so you can enjoy star-filled skies as you party. The lines here on the weekends are generally the longest of any club in Pacific Beach. There is plenty to see and do, from billiards and satellite TV sports to an interactive trivia game.

Coffeehouses

Brockton Villa Restaurant (✉ 1235 Coast Blvd., La Jolla, ☎ 858/454–7393), a palatial café overlooking La Jolla Cove, has indoor and outdoor seating, as well as scrumptious desserts and coffee drinks. It closes at 9 most nights, earlier on Sunday and Monday. **Claire de Lune** (✉ 2906 University Ave., North Park, ☎ 619/688–9845) won an award for its redesign of the historic Oddfellows building. The woodfloor hangout has sofas and armchairs for lounging as well as tables for studying. Local musicians and poets take the stage on various nights, and San Diego's most popular, and longest running, open-mic poetry night takes place every Tuesday. **Javanican** (✉ 4338 Cass St., Pacific Beach, ☎ 858/483–8035; ✉ 3719 Mission Blvd., Mission Beach, ☎ 858/488–8065) has two locations serving the young beach-community set. Adventurous musicians can sign up to play on the Pacific Beach location's stage on Tuesday night. The other location closes by 7 PM most evenings.

Comedy and Cabaret

Comedy Store La Jolla (✉ 916 Pearl St., La Jolla, ☎ 858/454–9176), like its sister establishment in Hollywood, hosts some of the best national touring and local talent. **Lips** (✉ 2770 5th Ave., Hillcrest, ☎ 619/295–7900) serves you dinner while female impersonators entertain. Their motto, "where the men are men and so are the girls," says it all.

Country-Western

In Cahoots (✉ 5373 Mission Center Rd., Mission Valley, ☎ 619/291–8635), with its great sound system, large dance floor, and DJ, is the destination of choice for cowgirls, cowboys, and city slickers alike. **Tio Leo's** (✉ 5302 Napa St., Bay Park, ☎ 619/542–1462) is a throwback to the days when lounges were dark and vinyl-filled. The lounge is within a Mexican restaurant, and an incredible variety of country, rockabilly, and swing acts grace the small stage.

Dance Clubs

Buffalo Joe's (✉ 600 5th Ave., Gaslamp Quarter, ☎ 619/236–1616) has a rocking dance floor. Retro disco and 1980s cover bands are the norm. Beware of the bachelorette parties. **E Street Alley** (✉ 919 4th Ave., Gaslamp Quarter, ☎ 619/231–9200) is a spacious, hotspot dance club with a DJ spinning Top 40 and club tunes. **Plan B** (✉ 945 Garnet Ave., Pacific Beach, ☎ 858/483–9920) has a stainless-steel dance floor and numerous places from which to view it. Plan B has the only permanent laser show in San Diego. **Sevilla** (✉ 555 4th Ave., Gaslamp Quarter, ☎ 619/233–5979) brings a Latin flavor to the Gaslamp. Get fueled up at the tapas bar before venturing downstairs for dancing. This is the best place in San Diego to take lessons in salsa and lambada.

Gay and Lesbian Nightlife

MEN'S BARS

Bourbon Street (⊠ 4612 Park Blvd., North Park, ☎ 619/291–0173) is a piano bar with live entertainment nightly. It resembles its New Orleans namesake with jazzy decor and a courtyard. **Brass Rail** (⊠ 3796 5th Ave., Hillcrest, ☎ 619/298–2233), a fixture since the early 1960s, is the oldest gay bar in San Diego. The club hosts dancing nightly, or you can just pass time playing pool on one of the three tables. **Flicks** (⊠ 1017 University Ave., Hillcrest, ☎ 619/297–2056), a hip video bar that's popular with the see-and-be-seen crowd, plays music and comedy videos on four big screens. Drink specials and videos vary each night.

WOMEN'S BARS

Club Bom Bay (⊠ 3175 India St., Middletown, ☎ 619/296–6789) occasionally has live entertainment and always attracts a dancing crowd. **The Flame** (⊠ 3780 Park Blvd., Hillcrest, ☎ 619/295–4163), fronted by a red neon sign resembling a torch, is a San Diego institution. The friendly dance club caters to lesbians most of the week. (Tuesday is Boys' Night.)

MIXED BARS

Club Montage (⊠ 2028 Hancock St., Middletown, ☎ 619/294–9590) is one of the largest and best clubs in town. The three-level club was originally oriented to the gay crowd, but now all types come for the high-tech lighting system and world-class DJs. For a breath of fresh air, step out to view the skyline and enjoy a drink from the rooftop bar.

Jazz

Crescent Shores Grill (⊠ 7955 La Jolla Shores Dr., La Jolla, ☎ 858/459–0541), perched on the top floor of the Hotel La Jolla, delivers an ocean view and a lineup of locally acclaimed jazz musicians Tuesday through Saturday. **Croce's** (⊠ 802 5th Ave., Gaslamp Quarter, ☎ 619/233–4355), the intimate jazz cave of restaurateur Ingrid Croce (singer-songwriter Jim Croce's widow), books superb acoustic-jazz musicians.Next door, Croce's **Top Hat** puts on live R&B nightly from 9 to 2. **Dizzy's** (⊠ 344 7th Ave., Gaslamp Quarter, ☎ 858/270–7467) late-night jazz jam is Friday after midnight. During the week are jazz, art, and spoken-word events. No alcohol. **Humphrey's by the Bay** (⊠ 2241 Shelter Island Dr., Shelter Island, ☎ 619/523–1010 for concert information), surrounded by water, is the summer stomping grounds for musicians such as Harry Belafonte and Chris Isaak. From June through September this dining and drinking oasis hosts the city's best outdoor jazz, folk, and light-rock concert series. The rest of the year the music moves indoors for some first-rate jazz most Sunday, Monday, and Tuesday nights, with piano-bar music on other nights. **Juke Joint Café** (⊠ 327 4th Ave., Gaslamp Quarter, ☎ 619/232–7685) has a bistro up front and a supper club in the back. Live music nightly is mainly jazz and R&B.

Night Bay Cruises

Bahia Belle (⊠ 998 W. Mission Bay Dr., Mission Bay, ☎ 619/539–7779) is a paddlewheeler that offers relaxing evening cruises along Mission Bay that include cocktails, dancing, and live music. The fare is less than most nightclub covers. **Hornblower Cruises** (⊠ 1066 N. Harbor Dr., Downtown, ☎ 619/686–8700) makes nightly dinner-dance cruises aboard the *Lord Hornblower*—passengers are treated to fabulous views of the San Diego skyline. **San Diego Harbor Excursion** (⊠ 1050 N. Harbor Dr., Downtown, ☎ 619/234–4111 or 800/442–7847) welcomes guests aboard with a glass of champagne as a prelude to nightly dinner-dance cruises.

Piano Bars

Hotel Del Coronado (✉ 1500 Orange Ave., Coronado, ☎ 619/435–6611), the famous fairy-tale hostelry, has piano music in its Crown Room and Palm Court. **Palace Bar** (✉ 311 Island Ave., Gaslamp Quarter, ☎ 619/544–1886), in the historical Horton Grand Hotel, is one of the most mellow lounges in the Gaslamp. **Top of the Hyatt** (✉ 1 Market Pl., Embarcadero, ☎ 619/232–1234) crowns the tallest waterfront building in California. The fantastic views and mood lighting make this one most romantic spots in town. **Top o' the Cove** (✉ 1216 Prospect St., La Jolla, ☎ 858/454–7779), also a magnificent Continental restaurant, has pianists playing show tunes and standards from the 1940s to the '80s.

Rock, Pop, Folk, World, and Blues

Belly Up Tavern (✉ 143 S. Cedros Ave., Solana Beach, ☎ 858/481–9022), a regular fixture on local papers' "best of" lists, has been hosting quality live entertainment, from reggae to folk to rock, since it opened in the mid-'70s. **Casbah** (✉ 2501 Kettner Blvd., Middletown,, ☎ 619/232–4355), near the airport, is a small club with a national reputation for showcasing up-and-coming acts. Nirvana, Smashing Pumpkins, and Alanis Morissette all played the Casbah on their way to stardom. **Dream Street** (✉ 2228 Bacon St., Ocean Beach, ☎ 619/222–8131) is the place to go to see local rock music on the heavy side. **Patrick's II** (✉ 428 F St., Gaslamp Quarter, ☎ 619/233–3077) serves up live New Orleans–style jazz, blues, and rock in an Irish setting.

OUTDOOR ACTIVITIES AND SPORTS

Updated by
Rob Aikins

At least one stereotype of San Diego is true—it is an active, outdoors-oriented community, thanks to the constant sunshine.

Beaches

San Diego's beaches—wide and sandy or narrow and rocky—are among its greatest natural attractions. The beaches below are listed from south to north.

Coronado

Silver Strand State Beach. This quiet Coronado beach is ideal for families. The water is relatively calm, lifeguards and rangers are on duty year-round, and there are places to rollerblade or ride bikes. Four parking lots provide plenty of room. Sites at an RV park ($12) are available on a first-come, first-serve basis; stays are limited to seven nights. ✉ *From San Diego–Coronado Bay Bridge, turn left onto Orange Ave., which becomes Rte. 75, and follow signs;* ☎ 619/435–5184.

Coronado Beach. With the famous Hotel Del Coronado as a backdrop, this stretch of sandy beach is one of San Diego County's largest and most picturesque. It's perfect for sunbathing, people-watching, or Frisbee. Other exercisers include Navy SEAL teams, as well as the occasional Marine Recon unit. ✉ *From the bridge, turn left on Orange Ave. and follow signs.*

Point Loma

Sunset Cliffs. Beneath the jagged cliffs on the west side of the Point Loma peninsula is a secluded beach popular with surfers and locals. Near Cabrillo Point, tide pools teeming with small sea creatures are revealed at low tide. A visit here is more enjoyable at low tide; check the local newspaper for tide schedules. ✉ *Take I–8 west to Sunset Cliffs Blvd. and head west.*

Mission Bay and the Beaches

Ocean Beach. This mile-long beach is a haven for volleyball players, sunbathers, and swimmers. The area around the municipal pier at the south end is a hangout for surfers and transients; the pier itself is open for fishing and has a restaurant at the middle. The beach is south of the Mission Bay channel. Limited parking is available. Swimmers should beware of unusually vicious rip currents. ⊠ *Take I–8 west to Sunset Cliffs Blvd. and head west. Turn right on Santa Monica Ave.*

Mission Beach. San Diego's most popular beach draws huge crowds on hot summer days. The 2-mi-long stretch extends from the north entrance of Mission Bay to Pacific Beach. The boardwalk is popular with walkers, runners, skaters, and bicyclists. Surfers, swimmers, and volleyball players congregate at the south end. Toward the north end, near the Belmont Park roller coaster, the beach narrows and the water becomes rougher. The crowds grow thicker and somewhat rougher as well. ⊠ *Exit I–5 at Garnet Ave. and head west to Mission Blvd. Turn south and look for parking.*

Pacific Beach. The boardwalk turns into a sidewalk here, but there are still bike paths and picnic tables along the beachfront. Pacific Beach runs from the north end of Mission Beach to Crystal Pier. North Pacific Beach extends from the pier north. The scene here is particularly lively on weekends. There are designated surfing areas, and fire rings are available. There's street parking, plus a big lot at Belmont Park near the south end. ⊠ *Exit I–5 at Garnet Ave. and head west to Mission Blvd. Turn north and look for parking.*

La Jolla

Tourmaline Surfing Park. This is one of the area's most popular beaches for surfing and sailboarding year-round. The parking lot is usually full by midday. ⊠ *Take Mission Blvd. north (it turns into La Jolla Blvd.) and turn west on Tourmaline St.*

Windansea Beach. The beach's sometimes towering waves (caused by an underwater reef) are truly world class. With its incredible views and secluded sunbathing spots set among sandstone rocks, Windansea is also one of the most romantic of West Coast beaches, especially at sunset. ⊠ *Take Mission Blvd. north (it turns into La Jolla Blvd.) and turn west on Nautilus St.*

Marine Street Beach. Wide and sandy, this strand of beach often teems with sunbathers, swimmers, walkers, and joggers. The water is good for surfing and bodysurfing, though you'll need to watch out for riptides. ⊠ *Accessible from Marine St., off La Jolla Blvd.*

Children's Pool/Shell Beach. Though you can't swim here, these two coves offer panoramic views and the chance to observe resident sea lions sunning themselves and frolicking in the water. ⊠ *Follow La Jolla Blvd. north. When it forks, stay to the left, then turn right onto Coast Blvd. Shell Beach is north of the Children's Pool along Coast Blvd.*

La Jolla Cove. This is one of the prettiest spots in the world. A palm-lined park sits on top of cliffs formed by the incessant pounding of the waves. At low tide the tide pools and cliff caves provide a destination for explorers. Divers and snorkelers can explore the underwater delights of the San Diego–La Jolla Underwater Ecological Reserve. The cove is also a favorite of rough-water swimmers. ⊠ *Follow Coast Blvd. north to signs, or take the La Jolla Village Dr. exit from I–5, head west to Torrey Pines Rd., turn left, and drive downhill to Girard Ave. Turn right and follow signs.*

La Jolla Shores. On summer holidays all access routes are usually closed to one of San Diego's most popular beaches. The lures here are a wide sandy beach and the most gentle waves in San Diego. A concrete boardwalk parallels the beach. Arrive early to get a parking spot in the lot at the foot of Calle Frescota. ⊠ *From I–5 take La Jolla Village Dr. west and turn left onto La Jolla Shores Dr. Head west to Camino del Oro or Vallecitos St. Turn right.*

Torrey Pines City Park Beach. The powerful waves at this beach, known as Black's Beach, attract surfers, and its relative isolation appeals to nudists (although by law nudity is prohibited). Access to parts of the shore coincides with low tide. There are no lifeguards on duty, and strong ebb tides are common—only experienced swimmers should take the plunge. The cliffs are dangerous to climb. ⊠ *Take Genesee Ave. west from I–5 and follow signs to Glider Port; easier access, via a paved path, available on La Jolla Farms Rd., but parking is limited to 2 hrs.*

Del Mar

Torrey Pines State Beach/Reserve. One of San Diego's best beaches contains 1,700 acres of bluffs, bird-filled marshes, and sandy shoreline. A network of trails leads through rare pine trees to the coast below. The large parking lot is rarely full. Lifeguards are on duty daily (weather permitting) from Memorial Day to Labor Day, and on weekends in May and September. ⊠ *Take the Carmel Valley Rd. exit west from I–5, turn left on Rte. S21;* ☎ *858/755–2063.* ⊠ *Parking $2.*

Del Mar Beach. The numbered streets of Del Mar, from 15th to 29th, end at a wide beach popular with volleyball players, surfers, and sunbathers. Parking can be a problem on nice summer days. The portions of Del Mar south of 15th Street are lined with cliffs and are rarely crowded. ⊠ *Take the Via de la Valle exit from I–5 west to Rte. S21 (also known as Camino del Mar in Del Mar) and turn left.*

Encinitas

Swami's. Extreme low tides expose tidepools that harbor anemones, starfish, and other sea life. Remember to look but don't touch; all sea life here is protected. The beach is also a top surfing spot; the only access is by a long stairway leading down from the cliff-top park. ⊠ *Follow Rte. S21 north from Cardiff, or exit I–5 at Encinitas Blvd., go west to Rte. S21, and turn left.*

Moonlight Beach. Large parking areas and lots of facilities make this beach, tucked into a break in the cliffs, a pleasant stop. To combat erosion sand is trucked in every year, making it a popular beach with sunbathers. The volleyball courts on the north end attract competent players, including a few professionals. ⊠ *Take the Encinitas Blvd. exit from I–5 and head west until you hit the Moonlight parking lot.*

Participant Sports

Bicycling

On any given summer day **Route S21** from La Jolla to Oceanside looks like a freeway for cyclists. Never straying more than a quarter-mile from the beach, it is easily the most popular and scenic bike route around.Local bookstores and camping stores sell guides to some challenging mountain-bike trails in outer San Diego County. A free comprehensive map of all county bike paths is available from the local office of the **California Department of Transportation** (⊠ 2829 Juan St., Old Town 92110, ☎ 619/688–6699). **Bicycle Barn** (⊠ 746 Emerald St., Pacific Beach, ☎ 858/581–3665) rents mountain bikes to beach cruisers. **Mission Beach Club** (⊠ 704 Ventura Pl. Mission Beach, ☎ 858/488–5050) is right on the boardwalk and rents bikes, skates, and boards of all types.

Boating, Jet Skiing, and Waterskiing

Most bay-side resorts rent equipment for on-the-water adventures. The **Bahia Resort Hotel** (✉ 998 W. Mission Bay Dr., Mission Bay, ☎ 858/539–7696) and its sister location, the **Catamaran Resort Hotel** (✉ 3999 Mission Blvd., Mission Beach, ☎ 858/488–2582) rent boats of all kinds and equipment. **H2O Jet Ski Rentals** (✉ 1617 Quivira Rd., Mission Bay, ☎ 619/226–2754) rents jet skis for use on Mission Bay. **Coronado Boat Rentals** (✉ 1715 Strand Way, Coronado, ☎ 619/437–1514) has kayaks, jet skis, fishing skiffs, and power boats from 15 ft to 19 ft in length as well as sailboats from 18 ft to 36 ft. The **Mission Bay Sports Center** (✉ 1010 Santa Clara Pl., Mission Bay, ☎ 858/488–1004) rents kayaks, catamarans, single-hull sailboats, and power boats. **Seaforth Boat Rentals** (✉ 1641 Quivira Rd., Mission Bay, ☎ 619/223–1681) rents jet skis, paddleboats, sailboats, and skiffs. Waveless Mission Bay and the small **Snug Harbor Marina** (☎ 760/434–3089), east of the intersection of Tamarack Avenue and I–5 in Carlsbad, are favorite spots.

Diving

Enthusiasts the world over come to San Diego to snorkel and scuba-dive off La Jolla and Point Loma. At La Jolla Cove you'll find the **San Diego–La Jolla Underwater Ecological Park.** Farther north, off the south end of Black's Beach, the rim of **Scripps Canyon** lies in about 60 ft of water. The canyon plummets to more than 900 ft in some sections. The HMCS *Yukon,* a decommissioned Canadian warship, was intentionally sunk off of **Mission Beach.** Beware and exercise caution: even experienced divers have become disoriented inside the wreck. **Sunset Cliffs** in Point Loma is best enjoyed by experienced divers, who mostly prefer to make their dives from boats. The *San Diego Union–Tribune* includes diving conditions on its weather page. For recorded diving information, contact the **San Diego City Lifeguard Service** (☎ 619/221–8824).

San Diego Divers Supply (✉ 4004 Sports Arena Blvd., Sports Arena, ☎ 619/224–3439) provides equipment and instruction, as well as boat trips and maps of local wrecks and attractions. **Diving Locker** (✉ 1020 Grand Ave., Pacific Beach, ☎ 858/272–1120) has been a fixture in San Diego since 1959.

Fishing

The Pacific Ocean is full of corbina, croaker, and halibut. No license is required to fish from a public pier, such as the Ocean Beach and Oceanside piers. A fishing license from the state **Department of Fish and Game** (✉ 4949 Viewridge Ave., San Diego 92123, ☎ 858/467–4201), available at most bait-and-tackle and sporting-goods stores, is required for fishing from the shoreline. **Fisherman's Landing** (✉ 2838 Garrison St., Point Loma, ☎ 619/221–8500) has a fleet of luxury vessels from 57 ft to 124 ft long, offering long-range multiday trips in search of yellowfin tuna, yellowtail, and other deep-water fish. **H&M Landing** (✉ 2803 Emerson St., Point Loma, ☎ 619/222–1144) schedules fishing trips December through March. **Helgren's Sportfishing** (✉ 315 Harbor Dr. S, Oceanside, ☎ 760/722–2133) is your best bet in North County, with trips departing from Oceanside Harbor.

Golf

The **Southern California Golf Association** (☎ 818/980–3630) publishes an annual directory ($15) with detailed and valuable information on all clubs. Another good resource, the **Southern California Public Links Golf Association** (☎ 714/994–4747) will answer questions over the phone or, for $5, will provide you with a roster of member courses.

The **Balboa Park Municipal Golf Course** (⌧ 2600 Golf Course Dr., Balboa Park, ☎ 858/570–1234) is in the heart of Balboa Park, making it convenient for downtown visitors. Greens fee: $33–$38. **Coronado Municipal Golf Course** (⌧ 2000 Visalia Row, Coronado, ☎ 619/435–3121) has 18 holes and views of San Diego Bay and the Coronado Bridge from the back nine holes. Greens fee: $20–$34. **Mission Bay Golf Resort** (⌧ 2702 N. Mission Bay Dr., Mission Bay, ☎ 858/490–3370) is an 18-hole, not-very-challenging course lighted for night play. Greens fee: $18–$22.

Torrey Pines Municipal Golf Course (⌧ 11480 N. Torrey Pines Rd., La Jolla, ☎ 800/985–4653), with 36 holes, is one of the best public golf courses in the United States. There are views of the Pacific from every hole and it's sufficiently challenging to host the Buick Invitational in February. Greens fee: $65–$105.

Aviara Golf Club (⌧ 7447 Batiquitos Dr., Carlsbad, ☎ 760/603–6900) has 18 holes (designed by Arnold Palmer) and views of the protected adjacent Batiquitos Lagoon and the Pacific Ocean. Greens fee: $175–$195. **La Costa Resort and Spa** (⌧ 2100 Costa del Mar Rd., Carlsbad, ☎ 760/438–9111 or 800/854–5000) has two 18-hole PGA-rated courses. One of the premier golf resorts in southern California, it hosts the Accenture World Match Play Championships each February. Greens fee: $195. **Rancho Bernardo Inn and Country Club** (⌧ 17550 Bernardo Oaks Dr., Rancho Bernardo, ☎ 858/675–8470 Ext. 1) has 45 holes. Guests can play three other golf courses at company-operated resorts: Mount Woodson, Temecula Creek, and Twin Oaks. Ken Blanchard's Golf University of San Diego, based here, is world famous. Greens fee: $85–$110.

Hiking and Nature Trails

Guided hikes are conducted regularly through Los Penasquitos Canyon Preserve and the Torrey Pines State Beach and Reserve. The **San Dieguito River Valley Regional Open Space** (⌧ 21 mi north of San Diego on I–5 to Lomas Santa Fe Dr., east 1 mi to Sun Valley Rd., north into park; Solana Beach, ☎ 619/235–5440) is a 55-mi corridor that begins at the mouth of the San Dieguito River in Del Mar, heading from the riparian lagoon area through coastal sage scrub and mountain terrain to end in the desert just east of Volcan Mountain near Julian. **Mission Trails Regional Parks** (⌧ 1 Father Junípero Serra Tr., Mission Valley, ☎ 619/668–3275, WEB www.mtrp.org), which encompasses nearly 6,000 acres of mountains, wooded hillsides, lakes, and riparian streams, is only 8 mi northeast of downtown. Trails range from easy to difficult; they include one with a superb city view from Cowles Mountain and another along a historic missionary path.

In-line and Roller-Skating

The sidewalks at **Mission Bay** are perfect for rollerblading and skating. **Bicycle Barn** (⌧ 746 Emerald St., Pacific Beach, ☎ 858/581–3665) rents blades for leisurely skates along the Pacific Beach boardwalk. **Mission Beach Club** (⌧ 704 Ventura Pl., Mission Beach, ☎ 858/488–5050) rents skates and everything else a beachgoer could need.

Surfing

If you're a beginner, consider paddling in the waves off Mission Beach, Pacific Beach, Tourmaline, La Jolla Shores, Del Mar, or Oceanside. More experienced surfers usually head for Sunset Cliffs, the La Jolla reef breaks, Black's Beach, or Swami's in Encinitas. **Surf Diva Surf School** (⌧ 2160-A Avenida de la Playa, La Jolla, ☎ 858/454–8273) offers clinics, surf camps, surf trips, and private lessons especially formulated for women. Many local surf shops rent both surf and bodyboards. **Mission Beach Club** (✉ 704 Ventura Pl., Mission Beach, ☎ 858/488–5050) is right on the boardwalk, just steps from the waves. **Star Surfing Company** (✉ 4652 Mission Beach, Pacific Beach, ☎ 858/273–7827) can get you out surfing around the Crystal Pier. **La Jolla Surf Systems** (✉ 2132 Avenida de la Playa, La Jolla, ☎ 858/456–2777) takes care of your needs if you want to surf the reefs or beachbreaks of La Jolla.

Volleyball

Ocean Beach, South Mission Beach, Del Mar Beach, Moonlight Beach, and the western edge of Balboa Park are major congregating points for volleyball enthusiasts. Contact the **San Diego Volleyball Club** (☎ 858/486–6885) to find out about organized games and tournaments.

Windsurfing

Also known as sailboarding, windsurfing is a sport best practiced on smooth waters, such as Mission Bay or the Snug Harbor Marina at the intersection of I–5 and Tamarack Avenue in Carlsbad. More experienced windsurfers will enjoy taking a board out on the ocean. Wave jumping is especially popular at the Tourmaline Surfing Park in La Jolla and in the Del Mar area. Sailboarding rentals and instruction are available at the **Bahia Resort Hotel** (✉ 998 W. Mission Bay Dr., Mission Bay, ☎ 858/488–0551), and the affiliated **Catamaran Resort Hotel. Mission Bay Sports Center** (✉ 1010 Santa Clara Pl., Mission Bay, ☎ 858/488–1004) can handle your windsurfing equipment needs. **Windsport** (✉ 844 W. Mission Bay Dr., Mission Bay, ☎ 858/488–4642) rents sailboards.

Spectator Sports

Baseball

The **San Diego Padres** (☎ 619/280–4636) has a strong fan base, which is largely why city voters passed a bill to build the team a new stadium, due to open April 2004.

Football

The **San Diego Chargers** (☎ 619/280–2121) of the National Football League fill Qualcomm Stadium from August through December.

Golf

The **Buick Invitational** brings the pros to the Torrey Pines Municipal Golf Course in mid-February (☎ 858/452–3226). The **Accenture World Match Play Championship** is held at the La Costa resort in February (☎ 760/438–9111).

SHOPPING

Downtown

Updated by
Lenore Greiner

Art galleries, antique stores, and boutiques fill the Victorian buildings and renovated warehouses of the lively **Gaslamp Quarter,** especially along 4th and 5th avenues. **Westfield Shoppingtown Horton Plaza** (Gaslamp Quarter, ☎ 619/238–1596) is a multilevel, open-air shopping, dining, and entertainment complex with a lively terra-cotta color scheme and flag-draped facades. There are department stores, fast-food counters, upscale restaurants, the Lyceum Theater, cinemas, and 140 other stores.

Seaport Village (✉ W. Harbor Dr. at Kettner Blvd., Embarcadero, ☎ 619/235–4014) is a waterfront complex of 75 shops and restaurants within walking distance of hotels. Aside from the shops, there are horse and carriage rides, an 1890 Looff carousel, and usually some form of public entertainment.

Coronado

The **Ferry Landing Marketplace** (✉ 1201 1st St., at B Ave.) has 30 shops plus a Tuesday-afternoon **Farmers Market. Orange Avenue** has six blocks lined with classy boutiques and galleries.

Hillcrest, North Park, Uptown

Although their boundaries blur, each of these three established neighborhoods north and northeast of downtown contains a distinct urban village with shops, many ethnic restaurants, and entertainment spots. Most of the activity is on University Avenue and Washington Street, and along the side streets connecting the two. Gay-popular and funky **Hillcrest,** north of Balboa Park, has many gift, book, and music stores. Retro rules in **North Park.** Nostalgia shops along Park Boulevard and University Avenue at 30th Street carry clothing, accessories, furnishings, wigs, and bric-a-brac of the 1920s–1960s. The **Uptown District,** an open-air shopping center on University Avenue, includes several furniture, gift, and specialty stores.

Old Town

The colorful Old Town historic district recalls a Mexican marketplace. Adobe architecture, flower-filled plazas, fountains, and courtyards decorate the shopping areas of Bazaar del Mundo and Old Town Esplanade, where you'll find international goods, toys, souvenirs, and arts and crafts. **Bazaar del Mundo** (✉ 2754 Calhoun St., ☎ 619/296–3161) has boutiques selling designer items, crafts, fine arts, and fashions from around the world. The best time to visit is during the annual Santa Fe Market in March, when you can browse collections of jewelry, replica artifacts, wearable-art clothing and accessories, pottery, and blankets—all crafted by Southwestern artists.

Mission Valley

The Mission Valley/Hotel Circle area, northeast of downtown near I–8 and Route 163, has a few major shopping centers. **Fashion Valley Center** (✉ 7007 Friars Rd.), with lush landscaping, a contemporary Mission theme, and over 200 shops and restaurants, is San Diego's upscale shopping mall. There's a San Diego Trolley station in the parking lot. The major department stores are Macy's, Nordstrom, Saks Fifth Avenue, Neiman Marcus, and Robinsons-May. **Park Valley Center** (✉ 1750 Camino de la Reina), across the street from Westfield Shoppingtown Mission Valley, is a U-shape strip mall, anchored by **OFF 5th** (☎ 619/296–4896), which offers last-season's fashions by Ralph Lauren, Armani, and Burberry once seen in Saks Fifth Avenue but at Costco prices. **Westfield Shoppingtown Mission Valley** (✉ 1640 Camino del Rio N), is San Diego's largest outdoor shopping mall, with department stores and discount stores carrying merchandise that might be found in the mall up the road at higher prices.

La Jolla

This seaside village has chic boutiques, art galleries, and gift shops lining narrow twisty streets, often celebrity soaked. On the east side of I–5, office buildings surround **Westfield Shoppingtown UTC** (✉ La Jolla Village Dr., between I–5 and I–805, ☎ 858/546–8858) has 155 shops, several department stores, a cinema, 25 eateries, and an ice-skating rink.

SIDE TRIPS TO THE NORTH COAST AND INLAND NORTH COUNTY

By Lenore
Greiner

San Diego County sprawls from the Pacific Ocean to Anza-Borrego Desert State Park on the eastern boundary. North County continues to draw multitudes of visitors to its lovely beach communities, the Legoland theme park, and father inland, the San Diego Wild Animal Park.

Numbers in the margin correspond to points of interest on the San Diego North County map.

Del Mar

23 mi north of downtown San Diego on I–5, 9 mi north of La Jolla on Rte. S21.

Del Mar is best known for its racetrack, chic shopping strip, celebrity visitors, and wide beaches. Along with its collection of shops, **Del Mar Plaza** also contains outstanding restaurants and landscaped plazas and gardens with Pacific views.

❶ The **Del Mar Fairgrounds** host the **Del Mar Thoroughbred Club** (✉ 2260 Jimmy Durante Blvd., ☎ 858/755–1141, WEB www.dmtc.com). Crooner Bing Crosby and his Hollywood buddies—Pat O'Brien, Gary Cooper, and Oliver Hardy, among others—organized the club in the 1930s, and Del Mar soon developed into a regular train stop for the stars of stage and screen. Even now the racing season here (usually July–September, Wednesday–Monday, post time 2 PM) is one of the most fashionable in California. Del Mar Fairgrounds hosts more than 100 different events each year, including the San Diego County Fair and a number of horse shows. ✉ *Head west at I–5's Via de la Valle Rd. exit,* ☎ *858/793–5555.*

Dining and Lodging

$$$–$$$$ ✕ **Pacifica Del Mar.** This lovely restaurant overlooks the sea from the plush precincts of Del Mar Plaza. Highly innovative, the restaurant frequently rewrites the menu to show off such show-stoppers as a tower of layered ahi sashimi and Dungeness crab, a house-smoked salmon terrine flavored with a dash of caviar, and a dry-aged New York steak served with a Gorgonzola-potato tart. ✉ *Del Mar Plaza, 1515 Camino del Mar,* ☎ *858/792–0476. AE, D, MC, V.*

$–$$$ ✕ **Jake's Del Mar.** This enormously popular oceanfront restaurant has a close-up view of the water and a menu of simple but well-prepared fare that ranges from a dressy halibut sandwich to crab-crowned swordfish Del Mar to mustard-crusted rack of lamb with port-flavored garlic sauce. A menu note reminds that the legendary, ice-cream stuffed hula pie is "what the sailors swam ashore for in Lahaina." ✉ *1660 Coast Blvd.,* ☎ *858/755–2002. AE, DC, MC, V.*

$$$$ 🏨 **L'Auberge Del Mar Resort and Spa.** Although it looks rather like an upscale condominium complex, L'Auberge is modeled on the Tudor-style hotel that once stood here, a playground for the early Hollywood elite. The beach is a three-minute walk downhill. Rooms are done in pink and green pastels and have marble bathrooms. Most rooms have balconies and gas fireplaces. Across the street are boutiques and restaurants at Del Mar Plaza. ✉ *1540 Camino del Mar 92014,* ☎ *858/259–1515 or 800/ 553–1336,* FAX *858/755–4940,* WEB *www.laubergedelmar.com. 112 rooms, 8 suites. Restaurant, bar, in-room data ports, cable TV, 2 pools, outdoor hot tub, massage, spa, 2 tennis courts, gym, meeting room. AE, D, DC, MC, V.*

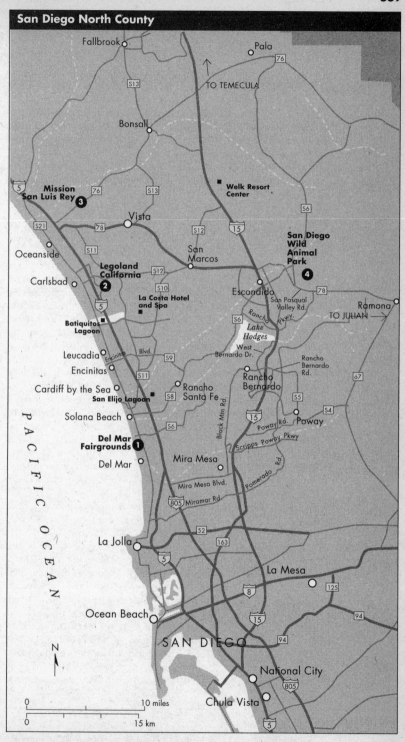

San Diego North County

Rancho Santa Fe

4 mi east of Solana Beach on Rte. S8 (Lomas Santa Fe Dr.), 29 mi north of downtown San Diego on I–5 to Rte. S8 east.

Groves of huge, drooping eucalyptus trees cover the hills of exclusive Rancho Santa Fe. East of I–5 on Via de la Valle Road, Rancho Santa Fe is horse country. It's common to see entire families riding the many trails that crisscross the hillsides. Lillian Rice, one of the first women to graduate with a degree in architecture from the University of California, designed the town, modeling it after villages in Spain. The challenging Rancho Santa Fe Golf Course, the original site of the Bing Crosby Pro-Am and considered one of the best courses in southern California, is open only to members of the Rancho Santa Fe community and guests of the inn.

Dining and Lodging

$$$$ ✕ **Mille Fleurs.** Mille Fleurs has a winning combination, from its lo-
★ cation in the heart of wealthy, horsey Rancho Santa Fe to the warm Gallic welcome extended by proprietor Bertrand Hug, and the talents of chef Martin Woesle. The quiet dining rooms are decorated like a French-Moroccan villa. Menus are written daily to reflect the market and Woesle's mood, but sometimes feature a soup of *musque de Provence* (pumpkin with cinnamon croutons), sautéed *lotte* (monkfish) with okra and curry sauce, stuffed quail with peaches, and oven-roasted baby lamb with summer vegetable ratatouille. ⊠ *Country Squire Courtyard, 6009 Paseo Delicias,* ☎ *858/756–3085. Reservations essential. AE, D, MC, V. No lunch weekends.*

$$$$ ✕🏨 **Rancho Valencia Resort.** One of southern California's hidden
★ treasures has luxurious accommodations in Spanish-style casitas scattered on 40 acres of landscaped grounds. Suites have corner fireplaces, luxurious Berber carpeting, and shuttered French doors leading to private patios. Rancho Valencia is one of the top tennis resorts in the nation and is adjacent to three well-designed golf courses. The inn's first-rate restaurant has a seasonal menu that might include a foie gras Napoleon; pasilla-chile crab cakes; farm-raised abalone steaks; and prime rib-eye steak in a Calvados-scented brown sauce. ⊠ *5921 Valencia Cir. 92067,* ☎ *858/756–1123 or 800/548–3664,* 🖷 *858/756–0165,* 🌐 *www.ranchovalencia.com. 43 suites. Restaurant, room service, bar, cable TV, minibars, 2 pools, health club, 3 outdoor hot tubs, spa, 18 tennis courts, croquet, hiking, bicycles. AE, DC, MC, V.*

$$–$$$ 🏨 **Inn at Rancho Santa Fe.** Understated elegance is the theme of this genteel old resort in the heart of the village. This is the sort of place where people don their "whites" and play croquet on the lawn Sunday afternoons. Most accommodations are in red-tile-roof cottages scattered about the property's 20 acres. The inn also maintains a beach house at Del Mar for guest use and has membership at the exclusive Rancho Santa Fe Golf Club and privileges at five other nearby, exclusive courses. ⊠ *5951 Linea del Cielo 92067,* ☎ *858/756–1131 or 800/ 843–4661,* 🖷 *858/759–1604,* 🌐 *www.theinnatranchosantafe.com. 73 rooms, 19 suites. Bar, dining room, room service, cable TV, pool, 18-hole golf course, 3 tennis courts, croquet, gym, library, meeting room. AE, DC, MC, V.*

Carlsbad

15 mi north of Rancho Santa Fe via Hwy. S9 to Hwy. S21, 36 mi north of downtown San Diego on I–5.

Since the Legoland California theme park moved in east of Carlsbad in 1999, this once laid-back Bavarian-inspired coastal community has enjoyed a thriving economy. The theme park is at the center of a tourist complex that includes resort hotels, a shopping mall, colorful flower fields, and golf courses. Carlsbad owes its name and Bavarian look to John Frazier, who lured people to the area a century ago with talk of the healing powers of mineral water bubbling from a coastal well. The water was found to have the same properties as water from the German mineral wells of Karlsbad—hence the name of the new community. Remnants from this era, including the original well and a monument to Frazier, are found at the **Alt Karlsbad Haus** (✉ 2802 Carlsbad Blvd., ☎ 760/434–1887), a stone building that houses a small day spa and the Carlsbad Famous Water Co., a 21st-century version of Frazier's waterworks.

★ ☙ ❷ **Legoland California** offers a full day of entertainment for pint-size fun-seekers and their parents. The experience is best appreciated by kids ages 2 to 10. Miniland, an animated collection of cities constructed entirely of Lego blocks, captures the imaginations of both kids and their adult companions. Other attractions include a castle; pint-size Dragon and Spellbound roller coasters; and Aquazone Wave Racers, the first power-ski water ride in North America. Kids can climb on and over, operate, manipulate, and explore displays and attractions constructed out of plastic blocks. ✉ *1 Lego Dr. (exit I–5 at Cannon Rd. and follow signs east ¼ mi),* ☎ *760/918–5346,* ⓦⓔⓑ *www.legolandca.com.* ✍ *$39; children $33.* ☉ *Mid-Sept.–mid-June, daily 10–5; mid-June–Labor Day, daily 9–9.*

In spring the hillsides are abloom at **Flower Fields at Carlsbad Ranch,** the largest bulb production farm in southern California, where you can walk through fields planted with thousands of ranunculus displayed against a backdrop of the blue Pacific Ocean. In 2001 a rose walk of fame was added, lined with examples of award-winning roses selected during the last half century, and a pair of demonstration gardens created by artists who normally work with paint and easels. The unusually large and well-stocked Armstrong Garden Center at the exit carries plants, garden accessories, and ranunculas bulbs. ✉ *5704 Paseo del Norte, east of I–5,* ☎ *760/431–0352,* ⓦⓔⓑ *www.theflowerfields.com.* ✍ *$5.* ☉ *Mar.–May, daily 10–6.*

★ ❸ **Mission San Luis Rey** was built by Franciscan friars in 1798 under the direction of Father Fermin Lasuen to help educate and convert local Native Americans. Once a location for filming Disney's *Zorro* TV series, the well-preserved mission is still owned by Franciscan friars. The San Luis Rey was the 18th and largest of California's missions. The *sala* (parlor), a friar's bedroom, a weaving room, the kitchen, and a collection of religious art convey much about early mission life. From the ocean, go east of I–5 on Route 76 then north on Rancho Del Oro Drive. ✉ *4050 Mission Ave., Oceanside,* ☎ *760/757–3651,* ⓦⓔⓑ *www.sanluisrey.org.* ✍ *$4.* ☉ *Daily 10–4:30.*

Dining and Lodging

$$$ ✗ **Bellefleur Restaurant.** This restaurant/winery at the north end of Carlsbad Company Stores serves specialties like mussels in broth with herbed rice, spinach ravioli with leek cream and scallops, veal chops, and single-portion pizzas. ✉ *5610 Paseo del Norte,* ☎ *760/603–1919. AE, D, DC, MC, V.*

$$$$ ✗▣ **Four Seasons Resort Aviara.** This hilltop resort sitting on 30 acres
★ overlooking Batiquitos Lagoon is one of the most luxurious in the San Diego area, with gleaming marble corridors, original artwork, crystal chandeliers, and enormous flower arrangements. Rooms, somewhat smaller than those in nearby resorts, have every possible amenity: oversize closets, private balconies or garden patios, and marble bath-

rooms with double vanities and deep soaking tubs. Vivace ($$–$$$) generates rave reviews for its innovative Italian cuisine. The Arnold Palmer–designed Aviara Golf Club is ranked among the top resort golf courses. ⊠ *7100 Four Seasons Point 92009,* ☎ *760/603–6800 or 800/332–3442,* FAX *760/603–6878,* WEB *www.fourseasons.com/aviara. 287 rooms, 44 suites. 4 restaurants, room service, in-room data ports, in-room safes, minibar, cable TV, 18-hole golf course, 6 tennis courts, 3 pools, health club, hair salon, massage, sauna, spa, steam room, bicycles, hiking, shops, baby-sitting, children's programs, laundry service, concierge, business services, meeting room, airport shuttle, car rental, some pets allowed (fee). AE, D, DC, MC, V.*

$$$$ ✕⊞ **La Costa Resort and Spa.** Don't expect glitz and glamour at this famous resort; it's surprisingly low-key, with low-slung buildings and vaguely Southwestern contemporary–style rooms. Rooms are large with opulent marble bathrooms; many have garden patios. There are two PGA championship golf courses and a golf school, plus a large tennis center. The spa provides nutritional counseling, and healthy cuisine is available in three restaurants. ⊠ *2100 Costa del Mar Rd. 92009,* ☎ *760/438–9111 or 800/854–5000,* FAX *760/931–7569,* WEB *www.lacosta.com. 397 rooms, 82 suites. 2 restaurants, bar, room service, in-room data ports, cable TV, driving range, 2 18-hole golf courses, 21 tennis courts, pro shop, 5 pools, health club, hair salon, hot tub, massage, sauna, steam room, spa, bicycles, croquet, hiking, shops, babysitting, children's programs (ages 5–12), laundry service, concierge, business services, meeting rooms, airport shuttle, car rental. AE, D, DC, MC, V.*

Escondido

8 mi north of Rancho Bernardo on I–15, 31 mi northeast of downtown San Diego on I–15.

Escondido is a thriving, rapidly expanding residential and commercial city of more than 120,000 people.

★ ☺ ❹ **San Diego Wild Animal Park** is an extension of the San Diego Zoo, a 35-minute drive south. The 1,800-acre preserve in the San Pasqual Valley is designed to protect endangered species of animals from around the world. Exhibit areas have been carved out of the dry, dusty canyons and mesas to represent the animals' natural habitats—North Africa, South Africa, East Africa, Heart of Africa, Australian Rain Forest, Asian Swamps, and Asian Plains.

The best way to see these preserves is on the 50-minute, 5-mi Wgasa Bushline Railway (included in the price of admission). The 1¼-mi-long **Kilimanjaro Safari Walk** winds through some of the park's hilliest terrain in the East Africa section, with observation decks overlooking the elephants and lions. A 70-ft suspension bridge spans a steep ravine, leading to the final observation point and a panorama of the entire park and the San Pasqual Valley. Along the trails of 32-acre **Heart of Africa** you can travel in the footsteps of an early explorer through forests and lowlands, across a floating bridge to a research station where an expert is on hand to answer questions; finally you arrive at Panorama Point where you capture an up-close-and-personal view of cheetahs, a chance to feed the giraffes, and a distant glimpse of the expansive savanna where rhinos, impalas, wildebeest, oryx, and beautiful migrating birds reside. The Wild Animal Park, which conducts captive breeding programs to save rare and endangered species, shows off one of its most successful efforts, the California Condor, at the **Condor Ridge** exhibit. The exhibit occupies nearly the highest point in the park. You can camp overnight in the park in summer on a Roar and Snore Campover

($105), take a Sunrise Safari in August, and celebrate the holidays during the annual Festival of Lights. Also in summer, the railway travels through the park after dark, and sodium-vapor lamps highlight the active animals. ✉ *15500 San Pasqual Valley Rd. Take I–15 north to Via Rancho Pkwy. and follow signs (6 mi),* ☎ *760/747–8702,* WEB *www.sandiegozoo.org/wap.* ✍ *$25.95, includes all shows and monorail tour; a $45 combination pass grants entry, within 5 days of purchase, to both the San Diego Zoo and the San Diego Wild Animal Park; parking $6. D, MC, V.* ☉ *Mid-June–Labor Day, daily 9–8; Mid-Sept.–mid-June, daily 9–4.*

Dining and Lodging

$$–$$$ ✕ **Vincent's Sirino's.** Try the grilled salmon with roasted garlic, the duck breast confit, or the rack of lamb; good homemade bread accompanies them. The wine list is serious, as are the desserts. ✉ *113 W. Grand Ave.,* ☎ *760/745–3835. AE, D, MC, V. Closed Sun.–Mon. No lunch Sat.*

$$ ⌂ **Welk Resort Center.** This resort sprawls over 600 acres of rugged, oak-studded hillside. Built by band leader Lawrence Welk in the 1960s, the resort includes a hotel, time-share condominiums, and a recreation and entertainment complex. A museum displays Welk memorabilia, a theater presents Broadway-style musicals year-round, and there are many shops on the premises. Hotel rooms, decorated with a Southwestern flair, have golf-course views. ✉ *8860 Lawrence Welk Dr. 92026,* ☎ *760/749–3000 or 800/932–9355,* FAX *760/749–6182,* WEB *www.welkresort.com. 137 rooms, 10 suites. In-room data ports, 3 restaurants, bar, grocery, cable TV, 6 pools, 7 hot tubs, 2 18-hole golf courses, 5 tennis courts, health club, shops, theater, children's programs, meeting room, travel services. AE, D, DC, MC, V.*

SAN DIEGO A TO Z

To research prices, get advice from other travelers, and book travel arrangements, visit www.fodors.com.

AIR TRAVEL

All major and some regional U.S. carriers serve San Diego International Airport. British Airways, Aero Mexico, and Air Canada are the only international carriers to San Diego. All others will require a connecting flight, usually in Los Angeles. Other connection points are Chicago, Dallas, and San Francisco. San Diego International Airport (SAN) is a five-minute drive from downtown. McClellan Palomar Airport serves North County. America West Express and United Express operate flights between here and Los Angeles International Airport. *See* Air Travel *in* Smart Travel Tips A to Z for airline phone numbers.

AIRPORTS AND TRANSFERS

➤ AIRPORT INFORMATION: **McClellan Palomar Airport** (✉ 2198 Palomar Airport Rd., Carlsbad, ☎ 760/431–4646).**San Diego International Airport** (☎ 619/231–2100, WEB www.portofsandiego.org).

➤ SHUTTLES AND BUSES: **Cloud 9 Shuttle** (☎ 800/974–8885 San Diego County, 858/974–8885 elsewhere, WEB www.cloud9shuttle.com).**San Diego Transit** (☎ 619/233–3004, WEB www.sdcommute.com).

BUS TRAVEL TO AND FROM SAN DIEGO

Greyhound operates 26 buses a day between San Diego and Los Angeles, connecting with buses to all major U.S. cities.

➤ BUS INFORMATION: **Greyhound** (✉ 120 W. Broadway, ☎ 619/239–8082 or 800/231–2222, WEB www.greyhound.com).

BUS AND TROLLEY TRAVEL WITHIN SAN DIEGO COUNTY

San Diego Transit buses connect with the San Diego Trolley light rail system and serve the cit, East County and North County from the Mexico border to Del Mar. The North County Transit District covers San Diego County from Del Mar north. Buses and trolleys run at about 15-minute intervals. Bus and trolley connections are posted at each station.

➤ BUS AND TROLLEY INFORMATION: **North County Transit District** (☎ 800/266–6883). **San Diego Transit** (☎ 619/233–3004; 619/234–5005 TTY/TDD, WEB www.sdcommute.com).

CAR RENTAL

All of the major car-rental companies have offices at San Diego International Airport. *See* Car Rental *in* Smart Travel Tips A to Z for national rental agency phone numbers.

CAR TRAVEL

Interstate 5 stretches from Canada to the Mexican border and bisects San Diego. Interstate 8 provides access from Yuma, Arizona, and points east. Drivers coming from Nevada and the mountain regions beyond can reach San Diego on I–15. Running parallel west of I–5 is Route S21, also known and sometime indicated as Highway 101, Old Highway 101, or Coast Highway 101, which never strays too far from the ocean.

EMERGENCIES

In case of emergency dial 911.

➤ HOSPITALS: **UCSD Medical Center–Hillcrest** (✉ 200 West Arbor Dr., ☎ 619/543–6222).

LODGING

San Diego Hotel Reservations is a free reservation service that can help you find a hotel anywhere in the county. San Diego Hotels specializes in discount rates at hotels in the city.

➤ RESERVATIONS: **San Diego Hotel Reservations** (☎ 800/728–3227, WEB www.sandiegohotelres.com). **San Diego Hotels** (☎ 800/311–5045, WEB www.san-diego-ca-hotels.com).

TOURS

BOAT TOURS

Three companies operate one- and two-hour harbor cruises. San Diego Harbor Excursion and Hornblower Invader Cruises boats depart from the Broadway Pier. No reservations are necessary for the $13–$18 voyages. Classic Sailing Adventures has morning, afternoon, and evening tours of the harbor and San Diego Bay for $60 per person. These companies also operate during whale-watching season from mid-December to mid-March.

➤ CONTACTS: **Classic Sailing Adventures** (✉ 1220 Rosecrans St. No. 137, ☎ 619/224–0800, WEB www.classicsailingadventures. com). **Hornblower Invader Cruises** (✉ 1066 N. Harbor Dr., ☎ 619/234–8687, WEB www.hornblower.com). **San Diego Harbor Excursion** (✉ 1050 N. Harbor Dr., ☎ 619/234–4111 or 800/442–7847, WEB www.harborexcursion.com).

BUS AND TROLLEY TOURS

Coach USA in San Diego runs a fleet of open-top, double-decker buses. For $25, you get an unlimited day pass that lets you hop on and off the bus at any of the stops. Old Town Trolley Historic Tours take you on narrated tours, and you can get on and off as you please at any stop, for $24. Grey Line San Diego offers a number of half- and full-day city tours. Rates are $25–$52, admissions to attractions included.

➤ FEES AND SCHEDULES: **Coach USA** (✉ 3500 Estudillo St., ☎ 619/527–4644, WEB www.sightseeingusa.com) **Gray Line Tours** (✉ 1775 Hancock St., No. 130, ☎ 619/491–0011; 800/331–5077 outside CA, WEB www.graylinesandiego.com). **Old Town Trolley** (✉ 2115 Kurtz St., ☎ 619/298–8687, WEB www.trolleytours.com).

TAXIS

You can generally hail a cab downtown, but in most cases you'll need to telephone for taxi service, and you might have to wait as much as an hour for your car to show up, depending on where you are. The Orange, Silver, and Yellow cab companies serve San Diego.

➤ TAXI COMPANY: **Orange Cab** (☎ 619/291–3333, WEB www.home. pacbell.net/orangesd). **Silver Cabs** (☎ 619/280–5555). **Yellow Cab** (☎ 619/234–6161, WEB www.driveu.com).

TRAIN TRAVEL

Amtrak serves downtown San Diego's Santa Fe Depot with daily trains to and from Los Angeles, Santa Barbara, and San Luis Obispo. Amtrak trains stop in San Diego North County at Solana Beach and Oceanside. The last train leaves San Diego at about 7 each night (9 on Friday; the last arrival is at about midnight).

Coaster commuter trains, which run between Oceanside and San Diego Monday–Saturday, stop at Del Mar, Solana Beach, Encinita, and Carlsbad.

➤ TRAIN INFORMATION: **Amtrak** (☎ 800/872–7245, WEB www.amtrak). **Coaster** (☎ 800/262–6883, WEB www.sdcommute.com). **Santa Fe Depot** (✉ 1050 Kettner Blvd., ☎ 619/239–9021).

VISITOR INFORMATION

➤ TOURIST INFORMATION: **Balboa Park Visitors Center** (✉ 1549 El Prado, ☎ 619/239–0512, WEB www.balboapark.org), open daily 9–4. **Carlsbad Convention and Visitors Bureau** (✉ 400 Carlsbad Village Dr., Carlsbad 92008, ☎ 760/434–6093 or 800/227–5722, WEB www.carlsbadca.org). **Coronado Visitor Center** (✉ 1100 Orange Ave., 92118, ☎ 619/437–8788, WEB www.coronadohistory.org/visitorcenter/). **Escondido Chamber of Commerce** (✉ 720 N. Broadway, Escondido 92025, ☎ 760/745–2125, WEB www.escondidochamber.org). **Greater Del Mar Chamber of Commerce** (✉ 1104 Camino del Mar, Del Mar 92014, ☎ 858/755–4844, WEB www.delmarchamber.org). **International Visitor Information Center** (✉ 11 Horton Plaza, at 1st Ave. and F St., ☎ 619/236–1212, WEB www.sandiego.org), open Monday–Saturday 8:30–5; June–Aug. and also Sun. 11–5 **San Diego Convention & Visitors Bureau** (✉ 401 B St., Suite 1400, San Diego, 92101, ✉ Herschel Ave. at Prospect St., ☎ 619/236–1212, WEB www.sandiego.org). **San Diego North Convention and Visitors Bureau** (✉ 360 N. Escondido Blvd., Escondido 92025, ☎ 760/745–4741). **San Diego Visitor Information Center** (✉ 2688 E. Mission Bay Dr., off I–5 at the Clairemont Dr. exit, ☎ 619/275–8259, WEB www. infosandiego.com/visitor), open daily 9–dusk.

17 PALM SPRINGS AND THE SOUTHERN CALIFORNIA DESERT

INCLUDING JOSHUA TREE NATIONAL PARK

Long known for their luxury resorts, championship golf courses, tennis stadiums, world-class shopping avenues, elegant spas, Palm Springs and the southern California desert hold natural as well as material treasures. Much of the desert remains a land of pristine beauty, tall mountain ranges, sheltering palms, and hot mineral springs. If you are looking for natural wonders and solitude, you need only travel to the wild desert to find them.

By Bobbi Zane

ONCE THE BOTTOM OF A VAST SEA, the desert of southern California is millions of years old. About 10 million years ago, the climate was hospitable to prehistoric mastodons, zebras, and camels. The Colorado River spilled into this basin intermittently as far back as 10,000 years ago, and Lake Cahuilla formed around 700 AD. The first human inhabitants of record in the area were members of the Agua Caliente band of Cahuilla Indians, who settled in and around the Coachella Valley (the northwestern portion of the Colorado Desert, between the San Jacinto and Little San Bernardino mountain ranges) about 1,000 years ago. Lake Cahuilla dried up about 300 years ago, but by then the Agua Caliente had discovered the hot springs and were making use of their healing properties during winter visits to the desert. The springs became a tourist attraction in 1871, when the tribe built a bathhouse (on a site near the current Spa Hotel in Palm Springs) to serve passengers on a pioneer stage highway. The Agua Caliente still own about 32,000 acres of desert, 6,700 of which lie within the city limits of Palm Springs.

In the last half of the 19th century farmers established a date-growing industry at the southern end of the Coachella Valley. By 1900 word had spread about the manifold health benefits of the area's dry climate, inspiring the gentry of the northern United States to come there to winter under the warm desert sun. Southeast of the Coachella, farmers began turning the barren Imperial Valley—home of the broad, brackish Salton Sea—into rich fields of tomatoes, corn, and grain in the mid-1900s. Until the 1970s, the Anza-Borrego Desert, which stretches from the southern end of the Coachella Valley nearly to the Mexican border, was a mostly unpopulated desert outpost occupied by a few hardy homesteaders and visited in winter by a few adventurous campers. Growth hit the Coachella Valley in the 1970s, when developers began to construct the world-class golf courses, country clubs, and residential communities that would draw celebrities, tycoons, and politicians. Communities sprang up south and east of Palm Springs, creating a sprawl of tract houses and strip malls and forcing nature lovers to push farther south into the sparsely settled Anza-Borrego Desert and the Imperial Valley.

Pleasures and Pastimes

Desert Wildlife

The southern California desert is a land of fascinating geology and wildlife. Explore the terrain at ground level at the Living Desert Zoo and Gardens. Other great places to learn about the natural history of the desert are the Palm Springs Desert Museum, Indian Canyons, Joshua Tree National Park, Anza-Borrego Desert, and along the shores of the Salton Sea.

Dining

Long a culinary wasteland, the desert now supports many trendy if not overly ambitious restaurants. Italian cuisine remains popular, but you can now dine at restaurants that serve fare that ranges from Thai to Indian, from seafood to vegetarian, and from classic French to contemporary Californian. You can find Mexican fare everywhere; in the smaller communities it may be your best choice. Dining throughout the region is casual. Many restaurants that were traditionally closed in summer are now opening on a limited basis: hours vary, so call in advance in the off season.

CATEGORY	COST*
$$$$	over $30
$$$	$22–$30
$$	$15–$21
$	under $15

per person for a main course at dinner, excluding tip and 7½% tax

Lodging

You can stay in the desert for as little as $40 or spend more than $1,000 a night. Rates vary widely by season: from low in summer to high in winter. January through April prices soar, and accommodations can be difficult to secure, so reserve as far ahead as you can. In any season it pays to inquire about hotel and resort packages that include extras such as golf or spa services. Discounts are sometimes given for extended stays. Hotel prices are frequently 50% less in summer than in winter and early spring. Year-round, budget lodgings are most easily found in Palm Springs and in the less glamorous towns of Cathedral City, Indio, Borrego Springs, El Centro, and in the Morongo Valley towns along Twentynine Palms Highway.

CATEGORY	COST*
$$$$	over $225
$$$	$160–$225
$$	$100–$159
$	under $100

All prices are for a standard double room, excluding 9%–11% tax.

Nightlife and the Arts

Nightlife is concentrated—and abundant—in the resort communities near Palm Springs. Options include a good jazz bar, a clutch of retro shows and glamour clubs, several dance clubs, and hotel entertainment. The *Fabulous Palm Springs Follies*—a vaudeville-style revue starring retired professional performers—is a must-see for most visitors. Arts festivals occur on a regular basis, especially during the winter and spring. The "Desert Guide" section of *Palm Springs Life* magazine (available at most hotels and visitor information centers) has nightlife listings, as does the "Weekender" pullout in the Friday edition of the *Desert Sun* newspaper. The gay scene is covered in the *Bottom Line* and in the *Gay Guide to Palm Springs*, published by the Desert Gay Tourism Guild.

Outdoor Activities and Sports

The Palm Springs area has an even 100 golf courses, many of which are familiar to golfing fans as the sites of championship and celebrity tournaments regularly seen on television. You can tee off where the pros play at PGA West, Mission Hills North, and La Quinta, all of which have instructors ready to help you finesse your swing. Even Borrego Springs and El Centro have golf courses.

The desert also holds a world of athletic opportunities for nongolfers. With almost 30,000 public and private pools in the region, swimming and sunning are a daily ritual. More than 35 mi of bike trails crisscross the mostly flat Palm Springs area alone. Indian Canyons, Mount San Jacinto State Park and Wilderness, Living Desert Zoo and Gardens, Joshua Tree National Park, Anza-Borrego Desert, and Big Morongo Canyon Preserve have scenic hiking trails. The Salton Sea attracts many migratory birds, especially in winter. Some of the best rock-climbing Highways in the world can be found in Joshua Tree National Park.

Whatever your sport, avoid outdoor activities midday during the hot season (roughly May through October). Any time of the year take precautions against the sun, such as wearing a hat and using sunscreen. Always drink plenty of water—at least a gallon of water per day (more if you are exercising)—to prevent dehydration.

Shopping

World-class designer boutiques, antiques shops, art galleries, vintage resale palaces, and a huge upmarket discount mall lure dedicated shoppers to the desert. Popular shopping venues include the Thursday-night Palm Springs Village Fest; El Paseo, in Palm Desert; Desert Hills Factory Stores, in Cabazon; and the consignment and resale shops in many desert communities.

Exploring the Southern California Desert

The desert resort cities of the Coachella Valley—Palm Springs, Cathedral City, Rancho Mirage, Palm Desert, Indian Wells, La Quinta, and Indio—are strung out along Highway 111, with Palm Springs at the northwestern end of this strip and Indio at the southeastern end. North of Palm Springs, between I–10 and Highway 62, is Desert Hot Springs. The towns of the Morongo Valley lie along Twentynine Palms Highway (Highway 62) northeast of Palm Springs, which leads to Joshua Tree National Park. Head south on Highway 86 from Indio to reach Anza Borrego State Park and the Salton Sea. All of the area's attractions are easy day trips from Palm Springs.

Numbers in the text correspond to numbers in the margin and on the Palm Springs and Southern California Desert maps.

Great Itineraries

IF YOU HAVE 1 DAY

If you've just slipped into the desert for a day, focus your activities around **Palm Springs.** Get an early morning scenic overview by taking the **Palm Springs Aerial Tramway** ① to the top of Mt. San Jacinto. In the afternoon head for **Palm Canyon Drive,** in Palm Springs, where you can have lunch alfresco at the Blue Coyote Grill and drop by the **Showbiz Museum** ⑤, at the Plaza Theater, to pick up tickets for an evening performance of the **Fabulous Palm Springs Follies** (better still, make reservations before your visit). In the afternoon visit **Palm Desert** ⑭, the trendiest of the desert cities, for a walk through the canyons and hillsides of the **Living Desert Zoo and Gardens** and a preshow dinner at a restaurant on **El Paseo.**

IF YOU HAVE 3 DAYS

🖬 **Palm Springs** ①–⑪ makes a good base for exploring the area. On your first day head to the **Palm Springs Aerial Tramway** ① in the morning and have lunch on **Palm Canyon Drive.** Spend the afternoon browsing through the Palm Canyon shops or (unless it's the height of the summer) hiking through the **Indian Canyons** ⑪. On day two take an early morning drive to **Joshua Tree National Park** ㉑, where you can explore the terrain, crawl through the entrance to Hidden Valley, and stop by the Oasis of Mara visitor center. Have a picnic lunch in the park or head back to **El Paseo,** in **Palm Desert** ⑭, for a midafternoon bite before exploring the chic shopping area. On the third morning take in the **Palm Springs Desert Museum** ④, where you can learn about the natural history of the desert and see some great art. In the afternoon pamper yourself at one of the spas for which Palm Springs is famous. Then have dinner and take in a performance of the **Fabulous Palm Springs Follies.**

If you have five days to spend in the desert, you'll have time to explore beyond the immediate ⌂ **Palm Springs** ①–⑪ area. On your first day take in a sweeping view of the Coachella Valley from the top of the **Palm Springs Aerial Tramway** ① in the morning and **Palm Canyon Drive** in the afternoon. On the second morning visit the **Palm Springs Desert Museum** ④, then grab a picnic lunch and head out to **Indian Canyons** ⑪, where you can dine by a waterfall. By evening you'll be ready to live it up at one of the desert's nightspots. Spend days three and four at **Joshua Tree National Park** ㉑. You can camp in the park or stay at a B&B in ⌂ **Twentynine Palms** ⑳, just outside the park. In the evening take an hour to gaze at the stars. On day five get an early start and complete your drive through the park so you can arrive back in the Palm Springs area for lunch. Check into a spa for the afternoon, and catch the **Fabulous Palm Springs Follies** on your last night.

Alternatively, you can spend days three and four in quiet ⌂ **Borrego Springs** ㉓, exploring the wonders of **Anza-Borrego Desert State Park** ㉒ and the **Salton Sea** ㉔. On the fifth morning drive to **Palm Desert** ⑭ to visit the **Living Desert Zoo and Gardens,** have lunch on **El Paseo,** do some shopping, and head back to your hotel for one last dip in the pool.

When to Tour the Desert

Because Palm Springs and the surrounding desert average 350 sunny days a year, you are almost assured a chance to get in a round or two of golf or some lounging around the pool whenever you visit. During the season (January–April), as everybody calls it, the desert weather is at its best, with daytime temperatures ranging between 70°F and 90°F. This is the time when you're most likely to see colorful displays of wildflowers and when most of the golf and tennis tournaments take place. The fall months are nearly as lovely, with the added bonus of being less crowded and less expensive. During summer daytime temperatures rise to 110°F or higher, though evenings cool to the mid-70s. Some attractions and restaurants, particularly those in the Borrego Springs area, close during this period.

THE DESERT RESORTS
Including Palm Springs

Around the desert resorts, privacy is the watchword. Celebrities flock to the desert from Los Angeles, and many communities are walled and guarded. Still, you might spot Hollywood stars, sports personalities, politicians, and other high-profile types in restaurants, out on the town, or on a golf course. For the most part the desert's social, sports, shopping, and entertainment scenes center around Palm Springs and Palm Desert.

Palm Springs

90 mi southeast of Los Angeles on I–10.

A tourist destination since the late 19th century, Palm Springs caught Hollywood's eye by the time of the Great Depression. It was an ideal hideaway: celebrities could slip into town, play a few sets of tennis, lounge around the pool, attend a party or two, and, unless things got out of hand, remain safely beyond the reach of gossip columnists. But it took a pair of tennis-playing celebrities to put Palm Springs on the map. In the 1930s actors Charlie Farrell and Ralph Bellamy bought 200 acres of land for $30 an acre and opened the Palm Springs Rac-

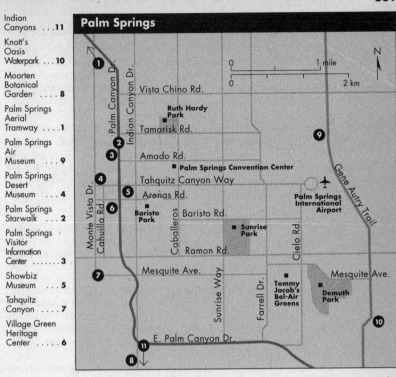

quet Club, which soon listed Ginger Rogers, Humphrey Bogart, and Clark Gable among its members.

The city of Palm Springs lost some of its luster in the 1970s as the wealthy moved on to newer down-valley communities. But Palm Springs reinvented itself, building on its history as a hideaway for Hollywood celebrities and cultivating a welcoming atmosphere for well-heeled gay visitors. You'll find reminders of the city's glamorous past in architecture, renovated hotels, restaurants, and shops. Formerly exclusive Palm Canyon Drive is now a lively avenue with coffeehouses, outdoor cafés and bars, and frequent special events.

Note: Ramon Road marks the division between north and south on major streets (e.g., North and South Palm Canyon Drive).

★ ☚ ➊ A trip on the **Palm Springs Aerial Tramway** provides a stunning 360-degree view of the desert through the picture windows of Rotair rotating tram cars. The 2½-mi ascent, the steepest vertical cable ride in the United States, brings you to an elevation of 8,516 ft in less than 20 minutes. On clear days, which are common, the view stretches 75 mi—from the peak of Mt. San Gorgonio, in the north, to the Salton Sea, in the southeast. At the top, a bit below the summit of Mt. San Jacinto, you'll find several diversions. Mountain Station has an observation deck, a restaurant, a cocktail lounge, apparel and gift shops, a theater that screens a 22-minute film on the history of the tramway, and picnic facilities. Ride-and-dine packages are available in late afternoon. The tram is a popular attraction, so lines can be long. ⊠ *1 Tramway Rd.,* ☎ *760/325–1440 or 888/515–8726,* WEB *www. pstramway.com.* ⊡ *$20.80; ride-and-dine package $27.80.* ☉ *Tram cars depart at least every 30 mins from 10 AM weekdays and 8 AM weekends; last car up leaves at 8 PM, last one down leaves Mountain Station at 9:45 PM.*

OFF THE
BEATEN PATH

MOUNT SAN JACINTO WILDERNESS STATE PARK, accessible only by hiking or via the Palm Springs Aerial Tramway, has camping and picnic areas and 54 mi of hiking trails. You can take guided wilderness mule rides during snow-free months. In winter the Nordic Ski Center rents cross-country ski equipment. You must get a free permit before coming for day or overnight wilderness hiking. ⊠ *Mountain Station,* ☎ *909/659–2607,* WEB *www.sanjac.statepark.org.* ☜ *Free.*

② A stroll down North and South Palm Canyon Drive, which is lined with shops, will take you past the **Palm Springs Starwalk,** whose nearly 200 bronze stars are embedded in the sidewalk (à la the Hollywood Walk of Fame). Most of the names you'll recognize (such as Elvis Presley, Marilyn Monroe, Lauren Bacall, and Liberace) have a Palm Springs connection; others are local celebs. ⊠ *Palm Canyon Dr. at Tahquitz Canyon Way.*

③ Stop at the **Palm Springs Visitor Information Center** for information on sights to see and things to do in the Palm Springs area. ⊠ *333 N. Palm Canyon Dr.,* ☎ *760/778–8415 or 800/347–7746,* WEB *www.palm-springs.org.* ☉ *Daily 10–6.*

★ ④ The exhibits at the **Palm Springs Desert Museum** span natural science, the visual arts, and the performing arts. The display on the natural history of the desert is itself worth a visit, and the grounds hold several striking sculpture courts. A modern-art gallery has works by artists such as Alberto Giacometti, Henry Moore, and Helen Frankenthaler. Of interest to movie fans might be the exhibits of the late actor William Holden's art collection and furniture designed and crafted by the late actor George Montgomery. The Annenberg Theater presents plays, concerts, lectures, operas, and other cultural events. ⊠ *101 Museum Dr.,* ☎ *760/325–7186,* WEB *www.psmuseum.org.* ☜ *$7.50; free 1st Fri. of month.* ☉ *Tues.–Sat. 10–5, Sun. noon–5.*

⑥ Three small museums at the **Village Green Heritage Center** illustrate pioneer life in Palm Springs. The **Agua Caliente Cultural Museum** (free) is devoted to the culture and history of the Cahuilla tribe. The **McCallum Adobe** ($2) holds the collection of the Palm Springs Historical Society. **Rudy's General Store Museum** (50¢) is a re-creation of a general store from the 1930s. ⊠ *221 S. Palm Canyon Dr.,* ☎ *760/327–2156.* ☉ *Hours vary; call ahead.*

⑦ Ranger-led tours of **Tahquitz Canyon** take you into a secluded, long-closed, and culturally sensitive canyon on the Agua Caliente Indian Reservation. Within the canyon are a spectacular 60-ft waterfall, rock art, ancient irrigation systems, native wildlife, and plants. A visitor center at the entrance to the canyon shows a video tour, displays artifacts, and sells maps. ⊠ *500 W. Mesquite,* ☎ *760/416–7044* WEB *www.indian-canyons.com.* ☜ *$12.50.* ☉ *Daily 7:30–5.*

⑧ Four-acre **Moorten Botanical Garden** nurtures more than 3,000 plant varieties in settings that simulate their original environments. Native American artifacts, rock, and crystal are exhibited. ⊠ *1701 S. Palm Canyon Dr.,* ☎ *760/327–6555.* ☜ *$2.50.* ☉ *Mon.–Sat. 9–4:30, Sun. 10–4.*

⑨ **Palm Springs Air Museum** showcases several dozen World War II aircraft, including a B-17 Flying Fortress bomber, a P-51 Mustang, a Lockheed P-38, and a Grumman TBF Avenger. ⊠ *745 N. Gene Autry Trail,* ☎ *760/778–6262,* WEB *www.air-museum.org.* ☜ *$8.* ☉ *Daily 10–5.*

☾ ⑩ For a break from the desert heat, head for **Knotts Soak City.** You'll find 13 water slides, a huge wave pool, an arcade, and other fun family attractions. ⊠ *1500 Gene Autry Trail,* ☎ *760/327–0499,* WEB *www. knotts.com.* ⊠ *$21.95.* ⊙ *Mid–Mar.–Labor Day, daily; Labor Day– Oct., weekends; weekdays 10–5, weekends 10–6.*

👆 ⑪ The **Indian Canyons** are the ancestral home of the Agua Caliente Band of Cahuilla Indians. You can see remnants of their ancient life: rock art, house pits and foundations, irrigation ditches, bedrock mortars, pictographs, and stone houses and shelters built atop high cliff walls. Four areas are open: Palm Canyon, noted for its stand of Washingtonia palms; Murray Canyon, home of Peninsula bighorn sheep and a herd of wild ponies; Andreas Canyon, where a stand of fan palms contrasts with sharp rock formations; and Tahquitz Canyon (☞ *above*). The trading post in Palm Canyon has hiking maps, refreshments, and Indian art, jewelry, and weavings. ⊠ *38–500 S. Palm Canyon Dr.,* ☎ *800/790–3398,* WEB *www.indian-canyons.com.* ⊠ *$6.* ⊙ *Daily 8–6.*

Dining and Lodging

$$$–$$$$
★
✕ **Le Vallauris.** In a tasteful old home with a beautiful garden, Le Vallauris serves California-accented French cuisine—dishes such as grilled veal chop with apples and Calvados and a grilled halibut with sun-dried-tomato crust and a lemon sauce. A pianist plays nightly. Sunday brunch is a hit. ⊠ *385 W. Tahquitz Canyon Way,* ☎ *760/325–5059. Reservations essential. AE, D, DC, MC, V. No lunch Wed.–Sat. in July–Aug.*

$$–$$$$
✕ **Otani Garden Restaurant.** Sushi, tempura, and *teppan* (grilled) specialties are served in a serene garden. A fresh Sunday brunch buffet includes tempura, stir-fried entrées, salads, and desserts. ⊠ *266 Avenida Caballeros,* ☎ *760/327–6700. AE, D, DC, MC, V. No lunch Sat.*

$$–$$$$
✕ **St. James at the Vineyard.** A multihue interior, an outdoor terrace with street views, and a bubbling modern fountain set a playful mood at this hot spot for dining and sipping cocktails. The eclectic menu roams the world: Colorado lamb chops, Saigon spring rolls, New Zealand green mussels, and penne *al* Bolognese. Some vegetarian items are also available. The service can be mildly chaotic on weekend nights in high season. ⊠ *265 S. Palm Canyon Dr.,* ☎ *760/320–8041. Reservations essential. AE, D, DC, MC, V. No lunch.*

$–$$$
★
✕ **Palmie.** The humble location in the back of a shopping arcade and the simple decor of Toulouse-Lautrec and other Gallic posters give nary a hint of the subtle creations prepared at this gem of a French restaurant. The two-cheese soufflé is one of several mouthwatering appetizers. Equally impressive are the duck confit and duck fillets entrée served with pear slices in red wine, and Palmie's signature dish, a perfectly crafted fish stew in a thin yet rich butter-cream broth. ⊠ *Galeria Henry Frank, 276 N. Palm Canyon Dr.,* ☎ *760/320–3375. AE, DC, MC, V. No lunch. Closed Aug.–mid-Sept.*

$–$$
★
✕ **Blue Coyote Grill.** Diners munch on burritos, tacos, and fajitas (or more unusual items, such as Yucatán lamb or orange chicken) at this casual restaurant. Choose between several flower-decked patios and indoor dining rooms. Two busy cantinas serve up tasty margaritas to a youngish crowd. ⊠ *445 N. Palm Canyon Dr.,* ☎ *760/327–1196. AE, DC, MC, V.*

$–$$
✕ **Thai Kitchen II.** This tidy corner storefront restaurant with attentive service serves up large portions of popular Thai items, including *pad thai,* crab cake, tamarind duck, and many curries. ⊠ *787 N. Palm Canyon Dr.,* ☎ *760/323–4527. AE, D, MC, V.*

$
✕ **Capra's.** Even if you're not hungry, this is the place to see a real Oscar; it's one presented to famed director Frank Capra, who made films such as *It's a Wonderful Life* and *You Can't Take It with You.* Capra's son runs this café filled with Hollywood memorabilia, including original movie posters and lobby cards, as well as awards. The menu lists sandwiches, soups and salads, chicken, pasta, veal, and a Capra original

called "spaghetti pie." ✉ *204 N. Palm Canyon Dr.,* ☎ *760/325–7030. MC, V. Closed Tues.*

$ ✕ **Edgardo's Cafe Veracruz.** For a sampling of Mayan and Aztec flavors, try some of the unique items on Edgardo's menu, such as soup made with *nopales* (cactus) and roast pork wrapped in banana leaves. The menu also has more familiar items, such as tamales and enchiladas. ✉ *494 N. Palm Canyon Dr.,* ☎ *760/320–3558. Reservations essential. AE, D, DC, MC, V.*

$–$$$ ✕🖾 **Ingleside Inn.** This hacienda-style inn attracts its share of Hollywood personalities, who appreciate the attentive service and relative seclusion. Many rooms have antiques, fireplaces, whirlpool tubs, stocked refrigerators, and private patios. The accommodations in the main building are dark and cool, even in summer. Melvyn's Restaurant at the Ingleside is one of the desert's best-known celebrity haunts. ✉ *200 W. Ramon Rd., 92264,* ☎ *760/325–0046 or 800/772–6655,* FAX *760/325–0710,* WEB *www.inglesideinn.com. 30 rooms. Restaurant, bar, refrigerators (some), pool, outdoor hot tub, concierge. AE, D, DC, MC, V. CP.*

$$$$ 🖾 **Palm Springs Hilton Resort and Racquet Club.** This venerable hotel across the street from the tented Spa Casino has aged gracefully. Rooms, decorated in soft desert colors, are fairly spacious but rather spare. All have private balconies or patios, some overlooking the hotel's lushly landscaped pool area. ✉ *400 E. Tahquitz Canyon Way, 92262,* ☎ *760/320–6868 or 800/522–6900,* FAX *760/320–2126,* WEB *www.hiltonpalmsprings.com. 260 rooms, 71 suites. Restaurant, 2 bars, golf privileges, 6 tennis courts, pool, health club, 2 outdoor hot tubs, children's programs (ages 4–16), concierge, business services, airport shuttle. AE, D, DC, MC, V.*

$$$$ 🖾 **Sundance Villas.** The two- and three-bedroom duplex homes in this complex have full kitchens, bathrooms with huge sunken tubs, outdoor pools and hot tubs, and laundry facilities. The villas are away from most desert attractions, in a secluded residential area at the north end of town. Rates, though high, cover up to six people. ✉ *303 W. Cabrillo Rd., 92262,* ☎ *760/325–3888 or 800/455–3888,* FAX *760/323–3029,* WEB *www.palmsprings.com. 19 villas. In-room VCRs, golf privileges, tennis court, pool, concierge. AE, D, DC, MC, V.*

$$$$ 🖾 **Willows Historic Palm Springs Inn.** This luxurious hillside B&B is within
★   walking distance of many village attractions. An opulent Mediterranean-style mansion built in the 1920s, it has natural hardwood and slate floors, stone fireplaces, fresco ceilings, hand-painted tiles, iron balconies, antiques throughout, and a 50-ft waterfall that splashes into a pool outside the dining room. There's even a private hillside garden planted with native flora, which affords one of the best views in the area. Guest rooms are decorated to recall the movies of Hollywood's golden era. ✉ *412 W. Tahquitz Canyon Way 92262,* ☎ *760/320–0771 or 800/966–9597,* FAX *760/320–0780,* WEB *www.thewillowspalmsprings.com. 8 rooms. Pool, outdoor hot tub. AE, D, DC, MC, V. BP.*

$$$–$$$$ 🖾 **Merv Griffin's Resort Hotel and Givenchy Spa.** Indulgence is the word
★   at this resort modeled after the Givenchy spa in Versailles. The mood is totally French, from the Empire-style rooms to the perfectly manicured rose gardens. Many rooms are one- or two-bedroom suites with separate salons, some with private patios and mountain or garden views. Personalized spa services include everything from facials to mud wraps to aromatherapy. The restaurants offer typical French fare as well as more heart-healthy options. ✉ *4200 E. Palm Canyon Dr., 92264,* ☎ *760/770–5000 or 800/276–5000,* FAX *760/324–6104,* WEB *www.merv.com. 63 rooms, 41 suites. 2 restaurants, golf privileges, 6 tennis courts, 4 pools, hair salon, health club, spa, croquet, concierge, business services, meeting room. AE, D, DC, MC, V.*

$$$–$$$$ 🗗 **Wyndham Palm Springs.** The main appeal of this hotel is its location adjacent to the Palm Springs Convention Center. The terra-cotta Spanish colonial–style building surrounds the largest swimming pool in Palm Springs. Because most customers are here on business, the vibe is more serious than at most other desert establishments. ⊠ *888 Tahquitz Canyon Way, 92262,* ☎ *760/322–6000 or 800/822–4200,* FAX *760/322–5351,* WEB *www.wyndham.com. 252 rooms, 158 suites. Restaurant, 2 bars, golf privileges, pool, wading pool, gym, hair salon, 2 outdoor hot tubs, sauna, business services, meeting room. AE, D, MC, V.*

$$–$$$$ 🗗 **Ballantine's Hotel.** Once known as the Mira Loma Hotel, this small property hosted Marilyn Monroe and Gloria Swanson in the late 1940s, when Monroe was still undiscovered and Swanson a big star. Both reportedly met lovers here, out of sight of gossip columnists. By the 1960s the glamour had disappeared and the hotel faded. Now renovation has recaptured the essence of the 1940s and 1950s, with furnishings by Eames, Biller, Bertoia, and Knoll. It's all quite retro—and a bit synthetic—with rotary dial phones, period appliances in kitchenettes, and a collection of classic films for your VCR. Amenities include private sunbathing patios and complimentary Continental breakfast. ⊠ *1420 N. Indian Canyon Dr. 92262,* ☎ *760/320–1178 or 800/780–3464,* FAX *760/320–5308,* WEB *www.palmsprings.com/ballantines. 14 rooms. Bar, kitchenettes, in-room VCRs, pool, dry cleaning, laundry service, concierge, business services. AE, MC, V. CP.*

$$–$$$$ 🗗 **Casitas Laquita.** A collection of Spanish-style bungalows occupying just over an acre, this small lodging caters to gay women. Rooms, decorated with a southwestern theme, have handcrafted furnishings; many have fireplaces. The innkeepers regularly host informal social activities. ⊠ *450 E. Palm Canyon Dr., 92264,* ☎ *760/416–9999 or 877/203–3410,* FAX *760/416–5415,* WEB *www.casitaslaquita.com. 12 rooms. Kitchenettes, pool. MC, V.*

$$$ 🗗 **Spa Hotel and Casino.** Rooms at this hotel, built over the original Agua Caliente springs, are infused with soft pinks and blues and filled with light-wood furniture. The hotel, owned by the Agua Caliente band of the Cahuilla tribe, appeals to an older crowd that appreciates its soothing waters and downtown location. The hotel's Spa Experience is a sampling of services that allows you to sink into a tub filled with naturally hot mineral water, rest in the cool white relaxation room, swim in the outdoor mineral pool, or let the sauna warm your spirits. ⊠ *100 N. Indian Canyon Dr., 92262,* ☎ *760/325–1461 or 800/854–1279,* FAX *760/325–3344,* WEB *www.sparesortcasino.com. 220 rooms, 10 suites. 2 restaurants, 2 bars, 18-hole golf course, pool, hair salon, 2 outdoor hot tubs, spa, steam room, casino, concierge, meeting room. AE, D, MC, V.*

$$–$$$ 🗗 **Harlow Hotel.** A resort that caters to gay men, this place is ideal for those seeking secluded accommodations in lush garden surroundings. Rooms in hacienda-style buildings surround a pool; many have fireplaces, private patios, and unusually large bathrooms. Crimson bougainvillea cascades from the rooftops, and date palms grow on the property, as do orange, tangerine, and grapefruit trees. There's a secluded clothing-optional sunbathing area. The room rates include breakfast and lunch. ⊠ *175 E. El Alameda, 92262,* ☎ *760/323–3977 or 888/547–7881,* FAX *760/320–1218,* WEB *www.harlowhotel.com. 15 rooms, 1 suite. Pool, gym, outdoor hot tub. AE, D, DC, MC, V. MAP.*

$$–$$$ 🗗 **Hyatt Regency Suites.** An enormous metal sculpture suspended from the ceiling dominates this hotel's six-story asymmetrical atrium lobby. One- and two-bedroom suites have private balconies and two TVs. The suites in the back have views of the pool and mountains. There's free underground parking, and you have golf privileges at Rancho Mirage Country Club and four other area courses. ⊠ *285 N. Palm Canyon Dr., 92262,* ☎ *760/322–9000 or 800/554–9277,* FAX *760/ 416–6588,* WEB *www.palmsprings.hyatt.com. 192 suites. 2 restaurants, snack bar, bar, golf privileges, pool, gym, hair salon, outdoor hot tub, spa, dry cleaning, laundry service, baby-sitting, concierge, business services, meeting room, airport shuttle. AE, D, DC, MC, V.*

$–$$$ 🖫 **Villa Royale Inn.** Now sparkling after a long period of neglect, this refurbished Mediterranean-style inn once again has lavish gardens. There are private entrances, secluded patios with gentle fountains, and courtyards filled with citrus trees, jasmine, and lavender. Rooms are appointed with European antiques and amenities. One- and two-room suites are large enough for an extended stay. Many of the suites have fireplaces, private outdoor patios, and fully equipped kitchens. ⊠ *1620 Indian Trail, 92264,* ☎ *760/327–2314 or 800/245–2314,* FAX *760/322–3794,* WEB *www.villaroyale.com. 24 rooms, 7 suites. Restaurant, bar, kitchens (some), 2 pools, outdoor hot tub, dry cleaning, laundry service. AE, D, DC, MC, V.*

$$ 🖫 **Park Inn.** This chain motel at the north end of Palm Springs offers views of Mt. San Jacinto. Appointments are basic, but there are barbecues for guest use. ⊠ *200 N. Palm Canyon Dr., 92262,* ☎ *760/320– 0555 or 800/732–7755,* FAX *760/320–2261,* WEB *www.parkinn.com. 93 rooms. Pool, outdoor hot tub, meeting room. AE, D, DC, MC, V. CP.*

$$ 🖫 **Santiago Resort.** This classy clothing-optional resort caters to gay men. Spacious rooms are stylishly decorated. An expansive pool area is surrounded by colorful tropical gardens. Rates include breakfast and lunch. ⊠ *650 San Lorenzo Rd., 92264,* ☎ *760/322–1300 or 800/710–7729,* FAX *760/416–0347,* WEB *www.santiagoresort.com. 23 rooms. Microwaves, refrigerators, pool, outdoor hot tub, sauna. AE, D, MC, V. MAP.*

$–$$ 🖫 **Casa Cody.** The service is personal and gracious at this large, western-style B&B a few steps from the Palm Springs Desert Museum. Spacious studios and one- and two-bedroom suites are furnished simply. Some have fireplaces, and most have kitchens. The homey rooms are situated in three buildings surrounding courtyards lushly landscaped with bougainvillea and citrus. There are also two historic adobe cottages, one of which was the desert home of opera singer Lawrence Tibbett. ⊠ *175 S. Cahuilla Rd., 92262,* ☎ *760/320–9346 or 800/231– 2639,* FAX *760/325–8610,* WEB *www.palm-springs.com/hotels/casacody. 14 rooms, 7 suites, 2 cottages. 2 pools, outdoor hot tub. AE, D, DC, MC, V. CP.*

$–$$ 🖫 **Inn Exile.** One of a cluster of a dozen motel-style accommodations near Warm Sands Drive that cater to gay men, the Inn Exile has attractive rooms decorated in southwestern motifs. The entire complex is clothing-optional. Ask for a room facing the main pool. ⊠ *545 Warm Sands Dr. 92264,* ☎ *760/327–6413 or 800/962–0182,* FAX *760/320– 5745,* WEB *www.innexile.com. 31 rooms. In-room VCRs, 4 pools, health club, 2 hot tubs, steam room, billiards. AE, D, DC, MC, V.*

$ 🖫 **Howard Johnson Lodge.** This typical Hojo motel is popular with tour groups. Set in a garden, the rooms are functional; some have private patios. Ask about special discounts. ⊠ *701 E. Palm Canyon Dr., 92264,* ☎ *760/320–2700 or 800/854–4345,* FAX *760/322–5354,* WEB *www.hojopalmsprings.com. 202 rooms, 1 suite. Refrigerators (some), pool, 3 outdoor hot tubs, laundry facilities, business services. AE, D, DC, MC, V.*

$ 🖫 **Vagabond Inn.** Rooms are smallish at this centrally located motel, but they're clean, comfortable, and a good value. ⊠ *1699 S. Palm Canyon Dr., 92264,* ☎ *760/325–7211 or 800/522–1555,* FAX *760/ 322–9269,* WEB *www.vagabondinns.com. 117 rooms, 3 suites. Coffee shop, pool, outdoor hot tub, 2 saunas. AE, D, DC, MC, V.*

Nightlife and the Arts

BARS AND CLUBS

Blue Guitar (⊠ 120 S. Palm Canyon Dr., ☎ 760/327–1549), owned by jazz artists Kal David and Lauri Bono, presents world-class jazz and blues. There are two shows nightly Friday and Saturday. **Hair of the Dog English Pub** (⊠ 238 N. Palm Canyon Dr., ☎ 760/323–9890) is a friendly bar popular with a young crowd that likes to tip back English ales and ciders. **Muriel's Supper Club** (⊠ 210 N. Palm Canyon Dr., ☎ 760/325–8839) is a sophisticated supper club with music, some name bands, and dancing. **Zelda's** (⊠ 169 N. Indian Canyon Dr., ☎ 760/325–2375) has two rooms, one featuring Latin sounds and another with Top 40 dance music and a male dance revue.

CASINOS

Casino Morongo (⊠ Cabazon off-ramp, I–10, ☎ 909/849–3080) is about 20 minutes west of Palm Springs. **Spa Resort Casino** (⊠ 140 N. Indian Canyon Dr., ☎ 800/258–2946) is in the middle of downtown.

GAY AND LESBIAN EVENTS

In late March, when the world's finest women golfers hit the links for the Annual Nabisco Championship in Rancho Mirage, thousands of gay women converge on Palm Springs for a four-day party popularly known as **Dinah Shore Weekend** (☎ 888/443–4624). The **White Party** (☎ 888/777–8886), held on Easter weekend, draws tens of thousands of gay men from around the country to the Palm Springs area for a round of parties and gala events.

THEATER

At the Palm Springs Desert Museum, the **Annenberg Theater** (⊠ 101 Museum Dr., ☎ 760/325–4490, WEB www.psmuseum.org) hosts Broadway shows, opera, lectures, Sunday-afternoon chamber concerts, and other events. The hottest ticket in the desert, **Fabulous Palm Springs Follies** (⊠ Plaza Theater, 128 S. Palm Canyon Dr., ☎ 760/327–0225, WEB www.palmspringsfollies.com) presents 10 sellout performances each week, November through May. The vaudeville-style revue stars extravagantly costumed, retired (but very fit) showgirls, singers, and dancers. Tickets are priced from $37 to $70.

Outdoor Activities and Sports

BICYCLING

Big Horn Bicycles (⊠ 302 N. Palm Canyon, ☎ 760/325–3367) operates bike tours to celebrity homes and Indian Canyons and also rents bikes. **Palm Springs Recreation Department** (⊠ 401 S. Pavilion Way, ☎ 760/323–8272, WEB www.ci.com-springs.ca.us) can provide you with maps of some city bike trails.

GOLF

Palm Springs hosts more than 100 golf tournaments annually. The Palm Springs Desert Resorts Convention and Visitors Bureau **Events Hotline** (☎ 760/770–1992) lists dates and locations. **Class A PGA** (☎ 760/324–5012) can match golfers with specific courses and arrange tee times. If you know which course you want to play, you can book tee times on-line at WEB www.PalmSpringsteetimes.com.

Tahquitz Creek Palm Springs Golf Resort (⊠ 1885 Golf Club Dr., ☎ 760/328–1005, WEB www.tahquitzcreek.com) has two 18-hole, par-72 courses and a 50-space driving range. The greens fee, including cart, runs $70–$90, depending on the course and day of the week. **Tommy Jacobs' Bel-Aire Greens Country Club** (⊠ 1001 S. El Cielo Rd., ☎ 760/322–6062, WEB www.ptclassics@aol.com) is a 9-hole executive course. The greens fee is $19 ($12 for replay).

Demuth Park (⊠ 4375 Mesquite Ave., ☎ no phone) has four lighted courts. **Ruth Hardy Park** (⊠ Tamarisk and Caballeros, ☎ no phone) has eight lighted courts.

Shopping

North Palm Canyon Drive is the main shopping destination in the city of Palm Springs. Its commercial core extends from Alejo Road south to Ramon Road. Anchoring the center of the drive is the Palm Springs Mall, with about 35 boutiques. The **Uptown Heritage District** (☎ 760/778–8415, WEB www.palm-springs.org), a collection of consignment and secondhand shops, galleries, and restaurants on North Palm Canyon Drive between Tachevah and Amado, assumes a festive mood on the first Friday of each month, when most of the shops remain open until 9. Every Thursday night the **Village Fest** (☎ 760/778–8415, WEB www.palm-springs.org) fills North Palm Canyon Drive between Tahquitz Canyon Way and Baristo Road with street musicians, a farmers' market, and stalls with food, crafts, art, and antiques.

East Palm Canyon Drive can be a source of great bargains. **Estate Sale Co.** (⊠ 4185 E. Palm Canyon Dr., ☎ 760/321–7628) is the biggest consignment store in the desert, with a warehouse of furniture, fine art, china and crystal, accessories, jewelry, movie memorabilia, and exercise equipment. Prices are set to keep merchandise moving. **Patsy's Clothes Closet** (⊠ 4121 E. Palm Canyon Dr., ☎ 760/324–8825) specializes in consignment high-fashion and designer clothing for women and men. Not far from Palm Springs proper is **Desert Hills Premium Outlets** (⊠ 48–650 Seminole Rd., Cabazon, ☎ 909/849–6641, WEB www.premiumoutlets.com), an outlet center with more than 150 brand-name discount fashion shops, among them Polo, Giorgio Armani, Nike, and Spa Gear.

The **Palms at Palm Springs** (⊠ 572 N. Indian Canyon Dr., Palm Springs, ☎ 760/325–1111; 800/753–7256 for reservations, WEB www.palmsspa.com) has a one-day spa program that begins with a 6 AM walk. The package includes a choice of 14 classes, the use of exercise equipment, admission to lectures, and individually designed low-calorie meals and snacks. Massage, facials, and wraps are among the options. **Spa du Jour** (⊠ 555 S. Sunrise Way, Suite 305, Palm Springs, ☎ 760/864–4150) offers spa regimens ranging from two to six hours, including aromatherapy wraps, massages, botanical and enzyme facials, and healthy lunches.

Hadley's Fruit Orchards (⊠ 48–980 Seminole Dr., Cabazon, ☎ 909/849–5255, WEB www.hadleyfruitorchards.com) sells dried fruit, nuts, date shakes, and wines.

Tours

Three thousand windmills churn mightily on the slopes surrounding Palm Springs, generating electricity used by southern California residents. Each windmill stands more than 150 ft high. **EV Adventures** conducts 1½-hour tours among the giant rotors, towers, and blades in what NASA declares is one of the most consistently windy places on earth. ⊠ 62–950 20th Ave., North Palm Springs, ☎ 760/251–1997, WEB www.windmilltours.com. ☜ $23. ☉ Mon.–Sat. 9–3.

Palm Springs Celebrity Tours conducts 1- and 2½-hour tours that cover Palm Springs–area history, points of interest, and celebrity homes. ⊠ 4751 E. Palm Canyon Dr., Palm Springs, ☎ 760/770–2700, WEB www.celebritytour.qpg.com. ☜ $17–$20. ☉ Daily 8–4.

Covered Wagon Tours can take you on a two-hour old-time exploration of the Coachella Valley Preserve with a cookout at the end of the journey. ⊠ *East end of Ramon Rd.,* ☏ *760/347–2161 or 800/367–2161,* WEB *www.coveredwagontours.com.* ⊠ *$60.*

Desert Safari Guides & Outfitters conducts tours of various lengths through the Indian Canyons and offers nighttime hiking excursions in the Palm Springs area. Pickups are at area hotels. ⊠ ☏ *760/325–4453 or 888/867–2327,* WEB *www.palmspringshiking.com.* ⊠ *$50–$70.*

Cathedral City

⑫ *2 mi east of Palm Springs on Rte. 111.*

One of the fastest-growing communities in the desert, Cathedral City is more residential than tourist oriented. However, the city has a number of good restaurants and entertainment venues with moderate prices.

Pickford Salon, a small museum inside the Mary Pickford Theater, showcases the life of the famed actress. On display is a selection of personal items contributed by family members, including her 1976 Oscar for contributions to the film industry, a gown she wore in the 1927 film *Dorothy Vernon of Haddon Hall,* and dinnerware from Pickfair. Two biographical video presentations about her life include one done by by Mary herself. ⊠ *36–850 Pickfair St.,* ☏ *760/328–7444,* WEB *marypickford14 @aol.com.* ⊠ *Free.* ☉ *10:30 AM–midnight.*

At **Camelot Park** you can play miniature golf, drive bumper boats, swing in the batting cages, test your skill in an arcade, and play video games. ⊠ *67–700 E. Palm Canyon Dr.,* ☏ *760/770–7522,* WEB *www. boomerspark.com.* ⊠ *$22.95; additional fee for some activities.* ☉ *Mon.–Thurs. 11–10, Fri. 11–midnight, Sat. 10–midnight, Sun. 10–10.*

Dining and Lodging

$–$$ ✕ **Oceans.** An unexpected discovery, this small bistro tucked into a back
★ corner of a shopping center offers a surprising selection of beautifully prepared seafood. Start with mussels Oceans, a bowl of tender bivalves in a creamy anisette broth. Entrées include perfectly grilled ahi tuna, blackened catfish with Cajun seasonings, and lobster ravioli with a saffron cream sauce. ⊠ *Canyon Plaza South, 67–555 E. Palm Canyon Dr.,* ☏ *760/324–1554. Reservations essential. AE, D, DC, MC, V. No lunch weekends.*

$$–$$$$ 🏨 **Doral Palm Springs Resort.** Rooms at this business hotel have picture-postcard views of surrounding golf courses and mountains. It's a well-kept older hotel with spacious rooms, many opening directly onto the pool area. Bathrooms are large, and rooms have separate vanity areas, capacious closets, and a soft desert-beige color scheme. The quiet property is close to I–10. ⊠ *67–967 Vista Chino, 92234,* ☏ *760/ 322–7000,* FAX *760/322–6853,* WEB *www.doralpalmsprings.com. 285 rooms. 2 restaurants, three 9-hole golf courses, putting green, 10 tennis courts, pool, 2 outdoor hot tubs, spa, racquetball, meeting rooms. AE, D, DC, MC, V.*

$$ 🏨 **Comfort Suites.** This chain motel is about as close as you can get to Rancho Mirage without paying sky-high prices. Public areas are spacious, modern, and attractively appointed. Some guest rooms are cramped, even though most accommodations are one- or two-bedroom suites. Noise can be a problem because the motel is on busy Highway 111. Continental breakfast is included in the price. ⊠ *69–151 E. Palm Canyon Dr., 92234,* ☏ *760/324–5939 or 800/862–5085,* FAX *760/324– 3034,* WEB *www.comfortsuites.com. 16 studios, 85 suites. Pool, outdoor hot tub, laundry facilities, meeting room. AE, D, DC, M, V. CP.*

Southern California Desert

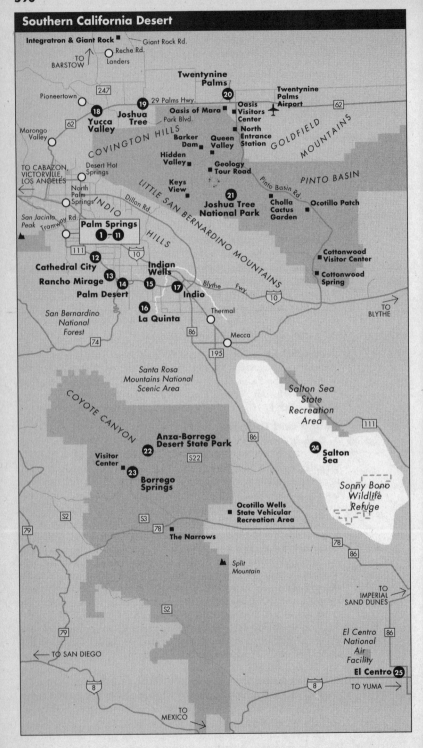

Integratron & Giant Rock ■ — Giant Rock Rd.
TO BARSTOW
Reche Rd.
Landers
Pioneertown
247
Twentynine Palms
29 Palms Hwy. **20**
Twentynine Palms Airport
62
Morongo Valley
62
18 Yucca Valley
19 Joshua Tree
Oasis of Mara
Park Blvd.
Oasis Visitors Center
North Entrance Station
GOLDFIELD MOUNTAINS
COVINGTON HILLS
Desert Hot Springs
Barker Dam ■
Queen Valley
Hidden Valley ■
Geology Tour Road
Keys View ■
PINTO BASIN
TO CABAZON, VICTORVILLE, LOS ANGELES
North Palm Springs
Dillon Rd.
21 Joshua Tree National Park
Cholla Cactus Garden ■
Pinto Basin Rd.
■ Ocotillo Patch
San Jacinto Peak ▲
Tramway Rd.
LITTLE SAN BERNARDINO MOUNTAINS
INDIO HILLS
Palm Springs **1** **11**
■ Cottonwood Visitor Center
■ Cottonwood Spring
111
12
10
Cathedral City
13 **14**
Rancho Mirage
Palm Desert
Indian Wells
15
17
Blythe Fwy.
10
TO BLYTHE
San Bernardino National Forest
16
La Quinta
Indio
Thermal
74
86
Mecca
195
Santa Rosa Mountains National Scenic Area
COYOTE CANYON
Salton Sea State Recreation Area
111
Anza-Borrego Desert State Park
22
S22
86
24 Salton Sea
Visitor Center
23
Borrego Springs
S2
S3
78
Ocotillo Wells State Vehicular Recreation Area ■
Sonny Bono Wildlife Refuge
79
■ The Narrows
78
86
Split Mountain ▲
S2
TO IMPERIAL SAND DUNES
79
El Centro National Air Facility
86
TO SAN DIEGO
El Centro **25**
8
TO MEXICO
8
TO YUMA

Nightlife and the Arts

Desert IMAX Theater (✉ Rte. 111 at Cathedral Canyon, ☎ 760/324–7333; 🎟 $5.50–$7.50), the only IMAX theater in the region, screens such popular big-screen films as *Ocean Oasis* and *Journey into Amazing Caves*. Once a venerable restaurant, the **Wilde Goose Cabaret** (✉ 67–938 E. Palm Canyon Dr., ☎ 760/328–5775) is now a dinner theater. Nightly entertainment ranges from jazz concerts to comedy acts to drag shows.

Tours

Desert Adventures takes to the wilds with two-to-four hour Jeep tours of Indian Canyons near Palm Springs, off-road in the Santa Rosa Mountains, and into a mystery canyon. Departures from Palm Springs and LaQuinta; hotel pickups available. ✉ *67-555 E. Palm Canyon Dr.* ☎ *760/324–5337,* WEB *www.red-jeep.com.* 🎟 *$59–$99.*

Rancho Mirage

⑬ *4 mi east Cathedral City on Rte. 111.*

Much of the scenery in exclusive Rancho Mirage is concealed behind the walls of gated communities and country clubs. The rich and famous live in estates and patronize elegant resorts and fine-dining establishments. The city's golf courses are the site of world-class tournaments. The Betty Ford Center, for those recovering from alcohol and drug addiction, is also here.

☺ The **Children's Discovery Museum of the Desert** contains instructive hands-on exhibits for children—a miniature rock-climbing area, a magnetic sculpture wall, make-it-and-take-it-apart projects, a rope maze, and an area for toddlers. ✉ *71–701 Gerald Ford Dr.,* ☎ *760/321–0602,* WEB *www.cdmod.org.* 🎟 *$5.* ☉ *Mon.–Sat. 10–5, Sun. noon–5.*

Dining and Lodging

$–$$$ ✗ **Shame on the Moon.** Old-fashioned ambience complete with big booths, friendly service, an eclectic menu, and modest prices make this one of the most popular restaurants in the desert. Entrées include salmon napoleon stacked with Portobellos, sautéed chicken coated with hazelnuts, veal short ribs, and Long Island duck with black figs. Portions leave you plenty to take home. ✉ *69–950 Frank Sinatra Dr.,* ☎ *760/324–5515. Reservations essential. AE, MC, V. No lunch.*

$–$$ ✗ **Las Casuelas Nuevas.** Hundreds of artifacts from Guadalajara, Mexico, lend festive charm to this casual restaurant with a garden patio. Tamales and shellfish dishes are among the specialties of the house. The margaritas will make you wish you'd brought your cha-cha heels. ✉ *70–050 Rte. 111,* ☎ *760/328–8844. AE, D, DC, MC, V.*

$$$$ 🏨 **Lodge at Rancho Mirage.** This hotel, formerly a Ritz-Carlton property and now part of the Rockresort chain, is tucked into a hillside in the Santa Rosa Mountains with sweeping views of the valley below. Gleaming marble and brass, original artwork, and plush carpeting create remarkable comfort. All rooms are spacious and meticulously appointed with antiques, fabric wall coverings, and often two phones and two TVs. Service provided by the multilingual staff is impeccable. The luxurious spa offers 30 treatments. ✉ *68–900 Frank Sinatra Dr., 92270,* ☎ *760/321–8282 or 866/518–6870,* FAX *760/770–7605,* WEB *www. rockresorts.com. 219 rooms, 21 suites. 3 restaurants, 2 bars, putting green, golf privileges, 10 tennis courts, pool, hair salon, health club, outdoor hot tub, spa, basketball, croquet, hiking, volleyball, shop, children's programs (ages 5–12), laundry service, concierge, concierge floor, business services, meeting room, car rental. AE, D, DC, MC, V.*

$$$$ ⊞ **Westin Mission Hills Resort.** A sprawling Moroccan-style resort on
★   360 acres, the Westin is surrounded by fairways and putting greens.
Rooms, in two-story buildings amid patios and fountains, are decorated
with soft desert colors. Paths and creeks meander through the complex,
and a lagoon-style swimming pool is encircled with a several-story
water slide. ⊠ *71–333 Dinah Shore Dr., 92270,* ☎ *760/328–5955 or
800/335–3545,* FAX *760/321–2607,* WEB *www.westin.com. 472 rooms,
40 suites. 2 restaurants, 3 snack bars, bar, 2 18-hole golf courses, 7 tennis courts, 3 pools, hair salon, health club, 4 outdoor hot tubs, spa, steam
room, croquet, shuffleboard, volleyball, recreation room, children's
programs (ages 4–12), convention center. AE, D, DC, MC, V.*

$$$–$$$$ ⊞ **Marriott Rancho Las Palmas Resort & Spa.** The aura is luxuriously
★   laid back at this family-oriented resort on 240 landscaped acres. A Span-
ish theme prevails throughout the public areas and guest accommoda-
tions. Rooms in the two-story buildings are unusually large; all have
sitting areas, private balconies or patios, and views of colorful gardens
or well-manicured fairways and greens. One of the swimming pools has
a 100-ft water slide. ⊠ *41–000 Bob Hope Dr., 92270,* ☎ *760/568–
2727 or 800/458–8786,* FAX *760/568–5845,* WEB *www.marriotthotels.com.
450 rooms, 22 suites. 4 restaurants, bar, 27-hole golf course, putting
green, 25 tennis courts, pro shop, 3 pools, hair salon, health club, 3 out-
door hot tubs, spa, bicycles, children's programs (ages 5–12), playground,
laundry facilities, laundry service, concierge, business services, con-
vention center, car rental. AE, D, DC, MC, V.*

$ ⊞ **Motel 6.** This motel may be bare-bones, but it puts you in tony Ran-
cho Mirage, right in the shadow of the Lodge at Rancho Mirage, up
the hill. Rooms come equipped with data ports, and you can help your-
self to free morning coffee. ⊠ *69–570 Rte. 111, 92270,* ☎ *760/324–
8475 or 800/466–8356,* FAX *760/328–0864,* WEB *www.motel6.com. 103
rooms. Pool, outdoor hot tub. AE, D, DC, M, V.*

Outdoor Activities and Sports

The best women golfers in the world compete in the **Annual Nabisco
Championship** (⊠ Mission Hills Country Club, ☎ 760/324–4546, WEB
www.nabiscochampionship.com; ⊠ $50), held in late March.

An 18-hole, par-70 course, **Pete Dye at the Westin Mission Hills Resort
Golf Club** (⊠ 71–501 Dinah Shore Dr., Rancho Mirage, ☎ 760/328–
3198, WEB www.troongolf.com), hosts a number of major tournaments.
The greens fee is $145 during peak season, including a mandatory cart;
off-season promotional packages during the summer are sometimes as
low as $60.

Shopping

Opened in 2002, the **River at Rancho Mirage** is a shopping/dining/en-
tertainment complex with a collection of high-end shops. Bang &
Olufsen, Bath and Body Works, Newport Clock Gallery, and many others
front a faux river with cascading waterfalls. The complex includes a
12-screen cinema, an outdoor amphitheater, and a collection of restau-
rants. ⊠ 71–800 Rte. 111, ☎ 760/341–2711.

Palm Desert

⓮ *2 mi east of Rancho Mirage on Rte. 111.*

Palm Desert is a thriving retail and business community, with some of
the desert's most popular restaurants, private and public golf courses,
and premium shopping.

West of and parallel to Highway 111, **El Paseo** (⊠ between Monterey
and Portola Aves., ☎ 877/735–7273, WEB www.elpaseo.com) is a mile-
long Mediterranean-style avenue with fountains and courtyards, French

and Italian fashion boutiques, shoe salons, jewelry stores, children's shops, restaurants, and nearly 30 art galleries. The pretty strip is a pleasant place to stroll, window-shop, people-watch, and exercise your credit cards. Along El Paseo is **Gardens of El Paseo** (✉ El Paseo at San Pablo, ☎ 760/862–1990, WEB www.thegardensonelpaseo.com), a shopping center anchored by Saks Fifth Avenue and populated by mainstream retailers such as Brooks Brothers, Ann Taylor, and Williams-Sonoma. Each November, the **Palm Desert Golf Cart Parade** (☎ 760/346–6111, WEB www.golfcartparade.com) celebrates golf with a procession of 100 carts disguised as floats buzzing up and down El Paseo.

★ ☟ Come eyeball to eyeball with wolves, coyotes, mountain lions, cheetahs, bighorn sheep, golden eagles, warthogs, and owls at the **Living Desert Zoo and Gardens.** Easy to challenging scenic trails traverse 1,200 acres of desert gardens populated with plants of the Mojave, Colorado, and Sonoran deserts. The 3-acre African Wa TuTu village centers on a traditional marketplace and exhibits camels, leopards, hyenas, and other African animals. Children can pet African domestic animals, including goats and guinea fowl, in a petting kraal. Elsewhere in the park an exhibit shows the path of the San Andreas earthquake fault across the Coachella Valley. Wildlife shows take place daily in Tennity Amphitheater; during the winter holidays the park presents "Wildlights," an evening light show. ✉ 47–900 Portola Ave., ☎ 760/346–5694, WEB *www.livingdesert.org.* ▭ *$8.50, $6.50 in summer.* ☉ *Sept.–mid-June, daily 9–5; mid-June–Aug., daily 8–1:30.*

The **Santa Rosa Mountains/San Jacinto National Monument,** administered by the Bureau of Land Management, protects Peninsula bighorn sheep and other wildlife on 272,000 acres of desert habitat. For an introduction to the site, stop by the visitor center—staffed by knowledgeable volunteers—for a look at exhibits illustrating the natural history of the desert. A landscaped garden displays native plants and frames a sweeping view. ✉ 51–500 Rte. 74, ☎ 760/862–9984, WEB *www.cablm.gov.* ▭ *Free.* ☉ *Daily 9–4.*

Dining

$$$–$$$$ ★ ✗ **Cuistot.** Chef-owner Bernard Dervieux trained with French culinary star Paul Bocuse, but he's taken a more eclectic approach at his own restaurant, tucked into the back of an El Paseo courtyard. Signature dishes include skillet-roasted veal chop with mushrooms and roasted garlic, live Maine lobster with baby asparagus, and handmade vegetable ravioli with white truffle oil. ✉ 73–111 El Paseo, ☎ 760/340–1000. *Reservations essential. AE, DC, MC, V. Closed Mon. No lunch Sun.*

$$–$$$$ ✗ **Doug Arango's.** Even the dish of liver and onions receives star treatment at this bistro with colorful sidewalk umbrellas and tomato-red walls. The entrées range from veal and pork ribs to an inventive seared foie gras. ✉ 73–520 El Paseo, ☎ 760/341–4120. *Reservations essential. AE, D, DC, MC, V. Closed Mon.; closed Sun. June–mid-Sept. No lunch June–mid-Sept.*

$$–$$$$ ✗ **Jillian's.** Husband-and-wife team Jay and June Trubee are the stars behind this fancy yet casual restaurant. He tends to the kitchen; she runs the dining rooms. Antiques and art fill the space, and the nighttime sky sets the mood in the center courtyard. Try the monumental appetizer called Tower of Crab (layers of crab, tomatoes, avocados, and brioche) and main dishes such as salmon baked in parchment and fettuccine with lobster. Save room for the popular Hawaiian cheesecake with macadamia-nut crust. Men will feel more comfortable wearing jackets. ✉ 74–155 El Paseo, ☎ 760/776–8242. *Reservations essential. AE, D, MC, V. Closed Sun. and mid-June–Oct. No lunch.*

$$–$$$$ ✕ **Morton's of Chicago.** Posh, clubby Morton's delivers not only enormous slabs of USDA prime steak but also seafood, veal, and lamb. All are served à la carte. The bar is always busy. Sinatra (and only Sinatra) plays softly in the background. ✉ 74–880 Country Club Dr., ☎ 760/340–6865. AE, D, MC, V. No lunch.

$$–$$$$ ✕ **Omri and Boni.** Chef Omri Siklai showed the same flair decorating this establishment that he displays nightly in the kitchen preparing an eclectic menu of contemporary Mediterranean dishes. Caesar salads, homemade pastas, chicken and veal dishes—even ostrich and kangaroo—are prepared with skill and imagination. Pastas and breads made on the premises are egg-free. ✉ 73–675 Rte. 111, ☎ 760/773–1735. Reservations essential. MC, V. Closed Tues. and July–Sept. No lunch.

$$–$$$$ ✕ **Ristorante Mamma Gina.** The greatest hits of Florence and Tuscany appear on the menu at this festive, upscale restaurant. The appetizers and salads are superb, but save room for pasta dishes or smartly crafted chicken, veal, and fish dishes. The wine selection favors Italian and California vintages. ✉ 73–705 El Paseo, ☎ 760/568–9898. Reservations essential. AE, D, MC, V. No lunch Sun. and in summer.

$$–$$$ ✕ **Augusta.** Artwork fills this noisy showplace. Two popular items on the eclectic menu are spit-roasted duck with cilantro sauce and Chilean sea bass marinated in sake. ✉ 73–951 El Paseo, ☎ 760/779–9200. Reservations essential. AE, DC, MC, V. Closed Aug. No lunch Sun.

$–$$$ ✕ **Café des Beaux Arts.** The café brings a little bit of Paris to the desert, with sidewalk dining, colorful flower boxes, and a bistro menu of French and Californian favorites, such as a hefty bouillabaisse and a broiled Portobello mushroom with grilled chicken and an artichoke heart, served with a sherry sauce. Leisurely dining is encouraged, which allows more time to savor the well-chosen French and domestic wines. ✉ 73–640 El Paseo, ☎ 760/346–0669. AE, D, DC, MC, V. Closed July–mid-Sept.

$–$$$ ✕ **Locanda Toscana.** Celebrities and celebrity watchers patronize this northern Italian–style restaurant known for excellent service, numerous antipasti choices, and fine soups. Popular dishes include breaded veal chop with lemon, osso buco Milanese, and homemade crab ravioli with vodka sauce. ✉ 72–695 Rte. 111, ☎ 760/776–7500. Reservations essential. AE, D, MC, V. Closed Aug. No lunch.

$–$$$ ✕ **Mayo's.** Bob Mayo presides over a snazzy retro supper club that has a private room dedicated to Hollywood's famed Rat Pack, decorated with larger-than-life photos of Frank Sinatra, Sammy Davis, and Dean Martin. The menu offers an updated version of Continental cuisine: pasta, Lake Superior whitefish, and filet mignon. ✉ 73–990 El Paseo, ☎ 760/346–2284. Reservations essential. AE, D, MC, V.

$–$$$ ✕ **Palomino.** One of the desert's longtime favorites specializes in grilled and roasted entrées: spit-roasted garlic chicken, oak-fired thin-crust pizza, paella, and oven-roasted prawns. Huge reproductions of famous French impressionist paintings cover the walls of the busy room. ✉ 73–101 Rte. 111, ☎ 760/773–9091. AE, D, DC, MC, V. No lunch.

$–$$ ✕ **Daily Grill.** A combination upscale coffee shop and bar, the Daily Grill serves good salads (the Niçoise is particularly scrumptious), a fine gazpacho, zesty pasta dishes, and various blue-plate specials. The sidewalk terrace invites people-watching. Sunday brunch is a weekly party. ✉ 73–061 El Paseo, ☎ 760/779–9911. AE, D, DC, MC, V.

$ ✕ **Bananaz Grill and Bar.** This large, boisterous eatery is exceedingly convivial. The food is cheap (for the area) and bountiful—husky sandwiches, roast chicken, and a dozen other options. The TVs and frequent live entertainment will keep you amused while you dine. Bananaz becomes a nightclub after 10, with live music and dancing. ✉ 72–291 Rte. 111, ☎ 760/776–4333. AE, D, DC, MC, V.

$$$$ ⊡ **Marriott's Desert Springs Resort and Spa.** This sprawling, convention-oriented hotel set on 450 landscaped acres has a dramatic U-shape design. The building wraps around the desert's largest private lake, into which an indoor stair-stepped waterfall flows. Rooms have lake or mountain views, balconies, and oversize bathrooms. It's a long walk from the lobby to the rooms; if you are driving, you might want to request a room close to the parking lot. ⊠ *74–855 Country Club Dr., 92260,* ☏ *760/341–2211 or 800/331–3112,* ℻ *760/341–1872,* ⓦⓔⓑ *www.desertspringsresort.com. 833 rooms, 51 suites. 11 restaurants, snack bar, 2 bars, minibars, driving range, 2 golf courses, putting green, 20 tennis courts, 5 pools, hair salon, health club, 4 outdoor hot tubs, spa, basketball, croquet, volleyball, shop, children's programs (ages 5–12), laundry service, business services, convention center, car rental. AE, D, DC, MC, V.*

$$–$$$ ⊡ **Mojave.** This tranquil inn is just steps from busy El Paseo. A 50-year-old motel, it's been transformed into a retro urban oasis. Rooms surround a lovely landscaped courtyard, where a small stream and pond are shaded by mature trees bearing oranges and grapefruit ripe for picking. Large rooms are furnished with 1940s-style chairs, armoires, and tables. Minibars come stocked with bottles of Nehi sodas, and there is a vintage video library. All rooms have outdoor sitting areas appointed with director's chairs. In-room spa services are available. Continental breakfast is included in the price. ⊠ *73721 Shadow Mountain Dr., 92260,* ☏ *760/346–6121 or 800/391–1104,* ℻ *760/674–9072,* ⓦⓔⓑ *www.hotelmojave.com. 22 rooms, 2 suites. In-room VCRs, pool, kitchens (some), outdoor hot tub, meeting rooms. AE, MC, V. CP.*

$$–$$$ ⊡ **Tres Palmas Bed & Breakfast.** Enormous windows, high open-beam ceilings, light wood, and textured peach-tile floors lend this contemporary inn near El Paseo a bright and spacious feel. The southwestern accents in common areas and guest rooms (which are more functional than luxurious) include old Navajo rugs from the innkeepers' collection. ⊠ *73–135 Tumbleweed La.,* ☏ *760/773–9858 or 800/770–9858,* ℻ *760/776–9159,* ⓦⓔⓑ *www.innformation.com/ca/trespalmas. 4 rooms. Pool, outdoor hot tub. AE, MC, V. CP.*

The Arts

McCallum Theatre (⊠ 73–000 Fred Waring Dr., ☏ 760/340–2787, ⓦⓔⓑ www.mccallumtheatre.com), the principal cultural venue in the desert, presents film, classical and popular music, opera, ballet, and theater. In mid-January the **Nortel Palm Springs International Film Festival** (☏ 760/322–2930, ⓦⓔⓑ www.psfilmfest.org) brings stars and more than 150 feature films from 25 countries, plus panel discussions, short films, and documentaries, to the McCallum and other venues.

Outdoor Activities and Sports

Big Wheel Bike Tours (⊠ Box 4185, 92261, ☏ 760/779–1837, ⓦⓔⓑ www.bigwheelbiketours.net) delivers rental mountain, three-speed, and tandem bikes to area hotels. **Desert Willow Golf Resort** (⊠ 38–500 Portola Ave., ☏ 760/346–7060, ⓦⓔⓑ www.desertwillow.com) is one of the newest golf resorts in the desert. A public course managed by the City of Palm Desert, it has two challenging 18-hole links. Greens fees are $167 including cart.

Fantasy Balloon Flights operates sunrise excursions over the southern end of the Coachella Valley. Flights run an hour to an hour and a half, followed by a traditional champagne toast. Pickups are available from area hotels. ⊠ 74-181 Parosella St. ☏ 760/568–0997, ⓦⓔⓑ www. fantasyballoonflights.com. ☏ $150.

Indian Wells

⑮ *5 mi east of Palm Desert on Rte. 111.*

For the most part a quiet residential community, Indian Wells hosts golf and tennis tournaments throughout the year, including the Pacific Life Open tennis tournament. You'll find most dining and shopping venues inside the two huge hotels that dominate the resort scene.

Lodging

$$$$ 🏨 **Hyatt Grand Champions Resort.** This stark white resort on 34 acres
★   specializes in pampering, with lavish accommodations and service provided by a multilingual staff. Huge suite-style rooms have balconies or terraces, sunken sitting areas, and minibars. The villas here may be the most luxurious accommodations in the desert. Resembling private residences, each has a secluded garden courtyard with outdoor whirlpool tub, a living room with fireplace, a dining room, and a bedroom. A private butler attends to your every whim. The pool area is a kind of garden water park, surrounded by palms and private cabanas. In 2002 the resort added a spa with 26 treatment rooms. ⊠ *44–600 Indian Wells La., 92210,* ☎ *760/341–1000 or 800/554–9288,* FAX *760/568–2236,* WEB *www.grandchampions.hyatt.com. 338 suites, 20 villas. 2 restaurants, bar, driving range, 2 golf courses, putting green, 12 tennis courts, pro shop, 5 pools, aerobics, hair salon, health club, 3 outdoor hot tubs, massage, sauna, spa, steam room, bicycles, shop, children's programs (ages 3–12), dry cleaning, laundry service, business services, convention center, meeting rooms. AE, D, DC, MC, V.*

$$$–$$$$ 🏨 **Renaissance Esmeralda Resort.** The centerpiece of this luxurious Mediterranean-style resort is an eight-story atrium lobby with a fountain whose water flows through a rivulet in the floor into cascading pools and outside to lakes surrounding the property. Given its size, the hotel has a surprisingly intimate feel. Spacious guest rooms—equipped with sitting areas, balconies, refreshment centers, two TV sets, and travertine vanities in the bathrooms—have light-wood furnishings and desert-color accents. One pool has a sandy beach. ⊠ *44–400 Indian Wells La., 92210,* ☎ *760/773–4444 or 800/331–3131,* FAX *760/773–9250,* WEB *www.marriotthotels.com. 560 rooms, 22 suites. 2 restaurants, snack bar, bar, minibars, 2 golf courses, putting green, 4 tennis courts, pro shop, 3 pools, wading pool, health club, 2 outdoor hot tubs, massage, sauna, spa, steam room, bicycles, basketball, volleyball, shop, children's programs (ages 5–12), laundry service, concierge, business services, meeting rooms, car rental. AE, D, DC, MC, V.*

Outdoor Activities and Sports

Next door to the Hyatt Grand Champions Resort, **Golf Resort at Indian Wells** (⊠ 44–500 Indian Wells La., Indian Wells, ☎ 760/346–4653) has two 18-hole Ted Robinson–designed championship courses: the 6,500-yard West Course and the 6,700-yard East Course. A public course, it has been named one of the country's top 10 resorts by *Golf Magazine.* Monday through Thursday greens fees are $130; Friday through Sunday they are $140 (fees may be discounted in summer). The resort also offers golf instruction through the Indian Wells Golf School.

The **Pacific Life Open** professional tennis tournament (☎ 760/360–3346, WEB www.master-series.com/indianwells) draws 200 of the world's top players to the Indian Wells Tennis Garden for two weeks in March. With more than 16,000 seats, the stadium is the second largest in the nation.

La Quinta

16 *4 mi east of Indian Wells on Rte. 111.*

The desert became a Hollywood hideout in the 1920s, when La Quinta Hotel (now the La Quinta Resort) opened, introducing the Coachella Valley's first golf course. Although there are a number of restaurants and strip malls in La Quinta, life here really revolves around the resort and its associated PGA West golf complex.

Dining and Lodging

$–$$ **✕ La Quinta Cliffhouse.** Sweeping mountain views at sunset and the
★ early California look of a western movie set draw patrons to this restaurant perched halfway up a hillside. The eclectic menu roams the globe: Caesar salad with grilled chicken, Szechuan-style ahi tuna, and, for dessert, Kimo's Hula Pie with house-made macadamia-nut ice cream. ⊠ *78–250 Rte. 111,* ☎ *760/360–5991. Reservations essential. AE, MC, V. No lunch.*

$$$$ **🏨 La Quinta Resort and Club.** Opened in 1926, the desert's oldest re-
★ sort is a lush green oasis. Broad expanses of lawn separate the adobe casitas that house some rooms; other rooms are in newer two-story units surrounding individual swimming pools and hot tubs set amid brilliant gardens. Fireplaces, stocked refrigerators, and fruit-laden orange trees contribute to a discreet and sparely luxurious air. A premium is placed on privacy, which accounts for La Quinta's continuing popularity with Hollywood celebrities. The resort can arrange access to some of the desert's most celebrated golf courses. ⊠ *49–499 Eisenhower Dr., 92253,* ☎ *760/564–4111 or 800/598–3828,* FAX *760/564–5768,* WEB *www.laquintaresort.com. 640 rooms, 244 suites. 6 restaurants, refrigerators, 5 golf courses, 23 tennis courts, 25 pools, hair salon, health club, 38 outdoor hot tubs, spa, children's programs (ages 4–16), concierge, business services, meeting room. AE, D, DC, MC, V.*

Nightlife and the Arts

The **La Quinta Arts Festival** (☎ 760/564–1244, WEB www.lqaf.com), normally held the third weekend in March, showcases painting, sculpture, photography, drawing, and printmaking. The show is accompanied by entertainment and food.

Outdoor Activities and Sports

PGA West (⊠ 49–499 Eisenhower Dr., ☎ 760/564–7170; 760/564–5729 for tee times, WEB www.pgawest.com) operates three 18-hole, par-72 championship courses and provides instruction and golf clinics. The greens fee (which includes a mandatory cart) ranges from $100 on weekdays in summer to $235 on weekends in February and March. Bookings are accepted 30 days in advance.

Indio

17 *5 mi east of Indian Wells on Rte. 111.*

More a farming community than a resort, Indio is the home of the date shake. The city and surrounding countryside generate 95% of the dates grown and harvested in the United States. If you take a hot-air balloon ride, you will likely drift over the tops of date palm trees.

Indio celebrates its raison d'être each February at the **National Date Festival and Riverside County Fair.** The mid-month festivities include an Arabian Nights pageant, camel and ostrich races, and exhibits of local dates. ⊠ *Riverside County Fairgrounds, 46-350 Arabia St.,* ☎ *760/863–8247 or 800/811–3247,* WEB *www.datefest.org.* 🎫 *$6.*

Displays at the **Coachella Valley Museum and Cultural Center,** in a former farmhouse, explain how dates are harvested and how the desert is irrigated for date farming. On the grounds you'll find a smithy and an old sawmill. ⊠ *82–616 Miles Ave.,* ☎ *760/342–6651.* ☒ *Free.* ☉ *Sept.–June, Wed.–Sat. 10–4, Sun. 1–4.*

A 100-mi drive from the Mexican border, Indio honors the influence of that culture at the **Indio International Tamale Festival** the first weekend in December. Centered around traditional Mexican Christmas food, the festival has tamale tastings, a parade, vendors, entertainment. ⊠ *Miles Park, 82–580 Miles Ave.,* ☎ *760/342–6532,* WEB *www.tamalefestival.org.* ☒ *Free.*

Dining and Lodging

$ ✕ **Ciro's Ristorante and Pizzeria.** This popular casual restaurant have been serving up pizza and pasta since the 1970s. The menu lists some unusual pizzas, such as western-style (loaded with sausage, pepperoni, Canadian bacon, and vegetables) and cashew with three cheeses. Daily pasta specials vary but might include red- or white-clam sauce or scallops with parsley and red wine. ⊠ *81–963 Rte. 111,* ☎ *760/347–6503,* WEB *www.cirospasta.com. AE, D, DC, MC, V. No lunch Sun.*

$ ☷ **Best Western Date Tree Inn.** Landscaped citrus and cactus gardens surround this hotel. Nicely appointed rooms are good for families, as are the pool-side barbecues. Continental breakfast is included in the price. ⊠ *81909 Indio Blvd., 92201,* ☎ *760/347–3421,* FAX *760/347–3421,* WEB *www.datetree.com. 119 rooms. Restaurant, in-room hot tubs (some), kitchens (some), microwaves, refrigerators, pool, exercise equipment, volleyball court, playground, laundry facilities. AE, D, DC, MC, V. CP.*

Nightlife

Fantasy Springs Casino (⊠ Golf Club Parkway off I–10, ☎ 760/342–5000, WEB www.fantasyspringsresort.com) has 850 Las Vegas–style gaming machines, off-track wagering, gaming tables, and a high-limit area, plus two restaurants and a cocktail lounge.

Outdoor Activities and Sports

The **Eldorado Polo Club** (⊠ 50–950 Madison St., ☎ 760/342–2223), known as the winter polo capital of the west, hosts world-class polo events. You can pack a picnic and watch practice matches for free during the week; there's a $6 per-person charge to picnic and watch matches on Sunday.

Shopping

Shields Date Gardens (⊠ 80–225 Rte. 111, ☎ 760/347–0996, WEB www.shieldsdates.com) sells date shakes, date gift packages, and delicious grapefruit in season. A continuous video illustrates the history of the date. You can buy a date shake at **Oasis Date Gardens** (⊠ 59–111 Rte. 111, Thermal, ☎ 760/399–5665, WEB www.oasisdategardens.com) as well as take a walking tour of the orchard (at 10:30 and 2:30 daily). On the tour you learn how dates are pollinated, grown, sorted, stored, and packed for shipping.

En Route   If you are headed for Joshua Tree National Park from the desert resorts area, you will pass **Desert Hot Springs,** 9 mi north of Palm Springs on Gene Autry Trail. The town's famous hot mineral waters, thought by some to have curative powers, bubble up from underground at temperatures of 90°F–148°F and flow into the wells of more than 40 hotel spas. Desert Hot Springs is the location of one of the desert's most exclusive resorts, **Two Bunch Palms Resort and Spa** (⊠ 67–425 Two Bunch Palms Trail, ☎ 760/329–8791 or 800/472–4334, WEB www.twobunchpalms.com). This gate-guarded resort (you must call for advance reservations) is the most romantic in the area and is the spa of choice for celebrities, who savor the mineral baths, the laid-back vibe, and the privacy. The landscaped grounds contain two rock-grotto mineral pools surrounded by palms, secluded picnic areas, meditation benches, tennis courts, hiking trails, and outdoor mud baths. As a guest here you can work out at the health club or take a Swedish-, Japanese-, or Native American–style massage, among other treatments. Accommodations include 19 hotel-style rooms with vintage 1920s accents and 26 villas with living rooms, kitchens, private whirlpool tubs, and private patios.

Once a Native American village and later a cattle ranch, **Big Morongo Canyon Preserve** is a serene oasis around a natural spring generated by snowmelt from the surrounding mountains. About 11 mi north of I–10 via Hwy. 62, the preserve attracts all manner of birds and animals to a riparian woodland filled with cottonwoods and willows. You're likely to spot great horned owls and many songbirds here any time of the year. A shaded meadow is a fine place for a picnic, and you can hike on several choice trails. No pets are permitted. ⊠ *East Dr., Morongo Valley,* ☎ *760/363–7190,* WEB *www.morongo.org.* ☏ *Free.* ☉ *Daily 7:30 AM–sunset.*

ALONG TWENTYNINE PALMS HIGHWAY

Including Joshua Tree National Park

The towns of Yucca Valley, Joshua Tree, and Twentynine Palms punctuate Twentynine Palms Highway (Highway 62), the northern Highway from the desert resorts to Joshua Tree National Park, and provide lodging and other visitor services to park goers. Flanked by Twentynine Palms Highway on the north and I–10 on the south, the park protects some of the southern California desert's most interesting and beautiful scenery. A visit to the park provides glimpse of the rigors of desert life in the Little San Bernardino Mountains. You can see the park highlights in a half day or take a daylong expedition into the backcountry.

Yucca Valley

⑱ *30 mi east of Palm Springs on Rte. 62 (Twentynine Palms Hwy.).*

One of the fastest-growing cities in the High Desert, Yucca Valley is emerging as a bedroom community for people who work as far away as Ontario, 85 mi to the west. In this sprawling suburb you can shop for necessities, get your car serviced, and chow down at the fast-food outlets. For some fun, head a few miles north to Pioneertown.

The **Hi-Desert Nature Museum** has a small zoo of animals that make their home in Joshua Tree, including scorpions, snakes, ground squirrels, and chuckawallas, a type of lizard. There's also a collection of rocks, minerals, and fossils from the Paleozoic era. ⊠ *57116 Twentynine Palms Hwy.,* ☎ *760/369–7212.* ☏ *Free.* ☉ *Tues.–Sun. 10–5.*

Roy Rogers, Gene Autry, and Russ Hayden built **Pioneertown,** an 1880s-style Wild West movie set, in 1946, complete with hitching posts, saloon, and an OK Corral. Today 250 people call the place home, even as film crews continue shooting. You can stroll past wooden and adobe storefronts and bowl at Pioneer Bowl, the oldest operating Brunswick Lanes in the country. Professional gunfights are staged April through November, Saturday at 1 and 2, and Sunday at 2:30. ⊠ *4 mi north of Yucca Valley on Pioneertown Rd.,* WEB *www.pioneertown.com.*

Dining and Lodging

$–$$ ✕ **Pappy & Harriet's Pioneertown Palace.** Smack in the middle of a western-movie-set town is this western-movie-set saloon where you can tuck into dinner, dance to live country-and-western tunes, or just relax with a drink at the bar. The food ranges from Tex-Mex to Santa Maria barbecue to steak and burgers—no surprises but plenty of fun. On Wednesday and Thursday nights you can take country dance lessons. Pappy & Harriet's may be in the middle of nowhere, but you'll need reservations for dinner on weekends. ⊠ *Pioneertown Rd., Pioneertown,* ☎ *760/365–5956. Closed Mon.–Tues. No lunch Wed.–Thurs. AE, D, MC, V.*

$ ✕ **Edchada's.** Rock climbers who spend their days scrambling up the rocks in Joshua Tree National Park gravitate to this Mexican restaurant, which has locations in Yucca Valley and Twentynine Palms. There are plenty of tacos and burritos on the menu, but locals swear by the blue corn enchiladas. ⊠ *56805 Twentynine Palms Hwy., Yucca Valley,* ☎ *760/365–7655;* ⊠ *73502 Twentynine Palms Hwy., Twentynine Palms,* ☎ *760/367–2131. AE, D, MC, V.*

$–$$ 🏠 **Rimrock Ranch Cabins.** These four circa-1940s housekeeping cabins have been restored to their original condition, complete with knotty-pine paneling, vintage Wedgwood stoves, artisan tiles, and antique furnishings. Owners Szu and Dusty Wakeman have added modern touches like personal espresso machines and outdoor fireplaces, making Rimrock a great place to work on a novel or enjoy a quiet vacation. Kitchens are fully equipped, and the grounds include a campfire pit and a deep pit barbecue. Gentle walking paths surround the property. ⊠ *Pioneertown Rd., Pioneertown,* ☎ *760/228–1297 or 818/404–3110,* ℻ *818/956–0268,* 🖥 *www.rimrockranchcabins.com. 4 cabins. Kitchens, pool. MC, V.*

$ 🏠 **Pioneertown Motel.** Built in 1946 as a bunkhouse for western film and TV stars shooting in Pioneertown, this motel sticks close to its roots. Each room, from the Cowboy Room to the Twilight Zone Room, has a theme that matches its name. The Flower room is all about buds and blooms. Hiking trails outside the motel lead into the desert. Bring your horse—there are corrals just for visiting animals. ⊠ *Pioneertown Rd., Pioneertown,* ☎ *760/365–4879,* ℻ *760/365–3127,* 🖥 *www.pioneertown.com. 18 rooms. Cable TV, in-room VCRs, kitchenettes. AE, D, MC, V.*

Joshua Tree

⑲ *8 mi east of Yucca Valley on Rte. 62 (Twentynine Palms Hwy.).*

Primarily a gateway to the national park, the town of Joshua Tree has basic services, a few fast-food outlets, and two lodgings of note.

★ ☺ Not far from the Joshua Tree town center, UFO fanatic George Van Tassel spent 18 years building the **Integratron,** a 38-ft-tall dome, which he completed in the early 1960s. Intended as a sort of combination cosmic fountain of youth and time machine, the structure contains a private "sound bath," where (by reservation) you can experience the dome's multiple-wave sound chamber in a floating sky chair. Don't miss the UFO landing strip nearby. Between the 1950s and 1970s Van Tassel drew thousands of believers to his UFO conventions and held weekly alien séances in the cave below **Giant Rock,** about 3 mi from the Integratron. The 23,000-ton freestanding boulder, one of the largest such rocks in the world, stands about 70 ft tall. The cave beneath the boulder was once the home of a prospector. To get to the Integratron from downtown Joshua Tree, take Sunburst Avenue north from Highway 62. When the pavement ends (at Golden), turn right and drive to Border, where you'll take a left. Drive about 6 mi to where the pavement ends and turn left onto Reche Road. Follow Reche Road about 6 mi into the town of Landers, and turn right onto Belfield Boulevard, which ends at Linn Road, in about a mile. The Integratron entrance is on the right. ✉ *Linn Rd. at Belfield Blvd., Landers,* ☎ *760/364–3126,* WEB *www.integratron.com.* ☞ *$5 for tour; $30 for sound bath.* ☉ *1st 3 wks of month, Fri.–Sun. noon–4.*

Dining and Lodging

$ ✗ **Arturo's.** Just outside Joshua Tree National Park's west entrance, this attractive restaurant serves traditional Mexican favorites. Try the combination burrito with moderately spicy beef-and-bean filling. ✉ *61695 Twentynine Palms Hwy.,* ☎ *760/366–2719. AE, D, DC, MC, V. Closed Mon.*

$ ✗ **Joshua Tree Park Center Café and Deli.** Buy a meal here and part of the profits benefit the Joshua Tree Association. Stoke up on a hearty breakfast, and order a box lunch before heading into the park. The café creates some unusual sandwiches, such as nutty chicken salad or roast beef and cheddar with Ortega chilies. ✉ *6554 Park Blvd.,* ☎ *760/366–3622. AE, D, MC, V. No dinner.*

$$$$ 🏠 **Mojave Rock Ranch Cabins.** If peace, solitude, and stunning desert views are what you seek, try this rustic retreat tucked away on a hillside north of town. From the hammock hung on your private porch you'll overlook gardens alive with barrel cactus, desert willow, and mesquite. The hilltop Bungalow has a hand-built stone-and-iron fireplace and a covered patio perfect for dining alfresco. The Homesteader, with a century-old wagon in the yard, is filled with western antiques. Each cabin sleeps four and has an enclosed dog run. ✉ *64976 Starlight Rd., 92252,* ☎ *760/366–8455,* FAX *760/366–1996,* WEB *www.mojaverockranch.com. 4 cabins. Kitchenettes, in-room hot tubs; no smoking. No credit cards.*

$–$$$ 🏠 **Joshua Tree Inn.** If these walls could talk: This 1950s motel-style B&B was popular with rock stars in the 1970s and early 1980s. The building's cinder-block construction is still visible, but now there's a nice garden. ✉ *61259 Twentynine Palms Hwy., 92252,* ☎ *760/366–1188 or 800/366–1444,* FAX *760/366–3805,* WEB *www.joshuatreeinn.com. 8 rooms, 2 suites. In-room data ports, pool. AE, D, DC, MC, V. BP.*

Outdoor Activities and Sports

Joshua Tree Rock Climbing School offers several programs, from one-day introductory classes to multiday programs for experienced climbers. The school provides all needed equipment. Beginning classes are limited to six people 13 years or over. ✉ *6535 Park Blvd.,* ☎ *800/890–4745,* WEB *www.rockclimbingschool.com.* ☞ *$80 for beginner class. Closed July.*

Vertical Adventures Climbing School trains about a thousand climbers each year in Joshua Tree National Park. Classes meet at a designated location in the park. All equipment is provided. ✉ *Box 7548 Newport Beach 92252,* ☎ *800/514–8785,* WEB *www.verticaladventures.com.* ☞ *$90-$95 per person for one-day classes. Closed July–Aug.*

Twentynine Palms

20 *16 mi east of Joshua Tree on Rte. 62 (Twentynine Palms Hwy.).*

The main gateway town to Joshua Tree National Park, Twentynine Palms is also the location of the U.S. Marine Air Ground Task Force Training Center. You can find services, supplies, and lodgings here.

The history and current life of Twentynine Palms is depicted in **Oasis of Murals,** a collection of 17 murals painted on the sides of buildings. If you drive around town, you can't miss them, but you can also pick up a free map from the Twentynine Palms Chamber of Commerce (⊠ 6455A Mesquite Ave., ☎ 760/367–3445, 🌐 www.oasisofmurals.com).

Dining and Lodging

$–$$$ ✕🏨 **29 Palms Inn.** The funky 29 Palms, on the Oasis of Mara, is the lodging closest to the entrance to Joshua Tree National Park. The collection of adobe and wood-frame cottages is scattered over 70 acres of grounds that are popular with birds and bird-watchers year-round. The contemporary fare at the inn's restaurant is more sophisticated than its Old West appearance might suggest. ⊠ 73950 Inn Ave., 92277, ☎ 760/367–3505, FAX 760/367–4425, 🌐 *www.29palmsinn.com. 15 rooms, 4 suites. Restaurant, pool, hot tub; no air-conditioning. AE, D, DC, MC, V. CP.*

$$–$$$ 🏨 **Homestead Inn.** A throwback to the old days in the desert, the Homestead is run by a salt-of-the-earth innkeeper who keeps a flock of road-runners as pets. The rooms are comfortable but not particularly stylish; a couple of them have their original bathroom tiles and fixtures. Three rooms have private patios; two have fireplaces and whirlpool tubs. The innkeeper will prepare dinners and picnic lunches with advance notice. ⊠ 74153 Two Mile Rd., 92277, ☎ 760/367–0030 or 877/367–0030, FAX 760/367–1108, 🌐 *www.joshuatreelodging.com. 7 rooms. Microwaves (some), refrigerators (some), in-room VCRs (some); no phones in some rooms. MC, V. Closed early July–Aug. BP.*

$$ 🏨 **Roughley Manor.** No expense was spared by the wealthy pioneer
★ who erected the stone mansion now occupied by this B&B. A 50-ft-long planked maple floor is the pride of the great room, the carpentry on the walls throughout is intricate, and huge stone fireplaces warm the house on the rare cold night. Original fixtures still gleam in the bathrooms, and the elegant bedrooms are furnished with pencil and canopy beds. An acre or so of gardens shaded by Washingtonia palms surrounds the house. ⊠ 74744 Joe Davis Rd., 92277, ☎ 760/367–3238, FAX 760/367–4483, 🌐 *www.roughleymanor.com. 2 suites, 6 cottages. Outdoor hot tub. DC, MC, V. BP.*

$ 🏨 **Best Western Gardens Motel.** This bright complex has smartly furnished rooms, some of which have coffeemakers and hot tubs. Continental breakfast is included in your room rate. ⊠ 71–487 Twentynine Palms Hwy., 92277, ☎ 760/367–9141, FAX 760/367–2584. 72 rooms, 12 suites. Microwaves (some), refrigerators (some), pool, outdoor hot tub, laundry facilities, business services. AE, D, DC, MC, V. CP.

Joshua Tree National Park

★ ☽ ㉑ *2 mi south of Twentynine Palms, off Rte. 62 (Twentynine Palms Hwy.).*

In part because it is so close to Los Angeles and San Diego, Joshua Tree National Park receives more than a million visitors each year. The 794,000-acre park contains complex, ruggedly beautiful scenery. Its mountains of jagged rock, natural cactus gardens, and lush oases shaded by tall fan palms mark the meeting place of the Mojave (high) and Colorado (low) deserts. This is prime hiking, rock-climbing, and exploring country, where coyotes, desert pack rats, and exotic plants like the white yucca, red-tipped ocotillo, and cholla cactus reside. Extensive stands of Joshua trees (they're actually shrubs, not trees) give the park its name. The plants reminded early white settlers of the biblical Joshua, with their thick, stubby branches representing his arms raised toward heaven. You can see portions of the park in a half-day excursion from Palm Springs or the other desert resort cities. A full-day driving tour allows time for a nature walk or two and stops at many of the 50 wayside exhibits, which provide insight into Joshua Tree's geology and rich vegetation.

The elevation in some areas of the park exceeds 4,000 ft, and light snow-falls and cold, strong north winds are common in winter. There are no services within the park and little water, so you should carry a gallon of water per person per day and use plenty of sunscreen any time of the year.

Joshua Tree National Park is open year-round, 24 hours a day, and the visitor centers are open daily 8–4:30. Admission to the park is $10 per vehicle, $5 if you enter on foot or bicycle. ☎ 760/367–5500, WEB *www.nps.gov/jotr.*

The **Oasis Visitor Center,** about 3 mi north of the north entrance to the park, has many free and inexpensive brochures, books, posters, and maps as well as several educational exhibits. Rangers are on hand to answer questions. A half mile's walk from the visitor center is **Oasis of Mara.** Inhabited first by Native Americans and later by prospectors and homesteaders, the oasis now provides a home for birds, small mammals, and other wildlife. ✉ *Utah Trail, ½ mi south of Rte. 62,* ☎ *760/ 367–5500,* WEB *www.nps.gov/jotr.*

Geology Tour Road, south of Queen Valley, is an 18-mi dirt road that winds through some of the park's most fascinating landscapes. It is recommended that you attempt this only in a four-wheel-drive vehicle. ✉ *Off Park Blvd., about 10 mi south of North Entrance Station.*

Drive east to west through **Queen Valley,** where the stands of Joshua trees are particularly alluring in spring. ✉ *Barker Dam Rd. off Park Blvd., about 10 mi from North Entrance Station.*

Hidden Valley, a boulder-strewn area, was once a cattle rustlers' hideout. You'll understand why the rustlers chose this spot when you crawl between the big rocks. A 1⅒-mi loop trail leads from Hidden Valley to **Barker Dam.** Built around 1900 by ranchers and miners to hold water for cattle and mining operations, the dam now serves the same purpose for wildlife. At Hidden Valley you can take the 60-minute guided **Desert Queen Ranch** walking tour (☎ 760/367–5555, WEB www.nps. gov/jotr, 🎫 $5). This ranger-led tour explores the homestead created by Joshua Tree pioneers William and Frances Keys and provides a glimpse of the 60 years the couple spent working to raise a family under extreme desert conditions. Bill Keys dug wells by hand and installed an irrigation system to water his vegetable gardens, fruit orchards, and wheat and alfalfa fields. The ranch has been restored to look much as it did when Bill died in 1969. The house, schoolhouse, store, and workshop still stand; the orchard has been replanted; and the grounds are full of old trucks, cars, and mining equipment. You must make reservations to take the tour, which is offered October–May, weekdays at 10 and 1, weekends at 10, 1, and 3. ✉ *Off Park Blvd., 2 mi north of intersection with western end of Barker Dam Rd.*

Survey all of Hidden Valley from **Keys View,** the most dramatic overlook in Joshua Tree National Park. At 5,185 ft, the spot has a view across the desert all the way to Mt. San Jacinto, near Palm Springs and, on clear days, as far south as the Salton Sea. Sunrise and sunset are magical times, when the light throws rocks and trees into high relief before (or after) bathing the hills in brilliant shades of red, orange, and gold. ✉ *Keys View Rd., 21 mi south of west entrance.*

If, instead of driving east through the park, you head south on **Pinto Basin Road** where it intersects with Park Boulevard, you will experience a stunning desert drive through Pinto Basin. At the **Cholla Cactus Gardens** (✉ Pinto Basin Rd., 10 mi southeast of junction with Park Blvd.) you can see a stand of Bigelow cholla, sometimes called the jumping cholla because its hooked spines seem to jump at you as you walk past. The chollas are best seen and photographed in late afternoon, when their backlighted spiky stalks stand out against a colorful sky. The **Ocotillo Patch** (⊠ Pinto Basin Rd., about 3 mi east of Cholla Cactus Gardens) has a roadside exhibit on the dramatic display made by the fiery red-tipped succulent following even the shortest rain shower. ⊠ *Off Park Blvd., 4 mi south of North Entrance Station.*

Follow Pinto Basin Road south toward **Cottonwood Visitor Center,** which has a small museum, picnic tables, drinking water, and rest rooms. A 1-mi trail leads from the visitor center to the **Cottonwood Spring Oasis.** Noted for its abundant birdlife, the palm-shaded oasis was an important water stop for prospectors, miners, and teamsters traveling between the small town of Mecca (to the southwest) and mines to the north. You can see the remains of an *arrastra*, a primitive type of gold mill, near the oasis, as well as the concrete ruins of two gold mines. Bighorn sheep frequent this area in winter. ⊠ *Pinto Basin Rd. 32 mi south of North Entrance Station,* ☎ *no phone.*

Dining and Camping

✕ **Picnic Areas.** There are no restaurants inside Joshua Tree, so you have to bring your own lunch. Picnic areas within the park are equipped with just the basics—picnic tables, fire pits, and primitive rest rooms. Only those near the entrances have water. There are picnic areas at the Cottonwood Spring visitor center and in Hidden Valley, as well as at Live Oak Springs, on Park Boulevard east of Jumbo Rocks.

⚠ **Cottonwood Campground.** In spring this campground is surrounded by some of the finest wildflower viewing in the desert. The park's southernmost campground, Cottonwood is often the last to fill up. Reservations are required for three group sites that hold up to 25 people each. *Flush toilets, dump station, fire pits, picnic tables, ranger station. 62 sites, 3 group sites.* ⊠ *Pinto Basin Rd., 32 mi south of North Entrance Station,* ☎ *760/367–5500,* WEB *www.nps.gov.jotr. D, MC, V. Reservations not accepted.*

⚠ **Hidden Valley Campground.** This is the most popular campground among rock climbers, who make their way up valley rock formations that have names like the Blob, Old Woman, and Chimney Rock. RVs are permitted, but there are no hook-ups. *Pit toilets, fire pits, picnic tables. 39 sites.* ⊠ *Off Park Blvd., 20 mi southwest of Oasis of Mara,* ☎ *760/367–5500,* WEB *www.nps.gov.jotr. Reservations not accepted.*

Outdoor Activities and Sports

The quarter-mile **Skull Rock Trail** (⊠ Jumbo Rocks Campground, just beyond loop E) is a hiking loop through boulder piles, desert washes, and a rocky alley. A fairly strenuous 4-mi round-trip hike on **Lost Horse Mine Trail** (⊠ At the parking area 1.25 mi east of Keys View Rd.) takes you along a former mining road to a well-preserved stamp mill, which was used to crush rock mined from the nearby mountain in search of gold. The operation was one of the most successful around, and the mine's cyanide settling tanks and stone buildings are the area's best preserved. From the mill area, a short but steep 10-minute side hike takes you to the top of a 5,278-ft mountain. Allow four hours for the hike.

ANZA-BORREGO DESERT

Largely uninhabited, the Anza-Borrego Desert is popular with those who love solitude, silence, space, light, and sweeping vistas. The desert lies south of the Palm Springs area, stretching along the western shore of the Salton Sea down to I–8 along the Mexican border. Isolated from the rest of California by mile-high mountains to the north and west, this desert is mostly occupied by Anza-Borrego Desert State Park, which at more than 600,000 acres is the largest state park in California. This is a place where you can escape the cares of the human world.

For thousands of years Native Americans of the Cahuilla and Kumeyaay tribes inhabited this area, spending their winters on the warm desert floor and their summers in the mountains. The first Europeans—a party led by Spanish explorer Juan Baptiste de Anza—crossed this desert in 1774. Anza, for whom the desert is named, made the trip through here twice. Seventy-five years later thousands of immigrants on their way to the goldfields up north crossed the desert on the Southern Immigrant Trail, remnants of which remain along Highway S2. Permanent settlers arrived early in the 20th century, and by the 1930s the first adobe resort cottage was built.

Anza-Borrego Desert State Park

㉒ *53 mi south of Indio, via Highway 86 and Highway S22 to Borrego Springs.*

One of the richest living museums in the nation, Anza-Borrego Desert State Park is a vast, nearly uninhabited wilderness where you can step through a field of wildflowers, cool off in a palm-shaded oasis, count zillions of stars in the black night sky, and listen to coyotes howl at dusk. The landscape, largely undisturbed by humans, reveals a rich natural history. There's evidence of a vast inland sea in the piles of oyster beds near Split Mountain and of the power of natural forces such as earthquakes and flash floods. In addition, scientists have also discovered the fossilized remains of mammoths and sites that were inhabited by early man. But the park lives in the present, too: following a wet winter, a stunning display of desert wildflowers blooms. Two new species of reptiles and a grove of 200 elephant trees are among the park's wild inhabitants.

Anza-Borrego Desert State Park is unusually accessible to visitors: Admission to the park is free, and few areas are off-limits. Unlike most parks in the country, Anza-Borrego lets you camp anywhere: just follow the trails and pitch a tent wherever you like. There are more than 500 mi of dirt roads, two huge wilderness areas, and 110 mi of riding and hiking trails. Many of the park's sites can be seen from paved roads, but some require driving on dirt roads. Rangers recommend that you use a four-wheel-drive vehicle on the dirt roads. When you do leave the pavement, carry the appropriate supplies: a shovel and other tools, flares, blankets, and plenty of water. The canyons are susceptible to flash flooding, so inquire about weather conditions (even on sunny days) before entering.

To get oriented and obtain information on current weather and wildlife conditions in the desert, stop by the **Visitors Information Center** in Borrego Springs. The place is designed to keep cool during the desert's blazing hot summers—it's built underground, beneath a demonstration desert garden. ⊠ *200 Palm Canyon Dr. (Rte. S22)*, ☎ *760/767–5311*, WEB *www.anzaborrego.statepark.org.* ☾ *Oct.–May, daily 9–5; June–Sept., weekends and holidays 9–5.*

At **Borrego Palm Canyon** a 1½-mi trail leads to a small oasis, one of the few native palm groves in North America. There are more than 1,000 native fan palms in the grove, and a stream and waterfall greet you at trail's end. The moderate hike is the most popular in the park. ⊠ *Palm*

Canyon Dr. (Rte. S22), about 1 mi west of the Visitors Information Center.

Coyote Canyon has a year-round stream and lush plant life. Portions of the canyon road follow a historic section of the old Anza Trail. The canyon is closed between June 15 and September 15 to allow native bighorn sheep undisturbed use of the water. Note that the dirt road that gives access to the canyon may be sandy enough to require a four-wheel-drive vehicle. ⊠ *Off DiGiorgio Rd., 4½ mi north Borrego Springs.*

The late afternoon view of the Borrego badlands from **Font's Point** is one of the most breathtaking you'll ever see in the desert, especially when the setting sun casts a golden glow on the eroded mountain slopes. The road from the Font's Point turnoff can be rough; inquire about its condition at the visitor center before starting out. Even if you can't make it out on the paved road, you can see some of the view from the highway. ⊠ *Off Salton Seaway (Hwy. S22), 13 mi east of Borrego Springs.*

Narrows Earth Trail is a short walk off the road east of Tamarisk Grove campground. Along the way you can see evidence of the many geologic processes involved in forming the canyons of the desert—a contact zone between two earthquake faults, sedimentary layers of metamorphic and igneous rock, and the like. ⊠ *Off Hwy. 78, 13 mi west of Borrego Springs.*

Geology students from all over the world visit the Fish Creek area of Anza-Borrego to explore a canyon known as **Split Mountain.** The narrow gorge with 600-ft walls was formed by an ancient stream. Fossils in this area indicate that a sea once covered the desert floor. ⊠ *Split Mountain Rd., 9 mi south of Hwy. 78 at Ocotillo Wells.*

Just a few steps off the paved road, **Carrizo Badlands Overlook** offers a view of eroded and twisted sedimentary rock that obscures the fossils of the mastodons, saber-tooths, zebras, and camels that roamed this region a million years ago. The route to the overlook through Earthquake Valley and Blair Valley parallels the historic Southern Emigrant Stage Route. ⊠ *Off Rte. S2, 40 mi south of Scissors Crossing (intersection of Hwy. S2 and Hwy. 78).*

Camping

⚠ **Borrego Palm Canyon.** This pleasant campground is near the Borrego Palm Canyon trailhead. There are two sections: one for recreational vehicles with hookups and another without hookups, designed for tent campers. Tent sites have ramadas for shade. *Flush toilets. Full hookups, drinking water, showers, fire pits, picnic tables, public telephone. 52 sites with full hookups, 65 tent sites.* ⊠ *Palm Canyon Dr. (Rte. S22), about 1 mi west of Visitors Information Center,* ☎ *760/767–5311; 800/ 444–7275 for reservations,* WEB *www.anzaborrego.statepark.org.*

⚠ **Tamarisk Grove.** Campsites are tucked under the shade of sprawling tamarisk trees at this campground across the road from the 1½-mi Yaqui Well Nature Trail, which has good bird- and wildlife watching. There are no hookups, but the sites can hold RVs up to 21 ft. *Flush toilets, drinking water, showers, fire pits, picnic tables. 27 sites. Yaqui Pass Rd., 13 mi west of Borrego Springs,* ☎ *760/767–5311, 800/444– 7275 for reservations,* WEB *www.anzaborrego.statepark.org.*

Outdoor Activities and Sports

The easy, mostly flat **Pictograph/Smuggler's Canyon Trail** (⊠ Blair Valley, 3½ mi east of S22 6 mi southeast of Hwy. 78 at Scissors Crossing) traverses a boulder–strewn trail. At the end you'll come to a collection of rocks covered with muted reds and yellows pictographs painted by

Native Americans within the last few hundred years. Walk about ½ mi beyond the pictures to reach Smuggler's Canyon, where an overlook provides views of the Vallecito Valley. The hike is 2–3 mi round-trip. **Yaqui Well Nature Trail** (⊠ Hwy. 78, across from Tamarisk Campground) takes you along a path to a desert water hole where birds and wildlife are abundant. It's also a good place to look for wildflowers in spring.

The sand dunes and rock formations at **Ocotillo Wells State Vehicular Recreation Area** (⊠ Hwy. 78, Ocotillo Wells, ☎ 760/767–5391, WEB www.ohv.parks.ca.gov) are a challenge for off-road enthusiasts with more than 40,000 acres of open desert to explore. Bring your own water, for none is available here. You can camp throughout the area, but there are no facilities.

Borrego Springs

❷❸ *Highway S22, 59 mi south of Indio via Rte. 86.*

The permanent population of Borrego Springs, set squarely in the middle of Anza-Borrego Desert State Park, hovers around 2,500. Long a quiet town, it is emerging as a laid-back destination for desert lovers. September through June, when temperatures hover in the 80s and 90s, you can engage in outdoor activities such as hiking, nature study, golf, tennis, horseback riding, and mountain biking. If winter rains cooperate, Borrego Springs puts on some of the best wildflower displays in the low desert. In some years the desert floor is carpeted with color: yellow dandelions and sunflowers, pink primrose, purple sand verbena, and blue phacelia. The bloom generally runs from late February through April. For current information on wildflowers around Borrego Springs, call ☎ 760/767–4684 or visit WEB www.borregosprings.com.

Dining and Lodging

$$–$$$ ✕ **La Pavilion at Rams Hill.** Colorful paintings add to the southwestern style of this spot known for prime rib and filet mignon. You can dine outdoors on the deck, which overlooks mountains and the adjacent golf course. Sunday brunch is served. ⊠ *1881 Rams Hill Rd.,* ☎ *760/767–0009. AE, D, DC, MC, V.*

$ ✕ **Bernard's.** In a single large room with a wall of windows overlooking the mall, chef-owner Bernard offers casual dining with an Alsatian flavor. Try sauerkraut Alsatian style, plus daily Alsatian specialties like bouillabaisse and roast leg of lamb. ⊠ *503 The Mall,* ☎ *760/767–5666. AE, D, DC, MC, V. Closed Sun.*

$$$$ ✕🏨 **La Casa del Zorro.** This resort owned by the Copley family con-
★ sists of a collection of casitas scattered about lushly landscaped grounds. You need walk only a few hundred yards from the resort to be alone under the sky, and you may well see roadrunners crossing the highway. Although the mood is laid-back, the resort is luxurious in every way, with accommodations ranging from ample standard rooms to private four-bedroom casitas, each with its own pool and outdoor hot tub. Service is excellent, and the Continental restaurant puts on a good Sunday brunch. ⊠ *3845 Yaqui Pass Rd., 92004,* ☎ *760/767–5323 or 800/ 824–1884,* FAX *760/767–5963,* WEB *www.lacasadelzorro.com. 4 rooms, 54 suites, 19 casitas. Restaurant, bar, 3 pools, 3 outdoor hot tubs, beauty salon, spa, putting green, 6 tennis courts, health club, hiking, horseback riding, horseshoes, jogging, volleyball, bicycles, business services, meeting room. AE, D, MC, V.*

$–$$$ 🏨 **Palm Canyon Resort.** One of the largest properties around, Palm Canyon Resort includes a hotel a quarter mile from the park visitor center, an RV park, a restaurant, a swimming pool, and other recreational facilities. The better rooms have refrigerators and balconies or patios. ⊠ *221 Palm Canyon Dr., 92004,* ☎ *760/767–5341 or 800/242–0044,*

FAX 760/767–4073, WEB *www.pcresort.com. 60 rooms, 1 suite. Restaurant, bar, refrigerators (some), 2 pools, 2 outdoor hot tubs, exercise equipment, shops, laundry facilities, meeting room. AE, D, DC, MC, V.*

$$ 🏨 **Borrego Springs Resort and Country Club.** This low-key resort is surrounded by expansive desert views, including one from every guest room. Contemporary style rules in the simply furnished rooms. Appointments include hair dryers and in-room coffee bars. ✉ *1112 Tilting T Dr., 92004,* ☎ *760/767–5700 or 888/826–7734,* FAX *760/767–5710,* WEB *www.borregospringsresort.com. 100 rooms, 32 suites. Restaurant, bar, microwaves, refrigerators, kitchenettes (some), 2 pools, outdoor hot tub, 18-hole golf course, putting green, 6 tennis courts, exercise equipment, meeting room. AE, D, MC, V.*

$$ 🏨 **Palms at Indian Head.** The Palms is the most recent establishment to occupy the site of the first lodging built in the Borrego Valley. That was the Hoberg Resort, which hosted many movie stars in the 1940s and 1950s before burning down in 1958. The Hoberg was replaced with the current two-story desert-modern building. Set at the base of Indian Head Mountain, where bighorn sheep roam, the B&B offers lovely desert views from guest rooms and common areas, plus jogging and walking trails. There's no smoking on the property. ✉ *2220 Hoberg Rd., 92004,* ☎ *760/767–7788 or 800/519–2624,* FAX *760/767–9717,* WEB *www.ramonamall.com/thepalms.html. 10 rooms. Restaurant, microwaves, refrigerators, cable TV, pool, outdoor hot tub; no room phones, no smoking. DC, MC, V. CP.*

Outdoor Activities and Sports

The 18-hole course at **Borrego Springs Resort and Country Club** (☎ 760/767–3330, WEB www.borregospringsresort.com) is open to the public. The greens fee is $25–$64, which includes a cart. The club is closed September 15–October 31. Also public is the 18-hole course at **Rams Hill Country Club** (☎ 760/767–5124, WEB www.ramshillgolf.com). The greens fee is $80–$120, which includes a mandatory cart. **Roadrunner Club** (☎ 760/767–5374) has an 18-hole, par-3 golf course. The greens fee is $15.

IMPERIAL VALLEY

From the Salton Sea to the Mexican Border

Imperial County, the southwesternmost in California, lies between the Colorado River, to the east, and the Anza-Borrego Desert, to the west. The area is both a great desert and one of the richest agricultural regions in the world, producing primarily winter vegetables and grains. The briny Salton Sea, California's largest lake, occupies a large portion of Imperial County. The sea is a vast inland water recreation area, while El Centro is the commercial and business heart of the valley. This is stereotypical desert, complete with miles and miles of sand dunes, an average annual rainfall of less than 1 inch, and summer temperatures soaring above 100°F.

Salton Sea

㉔ *30 mi south of Indio via Rte. 86 on the western shore and via Rte. 111 on the eastern shore; 29 mi east of Borrego Springs via S22.*

The Salton Sea, barely 100 years old, is the product of both natural and artificial forces. The sea occupies the Salton Basin, a remnant of prehistoric Lake Cahuilla. Over the centuries the Colorado River flooded the basin and the water drained into the Gulf of California. In 1905, a flood once again filled the Salton Basin. Because the exit to the gulf was now blocked, the flood waters remained in the basin. The resulting body of water was trapped 228 ft below sea level, creating a saline lake about 35 mi long and 15 mi wide, with a surface area of nearly 380 square mi. The lake has no real inflow, so over the years evaporation has made it 25% saltier than the ocean, creating a rare and splendid habitat for birds and fish. Lying along the Pacific Flyway, the sea supports 400 species of birds; four sport fish inhabit the Salton Sea: corvina, sargo, Gulf croaker, and tilapia. Fishing, boating, camping, and birding are popular activities year-round. However, efforts to develop expensive waterfront communities and resorts along the western shore have failed because the lake sometimes has a pungent odor. The remnants of the developments now resemble other desert ghost towns.

On the north shore of the sea, the huge **Salton Sea State Recreation Area** draws thousands each year to its playgrounds, hiking trails, fishing spots, boat launches, and swimming areas. The Headquarters Visitor Center contains exhibits and shows a short film on the history of the Salton Sea. Summer is the best time for fishing here. ⊠ *100–225 State Park Rd.,* ☎ *760/393–3052,* WEB *www.saltonsea.ca.gov.* ⊠ *$2.* ⊙ *Park daily, visitor center Oct.–Mar.*

The 1,785-acre **Sonny Bono National Wildlife Refuge** on the Pacific Flyway is a wonderful spot for viewing migratory birds. You might see eared grebes, burrowing owls, great blue herons, ospreys, yellow-footed gulls, white and brown pelicans, and snow geese heading south from Canada. Facilities include self-guided trails, observation platforms, and interpretive exhibits. Fishing and waterfowl hunting are permitted in season in designated areas. ⊠ *906 W. Sinclair Rd., Calipatria,* ☎ *760/348–5278,* WEB *www.fishandwildlife.com/regionone.* ⊠ *Free.* ⊙ *Daily sunrise–sunset.*

Camping

⚠ **Salton Sea State Recreation Area Headquarters.** A tree-shaded parking area for RVs, this campground is right on the sand just steps from the beach. It is adjacent to New Camp. *Flush toilets, dump station, drinking water, fire pits, picnic tables, playground. 27 sites with full hookups. 100–225 State Park Rd.,* ☎ *760/393–3052; 800/444–7275 for reservations,* WEB *www.saltonsea.ca.gov.*

⚠ **New Camp.** This campground near park headquarters is designed for tent campers. Sites have shaded ramadas and paved parking stalls. It's a short walk from here to the Varner Harbor boat-launching area and the park's prime fishing spots. *Flush toilets, drinking water, fire pits, picnic tables. 25 sites. 100–225 State Park Rd.,* ☎ *760/393–3052; 800/444–7275 for reservations,* WEB *www.saltonsea.ca.gov.*

Outdoor Activities and Sports

At this 350-square-mi sea in the middle of the desert, all sort of water sports are popular. You can water-ski, kayak, and canoe on the Salton Sea, or fish from the shore, from a boat, and from the jetty at Varner Harbor. Swimming is permitted at beaches anywhere along the shoreline, but be warned that the water is brackish. You can launch your boat at **Varner Harbor** (⊠ 100–225 State Park Rd., ☎ 760/393–3052; 800/444–7275 for reservations, WEB www.saltonsea.ca.gov), where a ramp and five docks are available. The fee is $2.

El Centro

㉕ *28 mi south of Salton Sea on Rte. 86.*

Bisected by I–8, El Centro lies close to the Mexican border at the southern end of the Imperial Valley. Primarily a commercial and business community, it occupies some of the richest farmland in California, with more than a half million acres in cultivation. Year-round the region produces bumper crops of lettuce, carrots, sugar beets, seed, and grain.

Naval Air Facility El Centro, the winter home of the Blue Angels aerobatic team, opens each March for a huge air show with stunt flying, displays of antique and experimental aircraft, a food fest ($5), and rides with civilian aerobatic performers. ⊠ *Bennett Rd.,* ☎ *760/339–2519,* WEB *www.nafec.navy.mil.* ⊡ *Free.*

The stately **Old Post Office Pavilion** once housed the local post office, but now it's the headquarters of the El Centro Arts Council. Frequently changing exhibits showcase local and national artists working in painting, sculpture, multimedia, and more. ⊠ *230 S. 5th St.,* ☎ *760/337–1777.* ⊡ *Free.* ☉ *Weekdays 8–5.*

OFF THE BEATEN PATH	**IMPERIAL SAND DUNES –** This 40-mi-long dune system east of El Centro is one of the largest in the United States. Formed from the windblown beach sands of the prehistoric Blake Sea, which once occupied this portion of the desert, some dune crests reach heights of more than 300 ft. The impressive vistas make the dunes a popular filming location. You can maneuver your four-wheel-drive or dune buggy up, down, and around the mountains of sand. To reach the dunes from El Centro, drive 15 mi north on Highway 86 to Brawley, then 23 mi east on Highway 78. ⊠ *Gecko Rd., ½ mi south of Rte. 78, Glamis,* ☎ *760/344–3919,* WEB *www.ca.blm.gov/elcentro.* ⊡ *Free.* ☉ *Park open daily year-round; Cahuilla ranger station open Oct.–May, Fri.–Sun. 7–5:30.*

Dining and Lodging

$$–$$$$ ✕ **Barbara Worth Restaurant.** The large windows of this country club restaurant provide a view of the ninth green and a lake. With orchids on the tables and bamboo chairs, the dining room has a Polynesian flavor, but the kitchen is strictly Continental. The restaurant is known for its beef Wellington, prime rib, and lamb chops. You can eat outside, a pleasant option for Sunday brunch. ⊠ *2050 Country Club Dr., Holtville,* ☎ *760/356–2806.* ☉ *Breakfast also available. AE, D, DC, MC, V.*

$ ✕ **Celia's.** The quesadillas and *carne asada* are standouts at this classic south-of-the-border-style, family-oriented restaurant. ⊠ *1530 W. Adams Ave.,* ☎ *760/352–4570. MC, V. Closed July–Aug.*

$–$$ 🛏 **Best Western John Jay Inn.** The federalist architecture of this three-story motel stands out in the desert environment, and the traditional theme is carried into the well-appointed rooms. Suites have coffeemakers, microwaves, and minibars. A complimentary Continental breakfast is available each morning. ⊠ *2352 S. 4th St., 92243,* ☎ *760/ 337–8677,* FAX *760/337–8693,* WEB *www.bestwestern.com. 50 rooms, 8 suites. In-room data ports, refrigerators, cable TV with movies, pool, hot tub, sauna, exercise equipment, laundry facilities, some pets allowed; no-smoking rooms. AE, D, DC, MC, V. BP.*

$ 🛏 **Barbara Worth Golf Resort and Convention Center.** Taking its name from the 1911 Harold Bell Wright book *The Winning of Barbara Worth,* about turning the desert into farmland by irrigation, this resort is a green spot in the desert. Low-lying buildings overlooking the golf course house pleasant rooms with exterior entrances. Evenings at the karaoke bar can be lively. ⊠ *2050 Country Club Dr., Holtville 92250,* ☎ *760/356–2806 or 800/356–3806,* FAX *760/356–4653,* WEB *www.bwresort.com. 103 rooms. Restaurant, bar, lounge, room service, microwaves, refrigerators, cable TV, 2 pools, hot tub, driving range, 18-hole golf course, putting green, meeting rooms. AE, D, DC, MC, V.*

$ ⌂ Vacation Inn and Suites The largest lodging facility in El Centro is this Spanish-style two-story motel with spacious rooms and suites. Rooms have coffeemakers, and complimentary Continental breakfast is included in the price. Local phone calls are free. The motel also has an RV park with showers and rest rooms. ⊠ *2015 Cottonwood Dr., 92243,* ☏ *760/ 352–9523 or 800/328–6289,* ℻ *760/352–7620. 160 rooms, 11 suites. Restaurant, bar, in-room data ports, kitchenettes, microwaves, refrigerators, cable TV, 2 pools, outdoor hot tub, business services, meeting rooms, airport shuttle, pets allowed; no-smoking rooms. AE, D, DC, MC, V. CP.*

PALM SPRINGS AND THE SOUTHERN CALIFORNIA DESERT A TO Z

To research prices, get advice from other travelers, and book travel arrangements, visit www.fodors.com.

AIR TRAVEL

Palm Springs International Airport is the major airport serving California's southern desert. The major airlines that fly to Palm Springs include Alaska, American/American Eagle, America West Express, Continental, SkyWest/Delta Connection, Northwest, and United/United Express. The airport is about 2 mi from downtown Palm Springs; most hotels provide shuttle service. SkyWest/Delta Connection serves Imperial County Airport. *See* Air Travel *in* Smart Travel Tips A to Z for airline phone numbers.

➤ AIRPORT INFORMATION: **Imperial County Airport** (☏ 760/355–7944). **Palm Springs International Airport** (☏ 760/318–3800, WEB www.palmspringsairport.com).

BUS TRAVEL

Greyhound provides service to the Palm Springs and El Centro depots. SunBus, operated by the SunLine Transit Agency, serves the entire Coachella Valley, from Desert Hot Springs to Mecca. Imperial County Transit provides bus service for the El Centro and Salton Sea communities.

➤ BUS INFORMATION: **Greyhound** (☏ 800/231–2222, WEB www. greyhound.com). **El Centro Depot** (⊠ 460 State St., ☏ 760/352–6363). **Palm Springs Depot** (⊠ 311 N. Indian Canyon Dr., ☏ 760/325–2053). **Imperial County Transit** (☏ 800/804–3050). **SunLine Transit** (☏ 760/ 343–3456 or 800/347–6828, WEB www.sunline.org).

CAR RENTAL

Most major car-rental companies are represented in the Palm Springs area; Budget and Enterprise have outlets in El Centro. *See* Car Rental *in* Smart Travel Tips A to Z for national car-rental agency phone numbers.

CAR TRAVEL

The desert resort communities occupy a 20-mi stretch between I–10, to the east, and Palm Canyon Drive (Highway 111), to the west. The area is about a two-hour drive east of Los Angeles and a three-hour drive northeast of San Diego. From Los Angeles take the San Bernardino Freeway (I–10) east to Highway 111. From San Diego I–15 heading north connects with the Pomona Freeway (Highway 60), leading to the San Bernardino Freeway (I–10) east. If you're coming from the Riverside area, you can also take Highway 74 east.

To reach Borrego Springs from Los Angeles, take I–10 east past the desert resorts area to Highway 86 South, and follow Highway 86 to the Borrego Salton Seaway (Highway S22). Drive west on S22 to Borrego Springs. You can reach the Borrego area from San Diego via I–8 to Highway 79 east through Cuyamaca State Park. This will take you to Highway 78 in Julian, which you follow east to Yaqui Pass Road (S3) into Borrego Springs.

The Imperial Valley lies south of S22 on Highway 86. Salton Sea attractions are on the south and east sides of the sea. El Centro is about a two-hour drive from San Diego via I–8.

EMERGENCIES

In the event of an emergency, dial 911.

Of course, it's best to avoid emergencies altogether. In the desert you can protect yourself by being prepared and taking a few simple safety precautions. Never travel alone. Always take a companion, especially if you are not familiar with the area. Let someone know about your trip, destination, and estimated time and date of return. Before setting out, make sure that your vehicle is in good condition. Carry a jack, tools, and tow rope or chain. Fill up your tank whenever you see a gas pump—it can be miles between service stations. Stay on main roads: If you drive even a few feet off the pavement, you could get you stuck in sand. Plus, venturing off-road is illegal in many areas. When driving, watch out for wild burros, horses, and range cattle. They roam free throughout much of the desert and have the right-of-way.

Drink at least one gallon of water per person, per day, preferably more (three gallons if you plan on hiking or other strenuous activity), even if you don't feel thirsty. Dress in layered clothing and wear comfortable, sturdy shoes and a hat. Keep snacks, sunscreen, and a first-aid kit on hand. If you suddenly have a headache or feel dizzy or nauseous, you could be suffering from dehydration. Get out of the sun immediately and drink plenty of water. Dampen your clothing to lower your body temperature.

Avoid canyons during rainstorms. Floodwaters can quickly fill up dry riverbeds and cover or wash away roads. Never place your hands or feet where you can't see. Rattlesnakes, scorpions, and black widow spiders may be hiding there.

➤ HOSPITALS: **Borrego Medical Center** (✉ 4343 Yaqui Pass Rd., Borrego Springs, ☎ 760/767–5051). **Desert Regional Medical Center** (✉ 1150 N. Indian Canyon Dr., Palm Springs, ☎ 760/323–6511). **El Centro Regional Medical Center** (✉ 509 S. 8th St., El Centro, ☎ 760/339–7100).

LODGING

The Palm Springs Visitor Information Center represents 85 properties in the desert resorts area and can help you arrange for lodgings there. Palm Springs Desert Resorts Authority can make accommodation reservations throughout the area (☞ Visitor Information, *below,* for both). McLean Company Rentals, Rental Connection, and ResortQuest arrange vacation rentals by the day, week, or month.

➤ LOCAL AGENTS: **McLean Company Rentals** (✉ 477 S. Palm Canyon Dr., Palm Springs 92262, ☎ 760/322–2500, WEB www.ps4rent.com). **Rental Connection** (✉ 190 E. Palm Canyon Dr., Palm Springs 92263, ☎ 760/320–7336 or 800/462–7256, WEB www.therentalconnection.com). **ResortQuest** (✉ 76–300 Country Club Dr., Palm Desert 92211, ☎ 800/869–1130, WEB www.resortquest.com).

TAXIS

A Valley Cabousine serves the Coachella Valley. Mirage Taxi serves the Coachella Valley and the Los Angeles and Ontario International airports. Fares in the Coachella Valley run about $2.25 per mile and up to $240 one-way to LAX. Yellow Cab of El Centro serves the Imperial Valley. Service within the El Centro city limits is $3.50 per trip.

➤ TAXI COMPANIES: **A Valley Cabousine** (☎ 760/340–5845). **Mirage Taxi** (☎ 760/772–1793). **Yellow Cab of El Centro** (☎ 760/352–3100).

TRAIN TRAVEL

The Amtrak *Sunset Limited,* which runs between Florida and Los Angeles, stops in Palm Springs and Indio.

➤ TRAIN INFORMATION: **Amtrak** (☎ 800/872–7245, WEB www. amtrak.com).

VISITOR INFORMATION

➤ TOURIST INFORMATION: **Borrego Springs Chamber of Commerce** (✉ 622 Palm Canyon Dr., 92004-0420 ☎ 760/767–5555 or 800/559–5524, WEB www.borregosprings.com). **El Centro Chamber of Commerce** (✉ 1095 S. 4th St., 92243, ☎ 760/352–3681, WEB www. elcentrochamber.com). **Joshua Tree National Park** (✉ 74–485 National Park Dr., Twentynine Palms 92277, ☎ 760/367–5500, WEB www. nps.gov/jotr). **Palm Springs Desert Resorts Authority** (✉ 69–930 Rte. 111, Suite 201, Rancho Mirage 92270, ☎ 760/770–9000 or 800/ 417–3529; 760/770–1992 for activities hot line, WEB www. palmspringsusa.com). **Palm Springs Visitor Information Center** (✉ 333 N. Palm Canyon Dr., 92262, ☎ 760/778–8415 or 800/347–7746, WEB www.palm-springs.org).

614

INDEX